EASTERN EUROPE OVERVIEW

The maps on the following pages show more detail.

0 km	100	200 km
0 miles	50	100 m

Baltic Sea

Gdynia
Sopot
Hel
Gdańsk
Malbork

WIELKOPOLSKA

Toruń

Berlin

Poznań

Warsaw

Wisła

GERMANY

POLAND

Łódź

MAZOVIA

Leipzig

Elbe

Dresden

Wrocław

Częstochowa

MAŁOPOLSKA

SILESIA

Katowice

Auschwitz

Wisła

Kraków

BOHEMIA

Labe

River

Prague

Olomouc

Ostrava

Zakopane

HIGH

Levoča

Plzeň

Vltava

CZECH
REPUBLIC

MORAVIA

Brno

TATRA
MTNS.

Poprad

Košice

Nürnberg

Danube

Český
Krumlov

SLOVAKIA

Eger

Melk

River

Vienna

Bratislava

DANUBE

Munich

AUSTRIA

Győr

BEND

Salzburg

Sopron

Budapest

Szombathely

Danube

TIROL

Innsbruck

Graz

Lake
Balaton

River

DOLOMITES

Klagenfurt

JULIAN

Maribor

HUNGARY

Bolzano

ALPS

Bled

Pécs

Lake
Bohinj

Lake
Bled

Ljubljana

Zagreb

Trieste

SLOVENIA

SLAVONIA

CROATIA

SERBIA

Piran

Venice

Motovun

Rijeka

Osijek

Po

River

Rovinj

ISTRIA

Pula

Plitvice Lakes
National Park

Bihać

Banja Luka

BOSNIA-
HERZEGOVINA

ITALY

Sarajevo

Florence

Mostar

Siena

Međugorje

MONTE-
NEGRO

Podgorica

Dubrovnik

Kotor

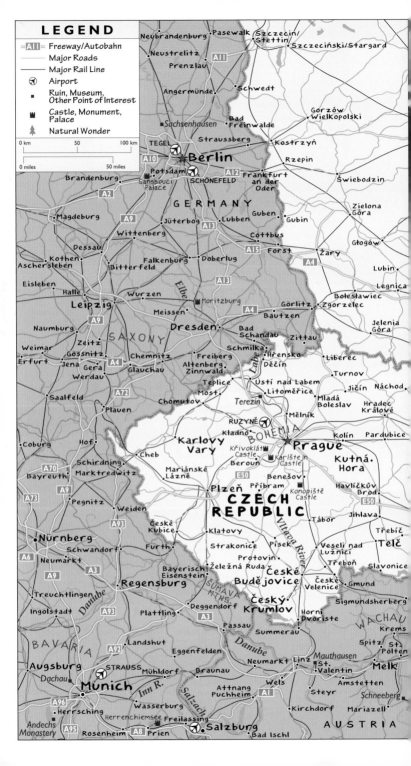

LEGEND

- **A11** = Freeway/Autobahn
- Major Roads
- Major Rail Line
- ✈ Airport
- ■ Ruin, Museum, Other Point of Interest
- ♜ Castle, Monument, Palace
- 🌲 Natural Wonder

0 km   50   100 km

0 miles   50 miles

Neubrandenburg • Pasewalk • Szczecin/Stettin • Szczeciński/Stargard

Neustrelitz • **A11**

Prenzlau

Angermünde • Schwedt

Gorzów Wielkopolski

■ Sachsenhausen • Bad Freinwalde

Straussberg • Kostrzyń

TEGEL ✈ • Berlin • Rzepin

Potsdam ✈ • SCHÖNEFELD • Frankfurt an der Oder • Świebodzin

Brandenburg • Sanssouci Palace ♜ • **A10**

A2 • GERMANY

Magdeburg • **A9** • Jüterbog • Lubben • Guben • Gubin • Zielona Góra

Wittenberg • **A13**

Kothen • Dessau • Bitterfeld • Falkenburg • Doberlug • Cottbus • **A15** • Forst • Żary • Głogów

Aschersleben • Lubin

Eisleben • Halle • Wurzen • **A13** • ■ Moritzburg • Görlitz • Zgorzelec • Bolesławiec • Legnica

Leipzig • **A9** • Meissen • **A4** • Bautzen

Naumburg • SAXONY • Dresden • Bad Schandau • Zittau • Jelenia Góra

Weimar • Zeitz • Chemnitz • Freiberg • Schmilka • Hřensko • Liberec

Erfurt • Gössnitz • Jena • Gera • Glauchau • Altenberg • Děčín • Turnov • Náchod

Werdau • Zinnwald • Teplice • Ústí nad Labem • Jičín • Hradec Králové

Saalfeld • **A72** • Most • Litoměřice • Mladá Boleslav

Coburg • Hof • Plauen • Chomutov • Terezín • Mělník

A70 • Schirnding • Cheb • RUZYNĚ ✈ • BOHEMIA • Kolín • Pardubice

Bayreuth • Marktredwitz • Kladno • Prague

A9 • Karlovy Vary • Křivoklát Castle ♜ • ★ Prague

A73 • Pegnitz • Mariánské Lázně • Beroun • Karlštejn Castle ■ • Kutná Hora

Weiden • **E50** • Benešov • Havlíčkův Brod

Nürnberg • Plzeň • Příbram • Konopiště Castle ■ • **E50**

A6 • Schwandorf • CZECH • Jihlava

Neumarkt • **A3** • Furth • Strakonice • Písek • REPUBLIC • Tábor • Třebíč

A9 • České Kubice • Klatovy • Protovin • Veselí nad Lužnicí • Telč

Treuchtlingen • Bayerisch Eisenstein • Železná Ruda • Třeboň • Slavonice

Ingolstadt • Regensburg • Danube • ŠUMAVA MTNS • České Budějovice • České Velenice • Gmund

A93 • Plattling • Deggendorf • Český Krumlov • Horní Dvořiste • WACHAU

BAVARIA • **A92** • Landshut • Passau • Summerau • Sigmundsherberg • Krems

Augsburg • Eggenfelden • Danube • Neumarkt • Linz • Mauthausen ■ • Spitz • St. Pölten

■ Dachau • STRAUSS ✈ • Mühldorf • Braunau • St. Valentin • Amstetten • Melk

A96 • Munich • Inn R. • Attnang Puchheim • **A1** • Wels • Steyr • Schneeberg

Herrsching • Wasserburg • Salzach • Kirchdorf • Mariazell

Andechs Monastery ■ • **A95** • Herrenchiemsee ♜ • Freilassing • ✈ Salzburg • Bad Ischl • AUSTRIA

Rosenheim • **A8** • Prien

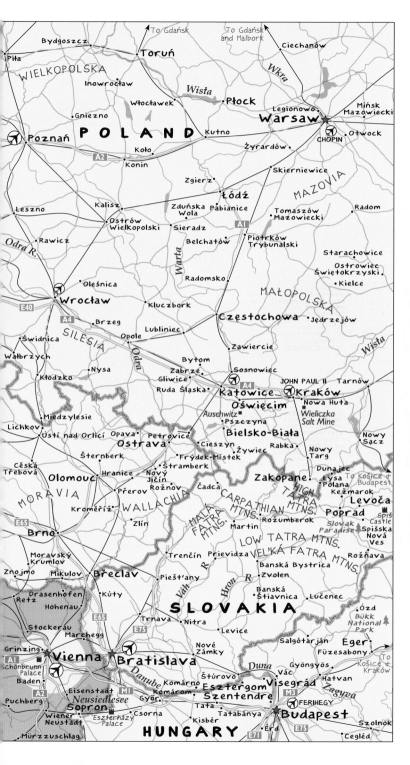

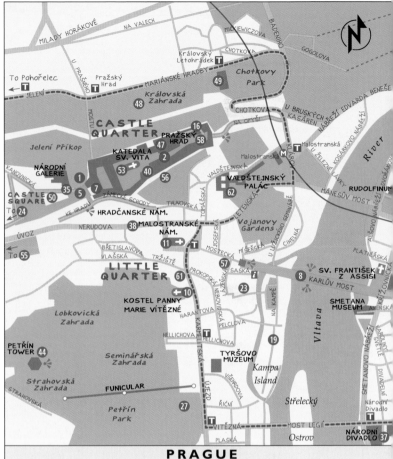

PRAGUE

1. Archbishop's Palace
2. Basilica of St. George and Convent
3. Bethlehem Chapel
4. Black Light Theater (3)
5. Castle Square
6. Ceremonial Hall
7. Changing of the Guard
8. Charles Bridge
9. Charles University
10. Church of St. Mary the Victorious
11. Church of St. Nicholas (in Little Quarter)
12. Church of St. Nicholas (in Old Town)
13. Convent of St. Agnes of Bohemia
14. To Dancing House
15. Estates Theatre
16. Golden Lane
17. Havelská Market
18. Jewish Quarter
19. Kampa Island
20. Karlova Street
21. Klaus Synagogue
22. Klementinum
23. Lennon Wall
24. To Loreta Church
25. Lucerna Gallery
26. Maisel Synagogue
27. Monument to Victims of Communism Who Survived
28. Mucha Museum
29. Municipal House
30. Mus. of Applied Arts
31. Mus. of Communism
32. Museum of Czech Cubism (in Black Madonna House)
33. Na Příkopě Street
34. Náprstek Museum of Asian, African & American Cultures
35. National Gallery in Sternberg Palace
36. National Museum
37. National Theatre
38. Nerudova Street
39. Old Jewish Cemetery
40. Old Royal Palace
41. Old Town Hall, Astronomical Clock, Tower & Chapel
42. Old Town Square & Jan Hus Memorial
43. Old-New Synagogue
44. Petřín Tower & Mus. of Jára Cimrman
45. Pinkas Synagogue
46. Powder Tower
47. Prague Castle
48. Royal Gardens
49. Royal Summer Palace
50. Schwarzenberg Palace
51. Spanish Synagogue
52. St. Martin in the Wall
53. St. Vitus Cathedral
54. St. Wenceslas Statue
55. To Strahov Monastery & Library
56. Terraced Gardens
57. Torture Museum
58. Toy and Barbie Museum
59. Týn Church
60. Ungelt Courtyard and House at the Golden Ring Gallery
61. Vrtba Garden
62. Wallenstein Palace & Garden
63. Wenceslas Square

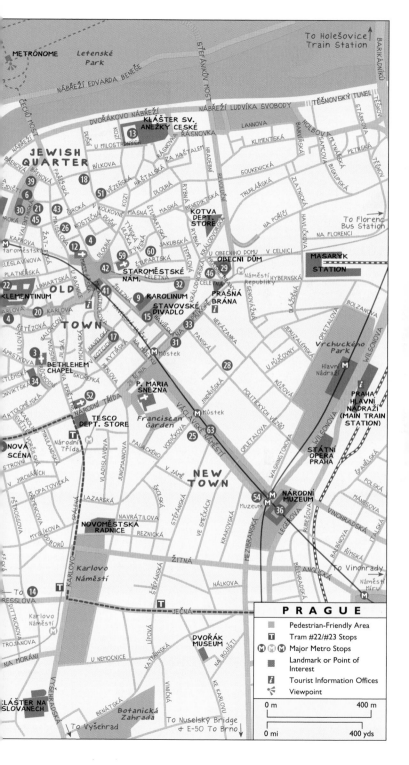

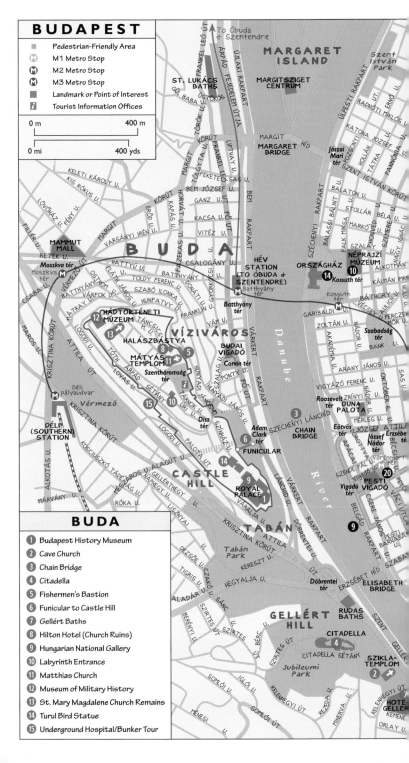

BUDAPEST

- ▪ Pedestrian-Friendly Area
- Ⓜ M1 Metro Stop
- Ⓜ M2 Metro Stop
- Ⓜ M3 Metro Stop
- ◼ Landmark or Point of Interest
- 𝒊 Tourist Information Offices

0 m	400 m
0 mi	400 yds

BUDA

1. Budapest History Museum
2. Cave Church
3. Chain Bridge
4. Citadella
5. Fishermen's Bastion
6. Funicular to Castle Hill
7. Gellért Baths
8. Hilton Hotel (Church Ruins)
9. Hungarian National Gallery
10. Labyrinth Entrance
11. Matthias Church
12. Museum of Military History
13. St. Mary Magdalene Church Remains
14. Turul Bird Statue
15. Underground Hospital/Bunker Tour

PEST

1. Museum of Trade and Tourism
2. Franz Liszt Square (Eateries)
3. Great Market Hall
4. Great Synagogue and Jewish Museum
5. Heroes' Square and Millennium Monument
6. To Holocaust Memorial Center
7. House of Terror Museum
8. Hungarian National Museum
9. Legenda Cruise Boats
10. Museum of Ethnography
11. Museum of Fine Arts
12. Opera House
13. Palace of Art
14. Parliament
15. Párisi Udvar Gallery
16. Postal Museum
17. St. István's Basilica
18. Széchenyi Baths
19. Vajdahunyad Castle
20. Vörösmarty Square, Gerbeaud Coffee House, and Start of Váci utca Pedestrian Street
21. Zoo

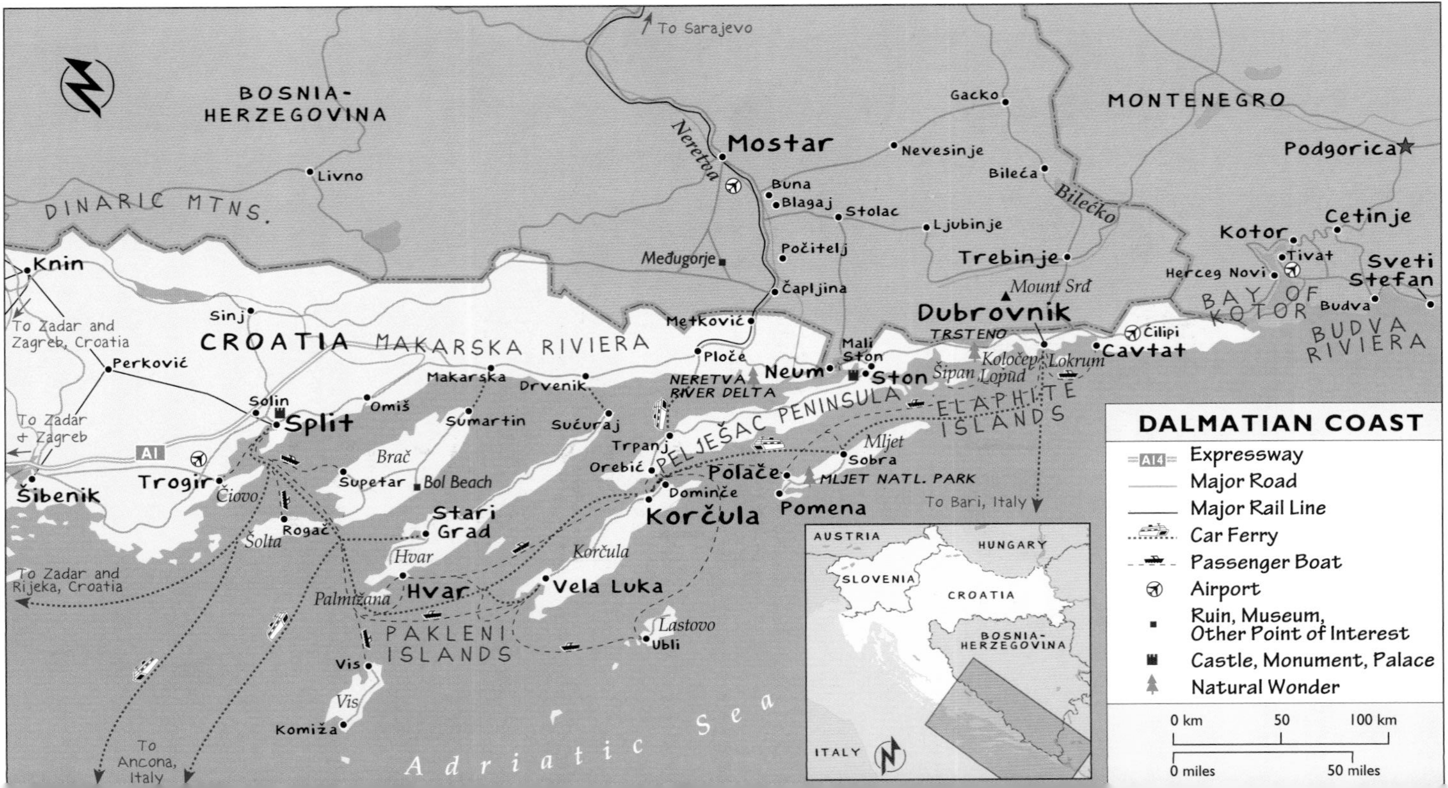
DALMATIAN COAST
Expressway
Major Road
Major Rail Line
Car Ferry
Passenger Boat
Airport
Ruin, Museum, Other Point of Interest
Castle, Monument, Palace
Natural Wonder
0 km
50
100 km
0 miles
50 miles
BOSNIA-HERZEGOVINA
MONTENEGRO
CROATIA
DINARIC MTNS.
MAKARSKA RIVIERA
To Sarajevo
Mostar
Neretva
Gacko
Nevesinje
Bileća
Bilećko
Podgorica
Livno
Buna
Blagaj
Stolac
Ljubinje
Cetinje
Kotor
Tivat
Herceg Novi
Sveti Stefan
Budva
BAY OF KOTOR
BUDVA RIVIERA
Međugorje
Počitelj
Čapljina
Trebinje
Mount Srđ
Dubrovnik
Čilipi
Cavtat
Knin
Sinj
To Zadar and Zagreb, Croatia
Perković
Metković
Ploče
Mali Ston
Ston
Neum
TRSTENO
Koločep
Lokrum
Šipan
Lopud
NERETVA RIVER DELTA
ELAPHITE ISLANDS
PELJEŠAC PENINSULA
Makarska
Drvenik
Solin
Split
Omiš
Sumartin
Sućuraj
To Zadar + Zagreb
A1
Trogir
Čiovo
Šibenik
Brač
Supetar
Bol Beach
Trpanj
Orebić
Mljet
Sobra
Polače
MLJET NATL. PARK
Dominče
Korčula
Pomena
To Bari, Italy
Stari Grad
Rogač
Šolta
Hvar
To Zadar and Rijeka, Croatia
Vela Luka
Palmižana
PAKLENI ISLANDS
Lastovo
Ubli
Vis
Komiža
To Ancona, Italy
Adriatic Sea
AUSTRIA
HUNGARY
SLOVENIA
CROATIA
BOSNIA-HERZEGOVINA
ITALY

Rick Steves'

EASTERN EUROPE

AVALON
TRAVEL

CONTENTS

TOP DESTINATIONS
IN EASTERN EUROPE

Baltic Sea

Gdańsk and the Tri-City

Pomerania

Warsaw

POLAND

100 Kilometers
100 Miles

Auschwitz-Birkenau

Kraków

Prague

Spiš Region

CZECH REPUBLIC

SLOVAKIA

Český Krumlov

Bratislava

Eger

Vienna

Danube Bend

Budapest

AUSTRIA

HUNGARY

Lake Bled

Julian Alps

Ljubljana

SLOV.

CROATIA

Zagreb

Rovinj

Plitvice Lakes

BOSNIA-HERZ.

Adriatic Sea

Split

Mostar

Korčula

Dubrovnik

INTRODUCTION

Until 1989, Eastern Europe was a foreboding place—a dark and gloomy corner of the "Evil Empire." But now the obligatory grays and preachy reds of communism live on only in history books, museums, and kitschy theme restaurants. Today's Eastern Europe is a traveler's delight, with low prices, friendly locals, lively squares, breathtaking sights, fascinating history, and a sense of pioneer excitement.

This book breaks Eastern Europe into its top big-city, small-town, and back-to-nature destinations. It then gives you all the information and suggestions necessary to wring the maximum value out of your limited time and money. If you're planning for a month or less in this region, this book is all you need.

Experiencing Europe's culture, people, and natural wonders economically and hassle-free has been my goal for three decades of traveling, tour guiding, and writing. With this book, I pass on to you all of the lessons I've learned.

You'll wander among Prague's dreamy, fairy-tale spires, bask in the energy of Kraków's Main Market Square, and soak with chess players in a Budapest bath. Ponder Europe's most moving Holocaust memorial at Auschwitz. Enjoy nature as you stroll on boardwalks through the Plitvice Lakes' waterfall wonderland or glide across Lake Bled to a church-topped island in the shadow of the Julian Alps. Taste a proud Hungarian vintner's wine and say, *"Egészségedre!"* (or stick with "Cheers!").

I've been selective, including only the top destinations and sights. For example, Poland has dozens of medieval castles—but Malbork is a cut above the rest.

The best is, of course, only my opinion. But after spending a third of my adult life exploring and researching Europe, I've developed a sixth sense for what travelers enjoy. Just thinking about the places featured in this book makes me want to polka.

What Is "Eastern Europe"?

"Eastern Europe" means different things to different people. To most Americans, Eastern Europe includes any place that was once behind the Iron Curtain, from the former East Germany to Moscow. But people who actually live in many of these countries consider themselves "Central Europeans." (To them, "Eastern Europe" is really eastern: Russia, Ukraine, Belarus, and Romania.)

In this book, I use the term "Eastern Europe" the way most Americans do—to describe the **Czech Republic, Slovakia, Poland, Hungary, Slovenia,** and **Croatia.** I've also thrown in two cities worth a detour: **Vienna** (in Austria) and **Mostar** (in Bosnia-Herzegovina). Vienna is a "gateway city" that feels more Western than Eastern, but it has important historical ties to the region. And Mostar—a mostly Muslim city a short drive or bus trip from Croatia's Dalmatian Coast—provides an opportunity to splice in some diversity.

So what do my six core "Eastern European" countries have in common? All of these destinations fell under communist control during the last half of the 20th century. More importantly, for centuries leading up to World War I, they were all part of the Austrian Hapsburg Empire. Before the Hapsburgs, the kings and emperors of these countries also frequently governed their neighbors. And all of these countries (except Hungary) are populated by people of Slavic heritage.

I hope that natives, sticklers, and historians will understand the liberties I've taken with the title of this book. But, after all, would you buy a book called *Rick Steves' Former Hapsburg Empire?*

About This Book

Rick Steves' Eastern Europe is a personal tour guide in your pocket. Better yet, it's actually two tour guides in your pocket: The co-author of this book is Cameron Hewitt, who writes and edits guidebooks and leads Eastern Europe tours for my travel company, Rick Steves' Europe Through the Back Door. Inspired by his Polish roots and by the enduring charm of the Eastern European people, Cameron has spent the last nine years closely tracking the exciting changes in this part of the world. Together, Cameron and I keep this book up-to-date and accurate (though for simplicity we've shed our respective egos to become "I" in this book).

This book is organized by destinations, each one a mini-vacation on its own, filled with exciting sights and convenient, affordable places to stay and eat. In the following chapters, you'll find this information:

Planning Your Time suggests a schedule with thoughts on

how best to use your limited time.

Orientation includes tourist information, tips on public transportation, local tour options, helpful hints, and an easy-to-read map designed to make the text clear and your arrival smooth.

Self-Guided Walks take you through interesting neighborhoods, with a personal tour guide in hand.

Sights provides a succinct overview of the most important sights, arranged by neighborhood, with ratings:

▲▲▲—Don't miss.
▲▲—Try hard to see.
▲—Worthwhile if you can make it.
No rating—Worth knowing about.

Sleeping describes my favorite hotels, from budget deals to splurges.

Eating serves up good-value restaurants, ranging from inexpensive take-out joints to fancier options.

Transportation Connections outlines your options for reaching nearby destinations by train, bus, and boat. In car-friendly regions, I've included route tips for drivers, with recommended roadside attractions along the way.

Country Introductions give you an overview of each country's culture, customs, money, history, current events, cuisine, language, and other useful practicalities.

The **Understanding Yugoslavia** chapter sorts out the various countries and conflicts, giving you a good picture of why Yugoslavia was formed, and why it broke apart.

The **appendix** is a traveler's tool kit, with a handy packing checklist, recommended books and films, instructions on how to use the telephone, useful phone numbers, and the procedure for dealing with lost credit cards. You'll also find detailed information on driving and public transportation, a climate chart, a festival list, and a hotel reservation form.

Study this book and put together the plan of your travel dreams. Then have a great trip! Traveling like a temporary local, and taking advantage of the information here, you'll enjoy the absolute most of every mile, minute, and dollar. As you travel the route I know and love, I'm happy that you'll be meeting some of my favorite Europeans.

PLANNING

Trip Costs

Traveling in Eastern Europe is a great value. While these countries are Westernizing at an astonishing rate, they remain at the poorer (and therefore cheaper) end of the European scale. Things that natives buy—such as food and transportation—are in line with

Eastern Europe: Best Three-Week Trip by Public Transportation

Day	Plan	Sleep in
1	Arrive in Prague	Prague
2	Prague	Prague
3	Prague; night train to Kraków	Night train
4	Kraków	Kraków
5	Kraków, day trip to Auschwitz	Kraków
6	Kraków, maybe side-trip to Wieliczka Salt Mine; night train to Eger	Night train
7	Eger	Eger
8	Early to Budapest	Budapest
9	Budapest	Budapest
10	Budapest	Budapest
11	To Ljubljana (catch direct 9-hr midday train; no night-train option)	Ljubljana
12	Ljubljana	Ljubljana
13	To Bled	Bled
14	Rent car for day trips around Julian Alps	Bled
15	To Zagreb, sightseeing, then early evening bus to Plitvice Lakes National Park	Plitvice
16	Plitvice hike in morning, then afternoon bus to Split	Split
17	Split	Split
18	Boat to Korčula	Korčula
19	Korčula	Korčula
20	Boat or bus to Dubrovnik	Dubrovnik
21	Dubrovnik	Dubrovnik
22	Side-trip to Mostar or fly home	

This ambitious, speedy, far-reaching itinerary works best by public transportation. Most of the time, you'll take the train. There are a few exceptions: Bled and Ljubljana are better connected by bus. To get from Bled to Plitvice, take the bus to Ljubljana, the train to Zagreb, and then the bus to Plitvice. To get from Plitvice to the coast, take the bus to Split. The Dalmatian Coast destinations are best connected to each other by boat or bus (no trains).

By **car,** this itinerary is exhausting, with lots of long road days. Instead, connect long-distance destinations by night train (e.g., Prague to Kraków, Kraków to Eger/Budapest), then strategically rent cars for a day or two in areas that merit having wheels (e.g., the Czech or Slovenian countryside). Also consider adding a side-trip to Croatia's Rovinj (and skip Zagreb). But remember that

international drop-off fees for rental cars can be astronomical, and plan accordingly (for example, you could drop off your rental car in Slovenia, train into Croatia, and then pick up a different rental car for your Croatia visit).

Vienna: The Austrian capital is a likely gateway between Western and Eastern Europe, but it's out of the way for the above itinerary. If you really want to see Vienna, give it two days between Budapest and Ljubljana (it also makes sense if you're going directly between Budapest and Prague).

Introduction

the local economy (that is, inexpensive). Hotels can be surprisingly expensive, but if you use my listings to find the best accommodations deals, a trip to these countries is substantially cheaper than visiting Italy, Germany, or France.

Five components make up your trip cost: airfare, surface transportation, room and board, sightseeing and entertainment, and shopping and miscellany. The prices I've listed below are more or less average for all of the destinations in this book. Prices are generally lower in Poland, Slovakia, and Mostar, and higher in Slovenia, Croatia, and Vienna; the Czech Republic and Hungary are in between. Of course, big cities (such as Prague and Budapest) are much more expensive than smaller towns (like Český Krumlov and Eger).

Airfare: A basic round-trip flight from the US to Prague should cost $700 to $1,200 (cheaper in winter), depending on where you fly from and when. Always consider saving time and money in Europe by flying "open jaw" (into one city and out of another). For example, the additional cost of flying into Prague and out of Dubrovnik is almost certainly cheaper than the added expense (and wasted time) of an overland return trip to Prague.

Surface Transportation: For the three-week whirlwind trip described on page 4, allow $300 per person for public transportation (train, bus, and boat tickets). Train travelers will probably save money by simply buying tickets along the way, rather than purchasing a railpass (see "Transportation," page 946). A basic car rental costs about $250 per person per week (based on two people splitting the cost of the car, tolls, gas, and insurance). Long-term car rental is cheapest when arranged in advance from the US, but exorbitant fees for dropping off in a different country can make long-term car rental prohibitively expensive for a multi-country itinerary (see "Car Rental," page 949).

Room and Board: You can thrive in Eastern Europe on an average of $90 a day per person for room and board. A $90-a-day budget per person allows $10 for lunch, $20 for dinner, and $60 for lodging (based on two people splitting the cost of a $120 double room that includes breakfast). That's doable. Students and tightwads eat and sleep for $40 a day ($20 per hostel bed, $20 for meals).

Sightseeing and Entertainment: Sightseeing is cheap here. Major sights generally cost $3 to $6, with some more expensive sights at around $10. Figure $10 to $25 for splurge experiences (e.g., going to concerts, taking a short Adriatic cruise, or soaking in a Budapest bath). You can hire your own private guide for four hours for about $100 to $150—a great value when divided among two or more people. An overall average of $20 a day works for most. Don't skimp here. After all, this category is the driving force behind your trip—you came to sightsee, enjoy, and experience Eastern Europe.

Shopping and Miscellany: Figure $1 per postcard, coffee, beer, and ice-cream cone. Shopping can vary in cost from nearly nothing to a small fortune. Good budget travelers find that this category has little to do with assembling a trip full of lifelong and wonderful memories.

When to Go

The "tourist season" runs roughly from May through September.

Summer has its advantages: the best weather, very long days (light until after 21:00), and the busiest schedule of tourist fun.

In spring and fall—May, June, September, and early October—travelers enjoy fewer crowds and milder weather. Cities are great at this time of year, but some small towns—especially resorts on the Croatian coast—are deserted and disappointing in May and October.

Winter travelers find concert season in full swing, with absolutely no tourist crowds (except in always-packed Prague), but some accommodations and sights are either closed or run on a limited schedule. Croatian coastal towns are completely dead in winter. Confirm your sightseeing plans locally, especially when traveling off-season. The weather can be cold and dreary, and night will draw the shades on your sightseeing before dinnertime. You may find the climate chart in the appendix helpful.

Sightseeing Priorities

Depending on the length of your trip, here are my recommended priorities. Assuming you're traveling by public transportation, I've taken geographical proximity into account.

3 days:	Prague
5 days, add:	Budapest
7 days, add:	Kraków and Auschwitz
9 days, add:	Český Krumlov
12 days, add:	Ljubljana and Bled
16 days, add:	Dubrovnik and Split
22 days, add:	Plitvice Lakes, Mostar, Eger, Rovinj

With more time or a special interest, choose among Vienna, Gdańsk, Pomerania, Toruń, Warsaw, the Danube Bend, Korčula, Zagreb, Slovakia's Spiš Region, and Bratislava.

The map on page 5 and the three-week itinerary on page 4 include most of the stops in the first 22 days.

Travel Smart

Your trip to Europe is like a complex play—easier to follow and really appreciate on a second viewing. While no one does the same

Know Before You Go

Your trip is more likely to go smoothly if you plan ahead.

Since **airline carry-on restrictions** are always changing, visit the Transportation Security Administration's website (www.tsa.gov/travelers) for an up-to-date list of what you can bring on the plane with you...and what you have to check. Remember to arrive with plenty of time to get through security.

Call your **debit and credit card companies** to let them know the countries you'll be visiting, so that they'll accept (and not deny) your international charges. Confirm your daily withdrawal limit; consider asking to have it raised so you can take out more cash at each ATM stop.

Be sure that your **passport** is valid at least six months after your ticketed date of return to the US. If you need to get or renew a passport, it can take up to three months (for more on passports, see www.travel.state.gov).

Book your rooms in advance if you'll be traveling during peak season (July and August), any major holidays and festivals (see page 955 of appendix), and definitely for your first night.

If you plan to hire a **local guide,** reserve ahead by email. Popular guides can get booked up.

If you're planning on **renting a car** in Eastern Europe, it's recommended that you carry an International Driver's Permit (available at your local AAA office for $15 plus two passport photos; www.aaa.com).

trip twice to gain that advantage, reading this book before your trip accomplishes much the same thing. As a practical matter (to avoid redundancy), many cultural or historical details are explained for one sight and not repeated for another—even if they would increase your understanding and appreciation of that second sight.

Design an itinerary that enables you to visit the various sights at the best possible times. As you read this book, make note of festivals, seasonal closures (especially in Croatia), and the days sights are closed. For example, most museums throughout Eastern Europe close on Mondays. Hotels are most crowded on Fridays and Saturdays, especially in resort towns.

Saturdays in Europe are virtually weekdays with earlier closing hours. Sundays have the same pros and cons as they do for travelers in the US: Sightseeing attractions are generally open; shops, banks, and markets are closed; public-transportation options are fewer; and city traffic is light. Rowdy evenings are rare on Sundays.

To give yourself a little rootedness, minimize one-night stands. It's worth a long drive after dinner to be settled into a town for two nights. People renting private rooms are also more likely to give a good price to someone staying more than one night.

Be sure to mix intense and relaxed periods in your itinerary. Every trip (and every traveler) needs at least a few slack days. Pace yourself. Assume you will return.

Reread this book as you travel, and visit local tourist information offices. Upon arrival in a new town, lay the groundwork for a smooth departure; write down the schedule for the train, bus, or boat you'll take when you depart.

Plan ahead for banking, laundry, picnics, and Internet stops. Get online at Internet cafés or your hotel to research transportation connections, confirm events, check the weather, and get directions to your next hotel. Buy a phone card (or carry a mobile phone) and use it for reservations, re-confirmations, and double-checking hours.

Connect with the culture. Enjoy the hospitality of the local people. Slow down and ask questions—most locals are eager to point you toward their idea of the right direction. Keep a notepad in your pocket for organizing your thoughts. Wear your money belt, familiarize yourself with the currency, and learn a simple formula to quickly estimate rough prices in dollars. Those who expect to travel smart, do.

Attitude Adjustment

Americans sometimes approach Eastern Europe expecting grouchy service, crumbling communist infrastructure, and grimy, depressing landscapes. Many Westerners think that independent travel in the East is reckless—or even dangerous. But those who visit are pleasantly surprised at the beauty, friendliness, safety, and ease of travel here. Travel in Eastern Europe today is nearly as smooth as travel in the West. The natives speak excellent English and are forever scrambling to impress their guests. Any remaining rough edges simply add to the charm and carbonate the experience.

The East-West stuff still fascinates us, but to locals, the Soviet regime is old news, Cold War espionage is the stuff of movies, and oppressive monuments to Stalin are a distant memory. Nearly two decades after the fall of the Iron Curtain, Eastern Europeans (or, as they prefer to be called, *Central* Europeans) think about communism only when tourists bring it up. Freedom is a generation old, and—for better or for worse—McDonald's, MTV, and mobile phones are every bit as entrenched here as anywhere else in Europe. Five of the six countries in this book are already part of the European Union, the sixth (Croatia) is on track to join soon... and all of them are looking optimistically to the future.

EU Enlargement and the "New Europe"

On May 1, 2004, the Czech Republic, Slovakia, Poland, Hungary, Slovenia, and five other countries joined the European Union. Though EU membership—and investment—should ultimately benefit everybody, old members and new members have both had their doubts.

For example, new EU member Poland survived the communist era without having to collectivize its small family farms. But now that they've joined the EU, collectivization is mandatory. Traditional Czech cuisine is also in jeopardy. EU hygiene standards dictate that cooked food can't be served more than two hours old. My Czech friend complained, "This makes many of our best dishes illegal." Czech specialties, often simmered, taste better the next day.

A wise Czech grandmother put it best. In her lifetime, she had lived in a country ruled from Vienna (Hapsburgs), Berlin (Nazis), and Moscow (communists). She said, "Now that we're finally ruled from Prague, why would we want to turn our power over to Brussels?"

For their part, longstanding EU members have been skeptical about taking on more countries. Wealthy nations have already spent vast fortunes to improve the floundering economies of poorer member countries (such as Portugal, Greece, and Ireland). Most of the new members expect a similar financial-aid windfall. Also on the financial front, Westerners are fretting about an influx of cheap labor from the East (see "The Polish Plumber Syndrome," page 20). Finally, Western Europeans worry about their political power being diluted. When the 10 new nations joined the EU, the geographical center of Europe shifted from Brussels to Prague. In this "New Europe," Poland or the Czech Republic might emerge with a leading role. The East eagerly embraces the future, intent on distancing itself from its painful recent history, while the West tentatively clings to the past, when its power was at its peak (and French, not English, was the world's language).

As the "New Europe" takes shape, players on both sides will continue to define their new roles and seek compromise. So far, the general consensus in the East is that joining Europe was the right move. In a few years, the Hungarians, Poles, Czechs, and their neighbors will all be working harder than ever and enjoying more coins jangling in their pockets...and those coins will be euros.

PRACTICALITIES

Red Tape: You need a passport—but no visa or shots—to travel in the countries covered in this book. Your passport must be valid for at least six months beyond the time you leave. Pack a photocopy of your passport in your luggage in case the original is lost or stolen.

Borders: All of the countries in this book, except Croatia and Bosnia-Herzegovina, have officially joined the open-borders Schengen Agreement. That means that there are no border checks between any of these countries, or between them and Western European countries such as Germany, Austria, and Italy. You'll simply zip through the border without stopping.

Croatia and Bosnia-Herzegovina, however, have not yet entered the Schengen Agreement. Upon entering or exiting these countries, you'll still have to stop. But whether traveling by car, train, or bus, you'll find that border crossings are generally a non-event—flash your passport, maybe wait a few minutes, and move on. You'll be quickly checked as many as four times—by the customs and immigration officers of the country you're leaving and, sometimes after continuing ahead a few yards, the one you're entering.

Even as borders fade, when you change countries, you must still change telephone cards, postage stamps, and underpants.

Time: In Europe—and in this book—you'll use the 24-hour clock. It's the same through 12:00 noon, then keep going—13:00, 14:00, and so on. For anything after 12, subtract 12 and add p.m. (14:00 is 2:00 p.m.).

The countries listed in this book are generally six/nine hours ahead of the East/West Coasts of the US. The exceptions are the beginning and end of Daylight Saving Time: Europe "springs forward" the last Sunday in March (two weeks after most of North America), and "falls back" the last Sunday in October (one week before North America). For a handy online time converter, try www.timeanddate.com/worldclock.

Medical Help: If you get sick, do as the locals do and go to a pharmacist. They can help you with almost any ailment. If you need more in-depth attention, ask your hotel for the nearest hospital.

Watt's Up? Europe's electrical system is different from North America's in two ways: the shape of the plug (two round prongs) and the voltage of the current (220 volts instead of 110 volts). For your North American plug to work in Europe, you'll need an adapter, sold inexpensively at travel stores in the US. As for the voltage, most newer electronics or travel appliances (such as hair dryers, laptops, and battery chargers) automatically convert the voltage—if you see a range of voltages printed on the item or its plug (such as "110–220"), it'll work in Europe. Otherwise, you can buy a converter separately in the US (about $20).

Just the FAQs, Please

Whom do I call in case of emergency?
In all the countries in this book, dial 112 for medical or other emergencies (except Bosnia-Herzegovina, where it's 124). For police, dial 112 in Slovakia, Hungary, Poland, or Austria; dial 158 in the Czech Republic; dial 113 in Slovenia; dial 92 in Croatia; and dial 122 in Bosnia-Herzegovina.

What if my credit card is stolen?
Act immediately. See "Damage Control for Lost Cards," page 934, for instructions.

How do I make a phone call to, within, and from Eastern Europe?
For detailed dialing instructions, refer to page 944.

How can I get tourist information about my destination?
Each Eastern European country has its own national tourist information office (see page 929). You'll also find smaller branch offices in virtually every city and town covered in this book. Note that Tourist Information is abbreviated **TI** in this book.

What's the best way to pack?
Light. For a recommended packing list, see page 960.

Does Rick have other resources that could help me?
For more on Rick's guidebooks, public television series, public radio show, website, guided tours, travel bags, accessories, and railpasses, see page 930.

News: Americans keep in touch in Europe with the *International Herald Tribune* (published almost daily via satellite throughout Europe). Big cities (such as Prague and Budapest) also have weekly English-language newspapers. Every Tuesday, the European editions of *Time* and *Newsweek* hit the stands with articles of particular interest to travelers. Sports addicts can get their fix from *USA Today*. News in English will be sold only where there's enough demand: in big cities and tourist centers. Good websites include www.europeantimes.com and http://news.bbc.co.uk. Many hotels have CNN or BBC television channels available.

MONEY

Banking

Throughout Europe, cash machines (ATMs) are the standard way for travelers to get local currency. Bring plastic—credit and/or debit cards—along with several hundred dollars in hard cash as an emergency backup. It's smart to bring two cards, in case one gets demagnetized or eaten by a temperamental machine. Traveler's

Are there any updates to this guidebook?
Check www.ricksteves.com/update for changes to the most recent edition of this book.

Can you recommend any good books or movies for my trip?
For suggestions, see pages 933–934.

Do you have information on driving, train travel, and flights?
See pages 946–955 in the appendix.

How much do I tip?
Relatively little. For tips on tipping, see page 935.

Will I get a student or senior discount?
While discounts are not listed in this book, youths (under 18) and students (with International Student Identity Cards) often get discounts—but only by asking.

How can I get a VAT refund on major purchases?
See the details on page 936.

Do Eastern European countries use the metric system?
Yes. A liter is about a quart, four to a gallon. A kilometer is six-tenths of a mile. I figure kilometers to miles by cutting them in half and adding back 10 percent of the original (120 km: 60 + 12 = 72 miles, 300 km: 150 + 30 = 180 miles). For more metric conversions, see page 958.

checks are a waste of time (long waits at slow banks) and a waste of money (in fees).

Because most of these countries still have different currencies, you'll likely wind up with leftover cash from the previous country. Coins can't be exchanged once you leave the country, so try to spend them before you cross the border. But bills are easy to convert to the "new" country's currency. Regular banks have the best rates for changing currency or traveler's checks (except in Poland, where *kantors*, or money-changing kiosks, generally offer good rates—check several to find the best). Post offices and train stations usually change money if you can't get to a bank.

Cash from ATMs

To use a cash machine (called a *Bankomat* in all of these countries) to withdraw money from your account, you'll need a debit card (ideally with a Visa or MasterCard logo for maximum usability), plus a PIN code. Know your PIN code in numbers; there are only numbers—no letters—on European keypads.

Before you go, verify with your bank that your card will work

Exchange Rates

Most of the countries in this book still use their traditional currencies...for now. In 2008, only Slovenia and Austria officially use the euro currency. Slovakia hopes to switch to euros in January of 2009. And within a few years, the rest will also adopt it.

In countries that don't officially use the euro, many businesses (especially hotels) quote prices in euros anyway. For maximum accuracy, I generally list the prices they gave me— so you'll notice that throughout this book, some prices are in euros while others are in the local currency. Even if places list prices in euros, they typically prefer payment in the local currency.

Here are the rough exchange rates for each country. Because of currency fluctuations, and to make things easier to convert in your head, these are very loose estimates (for the latest, see www.oanda.com):

1 euro (€) = about $1.40 (used in Slovenia, Austria, and—starting in 2009—Slovakia). To roughly convert prices in euros to dollars, add 40 percent: €20 is about $28, €50 is about $70, and so on.

20 Czech crowns (koruna, Kč) = about $1. To estimate prices in dollars, multiply by five and drop the last two digits (e.g., 1,000 Kč = about $50).

25 Slovak crowns (koruna, Sk) = about $1. To convert into dollars, multiply by four and drop the last two digits (e.g., 750 Sk = about $30).

3 Polish złoty (zł, or PLN) = about $1. To roughly convert into dollars, divide by three (e.g., 85 zł = about $30).

200 Hungarian forints (Ft, or HUF) = about $1. To figure dollars, divide by two and drop the last two digits (e.g., 10,000 Ft = about $50).

5 Croatian kunas (kn, or HRK) = about $1. To estimate dollars, multiply by two and drop one zero (e.g., 70 kn = about $14).

So, that 20-zł Polish woodcarving is about $7, the 5,000-Ft Hungarian dinner is about $25, and the 2,000-Kč taxi ride through Prague is...uh-oh.

overseas, and alert them that you'll be making withdrawals in Europe; otherwise, the bank may not approve transactions if it perceives unusual spending patterns. Using your credit and debit card in Europe—whether for ATM withdrawals or purchases— can cost you additional "international transaction" fees (of up to 3 percent plus $5 per transaction), so it makes sense to ask your bank or credit-card company about these fees to avoid unpleasant surprises.

When using an ATM, try to take out large sums of money to reduce your per-transaction bank fees: Push the "other amount" button and ask for a higher amount (though this is not always possible, especially in Poland and Croatia). If the machine refuses your request, don't take it personally. Just try again and select a smaller amount.

Bank machines often dispense high-denomination bills, which can be difficult to break (especially at odd hours). My strategy: Request an odd amount of money from the ATM (such as 2,800 Kč instead of 3,000 Kč); or, if that doesn't work, go as soon as possible to a bank or a large store (such as a supermarket) to break the big bills.

Keep your cash safe. Thieves target tourists. Use a money belt—a pouch with a strap that you buckle around your waist like a belt, and wear under your clothes. A money belt provides peace of mind, allowing you to carry lots of cash safely. Don't waste time every few days tracking down a cash machine—withdraw a week's worth of money, stuff it in your money belt, and travel!

Credit and Debit Cards

For purchases, Visa and MasterCard are more commonly accepted than American Express. Just like at home, credit or debit cards work easily at larger hotels, shops, and restaurants (though smaller businesses prefer payment in local currency). Note that some receipts show your credit-card number; don't toss these thoughtlessly.

SIGHTSEEING

Eastern Europe's dusty museums don't quite rank with the Louvre or the Prado. The best attractions here are new, modern museums that chronicle the communist regime and celebrate its demise (such as Budapest's House of Terror and Statue Park, and Gdańsk's "Roads to Freedom" exhibit). But some of the old-fashioned art and history museums are surprisingly good. Generally, you'll follow a confusing, one-way tour route through a maze of rooms with squeaky parquet floors, monitored by grumpy grannies who listlessly point you in the right direction. While many museums label exhibits in English, most don't post full explanations; you'll have to buy a book or borrow laminated translations. In some cases, neither option is available. Audioguides are just catching on.

Sightseeing can be hard work. Use these tips to make your visits to Eastern Europe's finest sights meaningful, fun, fast, and painless.

Plan Ahead

Set up an itinerary that allows you to fit in all your must-see sights. Most sights keep stable hours, but in some areas (especially Poland and coastal Croatia), hours tend to fluctuate from year to year and season to season. If you have your heart set on a particular attraction, it's always smart to confirm its hours at the local TI.

Don't put off visiting a must-see sight—you never know when a place will close unexpectedly for a holiday, strike, or restoration. If you'll be visiting during a holiday, find out if a particular sight will be open by phoning ahead or visiting its website.

When possible, visit key museums first thing (when your energy is best) and save other activities for the afternoon. Hit the highlights first, then go back to other things if you have the stamina and time.

Depending on the sight, there are ways to avoid crowds. Try visiting very early, at lunch, or very late. Evening visits are usually peaceful, with fewer crowds.

At the Sight

All sights have rules, and if you know about these in advance, they're no big deal.

Some important sights have metal detectors or conduct bag searches that will slow your entry.

Some museums require you to check daypacks and coats. They'll be kept safely. If you have something you can't bear to part with, stash it in a pocket or purse. If you don't want to check a small backpack, carry it under your arm like a purse as you enter. From a guard's point of view, a backpack is generally a problem, while a purse is not.

Cameras are normally allowed, but not flashes or tripods (without special permission). Flashes damage oil paintings and distract others in the room. Even without a flash, a handheld camera will take a decent picture (or buy postcards or posters at the museum bookstore).

Many museums have special exhibits in addition to their permanent collection. Some exhibits are included in the entry price, while others come at an extra cost (which you may have to pay even if you don't want to see the exhibit).

Expect changes—paintings can be on tour, on loan, out sick, or shifted at the whim of the curator. To adapt, pick up any available free floor plans as you enter, and ask museum staff if you can't find a particular painting.

Some attractions have an on-site café or cafeteria (usually a good place to rest and have a snack or light meal). The WCs are generally free and clean.

Museums have bookstores selling postcards and souvenirs.

Before you leave, scan the postcards and thumb through the biggest guidebook (or skim its index) to be sure you haven't overlooked something that you'd like to see.

Most sights stop admitting people 30–60 minutes before closing time, and some rooms close early (generally about 30 minutes before the actual closing time). Guards usher people out, so don't save the best for last.

Every sight or museum offers more than what is covered in this book. Use the information in this book as an introduction—not the final word.

SLEEPING

I like to list accommodations that are friendly, clean, comfortable, professional-feeling, centrally located, English-speaking, and family-run. Obviously, a place meeting every criterion is rare, and all of my recommendations fall short of perfection—sometimes miserably. But I've listed the best values for each price category. My favorites are small, family-run hotels (which aren't as prevalent in Eastern Europe as in the West), and friendly local people who rent "hotelesque" private rooms without a reception desk. I've also thrown in a few hostels and other cheap options for budget travelers.

Prices in Eastern Europe are generally low compared to the West...except for beds. You can uncover some bargains, but I think it's worth paying a little more for comfort and a good location. You can find a central, comfortable double for $100 just about anywhere. Plan on spending $90 to $130 per double in big cities, and $60 to $90 in smaller towns.

While most hotels listed in this book cluster at about $80 to $120 per double, they range from $15 bunks to $500-plus splurges (maximum plumbing and more). Three or four people can save money by requesting one big room. Traveling alone can be expensive: A single room is often only 20 percent cheaper than a double.

Remember that some hotels quote their rates in euros, while others use the local currency. For the sake of accuracy, I generally list the prices they gave me.

If asked whether they have non-smoking rooms, most hotels in Eastern Europe will say yes. When pressed, they'll sheepishly admit, "Well, *all* of our rooms are non-smoking"...meaning they air them out after a smoker has stayed there. I've described hotels as "non-smoking" only if they have specially designated rooms for this purpose. Be specific and assertive if you need a strictly non-smoking room.

For environmental reasons, towels are often replaced in hotels only when you leave them on the floor. In private accommodations

Sleep Code

To help you sort easily through the listings, I've divided the rooms into three categories based on the price for a standard double room with bath:

$$$ **Higher Priced**
$$ **Moderately Priced**
$ **Lower Priced**

Prices listed in this book are per room, not per person. Hotels usually accept credit cards and include a buffet breakfast (unless otherwise noted); private accommodations rarely do either. Virtually all of my recommended accommodations are run by people who speak English; if they don't, I mention it in the listing.

When there is a range of prices in one category, that means the price fluctuates with the season; the prices and seasons are posted at or near the hotel desk. To give maximum information in a minimum of space, I use the following code to describe the accommodations.

  S = Single room (or price for one person in a double).
  D = Double or twin. Double beds are usually big enough for non-romantic couples.
  T = Triple (often a double bed with a single).
  Q = Quad (usually two double beds).
  b = Private bathroom with toilet and shower or tub.
  s = Private shower or tub only (the toilet is down the hall).

According to this code, a couple staying at a "Db-2,700 Kč, cash only" place in Prague would pay a total of 2,700 Czech crowns (about $135) for a double room with a private bathroom. Credit cards are not accepted, but you can assume they speak English.

and some cheap hotels, they aren't replaced at all, so hang them up to dry and reuse. The cord that dangles over the tub or shower in big Croatian and Slovenian resort hotels is not a clothesline—you pull it if you've fallen and can't get up.

Before accepting a room, confirm your understanding of the complete price (including, for example, extra fees for short stays). Pay your bill the evening before you leave to avoid the time-wasting crowd at the reception desk in the morning, especially if you need to rush off to catch your train. The only tip my recommended accommodations would like is a friendly, easygoing guest. And, as always, I appreciate feedback on your experiences.

Private Rooms

A cheap option in Eastern Europe (especially in Croatia) is a room in a private home (*sobe* in Slovenia and Croatia; the German word *Zimmer* works there, too, and throughout Eastern Europe). These places are inexpensive, at least as comfortable as a cheap hotel, and a good way to get some local insight. The boss changes the sheets, so people staying several nights are most desirable—and those who stay less than three nights are often charged a lot more (typically 20–50 percent). For more on Croatian *sobe*, see page 616.

Hostels

For $15 to $25 a night, travelers of any age can stay at a youth hostel. While official hostels admit non-members for an extra fee, it's best to join the club and buy a youth hostel card before you go (call Hostelling International at US tel. 202/783-6161 or order online at www.hiayh.org). To increase your options, consider the many independent hostels that don't require a membership card (some of them are at www.hostels.com).

At any hostel, cheap meals are sometimes available, and kitchen facilities are usually provided for do-it-yourselfers. Expect crowds in the summer, snoring, and lots of youth groups giggling and making rude noises while you try to sleep. While many hostels have a few doubles or family rooms available upon request for a little extra money, plan on gender-segregated dorms with 4- to 20-beds per room.

Hosteling works well for those traveling solo: prices are per bed, not per room, and you'll have an instant circle of friends. More and more hostels are getting their business acts together, taking credit card reservations over the phone and leaving sign-in forms on the door for each available room. If you're serious about traveling cheaply, get a card, carry your own sheets, and cook in the members' kitchens.

However, if you're used to hosteling elsewhere in Europe, you may be unpleasantly surprised by some Eastern European hostels. In general, the official IYHF hostels are inconveniently located and particularly institutional, while independent hostels are more loosely run and grungier than the European norm. I've listed the best options I could find for most destinations...sometimes with lots of caveats.

Making Reservations

Given the erratic accommodations values in Eastern Europe—and the quality of the gems I've found for this book—I'd recommend that you reserve your rooms in advance, particularly if you'll be traveling during peak season. Finding accommodations as you travel is possible, but you're more likely to wind up in a poorly

The Polish Plumber Syndrome

You'll likely enjoy a taste of Eastern European culture on your next trip...to London or Dublin. When Eastern European countries joined the European Union in 2004, three EU members immediately welcomed their new comrades to work without a visa: Great Britain, the Republic of Ireland, and Sweden. This sparked a wave of immigration into these wealthy counties, as Eastern Europeans flocked to the land of plenty to find work. Many ended up in the hospitality industry.

The result has been mixed in each region. The transplants are enjoying more money and an irreplaceable cross-cultural experience. But Eastern Europe has seen a somewhat alarming "brain drain," as many of its youngest and most westward-thinking residents have rushed away. And in Britain and Ireland, tourists are encountering desk clerks who don't quite speak fluent English.

The other Western European countries are contemplating opening their borders, but it's controversial. One popular symbol—invented by a right-wing French politician—was an invading "Polish plumber" who'd put French plumbers out of a job. The Polish tourist board countered by putting up clever ads in France featuring an alluring Polish hunk stroking a pipe wrench, saying, "I'm staying in Poland...come visit me!"

This is just one more step in the Europe-wide process of integration. Europeans in their twenties have been dubbed the "Erasmus Generation"—after the Erasmus Student Network, an EU organization that fosters study-abroad opportunities within Europe. As European twentysomethings have grown up accustomed to attending universities in other counties, it seems natural for them to identify as "Europeans" rather than as Spaniards, Slovenes, or Swedes. Multilingualism, international résumés, and cross-cultural marriages are the norm.

As with all aspects of the EU enlargement, the resettlement of Poles, Czechs, and Hungarians to the bogs of Ireland will most likely ultimately be good for everyone, despite a few growing pains. It's just one more step in the evolution of a truly united Europe.

located and/or overpriced hotel than if you plan ahead.

To make a reservation in advance, contact hotels directly by email, phone, or fax. Email is the clearest and most economical way to make a reservation. In addition, many hotel websites now have online reservation forms. To ensure you have all the information you need for your reservation, use the form in this book's appendix (also at www.ricksteves.com/reservation).

I've taken great pains to list telephone numbers with long-distance instructions (see "Telephones" in the appendix). Use the telephone and the convenient phone cards. Simple English is usually fine; most hotels listed are accustomed to English-only speakers. If phoning from the US, be mindful of time zones (see page 11).

When you request a room in writing for a certain time period, use the European style for writing dates: day/month/year. Hoteliers need to know your arrival and departure dates. For example, for a two-night stay in July I would request: "2 nights, arrive 16/07/09, depart 18/07/09." Consider in advance how long you'll stay; don't just assume you can extend your reservation for extra days once you arrive.

If you don't get a reply to your email or fax, it usually means the place is already fully booked. If you get a response that gives room availability and rates, it's not a confirmation. You must tell them that you want that room at the given rate.

Some travelers make reservations as they travel, calling hotels a few days before their visit. If you prefer the flexibility of traveling without any reservations at all, you'll have greater success snaring rooms if you arrive at your destination early in the day. When you anticipate crowds, call hotels around 9:00 on the day you plan to arrive, when the hotel clerk knows who'll be checking out and just which rooms will be available.

Whether you reserve a few hours or a few months in advance, most hoteliers and B&B hosts will trust you and hold a room until 16:00 (4:00 p.m.) without a deposit, though some will ask for a credit-card number. While you can email your credit-card information (I do), some people prefer to share that personal info via phone call, fax, or secure online reservation form (if the hotel has one on its website).

If you must cancel your reservation, it's courteous to do so with as much advance notice as possible (simply make a quick phone call or send an email). Hoteliers and B&B hosts lose money if they turn away customers while holding a room for someone who doesn't show up. Understandably, some hoteliers bill no-shows for one night. Hotels sometimes have strict cancellation policies (for example, you might lose a deposit if you cancel within two weeks of your reserved stay, or you might be billed for the entire visit if you leave early); ask about cancellation policies before you book. Again, don't let these people down—I promised you'd call and cancel as early as possible if for some reason you won't show up.

Always reconfirm your room reservation a few days in advance from the road. If you'll be arriving later than 16:00, let them know.

On the small chance that a hotel loses track of your reservation, bring along a hard copy of their emailed or faxed confirmation.

EATING

Eastern Europe offers good food for very little money—especially if you venture off the main tourist trail. This is affordable sightseeing for your palate.

Slavic cuisine has a reputation for being heavy and hearty, with lots of pork, potatoes and cabbage...which is true. But the food here is also delicious, and there's a lot more diversity from country to country than you might expect. Tune in to the regional and national specialties and customs (see each country's introduction in this book for details).

Ethnic restaurants provide a welcome break from Slavic fare. Seek out vegetarian, Italian, Indian, Chinese, and other similar places. They're especially good in big cities such as Prague, Budapest, or Kraków (I've listed a few tasty options). Hungarian cuisine is rich and spicy (think paprika), while Slovenia and Croatia have delectable seafood and lots of Italian-style dishes (pastas and pizzas).

When restaurant-hunting, choose a spot filled with locals, not the place with the big neon signs boasting, "We Speak English and Accept Credit Cards." Most restaurants tack a menu onto their door for browsers and have an English menu inside. If the place isn't full, you can usually just seat yourself (get a waiter's attention to be sure your preferred table is OK)—the American-style "hostess," with a carefully managed waiting list, isn't common here. Once seated, feel free to take your time. In fact, it might be difficult to dine in a hurry. Only a rude waiter will rush you. Good service is relaxed (slow to an American). Europeans generally tip less than Americans do; for tips on tipping, see page 935.

When you're in the mood for something halfway between a restaurant and a picnic meal, look for take-out food stands, bakeries (with sandwiches to go), grocers willing to make you a sandwich, or simple little eateries for fast and easy sit-down restaurant food.

The Czech Republic is beer country, with Europe's best and cheapest brew. Poland also has fine beer, but the national drink is *wódka*. Hungary, Slovenia, and Croatia are known for their wines. Each country has its own distinctive liqueur, most of them a variation on *slivovice* (SLEE-voh-veet-seh)—a plum brandy so highly valued that it's the de facto currency of the Carpathian Mountains (often used for bartering with farmers and other mountain folk). Menus list drink size by the tenth of a liter, or deciliter (dl).

How Was Your Trip?

Were your travels fun, smooth, and meaningful? If you'd like to share your tips, concerns, and discoveries, please fill out the survey at www.ricksteves.com/feedback. I value your feedback. Thanks in advance—it helps a lot.

TRAVELING AS A TEMPORARY LOCAL

We travel all the way to Europe to enjoy differences—to become temporary locals. You'll experience frustrations. Certain truths that we find "God-given" or "self-evident," such as cold beer, ice in drinks, bottomless cups of coffee, hot showers, cigarette smoke being irritating, and bigger being better, are suddenly not so true. One of the benefits of travel is the eye-opening realization that there are logical, civil, and even better alternatives. A willingness to go local ensures that you'll enjoy a full dose of local hospitality.

Fortunately for you, hospitality is a local forte. The friendliness of the Eastern Europeans seems to have only been enhanced during the communist era: Tangible resources were in short supply, so an open door and a genial conversation were all that people had to offer. For many Eastern Europeans, the chance to chat with an American is still a delightful novelty. Even so, some people—hardened by decades of being spied on by neighbors and standing in long lines to buy food for their family—seem brusque at first. In my experience, all it takes is a smile and a little effort to befriend these residents of the former "Evil Empire."

If there is a negative aspect to the image Europeans have of Americans, it's that we are big, loud, aggressive, impolite, rich, superficially friendly, and a bit naive.

Americans tend to be noisy in public places, such as restaurants and trains. My European friends place a high value on speaking quietly in these same places. Listen while on the bus or in a restaurant—the place can be packed, but the decibel level is low. Try to remember this nuance, and soften your speaking voice as a way of respecting their culture.

While Europeans look bemusedly at some of our Yankee excesses—and worriedly at others—they nearly always afford us individual travelers all the warmth we deserve.

While updating my guidebooks, I hear over and over again that my readers are considerate and fun to have as guests. Thank you for traveling as temporary locals who are sensitive to the culture. It's fun to follow you in my travels.

Judging from all the happy feedback I receive from travelers

Introduction

who have used this book, it's safe to assume you'll enjoy a great, affordable vacation—with the finesse of an independent, experienced traveler.

Thanks, and happy travels!

BACK DOOR TRAVEL PHILOSOPHY
From *Rick Steves' Europe Through the Back Door*

Travel is intensified living—maximum thrills per minute and one of the last great sources of legal adventure. Travel is freedom. It's recess, and we need it.

Experiencing the real Europe requires catching it by surprise, going casual..."Through the Back Door."

Affording travel is a matter of priorities. (Make do with the old car.) You can travel—simply, safely, and comfortably—nearly anywhere in Europe for $100 a day plus transportation costs. In many ways, spending more money only builds a thicker wall between you and what you came to see. Europe is a cultural carnival, and, time after time, you'll find that its best acts are free and the best seats are the cheap ones.

A tight budget forces you to travel close to the ground, meeting and communicating with the people, not relying on service with a purchased smile. Never sacrifice sleep, nutrition, safety, or cleanliness in the name of budget. Simply enjoy the local-style alternatives to expensive hotels and restaurants.

Extroverts have more fun. If your trip is low on magic moments, kick yourself and make things happen. If you don't enjoy a place, maybe you don't know enough about it. Seek the truth. Recognize tourist traps. Give a culture the benefit of your open mind. See things as different but not better or worse. Any culture has much to share.

Of course, travel, like the world, is a series of hills and valleys. Be fanatically positive and militantly optimistic. If something's not to your liking, change your liking. Travel is addictive. It can make you a happier American as well as a citizen of the world. Our Earth is home to six and a half billion equally important people. It's humbling to travel and find that people don't envy Americans. Europeans like us, but, with all due respect, they wouldn't trade passports.

Globe-trotting destroys ethnocentricity. It helps you understand and appreciate different cultures. Regrettably, there are forces in our society that want you dumbed down for their convenience. Don't let it happen. Thoughtful travel engages you with the world—more important than ever these days. Travel changes people. It broadens perspectives and teaches new ways to measure quality of life. Rather than fear the diversity on this planet, travelers celebrate it. Many travelers toss aside their hometown blinders. Their prized souvenirs are the strands of different cultures they decide to knit into their own character. The world is a cultural yarn shop, and Back Door travelers are weaving the ultimate tapestry. Join in!

CZECH REPUBLIC

CZECH REPUBLIC

Česká Republika

Despite their difficult 20th-century experience, the Czechs managed to preserve their history. In Czech towns and villages, you'll find a simple joy of life—a holdover from the days of the Renaissance. The deep spirituality of the Baroque era still shapes the national character. The magic of Prague, the beauty of Český Krumlov, and the lyrical quality of the countryside relieve the heaviness caused by the turmoil that passed through here. Get beyond Prague and explore the country's medieval towns. These rugged woods and hilltop castles will make you feel like you're walking through the garden of your childhood dreams.

Of the Czech Republic's three main regions—Bohemia, Moravia, and small Silesia—the best known is Bohemia. It has nothing to do with beatnik bohemians, but with the Celtic tribe of Boheia that inhabited the land before the coming of the Slavs. A long-time home of the Czechs, Bohemia is circled by a naturally fortifying ring of mountains and cut down the middle by the Vltava River, with Prague as its capital. The wine-growing region of Moravia (to the east) is more hilly, Slavic, and colorful.

Tourists often conjure up images of Bohemia when they think of the Czech Republic. But the country consists of more than rollicking beer halls and gently rolling landscapes. It's also about dreamy wine cellars and fertile Moravian plains, with the rugged Carpathian Mountains on the horizon. Politically and geologically, Bohemia and Moravia are two distinct regions. The soils and climates in which the hops and wine grapes grow are very different...and so are the two regions' mentalities. The boisterousness of the Czech polka contrasts with the melancholy of the Moravian ballad; the political viewpoint of the Prague power broker is at odds with the spirituality of the Moravian bard.

Only a tiny bit of Silesia—around the town of Opava—is part of the Czech Republic today; the rest of the region is in Poland and Germany. (The Hapsburgs lost traditionally Czech Silesia to Prussia in the 1740s, and 200 years later, Germany in turn ceded most of it to Poland.) People in Silesia speak a wide variety of dialects that mix Czech, German, and Polish. Perhaps due to their

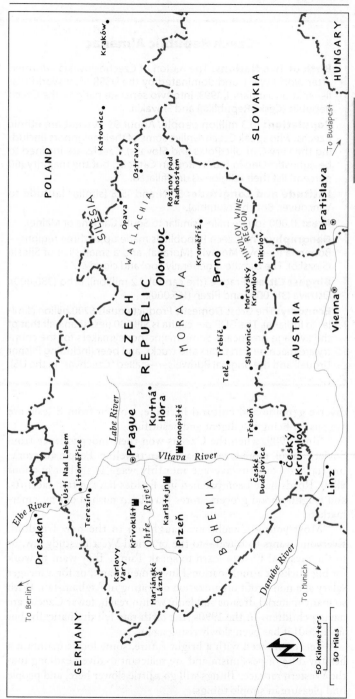

HUNGARY

Kraków

POLAND

Katowice

SLOVAKIA

Ostrava

To Budapest

Opava

SILESIA

Rožnov pod
Radhoštěm

WALLACHIA

Bratislava

Olomouc

Kroměříž

MIKULOV WINE
REGION

CZECH

Brno

Moravský
Krumlov

Mikulov

REPUBLIC

MORAVIA

Vienna

Telč

Třebíč

Slavonice

AUSTRIA

Labe River

Kutná
Hora

Prague

Konopiště

Třeboň

Ústí Nad Labem

Vltava River

Litoměřice

Český
Krumlov

Terezín

Karlštejn

České
Budějovice

Elbe River

Křivoklát

Ohře River

Linz

Dresden

BOHEMIA

Danube River

Karlovy
Vary

Plzeň

To Munich

To Berlin

Mariánské
Lázně

GERMANY

50 Kilometers

50 Miles

Czech Republic Almanac

Birth of Two Nations: The nation of Czechoslovakia—formed after World War I, and dominated by the USSR after World War II—split on January 1, 1993, into two separate nations: the Czech Republic (Česká Republika) and Slovakia.

Population: 10.3 million people. About 95 percent are ethnic Czechs, who speak Czech. Unlike some of their neighbors (including the very Catholic Poles and Slovaks), Czechs are inclined to be agnostic: One in four is Roman Catholic, but the majority (60 percent) list their religion as unaffiliated.

Latitude and Longitude: 50°N and 15°E (similar latitude to Vancouver, British Columbia).

Area: 31,000 square miles (similar to South Carolina or Maine).

Geography: The Czech Republic is made up of three regions—Bohemia (Čechy), Moravia (Morava), and a small slice of Silesia (Slezsko). The climate is generally cool and cloudy.

Biggest Cities: Prague (the capital, 1.2 million), Brno (380,000), Ostrava (318,000), and Plzeň (165,000).

Economy: The Gross Domestic Product equals $200 billion (similar to Indiana). The GDP per capita is $19,500 (less than half that of the average American). Some major moneymakers for the country are machine parts, cars and trucks, and beer (including Pilsner Urquell and the original Budweiser—called "Czechvar" in the US).

diverse genome and cultural heritage, women from Silesia are famous for being intelligent and beautiful.

Since 1989, when the Czechs won their independence from Soviet control, more Czechs have been traveling. People are working harder—but the average monthly wage is still only about $800. Roads have been patched up, facades have gotten facelifts, and neighborhood grocery stores have been pushed out by supermarkets.

Most young Czechs are caught up in the new freedom. Everyone wants to travel—to the practical West to study law, or to the mystical East to learn to speak Tamil. They want to work for big bucks at a multinational investment bank, or for a meager salary at a non-profit organization operating in Afghanistan. With so many material dreams suddenly within reach, fewer Czechs are having children. In the 1990s, the birth rate fell dramatically, but since 2001 it has been slowly rising again.

Yet, even faced with a bright future, some locals maintain a healthy dose of pessimism and are reluctant to dive headlong into the Western rat race. Things still go a little slower here, and people find pleasure in simple things.

More than a third of trade is with next-door-neighbor Germany. Privatization of formerly government-run industries goes on.

Currency: 20 Czech crowns (*koruna*, Kč) = about $1.

Government: Until 1989, Czechoslovakia was a communist state under Soviet control. Today, the Czech Republic is a member of the European Union (since 2004) and a vibrant democracy, with 68 percent of its eligible population voting in the 2006 election. Its parliament is made up of 200 representatives elected every four years and 81 senators elected for six years. No single political party dominates. The two big parties—the conservative Civic Democrats and the left-of-center Social Democrats—each won just a third of the vote in the 2006 election. The other three parties—the Communists, Christian Democrats, and the Greens—hold enough sway that the leader of the winning party typically heads a coalition government. The president (currently Václav Klaus, a conservative) is selected every five years by the legislators.

Flag: The Czech flag is red (bottom), white (top), and blue (a triangle along the hoist side).

The Average Czech: The average Czech has 1.2 kids (rising again, after the sharp decline that followed the end of communism), will live 76 years, and has one television in the house.

Czech children, adults, and grandparents delight in telling stories. In Czech fairy tales, there are no dwarfs and monsters. To experience the full absurdity and hilarity of Czech culture, you need a child's imagination and the understanding that the best fun comes from being able to laugh at yourself. Czech writers invented the robot, the pistol, and Black Light Theater (an absurd show of illusion, puppetry, mime, and modern dance—see page 109).

Literature and film are the most transparent window into the Czech soul. The most famous Czech literary figure is the title character of Jaroslav Hašek's *Good Soldier Švejk,* who frustrates the WWI Austro-Hungarian army he serves by cleverly playing dumb. Other well-known Czech writers include Václav Havel (playwright who went on to become Czechoslovakia's first post-communist president; he authored many essays and plays, including *The Garden Party*); Milan Kundera (author of *The Unbearable Lightness of Being,* set during the "Prague Spring" uprising); Bohumil Hrabal (stream-of-consciousness writer who captures the Czech spirit in *I Served the King of England* and *Too Loud a Solitude*); and Karel Čapek (novelist and playwright who created the robot in the play *R.U.R.*). But the most famous Czech writer of all is the existentialist great, Franz Kafka—a Prague Jew who wrote in German about a man turning into a giant cockroach *(The Metamorphosis)* and urbanites being pursued and persecuted for crimes they know nothing about *(The Trial).*

Ninety percent of the tourists who visit the Czech Republic see only Prague. But if you venture outside the capital, you'll enjoy traditional towns and villages, great prices, a friendly and gentle countryside dotted by nettles and wild poppies, and almost no Western tourists. Since the time of the Hapsburgs, fruit trees have lined the country roads for everyone to share. Take your pick.

Practicalities

Telephones: Dial 112 for emergencies, 158 for police. If an 0800 number doesn't work, replace the 0800 with 822. The basic, insertable Český Telecom phone card works well.

To call anywhere within the Czech Republic, dial the entire nine-digit number. To call the Czech Republic from another country, first dial the international access code (00 if calling from Europe or 011 from the US or Canada), then 420 (the Czech Republic's country code), then the nine-digit number. To call out of the Czech Republic, dial 00, the country code of the country you're calling (see chart in appendix), the area code if the country's phone system uses area codes (note that sometimes the initial zero is dropped depending on the country), and the local number.

Red Tape: You need a passport—but no visa or shots—to travel in the Czech Republic. Your passport must be valid for at least six months beyond the time you leave. Anyone planning to bring a rental car into the Czech Republic should check with their car-rental company first (see page 949). To drive on Czech highways, you'll need a toll sticker *(dálniční známka),* sold at borders, post offices, and gas stations (200 Kč/15 days, 300 Kč/2 months).

Transportation: If you have a Eurailpass, note that it doesn't cover the Czech Republic; you'll need to buy point-to-point train tickets for your travels to and from Prague (see page 948).

Czech History

The Czechs have always been at a crossroads of Europe—between the Slavic and Germanic worlds, between Catholicism and Protestantism, and between the Cold War East and West. As if having foreseen all of this, the mythical founder of Prague—the beautiful princess Libuše—named her city "Praha" (meaning "threshold" in Czech). Despite these strong external influences, the Czechs have retained their distinct culture...and a dark, ironic sense of humor to keep them laughing through it all.

Charles IV and the Middle Ages

Prague's castle put Bohemia on the map in the ninth century. About a century later, the region was incorporated into the German Holy

Roman Empire. Within a couple hundred years, Prague was one of Europe's largest and most highly cultured cities.

The 14th century was Prague's Golden Age, when Holy Roman Emperor Charles IV (1316–1378) ruled from here. Born to a Luxembourg nobleman and a Czech princess, Charles IV was a

dynamic man on the cusp of the Renaissance. He spoke five languages, counted Petrarch as a friend, imported French architects to make Prague a grand capital, founded the first university north of the Alps, and invigorated the Czech national spirit. (He popularized the legend of the good king Wenceslas to give his people a near mythical, King Arthur–type cultural standard-bearer.) Much of Prague's history and architecture (including the famous Charles Bridge, Charles University, and St. Vitus Cathedral) can be traced to this man's rule. Under Charles IV, the Czech people gained esteem among Europeans.

Jan Hus and Religious Wars

Jan Hus (c. 1370–1415) was a local preacher and professor who got in trouble with the Vatican a hundred years before Martin Luther. Like Luther, Hus preached in the people's language rather than Latin. To add insult to injury, he complained about Church corruption. Tried for heresy and burned in 1415, Hus became both a religious and a national hero. While each age has defined Hus to its liking, the way he challenged authority while staying true to himself has long inspired and rallied the Czech people. (For more on Hus, see the sidebar on page 62).

Inspired by the reformist ideas of Jan Hus, the Czechs rebelled against both the Roman Catholic Church and German political control. This burst of independent thought led to a period of religious wars, and ultimately the loss of autonomy to Vienna. Ruled by the Hapsburgs of Austria, Prague stagnated—except during the rule of King Rudolf II (1552–1612), a Holy Roman Emperor. With Rudolf living in Prague, the city again emerged as a cultural and intellectual center. Astronomers Johannes Kepler, Tycho de Brahe, and other scientists flourished, and much of the inspiration for Prague's great art can be attributed to the king's patronage.

Not long after this period, the Czech people entered one of their darkest spells. The Thirty Years' War (1618–1648) began

Notable Czechs

St. Wenceslas (907–935): Bohemian duke who allied the Czechs with the Holy Roman Empire. He went on to become the Czech Republic's patron saint, and is memorialized as a "good king" in the Christmas carol. See page 80.

Jan Hus (c. 1370–1415): Proto-Protestant Reformer who was burned at the stake. See page 62.

John Amos Comenius (1592–1670): "Teacher of Nations" and Protestant exile (Jan Amos Komenský in Czech), whose ideas paved the way for modern education.

Antonín Dvořák (1841–1904): Inspired by a trip to America, he composed his *New World Symphony*.

Tomáš Garrigue Masaryk (1850–1937): Sociology professor, writer, politician, and spiritual reformer. Idolized during his lifetime as the "dearest father" of the Czechoslovak democracy, an idea he was almost single-handedly responsible for. See page 100.

Jára Cimrman (c. 1853–1914): Illustrious inventor, explorer, philosopher, and all-around genius. Despite being overwhelmingly voted the "Greatest Czech of All Time" in a recent nationwide poll, he was not awarded the title; for details on the controversy, see page 92.

Alfons Mucha (1860–1939): You might recognize his turn-of-the-century Art Nouveau posters of pretty girls entwined in vines. Visit his museum in Prague (see page 83) and marvel at his stained-glass window in St. Vitus Cathedral (page 103).

Franz Kafka (1883–1924): While working for a Prague insurance firm, he wrote (in German) *The Metamorphosis* (man awakes as a cockroach), *The Trial,* and other psychologically haunting stories and novels.

Milan Kundera (1929–): Wrote the novel *The Unbearable Lightness of Being* (which became a film), among others.

Václav Havel (1936–): The country's first post-Soviet president, who's also known as a playwright and philosopher.

Martina Navrátilová (1956–): Tennis star of the 1980s. For more on Czech sports, see page 37.

in Prague when Czech Protestant nobles, wanting religious and political autonomy, tossed two Catholic Hapsburg officials out of the window of the castle. (This was one of Prague's many defenestrations—a uniquely Czech solution to political discord, in which offending politicians are thrown out the window.) The Czech Estates Uprising lasted for two years, ending in a crushing defeat of the Czech army in the Battle of White Mountain (1620), which marked the end of Czech freedom. Twenty-seven leaders of the uprising were executed (today commemorated by crosses on Prague's Old Town Square—see page 65), most of the old Czech nobility was dispossessed, and Protestants had to leave the country or convert to Catholicism. Often called "the first world war" because it engulfed so many nations, the Thirty Years' War was particularly tough on Prague. During this period, its population dropped from 60,000 to 25,000. The result of this war was 300 years of Hapsburg rule from afar, as Prague became a German-speaking backwater of Vienna.

Czech Nationalist Revival

The end of Prague as a "German" city came gradually. As the Industrial Revolution attracted Czech farmers and peasants into the cities, the demographics of the Czech population centers began to shift. Between 1800 and 1900, though it remained part of the Hapsburg Empire, Prague went from being an essentially German town to a predominantly Czech one. As in the rest of Europe, the 19th century was a time of great nationalism, as the age of divine kings and ruling families came to a fitful end. The Czech spirit was stirred by the completion of Prague's St. Vitus Cathedral, the symphonies of Antonín Dvořák, and the operas of Bedřich Smetana performed in the new National Theatre.

After the Hapsburgs' Austro-Hungarian Empire suffered defeat in World War I, their vast holdings broke apart and became independent countries. Among these was a union of Bohemia, Moravia, and Slovakia, the brainchild of a clever politician named Tomáš Garrigue Masaryk (see page 100). The new nation, Czechoslovakia, was proclaimed in 1918, with Prague as its capital.

Troubled 20th Century

Independence lasted only 20 years. In the notorious Munich Agreement of September 1938—much to the dismay of the Czechs and Slovaks—Great Britain and France peacefully ceded to Hitler the so-called "Sudetenland" (a fringe around the edge of Bohemia, populated mainly by people of German descent). It wasn't long before Hitler seized the rest of Czechoslovakia...and the Holocaust began.

For centuries, Prague's cultural make-up consisted of a rich mix of Czech, German, and Jewish people—historically about evenly divided. But only 5 percent of the Jewish population survived the Holocaust. After World War II ended, the three million people of Germanic descent who lived in Czechoslovakia were pushed into Germany. This forced resettlement—which led to the deaths of untold numbers of Germans—was the idea, among others, of Czechoslovak President Edvard Beneš, who had been ruling from exile in London throughout the war (see page 142). As a result of both of these policies (the Holocaust and the expulsion of Germans), today's Czech Republic is largely homogenous—about 95 percent Czechs.

Although Prague escaped the bombs of World War II, it went directly from the Nazi frying pan into the communist fire. A local uprising freed the city from the Nazis on May 8, 1945, but the Soviets "liberated" them on May 9.

The early communist chapter (1948–1968) was a mixture of misguided zeal, Stalinist repressions, and attempts to wed social-ism with democracy. The "Prague Spring" period—initiated by a young generation of reform-minded communists in 1968—came to an abrupt halt because of Soviet tanks.

The charismatic leader, Alexander Dubček, was exiled (and made a forest ranger in the backwoods), and the years following the unsuccessful revolt were particularly disheartening. In the late 1980s, the communists began constructing Prague's huge Žižkov TV tower (now the city's tallest structure)—not only to broadcast Czech TV transmissions, but also to jam Western signals. The Metro, built around the same time, was intended for mass transit, but was also designed to be a giant fallout shelter for protection against capitalist bombs.

But the Soviet empire crumbled. Czechoslovakia regained its freedom in the student- and artist-powered 1989 "Velvet Revolution" (so called because there were no casualties...or even broken windows). Václav Havel, a writer who had been imprisoned by the communist regime, became Czechoslovakia's first post-communist president. In 1993, the Czech and Slovak Republics agreed on the "Velvet Divorce" and became two separate countries (see sidebar on page 160).

The Czech Republic Today

President Havel ended his second (and, constitutionally, last) five-year term in 2003. While he's still admired by Czechs as a great thinker, writer, and fearless leader of the opposition movement during the communist days, many consider him less successful as a president. Some believe that the split of Czechoslovakia was partly caused by Havel's initial insensitivity to Slovak demands. The current president, Václav Klaus, was the pragmatic author of the economic reforms in the 1990s. Klaus' election in 2003 symbolized a change from revolutionary times, when philosophers became kings, to humdrum politics, when offices are gained by bargaining with the opposition (communist votes in the Parliament were the decisive factor in Klaus' election).

A major turning point occurred on May 1, 2004, when the Czech Republic joined the European Union. Today, while not

Czech Sports

Prague's top sports are soccer (that's "football" here) and hockey. Surprisingly, the Czechs are a world power in both.

The Czech **soccer** team reached the finals and semifinals of the 1996 and 2004 European Cups. In 2006, they made it to Round One of the World Cup, defeating the USA 3–0 before being eliminated with 0–2 defeats to Ghana and Italy. Within the Czech Republic, the two oldest and by far most successful soccer clubs are the bitter Prague rivals, Sparta and Slavia. Sparta's 1970s-era stadium is at Letná (behind the metronome ticking above the river). Slavia's brand-new stadium opens in March 2008 in Vršovice (tram #22 or #23 from the National Theatre).

The Czech national **hockey** team won four out of the last eight world championships. In 2006, the Czech team lost to Sweden in the final. Currently, more than 60 Czech players take the ice in America's NHL. Think Jaromír Jágr, one of the NHL's leading scorers. Sparta and Slavia also have hockey teams, but the rivalry is less jaded, as the teams from smaller towns are more than their equals. Slavia plays in the state-of-the-art Sazka Arena built for the 2004 world hockey championships in Prague (right at the Českomoravská Metro stop).

Back in the old days, ice hockey was the only battleground on which Czechoslovaks could seek revenge on their Russian oppressors. To this day, the hockey rink is where Czechs are proudest about their nationality. If you are in Prague in May during the hockey championships, join locals cheering their team in front of a giant screen on the Old Town Square (and other main squares around the country).

Ice hockey is also the most popular sport in Slovakia. To understand the friendly relationship between Czechs and Slovaks after their Velvet Divorce in 1989, just walk into any Czech or Slovak pub during the hockey championships. Unless the two teams are playing each other, all Czechs passionately support the Slovak team, and vice versa.

without its problems, the Czech Republic is enjoying a growing economy (up 6 percent in 2007) and a strong democracy, and Prague has emerged as one of the most popular tourist destinations in Europe.

Czech Food

Czech cuisine is heavy, hearty, and tasty. Expect lots of meat, potatoes, and cabbage. Still, there's more variety than you might expect. Ethnic restaurants provide a welcome break from Slavic fare. Seek out vegetarian, Italian, or Chinese (I've recommended several options).

After a sip of beer, ask for the *jídelní lístek* (menu). *Polévka* (soup) is the most essential part of a meal. The saying goes: "The soup fills you up, the dish plugs it up." Some of the thick soups for a cold day are *zelná* or *zelňačka* (cabbage), *čočková* (lentil), *fazolová* (bean), and *dršťková* (tripe—delicious if fresh, chewy as gum if not). The lighter soups are *hovězí* or *slepičí vývar s nudlemi* (beef or chicken broth with noodles), *pórková* (leek), and *květáková* (cauliflower). *Pečivo* (bread) is either delivered with the soup or you need to ask for it; it's always charged separately depending on how many *rohlíky* (rolls) or slices of *chleba* (yeast bread) you eat.

Main dishes are divided into *hotová jídla* (quick, ready-to-serve standard dishes, in some places available only during lunch hours, 11:30–14:30) and the more specialized *jídla na objednávku* or *minutky* (plates prepared when you order). Even the supposedly quick *hotová jídla* will take longer than fast food you're used to back home.

Hotová jídla (ready-to-serve dishes) come with set garnishes. The standard menu across the country includes *smažený řízek s bramborem* (fried pork fillet with potatoes), *svíčková na smetaně s knedlíkem* (beef tenderloin in cream sauce with dumplings), *vepřová s knedlíkem a se zelím* (pork with dumplings and cabbage), *pečená kachna s knedlíkem a se zelím* (roasted duck with dumplings and cabbage), *maďarský guláš s knedlíkem* (the Czech version of Hungarian goulash), and *pečené kuře s bramborem* (roasted chicken with potatoes). In this landlocked country, fish options are limited to *kapr* (carp) and *pstruh* (trout), prepared in a variety of ways and served with potatoes or fries. Vegetarians can go for the delicious *smažený sýr s bramborem* (fried cheese with potatoes) or default for *čočka s vejci* (lentils with fried egg). If you're spending the evening out with friends, have a beer and feast on the huge *vepřové koleno s hořčicí a křenem* (pork knuckle with mustard and horseradish sauce) with *chleba* (yeast bread).

The range of the *jídla na objednávku* (meals prepared to order) depends on the chef. You choose your starches and garnishes, which are charged separately.

Šopský salát, like a Greek salad, is usually the best salad option (a mix of tomatoes, cucumbers, peppers, onion, and feta cheese with vinegar and olive oil). The waiter will bring it with the main dish, unless you specify that you want it before.

For *moučník* (dessert), there are *palačinka* (crêpes served with fruit or jam), *lívance* (small pancakes with jam and curd), or *zmrzlinový pohár* (ice-cream sundae). Many restaurants will offer different sorts of *koláče* (pastries) and *štrůdl* (apple strudel), but it's much better to get these directly from a bakery.

No Czech meal is complete without a cup of strong *turecká*

Czech Beer

Czechs are among the world's most
enthusiastic beer *(pivo)* drinkers—each
adult drinks an average of 80 gal-
lons a year. The pub is a place to have
fun, complain, discuss art and politics,
talk hockey, and chat with locals and
visitors alike. The *pivo* that was drunk
in the country before the Industrial
Revolution was much thicker, providing
the main source of nourishment for the
peasant folk. Even today, it doesn't matter whether you're in a *restaurace* (restaurant), a *hostinec* (pub), or a *hospoda*
(bar)—a beer will land on your table
upon the slightest hint to the waiter,

and a new pint will automatically appear when the old glass
is almost empty. (You must tell the waiter *not* to bring more.)
Order beer from the tap (*točené* means "draft," *sudové pivo*
means "keg beer"). A *pivo* is large (.5 liter, or 17 oz); a *malé pivo*
is small (.3 liter, or 10 oz). Men invariably order the large size.
Pivo for lunch has me sightseeing for the rest of the day on
Czech knees.

The Czechs invented lager in nearby Plzeň ("Pilsen" in
German), and the result, Pilsner Urquell, is on tap in many
local pubs. But be sure to venture beyond this famous beer.

The Czechs produce plenty
of other good beers, includ-
ing Krušovice, Gambrinus,
Staropramen, and Kozel.
Budvar, from the town of
Budějovice ("Budweis" in
German), is popular with Anheuser-Busch's attorneys. The
Czech and the American breweries for years disputed the
"Budweiser" brand name. The solution: The original Czech
Budweiser is sold under its own name in Europe, China, and
Africa, while in America it markets itself as Czechvar.

The big degree symbol on bottles does not indicate the
percentage of alcohol content. Twelve degrees is about 4.2
percent alcohol, 10 degrees is about 3.5 percent alcohol, and 11
and 15 degrees are dark beers.

Each establishment has only one kind of beer on tap; to
try a particular brand, look for its sign outside. A typical pub
serves only one brand of 10-degree beer, one brand of 12-
degree beer, and one brand of dark beer. Czechs do not mix
beer with anything, and do not hop from pub to pub (in one
night, it is said, you must stay loyal to one lover and to one
beer). *Na zdraví* means "to your health" in Czech.

káva (Turkish coffee—finely ground coffee that only partly dissolves, leaving "mud" on the bottom, drunk without milk). Although espressos and instant coffees have made headway in the past few years, many Czechs regard them as a threat to their culture.

A good alternative to a beer is *minerálka* (mineral water). These healthy waters have a high mineral content. They're naturally carbonated because they come from the springs in the many Czech spas (Mattoni, the most common brand, is from Carlsbad). If you want plain water, ask for *voda bez bublinek* (water without bubbles). Tap water is generally not served. Water comes bottled and generally costs more than beer.

Bohemia is beer country (see sidebar, page 39), with Europe's best and cheapest brew. Locals also like the herb liquor *becherovka*. Moravians prefer wine and *slivovice* (SLEE-voh-veet-seh)—a plum brandy so highly valued that it's the de facto currency of the Carpathian Mountains (often used for bartering with farmers and other mountain folk). *Medovina* ("honey wine") is mead.

In bars and restaurants, you can go wild with memorable liqueurs, most of which cost about a dollar a shot. Experiment. *Fernet,* a bitter drink made from many herbs, is the leading Czech apéritif. *Absinthe,* made from wormwood and herbs, is a watered-down version of the hallucinogenic drink that's illegal in much of Europe. It's famous as the muse of many artists (including Henri de Toulouse-Lautrec in Paris more than a century ago). *Becherovka,* made of 13 herbs and 38 percent alcohol, was used to settle upset aristocratic tummies and as an aphrodisiac. This velvety drink remains popular today. *Becherovka* and tonic mixed together is nicknamed *beton* ("concrete"). If you drink three, you'll find out why.

You can stay in a pub as long as you want—no one will bring you an *účet* (bill) until you ask for it: *"Pane vrchní, zaplatím!"* ("Mr. Waiter, now I pay!").

Czech Language

Czech is a Slavic language closely related to its neighbors, Polish and Slovak. These days, English is commonly spoken, and you'll find the language barrier minimal. Among older people, German is a common second language.

Czech has a dizzying array of diacritical marks (little doo-hickeys over some letters that affect pronunciation). Most notably, some consonants can be topped with a *háček (č, š, ž, ň, ě)*. Here are some clues for Czech pronunciation:

j sounds like "y" as in "yarn"
c sounds like "ts" as in "cats"
č sounds like "ch" as in "chicken"

Czech Survival Phrases

English	Czech	Pronounced
Hello. (formal)	Dobrý den.	DOH-bree dehn
Hi. / Bye. (informal)	Ahoj.	AH-hoy
Do you speak English?	Mluvíte anglicky?	MLOO-vee-teh ANG-lits-kee
Yes. / No.	Ano. / Ne.	AH-no / neh
Please. / You're welcome. / Can I help you?	Prosím.	PROH-zeem
Thank you.	Děkuji.	DYACK-quee
I'm sorry. / Excuse me.	Promiňte.	PROH-meen-teh
Good.	Dobře.	DOHB-zhay
Goodbye.	Na shledanou.	nah SKLEH-dah-now
one / two	jeden / dva	YAY-dehn / dvah
three / four	tři / čtyři	tree / chuh-TEE-ree
five / six	pět / šest	pyeht / shehst
seven / eight	sedm / osm	SEH-dum / OH-sum
nine / ten	devět / deset	DEHV-yeht / DEH-seht
hundred	sto	stoh
thousand	tisíc	TYEE-seets
How much?	Kolik?	KOH-leek
local currency	koruna (Kč)	koh-ROO-nah
Where is...?	Kde je...?	gday yeh
...the toilet	...véce	vayt-SAY
men	muži	MOO-zhee
women	ženy	ZHAY-nee
water / coffee	voda / káva	VOH-dah / KAH-vah
beer / wine	pivo / víno	PEE-voh / VEE-noh
Cheers!	Na zdraví!	nah zdrah-VEE
The bill, please.	Účet, prosím.	OO-cheht PROH-zeem

š sounds like "sh" as in "shrimp"
ž sounds like "zh" as in "leisure"
ň sounds like "ny" as in "canyon"
ě sounds like "yeh" as in "yet"
ď sounds like the "dj" sound in "ledge"

Czech has one sound that occurs in no other language: ř (as in "Dvořák"), which sounds like a cross between a rolled "r" and "zh." It takes a lot of practice, but if you can master this sound, you'll impress the Czechs.

Vowels can be topped with an acute accent *(á, é, í, ó, ú, ý)*. Unlike in some languages (such as Spanish), this does *not* necessarily mean that the accented vowel gets the emphasis. Rather, it simply means that you linger on that vowel. For example, the word for "please" is *prosím*, with the emphasis on the first syllable but a long "i" sound at the end: PROH-seeeem.

Prague is flooded with tourists, most of whom don't bother to learn a single word of the local language. To ingratiate yourself to your hosts—not to mention, be a sensitive traveler—take some time to learn the Czech essentials.

PRAGUE

Praha

It's amazing what almost two decades of free-dom can do. Prague has always been historic. Now it's fun, too. No other place in Europe has become so popular so quickly. And for good reason: Prague—the only Central European capital to escape the bombs of the last century's wars—is one of Europe's best-preserved cities. It's filled with sumptuous Art Nouveau facades, offers tons of cheap Mozart and Vivaldi concerts, and brews the best beer in Europe. Beyond its architecture and traditional culture, it's an explosion of pent-up entrepreneurial energy jumping for joy after 40 years of communist rule. Its low prices can cause you to jump for joy, too. Travel in Prague is like travel in Western Europe...15 years ago and (except for hotels) for half the price.

Planning Your Time

Prague demands a minimum of two full days (with three nights, or two nights and a night train). From Budapest, Warsaw, or Kraków, it's a handy night train. From Munich, Berlin, and Vienna, Prague is a four- to six-hour train ride by day (you also have the option of a longer night train from Munich).

With two days in Prague, I'd spend a morning seeing the castle and a morning in the Jewish Quarter. Use your afternoons for loitering around the Old Town, Charles Bridge, and the Little Quarter, and split your nights between beer halls and live music. Keep in mind that Jewish Quarter sights close on Saturday. Some museums, mainly in the Old Town, are closed on Monday.

ORIENTATION

Locals call their town "Praha" (PRAH-hah). It's big, with 1.2 million people, but focus on its relatively compact old center during a quick visit. As you wander, take advantage of brown street signs directing you to tourist landmarks. Self-deprecating Czechs note that while the signs are designed to help tourists (locals never use them), they're only printed in Czech. Still—thanks to the little icons—the signs can help smart visitors who are sightseeing on foot.

The Vltava River divides the west side (Castle Quarter and Little Quarter) from the east side (New Town, Old Town, Jewish Quarter, Main Train Station, and most of the recommended hotels).

Prague addresses come with references to a general zone. Praha 1 is in the old center on either side of the river. Praha 2 is in the new city, southeast of Wenceslas Square. Praha 3 and higher indicate a location farther from the center. Virtually everything I list is in Praha 1 (unless noted otherwise).

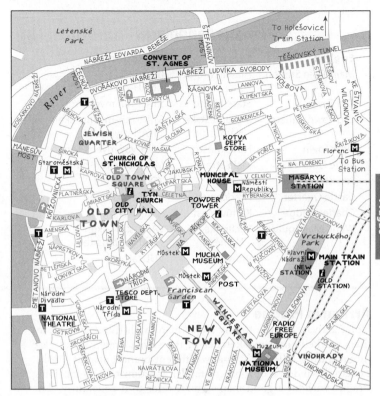

Tourist Information

TIs are at several key locations: **Old Town Square** (in the Old Town Hall, just to the left of the Astronomical Clock; Easter–Oct Mon–Fri 9:00–19:00, Sat–Sun 9:00–18:00; Nov–Easter Mon–Fri 9:00–18:00, Sat–Sun 9:00–17:00; tel. 224-482-018), **Main Train Station** (generally same hours as Old Town Square TI, but closed Sun), and the castle side of **Charles Bridge** (Easter–Oct daily 10:00–18:00, closed Nov–Easter). For general tourist information in English, dial 12444 (Mon–Fri 8:00–19:00) or check the TIs' useful website: www.prague-info.cz.

The TIs offer maps, phone cards, a useful transit guide, information on guided walks and bus tours, and bookings for private guides, concerts, hotel rooms, and rooms in private homes.

Several monthly event guides—all of them packed with ads—include the *Prague Guide* (29 Kč), *Prague This Month* (free), and *Heart of Europe* (free, summer only). The English-language weekly *Prague Post* newspaper is handy for entertainment listings and current events (60 Kč at newsstands).

Prague Landmarks

English	Czech	Pronounced
Main Train Station	Hlavní Nádraží	hlav-NEE NAH-drah-zhee
Old Town	Staré Město	STAH-reh myehs-toh
Old Town Square	Staroměstské Náměstí	STAR-roh-myehst-skeh NAH-myehs-tee
New Town	Nové Město	NOH-vay myehs-toh
Little Quarter	Malá Strana	MAH-lah strah-nah
Jewish Quarter	Josefov	YOO-zehf-fohf
Castle Quarter	Hradčany	HRAD-chah-nee
Charles Bridge	Karlův Most	KAR-loov most
Wenceslas Square	Václavské Náměstí	VAHT-slahf-skeh NAH-myehs-tee
Vltava River	Vltava	VUL-tah-vah

Arrival in Prague

Upon arrival, be sure to buy a city map, with trams and Metro lines marked and tiny sketches of the sights drawn in for ease in navigating (30–70 Kč, many different brands; sold at kiosks, exchange windows, or tobacco stands). It's a mistake to try doing Prague without a good map—you'll refer to it constantly. The *Kartografie Praha* city map, which shows all the tram lines and major landmarks, includes a castle diagram and a street index. It comes in two versions: 1:15,000 covers the city center, and 1:25,000 includes the whole city. The city center map is easier to navigate and sufficient unless you're staying in the suburbs.

By Train

Prague has two train stations. The Main Station (Hlavní Nádraží) serves all trains from Kraków, Frankfurt, Munich, and Salzburg; some trains from Budapest and Vienna; and most trains within the Czech Republic. The secondary station (Nádraží Holešovice) handles all trains from Berlin, most trains from Vienna and Budapest, and the high-speed SC Pendolino trains to the eastern Czech Republic.

Upon arrival, get money. The stations have ATMs (best rates) and exchange bureaus (rates are generally bad, but can vary—compare by asking at two windows what you'll get for $100, but keep in mind that many of the windows are run by the same company). Then buy your map and confirm your departure plans. Those arriving on an international train may be met at the tracks by room hustlers, trying to snare tourists for cheap rooms. These can be a good value.

Main Station (Hlavní Nádraží): This station's low-ceilinged hall contains a fascinating mix of travelers, kiosks, gamblers, loitering teenagers, and older riffraff. The creepy station ambience is the work of communist architects, who expanded a classy building to make it just big, painting it the compulsory dreary gray with reddish trim. An ATM is near the subway entrance. The station's baggage-storage counter is reportedly safer than the lockers.

At the Wasteels travel office, Jaroslav and Jaromír offer a helpful and friendly service. You can drop by here upon arrival to get a transit ticket without using the ATM (they take euro coins), and you can confirm and buy your outbound train tickets. They can help you figure out train connections, and they sell train tickets to anywhere in Europe—with domestic stopovers if you like—along with tickets for fast local trains and cheap phone cards (no commission; Mon–Fri 9:00–17:00 or later, Sat 9:00–16:00, closed Sun, tel. 972-241-954, www.wasteels.cz). You can even leave your bags here for a short time.

The information office for Czech Railways (downstairs on the left) is less helpful, and the ticket windows downstairs don't give schedule information. The windows marked *vnitrostátní* sell tickets within the Czech Republic.

The AVE office on the main floor books rooms in hotels and pensions, and sells taxi vouchers—for trips into town—at double the fair rate, but still better than you'd get directly from the cabbies themselves (daily 6:00–23:00; with your back to the tracks, walk down to the orange ceiling and past the "Meeting Point"—their office is in the left corner by the exit to the taxis; tel. 251-551-011, fax 251-555-156, www.avetravel.cz, ave@avetravel.cz).

If you're killing time at the station (or for a wistful glimpse of a more genteel age), go upstairs into the Art Nouveau hall. Here, under an elegant dome, you can sip coffee, enjoy music from the 1920s, watch boy prostitutes looking for work, and see new arrivals spilling into the city.

The station was originally named for Emperor Franz Josef. Later, it was renamed for President Woodrow Wilson (see the commemorative plaque in the main exit hall leading away from the tracks), because his promotion of self-determination led to the creation of the free state of Czechoslovakia in 1918. Under the communists (who weren't big fans of Wilson), it was bluntly renamed simply Hlavní Nádraží—literally, "Main Station."

Even though the Main Station is basically downtown, it can be a little tricky to get to your hotel. The biggest challenge is that the **taxi** drivers at the train station are a gang of no-neck mafia thugs who wait around to charge an arriving tourist five times the

Rip-Offs in Prague

Prague's new freedom comes with new scams. There's no particular risk of violent crime, but green, rich tourists do get taken by con artists. Simply be on guard, particularly when traveling on trains (thieves thrive on overnight trains), changing money (tellers with bad arithmetic and inexplicable pauses while counting back your change), dealing with taxis (see "By Taxi," page 56), paying in restaurants (see "Eating," page 122), and in seedy neighborhoods.

Anytime you pay for something, make a careful note of how much it costs, how much you're handing over, and how much you expect back. Count your change. Someone selling you a phone card marked 190 Kč might first tell you it's 790 Kč, hoping to pocket the difference. If you call his bluff, he'll pretend that it never happened.

Plainclothes policemen "looking for counterfeit money" are con artists. Don't show them any cash or your wallet. If you're threatened with an inexplicable fine by a "policeman," conductor, or other official, you can walk away, scare him away by saying you'll need a receipt (which real officials are legally required to provide), or ask a passerby if the fine is legit. On the other hand, do not ignore the plainclothes inspectors on the Metro and trams who have shown you their badges.

Pickpockets can be little children or adults dressed as professionals—or even as tourists. They target Western visitors. Many thieves drape jackets over their arms to disguise busy fingers.

regular rate. To get an honest cabbie, I'd walk a few blocks and hail one off the street; pay a premium for a voucher at the AVE office (see above); or call AAA Taxi (tel. 233-113-311) or City Taxi (tel. 257-257-257). A taxi should get you to your hotel for no more than 200 Kč (see "By Taxi," page 56).

A better option may be to take the **Metro.** It's dirt-cheap and easy, with very frequent departures. Once you're on the Metro, you'll wonder why you would ever bother with a taxi (inside station, look for the red M with two directions: Háje or Letňany). To get to hotels in the Old Town, catch a Háje-bound train to the Muzeum stop, then transfer to the green line (direction: Dejvická) and get off at either Můstek or Staroměstská; these stops straddle the Old Town.

Or, if your hotel is close enough, consider **walking** (Wenceslas Square, a downtown landmark, is about a 10-minute walk away—turn left out of the station and follow Wilsonova street to the huge National Museum).

Holešovice Station (Nádraží Holešovice): This station,

Thieves work the crowded and touristy places in teams. They use mobile phones to coordinate their bumps and grinds. Be careful if anyone creates a commotion at the door of a Metro or tram car (especially around the Národní Třída and Vodičkova tram stops, or on the made-for-tourists trams #22 and #23)—it's a smoke-screen for theft.

Car theft is also a big problem in Prague (many Western European car-rental companies don't allow their rentals to cross the Czech border). Never leave anything valuable in your car—not even in broad daylight on a busy street.

The sex clubs on Skořepka street, just south of Havelská Market, routinely rip off naive tourists and can be dangerous. They're filled mostly with young Russian women and German and Asian men. Lately this district has become the rage for British "stag" parties, for guys who are happy to fly cheaply to get to cheap beer and cheap thrills.

This all sounds intimidating. But Prague is safe. It has its share of petty thieves and con artists, but very little violent crime. Don't be scared—just be alert.

slightly farther from the center, is suburban mellow. The main hall has all the services of the Main Station in a more compact area. On the left are international and local ticket windows (open 24 hours), an information office, and an AVE office with last-minute accommodations (daily 12:00–20:00, tel. 972-224-660). On the right is a little-frequented café with Internet access (1 Kč/min, daily 8:00–19:30). Two ATMs are immediately outside the first glass doors, and the Metro is 50 yards to the right (follow signs toward *Vstup*, which means "entrance"; it's three stops to Hlavní Nádraží—the Main Station—or four stops to the city-center Muzeum stop). Taxis and trams are outside to the right (allow 200 Kč for a cab to the center). The airport bus (45 Kč, runs 2/hr) is outside to the left.

By Plane

Prague's modern, tidy, low-key **Ruzyně Airport,** located 12 miles (about 30 min) west of the city center, is as user-friendly as any airport in Western Europe or the US. The airport has ATMs (avoid the change desks); desks promoting their transportation services (such as city transit and shuttle buses); kiosks selling city maps and phone cards; and a tourist service with few printed materials. Airport info: tel. 220-113-314, operator tel. 220-111-111.

Getting to and from the airport is easy. Leaving the airport, you have four options:

Dirt Cheap: Take bus #119 to the Dejvická Metro station, or #100 to the Zličín Metro station (20 min), then take the Metro into the center (20 Kč, info desk in airport arrival hall).

Cheap: Take the Čedaz minibus shuttle to Náměstí Republiky, across from Kotva department store, on the edge of the Old Town (daily 5:30–21:30, 2/hr, pay 120 Kč directly to driver, info desk in arrival hall).

Moderate: Take a Čedaz minibus directly to your hotel, with a couple of stops likely en route (480 Kč for a group of up to four, tel. 220-114-286).

Expensive: Catch a taxi. Cabbies wait at the curb directly in front of the arrival hall. Airport taxi cabbies are honest but more expensive. Carefully confirm the complete price before getting in. It's a fixed rate of 600–700 Kč, with no meter.

Helpful Hints

Medical Help: A 24-hour pharmacy is at Palackého 5 (a block from Wenceslas Square, tel. 224-946-982). For standard assistance, there are two state hospitals in the center: the **General Hospital** (open daily 24 hours, moderate wait time, right above Karlovo Náměstí at U Nemocnice 2, Praha 2, use entry G, tel. 224-962-564); and the **Na Františku Hospital** (on the embankment next to Hotel InterContinental, Na Františku 1, go to the main entrance, for English assistance call Mr. Hacker between 8:00–14:00, tel. 222-801-278 or tel. 222-801-371—serious problems only). The reception staff may not speak English, but doctors do.

For better-than-standard assistance in English (including dental service), consider the top-quality **Hospital Na Homolce** (less than 1,000 Kč for an appointment, from 8:00–16:00 call 252-922-146, for after-hours emergencies call 257-211-111; bus #167 from Anděl Metro station, Roentgenova 2, Praha 5).

Internet Access: Internet cafés are well-advertised and scattered through the Old and New towns. Consider **Bohemia Bagel** near the Jewish Quarter (see page 128). **Káva Káva Káva Coffee,** on the boundary between the Old and New towns, is in the Platýz courtyard off Národní 37.

Bookstores: Prague has several enjoyable bookshops with English titles. **Anagram Bookshop,** in the Ungelt courtyard behind the Týn Church, sells books in English on a wide range of topics (Mon–Sat 10:00–20:00, Sun 10:00–19:00, Týn 4, tel. 224-895-737). **V Ráji,** next to Maisel Synagogue in the Jewish Quarter, is the flagship store of a small publishing house dedicated to books about Prague. They offer an assortment of photo publications, fairy tales, and maps (Maiselova 12, tel. 222-326-925). **Kiwi Map Store,** near Wenceslas Square, is one of Prague's best sources for maps (Mon–Fri 9:00–19:00, Sat 9:00–14:00, closed Sun, Jungmanova 23, tel. 224-948-455). For suggestions on specific maps to look for, see page 932.

Laundry: A full-service laundry near most of the recommended hotels is at Karolíny Světlé 11 (200 Kč/8-pound load, wash and dry in 2 hours, Mon–Fri 7:30–19:00, closed Sat–Sun, 200 yards from Charles Bridge on Old Town side). Or surf the Internet while your undies tumble-dry at Korunní 14 (160 Kč/load wash and dry, Internet access-2 Kč/min, daily 8:00–20:00, near Náměstí Míru Metro stop, Praha 2).

Local Help: Magic Praha is a tiny travel service run by hard-working Lída Jánská. A charming Jill-of-all-trades who takes her clients' needs seriously, she's particularly help-ful with accommodations and transfers throughout the Czech Republic, as well as private tours and side-trips to historic towns (tel. 235-325-170, mobile 604-207-225, www.magicpraha.cz, magicpraha@magicpraha.cz). Lída also speaks Spanish and Portuguese.

Car Rental: All of the biggies have offices in Prague (check each company's website, or ask at the TI). For a local alterna-tive, consider **Alimex,** which features a wide variety of new vehicles (tel. 233-350-001, toll-free tel. 800-150-170, www.alimexcr.cz). The cheapest model, a Škoda Fabia, is a great value (450 Kč/day with basic insurance, plus 238 Kč/day for full theft and damage insurance; additional fees: 500-Kč tax for airport pickup, 357 Kč for delivery to your hotel; discounts if you book online, smart to reserve up to a week ahead in peak season). Note that the cheapest cars sometimes have giant ads pasted on the side. They have branches at the air-port (daily 8:00–22:00) and near the Holešovice Station (daily 8:00–18:00).

Best Views: Enjoy the "Golden City of a Hundred Spires" dur-ing the early evening, when the light is warm and the colors are rich. Good viewpoints include the terrace at the Strahov Monastery (above the castle), the top of St. Vitus Cathedral (at the castle), the top of either tower on Charles Bridge, the Old Town Square clock tower (has an elevator), the Restaurant u Prince Terrace (see page 129), and the steps of the National Museum overlooking Wenceslas Square.

Prague

Getting Around Prague

You can walk nearly everywhere. But after you figure out the public transportation system, you'll realize that the Metro is slick, the trams fun, and the taxis quick and easy. For details, pick up the handy transit guide at the TI. City maps show the tram, bus, and Metro lines.

By Metro and Tram

Affordable and excellent public transit is perhaps the best legacy of the communist era (locals ride all month for 460 Kč). The three-line Metro system is handy and simple, but doesn't always get you right to the tourist sights (landmarks such as the Old Town Square and Prague Castle are several blocks from the nearest Metro stops). The trams rumble by every two or three minutes and take you just about anywhere.

Tickets: The trams and Metro work on the same tickets (but expect price increases):

- 20-minute basic ticket with limited transfer options—14 Kč *základní s omezenou přestupností*. With this ticket, no transfers are allowed on trams and buses, but on the Metro, you can go up to five stops with one transfer (not valid for night trams or night buses).
- 75-minute transfer ticket with unlimited transfers *(základní přestupní)*—20 Kč.
- 24-hour pass *(jízdenka na 24 hodin)*—80 Kč.
- 3-day pass *(jízdenka na 3 dny)*—220 Kč.
- 7-day pass *(jízdenka na 7 dní)*—280 Kč.

Buy tickets from your hotel, at newsstand kiosks, or from automated machines (select ticket price, then insert coins). For convenience, buy all the tickets that you think you'll need—but estimate conservatively. Remember, Prague is a great walking town, so unless you're commuting from a hotel far outside the center, you will likely find that individual tickets work best. Be sure to validate your ticket on the tram, bus, or Metro by sticking it in the machine (which stamps a time on it—watch locals and imitate). Inspectors routinely ambush ticketless riders (including tourists) and fine them 500 Kč on the spot.

Tips: Navigate by signs that list the end stations. When you come to your stop, push the yellow button if the doors don't automatically open. Although it seems that all Metro doors lead to the neighborhood of Výstup, that's simply the Czech word for "exit." When a tram pulls up to a stop, two different names are announced: first, the name of the stop you're currently at, followed by the name of the stop that's coming up next. Confused tourists, thinking they've heard their stop, are notorious for rushing off the tram one stop too soon. Trams run every 5–10 minutes in

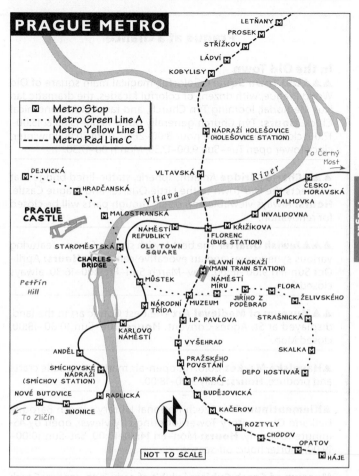

PRAGUE METRO

Metro Stop
···· Metro Green Line A
—— Metro Yellow Line B
- - - Metro Red Line C

LETŇANY
PROSEK
STŘÍŽKOV
LÁDVÍ
KOBYLISY
NÁDRAŽÍ HOLEŠOVICE (HOLEŠOVICE STATION)
To Černý Most
DEJVICKÁ
HRADČANSKÁ
VLTAVSKÁ
ČESKO-MORAVSKÁ
PALMOVKA
INVALIDOVNA
KŘIŽÍKOVA
FLORENC (BUS STATION)
HLAVNÍ NÁDRAŽÍ (MAIN TRAIN STATION)
NÁMĚSTÍ MÍRU
FLORA
JIŘÍHO Z PODĚBRAD
ŽELIVSKÉHO
STRAŠNICKÁ
SKALKA
DEPO HOSTIVAŘ
PRAGUE CASTLE
MALOSTRANSKÁ
NÁMĚSTÍ REPUBLIKY
STAROMĚSTSKÁ
OLD TOWN SQUARE
CHARLES BRIDGE
MŮSTEK
Petřín Hill
NÁRODNÍ TŘÍDA
MUZEUM
I.P. PAVLOVA
KARLOVO NÁMĚSTÍ
ANDĚL
VYŠEHRAD
PRAŽSKÉHO POVSTÁNÍ
PANKRÁC
SMÍCHOVSKÉ NÁDRAŽÍ (SMÍCHOV STATION)
BUDĚJOVICKÁ
NOVÉ BUTOVICE
RADLICKÁ
JINONICE
KAČEROV
To Zličín
ROZTYLY
CHODOV
OPATOV
HÁJE
NOT TO SCALE

Vltava
River

Prague

the daytime (a schedule is posted at each stop). The Metro closes at midnight, and the nighttime tram routes (identified with white numbers on blue backgrounds at tram stops) run all night at 30-minute intervals. There's more information and a complete route planner at www.dp-praha.cz.

Handy Trams: Trams #22 and #23 are practically made for sightseeing, using the same route to connect the New Town with the Castle Quarter (find the line marked on the color map at beginning of this book). The trams use some of the same stops as the Metro (making it easy to get to—or travel on from—the tram route). Of the many stops these trams make, the most convenient are two in the New Town (Národní Třída Metro stop, between the bottom of Wenceslas Square and the river; and Národní Divadlo, at the National Theatre), one stop in the Little Quarter

Prague at a Glance

In the Old Town

▲▲▲**Old Town Square** Colorful, magical main square of Old World Prague, with dozens of colorful facades, the dramatic Jan Hus Memorial, looming Týn Church, and fanciful Astronomical Clock. **Hours:** Týn Church generally open 10:00–13:00 & 15:00–17:00; clock strikes on the hour 8:00–21:00, until 20:00 in winter; clock tower open Tue–Sun 9:00–17:30, Mon 11:00–17:30.

▲▲▲**Charles Bridge** An atmospheric, statue-lined bridge that connects the Old Town to the Little Quarter and Prague Castle. **Hours:** Always viewable and open, though parts will be closed for renovation.

▲▲▲**Jewish Quarter** The best Jewish sight in Europe, featuring various synagogues and an evocative cemetery. **Hours:** April–Oct Sun–Fri 9:00–18:00, Nov–March Sun–Fri 9:00–16:30, always closed Sat.

▲▲**Museum of Medieval Art** The best Gothic art in the land, displayed at St. Agnes Convent. **Hours:** Tue–Sun 10:00–18:00, closed Mon.

▲**Havelská Market** Colorful open-air market that sells crafts and produce. **Hours:** Daily 9:00–18:00.

▲**Klementinum** The Czech National Library's lavish Baroque Hall and Observatory Tower (offering city views), open by 45-minute tour only. **Hours:** Mon–Fri 14:00–19:00, Sat–Sun 10:00–19:00, shorter hours off-season.

Museum of Czech Cubism Exhibit of early-20th-century Czech artistic school, in the Old Town's interesting Black Madonna House. **Hours:** Tue–Sun 10:00–18:00, closed Mon.

In the New Town

▲▲**Wenceslas Square** Lively boulevard at the heart of modern Prague. **Hours:** Always open.

▲▲**Mucha Museum** Likeable collection of Art Nouveau works by Czech artist Alfons Mucha. **Hours:** Daily 10:00–18:00.

▲▲**Municipal House** Pure Art Nouveau architecture, including Prague's largest concert hall and several eateries. **Hours:** Daily 10:00–18:00.

▲▲**Museum of Communism** The rise and fall of the regime, from start to Velvet finish. **Hours:** Daily 9:00–21:00.

Dancing House Frank Gehry–designed building on the Vltava riverbank, depicting a pair of Czech patriots...or Fred and Ginger. **Hours:** Always viewable.

In the Little Quarter
Church of St. Nicholas Jesuit centerpiece of Little Quarter Square, with ultimate High Baroque decor and a climbable bell tower. **Hours:** Church—daily 9:00–17:00; tower—April–Oct daily 10:00–18:00, closed Nov–March.

Petřín Hill Little Quarter hill with public art, a funicular, a replica of the Eiffel Tower, and the quirky museum of a nonexistent Czech hero. **Hours:** Funicular—daily 8:00–22:00; tower and museum—daily 10:00–22:00.

In the Castle Quarter
▲▲▲**St. Vitus Cathedral** The Czech Republic's most important church, featuring a climbable tower and a striking stained-glass window by Art Nouveau artist Alfons Mucha. **Hours:** Daily April–Oct 9:00–17:00, Nov–March 9:00–16:00, but closed Sunday mornings year-round for Mass.

▲▲**Prague Castle** Traditional seat of Czech rulers, with St. Vitus Cathedral (see above), Old Royal Palace, Basilica of St. George, shop-lined Golden Lane, and lots of crowds. **Hours:** Castle sights—daily April–Oct 9:00–17:00, Nov–March 9:00–16:00; castle grounds—daily 5:00–23:00.

▲**Strahov Monastery and Library** Baroque center of learning, with ornate reading rooms and old-fashioned science exhibits. **Hours:** Daily 9:00–12:00 & 13:00–17:00.

Loreta Church Baroque church that supposedly features the actual house of the Virgin Mary. **Hours:** Tue–Sun 9:00–12:15 & 13:00–16:30, closed Mon.

Toy and Barbie Museum Several centuries of toys, starring an army of Barbies. **Hours:** Daily 9:30–17:30.

Prague

(Malostranská Metro stop), and three stops above Prague Castle (Královský Letohrádek, Pražský Hrad, and Pohořelec; for details, see "Getting to Prague Castle—By Tram" on page 95).

By Taxi

Prague's taxis—notorious for hyperactive meters—are being tamed. New legislation is in place to curb crooked cabbies, and police will always take your side in an argument. Many cabbies are crooks who consider it a good day's work to take one sucker for a ride. You'll make things difficult for a dishonest cabbie by challenging an unfair fare.

While most hotel receptionists and guidebooks advise that you avoid taxis, I find Prague to be a great taxi town and use them routinely. With the local rate, they're cheap (read the rates on the door: drop charge starts at 36 Kč; per-kilometer charge—29 Kč; and waiting time per minute—5 Kč). The key is to be sure the cabbie turns on the meter at the #1 tariff (look for the word *sazba*, meaning "tariff," on the meter). Avoid cabs waiting at tourist attractions and train stations. To improve your odds of getting a fair meter rate—which starts only when you take off—call for a cab (or have your hotel or restaurant call one for you). AAA Taxi (tel. 233-113-311) and City Taxi (tel. 257-257-257) are the most likely to have English-speaking staff—and honest cabbies. I also find that hailing a passing taxi usually gets me a decent price.

If a cabbie surprises you at the end with an astronomical fare, simply pay 200 Kč, which should cover you for a long ride anywhere in the center. Then go into your hotel. On the miniscule chance that he follows you, the receptionist will back you up.

TOURS

Walking Tours—Many small companies offer walking tours of the Old Town, the castle, and more. For the latest, pick up the walking-tour fliers at the TI. Since guiding is a routine side-job for local university students, you'll generally get hardworking young guides at good prices. While I'd rather go with my own private guide (see below), public walking tours are cheaper, cover themes you might not otherwise consider, connect you with other English-speaking travelers, and allow for spontaneity. **Prague Walks** is as good as any (250–1,000 Kč, 1.5–6 hours; tours depart at 11:00, 14:00, and 19:00 from Astronomical Clock; tel. 222-322-309, mobile 608-339-099, www.praguewalks.com, pwalks@comp.cz). By request, they can organize a clever Good Morning Walk, which starts at 8:00 (April–Aug only), before the crowds hit.

Private Guides—In Prague, hiring a local guide is particularly smart—they're twice as helpful for half the price compared to guides in Western Europe. Because prices are usually per hour (not per person), small groups can inexpensively hire a guide for several days. Guides meet you wherever you like, and tailor the tour to your interests. Visit their websites in advance for details on various walks, airport transfers, countryside excursions, and other services offered, and then make arrangements by email.

Šárka Kačabová and her team of guides have a knack for making popular Czech culture easily comprehensible in a short time (400 Kč/hr for one or two people, 600 Kč/hr for three or more, mobile 777-225-205, www.prague-guide.info, saraguide @volny.cz). **Katka Svobodová,** an anthropologist and historian, is a hardworking guide who knows her stuff and speaks excellent English (400 Kč/hr, 3-hour minimum, mobile 603-181-300, www .praguewalker.com, katerina@praguewalker.com). **Jana Hronková** has a natural style—a welcome change from the more-strict professionalism of some of the busier guides (mobile 732-185-180, janahronkova@hotmail.com).

My readers have recommended **Renata Blažková,** who has a special interest in the history of Prague's Jewish Quarter (tel. 222-716-870, mobile 602-353-186, blazer@volny.cz) and **Martin Bělohradský,** whose main area of expertise lies in fine arts and architecture (mobile 723-414-565, martinb@uochb.cas.cz).

The **TI** also has plenty of private guides (rates for a 3-hour tour: 1,200 Kč/1 person, 1,400 Kč/2 people, 1,600 Kč/3 people, 2,000 Kč/4 people; desk at Old Town Square TI, arrange and pay in person at least 2 hours in advance, tel. 224-482-562, guides@pis .cz). For a listing of more private guides, see www.guide-prague.cz.

Jewish-Themed Tours: Sylvie Wittmann, a native Czech Jew, has developed a diverse group of knowledgeable guides who aspire to bring Jewish traditions back to life in Prague. Consider her three-hour walking tour of the Jewish Quarter (630 Kč includes entry to the synagogues of the Jewish Museum, May–Oct Sun–Fri at 10:30 and 14:00, Nov–April Sun–Fri at 10:30 only, no tours on Sat) or her six-hour trip to Terezín's Concentration Camp (1,150 Kč includes transportation and all entries, departs May–Oct daily at 10:00; mid-March–April and Nov–Dec no Mon, Wed, or Fri tours; Jan–mid-March by appointment only). All tours require prior reservation and meet in front of Hotel InterContinental at the end of Pařížská Street (tel. & fax 222-252-472, mobile 603-168-427, www.wittmann-tours.com, sylvie @wittmann-tours.com). Sylvie also offers trips to lesser-known destinations, as well as tours of the Czech Republic and Eastern Europe from a Jewish point of view.

Outside Prague: To get beyond sights listed in most guidebooks, call Thomas Zahn, who runs **Pathways Guided Travel.** Thomas, an American who married into the Czech Republic,

Prague

Prague's Four Towns

Until about 1800, Prague was actually four distinct towns with four town squares, all separated by fortified walls. Each town had a unique character, which came from the personality of the people who initially settled it. Today, much of Prague's charm survives in the distinct spirit of each of its towns.

Castle Quarter (Hradčany): Since the ninth century, when the first castle was built on the promontory overlooking a ford across the Vltava River, Castle Hill has been occupied by the ruling class. When Christianity arrived in the Czech lands, this hilltop—oriented along an east–west axis—proved a perfect spot for a church and, later, the cathedral (which, according to custom, must be built with the altar pointing east). Finally, the nobles built their representative palaces in proximity to the castle to compete with the Church for influence on the king. Even today, you feel like clip-clopping through this neighborhood in a fancy carriage. The Castle Quarter—which hosts the offices of the president and the foreign minister—has high art and grand buildings, little commerce, and few pubs.

Little Quarter (Malá Strana): This Baroque town of fine palaces and gardens rose from the ashes of a merchant settlement that burned down in the 1540s. The Czech and European nobility who settled here took pride in the grand design of their gardens. In the 1990s, after decades of decay, the gardens were carefully restored. While some are open only to the successors of the former nobility—including the Czech Parliament and the American, German, and Polish Embassies—many are open to visitors.

Old Town (Staré Město): Charles Bridge connects the Little Quarter with the Old Town. A boomtown since the 10th century, this area has long been the busy commercial quarter—filled with merchants, guilds, and supporters of Jan Hus (who wanted a Czech-style Catholicism). Trace the walls of this town in the modern road plan (the Powder Tower is a remnant of a wall system that completed a fortified ring, half provided by the river). The marshy area closest to the bend—least inhabitable and therefore allotted to the Jewish community—became the ghetto (today's Josefov, or Jewish Quarter).

New Town (Nové Město): The New Town rings the Old Town—cutting a swath from riverbank to riverbank—and is forti-

specializes in helping Americans of Czech descent find their roots. On short notice, Thomas might be able to get you to the village where your ancestors emigrated from. But if you're serious about locating your actual ancestral home and maybe even meeting with newly discovered relatives, you'll need to call Thomas three to four months in advance so you both can begin the research. Thomas also organizes and leads creative, affordable (typically one- to

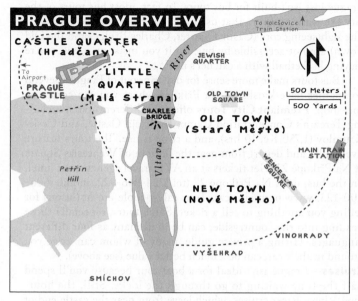

fied with Prague's outer wall. In the 14th century, the king created this town, tripling the size of what would become Prague. Wenceslas Square was once the horse market of this busy working-class district. Even today, the New Town is separated from the Old Town by a "moat" (the literal meaning of the street called Na Příkopě). As you cross bustling Na Příkopě, you leave the glass and souvenir shops behind, and you enter a town of malls and fancy shops that cater to locals and visitors alike.

The Royal Way: Cutting through the four towns—from St. Vitus Cathedral down to the Charles Bridge, and then from the bridge to the Powder Tower—is the Royal Way (Královská Cesta), the ancient path of coronation processions. Today, this city spine is marred by tacky trinket shops and jammed by tour groups. Use it for orientation only—try to avoid it if you want to see the real Prague.

two-day) excursions from Prague, during which you'll ideally learn how to navigate the off-the-beaten-track destinations in the Czech Republic by yourself. Thomas is raising his three children in the Czech Republic, and has good ideas about how to make Prague and the surrounding area fun for your kids. Explore Thomas' website for ways to connect with the Czech countryside (tel. 257-940-113, mobile 603-758-983, www.pathfinders.cz).

Bus Tours—While I generally recommend cheap big-bus orientation tours for an efficient, once-over-lightly look at great cities, Prague just isn't built for bus tours. In fact, most bus tours of the city are walking tours that use buses for pick-ups and transfers. The sightseeing core (Castle Quarter, Charles Bridge, and the Old Town) are not accessible by bus. So if you insist on a bus, you're playing basketball with a catcher's mitt.

Bus tours make more sense for day trips out of Prague. Several companies have kiosks on Na Příkopě where you can comparison-shop. **Premiant City Tours** offers 20 different tours, including Terezín's Concentration Camp, Karlštejn Castle, and Český Krumlov (1,750 Kč, 10 hrs), and a river cruise. The tours feature live guides and depart from near the bottom of Wenceslas Square at Na Příkopě 23. Get tickets at an AVE travel agency, your hotel, on the bus, or at Na Příkopě 23 (tel. 224-946-922, mobile 606-600-123, www.premiant.cz). Tour salespeople are notorious for telling you anything to sell a ticket. Some tours, especially those heading into the countryside, can be in as many as four different languages. Hiring a private guide, many of whom can drive you around in their car, can be a much better value (see above).

Cruises—Prague isn't ideal for a boat tour because you'll spend half the time waiting to go through the locks. Still, the hour-long Vltava River cruises, which leave from near the castle end of Charles Bridge about hourly, are scenic and relaxing, though not informative (100–150 Kč).

▲**Paddleboat Cruises**—Renting a rowboat or paddleboat on the island by the National Theatre is a better way to enjoy the river. You'll float at your own pace among the swans and watch local lovers cruise by in their own paddleboats (40–60 Kč/hr, bring photo ID for deposit).

SIGHTS

I've arranged these sights according to which of Prague's four towns you'll find them in (see sidebar): Old Town, New Town, Little Quarter, or Castle Quarter.

The Old Town (Staré Město)

From Prague's dramatic centerpiece, the Old Town Square, sightseeing options fan out in all directions. Get oriented on the square before venturing onward. You can find out about Jewish heritage in the Jewish Quarter (Josefov), a few blocks from the Old Town Square. Closer to the square, you'll find the quaint and historic Ungelt courtyard and Celetná street, which leads to the Museum of Czech Cubism and the landmark Estates Theatre. Nearby, Karlova street funnels all the tourists to the famous Charles Bridge. All

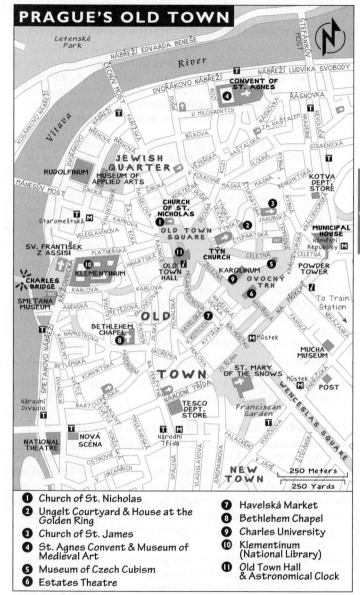

PRAGUE'S OLD TOWN

1. Church of St. Nicholas
2. Ungelt Courtyard & House at the Golden Ring
3. Church of St. James
4. St. Agnes Convent & Museum of Medieval Art
5. Museum of Czech Cubism
6. Estates Theatre
7. Havelská Market
8. Bethlehem Chapel
9. Charles University
10. Klementinum (National Library)
11. Old Town Hall & Astronomical Clock

Jan Hus and Martin Luther

The word *catholic* means "universal." The Roman Catholic Church—in many ways the administrative ghost of the Roman Empire—is the only organization to survive from ancient times. For more than a thousand years, it enforced its notion that the Vatican was the sole interpreter of God's word on earth, and the only legitimate way to be a Christian was as a Roman Catholic.

Jan Hus (c. 1369–1415) lived and preached a century before Martin Luther. Both were college professors, as well as priests. Both drew huge public crowds as they preached in their university chapels. Both condemned Church corruption and promoted a local religious autonomy. Both helped establish their national languages. (Hus gave the Czechs their unique accent marks so that the letters could fit the sounds.) And both got in big trouble.

While Hus was burned, Luther survived. Living after Gutenberg, Luther was able to spread his message more cheaply and effectively, thanks to the new printing press. Since Luther was high-profile and German, killing him would have caused major political complications. While Hus may have loosened Rome's grip on Christianity, Luther orchestrated the Reformation that finally broke it. Today, both are honored as national heroes as well as religious reformers.

of the sights described here are within a five-minute walk of the magnificent Old Town Square.

▲▲▲Old Town Square (Staroměstské Náměstí)

The focal point for most visits, Prague's Old Town Square is one of its top sights. This has been a market square since the 11th century. It became the nucleus of the Old Town (Staré Město) in the 13th century, when its Town Hall was built. Today, the old-time market stalls have been replaced by outdoor cafés and touristy horse buggies. But under this shallow surface, the square hides a magic power to evoke the history that has passed through here. The square's centerpiece is a memorial to Jan Hus.

• *Gawk your way to the square's centerpiece, the...*

Jan Hus Memorial: This monument, erected in 1915 (500 years after the Czech reformer's martyrdom by fire), symbolizes the long struggle for Czech freedom (see sidebar above). Walk around the memorial. Jan Hus stands tall between two groups of people: victorious Hussite patriots and Protestants defeated by the Hapsburgs in 1620. One of the patriots holds a chalice (cup); in the medieval Church, only priests could drink the wine at Communion. Since the Hussites fought for their right to take both

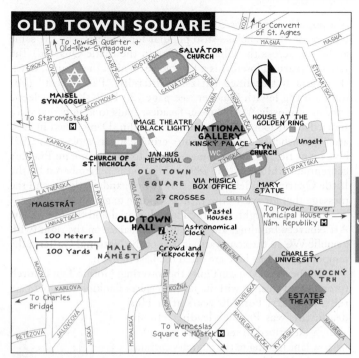

OLD TOWN SQUARE

To Convent of St. Agnes

KOŽÍ

MASNÁ

MASNÁ

ŠTUPARTSKÁ

To Jewish Quarter & Old-New Synagogue

ŠIROKÁ

MAISELOVA

PAŘÍŽSKÁ

KOSTEČNÁ

DUŠNÍ

SALVÁTOR CHURCH

SALVÁTORSKÁ

DLOUHÁ

TÝNSKÁ ULIČKA

MAISEL SYNAGOGUE

JÁCHYMOVA

To Staroměstská Ⓜ

KAPROVA

ZÁTECKÁ

CHURCH OF ST. NICHOLAS

IMAGE THEATRE (BLACK LIGHT)

JAN HUS MEMORIAL

NATIONAL GALLERY KINSKÝ PALACE

WC

HOUSE AT THE GOLDEN RING

Ungelt

TÝN CHURCH

ŠTUPARTSKÁ

OLD TOWN SQUARE

VIA MUSICA BOX OFFICE

MARY STATUE

PLATNÉŘSKÁ

U RADNICE

MIKULÁŠSKÁ

27 CROSSES

CELETNÁ

MAGISTRÁT

LINHARTSKÁ

OLD TOWN HALL

Pastel Houses

Astronomical Clock

To Powder Tower, Municipal House & Nám. Republiky Ⓜ

100 Meters

100 Yards

MALÉ NÁMĚSTÍ

Crowd and Pickpockets

ŽELEZNÁ

CHARLES UNIVERSITY

OVOCNÝ TRH

HUSOVA

KARLOVA

To Charles Bridge

JALOVCOVÁ

JILSKÁ

KOŽNÁ

PELLATRICHOVA

MICHALSKÁ

To Wenceslas Square & Můstek Ⓜ

HAVELSKÁ

HAVELSKÁ ULIČKA

ESTATES THEATRE

RYTÍŘSKÁ

HAVÍŘSKÁ

ŘETĚZOVÁ

Prague

the wine and the bread, the cup is their symbol. Hus looks proudly at the Týn Church (described below), which became the headquarters and leading church of his followers. A golden chalice once filled the now-empty niche under the gold bas-relief of the Virgin Mary on the church's facade. After the Hapsburg (and, therefore, Catholic) victory over the Czechs in 1620, the Hussite chalice was melted down and made into the image of Mary that shines from that spot high over the square today.

Behind the statue of Jan Hus, the bronze statue of a mother with her children represents the ultimate rebirth of the Czech nation. Because of his bold stance for independence in the way common people worship God, Hus was excommunicated and burned in Germany a century before the age of Martin Luther.

• Standing by Jan Hus, get oriented with a...

Spin-Tour: Whirl clockwise to get a look at Prague's diverse architectural styles: Gothic, Renaissance, Baroque, Rococo, and Art Nouveau. Start with the green domes of the Baroque **Church of St. Nicholas.** Originally Catholic, now Hussite, this church is a popular venue for concerts. (There's another green-domed Church of St. Nicholas—also popular for concerts—by the same architect, across the Charles Bridge in the Little Quarter.) The Jewish Quarter (Josefov) is a few blocks behind the church, down the uniquely tree-lined Pařížská—literally, "Paris street." (For more on the Jewish Quarter, see page 72.) Pařížská, an eclectic cancan of mostly Art Nouveau facades, leads to a bluff that once sported a 100-foot-tall stone statue of Stalin. Demolished in 1962 after Khrushchev exposed Stalin's crimes, it was replaced in 1991 by a giant ticking **metronome**—partly to commemorate Prague's centennial exhibition (the 1891 exhibition is remembered by the Little Quarter's Eiffel-esque Petřín Tower), and partly to send the message that for every power, there's a time to go.

Spin to the right, past the Hus Memorial and the fine yellow Art Nouveau building. The large Rococo palace on the right (with a public WC in the courtyard) is part of the **National Gallery;** the temporary exhibits here are often the best in town.

To the right, you can't miss the towering, Gothic **Týn Church** (pronounced "teen"), with its fanciful spires flanking the gold bas-relief of Mary. For 200 years after Hus' death, this was Prague's leading Hussite church (described in more detail below). A narrow lane leading to the church's entrance passes the **Via Musica,** the most convenient ticket office in town (see page 108). Behind the Týn Church is a gorgeously restored medieval courtyard called **Ungelt** (see page 67). The row of pastel houses in front of Týn Church has a mixture of Gothic, Renaissance, and Baroque facades. To the right of these buildings, shop-lined **Celetná street** leads to a square called Ovocný Trh (with the Estates Theatre and Museum of Czech Cubism—see page 68), and beyond that, to the Municipal House and Powder Tower in the New Town (see page 84 and page 85).

Continue spinning right—with more gloriously colorful architecture—until you reach the pointed 250-foot-tall spire marking the 14th-century **Old Town Hall** (which has the only elevator-accessible tower in town—see below). The chunk of pink building attached to the tower of the Neo-Gothic City Hall is the town's memorial to bad losers. The building once stretched all the way to the Church of St. Nicholas. Then, in the last days of World War II (May 1945), German tanks knocked off this landmark—to the joy of many Prague citizens who considered it an ugly, oversized 19th-century stain on the medieval square. Across the square from the Old Town Hall (opposite the Astronomical Clock), touristy

Melantrichova street leads directly to the New Town's Wenceslas Square (see page 78), passing the craft-packed Havelská Market (see page 69) along the way.

• *Now wander across the square, toward the Old Town Hall Tower. Embedded in the pavement at the base of the tower (near the snack stand), you'll see...*

Twenty-Seven Crosses: These white inlaid crosses mark the spot where 27 Protestant nobles, merchants, and intellectuals were beheaded in 1621 after rebelling against the Catholic Hapsburgs. The execution ended Czech independence for 300 years—and it's still one of the grimmest chapters in its history.

• *Looming behind the crosses is the Old Town Hall. Near the base of the tall tower, around the corner to the left, is Prague's famous...*

Astronomical Clock: Join the gang for the striking of the hour on the Town Hall clock, worth ▲▲ (daily 8:00–21:00, until 20:00 in winter). As you wait, see if you can figure out how the clock works.

With revolving disks, celestial symbols, and sweeping hands, this clock keeps several versions of time. Two outer rings show the hour: Bohemian time (gold Gothic numbers on black background, counts from sunset—find the zero, between 23 and 1...supposedly the time of tonight's sunset) and modern time (24 Roman numerals, XII at the top being noon, XII at the bottom being midnight). Five hundred years ago, everything revolved around the earth (the fixed middle background—with Prague marking the center, of course).

To indicate the times of sunrise and sunset, arcing lines and moving spheres combine with the big hand (a sweeping golden sun) and the little hand (a moon that spins to show various stages). Look for the orbits of the sun and moon as they rise through day (the blue zone) and night (the black zone).

If this seems complex to us, it must have been a marvel 500 years ago. Because the clock was heavily damaged during World War II, much of what you see today is a reconstruction. The circle below (added in the 19th century) shows the signs of the zodiac, scenes from the seasons of a rural peasant's life, and a ring of saints' names—one for each day of the year, with a marker showing today's special saint (at top).

Four statues flanking the clock represent the 15th-century outlook on time and prejudices. A Turk with a mandolin symbolizes hedonism, a Jewish moneylender is greed, and the figure staring into a mirror stands for vanity. All these worldly goals are vain in the face of Death, whose hourglass reminds us that our time is unavoidably running out.

At the top of the hour (don't blink—the show is pretty quick): First, Death tips his hourglass and pulls the cord, ringing the bell; then the windows open and the 12 apostles parade by, acknowledging the gang of onlookers; then the rooster crows; and then the hour is rung. The hour is often off because of daylight saving time (completely senseless to 15th-century clockmakers). At the top of the next hour, stand under the tower—protected by a line of banner-wielding concert salespeople in powdered wigs—and watch the tourists.

• *To the left of the clock is Prague's main TI, which has an information desk and sells tickets for a pair of activities...*

Clock Tour and Tower Climb: The main TI, to the left of the Astronomical Clock, contains an information desk and sells tickets for these two options: zipping up the Old Town Hall tower via elevator (60 Kč, Tue–Sun 9:00–17:30, Mon 11:00–17:30, fine views); or taking a 45-minute tour of the Old Town Hall, which includes a Gothic chapel and a close-up look at the inner guts of the Astronomical Clock (plus its statues of the 12 apostles; 50 Kč, 2/hr).

• *Now that you're oriented, you can use this delightful square as your launchpad for the rest of Prague's Old Town sights.*

▲Týn Church

While this church has a long history, it's most notable for its 200-year-stint as the leading church of the Hussite movement (generally open daily 10:00–13:00 & 15:00–17:00). It was Catholic before the Hussites, and returned to Catholicism after the Hussites were defeated. As if to insult Hus and his doctrine of simplicity, the church's once elegant and pure Gothic columns are now encrusted with noisy Baroque altars. Although Gothic, the church interior is uncharacteristically bright because of its Baroque clear windowpanes and whitewash. Read the church's story (posted in English, rear-left side) for a Catholic spin on the church's events—told with barely a mention of Hus. The fine 16th-century carved John the Baptist altar (right aisle) is worth a look.

Outside, on the side of the church facing Celetná street, find a statue of St. Mary resting on a temporary column against the wall. The Catholics are still waiting for a chance to reinstall St. Mary in the middle of the Old Town Square, where she stood for about 250 years until being torn down in 1918 by a mob of anti-Hapsburg (and therefore anti-Catholic) demonstrators.

Behind Týn Church

▲**Ungelt Courtyard (Týnský Dvůr)**—Ever since the Old Town was established, the Ungelt courtyard—located directly behind the Old Town Square's Týn Church—has served as a hostel for foreign merchants, much like a Turkish caravanserai. Here the merchants (usually German) would store their goods and pay taxes before setting up stalls on the Old Town Square. Notice that there are only two entrances into the complex, for the purpose of guaranteeing the safety of goods and merchants. After decades of disuse, the courtyard had fallen into such disrepair by the 1980s that authorities considered demolishing it. Marvelously restored a few years ago, the Ungelt courtyard is now the most pleasant area in the Old Town for an outdoor coffee (such as at Ebel Coffee House—see page 130), sorting through wooden crafts, and paging through English books (at Anagram Bookshop, described on page 50).

Church of St. James (Kostel Sv. Jakuba)—Perhaps the most beautiful church in the Old Town, the Church of St. James is just beyond Ungelt courtyard. The Minorite Order has occupied this church and the adjacent monastery almost as long as merchants have occupied Ungelt. A medieval city was a complex phenomenon: Side-by-side, there existed commerce, brothels, and a life of contemplation. (I guess it's not that much different from today.) Artistically, St. James (along with the Church of the Ascension of St. Mary at Strahov Monastery—see page 95) is a stunning example of how simple Gothic spaces could be transformed into sumptuous feasts of Baroque decoration. The blue light in the altar highlights one of Prague's most venerated treasures—the bejeweled Madonna Pietatis. Above the *pietà*, as if held aloft by hummingbird-like angels, is a painting of the martyrdom of St. James (free, daily 9:30–12:00 & 14:00–16:00).

As you leave, find the black and shriveled-up arm with clenched fingers (15 feet above and to the left of the door). According to legend, a thief attempted to rob the Madonna Pietatis from the altar, but his hand was frozen the moment he touched the statue. The monks had to cut off the arm in order for it to let go. The desiccated arm now hangs here as a warning—and the entire delightful story is posted nearby in English.

North of the Old Town Square, near the River

▲▲**Museum of Medieval Art**—The St. Agnes Convent houses the Museum of Medieval Art in Bohemia and Central Europe (1200–1550). The 14th century was Prague's Golden Age, and the religious art displayed in this Gothic space is a testament to the rich cultural life of the period. Each exquisite piece is well lit and thoughtfully described in English. Follow the arrows on a chronological sweep through Gothic art history. The various Madonnas and saints were gathered here from churches all over Central Europe (100 Kč, Tue–Sun 10:00–18:00, closed Mon, 2 blocks northeast of the Spanish Synagogue, along the river at Anežská 12).

Princess Agnes founded this Clarist convent in the 13th century as the first hospital in Prague. Agnes was canonized by Pope John Paul II (who loved to promote the Slavic faithful) in 1989. Since local celebrations of her sainthood on November 26 coincided with the Velvet Revolution (the peaceful overthrow of the Communist government in 1989), Agnes has since been regarded as the patron of the renascent Czech democracy (you'll see her on the 50-Kč bill).

On Celetná Street, toward the New Town

Celetná, a pedestrian-only street, is a convenient and relatively untouristy way to get from the Old Town Square to the New Town (specifically the Municipal House, page 84, and Powder Tower, page 85). Along the way, at the square called Ovocný Trh, you'll find these sights.

Museum of Czech Cubism—Cubism was a potent force in Prague in the early 20th century. The fascinating Museum of Czech Cubism in the Black Madonna House (Dům u Černé Matky Boží) offers the complete Cubist experience: Cubist architecture (stand back and see how masterfully it makes its statement while mixing with its neighbors...then get up close and study the details), a great café (upstairs), a ground-floor shop, and, of course, a museum. On three floors, you'll see paintings, furniture, graphics, and architectural drafts by Czech Cubists. This building is an example of what has long been considered the greatest virtue of Prague's architects: the ability to adapt their grandiose plans to the existing cityscape (museum entry-100 Kč, Tue–Sun 10:00–18:00, closed Mon, corner of Celetná and Ovocný Trh at Ovocný Trh 19, tel. 224-301-003). If you're not interested in touring the museum itself, consider a drink in the similarly decorated upstairs Grand Café Orient (see page 130).

Estates Theatre (Stavovské Divadlo)—Built by a nobleman in the 1770s, this Classicist building—gently opening its greenish walls onto Ovocný Trh—was the prime opera venue in Prague at a time when an Austrian prodigy was changing the course of music. Wolfgang Amadeus Mozart premiered *Don Giovanni* in this building, and personally directed many of his works here. Prague's theatergoers would whistle arias from Mozart's works on the streets the morning after they premiered. Today, part of the National Theatre group, the Estates Theatre, continues to produce *The Marriage of Figaro, Don Giovanni,* and occasionally *The Magic Flute.* For a more intimate encounter with Mozart, go to Villa Bertramka (see page 110).

On Melantrichova Street

▲**Havelská Market**—Skinny, tourist-clogged Melantrichova street leads directly from the Old Town Square's Astronomical Clock to the bottom of Wenceslas Square. But even along this most crowded of streets, a genuine bit of Prague remains: Havelská Market, offering crafts and produce. The open-air market was set up in the 13th century for the German trading community. Though heavy on souvenirs these days, the market still keeps hungry locals and vagabonds fed cheaply. It's ideal for a healthy snack; merchants are happy to sell a single vegetable or piece of fruit; and you'll find a washing fountain and plenty of inviting benches midway down the street. The market is also a fun place to browse for crafts. It's a homegrown, homemade kind of place; you'll often be dealing with the actual artist or farmer (market open daily 9:00–18:00, produce best on weekdays; more souvenirs, puppets, and toys on weekends). The many cafés and little eateries circling the market offer a fine and relaxing vantage point from which to view the action.

From Old Town Square to Charles Bridge

Karlova Street—Karlova street winds through medieval Prague from the Old Town Square to the Charles Bridge (it zigzags...just follow the crowds). This is a commercial gauntlet, and it's here that the touristy feeding frenzy of Prague is most ugly. Street signs keep you on track, and *Karlův most* signs point to the bridge. Obviously, you'll find few good values on this drag. Two favorite places providing a quick break from the crowds are just a few steps off Karlova on Husova street: **Cream and Dream Ice Cream** (Husova 12) and **U Zlatého Tygra,** a colorful pub that serves great, cheap beer in a classic and untouristy setting (Husova 17; see page 125).

▲**Klementinum**—The Czech Republic's massive National Library borders touristy Karlova street. The contrast could not be starker: Step out of the most souvenir-packed stretch of Eastern Europe, and enter into the meditative silence of Eastern Europe's biggest library. The Klementinum was built to house a college in the 1600s by the Jesuits, who had been invited to Prague by the Catholic Hapsburgs to offset the influence of the predominantly Protestant

Charles University nearby. The building was transformed into a library in the early 1700s, when the Jesuits took firm control of the university. Their books, together with the collections of several noble families (written in all possible languages...except Czech), form the nucleus of the National and University Library, which is now six million volumes strong. (Note that the Klementinum's Chapel of Mirrors is a popular venue for evening concerts.)

▲▲▲Charles Bridge (Karlův Most)

Among Prague's defining landmarks, this much-loved bridge offers one of the most pleasant and entertaining 500-plus-yard strolls in Europe. Enjoy the bridge at different times of day. The bridge is most memorable early—before the crowds—and late, during that photographers' "magic hour" when the sun is low in the sky.

At the Old Town end of the bridge, in a little square, is a statue of the bridge's namesake, **Charles IV.** This Holy Roman Emperor (*Karlo Quatro*—the guy on the 100-Kč bill) ruled his vast empire from Prague in the 14th century. He's holding a contract establishing Prague's university, the first in Northern Europe. This statue was erected in 1848 to celebrate the university's 500th birthday. The women around Charles' pedestal symbolize the university's four subjects: the arts, medicine, law, and theology. (From the corner by the busy street, many think the emperor's silhouette makes it appear as if he's peeing on the tourists. Which reminds me—public WCs are in the passageway opposite the statue.)

Bridges had been built on this spot before, as the remnant tower from Judith Bridge testifies (see the smaller of the two bridge towers at the far end). All were washed away by floods. After a major flood in 1342, Emperor Charles IV decided to commission an entirely new structure rather than repair the old one. Until the 19th century, this was Prague's only bridge crossing the river.

Charles Bridge has long fueled a local love of legends—including one tied to numbers. According to medieval record, the founding stone was laid in 1357, on the 9th of July at 5:31 (it's a palindrome: 135797531). It's said that Charles must have chosen that precise moment (which also coincides with a favorable positioning of the earth and Saturn) to lay the foundation stone of the bridge. Further "corroboration" of this remarkable hypothesis was provided by the discovery that the end of the bridge on the Old Town side aligns perfectly with the tomb of St. Vitus (in the cathedral across the river) and the setting sun at summer solstice.

Charles Bridge Reconstruction

Talked about for many years, financed by the city of Prague, and scheduled to last over a decade, the long-overdue reconstruction of the Charles Bridge finally began in the summer of 2007, days after people celebrated the bridge's 650-year anniversary.

Aware of the problem that closing the entire bridge would deal to the tourist industry, the city chose a more costly and technologically challenging "chessboard" strategy. With this plan, only a short partial section is closed at any time, allowing people to still use the bridge for crossing over. Moreover, to give everyone the opportunity to peek inside the centuries-old structure, and thus turn the bridge renovation into Prague's new attraction, the mayor requested (to the dismay of many archaeologists) that the construction site be at all times surrounded only by light, transparent fences.

The reconstruction is planned in two stages. In the first major stage—preceded by archaeological excavations and scheduled to be completed by 2010—gas lighting will return to the bridge, and the sewage system, insulation, and pavement will be installed. In the next stage, many of the deteriorated sandstone pieces will be replaced by new ones. In the past, builders often chose poor-quality sandstone, and this is precisely the mistake current workers want to avoid. To minimize impact on the nearby areas, most of the building material will be transported by river.

In the absence of accurate 14th-century records, this intriguing proposition has delighted the modern Czech imagination.

The magically aligned spot on the Old Town side is now occupied by the **bridge tower,** considered one of the finest Gothic

gates anywhere. Contemplate the fine sculpture on the Old Town side of the tower, showing the 14th-century hierarchy of kings, bishops, and angels. Climbing the tower rewards you with wonderful views over the bridge (40 Kč, daily 10:00–19:00, as late as 22:00 in summer).

In the 17th century, there were no statues on the bridge—only a **cross,** which you can still see as part of the third sculpture on the right. The gilded Hebrew inscription celebrating Christ was paid for by a fine imposed on a Jew for mocking the cross.

The bronze Baroque statue depicting **John of Nepomuk**—a saint of the Czech people—draws a crowd (look for the guy with the five golden stars around his head, near the Little Quarter end of the bridge on the right). John of Nepomuk was a 14th-century priest to whom the queen confessed all her sins. According to a 17th-century legend, the king wanted to know his wife's secrets, but Father John dutifully refused to tell. He was tortured and eventually killed by being tossed off the bridge. When he hit the water, five stars appeared. The shiny plaque at the base of the statue depicts the heave-ho. Devout pilgrims—from Mexico and Moravia

alike—touch the engraving to make a wish come true. You get only one chance in life for this wish, so think carefully before you touch the saint. Notice the date on the inscription: This oldest statue on the bridge was unveiled in 1683, on the supposed 300th anniversary of the martyr's death. You'll find statues like this one on squares and bridges throughout the country. The actual spot of the much-talked-about heave-ho is a few steps farther away from the castle—find the five points of the Orthodox cross between two statues on the bridge railing.

Most of the other Charles Bridge statues date from the late 1600s and early 1700s. Today, half of them are replicas—the originals are in city museums, out of the polluted air. At the far end of Charles Bridge, you reach the **Little Quarter**. For sights in this neighborhood, see page 88.

▲▲▲Jewish Quarter (Josefov)

Prague's Jewish Quarter neighborhood and its well-presented, profoundly moving museum tell the story of this region's Jews. For me, this is the most interesting collection of Jewish sights in Europe and well worth seeing. The Jewish Quarter is an easy walk from Old Town Square, up delightful Pařížská street (next to the green-domed Church of St. Nicholas).

As the Nazis decimated Jewish communities in the region, Prague's Jews were allowed to collect and archive their treasures here. Although the archivists were ultimately killed in concentration camps, their work survives. Seven sights scattered over a three-block area make up the tourists' Jewish Quarter. Six of the sights—all except the Old-New Synagogue—are called "The Museum" and are covered by one admission ticket. Your ticket comes with a map that locates the sights and lists admission appointments—the times you'll be let in if it's very busy. (Ignore

PRAGUE'S JEWISH QUARTER

the times unless it's really crowded.) You'll notice plenty of security (stepped up since 9/11).

Cost, Hours, Tours: To visit all seven sights, you'll pay 500 Kč (300 Kč for the six sights that make up the Museum, plus 200 Kč for the Old-New Synagogue—hours on page 77). Museum sights open April–Oct Sun–Fri 9:00–18:00; Nov–March Sun–Fri 9:00–16:30; closed year-round on Sat—the Jewish Sabbath—and on Jewish holidays. Each sight is thoroughly and thoughtfully described in English, making a guided tour unnecessary for most visitors. Occasional guided walks in English start at the Maisel Synagogue (50 Kč, 3 hours, tel. 222-317-191).

Cemetery: The Old Jewish Cemetery—with its tightly packed, topsy-turvy tombstones—is, for many, the most evocative part of the experience. Unfortunately, there's no ticket just to see the cemetery, and they've closed off most free viewpoints. If the 300-Kč museum ticket is too steep for you and you just want a free peek at the famous cemetery, climb the steps to the covered porch of the Ceremonial Hall (but don't rest your chin on the treacherous railing).

Planning Your Time: The most logical start (if you'll be seeing everything) is to buy your ticket at Pinkas Synagogue and visit this most powerful memorial of the museum complex first. From there, walk through the Old Jewish Cemetery, which leads to the Ceremonial Hall and Klaus Synagogue. After visiting those, head

Prague's Jewish Heritage

The Jewish people from the Holy Land (today's Israel) were dispersed by the Romans 2,000 years ago. Over the centuries, their culture survived in enclaves throughout the world: "The Torah was their sanctuary which no army could destroy." Jews first came to Prague in the 10th century. The Jewish Quarter's main intersection (Maiselova and Široká streets) was the meeting point of two medieval trade routes.

During the Crusades in the 12th century, the pope declared that Jews and Christians should not live together. Jews had to wear yellow badges, and their quarter was walled in. It became a ghetto. In the 16th and 17th centuries, Prague had one of the biggest ghettos in Europe, with 11,000 inhabitants. Within its six gates, Prague's Jewish Quarter was a gaggle of 200 wooden buildings. It was said that "Jews nested rather than dwelled."

The "outcasts" of Christianity relied mainly on profits from money lending (forbidden to Christians) and community solidarity to survive. While their money bought them protection (the kings highly taxed Jewish communities), it was often also a curse.

over to the Old-New Synagogue, have a coffee break (Pekařství bakery or Franz Kafka Café, both described on page 128, are nearby). Next, visit the museum-like Maisel Synagogue, and finally the Spanish Synagogue. (Note that Prague's fine Museum of Medieval Art, described on page 67, is only a few blocks from the Spanish Synagogue.)

Art Nouveau and the New Josefov: Going from sight to sight in the Jewish Quarter, you'll walk through perhaps Europe's finest Art Nouveau neighborhood. Make a point to enjoy the circa-1900 buildings with their marvelous trimmings and oh-wow entryways. While today's modern grid plan has replaced the higgledy-piggledy medieval streets of old, Široká ("Wide Street") was and remains the main street of the ghetto.

Pinkas Synagogue (Pinkasova Synagóga)—A site of Jewish worship for 400 years, this synagogue is a poignant memorial to the victims of the Nazis. The walls are covered with the handwritten names of 77,297 Czech Jews who were sent from here to the gas chambers at Auschwitz and other camps. (As you ponder this sad sight, you'll hear the somber reading of the names alter-

Throughout Europe, when times got tough and Christian debts to the Jewish community mounted, entire Jewish communities were evicted or killed.

In the 1780s, Emperor Josef II, motivated more by economic concerns than philanthropy, eased much of the discrimination against Jews. In 1848, the Jewish Quarter's walls were torn down, and the neighborhood—named Josefov in honor of the emperor who provided this small measure of tolerance—was incorporated as a district of Old Town.

In 1897, ramshackle Josefov was razed and replaced by a new modern town—the original 31 streets and 220 buildings became 10 streets and 83 buildings. This is what you'll see today: an attractive neighborhood of pretty, mostly Art Nouveau buildings, with a few surviving historic Jewish structures. By the 1930s, Prague's Jewish community was hugely successful, thanks largely to their ability to appreciate talent—a rare quality in the small Central European countries whose citizens, as the great Austrian novelist Robert Musil put it, "were equal in their unwillingness to let one another get ahead."

Of the 120,000 Jews living in the area in 1939, just 10,000 survived the Holocaust to see liberation in 1945. Today, only a few thousand Jews remain in Prague...but the legacy of their ancestors lives on.

nating with a cantor singing the Psalms.) Hometowns are in gold and family names are in red, followed in black by the individual's first name, birthday, and last date known to be alive. Notice that families generally perished together. Extermination camps are listed on the east wall. Climb eight steps into the women's gallery. When the communists moved in, they closed the synagogue and erased virtually everything. With freedom, in 1989, the Pinkas Synagogue was reopened and the names were rewritten (The names in poor condition near the ceiling are original.) Note that large tour groups may disturb this small memorial's compelling atmosphere between 10:00 and 12:00.

Upstairs is the **Terezín Children's Art Exhibit** (very well-described in English), displaying art drawn by Jewish children who were imprisoned at Terezín Concentration Camp and later perished. Terezín makes an emotionally moving day trip from Prague (get details from TI).

Old Jewish Cemetery (Starý Židovský Hřbitov)—From the Pinkas Synagogue, you enter one of the most wistful scenes in Europe—Prague's Old Jewish Cemetery. As you wander among

12,000 evocative tombstones, remember that from 1439 until 1787, this was the only burial ground allowed for the Jews of Prague.

Tombs were piled atop each other because of limited space, the sheer number of graves, and the Jewish belief that the body should not be moved once buried. With its many layers, the cemetery became a small plateau. And as things settled over time, the tombstones got crooked. The Jewish word for cemetery means "House of Life." Many Jews believe that death is the gateway into the next world. Pebbles on the tombstones are "flowers of the desert," reminiscent of the old days when rocks were placed upon the sand gravesite to keep the body covered. Wedged under some of the pebbles are scraps of paper that contain prayers.

Ceremonial Hall (Obřadní Síň)—Leaving the cemetery, you'll find a Neo-Romanesque mortuary house built in 1911 for the puri-

fication of the dead (on left). It's filled with a worthwhile exhibition, described in English, on Jewish medicine, death, and burial traditions. A series of crude but instructive paintings (hanging on walls throughout the house) show how the "burial brotherhood" took care of the ill and buried the dead. As all are equal before God, the rich and poor alike were buried in embroidered linen shrouds similar to the one you'll see on display.

Klaus Synagogue (Klauzová Synagóga)—This 17th-century synagogue (also near the cemetery exit) is the final wing of a museum devoted to Jewish religious practices. Exhibits on the ground floor explain the Jewish calendar of festivals. The central case displays a Torah (the first five books of the Bible) and solid silver pointers used when reading—necessary since the Torah is not to be touched. Upstairs is an exhibit on the rituals of Jewish life (circumcisions, bar and bat mitzvahs, weddings, kosher eating, and so on).

Old-New Synagogue (Staronová Synagóga)—For more than 700 years, this has been the most important synagogue and the central building in Josefov. Standing like a bomb-hardened bunker, it feels as though it has survived plenty of hard times. Stairs take you down to the street level of the 13th century and into the Gothic interior. Built in 1270, it's the oldest synagogue in Eastern

Europe (separate 200-Kč admission includes worthwhile 10-minute tour—ask about it, Sun–Thu 9:30–18:00, Fri 9:30–17:00, closed Sat). Snare an attendant who is likely to love showing visitors around. The steep admission keeps many away, but even if you decide not to pay, you can see the exterior and a bit of the interior. (Go ahead...pop in and crane your cheapskate neck.)

The lobby (down the stairs, where you show your ticket) has two fortified old lockers—in which the most heavily taxed com-

munity in medieval Prague stored its money in anticipation of the taxman's arrival. As 13th-century Jews were not allowed to build, the synagogue was erected by Christians (who also built the St. Agnes Convent nearby). The builders were good at four-ribbed vaulting, but since that resulted in a cross, it wouldn't work for a synagogue. Instead, they made the ceiling using clumsy five-ribbed vaulting.

The interior is pure 1300s. The Shrine of the Ark in front is the focus of worship. The holiest place in the synagogue, it holds the sacred scrolls of the Torah. The old rabbi's chair to the right remains empty (notice the thin black chain) out of respect. The red banner is a copy of the one that the Jewish community carried through town during medieval parades. Notice the yellow-pointed hat within the Star of David (on the banner), which the pope ordered all Jewish men to wear in 1215. Twelve is a popular number (e.g., windows), because it symbolizes the 12 tribes of Israel. The horizontal slit-like windows are an 18th-century addition, allowing women to view the male-only services.

Maisel Synagogue (Maiselova Synagóga)—This synagogue was built as a private place of worship for the Maisel family during the 16th-century Golden Age of Prague's Jews. Maisel, the financier of the Hapsburg king, had lots of money. The synagogue's interior is decorated Neo-Gothic. In World War II, it served as a ware-

house for the accumulated treasures of decimated Jewish communities that Hitler planned to use for his "Museum of the Extinct Jewish Race." The one-room exhibit shows a thousand years of Jewish history in Bohemia and Moravia. Well-explained in English, topics include the origin of the Star of David, Jewish mysticism, the history of discrimination, and the creation of

Prague's ghetto. Notice the eastern wall, with the Holy Ark containing the scroll of the Torah. The central case shows the silver ornamental Torah crowns that capped the scroll.

Spanish Synagogue (Španělská Synagóga)—Displays of Jewish history through the 18th, 19th, and tumultuous 20th centuries continue in this ornate, Moorish-style synagogue built in the 1800s. The upstairs is particularly intriguing, with circa-1900 photos of Josefov, an exhibit on the fascinating story of this museum and its relationship with the Nazi regime, and life in Terezín. The Winter Synagogue (also upstairs) shows a trove of silver worshipping aids gathered from countryside Jewish neighborhoods that were depopulated in the early 1940s, thus giving a sense of what the Nazis stockpiled.

The New Town (Nové Město)

Enough of pretty, medieval Prague—let's leap into the modern era. The New Town, with Wenceslas Square as its focal point, is today's urban Prague. This part of the city offers bustling boulevards and interesting neighborhoods. The New Town is the best place to view Prague's remarkable Art Nouveau art and architecture and to learn more about its recent communist past.

▲▲Wenceslas Square

More a broad boulevard than a square (until recently, trams rattled up and down its park-like median strip), this city landmark is named for King Wenceslas—featured both on the 20-Kč coin and the equestrian statue that stands at the top of the boulevard. Wenceslas Square (Václavské Náměstí) functions as a stage for modern Czech history: The creation of the Czechoslovak state was celebrated here in 1918; in 1968, the Soviets put down huge popular demonstrations here; and, in 1989, more than 300,000 Czechs and Slovaks converged here to claim their freedom.

❷ **Self-Guided Walk:** Let's take a stroll down Prague's urban centerpiece. Start near the Wenceslas statue at the top (Metro: Muzeum), and look to the building crowning the top of the square.

National Museum (Národní Muzeum): While its collection is dull, the building offers a powerful view, and the interior is richly decorated in the Czech Revival Neo-Renaissance style that heralded the 19th-century rebirth of the Czech nation. The light-colored patches in the museum's columns fill holes where Soviet bullets hit during the crackdown against the 1968 Prague Spring uprising. Masons—defying their communist bosses, who wanted the damage to be forgotten—showed their Czech spirit by intentionally mismatching their patches (80 Kč, daily May–Sept 10:00–18:00, Oct–April 9:00–17:00, halls of Czech fossils and animals).

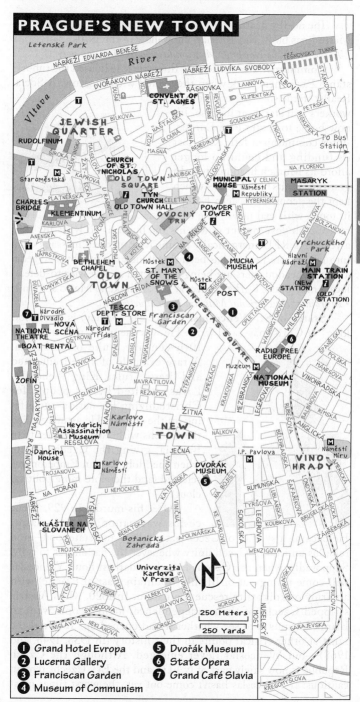

PRAGUE'S NEW TOWN

Letenské Park

NÁBŘEŽÍ EDVARDA BENEŠE

River

TĚČNOVSKY TUNNEL

STÁRKOVA

NÁBŘEŽÍ LUDVÍKA SVOBODY

DVOŘÁKOVO NÁBŘEŽÍ

RÁSNOVKA

LANNOVA

HOLBOVA

Vltava

DUŠNÍ

KRÁSNOVKA

REVOLUČNÍ

KLIMENTSKÁ

BISKUPSKÁ

CONVENT OF ST. AGNES

HRADEBNÍ

PETRSKÁ

JEWISH QUARTER

BÍLKOVA

KOZÍ

NA POŘÍČÍ

To Bus Station

RUDOLFINUM

NÁSTALSKÁ

DLOUHÁ

RYBNÁ

SOUKENICKÁ

ZLATNICKÁ

NA FLORENCI

Staroměstská

ŠIROKÁ

VALENTÍNSKÁ

MASNÁ

BENEDIKTSKÁ

MASARYK STATION

MAISELOVA

KAPROVA

CHURCH OF ST. NICHOLAS

JAKUBSKÁ

RYBNÁ

TEMPLOVÁ

MUNICIPAL HOUSE

V CELNICI

CHARLES BRIDGE

PLATNÉŘSKÁ

U RADNICE

OLD TOWN SQUARE

JILSKÁ

CELETNÁ

Náměstí Republiky

HYBERNSKÁ

KLEMENTINUM

KARLOVA

TÝN CHURCH

OLD TOWN HALL

OVOCNÝ TRH

POWDER TOWER

SENOVÁŽNÁ

OPLETALOVA

BOLZANOVA

ANENSKÁ

Vrchuckého Park

NÁPRSTKOVA

MICHALSKÁ

U PRÍKOPE

PANSKÁ

NEKÁZANKA

Hlavní Nádraží

MAIN TRAIN STATION (NEW STATION)

BETHLEHEM CHAPEL

KONVIKTSKÁ

PERLOVÁ

KOŽNÁ

Můstek

ST. MARY OF THE SNOWS

MUCHA MUSEUM

RŮŽOVÁ

OLD TOWN

DIVADELNÍ

NÁRODNÍ TŘÍDA

Můstek

POST

OPLETALOVA

(OLD STATION)

TESCO DEPT. STORE

Franciscan Garden

Národní Divadlo

NOVÁ SCÉNA

Národní Třída

4

3

1

WASHINGTONOVA

WILSONOVA

NATIONAL THEATRE

OSTROVNÍ

SPÁLENÁ

2

OPLETALOVA

ŠPANĚLSKÁ

BOAT RENTAL

OPATOVICKÁ

VLADISLAVOVA

JUNGMANNOVA

WENCESLAS SQUARE

POLSKÁ

ŽOFÍN

LAZARSKÁ

VE SMEČKÁCH

Muzeum

MÁNESOVA

MASARYKOVO NÁBŘEŽÍ

DITTRICHOVA

KARLOVO

MYSLÍKOVA

NAVRÁTILOVA

ŠTĚPÁNSKÁ

KRAKOVSKÁ

MEZIBRANSKÁ

6

RADIO FREE EUROPE

VINOHRADSKÁ

REZNICKÁ

NATIONAL MUSEUM

RUBEŠOVA

RÍMSKÁ

Karlovo Náměstí

ŽITNÁ

LEGEROVA

BALBÍNOVA

Heydrich Assassination Museum

RESSLOVA

NEW TOWN

HÁLKOVA

BĚLEHRADSKÁ

ANGLICKÁ

Dancing House

KARLOVO

JEČNÁ

I.P. Pavlova

Náměstí Míru

RAŠÍNOVO NÁBŘEŽÍ

TROJANOVA

Karlovo Náměstí

LIPOVÁ

I.P. Pavlova

VINO-HRADY

BELGICKÁ

NA MORÁNI

U NEMOCNICE

KATEŘINSKÁ

DVOŘÁK MUSEUM

RUMUNSKÁ

ONDRÍČKOVA

MÁNESLICKÁ

5

NA BOJIŠTI

TYRŠOVA

LUBLAŇSKÁ

ŠAFARÍKOVA

KOUBKOVA

BRUSELSKÁ

KLÁŠTER NA SLOVANECH

VYŠEHRADSKÁ

BENÁTSKÁ

VINIČNÁ

APOLINÁŘSKÁ

KE KARLOVU

LEGEROVA

SOKOLSKÁ

ZÁHŘEBSKÁ

TROJICKÁ

Botanická Zahrada

WENZIGOVA

PODSKALSKÁ

NA SLUPI

SVOBODOVA

Univerzita Karlova V Praze

STUDNIČKOVA

HORSKÁ

FRIČOVA

N

BĚLEHRADSKÁ

BOTIČSKÁ

ALBERTOV

HLAVOVA

NUSELSKÝ MOST

SARAJEVSKÁ

VNISLAVOVA

NEKLANOVA

250 Meters

250 Yards

KŘESOMYSLOVA

1 Grand Hotel Evropa   **5** Dvořák Museum

2 Lucerna Gallery   **6** State Opera

3 Franciscan Garden   **7** Grand Café Slavia

4 Museum of Communism

Prague

The nearby Metro stop (Muzeum) is the crossing point of two Metro lines built with Russian know-how in the 1970s.

• *To the left of the National Museum (as you face it) is an ugly...*

Communist-Era Building: This structure housed the rubber-stamp Parliament back when they voted with Moscow. A Social Realist statue showing triumphant workers still stands at its base. It's now home to Radio Free Europe. After communism fell, RFE lost its funding and could no longer afford its Munich headquarters. In gratitude for its broadcasts—which kept the people of Eastern Europe in touch with real news—the cur-

rent Czech government now rents the building to RFE for 1 Kč a year. (As RFE energetically beams its American message deep into Islam from here, it has been threatened recently by al-Qaeda, and new headquarters are being completed at an easier-to-defend locale near Franz Kafka's grave, at the Želivského Metro station.)

• *In front of the National Museum is the equestrian...*

Statue of St. Wenceslas: Wenceslas (Václav) is the "good king" of Christmas-carol fame. He was the wise and benevolent

10th-century Duke of Bohemia. A rare example of a well-educated and literate ruler, King Wenceslas I was credited by his people for Christianizing his nation and lifting up the culture. He astutely allied the Czechs with Saxony, rather than Bavaria, giving the Czechs a vote when the Holy Roman Emperor was selected (and therefore more political clout).

After his murder in 929, Wenceslas was canonized as a saint.

He became a symbol of Czech nationalism and statehood—and remains an icon of Czech unity whenever the nation has to rally. Supposedly, when the Czechs face their darkest hour, Wenceslas will come riding out of Blaník Mountain (east of Prague) with an army of knights to rescue the nation. In 1620, when Austria stripped Czechs of their independence, many people went to Blaník Mountain to see whether it had opened up. They did the same at other critical points in their history (in 1938, 1948, and 1968)—but Wenceslas never emerged. Although the Czech Republic is now safely part of NATO and the EU, Czechs remain cautious: If Wenceslas hasn't come out yet, the worst times must still lie ahead...

Study the statue. Wenceslas, on the horse, is surrounded by the four other Czech patron saints. Notice the focus on books. A small nation without great military power, the Czech Republic chose national heroes who enriched the culture by thinking, rather than fighting. This statue is a popular meeting point. Locals say, "I'll see you under the tail."

• *Now begin walking down the square. Thirty yards below the big horse is a small garden with a low-key...*

Memorial: This commemorates victims of communism, such as Jan Palach. In 1969, a group of patriots decided that an act of self-immolation would stoke the fires of independence. Jan Palach, a philosophy student who loved life—but wanted to live in freedom—set himself on fire on the steps of the National Museum for the cause of Czech independence. He died a few days later in a hospital ward. Czechs are keen on anniversaries, and huge demonstrations swept the city on the 20th anniversary of Palach's death. These protests led, 10 months later, to the overthrow of the Czech communist government in 1989.

This grand square is a gallery of modern architectural styles. As you wander downhill, notice the fun mix, all post-1850: Romantic Neo-Gothic, Neo-Renaissance, and Neo-Baroque from the 19th century; Art Nouveau from about 1900; ugly Functionalism from the mid-20th century (the "form follows function" and "ornamentation is a crime" answer to Art Nouveau); Stalin Gothic from the 1950s "communist epoch" (a good example is the Jalta building, halfway downhill on the right); and the glass-and-steel buildings of the 1970s.

• *Walk a couple of blocks downhill through the real people of Prague (not tourists) to* **Grand Hotel Evropa**, *with its hard-to-miss, dazzling Art Nouveau exterior and plush café interior full of tourists. Stop for a moment to ponder the events of...*

November of 1989: This huge square was filled every evening with more than 300,000 ecstatic Czechs and Slovaks who believed freedom was at hand. Assembled on the balcony of the building opposite Grand Hotel Evropa (look for the *Marks & Spencer* sign) were a priest, a rock star (famous for his unconventional style, which constantly unnerved the regime), Alexander Dubček (hero of the 1968 revolt), and Václav Havel (the charismatic playwright, newly released from prison, who was every freedom-loving

Czech's Nelson Mandela). Through a sound system provided by the rock star, Havel's voice boomed over the gathered masses, announcing the resignation of the Politburo and saying that the Republic of Czechoslovakia's freedom was imminent. Picture that cold November evening, with thousands of Czechs jingling their keychains in solidarity, chanting at the government, "It's time to go now!" (To quell this revolt, government tanks could have given it the Tiananmen Square treatment—which had spilled patriotic blood in China just six months earlier. Locals believe that the Soviet statesman, Mikhail Gorbachev, must have made a phone call recommending that blood not be shed.) For more on the events leading up to this climactic rally, see "Národní Třída and the Velvet Revolution" on page 87.

• *Immediately opposite Grand Hotel Evropa is the Lucerna Gallery (use entry marked* Palác Rokoko *and walk straight in).*

Lucerna Gallery: This grand mall retains some of its Art Deco glamour from the 1930s, with shops, theaters, a ballroom in the basement, and the fine Lucerna Café upstairs. You'll see a sculpture—called *Wenceslas Riding an Upside-Down Horse*—hanging like a swing from a glass dome. David Černý, who created the statue in 1999, is the Czech Republic's most original contemporary artist. Always aspiring to provoke controversy, Černý has painted a menacing Russian tank pink, attached crawling babies to the rocket-like Žižkov TV tower, defecated inside the National Gallery to protest the policies of its director, and sunk a shark-like Saddam Hussein inside an aquarium for a 2005 exhibition. Inside are also a **Ticketpro box office** (with all available tickets, daily 9:30–18:00), a lavish 1930s Prague cinema (under the upside-down horse, shows artsy films in Czech with English subtitles, or vice versa, 110 Kč).

Directly across busy Vodičkova street (with a handy tram stop) is the Světozor mall. Inside, you'll find the **World of Fruit Bar Světozor,** every local's favorite ice-cream joint. True to its name, the bar tops its ice cream with every variety of fruit. They sell cakes and milkshakes, too. Ask at the counter for an English menu.

• *Farther down the mall on the left is the entrance to the peaceful...*

Franciscan Garden (Františkánská Zahrada): Its white benches and spreading rosebushes are a universe away from the fast beat of the city, which throbs behind the buildings that surround the garden.

Back on Wenceslas Square, if you're in the mood for a mellow hippie teahouse, consider a break at **Dobrá Čajovna** ("Good Teahouse") near the bottom of the square (#14—see page 131). Or, if you'd like an old-time wine bar, pop into the plain **Šenk Vrbovec** (nearby at #10); it comes with a whiff of the communist days, embracing the faintest bits of genteel culture from an age when refinement was sacrificed for the good of the working class.

They serve traditional drinks, Czech keg wine, Moravian wines (listed on blackboard outside), *becherovka* (the 13-herb liqueur), and—only in autumn—*burčák* (this young wine tastes like grape juice turned halfway into wine).

The bottom of Wenceslas Square is called **Můstek,** which means "Bridge"; a bridge used to cross a moat here, allowing entrance into the Old Town (you can still see the original Old Town entrance down in the Metro station).

• *Running to the right from the bottom of Wenceslas Square is the street called...*

Na Příkopě: Meaning "On the Moat," this busy boulevard follows the line of the Old Town wall, leading to one of the wall's former gates, the Powder Tower. Along the way, it passes the Museum of Communism (see page 85) and a couple of Art Nouveau sights (see below). City tour buses (see page 60) leave from along this street, which offers plenty of shopping temptations (such as these malls: Slovanský Dům at Na Příkopě 22, and Černá Růže at Na Příkopě 12, next door to Moser, which has a crystal showroom upstairs).

Na Příkopě: Art Nouveau Prague

Stroll up Na Příkopě to take in two of Prague's best Art Nouveau sights. The first one is on the street called Panská (turn right up the first street you reach as you walk up Na Příkopě from Wenceslas Square); the second is two blocks farther up Na Příkopě, next to the big, Gothic Powder Tower.

▲▲**Mucha Museum**—This is one of Europe's most enjoyable little museums. I find the art of Alfons Mucha (MOO-kah, 1860–1939) insistently likeable. See the crucifixion scene he painted as an eight-year-old boy. Read how this popular Czech artist's posters, filled with Czech symbols and expressing his people's ideals and aspirations, were patriotic banners that aroused the national spirit. And check out the photographs of his models. With the help of an abundant supply of slinky models, Mucha was a founding father of the Art Nouveau movement. Partly overseen by Mucha's grandson, the museum is two blocks off Wenceslas Square and wonderfully displayed on one comfortable floor (120 Kč, daily 10:00–18:00, well described in English, Panská 7, tel. 224-233-355, www.mucha.cz). The included 30-minute video is definitely worthwhile (in English, generally at :15 and :45 past the hour—ask for the starting time); it describes the main project of Mucha's life—the *Slav Epic,* currently on display in Moravský Krumlov (a small town in the eastern Czech Republic).

• *Coming back to Na Příkopě and continuing toward the Powder Tower, notice the Neo-Renaissance* **UniCredit Bank** *(formerly Živnostenská Banka, Prague's oldest banking institution) building on the corner of*

Art Nouveau

Prague is the best Art Nouveau town in Europe, with fun-loving facades gracing streets all over town. Art Nouveau, born in Paris, is "nouveau" because it wasn't inspired by Rome. It's neo-nothing...a fresh answer to all the revival styles of the later 19th century and an organic response to the Eiffel Tower art of the Industrial Age. The style liberated the artist in each architect. Notice the unique curves and motifs expressing originality on each Art Nouveau facade. Artists such as Alfons Mucha believed that the style should include all facets of daily life. They designed everything from buildings and furniture to typefaces and cigarette packs.

Prague's three top Art Nouveau architects are Jan Koula, Josef Fanta, and Osvald Polivka (whose last name sounds like the Czech word for "soup"). Think "Cola, Fanta, and Soup"—easy to remember and impress your local friends.

Prague's Art Nouveau highlights include the facades lining the streets of the Jewish Quarter, the Mucha window in St. Vitus Cathedral, and Grand Hotel Evropa on Wenceslas Square. The top two sights for Art Nouveau fans are the Mucha Museum and the Municipal House.

Nekázanka. It houses a modern bank with classy circa-1900 ambience (enter and peek into the main hall upstairs).

At the end of Na Příkopě, you'll arrive at the...

▲▲**Municipal House (Obecní Dům)**—The Municipal House is the "pearl of Czech Art Nouveau." Financed by cultural and artistic leaders, it was built (1905–1911) as a ceremonial palace to reinforce the self-awareness of the Czech nation. It features Prague's largest concert hall, a recommended Art Nouveau café (Kavárna Obecní Dům, see page 129), and two other restaurants. Pop in and wander around the lobby of the concert hall. Walk through to the ticket office on the ground floor. For the best look, including impressive halls and murals you won't see otherwise, take one of the regular hour-long **tours** (open daily 10:00–18:00; tours—150 Kč; generally at 10:15, 12:00, 14:00, and 16:00; in English 2/day, buy ticket from ground-floor shop where tour departs; tel. 222-002-101).

Standing in front of the Municipal House, you can survey four different styles of architecture. First, enjoy the pure Art

Nouveau of the Municipal House itself. Featuring a goddess-like Praha presiding over a land of peace and high culture, the *Homage to Prague* mosaic on the building's striking facade stoked cultural pride and nationalist sentiment. Across the street, the classical fixer-upper from 1815 was the customs house, which has recently been turned into a giant stage for Broadway-style musicals. The stark national bank building (Česká Národní Banka) is textbook Functionalism from the 1930s. Farther away, across the square, former Neo-Romanesque barracks have been transformed into central Prague's biggest shopping mall and underground parking lot.

Powder Tower: The big, black Powder Tower (not worth touring inside) was the Gothic gate of the town wall, built to house the city's gunpowder. The decoration on the tower, portraying Czech kings, is the best 15th-century sculpture in town. If you go through the tower, you'll reach Celetná street, which leads past a few sights to the Old Town Square (see page 68).

Národní Třída: Communist Prague

From Můstek at the bottom of Wenceslas Square, you can head west on Národní Třída (in the opposite direction from Na Příkopě and the Art Nouveau sights) for an interesting stroll through urban Prague to the National Theatre and the Vltava River. But first, consider dropping into the Museum of Communism, a few steps down Na Příkopě (on the right).

▲▲**Museum of Communism**—This museum traces the story of communism in Prague: the origins, dream, reality, and nightmare; the cult of personality; and finally, the Velvet Revolution (see sidebar on page 86). Along the way, it gives a fascinating review of the Czech Republic's 40-year stint with Soviet economics, "in all its dreariness and puffed-up glory." You'll find propaganda posters, busts of communist All-Stars (Marx, Lenin, Stalin), and a photograph of the massive stone Stalin that overlooked Prague until 1962. Slices of communist life are re-created here, from a bland store counter to a typical classroom (with textbooks using Russia's Cyrillic alphabet—no longer studied—and a poem on the chalkboard that extols the virtues of the tractor). Don't miss the Jan Palach exhibit and the 20-minute video (plays continuously, English subtitles) that shows how the Czech people chafed under the big Red yoke from the 1950s through 1989 (180 Kč, daily 9:00–21:00, Na Příkopě 10, above a McDonald's and next to a casino—Lenin is turning over in his grave, tel. 224-212-966, www.museumofcommunism.com).

• *Now head for the river (with your back to Wenceslas Square, go left down 28 Října to Národní Třída). Along the way, Národní Třída has a story to tell.*

The Velvet Revolution of 1989

On the afternoon of November 17, 1989, 30,000 students gathered in Prague's New Town to commemorate the 50th anniversary of the suppression of student protests by the Nazis, which had led to the closing of Czech universities through the end of World War II. The 1989 demonstration—initially planned by the Communist Youth as a celebration of the communist victory over fascism—spontaneously turned into a protest *against* the communist regime. "You are just like the Nazis!" shouted the students. The demonstration was planned to end in the National Cemetery at Vyšehrad (the hill just south of the New Town). But when the planned events concluded in Vyšehrad, the students decided to march on toward Wenceslas Square, making history.

As they worked their way north along the Vltava River, the students were careful to keep their demonstration peaceful. Any hint of violence, the demonstrators knew, would incite brutal police retaliation. Instead, as the evening went on, the absence of police became conspicuous. (In the 1980s, the police never missed a chance to participate in any demonstration...preferably outnumbering the demonstrators.) At about 20:00, as the students marched down this stretch of Národní Třída street toward Wenceslas Square, three rows of policemen suddenly blocked the demonstration at the corner of Národní and Spálená streets. A few minutes later, military vehicles with fences on their bumpers (having crossed the bridge by the National Theatre) appeared behind the marching students. This new set of cops compressed the demonstrators into the stretch of Národní Třída between Voršilská and Spálená. The end of Mikulandská street was also blocked, and policemen were hiding inside every house entry. The students were trapped.

At 21:30, the "Red Hats" (a special anti-riot commando force known for its brutality) arrived. The Red Hats lined up on both sides of this corridor. To get out, the trapped students had to run through the passageway as they were beaten from the left and right. Police trucks ferried captured students around the corner to the police headquarters (on Bartolomějská) for interrogation.

The next day, university students throughout Czechoslovakia decided to strike. Actors from theaters in Prague and Bratislava joined the student protest. Two days later, the students' parents—shocked by the attacks on their children—marched into Wenceslas Square. Sparked by the events of November 17, 1989, the wave of peaceful demonstrations ended later that year on December 29, with the election of Václav Havel as the president of a free Czechoslovakia.

Národní Třída and the Velvet Revolution—Národní Třída ("National Street") is where you feel the pulse of the modern city.

The street, which connects Wenceslas Square with the National Theatre and the river, is a busy thoroughfare running through the heart of urban Prague. In 1989, this unassuming boulevard played host to the first salvo of a Velvet Revolution that would topple the communist regime.

Make your way down Národní Třída until you hit the tram tracks (just beyond the Tesco department store). On the left, look for the photo of Bill Clinton playing saxophone, with Václav Havel on the side (this is the entrance to Reduta, Prague's best jazz club; next door are two recommended eateries, Café Louvre and Le Patio—see pages 130 and 127). Just beyond that, you'll come to a short corridor with white arches. Inside this arcade is a simple memorial to the hundreds of students injured here by the police on November 17, 1989 (see sidebar on facing page).

Along the Vltava River

I've listed these sights from north to south, beginning at the grand, Neo-Renaissance National Theatre, which is five blocks south of Charles Bridge and stands along the riverbank at the end of Národní Třída.

National Theatre (Národní Divadlo)—Opened in 1883 with Smetana's opera *Libuše,* this theater was the first truly Czech venue in Prague. From the very start, it was nicknamed the "Cradle of Czech Culture." The building is a key symbol of the Czech national revival that began in the late 18th century. In 1800, "Prag" was predominantly German. The Industrial Revolution brought Czechs from the countryside into the city, their new urban identity defined by patriotic teachers and priests. By 1883, most of the city spoke Czech, and the opening of this theater represented the birth of the modern Czech nation. It remains an important national icon: The state annually pours more subsidies into this theater than into all of Czech film production. It's the most beautiful venue in town for opera or ballet, often with world-class singers (see page 111).

Next door (just inland, on Národní Třída) is the boxy, glassy facade of the **Nová Scéna.** This "New National Theatre" building, dating from 1983 (the 100th anniversary of the original National Theatre building), reflects the bold and stark communist aesthetic.

Across the street from the National Theatre is the former haunt of Prague's intelligentsia, **Grand Café Slavia,** a Viennese-style coffeehouse that is fine for a meal or drink with a view of the river (see page 129).

•Just south of the National Theatre in the Vltava, you'll find...

Prague's Islands—From the National Theatre, the Legions' Bridge (Most Legií) leads across the island called **Střelecký Ostrov.** Covered with chestnut trees, this island boasts Prague's best beach (on the sandy tip that points north to Charles Bridge). You might see a fisherman pulling out trout from a river that's now much cleaner than it used to be. Bring a swimsuit and take a dip just a stone's throw from Europe's most beloved bridge. In summer, the island hosts open-air movies (most in English or with English subtitles, nightly mid-July–early Sept at about 21:00, www.strelak.cz).

In the mood for boating instead of swimming? On the next island up, on **Slovanský Ostrov,** you can rent a boat (40 Kč/hr for rowboats, 60 Kč/hr for paddleboats, bring a picture ID as deposit). A lazy hour paddling around Střelecký Ostrov—or just floating sleepily in the middle of the river surrounded by this great city's architectural splendor—is a delightful experience on a sunny day. It's cheap, easy, fun (and it's good for you).

• A 10-minute walk (or one stop on tram #17) from the National Theatre, beyond the islands, is Jirásek Bridge (Jiráskův Most), where you'll find the...

Dancing House (Tančící Dům)—If ever a building could get your toes tapping, it would be this one, nick-named "Fred and Ginger" by American architecture buffs. This metallic samba is the work of Frank Gehry (who designed the equally striking Guggenheim Museum in Bilbao, Spain, and Seattle's Experience Music Project). Eight-legged Ginger's wispy dress and Fred's metal mesh head are easy to spot. The building's top-floor res-taurant, La Perle de Prague, is a fine place for a fancy French meal (VIPs often eat and drink here, reservation needed even to get into the elevator, tel. 221-984-160).

The Little Quarter (Malá Strana)

This charming neighborhood, huddled under the castle on the west bank of the river, is low on blockbuster sights but high on ambience. The most enjoyable approach from the Old Town is across Charles Bridge. From the end of the bridge (TI in tower), Mostecká street leads two blocks up to the Little Quarter Square (Malostranské Náměstí) and the huge Church of St. Nicholas. But before you head up there, consider a detour to Kampa Island (all described on next page).

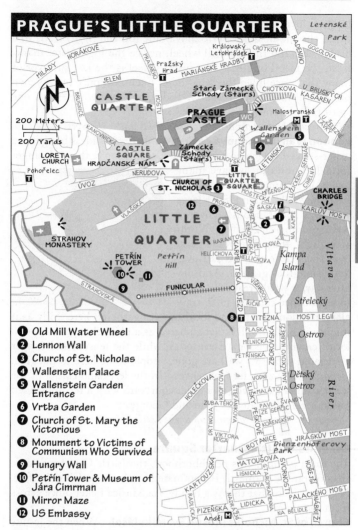

PRAGUE'S LITTLE QUARTER

1. Old Mill Water Wheel
2. Lennon Wall
3. Church of St. Nicholas
4. Wallenstein Palace
5. Wallenstein Garden Entrance
6. Vrtba Garden
7. Church of St. Mary the Victorious
8. Monument to Victims of Communism Who Survived
9. Hungry Wall
10. Petřín Tower & Museum of Jára Cimrman
11. Mirror Maze
12. US Embassy

Between Charles Bridge and Little Quarter Square

Kampa Island—One hundred yards before the castle end of the Charles Bridge, stairs on the left lead down to the main square of Kampa Island (mostly created from the rubble of the Little Quarter, which was destroyed in a 1540 fire). The island features relaxing pubs, a breezy park,

hippies, lovers, a fine contemporary art gallery, and river access. From the main square, Hroznová lane (on the right) leads to a bridge. Behind the old mill wheel, notice the high-water marks from the flood of 2002. The water wheel is the last survivor of many that once lined the canal here. Each mill once had its own protective water spirit *(vodník)*. Today, only one wheel—and one spirit (Mr. Kabourek)—remains.

• *Fifty yards beyond the bridge (on the right, under the trees) is the...*

Lennon Wall (Lennonova Zeď)—While Lenin's ideas hung like a water-soaked trench coat upon the Czech people, the rock singer

John Lennon's ideas gave many locals hope and a vision. When Lennon was killed in 1980, a large wall was spontaneously covered with memorial graffiti. Night after night, the police would paint over the "All You Need Is Love" and "Imagine" graffiti. And day after day, it would reappear. Until independence came in 1989, trav-elers, freedom-lovers, and local hippies gathered here. Silly as it might seem, this wall is remembered as a place that gave hope to locals craving freedom. Even today, while the tension and danger associated with this wall are gone, people come here to imagine. *"John žije"* is Czech for "John lives." In the left-hand corner of the wall, a small gate leads to a quiet courtyard with a recommended outdoor café dedicated to John and George.

• *From here, you can continue up to the Little Quarter Square.*

On or near Little Quarter Square

The focal point of this neighborhood, the Little Quarter Square (Malostranské Náměstí) is dominated by the huge Church of St. Nicholas. Note that there's a handy Via Musica ticket office across from the church.

Church of St. Nicholas (Kostel Sv. Mikuláše)—When the Jesuits came to Prague, they found the perfect piece of real estate for their church and its associated school—right on Little Quarter Square. The church (built 1703–1760) is the best example of High Baroque in town. It's giddy with curves and illusions. The altar features a lavish gold-plated Nicholas, flanked by the two top Jesuits: the founder, St. Ignatius Loyola and his missionary follower, St. Francis Xavier. Climb up the **gallery** through the staircase in the left transept for a close-up look at a collection of large canvases and illusionary frescoes by Karel Škréta, the greatest Czech Baroque painter. Notice that at first glance, the canvases are utterly dark. But as sunbeams shine through the window, various parts of the painting brighten up. Like a looking-glass, it reflects the light, creating a play of light and darkness. This painting technique reflects a central Baroque belief: The world is full of darkness, and the only hope that makes it come alive comes from God. The church walls seem to nearly fuse with the sky, suggesting that happenings on earth are closely connected to heaven. Find St. Nick with his bishop's miter in the center of the ceiling, on his way to heaven (60 Kč, church open daily 9:00–17:00, opens at 8:30 for prayer).

Tower Climb: For a good look at the city and the church's 250-foot dome, climb 215 steps up the bell tower (50 Kč, April–Oct daily 10:00–18:00, closed Nov–March, tower entrance is outside the right transept).

Concerts: The church is also an evening concert venue; tickets are generally on sale at the door (450 Kč, generally nightly except Tue at 18:00, www.psalterium.cz).

• *From here, you can hike 10 minutes uphill to the castle (and five more minutes to the Strahov Monastery). For information on these sights, see "The Castle Quarter," later in this chapter. If you're walking up to the castle, consider going via...*

Nerudova Street—This steep, cobbled street, leading from Little Quarter Square to the castle, is named for Jan Neruda, a gifted 19th-century journalist (and somewhat less talented fiction writer). It's lined with old buildings still sporting the characteristic doorway signs (e.g., the lion, three violinists, house of the golden suns) that once served as street addresses. The surviving signs are carefully restored and protected by law. They represent the family name, the occupation, or the various passions of the people who once inhabited the houses. (If you were to replace your house number with a symbol, what would it be?) In 1777, in order to collect taxes more effectively, Hapsburg Empress Maria Theresa decreed that numbers be used instead of these quaint house names. This neighborhood is filled with old noble palaces, now generally used as foreign embassies and offices of the Czech parliament.

South of Little Quarter Square, to Petřín Hill

Karmelitská street, leading south (along the tram tracks) from Little Quarter Square, is home to these sights.

Church of St. Mary the Victorious (Kostel Panny Marie Vítězné)—This otherwise ordinary Carmelite church displays Prague's most worshiped treasure, the Infant of Prague (Pražské Jezulátko). Kneel at the banister in front of the tiny, lost-in-gilded-Baroque altar, and find the prayer in your language (of the 13 in the folder). Brought to Czech lands during the Hapsburg era by a Spanish noblewoman who came to marry a Czech nobleman, the Infant has become a focus of worship and miracle tales in Prague and Spanish-speaking countries. South Americans come

Jára Cimrman:
When Optimists Should Be Shot

"I am such a complete atheist that I am afraid God will punish me." Such is the pithy wisdom of Jára Cimrman, the man overwhelmingly voted the "Greatest Czech of All Time" in a nationwide poll in 2005. Who is Jára Cimrman? A philosopher? An explorer? An inventor? He is all of these things, yes, and much more. Today, a museum celebrates his life (see page 94).

Born in the mid-19th century to a Czech tailor of Jewish descent and an Austrian actress, Cimrman studied in Vienna before starting off on his journeys around the world. He traversed the Atlantic by a steamboat he designed himself, taught drama to peasants in Peru, and drifted across the Arctic Sea on an iceberg. Other astounding feats soon followed. Cimrman was the first to come within 20 feet of the North Pole. He was the first to invent the light bulb (unfortunately, Edison beat him to the patent office by five minutes). It was he who suggested to the Americans the idea for a Panama Canal, though, as usual, he was never credited. Indeed, Cimrman surreptitiously advised many of the world's greats: Eiffel on his tower, Einstein on his theories of relativity, Chekhov on his plays. ("You can't just have *two* sisters," Cimrman told the playwright. "How about three?") In 1886, long before the world knew of Sartre or Camus, Cimrman was writing tracts such as *The Essence of the Existence,* which would become the foundation for his philosophy of "Cimrmanism," also known as "non-existentialism." (Its central premise: "Existence cannot not exist.")

This man of unmatched genius would have won the honor of "Greatest Czech of All Time" if not for the bureaucratic narrow-mindedness of the poll's sponsors, who had a single objection to Cimrman's candidacy: He's not real. Jára Cimrman is the brainchild of two Czech humorists—Zdeněk Svěrák and Jiří Šebánek—who brought their patriotic Renaissance man to life in 1967 in a satirical radio play. So, even though Cimrman handily won the initial balloting in January of 2005, Czech TV officials—blatantly biased against his non-existentialism—refused to let him into the final rounds of the competition.

How should we interpret the fact that the Czechs would

on pilgrimage to Prague just to see this one statue. An exhibit upstairs shows tiny embroidered robes given to the Infant, including ones from Hapsburg Empress Maria Theresa of Austria (1754) and Vietnam (1958), as well as a video showing a nun lovingly dressing the doll-like sculpture (free, Mon–Sat 9:30–17:30, Sun 13:00–17:00, English-language Mass Sun at 12:00, Karmelitská 9, www.pragjesu.com).

rather choose a fictional character as their greatest countryman over any of their flesh-and-blood national heroes—say, Charles IV (the 14th-century Holy Roman Emperor who established Prague as the cultural and intellectual capital of Europe), Jan Hus (the 15th-century religious reformer who challenged the legitimacy of the Catholic Church), Comenius (the 17th-century educator and writer considered one of the fathers of modern education), or Martina Navrátilová (someone who plays a sport with bright-green balls)? The more cynically inclined—many Czechs among them—might point out that the Czech people have largely stayed behind their mountains for the past millennia, with little interest in, or influence on, happenings elsewhere in the world. Perhaps Cimrman is so beloved because he embodies that most prickly of ironies: a Czech who was greater than all the world's greats, but who for some hiccup of chance has never been recognized for his achievements.

Personally, I like to think that the vote for Cimrman says something about the country's rousing enthusiasm for blowing raspberries in the face of authority. Throughout its history—from the times of the Czech kings who used crafty diplomacy to keep the German menace at bay, to the days of Jan Hus and his questioning of the very legitimacy of any ruler's power, to the flashes of anti-communist revolt that at last sparked the Velvet Revolution in 1989—the Czechs have maintained a healthy disrespect for those who would tell them what is best or how to live their lives. Other countries soberly choose their "Greatest" from musty tomes of history, but the Czechs won't play this silly game. Their vote for a fictional personage, says Cimrman's co-creator Svěrák, says two things about the Czech nation: "That it is skeptical about those who are major figures and those who are supposedly the 'Greatest.' And that the only certainty that has saved the nation many times throughout history is its humor."

Cimrman would agree. A man of greatness, he was always a bit skeptical of those who saw themselves as great, or who marched forward under the banner of greatness. As Cimrman liked to say, "There are moments when optimists should be shot."

• *Continue a few more blocks down Karmelitská to the south end of the Little Quarter (where the street is called Újezd, roughly across the Legions' Bridge from the National Theatre). Here you find yourself at the base of...*

Petřín Hill—This hill, topped by a replica of the Eiffel Tower, features several unusual sights.

The figures walking down the steps in the hillside make up

the **Monument to Victims of Communism Who Survived.** The monument's figures are gradually atrophied by the totalitarian regime. They do not die, but slowly disappear, one limb at a time. The statistics say it all: In Czechoslovakia alone, 205,486 people were imprisoned, 248 were executed, 4,500 died in prison, 327 were shot attempting to cross the border, and 170,938 left the country. To the left of the monument is the **Hungry Wall,** Charles IV's 14th-century equivalent of FDR's work-for-food projects. On the right (50 yards away) is the base of a handy **funicular**—hop on to reach Petřín Tower (uses 20-Kč tram/Metro ticket, runs daily, every 10–15 min from 8:00–22:00).

The summit of Petřín Hill is considered the best place in Prague to take your date for a romantic city view. Built for an exhibition in 1891, the 200-foot-tall **Petřín Tower** is a fifth the height of its Parisian big brother, which was built two years earlier. But, thanks to this hill, the top of the tower sits at the same elevation as the real Eiffel Tower. Climbing the 400 steps rewards you with amazing views over the city. Local wives drag their men to Petřín Hill each May Day to reaffirm their love with a kiss under a blooming sour-cherry tree.

In the tower's basement is the funniest sight in Prague, the **Museum of Jára Cimrman, Genius Who Did Not Become Famous.** The museum traces Cimrman's (fictional) life, including pictures and English descriptions of the thinker's overlooked inventions (50 Kč includes tower and Cimrman museum, daily 10:00–22:00). For more on the mysterious Cimrman, see the sidebar on page 92.

The **mirror maze** next door is nothing special, but fun to quickly wander through since you're already here (50 Kč, daily 10:00–22:00).

The Castle Quarter (Hradčany)

Looming above Prague, dominating its skyline, is the Castle Quarter. Prague Castle and its surrounding sights are packed with Czech history, as well as with tourists. In addition to the castle itself, I enjoy visiting the nearby Strahov Monastery—which has a fascinating old library and beautiful views over all of Prague.

Castle Square (Hradčanské Náměstí)—right in front of the castle gates—is at the center of this neighborhood. Stretching along the promontory away from the castle is a regal neighborhood that ends at the Strahov Monastery. Above the castle are the Royal Gardens, and below the castle are more gardens and lanes leading down to the Little Quarter.

Getting to Prague Castle

If you're not up for a hike, the tram offers a sweat-free ride up to the castle. Taxis are expensive, as they have to go the long way around (200 Kč).

By Foot: Begin in the Little Quarter, just across Charles Bridge from the Old Town. Hikers can follow the main cobbled road (Mostecká) from Charles Bridge to Little Quarter Square, marked by the huge, green-domed Church of St. Nicholas. (The nearest Metro stop is Malostranská, from which Valdštejnská street leads down to Little Quarter Square.) From Little Quarter Square, hike uphill along Nerudova street (described on page 91). After about 10 minutes, a steep lane on the right leads to the castle. (If you continue straight, Nerudova becomes Úvoz and climbs to the Strahov Monastery.)

By Tram: Trams #22 and #23 take you up to the castle. While you can catch the tram in various places, these three stops are particularly convenient: at the Národní Třída Metro stop (between Wenceslas Square and the National Theatre in the New Town); in front of the National Theatre (Národní Divadlo, on the riverbank in the New Town); and at Malostranská (the Metro stop in the Little Quarter). After rattling up the hill, these trams make three stops near the castle: Get off at **Královský Letohrádek** for the scenic approach to the castle (through the Royal Gardens—free entry, open April–Oct daily 10:00–18:00, closed Nov–March); or stay on one more stop to get off at **Pražský Hrad** (most direct but least interesting—simply walk along U Prašného Mostu over the bridge into the castle); or go yet two more stops to **Pohořelec** to visit the Strahov Monastery before hiking down to the castle. To get to the monastery from this tram stop, follow the tram tracks uphill for 50 yards, enter the fancy gate on the left near the tall redbrick wall, and you'll see the twin spires of the monastery. The library entrance is in front of the church on the right.

Tram Tips: When you're choosing which of the castle's three tram stops to get off at, consider the time of day. The castle is plagued with crowds. If you're visiting in the morning, use the Pražský Hrad tram stop for the quickest commute to the castle. Be at the door of St. Vitus Cathedral when it opens at 9:00 (just 10–15 minutes later, it'll be swamped with tour groups). See the castle sights quickly, then move on to the Strahov Monastery. I'd avoid the castle entirely mid-morning, but by mid-afternoon, the tour groups are napping and the grounds are (relatively) uncrowded. If you're going in the afternoon, take the tram to the Pohořelec stop, see the Strahov Monastery first, then wander down to the castle.

▲Strahov Monastery and Library

Twin Baroque domes high above the castle mark the Strahov Monastery. This complex is best reached from the Pohořelec stop on tram #22 or #23 (from the stop, go up the red-railed ramp and

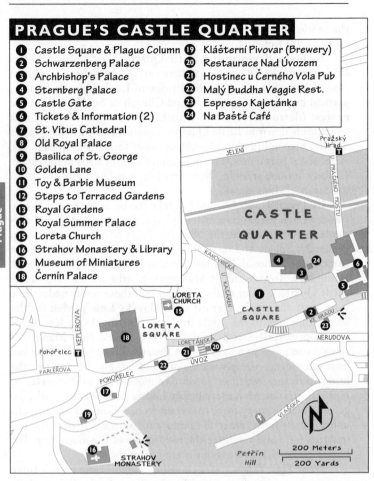

PRAGUE'S CASTLE QUARTER

❶ Castle Square & Plague Column
❷ Schwarzenberg Palace
❸ Archbishop's Palace
❹ Sternberg Palace
❺ Castle Gate
❻ Tickets & Information (2)
❼ St. Vitus Cathedral
❽ Old Royal Palace
❾ Basilica of St. George
❿ Golden Lane
⓫ Toy & Barbie Museum
⓬ Steps to Terraced Gardens
⓭ Royal Gardens
⓮ Royal Summer Palace
⓯ Loreta Church
⓰ Strahov Monastery & Library
⓱ Museum of Miniatures
⓲ Černín Palace

⓳ Klášterní Pivovar (Brewery)
⓴ Restaurace Nad Úvozem
㉑ Hostinec u Černého Vola Pub
㉒ Malý Buddha Veggie Rest.
㉓ Espresso Kajetánka
㉔ Na Baště Café

through the gate into the monastery grounds). If you're coming on foot from the Little Quarter, allow 15 minutes for the uphill hike. After seeing the monastery, hike down to the castle (a 5-min walk).

Monastery: The monastery (Strahovský Klášter Premonstrátů) had a booming economy of its own in its heyday, with vineyards, brewery, and a sizeable beer hall—all still open. Its main church, dedicated to the Assumption of St. Mary, is an originally Romanesque structure decorated by the monks in textbook Baroque (usually closed, but look through the window inside the front door to see its interior).

Library: The adjacent library (Strahovská Knihovna) offers a peek at how enlightened thinkers in the 18th century influenced learning (80 Kč, daily 9:00–12:00 & 13:00–17:00). Cases in the

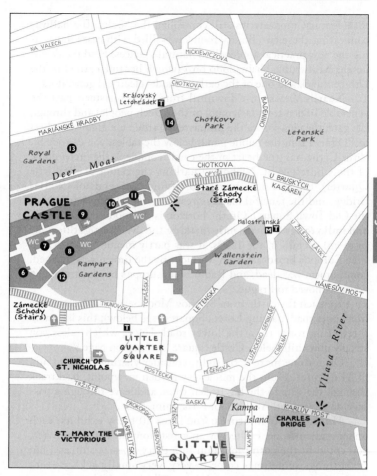

library gift shop show off illuminated manuscripts (described in English). Some are in old Czech, but these are rare. Because the Enlightenment believed in the universality of knowledge, there was little place for vernaculars—therefore, few books here are in the Czech language. Two rooms (seen only from the door) are filled with 10th- to 17th-century books, shelved under elaborately painted ceilings. The theme of the first and bigger hall is philosophy, with the history of man's pursuit of knowledge painted on the ceiling. The other hall focuses on theology. Notice the gilded locked case containing the *libri prohibiti* (prohibited books) at the end of the room. Only the abbot had the key, and you had to have his blessing to read these books—by writers such as Nicolas Copernicus and Jan Hus, and even including the French encyclopedia. As the Age of Enlightenment began to take hold in Europe at the end of the

18th century, monasteries still controlled the books. The hallway connecting these two library rooms was filled with cases illustrating the new practical approach to natural sciences. Find the dried-up elephant trunks, baby dodo bird (which became extinct in the 17th century), and one of the earliest-model electrical generators.

Nearby Views: Just downhill from the monastery, past the venerable linden trees (a symbol of the Czech people) and through the gate, the views from the **monastery garden** are among the best in Prague. From the public perch below the tables, you can see St. Vitus Cathedral (the heart of the castle complex), the green dome of the Church of St. Nicholas (marking the center of the Little Quarter), the two dark towers fortifying both ends of Charles Bridge, and the fanciful black spires of the Týn Church (marking the Old Town Square). On the horizon is the modern **Žižkov TV and radio tower** (conveniently marking the liveliest nightlife zone in town). Begun in the 1980s, it was partly meant to jam Radio Free Europe's broadcast from Munich. By the time it was finished, communism was dead, and Radio Free Europe's headquarters had actually moved to Prague.

To reach the castle from Strahov Monastery, take Loretánská (the upper road, passing Loreta Square—see below); this is a more interesting route than the lower road, Úvoz, which takes you steeply downhill, below Castle Square (see map on page 96).

Or, for one more little sight, consider visiting the Museum of Miniatures. From the monastery garden viewpoint, backtrack through the gate to the big linden trees, and leave through a passage on your right. At the door is the miniscule...

Museum of Miniatures: You'll see 40 teeny exhibits, each under a microscope, crafted by an artist from St. Petersburg. Yes, you could fit the entire museum in a carry-on-size suitcase, but good things sometimes come in very, very small packages—it's fascinating to see minutiae such as a padlock on the leg of an ant. An English flier explains it all (entry-50 Kč, kids-20 Kč, daily 9:00–17:00).

On Loreta Square, Between Strahov Monastery and Castle Square

From the monastery, take Loretánská street to Loreta Square (Loretánské Náměstí). As you wander this road, you'll pass several mansions and palaces, and an important pilgrimage church.

Loreta Church—This church has been a hit with pilgrims for centuries, thanks to its dazzling bell tower, peaceful yet plush cloister, sparkling treasury, and much-venerated "Holy House" (110 Kč, Tue–Sun 9:00–12:15 & 13:00–16:30, closed Mon).

Once inside the entry, follow the one-way clockwise route. Strolling along the cloister, notice that the ceiling is painted with the many places Mary has miraculously appeared to the faithful in Europe.

In the garden-like center of the cloister stands the ornate **Santa Casa (Holy House),** considered by some pilgrims to be part of Mary's home in Nazareth. Because many pilgrims returning from the Holy Land docked at the Italian port of Loreto, it's called the Loreta Shrine. The Santa Casa is the "little Bethlehem" of Prague. It is the traditional departure point for Czech pilgrims setting out on the long, arduous journey to Europe's most important pil-

grimage site, Santiago de Compostela, in northwest Spain. Inside, on the left wall, hangs what some consider to be an original beam from the house of Mary. It's overseen by a much venerated statue of the "Black Virgin." The Santa Casa itself might seem like a bit of a letdown, but consider that you're entering the holiest spot in the country for generations of believers.

The small Baroque church behind the Santa Casa is one of the most beautiful in Prague. The decor looks rich—but the marble and gold is all fake (tap the columns). From the window in the back, you can see a stucco relief on the Santa Casa that shows angels rescuing the house from a pagan attack in Nazareth and making a special delivery to Loreto in Italy.

Continue around the cloister. In the last corner is St. Bearded Woman (Svatá Starosta). This patron saint of unhappy marriages is a woman whose family arranged for her to marry a pagan man. She prayed for an escape, sprouted a beard...and the guy said, "No way." While she managed to avoid the marriage, it angered her father, who crucified her. The many candles here are from people suffering through unhappy marriages.

Take a left just before the exit and head upstairs, following signs to the treasury—a room full of jeweled worship aids (well described in English). The highlight here is a monstrance (Communion wafer holder) from 1699, with more than 6,000 diamonds.

Enjoy the short carillon concert at the top of the hour; from the lawn in front of the main entrance, you can see the racks of bells being clanged. (At the exit, you'll see a schedule of English-language Masses and upcoming *pout'*—pilgrimage—departing from here.)

Castle Square (Hradčanské Náměstí)

This is the central square of the Castle Quarter. Enjoy the awesome city view and the two entertaining bands that play regularly

Tomáš Garrigue Masaryk
(1850–1937)

Tomáš Masaryk was the George Washington of Czechoslovakia. He founded the first democracy in Eastern Europe at the end of World War I, uniting the Czechs and the Slovaks to create Czechoslovakia. Like Václav Havel 70 years later, Masaryk was a politician whose vision extended far beyond the mountains enclosing the Bohemian basin.

Masaryk was born into a poor servant family in southern Moravia. After finishing high school, the village boy set off to attend university in Vienna. Masaryk earned his Ph.D. in sociology just in time for the opening of the Czech-language university in Prague. By that time, he was already married to an American music student named Charlotta Garrigue, who came from a prominent New York family. (The progressive Tomáš actually took her family name as part of his own.) Charlotta opened the doors of America's high society to Masaryk. Among the American friends he made was a young Princeton professor named Woodrow Wilson.

Masaryk was greatly impressed with America, and his admiration for its democratic system became the core of his gradually evolving political creed. He traveled the world and went to Vienna to serve in the parliament. By the time World War I broke out in 1914, Masaryk was 64 years old and—his friends thought—

at the gate. (If the Prague Castle Orchestra is playing, say hello to friendly, mustachioed Josef, and consider getting the group's terrific CD.) A café with dramatic city views called Espresso Kajetánka hides a few steps down, immediately to the right as you face the castle (see page 133). From here, stairs lead into the Little Quarter.

Castle Square was a kind of medieval Pennsylvania Avenue—the king, the most powerful noblemen, and the archbishop lived here. Look uphill from the gate. The Renaissance **Schwarzenberg Palace** (on the left, with the big rectangles scratched on the wall, now under renovation) was where the Rožmberks "humbly" stayed when they were in town from their Český Krumlov estates. The Schwarzenberg family inherited the Krumlov estates and aristocratic prominence in Bohemia, and stayed in the palace until the 20th century.

The archbishop still lives in the yellow Rococo **palace** across the square (with the three white goose necks in the red field—the ready for retirement. But while most other Czech politicians stayed in Prague and supported the Hapsburg Empire, Masaryk went abroad in protest and formed a highly original plan: to create an independent, democratic republic of Czechs and Slovaks. Masaryk and his supporters recruited an army of 100,000 Czechs and Slovak soldiers who were willing to fight with the Allies against the Hapsburgs...establishing a strong case to put on his friend Woodrow Wilson's Oval Office desk.

On the morning of October 28, 1918, news of the unofficial capitulation of the Hapsburgs reached Prague. Local supporters of Masaryk's idea quickly took control of the city and proclaimed the free republic. As the people of Prague tore down double-headed eagles (a symbol of the Hapsburgs), Czechoslovakia was born.

On November 11, 1918, four years after he had left the country as a political nobody, Masaryk arrived in Prague as the greatest Czech hero since the revolutionary priest Jan Hus. The dignified old man rode through the masses of cheering Czechs on a white horse. He told the jubilant crowd, "Now go home—the work has only started." Throughout the 1920s and 1930s, Masaryk was Europe's most vocal defender of democratic ideals against the rising tide of totalitarian ideologies.

In 2001, the US government honored Masaryk's dedication to democracy by erecting a monument to him in Washington, DC—he is one of only three foreign leaders (along with Gandhi and Churchill) to have a statue in the American capital.

coat of arms of Prague's archbishops).

Through the portal on the left-hand side of the palace, a lane leads to the **Sternberg Palace** (Šternberský Palác), filled with the National Gallery's skippable collection of European paintings—including minor works by Albrecht Dürer, Peter Paul Rubens, Rembrandt, and El Greco (100 Kč, Tue–Sun 10:00–18:00, closed Mon).

The black Baroque sculpture in the middle of the square is a **plague column,** erected as a token of gratitude to the saints who saved the population from the epidemic, and an integral part of the main square of many Hapsburg towns.

The statue marked *TGM* honors **Tomáš Garrigue Masaryk** (1850–1937), a university prof and a pal of Woodrow Wilson. At the end of World War I, Masaryk united the Czechs and the Slovaks into one nation and became its first president (see sidebar).

Prague Castle (Pražský Hrad)

For more than a thousand years, Czech leaders have ruled from Prague Castle. Today, Prague's Castle is, by some measures, the biggest on Earth. Four stops matter, and all are explained here: St. Vitus Cathedral, Old Royal Palace, Basilica of St. George, and the Golden Lane.

Hours: Castle sights are open daily April–Oct 9:00–17:00, Nov–March 9:00–16:00, last entry 15 minutes before closing; grounds are open daily 5:00–23:00. St. Vitus Cathedral is closed Sunday mornings for Mass. Be warned that the cathedral can be unexpectedly closed due to special services—consider calling ahead to confirm (tel. 224-373-368 or 224-372-434). If you're not interested in entering the museums, you could try a nighttime visit—the castle grounds are safe, peaceful, floodlit, and open late.

Tickets: When you visit, the cathedral may have a new, moderately priced 50-Kč fee (which was being discussed by the Church and the president at the time of publication). If this fee becomes official, cathedral tickets (which will get you past the main tower) will be sold in the TIs outside the cathedral, just like the castle combo-tickets described below. The front of the cathedral will remain free.

For the other castle sights, rather than buying the comprehensive long-tour ticket (350 Kč), I recommend getting the short-tour ticket (250 Kč, covers the Old Royal Palace, Basilica of St. George, and the Golden Lane at peak hours; buy in palace, Basilica, or the ticket offices on the two castle squares). If you want to save time, skip the packed Golden Lane during the day, and return at night for a romantic, crowd-free visit (free in the morning and evening).

Tours: Hour-long tours in English depart from the main ticket office about three times a day, but cover only the cathedral and Old Royal Palace (90 Kč plus ticket, tel. 224-373-368). You can rent an **audioguide** for 200 Kč (good all day) by picking it up at the main desk in the TI, located across from the cathedral entrance—show this book for this rate (promised through 2009 by the manager). The audioguide also entitles you to priority entrance into the cathedral—when the line in front of the entrance is long, walk to the exit door on the right and show the audioguide to the guard to be let in.

Crowd-Beating Tips: Huge throngs of tourists turn the castle grounds into a sea of people during peak times (9:30–12:30). St. Vitus Cathedral is the most crowded part of the castle complex. If you're visiting in the morning, be at the cathedral entrance promptly at 9:00, when the doors open. For 10 minutes, you'll have the sacred space for yourself (after about 9:15, tour guides jockeying unwieldy groups from tomb to tomb turn the church into a noisy human traffic jam). Late afternoon is least crowded.

Castle Gate and Courtyards—Begin at Castle Square. From here, survey the castle—the tip of a 1,500-foot-long series of

courtyards, churches, and palaces. The guard changes on the hour (5:00–23:00), with the most ceremony and music at noon.

Walk under the fighting giants, under an arch, through the passageway, and into the courtyard. The modern green awning with the golden-winged cat (just past the ticket office) marks the offices of the Czech president, who, according to the constitution, is more of a figurehead than a power broker. The most recent president—and at the time of this writing the favorite for the 2008 election—is Václav Klaus. He's popular with members of the older generation (who like consistency), but is bitterly resented by most younger people, many of whom see him as incapable of considering points of view other than his own. Outside the Czech Republic, Klaus is known for his unconstructive criticism of the European Union, and more recently, for his denunciation of the campaign against global warming (the reality of which he denies). In the fall of 2007, Klaus—who in his most recent book argues that the "environmental hysteria" fundamentally endangers the freedom of the individual—became the face of the Exxon-sponsored campaign in the American media that preceded a UN conference on global warming.

As you walk through another passageway, you'll find yourself facing...

▲▲▲St. Vitus Cathedral (Katedrála Sv. Víta)—The Roman Catholic cathedral symbolizes the Czech spirit—it contains the tombs and relics of the most important local saints and kings, including the first three Hapsburg kings.

❍ Self-Guided Tour: The following commentary will bring meaning to your cathedral visit.

Cathedral Facade: Before entering, check out the facade. What's up with the guys in suits carved into the facade below the big round window?

They're the architects and builders who finished the church. Started in 1344, construction was stalled by wars and plagues. But, fueled by the 19th-century rise of Czech nationalism, Prague's top church was finished in 1929 for the 1,000th anniversary of the death of St. Wenceslas. While it looks all Gothic, it's actually two distinct halves: the original 14th-century Gothic around the high altar, and the modern Neo-Gothic nave. For 400 years, a temporary wall sealed off the functional, yet unfinished, cathedral.

Mucha Stained-Glass Window: Go inside, buy your ticket, show your ticket at the fenced-off area, and find the third window on the left. This masterful 1931 Art Nouveau window is by Czech artist Alfons Mucha (if you like this, you'll love the Mucha Museum in the New Town—see page 83).

(see page 83)

Notice Mucha's stirring nationalism: Methodius and Cyril, widely considered the fathers of Slavic-style Christianity, are top and center.

Cyril—the monk in black holding the Bible—brought the word of God to the Slavs. They had no written language in the ninth century—so he designed the necessary alphabet (Glagolitic, which later developed into Cyrillic). Methodius, the bishop, is shown baptizing a mythic, lanky, long-haired Czech man—a reminder of how he brought Christianity to the Czech people. Scenes from the life of Cyril on the left and scenes from the life of Methodius on the right bookend the stirring and epic Slavic scene. In the center are a kneeling boy and a prophesying elder—that's young St. Wenceslas and his grandmother, St. Ludmila. In addition to being specific historical figures, these characters are also symbolic: The old woman, with closed eyes, stands for the past and memory, while the young boy, with a penetrating stare, represents the hope and future of a nation. Notice how master designer Mucha draws your attention to these two figures through the use of colors—the dark blue on the outside gradually turns into green, then yellow, and finally the gold of the woman and the crimson of the boy in the center. In Mucha's color language, blue stands for the past, gold for the mythic, and red for the future. Besides all the meaning, Mucha's art is simply a joy to behold. (And on the bottom, the tasteful little ad for *Banka Slavie*, which paid for the work, is hardly noticeable.)

Relief of Prague: Continue circulating around the apse. As you walk around the high altar, study the fascinating carved-wood relief of Prague. It depicts the victorious Hapsburg armies entering the castle after the Battle of White Mountain, while the Protestant king Frederic escapes over the Charles Bridge (before it had any statues). Carved in 1630, 10 years after the famous event occurred, the relief also gives you a peek at Prague in 1620, stretching from the Týn Church to the cathedral (half-built at that time, up to where you are now). Notice that back then, the Týn Church was Hussite, so the centerpiece of its facade is not the Virgin Mary—but a chalice, symbol of Jan Hus' ideals. The old city walls—now replaced by the main streets of the city—stand strong. The Jewish Quarter (the slummy, muddy zone along the riverside below the bridge on the left) fills land no one else wanted.

Apse: Circling around the high altar, you pass graves of bishops, including the tomb of St. Vitus (behind the chair of the bishop). The stone sarcophagi contain kings from the Přemysl dynasty (12th to 14th centuries). Locals claim the gigantic, shiny tomb of St. John of Nepomuk has more than a ton of silver (for more on St. John of Nepomuk, see page 72). After the silver tomb, look up at the royal box from where the king would attend Mass in his jammies (an elevated corridor connected his private apartment with his own altar-side box pew).

Look for the finely carved wood panel that gives a Counter-Reformation spin on the Wars of Religion. It shows the "barbaric" Protestant nobles destroying the Catholic icons in the cathedral after their short-lived victory.

Wenceslas Chapel: A fancy roped-off chapel (right transept) houses the tomb of St. Wenceslas, surrounded by precious 14th-century murals showing scenes of his life (see description on page 80), and a locked door leading to the crown jewels. The Czech kings used to be crowned right here in front of the coffin, draped in red. The chapel is roped off because the wallpaper is encrusted with precious and semiprecious stones. (Lead us not into temptation.) You can view the chapel from either door (if the door facing the nave is crowded, duck around to the left to find a door that is most likely open).

Spire: You can climb 287 steps up the spire for one of the best views of the whole city (included in cathedral ticket, April–Oct daily 9:00–17:00 except Sun morning, last entry 45 minutes before closing, closes at 16:00 Nov–March).

Back Outside the Cathedral: Leaving the cathedral, turn left (past the public WC). The **obelisk** was erected in 1928—a single piece of granite celebrating the 10th anniversary of the establishment of Czechoslovakia. It was originally much taller, but broke in transit—an inauspicious start for a nation destined to last only 70 years. Up in the fat, green tower of the cathedral is the Czech Republic's biggest bell, nicknamed "Zikmund." In June of 2002, it cracked—and two months later, the worst flood in recorded history hit the city. As a nation sandwiched between great powers,

Czechs are deeply superstitious when it comes to the tides of history. Often feeling unable to influence the course of their own destiny, they helplessly look at events as we might look at the weather and other natural phenomena—trying to figure out what fate has in store for them next.

Find the 14th-century **mosaic** of the Last Judgment outside on the right transept. It was commissioned Italian-style by King Charles IV, who was modern, cosmopolitan, and ahead of his time. Jesus oversees the action, as some go to heaven and some go to hell. The Czech king and queen kneel directly below Jesus and the six patron saints. On coronation day, they would walk under this arch, which would remind them (and their subjects) that even those holding great power are not above God's judgment. The royal crown and national jewels are kept in a chamber (see the grilled windows) above this entryway, which was the cathedral's main entry for centuries while the church remained uncompleted.

Across the square and 20 yards to the right, a door leads into the Old Royal Palace (in the lobby, there's a WC with a window shared by the men's and women's sections—meet your partner to enjoy the view).

Old Royal Palace (Starý Královský Palác)—Starting in the 12th century, this was the seat of the Bohemian princes. While extensively rebuilt, the **large hall** is late Gothic, designed as a multipurpose hall for the old nobility. It's big enough for jousts—even the staircase was designed to let a mounted soldier gallop in. It was filled with market stalls, giving nobles a chance to shop without actually going into town. In the 1400s, the nobility met here to  elect their king. This tradition survived until modern times, as the parliament crowded into this room until the late 1990s to elect the Czechoslovak (and later Czech) president. (The last three elections happened in another, far more lavish hall in the castle.) Look up at the flower-shaped, vaulted ceiling.

On your immediate right, enter the two small Renaissance rooms known as the **"Czech Office."** From these rooms (empty today except for their 17th-century porcelain heaters), two governors used to oversee the Czech lands for the Hapsburgs in Vienna. In 1618, angry Czech Protestant nobles poured into these rooms and threw the two Catholic governors out of the window. An old law actually permits "defenestration"—throwing people (usually bad politicians) out of windows when necessary. Old prints on the wall show the second of Prague's many defenestrations. The two governors landed—fittingly—in a pile of horse manure. Even though they suffered only broken arms and bruised egos, this event kicked off the huge and lengthy Thirty Years' War.

Look down on the chapel from the end, and go out on the balcony for a fine Prague view. Is that Paris' Eiffel Tower in the distance? No, it's Petřín Tower—a fine place for a relaxing day at the park, offering sweeping views over Prague (see page 94).

As you exit through the side door, pause at the door to consider the subtle yet racy little Renaissance knocker. Go ahead—play with it for a little sex in the palace (be gentle).

Across from the palace exit is the...

Basilica and Convent of St. George (Bazilika Sv. Jiří)—Step into the beautiful-in-its-simplicity Basilica of St. George to see Prague's best-preserved Romanesque church. Notice the characteristic double windows on the gallery, as well as the walls made of limestone (the rock that Prague rests on). In those early years, the building techniques were not yet advanced, and the ceiling is made of wood, rather than arched with stone. St. Wenceslas' grandmother, St. Ludmila, who had established this first Bohemian convent, was reburied here in 973. Look for Gothic frescoes depicting this cultured woman (to the right of the altar space). The Baroque front—which dates from much later—was added on the exterior at the same time as the St. John of Nepomuk chapel (through which you exit the church). The scary-looking bones under the chapel altar are replicas—neither St. John's nor real.

Today, the **convent** next door houses the National Gallery's Collection of Old Masters, featuring the best Czech paintings from the Mannerist and Baroque periods (100 Kč, Tue–Sun 10:00–18:00, closed Mon).

Continue walking downhill through the castle grounds. Turn left on the first street, which leads into the...

Golden Lane (Zlatá Ulička)—This street of old buildings, which originally housed goldsmiths, is jammed with tourists during the day and lined with overpriced gift shops. Franz Kafka lived briefly at #22. There's a deli/bistro at the top. In the morning (before 9:00) and at night (after 17:00 in summer, 16:00 in winter), the tiny street is free, empty, and romantic. Exit the lane through a corridor at the last house (#12).

Toy and Barbie Museum (Muzeum Hraček)—At the bottom of the castle complex, just after leaving the Golden Lane, a long, wooden staircase leads to two entertaining floors of old toys and dolls thoughtfully described in English. You'll see a century of teddy bears, 19th-century model train sets, and an incredible Barbie collection (the entire top floor). Find the buxom 1959 first edition, and you'll understand why these capitalistic sirens of material discontent weren't allowed here until 1989 (60 Kč, 120 Kč per family, not included in any castle tickets, daily 9:30–17:30, WC next to entrance).

After Your Castle Visit: Tourists squirt slowly through a fortified door at the bottom end of the castle. From there, you can follow the steep lane directly back to the riverbank (and the Malostranská Metro station).

Or you can take a hard right and stroll through the long, delightful park. Along the way, notice the modernist design of the **Na Valech Garden,** which was carried out by the "court architect" of the 1920s, Jože Plečnik of Slovenia (see page 552).

Halfway through the long park is a viewpoint overlooking **terraced gardens;** you can zigzag down through these gardens into the Little Quarter (80 Kč, April–Oct daily 10:00–18:00, closed Nov–March).

If you continue through the park all the way to Castle Square, you'll find two more options: a staircase leading down into the Little Quarter, or a cobbled street taking you to historic Nerudova street (described on page 91).

Congratulations. You've conquered the castle.

ENTERTAINMENT

Prague booms with live and inexpensive theater, classical music, jazz, and pop entertainment. Everything is listed in several monthly cultural events programs (free at TI) and in the *Prague Post* newspaper (60 Kč at newsstands).

You'll be tempted to gather fliers as you wander through the town. Don't bother. To really understand all your options (the street Mozarts are pushing only their concerts), drop by a **Via Musica** box office. There are two:

One is next to Týn Church on the Old Town Square (daily 10:30–19:30, tel. 224-826-969), and the other is in the Little Quarter across from the Church of St. Nicholas (daily 10:30–18:00, tel. 257-535-568). The event schedule posted on their wall clearly shows everything that's playing today and tomorrow, including tourist concerts, Black Light Theater, and marionette shows, with photos of each venue and a map locating everything (www.viamusica.cz).

Ticketpro sells tickets for the serious concert venues and most music clubs (daily 8:00–12:00 & 12:30–16:30, Rytířská 31, between Havelská Market and Estates Theatre; also has a booth in Tourist Center at Rytířská 12, daily 9:00–20:00; English-language reservations tel. 296-329-999).

Consider buying concert tickets directly from the actual venues. You won't save money, but more of your money will go to the musicians.

Locals dress up for the more "serious" concerts, opera, and ballet, but many tourists wear casual clothes—as long as you don't show up in shorts, sneakers, or sandals you'll be fine.

Black Light Theater

A kind of mime/modern dance variety show, Black Light Theater has no language barrier and is, for many, more entertaining than a classical concert. Unique to Prague (though somewhat comparable to a very low-budget Cirque du Soleil), Black Light Theater originated in the 1960s as a playful and mystifying theater of the absurd. These days, some aficionados lament that it's becoming a cheesy variety show, while others are uncomfortable with the sexual flavor of some acts. Still, it's an unusual theater experience that most enjoy. Shows last about 90 minutes. Avoid the first four rows, which get you so close that it ruins the illusion. Each theater has its own personality:

Ta Fantastika is traditional and poetic, with puppets and a little artistic nudity (*Aspects of Alice* nightly at 21:30, 620 Kč, reserved seating, near east end of Charles Bridge at Karlova 8, tel. 222-221-366, www.tafantastika.cz).

Image Theatre has more mime and elements of the absurd, with shows including *Clonarium, Fiction,* and *The Best of Image:* "It's precisely the fact that we are all so different that unites us" (shows nightly at 18:00 and 20:00, 480 Kč, open seating—arrive early to grab a good spot, just off Old Town Square at Pařížská 4, tel. 222-314-448, www.imagetheatre.cz).

Laterna Magica, in the big, glassy building next to the National Theatre, mixes Black Light techniques with film projection into a multimedia performance that draws Czech audiences (*Wonderful Circus, Rendezvous, Graffiti,* shows Mon–Sat at 20:00, no shows on Sun, 680 Kč, tel. 224-931-482, www.laterna.cz).

The other Black Light theaters advertised around town aren't as good.

Concerts

Each day, six to eight classical concerts designed for tourists fill delightful Old World halls and churches with music of the crowd-pleasing sort: Vivaldi, Best of Mozart, Most Famous Arias, and works by the famous Czech composer Antonín Dvořák. Concerts typically cost 400–1,000 Kč, start anywhere from 13:00 to 21:00, and last about an hour. Common venues are two buildings on the Little Quarter Square (the Church of St. Nicholas and the Prague Academy of Music in Liechtenstein Palace); in the Klementinum's Chapel of Mirrors; at the Old Town Square (in a different Church of St. Nicholas); and in the stunning Smetana Hall in the Municipal House (see page 84). The artists vary from excellent to amateur.

A sure bet is the jam session held every Monday at 17:00 at **St. Martin in the Wall,** where some of Prague's best musicians gather to tune in and chat with each other (400 Kč, Martinská street, just north of the Tesco department store in the Old Town).

The **Prague Castle Orchestra,** one of Prague's most entertaining acts, performs regularly on Castle Square. This trio—Josef on flute, Radek on accordion, and Zdeněk on bass—plays a lively Czech mélange of Smetana, swing, old folk tunes, and 1920s cabaret songs. Look for them if you're visiting the castle (see page 102) and consider picking up their fun CD. They're also available for private functions (mobile 603-552-448, josekocurek@volny.cz).

Serious music-lovers should consider Prague's two top ensembles: The **Czech Philharmonic,** which performs in the Neo-Renaissance Rudolfinum (on Palachovo Náměstí, in the Jewish Quarter on the Old Town side of Mánes Bridge, 250–1,000 Kč, ticket office open Mon–Fri 10:00–18:00, and until just before the show starts on concert days, tel. 227-059-352, www.ceskafilharmonie.cz, info@cfmail .cz), and the **Prague Symphony Orchestra,** based in the gorgeous Art Nouveau Municipal House (ticket office on U Obecního Domu street opposite Hotel Paris, open Mon–Fri 10:00–18:00, tel. 222-002-336, www.fok.cz, pokladna@fok.cz). Both orchestras perform in their home venues about five nights a month from September through June. Most other nights these spaces are rented to agencies that organize tourist concerts of varying quality for double the price (see the top of this section). Check first whether your visit coincides with either ensemble's performance.

During his frequent visits to Prague, Mozart (1756–1791) stayed with his friends in the beautiful, small, Neoclassical **Villa Bertramka,** now the Mozart Museum. Surrounded by a peaceful garden, the villa preserves the time when the Salzburg prodigy felt more appreciated in Prague than in Austria. Intimate concerts are held some afternoons and evenings, either in the garden or in the small concert hall (110 Kč, daily April–Oct 9:30–18:00, Nov–March 9:30–17:00, Mozartova 169, Praha 5; from Metro: Anděl, it's a 10-min walk—head to Hotel Mövenpick and then go up alley behind hotel; tel. 257-317-465, www.bertramka.cz).

Opera and Ballet

The **National Theatre** (Národní Divadlo, on the New Town side of Legií Bridge)—with a must-see Neo-Renaissance interior (see page 87)—is best for opera and ballet (shows from 19:00, 300–1,000 Kč, tel. 224-912-673, www.nationaltheatre.cz). The **Estates Theatre** (Stavovské Divadlo) is where Mozart premiered and personally directed many of his most beloved works (see page 69). *Don Giovanni*, *The Marriage of Figaro*, and *The Magic Flute* are on the program a couple of times each month (shows from 20:00, 800–1,400 Kč, between the Old Town Square and the New Town on a square called Ovocný Trh, tel. 224-214-339, www.estatestheatre.cz). A handy ticket office for both of these theaters is in the little square (Ovocný Trh) behind the Estates Theatre, next to a pizzeria.

The **State Opera** (Státní Opera) operates on a smaller budget and is also not as architecturally rewarding as the National Theatre (shows at 19:00 or 20:00, 400–1,200 Kč, buy tickets at the theater, on 5 Května—the busy street between the Main Train Station and Wenceslas Square, see map on page 79, tel. 224-227-693, www.opera.cz).

Festivals

World-class musicians are in town during these musical festivals: **Prague Spring** (last three weeks of May, www.festival.cz), **Prague Autumn** (last half of Sept, www.pragueautumn.cz), and the newer **Prague Proms** (July–Aug, www.pragueproms.cz).

SHOPPING

Prague's entire Old Town seems designed to bring out the shopper in visitors. Puppets, glass, and ceramics are traditional. Shop your way from the Old Town Square up Celetná street to the Powder Tower, then along Na Příkopě to the bottom of Wenceslas Square (Václavské Náměstí). The city center is tourist-oriented—most locals do their serious shopping in the suburbs. For information on VAT refunds (for purchases of more than 2,000 Kč—about $100) and customs regulations, see page 937 in the appendix.

Celetná is lined with big stores selling all the traditional Czech goodies. Tourists wander endlessly here, mesmerized by the window displays. Celetná Crystal, about midway down the street, offers the largest selection of affordable crystal. You can have the glass safely shipped home directly from the shop.

Na Příkopě has a couple of good modern malls. The best is Slovanský Dům (daily 10:00–20:00, Na Příkopě 22), where you wander deep past a 10-screen multiplex into a world of classy restaurants and designer shops surrounding a peaceful, park-like inner courtyard. Another modern mall is Černá Růže (daily

10:00–20:00, Na Příkopě 12). Next door is Moser, which has a museum-like crystal showroom upstairs (mentioned below).

Národní Třída (National Street) is less touristy and lined with some inviting stores. The big Tesco department store in the middle sells anything you might need, from a pin for a broken watchband to a swimsuit (generally daily 9:00–21:00, Národní Třída 26).

Crystal: Along with shops on Celetná and Na Příkopě, a small square just off the Old Town Square, Malé Náměstí, is ringed by three major crystal retailers (generally open daily 10:00–20:00): Moser, Rott Crystal, and Crystalex (which claims to have "factory-direct" prices, at #6 on the square).

Czech Garnets: This extraordinary stone of fiery red color, which has unique refractive and (some claim) even curative properties, is found only in Bohemia. The characteristic design of garnet jewelry, with the jewels overwhelming the metal setting, became popular in the 1890s and remains so today. Although garnet jewelry is sold in most crystal shops, the **Turnov Granát Co-op** has the largest selection (with shops at Dlouhá 30 and Panská 1, www .granat.eu). It oversees its own mining and represents over 300 traditional goldsmiths and jewelers. Make sure to ask your vendor for a certificate of authenticity, as many shops sell glass imitations.

SLEEPING

Peak season for hotels in Prague is late April, May, June, September, and early October. Easter and Christmas are the most crowded times, when prices are jacked up a bit. I've listed peak-time prices—if you're traveling in July or August, you'll find rates generally 15 percent lower, and from November through March, about 30 percent lower.

Room-Booking Services

Prague is awash with fancy rooms on the push list; private, small-time operators with rooms to rent in their apartments; and roving agents eager to book you a bed and earn a commission. You can save about 30 percent by showing up in Prague without a reservation and finding accommodations upon arrival. However, it is a hustle, and you will not necessarily get your first choice. If you're coming in by train or car, you'll encounter booking agencies. They can almost always find you a reasonable room, and, if it's a private guest house, your host can even come and lead you to the place.

Athos Travel has a line on 200 properties (ranging from hostels to 5-star hotels), 90 percent of which are in the historical center. To book a room, call them or use their handy website, which allows you to search for a room, based on various criteria (best to arrange in advance during peak season, can also help with

Sleep Code

(20 Kč = about $1, country code: 420)
S = Single, **D** = Double/Twin, **T** = Triple, **Q** = Quad, **b** = bathroom, **s** = shower only. Unless otherwise noted, credit cards are accepted, and breakfast and tax are included. Everyone listed here speaks English.

To help you sort easily through these listings, I've divided the rooms into three categories based on the price for a standard double room with bath:

$$$ Higher Priced—Most rooms 4,000 Kč or more.
$$ Moderately Priced—Most rooms between
                3,000–4,000 Kč.
$ Lower Priced—Most rooms 3,000 Kč or less.

last-minute booking off-season, tel. 241-440-571, fax 241-441-697, www.a-prague.com, info@a-prague.com). Readers report that Athos is aggressive with its business policies—while there's no fee to cancel well in advance, they strictly enforce penalties on cancellations within 48 hours.

AVE, at the Main Train Station (Hlavní Nádraží), is another booking service (daily 6:00–23:00). With the tracks at your back, walk down to the orange ceiling and past the "Meeting Point" (don't go downstairs)—their office is in the left corner by the exit to the rip-off taxis. Their display board shows discounted hotels, and they have a slew of hotels and small pensions available (2,000-Kč pension doubles in old center, 1,500-Kč doubles a Metro ride away). You can reserve by email, using your credit card as a deposit (tel. 251-551-011, fax 251-555-156, www.avetravel.cz, ave@avetravel .cz), or just show up at the office and request a room. Be clear on the location before you make your choice. They sell taxi vouchers for those who want the convenience of a ride from the train station's taxi stand, though they cost double the fair rate.

For a more personal touch, Lída Jánská's **Magic Praha** helps with accommodations (tel. 235-325-170, mobile 604-207-225, www.magicpraha.cz, magicpraha@magicpraha.cz; see "Helpful Hints," page 51). Lída rents a well-located apartment with a river view near the Jewish Quarter.

Web-booking services, such as Priceline.com and Biddingfortravel.com, enable budget travelers to snare fancy rooms on the push list for half the rack rate. It's not unusual to find a room in a four-star hotel for 1,300 Kč—but keep in mind that many of these international business-class hotels are far from the city center.

Old Town Hotels and Pensions

You'll pay higher prices to stay in the Old Town, but for many travelers, the convenience is worth the expense. These places are all within a 10-minute walk of the Old Town Square.

$$$ Hotel Maximilian is a sleek, mod, 70-room place with Art Deco black design; big, plush living rooms; and all the business services and comforts you'd expect in a four-star hotel. It faces a church on a perfect little square just a short walk from the action (Db-4,500 Kč, extra bed-1,500 Kč, their "preferred rate" gives you a 14 percent discount if you lock in a reservation with no cancellation option, check online for lower rates, Haštalská 14, tel. 225-303-111, fax 225-303-110, www.maximilianhotel.com, reservation@maximilianhotel.com).

$$$ Residence Řetězová is on a central but delightfully quiet cobbled lane. Its medieval shell has been remodeled into nine elegant, plush, and spacious apartments—each one is unique. You can enjoy the mystery and ambience of old Prague with all the modern comforts (Db-4,100–5,600 Kč, large apartment-10,200 Kč for up to 6 people; 20 percent discount with advance reservation, this book, and cash; check online for lower, last-minute rates and to choose your room; free Internet access, Řetězová 9, tel. & fax 222-221-800, www.residenceretezova.com, info@residenceretezova.com).

$$ Hotel Haštal is next to Hotel Maximilian (first listing) on the same quiet, hidden square in the Old Town. A popular hotel back in the 1920s, it was tactfully renovated to complement the neighborhood's vibrant circa-1900 architecture. Its 24 rooms are comfortable, but the walls are a bit thin (Sb-2,900 Kč, Db-3,600 Kč, extra bed-550 Kč, 20 percent discount when booking online, air-con, Haštalská 16, tel. 222-314-335, www.hastal.com, info @hastal.com). The hotel's small restaurant is understandably popular with locals for its reasonably priced lunch specials and draft beer.

$$ Pension u Medvídků ("By the Bear Cubs") has 31 comfortably renovated rooms in a big, rustic, medieval shell with dark wood furniture. Upstairs, you'll find lots of beams—or, if you're not careful, they'll find you (Sb-2,300 Kč, Db-3,500 Kč, Tb-4,500 Kč, extra bed-500 Kč, "historical" rooms 10 percent more, apartment for 20 percent more, manager Vladimír promises readers of this book a 10 percent discount with cash if you book direct, Internet access, Na Perštýně 7, tel. 224-211-916, fax 224-220-930, www .umedvidku.cz, info@umedvidku.cz). The pension runs a popular beer-hall restaurant with live music most Fridays and Saturdays until 23:00—request an inside room for maximum peace.

$$ Green Garland Pension (U Zeleného Věnce), on the same quiet pedestrian street as Residence Řetězová, has a warm and personal feel rare in the Old Town. Located in a thick 14th-century building with open beams, it has a blond-hardwood

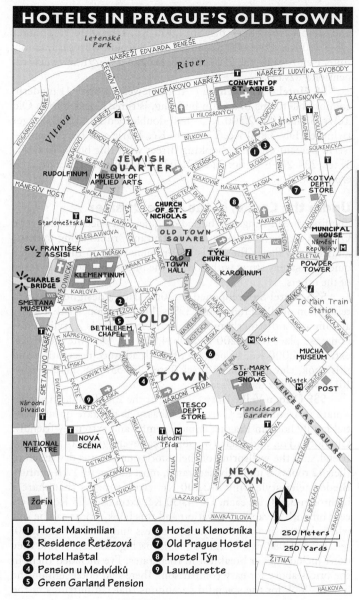

HOTELS IN PRAGUE'S OLD TOWN

1. Hotel Maximilian
2. Residence Řetězová
3. Hotel Haštal
4. Pension u Medvídků
5. Green Garland Pension
6. Hotel u Klenotníka
7. Old Prague Hostel
8. Hostel Týn
9. Launderette

Prague

charm decorated with a woman's touch. Its nine rooms are clean and simply furnished (big Sb-2,900 Kč, Db-3,400 Kč, bigger Db-3,700 Kč, Tb-4,400 Kč, 10 percent discount with cash, family suite, Řetězová 10, tel. 222-220-178, fax 224-248-791, www.uzv.cz, pension@uzv.cz).

$$ Hotel u Klenotníka ("At the Jeweler"), with 11 modern, comfortable rooms in a plain building, is three blocks off the Old Town Square (Sb-2,500 Kč, small double-bed Db-3,300, bigger twin-bed Db–3,800 Kč, Tb-4,500 Kč, Marie and Helena promise 10 percent off when booking direct with this book, Rytířská 3, tel. 224-211-699, fax 224-221-025, www.uklenotnika.cz, info @uklenotnika.cz).

Under the Castle, in the Little Quarter

The first three listings are buried on quiet lanes deep in the Little Quarter, among cobbles, quaint restaurants, rummaging tourists, and embassy flags. The last is a 10-minute walk up the river on a quiet and stately street with none of the intense medieval cityscape of the others.

$$$ Hotel Sax reopened in 2008 after a designer-planned renovation of all 22 rooms in a 1950s–1960s fashion. With a fruity atrium and a distinctly modern, stark feel, this is a stylish, no-nonsense place (Sb-4,200 Kč, Db-4,900 Kč, Db suite-5,600 Kč, extra bed-1,000 Kč, 10 percent off with advance reservation and this book, elevator, Jánský Vršek 3, tel. 257-531-268, fax 257-534-101, www.sax.cz, hotel@sax.cz).

$$$ Dům u Velké Boty ("House at the Big Boot"), on a quiet square in front of the German Embassy, is the rare quintessential family hotel in Prague: homey, comfy, and extremely friendly. Charlotta, Jan, and their two sons treat every guest as a (thirsty) friend, and the wellspring of their stories never runs dry. Each of their 12 rooms is uniquely decorated, most in tasteful 19th-century Biedermeier style (tiny S-2,100 Kč, two D rooms that share a bathroom-3,400 Kč each, Db-4,450 Kč, extra bed-725 Kč, 10 percent off with advance reservation and this book, prices can be soft when slow, cash only, free Internet access and Wi-Fi, Vlašská 30, tel. 257-532-088, www.bigboot.cz, info@bigboot.cz). While they don't include tax or breakfast in their rates, I've included them in the prices above for easy comparison. There's no hotel sign on the house—look for the splendid geraniums that Jan nurtures in the windows.

$$ Hotel Julián is an oasis of professional, predictable decency in an untouristy neighborhood. Its 32 spacious, fresh, well-furnished rooms and big, homey public spaces hide behind a noble Neoclassical facade. The staff is friendly and helpful (Sb-3,680 Kč, Db-3,980 Kč, Db suite-4,800 Kč, extra bed-900 Kč,

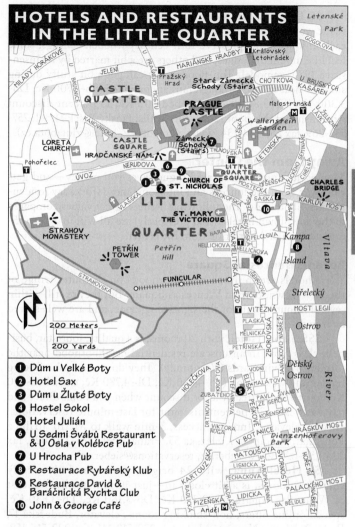

HOTELS AND RESTAURANTS IN THE LITTLE QUARTER

1. Dům u Velké Boty
2. Hotel Sax
3. Dům u Žluté Boty
4. Hostel Sokol
5. Hotel Julián
6. U Sedmi Švábů Restaurant & U Osla v Kolébce Pub
7. U Hrocha Pub
8. Restaurace Rybářský Klub
9. Restaurace David & Baráčnická Rychta Club
10. John & George Café

discount for booking online, 15 percent discount off rack rate with this book, free tea and coffee in room, air-con, elevator, plush and inviting lobby, parking lot; Metro: Anděl, then an 8-min walk; or take tram #6, #9, #12, #20, or #58 for two stops; Elišky Peškové 11, Praha 5, reservation tel. 257-311-150, reception tel. 257-311-145, fax 257-311-149, www.julian.cz, casjul@vol.cz). Free lockers and a shower are available for those needing a place to stay after checkout (for example, while waiting for an overnight train). Mike's Chauffeur Service, based here, is reliable and affordable (see page 134).

$$ Dům u Žluté Boty ("House at the Yellow Boot") hides rustic wooden interiors behind colorful walls. Its seven rooms are each unique: Some preserve 16th-century wooden ceilings; some feel like mountain lodges; and others are a bit marred by an insensitive 1970s remodel. Top-floor rooms can get a bit stuffy during summer heat waves, although fans are provided (Sb-2,700 Kč, Db-3,300 Kč, Tb-3,800 Kč, extra bed-500 Kč, 15 percent discount with cash and this book, some thin walls, Jánský Vršek 11, tel. 257-532-269, fax 257-534-134, www.zlutabota.cz, hotel@zlutabota.cz).

Away from the Center

Moving just outside central Prague saves you money—and gets you away from the tourists and into some more workaday residential neighborhoods. The following listings (great values compared to the downtown hotels listed previously) are all within a 5- to 15-minute tram or Metro ride from the center.

Beyond Wenceslas Square

These hotels are in urban neighborhoods on the outer fringe of the New Town, beyond Wenceslas Square. But they're still within several minutes' walk of the sightseeing zone, and are well-served by trams.

$$$ Sieber Hotel, with 20 rooms, is a quality, four-star, business-class hotel in an upscale residential neighborhood near the former royal vineyards (Vinohrady). They do a good job of being homey and welcoming (Sb-4,480 Kč, Db-4,780 Kč, extra bed-990 Kč, fourth night free, ask for discount when you book direct and pay with cash, 30 percent discount for last-minute reservations, air-con, elevator, Internet access, 3-min walk to Metro: Jiřího z Poděbrad, or tram #11, Slezská 55, Praha 3, tel. 224-250-025, fax 224-250-027, www.sieber.cz, reservations@sieber.cz).

$$ Hotel Anna, with 24 bright, pastel, and classically charming rooms, is a bit closer in—just 10 minutes by foot east of Wenceslas Square (Sb-2,350 Kč, Db-3,160 Kč, Tb-3,830 Kč, special online offers, non-smoking rooms, elevator, Budečská 17, Praha 2, Metro: Náměstí Míru, tel. 222-513-111, fax 222-515-158, www.hotelanna.cz, sales@hotelanna.cz). They run a similar hotel (same standards and prices) nearby.

$$ Hotel 16 is a sleek and modern business-class place with an intriguing Art Nouveau facade, polished cherry-wood elegance, high ceilings, and 14 fine rooms (Sb-2,800 Kč, Db-3,500 Kč, bigger Db-3,700 Kč, Tb-4,700 Kč, 10 percent discount with this book, triple-paned windows, back rooms facing the garden are quieter, air-con, elevator, Internet access, 10-min walk south of Wenceslas Square, Metro: I. P. Pavlova, Kateřinská 16, Praha 2, tel. 224-920-636, fax 224-920-626, www.hotel16.cz, hotel16@hotel16.cz).

The Best Values, Farther from the Center

These accommodations are a 10- to 20-minute tram ride from the center, but once you make the trip, you'll see it's no problem—and you'll feel pretty smug saving $50–100 a night per double by not sleeping in the Old Town. The Adalbert is on the grounds of an ancient monastery and the Větrník is adjacent, with two of Prague's best-preserved natural areas (Star Park and Šárka) just a short walk away. The Šemíka and Lída are within a stone's throw of peaceful Vyšehrad park, with a legendary castle on a cliff overlooking the Vltava River.

$$ Hotel Adalbert occupies an 18th-century building in the Břevnov Monastery (one of the Czech Republic's oldest monastic institutions, founded in 993). Meticulously restored after the return of the Benedictine monks in the 1990s, the monastery complex is the ultimate retreat for those who come to Prague for soul-searching or just wanting a quiet place away from the bustle. Join the monks for morning (7:00) and evening (18:00) Mass in the St. Margaret Basilica, a large and elegant Baroque church executed with unusual simplicity. You can help yourself in the monastery fruit orchard, and eat in the atmospheric monastery pub (Klášterní Šenk). The hotel itself caters primarily to business clientele and takes ecology seriously: recycling, water conservation, and free tram tickets for guests (Sb-2,600 Kč, Db-3,600 Kč, extra bed-1,050 Kč, ask for a first-floor room as some of the attic rooms—room numbers in the 200s—feel a bit cramped, Wi-Fi, free parking, ask for 10 percent Rick Steves discount when you reserve, halfway between city and airport at Markétská 1, Praha 6, tram #22 to Břevnovský Klášter; 5 min by tram beyond the castle, 20 min from Old and New Towns; tel. 220-406-170, fax 220-406-190, www.hoteladalbert.cz, info@hoteladalbert.cz).

$ Pension Větrník fills an attractive white-and-orange former 17th-century windmill in one of Prague's most popular residential areas, right next to the Břevnov Monastery and midway between the airport and the city. Owner Miloš Opatrný is a prizewinning Czech chef who sailed the world feeding cruise-ship passengers. On request, Miloš will prepare a feast you'll never forget. The six rooms here are the pride of the Opatrný family, who live on the upper floors. The garden has a good-hearted bear of a dog and a tennis court—rackets and balls are provided (Db-2,200 Kč, suite-3,300 Kč, extra bed-550 Kč, U Větrníku 4, Praha 6; airport bus #179 stops right in front of the house, tram #18 goes straight to Charles Bridge, both take 20 min; tel. 220-612-404, fax 235-361-406, www.pensionvetrnik.wz.cz).

$ Hotel u Šemíka, named for a heroic mythical horse, offers 25 rooms in a quiet residential neighborhood just below Vyšehrad Castle and the Slavín cemetery where Dvořák, Mucha, and Čapek

HOTELS AND RESTAURANTS IN THE NEW TOWN AND BEYOND

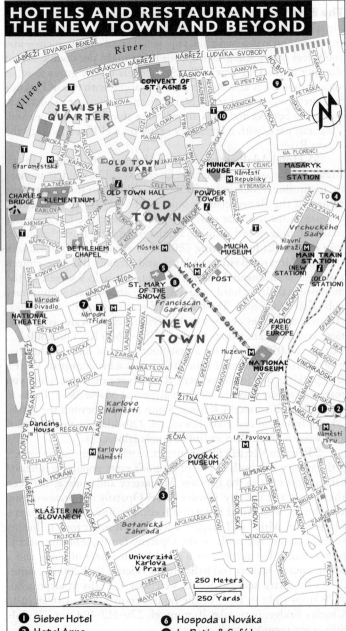

1. Sieber Hotel
2. Hotel Anna
3. Hotel 16
4. Hostel Elf
5. Restaurace u Pinkasů
6. Hospoda u Nováka
7. Le Patio & Café Louvre
8. Dobrá Čajovna Teahouse
9. Restaurant Červená Tabulka
10. Himalaya Restaurant

are buried. It's a 10-minute tram ride south of the Old Town (Sb-2,000 Kč, Db-2,650 Kč, apartment-3,350–3,700 Kč for 2–4 people, extra bed-600 Kč, ask for the "direct booking" Rick Steves 10 percent discount; from the center, take trams #3, #17, or #21 to Výtoň, go under rail bridge, and walk 3 blocks uphill to Vratislavova 36; Praha 2, tel. 224-920-736, fax 224-911-602, www.usemika.cz, usemika@usemika.cz).

$ Guest House Lída, with 12 homey and spacious rooms, fills a big house in a quiet residential area farther inland, a 15-minute tram ride from the center. Jan, Jiří, and Jitka Prouza, who run the place, are a wealth of information and know how to make people feel at home (Sb-1,380 Kč, small Db-1,440 Kč, Db-1,760 Kč, Tb-2,110 Kč, Qb-2,530 Kč, cash only, family rooms, top-floor family suite with kitchenette, Internet access, parking garage-200 Kč/day, Metro: Pražského Povstání; exit Metro and turn left on Lomnického between the Metro station and big blue-glass ČSOB building, follow Lomnického for 500 yards, then turn left on Lopatecká, go uphill and ring bell at Lopatecká #26, no sign outside; Praha 4, tel. & fax 261-214-766, www.lidabb.eu, lidabb@seznam.cz). The Prouza brothers also rent four apartments across the river, an equal distance from the center (Db-1,600 Kč, Tb-1,900 Kč, Qb-2,100 Kč).

Hostels in the Center

It's tough to find a double for less than 3,000 Kč in the old center. But Prague has an abundance of fine hostels—each with a distinct personality, and each excellent in its own way for anyone wanting a 400-Kč dorm bed or an extremely simple, twin-bedded room for about 1,300 Kč.

$ Old Prague Hostel is a small and very friendly place with 70 beds on the second and third floors of an apartment building on a back alley near the Powder Tower. The spacious rooms were once apartment bedrooms, so it feels less institutional than most hostels. Hanging out in the comfy TV lounge/breakfast room, you'll feel like part of an international family. Older travelers would feel comfortable in this mellow place (six D-1,360 Kč, bunk in 3- to 8-person room-450–530 Kč; includes breakfast, sheets, towels, lockers, and free Internet access; in summer reserve one month ahead, Benediktská 2, see map on page 115 for location, tel. 224-829-058, fax 224-829-060, www.oldpraguehostel.com, oldpraguehostel@seznam.cz).

$ Hostel Týn is hidden in a silent courtyard two blocks from the Old Town Square. Because the management is aware of its value, they don't bother being too friendly (D-1,200 Kč, T-1,400 Kč, bunk in 4- to 5-bed co-ed room-400 Kč, lockers, reserve one week ahead, Týnská 19, see location on map on page 115, tel.

Prague

224-828-519, mobile 776-122-057, www.hostel-tyn.web2001.cz, backpacker@razdva.cz).

$ Hostel Elf, a 10-minute walk from the Main Train Station or one bus stop from the Florenc Metro station, is fun-loving, ramshackle, covered with noisy, self-inflicted graffiti, and the wildest of these hostels. They offer cheap, basic beds, a helpful staff, and lots of creative services—kitchen, free luggage room, free Internet access, laundry, no lockout, free tea, cheap beer, a terrace, and lockers (120 beds, D-900 Kč, bunk in 6- to 11-person room-320 Kč, includes sheets and breakfast, cash only, reserve four days ahead, Husitská 11, Praha 3, take bus #133 or #207 from Florenc Metro station for one stop to U Památníku, tel. 222-540-963, www.hostelelf.com, info@hostelelf.com).

$ Hostel Sokol, plain and institutional with 100 beds, is peacefully located just off park-like Kampa Island in the Tyrš House buildings (the seat of the Czech Sokol Organization). Big WWI hospital–style rooms are lined with single beds and lockers (bunk in 8- to 14-person room-350 Kč, cash only, no breakfast, easy to reserve without deposit by phone or email, open 24/7, kitchen, Nosticova 2, see location on map on page 117, tel. 257-007-397, fax 257-007-340, www.sokol-cos.cz/index_en.htm, hostel@sokol-cos.cz). From the Main Train Station, ride tram #9 to Újezd. From the Holešovice station, take tram #12 to Hellichova. From either tram stop, walk 200 yards to the hostel.

EATING

A big part of Prague's charm is found in wandering aimlessly through the city's winding old quarters, marveling at the architecture, watching the people, and sniffing out fun restaurants. You can eat well here for very little money. What you'd pay for a basic meal in Vienna or Munich will get you a feast in Prague. In addition to meat-and-potatoes Czech cuisine (see "Czech Food," page 37), you'll find trendy, student-oriented bars and lots of fine ethnic eateries. For ambience, the options include traditional, dark Czech beer halls; elegant Art Nouveau dining rooms; or hip and modern cafés.

Watch out for scams. Many restaurants put more care into ripping off green tourists (and even locals) than into their cooking. Tourists are routinely served cheaper meals than what they ordered, given a menu with a "personalized" price list, charged extra for things they didn't get, or shortchanged. Speak Czech. Even saying "Hello" in Czech (see phrases on page 41) will get you better service. Avoid any menu without clear and explicit prices. Be careful of waiters padding the tab. Carefully examine your itemized bill and understand each line (a 10 percent service charge is sometimes added—in that case, there's no need to tip extra). Tax is always included in the price, so it shouldn't be tacked on later. Part with very large bills only if necessary, and deliberately count your change. Never let your credit card out of your sight. Make it a habit to get cash from an ATM to pay for your meals. (Credit cards can cost merchants as much as 10 percent.) Remember, there are two parallel worlds in Prague: the tourist town and the real city. Generally, if you walk two minutes away from the tourist flow, you'll find better value, ambience, and service.

I've listed these eating and drinking establishments by neighborhood (see "Prague's Four Towns," page 58). The most options—and highest prices—are in the Old Town. If you want a memorable splurge, see "Dining with Style" on page 133. For a light meal, consider one of Prague's many cafés (see "Cafés" on page 129). Many of the places listed here are handy for an efficient lunch, but may not offer fine evening dining. Others make less sense for lunch, but are great for a slow, drawn-out dinner. Read the descriptions to judge which is which.

Fun, Touristy Neighborhoods: Several areas are pretty and well-situated for sightseeing, but lined only with touristy restaurants. While these places are not necessarily bad values, I've listed only a few of your many options—just survey the scene in these spots and choose whatever looks best. Kampa Square, just off the Charles Bridge, feels like a small-town square. Havelská Market is surrounded by colorful little eateries, any of which give a fine perch for viewing the market scene while you munch. The massive Old Town Square is *the* place to nurse a drink or enjoy a meal while watching the tide of people, both tourists and locals, sweep back and forth. There's often some event on the main square, and its many restaurants provide tasty and relaxing vantage points.

Dining with a View: For great views, consider these options: **U Prince Terrace** (rooftop dining above a fancy hotel, completely touristy but awesome views, recommended and described on page 129); the **Bellavista Restaurant** at Strahov Monastery; **Petřínské Terasy** and **Nebozízek** next to the funicular stop halfway up Petřín Hill; and the many overpriced but elegant places serving scenic meals along the riverbanks. For the best cheap riverside dinner, have a picnic on a paddleboat (see page 60). There's nothing like drifting down the middle of the Vltava River as the sun sets, while munching on your picnic meal and sipping beer with your favorite travel partner.

In or near the Old Town
Characteristically Czech Places

With the inevitable closing of cheap student pubs (replaced by shops and hotels that make more money), it's getting difficult to

RESTAURANTS IN THE OLD TOWN

Letenské Park

NÁBŘEŽÍ EDVARDA BENEŠE

River

Vltava

CONVENT OF ST. AGNES

JEWISH QUARTER

RUDOLFINUM

MUSEUM OF APPLIED ARTS

CHURCH OF ST. NICHOLAS

Staroměstská

SV. FRANTIŠEK Z ASSISI

CHARLES BRIDGE

SMETANA MUSEUM

KLEMENTINUM

OLD TOWN SQUARE

OLD TOWN HALL

TÝN CHURCH

OLD

TOWN

BETHLEHEM CHAPEL

KAROLINUM

OVOCNÝ TRH

POWDER TOWER

MUNICIPAL HOUSE

Náměstí Republiky

To Main Train Station

Kotva Dept. Store

Mústek

MUCHA MUSEUM

ST. MARY OF THE SNOWS

Mústek

POST

Národní Divadlo

Tesco Dept. Store

Franciscan Garden

WENCESLAS SQUARE

NATIONAL THEATRE

NOVÁ SCÉNA

Národní Třída

NEW TOWN

200 Meters

200 Yards

ŽOFÍN

❶	Plzeňská Rest. u Dvou Koček	⓬	Chez Marcel
❷	Restaurace u Provaznice	⓭	La Casa Blú
❸	U Medvídků Beer Hall	⓮	Molly Malone's Irish Pub
❹	U Zlatého Tygra Pub	⓯	Bohemia Bagel
❺	Restaurace u Betlémské Kaple	⓰	Restaurace u Prince Terrace
❻	Česká Kuchyně	⓱	Municipal House Eateries
❼	Restaurace Mlejnice	⓲	Grand Café Slavia
❽	Country Life Veggie Restaurant	⓳	Grand Café Orient
❾	Lehká Hlava Veggie Restaurant	⓴	Café Montmartre
❿	Klub Architektů	㉑	Ebel Coffee House
⓫	Dahab	㉒	Havelská Market

find a truly Czech pub in the historic city center. Most Czechs no longer go to "traditional" eateries, preferring the cosmopolitan taste of the world to the mundane flavor of sauerkraut. As a result, ancient institutions with "authentic" Czech ambience have become touristy—but they're still great fun, a good value, and respected by Czechs. Expect wonderfully rustic spaces, smoke, surly service, and reasonably good, inexpensive food. Understand every line on your bill.

Plzeňská Restaurace u Dvou Koček ("By the Two Cats") is a typical Czech pub with cheap, no-nonsense, hearty Czech food and beer. Sandwiched between the two red-light-district streets, and now filled with tourists rather than Czechs, the restaurant somehow maintains its charm (200 Kč for three courses and beer, serving original Pilsner Urquell, piano or accordion music nightly until 23:00, under an arcade, facing a tiny square between Perlová and Skořepka stréets).

Restaurace u Pinkasů, with a menu that reads like a 19th-century newspaper, is a Prague institution, founded in 1843. It's best in summer, when you sit in the garden behind the building, in the shade of the Gothic buttresses of the St. Mary of the Snows Church. But its waiters could win the award for the rudest service in town (daily 9:00–24:00, tucked in a courtyard near the bottom of Wenceslas Square, on the border between Old and New towns, see location on map on page 120, Jungmannovo Náměstí 16, tel. 221-111-150).

Restaurace u Provaznice ("By the Ropemaker's Wife") has all the Czech classics, peppered with the story of a once-upon-a-time-faithful wife. (Check the menu for details of the gory story.) It's less touristed and less expensive than the other restaurants in this area. Natives congregate here for their famously good "pig leg" with horseradish and Czech mustard (daily 11:00–24:00, a block into the Old Town from the bottom of Wenceslas Square at Provaznická 3, tel. 224-232-528).

U Medvídků ("By the Bear Cubs"), which started out as a brewery in 1466, is now a flagship beer hall of the Czech Budweiser. The one large room is bright, noisy, touristy, and a bit smoky (daily 11:30–23:00, a block toward Wenceslas Square from Bethlehem Square at Na Perštýnì 7, tel. 224-211-916). The small beer bar next to the restaurant (daily 16:00–3:00 in the morning) is used by university students during emergencies—such as after most other pubs have closed.

U Zlatého Tygra ("By the Golden Tiger") has long embodied the proverbial Czech pub, where beer turns strangers into kindred spirits, who cross the fuzzy line between memory and imagination as they tell their hilarious life stories to each other. Today, "the Tiger" is a buzzing shrine to one of its longtime regulars, the writer Bohumil Hrabal, whose fictions immortalize many of the colorful characters that once warmed the wooden benches here (daily 15:00–23:00, often jam-packed, just south of Karlova at Husova 17).

Hospoda u Nováka, behind the National Theatre (i.e., not so central), is emphatically Czech, with few tourists. It takes good care of its regulars (you'll see the old monthly beer tabs in a rack just inside the door). Nostalgic communist-era signs are everywhere. During that time, pubs like this were close-knit communities where regulars escaped from the depression of daily life. Today, the U Nováka is a bright and smoky hangout where you can still happily curse whatever regime you happen to live under. While the English menu lists the well-executed Czech classics, it doesn't list the cheap daily specials (daily 10:00–23:00, V Jirchářích 2, see map on page 120, tel. 224-930-639).

Restaurace u Betlémské Kaple, behind Bethlehem Chapel, is not "ye olde" Czech. It has light wooden decor, cheap lunch deals, and fish specialties that attract natives and visitors in search of a good Czech bite for Czech prices (daily 11:00–23:00, Betlémské Náměstí 2, tel. 222-221-639).

Česká Kuchyně ("Czech Kitchen") is a blue-collar cafeteria serving steamy old Czech cuisine to a local clientele. It's fast, practical, cheap, and traditional as can be. There's no English inside, so—if you want apple charlotte, but not tripe soup—be sure to review the small English menu in the window outside before entering. Note the numbers of your preferred dishes, because they correspond to the Czech menu that you'll see inside. Pick up your tally sheet as you enter, grab a tray, point liberally to whatever you'd like, and keep the paper to pay as you exit. It's extremely cheap...unless you lose your paper (daily 9:00–20:00, very central, across from Havelská Market at Havelská 23, tel. 224-235-574).

Restaurace Mlejnice ("The Mill") is a fun little pub strewn with farm implements and happy eaters, located just out of the tourist crush two blocks from the Old Town Square. They serve hardy traditional and modern Czech plates for 150–180 Kč. Reservations are smart in the evening (daily 11:00–24:00, between Melantrichova and Železná at Kožná 14, tel. 224-228-635).

Hip Restaurants
Country Life Vegetarian Restaurant is a bright, easy, non-smoking cafeteria with a well-displayed buffet of salads and hot veggie dishes. It's midway between the Old Town Square and the bottom of Wenceslas Square. They're serious about their vegetarianism, serving only plant-based, unprocessed, and unrefined food. Its dining area is quiet and elegantly woody for a cafeteria, with three tables and wicker chairs outside in the courtyard (Sun–Thu

9:00–20:30, Fri 9:00–17:00, closed Sat, through courtyard at Melantrichova 15/Michalská 18, tel. 224-213-366).

Lehká Hlava Vegetarian Restaurant ("Clear Head"), tucked away on a cul-de-sac, has a mission to provide a "clear atmosphere for enjoying food." Sitting as if in an enchanted forest, diners enjoy dishes from around the world. Reserve in advance for evenings (100–150-Kč plates, two-course 90-Kč daily special, no eggs, no smoke, lots of vegan dishes, daily 11:30–23:30, between Bethlehem Chapel and the river at Boršov 2, tel. 222-220-665).

Klub Architektů, next to Bethlehem Chapel, is a modern hangout in a medieval cellar that serves excellent original dishes, hearty salads, Moravian wines, and Slovak beer (daily, Betlémské Náměstí 169, tel. 224-401-214).

At **Le Patio,** on the big and busy Národní Třída, the first thing you'll notice are the many lanterns suspended from the ceiling—and the big ship moored out back (okay, just its hulking bow). Le Patio has a hip, continental feel, but for a place that also sells furniture (head straight back, and down the stairs), it definitely needs comfier dining chairs. The atmosphere is as pleasant and carefully designed as the dishes, with international fare from India, France, and points in between. There's always a serious vegetarian option available (200–350-Kč plates, daily 8:00–23:00, Národní 22, see "New Town" map on page 120, tel. 224-934-375). Diners enjoy live music on Friday and Saturday nights (19:30–22:30).

Ethnic Eateries on or near Dlouhá Street

Dlouhá, the wide street leading away from the Old Town Square behind the Jan Hus monument (left of Týn Church), is lined with ethnic restaurants catering mostly to cosmopolitan locals. Within a couple of blocks, you can eat your way around the world. From Dlouhá, wander the Rámová/Haštalská area to survey a United Nations of eateries: You'll find Moroccan (**Dahab,** with some interesting hubbly-bubbly action at Dlouhá 33), French (**Chez Marcel** at Haštalská 12 is understandably popular—with a fun-loving waitstaff), Thai, Afghan, Italian, and these four, which deserve special consideration:

Indian: At **Himalaya,** Slovak waitresses dressed in *salwar kameez* serve their decidedly North Indian chef's vegetarian platters and tandoori meats with Pilsner beer to a Bollywood beat for Czech prices (Mon–Fri 11:00–23:00, Sat–Sun 12:00–23:00, Soukenická 2, at the end of Dlouhá across Revoluční, tel. 233-353-594).

Irish: **Molly Malone's Irish Pub,** hidden in a forgotten corner of the Jewish Quarter, may seem a strange recommendation in Prague—home of some of the world's best beer—but it has the kind of ambience that locals (and few tourists) seek out. Molly

Malone's has been the expat and local favorite for Guinness ever since the Velvet Revolution enabled the Celts to return to one of their homelands. Worn wooden floors, dingy walls, and the Irish manager transport you right into the heart of blue-collar Dublin—which is, after all, a popular place for young Czechs to find jobs in the high-tech industry (Sun–Thu 11:00–1:00 in the morning, Fri–Sat 11:00–2:00 in the morning, U Obecního Dvora 4, tel. 224-818-851).

Latin American: **La Casa Blů,** with cheap lunch specials, Mexican plates, Staropramen beer, and greenish *mojitos,* is your Spanish village in Prague and one of the last student bastions in the Old Town. Painted in warm orange-and-red and guarded by creatures from Mayan mythology, La Casa Blů is packed nightly with smoke, guitar music, and a fusion of Czechs and Chileans (Mon–Sat 11:00–23:00, Sun 14:00–23:00, on the corner of Kozí and Bílkova, tel. 224-818-270).

North American: **Bohemia Bagel** is hardly authentic—exasperated Czechs insist that bagels have nothing to do with Bohemia. Owned by an American, this practical café caters mostly to youthful tourists, with good sandwiches (100–125 Kč), a little garden out back, and Internet access (1.50 Kč/min). If homesick, you'll love the menu, with everything from a Philly cheesesteak to bacon and eggs (daily 7:00–24:00, Masná 2, tel. 224-812-560).

In the Jewish Quarter

These four eateries are well located to break up a demanding tour of the Jewish Quarter—all within two blocks of each other on or near Široká (see map on page 73). Also consider the nearby ethnic eateries listed above.

Kolkovna, the flagship of a franchise owned by Pilsner Urquell, is big and woody, yet modern, serving a fun mix of Czech and international cuisine—ribs, salads, cheese plates, and good beer (a bit overpriced but good energy, daily 11:00–24:00, across from Spanish Synagogue at V Kolkovně 8, tel. 224-819-701).

Franz Kafka Café, with a cool, dark, and woody interior strewn with historic photos of the ghetto and a few good sidewalk tables, is great for a relaxing salad, sandwich, snack, or drink (150-Kč salads, daily 10:00–21:00, a block from the cemetery at Široká 12).

Pekařství ("Bakery") is a little deli with fresh sandwiches, greasy microwavable meat pies, tempting cakes, yogurt, and a cooler full of drinks. It's self-serve and dirt-cheap, with plain circa-1960 linoleum loft seating upstairs (daily 7:00–22:30, Široká 10, near the Pinkas Synagogue). Head upstairs to see the insane director of the National Gallery throwing paint on a nude woman.

Restaurace U Knihovny ("By the Library"), situated steps away from the City and National Libraries as well as the Pinkas Synagogue, is a favorite lunch spot for Czechs who work nearby. Their cheap daily lunch specials consist of seven imaginative variations on traditional Czech themes, the service is friendly, and the stylish redbrick interior is warm. Smoking is not permitted during lunch (daily 11:00–23:00, on the corner of Veleslavínova and Valentinská, mobile 732-835-876).

Dining with an Old Town Square View

Restaurant u Prince Terrace, in the five-star U Prince Hotel facing the Astronomical Clock, is designed for foreign tourists. A sleek elevator takes you to its rooftop, where every possible inch is used to serve good food (international with plenty of fish) from their open-air grill. The view is arguably the best in town—especially at sunset. The menu is a fun but overpriced mix, with photos that make ordering easy. Being in such a touristy spot, waiters are experts at nicking you with confusing menu charges; don't be afraid to confirm exact prices before ordering. This place is also great for just a drink at sunset or late at night (fine salads, 240–300-Kč plates, daily until 24:00, brusque staff, outdoor heaters when necessary, Staroměstské Náměstí 29, tel. 224-213-807—but no reservations possible).

Art Nouveau Splendor in the Municipal House

The **Municipal House** (Obecní Dům), the sumptuous Art Nouveau concert hall, has three restaurants: a café, a French restaurant, and a beer cellar (all at Náměstí Republiky 5). The dressy café, **Kavárna Obecní Dům,** is drenched in chandeliered, Art Nouveau elegance and offers the best value and experience here (light, pricey meals and drinks with great atmosphere and bad service, 250-Kč three-course special daily for lunch or dinner, open daily 7:30–23:00, live piano or jazz trio 16:00–20:00, tel. 222-002-763). The fine and formal French restaurant in the next wing oozes Mucha elegance (700–1,000-Kč meals, daily 12:00–16:00 & 18:00–23:00, tel. 222-002-777). The overpriced, touristy beer cellar is open daily 11:30–23:00.

Cafés

Dripping with history, these places are as much about the ambience as they are about the coffee. Most cafés also serve sweets and light meals.

Grand Café Slavia, across from the National Theatre (facing the Legií Bridge on Národní street), is a fixture in Prague, famous as a hangout for its literary elite. Today, it's tired and clearly past its prime, with an Art Deco interior, lousy piano entertainment, and celebrity photos on the wall. But its iconic status makes it a fun stop for a coffee—skip the food (daily 8:00–23:00, sit as near the river as possible). Notice the *Drinker of Absinthe* painting on the wall (and on the menu for 55 Kč)—with the iconic Czech writer struggling with reality.

Café Louvre is a longtime elegant favorite (opened in 1902) that still draws an energetic young crowd. From the big and busy Národní street, you walk upstairs into a venerable world of newspapers on sticks (including some in English) and waiters in vests and aprons. The back room has long been the place for billiard tables (100 Kč/hr). An English flier tells its history (200-Kč plates, 120-Kč two-course lunch offered 11:00–15:00, open daily 8:00–23:30, Národní 22, see "New Town" map on page 120, tel. 224-930-949).

Grand Café Orient is just two flights up off busy Celetná street, yet a world away from the crush of tourism below. Located in the Black Madonna House, the café is upstairs from the Museum of Czech Cubism (see page 68) and fittingly decorated with a Cubist flair. With its stylish old circa-1910 decor toned to dark green, this space is full of air and light—and a good value as well (salads, sandwiches, great balcony seating, Mon–Fri 9:00–22:00, Sat–Sun 10:00–22:00, Ovocný Trh 19, at the corner of Celetná near the Powder Tower, tel. 224-224-240).

Café Montmartre, on a small street parallel to Karlova, combines Parisian ambience with unbeatable Czech prices. Dreamy Czech minds found their asylum here after Grand Café Slavia (see above) and other long-time favorites either closed down or became stuck in their past. The main room is perfect for discussing art and politics, while the intimate room behind the courtyard is where you recite poetry to your date (Mon–Fri 9:00–23:00, Sat–Sun 12:00–23:00, Řetězová 7, tel. 222-221-244).

Ebel Coffee House, in the Ungelt courtyard behind the Týn Church, is the local Starbucks—priding itself on its wide assortment of fresh coffee from every coffee-growing country in the world, inviting cakes, and a colorful setting that delights the mind as much as the caffeine (daily 9:00–22:00, Týn 1, tel. 224-895-788).

John & George Café, in the courtyard on the other side of the Lennon Wall, is a secluded spot serving raspberry drinks, fresh sandwiches, and Italian coffee next to a flower garden, an English lawn, and one of the oldest trees in Prague (daily 11:00–22:00, Velkopřevorské Náměstí 4, look for small gate at left end of Lennon Wall, entrance to indoor seating area is another 20 yards to the left, see "Little Quarter" map on page 117, tel. 257-217-736).

Teahouses

Many Czech people are bohemian philosophers at heart and prefer the mellow, smoke-free environs of a teahouse to the smoky, traditional beer hall. Young Czechs are much more interested in traveling to exotic destinations like Southeast Asia, Africa, or Peru than to Western Europe, so the Oriental teahouses set their minds in vacation mode.

While there are teahouses all over town, a fine example in a handy locale is Prague's original one, established in 1991. **Dobrá Čajovna** ("Good Teahouse"), just a few steps off the bustle of Wenceslas Square, takes you into a very peaceful world that elevates tea to an almost religious ritual. At the desk, you'll be given an English menu and a bell. Grab a seat and study the menu, which lovingly describes each tea. The menu lists a world of tea (very fresh, prices by the small pot), "accompaniments" (such as Exotic Miscellany), and light meals "for hungry tea drinkers." When you're ready to order, ring your bell to beckon a tea monk—likely a member of the Lovers of Tea Society (Mon–Sat 10:00–21:30, Sun 14:00–21:30, near the base of Wenceslas Square, opposite McDonald's at Václavské Náměstí 14, www.cajovna.com).

In the Little Quarter

These characteristic eateries are handy for a bite before or after your Prague Castle visit. For locations, see the map on page 117.

U Sedmi Švábů ("By the Seven Roaches") is a touristy den where even the cuisine is medieval. Since America had not yet been discovered in the Middle Ages, you won't find any corn, potatoes, or tomatoes on the menu. The salty yellow things that come with the Krušovice beer are chickpeas. Carnivores thrive here: Try the skewered meats *(špíz u Sedmi Švábů)*, flaming beef *(flambák)*, or pork knuckle (daily 11:00–23:00, Janský Vršek 14, tel. 257-531-455).

U Osla v Kolébce ("By the Donkey in the Cradle") fills a peaceful courtyard just a minute off the touristy hubbub of Nerudova. The laid-back scene consists of two restaurants with nearly identical simple menus, dominated by tasty sausages and salads (daily 10:00–22:00, Jánský Vršek 8, below Nerudova, next door to U Sedmi Švábů, tel. 731-407-036).

U Hrocha ("By the Hippo"), a very authentic little pub packed with beer-drinkers and smoke, serves simple, traditional meals— basically meat starters with bread. Just below the castle near Little Quarter Square (Malostranské Náměstí), it's actually the haunt of many members of Parliament, which is located just around the corner (daily 12:00–23:00, chalkboard lists daily meals in English, Thunovská 10).

Restaurace Rybářský Klub, on Kampa Island overlooking the river, is run by the Society of Czech Fishermen and serves one of the widest and tastiest selections of freshwater fish in Prague at reasonable prices. Dine on fish-cream soup, pike, trout, carp, or catfish under the imaginative artwork of Little Quarter painter Mr. Kuba. On warm evenings, late May through October, the society fills its dock with tables and offers my choice for the best riverside dining in town (three-course meal for around 400 Kč, riverside menu not as extensive as indoor restaurant menu, daily 12:00–23:00, U Sovových Mlýnů 1, tel. 257-534-200).

In the Castle Quarter

To locate the following restaurants, see the map on page 96.

Klášterní Pivovar ("Monastery Brewery"), founded by an abbot in 1628 and re-opened in 2004, has two large rooms and a pleasant courtyard. This is the place to enjoy rare unpasteurized yeast beer, brewed on the premises. The wooden decor and circa-1900 newspaper clippings (including Hapsburg Emperor Franz Josef's "Proclamation to My Nations," announcing the beginning of the First World War) evoke the era when Vienna was Europe's artistic capital, Prague was building its Eiffel Tower, and life moved much slower than today. To accompany the beer, try the beer-flavored cheese served on toasted black-yeast bread (daily 10:00–22:00, Strahovské Nádvoří 301, tel. 233-353-155, www.klasterni-pivovar.cz). It's directly across from the entrance to the Strahov Library (not to be confused with the enormous, group-oriented Klášterní Restaurace next door, to the right).

Restaurace Nad Úvozem is hidden in the middle of a staircase that connects Loretánská and Úvoz streets. This secret spot, which boasts super views of Prague, offers excellent food for surprisingly low prices, given its location. Try the roast beef in plum sauce (170 Kč). The service is slower when the restaurant is full, as the kitchen has limited space (daily 12:00–21:00; as you go down Loretánská watch for pans, scoops, and spoons hanging on chains on your right at #15; tel. 220-511-532). To discourage pub-goers from mingling with diners, the beer here is terribly overpriced (69 Kč).

Hostinec u Černého Vola ("By the Black Ox") is a smoky, dingy old-time pub—its survival in the midst of all the castle splendor and tourism is a marvel. It feels like a kegger on the banks of the river Styx, with classic bartenders serving up Kozel beer (traditional "goat" brand with excellent darks) and beer-friendly light meals. The pub is located on Loretánská (no sign outside, sniff for cigarette smoke and look for the only house on the block without an arcade—or see map on page 96, daily 10:00–22:00, English menu on request).

Malý Buddha ("Little Buddha") serves delightful food—especially vegetarian—and takes its theme seriously. You'll step into a mellow, low-lit escape of bamboo and peace to be served by people with perfect complexions and almost no pulse (Tue–Sun 13:00–22:30, closed Mon, non-smoking, between the castle and

Strahov Monastery at Úvoz 46, tel. 220-513-894).

Espresso Kajetánka, just off Castle Square, has magnificent city views. It's a good-if-overpriced place for a drink or snack as you start or end your castle visit (daily 10:00–20:00, Ke Hradu, tel. 257-533-735).

Na Baště, more convenient but not as scenic, is in a garden through the gate to the left of the main castle entry. The outdoor seating, among Jože Plečnik's ramparts and obelisks, is the castle at its most peaceful (Sun–Thu 11:00–23:00, Fri–Sat 11:00–24:00, tel. 281-933-010).

Dining with Style

In Prague, a fancy candlelit dinner with fine wines and connoisseur-approved dishes costs more than most locals can afford—but it's still a bargain in comparison to similar restaurants in Paris or Dallas. I list only two such splurges: one aristocratic, Old World, and under the castle; one more modern, untouristy, and near the Old Town Square.

Restaurace David, with two little 18th-century rooms hiding on a small cobblestone street opposite the American Embassy in the Little Quarter, is my choice for a romantic splurge. The exquisite cuisine, a modern incarnation of traditional Czech with French and European influences, ranges from game to roasted duck and liver. Your meal comes with the gourmet quotient of knives and fancy glasses, and graceful waiters serve you like an aristocrat—appropriate, considering the neighborhood. Reservations are recommended (most meals 600–1,000 Kč, open daily, Tržiště 21, see "Little Quarter" map on page 117, tel. 257-533-109).

Restaurant Červená Tabulka ("Red Chalkboard") is in a low, nondescript townhouse in a quiet neighborhood outside of the tourist circus. Sit in the dressy candlelit interior or on the quiet and breezy cobbled courtyard. Either way, there's not a dumpling in sight. The menu features modern international dishes with a focus on fish (fine 300-Kč plates and gourmet presentation). The wines are excellent and a great value (daily 11:30–23:00, Lodecká 4, tel. 224-810-401). To get to the restaurant from the Municipal House, cross Náměstí Republiky and turn right onto Truhlářská; it's 200 yards down the street on the corner of quiet Petrské Náměstí square, see "New Town" map on page 120.

TRANSPORTATION CONNECTIONS

Getting to Prague: Centrally located Prague is a logical gateway between Eastern and Western Europe. Prague is connected by convenient night trains with Budapest, Kraków, and Warsaw (see next page). From the West, direct overnight trains connect Prague to

Munich, and frequent day trains leave from Berlin and Vienna. For information on Prague's airport, see page 49.

If you're using a Eurailpass, keep in mind that it doesn't cover the Czech Republic. You need to buy a ticket for the Czech portion of the trip (if you're coming from Vienna, however, it's cheaper to buy a ticket for the whole route and not use up a travel day of a flexipass). You can either buy that in the station before leaving a Eurailpass-covered country, or save about €5 by buying it directly from the Czech conductor (German stations, for example, charge twice what Czechs do for Czech tickets; note that you can only buy tickets on board on long-distance trains—if you go to Prague indirectly via a milk-run train, you can be fined heavily for boarding without a ticket).

You'll find handy Czech train and bus schedules at www .vlak-bus.cz (train info tel. 221-111-122, little English spoken). Remember that for all train connections, it's important to confirm which of Prague's stations to use.

From Prague by Train to: Český Krumlov (8/day, 1/day direct, 4 hrs—bus is faster, cheaper, and easier), **Budapest** (3/day, 7 hrs; 2 overnight trains, 9 hrs), **Kraków** (1 direct train/day, 7 hrs; 2 more with 1–2 changes, 8 hrs), **Warsaw** (2/day direct including 1 night train, 8.5–9.5 hrs), **Vienna** (5/day direct, 4.5 hrs, 5 more with 1 change, 5–6 hrs), **Berlin** (7/day, 4.5–5 hrs), **Munich** (2/day direct, 6 more with changes, 6–7.5 hrs, 1/night, 10 hrs), **Frankfurt** (8/day, 7–8 hrs, 1 change in Dresden or Nürnberg).

By Bus to: Terezín (hourly, 1 hr, from Florenc station), **Český Krumlov** (7/day, 3.5 hrs, from Florenc station; an easy direct 3-hr bus leaves at about 9:00).

By Car with a Driver: Mike's Chauffeur Service is a reliable family-run company with fair and fixed rates for around town and beyond. Friendly Mike's motto is "We go the extra mile for you" (round-trip fares with waiting time included, guaranteed through 2009 with this book: Český Krumlov-3,800 Kč, Terezín-1,900 Kč, Karlštejn-1,700 Kč, these prices for up to 4 people, minivan for up to 6 and brand-new minibus for 7 also available, tel. 241-768-231, mobile 602-224-893, www.mike-chauffeur.cz, mike.chauffeur @cmail.cz). On the way to Krumlov, Mike will stop at no extra charge at Hluboká Castle or České Budějovice, where the original Bud beer is made. Mike offers a "Panoramic Transfer to Vienna" for 7,000 Kč (depart Prague at 8:00, arrive Český Krumlov at 10:00, stay up to 6 hrs, 1-hr scenic Czech riverside-and-village drive, then a 2-hr autobahn ride to your Vienna hotel, maximum 4 people). Mike also offers a similar "Panoramic Transfer to Budapest" for 10,000 Kč (2 hrs to Český Krumlov, then 1-hr scenic drive to Linz, followed by 5–6 hrs on expressway to Budapest).

ČESKÝ KRUMLOV

Lassoed by its river and dominated by its castle, this enchanting town feels lost in a time warp. While Český Krumlov is the Czech Republic's answer to Germany's Rothenburg, it has yet to be turned into a medieval theme park. When you see its awe-inspiring castle, delightful Old Town of shops and cobbled lanes, characteristic little restaurants, and easy canoeing options, you'll understand why having fun is a slam-dunk here.

Český Krumlov (CHESS-key KROOM-loff) means, roughly, "Czech Bend in the River." Calling it "Český" for short sounds silly to Czech-speakers (since dozens of Czech town names begin with "Český"). "Krumlov" for short is okay.

Since Krumlov is the second-most-visited town (1.5 million visits annually) in the Czech Republic, there's enough tourism to make things colorful and easy—but not so much that it tramples the place's charm. This town of 15,000 attracts a young, bohemian crowd, drawn here for its simple beauty, cheap living, and fanciful bars.

Planning Your Time

Because the castle and theater can be visited only with a guide (and English-language tours are offered just a few times a day), serious sightseers should reserve both tours first thing in the morning in person at the castle and theater (or call the castle), and then build their day around the tour times. Those who hate planning ahead on vacation can join a Czech tour anytime with an English information sheet.

A paddle down the river to Zlatá Koruna Abbey is a highlight (three hours, see "Canoeing and Rafting the Vltava," page 147),

Český Krumlov

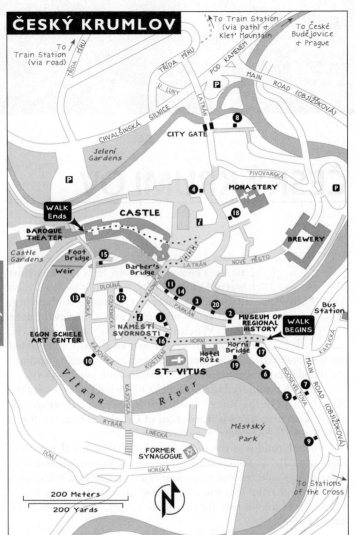

ČESKÝ KRUMLOV

1. Castle View Apts.
2. Hotel Mlýn
3. Pension Olšakovský & Pension u Vltavy
4. Lobo Pension & Pension Danny
5. Little Pension Teddy
6. Pension Myší Díra & Maleček Boat Rental
7. Pension Anna
8. Hostel 99 & Hospoda 99 Rest.
9. Krumlov House Hostel
10. Na Louži Restaurant
11. Krčma u Dwau Maryí
12. Cikánská Jizba
13. Rest. u Dobráka
14. Laibon Restaurant
15. Rybářská Restaurace
16. Krčma v Šatlavské
17. Restaurace Barbakán
18. Dobrá Čajovna Teahouse
19. Start Short River Float
20. End Short River Float & Start Zlatá Koruna Float

and a 20-minute walk up to the Křížový Vrch (Hill of the Cross) rewards you with a fine view of the town and its unforgettable riverside setting (see "Hiking," page 148). Other sights are quick visits and worthwhile only if you have a particular interest (Egon Schiele, puppets, torture, and so on).

The town itself is the major attraction. Evenings are for atmospheric dining and drinking. Sights are generally open 10:00–17:00 and closed on Monday.

ORIENTATION

Český Krumlov is extremely easy to navigate. The twisty Vltava River, which makes a perfect S through the town, ropes the Old Town into a tight peninsula. Above the Old Town is the Castle Town. Český Krumlov's one main street starts at the isthmus and heads through the peninsula. It winds through town and continues across a bridge before snaking through the Castle Town, the castle complex (a long series of courtyards), and the castle gardens high above. The main square, Náměstí Svornosti—with the TI, ATMs, and taxis—dominates the Old Town and marks the center of the peninsula. All recommended restaurants and hotels are within a few minutes' walk of this square. No sight in town is more than a five-minute stroll away.

Tourist Information

The helpful TI is on the main square (daily 9:00–19:00, July–Aug until 20:00, shorter hours in winter, tel. 380-704-622, www .ckrumlov.cz). Pick up the free city map. The 129-Kč *City Guide* book explains everything in town and includes a fine town and castle map in the back. The TI can check train, bus, and flight schedules. Ask about concerts, city walking tours in English, and canoe trips on the river. A second, less-crowded TI—actually a private business—is just below the castle (daily 9:00–19:00, tel. 380-725-110).

Arrival in Český Krumlov

By Train: The train station is a 20-minute walk from town (turn right out of the station, then walk downhill onto a steep cobbled path leading to an overpass into the town center). Taxis are standing by to zip you to your hotel (about 100 Kč), or call 602-113-113 to summon one.

By Bus: The bus station is just three blocks away from the Old Town (from the bus station lot, drop down to main road and turn left, then turn right at Potraviny grocery store to reach the center). Figure on 60 Kč for a taxi from the station to your hotel.

Český Krumlov

Český Krumlov History

With the natural moat provided by the sharp bend in the Vltava, it's no wonder this has been a choice spot for eons. Celtic tribes first settled here a century before Christ. Then came German tribes. The Slavic tribes arrived in the ninth century. The Rožmberks—Bohemia's top noble family—ran the city from 1302 to 1602. You'll see their rose symbol all over town. In many ways, the 16th century was the town's Golden Age, when Český Krumlov hosted artists, scientists, and alchemists from all over Europe. In 1588, the town became home to an important Jesuit college. The Hapsburgs bought the region in 1602, ushering in a more Germanic period. (After that, as many as 75 percent of the town's people were German—until 1945, when most Germans were expelled.)

The rich mix of Gothic, Renaissance, and Baroque buildings is easy to under-appreciate. As you wander, look up...notice the surviving details in the stonework. Step into shops. Snoop into back lanes and tiny squares. Gothic buildings curve with the winding streets. Many precious Gothic and Renaissance frescoes were whitewashed in Baroque times (when the colorful trimmings of earlier periods were way out of style). Today, these precious frescoes are being rediscovered and restored.

With its rich German heritage, it was easy for Hitler to claim that this region—the Sudetenland—was rightfully part of Germany, and in 1938, the infamous Munich Agreement made it his. Americans liberated the town in 1945. Due to Potsdam Treaty–

Helpful Hints

Internet Access: Fine Internet cafés are all over town and in many of the accommodations. The TI on the main square has several fast, cheap, stand-up stations. Perhaps the best cybercafé is behind the TI by the castle (tel. 380-725-117). **Pension Teddy** has Internet access in its bar (1 Kč/min, open long hours daily, Rooseveltova street).

Bookstore: Shakespeare and Sons is a good little English-language bookstore (daily 11:00–20:00, a block below the main square at Soukenická 44, tel. 380-711-203).

Laundry: Pension Lobo runs a self-service launderette under the castle. Since there are only a few machines, you may have to wait (200 Kč to wash and dry, includes soap, daily 9:00–20:00, Latrán 73).

Festivals: Locals drink oceans of beer and celebrate their medieval roots at big events such as the Celebration of the Rose (Slavnosti Růže), where blacksmiths mint ancient coins, jugglers swallow fire, mead flows generously, and pigs are roasted approved ethnic cleansing, three million Germans in Czech lands were sent west to Germany. Emptied of its German citizenry, Český Krumlov turned into a ghost town, partially inhabited by Roma (Gypsies).

In the post-WWII world planned by Stalin and FDR, the border of the Soviet and American spheres of influence fell about here. While the communist government established order, the period from 1945 to 1989 was a smelly time capsule, as the town was infamously polluted. Its now-pristine river was foamy with pollutants from the paper mill just upstream, while the hills around the town were marred with blocks of prefabricated concrete. The people who moved in never fully identified with the town—in Europe, a place without ancestors is without life-giving roots. But the bleak years of communism paradoxically provided a cocoon to preserve the town. There was no money, so little changed, apart from a build-up of grime.

In the early 1990s, tourists discovered Český Krumlov, and the influx of money saved the buildings from ruin. Color returned to the facades, waiters again dressed in coarse linen shirts, and the main drag was flooded with souvenir shops.

With its new prosperity, today's Český Krumlov looks like a fairy-tale town. In fact, movie producers consider it ideal for films. *The Adventures of Pinocchio* was filmed here in 1995, as was the opening sequence for the 2006 film *The Illusionist*.

on open fires (June 19–21 in 2008, June 18–22 in 2009). The summer also brings a top-notch international jazz and alternative music festival to town, performed in pubs, cafés, and the castle gardens (July 18–Aug 23 in 2008, July 17–Aug 22 in 2009). During the St. Wenceslas celebrations, the square becomes a medieval market and the streets come alive with theater and music (Sept 26–28 in 2008, Sept 25–28 in 2009). Reserve a hotel well in advance if you'll be in town for these events (for more details, see www.ckrumlov.cz).

TOURS

Walking Tours—Since the town itself, rather than its sights, is what it's all about here, taking a guided walk is key for a meaningful visit. The TI sponsors three different guided walks. They are cheap, in English, and time well-spent. All meet in front of the TI on the main square. No reservations are necessary—just drop in and pay the guide. The **Historic Town Walk** offers the best general town introduction and is most likely to run (225 Kč, daily at 10:00, 90 min). The **Rose Tour** covers the Renaissance and town architecture (160 Kč, daily at 14:00, 60 min). The **Brewing History Tour,** which is the most intimate of the many brewery tours in this land that so loves its beer, takes you through the Eggenberg Brewery (150 Kč, daily at 12:30, 90 min). For a self-guided town walk, consider renting an **audioguide** from the TI (60 Kč/hr).

Private Guides—Oldřiška Baloušková is a hardworking, excellent, young English-speaking guide who can show you around her hometown (400 Kč/hr, mobile 737-920-901, krumlovguide @hotmail.com). Jiří (George) Václavíček, a gentle and caring man who perfectly fits mellow Český Krumlov, is a joy to share this town with (350 Kč/hr, tel. 380-726-813, mobile 603-927-995, jiri .vaclavicek@seznam.cz). Karolína Kortušová is an enthusiastic woman with great organizational skills. Her company, Krumlov Tours, can set you up with a good local tour guide, palace and theater admissions, river trips, and more (guides-400 Kč/hr, mobile 723-069-561, www.krumlovtours.com, info@krumlovtours.com).

SELF-GUIDED WALK

▲▲▲Welcome to Český Krumlov

The town's best sight is its cobbled cityscape, surrounded by its babbling river and capped by a dramatic castle. All of Český Krumlov's meager sights are laced together in this charming walk from the top of the Old Town, down its spine, across the river, and up to the castle.

• *Start at the bridge over the isthmus, once the fortified grand entry gate to the town.*

Horní Bridge: From this "Upper Bridge," note the natural fortification provided by the tight bend in the river. The last building in town (just over the river) is the Eggenberg Brewery (with daily tours—see "Tours," above). Behind that, on the horizon, is a pile of white apartment high-rises—built in the last decade of the communist era and considered the worst places in town to call home. Left of the brewery stands the huge monastery (not generally open to the public). Behind that on Kleť, the highest hilltop, stands a TV tower that locals say was built to jam Voice of America broadcasts. Facing the town, on your left, rafters take to the river for the sloppy half-hour float around town to the take-out spot just on your right.

• *A block downhill on Horní (Upper) street is the...*

Museum of Regional History: This small museum gives you a quick look at regional costumes, tools, and traditions. When you pay, pick up the English translation of the displays (it also includes a lengthy history of Krumlov). Start on the top floor, where you'll see a Bronze Age exhibit, old paintings, a glimpse of noble life, and a look at how the locals rafted lumber from Krumlov all the way to Vienna. Don't miss the fun-to-study ceramic model of Český Krumlov in 1800 (note the extravagant gardens high above the town). The lower floor comes with fine folk costumes and domestic art (50 Kč, daily 10:00–17:00, until 18:00 in July–Aug, Horní 152, tel. 380-711-674).

• *Below the museum, a little garden overlook affords a fine castle view. Immediately across the street, notice the Renaissance facade of...*

Hotel Růže: This former Jesuit college hides a beautiful courtyard. Pop inside to see a couple of bronze busts that stand like a shrine to the founders of Czechoslovakia. The one on the right, dedicated by the Czech freedom fighters, commemorates the first Czechoslovak president, Tomáš Garrigue Masaryk (in office 1918–1934; see sidebar on page 100). The bust on the left recalls Masaryk's successor, Edvard Beneš (in office 1934–1948; see sidebar on page 142).

• *Walk another block down the main drag, until you reach steps on the left leading to the...*

Church of St. Vitus: Český Krumlov's main church was built as a bastion of Catholicism in the 15th century, when the Roman Catholic Church was fighting the Hussites. The 17th-century Baroque high altar shows a totem of religious figures: the Virgin Mary (crowned in heaven), St. Vitus (above Mary), and way up on top, St. Wenceslas, the patron saint of the Czech people—long considered their ambassador in heaven. The canopy in the back, while empty today, once supported a grand statue of a Rožmberk atop a horse. The statue originally stood at the high altar. Too egotistical for Jesuits, it was later moved to the rear of the nave, and then lost for good. As you listen to the river, notice the empty organ case. While the main organ is out for restoration, the cute little circa-1716 Baroque beauty is getting plenty of use (see photos of the restoration work on the far wall, church open daily 10:00–19:00, Sunday Mass at 9:30, tel. 380-711-336).

• *Continuing on Horní street, you'll come to the...*

Main Square (Náměstí Svornosti): Lined by a mix of Renaissance and Baroque homes of burghers (all built upon 12th-century Gothic foundations), the main square has a grand charm. There's continuity here. Lékárna, with the fine, red, Baroque facade on the lower corner of the square, is still a pharmacy, as it has been since 1620. McDonald's tried three times to get a spot here but

Edvard Beneš and the German Question

Czechoslovakia was created in 1918, when the vast, multiethnic Hapsburg Empire broke into smaller nations after losing World War I. The principle that gave countries such as Poland, Czechoslovakia, and Romania independence was called "self-determination": Each nation had the right to its own state within the area where its people were in the majority. But the peoples of Eastern Europe had mixed over the centuries, making it impossible to create functioning states based purely on ethnicity. In the case of Czechoslovakia, the borders were drawn along historical rather than ethnic boundaries. While the country was predominantly Slavic, there were also areas with overwhelmingly German and Hungarian majorities. One of these areas—a fringe around the western part of the country, mostly populated by Germans—was known as the Sudetenland.

At first, the coexistence of Slavs and Germans in the new republic worked fine. German parties were important power brokers and participated in almost every coalition government. Hitler's rise to power, however, led to the growth of German nationalism, even outside Germany. Soon 70 percent of Germans in Czechoslovakia voted for the Nazis. In September 1938, the Munich Agreement ceded the Sudetenland to Germany—and the Czech minority had to leave.

Edvard Beneš was the first Czechoslovak secretary of state (1918–1934) and later became the country's second president (1934–1948). Beneš led the Czechoslovak exile government in London during World War II. Like most Czechs and Slovaks, Beneš believed that after the hard feelings produced by the Munich Agreement, peaceful coexistence of Slavs and Germans in a single state was impossible. His postwar solution: move the Sudeten Germans to Germany, much as the Czechs had been forced out of the Sudetenland before. Through skillful diplomacy, Beneš got

was turned away. The Town Hall flies the Czech flag and the town flag, which shows the rose symbol of the Rožmberk family, who ruled the town for 300 years.

Imagine the history that this square has seen: In the 1620s, the rising tide of Lutheran Protestantism threatened Catholic Europe. Krumlov was a seat of Jesuit power and learning, and the intellectuals of the Roman church allegedly burned books on this square. Later, when there was a bad harvest, locals blamed witches—and burned them, too. Every so often, terrible plagues rolled through the countryside. In a nearby village, all but two residents were killed by a plague.

But the plague stopped before devastating the people of Český Krumlov, and in 1715—as thanks to God—they built the plague the Allies to sign on to this idea.

Shortly after the end of World War II, three million people of German ancestry were forced to leave their homes. Millions of Germanic people in Poland, Romania, Ukraine, and elsewhere met with a similar fate. Many of these families had been living in these areas for centuries. The methods employed to expel them included murder, rape, and plunder. (Today, we'd call it "ethnic cleansing.")

In 1945, Český Krumlov lost 75 percent of its population, and Czechs moved into vacated German homes. Having easily acquired the property, the new residents didn't take much care of the houses. Within a few years, the once-prosperous Sudetenland was reduced to shabby towns and uncultivated fields—a decaying, godforsaken region. After 1989, displaced Sudeten Germans—the majority of whom now live in Bavaria—demanded that the Czechoslovak government apologize for the violent way in which the expulsion was carried out. Some challenged the legality of the decrees, and for a time the issue threatened otherwise good Czech–German relations.

Although no longer such a hot-button diplomatic issue, the so-called Beneš Decrees remain divisive in Czech politics. While liberals consider the laws unjust, many others—especially the older generations—see them as fair revenge for the behavior of the Sudeten Germans prior to and during the war. In the former Sudetenland, where Czech landowners worry that the Germans will try to claim back their property, Beneš is a hugely popular figure. His bust in Český Krumlov's Hotel Růže is one of the first memorials to Beneš in the country. The bridge behind the Old Town has been named for Beneš since the 1990s. The main square—the center of a thriving German community 70 years ago—is now ironically called "Square of Concord."

monument that stands on the square today. Much later, in 1938, Hitler stood right here before a backdrop of long Nazi banners to celebrate the annexation of the Sudetenland. And in 1968, Russian tanks spun their angry treads on these same cobblestones to intimidate locals who were demanding freedom. Today, thankfully, this square is part of an unprecedented time of peace and prosperity for the Czech people.

• *The following three museums are grouped around the main square.*

Puppet Museum: You'll see fascinating displays in three small rooms of more than 300 movable creations (overwhelmingly of Czech origin, but also some from Burma and Rajasthan). At the model stage, children of any age can try their hand at pulling the strings on their favorite fairy tale (80 Kč, daily 10:00–21:00,

Radniční 29, tel. 380-713-422, www.inspirace.krumlov.cz).

Torture Museum: This is just a lame haunted house: dark, with sound effects, cheap modern models, and prints showing off the cruel and unusual punishments of medieval times (80 Kč, daily 9:00–20:00, English descriptions, Náměstí Svornosti 1, tel. 380-766-343).

Egon Schiele Art Center: This classy contemporary art gallery has temporary exhibits, generally featuring 20th-century Czech artists. The top-floor permanent collection celebrates the Viennese artist Egon Schiele (pronounced "Sheila"), who once spent a few weeks here during a secret love affair. A friend of Gustav Klimt and an important figure in the Secessionist movement in Vienna, Schiele lived a short life, from 1890–1918. His cutting-edge lifestyle and harsh art of graphic nudes didn't always fit the conservative, small-town style of Český Krumlov, but townsfolk are happy enough today to charge you to see this relatively paltry collection (180 Kč, daily 10:00–18:00, Široká 70, tel. 380-704-011). The Schiele collection in Vienna's Belvedere Palace is far better (see page 882).

• *From the main square, walk up Radniční street and cross the...*

Barber's Bridge (Lazebnicky Most): This wooden bridge, decorated with two 19th-century statues, connects the Old Town and the Castle Town. In the center stands a statue of St. John of Nepomuk, who's also depicted by a prominent statue on Prague's Charles Bridge (see page 72). Among other responsibilities, he's the protector against floods. In the great floods of August 2002, the angry river submerged the bridge (but removable banisters minimized the damage). Stains just above the windows of the adjacent building show how high the water rose.

• *After crossing the bridge, hike on up the hill. Your next stop is Krumlov Castle.*

SIGHTS

▲▲Krumlov Castle (Krumlovský Zámek)

No Czech town is complete without a castle—and now that the nobles are gone, their mansions are open to us common folk. The Krumlov Castle complex includes bear pits, the castle itself, a rare Baroque theater, and groomed gardens (www.castleckrumlov.cz).

Round Tower (Zámecká Věž)—The strikingly colorful round tower marks the location of the first castle, built here to guard the medieval river crossing. With its 16th-century Renaissance paint job colorfully restored, it looks exotic, featuring fancy astrological decor, terra-cotta symbols of the zodiac, and a fine arcade. Climb its 162 steps for a great view (30 Kč, daily 9:00–18:00, last entry 17:30).

Bear Pits—At the site of the castle drawbridge, the bear pits hold a family of European brown bears, as it has since the Rožmberks added bears to their coat of arms in the 16th century to demonstrate their (fake) blood relation to the distinguished Italian family of Orsini (the name means "bear-like").

Castle—The immense castle is a series of courtyards with shops, contemporary art galleries, and tourist services. The interior is accessible only by tour, which gives you a glimpse of the places where the Rožmberks, Eggenbergs, and Schwarzenbergs dined, studied, worked, prayed, entertained, and slept. (By European

standards, the castle's not much, and the tours move slowly.) Imagine being an aristocratic guest here, riding the dukes' assembly line of fine living: You'd promenade through a long series of elegant spaces and dine in the sumptuous dining hall before enjoying a concert in the Hall of Mirrors, which leads directly to the Baroque Theater (described next). After the play, you'd go out into the château garden for a fireworks finale.

Cost, Hours, and Tours: To see the interior, you must take a 60-minute escorted tour: Tour I (Gothic and Renaissance rooms, of the most general interest) or Tour II (19th-century castle life). Tours run June–Aug Tue–Sun 9:00–12:00 & 13:00–18:00, spring and fall until 17:00, closed Mon and Nov–March. Tours in Czech cost 90 Kč, leave regularly, and include an adequate flier in English that contains about half the information imparted by the guide (most likely a student who's just memorized the basic script). English tours are preferable, but cost more (160 Kč), run less frequently, and are often booked solid. Make your reservation when you arrive in town—just walk up to the castle office—or you can call 380-704-721, though the number is often busy. You'll be issued a ticket with your tour time printed on it. Be in the correct courtyard at that time, or you'll be locked out.

▲▲**Baroque Theater (Zámecké Divadlo)**—Europe once had several hundred fine Baroque theaters. Using candles for light and fireworks for special effects, most burned down. Today, only two survive in good shape and are open to tourists: one at Stockholm's Drottningholm Palace, and one here, at Krumlov Castle. During the 45-minute tour, you'll sit on benches in the theater and then go under the stage to see the wood-and-rope contraptions that enabled scenes to be scooted in and out within seconds (while fireworks and smoke blinded the audience). Due to the theater's fragility, the number of visitors is strictly regulated. There are only five English tours a day, limited to 25 people per group and generally sold out in advance. While it's a lovely little theater with an impressive 3-D effect that makes the stage look deeper than it really is, I wouldn't bother with the tour unless you can snare a spot on an English one. The theater is used only once a year for an actual performance, with attendance limited to Baroque theater enthusiasts. You can call 380-704-721 to establish English-language tour times and reserve a space; but as with the castle tour, you will likely do best by visiting the ticket office in person (180 Kč, tours daily May–Oct only; English departures at 10:00, 11:00, 13:00, 14:00 and 15:00; buy theater tour tickets at castle ticket office).

Castle Gardens—This 2,300-foot-long garden crowns the castle complex. It was laid out in the 17th century, when the noble family would light it with 22,000 oil lamps, torches, and candles for special occasions. The lower part is geometrical and symmetrical—French-style. The upper is rougher—English-style (free, May–Sept daily 8:00–19:00, April and Oct daily 8:00–17:00, closed Nov–March).

Near Český Krumlov

Zlatá Koruna Abbey—Directly above the river at the end of a three-hour float by raft or canoe (see "Activities," next section), this abbey was founded by the king in the 13th century to counter the growing influence of the Vítek family, the ancestors of the mighty Rožmberks. As you enter the grounds, notice the central linden tree, with its strange, cape-like leaves; it's said to have been used by the anti-Catholic Hussites when they hanged the monks. The short guided abbey tour takes you through the rare two-storied Gothic Chapel of the Guardian Angel, the main church, and the cloister. After the order was dissolved in 1785, the abbey functioned shortly as a village school, before being turned into a factory during the Industrial Revolution. Damage from this period is visible on the cloister's crumbling arches. The abbey was restored in the 1990s and opened to the public only a few years ago (85 Kč, tours in Czech run every 45 minutes, Tue–Sun 9:00–15:15, until 16:15 June–Aug, closed Mon and Oct–March, call 380-743-126 to pre-arrange an English tour, access via river float).

ACTIVITIES

Český Krumlov lies in the middle of a valley popular for canoeing, rafting, hiking, and horseback riding. Boat-rental places are convenient to the Old Town, and several hiking paths start right in town.

▲▲▲Canoeing and Rafting the Vltava

Splash a little river fun into your visit by renting a rubber raft or hard plastic canoe for a quick 30-minute spin around Český

Krumlov. Or go for a three-hour float and paddle through the Bohemian forests and villages of the nearby countryside. You'll end up at Zlatá Koruna Abbey (described above), where the rafting company will shuttle you back to town—or provide you with a bicycle to pedal back on your own along a bike path. This is a great hot-weather activity. Though the river is far from treacherous, be prepared to get wet.

On any trip, you'll encounter plenty of inviting pubs and cafés for breaks along the way. There's a little white water, but the river is so shallow that if you tip, you simply stand up and climb back in. (When that happens, pull the canoe up onto the bank to empty it, since you'll never manage to pour the water out while still in the river.)

Choose from a kayak, a canoe (fastest, less work, more likely to tip), or an inflatable raft (harder rowing, slower, but very stable). Prices are per boat (2–6 people) and include a map, a waterproof container, and transportation to or from the start and end points. Here are your options:

Quickie Circle-the-Town Float: The easiest half-hour experience is to float around the city's peninsula, starting and ending at opposite sides of the tiny isthmus. Heck, you can do it twice (350 Kč for 1 or 2 people in a canoe or raft).

Three-Hour Float to Zlatá Koruna Abbey: This is your best basic trip, with pastoral scenery, a riverside pub on the left after two hours, and a beautiful abbey as your destination (about 9 miles, 700 Kč for 1 or 2 people). From there you can bike back or catch a shuttle bus home—simply arrange a return plan with the rental company. For more on the abbey, see previous page.

Longer and Faster Trips: If you start upriver from Krumlov (direction: Rožmberk), you'll go faster with more white water, but the river parallels a road so it's a little less idyllic. Longer trips in either direction involve lots of paddling, even though you're going downstream. Rafting companies can review the many day-trip options with you.

Rental Companies: Several companies offer this lively activity. Perhaps the handiest are **Půjčovna Lodí Maleček Boat Rental** (open long hours daily April–Oct, closed Nov–March, at recommended Pension Myší Díra, Rooseveltova 28, tel. 380-712-508, www.malecek.cz, lode@malecek.cz) and **Cestovní Agentura Vltava** (April–Oct daily 9:00–18:00, closed Nov–March, in Pension Vltava at Kájovská 62, tel. 380-711-988, www.ckvltava.cz). Vltava also rents mountain bikes (320 Kč per day) and can bring a bike to the abbey for you to ride back.

Hiking

For an easy 20-minute hike to Křížový Vrch (Hill of the Cross), walk to the end of Rooseveltova street, cross at the traffic light, then head straight for the first (empty) chapel-like Station of the Cross. Turning right, it's easy to navigate along successive Stations of the Cross until you reach the white church on the hill (closed), set in the middle of wild meadows. Looking down into the valley at the medieval city nestled within the S-shaped river, framed by the rising hills, it's hard to imagine any town with a more powerful *genius loci* (spirit of the place). The view is best at sunset.

SLEEPING

Krumlov is filled with small, good, family-run pensions offering doubles with baths from 1,000–1,500 Kč and hostel beds for 300 Kč. Summer weekends and festivals (see page 138) are busiest and most expensive; reserve ahead when possible. Hotels (not a Krumlov forte) speak some English and accept credit cards;

Sleep Code

(20 Kč = about $1, country code: 420)
S = Single, **D** = Double/Twin, **T** = Triple, **Q** = Quad, **b** = bathroom, **s** = shower only. Unless otherwise noted, prices include breakfast.

To help you sort easily through these listings, I've divided the rooms into three categories based on the price for a standard double room with bath:

$$$ **Higher Priced**—Most rooms 1,500 Kč or more.
$$ **Moderately Priced**—Most rooms between
                        1,000–1,500 Kč.
$ **Lower Priced**—Most rooms 1,000 Kč or less.

pensions rarely do either. While you can find a room upon arrival here, it's better to book at least a few days ahead if you want to stay in the heart of town. Cars are not very safe overnight—locals advise paying for a garage.

In the Old Town

$$$ Castle View Apartments, run by local guide Jiří Václavíček, rents seven apartments. These are the plushest and best-equipped rooms I found in town—the bathroom floors are heated, all come with kitchenettes, and everything's done just right. Their website describes each of the stylish apartments (1,800–4,000 Kč depending on size, view, and season; the big 4,000-Kč apartment sleeps up to six, complex pricing scheme, reserve direct with this book in 2008 and 2009 to claim a 10 percent discount off their online prices, fourth night free, non-smoking, voucher for breakfast at next-door Grand Hotel, Šatlavská 140, tel. 380-726-813, www .castleview.cz, info@castleview.cz).

On Parkán Street, Below the Square

Secluded Parkán street, which runs along the river below the square, has a row of pensions with three to five rooms each. These places have a family feel and views of the looming castle above.

$$$ Hotel Mlýn, at the end of Parkán, is a newly opened and tastefully furnished hotel with more than 30 rooms and all the amenities (Sb-2,200 Kč, Db-2,800 Kč, elevator, parking extra, Parkán 120, tel. 380-731-133, fax 380-747-054, www.hotelmlyn.eu, info@hotelmlyn.eu).

$$ Pension Olšakovský, which has a delightful breakfast area on a terrace next to the river, treats visitors as family guests (Db-1,050–1,250 Kč, includes parking, Parkán 114, tel. & fax 380-714-333, mobile 604-430-181, www.ckrumlov.cz/penzionekolsakovsky, J.Olsakovsky@post.cz). **Pension u Vltavy,** next door, is similar (Db-1,000–1,300 Kč, tel. & fax 380-716-396, mobile 605-175-758, www.ckrumlov.cz/uvltavy).

On Latrán Street, at the Base of the Castle

A quiet, cobbled pedestrian street (Latrán) runs below the castle just over the bridge from the Old Town. It's a 10-minute walk downhill from the train station. Lined with characteristic shops, the street has a couple of fine little family-run, eight-room pensions.

$$ Lobo Pension fills a modern, efficient, concrete building with eight fresh, spacious rooms. The pension operates a shuttle bus to Linz for 450 Kč per person (Db-1,100 Kč, Tb-1,500 Kč, includes parking, Latrán 73, tel. & fax 380-713-153, www .pensionlobo.cz, pensionlobo@cmail.cz).

$ Pension Danny is a little funkier, with homier rooms and a tangled floor plan above a restaurant (Db-990 Kč, apartment Db-1,190 Kč, breakfast in room, Latrán 72, tel. 380-712-710, www.pensiondanny.cz, pensiondanny@tiscali.cz).

On Rooseveltova Street, Between the Bus Station and the Old Town

Rooseveltova street, midway between the bus station and the Old Town (a four-minute walk from either), is lined with several fine little places, each with easy free parking. The key here is tranquility—the noisy bars of the town center are out of earshot.

$$ Little Pension Teddy has seven decent riverview rooms that share a common balcony (Db-1,200 Kč with this book in 2008, cash only, a bit smoky, Internet access in the bar—1 Kč/min, Rooseveltova 38, tel. 380-711-595, www.teddy.cz, info@teddy.cz).

$$ Pension Myší Díra ("Mouse Hole") hides eight sleek, spacious, bright, and woody Bohemian contemporary rooms overlooking the Vltava River just outside the Old Town (Db-1,000–1,690 Kč, bigger deluxe riverview Db-1,200–1,990 Kč, prices depend on day and season, breakfast in your room, Rooseveltova 28, tel. 380-712-853, fax 380-711-900, www.malecek.cz). The no-nonsense reception, which closes at 20:00, runs the recommended boat rental company (Půčovna Lodí Malaček, at the same address), along with three similar pensions with comparable prices: Pension Wok down by the river, Pension Margarita farther along Rooseveltova, and Pension u Hada.

$$ Pension Anna is well-run, with two doubles, five apartments, and a restful little garden. Its apartments are spacious suites, with a living room and stairs leading to the double-bedded loft (Db-1,250 Kč, Db apartment-1,550 Kč, extra bed-350 Kč, Rooseveltova 41, tel. & fax 380-711-692, pension.anna@quick.cz). If you book a standard Db and they bump you up to an apartment, don't pay more than the Db rate.

Hostels

There are several hostels in town. Hostel 99 (closest to the train station) is clearly the high-energy, youthful party hostel. Krumlov House (closer to the bus station) is more mellow. Both are well managed and each is a five-minute walk from the main square.

$ Hostel 99's picnic-table terrace looks out on the Old Town. While the gentle sound of the river gurgles outside your window, late at night you're more likely to hear a youthful international crowd having a great time. The hostel caters to its fun-loving young guests, offering free inner tubes for river floats, rental bikes, and a free keg of beer each Wednesday. The adjacent and recommended Hospoda 99 restaurant serves good and cheap soups, salads, and meals

(65 beds in 4- to 10-bed coed rooms-300 Kč, D-700 Kč, T-990 Kč, Internet access-1 Kč/minute, laundry-200 Kč/load, use the lockers, no curfew or lockout, 10-min downhill walk from train station or two bus stops to Spicak, Vezni 99, tel. & fax 380-712-812, www .hostel99.com, hostel99@hotmail.com).

$ Krumlov House Hostel is take-your-shoes-off-at-the-door, shiny, hardwood-with-throw-rugs mellow. Efficiently run by a Canadian, it has a hip and trusting vibe and feels welcoming to travelers of any age (24 beds, 6 beds in two dorms-300 Kč per bed, Db-800 Kč, 2-person apartment-900 Kč, family room, no breakfast but there is a guests' kitchen, DVD library, laundry facilities, Rooseveltova 68, tel. 380-711-935, www.krumlovhostel.com).

EATING

Krumlov, with a huge variety of creative little restaurants, is a fun place to eat. In peak times, the good places fill fast, so make reservations or eat early.

Na Louži seems to be everyone's favorite little Czech bistro, with 40 seats in one 1930s-style room decorated with funky old advertisements. They serve inexpensive, tasty Czech cuisine and hometown Eggenberg beer on tap. If you've always wanted to play the piano for an appreciative Czech crowd in a colorful little tavern...do it here (daily 10:00–23:00, Kájovská 66, tel. 380-711-280).

Krčma u Dwau Maryí ("Tavern of the Two Marys") is a characteristic old place with idyllic riverside picnic tables, serving ye olde Czech cuisine and drinks. The fascinating menu explains the history of the house and makes a good case that the food of the poor medieval Bohemians was tasty and varied. Buck up for buckwheat, millet, greasy meat, or the poor-man's porridge (daily 11:00–23:00, Parkán 104, tel. 380-717-228).

Cikánská Jizba ("Gypsy Pub") is a Roma tavern filling one den-like, barrel-vaulted room. The Roma staff serves Slovak-style food (Slovakia is where most of the Czech Republic's Roma population came from). Krumlov has a long Roma history, and even today 1,000 Roma people live in the town. While this rustic little restaurant—which packs its 10 tables under a mystic-feeling Gothic vault—won't win any cuisine awards, you never know what festive and musical activities will erupt, particularly on Friday nights when the owner's son's band Cindži Renta ("Wet Rag") performs here (Mon–Sat 15:00–24:00, closed Sun, 2 blocks toward castle from main square at Dlouhá 31, tel. 380-717-585). For more on the Roma of Eastern Europe, see page 178.

Restaurace u Dobráka ("Good Man") is like eating in a medieval garage, with a giant poster of Karl Marx overseeing the action. Lojza, who's been tossing steaks on his open fire for years, makes sure you'll eat well. Locals know it as the best place for grilled steak and fish—expect to pay 350 Kč for a full meal. He charges too much for his beer in order to keep the noisy beer-drinkers away (open daily 17:30–24:00 from Easter until Lojza "has a shoebox full of money," Široká 74, tel. 380-717-776).

Laibon is the modern vegetarian answer to the carnivorous Middle Ages. Settle down inside or head out onto the idyllic river terrace, and lighten up your pork-loaded diet with soy goulash or Mútábúr soup (daily 11:00–23:00, Parkán 105).

Rybářská Restaurace ("Fisherman's Restaurant") doesn't look particularly inviting from outside, but don't get discouraged. This is *the* place in town to taste freshwater fish you've never heard of (and never will again). Try eel, perch, shad, carp, trout, and more. Choose between indoor tables under fishnets or riverside picnic benches outside (daily 11:00–22:00, on the island by the mill-wheel).

Krčma v Šatlavské is an old prison gone cozy, with an open fire, big wooden tables under a rustic old medieval vault, and tables outdoors on the pedestrian lane. It's great for a late drink or game cooked on an open spit. *Medovina* is the hot honey wine (daily 12:00–24:00, on Šatlavská, follow lane leading to the side from TI on main square, mobile 608-973-797).

Restaurace Barbakán is built into the town fortifications, with a terrace hanging high over the river. It's a good spot for old-fashioned Czech cooking and beer, at the top of town and near the recommended Rooseveltova street accommodations (open long hours daily, reasonable prices, Horní 26, tel. 380-712-679).

Hospoda 99 Restaurace serves good and cheap soups, salads, and meals. It's the choice of hostelers and locals alike for its hamburgers, vegetarian food, Czech dishes, and cheap booze (meals served 10:00–22:00, bar open until 24:00, at Hostel 99, Vezni 99, tel. 380-712-812). This place is booming until late, when everything else is hibernating.

Dobrá Čajovna is a typical example of the quiet, exotic-feeling teahouses that flooded Czech towns in the 1990s as alternatives to smoky, raucous pubs. While directly across from the castle entrance, it's a world away from the touristic hubbub. As is so often the case, if you want to surround yourself with locals, don't go to a traditional place...go ethnic. With its meditative karma inside and a peaceful terrace facing the monastery out back, it provides a relaxing break (daily 13:00–22:00, Latrán 54, mobile 777-654-744).

TRANSPORTATION CONNECTIONS

Almost all trains to and from Český Krumlov require a transfer in the city of České Budějovice, a transit hub just to the north. České Budějovice's bus and train stations are next to each other.

From Český Krumlov by Train to: České Budějovice (6/day, 1 hr), **Prague** (8/day, change usually required, 4 hrs—bus is faster, cheaper, and easier), **Vienna** (5/day, with at least one change, 5–6 hrs; overnight possible, 10 hrs), **Budapest** (4/day with at least one change, 11–13 hrs).

From Český Krumlov by Bus to: Prague (7/day, 3.5 hrs, 180 Kč; 2 of the daily departures—12:00 and 16:45—can be reserved and paid for at TI, or simply buy tickets from driver), **České Budějovice** (transit hub for other destinations; about 2/hr, 30–50 min, 30 Kč). The Český Krumlov bus station, a five-minute walk out of town, is just a big parking lot with numbered stalls for various buses (bus info tel. 380-711-190, timetables online at http://jizdnirady.atlas.cz).

By Shuttle Bus or Private Car to Linz and Beyond: If you get to Linz, Austria, by bus or car, you'll have your choice of fast trains that run hourly from Linz to Munich, Salzburg, and Vienna. **Pension Lobo** in Český Krumlov runs a shuttle bus service to Linz (450 Kč, 90 min, departs daily at 11:00, 2 people minimum, tel. 380-713-153). A taxi to Linz costs 2,000 Kč (sometimes less). If money is no object, hiring a private car can be efficient, especially to Budapest (the TI has referrals).

Český Krumlov

SLOVAKIA

SLOVAKIA

Slovensko

Slovakia is the West Virginia of Central Europe—poor, relatively undeveloped, but spectacularly beautiful in its own rustic way. Sitting quietly in the very center of Central Europe, wedged between stronger and more prosperous nations (the Czech Republic, Hungary, and Poland), Slovakia was brutally disfigured by the communists, then overshadowed by the Czechs. But in recent years, this fledgling republic has begun to find its wings. Thanks to EU funding and international business investment, Slovakia is enjoying an economic boom. Today two very different Slovakias are emerging: the modern, industrialized, relatively affluent west, centered on the capital of Bratislava; and the remote, poorer, "backwards" east, with high unemployment and more traditional lifestyles.

Slovakia is far more ethnically diverse than its neighbors. Among Slovakia's large minority groups are Hungarians, many of whom still cling to the century-old glory days when this was called Upper Hungary and ruled from Budapest. Many Slovaks resent the cultural chauvinism of Hungarians, and still harbor hard feelings toward their former oppressors. Another large group is the Roma (Gypsies; see page 178). Rounding out the cultural cocktail are Czechs, Ruthenians (Carpathian Mountain peasants of Ukrainian origin), and a smattering of Germans.

Though the Slovaks are more closely associated with their former countrymen, the Czechs, they actually have more culturally in common with their other neighbors, the Poles. While the Czechs take pride in a marked agnosticism, the Slovaks tend to be more devout Catholics. Also like the Poles, the Slovaks have a strong agricultural (rather than industrial) heritage. And the Slovak and Polish languages are surprisingly similar.

Among travelers, there seem to be two schools of thought

on Slovakia. Some people adore the country for its stark natural beauty and because it's an exciting cultural detour off the prettified tourist mainstream. Slovakia gives more adventurous travelers the opportunity to feel the pulse of a nation that's still struggling to transition into democracy—and yet is stable and safe enough for a comfortable visit. These people enjoy hiking along Slovakia's glorious mountain trails, driving through its humble villages, interacting with its kind people, and pondering the blemishes that communism left on its pastoral landscape.

Other people can't wait to leave Slovakia, turned off by its drab industrial skeletons, relative poverty, and dearth of must-see sights compared to the rest of Eastern Europe. Tourists focusing on pretty-as-a-postcard Eastern Europe will want to spend more time elsewhere...and should.

What is clear is that Slovakia is not your standard European country. With lots of pleasant surprises, Slovakia is worth a peek for more adventurous travelers.

The country's capital, Bratislava, is perfectly situated at the western tip of the country, right on the train line between Budapest and Vienna. Up in the north—not far from the Polish border—are the most beautiful parts of this mountainous nation: the rolling hills of the Spiš Region and the jagged peaks of the High Tatras.

Practicalities

Telephones: Insertable telephone cards, sold at newsstands and kiosks everywhere, get you access to the modern public phones.

When calling locally, dial the number without the area code. To make a long-distance call within the country, start with the area code (which begins with 0). To call a Slovak number from abroad, dial the international access number (00 if calling from Europe, 011 from the US or Canada), followed by 421 (Slovakia's country code), then the area code (without the initial 0) and the number.

Slovakia Almanac

Official Name: Slovenská Republika, though locals call it Slovensko. The nation is the eastern half of the former Czecho-slovakia (split peaceably in 1993).

Population: 5.4 million people. The majority are native Slovaks who are Roman Catholic and speak Slovak. But one in 10 has Hungarian roots, and an estimated one in 10 is Roma (Gypsy).

Latitude and Longitude: 48°N and 20°E (similar latitude to Paris or Vancouver, BC).

Area: 19,000 square miles (the size of Massachusetts and New Hampshire put together).

Geography: The northeastern half of Slovakia features the beautiful rolling hills and spiky, jagged peaks of the Carpathian Mountains. The southwestern half is quite flat—a continuation of the Hungarian Plain. The climate is generally cool and cloudy.

Biggest Cities: Only two cities have more than 100,000 inhabit-ants: Bratislava in the west (the capital, 450,000) and Košice in the east (235,000).

Economy: The Gross Domestic Product is about $100 billion (less than half that of the Czech Republic), and the GDP per capita is $18,200 (less than the average Czech and roughly half that of the average German). Despite a recent economic upturn, unemploy-ment hovers at about 10 percent.

Currency: In 2008, Slovakia retains its traditional currency, the Slovak koruna (Sk; 25 Sk = about $1). In 2009, Slovaks hope to

To call out of Slovakia, dial 00, the country code of the country you're calling (see chart in appendix), the area code if applicable (you may need to drop the initial zero), and the local number.

Information: For more in-depth information about Slovakia, pick up a copy of *Spectacular Slovakia,* an excellent annual maga-zine produced by the English-language newspaper in Bratislava (www.spectacularslovakia.sk).

Slovak History

Even though it's more recently associated with the Czech Republic, Slovakia was for centuries ruled from Budapest and known as Upper Hungary. While the Ottomans occupied most of Hungary in the 16th and 17th centuries, the Hungarians moved their capi-tal to Bratislava. But even throughout the long era of Hungarian domination, most people living in Slovakia were Slavs.

Czechoslovakia was formed at the end of World War I, when the Austro-Hungarian Empire was splitting into pieces. During this flurry of new nation-building, a small country of 10 million adopt the euro: €1 = about $1.40. For simplicity, I've listed some prices in both currencies. Under the official exchange rate, €1 = 35 Sk.

Government: President Ivan Gašparovič heads a government that isn't dominated by any single political party. Slovakia also has a 150-seat National Council (like a parliament).

Flag: Horizontal bands of white, blue, and red with a shield bearing a "patriarchal cross" (with two cross-bars instead of one) atop three humps. The three humps represent three historic mountain ranges of Slovakia: Mátra (now in northern Hungary, near Eger), Fatra, and Tatra. The double-barred cross represents St. Stephen  (István) of Hungary, commemorating the many centuries that Slovakia was part of Hungary.

Slovaks You May Recognize: Andy Warhol (American Pop artist who gained more than his 15 minutes of fame; born to Slovak immigrants), Martina Hingis (Swiss tennis player born in Slovakia), Štefan Bani (emigrated to America and invented the parachute).

Czechs or five million Slovaks was unlikely to survive. The Czechs were concerned about the huge number of Germans in their territory (the Sudetenland), while the Slovaks—who had endured relatively oppressive conditions under the Hungarian half of the empire—were unsure of their ability to steer their own nation.

And so these two Slavic peoples decided there was safety in numbers. (It was a delicate balance—there were more Sudeten Germans in Czechoslovakia than there were Slovaks.) The union was logical enough—especially in the eyes of Tomáš Masaryk, Czechoslovakia's first president (and a buddy of Woodrow Wilson's from Princeton). Masaryk was from the border of the two regions and spoke a dialect that mixed elements of Czech and Slovak. Czechoslovakia was born.

The Czechs and the Slovaks were constantly reminded that they were countrymen in name only. In a prelude to World War II, these two peoples were again split along the cultural fault that always divided them: Today's Czech Republic was absorbed into Germany, while much of the Slovak land went

It's Not You, It's Me: The Velvet Divorce

In the autumn of 1989, hundreds of thousands of Czechs and Slovaks streamed into Prague to demonstrate on Wenceslas Square. Their "Velvet Revolution" succeeded, and Czechoslovakia's communist regime peacefully excused itself.

Almost immediately, the union began to splinter. Ever since they joined with the Czechs in 1918, the Slovaks felt they were ruled from Prague (unmistakably the political, economic, and cultural center of the country) rather than from their own capital. And the Czechs, for their part, resented the financial burden of their poorer neighbors to the east. In the post-communist world, the Czechs found themselves with a 10 percent unemployment rate...compared to 20 or 30 percent unemployment in the Slovak lands. In this new world of flux and freedom, long-standing tensions came to a head.

The dissolution of Czechoslovakia began over a hyphen, as the Slovaks wanted to rename the country Czecho-Slovakia. Ideally, this symbolic move would come with a redistribution of powers: two capitals and two UN reps, but one national bank and a single currency. The Slovaks were also less enthusiastic about abandoning the communist society altogether, since the Soviet regime had left them with a heavily industrialized economy that depended on a socialist element for survival.

Initially, many Czechs couldn't understand the Slovaks' demands. The first post-communist president of Czechoslovakia,

to Nazi-allied Hungary.

During the communist era, the regime decided to convert the Slovak economy from a low-key agricultural model to a base of heavy industry. But the industry was centrally planned for communist purposes (relying on raw materials imported from elsewhere within the Eastern Bloc)—so it made sense only as a cog in the communist machine. Many of Slovakia's factories built heavy arms, making the country the biggest producer of tanks in the world. Slovakia became one of the ugliest and most polluted corners of Eastern Europe. The Slovak environment—and economy—are still recovering.

When the wave of uprisings spread across Eastern Europe in 1989, Czechoslovakia peacefully achieved its own freedom with the Velvet Revolution. Then, on January 1, 1993, Czechoslovakia amicably split into two nations: the Czech and Slovak Republics (see sidebar). At first, many Slovaks weren't sure this was so wise. But more recently, it seems that the Czechs and Slovaks are getting along better than ever—by choice, not because they're compelled to. Czechs root for the Slovak hockey team, and Slovaks cheer on the Czech Václav Havel, made matters worse when he took a rare trip to the Slovak half of his country in 1990. In a fit of terrible judgment, Havel boldly promised he'd close the ugly, polluting Soviet factories in Slovakia...seemingly oblivious to the fact that many Slovaks still depended on these factories for survival. Havel left in disgrace and visited the Slovak lands only twice more in the next two and a half years.

In June 1992, the Slovak nationalist candidate Vladimír Mečiar fared surprisingly well in the elections—suggesting that the Slovaks were serious about secession. The politicians plowed ahead, getting serious about the split in September 1992. The transition took only three months, from start to finish.

The people of Czechoslovakia never actually voted on the separation; in fact, public opinion polls in both regions were two-thirds *against* the split. This makes Slovakia quite possibly the only country in the history of the world to gain independence... even though it didn't want it.

The Velvet Divorce became official on January 1, 1993, and each country ended up with its own capital, currency, and head of state. The Slovaks let loose a yelp of excitement, and the Czechs emitted a sigh of relief. The divorce dissolved the tensions, and a decade and a half later, most Czechs and Slovaks still feel closer to each other than to any other nationality.

the Czech soccer powerhouse...unless, of course, their teams are playing against each other.

After the so-called Velvet Divorce, the first president of Slovakia was a former boxer named Vladimír Mečiar, whose authoritarian rule was not much better than the communists'. Mečiar was frequently accused of corruption (including pulling issues off the ballot when the polls seemed to be going against him), and people suspect he was involved in the kidnapping, torture, and humiliation of one of his political opponent's sons in 1995. He was also notorious for making offensive statements about his country's substantial Hungarian and Roma minorities. Mečiar drew criticism from neighboring Eastern and Western European nations, as well as the US. He was finally defeated at the polls in 2000, but—like a bad penny—he kept turning up, nearly winning elections in 2002 and 2004. And now, once again, Mečiar plays a minor role in government, as leader of a small fringe party that has a share in Slovakia's current government coalition.

But, as Mečiar (and his voting base) gets along in years, Slovakia appears to be turning to more mainstream politics.

Key Slovak Phrases

English	Slovak	Pronounced
Hello. (formal)	*Dobrý deň.*	DOH-bree dyehn
Hi. / Bye. (informal)	*Ahoj.*	AH-hoy
Do you speak English?	*Hovoríte po anglicky?*	hoh-VOH-ree-teh poh ANG-lits-kee
Yes. / No.	*Áno. / Nie.*	AH-no / nyeh
Please. / You're welcome. / Can I help you?	*Prosím.*	PROH-seem
Thank you.	*Ďakujem.*	DYAH-koo-yehm
I'm sorry. / Excuse me.	*Prepáčte.*	preh-PAHCH-teh
Good.	*Dobro.*	DOH-broh
Goodbye.	*Do videnia.*	doh vih-DAY-neeah
one / two	*jeden / dva*	YAY-dehn / dvah
three / four	*tri / štyri*	tree / SHTEE-ree
five / six	*päť / šesť*	peht / shehst
seven / eight	*sedem / osem*	SEH-dyehm / OH-sehm
nine / ten	*deväť / desať*	DYEH-veht / DYEH-saht
hundred	*sto*	stoh
thousand	*tisíc*	TYEE-seets
How much?	*Koľko?*	KOHL-koh
local currency (until 2009)	*koruna (Sk)*	koh-ROO-nah
Where is...?	*Kde je...?*	gday yeh
...the toilet	*...záchod*	ZAH-khohd
men	*muži*	MOO-zhee
women	*ženy*	ZHAY-nee
water / coffee	*voda / káva*	VOH-dah / KAH-vah
beer / wine	*pivo / víno*	PEE-voh / VEE-noh
Cheers!	*Na zdravie!*	nah ZDRAH-vyeh
the bill	*účet*	OO-cheht

Slovakia joined the European Union in May of 2004. As one of the poorest EU members, Slovakia quickly became one of the EU's greatest beneficiaries. Low labor costs and an unbeatable location have attracted many foreign automakers to build plants here, leading the *New York Times* to dub Slovakia "the European Detroit." In fact, Slovakia is currently the world's biggest car producer...per capita, of course. Ireland's "Celtic Tiger" economic boom has led people to make comparisons with Slovakia, even predicting the coming of a "Tatra Tiger" (named for the Slovak mountain range).

Inspired by the model of Ireland—another poor country that has enjoyed phenomenal economic growth since joining the EU—Slovaks seem poised to pounce on the future. The Slovak economy has gone from worst to first, and Slovaks are on track to become only the second Eastern European country (after Slovenia) to adopt the euro, likely in January of 2009.

Slovak Food
Slovak cuisine is similar to Czech cuisine—with lots of starches and gravy, and plenty of pork, cabbage, and potatoes (see "Czech Food," page 37). If there's anything distinctive about Slovak food, it's the slight Hungarian influence—Slovaks use more paprika than their Czech cousins. Slovakia also has a strong tradition of grilling pickled meats. Also keep an eye out for Slovakia's national dish, *bryndzové halušky* (small potato dumplings with sheep's cheese and bits of bacon). Like the Czechs, the Slovaks produce fine beer *(pivo)*. One of the top brands is Zlatý Bažant ("Golden Pheasant").

Slovak Language
Many people assume Slovak is virtually the same as Czech. To be sure, there are similarities—but they're hardly identical.

Slovak is handy as a sort of a lingua franca of Slavic tongues. Czechs can understand Poles, but not Slovenes; Poles can understand Croatians, but not Czechs. But Slovak speakers generally find they can understand—and be understood in—any of these languages.

Slovak's similarity to Czech was exaggerated during the 75 years that they shared a country. Soccer games would be broadcast with two commentators—one spoke Czech, and the other spoke Slovak. Anyone growing up in this era grew comfortable using the languages interchangeably. But today's teenagers—who have only spoken exclusively Czech or Slovak—find they have trouble understanding each other.

BRATISLAVA

For centuries, Bratislava—known as "Pressburg" to its German inhabitants—was a complex and beautiful city, with deep roots in many different cultures: Slovak, German/Austrian, Hungarian, Jewish, Romanian, and Roma (Gypsy). The Hungarians used the city—which they called "Poszony"—as their capital during the century and a half that Buda and Pest were occupied by Ottoman invaders. Later, Bratislava was one of Hapsburg empress Maria Theresa's favorite places. Everyone from Hans Christian Andersen to Casanova sang the wonders of this bustling burg on the Danube. When Czechoslovakia was formed at the end of World War I, the city shed its German and Hungarian names, proudly taking the new Slavic name "Bratislava"—meaning roughly "City of Slavic Brotherhood."

In the 20th century, Bratislava became the textbook example of a historic city whose multilayered charm and delicate cultural fabric were destroyed and shrouded in gray by the communist regime. The communists were more proud of their ultramodern suspension bridge, New Bridge (a.k.a. Most SNP), than of the historic Jewish quarter they razed to make way for it. Now the bridge and its highway slice through the center of the Old Town, and the heavy traffic rattles the stained-glass windows of St. Martin's Cathedral.

But the most recent chapter in Bratislava's story is one of great success. Over the last decade, the city has gone from being a desolate, gloomy victim of communism to a thriving economic center and social hub. Its population of 450,000 includes some 70,000 students (at the city's six universities), creating an atmosphere of youthful energy and optimism. The increasingly rejuvenated

Old Town is traffic-free, giving it an almost Mediterranean ambience on sunny summer days, when Bratislava's outdoor cafés hum with life.

Planning Your Time

Bratislava is blessed with a priceless location on the Danube (and the tourist circuit), smack-dab between Budapest and Vienna. On the plus side, the ambience in the Old Town is enjoyable. On the other hand, actual sightseeing options are disappointing, and a busy traveler—one more interested in seeing museums than in sipping coffee—gets bored here quickly. On my list of priorities, time spent in Budapest and Vienna is more precious. But if you're passing through and you're curious, Bratislava merits a quick sightseeing sprint. Head straight for the Old Town, wander through to the river, and—if time allows—hike up to the castle.

I've listed no hotels in Bratislava; beds are better in nearby Vienna and Budapest.

ORIENTATION

(area code: 02)

Bratislava, with nearly half a million residents, is Slovakia's capital and biggest city. It has a small, colorful Old Town (Staré Mesto) surrounded by the ugly communist sprawl of the New Town and suburbs. The Old Town and the castle above it are the only parts of Bratislava worth visiting.

Bratislava's grim Stalinist vibe isn't all bad. It offers hardy travelers an opportunity for a cultural scavenger hunt deep into the guts of apartment-block neighborhoods, where the average Josefs of the "Evil Empire"—from here to Vladivostok—eked out their lives. Across the river from the Old Town, the suburb called Petržalka is gloomy and harrowing, in a *1984*-comes-to-life sort of way.

Beware: Bratislavans in the tourist zone sometimes try to short-change and otherwise rip off their city's visitors as brazenly as their Prague cousins do. Check your bill and count your change carefully.

Tourist Information

The TI, called the Bratislava Culture and Information Centre, has two branches in the heart of the city. There's a small window in the **train station** (Mon–Fri 9:00–17:00, Sat–Sun 9:00–14:00; tel. 02/5249-5906). The **main branch** is across the square from the back of the Old Town Hall on Primaciálne Námestie (June–Sept Mon–Fri 8:30–19:00, Sat 9:00–18:00, Sun 10:00–18:00; Oct–May Mon–Fri 8:30–18:00, Sat 9:00–15:00, Sun 10:00–15:00; Klobučnícka 2,

Bratislava

tel. 02/5443-3715, www.bkis.sk and www.bratislava.sk). Pick up the free map and browse their brochures; they can also help you find a room for a modest fee. The **Bratislava City Card** is worthwhile only if you're doing the Old Town walking tour (see "Tours," below; 350 Sk/€10 for 1 day, includes walking tour May–Oct, 50 percent discount on tour Nov–April, sold at TI).

Arrival in Bratislava

By Train: Bratislava's Main Train Station, called Bratislava Hlavná Stanica, is about a half-mile north of the Old Town. As you emerge from the tracks, the TI is down the hall to your left, and the luggage-check desk is to your right (look for *ú schovňa batožín;* there are no lockers, and the check desk usually closes for 30-min lunch and dinner breaks—try to confirm that they'll be there when you get back if you'll be rushing to catch a train).

It's an easy 15-minute **walk** to the center. Leave through the front door and head along the communist-style arcade (on the right) past the buses to the busy street. Take the overpass across the street, and continue straight on Štefánikova. This formerly elegant old street is lined with rotting facades from Bratislava's high-on-the-hog Hapsburg era. After about 10 minutes, you'll pass the nicely manicured presidential gardens on your left, then the Grassalkovich Palace, Slovakia's "White House." Continue straight through the busy intersection, and head for the green onion-domed steeple. This is St. Michael's Gate, at the start of the Old Town (described below).

If you want to shave a few minutes off the trip, you can go part of the way by **tram** (from train station's main hall, with tracks at your back, look for signs to *električky* on left; take escalator down, buy a 14-Sk "basic ticket" from the machine, and hop on tram #1).

By Plane: Some budget carriers—especially SkyEurope—fly into Bratislava Airport (Letisko Bratislava, airport code: BTS, www.letiskobratislava.sk). This airport is marketed as "Vienna-Bratislava," thanks to its proximity to both capitals. Located six miles northeast of downtown Bratislava, the airport is officially named for Milan Rastislav Štefánik, who worked toward the creation of Czechoslovakia at the end of World War I. The airport has easy bus connections into Bratislava's Main Train Station (bus #61, 6/hr in peak time, 3/hr in slow times, trip takes 30 min; to reach the bus stop, exit straight out of the arrivals hall, cross the street, buy a ticket at the kiosk, and look for the bus stop on your right). To get to Vienna, you can take a taxi (figure €60–90, depending on whether you use a cheaper Slovak or more expensive Austrian cab).

TOURS

The main TI shares an office with the Bratislava **tour guide association** (tel. 02/5443-4059, guides@bkis.sk). They offer a one-hour Old Town walking tour in English every day at 14:00 (400 Sk/€12, free with Bratislava City Card—see page 166, 2-person minimum, call ahead to confirm).

For a more extensive (and expensive) look at the city, join a longer **Bratislava Sightseeing** city tour. There are three itineraries: Discover Bratislava (1,290 Sk/€37, 4 hours, almost daily, minibus tour to outlying sights, then walking tour of Old Town), Communist Bratislava (1,150 Sk/€33, 3 hours, 1/week, sights from the Red old days), and Little Carpathians (1,980 Sk/€57, 5 hours, 2/week, wine road and other sights in the countryside). All tours depart from the Hotel Devin (facing the Danube a few steps down from the long, skinny Hviezdoslavovo Square, look for fliers locally for schedule, or visit www.visitbratislava.info; best to reserve in advance).

Martin Sloboda, one of Bratislava Sightseeing's owners, is a can-do entrepreneur who writes local guidebooks and runs his own guiding agency. Martin can set you up with a good local guide (€120/3 hours, €150/4 hours), and can help you track down your Slovak roots (tel. 02/5464-1467, www.msagency.sk, info @msagency.sk).

Bratislava

SIGHTS

On a short visit, it's enough to simply wander the Old Town, enjoy a drink at an outdoor café, and soak in Slovakia. If you need more diversion than that, you can hike up to the castle. More low-impact sightseeing options include a pair of dusty, sleepy museums in the heart of the Old Town (described below). If you're interested in museums beyond the ones I mention, check out www.snm.sk.

▲**Old Town Wander**—This self-guided stroll takes you through the heart of old Bratislava. If you're coming from the station, make

your way toward the green onion-domed steeple of St. Michael's Gate (explained in "Arrival in Bratislava," above). Before going through the passage into the Old Town, peek over the railing on your left to the inviting garden below—once part of the city moat.

Step through the passageway into the delightfully traffic-free **Old Town.** Pretty as it is now, the Old Town was a decrepit ghost town during the communist era. Locals avoided this desolate corner of the city, preferring to spend time in the Petržalka suburb across the river. But after the fall of communism, city leaders decided to revitalize this zone. They replaced all of the cobbles, spruced up the public buildings, and encouraged the new private owners of other buildings to invest in careful restoration. It worked: Today the Old Town is gleaming, and packed with locals and tourists alike.

Continue through the onion-domed **St. Michael's Gate** (Michalská Brána), the last remaining tower of the city wall. As you pass under the gate, notice the "kilometer zero" plaque in the ground, marking the point from which distances in Slovakia are measured.

Coming through the gate, you're at the head of **Michalská street.** The cafés and restaurants that line this street are inviting, especially in summer. But if you don't look beyond the facades and outdoor tables, you'll miss much of Bratislava's charm. Courtyards and galleries—most of them open to the public—burrow through the city's buildings. For example, just inside St. Michael's Gate on the right, the gallery at #7 is home to several fashion designers.

As you stroll down Michalská, think about which of these places you'd like to circle back to later for a drink or a meal. The **chocolate shop** at #6 (on the left) is highly regarded among locals. Look over the shop's entrance and find the cannonball embedded in the wall above the seal. This commemorates the fact that Napoleon laid siege to the city twice, causing massive devastation—even worse than the city suffered during World War II. Keep an eye out for these cannonballs all over town...somber reminders of one of Bratislava's darkest times.

Noticing a lot of skin? Slovak women are known for their provocative dress. When pressed for a reason for this, local men smirk and say, "That's just the way it is."

Two blocks down from St. Michael's Gate, the name of this main drag changes to Ventúrska, the street jogs to the right, and the café scene continues. This is a good time for you to detour left (along Sedlárska) and head for the **Main Square** (Hlavné Námestie)—the bustling centerpiece of Old World Bratislava. Virtually every building around this square dates from a different architectural period, from Gothic (the yellow tower) to Art Nouveau (the fancy facade facing it from across the square). When these buildings were restored a few years ago, great pains were taken to achieve authenticity—each one even matches the color most likely used when it was originally built.

Peering over one of the benches is a cartoonish statue of **Napoleon** (notice the French flag marking the embassy right behind him). With bare feet and a hat pulled over his eyes, it's hardly a flattering portrait—you could call it the Slovaks' revenge for the difficulties they faced at his armies' hands. Napoleon is just the first we'll see of many whimsical statues that dot Bratislava's Old Town. Most of these date from the late 1990s, when city leaders wanted to entice locals back into the newly prettied-up Old Town.

At the top of the Main Square is the impressive **Old Town Hall** (Stará Radnica), marked by a bold yellow tower. Near the bottom of the tower, notice the cannonball embedded in the facade—yet another reminder of Napoleon's impact on Bratislava. Over time, the Old Town Hall gradually grew, annexing the buildings next to it—creating a mishmash of architectural styles along this side of the square. Step through the passageway into the Old Town Hall's gorgeously restored courtyard with Renaissance arcades.

The Old Town Hall houses a ho-hum **City History Museum** (Mestské Múzeum), with a tower you can climb and a museum on torture (a.k.a. "feudal justice") in the basement (50 Sk/€1.50, Tue–Fri 10:00–17:00, Sat–Sun 11:00–18:00, closed Mon, Primaciálne Námestie 3, tel. 02/5920-5130, www.muzeum.bratislava.sk).

On the other side of the Old Town Hall is Bratislava's most interesting museum, the **Primate's House** (Primaciálny Palác, 40 Sk/€1.25, Tue–Fri 10:00–17:00, Sat–Sun 11:00–18:00, closed Mon). This grand mansion, gradually expanded and glorified over several centuries by a series of archbishops who lived here, features fancy

Bratislava

apartments, a Mirror Hall for concerts and meetings, a striking marble chapel, and a series of six English tapestries.

Backtrack to the Main Square. With your back to the Old Town Hall, go to the end of the square and follow the street to the left (Rybárska Brána). A block

down this street, you'll come to a jovial chap doffing his top hat. This is a statue of **Schöner Náci,** who lived in Bratislava until the 1960s. This eccentric old man, a poor carpet cleaner, would dress up in his one black suit and top hat, and go strolling through the city, offering gifts to the women he fancied. (He'd often whisper *"schön"*—German for "pretty"—to the women, which is how he got his nickname.) After spending his life cheering up the gloomy streets of communist Bratislava, Schöner Náci now gets to spend eternity greeting visitors in front of his favorite café.

As a sad epilogue, Schöner Náci's arm was broken off recently by a bunch of drunks. As Prague gets more expensive, Bratislava is becoming the cheaper alternative for weekend "stag parties," popular with Brits lured here by cheap flights and cheap beer. Locals hope this is a short-lived trend, and that those rowdy louts will move farther east before long.

Continue down Rybárska. A block farther on, at the intersection of Panská and Rybárska, keep an eye out for **Čumil** ("the

Peeper"), grinning at passersby from a manhole. This was the first and still the favorite of Bratislava's statues. There's no story behind this one—the artist simply wanted to create a fun icon, and let the townspeople make up their own tales. Čumil has survived being driven over by a truck—twice—and he's still grinning.

Continuing past Čumil, you'll reach the long, skinny square called **Hviezdoslavovo Námestie**—another part of Bratislava that has undergone much-needed rejuvenation recently. The landscaped park in the center is particularly inviting, with more fun sculptures (including, at the far end to the right, Hans Christian Andersen) and a life-size chessboard. At this end of the square is the impressive, silver-topped Slovak National Theater (Slovenské Národné Divadlo)—evidence of Bratislava's strong theatrical tradition.

Right in front of the theater (by the McDonald's), look down into the glass **display case** to see the foundation of the one-time Fishermen's Gate into the city. Surrounding the base of the gate is water. This entire square was once a tributary of the Danube, and the Carlton Hotel across the way was a series of inns on different islands. The buildings along the Old Town side of the square mark where the city wall once stood.

From here, it's just a block to the Danube—passing the Slovak National Gallery, for those fascinated by Slovak art (big green building). Once at the Danube, you'll get a good look at the communists' pride and joy, the **New Bridge** (Nový Most, a.k.a. Most SNP). As with many Soviet-era landmarks around Eastern Europe, many locals aren't crazy about this structure—not only for the questionable starship *Enterprise* design, but also because of the oppressive regime it represents. However, the restaurant and observation deck up top—long a stale holdover from communist times—was recently renovated into a posh eatery with see-through tables.

If you follow the Danube toward the bridge, before long you'll spot big **St. Martin's Cathedral** (Dóm Sv. Martina) on the right.

This historic church isn't looking too sharp these days—and the highway thundering a few feet in front of its door (courtesy of the Soviets) doesn't help matters. If it were any closer, the off-ramp would go through the nave. Sad as it is now, the cathedral has been party to some pretty important history. While Buda and Pest were occupied by Ottomans for a century and a half, Bratislava was the capital of Hungary. Many Hungarian kings and queens were crowned in this church. A replica of the Hungarian crown still tops the steeple.

If you walk under the highway, then start climbing the stairs marked *Zámocké Schody*, you'll wind up at...

Bratislava Castle (Bratislavský Hrad)—This imposing fortress, nicknamed the "upside-down table," is the city's most prominent landmark. The castle saw its finest days when Hapsburg empress Maria Theresa took a liking to Bratislava in the 18th century, and decided she wanted to have a nice place to hold court here. But M. T.'s castle burned to the ground in an 1811 fire, and it was left as a ruin for a

Bratislava

century and a half—not reconstructed until 1953. The communist rebuild—especially inside the courtyard, which feels like a prison exercise yard—is drab and uninviting. The castle houses a few dull museums (history, musical instruments) and the chance to toss a coin down an incredibly deep well (280 feet before you hear the plop—the same distance as to the Danube; find entrance at far left corner as you enter main courtyard). But the best reason to visit the castle is for the views—especially of the New Bridge and the endless communist apartment blocks of the Petržalka suburb across the river.

By the way, the huge, pointy monument back toward the train station is **Slavín,** where more than 6,800 Soviet soldiers who fought to liberate Bratislava from the Nazis are buried. A nearby church had to take down its steeple so as not to draw attention away from the huge Soviet soldier on top of the monument.

TRANSPORTATION CONNECTIONS

From Bratislava by Train to: Vienna (2–3/hr, 1 hr), **Budapest** (4/day direct, more with transfers, 2.25–4 hrs), **Prague** (3/day direct, 4.25–5.5 hrs).

You can also connect to both Budapest and Vienna by **boat** (see page 485 and 889, respectively).

THE SPIŠ REGION

The most beautiful part of Slovakia is the mountainous north-central region, comprising the jagged High Tatras and the Spiš Region. The dramatic Carpathian Mountains slice through Eastern Europe here, dividing the Poles and Czechs in the north from the Hungarians and Yugoslavs in the south. With these Carpathian peaks as a backdrop, this region offers fine high-mountain scenery; easy river-rafting trips with fun-loving guides through a breathtaking gorge; a classic, Old World walled town with one of Europe's finest Gothic altarpieces; a glimpse at Slovakia's complicated ethnic mix; and treacherous but legendary hiking trails in a place so pretty, they call it "paradise."

Planning Your Time

The Spiš Region is a handy place for drivers to break up the long journey between Kraków and Hungary—on this route, Levoča is worth an overnight to recharge and get a taste of rural Slovakia. But unless you have a special interest, don't go out of your way to reach this area. Train travelers or those on a speedy itinerary should skip it (sleep through Slovakia on the night train).

Getting to the Spiš Region

Seeing the Spiš Region is a real headache without a car. If you're going between Kraków and Hungary (Eger or Budapest), the train line veers around Levoča far to the east, through Košice. From Košice, trains will get you to Prešov or Spišská Nová Ves, and the bus will take you the rest of the way to Levoča. From the west, buses run between Bratislava and Levoča (though it's often

SPIŠ REGION

faster to take the train to Poprad, then bus to Levoča). For specific schedules, see www.cp.sk.

Levoča

Levoča (LEH-voh-chah) is a diamond in the rough. If you can look past the crumbling facades and potholed roads, you'll see Slovakia's finest small town—with a mostly intact medieval wall, a main square ringed by striking Renaissance facades, and one of the greatest Gothic altarpieces in all of Europe.

Levoča boomed in the Middle Ages, when trade between Hungary and Poland brought abundant merchant traffic through its gates. In the 15th century, the town's centerpiece was built: St. James Church. A local woodcarver named Master Pavol packed the church with one of the most impressive collections of altarpieces in the world—including the pièce de résistance, an exquisite 60-foot-high main altar.

In the 19th century, Levoča vied with a neighboring town, Spišská Nová Ves (eight miles south), to host a station on an important rail line that was being built. S.N.V. won, and became a transportation hub for the region. While unfortunate for Levoča's economy at the time, this lack of train access has allowed Levoča to remain a wonderfully well-preserved Old World village of 10,000. If all of this makes Levoča feel off the beaten track, so much the better.

ORIENTATION

(area code: 053)

Levoča is small—you can walk from one end of the walled burg to the other in 15 minutes—and all roads lead to the town's main square, which is named for the important woodcarver Master Pavol (Námestie Majstra Pavla). The **TI** can answer your questions about the town, and put you in touch with a local guide (Mon–Fri 9:00–17:00, Sat 10:00–14:00, on the main square at #58, tel. 053/451-3763, www.levoca.sk).

SIGHTS AND ACTIVITIES

▲**Church of St. James (Chrám Sv. Jakuba)**—This huge Gothic church, dominating Levoča's main square, contains 11 ornately decorated altars—including the tallest wooden altarpiece in the world.

The church dates from the 14th century. In the late 15th century, neighboring VIPs visited here. The greatest Hungarian king, Mátyás Corvinus, came in 1474 (for more on Corvinus, see sidebar on page 424). Two decades later, representatives of Poland's powerful Jagiellonian dynasty paid a visit. These important guests—both commemorated inside the church—are a reminder that Slovakia has long been at a crossroads of Eastern Europe.

In the early 16th century, the great sculptor Master Pavol left his mark on the church. Master Pavol's unique, almost cartoonish style features figures with too-big heads, strangely weepy eyes, and honest-to-goodness personalities. Pavol's masterpiece is the church's single most impressive sight: the 60-foot-tall **main altar,** carved out of linden wood and bathed in gold paint. The large central figures represent Mary and the Baby Jesus, flanked by St. James (the church's namesake, on left) and St. John the Evangelist (on right). The four panels surrounding these figures depict scenes from James' and John's lives and deaths. Beneath them is a depiction of the Last Supper. Unusual in Gothic art, each apostle has his own individual features (based on the local merchants who financed the work). With this and his other carvings, Master Pavol

History of the Spiš Region

The Spiš (pronounced "speesh") region is one of the most historic and scenic corners of Slovakia. The area was named Szepes ("beautiful") by the Hungarians, who controlled this area in the Middle Ages. After the Tatars swept through in the 13th century, decimating the local population, the Hungarians invited Saxons (from the region of today's Germany around Dresden) to come and resettle the land. Silver, copper, and iron ore were discovered, and the Spiš became a prosperous mining region, with 24 bustling, richly decorated Saxon towns (including Levoča). The region became a showcase of Gothic and, later, Renaissance architecture.

For centuries, the Spiš was populated by a colorful mix of Saxons, Jews, and Slovaks. But after World War II, Czechoslovakia forced out people of German heritage—including descendents of those Saxon settlers who arrived here centuries before. Spiš was abandoned, and many towns were repopulated by Slovaks, while others were settled by Roma (Gypsies; see page 178).

Today's Spiš, while still suffering from economic ills, is emerging as a popular tourist destination.

was knocking on the door of the Renaissance.

The nave is lined with several other altarpieces—some by Master Pavol, some by others. At the front of the right nave (right-hand corner), look for the altar depicting the **Passion of Christ,** carved for the 1474 visit of Hungarian King Mátyás Corvinus. Jesus looks like Mátyás, Mary resembles his Italian wife, and the altar was supposed to bring the couple good luck in having a child.

To the left as you view the main altar, notice the interesting medieval **frescoes** on the wall (splotchy from a bad 19th-century renovation). The frescoes on the left depict the life of St. Dorothy. On the right are two strips. The upper strip shows a couple performing good deeds (feeding the hungry, visiting prisoners, burying the dead, and so on). In the lower strip, they sit on animals representing the mortal sins.

As you leave, at the back of the left nave, look for another Master Pavol altar with an iconic statue of **Mary.** When the Reformation swept Europe in the 16th century, locals hid statues such as Mary (who was tucked away in the Town Hall) to protect them from iconoclasts who destroyed religious symbols to unclutter their communion with God. Two centuries later, the long-forgotten statues were miraculously discovered and brought back to the church...for you to enjoy. (Slovaks love this emotive depiction of Mary so much, they put her on the 100-Sk note.)

Cost, Tours, Hours: The cost is 50 Sk, and you can visit only at the times posted on the door of the church office, across the street from the church entrance (on the north side of the church, facing the top of the square). You'll be accompanied by a guide, but you don't have to listen to her spiel (usually Slovak only—but try asking for English). Use the above information to appreciate the church, or find the talking box in the back of the nave and insert a coin for English. The church is open July–Aug Tue–Sat 9:00–17:00, Sun 13:00–17:00, Mon 11:00–17:00, tours every 30 min; Sept–Oct and Easter–June Tue–Sat 8:30–16:00, Sun 13:00–16:00, Mon 11:30–16:00, tours roughly hourly, though not always at the top of the hour; Nov–Easter Tue–Sat 8:30–16:00, closed Sun–Mon, tours roughly hourly. Tel. 053/451-2347, mobile 0907-521-673, www .chramsvjakuba.sk.

House of Master Pavol—The downside of the Church of St. James is that you can see the breathtaking altarpieces only from a distance, so you can't get a sense of what made Pavol the Master. At this museum, replicas of the statues allow you to look Pavol's creations right in their big, weepy eyes (40 Sk/€1.25, daily 9:00–17:00, tel. 053/451-3496).

Levoča Town Hall (Radnica v Levoči)—The huge, Renaissance-

style building behind the Church of St. James used to be the Town Hall; now it's a museum featuring the town and region's history and colorful folk cultures. You'll watch a movie in English before wandering though a grand, wood-carved meeting hall (with a beautifully painted ceiling) and rooms of maps of historic Levoča and the Spiš Region (50 Sk/€1.50, skimpy English information, daily 9:00–17:00, tel. 053/451-2786).

Mariánska Hora—This humble church, overlooking Levoča from a perch on a nearby hill, has been an important site for pilgrimages for centuries. Every year, on the first weekend of July, hundreds of thousands of Slovaks flock to the hill from the surrounding countryside—many walking as far as 30 miles. In 1995, Pope John Paul II made a pilgrimage here, saying Mass in front of some 650,000 people.

Near Levoča

Spiš Castle (Spišský Hrad)—Just a few miles from Levoča lies one of Europe's largest castles. Spiš Castle watches over the region from high on a bluff, overlooking a desolate terrain. Though there

The "Gypsy Question"

Eastern Europe is home to a silent population—mostly in Romania, Bulgaria, Hungary, and this part of Slovakia—of millions of dark-skinned people who speak an Indian-based dialect and follow their own, decidedly non-European culture. The most common name for Europe's overlooked culture, "Gypsy," is a holdover from the time when these people were thought to have come from Egypt. While the term isn't overtly offensive to most, it's both geographically mistaken and politically incorrect. (It's also taken on a negative connotation—as with the ethnic slur, "I've been gypped!") Today's preferred term for these people is "Roma."

The Roma most likely originated in today's India. In fact, the language still spoken by about two-thirds of today's European Roma—called Romany—is related to contemporary Indian languages. The Roma migrated into Europe through the Ottoman Empire (today's Turkey), arriving in the Balkan Peninsula in the 1300s. Traditionally, Roma earned their livelihood as entertainers (fortune telling, music and dancing, horse shows, dancing bears); as thieves; and as metalworkers (which is why they tended to concentrate in mining areas, like Slovakia and Kosovo).

Roma were initially not allowed to enter Austrian territory, but as the Hapsburgs recaptured lands once controlled by the Ottomans (such as Slovakia and Hungary), they permitted the Roma already living there to stay. In the 18th and 19th centuries, as "Gypsy music" funneled into the theaters of Vienna and Budapest, a romantic image of the Roma emerged: a happy-go-lucky nomadic lifestyle; intoxicating music, with dancers swirling around a campfire; mystical, or even magical, powers over white Europeans; and alluring, sultry women. But white Europe's image of the Roma also had a sinister side. Even today, Europeans and Americans alike might warn their children, "If you don't behave, I'll sell you to the Gypsies!" This widespread bigotry culminated in the Holocaust—when half a million Roma people were murdered in Nazi concentration camps.

Today's Roma are Europe's forgotten population—estimates range from 6 to 12 million throughout the continent. Many Roma do their best to integrate with their white neighbors. But Roma who hold down jobs and send their kids to school often find themselves shunned both by their fellow Roma, and by the white Europeans they're emulating. Other Roma resist assimilation. For example, in the Spiš Region, some Roma live in small, remote, self-contained villages—a long walk up a dirt road away from the mainstream "civilization." Polygamy is not uncommon, and some girls marry and begin having children at a very early age. Most children start attending school, but a high percentage drop out after just a few years.

Largely because of their unconventional lifestyle, Roma are subject to a pervasive prejudice unparalleled in today's Europe. Local news anchors—hardly fair or balanced—pointedly scapegoat the Roma for problems. A small town in the Czech Republic tried to build a wall between its wealthy neighborhood and the Roma ghetto. Schools are sometimes carefully segregated, with signs reading, "Whites Only." And recently, obstetricians in the Czech Republic were accused of sterilizing their female Roma patients without their informed consent.

It's easy to criticize these seemingly closed-minded attitudes. But, in the eyes of white Europeans, the Roma's poor reputation is at least partly deserved. While many Roma are upstanding citizens, others do turn to thievery for survival. The tour-guide refrain, "Watch out for Gypsy thieves!" might seem racist—but it's also good advice. As politically incorrect as it sounds to say so, many visitors have learned the hard way that it's downright foolish not to keep a close eye on a Roma person loitering in a tourist zone.

The large Roma population also puts an enormous strain on the already overtaxed social-welfare networks in these countries. Unemployment in the Spiš Region is near 30 percent—but among Roma, it's more like 50 percent in the summer (when some seasonal work is available) to 80 percent in the winter. To a white Slovak struggling to succeed in the tough times of post-communist Eastern Europe, Roma people are often seen as freeloaders.

What emerges is a seemingly unsolvable problem—a fundamental cultural misunderstanding, tinged with racist undertones, that separates the people of this region. So far, the Roma haven't produced a Martin Luther King Jr. to mobilize the culture and demand equal rights—and many experts think they likely never will. The greatest "crossover" success stories are musicians and artists, with no political aspirations.

But the white European community is beginning to take note. The Decade of Roma Inclusion—launched in 2005 by Hungarian-American businessman George Soros—is an initiative being undertaken by nine Eastern European countries to better address the human rights of their Roma citizens (www.romadecade.org). Many are hopeful, too, that with the EU's increased focus on cooperation and human rights, the Roma will find a welcome home in the new, united Europe.

have been castles on this strategic spot for as long as people
have lived here, the current
version was built during the
15th century. Since its destruction in 1781, only evocative,
photogenic ruins remain.

The interior is tourable,
though anyone you ask will tell you it's pretty dull in there (100
Sk/€3, daily May–Sept 9:00–19:00, Oct 9:00–18:00, last entry 45
min before closing, closed Nov–April, tel. 053/454-1336, www
.spisskyhrad.sk). However, views of the castle from the surrounding countryside are majestic.

Spiš Castle is the centerpiece of a cluster of interesting sights.
The town just below the castle is **Spišské Podhradie** ("Under the
Spiš Castle"). On a ridge opposite Spiš Castle is **Spišská Kapitula,**
the site of the Spiš Region's cathedral, surrounded by a modest village and an imposing 14th-century wall. And tucked behind Spiš
Castle is **Žehra,** a village with a simple, onion-domed church that
contains some 13th- to 15th-century wall paintings.

Getting There: From Levoča, take the main road (E50) east.
After 7.5 miles, you'll see the first turnoff, which takes you scenically past Spišská Kapitula and through Spišské Podhradie (park
near town and hike all the way up, or cut through town back to the
main road and wind around to the second exit). To get to the castle
more directly, stay on E50 past the first exit, and go another two
miles, where there'll be another turnoff to the right leading up to
the parking lot behind the castle.

Slovak Paradise (Slovenský Raj)—Outdoors enthusiasts from
all over Eastern Europe flock to this national park, and for good
reason—it features steep river gorges lined with waterfalls, and
plateaus pocked by caves, offering some of the most enjoyable hikes
this side of the Plitvice Lakes (see page 781). The Slovak Paradise
is known for its seemingly treacherous trails—one often-photo-
graphed stretch features ladders laid at sharp uphill angles, spanning a gaping gorge. The faint of heart should steer clear of these
more challenging hikes, but in other parts of the park, you'll find
trails suitable for any hiker (www.slovenskyraj.sk). Spišská Nová
Ves is the handiest gateway, on the northeastern fringe of the park
(and with a convenient train station).

River Rafting in the Pieniny—A few miles north of Levoča, at
the border with Poland, is the Pieniny region (www.pieniny.sk).
Here, the Dunajec (DOO-nah-yets) River flows through a dramatic gorge in the shadow of sheer limestone cliffs, with Poland
on one bank and Slovakia on the other—like scenery from *The
Lord of the Rings.*

The best way to experience the Pieniny is on a boat cruise. You'll board a *plt'*—a strange, pontoon-type raft made up of five

canoe-like skiffs lashed together and bridged with long benches— and ply the waters of the Dunajec River. Your lively conductor is dressed in the traditional costume of the Góral folk who populate this region. The trip is generally smooth—no whitewater to speak of—and offers a lazy chance to enjoy the scenery.

Rafting trips go roughly from early May through late October, weather permitting (daily 8:30–17:00, until 15:00 Sept–Oct, about 300 Sk/€9 per person, float lasts about 1 hour). The best stretch of river is 5.5-mile-long, U-shaped **Dunajec Canyon,** that begins near the town of **Červený Kláštor** ("Red Cloister"—this old building is near the town itself) and ends at the town of **Lesnica.** Hop on at a raft landing—marked as *prístav plt'í* on signs and maps. When you reach Lesnica, catch the bus back to your starting point...or hike the three miles back to Červený Kláštor.

SLEEPING

All of the presidents of Central European countries converged on Levoča for a conference in 1998, and you'll see photos of many of them decorating the few proud hotels in town. All of these hotels are right on the main square, Námestie Majstra Pavla.

$$ Hotel Satel is a plush, swanky place that caters to tour groups. Its 23 frou-frou rooms are all pastel pinks, spread around

---

Sleep Code

(25 Sk = about $1, €1 = about $1.40, country code: 421, area code: 053)

S = Single, **D** = Double/Twin, **T** = Triple, **Q** = Quad, **b** = bathroom, **s** = shower only. Credit cards are accepted and English is spoken at each place. For the convenience of their international guests, Levoča's hotels generally quote prices in euros. These rates do not include breakfast.

To help you sort easily through these listings, I've divided the rooms into two categories, based on the price for a standard double room with bath:

  $$ Higher Priced—Most rooms €50 or more.
   $ Lower Priced—Most rooms less than €50.

---

a beautifully restored inner courtyard (Sb-€70, Db-€80, 20 percent cheaper Nov–March, breakfast-€6, elevator to some rooms,
Námestie Majstra Pavla 55, tel. 053/451-2943, fax 053/451-4486,
www.hotelsatel.com, satel-le@hotelsatel.com).

$ **Hotel Barbakan,** near the top of the main square, feels
traditional. Though its 15 rooms are darkly furnished, it's a decent
option for the price (Sb-€35, Db-€46, suite-€52, 15 percent
cheaper Oct–April, extra bed-€12, breakfast-€5, lots of stairs with
no elevator, Košická 15, tel. 053/451-4310, fax 053/451-3609, www
.barbakan.sk, recepcia.hot@barbakan.sk).

$ **Hotel Arkada,** popular with tours, has 32 nondescript
rooms (Sb-€35, Db-€50, suite-€62, 20 percent cheaper mid-Oct–
April, extra bed-€12, breakfast-€4, Námestie Majstra Pavla 26,
tel. 053/451-2372, fax 053/451-2255, www.arkada.sk, hotelarkada
@arkada.sk).

EATING

Hotel Satel and **Hotel Barbakan,** listed above, both have restaurants. But **Reštaurácia u 3 Apoštolov** ("Three Apostles"),
also right on the square, is a cut above, serving tasty Slovak cuisine. The decor is nothing special, but the food is delicious and
cheap: pungent garlic soup, excellent trout, and the tasty "Apostle
Specialty"—sautéed beef and vegetables in a spicy sauce, wrapped
in a potato pancake (main dishes around 200 Sk/€6, long hours
daily, Námestie Majstra Pavla 11, tel. 053/451-2302).

The High Tatras (Vysoké Tatry)

While not technically in the Spiš Region, Slovakia's most breathtaking mountain range is nearby. The High Tatras mountain range
is small but mighty—dramatic, nearly 9,000-foot-tall granite peaks
spike up from the plains, covering an area of only about 100 square
miles. The High Tatras are the northernmost and highest part
of the Carpathian Mountains, which stretch across the heart of
Eastern Europe all the way to Romania. These cut-glass peaks have
quickly become legendary among hardy, in-the-know travelers for
their remarkably inexpensive hiking and skiing opportunities.

The High Tatras make up the Polish–Slovak border. Without
a car, the most accessible approach is from the Polish resort town
of **Zakopane** (an easy 1.5-hour bus or train connection from
Kraków). But for more rugged beauty, head to the southern part of
the range, in Slovakia.

The mid-sized city of **Poprad**—located on a plain about 10 miles from the mountains—is the most convenient launchpad for venturing into Slovakia's High Tatras. Along the base of the High Tatras are various modest resort towns (including the biggest, Starý Smokovec). There's no shortage of scenic hikes all over the region (good maps and guidebooks available locally). The best no-sweat high-altitude option is to take the **cable car** from the resort village of Tatranská Lomnica up to the viewpoint at Lomnický Štít (8,640 feet; popular and crowded, so visit early).

By car, take road 537 along the base of the High Tatras to connect the various towns. By public transportation, you'll commute by electric trains *(električky)* from Poprad into Starý Smokovec. (There are also direct, one-hour buses from Levoča to Starý Smokovec.) From Starý Smokovec, you can continue by electric train on to Tatranská Lomnica and other villages. Each town has its share of simple resort-type hotels, but serious hikers enjoy staying in the High Tatras' many *chaty* (mountain huts). For more details on the High Tatras, visit www.tanap.sk or www.tatry.net. *Spectacular Slovakia* magazine, mentioned on page 158, also has good coverage of the region (www.spectacularslovakia.sk).

POLAND

POLAND

Polska

Americans who think of Poland as run-down—full of rusting factories, smoggy cities, and gloomy natives—are speechless when they step into Kraków's vibrant main square, Gdańsk's colorful pedestrian drag, or Warsaw's lively Old Town. While parts of the country are still cleaning up the industrial mess left by the Soviets, Poland also has some breathtaking medieval cities that show off its warm and welcoming people, dynamic history, and unique cultural fabric.

The Poles are a proud people—as moved by their spectacular failures as by their successes. Their quiet elegance has been tempered by generations of abuse by foreign powers. The Poles place a lot of importance on honor, and you'll find fewer scams and con artists here than in other countries.

In a way, there are two Polands: lively, cosmopolitan urban centers, and countless tiny farm villages in the countryside. City-dwellers often talk about the "simple people" of Poland—those descended from generations of farmers, working the same plots for centuries and living an uncomplicated, traditional lifestyle. This large contingent of old-fashioned, salt-of-the-earth folks—who like things the way they are—is a major reason why Poland was so hesitant to join the European Union (see page 196).

Poland is the poorest of the countries that joined the European Union in 2004. While the most important tourist centers have been prettied up admirably, you only need venture a few blocks, or drive through the countryside, to see unmistakable signs of poverty. It's the little things that aren't quite up to Western snuff: parks with patches of mud instead of grass, ramshackle farmhouses with overgrown yards, and rough-around-the-edges infrastructure (rusted railings, potholed roads, and so on). These finer points are expensive to cultivate—unnecessary niceties that the Poles simply can't afford yet. But with the Poles' ambitious spirit and new EU investment, it shouldn't be long before Poland starts to look more like the wealthy West.

Poland is one of Europe's most devoutly Catholic countries. Catholicism defines these people, holding them together through times when they had little else. Squeezed between Protestant Germany (originally Prussia) and Orthodox Russia, Poland wasn't even a country for generations (1795–1918). Its Catholicism helped keep its spirit alive. In the last century, while "under communism" (as that age is referred to), Poles found their religion a source of strength as well as rebellion—they could express dissent by going to church. Some of Poland's best sights are churches, usually filled with locals praying silently. While these church interiors are worth a visit, be especially careful to show the proper respect (maintain silence, keep a low profile, and snap pictures discreetly).

Visitors are sometimes surprised at how much of Poland's story is a Jewish story. Before World War II, 80 percent of the world's Jews lived in Poland. Warsaw was the world's second-largest Jewish city (after New York) with 380,000 Jews (out of a total population of 1.2 million). Poland was a magnet for Jews because of its relatively welcoming policies. Still, Jews were forbidden from owning land; that's why they settled mostly in the cities. But the Holocaust (and a later Soviet policy of sending "troublemaking" Jews to Israel) decimated the Jewish population. This tragic chapter, combined with postwar border shifts and population movements, made Poland one of Europe's most ethnically homogenous countries. Today, virtually everyone in the country speaks Polish, and only a few thousand Polish Jews remain.

Poland is historically extremely pro-American. Of course, their big neighbors (Russia and Germany) have been their historic enemies. And when Hitler invaded in 1939, the Poles felt let down by their supposed European friends (France and Britain), who declared war on Germany but provided virtually no military support. America has always been regarded as the big ally from

Poland Almanac

Official Name: Rzeczpospolita Polska (Republic of Poland), or Polska for short.

Snapshot History: This thousand-year-old country has been dominated by foreigners for much of the last two centuries, finally achieving true independence (from the Soviet Union) in 1989.

Population: Nearly 39 million people, slightly more than California. About 97 percent are ethnically Polish and speak Polish (though English is also widely spoken). Three out of every four Poles are practicing Catholics. The population is younger than most European countries, with an average age of 37 (Germany's is 42).

Latitude and Longitude: 52°N and 20°E (similar latitude to Berlin, London, and Edmonton, Alberta).

Area: 122,000 square miles, the same as New Mexico (or Illinois and Iowa put together).

Geography: Because of its overall flatness, Poland has been a corridor for invading armies since its infancy. The Vistula River (680 miles) runs south-to-north up the middle of the country, passing through Kraków and Warsaw, and emptying into the Baltic Sea at Gdańsk. Poland's climate is generally cool and rainy—40,000 storks love it.

Biggest Cities: Warsaw (the capital, 1.7 million), Łódź (790,000), and Kraków (757,000).

Economy: The Gross Domestic Product is $554 billion (a little more than the state of Ohio), but the GDP per capita is $14,400—less than a third what the average Ohioan makes. The 1990s saw an aggressive—and very successful—transition from state-run socialism to privately owned capitalism. Still, Poland's traditional potato-and-pig-farming society is behind the times, with 16 percent of the country's workers producing less than 3 percent of its GDP. One in seven Poles is unemployed, and nearly one in five lives in poverty. Poland's entry into the European Union in 2004 brought substantial financial aid that should improve things.

across the ocean. In 1989, when Poland finally won its freedom, many Poles only half-joked that they should apply to become the 51st state of the United States.

On my first visit to Poland, I had a poor impression of Poles, who seemed brusque and often elbowed ahead of me in line. I've since learned that all it takes is a smile and a cheerful greeting—preferably in Polish—to break through the thick skin that helped these kind people survive the difficult communist times. With a

Currency: 1 złoty (zł, or PLN) = 100 groszy (gr) = about 30 cents; 3 zł = about $1.

Real Estate: A typical one-bedroom apartment in Warsaw (250 square feet) rents for roughly $600 a month.

Government: Poland's mostly figurehead president selects the prime minister and Cabinet, with legislators' approval. They govern along with a two-house legislature (Sejm and Senat) of 560 seats. Donald Tusk, leader of the centrist Civic Platform, became prime minister in 2007. Current president Leck Kaczyński's five-year term expires in 2010. (For more on Polish politics, see page 197.)

Flag: The upper half is white, and the lower half is red—the traditional colors of Poland. Poetic Poles claim the white represents honor, and the red represents the enormous amounts of blood spilled by the Poles to honor their nation. The flag sometimes includes a coat of arms with a crowned eagle (representing Polish sovereignty). Under Poland's many oppressors (including the Soviets), the crown was removed from the emblem, and its talons were trimmed. On regaining its independence, Poland coronated its eagle once more.

The Average Pole: New prosperity aside, the average Pole spends just 4 percent of what a German spends on personal consumption. One in four Poles uses the Internet, and the average Pole will live to about age 75. The average woman gets married at 24 and will have 1.25 children.

Not-so-Average Poles: Despite the many "Polack jokes" you've heard (and maybe repeated), you actually know of many famous Polish intellectuals—you just don't realize they're Polish. The "Dumb Polack" Hall of Fame includes Karol Wojtyła (Pope John Paul II), Mikołaj Kopernik (Nicolas Copernicus), composer Fryderyk Chopin, scientist Marie Curie (née Skłodowska), writer Teodor Józef Korzeniowski (better known as Joseph Conrad, author of *Heart of Darkness*), filmmaker Roman Polański *(Chinatown, The Pianist)*, politician Lech Wałęsa...and one of this book's co-authors.

friendly hello *(Dzień dobry!)*, you'll turn any grouch into a new friend.

Practicalities

Restroom Signage: To confuse tourists, the Poles have devised a secret way of marking their WCs. You'll see doors marked with *męska* (men) and *damska* (women)—but even more often, you'll simply see a triangle (for men) or a circle (for women). Likewise, a

Top 10 Dates That Changed Poland

A.D. 966—The Polish king, Mieszko I, is baptized a Christian, symbolically uniting the Polish people and founding the nation.

1385—The Polish queen (called a "king" by sexist aristocrats of the time) marries a Lithuanian duke, starting the two-century reign of the Jagiełło family.

1410—Poland defeats the Teutonic Knights at the Battle of Grunwald, part of a Golden Age of territorial expansion and cultural achievement.

1572—The last Jagiellonian king dies, soon replaced by bickering nobles and foreign kings. Poland declines.

1795—In the last of three partitions, the country is divvied up by its more-powerful neighbors: Russia, Prussia, and Austria.

1918—Following World War I, Poland gets back its land and sovereignty.

1939—Gdańsk (then called Danzig) is invaded by Nazi Germany, starting World War II. At war's end, the country is "liberated" (i.e., occupied) by the Soviet Union.

1980—Lech Wałęsa leads a successful strike, demanding more freedom from the communist regime.

1989—The Berlin Wall falls, and Poland soon gains independence under its first president...Lech Wałęsa.

2004—Poland joins the European Union, pedaling fast to catch up to its more-prosperous neighbors.

sign with a triangle, a circle, and an arrow is directing you to the closest WCs.

Pay to Pee: To irritate tourists, Polish bathrooms often charge a small fee. Sometimes you'll even be charged at a restaurant where you're paying to dine. Sadly, many American visitors let this minor inconvenience interfere with their enjoyment of the trip. My advice: You don't have to like it, but get used to it—it's a hassle, but it's cheap (usually around 1 zł).

Train Station Lingo: "PKP" is the abbreviation for Polish National Railways ("PKS" is for buses). In larger towns with several train stations, you'll usually use the one called Główny (meaning "Main"—except in Warsaw, where it's Centralna). Underneath the stations are often mazes of walkways—lined with market stalls—that lead to platforms *(peron)* and exits *(wyjście)*. Most stations have several platforms, each of which has two tracks *(tor)*. Departures are generally listed by the *peron*, so keep your eye on both tracks for your train. Arrivals are *przyjazdy*, and departures are *odjazdy*.

Left-luggage counters or lockers are marked *przechowalnia bagażu*. *Kasy* are ticket windows. "Information" windows are more often than not staffed by monolingual grouches. Smile sweetly, write down your destination and time, and hang onto your patience. The line you choose will invariably be the slowest one—leave plenty of time to buy your ticket before your train departs (or, if you're running out of time, buy it on board for a few dollars extra). You'll likely be given two separate tickets: one for the journey, and the other for your seat assignment. On arriving at a station, to get into town, follow signs for *wyjście do centrum* or *wyjście do miasta*.

Museum Tips: Virtually every museum in Poland is closed on Monday. The ticket window for any museum closes a half-hour before the museum's closing time, and this last-entry deadline is strictly enforced. Poland's museums are notorious for constantly tweaking their opening times. I've tried to list the correct hours, but be aware that they're virtually impossible to predict—try to confirm locally if you have your heart set on a particular place.

Polish Artists: Though Poland has produced world-renowned scientists, musicians, and writers, the country isn't known for its artists. Polish museums greet foreign visitors with fine artwork by unfamiliar names. If you're planning to visit any museums in Poland, there are two artists worth remembering: **Jan Matejko,** a 19th-century positivist who painted grand historical epics (see page 302); and one of his students, **Stanisław Wyspiański,** a painter and playwright who led the charge of the Młoda Polska movement (the Polish answer to Art Nouveau—see page 219) in the early 1900s.

Telephones: Insertable telephone cards, sold at newsstands and kiosks everywhere, get you access to the modern public phones. Cheap international phone cards for calling the US have only recently begun to appear (often sold at Internet cafés or youth hostels; see page 940 for details).

To summon the police, call 997; for an ambulance, dial 999; for the fire department, it's 998. Remember these prefixes: 0800 is toll-free, and 0700 is expensive (like phone sex). Many Poles use mobile phones (which come with 060 and 050 prefixes).

Poland uses a direct-dial system, which means you call the same number whether dialing across the street or across the country. To call Poland from another country, first dial the international access number (00 if you're calling from Europe, or 011 from the US and Canada), followed by 48 (Poland's country code), then the number (without the initial 0). To call out of Poland, dial 00, the country code of the country you're calling (see chart in appendix), the area code if applicable (may need to drop initial zero), and the local number (see page 944 for details).

Polish History

Poland is flat. Take a look at a topographical map of Europe, and you can see the Poles' historical dilemma: The path of least resistance from northern Europe to Russia is right through Poland. Over the years, many invaders—including Napoleon and Hitler—have taken advantage of Poland's strategic location. The country is nicknamed "God's playground" for the many wars that have rumbled through its territory. Poland has been invaded by

Soviets, Nazis, French, Austrians, Russians, Prussians, Swedes, Teutonic Knights, Tatars, Bohemians, Magyars—and, about 1,300 years ago, Poles.

Medieval Greatness

The first Poles were a tribe called the Polonians ("people of the plains"), a Slavic band that showed up in these parts in the eighth century. In 966, Mieszko I, Duke of the Polonian tribe, adopted Christianity and founded the Piast dynasty (which would last for more than 400 years). Poland was born.

Poland struggled with two different invaders in the 13th century: the Tatars (Mongols who ravaged the south) and the Teutonic Knights (Germans who conquered the north—see page 370). But despite these challenges, Poland persevered. The last king of the Piast dynasty was also the greatest: Kazimierz the Great, who famously "found a Poland made of wood and left one made of brick and stone"—bringing Poland (and its capital, Kraków) to international prominence (see page 217). The progressive Kazimierz also invited Europe's much-persecuted Jews to settle here, establishing Poland as a haven for the Jewish people—which it would remain until the Nazis arrived.

Kazimierz the Great died at the end of the 14th century without a male heir. His grand-niece, Jadwiga, became "king" (the Poles weren't ready for a "queen") and married Lithuanian Prince Władysław Jagiełło, uniting their countries against a common enemy, the Teutonic Knights. Their marriage marked the beginning of the Jagiellonian dynasty and set the stage for Poland's Golden Age. With territory spanning from the Baltic Sea to the Black Sea, Poland flourished.

Foreign Kings and Partitions

When the Jagiellonians died out in 1572, political power shifted to the nobles. Poland became a nation governed by its wealthiest

10 percent—the *szlachta,* or nobility, who elected a series of foreign kings. Many of these kings made bad diplomatic decisions and squandered the country's resources. To make matters worse, the Polish Parliament (Sejm) introduced the concept of *liberum veto,* whereby any measure could be vetoed by a single member of parliament. This policy—which effectively demanded unanimous approval for any law to be passed—paralyzed the Sejm's waning power.

By the late 18th century, Poland was floundering—and surrounded by three land-hungry empires (Russia, Prussia, and Austria). Over the course of less than 25 years, these countries divided Poland's territory among themselves in a series of three partitions. In 1795, "Poland" (nicknamed "the cake of kings"—to be sliced and eaten at will) disappeared from Europe's maps, not to return until 1918.

Even though Poland was gone, the Poles wouldn't go quietly. As the partitions were taking place, Polish soldier Tadeusz Kościuszko (a hero of the American Revolution) returned home to lead an unsuccessful military resistance against the Russians. After another failed uprising against Russia in 1830, many of Poland's top artists and writers fled to Paris—including pianist Fryderyk Chopin and Romantic poet Adam Mickiewicz (whose statue adorns Kraków's main square and Warsaw's Royal Way). These Polish artists tried to preserve the nation's spirit with music and words; those who remained in Poland continued to fight with swords and fists. By the end of the 19th century, the image of the Pole as a tireless, idealistic insurgent emerged. During this time, some Romantics—with typically melodramatic flair—dubbed Poland "the Christ of nations" for the way it was misunderstood and persecuted by the world.

At the end of World War I, Poland finally regained its independence...but the peace didn't last long.

Saddle on a Cow: World War II and Communism

In the early 20th century, Poland enjoyed a diverse ethnic mix—including Germans, Russians, Ukrainians, Lithuanians, and an enormous Jewish minority. A third of Poland spoke no Polish. But then, on September 1, 1939, Hitler began World War II by attacking the Baltic port city of Gdańsk. With six million deaths in the next six years, Poland suffered the worst per-capita WWII losses of any nation.

At the war's end, as the victorious Allies shifted Poland's borders significantly westward, a massive movement of populations took place: Germans from western Poland were forced into Germany, and Poles from what would become Ukraine were transplanted to Poland proper. After millions died in the war, millions

The Heritage of Communism

While Poland has been free, democratic, and capitalist since 1989, even young adults carry lots of psychological baggage from living under communism. Although the young generally embrace the fast new affluence with enthusiasm, many older people tend to be nostalgic about that slower-paced time that came with more security. And even young professionals, with so much energy and hope now, don't condemn everything about that stretch of history. A friend who was 13 in 1989 recalled those days this way:

"My childhood is filled with happy memories. Under communism, life was family-oriented. Careers didn't matter. There was no way to get rich, no reason to rush, so we had time. People always had time.

"But there were also shortages—many things were 'in deficit.' Sometimes my uncle would bring us several toilet paper rolls, held together with a string—absolutely the best gift anyone could give. I remember my mother and father had to 'organize' for special events...somehow find a good sausage and some Coca-Cola.

"Boys in my neighborhood collected pop cans. Since drinks were very limited in Poland, cans from other countries represented a world of opportunities beyond our borders. Parents could buy their children these cans on the black market, and the few families who were allowed to travel returned home with a treasure trove of cans. One boy up the street from me went to Italy, and proudly brought home a Pepsi can. All of the boys in the neighborhood wanted to see it—it was a huge status symbol. But a month later, communism ended, you could buy whatever you wanted, and everyone's can collections were worthless.

"We had real chocolate only for Christmas. The rest of the year, for treats we got something called 'chocolate-like product', which was sweet, dark, and smelled vaguely of chocolate. And we had oranges from Cuba for Christmas, too. Everybody was excited when the newspapers announced, 'The boat with the oranges from Cuba is just five days from Poland.' We waited with excitement all year for chocolate and those oranges. The smell of Christmas was so special. Now we have that smell every day. Still, my happiest Christmases were under communism."

more were displaced from their ancestral homes. When the dust settled, Poland was in rubble...and almost exclusively Polish.

Poland was arguably hit harder by the Soviet regime than the other countries in this book. As conditions worsened in the 1970s, food shortages were the norm. Stores were marked by long lines stretching around the block. Poles were issued ration coupons for food staples, and cashiers clipped off a corner when a purchase was made...assuming, of course, the item was in stock. It often wasn't.

The little absurdities of communist life—which today seem almost comical—made every day a struggle. For years, every elderly woman in Poland had hair the same strange magenta color. There was only one color of dye available, so the choice was simple: Let your hair grow out (and look clownishly half red and half white), or line up and go red.

During these difficult times, the Poles often rose up—staging major protests in 1956, 1968, 1970, and 1976. Stalin famously noted that introducing communism to the Poles was like putting a saddle on a cow.

When an anti-communist Polish cardinal named Karol Wojtyła was elected Pope in 1978, it was a sign to his countrymen that change was in the air. (For more on Pope John Paul II, see page 222.) In 1980, Lech Wałęsa, an electrician at the shipyards in Gdańsk, became the leader of the Solidarity movement, the first workers' union in communist Eastern Europe. After an initial 18-day strike at the Gdańsk shipyards, the communist regime gave in, legalizing Solidarity (for more on Solidarity, see page 342).

But the union grew too powerful, and the communists felt their control slipping away. On Sunday, December 13, 1981, Poland's head of state, General Wojciech Jaruzelski, declared martial law in order to "forestall Soviet intervention." (Whether the Soviets actually would have intervened remains a hotly debated issue.) Tanks ominously rolled through the streets of Poland on that snowy December morning, and the Poles were terrified.

Martial law would last until 1983. Each Pole has his or her own chilling memories of this frightening time. During riots, the people would flock into churches—the only place they would be safe from the ZOMO, or riot police. But Solidarity struggled on, going underground and becoming a united movement of all demographics, 10 million members strong (more than a quarter of the population).

In July 1989, the ruling Communist Party agreed to hold open elections (reserving 65 percent of representatives for themselves). Their goal was to appease Solidarity, but the plan backfired: Communists didn't win a single seat. These elections helped spark the chain reaction across Eastern Europe that eventually tore down the Iron Curtain. Lech Wałęsa became

Polish Jokes

Through the dreary communist times, the Poles managed to keep their sense of humor. A popular target of jokes was the riot police, or ZOMO. Here are just a few of the things Poles said about these unpopular cops:

- It's better to have a sister who's a whore than a brother in the ZOMO.
- ZOMO police are hired based on the 90–90 principle: They have to weigh at least 90 kilograms (200 pounds), and their I.Q. must be less than 90.
- ZOMO would be dispatched in teams of three: one who could read, one who could write, and a third to protect those other two smart guys.
- A ZOMO policeman was sitting on the curb, crying. Someone came up to him and asked what was wrong. "I lost my dog!" he said. "No matter," the person replied. "He's a smart police dog. I'm sure he can find his way back to the station." "Yes," the ZOMO said. "But without him, I can't!"

The communists gave their people no options at elections: If you voted, you voted for the regime. Poles liked to joke that in some ways, this made communists like God—who created Eve, then said to Adam, "Now choose a wife." The communists could run a pig as a candidate, and it would still win. A popular symbol of dissent became a pig painted with the words, "Vote Red."

There were even jokes about jokes. Under communism, Poles noted that there was a government-sponsored prize for the funniest political joke: 15 years in prison.

Poland's first post-communist president. (For more on Lech Wałęsa, see page 344.)

Poland in the 21st Century: The European Union

When 10 new countries joined the European Union in May 2004, Poland was the most ambivalent of the bunch. After centuries of being under other empires' authority, the Poles were hardly eager to relinquish some of their hard-fought autonomy to Brussels. Many Poles thought that EU membership would make things worse (higher prices, a loss of traditional lifestyles) before they got better. But most people agreed that their country had to join to survive in today's Europe. Now, a few years later, most begrudgingly acknowledge that the benefits of EU membership have outweighed the drawbacks.

While other countries were planning their fireworks displays to celebrate EU enlargement on May 1, 2004, Poland was seized

Poland

by a strange sort of mass hysteria. The country buzzed with rumors of increased prices. When the news reported that sugar would be subject to a higher tax rate, there was a run on the stores, as the Poles bought up as much sugar as they could stockpile. The result? A shortage of sugar...and higher prices, even before May 1. (If this sounds like a bad Polish joke come to life, remember the days after September 11, 2001, when US stores ran out of tarp, duct tape, and bottled water.)

The most obvious impact of EU membership so far has been the tremendous migration of young Poles seeking work in other EU countries (mostly Britain, Ireland, and Sweden, which waive visa requirements for Eastern European workers). Many of them find employment at hotels and restaurants. Visitors to London and Dublin are noticing a surprising language barrier at the front desks of hotels, and Polish expat newspapers are joining British gossip rags on newsstands. Those who remain in Poland are becoming concerned about the "brain drain" of bright young people flocking out of their country. For more on this phenomenon, see "The Polish Plumber Syndrome" on page 20.

Poland is by far the most populous of the recent EU members, with 39 million people (about the same as Spain, or about half the size of Germany). This makes Poland the sixth-largest of the 27 EU member states—giving it serious political clout, which it has already asserted in shaping a new EU constitution. As the EU learns to live with its new Eastern European comrades, Poland looks poised to take a leading role in the "New Europe."

The Kaczyński Brothers: Those Two Who Would Lead Poland

Poland's political process took a surprising turn in the 2005 presidential election, won by Lech Kaczyński and his conservative Law and Justice party. The party's platform is pro-tax cuts, fiercely Euroskeptic (anti-EU), and very Catholic. This suits the Poles fine. Like a nation of Newt Gingriches, Poles are phobic when it comes to "big government," since they've been subjugated and manipulated so much by foreign oppressors over the centuries. This is partly why the infrastructure here still lags somewhat behind other Eastern European countries (lower taxes = less investment in roads). On the American spectrum, Poland may be the most politically "conservative" country in Europe.

In a queasy twist, several months after his election, President Lech Kaczyński took the controversial step of appointing his identical twin brother (and Law and Justice party co-founder) Jarosław as Poland's prime minister. The Kaczyński brothers were child actors who appeared in several popular movies together—their biggest hit was titled *Those Two Who Would Steal the Moon*. As teenagers,

Poland

they would switch identities and take tests for each other. Today the 45-minute-older, unmarried, and slightly more handsome Jarosław, who still lives with the twins' mother, is considered one of Poland's most eligible bachelors. (You can't make this stuff up.)

The political pendulum took a hard swing back to the center in October of 2007, when the Kaczyński brothers' main political rival, the pro-EU Donald Tusk, led his Civic Platform party to victory in the parliamentary elections. Tusk was named prime minister, though Lech Kaczyński remains president through at least 2010. As Poland marches into the 21st century, its future will be guided by Donald Tusk and the Kaczyńskis—the yin and yangs of Polish politics. The name Kaczyński loosely means "duck"—so the Poles, always quick with a joke about their political fortunes, quip that they're led by "Donald and the Ducks."

Polish Food

Polish food is hearty and tasty. Since Poland is north of the Carpathian Mountains, its weather tends to be chilly, which limits the kinds of fruits and vegetables that flourish here. Like other northern European countries (such as Russia or Scandinavia), dominant staples include potatoes, dill, berries, beets, and bread. Much of what you might think of as "Jewish food" turns up on Polish menus (gefilte fish, potato pancakes, chicken soup, and so forth)—not necessarily because either group influenced the other, but because they lived in the same area for centuries under the same climatic and culinary influences.

Polish soups are a highlight. The most typical are *żurek* and *barszcz*. Żurek (often translated as "sour soup" on menus) is a light-colored soup made from a sourdough base, usually containing a hard-boiled egg and pieces of *kiełbasa* (sausage). Barszcz, better known to Americans as borscht, is a savory beet soup. There are various types of borscht: *Barszcz czerwony* (red borscht) is a broth with a deep red color, sometimes containing dumplings or a hard-boiled egg. *Barszcz ukraiński* (Ukrainian borscht) is similar, but has vegetables mixed in (usually cabbage, beans, and carrots). In summer, try the "Polish gazpacho"—*chłodnik*, a cream soup with beets, onions, and radishes that's served cold.

Another familiar Polish dish is pierogi. These ravioli-like dumplings come with various fillings. The most traditional are minced meat, sauerkraut, mushroom, cheese, and blueberry, but many restaurants experiment with more exotic fillings. Pierogi are often served with specks of fatty bacon to add flavor. Pierogi are a budget traveler's dream: Restaurants serving them are everywhere, and they're generally cheap, filling, and tasty.

Bigos is a rich and delicious sauerkraut stew cooked with meat, mushrooms, and whatever's in the pantry. *Gołąbki* is cabbage leaves

Bar Mleczny (Milk Bar)

When you see a "bar" in Poland, it doesn't mean alcohol—it means cheap grub. Eating at a *bar mleczny* is an essential Polish sightseeing experience. These cafeterias, which you'll see all over the country, are an incredibly cheap way to get a good meal...and, with the right attitude, a fun cultural experience.

In the communist era, the government subsidized the food at milk bars, allowing lowly workers to enjoy a meal out. The tradition continues, and today, Poland still foots the bill for most of your milk-bar meal. Prices are astoundingly low—my bill for a full meal usually comes to about $4–5—and, while communist-era fare was gross, today's milk-bar cuisine is usually quite tasty.

Milk bars usually offer many of the traditional tastes listed in the "Polish Food" section. Common items are soups (like *żurek* and *barszcz*), a variety of cabbage-based salads, *kotlet* (fried pork chops), pierogi (like ravioli, with various fillings), and *naleśniki* (pancakes). You'll often see glasses of juice and (of course) milk, but most milk bars also stock bottles of water and Coke.

There are two general types of milk bars: updated, modern cafeterias that cater to tourists (English menus), add some modern twists to their traditional fare, and charge about 50 percent more; and time-machine dives that haven't changed for decades. At truly traditional milk bars, the service is aimed at locals—no English menu and a confusing ordering system.

Every milk bar is a little different, but here's the general procedure: Head to the counter, wait to be acknowledged, and point to what you want. Handy vocabulary: *to* (sounds like "toe") means "that"; *i* (pronounced "ee") means "and."

If the milk-bar lady asks you any questions, you have three options: nod stupidly until she just gives you something; repeat one of the things she just said (assuming she's asked you to choose between two options, like meat or cheese in your pierogi); or hope that a kindly English-speaking Pole in line will leap to your rescue. If nothing else, ordering at a milk bar is an adventure in gestures. Smiling seems to slightly extend the patience of milk-bar staffers.

Once your tray is all loaded up, pay the cashier, do a double-take when you realize how cheap your bill is, then find a table. After the meal, it's generally polite, if not expected, to bus your own dishes (watch locals and imitate).

stuffed with minced meat and rice in a tomato or mushroom sauce. *Kotlet schabowy* (fried pork chops)—once painfully scarce in communist Poland—remain a local favorite to this day. *Kaczka* (duck) is popular, as is fish: Look for *pstrąg* (trout), *karp* (carp, beware of bones), and *węgorz* (eel). Poles eat lots of potatoes, which are served with nearly every meal. The bagel-like rings you'll see on the street, *obwarzanki*, are fresh, tasty, and cheap.

Poland has good pastries. A *piekarnia* is a bakery specializing in breads. But if you really want something special, look for a *cukiernia* (pastry shop). The classic Polish treat is *pączki*, glazed jelly doughnuts. They can have different fillings, but most typical is a wild-rose jam. *Szarlotka* is apple cake—sometimes made with chunks of apples (especially in season), sometimes with apple filling. *Sernik* is cheesecake, and *makowiec* is poppy-seed cake. *Winebreda* is an especially gooey Danish. *Babeczka* is like a cupcake filled with pudding. You may see *jabłko w cieście*—slices of apple cooked in dough, then glazed. *Napoleonka* is a French-style treat with layers of crispy wafers and custard.

Lody (ice cream) is popular. The most beloved traditional candy is *ptasie mleczko* (birds' milk), which is like a semi-sour marshmallow covered with chocolate. E. Wedel is the country's top brand of chocolate, with outlets in all the big cities (see page 318).

Thirsty? *Woda* is water, *woda mineralna* is bottled water (*gazowana* is with gas/carbonation, *niegazowana* is without), *kawa* is coffee, *herbata* is tea, *sok* is juice, and *mleko* is milk. Żywiec and Okocim are the best-known brands of *piwo* (beer).

Wódka (vodka) is a Polish staple—the name means, roughly, "precious little water." Żubrówka, the most famous brand of vodka, comes with a blade of grass from the bison reserves in eastern Poland (look for the bottle with the bison). The bison "flavor" the grass...then the grass flavors the vodka. Poles often mix Żubrówka with apple juice, and call this cocktail *szarlotka* ("apple cake"). For "Cheers!" say, "*Na zdrowie!*" (nah ZDROH-vyeh).

Unusual drinks to try if you have the chance are *kwas* (a cold, fizzy, Ukrainian-style non-alcoholic beverage made from day-old rye bread) and *kompot* (a hot drink made from stewed berries). Poles are unusually fond of carrot juice (often cut with fruit juice); Kubuś is the most popular brand.

"Bon appétit" *is* "*Smacznego*" (smatch-NEH-goh). To pay, ask for the *rachunek* (rah-KHOO-nehk).

Polish Language

Polish is closely related to its neighboring Slavic languages (Slovak and Czech), with the biggest difference being that Polish has lots of fricatives (hissing sounds—"sh" and "ch"—often in close proximity). Consider the opening line of Poland's most famous

Key Polish Phrases

English	Polish	Pronounced
Hello. (formal)	*Dzień dobry.*	jehn DOH-bree
Hi. / Bye. (informal)	*Cześć.*	cheshch
Do you speak English? (asked of a man)	*Czy Pan mówi po angielsku?*	chee pahn MOO-vee poh ahn-GYEHL-skoo
Do you speak English? (asked of a woman)	*Czy Pani mówi po angielsku?*	chee PAH-nee MOO-vee poh ahn-GYEHL-skoo
Yes. / No.	*Tak. / Nie.*	tahk / nyeh
Please. / You're welcome. / Can I help you?	*Proszę.*	PROH-sheh
Thank you.	*Dziękuje.*	jehn-KOO-yeh
I'm sorry. / Excuse me.	*Przepraszam.*	pzheh-PRAH-shahm
Good.	*Dobrze.*	DOHB-zheh
Goodbye.	*Do widzenia.*	doh veed-ZAY-nyah
one / two	*jeden / dwa*	YEH-dehn / dvah
three / four	*trzy / cztery*	tzhee / chuh-TEH-ree
five / six	*pięć / sześć*	pyench / sheshch
seven / eight	*siedem / osiem*	SYEH-dehm / OH-shehm
nine / ten	*dziewięć / dziesięć*	JEH-vyench / JEH-shench
hundred	*sto*	stoh
thousand	*tysiąc*	TEE-shanch
How much?	*Ile?*	EE-leh
local currency	*złoty (zł)*	ZWOH-tee
Where is...?	*Gdzie jest...?*	gdzeh yehst
...the toilet	*...toaleta*	toh-ah-LEH-tah
men	*męska*	MEHN-skah
women	*damska*	DAHM-skah
water / coffee	*woda / kawa*	VOH-dah / KAH-vah
beer / wine	*piwo / wino*	PEE-voh / VEE-noh
Cheers!	*Na zdrowie!*	nah ZDROH-vyeh
the bill	*rachunek*	rah-KHOO-nehk

tongue-twisting nursery rhyme: *W Szczebrzeszynie chrzaszcz brzmi w trzcinie* ("In Szczebrzeszyn, a beetle is heard in the reeds"—pronounced vuh shih-chehb-zheh-shee-nyeh khzhahshch bzh-mee vuh tzhuh-cheen-yeh...or something like that).

Polish intimidates Americans with long, difficult-to-pronounce words. But if you take your time and sound things out, you'll quickly develop an ear for it. One helpful rule of thumb: The stress is always on the next-to-last syllable.

Polish has some letters that don't appear in English, and some letters and combinations are pronounced differently than in English:

ć, ci, and **cz** all sound like "ch" as in "church"
ś, si, and **sz** all sound like "sh" as in "short"
ż, zi, and **rz** all sound like "zh" as in "leisure"
ń and **ni** sound like "ny" as in "canyon"
ę and **ą** are pronounced nasally, as in French: "en" and "an"
c sounds like "ts" as in "cats"
j sounds like "y" as in "yellow"
w sounds like "v" as in "Victor"
ł sounds like "w" as in "with"

So to Poles, "Lech Wałęsa" isn't pronounced "lehk wah-LEH-sah," as Americans tend to say—but "lehkh vah-WEHN-sah."

As you're tracking down addresses, these words will help: *miasto* (town), *plac* (square), *rynek* (big market square), *ulica* (road), *aleja* (avenue), and *most* (bridge).

KRAKÓW

Kraków is easily Poland's best destination: a beautiful, old-fashioned city buzzing with history, enjoyable sights, tourists, and college students. Even though the country's capital moved from here to Warsaw 400 years ago, Kraków remains Poland's cultural and intellectual center. Of all of the Eastern European cities laying claim to the boast "the next Prague," Kraków is for real.

Kraków grew wealthy from trade in the late 10th and early 11th centuries. Traders who passed through were required to stop here for a few days and sell their wares at a reduced cost. Local merchants turned around and sold those goods with big price hikes...and Kraków thrived. In 1038, it became Poland's capital.

Tatars invaded in 1241, leaving the city in ruins. Krakovians took this opportunity to rebuild their streets in a near-perfect grid, a striking contrast to the narrow, mazelike lanes of most medieval towns. The destruction also paved the way for the spectacular Main Market Square—still Kraków's best attraction.

King Kazimierz the Great sparked Kraków's Golden Age in the 14th century (see page 217). In 1364, he established the university that still defines the city (and counts Copernicus and Pope John Paul II among its alumni).

But Kraków's power waned as Poland's political center shifted to Warsaw. In 1596, the capital officially moved north. At the end of the 18th century, three neighboring powers—Russia, Prussia, and Austria—partitioned Poland, annexing all of its territory and dividing it among themselves. Warsaw ended up as a satellite of oppressive Moscow, and Kraków became a poor provincial backwater of Vienna. But despite Kraków's reduced prominence,

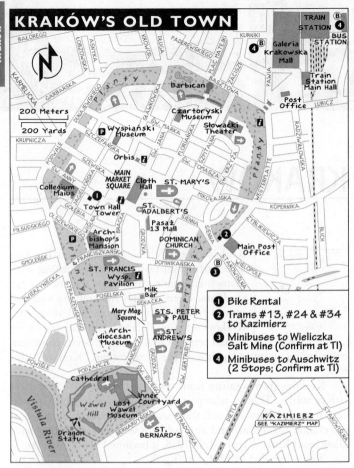

KRAKÓW'S OLD TOWN

200 Meters
200 Yards

❶ Bike Rental
❷ Trams #13, #24 & #34 to Kazimierz
❸ Minibuses to Wieliczka Salt Mine (Confirm at TI)
❹ Minibuses to Auschwitz (2 Stops; Confirm at TI)

Austria's comparatively liberal climate helped turn the city into a haven for intellectuals and progressives (including a young revolutionary thinker from Russia named Vladimir Lenin).

Kraków emerged from World War II virtually unscathed. But when the communists took over, they decided to give intellectual (and potentially dissident) Kraków an injection of good Soviet values—in the form of heavy industry. They built Nowa Huta, an enormous steelworks and planned town for workers, on Kraków's outskirts—dooming the city to decades of smog. Thankfully, Kraków is now much cleaner than it was 20 years ago.

Pope John Paul II was born (as Karol Wojtyła) in nearby Wadowice, and served as archbishop of Kraków before being called to Rome. Kraków might be the most Catholic town in Europe's most Catholic country—so be sure to visit a few of its many

Kraków Essentials

English	Polish	Pronounced
Main Train Station	Kraków Główny	KROCK-oof GWOHV-nee
Old Town	Stare Miasto	STAH-reh mee-AH-stoh
Main Market Square	Rynek Główny	REE-nehk GWOHV-nee
Cloth Hall	Sukiennice	soo-kyeh-NEET-seh
Floriańska Street	Ulica Floriańska	OOH-leet-suh floh-ree-AHN-skah
Park around the Old Town	Planty	PLAHN-tee
Castle Hill	Wawel	VAH-vehl
Jewish Quarter	Kazimierz	kah-ZHEE-mehzh
Vistula River	Wisła	VEES-wah
Salt Mine	Wieliczka	vee-LEECH-kah
Planned Communist Suburb	Nowa Huta	NOH-vah HOO-tah

churches. University life, small but thought-provoking museums, great restaurants, sprawling parks, and Jewish history round out the city's appeal.

Over the last few years, I've watched the number of visitors to Kraków skyrocket. Yet despite its overwhelming popularity, the natives remain welcoming and competition keeps prices delightfully low. These days, Kraków is a tourist town, but it's a real town, too—enjoy it.

Planning Your Time

Kraków and its important side-trips deserve at least two full days on the busiest itinerary. Most people can easily fill three days. The city's sights are quickly exhausted, but more than any town in Europe, Kraków is made for aimless strolling.

Ideally, spend two full days in Kraków itself, plus a visit to Auschwitz (either as a side-trip on the third day, or en route to or from Kraków). In a pinch, spend one day sightseeing in Kraków, another at Auschwitz, and two evenings on the Main Market Square.

With only one full day in Kraków, follow this plan: Take my self-guided walk of Kraków's Royal Way to cover the city's core. Visit any Old Town museums that interest you (Wyspiański Museum, Czartoryski Museum, Jagiellonian University Museum,

Gallery of 19th-Century Polish Art), and have lunch on or near the Main Market Square. Spend the afternoon at Wawel Castle (note that many castle sights close at 15:00). Savor the Main Market Square over dinner or a drink, or enjoy traditional Jewish music and cuisine in Kazimierz.

With more time in Kraków, explore Kazimierz, the former Jewish Quarter—a must for those interested in Jewish heritage, and illuminating for anyone. Or, if you're intrigued by the architecture of the communist era, head for the Nowa Huta suburb.

Auschwitz, an essential side-trip, requires the better part of a day for a round-trip visit (see next chapter). If you have more time, the Wieliczka Salt Mine nearby makes another good day trip. It's conceivably possible to fit Auschwitz and Wieliczka into the same day, especially with an early start and a local driver—but it's far more reasonable to do them on separate days.

ORIENTATION

(area code: 012)
Kraków (KROCK-oof, sometimes spelled "Cracow" in English) is mercifully compact, flat, and easy to navigate. While the urban sprawl is big (with about 757,000 people), the tourist's Kraków feels small. You can walk from the northern edge of the Old Town to the southern edge (Wawel Hill) in about 15 minutes.

Most sights—and almost all recommended hotels and restaurants—are in the Old Town (Stare Miasto), which is surrounded by a greenbelt called the Planty. In the center of the Old Town lies the Main Market Square (Rynek Główny). From the Main Market Square, the Main Train Station is a 15-minute walk to the northeast; Kazimierz (the Jewish quarter) is a 20-minute walk to the southeast; and Wawel Hill (with a historic castle, museums, and Poland's national church) is a 10-minute walk south. Just beyond Wawel is the Vistula River.

Tourist Information

Kraków has several helpful TIs. Four are in the Old Town: in the **Planty** park, between the Main Train Station and Main Market Square (daily June–Sept 9:00–19:00, Oct–May 9:00–17:00, in round kiosk at ulica Szpitalna 25, tel. 012-432-0110); just north of the Main Market Square on **ulica Św. Jana** (specializes in concert tickets, Mon–Sat 10:00–18:00, closed Sun, at #2, tel. 012-421-7787); in the **Old Town Hall Tower** right on the Main Market Square (daily June–Sept 9:00–19:00, Oct–May 10:00–18:00, tel. 012-433-7310); and in the new **Wyspiański Pavilion** just south of the square on ulica Grodzka (daily 10:00–20:00, plac Wszystkich Świętych 3, tel. 012-616-1886). Other branches are in **Kazimierz** (Mon–Fri

9:00–17:00, closed Sat–Sun, ulica Józefa 7, tel. 012-422-0471), **Nowa Huta** (Tue–Sat 10:00–14:00, closed Sun–Mon, os. Słoneczne 16, tel. 012-643-0303), and the **airport** (daily 10:00–18:00, tel. 012-285-5341). The website for all TIs is www.krakow.pl.

At any TI, ask what's new in fast-changing Kraków, browse the brochures, and pick up the free one-page map and the *Kraków Tourist Information Compendium* booklet. The TIs also offer a free room-finding service, and sell tickets for walking and bus tours (see "Tours," later in this chapter).

I'd skip the TI's **Kraków Tourist Card,** which covers public transportation in Kraków, admission to several city museums, and moderate discounts to outlying sights and tours (50 zł/2 days, 65 zł/3 days). Since public transportation is mostly unnecessary and museums are so cheap, this card doesn't make sense for most visitors.

Arrival in Kraków

By Train: Kraków's Main Train Station (called "Kraków Główny") is just northeast of the Old Town. It shares a broad plaza (plac Dworcowy) with the new, giant Galeria Krakowska shopping mall.

Taxis from the station are cheap and easy (from the tracks, take the elevator or stairs to the rooftop above you, where you'll find a giant parking lot where taxis wait; the fair metered rate to downtown is a reasonable 10–15 zł).

Most hotels are within easy **walking** distance. It's about a 15-minute stroll to the Main Market Square—just follow signs to the center (*wyjście do centrum* or *miasta*). From the tracks, you'll first walk down some stairs and pass through a tunnel, which dead-ends at an entrance to the Galeria Krakowska shopping mall. Ignore this, since once you get inside this enormous mall, it's confusing to find your way back out the other end. Instead, turn left up the stairs, then walk under the long green canopy to the yellow main terminal building. Exiting on the other side of the main terminal, you'll emerge into the wide-open plaza called plac Dworcowy, fronted by the Galeria Krakowska mall and a yellow post office. Beyond the post office, several flights of stairs feed into a pedestrian underpass beneath the busy ring road; as you emerge from this underpass, bear right (following signs for *Rynek Główny/ Main Market*) and head into the Planty park. You'll see the round TI kiosk on your left, and the Main Market Square is a few blocks straight ahead.

By Bus: The new, slick bus station is right behind the train station. To get into town, use the tunnel that takes you under the train tracks (following signs for *PKP*—the train station—and *centrum*). Once at the train station, follow the directions above.

To get *to* the bus station from the Old Town (such as to catch a bus to Auschwitz), first head to the train station (go through the Planty park and use the underpass). From the train station's main terminal, walk under the long green canopy to the train platforms. Use the pedestrian underpass to go under the tracks (following signs for *dojście do dworca autobusowego*); when you emerge on the other side, the bus station is the blocky, modern building on your left (marked *RDA Dworzec Autobusowy*). Inside are the standard amenities (lockers and toilets), domestic and international ticket windows, and an electronic board showing the next several departures. Some bus departures, marked on the board with a *G*, leave from the upper *(gorna)* stalls, which you can see out the window. Other bus departures, marked with a *D*, leave from the lower *(dolna)* stalls; to find these, go down the easy-to-miss stairs (marked *zejście na dolna płytę*) on the left just beyond the ticket windows.

By Car: *Centrum* signs lead you into the Old Town—you'll know you're there when you hit the ring road that surrounds the Planty park. Parking garages surround the Old Town. Your hotel can advise you on directions and parking.

By Plane: The small, modern **John Paul II Kraków-Balice Airport** is about 10 miles west of the center. A new train station near the airport allows you to zip quickly downtown (catch the blue shuttle bus in front of the terminal, which will take you to the station nearby; then buy the 7.50-zł ticket on the train—cheaper if you buy it at the station before boarding—for the 15-min trip to Kraków's Main Train Station; then see train arrival instructions above). You can also catch public bus #192 in front of the airport to Kraków's main bus station (covered by normal 3.10-zł bus ticket, does not run in the winter, see bus station arrival instructions above). Or, for door-to-door service, catch a cab from the taxi stand in front of the terminal (around 60–70 zł, more expensive at night, about 30 min). You can also arrange a taxi transfer in advance (such as with recommended driver Adrzej Durman, listed on page 212). Airport info: tel. 012-295-5800, www.lotnisko-balice.pl.

Note that many budget flights—including those on Wizz Air, SkyEurope, Centralwings, easyJet, and Ryanair—use the **International Airport Katowice in Pyrzowice** (Międzynarodowy Port Lotniczy Katowice w Pyrzowicach, www.gtl.com.pl). This airport serves the city of Katowice, about 50 miles west of Kraków. Direct buses run sporadically between Katowice Airport and Kraków's Main Train Station (50 zł, about 4/day, trip takes 1.75 hrs). You can also take the bus from Katowice Airport into the Katowice train station (hourly, 50 min), then take the train to Kraków (hourly, 1.5 hrs). Wizz Air's website is useful for figuring out your connection: www.wizzair.com.

Helpful Hints

Sightseeing Schedules: Most Old Town museums are closed Monday, which is a good time to visit Kazimierz, where everything's open. Conversely, Kazimierz is very quiet on Saturdays. Hours at museums tend to change frequently, and museums tend to close unexpectedly for renovation. It's important to carefully confirm the opening times of sights at the TI.

Internet Access: Kraków's many Internet cafés—it seems there's one on every corner—charge around 2 zł for 15 min.

Post Office: The main post office (Poczta Główna) is at the intersection of Starowiślna and the Westerplatte ring road, a few blocks east of the Main Market Square.

Bookstore: For used English books, try **Massolit Books,** just west of the Old Town (Sun–Thu 10:00–20:00, Fri–Sat 10:00–22:00, ulica Felicjanek 4, tel. 012-432-4150).

Laundry: Doing laundry in Kraków is frustrating. There's no good self-service launderette in the center, unless you're staying at a hostel. Your hotel can do your wash, but it's expensive. If you must have something laundered, a central option is **Betty Clean** (about 9 zł per shirt, 12 zł for pants, takes 24 hours, pay 50 percent more for express 3-hour service, Mon–Fri 7:30–19:30, Sat 8:00–15:30, closed Sun, just outside the Planty park at ulica Zwierzyniecka 6, tel. 012-423-0848).

Travel Agencies: Orbis, at the top of the Main Market Square, books bus tours, changes money, and sells train, plane, and international bus tickets (May–Sept Mon–Fri 9:00–19:00, Sat 9:00–15:00, closed Sun, closes 1 hour earlier Oct–April, Rynek Główny 41, www.orbis.krakow.pl, tel. 012-619-2449). The agency posts a handy complete train schedule in their window. Buy your train tickets in this central location (no fee, English spoken) to avoid the trip to (and often long lines at) the station.

Also on the square—right in the Cloth Hall—is **MCIT** (Małopolskie Centrum Informacji Turystycznej), which sells maps and guidebooks, books tours, arranges transportation and car rentals, and has a room-finding service (generally open summer Mon–Fri 9:00–20:00, Sat 9:00–18:00, Sun 9:00–16:00, open later during busy times; winter Mon–Fri 9:00–17:00, Sat 9:00–14:00, usually closed Sun in winter; in middle of Cloth Hall facing St. Mary's Church at Rynek Główny 1–3, tel. 012-421-7706, www.mcit.pl).

Getting Around Kraków

Kraków's top sights and best hotels are easily accessible by foot. You'll only need wheels if you're going to the Kazimierz Jewish

Kraków at a Glance

Be Warned: Kraków's museum hours tend to fluctuate. If you want to be sure to get into a certain sight, confirm the hours in advance.

▲▲▲**Main Market Square** Stunning heart of Kraków and a people magnet any time of day. **Hours:** Always open. See page 216.

▲▲**Planty** Once a moat, now a scenic park encircling the city. **Hours:** Always open. See page 214.

▲▲**St. Mary's Church** Landmark church with extraordinary wood-carved Gothic altarpiece. **Hours:** Mon–Sat 11:30–18:00, Sun 14:00–18:00. See page 215.

▲▲**Cloth Hall** Fourteenth-century market hall with 21st-century souvenirs. **Hours:** Summer Mon–Fri 9:00–18:00, Sat–Sun 9:00–15:00, sometimes later; winter Mon–Fri 9:00–16:00, Sat–Sun 9:00–15:00. See page 218.

▲▲**St. Francis' Basilica** Lovely Gothic church with some of Poland's best Art Nouveau. **Hours:** Open long hours daily. See page 221.

▲▲**Wawel Cathedral** Poland's splendid national church, with tons of tombs, a crypt, and a climbable tower. **Hours:** Ticket sales for crypt and tower May–Sept Mon–Sat 9:00–17:15, Sun 12:30–17:15; Oct–April Mon–Sat 9:00–15:45, Sun 12:30–15:45. See page 226.

▲▲**Wawel Castle Grounds** Historic hilltop with views, castle, cathedral, courtyard with chakras, and a passel of museums. **Hours:** Grounds open daily 6:00 until dusk. See page 229.

▲▲**Jewish Cemeteries** Two touching burial sites—the Old (1552–1800) and New (post-1800)—in Kazimierz. **Hours:** Old

quarter or the Nowa Huta suburbs.

By Public Transit: Trams and buses zip around Kraków's urban sprawl. While most trams are new and modern, a few rickety old trams with big windows (dubbed "aquariums" by locals) also rattle around the city. The same tickets are used for both trams and buses, and can be purchased at most kiosks, at the new automated machines at major stops, or—for 0.50 zł extra—from the driver. There are three kinds of tickets: A *bilet jednoprzejazdowy* (basic single ticket, no transfers) costs 2.50 zł at a kiosk. Technically, if

Cemetery—Sun–Fri 9:00–16:00, sometimes until 18:00 in summer, closes earlier in winter and at sundown on Fri, always closed Sat; New Cemetery—Sun–Fri 8:00–18:00, until 16:00 in winter, closed Sat. See page 241.

▲▲**Gallery of 19th-Century Polish Art** Worthwhile collection of paintings by should-be-famous artists (may be under renovation). **Hours:** Should be similar to those of Czartoryski Museum, below. See page 236.

▲**Czartoryski Museum** Varied collection, with European paintings (da Vinci and Rembrandt) and Polish armor, handicrafts, and decorative arts. **Hours:** May–Oct Tue and Thu 10:00–16:00, Wed and Fri–Sat 10:00–19:00, Sun 10:00–15:00, closed Mon; Nov–April Tue, Thu, and Sun 10:00–15:30, Wed and Fri–Sat 10:00–18:00, closed Mon. See page 233.

▲**Wyspiański Museum** Art by the talented leader of the Młoda Polska Art Nouveau movement. **Hours:** May–Oct Wed and Sat 10:00–19:00, Thu–Fri 10:00–16:00, Sun 10:00–15:00; Nov–April Wed–Thu and Sat–Sun 10:00–15:30, Fri 10:00–18:00; closed Mon–Tue year-round. See page 235.

▲**Polish Folk Museum** Traditional rural Polish life on display—an open-air museum moved inside. **Hours:** May–Sept Mon and Wed–Fri 10:00–17:00, Sat–Sun 10:00–14:00, closed Tue; Oct–April Mon 10:00–18:00, Wed–Fri 10:00–15:00, Sat–Sun 10:00–14:00, closed Tue. See page 243.

▲**Pharmacy Under the Eagle** Small Podgórze exhibit about the Holocaust in Kraków, including three evocative historic films. **Hours:** May–Oct Mon 10:00–14:00, Tue–Sat 9:30–17:00, closed Sun; Nov–April Mon 10:00–14:00, Tue–Thu and Sat 9:00–16:00, Fri 10:00–17:00, closed Sun. See page 244.

you're using this cheap ticket, you have to buy a separate ticket for your bag (or risk a fine). So you might as well get a *bilet godzinny*—good for an hour, and allowing transfers and luggage (3.10 zł). Always validate your ticket when you board the bus or tram. You can also get longer-term tickets for 24 hours (10.40 zł), 48 hours (18.80 zł), and 72 hours (25 zł). These must be validated the first time you use them, and can only be purchased at the new automated machines at some stops, or at special MPK ticket booths (the handiest is in the Planty park near the TI).

By Taxi: Just as in other Eastern European cities, only take cabs that are clearly marked with a company logo and telephone number. Kraków taxis start at 5 zł and charge 2–3 zł per kilometer. Rides are very short and generally run less than 10 zł. You're more likely to get the fair metered rate by calling or hailing a cab, rather than taking one waiting at tourist spots. To call a cab, try **Radio Taxi** (tel. 012-9191).

By Bike: Biking the Planty park and along the riverside promenades gets you out of the prettied-up Old Town to see a slice of untouristy Kraków. **Wypożyczalnia Rowerów Rent-a-Bike,** half a block off the Main Market Square, is run by easygoing Michał Bisping (5 zł/hr, 35 zł/day, April–Oct daily 9:00–dusk, less in bad weather, closed Nov–March, ulica Św. Anny 4, mobile 0501-745-986).

TOURS

You can buy tickets for the walking tours and bus tours at any TI.

Local Guides—Kraków has several affordable guides. I've enjoyed working with two in particular, both of whom can show you the sights in Kraków and also have cars (for driving you on day trips, or for taking you into the countryside to help you track down your Polish roots): **Marta Chmielowska** (250 zł/half-day, 300 zł with her car, full day just a little more, 500 zł to Auschwitz, mobile 0603-668-008, martachm@op.pl) and **Anna Gega** (by foot: 250 zł/4 hrs, 350 zł/day; by car: 300 zł/4 hrs, 500 zł/day—maybe more for long-distance trips; mobile 0604-151-293, leadertour@wp.pl). Note that since only official Auschwitz guides can give tours at the concentration camp museum, Marta or Anna can drive you there—but generally can't lead you around once at the camp. Instead, they can arrange for an official guide or help you join a scheduled tour.

Driver—Since Kraków is such a useful home base for day trips, it can be handy to splurge on a private driver for door-to-door service. **Andrzej (Andrew) Durman,** a Pole who lived in Chicago and speaks great English, is a friendly and can-do driver. While not technically a guide, he provides casual commentary while you roll (prices are for up to four people if you book direct: 380 zł to Auschwitz, 180 zł to Wieliczka Salt Mine, 50 zł for transfer from Kraków airport, 350 zł for transfer from Katowice airport, 600 zł for an all-day trip into the countryside—such as into the High Tatras or to track down your Polish roots, maybe more to cover gas costs for long-distance trips, mobile 0602-243-306, tel. 012-411-5630, www.tour-service.pl, andrew@tour-service.pl). The local guides listed above can also drive you on day trips.

Walking Tours—Various companies run city walking tours in English daily in summer. Most do a 2.5-hour tour of the Old Town as well as a 2.5-hour tour of Kazimierz, the Jewish district (40–60 zł per tour, depending on company). Because the scene is continually evolving, it's best to pick up fliers locally (at the TI or your hotel) and choose the one that fits your interests and schedule. Four people can hire their own great local guide for about the same amount of money.

Crazy Guides—This irreverent company offers tours to the communist suburb of Nowa Huta and other outlying sights. For details, see page 247.

Bus Tours—Various tour companies run bus-plus-walking itineraries (each of them around 100–130 zł), including a general city overview (3 hrs), Auschwitz (6 hrs), Wieliczka Salt Mine (4 hrs), and other regional side-trips. There's also a new hop-on, hop-off bus tour with eight stops (in the Old Town and Kazimierz; 50 zł/1 day, 65 zł/2 days, buses go about once hourly 10:00–16:00, buy tickets on bus or at TI, www.tourbus.pl). Get information on all tour companies at the TI.

Buggy Tours—Romantic, horse-drawn buggies trot around Kraków from the Main Market Square. The going rate is a hefty 100 zł for a 30-minute tour.

Golf-Cart Tours—Several outfits around town (including on the Main Market Square) offer tours on a golf cart with recorded commentary (prices are for up to 4 people: 100 zł for half-hour tour of Old Town or Kazimierz, 170 zł for hour-long tour of both the Old Town and Kazimierz).

SIGHTS

Kraków's Royal Way Walk

Most of Kraków's major sights are conveniently connected by this self-guided walking tour. This route is known as the "Royal Way" because the king used to follow this same path when he returned to Kraków after a journey. After the capital moved to Warsaw, most kings were still coronated and buried in Wawel Cathedral at the far end of town—and they followed this same route for both occasions. You could sprint through this walk in under an hour (less than a mile altogether), but it's much more fun if you take it slow.

• *Begin just outside the main gate at the north end of the Old Town.*

▲Barbican (Barbakan), Florian Gate (Brama Floriańska), and City Walls

Tatars invaded Kraków three times in the 13th century. After the first attack destroyed the city in 1241, Krakovians built this wall.

The original rampart had 47 watchtowers and eight gates. The big, round defensive fort standing outside the wall is a barbican. Structures like this provided extra fortification to weak sections. Imagine how it looked in 1500, when this barbican stood outside the town moat with a long bridge leading to the Florian Gate—the city's main entryway. Today you can pay 6 zł to scramble along the passages and fortifications of the barbican (May–Oct daily 10:30–18:00, last entry 30 min before closing, closed Nov–April). There's little to see inside...except for once a month in the summer, when a battle of knights is staged here (get details at TI). The same ticket also lets you climb up onto the surviving stretch of Old Town walls flanking the Florian Gate (entry from inside walls).

• *Before entering the Old Town, look to the left and right of the barbican to see the...*

▲▲Planty

By the 19th century, Kraków's no-longer-necessary city wall had fallen into disrepair. Krakovians decided to tear down what remained, fill in the moat, and plant trees. (The name comes not from the English "plant," but from the Polish *plantovac*, or "flat"—since they flattened out this area to create it.) Today, the Planty is a beautiful park that stretches 2.5 miles around the entire perimeter of Kraków's Old Town.

• *Go through the Florian Gate into the Old Town. Inside the gate, notice the little chapel with a replica of the famous Black Madonna of Częstochowa, a town just north of here. Once through the gate, you're standing at the head of Kraków's historic (and now touristic) gamut...*

▲Floriańska Street (Ulica Floriańska)

On the inside of the city wall, you'll see a makeshift **art gallery,** where starving students hawk the works they've painted at the Academy of Fine Arts (across the busy street from the barbican). Portraits, still lifes, landscapes, local scenes, nudes...this might just be Kraków's best collection of art. If you were to detour along the gallery (to the left as you face the gate), in a block you'd arrive at another fine collection—the eclectic Czartoryski Museum, home to a rare Leonardo da Vinci oil painting (see "National Museum Branches," page 233).

Walking down Floriańska street, you can't miss the **McDonald's** on the left. When renovating this building, they dis-covered a Gothic cellar—so they excavated it and added seating. Today, you can super-size your ambience by dining on a Big Mac and fries under a medieval McVault.

About halfway down the long block, on the left (at #45), look for **Cukiarnia Jama Michalika** ("Michael's Cave"). This dark, atmospheric café, popular with locals for its coffee and pastries, began in 1895 as a simple bakery in a claustrophobic back room. A brothel upstairs scared off respectable patrons, so the owner attracted students by creating a cabaret act called "The Green Balloon." To this day, the cabaret—political satire set to music—still runs (in Polish only, Sun at 12:00). Around the turn of the 20th century, this was a hangout of the Młoda Polska (Young Poland) movement—the Polish answer to Art Nouveau (explained on page 219). The walls are papered with sketches from poor artists who couldn't pay their tabs. Poke around inside, and see how many green balloons you can spot. Consider having coffee and dessert here (Sun–Thu 9:00–22:00, Fri–Sat 9:00–23:00), but expect a grouchy greeting and a fee for the coat-check and miserable bathrooms.

Continue strolling down Floriańska street. Two blocks ahead on the left (at #3, 50 yards before the big church), you'll see **Jazz Club u Muniaka.** In the 1950s, Janusz Muniak was one of the first Polish jazzmen. Now he owns this place, and jams regularly here in a cool cellar surrounded by jazzy art. If you hang around the bar before the show, you might find yourself sitting next to Janusz himself, smoking his pipe...and getting ready to smoke on the saxophone (for details, see "Entertainment" on page 250).

• *Continue into the Main Market Square, where you'll run into...*

▲▲St. Mary's Church (Kościół Mariacki)

A church has stood on this spot for 800 years. The original church was destroyed by the first Tatar invasion in 1241, but all subsequent versions—including the current one—have been built on the same foundation. You can look down the sides to see how the Main Market Square has risen about seven feet over the centuries.

How many church towers does St. Mary's have? Technically, the answer is one. The shorter tower belongs to the church; the taller one is a municipal watchtower, from which you'll hear a bugler playing the hourly *hejnał* song. According to Kraków's favorite legend, during that first Tatar invasion, a town watchman saw the enemy approaching and sounded the alarm. Before he could finish the tune, an arrow pierced his throat—which is why, even today, the *hejnał* stops *subito* partway through. Today's buglers—12 in all—are firemen first, musicians second. Each one works a 24-hour shift up there, playing the *hejnał* on the hour, every hour (broadcast on national Polish radio at noon).

In the summer, you can actually climb up the 239 stairs to the top of the taller **tower** to visit the *hejnał* fireman. While it's a huff—with some claustrophobic stone stairs, followed by some steep, acrophobic wooden ones—the view up top is the best you'll find of the square (5 zł, buy ticket at little kiosk next to front door, May–Sept Tue, Thu, and Sat 9:00–11:30 & 13:00–17:30, closed Oct–April).

To get inside, the church's front door is open 14 hours a day and is free to those who come to pray. Tourists use the door around the right side (6 zł, buy ticket across the little square, Mon–Sat 11:30–18:00, Sun 14:00–18:00). The rusty neck-stock (behind the tourists' left door) was used for public humiliation until the 1700s. The church's highlight, its wooden altarpiece, is open daily between noon and 18:00. Try to be here by 11:50 for the ceremonial opening or at 18:00 for the closing.

Inside, you're drawn to one of the best medieval woodcarvings in existence—the exquisite, three-part Gothic **altarpiece** by German Veit Stoss (Wit Stwosz in Polish). Carved in 12 years and completed in 1489, it's packed with emotion rare in Gothic art. Stoss used oak for the structural parts and linden trunks for the figures. When the altar doors are closed, you see scenes from the lives of Mary and Jesus. The open altar depicts the Dormition (death) of the Virgin. The artist catches the apostles (11, without Judas) around Mary, reacting in the seconds after she collapses. Mary is depicted in three stages: dying, being escorted to heaven by Jesus, and (at the very top) being crowned in heaven (flanked by two Polish saints—Adalbert and Stanisław). The six scenes on the sides are the Annunciation, birth of Jesus, visit by the Three Magi, Jesus' Resurrection, his Ascension, and Mary becoming the mother of the apostles at Pentecost.

There's more to St. Mary's than the altar. While you're admiring this church's art, notice the flowery Neo-Gothic painting covering the choir walls. Stare up into the starry, starry blue ceiling. As you wander around, consider that the church was renovated a century ago by three Polish geniuses from two very different artistic generations: the venerable positivist Jan Matejko and his Art Nouveau students, Stanisław Wyspiański and Józef Mehoffer (we'll learn more about these two later on our walk). The huge silver bird under the organ loft in back is a crowned eagle, the symbol of Poland.

• *Leaving the church, enjoy the...*

▲▲▲Main Market Square (Rynek Główny)

Kraków's marvelous Square, one of Europe's most gasp-worthy public spaces, bustles with street musicians, colorful flower stalls, cotton-candy vendors, loitering teenagers, businesspeople

Kazimierz the Great
(1333–1370)

Out of the many centuries of Polish kings, only one earned the nickname "great," and he's the only one worth remembering: Kazimierz the Great.

K. the G., who ruled Poland from Kraków in the 14th century, was one of those larger-than-life medieval kings who left his mark on all fronts—from war to diplomacy, art patronage to womanizing. His scribes bragged that Kazimierz "found a Poland made of wood, and left one made of brick and stone." He put Kraków on the map as a major European capital. He founded many villages (some of which still bear his name) and replaced wooden structures with stone ones (such as Kraków's Cloth Hall). Kazimierz also established the Kraków Academy (today's Jagiellonian University), the second-oldest university in Central Europe. And to protect all these new building projects, he heavily fortified Poland by building a series of imposing forts and walls around its perimeter.

Most of all, Kazimierz is remembered as a progressive, tolerant king. In the 14th century, other nations were deporting—or even interning—their Jewish subjects, who were commonly scapegoated for anything that went wrong. But the enlightened and kindly Kazimierz actively encouraged Jews to come to Poland by granting them special privileges, often related to banking and trade—establishing the country as a safe haven for Jews in Europe.

Kazimierz the Great was the last of Poland's long-lived Piast dynasty. Although he left no male heir—at least, no legitimate one—Kazimierz's advances set the stage for Poland's Golden Age (14th–16th centuries). After his death, Poland united with Lithuania (against the common threat of the Teutonic Knights), the Jagiellonian dynasty was born, and Poland became one of Europe's mightiest medieval powers.

commuting by foot, gawking tourists, and the lusty coos of pigeons. This Square is where Kraków lives. On my last visit, local teens practiced break-dancing moves at one end of the Square while farmers protested Poland's EU membership at the other.

The Square was established in the 13th century, when the city had to be rebuilt after being flattened by the Tatars. At the time, it was the biggest square in medieval Europe. It was illegal to sell anything on the street, so everything had to be sold here on the Main Market Square. It was divided into smaller markets, such as the butcher stalls, the ironworkers' tents, and the Cloth Hall (see next page). Recent work to renovate the Square's pavement has revealed a wealth of remains from previous structures (which may someday be turned into an "underground museum" of excavations).

The statue in the middle of the Square is of Romantic poet **Adam Mickiewicz** (1789–1855). His epic masterpiece, *Pan Tadeusz,* is still regarded as one of the greatest works in Polish, and Mickiewicz is considered the "Polish Shakespeare." A wistful, nostalgic tale of Polish-Lithuanian nobility, *Pan Tadeusz* stirred patriotism in a Poland that had been dismantled by surrounding empires.

Near the end of the Square, you'll see the tiny, copper-domed **Church of St. Adalbert,** the oldest church in Kraków (10th century). This Romanesque structure predates the Square. Like St. Mary's (described above), it seems to be at an angle because it's aligned east–west, as was the custom when it was built. (In other words, the churches aren't crooked—the Square is.)

Drinks are reasonably priced at cafés on the Square (most around 10 zł). Find a spot where you like the view and the chairs, then sit and sip. Enjoy the folk band. Tip them, and you can photograph their traditional Kraków garb up close. (A big tip gets you *The Star-Spangled Banner.*)

As the Square buzzes around you, imagine this place before 1989. There were no outdoor cafés, no touristy souvenir stands, and no salesmen hawking cotton candy and quacking mouthpieces. The communist government shut down all but a handful of the businesses. They didn't want people to congregate here—they should be at home, resting, because "a rested worker is a productive worker." The buildings were covered with soot from the nearby Lenin Steelworks in Nowa Huta. (The communists denied the pollution, and when the student "Green Brigades" staged a demonstration in this Square to raise awareness in the 1970s, they were immediately arrested.)

• *The huge, yellow building right in the middle of the Square is the…*

▲▲Cloth Hall (Sukiennice)

In the Middle Ages, this was the place that cloth-sellers had their market stalls. Kazimierz the Great turned the Cloth Hall into a permanent structure in the 14th century. In 1555, it burned down, and was replaced by the current building. The letter *S* (at the top of the gable above the entryway) stands for King Sigismund the Old, who commissioned this version of the hall. As Sigismund fancied all things Italian (including women—he married an

Młoda Polska (Young Poland)

Polish art in the late 19th century was ruled by positivism, a school with a very literal, straightforward focus on Polish history (Jan Matejko led the charge; see page 302). But when the new generation of Kraków's artists came into their own in the early 1900s, they decided that the old school was exactly that. Though moved by the same spirit and goals as the previous generation—evoking Polish patriotism at a time when their country was being occupied—these new artists used very different methods. They were inspired by a renewed appreciation of folklore and peasant life. Rather than being earnest and literal (an 18th-century Polish war hero on horseback), the new art was playful and highly symbolic (the artist frolicking in a magical garden in the idyllic Polish countryside). This movement became known as Młoda Polska (Young Poland)—Art Nouveau with a Polish accent.

Stanisław Wyspiański (vees-PAYN-skee, 1869–1907) was the leader of Młoda Polska. He produced beautiful artwork, from simple drawings to the stirring stained-glass images in Kraków's St. Francis' Basilica. Wyspiański was an expert at capturing human faces with realistic detail, emotion, and personality. The versatile Wyspiański was also an accomplished stage designer and writer. His patriotic play *The Wedding*—about the nuptials of a big-city artist and a peasant girl—is regarded as one of Poland's finest dramas. The largest collection of Wyspiański's art is in Kraków's Wyspiański Museum, but you'll also see examples in Kraków's St. Francis' Basilica and Warsaw's National Museum.

Józef Mehoffer (may-HOH-fehr), Wyspiański's good friend and rival, was another great Młoda Polska artist. Mehoffer's style is more expressionistic and abstract than Wyspiański's, often creating an otherworldly effect. See Mehoffer's work in Kraków's St. Francis' Basilica and at the artist's former residence; and in Warsaw, at the National Museum.

Other names to look for include **Jacek Malczewski** (mahl-CHEHV-skee), who specialized in self-portraits, and **Olga Boznańska** (bohz-NAHN-skah), the movement's only prominent female artist. Both are featured in Warsaw's National Museum.

Italian princess), this structure is in the Italianate Renaissance style. Sigismund kicked off a nationwide trend, and you'll still see Renaissance buildings like this one all over the country—making the style as typically Polish as it is typically Italian. We'll see more works by Sigismund's imported Italian architects at Wawel Castle.

The Cloth Hall is still a functioning market—mostly souvenirs, including wood carvings, chess sets, jewelry (especially amber), painted boxes, and trinkets (summer Mon–Fri 9:00–18:00, Sat–Sun 9:00–15:00, sometimes later; winter Mon–Fri 9:00–16:00, Sat–Sun 9:00–15:00). Cloth Hall prices are slightly inflated, but still cheap by American standards. You're paying a little extra for the convenience and the atmosphere, but you'll see locals buying gifts here, too.

WCs and telephones are at each end of the Cloth Hall. The upstairs of the Cloth Hall is home to the very good **Gallery of 19th-Century Polish Art.** The collection was moved to a castle outside of town during a recent renovation, but it might be back here again for your visit (see page 236).

• *Browse through the Cloth Hall passageway. As you emerge into the other half of the square, the big tower on your left is the...*

Town Hall Tower

This is all that remains of a Town Hall building from the 14th century—when Kraków was the powerful capital of Poland. After the 18th-century partitions of Poland, Kraków's prominence took a nosedive. By the 19th century, Kraków was Nowheresville. As the town's importance crumbled, so did its Town Hall. It was cheaper to tear down the building than to repair it, and all that was left standing was this nearly 200-foot-tall tower. In summer, you can climb the tower, stopping along the way to poke around an exhibit on Kraków history—but the views from up top are disappointing (6 zł, May–Oct daily 10:30–14:00 & 14:30–18:00, closed Nov–April). In the bottom of the tower is a TI, where you buy your ticket for the tower.

The **gigantic head** you may see at the base of the Town Hall Tower (the opposite end from the Cloth Hall) is a sculpture by contemporary artist Igor Mitoraj, who studied here in Kraków. Typical of Mitoraj's works, the head is an empty shell that appears to be wrapped in cloth. It was originally intended to be placed near the train station (where they might have moved it, if you don't see it here). But because of construction delays at the station, it found a home here on the square. While some locals enjoy having a work by their fellow Krakovian in such a prominent place, others disapprove of its sharp contrast with the square's genteel Old World ambience.

• *When you're finished on the square, we'll head toward Wawel Hill. But we'll take a one-block detour from the Royal Way to introduce you* to one of Kraków's best churches. Leave on the street called ulica Bracka, in the middle of the bottom of the square (next to the Deutsche Bank, at the end of the Cloth Hall). Follow this one long block (and across the busy Franciszkańska street) directly to the side door of a big red-brick church. Go ye.

▲▲St. Francis' Basilica (Bazylika Św. Franciszka)

This beautiful Gothic church, which was Pope John Paul II's home church while he was archbishop of Kraków, features some of Poland's best Art Nouveau *in situ* (in the setting for which it was intended). After an 1850 fire, it was redecorated by the two leading members of the Młoda Polska (Young Poland) movement: Stanisław Wyspiański and Józef Mehoffer. These two talented and fiercely competitive Krakovians were friends who apprenticed together under Poland's greatest painter, Jan Matejko. The glorious decorations of this church are the result of their great rivalry run amok. (For more Wyspiański or Mehoffer, visit their museums—see "National Museum Branches," page 233.)

● Self-Guided Tour: Entering through the side door, turn left into the altar area to enjoy the paintings and stained-glass windows by **Stanisław Wyspiański.** The windows flanking the high altar represent the Blessed Salomea (left, the church's founder, buried in a side chapel) and St. Francis (right, the church's namesake). Salomea was a medieval Polish woman who became queen of Hungary, but later returned to Poland and entered a convent after her husband's death. Notice she's dropping a crown—repudiating the earthly world and giving herself over to the simple, stop-and-smell-God's-roses lifestyle of St. Francis. As you face the back of the church, look at the window in the rear of the nave: *God the Father Let It Be*, Wyspiański's finest masterpiece. The colors beneath the Creator change from yellows and oranges (fire) to soothing blues (water), depending on the light. Wyspiański was supposedly inspired by Michelangelo's vision of God in the Sistine Chapel, though he used a street beggar to model the specific features of God. Wyspiański also painted the delightful floral designs decorating the walls of the nave—fitting for a church dedicated to a saint so famous for his spiritual connection to nature. (For more on Wyspiański, see page 219.)

The chapel on the right side of the nave (as you face the back of the church) contains some evocative Stations of the Cross. This is **Józef Mehoffer**'s response to Wyspiański's work. The centerpiece of the room is a replica of the Shroud of Turin—which, since it touched the original shroud, is also considered a holy relic.

The modern painting (with an orange background, midway up the nave on the left as you face the back of the church) depicts **St. Maksymilian Kolbe,** the Catholic priest who traded his own

Karol Wojtyła (1920–2005): The Life and Death of the Greatest Pole

Karol Wojtyła was born to a humble family in the town of Wadowice (near Kraków) on May 18, 1920. Karol's mother died when he was a young boy. When he was older, he moved with his father to Kraków to study philosophy and drama at Jagiellonian University. Young Karol was gregarious and athletic—an avid skier, hiker, swimmer, and soccer goalie. During the Nazi occupation in World War II, he was forced to work in a quarry. In defiance of the oppressive Nazis, he secretly studied theology and appeared in illegal underground theatrical productions. When the war ended, he resumed his studies, this time at the theology faculty.

After graduating in 1947, Wojtyła swiftly rose through the ranks of the Catholic Church hierarchy. By 1964, he was archbishop of Kraków, and just three years later, he became the youngest cardinal ever in the Roman Catholic Church. Throughout the 1960s, he fought an ongoing battle with the regime when they refused to allow the construction of a church in the Kraków suburb of Nowa Huta. After years of saying Mass for huge crowds in open fields, Wojtyła finally convinced the communists to allow the construction of the Lord's Ark Church in 1977 (see page 249). A year later, just as Poland was facing its darkest hour, Karol Wojtyła was called to the papacy—the first non-Italian pope in more than four centuries.

Imagine you're Polish in the 1970s. Your country was devastated by World War II, and has struggled under an oppressive regime ever since. Food shortages are epidemic. Lines stretch around the block even to buy a measly scrap of bread. Life is bleak, oppressive, and hopeless. Then someone who speaks your language—someone you've admired your entire life, and one of the only people you've seen successfully stand up to the regime—becomes one of the world's most influential people. A Pole like you is the leader of a billion Catholics. He makes you believe that the impossible can happen. He says to you again

life to save a fellow inmate at Auschwitz (see his story on page 272). Kolbe is particularly beloved here, as he actually served at this church.

Just before going out the back door (below Wypiański's stained-glass window), find the **silver plate** labeled "Jan Paweł II" on the second pew from the last (on right); this was Pope John Paul II's favorite place to pray when he lived in the Archbishop's Palace across the street.

• *Stepping outside (through the back door), look to the right. The light-yellow building across the street is the...*

and again: *"Nie lękajcie się"*—"Have no fear." And you begin to believe it.

In addition to encouraging his countrymen, the Pope had a knack for challenging the communists. He'd push at them strongly enough to get his point across, but never went so far as to jeopardize the stature of the Church in Poland. Gentle but pointed wordplay was his specialty. The inspirational role he played in the lives of Lech Wałęsa and the other leaders of Solidarity gave them the courage to stand up to the communists (for more on Solidarity, see page 342). Many people (including Mikhail Gorbachev) credit Pope John Paul II for the collapse of Eastern European communism.

Even as John Paul II's easy charisma attracted new worshippers to the Church (especially young people), his conservatism on issues such as birth control, homosexuality, and female priests pushed away many Catholics. Under his watch, the Church struggled with embarrassing pedophilia scandals in the US. By the end of his papacy, John Paul II's failing health and old-fashioned politics had caused him to lose stature in worldwide public opinion. And yet, approval of the Pope never waned in Poland. His countrymen—even the relatively few atheists and agnostics—saw John Paul II both as the greatest hero of their people...and as a member of the family, like a kindly grandfather.

When Pope John Paul II died on April 2, 2005, the mourning in Poland was deep and sustained. Though the Pope's passing was hardly unexpected, it created an overwhelming wave of grief that flooded the country for weeks. Musical performances of all kinds were cancelled for a week after his death, and the irreverent MTV-style music channel simply went off the air out of respect.

Karol Wojtyła has already been fast-tracked for sainthood. Out of 265 popes, only two have been given the title "great." There's already talk in Rome of increasing that number to three. Someday soon we may speak of this remarkable soul as "John Paul the Great." His countrymen already do.

Archbishop's Palace

This building (specifically, the window over the stone entryway) was Pope John Paul II's residence when he was the archbishop of Kraków. When he became Pope, it remained his home-away-from-Rome for visits to his hometown. After a long day of saying formal Mass during his visits to Kraków, he'd wind up here. Weary as he was, before going to bed he'd stand in the window for hours, chatting casually with the people assembled below—about religion, but also about sports, current events, and whatever was on their minds. In 2005, when the Pope's health deteriorated, this street filled with his supporters, even though the Pope was in Rome. For days, somber locals focused their vigil on this same window, their eyes fixed on a black crucifix that had been placed here. At 21:37 on the night of April 2, 2005, the Pope passed away in Rome. Ten thousand Krakovians were in this street, under this window, listening to a Mass broadcast on loudspeakers from the church. When the priest announced the Pope's death, every single person simultaneously fell to their knees in silence. For the next several days, thousands of the faithful continued to stand in this street, staring intently at the window where they last saw the man they considered to be the greatest Pole.

• *Now turn right, walk along the side of the church, pass a few monuments and a tram stop, and turn right again down busy...*

Grodzka Street

Now you're back on the Royal Way proper. At the corner of Grodzka street sits the modern, copper-colored **Wyspiański Pavilion.** In addition to housing a handy TI and a conference center, this building features three new stained-glass windows based on designs Wyspiański once submitted for a contest to redecorate Wawel Cathedral. While these designs were rejected back then, they were finally realized on the hundredth anniversary of his death (in 2007). Visible from inside the building during the day (step inside to see them), and gloriously illuminated to be seen outside the building at night, they represent three Polish historical figures: The gaunt St. Stanisław (Poland's first saint), the skeletal Kazimierz the Great (in the middle), and the swooning King Henry the Pious.

Now continue down Grodzka street. This lively thoroughfare, connecting the square with Wawel, is teeming with shops—and some of Kraków's best restaurants (see "Eating," page 258). Survey your options now, and choose (and maybe reserve) your favorite for dinner tonight.

This is also a good street to find some of Kraków's **milk bars** (three are listed under "Eating" on page 260). The most traditional one is about two blocks down, on the right (at #45), with a simple *Bar Mleczny* sign. These government-subsidized cafeterias are the locals' choice for a quick, cheap, filling, lowbrow lunch. Prices are deliriously cheap (soup costs less than a dollar), and the food isn't bad. For more on milk bars, see page 199. Or, for an even quicker bite, buy an *obwarzanki* (typically fresh ring-shaped roll) from a street vendor.

• *One more block ahead, the small square on your right is...*

Mary Magdalene Square (Plac Św. Marii Magdaleny)

Back when Kraków was just a village, this was its main square.

Today it offers a great visual example of Kraków's religious nature. In the Middle Ages, Kraków was known as "Small Rome" for its many churches. Today, there are 142 churches and monasteries within the city limits (32 in the Old Town alone)—more per square mile than anywhere outside Rome. You can see several of them from this spot: The nearest, with the picturesque white facade and red dome, is the **Church of Saints Peter and Paul** (Kraków's first Baroque church, and a popular tourist concert venue). The statues lining this church's facade are the 11 apostles (minus Judas), plus Mary Magdalene—hence the name of the square. The next church to the right, with the twin towers, is the Romanesque **St. Andrew's** (now with a Baroque interior). According to legend, a spring inside this church provided water to citizens who holed up here during Tatar invasions in the 13th century. If you look farther down the street, you can see three more churches. And the square next to you used to be a church, too—it burned in 1855, and only its footprint survives.

• Go through the square (admiring the sculpture on the column that won Kraków's distinguished "ugliest statue" award in 2002), and turn left down...

Kanonicza Street (Ulica Kanonicza)
With so many churches around here, the clergy had to live somewhere. Many lived on this well-preserved street—supposedly the oldest street in Kraków. As you walk, look for the cardinal hats over three different doorways. The Hotel Copernicus, on the left, has hosted visitors both famous (Copernicus himself) and infamous (George W. Bush). Find the yellow house on the right (#19), where Karol Wojtyła lived for 10 years after World War II—long before he became Pope John Paul II. Today this building houses Kraków's only museum dedicated to its favorite son, worth visiting if you're a fan of the late pontiff (for more on the museum, see page 237).

• At the end of Kanonicza street, a ramp leads up to the most important piece of ground in all of Poland.

Wawel Hill
Wawel (VAH-vehl), a symbol of Polish royalty and independence, is sacred territory to every Polish person. A castle has stood here since the beginning of recorded history. Today, Wawel—awash in tourists—is the most visited sight in the country. Crowds and an overly complex admissions system for the hill's many historic sights can be exasperating. Thankfully, a stroll through the cathedral and around the castle grounds requires no tickets, and—with the help of the following commentary—is enough. The many museums on Wawel (described below) are mildly interesting, but can be skipped

(grounds open daily from 6:00 until dusk, inner courtyard closes 30 min earlier).

Entry Ramp to the Castle

Walk up the long ramp to the castle entry. When Kraków was part of the Hapsburg Empire in the 19th century, the Austrians turned this castle complex into a fortress—destroying much of its delicate beauty. When Poland regained its independence after World War I, the castle was returned to its former glory. The bricks you see on your left as you climb the ramp bear the names of Poles from around the world who donated to the cause.

The jaunty equestrian statue ahead is **Tadeusz Kościuszko** (1746–1817)—a familiar name to American history buffs. Kościuszko was a hero of the American Revolution and helped design West Point. When he returned to Poland, he fought bravely but unsuccessfully against the Russians (during the partitions that would divide Poland's territory among three neighboring powers).

• *Hiking through the Heraldic Gate next to Kościuszko, you pass the ticket office (if you'll be going into the museums, use the other ticket office, with shorter lines, on top of the hill—see "Tickets and Reservations," page 229). As you crest the hill, on your left is...*

▲▲Wawel Cathedral

Poland's national church is its Westminster Abbey. While the history buried here is pretty murky to most Americans, to Poles, this church is *the* national mausoleum. It holds the tombs of nearly all of Poland's most important rulers and greatest historical figures.

Cathedral Exterior—Go around to the far side of the cathedral to take in its profile. This uniquely eclectic church is the product of centuries of haphazard additions...yet somehow, it works. It began as a simple, stripped-down Romanesque church in the 12th century. (The white base of the nearest tower is original. In fact, anything at Wawel that's made of white limestone like this was probably part of the earliest Romanesque structures.)

Kazimierz the Great and his predecessors gradually surrounded the cathedral with some 20 chapels, which were further modified over the centuries—making this beautiful church a happy hodge-podge of styles. To give you a sense of the historical sweep, scan the chapels from left to right: 14th-century Gothic, 12th-century Romanesque (the base of the tower), 17th-century Baroque (the inside is Baroque, though the exterior is a copy of its Renaissance neighbor), 16th-century Renaissance, and 18th- and 19th-century Neoclassical. (This variety in styles is even more evident in the chapels' interiors.)

Pay attention to the two particularly interesting domed chapels to the right of the tall tower. The gold one is the Sigismund's Chapel, housing memorials to the Jagiellonian kings—including Sigismund the Old, who was responsible for Kraków's Renaissance renovation in the 16th century. Poles consider this chapel, made with 80 pounds of gold, to be the finest Renaissance chapel north of the Alps. The green chapel next to it, home to the Swedish Waza dynasty, resembles its neighbor (but it's a copy built 150 years later, and without all that gold). The tallest tower, called the Sigismund Tower, has a clock with only an hour hand.

Go back around and face the front entry for more architectonic silliness. You see Gothic chapels flanking the door, a Renaissance ceiling, lavish Baroque decoration over the door, and some big bones (thought to come from extinct animals). Years ago, these were taken for the bones of giants and put here as an oddity to be viewed by the public. (Back then, there were no museums, so notable items like these were used to lure people to the church.) It's said that as long as the bones hang here, the cathedral will stand. The door is the original from the 14th century, with fine wrought-iron work. The *K* with the crown stands for Kazimierz the Great. The black marble frame is made of Kraków stone from nearby quarries.

Cathedral Interior—The cathedral interior is slathered in Baroque memorials and tombs, decorated with tapestries, and soaked in Polish history.

Cost and Hours: Visitors can usually walk around the main part of the church for free. You must buy a 10-zł ticket to climb up the tallest tower or visit the crypt and the royal tombs, and you might be told to buy this ticket even to enter the main part of the church. You can buy the ticket at the house across from the cathedral entry. The cathedral is open May–Sept Mon–Sat 9:00–17:00, Sun 12:30–17:00; Oct–April Mon–Sat 9:00–16:00, Sun 12:30–16:00; last entry always 15 min before closing.

❺Self-Guided Tour: After you step inside, you'll follow the one-way route that leads you through the choir, then around the back of the apse, then back to the entry.

At the entry, look straight ahead to see the silver tomb under a **canopy,** inspired by the one in St. Peter's at the Vatican. It contains the remains of the first Polish saint, Stanisław (from the 11th century).

Go behind this canopy into the ornately carved **choir** area. For 200 years, the colorful chair to the right of the high altar has been the seat of Kraków's archbishops, including Karol Wojtyła, who served here for 14 years before becoming pope.

Now you'll continue into the left nave. From here, if you have a ticket, you can enter two of the optional attractions: Claustrophobic wooden stairs lead up to the 11-ton **Sigismund Bell** and pleasant views of the steeples and spires of Kraków. Then, a little farther back, descend into the little **crypt** (with a rare, purely Romanesque interior), which houses the remains of Adam Mickiewicz—the Romantic poet whose statue dominates the Main Market Square.

Now continue around the apse (behind the main altar). After curving around to the right, look for the red-marble tomb (on the right) of The Great One—**Kazimierz,** of course. (Look for *Kazimierz Wielki*—at his feet is what appears to be a beaver.) A few more steps toward the entrance, on the right, is the white sarcophagus of **St. Jadwiga** (with a dog at her feet). This 14th-century "King of Poland" helped Christianize Lithuania, fought the Teutonic Knights, kicked off the grand Jagiellonian dynasty, and was sainted by Pope John Paul II in 1997. (The sexist bigwigs of the time begrudgingly allowed her to take the throne, but refused to call her "Queen.") All the flowers here prove she's popular with Poles today. Across from Jadwiga, peek into the gorgeous 16th-century **Sigismund Chapel,** with its silver altar (this is the gold-roofed chapel you just saw from outside).

Just beyond the Sigismund Chapel is a door leading back outside. But first, consider continuing on for a look at the **Gothic chapel** to the left of the main door, with its Orthodox-style 14th-century frescoes.

If you don't have a ticket, your tour is finished. But those with a ticket can circle around, past the main door. In the back corner of the church is the entrance to the **royal tombs.** The first big room houses Poland's greatest war heroes: Kościuszko (of American Revolution fame), Jan III Sobieski (who successfully defended Vienna from the Ottomans; in the simple black coffin with the gold inscription *J III S*), Sikorski, Poniatowski, and so on. Then you'll wander through several rooms of second-tier Polish kings, queens, and their kids. Marshal Józef Piłsudski, the WWI hero who ruled Poland from 1926 to 1935, has the last grave (in the room on the right, just before you exit). His tomb was moved here so the rowdy soldiers who came to pay their respects wouldn't disturb the others. You may notice that there's one VIP (Very Important Pole) who's missing...Karol Wojtyła, a.k.a. John Paul II, once the bishop of this cathedral. John Paul II left no specific requests for his body, and the Vatican controversially (to Poles, at least) chose to entomb him under St. Peter's Basilica, instead of sending him back home to Wawel.

• *Up the little staircase across from the cathedral entry is the...*

Cathedral Museum—This small museum features various holy robes and replicas of what's buried with the kings, plus the Sigismund Bell's original clapper (covered by 10-zł cathedral ticket, Tue–Sun 10:00–15:00, closed Mon).

• *When you're finished in the cathedral, stroll around the...*

▲▲Wawel Castle Grounds

In the rest of the castle, you'll uncover more fragments of Kraków's history, and have the opportunity to visit several museums. While I consider the museums skippable, if you want to visit them, buy tickets before you enter the inner courtyard (since you can't buy tickets or backtrack once inside). Read the descriptions on page 231 to decide which museums appeal to you.

Tickets and Reservations: Tickets are sold at several points around the Wawel grounds. Most people line up at the top of the entry ramp, but it's faster to buy tickets at the Tourist Centre at the far corner of the castle grounds (across the field from the cathedral, near the café). A limited number of tickets are sold for the Royal State Rooms, Crown Treasury and Armory, and Royal Private Apartments (which can be visited only with a tour). Boards show how many tickets for each of these are still available on the day you're there. Tickets come with an assigned entry time (though you can usually sneak in before your scheduled appointment). In the summer, ticket lines can be long, and sights can sell out by midday. You can reserve tickets ahead for the tour of the Royal Private Apartments (no fee) and the Royal State Rooms and the Crown Armory and Treasury (16-zł reservation fee for up to 9 people; tel. 012-422-1697). Frankly, the sights aren't worth all the fuss—if they're sold out, you're not missing much.

◑ Self-Guided Tour: This tour, which doesn't enter any of the attractions, is plenty for most visitors.

This hilltop has seen lots of changes over the years. Kazimierz the Great turned a small fortress into a mighty Gothic castle in the 14th century. Today, you'll see the cathedral and a castle complex, but little remains of Kazimierz's grand fortress, which burned to the ground in 1499. In the grassy field across from the cathedral, you'll see the **foundations** of two Gothic churches that were destroyed when the Austrians took over Wawel in the 19th century and needed a parade ground for their troops. (They built the red-brick hospital building beyond the field, now used by Wawel administration.)

• *Head across to the gap in the buildings beyond the field.*

Beyond this castle complex is a viewpoint over the Vistula and Kraków's outskirts. From here, you can see some unusual landmarks, including the odd wavy-roofed building just across the river (which houses the Manggha Japanese art gallery) and the symmetrical little bulge that tops the highest hill on the horizon. This is the **Kościuszko Mound**, erected in 1823 to honor the Polish and American military hero.

Now look directly below you, along the riverbank, to find a fire-belching monument to the **dragon** that was instrumental in the founding of Kraków...

Once upon a time, a prince named Krak founded a town on Wawel Hill. It was the perfect location—except for the fire-breathing dragon who lived in the caves under the hill and terrorized the town. Prince Krak had to feed the dragon all of the town's livestock to keep the monster from going after the townspeople. But Krak, with the help of a clever shoemaker, came up with a plan. They stuffed a sheep's skin with sulfur and left it outside the dragon's cave. The dragon swallowed it, and before long, developed a terrible case of heartburn. To put the fire out, the dragon started drinking water from the Vistula. He kept drinking and drinking until he finally exploded. The town was saved, and Kraków thrived.

If you want to head down to see the Vistula and the dragon close up, take a shortcut through the nearby **Dragon's Den** (Smocza Jama). It's just a 135-step spiral staircase and a few underground caverns—worthwhile only as a quick way to get from the top of Wawel down to the banks of the Vistula (3 zł, pay at machine—coins only, April–Oct daily 10:00–17:00, July–Aug until 18:00, closed Nov–March).

• *Now head back the way you came, to the big square in front of the cathedral. Once you go into the next area, you'll have to exit out into the real world (or you'll have to backtrack 10 minutes around the hill to get back to this spot). Remember, if you want to see any of the museums inside the inner courtyard (see "Wawel Castle Museums," below), you must buy tickets now. The only major Wawel museum outside the inner courtyard is the* **Lost Wawel** *exhibit, near the snack bar directly across the square from the long side of the cathedral (possibly closed for renovation; described on page 232). If you want to see this, do it now.*

Behind the cathedral, a grand green-and-pink entryway—with a strict security checkpoint—leads into the palace's dramatically Renaissance-style...

▲**Inner Courtyard**—If this space seems to have echoes of Florence, that's because it was designed and built by young Florentines after Kazimierz's original castle burned down. Notice the three distinct levels: The ground floor housed the private apartments of the higher nobility (governors and castle administrators); the middle level held the private apartments of the king; and the top floor—much taller, to allow more light to fill its large spaces—were the public state rooms of the king. The ivy-covered wing to the right of where you entered served as the headquarters of the notorious Nazi

governor of German-occupied Poland, Hans Frank. (He was tried and executed in Nürnberg after the war.) The wall at the far end of the courtyard is a false wall, designed to create a pleasant Renaissance symmetry, and also to give the illusion that the castle is bigger than it is. Looking through the windows, notice that there's nothing but air on the other side. When foreign dignitaries visited, these windows could be covered to complete the illusion. The entrances to most Wawel museums are around this courtyard, and some believe that you'll find something even more special: chakra.

Adherents to the Hindu concept of **chakra** believe that a powerful energy field connects all living things. Mirroring the seven chakra points on the body (from head to groin), there are seven points on the surface of the earth where this energy is most concentrated: Delhi, Delphi, Jerusalem, Mecca, Rome, Velehrad... and Wawel Hill—specifically over there in the corner (immediately to your left as you enter the courtyard). Look for peaceful people (here or elsewhere on the castle grounds) with their eyes closed. One thing's for sure: They're not thinking of Kazimierz the Great. The smudge marks on the wall are from people pressing up against this corner, trying to absorb some good vibes from this chakra spot.

The Wawel administration seems creeped out by all this. They've done what they can to discourage this ritual (such as putting up information boards right where the power is supposedly most focused), but believers still gravitate from far and wide to hug the wall. Give it a try...and let the Force be with you. (Just for fun, ask a Wawel tour guide about the chakra, and watch her squirm—they're forbidden to talk about it.)

• Now's the time to visit some of the castle museums. When you're finished, you can exit through the door at the far end of the courtyard. Your Wawel tour is finished.

Wawel Castle Museums—There are five museums and exhibits in Wawel Castle (not including the cathedral and Cathedral Museum). Each has its own admission (hours for all museums, unless otherwise noted: April–Oct Mon 9:30–13:00, Tue and Fri 9:30–17:00, Wed–Thu 9:30–16:00, Sat–Sun 11:00–16:00; Nov–March Tue–Sat 9:30–16:00, Sun 10:00–16:00, closed Mon, last entry 1 hour before closing, tel. 012-422-5155, ext. 219, www.wawel.krakow.pl). Notice that in the high season (April–Oct), visiting on Monday has both advantages (Royal State Rooms and Crown Treasury and Armory are both free) and disadvantages (Royal Private Apartments and Oriental Art are closed, and the others close at 13:00). Off-season (Nov–March), everything is closed on Monday—except sometimes the Lost Wawel exhibit (though it may be closed altogether for renovation during your visit).

The **Royal State Rooms** (Komnaty Królewskie), while precious to Poles, are mediocre by European standards. Still, this is the best of the Wawel museums (15 zł, free on Mon April–Oct, free on Sun Nov–March, enter through courtyard). First you'll wander through some ho-hum halls to get to the Throne Room, with 30 carved heads in the ceiling. According to legend, one of these heads got mouthy when the king was trying to pass judgment—so its mouth has been covered to keep it quiet. Then you'll walk along the outdoor gallery (enjoying views down into the courtyard) before heading upstairs. These top-floor rooms are best, with remarkably decorated wooden ceilings, gorgeous leather-tooled walls, and 16th-century Brussels tapestries (140 of the original series of 300 survive). Wandering these halls (with their period furnishings), you get a feeling for the 16th- and 17th-century glory days of Poland, when it was a leading power in Eastern Europe. The Senate Room, with its throne and fine tapestries, is the climax.

The **Royal Private Apartments** (Prywatne Apartamenty Królewskie) are more of the same, and the only part of the complex that must be visited with a guided tour (20 zł, enter through courtyard; April–Oct closed Mon, opens at 9:30 Sat–Sun, English tours Tue–Sun at 10:50, 12:00, and 13:10, often more; Nov–March closed Sun–Mon, English tours Tue–Sat at 12:00, usually plus others).

The **Crown Treasury and Armory** (Skarbiec i Zbrojownia) is a decent collection of swords, saddles, and shields; ornately decorated muskets and crossbows; and cannons in the basement (15 zł, April–Oct opens at 9:30 Sat–Sun and is free on Mon, free on Sun Nov–March, enter through courtyard).

The small **Oriental Art** (Sztuka Wschodu) exhibit displays swords, carpets, vases, and remarkable Turkish tents (upstairs, next to the Senate Room) used by the Ottomans during the 1683 Battle of Vienna. These are trophies of Jan III Sobieski, the Polish king who led a pan-European army to victory in that battle (7 zł, tickets sold at the door, April–Oct closed Mon but open until 18:00 Sat–Sun, closed Sun–Mon Nov–March, enter through courtyard, don't miss entry on your way back downstairs from Royal State Rooms).

The **Lost Wawel** (Wawel Zaginiony) exhibit—which might be closed for renovation—traces the history of this hill and its various churches and castles. The one-way route leads through excavations of a 10th-century church, and exhibits include a model of the cathedral in its original Romanesque form (much simpler, before all the colorful, bulbous domes, chapels, and towers were added). There's also a replica of the entire castle complex in the 18th century (pre-Austrian razing). A display shows fascinating decorative tiles from 16th-century stoves that once heated the place, plus some medieval artifacts (likely cost and hours if open: 7 zł, tickets sold at the door, free on Mon April–Oct, free on Sun Nov–March; Nov–March open Mon but closed Tue, enter near snack bar across from side of cathedral).

National Museum Branches

Kraków's **National Museum** (Muzeum Narodowe) is made up of a series of small but interesting museums scattered throughout the city. Oddly enough, the main branch (Gmach Główny) is the least worth visiting, with 20th-century Polish art and temporary exhibits (west of Main Market Square at aleja 3 Maja 1, www.muzeum .krakow.pl). I've listed the best of the National Museum's branches below.

All of the branches are covered by a single 22-zł **"Jubilee Ticket."** This ticket isn't worth it unless you're going to at least three branches.

Be warned: The **hours** of these museums can be maddeningly sporadic. If you have your heart set on a particular museum, confirm the opening times carefully before you visit.

▲**Czartoryski Museum (Muzeum Czartoryskich)**—This eclectic collection, displaying armor, handicrafts, decorative arts, and paintings, is one of Kraków's best-known (and most overrated) museums. While it's mostly just dull historical bric-a-brac, two world-class paintings—a da Vinci and a Rembrandt—make it worth ▲▲ for art-lovers. A warning: The museum's major attractions are often not displayed (on loan to other museums), and this disappointing fact isn't well-advertised before you buy your ticket. Try to confirm that the two famous paintings are actually there before you enter.

Cost, Hours, Location: 10 zł, more for special exhibits; May–Oct Tue and Thu 10:00–16:00, Wed and Fri–Sat 10:00–19:00, Sun 10:00–15:00, closed Mon; Nov–April Tue, Thu, and Sun 10:00–15:30, Wed and Fri–Sat 10:00–18:00, closed Mon; last entry 30 min before closing, 2 blocks north of the Main Market Square at ulica Św. Jana 19, tel. 012-422-5566.

Audioguide: The exhibits are poorly described in English. The dense, dry, but informative 15-zł audioguide helps make things meaningful. Or, for the basics, follow my self-guided tour (below).

Background: Inspired by Poland's 1791 constitution (Europe's first), Princess Izabela Czartoryska began collecting bits of Polish history and culture. She fled with the collection to Paris after the

1830 insurrection, and 45 years later, her grandson returned it to its present Kraków location. When he ran out of space, he bought part of the monastery across the street, joining the buildings with a fancy passageway. The Nazis took the collection to Germany, and although most of it has been returned, some pieces are still missing.

❂ **Self-Guided Tour:** Buy your ticket and walk up to the second floor. You'll wander through rooms of paintings, armor (the ceremonial Turkish tent—from the 1683 siege of Vienna—and feathered Hussar armor are memorable), tapestries, treasury items, majolica, and Meissen porcelain figures.

At the end of the first series of rooms, you can detour left and across the passageway, into the former monastery, where you'll see more armor (with some beautifully ornate saddles), Czartoryski family portraits, and ancient art (mostly sculptures and vases).

Then backtrack and climb up to the third floor, which is devoted to European art. After a few halls of also-rans (the long Italian Hall that also features some Dutch painters; then the Corner Room with Italian, French, and Dutch High Renaissance and Baroque works), you'll come to the museum's prize possessions.

First, alone in its own room, is *Lady with an Ermine,* by Leonardo da Vinci. This small (21" x 16"), simple portrait of a teenage girl is one of the most influential paintings in art history and a rare surviving work by one of history's greatest minds. The girl is likely Cecilia Gallerani, the young mistress of the Duke of Milan, Leonardo's employer. The ermine (white during winter) suggests several overlapping meanings, including a symbol of chastity (thus praising Cecilia's questioned virtue) and a naughty reference to the Duke's nickname, "Ermellino"—notice that his mistress is sensually, um, "stroking the ermine."

Painted before the *Mona Lisa,* the portrait was immediately recognized as revolutionary. Cecilia turns to look off-camera at someone, catching her in an unguarded moment, a behind-the-scenes look unheard-of in the days of the posed, front-facing formal portrait. Her simple gestures and faraway gaze speak volumes about her inner thoughts and personality. Leonardo tweaks the generic Renaissance "pyramid" composition by turning it to three-quarters angle and softening it with curved lines—from her eyes, down her cheek and sloping shoulders, then doubling back across her folded arms. The background—once gray and blue—was painted black in the 19th century.

Lady with an Ermine is one of only three surviving oil paintings by Leonardo. It's better preserved than her famous cousin in Paris *(Mona Lisa),* and—many think—simply more beautiful. Can we be sure it's really by the enigmatic Leonardo? Well, recently they found the master's fingerprint—literally—pressed into the paint.

On the wall opposite the lady and her ermine, notice the empty frame with a print of a Rembrandt portrait inside. This is one of the pieces the Nazis didn't give back.

Two rooms later—after the Portrait Room—is the museum's other highlight, Rembrandt's *Landscape with the Good Samaritan* (1638). This small, remarkably detailed painting depicts the popular parable. On the right, the barely visible Samaritan helps the wounded, half-naked man onto his horse (as a little boy and girl look on). To the left, much farther down the road (just beyond the waterfall and bridge), find the two tiny figures walking: the priest and the Levite who had passed the injured man by. The churning sky—with bright sunlight clashing against black clouds—seems to reflect the inner conflict that comes with doing the right thing... or not. Instead of using a strict interpretation of the parable's Holy Land setting, Rembrandt chooses to combine disparate elements—such as the juxtaposition of classic Dutch windmills with the domed city of Jericho in the distance—to make the parable feel even more universal and immediate.

▲**Wyspiański Museum (Muzeum Wyspiańskiego)**—If you enjoyed Stanisław Wyspiański's stained glass and wall paintings in St. Francis' Basilica, visit the museum that collects his work. Housed in a renovated mansion, this museum traces the personal history and artistic development of the Młoda Polska poster boy.

Cost, Hours, Location: 8 zł, more for special exhibits, dry 15-zł English audioguide basically repeats the good English descriptions posted in most rooms; May–Oct Wed and Sat 10:00–19:00, Thu–Fri 10:00–16:00, Sun 10:00–15:00; Nov–April Wed–Thu and Sat–Sun 10:00–15:30, Fri 10:00–18:00; closed Mon–Tue year-round, last entry 30 min before closing, 1 block northwest of the Main Market Square at ulica Szczepańska 11, tel. 012-292-8183.

◐ Self-Guided Tour: Buy your ticket and climb the stairs. The museum layout is frequently rearranged, so keep your eyes open for these highlights. On the second floor, you'll likely see works from Wyspiański's youthful collaboration with his teacher Jan Matejko and his friend Józef Mehoffer; together they renovated St. Mary's Church (including designs for beautiful stained-glass windows). You'll also see a display of Wyspiański's precocious childhood sketchbooks, and the design for the dramatic stained-glass *Apollo,* which hangs in the House of the Medical Society (which, unfortunately, is closed to the public). Rounding out this floor are portraits and self-portraits, serene landscapes, the costumes and sets Wyspiański designed for his own plays, and copies of Wyspiański's printed works (which he also designed himself).

In the stairwell up to the third floor are more stained-glass designs, this time for Wyspiański's masterpiece, *God the Father Let It Be,* from St. Francis' Basilica. On the top floor, find the model of the elaborate acropolis Wyspiański planned for the top of Wawel Hill, with a domed palace, an amphitheater, and a circus maximus. Nearby is a haunting painting of the Planty in winter, with Wawel Castle hovering in the background. The next few rooms contain more stained-glass designs. Then, filling another room, are portraits of Wyspiański's family—including his daughter Helenka just waking up, and his wife breast-feeding their son Staś. Helenka circles around to get good views of both of them, appearing twice in the painting.

▲▲**Gallery of 19th-Century Polish Art (Galeria Sztuki Polskiej XIX Wieku)**—This surprisingly enjoyable collection of works by obscure Polish artists is usually displayed on the upper level of the Cloth Hall. It was recently relocated to a faraway countryside castle during a renovation, but it may be back here again and open for your visit. If so, it's worth a look (likely 10 zł, similar hours to Czartoryski Museum—see page 233, entrance on side of Cloth Hall facing Adam Mickiewicz statue, tel. 012-422-1166).

While you probably won't recognize any of the names in here, some of these paintings are just plain good. The biggest works are by the historical painter Jan Matejko (for more on Matejko, see page 302). One of Matejko's paintings depicts Tadeusz Kościuszko—a hero of the American Revolution, now back in his native Poland fighting the Russians—doffing his hat after his unlikely victory at the battle at Racławice. Another Matejko painting shows the last Grand Master of the fearsome Teutonic Knights swearing allegiance to the Polish king in 1525. This historic ceremony took place in the Main Market Square of the capital at the time, Kraków. Notice the Cloth Hall and the spires of St. Mary's Church in the background. Matejko has painted his own face on one of his favorite historical figures, the jester Stańczyk (at the foot of the throne; for more on Stańczyk, see page 304).

Other excellent, but more obscure, painters are also represented. Find Józef Chełmoński's energy-charged *Four-in-Hand* (depicting a Ukrainian horseman giving a lift to a pipe-smoking nobleman) and misty *Cranes.* And my favorite: Władysław Podkowiński's gripping *Frenzy,* with a pale, sensuous woman clutching an all-fired-up black stallion. The painting caused a frenzy indeed at its 1894 unveiling—leading the unbalanced artist to attack his creation with a knife.

More National Museum Branches—You can also check out the museum of Wyspiański's friend and rival, the **Józef Mehoffer House** (Dom Józefa Mehoffera, 6 zł, ulica Krupnicza 26, tel. 012-421-1143), and the former residence of their mentor, the **Jan Matejko House** (Dom Jana Matejki, 6 zł, ulica Floriańska 41, tel.

012-422-5926). Both have opening hours similar to the Wyspiański Museum.

Other Museums

The following sights, while not part of the National Museum and therefore not covered by the combo-ticket, are worth considering if you're looking to fill out your Kraków sightseeing experience.

Jagiellonian University Museum: Collegium Maius—Kraków had the second university in Central Europe (after Prague), boasting over the centuries such illustrious grads as Copernicus and Pope John Paul II. With around 150,000 students, this city is still very much a university town, and Jagiellonian University proudly offers tours of its historic oldest building, the 15th-century Collegium Maius (one block west of the Main Market Square at ulica Jagiellońska 15). In the Middle Ages, professors were completely devoted to their scholarly pursuits. They were unmarried, and lived, ate, and slept here in an almost monastic environment. They taught downstairs and lived upstairs. In many ways, this building feels more like a monastery than a university.

Student guides lead visitors through the musty and mildly interesting interior of the complex. You'll choose between two different guided tours. The shorter 30-minute "main exhibition" route includes the library, refectory (with a gorgeously carved Baroque staircase), treasury (including Polish filmmaker Andrzej Wajda's honorary Oscar), assembly hall, and some old scientific instruments (12 zł, or 6 zł on Sat, a few tours per day in English, leaves every 20 min Mon, Wed, and Fri 10:00–14:20, Tue and Thu 10:00–17:20, Sat 10:00–13:20, none Sun). The one-hour deluxe version adds some more interiors, room after room of more old scientific instruments, medieval art (mostly church sculptures), a Rubens, a small landscape from the shop of Rembrandt, and Chopin's piano (16 zł, usually in English, Mon–Fri at 13:00, none Sat–Sun). It's smart to call ahead to find out when the shorter tour is scheduled in English, and to reserve for either tour (tel. 012-663-1307). The shorter tour is especially popular and books up long in advance (20 people maximum), particularly on Saturdays, when it's half-price.

Aside from the courtyard, the only part of the Colleguim Maius you can see without a tour is an interactive exhibit that allows you to tinker with replicas of old scientific tools (7 zł, or 5 zł on Sat, open Mon–Sat 9:00–13:30, closed Sun).

Before you leave, enjoy a cup of hot chocolate at the chocolate shop—widely regarded as the best in town.

Archdiocesan Museum (Muzeum Archidiecejalne)—Kraków does not yet have a comprehensive museum devoted to its most famous resident, Pope John Paul II. But this museum, in a building where JPII lived both as a priest and as a bishop, does its best to capture some of his story. The museum consists of several parts: the underwhelming ground-floor collection of sacral art (with altars, paintings, and vestments); various temporary exhibits; and the top-floor museum devoted to John Paul II. Wandering past the scores of paintings and photographs, JPII's cult of personality is almost palpable. Unfortunately, since the collection mostly consists of elaborate gifts received by the Holy Father from around the world, it offers little intimacy or insight into the man himself. Still, it'll be appreciated by JPII admirers (5 zł, Tue–Fri 10:00–16:00, Sat–Sun 10:00–15:00, closed Mon, Kanonicza 19–21, tel. 012-421-8963).

Kazimierz (Jewish Quarter)

The neighborhood of Kazimierz (kah-ZHEE-mezh), 20 minutes by foot southeast of Kraków's Old Town, is the historic heart of Kraków's once-thriving Jewish community. After years of neglect, the district is today being rediscovered by Krakovians and tourists alike. Visitors expecting a polished, touristy scene like Prague's Jewish Quarter will be surprised...and maybe disappointed. This is basically a local-feeling, slightly run-down neighborhood with a handful of Jewish cemeteries, synagogues, and restaurants, and often a few pensive Israeli tour groups wandering the streets. But for me, the lack of crowds makes it an even more evocative experience than the Prague alternative.

Try to visit any day except Saturday, when only the Old Synagogue and Galicia Jewish Museum are open. Note that it's respectful for men to cover their heads while visiting a Jewish cemetery or synagogue. While some of these sights offer loaner yarmulkes, it's easiest to just bring your own hat.

Getting to Kazimierz: From the Old Town, it's about a 20-minute **walk,** which gets you out of the fairy-tale tourist zone, and into the real, soot-stained, workaday Kraków (that's a good thing). From the Main Market Square, walk down ulica Sienna (near St. Mary's Church). At the fork, bear right through the Planty park. At the intersection with the busy Westerplatte ring road, you'll continue straight ahead (bear right at fork, then continue straight across the busy ring road) down Starowiślna for 15 more minutes. To hop the **tram,** go to the stop on the left-hand side of ulica Sienna (at the intersection with Westerplatte, across the street from the Poczta Główna, or Main Post Office). Catch tram #13, #24, or #34 and go two stops to Miodowa. Walking or by tram, at the intersection of Starowiślna and Miodowa, you'll see a small park across the street and to the right. To reach the heart of Kazimierz—ulica Szeroka—cut through this park. To get back into the Old Town, catch tram #13, #24, or #34 from the intersection of Starowiślna and Miodowa (kitty-corner from where you got off the tram) and go two stops back to the Poczta Główna stop.

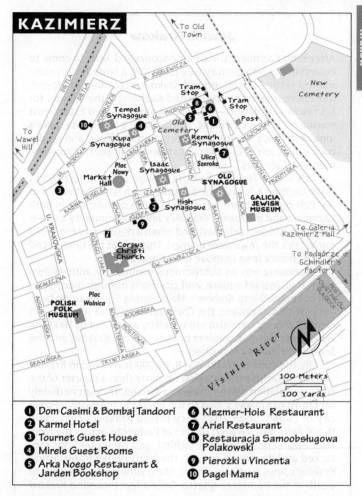

KAZIMIERZ

To Old Town

To Wawel Hill

Tempel Synagogue

Kupa Synagogue

Old Cemetery

Remu'h Synagogue

Ulica Szeroka

Plac Nowy

Isaac Synagogue

Market Hall

OLD SYNAGOGUE

High Synagogue

GALICIA JEWISH MUSEUM

Corpus Christi Church

Polish Folk Museum

Plac Wolnica

New Cemetery

Post

Tram Stop

Tram Stop

To Galeria Kazimierz Mall

To Podgórze & Schindler's Factory

Vistula River

100 Meters
100 Yards

❶ Dom Casimi & Bombaj Tandoori
❷ Karmel Hotel
❸ Tournet Guest House
❹ Mirele Guest Rooms
❺ Arka Noego Restaurant & Jarden Bookshop
❻ Klezmer-Hois Restaurant
❼ Ariel Restaurant
❽ Restauracja Samoobsługowa Polakowski
❾ Pierożki u Vincenta
❿ Bagel Mama

Orientation: Start your visit to Kazimierz on **ulica Szeroka,** which is more of a long, parking-lot square than a street, surrounded by Jewish restaurants, hotels, and synagogues.

Check in at the **Jarden Bookshop** at the top of the square (Mon–Fri 9:00–18:00, Sat–Sun 10:00–18:00, ulica Szeroka 2, tel. 012-429-1374, www.jarden.pl, jarden@jarden.pl). While there are many new bookstores in Kazimierz (mostly inside the various museums and synagogues), this is the original. It serves as a sort of tourist information center for the neighborhood, and sells a wide variety of fairly priced books on Kazimierz and Jewish culture in the region (including a good 3.50-zł Kazimierz map and well-illustrated 18-zł *Jewish Kraków* guidebook). They also run several tours (prices based on the number of people; I've listed the

Jewish Kraków

After King Kazimierz the Great encouraged Jews to come to Poland in the 14th century (see page 217), a large Jewish community settled in and around Kraków. According to legend, Kazimierz (the king) established Kazimierz (the village) for his favorite girlfriend—a Jewish woman named Ester—just southeast of the city walls. (If you have a 50-zł note, take a look at it: that's Kazimierz the Great on the front, and on the back is his capital, Cracovia, and the most important town he founded, Casmirus.)

It's a cute legend, but the village of Kazimierz didn't really become a Jewish enclave until much later. By the end of the 15th century, there were large Jewish populations in both Kazimierz and in Kraków. Kraków's Jewish community and the university students clashed, and when a destructive fire broke out in 1495, the Jews were blamed. The king at the time forced all of Kraków's Jews to move to Kazimierz.

Kazimierz was an autonomous community, with its own Town Hall, market square, and city walls (though many Jews still commuted into Kraków's Main Market Square to do business). Within Kazimierz, the Christian (west) and Jewish (east) neighborhoods were also separated by a wall. But by 1800, the walls came down, Kazimierz became part of Kraków, and the Jewish community flourished.

By the start of World War II, 65,000 Jews lived in Kraków (mostly in Kazimierz)—making up more than a quarter of the city's population. When the Nazis arrived, they immediately sent most of Kraków's Jews to the ghetto in the eastern Polish city of Lublin. Soon after, they forced Kraków's remaining 15,000 Jews into a walled ghetto at Podgórze, across the river. The Jews' cemeteries were defiled, and their buildings ransacked and destroyed. In 1942, the Nazis began transporting Kraków's Jews to death camps. Many others were worked to death in the Podgórze ghetto. Only a few thousand Kraków Jews survived the war.

Today's Kraków has only about 200 Jewish residents. During the communist era, this waning population was ignored or mistreated. But in recent years, Kazimierz has enjoyed a renaissance of Jewish culture—thanks largely to the popularity of *Schindler's List* (which was partly filmed here). Look for handwritten letters from Steven Spielberg and the cast in local restaurants (such as Ariel) and hotels. These have more recently been joined by autographs from *The Pianist* director Roman Polański. While few Jews live here now, the spirit of the Jewish tradition lives on in the many synagogues, as well as in the soulful cemeteries.

price per person for 2 people): Jewish Kazimierz overview (55 zł, 2 hrs, walking tour), Kazimierz and the WWII ghetto (70 zł, 3 hrs, walking, the best overview), *Schindler's List* sights (100 zł, 2 hrs, by car), and Auschwitz-Birkenau (180 zł, 6–7 hrs, by car). Call to reserve ahead, as tours are by appointment only. Tours will run if a minimum of three people sign up, but pairs or singles can join an already scheduled tour.

Note that an official **TI** is just a few blocks off the bottom of ulica Szeroka, at ulica Józefa 7 (Mon–Fri 9:00–17:00, closed Sat–Sun, tel. 012-422-0471). For hotel and restaurant suggestions, see page 257 of "Sleeping" and page 261 of "Eating." Several restaurants offer live traditional Jewish klezmer music nightly in summer.

▲▲**Jewish Cemeteries**—Kazimierz has two Jewish cemeteries, far less touristy and, to me, at least as powerful as the famous one in Prague.

The small **Old Cemetery** (Stary Cmentarz) was used to bury members of the Jewish community from 1552 to 1800. It has

been renovated—so in a way, it actually feels "newer" than the New Cemetery. After the New Cemetery (described in next paragraph) was opened in 1800, this cemetery gradually fell into disrepair. What remained was further desecrated by the Nazis during World War II. In the 1950s, it was discovered, excavated, and put back together as you see here. Shattered gravestones form a mosaic wall around the perimeter. As in all Jewish cemeteries, you may see small stones stacked on the graves (originally placed over desert graves to cover the body and prevent animals from disturbing it). Behind the little synagogue to the left, the tallest tombstone next to the tree belonged to Moses Isserle (a.k.a. Remu'h), an important 16th-century rabbi. He is believed to be a miracle worker, and his grave was one of the only ones that remained standing after World War II. The knee-high metal receptacle nearby is for written prayers (5 zł, very sporadic hours according to demand—especially outside of peak season—but generally open Sun–Fri 9:00–16:00, can be open until 18:00 in summer, closes earlier off-season and by sundown on Fri, always closed Sat, enter through Remu'h Synagogue at ulica Szeroka 40).

The much larger **New Cemetery** (Nowy Cmentarz) has graves of those who died after 1800. Nazis vandalized this cemetery, selling many of its gravestones to stonecutters, and using others as pavement in their concentration camps. Many of the gravestones have since been returned to their original positions. Other headstones could not be replaced, and were used to create the moving mosaic wall and Holocaust monument (on the right as you enter). Most gravestones are in one of three languages: Hebrew (generally the oldest, especially if there's no other language); Yiddish (which looks like German); and Polish (from Jews who assimilated into the Polish community). The earliest graves are simple stones, while later ones imitate graves in Polish Catholic cemeteries—larger, more elaborate, and with a long stone jutting out to cover the body. Notice that some new-looking graves have old dates. These were most likely put here well after the Holocaust (or even after communism) by relatives of the dead (free, Sun–Fri 8:00–18:00, until 16:00 in winter, closed Sat, tricky to find—go under railway bridge at east end of ulica Miodowa, jog left as you emerge, cemetery is to your right, enter through gate with small *cmentarz żydowski* sign).

Synagogues—Six different synagogues in Kazimierz welcome visitors. Each of the interiors is a variation on the same theme: A large central prayer hall, often with an altar (facing east, toward Jerusalem) where the Torah is kept. The elevated platform in the center, sometimes surrounded by a cage-like structure, is the equivalent of a pulpit in a Christian church. You may see separate areas (often a balcony or an arcade) where women would worship, separately from men. Some synagogues have been converted into museums, while others are still used for services. The first two synagogues listed below are on Kazimierz's main square, ulica Szeroka; the next four are all within three blocks to the west (all are shown on the map on page 239).

Remu'h Synagogue, from 1553, has been carefully renovated and is fully active (included in 5-zł entry fee for Old Cemetery, same unpredictable hours as Old Cemetery, ulica Szeroka 40).

The **Old Synagogue** (Stara Synagoga), the oldest surviving Jewish building in Poland, is now a three-room museum on local Jewish culture, with English descriptions. Most of the exhibits are displayed in the impressive main prayer hall (7 zł, free on Mon; April–Oct Mon 10:00–14:00, Tue–Sun 10:00–17:00; Nov–March Mon 10:00–14:00, Wed–Thu and Sat–Sun 9:00–16:00, Fri 10:00–17:00, closed Tue; ulica Szeroka 24).

The recently renovated **High Synagogue**—so called because its prayer room is upstairs—displays a photo exhibition of the people who lived here before and after the Holocaust (7 zł, daily 9:00–19:00, just around the corner from the Old Synagogue at ulica Józefa 38).

Isaac Synagogue (Synagoga Izaaka), Kraków's biggest, was built in the 17th century. On the walls in the prayer hall are giant wall paintings of prayers (for worshippers who couldn't afford to buy books). As it was recently bought by a Hasidic group, with plans to convert it into a fully functioning synagogue, its cost and opening hours are likely to change (possibly 5 zł, Sun–Fri 9:00–19:00, July–Aug until 20:00, closed Sat, closes at sundown on winter Fri—as early as 15:00 in Dec, a block west of ulica Szeroka at ulica Kupa 18, tel. 012-430-5577).

Tempel Synagogue (Synagoga Templu) has the grandest interior—big and dark, with elaborately decorated, gilded ceilings and balconies—and the most lived-in feel of the bunch (5 zł, Sun–Fri 10:00–16:00, sometimes until 18:00, closed Sat, corner of ulica Miodowa and ulica Podbrzezie).

The smaller **Kupa Synagogue** (Synagoga Kupa), clean and brightly decorated, sometimes hosts temporary exhibits (Miodowa 27).

Galicia Jewish Museum (Galicja Muzeum)—This museum focuses on the present rather than the past. With a series of photographs displayed around a restored Jewish furniture factory, the exhibit shows today's remnants of yesterday's Judaism in the area around Kraków (a region known as "Galicia"). From forgotten synagogues to old Jewish gravestones flipped over and used as doorsteps, these giant postcards of Jewish artifacts (with good English descriptions) ensure that an important part of this region's heritage won't be forgotten. Complementing this permanent collection are good temporary exhibits (7 zł, daily March–Oct 9:00–19:00, Nov–Feb 9:30–17:30, 1 block east of ulica Szeroka at ulica Dajwór 18, tel. 012-421-6842, www.galiciajewishmuseum.org). The museum also serves as a sort of cultural center, with a good bookstore, café, and programming that caters to both locals and visitors (such as Jewish dancing lessons on Saturday mornings).

Kazimierz Market Square (Plac Nowy)—The natives shop at plac Nowy's market stalls. This is a gritty, factory-workers-on-lunch-break contrast to Kraków's touristy Main Market Square (stalls open Tue–Sun 6:00–14:00, a few also open later, closed Mon). Consider dropping by here for some shopping, people-watching, or a quick, cheap, and local lunch (see "Eating," page 261). More recently, several trendy bars and nightclubs have popped up around this square.

▲Polish Folk Museum (Muzeum Etnograficzne)—This clever and refreshingly good museum hides a few blocks west of the Jewish area of Kazimierz, in the former town hall. The square it's on, plac Wolnica, was Kazimierz's primary market square, once almost as big as Kraków's. Inside the museum, you'll find models of traditional rural Polish homes, as well as musty replicas of the interiors (like an open-air folk museum—but inside). On the second floor are traditional Polish folk costumes, holiday celebrations (including Christmas decorations), and traditional instruments (such as a "Polish bagpipe" you don't have to blow into—no kidding). The top floor features folk art, past and present (6.50 zł, free on Sun; May–Sept Mon and Wed–Fri 10:00–17:00, Sat–Sun 10:00–14:00, closed Tue; Oct–April Mon 10:00–18:00, Wed–Fri 10:00–15:00, Sat–Sun 10:00–14:00, closed Tue; ulica Krakowska 46, tel. 012-430-6023).

Near Kazimierz: Podgórze

This neighborhood, directly across the Vistula from Kazimierz, is where the Nazis forced Kraków's Jews into a ghetto in early 1941. (*Schindler's List* and the films in the Pharmacy Under the Eagle museum depict the sad scene of the Jews loading their belongings onto carts and trudging over the bridge into Podgórze.) The ghetto was surrounded by a wall with a fringe along the top that resembled Jewish gravestones—a chilling premonition of what was to come. (A short section of this wall is still standing along Lwowska street.) **Ghetto Heroes' Square** (plac Bohaterow Getta) is the focal point of the visitor's Podgórze. It was on this square—now decorated with a recent monument consisting of several empty metal chairs—that many Jews waited to be sent to concentration camps.

Getting There: To get to Ghetto Heroes' Square, continue through Kazimierz on tram #13, #24, or #34 (described under "Getting to Kazimierz" on page 238) to the stop called plac Bohaterow Getta. You can also simply continue walking along Starowiślna, about 10 minutes past the other Kazimierz sights—it's just across the bridge.

▲Pharmacy Under the Eagle (Apteka pod Orłem)—This modest museum, on Ghetto Heroes' Square, tells the story of Tadeusz Pankiewicz, a Polish Catholic pharmacist who chose to remain in Podgórze when it became a Jewish ghetto. During this time, the pharmacy was an important meeting point for the ghetto residents, and Pankiewicz and his staff heroically aided and hid Jewish victims of the Nazis. (Pankiewicz survived the war and was later acknowledged by Israel as one of the "Righteous Among the Nations"). Today the pharmacy hosts a small exhibit about the Jewish ghetto. Three video screens display footage from that era: One shows Kazimierz before the Nazis arrived; another documents the forced transition to the Podgórze ghetto; and a third is secret surveillance footage of Płaszów Concentration Camp, on Kraków's outskirts (4 zł, free on Mon, some English descriptions, good 10-zł audioguide; May–Oct Mon 10:00–14:00, Tue–Sat 9:30–17:00, closed Sun; Nov–April Mon 10:00–14:00, Tue–Thu and Sat 9:00–16:00, Fri 10:00–17:00, closed Sun; plac Bohaterow Getta 18, tel. 012-656-5625).

Most people coming to Podgórze are actually looking for...

Schindler's Factory—Fans of the Holocaust movie and book—and the compassionate Kraków businessman who did his creative best to save the lives of his Jewish workers—can see Oskar Schindler's actual factory. This is where Schindler worked, and where Spielberg filmed much of *Schindler's List*. The factory went bust a few years back, but now the abandoned buildings are gradually being converted into a new museum. The exhibit (which may be partly finished during your visit) will have two parts: In the main building will be an exhibit on Schindler and other people of the so-called "Righteous Among the Nations"—non-Jews who risked their lives to help the Nazis' victims during World War II. Just inside the gate (on the left) is the long staircase—immortalized in a scene from *Schindler's List*—that leads to a replica of Oskar Schindler's office. Gestapo agents and other Nazi troops were also stationed in this building to keep an eye on Schindler and his workers. Just behind the main building are several factory buildings, which will most likely be converted into the second part of the museum: a gallery for modern art. Check with the TI or ask around Kazimierz before making the long trek out here to find out what (if anything) there is to see, as well as cost and hours.

Getting There: It's in a depressed industrial area a five-minute walk from Ghetto Heroes' Square (plac Bohaterow Getta): Head up Kącik street (to the left of the big, glass skyscraper), go under the railroad underpass marked *Kraków-Zabłocie*, and continue two blocks to the second big building on the left (ulica Lipowa 4, marked *Fabryka Oskara Schindlera—Emalia*).

Closer to the center, **Schindler's apartment** is a block from Wawel Castle at ulica Straszewskiego 7 (unmarked and not available for tours).

▲▲Wieliczka Salt Mine (Kopalnia Soli Wieliczka)

Wieliczka (vee-LEECH-kah), 10 miles southeast of Kraków, is beloved by Poles. Though it's a bit overrated, it's unique and practically obligatory if you're in Kraków for at least two days.

This remarkable mine has been producing salt since at least the 11th century. Under Kazimierz the Great, one-third of Poland's income came from these precious deposits. Wieliczka miners spent much of their lives underground, leaving for work before daybreak and returning after sundown, rarely emerging into daylight. To pass the time, and to immortalize their national pride and religiosity in art, 19th-century miners began to carve figures, chandeliers, and eventually even an elaborate chapel out of the salt. Until a few years ago, the mine still produced salt. Today's miners—about 400 of them—work on maintaining the 200 miles of chambers. This entire network is supported by wooden beams (because metal would rust).

From the lobby, your guide leads you 210 feet down a winding staircase. From this spot, you begin a 1.5-mile generally downhill stroll (more than 800 steps down all together) past 20 of the mine's 2,000 chambers (with signs explaining when they were dug), finishing 443 feet below the surface. When you're done, an elevator beams you back up.

The tour shows how the miners lived and worked, using horses who spent their whole lives without ever seeing the light of day. It takes you through some vast underground caverns past subterranean lakes, and introduces you to some of the mine's many sculptures (including one of Copernicus—who actually visited here in the 15th century—as well as an army of salt elves, and this region's favorite son, Pope John Paul II). Your jaw will drop as you enter the enormous **Chapel of St. Kinga,** carved over three decades in the early 20th century. Look for the salt-relief carving of the Last Supper (its 3-D details are astonishing, considering it's just six inches deep).

While advertised as two hours, your tour finishes in a deep-down shopping zone 90 minutes after you started (they hope you'll hang out and shop). Note when the next elevator departs (just 3/hr), and you can be outta there on the next lift. Zip through the shopping zone in two minutes, or step over the rope and be immediately in line for the great escape (you'll be escorted 300 yards to the skinny industrial elevator, into which you'll be packed like mine workers).

Cost and Hours: Visits are by tour only (65 zł to join a guided tour). English tours are generally daily year-round at 10:00, 11:30, 12:30, 13:45, 15:00, and 17:00; April–June and Sept also at 16:00; June and Sept also at 9:00; and July–Aug every half-hour between 8:30 and 18:00. If you miss the English-language tour (or decide to just show up and take whatever's going next), buy the informative guidebook, which narrates the exact route the tours do (daily April–Oct 7:30–19:30, Nov–March 8:00–17:00, ulica Daniłowicza 10, tel. 012-278-7302, www.kopalnia.pl). You'll pay an extra 10 zł for permission to use your camera—but be warned that flash photos often don't turn out, thanks to the irregular reflection of the salt crystals. Dress warmly—the mine is a constant 57 degrees Fahrenheit.

Mine Museum: Your ticket includes a dull mine museum at the end of the tour. It adds an hour to the mine tour and is discouraged by locals ("1.5 miles more walking, colder, more of the same"). Make it clear when you buy your ticket that you're not interested in the museum.

Getting to Wieliczka: The salt mine, 10 miles from Kraków, is best reached by minibus (2.50 zł, 4/hr or with demand). These minibuses (with *Wieliczka Soli* sign in window) leave from various points around Kraków, usually near the Main Post Office (Poczta Główna; it's east of Main Market Square, just beyond the Planty park, at the start of Starowiślna street). The departure point changes occasionally—confirm at the TI. This is better than taking the train or bus, which deposit you in the town of Wieliczka, far from the mine.

A different minibus, operated by the salt mine, charges more and departs about hourly from Royal Hotel on Grodzka street in Kraków (75-zł ticket includes 65 zł for the mine and 10 zł round-trip for the minibus).

▲Nowa Huta

Nowa Huta ("New Steel Works"), an enormous planned workers' town, offers a glimpse into the stark, grand-scale aesthetics of the communists. Since it's five miles east of central Kraków and a little tricky to see on your own, skip it unless you're determined. But architects and communists may want to make a pilgrimage here.

Getting There: Tram #4 and #15 go from near Kraków's Old Town (catch it on the ring road near Kraków's Main Train Station, at the Basztowa stop) along Pope John Paul II Avenue (aleja Jana Pawła II) to Nowa Huta's main square, plac Centralny (about 30 min total). From there, tram #4 (but not #15) continues a few minutes farther to the main gate of the Tadeusz Sendzimir Steelworks, and then it returns to Kraków.

Tours: True to its name, Mike Ostrowski's **Crazy Guides** is a very loosely run operation that takes tourists to Nowa Huta in genuine communist-era vehicles (mostly Trabants and Polski Fiats). While the content is good, be warned that Mike and his comrades are laid-back, very informal, and sometimes crude. If you're offended by a foul-mouthed guide who reminds you of a scruffy college student, or if you don't like the idea of careening down the streets of Kraków in a car that feels like a cardboard box with a lawnmower engine, skip this tour. For the rest of us, it's a fun and convenient way to experience Nowa Huta (119 zł per person for 2.5-hr Nowa Huta tour; 169 zł per person for 4-hr Communism Deluxe tour that also includes their makeshift "museum"—a communist-era apartment that's decorated to give you a taste of the way things were; 159 zł per person for 4-hr Real

Kraków tour that covers the basic Nowa Huta trip plus other outlying sights; other crazy experiences also available, cash only, reserve ahead and they'll pick you up at your hotel, mobile 0500-091-200, www.crazyguides.com, mike@crazyguides.com).

History: Nowa Huta was the communists' idea of paradise. It's one of only three towns outside the Soviet Union that were custom-built to showcase socialist ideals. (The others are Dunaújváros—once called Sztálinváros—south of Budapest, Hungary; and Eisenhüttenstadt—once called Stalinstadt—near Brandenburg, Germany.) Completed in just 10 years (1949–1959), Nowa Huta was primarily built because the Soviets felt that smart and sassy Kraków needed a taste of heavy industry. Farmers and villagers were imported to live and work in Nowa Huta. Many of the new residents weren't accustomed to city living, and brought along their livestock (who grazed in the fields around unfinished buildings). For commies, it was downright idyllic: Dad would cheerily ride the tram into the steel factory, mom would dutifully keep house, and the kids could splash around at the man-made beach and learn how to cut perfect red stars out of construction paper. But Krakovians had the last laugh: Nowa Huta, along with Lech Wałęsa's shipyard in Gdańsk, was one of the home bases of the Solidarity strikes that eventually brought down the regime. Now, with the communists long gone, Nowa Huta remains a sooty suburb of Poland's cultural capital, with a whopping 200,000 residents.

Sights: Nowa Huta's focal point used to be known simply as **Central Square** (plac Centralny), but in a fit of poetic justice, it was recently renamed for the anti-communist Ronald Reagan (plac Centralny im. Ronalda Reagana). This square is the heart of the planned town. A map of Nowa Huta looks like a clamshell: a semi-circular design radiating out from Central/Reagan Square. Numbered streets fan out like spokes on a wheel, and trolleys zip workers directly to the immense factory.

Believe it or not, the inspiration for Nowa Huta was the Renaissance (which, thanks to the textbook Renaissance design of the Cloth Hall and other landmarks, Soviet architects considered typically Polish). Note the elegantly predictable arches and galleries that would make Michelangelo proud. When first built (before it was layered with grime), Nowa Huta was delightfully orderly, primly painted, impeccably maintained, and downright beautiful... if a little boring. It was practical, too: Each of the huge apartment blocks is a self-contained unit, with its own grassy inner courtyard, school, and shops. Driveways (which appear to dead-end at underground garage doors) lead to vast fallout shelters.

Today's Nowa Huta is a far cry from its glory days. Wander around. Poke into the courtyards. Reflect on what it would be like

Kraków

to live here. It may not be as bad as you imagine. Ugly as they seem from the outside, these buildings are packed with happy little apartments filled with color, light, and warmth.

The wide boulevard running northeast of Central/Reagan Square, Solidarity Avenue (aleja Solidarności, lined with tracks for tram #4), leads to the **Tadeusz Sendzimir Steelworks.** Originally named for Lenin, this factory was supposedly built using plans stolen from a Pittsburgh plant. It was designed to be a cog in the communist machine—reliant on iron ore from Ukraine, and therefore worthless unless Poland remained in the Soviet Bloc. Down from as many as 40,000 workers at its peak, the steelworks now employs only about 10,000. Today there's little to see other than the big sign, stern administration buildings, and smokestacks in the distance. Examine the twin offices flanking the sign—topped with turrets and a decorative frieze inspired by Italian palazzos, these continue the Renaissance theme of the housing districts.

Another worthwhile sight in Nowa Huta is the **Lord's Ark Church** (Arka Pana, several blocks northwest of Central/Reagan Square on ulica Obrońców Krzyża). Back when he was archbishop of Kraków, Karol Wojtyła fought for years to build a church in this most communist of communist towns. When the regime refused, he insisted on conducting open-air Masses before crowds in fields—until the communists finally capitulated. Consecrated on May 15, 1977, the Lord's Ark Church has a Le Corbusier–esque design that looks like a fat, exhausted Noah's Ark resting on Mount Ararat—encouraging Poles to persevere through the floods of communism. While architecturally interesting, the church is mostly significant as a symbol of an early victory of Catholicism over communism.

SHOPPING

Two of the most popular Polish souvenirs—amber and pottery—come from areas far from Kraków. Amber *(bursztyn)* is found on northern Baltic shores (see page 335). "Polish pottery," the distinctive blue-and-white pieces, is made in the region of Silesia, west of Kraków (mostly in the town of Bolesławiec). Because neither of these items actually comes from Kraków, you won't find any great bargains. Somewhat more local are the many wood carvings you'll see.

The **Cloth Hall,** smack-dab in the center of the Main Market Square, is the most convenient place to pick up any Polish souvenirs. It has a great selection, respectable prices, and the city's highest concentration of pickpockets (summer Mon–Fri 9:00–18:00, Sat–Sun 9:00–15:00, sometimes later; winter Mon–Fri 9:00–16:00, Sat–Sun 9:00–15:00).

A small but swanky mall called **Pasaż 13** is a few steps off the southeast corner of the Main Market Square, where Grodzka street enters the square. Enter the mall under the balcony marked *Pasaż 13* (next to the Benetton store; Mon–Sat 9:00–21:00, Sun 9:00–17:00).

Two new, enormous shopping malls lie just beyond the tourist zone. The gigantic **Galeria Krakowska,** with 270 shops, shares a square with the train station (Mon–Sat 9:00–22:00, Sun 10:00–21:00, can't miss it right next to the Main Train Station). Note that nearby landmarks are signposted inside this massive, labyrinthine mall (*PKP/PKS* leads to the train and bus stations; *Stare Miasto* goes to the Old Town). Only slightly smaller is the **Galeria Kazimierz** (Mon–Sat 10:00–22:00, Sun 10:00–20:00, just a few blocks east of the Kazimierz sights, along the river at Podgórska 24).

ENTERTAINMENT

As a town full of both students and tourists, Kraków has plenty of entertainment options.

Concerts—You'll find a wide range of musical events, from tourist-oriented "Chopin's greatest hits" in quaint old ballrooms, to folk-dancing shows, to serious philharmonic performances. Popular venues include various churches (such as the Church of Sts. Peter and Paul on ulica Grodzka, or the Church of St. Bernard near Wawel Castle), various gardens around town (July–Aug only), and the Polonia House (Dom Polonii) on the Main Market Square (at #14, near ulica Grodzka). Because Kraków's live-music scene is continually evolving, it's best to inquire locally about what's on during your visit. Hotel lobbies are stocked with fliers for upcoming concerts. But to get all of your options, visit the TI on ulica Św. Jana, which specializes in cultural events (Mon–Sat 10:00–18:00, closed Sun, just off the Main Market Square at ulica Św. Jana 2, tel. 012-421-7787). They can tell you what's happening in Kraków, book tickets for most concerts (no extra fee), and tell you how to get tickets for the others. The monthly *Karnet* cultural events book lists everything (4 zł, half in Polish and half in English, also online at www.karnet.krakow.pl).

Jazz—For something a little more edgy, delve into Kraków's thriving jazz scene. Several popular clubs hide on the streets surrounding the Main Market Square (open nightly, most shows start around 21:30). The most famous and best for all-around jazz in a sophisticated cellar environment is **Jazz Club u Muniaka** (10–20-zł cover, open nightly 19:00–1:00 in the morning, live music nightly from 21:30, best music when the owner Janusz plays on Thu–Sat, ulica Floriańska 3, tel. 012-423-1205; described on my

Kraków

self-guided walk—see page 215). **Harris Piano Jazz Bar,** right on the Main Market Square (at #28), is more casual and offers a mix of traditional and updated "fusion" jazz (free or 5-zł cover most nights, 15–35-zł cover for more serious shows on Sat, music nightly from 21:30, tel. 012-421-5741, www.harris.krakow.pl). **Stalowa Magnolia** is a bit more youthful, clubby-feeling, and snooty, with jazz about two nights a week and rock or pop the other nights (5-zł cover to sit in music room on weeknights, on weekends 15-zł cover for men and free for women, music nightly from 21:30, ulica Św. Jana 15, www.stalowemagnolie.com).

Nightlife in Kazimierz—Young people willing to venture farther afield enjoy the lively nightlife in Kazimierz. Because the neighborhood has more affordable rents than the Old Town and it's not too far away (a 20-min walk or a 5-min tram ride), it has emerged as a cutting-edge after-hours mecca. Especially around plac Nowy, the streets teem with innovative, trendy pubs and nightclubs. Ask locals for tips on this always-evolving scene.

Klezmer Music in Kazimierz—For something a bit more sedate and cultured, consider the nightly klezmer music concerts of traditional Jewish music, also in Kazimierz (described on page 238).

SLEEPING

Healthy competition—with new, cleverly run places cropping up all the time—keeps Kraków's accommodation prices reasonable and makes choosing a hotel fun rather than frustrating. I've focused my accommodations on two areas: in and near the Old Town; and in Kazimierz, which is a local-style, more affordable neighborhood that is home to both the old Jewish quarter and Kraków's most happening nightlife.

Sleep Code

(3 zł = about $1, country code: 48)
S = Single, **D** = Double/Twin, **T** = Triple, **Q** = Quad, **b** = bathroom, **s** = shower only. Breakfast is included, credit cards are accepted, and English is spoken (unless otherwise noted).

To help you sort easily through these listings, I've divided the rooms into three categories, based on the price for a standard double room with bath:

  $$$ **Higher Priced**—Most rooms 400 zł or more.
  $$ **Moderately Priced**—Most rooms between 300–400 zł.
  $ **Lower Priced**—Most rooms 300 zł or less.

Rates are soft. Hoteliers don't need much of an excuse to offer you 10 to 20 percent off, especially on weekends or in the off-season. If you're traveling with a laptop, most places will let you get online in your room for free—some with Wi-Fi, others with a cable (which they can loan you).

In the Old Town

While you could stay away from the center, accommodations values here are so good that there's little sense in sleeping beyond the Planty park. Most of my listings are inside (or within a block or two of) the former city walls.

The Old Town has four basic types of accommodations: small, well-run guest houses (my favorite); big hotels (comfortable but overpriced); apartments (cheap, but you're on your own); and upstart youth hostels. I've listed the best of each type.

Guest Houses

These good-value pensions almost invariably come with lots of stairs (no elevators), and are run by smart, can-do, entrepreneurial owners. They're all located in the heart of the Old Town along busy pedestrian streets, and most don't have air-conditioning—so they can be noisy with the windows open in the summer, especially on weekends. (Light sleepers should request quiet rooms.) These places book up fast, especially in summer—reserve as far ahead as possible. Don't expect a 24-hour reception desk. I've listed the times the reception is officially open, but if you're arriving later, tell them and they'll wait up for you.

$$ Golden Lion Apartments, actually more of a guest house, has 12 smallish rooms with modern flair on a bustling (and often noisy) pedestrian street a block off the Main Market Square (S-180 zł, Sb-200–250 zł, D-270 zł, Db-300–350 zł, price depends on size, 10 percent cheaper Nov–Feb, free Wi-Fi, guest kitchen, ulica Szewska 19, tel. 012-422-9323, fax 012-421-9775, www.goldenlion .pl, reservation@goldenlion.pl, Anna and the Łodziński family).

$ At Pensjonat Trecius, Michał Palarczyk offers surprising class for low prices. Hiding upstairs in a nondescript building overlooking the bustling (and sometimes noisy) Floriańska pedestrian street, its eight rooms are nicely decorated, except for the two cheaper, unrenovated rooms on the top floor (S-120 zł, Sb-150–220 zł depending on size, D-150 zł, Db-200–300 zł depending on size, extra bed-50 zł, 5 percent cheaper if you pay cash, continental breakfast-8 zł, full breakfast-16 zł, non-smoking, reception open Mon–Fri 8:00–20:00, Sat–Sun 8:00–15:00, free cable Internet, 2 blocks from the Main Market Square at ulica Św. Tomasza 18, tel. 012-421-2521, fax 012-426-8730, www.trecius.krakow.pl, hotel @trecius.krakow.pl).

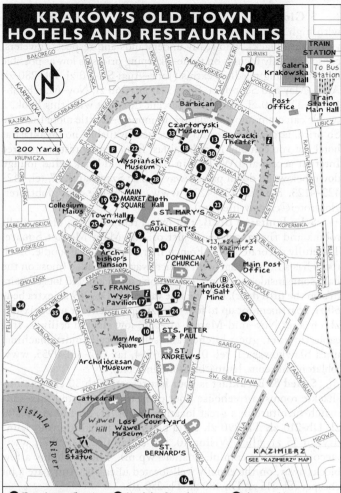

KRAKÓW'S OLD TOWN HOTELS AND RESTAURANTS

1. Pensjonat Trecius
2. Globtroter Guest House
3. La Fontaine B&B
4. Golden Lion Apts.
5. Bed & Breakfast
6. Hotel Maltański
7. Hotel Pugetów
8. Hotel Gródek
9. Wentzl Hotel, Rest. & Słodki
10. Hotel Senacki & Bar Grodzki
11. Hotel Classic
12. Hotel Wawel
13. Kraków City Apts.
14. Grodzka Apt. House
15. Mama's Hostel
16. Nathan's Villa Hostel
17. Restauracja pod Aniołami
18. Restauracja Farina
19. Farinella Rest. & Chimera Cafeteria
20. Miód Malina Restaurant
21. Restauracja Jarema
22. Polskie Smaki
23. Cyklop Pizza
24. Pizzeria Trzy Papryczki
25. Aqua e Vino
26. Kwandras Lunch Bar
27. Bar Mleczny
28. Restauracja Redolfi
29. Restauracja Hawełka
30. Cukiarnia Jama Michalika
31. Jazz Club u Muniaka
32. Harris Piano Jazz Bar
33. Stalowa Magnolia
34. Massolit Books
35. Betty Clean Laundry

$ Globtroter Guest House offers 15 rustic-feeling rooms with high ceilings and big beams around a serene garden courtyard. Jacek (Jack), who really understands and respects travelers, conscientiously focuses on value—keeping prices as low as possible by not offering needless extras (June–Aug: Sb-170 zł, Db-280 zł; April–May and Sept–Oct: Sb-155 zł, Db-260 zł; Nov–March: Sb-150 zł, Db-210 zł; ask for 10 percent discount with this book, 2 people can cram into a single to save money—a little more than the Sb price, larger suites for up to five also available, no breakfast at hotel but you can buy 14-zł breakfast from nearby restaurant, free Internet access and Wi-Fi, fun 700-year-old brick cellar lounge down below, go down passageway at plac Szczepańska 7, tel. 012-422-4123, fax 012-422-4233, www.cracow-life.com/globtroter, globtroter@cracow-life.com).

$ La Fontaine B&B, run by a French family, offers eight rooms and five apartments just off the Main Market Square. Tastefully decorated with French flair, it's cute as a poodle. Each room has a little lounge with a microwave and fridge (most on the hall, some inside the room). If you don't mind lots and lots of stairs (it's on the fifth floor), this is a fine value (Sb/Db-269 zł, extra bed-60 zł, apartment for up to four-460 zł, apartment for up to six-659 zł, cheaper Nov–mid-March, air-con, low slanted ceilings, free cable Internet, guest kitchen and self-service laundry machine, ulica Sławkowska 1, tel. 012-422-6564, fax 012-431-0955, www.bblafontaine.com, biuro@bblafontaine.com).

$ Bed & Breakfast is your last resort, with 30 cheap, ramshackle rooms, a treehouse floor plan, thin walls, and mix-and-match furniture in a great location (S-100 zł, Sb-130 zł, D-190 zł, Db-210 zł, Tb-290 zł, extra bed-70 zł, they'll do your laundry for 15 zł, ulica Wiślna 10, tel. & fax 012-421-9871, www.accommodation.com.pl, wislna@wp.pl). The 10 rooms a few blocks away, on the equally well-located ulica Św. Anny, are a bit cheaper (Sb-115 zł, Db-180 zł, Tb-250 zł).

Hotels
$$$ Donimirski Boutique Hotels, with three different locations in or near Kraków's Old Town, set the bar for splurge hotels in Kraków (website for all: www.donimirski.com). All Donimirski hotels offer my readers a 15 percent discount. You can expect any of these hotels to have some of the friendliest staff in Kraków and all of the classy little extras that add up to a memorable hotel experience (like a fluffy white bathrobe for every guest). **Hotel Maltański**—my home away from home in Kraków—has 16 rooms in the beautifully renovated former royal stables, just outside the Planty park and only two blocks from Wawel Castle (Sb-560 zł, Db-590 zł, cheaper Nov–March, parking-30 zł/day, ulica Straszewskiego 14,

tel. 012-431-0010, fax 012-431-0615, maltanski@donimirski.com). **Hotel Pugetów,** with seven plush rooms and a fun breakfast cellar, is on the other side of town, in a slightly dingy but convenient neighborhood between the Main Market Square and Kazimierz (Sb-350 zł, Db-510 zł, Db suite-790 zł, cheaper Nov–March, ulica Starowiślna 13–15, tel. 012-432-4950, pugetow@donimirski .com). **Hotel Gródek**—by far the fanciest and most central of the bunch—offers 23 rooms a three-minute walk behind St. Mary's Church on a quiet dead-end street overlooking the Planty park. This place is easily the best splurge in town, with a handy location, gorgeously decorated rooms, and a top-notch breakfast surrounded by a mini-museum of artifacts discovered while they were building the place (Sb-700 zł, bigger "deluxe" Sb-850 zł, Db-740 zł, bigger "deluxe" Db-890 zł, cheaper Nov–March, free Internet access and cable Internet, good Cul-de-Sac restaurant serves tasty international cuisine from a prizewinning chef in the cellar, parking-50 zł/day, Na Gródku, tel. 012-431-9030, grodek@donimirski .com). If you have a car, ask about rooms at their countryside castle, Zamek Korzkiew.

$$$ Wentzl Hotel is your splurge-right-on-the-Square option. Many of its 18 rooms overlook the Main Market Square (request when you reserve), but two layers of double-paned windows keep things quiet. The decor is classy Old World with modern touches, like state-of-the-art TVs and bathrooms (Sb-650 zł, Db-700 zł, bigger "deluxe" rooms cost 40 zł more, all rooms 40 zł cheaper Nov–March, elevator, air-con, free Wi-Fi, Rynek Główny 19, tel. 012-430-2664, fax 012-430-2665, www.wentzl.pl, hotel@wentzl.pl).

$$$ Hotel Senacki is a business-class place renting 20 tasteful rooms between Wawel Castle and the Main Market Square. Nine of the rooms have air-conditioning for no extra charge—if you'll be here in summer, request this when you reserve (Sb-400 zł, Db-450–550 zł, lower price is for "attic" rooms with skylight windows and a flight of stairs after the elevator, deluxe Db-600 zł, extra bed-100 zł, all rates 40 zł cheaper Fri–Sun, 15 percent cheaper Nov–March, parking-55 zł/day, non-smoking rooms, elevator—but doesn't go to "attic" rooms, free cable Internet, ulica Grodzka 51, tel. 012-421-1161, fax 012-422-7934, www.senacki .krakow.pl, recepcja@senacki.krakow.pl).

$$$ Hotel Classic, a modern home in old Kraków (on a peaceful street just inside the Planty park), has 30 rooms, a sleek marble lobby, professional staff, reasonable prices, and little character (April–Oct: Sb-425 zł, Db-450 zł, suite-600 zł; Nov–March: Sb-300 zł, Db-325 zł, suite-500 zł; Rick Steves readers get a 20 percent discount on weekdays and 25 percent discount Fri–Sun with a 2-night minimum stay, non-smoking floor, air-con, elevator, free cable Internet, ulica Św. Tomasza 32, tel. 012-424-0303, fax 012-429-3680, www.hotel-classic.pl, hotel@hotel-classic.pl).

$$$ **Hotel Wawel,** with a swanky marble lobby and the history of the hotel painted on the walls, has 39 rooms in a good location. Some of the rooms are nicely renovated, a great value, and cost the same as the slightly musty older rooms—but it's a crapshoot, since they can't assign your room until you check in (Sb-300 zł, Db-430 zł, big "retro" Db-520 zł, Tb-450 zł, 30 zł extra to turn on air-con—but not in all rooms, elevator—but doesn't go to top floor, ulica Poselska 22, tel. 012-424-1300, fax 012-424-1333, www.hotelwawel.pl, hotel@hotelwawel.pl).

Apartments

You can save money by staying in your own apartment rather than a hotel. Apartments come with great locations, simple kitchens, and relatively low prices, but no reception desk or big-hotel services (such as having your room cleaned daily)...you're on your own. Apartments aren't just for long stays—these places welcome even one-nighters. While the apartments themselves are neat and modern, most of these are in old buildings with dreary entryways and stairways. I've listed hours that the "reception" is open for each one; if arriving outside of these times, you can call ahead to arrange when to pick up the keys.

$$ **Kraków City Apartments,** run by Andzej and Katarzyna, is six clean, modern, sleek apartments tucked away in a quiet courtyard at the corner of the Old Town (Db-340 zł, bigger apartment for 400 zł, 15 percent cheaper Oct–mid-April, nonsmoking, elevator, free cable Internet, ulica Szpitalna 34, tel. 012-431-0041, mobile 0501-274-755, www.krakowapartments.info, info @krakowapartments.info). They also have two more apartments for about 60 zł less a few blocks south on Stolarska street (still in the Old Town).

$ **Grodzka Apartment House** offers 11 new-feeling, stylishly decorated apartments around a courtyard along one of Kraków's most happening streets, just a few steps off the Main Market Square. The studio apartments are as nice as a hotel room for a fraction of the price (studio-230 zł, 1-bedroom-260–300 zł, 2-bedroom-400 zł, prices soft—especially for advance booking, no breakfast but can buy a 15-zł breakfast at nearby café, reception open daily 11:00–21:00, some apartments have street noise—light sleepers ask for quiet room, free cable Internet, go down the passage at Grodzka 4, mobile 066-054-1085, www.grodzka.net.pl, info@grodzka.net.pl, Mikołaj and Sebastian). They also have more apartments (though not quite as nice) in two other Old Town buildings.

Hostels

New hostels are born—and go extinct—every other day in Kraków. But these two are the real deal. Accept no substitutes. My first listing is just steps off the Main Market Square; the second one is in an up-and-coming neighborhood between Wawel Hill and Kazimierz.

$ Mama's Hostel is ideally located and more dignified than most hostels—like an old apartment taken over by vagabonds with good manners, but who still know how to have a good time. With 50 beds in seven rooms and mellow public spaces, it's a winner (60 zł per person in a 6-bed room, 55 zł in an 8-bed room, 50 zł in a 10-bed room, 45 zł in a 12-bed room, D-160 zł; includes sheets, breakfast, laundry, and lockers; non-smoking, no curfew, free Internet and Wi-Fi, kitchen, lots of stairs with no elevator, ulica Bracka 4, tel. & fax 012-429-5940, www.mamashostel.com .pl, hostel@mamashostel.com.pl).

$ Nathan's Villa Hostel is well-run by an energetic young Bostonian and his wife. It's loose, easygoing, and fun, with 120 beds in 21 cleverly painted rooms, a bar, a beer garden, an art gallery, a cheap BBQ every night in summer, and plenty of backpacker bonding. Their advertising promises advice on how to "get hammered," and the bar has regular drinking contests...if that's not your scene, sleep elsewhere (bunk in 4-bed room-65 zł, in 6-bed room-60 zł, in 8-bed room-55 zł, in 10-bed room-50 zł, D-160 zł, Db-180 zł, 5 zł less Nov–Feb; includes breakfast, sheets, laundry facilities, and lockers; free Internet access, non-smoking, no curfew or lockout time, ulica Św. Agnieszki 1, tel. 012-422-3545, www.nathansvilla.com, krakow@nathansvilla.com).

In Kazimierz

Sleep in Kazimierz to be close to Kraków's Jewish heart—or simply to experience a cheaper, less touristy, more local-feeling neighborhood outside the Old Town. With the highest concentration of pubs and nightclubs in town, Kazimierz is *the* spot for nightlife—which means that all of these places can be subject to some noise, especially on weekends. The downside: You are a 20-minute walk or a five-minute tram ride from the medieval ambience of Kraków's old center (for details on getting to Kazimierz from the Old Town, see page 238). Some of the klezmer music restaurants listed in "Eating" also rent rooms, but they're generally an afterthought to the food and music, and not a good value. For locations, see the map on page 239.

$$ Dom Casimi is nicely located, with 12 rooms at the top of ulica Szeroka in the heart of Jewish Kazimierz (Sb-190–260 zł, Db-290–370 zł, Tb-330–430 zł, price depends on size and style of room, 15 percent cheaper Oct–March, stairs with no elevator, free Wi-Fi, ulica Szeroka 7/8, tel. 012-426-1193, fax 012-426-1194, www.casimi.pl, casimi@casimi.pl).

$ Karmel Hotel, with 11 rooms on a pleasant side street near the heart of Kazimierz, feels elegant for the price (Sb-240 zł, tight twin Db-298 zł, more spacious "komfort plus" Db with one big bed-398 zł, pricier suites also available, extra bed-50 zł, about 15–20 percent less Nov–March, upstairs with no elevator, free cable Internet, ulica Kupa 15, tel. 012-430-6697, fax 012-430-6726, www.karmel.com.pl, hotel@karmel.com.pl).

$ Tournet Guest House, well-run by friendly Piotr and Sylwia Działowy, offers 17 cheap, clean, colorful rooms near the edge of Kazimierz toward Wawel Hill. The "basic" rooms don't include breakfast (7 zł extra) or TV sets (basic Sb-110 zł, standard Sb-150 zł, basic Db-140 zł, standard Db-200 zł, Tb-250 zł, extra bed-50 zł, 20 zł less Nov–March, lots of stairs with no elevator, free Wi-Fi, reception open 7:00–22:00, ulica Miodowa 7, tel. 012-292-0088, fax 012-292-0089, www.accommodation.krakow.pl, tournet@accommodation.krakow.pl).

$ Mirele Guest Rooms offers 11 simple but comfortable rooms surrounding the 17th-century Kupa Synagogue—not unlike a convent-type accommodation. You can literally walk through the balconies overlooking the synagogue's prayer hall (S-110 zł, Sb-150 zł, D-170 zł, Db-190 zł, T-240 zł, cash only, breakfast-15 zł extra, non-smoking, guest kitchen, free Wi-Fi, some nightclub noise on weekends—ask for quiet room, ulica Miodowa 27, tel. 012-422-6151, www.mirele.krakow.pl, mirele@sezam.pl, Wasilewski family).

EATING

Kraków has a wide array of excellent restaurants—for every one I've listed, there are two or three nearly as good. The Old Town is very strong on traditional Polish and Italian, but less successful with other cuisines. Kazimierz has a more diverse selection, including Jewish restaurants with live klezmer music.

In the Old Town

Kraków's Old Town is littered with great restaurants. Prices are reasonable even on the Main Market Square. And a half-block away, they get even better. All of these eateries (except the milk bars) are likely to be booked up on weekends—always reserve ahead.

Restauracja pod Aniołami ("Under Angels") offers a dressy, candlelit atmosphere on a covered patio, or in a deep, steep, romantic cellar with rough wood and medieval vaults. The cuisine is traditional Polish, with an emphasis on grilled meats and trout (on a wood-fired grill). Don't go here if you're in a hurry—only if you want to really slow down and enjoy your dinner (main dishes 25–50 zł, daily 13:00–24:00, reservations smart, ulica Grodzka 35, tel. 012-421-3999). If you want a fast, cheap, and tasty lunch, drop by their tiny **sandwich bar** for sandwiches to take away or enjoy at their sidewalk tables (2–3 zł for mini-open-faced sandwiches, 5 zł for more filling roll sandwiches, Mon–Fri 9:00–19:00, Sat 9:00–18:00, closed Sun, shorter hours off-season).

Restauracja Farina, with a fish-and-bottles theme, features a welcoming atmosphere, friendly service, and Polish and Mediterranean cuisine with an emphasis on fresh fish (20–30-zł pastas, 25–55-zł main dishes). They serve some special seafood dishes (60–90 zł or more) only Thursday through Sunday—when they've just gotten their fresh delivery (open daily 12:00–23:00, 2 blocks north of the square at ulica Św. Marka 16, at intersection with ulica Św. Jana, tel. 012-422-1680). They have a smaller branch, called **Farinella,** with a similar menu and prices, but more Spanish flair (including a small selection of tapas; daily 10:00–23:00, ulica Św. Anny 5, tel. 012-422-2121).

Miód Malina ("Honey Raspberry") is a delightful Polish-Italian fusion restaurant well located on bustling Grodzka street. The menu is half Polish and half Italian—yet, remarkably, they do both cuisines equally well. You can start with borscht and follow it with spaghetti Bolognese, or have a caprese salad before downing a dish of wood-fired pierogi. Sit in the cozy, warmly painted interior, or out in the courtyard (16-zł pierogi, 16–30-zł wood-fired pizzas and pastas, 25–45-zł main dishes, daily 12:00–23:00, ulica Grodzka 40, tel. 012-430-0411).

Restauracja Jarema (yah-RAY-mah) offers a tasty reminder that Kraków used to rule a large swath of Ukraine and Lithuania. They serve eastern Polish/Ukrainian cuisine (with well-described specialties) amid 19th-century aristocratic elegance—you'll feel like you're dining in an old mansion (main dishes 30–70 zł, several good vegetarian options, daily 12:00–22:00, usually live music from 19:00, reservations wise, across the street from barbican at plac Matejki 5, tel. 012-429-3669).

Polskie Smaki ("Polish Flavors") is a homey little self-service cafeteria with a surprisingly elegant interior—sort of a dressed-up milk bar. They serve fast, inexpensive, and tasty traditional meals a block off the Main Market Square, with good borscht and *gołąbki* (stuffed cabbage rolls) at a fraction of what you'd pay elsewhere (main dishes 7–12 zł, daily 9:00–22:00, ulica Św. Tomasza 5, tel. 012-422-4822).

Chimera, just off the Main Market Square, is a cafeteria that serves fast traditional meals to a steady stream of students, either outside on their quiet courtyard, or inside in what seems like a fake Old World stage set (good salad buffet: small plate-10 zł, big plate-14 zł, good for vegetarians, daily 9:00–23:00, near university at ulica Św. Anny 3, it's the second restaurant marked *Chimera* as you approach from the square). I'd skip their expensive full-service restaurant (main dishes 35–60 zł, daily 12:00–24:00, next door and slightly closer to the square).

Pizza: **Cyklop,** with 10 tables wrapped around the cook and his busy oven, has excellent wood-fired pizzas (one-person pizzas for 11–16 zł, two-person pizzas for 13–20 zł, daily 11:30–22:00, near St. Mary's Church at Mikołajska 16, tel. 012-421-6603). **Pizzeria Trzy Papryczki** ("Three Peppers")—also dishing out wood-fired pizzas (though not quite as good as Cyklop's)—has better ambience, either inside or out in the welcoming garden (one-person pizzas for 15–25 zł, two-person pizzas for 20–30 zł, daily 11:00–24:00, ulica Poselska 17, tel. 012-292-5532).

Serious Italian: The Italian-owned **Aqua e Vino** offers good food in a mellow, mod, black-and-white cellar decorated with giant stills from old movies. Probably the most authentic Italian eatery in town, it has a loyal following among the Italian expat community (25–35-zł pastas, 40–50-zł main dishes, daily 12:00–24:00, ulica Wiślna 5/10, tel. 012-421-2567).

Milk Bars on Grodzka Street

Ulica Grodzka, the busy street that cuts south from the Main Market Square, has a convenient little pocket of three milk bars within a few steps of each other (all are open daily for lunch and dinner, but only until 19:00 or 20:00, sometimes later in summer). Survey all three options before you dive in. For pointers on eating at a milk bar, review the sidebar on page 199.

Approaching from the square, the first one you'll come to (just after the modern copper-colored Wyspiański Pavilion, on the left) is the most modern and "trendy" of the three, more popular with students than with their grandparents: **Kwandras Lunch Bar** ("Quarter"—as in, you can eat here in a quarter-hour; pierogi and other dishes for 7–10 zł, full dinner for 12 zł, ulica Grodzka 32, tel. 012-294-2222).

A few steps down the street and on the right is the most basic and traditional, with a blue-and-white sign reading simply **Bar Mleczny** ("Milk Bar"; low-profile sign over the door reads *Restauracja "pod Temidą"*). The next best thing to a time machine to the communist era, this place has grumpy monolingual service, a mostly local clientele, and cheap but good food (5–10-zł mains).

A few more steps down, also on the right (just before the two churches), is **Bar Grodzki,** a single tight little room with shared tables. In addition to the standard milk-bar fare, Bar Grodzki

specializes in tasty potato pancake dishes *(placki ziemniaczane).*
Try the rich and hearty "Hunter's Delight"—potato pancake with
sausage, beef, melted cheese, and spicy sauce for 15 zł. The English
menu posted by the counter makes ordering easy. Order, sit, and
wait to be called to fetch your food (most main dishes 8–15 zł).

Splurging on the Main Market Square

You'll find plenty of relatively expensive, tourist-oriented restaurants on the Square. While all of these places have rich interiors, there's not much point in paying a premium to dine here
unless you're sitting outside on the square (one exception is Pod
Krzyżkiem at #39, with a surrealistic interior that boldly attempts
to one-up Eastern Europe's top square). While tourists go for the
ye olde places, natives hang out at pizza joints (like Sphinx, part
of a wildly popular Poland-wide chain). Poles generally afford this
zone on their meager incomes by just having a drink on the square
after eating at home.

Restauracja Redolfi comes with my favorite square view,
great salads, French cuisine, and a wide selection of desserts (30-zł
salads, 40–60-zł main dishes, daily 9:00–24:00, Rynek Główny
38, tel. 012-423-0579).

Wentzl Restauracja has a tidy little "garden" with a different,
but equally classic, square view (near St. Adalbert's Church and
Grodzka street). Serving modern Polish and French fare, it also has
a spacious and classy interior upstairs, with big windows overlooking the square (30–65-zł main dishes, daily 13:00–23:00, at #19,
tel. 012-429-5712). **Wentzl Słodki** ("Sweets"), a few doors down, is
a local favorite for enjoying dessert on the Square. Consider dining
more cheaply elsewhere, then finishing up with coffee, ice cream,
or cake here (10–15-zł desserts, daily 11:00–23:00).

Restauracja Hawełka is an old institution serving tired but
reliable traditional Polish cuisine (rather than the trendy, international angle most other Square restaurants take). This was a rowdy
pub in the communist days, but now the interior has a crusty,
genteel painting-gallery ambience (main dishes 30–70 zł, daily
11:00–23:00, near the corner of Szczepańska at Rynek Główny 34,
tel. 012-422-0631).

In Kazimierz

The entire district is bursting with lively cafés and bars—it's a happening night scene. Jewish food is the specialty here, but in general
the neighborhood offers more diversity than the Old Town (such
as bagels and Indian cuisine, described below). The non-Jewish
places I've listed are fast, cheap, and convenient. For locations, see
the map on page 239.

Klezmer Concerts and Jewish Food

Kazimierz is a hub of Jewish restaurants, featuring cuisine and music that honors the neighborhood's Jewish heritage (and caters to its Jewish visitors). On a balmy summer night, the air is filled with the sound of klezmer music—traditional Jewish music from 19th-century Poland, generally with violin, string bass, clarinet, and accordion. Skilled klezmer musicians can make their instruments weep or laugh like human voices. Several places on ulica Szeroka (Kazimierz's main square) offer klezmer concerts around 20:00. All of these have several rooms, which the musicians move between as the evening goes on. While most places claim to do concerts nightly year-round, in reality they can be canceled anytime it's slow (especially off-season). For this reason—and because these places fill up—it's important to reserve ahead. (If you're in Kazimierz for some daytime sightseeing, visit several, pick your favorite, and reserve dinner.) Each restaurant has a similar menu, with main dishes for 20–40 zł. You'll pay an additional cover charge just for the music (about 20 zł per person).

Arka Noego ("Noah's Ark") has a good reputation for its music and its food (daily 9:00–2:00 in the morning, shares building with Jarden Bookshop at #2, tel. 012-429-1528).

At **Klezmer-Hois,** which fills a venerable former Jewish ritual bathhouse, you'll feel like you're dining in a rich grandparent's home (food is a bit more expensive here than at the other Kazimierz restaurants, daily 8:00–22:00, at #6, tel. 012-411-1245, www.klezmer.pl).

Ariel is popular but has gone downhill in recent years, and receives mixed reviews for its food (daily 10:00–24:00, music in up to four different rooms, best upstairs in the larger dining hall, at #18, tel. 012-421-7920).

Inexpensive Polish Food

Restauracja Samoobsługowa Polakowski is a glorified milk bar with country-kitchen decor and cheap and tasty Polish fare. Curt service...cute hats (main dishes about 7–11 zł, borrow the English menu and/or point to what you want, daily 9:00–22:00, just behind the top of ulica Szeroka at ulica Miodowa 39).

Pierożki u Vincenta is a tiny, Vincent van Gogh–inspired eatery serving great pierogi (Polish-style ravioli) with both traditional fillings and creative new-fangled versions (most around 10 zł, Sun–Thu 12:00–21:00, Fri–Sat 12:00–22:00, closes 1 hour earlier in winter, ulica Józefa 11, tel. 012-430-6834).

The **plac Nowy market** offers a fully authentic, very cheap, blue-collar Polish experience—join the workers on their lunch break at the little food windows on Kazimierz's market square.

Nearby, the ice-cream window at the corner of ulica Rabina Meiselsa is a local favorite.

Other Options

Bagel Mama, run by an American named Nava, is a casual New York–style deli with bagels, soups, salads, wraps, and tasty burritos. The bagels come dressed with a wide variety of spreads, from simple cream cheese or peanut butter to lox, tuna, or curry chicken. You can dine at one of the few small tables, or get it to go (most items around 15 zł, Tue–Sat 10:00–21:00, Sun 10:00–19:00, closed Mon; also closed mid-May–mid-June during the French Open, which Nava caters; behind Tempel Synagogue at ulica Podbrzezie 2, tel. 012-431-1942).

Bombaj Tandoori offers a decent tandoori-and-naan fix at the top of ulica Szeroka, with ample outdoor seating (15–35-zł main dishes, Sun–Thu 12:00–23:00, Fri–Sat 12:00–24:00, at #7/8, tel. 012-422-3797).

TRANSPORTATION CONNECTIONS

For getting between Kraków and **Auschwitz,** see page 277 in the next chapter.

From Kraków by Train to: Warsaw (hourly, 2.75 hrs, see below), **Gdańsk** (4/day direct, 7–8 hrs; plus 1 direct night train, 11 hrs; more with transfer in Warsaw), **Toruń** (1/day direct, 7.75 hrs; better to transfer at Warsaw's Zachodnia station: 4/day, 5.75–6.5 hrs), **Prague** (1/night direct, 8.5 hrs; 3 decent daytime options, 6.75 hrs direct or 8 hrs with 1–2 changes), **Berlin** (2/day direct, including 1 night train, 9.5–10.5 hrs; otherwise transfer in Warsaw, 9–11 hrs), **Budapest** (1 direct night train/day, 11 hrs; otherwise transfer in Katowice, Poland, or Břeclav, Czech Republic, 9–10 hrs), and **Vienna** (1/night direct, 7.5 hrs; 3 decent daytime options, 6.25 hrs direct or 7–8.5 hrs with 1–3 changes).

The train to **Warsaw** is particularly pleasant: A speedy 2.75 hours without stopping, from city center to city center. You'll be offered a free drink and snack to nibble on as you enjoy the pastoral scenery.

AUSCHWITZ-BIRKENAU

The unassuming regional capital of Oświęcim (ohsh-VEENCH-im) was the site of one of humanity's most unspeakably horrifying tragedies: the systematic murder of at least 1.1 million innocent people. From 1941 until 1945, Oświęcim was the home of Auschwitz, the biggest, most notorious concentration camp in the Nazi system. Today, Auschwitz is the most poignant memorial anywhere to the victims of the Holocaust.

A visit here is obligatory for Polish 14-year-olds; students usually come again during their last year of school, as well. You'll often see Israeli high school groups walking through the grounds waving their Star of David flags. Many visitors, including Germans, leave flowers and messages. One of the messages reads, "Nations who forget their own history are sentenced to live it again."

ORIENTATION

"Auschwitz" actually refers to a series of several camps in Poland—most importantly Auschwitz I, in the village of Oświęcim (50 miles, or a 75-minute drive, west of Kraków), and Auschwitz II, a.k.a. Birkenau (about 2 miles west of Oświęcim). Those visiting Auschwitz generally see both parts. **Auschwitz I,** where public transportation from Kraków arrives, has the main museum building, the *Arbeit Macht Frei* gate, and indoor museum exhibits in former prison buildings. Then a brief shuttle-bus ride takes visitors to **Birkenau**—on a much bigger scale and mostly outdoors, with the famous guard tower (with another bookshop and more WCs), a vast field with ruins of barracks, a few tourable rough barracks, the notorious "dividing platform," and a giant monument flanked

Auschwitz

Why Visit Auschwitz?

Why visit a notorious concentration camp on your vacation? Auschwitz-Birkenau is one of the most moving sights in Europe, and certainly the most important of all the Holocaust memorials. Seeing the camp can be difficult: Many visitors are overwhelmed by a combination of sadness and anger over the tragedy, as well as inspiration at the remarkable stories of survival. But Auschwitz survivors and victims' families want tourists to come here and experience the scale and the monstrosity of the place. In their minds, a steady flow of visitors will ensure that the Holocaust is always remembered—so it never happens again.

Auschwitz isn't for everyone. But I've never met anyone who toured Auschwitz and regretted it. For many, it's a profoundly life-altering experience—and at the very least, it will forever affect the way you think about the Holocaust.

---

by remains of destroyed crematoria.

Begin at **Auschwitz I.** The museum's main building has ticket booths (to pay for a tour or to make a donation), bookshops (consider the good *Guide-Book* brochure or the bigger laminated map), exchange offices, WCs, and eateries. You'll also find maps of the camp (posted on the walls) and a theater that shows a powerful film. A helpful **information desk**—where you can ask questions, buy tickets for the tour (see "Tours"), and find out about bus schedules for the return trip to Kraków—is halfway down the main entrance hall on the right, in the back corner behind the little tables.

Cost, Hours, Information: Entrance to the camp is free, but donations are gladly accepted. The museum opens every day at 8:00, and closes June–Aug at 19:00, May and Sept at 18:00, April and Oct at 17:00, March and Nov at 16:00, and Dec–Feb at 15:00. Information: tel. 033-844-8100, www.auschwitz.org.pl.

Getting There: For details on getting between Kraków and Auschwitz, see "Transportation Connections" on page 277.

Getting from Auschwitz I to Birkenau: Buses shuttle visitors two miles between the camps nearly hourly (free, hourly mid-May–Oct, leaving Auschwitz I at the bottom of the hour and Birkenau at the top of the hour, times posted at the bus stop outside the main building of each site; Nov–mid-May only 1–4/day to correspond with tours). Taxis are also standing by (about 15 zł). Many visitors, rather than wait for the next bus, decide to walk the 20 minutes between the camps—offering a much-needed chance for reflection. Along the way, you'll pass the Judenrampe, a new exhibit featuring an old train car like the ones used to transport

On the Way to Auschwitz: The Polish Countryside

You'll spend about an hour gazing out the window as you drive or ride to Auschwitz. This may be your only real look at the Polish countryside. Ponder these thoughts about what you're passing...

The small houses you see are traditionally inhabited by three generations at the same time. Nineteenth-century houses (the few that survive) often sport blue stripes. Back then, parents announced that their daughters were now eligible by getting out the blue paint. Once they saw these blue lines, local boys were welcome to come a-courtin'.

Big churches mark small villages. Tiny roadside memorials and crosses indicate places where fatal accidents have occurred.

Polish farmers traditionally had small lots that were notorious for not being very productive. These farmers somewhat miraculously survived the communist era without having to merge their farms. For years, they were Poland's sacred cows: producing little, paying almost no tax, and draining government resources. But since Poland joined the European Union in 2004, they're being forced to get up to snuff...and, in many cases, collectivize their farms after all.

Since most people don't own cars, bikes are common and public transit is excellent. There are lots of bus stops, as well as minibuses that you can flag down anywhere for a 2-zł ride. The bad roads are a legacy of communist construction, exacerbated by heavy truck use and brutal winters.

Poland has more than 2,000 counties, or districts, each with its own coat of arms; you'll pass several along the way. The forests are state-owned, and locals enjoy the right to pick berries in the summer and mushrooms in the autumn (you may see people—often young kids—selling their day's harvest by the side of the road). The mushrooms are dried and then boiled to make tasty soups in the winter.

prisoners, explained by an informational sign.

Film: The 17-minute movie (too graphic for children) was shot by Ukrainian troops days after the Red Army liberated the camp (3.50 zł, buy ticket on arrival; always in English at 10:00, 11:00, 13:00, and 15:00, sometimes more—ask when you arrive).

Photography: Because the philosophy of the camp is to spread the story of Auschwitz, taking photographs of anything outside is encouraged. However, to ease the movement of visitors, photography is not allowed inside the museum buildings.

Eating: There's a café and decent cafeteria (Bar Smak) at the main Auschwitz building. More options are in the commercial complex across the street.

TOURS

Round-trip **tours** from Kraków to Auschwitz take care of transportation for you (see "Tours" in the Kraków chapter, page 212). But with a tour, you pay triple and have to adhere to a strict schedule. The most rewarding way to visit is to go by yourself, take one of the camp's organized tours, and then explore the grounds on your own.

The Auschwitz Museum has a network of excellent guides who are serious and frank, and feel a strong sense of responsibility about sharing the story of the camp. Appropriately, these well-trained guides are more historians than entertainers. The 3.5-hour **English tour** covers Auschwitz, Birkenau, and the film (26 zł, buy ticket halfway down the main entry hall, on the right, in the back corner behind the tables). Most of the year, there are generally at least four English tours scheduled each day. You'll watch the film first, and the actual tour begins 30 minutes later (film at 10:00, 11:00, 13:00, and 15:00; possibly more with demand—as soon as 10 English-speakers gather, ask for a tour; in winter generally at 11:00 and 13:00, maybe also at 15:00). Try to arrive at least 20 minutes ahead, because if the tour's full, you might have to wait until the next one.

You can also hire your own **private official museum guide** for the basic 3.5-hour tour of the camp (210 zł), or for a longer "study tour" (277 zł/4 hrs at Auschwitz I only; 410 zł/6 hrs for Auschwitz I and Birkenau; 534 zł/8 hrs spread over 2 days). This guide service is an exceptional value and worthwhile if you have special interest in the camp. But because English guides are limited, it's essential to reserve as far ahead as possible (fill out the online form at www.auschwitz.org.pl, or call 033-844-8099 or 033-844-8100). Individuals can't reserve a private guide between 10:00 and 14:00, when they're needed for bigger groups.

Local guides from Kraków can drive you to Auschwitz, but—since they're not officially registered museum guides—generally can't show you around the site. In these cases, they will most likely arrange a museum guide for you, or time your visit so you can join the English tour described above. This can still be a good value, as you'll have door-to-door service to the camp—and three hours in the car with a local expert (see "Tours" in the Kraków chapter, page 212).

Visiting without a guide works just fine, given the abundance of English descriptions and the self-guided tour, offered at both camps, described next.

Auschwitz Renovation

In December of 2006, the International Auschwitz Council announced plans to renovate the site over the next several years. The museum at Auschwitz I, widely considered the oldest Holocaust exhibit in the world, has been largely unchanged in the more than 50 years since it opened. Now the museum displays will be modernized, and better organized to accommodate the growing number of visitors. The key elements described in this chapter (such as the displays of human hair, eyeglasses, and suitcases) will still be part of the exhibit, but will likely be spread into more buildings (mostly on the ground floor, to avoid congestion on stairways). At Birkenau, restorers will build retaining walls to prevent the remains of the huge crematoria—key evidence of Nazi crimes—from slowly sinking into the ground.

Because of the renovation, be aware that the information in this chapter (especially the locations of exhibits on the self-guided tour) is subject to change. Ask about recent developments when you arrive at the camp.

SELF-GUIDED TOUR

Auschwitz I

Before World War II, this camp was a base for the Polish army. When Hitler occupied Poland, he took over these barracks and turned it into a concentration camp for his Polish political enemies. The location was ideal, with a nearby rail junction and rivers providing natural protective boundaries. In 1942, Auschwitz became a death camp for the extermination of European Jews and others whom Hitler considered "undesirable." By the time the camp was liberated in 1945, at least 1.1 million people had been murdered here—approximately 960,000 of them Jewish.

As you exit the entry building's back door and go toward the camp, you see the notorious gate with the cruel message, *Arbeit Macht Frei* ("Work Sets You Free"). Note that the B was welded on upside down by belligerent inmates. On their arrival, new prisoners were told the truth: The only way out of the camp was through the crematorium chimneys.

Just inside the gate and to the right, the camp orchestra (made up of prisoners) used to play marches; having the prisoners march

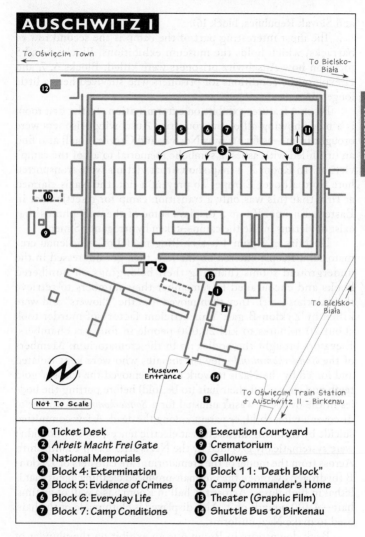

AUSCHWITZ I

To Oświęcim Town ←

To Bielsko-Biała →

⑫

④ ⑤ ⑥ ⑦ ⑪

③ ⑧

⑩

⑨

②

⑬
ℹ
①

To Bielsko-Biała →

Museum Entrance

⑭

Not To Scale

P

To Oświęcim Train Station & Auschwitz II – Birkenau

Auschwitz

① Ticket Desk
② *Arbeit Macht Frei* Gate
③ National Memorials
④ Block 4: Extermination
⑤ Block 5: Evidence of Crimes
⑥ Block 6: Everyday Life
⑦ Block 7: Camp Conditions
⑧ Execution Courtyard
⑨ Crematorium
⑩ Gallows
⑪ Block 11: "Death Block"
⑫ Camp Commander's Home
⑬ Theater (Graphic Film)
⑭ Shuttle Bus to Birkenau

made them easier to count.

The main road leads past the barracks. An average of 14,000 prisoners were kept at this camp at one time. (Birkenau could hold up to 100,000.) The first row of barracks contains the **National Memorials,** created by the home countries of the camps' victims. The most worthwhile are the "Suffering, Struggle, and Destruction of the Jews" exhibit (block 27) and the nearby Roma (Gypsy) exhibit. Most of the other national memorials were created during the communist era, so they have a decidedly socialist spin; some have been updated (including Hungary, block 18, and the Czech and Slovak Republics, block 16).

The most interesting part of the camp is the second row of barracks, which holds the museum exhibitions. Blocks 4 and 5 focus on how Auschwitz prisoners were killed. Blocks 6, 7, and 11 explore the conditions for prisoners who survived here a little longer than most.

Block 4 features exhibits on **extermination.** In the first room is a map showing all of the countries Auschwitz prisoners were brought from—as far away as Norway and Greece. You'll also find an urn filled with ashes, a symbolic memorial to all of the camp's victims. In Room 2, a map shows that victims were transported here from all over Europe. To prevent a riot, the Nazis claimed at first that this was only a transition camp for resettlement in Eastern Europe. Room 3 displays some of the only photos that exist of victims inside the camp—taken by arrogant SS men.

Upstairs in Room 4 is a chilling model of a Birkenau crematorium. People entered on the left, then got undressed in the underground rooms (hanging their belongings on numbered hooks and encouraged to remember their numbers to retrieve their clothes later). They then moved into the "showers" and were killed by Zyklon-B gas. This efficient factory of murder took about 20 minutes to kill 20,000 people in four gas chambers. Elevators brought the bodies up to the crematorium. Members of the *Sonderkommand*—Jewish inmates who were kept isolated and forced by the Nazis to work here—removed the corpses' gold teeth and shaved off their hair (to be sold) before putting the bodies in the ovens. It wasn't unusual for a *Sonderkommand* worker to discover a wife, child, or parent among the dead. A few committed suicide by throwing themselves at electric fences; those who didn't were systematically executed by the Nazis after a two-month shift. Across from the model of the crematorium are canisters of Zyklon-B (hydrogen cyanide), the German-produced cleaning agent that is lethal in high doses. Across the hall in Room 5 is a wall of victims' hair—4,400 pounds of it. Also displayed is cloth made of the hair, used to make Nazi uniforms.

Back downstairs in Room 6 is an exhibit on the plunder of victims' personal belongings. People being transported here were encouraged to bring luggage—and some victims had even paid in advance for houses in their new homeland. After they were killed, everything of value was sorted and stored in warehouses that prisoners named "Canada" (after a country they associated with great wealth). Although the Canada warehouses were destroyed, you can see a few of these items in the next building.

Block 5 focuses on **material evidence** of the crimes that took place here. It consists mostly of piles of the victims' goods, a tiny fraction of everything the Nazis stole. As you wander through the

Chilling Statistics: The Holocaust in Poland

The majority of people murdered by the Nazis during the Holocaust were killed right here in Poland. For centuries, Poland was known for its tolerance of Jews, and right up until the beginning of World War II, Poland had Europe's largest concentration of Jews: 3,500,000. Throughout the Holocaust, the Nazis murdered 4,500,000 Jews in Poland (many of them brought in from other countries) at camps, including Auschwitz, and in ghettos such as Warsaw's.

By the end of the war, only 300,000 Polish Jews had survived—less than 10 percent of the original population. Many of these survivors were granted "one-way passports" (read: deported) to Israel by the communist government in 1968 (following a big student demonstration with a strong Jewish presence). Today, only a few thousand Jews live in all of Poland.

rooms, you'll see eyeglasses; fine Jewish prayer shawls; crutches and prosthetic limbs (the first people the Nazis ever exterminated were mentally and physically ill German citizens); a seemingly endless mountain of shoes; and suitcases with names of victims—many marked *Kind,* or "child." Visitors often wonder if the suitcase with the name "Frank" belonged to Anne, one of the Holocaust's most famous victims. After being discovered in Amsterdam by the Nazis, the Frank family was transported here to Auschwitz, where they were split up. Still, it's unlikely this suitcase was theirs. Anne Frank and her sister Margot were sent to the Bergen-Belsen camp in northern Germany, where they died of typhus shortly before the war ended. Their father, Otto Frank, survived Auschwitz and was found barely alive by the Russians, who liberated the camp in January of 1945.

Although the purpose of Auschwitz was to murder its inmates, not all of them were killed immediately. After an initial evaluation, some prisoners were registered and forced to work. (This did not mean they were chosen to live—but rather to die later.) In Block 6, you see elements of the **everyday life** of prisoners. The halls are lined with photographs of victims. Notice the dates of arrival *(przybył)* and death *(zmarł)*—those who were registered survived here an average of two to three months. (Flowers are poignant reminders that these victims are survived by loved ones.) Room 1 displays drawings of the arrival process—sketched by survivors of the camp. After the initial selection, those chosen to work were showered, shaved, and photographed. After a while, photographing each prisoner got to be too expensive, so prisoners were tattooed instead (see photographs): on the chest, on the arm,

St. Maksymilian Kolbe
(1894–1941)

Among the many inspirational stories of Auschwitz is that of a Polish priest named Maksymilian Kolbe. Before the war, Kolbe traveled as a missionary to Japan, then worked in Poland for a Catholic newspaper. While he was highly regarded for his devotion to the Church, some of his writings had an unsettling anti-Semitic sentiment. But during the Nazi occupation, Kolbe briefly ran an institution that cared for refugees—including Jews.

In 1941, Kolbe was arrested and interned at Auschwitz. When a prisoner from Kolbe's block escaped in July of that year, the Nazis punished the remaining inmates by selecting 10 of them to put in the Starvation Cell until they died—based on the Nazi "doctrine of collective responsibility." After the selection had been made, Kolbe offered to replace a man who expressed concern about who would care for his family. The Nazis agreed. (The man Kolbe saved is said to have survived the Holocaust.)

All 10 of the men—including Kolbe—were put into Starvation Cell 18. Two weeks later, when the door was opened, only Kolbe had survived. The story spread through-out the camp, and Kolbe became an inspiration to the inmates. To squelch the hope he had given the others, Kolbe was executed by lethal injection.

In 1982, Kolbe was canonized by the Catholic Church. Some critics—mindful of his earlier anti-Semitic rhetoric—still consider Kolbe's sainthood controversial. But most Poles feel he redeemed himself for his earlier missteps through this noble act at the end of his life.

or—for children—on the leg. A display shows the symbols that prisoners had to wear to show their reason for internment—Jew, Roma (Gypsy), homosexual, political prisoner, and so on.

Room 4 shows the starvation that took place. The 7,500 survivors that the Red Army found here when the camp was liberated were living skeletons (the healthier ones had been forced to march to Germany). Of those liberated, 20 percent died soon after of disease and starvation. Look for the prisoners' daily ration (in the glass case): a pan of tea or coffee in the morning; thin vegetable soup in the afternoon; and a piece of bread (often made with sawdust or chestnuts) for dinner. This makes it clear that Auschwitz was never intended to be a "work camp," where people were kept alive, healthy, and efficient to do work. Rather, people were meant to die here—if not in the gas chambers, then through malnutrition and overwork.

You can see scenes from the prisoner's workday (sketched by survivors after liberation) in Room 5. Prisoners worked as long as the sun shone—eight hours in winter, up to twelve hours in summer—mostly on farms or in factories. Room 6 is about Auschwitz's child inmates, 20 percent of the camp's victims. Blond, blue-eyed children—like the girl in the bottom row on the right—were either "Germanized" in special schools or, if younger, adopted by German families. Dr. Josef Mengele conducted experiments on children, especially twins and triplets, to try to figure out ways to increase fertility for German mothers.

Block 7 shows **living and sanitary conditions** at the camp—which you'll see in more detail later at Birkenau. Blocks 8–10 are vacant (medical experiments were carried out in Block 10).

Step into the **courtyard** between Blocks 10 and 11. The wall at the far end is where the Nazis shot several thousand political prisoners, leaders of camp resistance, and religious leaders. Notice that the windows are covered, so that nobody could witness the executions. Also take a close look at the memorial—the back of it is made of a material designed by Nazis to catch the bullets without a ricochet. Inmates were shot at short range—about three feet. The pebbles represent prayers from Jewish visitors.

The most feared place among prisoners was the **"Death Block" (#11),** from which nobody ever left alive. In Room 5, you can see how prisoners lived in these barracks—three-level bunks, with three prisoners sleeping in each bed (they had to sleep on their sides so they could fit). Death here required a trial (the room in which sham trials were held—lasting about 2 minutes each—is on display). In Room 6, people undressed before they were executed. In the basement, you'll see several different types of cells. The Starvation Cell (#18) held prisoners selected to starve to death when a fellow prisoner escaped; Maksymilian Kolbe spent two weeks here to save a man's life (see sidebar). In the Dark Cell (#20), which held up to 30, people had only a small window for ventilation—and if it became covered with snow, the prisoners suffocated. At the end of the hall in Cell 21, you can see where a prisoner scratched a crucifix (left) and image of Jesus (right) on the wall. In the Standing Cells (#22), four people would be forced to stand together for hours at a time (of course, the bricks went all the way to the ceiling then). Upstairs is an exhibit on resistance within the camp.

Before you leave Auschwitz, visit the **crematorium** (from Block 11, exit straight ahead and go past the first row of barracks, then turn right and go straight on the road between the two rows of barracks; pass through the gap in the fence and look for the chimney on your left). People undressed outside, or just inside the

Auschwitz

door. Up to 700 people at a time could be gassed here. Inside the door, go into the big room on the right. Look for the vents in the ceiling—this is where the SS men dropped the Zyklon-B. Through the door is a replica of the furnace. This facility could burn 340 bodies a day—so it took two days to burn all of the bodies from one round of executions. The Nazis didn't like this inefficiency, so they built four more huge crematoria at Birkenau.

Shortly after the war, camp commander Rudolf Höss was tried, convicted, and sentenced to death. Survivors requested that he be executed at Auschwitz. In 1947, he was hanged. These gallows are preserved behind the crematorium (about a hundred yards from his home where his wife—who loved her years here—read stories to their children, very likely by the light of a human-skin lampshade).

Take your time with Auschwitz I. When you're ready, continue to the second stage of the camp—Birkenau (see "Getting from Auschwitz I to Birkenau," page 265).

Auschwitz II—Birkenau

In 1941, when the original Auschwitz camp got to be too small for the capacity the Nazis envisioned, they began a second camp in some nearby farm fields. The original plan was for a camp that could hold 200,000 people, but at its peak, Birkenau (Brzezinka) held only about 100,000. They were still adding onto it when the camp was liberated in 1945.

Train tracks lead past the main building and into the camp. The first sight that greeted prisoners was the guard tower (familiar to many visitors from the stirring scenes in *Schindler's List*). Climb to the top of the entry building (also houses WCs and bookstore) for an overview of the massive camp. As you look over the camp, you'll see a vast field of chimneys and a few intact wooden and brick barracks. The train tracks lead straight back to the dividing platform, and then dead-end at the ruins of the crematorium and camp monument at the far side.

Some of the barracks were destroyed by Germans. Most were dismantled to be used for fuel and building materials shortly after the war. But the first row has been reconstructed (using components from the original structures). Visit the barracks on the right.

The first of these barrack buildings was the **latrine:** The front half of the building contained washrooms, and the back was a row of toilets. There was no running water; prisoners were in charge of keeping these clean. Because of the unsanitary conditions, the

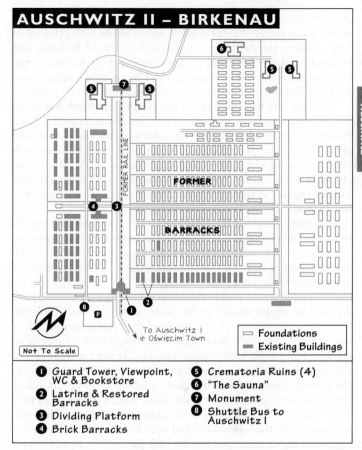

AUSCHWITZ II – BIRKENAU

FORMER RAIL LINE

FORMER

BARRACKS

P

To Auschwitz I
& Oświęcim Town

Not To Scale

☐ Foundations
■ Existing Buildings

1 Guard Tower, Viewpoint, WC & Bookstore
2 Latrine & Restored Barracks
3 Dividing Platform
4 Brick Barracks

5 Crematoria Ruins (4)
6 "The Sauna"
7 Monument
8 Shuttle Bus to Auschwitz I

Auschwitz

Nazis were afraid to come in here—so it was the heart of the black market and the inmates' resistance movement.

The fourth barrack was a **bunk** building. Each inmate had a personal number, a barrack number, and a bed number. Inside, you can see the beds (angled so that more could fit). An average of 400 prisoners—but up to 1,000—would be housed in each of these buildings. These wooden structures, designed as stables by a German company (look for the horse-tying rings on the wall), came in prefab pieces that made them cheap and convenient. Two chimneys connected by a brick duct provided a little heat. The bricks were smoothed by inmates who sat here to catch a bit of warmth.

Follow the train tracks toward the monument about a half-mile away, at the back end of Birkenau. At the intersection of these tracks and the perpendicular gravel road (halfway to the monument) was the gravel **dividing platform.** A Nazi doctor would stand facing the guard tower and evaluate each prisoner. If he pointed to the right, the prisoner was sentenced to death, and trudged—unknowingly—to the gas chamber. If he pointed to the left, the person would be registered and live a little longer. It was here that families from all over Europe were torn apart forever.

On the left-hand side of the tracks are some **brick barracks.** The supervisors lived in the two smaller rooms near the door. Farther in, most barracks still have the wooden bunks that held about 700 people per building. Four or five people slept on each bunk, including the floor—reserved for new arrivals. There were chamber pots at either end of the building. After a Nazi doctor died of typhus, sanitation improved, and these barracks got running water.

As you walk along the camp's only road, which leads along the tracks to the crematorium, imagine the horror of this place—no grass, only mud, and all the barracks packed with people, with smoke blowing in from the busy crematoria. This was an even worse place to die than Auschwitz I.

The train tracks lead to the camp memorial and crematorium. At the end of the tracks, go 50 yards to the left and climb the three concrete steps to view the ruin of the **crematorium.** This is one of four crematoria here at Birkenau, each with a capacity to cremate more than 4,400 people per day. At the far-right end of the ruins, see the stairs where people entered the rooms to undress. People were given numbered lockers, conning them into thinking they were coming back. (The Nazis didn't want a panic.) Then they piled into the "shower room"—the underground passage branching away from the memorial—and were killed. Their bodies were burned in the crematorium (on the left), giving off a scent of sweet almonds (the Zyklon-B). Beyond the remains of the crematorium is a hole—once a gray lake where tons of ashes were dumped. This efficient factory of death was destroyed by the Nazis as the Red Army approached, leaving today's evocative ruins.

With more time, you could continue deeper into the camp—to the reception and disinfection building that prisoners called **"the sauna,"** and to the remains of the other two destroyed **crematoria.**

The Soviets arrived on January 27, 1945, and the nightmare of Auschwitz was over. The Polish parliament voted to turn these grounds into a museum, so that the world would understand, and never forget, the horror of what happened here. The **monument** at the back of the camp, built in 1967 (by the communist government in its heavy "Social Realist" style), represents gravestones and the chimney of a crematorium. The plaques, written in each of the languages spoken by camp victims (including English, far right), explain that the memorial is "a cry of despair and a warning to humanity."

TRANSPORTATION CONNECTIONS

Remember that the Auschwitz Museum is in the town of Oświęcim, about 50 miles west of Kraków.

From Kraków to Auschwitz

The easiest way to reach Auschwitz is with a package tour or private guide (described on page 212). But if you're using public transportation, here are your options:

Frequent **buses** connect Kraków and Auschwitz, mostly run by PKS Oświęcim (7 zł, at least hourly, 1.75 hrs, get the most recent schedule at any Kraków TI, buses depart from Kraków's new bus station behind the train station—see page 210). Buy a one-way ticket from the driver to leave your options open for getting home (described on next page). Note that these buses can be full, and since most come from other towns, there's no way to reserve a seat—so line up early. If you don't get on a bus, you'll have to wait for the next one. Once in the town of Oświęcim, buses from Kraków stop first at the train station, then continue on to one of two stops near the museum: About half of the buses go directly into the parking lot at the museum itself, while the rest use a low-profile bus stop on the edge of the Auschwitz camp grounds (you'll see a small *Muzeum Auschwitz* sign on the right just before the stop, and a blue *Oświęcim Muzeum PKS* sign on the stop itself). From this bus stop, follow the sign down the road and into the parking lot; the main museum building is across the lot on your left. Note that since some buses don't actually go into the museum's parking lot, the Auschwitz stop can be easy to miss—don't be shy about letting your driver know where you want to go: *"Muzeum?"*

Several **minibuses** from Kraków head for Auschwitz (7 zł, 1–2/hr, 1.75 hrs). Like the buses, some go right to the museum, while others use the bus stop at the edge of camp (see above). The departure point in Kraków changes frequently. You'll most likely find the minibuses in two areas near the train station: behind the Galeria Krakowska mall on Ogrodwa street; or from the parking lot behind the bus station. Carefully confirm these locations (which tend to change) at a Kraków TI before you go looking for these minibuses.

You could ride the **train** to Oświęcim, but it's less convenient than the bus because it leaves you at the train station, farther from the museum (8/day, less Sat–Sun, 1.5 hrs, 11 zł).

If you wind up at the Oświęcim **train station,** it's about a 20-minute walk to the camp (turn right out of station, go straight,

then turn left at roundabout, camp is several blocks ahead on left).
Or you can take a taxi (around 15 zł).

Returning from Auschwitz to Kraków

Upon arrival at Auschwitz I, visit the information window inside
the main building (halfway down the main entry hall, on the right,
in the back corner behind the tables). They can give you a schedule
of departures and explain where the bus or minibus leaves from. (If
you'll be staying late into the afternoon, make a point of figuring
out the last possible bus or train back to Kraków, and plan accordingly.) Remember to allow enough time to make it from Birkenau
back to Auschwitz I to catch your bus.

Some buses and minibuses back to Kraków do not leave
from the camp parking lot itself (though some buses do). Instead,
you'll most likely catch the bus from the stop on the edge of the
Auschwitz I grounds. To reach this bus stop, leave the Auschwitz
I building through the main entry and walk straight along the
parking lot, then turn right on the road near the end of the lot.
At the dead end, cross the street to the little bus stop (with a blue
Oświęcim Muzeum PKS sign). Don't be distracted by the ads for
a nearby travel agency—you can buy tickets on board. Note that
there's no public transportation back to Kraków from Birkenau,
where most people end their tours; you'll have to take the shuttle
bus back to Auschwitz I first.

WARSAW

Warszawa

Warsaw (Warszawa, vah-SHAH-vah in Polish) is Poland's capital and biggest city. It's huge, famous, and important...but not particularly romantic. If you're looking for Old World quaintness, head for Kraków. If you're tickled by spires and domes, get to Prague. But if you want to experience a truly 21st-century city, Warsaw's your place.

Stroll down revitalized boulevards that evoke the city's glory days, pausing at an outdoor café to sip coffee and nibble at a *pączki* (the classic Polish jelly doughnut). Commune with the soul of Poland through its artists (at the National Museum), its favorite composer (at the Chopin Museum), its dramatic history (at the Warsaw Historical Museum and Warsaw Uprising Museum), and its Jewish story (in the former Jewish Ghetto). And ponder the wide range of Warsaw's postwar urban architecture, from dreary communist monstrosities to cutting-edge designer shopping malls.

Like Berlin, Warsaw is modernizing—fast. Mindful of its history, yet optimistic about the future, Warsaw has happily emerged from a long hibernation. Varsovians are embracing their role as the capital city of an influential nation in the "New Europe." The European Union has two universities aimed at educating future political leaders (or "Eurocrats"). One is in Bruges, Belgium, just down the road from the EU capital of Brussels. The other one is right here. You can almost feel Warsaw peeling back the layers of communist grime as it replaces pot-holed highways with pedestrian-friendly parks. Today's Warsaw also has gleaming new skyscrapers and street signs, stylishly dressed locals, cutting-edge shopping malls, swarms of international businesspeople, and a gourmet coffee shop on every corner.

Warsaw has good reason to be a city of the future: The past hasn't been very kind. Since becoming Poland's capital in 1596, Warsaw has seen wave after wave of foreign rulers and invasions—especially during the last hundred years. But in this horrific crucible, the enduring spirit of the Polish people was forged. As one proud Varsovian told me, "Warsaw is ugly because its history is so beautiful."

The city's darkest days came during the Nazi occupation of World War II. First, its Jewish residents were forced into a tiny ghetto. They rose up...and were slaughtered. Then, its Polish residents rose up...and were slaughtered. Hitler sent word to systematically demolish this troublesome city. At the war's end, Warsaw was devastated. An estimated 800,000 residents were dead—almost two out of every three Varsovians.

The Poles almost gave up on what was then a pile of rubble to build a brand-new capital city elsewhere. But ultimately they decided to rebuild, creating a city of contrasts: painstakingly restored medieval lanes, crumbling communist apartment blocks (*bloki* in Polish), and sleek, super-modern, glass-and-steel skyscrapers. Between the buildings, you'll find fragments of a complex, sometimes tragic, and often inspiring history.

A product of its complicated past, sprinkled with the big-city style and sophistication of the present, while remaining quintessentially Polish, Warsaw is a place worth grappling with to understand the Poland of today...and the Europe of tomorrow.

Planning Your Time

Warsaw can easily fill two or three days, but for a first visit, one full day is enough for most people. Get your bearings by taking a stroll through Polish history on the Royal Way, using my self-guided walk (see page 286). Then enjoy the Old Town area. Visit other sights according to your interests: Polish artists, Holocaust history, the Warsaw Uprising, Polish royalty, or Chopin. To slow down and take a break from the city, relax in Łazienki Park.

ORIENTATION

(area code: 022)

Warsaw sprawls with 1.7 million residents. Everything is on a big scale—it seems to take forever to walk just a few "short" blocks. Get comfortable with public transportation and plan your sightseeing wisely to avoid backtracking.

Virtually everything of interest to travelers is on a mild hill on the west bank of the Vistula River. The city's Central Train Station (Warszawa Centralna) is in the shadow of its biggest landmark:

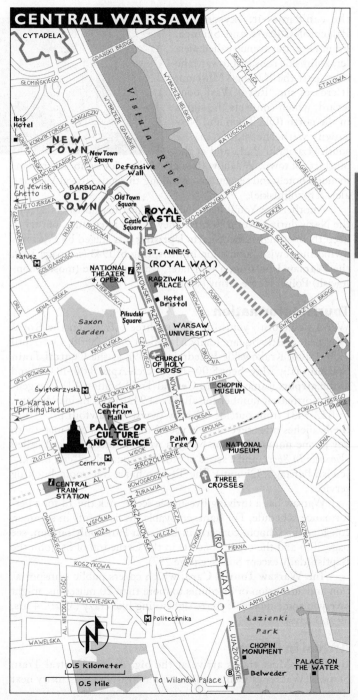

CENTRAL WARSAW

CYTADELA

SŁOMIŃSKIEGO

GDAŃSKI BRIDGE

WYBRZEŻE GDAŃSKIE

Vistula River

SKOCZYLASA

STALOWA

WYBRZEŻE HELSKIE

RATUSZOWA

JAGIELLOŃSKA

KONWIKTORSKA SANGUSZKI

Ibis Hotel

BONIFRATERSKA

NEW TOWN

New Town Square

FRANCISZKAŃSKA

FRETA

Defensive Wall

To Jewish Ghetto

BARBICAN

ŚWIĘTOJERSKA

OLD TOWN

Old Town Square

GEN. ANDERSA

ŚLĄSKO-DĄBROWSKI BRIDGE

OKRZEI

WYBRZEŻE SZCZECIŃSKIE

Castle Square

ROYAL CASTLE

DŁUGA

MIODOWA

Ratusz M

SOLIDARNOŚCI

ST. ANNE'S

(ROYAL WAY)

KAROWA

ŚWIETOKRZYSKI BRIDGE

ORLA

SENATORSKA

NATIONAL THEATER & OPERA

WIERZBOWA

KRAKOWSKIE PRZEDMIEŚCIE

RADZIWIŁŁ PALACE

Hotel Bristol

BEDNARSKA

DOBRA

PTASIA

Saxon Garden

Piłsudski Square

KRÓLEWSKA

WARSAW UNIVERSITY

OBOŻNA

CZACKIEGO

CZĘSTA

GRZYBOWSKA

CHURCH OF HOLY CROSS

NOWY

ŚWIAT

TAMKA

Świętokrzyska M

ŚWIĘTOKRZYSKA

CHOPIN MUSEUM

To Warsaw Uprising Museum

Galeria Centrum Mall

FOKSAL

PONIATOWSKIEGO BRIDGE

CHMIELNA

PALACE OF CULTURE AND SCIENCE

SMOLNA

Palm Tree

ZŁOTA

E. PLATER

Centrum M

WIDOK

JEROZOLIMSKIE

NATIONAL MUSEUM

LUDNA

CENTRAL TRAIN STATION

AL.

NOWOGRODZKA

THREE CROSSES

CHAŁUBIŃSKIEGO

ŻURAWIA

MARSZAŁKOWSKA

WSPÓLNA

KRUCZA

ROZBRAT

HOŻA

WILCZA

POKORNA

(ROYAL WAY)

PIĘKNA

KOSZYKOWA

NOWOWIEJSKA

AL. ARMII LUDOWEJ

WAWELSKA

AL. NIEPODLEG ŁOŚCI

Politechnika M

Łazienki Park

N

CHOPIN MONUMENT

AL. UJAZDOWSKIE

PALACE ON THE WATER

0.5 Kilometer

0.5 Mile

Belweder

(B)

To Wilanów Palace

Warsaw

Warsaw

the can't-miss-it, skyscraping
Palace of Culture and Science.
From here, the avenue called aleja
Jerozolimskie runs east toward the
river, past the National Museum.
It crosses the "Royal Way" boulevard, which connects the sights
in the north (Old Town and New
Town) with the sights in the
south (Łazienki Park, and at the
outskirts of town, Wilanów Palace). Most major sights and recommended hotels and restaurants are along this axis (Royal Way and
aleja Jerozolimskie).

Another tip: You'll hear about two distinct uprisings against
the Nazis during World War II. They're easy to confuse, but try to
keep them straight: the **Ghetto Uprising** was staged by Warsaw's
dwindling Jewish population in the spring of 1943 (see page 306);
the **Warsaw Uprising,** a year later, was led by the (mostly non-
Jewish) Polish Home Army (see page 310).

Tourist Information

Warsaw's helpful, youthful TI has three offices: on the **Royal
Way** near Castle Square (daily May–Sept 9:00–20:00, Oct–April
9:00–18:00, Krakowskie Przedmieście 39), at the **Central Train
Station** (daily May–Sept 8:00–20:00, Oct–April 8:00–18:00), and
at the **airport** (same hours as Central Train Station TI). The general information number for all TIs is 9431 from inside Warsaw,
or 022-9431 from outside Warsaw (www.warsawtour.pl). All of
the branches offer several free, useful materials: a city map (with
key phone numbers on the back), a well-produced booklet called
Warsaw: In Short, and a series of brochures on sights ("city breaks,"
Jewish heritage, Chopin). The TI also has a free room-booking
service.

Warsaw has a thriving live-music scene. Ask the TI for a performance schedule. For light, enjoyable music events in summer,
consider the Chopin concerts in Łazienki Park (only on Sun, see
page 305) and the organ concerts in the Cathedral of St. John the
Baptist (daily except Sun, see page 297).

The **Warsaw Tourist Card,** which covers public transportation and admission or discounts to more than 20 museums, might
save you some money if you're sightseeing like crazy (35 zł/24 hrs,
65 zł/3 days).

Arrival in Warsaw

By Train: Most trains arrive at the big, dreary Central Train
Station (Warszawa Centralna), a communist-era monstrosity next

Warsaw Essentials

English	Polish	Pronounced
Warsaw	Warszawa	vah-SHAH-vah
Central Train Station	Warszawa Centralna	vah-SHAH-vah tsehn-TRAHL-nah
Palace of Culture and Science	Pałac Kultury i Nauki (or simply "Pałac")	PAH-wahts nah-OO-kee
New Town	Nowe Miasto	NOH-vay mee-AH-stoh
Old Town	Stare Miasto	STAH-reh mee-AH-stoh
Old Town Market Square	Rynek Starego Miasta	REE-nehk stah-RAY-goh mee-AH-stah
Royal Way	Szłak Królewski	shwock kroh-LEHV-skee
Popular restaurant street on Royal Way	Nowy Świat	NOH-vee SHVEE-aht
Attraction-lined street on Royal Way	Krakowskie Przedmieście	krah-KOHV-skyeh pzhehd-MYESH-cheh
Royal Castle	Zamek Królewski	ZAH-mehk kroh-LEHV-skee
Castle Square	Plac Zamkowy	plahts zahm-KOH-vee
Piłsudski Square	Plac Marszałka Józefa Piłsudskiego	plahts mar-SHAW-kah yoh-ZEH-fah pew-sood-SKYAY-goh
Łazienki Park	Park Łazienkowski	park wah-zhehn-KOV-skee
Vistula River	Wisła	VEES-wah

to the Palace of Culture and Science. You'll emerge from your platform *(peron)* into a labyrinth of passageways—made even more confusing because each platform has several exits. **Lockers** are in this underground level; find the long passage beyond and parallel to *peron* 4 (look for *przechowalnia bagażu*).

To get your bearings, head to the **main arrival hall** (follow signs to *Hala Główna*). Lining one wall of this hall are **ticket**

windows, some of which are designated for international tickets *(kasa międzynarodowa)*. A rail service center is in the corner (under the big, orange *Apteka Non Stop* sign). If the lines at the main hall ticket windows are way too long, you can find more ticket windows in the maze of corridors under the station. Allow yourself plenty of time to wait in line to buy tickets. Some locals bypass these lines altogether and buy their tickets on the train for an extra charge (about 7 zł extra). Train info: tel. 9436, or 022-9436 from outside Warsaw.

From the station, **bus #175** takes you to the Royal Way and Old Town in about 10 minutes (see "Getting Around Warsaw"). You can catch this bus—and others going in the same direction—in front of the skyscraper with the LOT airlines office and Hotel Marriott across busy aleja Jerozolimskie from the station. Follow signs to exit at *Al. Jerozolimskie*. (The easiest way across this street is via a pedestrian underpass—follow *Hotel Marriott* signs.)

Taxis wait outside the main hall (many are crooked—look for one with a company logo and telephone number, and ask for an estimate up front; the fare should be about 15–20 zł for most of my recommended hotels).

By Car: Warsaw is a stressful city to drive and park in. Arrange parking with your hotel, and get around by foot or public transit. You must pay to park in the city Mon–Fri 8:00–18:00. Park your car (likely on a sidewalk), find the parking pay station, and insert coins until the proper amount of time appears in the left-hand window (about 2 zł/hr). Press the green button, wait for your ticket, and put it on your dashboard. Sometimes public parking areas are monitored by "attendants"—unemployed creeps who kindly help you find a spot, then ask if you want them to "watch your car" for you. Try to avoid parking where you see these crooks, but if you do, 1–2 zł is a small investment to prevent the car from being damaged.

By Plane: Warsaw's **Fryderyk Chopin International Airport** (Port Lotniczy im. Fryderyk Chopina) is about six miles southwest of the center. The two main terminals are next to each other: Terminal 1 and the new Terminal 2 (which handles most arrivals for both terminals). A third terminal, called Etiuda, is used by discount airlines. At the airport, you'll find a TI, ATMs, and exchange offices *(kantor)*. From any terminal, bus #175 runs into the center (Central Train Station, Royal Way, and Old Town; tickets sold for 2.40 zł at kiosk, or 3 zł from driver, 4–6/hr, fewer Sat–Sun, 30–45 min). The 30-minute taxi ride to the center shouldn't cost you more than 40 zł (though hucksters who approach you offering a ride may try to charge you astronomical rates—ask for an estimate, and if it's more than 40 zł, ask the next guy). The trip into town can take much longer during rush hour, because only one main thoroughfare connects the airport to the center. Airport info: tel. 022-650-4100, www.lotnisko-chopina.pl.

Getting Around Warsaw

By Public Transit: In this big city, it's essential to get a handle on public transportation. Ignore the Metro (which is useless to most tourists), but take advantage of the buses and trams. All three systems use the same tickets. A single ticket costs 2.40 zł (called *bilet jednorazowy*, good for one trip, no transfers); a one-day ticket costs 7.20 zł (*bilet dobowy*, good for 24 hours); and a three-day ticket is 12 zł (*bilet trzydniowy*). Buy your ticket at any kiosk with a *RUCH* sign, and be sure to validate it as you board by inserting it in the little yellow box (24-hour and 3-day tickets need only be validated the first time you ride). While you can usually buy the basic one-ride tickets from your bus or tram driver for an extra 0.60 zł, it isn't always possible, so it's best to buy a ticket before boarding.

Most of the city's major attractions line up on a single axis, the Royal Way, which is served by several different buses (but no trams). The designed-for-tourists **bus #180** conveniently connects virtually all of the significant sights and neighborhoods: the former Jewish Ghetto, Castle Square/Old Town, the Royal Way, Łazienki Park, and Wilanów Palace (south of the center). This particularly user-friendly bus lists sights in English on the posted schedule inside (other buses don't). **Bus #175** links the airport, the Central Train Station, the Royal Way, and Old Town. Those two buses, as well as buses #116, #122, #195, and #503, go along the most interesting stretch of the Royal Way (between aleja Jerozolimskie and Castle Square in the Old Town). Bus routes beginning with "E" are express, so they go long distances without stopping.

Note that on Saturdays and Sundays in summer (June–Oct), the Nowy Świat section of the Royal Way is closed to buses, so the above buses detour along a parallel street.

By Taxi: As in most big Eastern European cities, it's wise to use only cabs that are clearly marked with a company logo and telephone number (or call your own: Locals like MPT Radio Taxi, tel. 9191; or Elle taxi, tel. 022-811-1111). All official taxis have similar rates: 6 zł to start, then 2–3 zł per kilometer (more after 22:00 or in the suburbs). The drop fee may be higher if you catch the cab in front of a big, fancy hotel.

TOURS

Each year, new companies crop up offering **walking tours** in Warsaw. As none is well-established yet, get the latest advice from the TI. Various companies offer **bus tours** (which include some walking; short version-40 zł/1.5 hrs; long version-120–140 zł/3–4.5 hrs; get information at TI). A **tourist train** does a 30-minute circuit, leaving from in front of the Royal Castle (20 zł, daily May–Oct, doesn't run Mon Nov–April).

SELF-GUIDED WALK

▲▲Warsaw's Royal Way

The Royal Way (Szłak Królewski) is the six-mile route that the kings of Poland used to take from their main residence (at Castle Square in the Old Town) to their summer home (Wilanów Palace, south of the center and not worth visiting). In the heart of the city, the Royal Way is a busy boulevard with two different names: hip and vibrant **Nowy Świat** (at the south end), which offers lots of shops and restaurants, and a good glimpse of urban Warsaw; and **Krakowskie Przedmieście** (at the north end, ending at the Old Town), lined with historic landmarks and better for sightseeing.

Since this spine connects most hotels, restaurants, and sights, you'll almost certainly use it—on foot or by bus—sometime during your trip (key buses are noted under "Getting Around Warsaw," above). This self-guided walk should make your commute more interesting. Not counting sightseeing stops, figure about 10 minutes to walk along Nowy Świat ("Part 1"), then another 20 minutes along Krakowskie Przedmieście to the Old Town ("Part 2").

Royal Way Walk Part 1: Nowy Świat

Begin at the head of the boulevard called Nowy Świat, at the intersection with busy **aleja Jerozolimskie** ("Jerusalem Avenue"). This street once led to a Jewish settlement called New Jerusalem. Like so much else in Warsaw, it's changed names many times. Between the World Wars, it became "May 3rd Avenue," celebrating Poland's 1791 constitution (Europe's first). But this was too nationalistic for the occupying Nazis, who called it simply Bahnhofstrasse ("Train Station Street"). Then the communists switched it back to "Jerusalem"—strangely disregarding the religious connotations of that name. (Come on, guys—what about a good, old-fashioned "Stalin Avenue"?)

You can't miss the giant, out-of-place **palm tree** in the middle of aleja Jerozolimskie. When a local artist went to the real Jerusalem, she was struck at how many palm trees she saw there. She decided it was only appropriate that one should grace Warsaw's own little stretch of "Jerusalem." This model palm tree—with a trunk from France and leaves from California, where theme parks abound with such fake trees—went up a few years ago as a temporary installation. It was highly controversial, dividing the neighborhood. One snowy

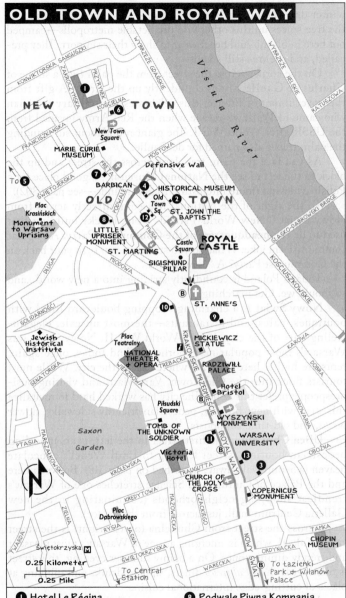

OLD TOWN AND ROYAL WAY

Warsaw

① Hotel Le Régina
② Old Town Apts. Office
③ Hotel Harenda
④ Duval Apartments
⑤ To Ibis Warszawa Stare Miasto
⑥ Dom Przy Rynku Hostel
⑦ Restauracja pod Samsonem
⑧ Podwale Piwna Kompania
⑨ Pierogarnia na Bednarskiej
⑩ Siedem Grzechów Restaurant
⑪ BrowArmia Brewpub
⑫ U Fukiera & Gessler Restaurants
⑬ Uniwersytecky Milk Bar

winter day, the pro–palm tree faction—who appreciate the way the tree spices up this otherwise predictable metropolis—camped out here in bikinis and beachwear to show their support. They prevailed, and the tree still stands.

On the corner across the street from the palm tree, a statue of **Charles de Gaulle** strides confidently up the street. A gift from the government of France, this celebrates the military tactician who came to Warsaw's rescue when the Red Army invaded from the USSR after World War I. The giant roundabout surrounding the palm tree is also named for de Gaulle.

As you face the palm tree, look across the street and up the block to the left to see the **National Museum**—a good place for a Polish art lesson (more interesting than it sounds—see page 302).

To the right of the National Museum, directly across from Nowy Świat ("New World") stands a big, blocky building that used to be the **headquarters of the Communist Party.** A popular communist-era joke: What do you see when you turn your back on the Communist Party? A "New World."

Today's Poland is confidently striding into a new world...and so should we. Get marching.

Nowy Świat is a charming shopping boulevard lined with boutiques, cafés, and restaurants—the most upscale, elegant-feeling part of the city. Before World War II, Nowy Świat was Warsaw's most popular neighborhood. And today, once again, rents are higher here than anywhere else in the city. While most tourists flock into the Old Town, Varsovians and visiting businesspeople prefer this zone. The city has worked hard to revitalize this strip with new, broader, pedestrian-friendly sidewalks, flower boxes, and old-time lampposts.

Ulica Chmielna, the first street to the left, is an appealing pedestrian boutique street leading to Emil Wedel's chocolate heaven (a 5-min walk away; described on page 318). Between here and the Palace of Culture and Science stretches one of Warsaw's trendiest shopping neighborhoods (culminating in the new Galleria Centrum mall, just across from the Palace).

Across the street from Chmielna (on the right) is the street called **Foksal,** which is emerging as one of Warsaw's most pleasant and trendy dining zones. On a balmy summer evening, this street is filled with chatty *al fresco* diners, sipping drinks and nibbling at plates of cutting-edge international cuisine.

A few steps down Nowy Świat, on the left, don't miss the **A. Blikle** pastry shop and café—*the* place in Poland to buy sweets, especially *pączki* (rose-flavored jelly doughnuts—for more on this popular spot, see page 317.) If you're homesick for Starbucks, drop into one of the many gourmet coffee shops that line this stretch of Nowy Świat—with American-style lattes "to go."

The next three blocks are more of the same. Eat and shop your way up Nowy Świat, until you reach the big Copernicus statue.

Royal Way Walk Part 2: Krakowskie Przedmieście

The street name changes to Krakowskie Przedmieście (roughly translated as "Suburb in the Direction of Kraków") at the big

 statue of **Copernicus,** in front of the Polish Academy of Science. Mikołaj Kopernik (1473–1543) was born in Toruń (see page 377) and went to college in Kraków. The Nazis stole this statue and took it to Germany (which, like Poland, claims Copernicus as its own). Now it's back where it belongs. Nearby, find the Canaletto painting of this same street scene in 1778, and compare it to today's reality. (It looks similar because paintings like this were used to rebuild the city after World War II.)

We'll pass many churches along this route, but the **Church of the Holy Cross** is unique (Kościół Św. Krzyża, across from Copernicus, free entry). Composer Fryderyk Chopin's heart is inside one of the pillars of the nave (second big pillar on the left, look for the marker). After two decades of exile in France, Chopin's final wish was to have his heart brought back to his native Poland. During World War II, the heart was hidden away in the countryside for safety. Chopin's organs aside, this church feels more alive than most. Locals often drop in. Check out the bright gold chapel, located on the left as you face the altar, near the front of the church. It's dedicated to a saint whom Polish Catholics believe helps them with "desperate and hopeless causes." People praying here are likely dealing with some tough issues. The beads draped from the altarpieces help power their prayers, and the many little brass plaques are messages of thanks for prayers answered. In the back-right corner (as you face the altar), behind the giant barbed wire, is a memorial to the 20,000 Polish POWs—mostly officers and prominent civilians—massacred by Soviet soldiers in 1940 near Katyń, a village in today's Russia.

Leave the church and cross the street (appreciating how pedestrian-friendly it's become in recent years). At #20, look for the Uniwersytecky Bar, a classic **milk bar** *(bar mleczny)*—a government-subsidized cafeteria filled with students and anyone who wants a bargain (for more about milk bars, see page 199).

Cheap grub is a reliable indicator that you're entering the university district. Sure enough, about a block up the street on the right, you'll see the gates (marked *Uniwersytet*) to the main campus of **Warsaw University,** founded in 1816. This area is a lively student district with plenty of bookstores and cafés.

The 18th century was a time of great political decline for Poland, as a series of incompetent foreign kings mishandled crises and squandered funds. But ironically, it was also Warsaw's biggest economic boom time. Along this boulevard, aristocratic families of the period built **mansions**—most of them destroyed during World War II and rebuilt since, some with curious flourishes. (Just past the university on the right, look for the doorway supported by four bearded brutes admiring their overly defined abs.) Over time, many of these families donated their mansions to the university.

The yellow church a block up from the university is the Church of the Nuns of the Visitation (Kościół Sióstr Wizytek). The monument in front commemorates **Cardinal Stefan Wyszyński,** who was the Polish primate (the head of the Polish Catholic Church) from 1948 to 1981. He took this post soon after the arrival of the communists, who opposed the Church, but also realized it would be risky for them to shut down the churches in such an ardently religious country. The Communist Party and the Catholic Church coexisted tensely in Poland, and when Wyszyński protested a Stalinist crackdown in 1953, he was arrested and imprisoned. Three years later, in a major victory for the Church, Wyszyński was released. He continued to fight the communists, becoming a great hero of the Polish people in their struggle against the regime.

Farther up, you'll see the elegant, venerable **Hotel Bristol.** Leave the Royal Way briefly here to reach Piłsudski Square (a block away on the left, up the street opposite Hotel Bristol).

The vast, empty-feeling **Piłsudski Square** (Plac Marszałka Józefa Piłsudskiego) has been important Warsaw real estate for centuries, constantly changing with the times. In the 1890s, the Russians who controlled this part of Poland began construction of a huge and magnificent Orthodox cathedral on this spot. But soon after it was completed, Poland regained its independence, and anti-Russian sentiments ran hot. So in the 1920s, just over a decade after the cathedral went up, it was torn down again. During the Nazi occupation, this square took the name "Adolf-Hitler-Platz." Under the communists, it was Zwycięstwa, meaning "Victory" (of the Soviets over Hitler's fascism). When the regime imposed martial law in 1981, the people of Warsaw silently protested by filling the square with a giant cross made of flowers. The huge plaque in the ground near the road commemorates two monumental communist-era Catholic events on this square: John Paul II's first visit as pope to his homeland on June 2, 1979, and the funeral on May 31, 1981, of Cardinal Stefan Wyszyński, whom we met across the street.

Stand near this giant plaque, with the Royal Way at your

back, for this quick spin-tour orientation: Ahead are the Tomb of the Unknown Soldier and Saxon Garden (explained below); to the right is the old National Theater, eclipsed by a modern business center/parking garage; 90 degrees to the right is a statue of Piłsudski (which you passed to get here—described below); and 90 more degrees to the right—past the big gray Polish Ministry of Defense building—is the Victoria Hotel, the ultimate plush, top-of-the-top hotel where all communist-era VIPs stayed. To the right of the hotel, on the horizon, you can see Warsaw's newly emerging skyline. The imposing Palace of Culture and Science, which once stood alone over the city, is being joined by a cluster of brand-new skyscrapers, giving Warsaw a Berlin-esque vibe befitting its important role as a business center of the "New Europe."

Walk to the fragment of colonnade by the park that marks the **Tomb of the Unknown Soldier** (Grób Nieznanego Żołnierza). The colonnade was once part of a much larger palace built by the Saxon prince electors (Dresden's Augustus the Strong and his son), who became kings of Poland in the 18th century. After the palace was destroyed in World War II, this fragment was kept to memorialize Polish soldiers. The names of key battles are etched into the columns, the urns contain dirt from major Polish battlefields, and the two soldiers are pretty stiff.

Just behind the Tomb is the stately **Saxon Garden** (Ogród Saski), inhabited by genteel statues and a spurting fountain. This park was also built by the Saxon kings of Poland. Like most foreign kings, Augustus the Strong and his son cared little for their Polish territory, building gardens like these for themselves instead of investing in more pressing needs. Poles say that foreign kings such as Augustus did nothing but "eat, drink, and loosen their belts" (it rhymes in Polish). According to Poles, these selfish absentee kings are the culprits for Poland's eventual decline.

Walk back out toward the Royal Way, stopping at the statue you passed earlier. In 1995, the square was again renamed—this time for **Józef Piłsudski** (1867–1935), the guy with the big walrus moustache. With the help of the French General de Gaulle (whom we met earlier), Piłsudski forced the Russian Bolsheviks out of Poland in 1920 in the so-called Miracle on the Vistula. Piłsudski is credited with creating a once-again-independent Poland after over a century of foreign oppression, and he essentially ran Poland after World War I. Of course, under the communists, Piłsudski was swept under the rug, but today he's enjoying a renaissance as Poland's favorite prototype anti-communist hero (his name adorns streets, squares, and bushy-mustachioed monuments all over the country).

Return to Hotel Bristol, turn left, and continue your Royal Way walk. Next door to the hotel, you'll see the huge **Radziwiłł Palace.**

Warsaw at a Glance

▲▲**Old Town Market Square** Re-creation of Warsaw's glory days, with lots of colorful architecture. **Hours:** Always open. See page 297.

▲▲**National Museum** Collection of mostly Polish art, with unknown but worth-discovering works by Jan Matejko and the Młoda Polska (Art Nouveau) crew. **Hours:** Tue–Thu 10:00–16:00, Fri 10:00–20:00, Sat–Sun 10:00–17:00, closed Mon. See page 302.

▲**Castle Square** Colorful spot with whiffs of old Warsaw—Royal Castle (next), monuments, and a chunk of the city wall, with cafés just off the square. **Hours:** Always open. See page 294.

▲**Royal Castle** Warsaw's best palace, rebuilt after World War II, but stocked with original furnishings (hidden during the war). **Hours:** Tour hours vary with season: May–Sept Mon 11:00–16:00, Tue–Sun 10:00–18:00; Oct–April Tue–Sat 10:00–16:00, Sun 11:00–16:00, closed Mon; permanent exhibition closed on Sun year-round and closed Mon in winter. See page 295.

▲**Chopin Museum** Elegant old mansion with Chopin bric-a-brac and occasional piano concerts. **Hours:** May–Sept Mon, Wed, and Fri 10:00–17:00, Thu 12:00–18:00, Sat–Sun 10:00–14:00, closed Tue; Oct–April Mon–Wed and Fri–Sat 10:00–14:00, Thu 12:00–18:00, closed Sun. See page 304.

The Warsaw Pact was signed here in 1955, officially uniting the Soviet satellite states in a military alliance against NATO. This building also serves as the Polish "White House," with the offices of Poland's figurehead president, Lech Kaczyński. For more on Kaczyński—and his identical twin brother Jarosław—see "The Kaczyński Brothers: Those Two Who Would Lead Poland" on page 197.

Beyond Radziwiłł Palace, you'll reach a statue (on a pillar) of **Adam Mickiewicz,** Poland's national poet. Polish high school students have a big formal ball (like a prom) 100 days before graduation. After the ball, if students come here and hop around the statue on one leg, it's supposed to bring them good luck on their finals. Mickiewicz, for his part, looks like he's suffering from a heart attack—perhaps in response to the impressively ugly National Theater and Opera a block in front of him.

Continue to the end of the Royal Way, marked by the big pink palace. For a scenic finale to your Royal Way stroll, climb the 150 steps of the view tower by **St. Anne's Church** (3 zł, sporadic hours but generally open daily 10:00–18:00, until 20:00 or 21:00 in

▲**Łazienki Park** Lovely, sprawling green space with Chopin statue, peacocks, and Neoclassical buildings. **Hours:** Always open. See page 305.

▲**Warsaw Uprising Museum** High-tech exhibit tracing the history of the Uprising and celebrating its heroes. **Hours:** Mon, Wed, and Fri 8:00–18:00, Thu 8:00–20:00, Sat–Sun 10:00–18:00, closed Tue. See page 309.

Warsaw Historical Museum Glimpse of the city before and after World War II, with excellent movie in English. **Hours:** Museum—Tue and Thu 11:00–18:00, Wed and Fri 10:00–15:30, until 18:00 mid-July–Sept, Sat–Sun 10:30–16:30, closed Mon, also closed one Sat–Sun a month; Movie—Tue–Sun at noon. See page 298.

Palace of Culture and Science Huge "Stalin Gothic" skyscraper with a more impressive exterior than interior, housing theaters, multiplex cinema, observation deck, and more. **Hours:** Observation deck—daily June–Sept 9:00–20:00, Fri–Sat until 23:45; Oct–May 9:00–18:00. See page 300.

Jewish Ghetto: Path of Remembrance Pilgrimage from Ghetto Heroes Square to the infamous Nazi "transfer spot" where Jews were sent to death camps. **Hours:** Always open. See page 308.

summer, on the right just before Castle Square). You'll be rewarded with a great view of the Old Town, river, and Warsaw's skyline.

From St. Anne's Church, it's just another block—past inviting art galleries and restaurants—to the Castle Square, the TI, and the start of the Old Town.

SIGHTS

The Old Town

In 1945, not a building remained standing in Warsaw's "Old" Town (Stare Miasto). Everything you see is rebuilt, mostly finished by 1956. Some think the Old Town feels artificial and phony, in a Disney World kind of way. For others, the painstaking postwar reconstruction just feels right, with Old World squares and lanes charming enough to give Kraków a run for its money. Before 1989, stifled by communist repression and choking on smog, the Old Town was an empty husk of its historic self. But now, the outdoor restaurants and market stalls have returned, and the locals and tourists are out strolling.

These sights are listed in order from south to north, beginning at the Castle Square and ending at the entrance to the New Town. For the best route from the Central Train Station to the Old Town, see the "Royal Way" self-guided walk, above.

▲**Castle Square (Plac Zamkowy)**—This lively square is dominated by the big, pink Royal Castle, the historic heart of Warsaw's political power.

After the second great Polish dynasty—the Jagiellonians—died off in 1572, the Republic of Nobles (about 10 percent of the population) elected various foreign kings to their throne. The guy on the 72-foot-tall **pillar** is Sigismund III, the first Polish king from the Swedish Waza family. In 1596, he relocated the capital from Kraków to Warsaw. This move made sense, since Warsaw was closer to the center of 16th-century Poland (which had expanded to the east), and because the city had been gaining political importance as the meeting point of the Sejm, or parliament of nobles, over the preceding 30 years. Along the right side of the castle, notice the two previous versions of this pillar lying on a lawn. The first one, from 1644, was falling apart and had to be replaced in 1887 by a new one made of granite. In 1944, a Nazi tank broke this second pillar—a symbolic piece of Polish heritage—into the four pieces (still pockmarked with bullet holes) that you see here today. As Poland rebuilt, its citizens put Sigismund III back on his pillar.

Across the square from the castle, you'll see the partially reconstructed defensive wall. This rampart once enclosed the entire Old Town. Situated at the crossroads of Eastern Europe, Warsaw—like all of Poland—has seen invasion from all sides.

Explore the café-lined lanes that branch downhill off Castle Square. Street signs indicate the year that each street was originally built.

The first street leading off the square is **ulica Piwna** ("Beer Street"), where you'll find **St. Martin's Church** (Kościół Św. Martina, on the left). Run by Franciscan nuns, this church has a simple, modern interior. Notice the partly destroyed crucifix—all that survived World War II. Across the street and closer to Castle Square, admire the carefully carved doorway of Restauracja pod Gołębiami ("Under Doves")—dedicated to the memory of an old woman who fed birds amidst the Old Town rubble after World War II.

Back on the Castle Square, find the white **plaque** in the

middle of the second block (by plac Zamkowy 15/19). It explains that 50 Poles were executed by Nazis on this spot on September 2, 1944. You'll see plaques like this all over the Old Town, each one commemorating victims or opponents of the Nazis. The brick planter under the plaque is often filled with fresh flowers to honor the victims.

▲**Royal Castle (Zamek Królewski)**—There has been a castle here since the Mazovian dukes built a wooden version in the 14th century. It has shifted shape with the tenor of the times, being rebuilt and remodeled by many different kings. When Warsaw became the capital in 1596, this massive building was used both as the king's residence and as the meeting place of the parliament (Sejm). After it was destroyed in World War II, rebuilding began again in the 1950s and was not completed until the 1970s.

Of all of Warsaw's many castles, this one is most interesting to tour—which isn't saying much. While the exterior is entirely

reconstructed, many of the furnishings are original (hidden away when it became clear the city would be demolished). Each room is well described in English.

The castle makes a great Polish history textbook. In fact, you'll likely see grade-school classes sitting cross-legged on the floors. Watching the teachers quizzing eager young history buffs, you can only imagine what it's like to be a young Pole, with such a tumultuous recent history.

Warning: The castle opening times, tour routes, and even the castle layout are maddeningly unpredictable. Things frequently change, depending on special events, temporary exhibitions, the direction the wind is blowing, and the inexplicable whims of palace administrators.

Touring the Castle: The castle has various parts, each with separate tickets. For a basic visit, you'll choose between two completely different tour routes: **Route I,** which is unguided and available only at the top of each hour (12 zł); or **Route II,** which includes a mandatory tour with a Polish-speaking guide (20 zł, tour departs about every 10 min). Route I, which includes the Senators' Chamber and the Matejko rooms, is the better option. Castle entry is free one day a week (Mondays in summer, Sundays in winter), with a "greatest hits" tour combining both routes.

Tour hours change with the season: May–Sept (Route I—Tue–Sun 10:00–16:00; Route II—Tue–Sat 10:00–18:00, Sun 11:00–18:00; on Mon "greatest hits" route free and open 11:00–16:00) and Oct–April (Route I and II open Tue–Sat 10:00–16:00, closed Mon;

on Sun "greatest hits" route free and open 11:00–16:00). The last entry for either route is one hour before closing.

There's also an often-closed **permanent exhibition** that includes decorative arts (17th and 18th centuries), a porcelain gallery, a coin collection, some paintings (including a pair of Rembrandts), and various exhibits of interest only to Polish historians (10 zł, possibly Tue–Sat 10:00–16:00, likely closed Mon in winter and Sun year-round). Rounding out the attractions is a series of temporary exhibitions. The palace is at Plac Zamkowy 4 (tel. 022-355-5170, www.zamek-krolewski.com.pl). A public WC is on the courtyard just around the corner of the castle.

Route I Highlights: The **Parliament Chambers** are a reminder that this "castle" wasn't just the king's house, but also the meeting place of the legislature. The grand **Senators' Chamber,** with the king's throne, is surrounded by different coats of arms. Each one represents a region that was part of Poland during its Golden Age, back when it was united with Lithuania and its territory stretched from the Baltic to the Black Sea. In this room, Poland adopted its 1791 constitution. It was the first in Europe, written soon after America's and just months before France's. And, like the Constitution of the United States, it was very progressive, based on the ideals of the Enlightenment. But when the final partitions followed in 1793 and 1795, Poland was divided between neighboring powers and disappeared from the map until 1918—so the constitution was never really put into action. The next room features paintings by **Jan Matejko** that capture the excitement surrounding the adoption of this ill-fated constitution (for more on Matejko, see page 302).

Route II Highlights: You'll see two different types of royal apartments: public state rooms and private chambers. In the **Throne Room,** note the crowned eagle, the symbol of Poland, decorating the banner behind the throne. The Soviets didn't allow anything royal or aristocratic, so postwar restorations came with crown-less eagles. Only after 1989 were the crowns replaced (in the case of this banner, sewn on). A few rooms later is the **Canaletto Room,** filled with canvases of late-18th-century Warsaw painted in exquisite detail by this talented artist. These paintings came in handy when the city needed to be rebuilt. (This Canaletto, also known for his panoramas of Dresden, was the nephew of another artist with the same nickname, famous for painting Venice's canals.) Continue wandering through the sumptuous halls, saying hello to US Constitution co-signer Ben Franklin (by the door in the Green Room) and gaping at the Marble Room (with portraits of Polish kings around the ceiling—find your favorite).

• *After you finish touring the castle and you're ready to resume exploring the Old Town, turn left at the end of the square onto...*

St. John's Street (Świętojańska)—On the plaque under the street name sign, you can guess what the dates mean, even if you don't know Polish: This building was constructed 1433–1478, destroyed in 1944, and rebuilt 1950–1953.

• *Partway down the street on the right, you'll come to the big brick...*

Cathedral of St. John the Baptist (Katedra Św. Jana Chrzciciela)—This cathedral-basilica is the oldest (1339) and most important church in Warsaw. Poland's constitution was consecrated here on May 3, 1791. Much later, this church became the final battleground of the 1944 Warsaw Uprising—when a Nazi tank (appropriately named *Goliath*) drove into the church and intentionally exploded, massacring the rebels. You can still see part of that tank's tread hanging on the outside wall of the church (through the passage on the right side, near the end of the church).

Despite the church's historical significance, its interior is pretty dull (free, open to tourists daily 10:00–13:00 & 15:00–17:30, closed during services). Typical of brick churches, it has a "hall church" design, with three naves of equal height. Look for the crucifix ornamented with real human hair (chapel left of high altar). The high altar holds a copy of the Black Madonna—proclaimed "everlasting queen of Poland" after a victory over the Swedes in the 17th century. The original Black Madonna is in Częstochowa (125 miles south of Warsaw)—a mecca for Slavic Catholics, who visit in droves in hopes of a miracle.

The cathedral also hosts organ **concerts** in summer (8 zł, May–mid-Sept Mon–Sat at 12:00, 25 min, no concerts Sun or mid-Sept–April).

• *Continue up the street and enter Warsaw's grand...*

▲▲**Old Town Market Square (Rynek Starego Miasta)**—Seventy years ago, this was one of the most happening spots in Central Europe. Sixty years ago, it was rubble. And today, like a phoenix from the ashes, it reminds residents and tourists alike of the prewar glory of the Polish capital.

Go to the **mermaid fountain** in the middle of the square. The mermaid is an important symbol in Warsaw—you'll see her everywhere. Legend has it that a mermaid *(syrenka)* lived in the Vistula River and protected the townspeople. While this siren supposedly serenaded the town, Varsovians like her more for her strength (hence the sword). In fact, the woman who modeled for this sculpture, Krystyna Krahelska (code name: "Danuta"), served as a paramedic for the Polish Home Army during the Warsaw Uprising. On the second day of the fighting, she was shot in the chest and died, becoming a martyr for the Polish people.

Each of the square's four sides is named for a prominent 18th-century Varsovian: Kołłątaj, Dekert, Barss, and Zakrzewski. These men served as "Presidents" of Warsaw (more or less the mayor), and Kołłątaj was also a framer of Poland's 1791 constitution. Take some time to explore the square. Enjoy the colorful architecture. Notice that many of the buildings were intentionally built to lean out into the square—to simulate the higgledy-piggledy wear and tear of the original buildings.

• On the Dekert (north) side of the square is the...

Warsaw Historical Museum (Muzeum Historyczne Warszawy)—This labyrinthine museum rambles through several reconstructed buildings fronting the Old Town Market Square. With limited descriptions in English, the museum is difficult to appreciate. You'll twist your way through room after room of historical bric-a-brac. The exhibits near the end—photos of the Old Town before and immediately after its WWII destruction—are the most interesting (6 zł, free entry on Sun but must pay 6 zł for optional but recommended movie, open Tue and Thu 11:00–18:00, Wed and Fri 10:00–15:30—until 18:00 mid-July–Sept, Sat–Sun 10:30–16:30, closed Mon, also closed one Sat–Sun a month, last entry 45 min before closing, Rynek Starego Miasta 28/42, tel. 022-635-1625).

The museum's saving grace is its excellent 20-minute **film** in English, worth ▲▲ and the price of admission alone; unfortunately, it runs only at 12:00. With somber narration and black-and-white scenes from before, during, and after the wartime devastation, this film is best appreciated after you've had a chance to see some of today's Warsaw (especially along the Royal Way). The movie ends with, "They say that there are no miracles. Then what is this city on the Vistula?" Emotionally drained, you can only respond, "Amen."

• Leave the square on Nowomiejska (at the mermaid's 2 o'clock, by the second-story niche sculpture of St. Anne). After a block, you'll reach the...

Barbican (Barbakan)—This defensive gate of the Old Town, similar to Kraków's, protected the medieval city from invaders. Just outside the gate, you may be accosted by a pair of village idiots, dressed as **medieval executioners.** These unemployed (but undeniably creative) punks, in a sort of aggressive, costumed panhandling, will steer you to their "executioner's block" and playfully threaten to liberate your head from your body until you give them some pocket change. Actually, these guys speak English, and if you talk to them, they'll explain that at least two buildings within the Old Town actually were used for executions once upon a time.

• Once you've crossed through the Barbican and have been granted a stay *of execution, you're officially in Warsaw's...*

New Town (Nowe Miasto)—This 15th-century neighborhood is "new" in name only: It was the first part of Warsaw to spring up outside of the city walls (and therefore slightly newer than the Old Town). The New Town is a fun place to wander: Only a little less charming than the Old Town, but with a more real-life feel—like people live and work here. It also has some good Polish restaurants that are cheaper than the Old Town options (see "Eating," page 315). Its centerpiece is the **New Town Square** (Rynek Nowego Miasta), watched over by the distinctive green dome of St. Kazimierz Church.

Scientists might want to pay homage at the museum for Warsaw native **Marie Skłodowska-Curie** (at her birthplace, ulica Freta 16; overpriced at 8 zł, Tue 8:30–16:00, Wed–Fri 9:30–16:00, Sat 10:00–16:00, Sun 10:00–15:00, closed Mon). This Nobel Prize winner was the world's first radiologist—discovering both radium and polonium (named for her native land) with her husband, Pierre Curie. Since she lived at a time when Warsaw was controlled by oppressive Russia, she conducted her studies in France. The museum—with photos, furniture, artifacts, and a paucity of English information—is a bit of a snoozer, best left to true fans.

From the New Town to Castle Square: You can backtrack the way you came, or, to get a look at Warsaw's back streets, consider this route from the big, round Barbican gate (where the New Town meets the Old): Go back through the Barbican and over the little bridge, turn right, and walk along the houses that line the inside of the wall. You'll pass a leafy garden courtyard on the left—a reminder that people actually live in the tourist zone within the Old Town walls. Just beyond the garden on the right, look for the carpet-beating rack, used to clean rugs (these are common fixtures in people's backyards). Go left into the square called Szeroki Dunaj ("Wide Danube") and look for another mermaid (over the Thai restaurant). Continue through the square and turn right at Wąski Dunaj ("Narrow Danube"). After about 100 yards, you pass the city wall. Just to the right (outside the wall), you'll see the monument to the **Little Upriser** of 1944, an imp wearing a grown-up's helmet and too-big boots, and carrying a machine gun. Children—and especially Scouts (Harcerze)—played a key role in the resistance against the Nazis. Their job was mainly carrying messages and propaganda.

Now continue around the wall (the upper, inner part is more pleasant)—admiring more public art—back to Castle Square.

Near Nowy Świat and the Central Train Station

These sights are near Nowy Świat, within a few blocks of the Central Train Station.

NEAR WARSAW'S CENTRAL TRAIN STATION

Palace of Culture and Science (Pałac Kultury i Nauki, or PKiN)

—This massive skyscraper, dating from the early 1950s, is Poland's tallest building (760 feet). It was a "gift" from Stalin that the people of Warsaw couldn't refuse. Varsovians call it "Stalin's Penis"...using cruder terminology than that. (There were seven such "Stalin Gothic" erections in Moscow.) Because it was to be "Soviet in substance, Polish in style," Soviet architects toured Poland to absorb local culture before starting the project. Notice the frilly decorative friezes that top each level—evocative of Poland's many Renaissance buildings (such as Kraków's Cloth Hall). The clock was added in 1999 as part of the millennium celebrations. Since the end of communism, the younger generation doesn't mind the structure so much—and some even admit to liking it for the way it enlivens the new, predictable, glass-and-steel

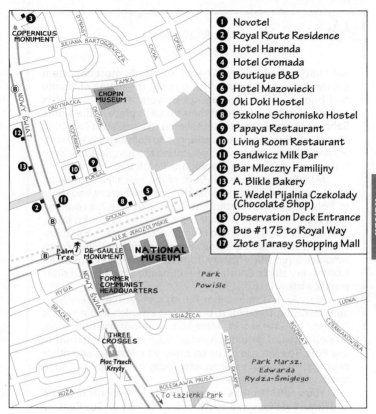

Map legend:

1. Novotel
2. Royal Route Residence
3. Hotel Harenda
4. Hotel Gromada
5. Boutique B&B
6. Hotel Mazowiecki
7. Oki Doki Hostel
8. Szkolne Schronisko Hostel
9. Papaya Restaurant
10. Living Room Restaurant
11. Sandwicz Milk Bar
12. Bar Mleczny Familijny
13. A. Blikle Bakery
14. E. Wedel Pijalnia Czekolady (Chocolate Shop)
15. Observation Deck Entrance
16. Bus #175 to Royal Way
17. Złote Tarasy Shopping Mall

skyline springing up around it.

Everything about the Pałac is big. It's designed to show off the strong, grand-scale Soviet aesthetic and architectural skill. The Pałac contains various theaters (the Culture), museums of evolution and technology (the Science), a congress hall, a multiplex (showing current movies), an observation deck, and lots of office space. With all of this Culture and Science under one roof, it's a shame that none of it makes for worthwhile sightseeing. While the interior is highly skippable, viewing the building from the outside is a quintessential Warsaw experience, worth ▲▲.

If you're killing time between trains, you could zip up to the observation deck in 20 seconds on the retrofitted Soviet elevators. Better yet, snap a photo from down below and save your money—it's overpriced and the view's a letdown. While you'll get a nice overview of Warsaw's forest of new skyscrapers, you can hardly see the Old Town, and Warsaw's most prominent big building—the Pałac itself—is missing (20 zł, includes Polish-oriented special exhibitions; daily June–Sept 9:00–20:00, Fri–Sat 20:00–23:45

Jan Matejko
(1838–1893)

Jan Matejko (yawn mah-TAY-koh) is Poland's most important painter, period. In the late 19th century, the nation of Poland had been dissolved by foreign powers, and Polish artists struggled to make sense of their people's place in the world. Rabble-rousing Romanticism seemed to have failed (inspiring many brutally suppressed uprisings), so Polish artists and writers turned their attention to educating the people about their history, with the goal of keeping the Polish traditions alive.

Matejko was at the forefront of this so-called "positivist" movement. Matejko saw what the tides of history had done to Poland, and was determined to make sure his countrymen learned from it. He painted two types of works: huge, grand-scale epics depicting monumental events in Polish history; and small, intimate portraits of prominent Poles. Polish schoolchildren study history from books with paintings of virtually every single Polish king—all painted by the incredibly prolific Matejko.

Matejko is admired not for his technical mastery (he's an unexceptional painter), but for the emotion behind—and inspired by—his works. Matejko's paintings are utilitarian, straightforward, and dramatic enough to stir the patriot in any Pole. The intense focus on history by Matejko and other positivists is one big reason why today's Poles are still so in touch with their heritage.

You'll see Matejko's works in Warsaw's National Museum and Royal Castle, as well as in Kraków's Gallery of 19th-Century Polish Art (above the Cloth Hall). You can also visit his former residence in Kraków.

for 5 zł more; Oct–May 9:00–18:00, enter through main door on east side of Pałac—opposite from train station, tel. 022-656-7600, www.pkin.pl).

Złote Tarasy Shopping Mall—Tucked behind the train station, "Golden Terraces" is a new, super-modern shopping mall with a funky, undulating glass-and-steel roof. Even though you didn't come all the way to Poland to visit a shopping mall, it's worth detouring here to get a taste of Poland's race into the future. In many ways, this—and not humble farmers munching pierogi—is the face of today's Poland (Mon–Sat 10:00–22:00, Sun 10:00–20:00, lots of designer shops, good food court on top level, www.zlotetarasy.pl).

▲▲National Museum (Muzeum Narodowe)—This museum, while short on big-name pieces, interests art-lovers and offers a good, accessible introduction to some talented Polish artists unknown outside their home country.

Cost, Hours, Location: 12 zł, more for temporary exhibits, permanent collection free on Sat, open Tue–Thu 10:00–16:00, Fri 10:00–20:00, Sat–Sun 10:00–17:00, closed Mon, last entry 45 min before closing, 1 block east of Nowy Świat at aleja Jerozolimskie 3, tel. 022-629-3093, www.mnw.art.pl.

◆ Self-Guided Tour: On the ground floor are exhibits of ancient art (from Egyptian and Greek pieces to works by early Polish tribes), as well as room upon room of medieval altarpieces and crucifixes (including some of the most graphic I've seen). The upper floors have temporary exhibits and collections of Polish and European decorative arts and European paintings. But the reason we're here is the Gallery of Polish Painting, one floor up. Focus on the two most important eras, at opposite ends of the building.

First, find the **Jan Matejko** room. From the lobby, take the left staircase up one level, then walk along the railing and go in the door on the left. Bear right through this door, then walk to the very back of this wing, where Matejko hides (if you can't find him, ask the guards, "mah-TAY-koh?"). On the way, you'll pass through a whole room of Napoleon portraits. The Poles loved Napoleon, who bravely marched on Russia in an era when this part of Poland was occupied and oppressed by the Russians... sadly, not for the last time.

The Matejko room is dominated by the enormous *Battle of Grunwald*. This epic painting commemorates one of Poland's high-water marks—the dramatic victory of a Polish-Lithuanian army over the Teutonic Knights, who had been terrorizing northern Poland for decades (for more on the Teutonic Knights, see page 370). On July 15, 1410, some 40,000 Poles and Lithuanians (led by the sword-waving Lithuanian in red, Grand Duke Vytautas) faced off against 27,000 Teutonic Knights (under their Grand Master, in white) in one of the medieval world's bloodiest battles. Matejko plops us right in the thick of the battle's chaos, painting life-size figures and framing off a 32-foot-long slice of the actual two-mile battle line.

In the center of the painting, the Teutonic Grand Master is about to become a shish kebab. Duke Vytautas, in red, leads the final charge. And waaaay up on a hill (in the upper right-hand corner, on horseback, wearing a silver knight's suit) is Władysław Jagiełło, the first king of the Jagiellonian dynasty...ensuring his bloodline will survive another 150 years.

Matejko spent three years covering this 450-square-foot canvas in paint. The canvas was specially made in a single seamless piece. At the unveiling, this was such a popular work that there were almost as many fans as there are figures in the painting.

From Poland's high point in the *Battle of Grunwald*, turn to the canvas immediately to the left, *Stańczyk after the Loss of Smolensk,* to see how Poland's fortunes shifted drastically a century later. This smaller, more intimate portrait by Matejko depicts a popular Polish figure: the court jester Stańczyk, who's smarter than the king, but not allowed to say so. This complex character, representing the national conscience, is a favorite symbol of Matejko's. Stańczyk slumps in gloom. He's just read the news (on the table beside him) that the city of Smolensk has fallen to the Russians after a three-year siege (1512–1514). The jester had tried to warn the king to send more troops, but the king was too busy partying (behind the curtain). The painter Matejko—who may have used his own features for Stańczyk's face—also blamed the nobles of his own day for fiddling while Poland was partitioned.

Other Matejko paintings include one depicting the tragic couple of the last Jagiellonian king, Stanisław August Poniatowski (here identified as Sigismund Augustus), and his wife, Barbara—whom the king loved deeply, even though she couldn't bear him an heir. (In the next room, see the painful end to their sad tale: Barbara on her deathbed.)

Next, take a look at the **Młoda Polska** ("Young Poland") collection, featuring paintings from Poland's version of Art Nouveau (see page 219). It's in the same position on the opposite side of the building: From the lobby, take the right staircase up, then go in the right-hand door, bear left, and work around all the way to the back. In addition to a room of works by movement headliner Stanisław Wyspiański, you'll see the hypnotic *Strange Garden* by Wyspiański's friend and rival, Józef Mehoffer. In the next room are several paintings by Jacek Malczewski, many of them depicting the goateed, close-cropped artist in a semi-surrealistic, Polish countryside contexts. There's also a room of canvases by the only prominent female Polish painter, Olga Boznańska (past the Wyspiański room)—with a softer and more impressionistic touch than her male Młoda Polska counterparts.

▲**Chopin Museum (Muzeum Fryderyka Chopina)**—The reconstructed Ostrogski Castle houses this modest museum honoring Poland's most famous composer. Everything of interest is upstairs: manuscripts, letters, and original handwritten compositions. You'll also see Chopin's last piano, which he used for composing during the final two years of his life (1848–1849). Nearby, flip through the guest book. Chopin's music is popular in Japan, and Japanese music-lovers flock here, almost as a pilgrimage. In the next room, find Chopin's bronze death mask and admire his distinctively Polish nose, shaped like an eagle's beak (10 zł; May–Sept Mon, Wed, and Fri 10:00–17:00, Thu 12:00–18:00, Sat–Sun 10:00–14:00, closed Tue; Oct–April Mon–Wed and Fri–Sat 10:00–14:00, Thu 12:00–18:00, closed Sun; 3 blocks east of Nowy Świat at ulica

Okólnik 1, tel. 022-827-5473).

The top floor has a **concert hall,** open only for special concerts. If you're in town for one, go. There's nothing like hearing Chopin's music fill this fine mansion, passionately played by a teary-eyed Pole who really feels the music (call museum to ask for concert schedule).

The **Ostrogski Castle** was destroyed down to the brick cellar in World War II. A plaque by the staircase around back notes that it was "voluntarily reconstructed" by the communists in 1970 "to celebrate the 25th anniversary of the People's Republic of Poland." In the courtyard behind is a statue of a golden duck *(złota kaczka)*, a mythical creature that supposedly lived in the castle's cellar. An often-repeated but strangely anticlimactic parable explains that this duck gave a cobbler's apprentice a huge amount of money, telling him that if he frittered it away by the end of the day, he'd win great rewards. The boy gave some to a beggar, which didn't fit the duck's idea of "frittering"—but the boy found happiness anyway.

Chopin's tourable birth house is in **Żelazowa Wola,** 34 miles from Warsaw. On weekends in summer, a bus leaves from in front of the Chopin Museum to go to Żelazowa Wola and back (23 zł round-trip, departs Sat at 10:30, Sun at 13:30, 2.5 hours at Żelazowa Wola before returning). While interesting to Chopin devotees, it's not worth the trek for most (house open May–Sept Tue–Sun 9:30–17:30, Oct–April Tue–Sun 10:00–16:00, always closed Mon).

South of the Center

▲**Łazienki Park (Park Łazienkowski)**—This huge, idyllic park is where Varsovians go to play. The park is sprinkled with fun Neoclassical buildings, strutting peacocks, and young Poles in love. It was built by Poland's very last king (before the final partition), Stanisław August Poniatowski, to serve as his summer residence and provide a place for his citizens to relax.

On the edge of the park (along Belwederska) is a **monument to Fryderyk Chopin.** The monument, in a rose garden, is flanked by platforms, where free summer piano **concerts** are given weekly

(mid-May–mid-Sept only, generally Sun at 12:00 and 16:00—confirm at TI). The statue shows Chopin sitting under a windblown willow tree. While he spent his last 20 years and wrote most of his best-known music in France, his inspiration came from wind blowing through the willow trees of his native land, Poland. The

Warsaw's Jews and the Ghetto Uprising

From the Middle Ages until World War II, Poland was a safe haven for Europe's Jews. While other kings were imprisoning and deporting Jews in the 14th century, the progressive king Kazimierz the Great welcomed Jews into Poland, even granting them special privileges (see page 217).

By the 1930s, there were more than 380,000 Jews in Warsaw—nearly a third of the population (and the largest concentration of Jews in the world). The Nazis arrived in 1939. Within a year, they had pushed all of Warsaw's Jews into one neighborhood and surrounded it with a wall, creating a miserably overcrowded ghetto (crammed full of half a million people, including many from nearby towns). Over the next year, the Nazis brought in more Jews from throughout Poland, and the number grew by a million.

By the summer of 1942, more than a quarter of the Jews in the ghetto had already died of disease, murder, or suicide. The Nazis started moving Warsaw's Jews (at the rate of 5,000 a day) into what they claimed were "resettlement camps." Most of these people were actually murdered at Treblinka or Auschwitz. After hundreds of thousands of Jews had been taken away, the waning population—now about 60,000—began to get word from concentration camp escapees about what was actually going

Nazis melted the original statue (from 1926) down for its metal. Today's copy was recast after World War II. Savor this spot; it's great in summer, with roses wildly in bloom, and in autumn, when the trees provide a golden backdrop for the black, romantic statue.

Venture to the center of the park, where (after a 10-min hike) you'll find King Poniatowski's striking **Palace on the Water** (Pałac na Wodzie)—literally built in the middle of a river. Nearby, you'll spot a clever amphitheater with seating on the riverbank and the stage on an island. The king was a real man of the Enlightenment, hosting weekly dinners here for artists and intellectuals. But Poland's kings are long gone, and proud peacocks now rule this roost.

Getting There: The park is just south of the city center on the Royal Way. Buses #116, #180, and #195 run from Castle Square in the Old Town along the Royal Way directly to the park (get off at the stop called Łazienki Królewskie, by Belweder Palace—you'll see Chopin squinting through the trees on your left). Maps at park entrances locate the Chopin monument, Palace on the Water, and other park attractions.

on there. Spurred by this knowledge, Warsaw's surviving Jews staged a dramatic uprising.

On April 19, 1943, the Jews attacked Nazi strongholds and had some initial success—but within a month, the Nazis crushed the Ghetto Uprising. The ghetto's residents and structures were "liquidated." About 300 of Warsaw's Jews survived, thanks in part to a sort of "underground railroad" of courageous Varsovians.

Warsaw's Jewish sights are moving, but even more so if you know some of their stories. You may have heard of **Władysław Szpilman,** a Jewish concert pianist who survived the war with the help of Jews, Poles, and even a Nazi officer. Szpilman's life story was turned into the highly acclaimed, Oscar-winning 2002 film *The Pianist,* which powerfully depicts events in Warsaw during World War II.

Less familiar to non-Poles—but equally affecting—is the story of Henryk Goldszmit, better known by his pen name, **Janusz Korczak.** Korczak wrote imaginative children's books that are still enormously popular among Poles. He worked at an orphanage in the Warsaw ghetto. When his orphans were sent off to concentration camps, the Nazis offered the famous author a chance at freedom. Korczak turned them down, and chose to die at Treblinka with his children.

Jewish Warsaw

After centuries of living peacefully in Poland, Warsaw's Jews suffered terribly at the hands of the Nazis (see sidebar, above). You can visit several sights in Warsaw that commemorate those who were murdered, and those who fought back. Because the Nazis leveled the ghetto, there is literally nothing left except the street plan, some monuments, and the heroic spirit of its former residents.

Ghetto Walking Tour—For a quick walking tour of the former ghetto site, begin at **Ghetto Heroes Square** (plac Bohaterow Getta). To get here from the Old Town you can hop a taxi (10 zł), take a bus (to Nalewki stop, bus #180 is particularly useful), or walk (go through Barbican gate two blocks into New Town, turn left on Świętojerska, and walk straight 10 min—passing the new green-glass Supreme Court building—until you reach a grassy park on Zamenhofa Street). The square is in the heart of what was the Jewish ghetto—now surrounded by bland Soviet-style apartment blocks. After the Uprising, the entire ghetto was reduced to dust by the Nazis—leaving the communists to rebuild to their own specifications. The district is called Muranów ("Rebuilt") today.

The **monument** in the middle of the square commemorates those who fought and died, "for the dignity and freedom of the

Jewish Nation, for a free Poland, and for the liberation of humankind." The big park across the street is the future site of the Museum of the History of Polish Jews. This project has been in the works for years. Officials have agreed on a design, but it will likely be a while before the museum is complete (for the latest, see www.jewishmuseum .org.pl).

Facing the monument, head left (with the park on your left) up Zamenhofa—which, like many streets in this neighborhood, is named for a hero of the Ghetto Uprising. From the monument, you'll follow a series of three-foot-tall black stone monuments to Uprising heroes—the **Path of Remembrance.** Like Stations of the Cross, each recounts an event of the uprising. Every April 19th (the day the Uprising began), huge crowds follow this path. In a block, at the corner of Miła (partly obscured by some bushes), you'll find a **bunker** where organizers of the Uprising hid out (and where they committed suicide when the Nazis discovered them on May 8, 1943).

Continue following the black stone monuments up Zamenhofa (which becomes Dubois), then turn left at the corner and, later on that same block, cross busy Stawki street. A long block up Stawki and on the right, you'll see the **Umschlagplatz** monument—shaped like a cattle car. That's German for "transfer place," and it marks the spot where the Nazis brought Jewish families to prepare them to be loaded onto trains bound for Treblinka or Auschwitz (a harrowing scene vividly depicted in *The Pianist*). In the walls of the monument are inscribed the first names of some of the victims.

Jewish Historical Institute of Poland (Żydowski Instytut Historyczny)—For more in-depth information about Warsaw's Jewish community, including the Ghetto Uprising, visit this museum housed in the former Jewish Library building. The main floor displays well-described old photos. The 37-minute movie about life and death in the ghetto—played in English upon request—is graphic and powerful. Upstairs, you'll find more on Jewish art, culture, and temporary exhibits (10 zł, Mon–Wed and Fri 9:00–16:00, Thu 11:00–18:00, closed Sat–Sun, last entry 1 hour before closing, just north of Saxon Garden at ulica Tłomackie 3/5, tel. 022-827-9221, www.jewishinstitute.org.pl).

The Peugeot building next door—appropriately dubbed "the blue tower" by locals—was built on the former site of Warsaw's biggest synagogue, destroyed by the Nazis as a victorious final kick.

The Warsaw Uprising

While the 1944 Warsaw Uprising (see sidebar on page 310) is a recurring theme in virtually all Warsaw sightseeing, two sights in particular—one a monument, the other a museum—are worth a visit for anyone with a special interest. Neither is right on the main tourist trail; the monument is closer to the sightseeing action, while the museum is a tram or taxi ride away.

Warsaw Uprising Monument—The most central sight relating to the Warsaw Uprising is the monument at plac Krasińskich (intersection of ulica Długa and Miodowa, a few blocks northwest of the New Town). Larger-than-life soldiers and civilians race for the sewers in a desperate attempt to flee the Nazis. Just behind the monument is the rusting copper facade of Poland's Supreme Court.

▲Warsaw Uprising Museum (Muzeum Powstania Warszawskiego)—This new museum opened on August 1, 2004—the 60th anniversary of the Warsaw Uprising. Thorough, well-presented, and packed with Polish field-trip groups, the museum celebrates the heroes of the Uprising. The location is inconvenient (a 10-min tram ride west of Central Train Station), and probably not worth the trip for those with a casual interest. But for history buffs, it's Warsaw's single best museum.

Cost and Hours: 4 zł, Mon, Wed, and Fri 8:00–18:00, Thu 8:00–20:00, Sat–Sun 10:00–18:00, closed Tue, last entry 30 min before closing, tel. 022-539-7901, www.1944.pl.

Getting There: It's on the west edge of downtown at ulica Przyokopowa 28. Take tram #24 from near the Central Train Station (from the underground passageways, follow signs for *Ochota* to find the tram tracks), or from across the street from the National Museum (near the start of Nowy Świat). Get off at the stop called Muzeum Powstania Warszawskiego, cross the tracks and the busy street, walk straight one short block up Grzybowska, and take a left on Przyokopowa. The museum is the big, red-brick building on the left. You can also get to the museum by taking bus #105 (meet it across the street from the Central Train Station—in front of the Palace of Culture and Science; get off at the Rondo Daszyńskiego stop); or, from the Old Town, by hopping on tram #32 (down the stairs between St. Anne's Church and the Royal Castle).

➲Self-Guided Tour: The museum has several parts. The beautifully restored 1905 red-brick building, once an electrical plant, houses the permanent exhibition. The more recent gray addition behind it displays temporary exhibitions. And the park stretching around the back of the complex also has some moving sights. Buy your ticket at the little house on the left (marked *kasa*), then head into the main hall.

Warsaw

The Warsaw Uprising

By the summer of 1944, it was becoming clear that the Nazis' days in Warsaw were numbered. The Red Army drew near, and by late July, Soviet tanks were within 25 miles of downtown Warsaw.

The Varsovians could have simply waited for the Soviets to cross the river and force the Nazis out. But they knew that Soviet "liberation" would also mean an end to Polish independence. The Polish Home Army numbered 400,000—30,000 of them in Warsaw alone—and was the biggest underground army in military history. The uprisers wanted Poland to control its own fate, and they took matters into their own hands. The resistance's symbol was an anchor made up of a P atop a W (which stands for *Polska Walcząca*, or "Poland Fighting"—you'll see this icon all around town). Over time, the Home Army had established an extensive network of underground tunnels and sewers, which allowed them to deliver messages and move around the city without drawing the Nazis' attention. These tunnels gave the Home Army the element of surprise.

On August 1, 30,000 Polish resistance fighters launched an attack on their Nazi oppressors. They poured out of the sewers and caught the Nazis off guard, initially having great success.

But the Nazis regrouped quickly, and within a few days, they had retaken several areas of the city—murdering tens of thousands of innocent civilians as they went. In one notorious incident, some 5,500 Polish soldiers and 6,000 civilians who were surrounded by Nazis in the Old Town were forced to flee through the sewers; many drowned or were shot. (This scene is depicted in the Warsaw Uprising Monument on plac Krasińskich—see page 309.)

Just two months after it had started, the Warsaw Uprising was over. The Home Army called a cease-fire. About 18,000 Polish uprisers had been killed, along with nearly 200,000 innocent civilians. An infuriated Hitler ordered that the city be destroyed—which it was, systematically, block by block, until virtually nothing remained.

Through all of this, the Soviets stood still, watched, and waited. When the smoke cleared and the Nazis left, the Red Army marched in and claimed the wasteland that was once called Warsaw. After the war, General Dwight D. Eisenhower said that the scale of destruction here was the worst he'd ever seen.

Depending on whom you talk to, the desperate uprising of Warsaw was incredibly brave, stupid, or both. As for the Poles, they remain fiercely proud of their struggle for freedom. The city of Warsaw has recently commemorated this act of bravery with the new Warsaw Uprising Museum.

The high-tech **main exhibit** sprawls through three floors. It chronologically tells the story of the Uprising, with a keen focus on military history. While it's easy to get turned around, look for directional signs and don't be afraid to explore. Everything is well-described in English; also look for the printed pages of English information. The ground floor focuses on Germany's invasion and occupation of Poland. Then you'll take the elevator up to the top floor (signed 2), which features exhibits on the Uprising itself. After walking through a simulated sewer—reminiscent of the one that many Home Army soldiers and civilians used to evade the Germans—you'll head downstairs into an exhibit on the Uprising's aftermath. A chilling section describes how Warsaw became a "city of graves," with burial mounds and makeshift crosses scattered everywhere. Occupying the center of the main hall are two large-scale exhibits: a replica of an RAF Liberator B-24 J, used for airborne surveillance of wartime Warsaw; and a giant movie screen showing fascinating newsreels assembled by the Home Army's own propaganda unit during the Uprising. Under the screen, behind the black curtains, is yet another exhibit, this one about life in Nazi-occupied Warsaw (with another, more claustrophobic walk-through sewer).

The **park** features several thought-provoking sights. Around the right side are several monuments, with photographs along the side wall showing the history of the museum building. Along the back is the Wall of Memory, a Vietnam Wall–type monument to soldiers of the Polish Home Army who were killed in action. You'll see their rank and name, followed by their codename, in quotes. The Home Army observed a strict policy of anonymity, forbidding members from calling each other anything but their codenames. The bell in the middle is dedicated to the commander of the uprising, Antoni Chruściel (codename "Monter"). Near the ticket-selling house, look for the reconstructed German bunker, used by the Nazis during the occupation.

The museum also has an observation deck (in the temporary exhibits building) and a café with drinks and light snacks, decorated in pre-war Warsaw style.

SLEEPING

The accommodations scene in central Warsaw is difficult, with an abundance of overpriced business hotels and cheap hostel-type accommodations, but little in between. Desk clerks do their best to reinforce the communist-era stereotype of grouchy, incompetent service. Thankfully, there are a few happy exceptions—such as Boutique B&B and Duval Apartments, easily the best options in Warsaw. Since this is a convention town, prices can go up during

Sleep Code

(3 zł = about $1, country code: 48)
S = Single, **D** = Double/Twin, **T** = Triple, **Q** = Quad, **b** = bathroom,
s = shower only. Unless otherwise noted, English is spoken,
breakfast is included, and credit cards are accepted.

To help you sort easily through these listings, I've divided
the rooms into three categories, based on the price for a standard double room with bath:

$$$ **Higher Priced**—Most rooms 400 zł or more.
  $$ **Moderately Priced**—Most rooms between
                                  300–400 zł.
   $ **Lower Priced**—Most rooms 300 zł or less.

convention times and way down on weekends. For locations, see
the maps on pages 287 and 300.

$$$ Hotel Le Régina is a tempting splurge buried in the
quiet and charming New Town (just beyond the Old Town). From
its elegant public spaces to its 61 top-notch rooms, everything here
is done with class. Choose between plenty nice "standard rooms,"
or pay an extra 200 zł for bigger "superior" rooms, with hand-
painted frescoes over each bed. While the rack rates are sky-high
(standard Db-1,200 zł, superior Db-1,400 zł), you'll often find far
better deals on their website (for a standard room in summer figure
Db-550–650 zł on weekdays, Db-400–500 zł on weekends, prices
change constantly in summer—check online for latest deals, more
expensive during winter convention season, prices don't include tax
or optional 100-zł breakfast, pricier suites, elevator, non-smoking
floor, free Wi-Fi, gym, pool, Kościelna 12, tel. 022-531-6000,
www.leregina.com, info@leregina.com).

$$$ Novotel, with 733 rooms across the street from the
Palace of Culture and Science, overlooks Poland's busiest intersec-
tion. Recently renovated inside and out, this is a good option for a
big, business-class, downtown hotel (official rate is Sb/Db-550 zł,
but in slow times—especially weekends—you may pay 300–450
zł, best deals are online, optional breakfast-60 zł, non-smoking
rooms, elevator, pay Internet access and Wi-Fi, Marszałkowska
94/98, tel. 022-621-0271, fax 022-625-0476, www.orbis.pl, nov
.warszawa@orbis.pl).

$$ Old Town Apartments offers 32 studio, one-bedroom,
and two-bedroom apartments (all with kitchen) inside Warsaw's
Old Town. The prices are good and the location is excellent, but
you're pretty much on your own (no real reception, no breakfast).
View the apartments on their website, pick the one that looks best,

and set up a meeting to get the keys at their office (prices flex with demand, but figure studio-300 zł, 1-bedroom-350 zł, 2-bedroom-450 zł, some more expensive "featured" apartments on the square also available, slightly cheaper Oct–April and last-minute, skip their overpriced airport transfer, tel. 022-887-9800, fax 022-831-4956, www.warsawshotel.com, warsaw@bookaa.net). They have an office right on the Old Town Market Square that acts as a sort of reception desk (Mon–Fri 9:00–20:00, Sat–Sun 9:00–17:00, Rynek Starego Miasta 12/14 #2). They also rent 15 pricey apartments on Nowy Świat, called **Royal Route Residence** (studio-400 zł, 1-bedroom-500 zł, 2-bedroom-600 zł, breakfast-25 zł, corner of Nowy Świat and Chmielna, office open Mon–Fri 10:00–18:00—at other times arrange a meeting to get the keys, tel. 022-962-8495, same booking info as above).

$$ Hotel Harenda rents 43 rooms with leatherbound doors on the second and third floors of an office building right in the middle of the Royal Way, by the Copernicus monument. The tired, communist-era rooms are crying out for a renovation, but the location is convenient, and the ground-floor pub is a popular hangout spot (March–June and Sept–Oct: Sb-310 zł, Db-340 zł; July–Aug and Nov–Feb: Sb-295 zł, Db-315 zł; breakfast-20 zł, second night is free Fri–Sun, some rowdy street noise—especially on weekends—so request a quiet room, lots of stairs with no elevator, free Internet access and Wi-Fi, Krakowskie Przedmieście 4/6, tel. & fax 022-826-0071, www.hotelharenda.com.pl, rezerwacja @hotelharenda.com.pl).

$$ Hotel Gromada, a 320-room conference hotel, has a dreary communist exterior, but the lobby and most rooms have been refurbished. There are three types of rooms, all of which are pretty similar: "tourist" (lightly renovated since the communist days); "standard" (a little nicer, with newer bathrooms, but still scruffy); and "plus" (much better and in a newer building). While the place is dull, it has a fine location—between the Palace of Culture and Science and Nowy Świat (tourist rooms: Sb-250 zł, Db-300 zł; standard rooms: Sb-320 zł, Db-350 zł; plus rooms: Sb-420 zł, Db-450 zł; about 25 percent cheaper Fri–Sat, non-smoking rooms, elevator, plac Powstańców Warszawy 2, tel. 022-582-9900, fax 022-582-9527, www.hotele.gromada.pl, warszawahotel .centrum@gromada.pl).

$ Boutique B&B offers more comfort and class than a hotel twice its price, in a beautifully renovated and well-located old building. Jarek Chołodecki, who lived near Chicago for many years, returned to Warsaw and converted apartments into this wonderful bed-and-breakfast with six rooms. It's a friendly, casual, stylish place, creatively decorated and impeccably maintained. You'll feel like you're staying with your Warsaw sophisticate cousin—quirky, charismatic Jarek loves to chat with his guests around the family-style breakfast table, and his many return guests become good friends (standard Db-280 zł, junior suite-320 zł, big suite-420 zł, elevator, free Wi-Fi, ulica Smolna 14, tel. 022-829-4801, fax 022-829-4802, www.bedandbreakfast.pl, office@bedandbreakfast.pl). Let Jarek know what time you're arriving. To make things easier, he can arrange for a no-stress ride in from the airport for the same price as a taxi (40 zł, more at night, request when you reserve your room).

$ Duval Apartments, named for a French woman who supposedly had an affair with the Polish king in this building, offers four beautifully appointed rooms above a restaurant (called Same Fusy) a few steps off the square in the Old Town. Each room has a different theme: traditional Polish, Japanese, glass, or retro (Sb-275 zł, Db-300 zł, Tb-350 zł, more for 1-night stays, includes breakfast, lots of stairs with no elevator, some restaurant noise—light sleepers should request a quiet room, free Wi-Fi, Nowomiejska 10, tel. & fax 022-831-9104, mobile 0608-679-346, www.duval .net.pl, duval@duval.net.pl). There's no reception, and the rooms aren't affiliated with the restaurant, so arrange a meeting time with Agnieszka when you reserve. On arrival, go up the stairs and ring doorbell #5.

$ Ibis Warszawa Stare Miasto, with 333 cookie-cutter rooms, is the place for predictable comfort with zero personality. This hotel, part of the popular European chain, overlooks a WWII memorial in a nondescript, businessy-feeling neighborhood a 10-minute walk north of the Old Town (Sb/Db-279 zł, or 219 zł Fri–Sun, sometimes better deals online, breakfast-28 zł, air-con, non-smoking rooms, elevator, Muranowska 2, tel. 022-310-1000, fax 022-310-1010, www.ibishotel.com, h3714@accor.com).

$ Hotel Mazowiecki is a communist throwback on a drab urban street between the Palace of Culture and Science and Nowy Świat. Its 56 rooms are old and basic (though some rooms with bathrooms have been lightly renovated), but well located for the price. As there are some popular nightclubs nearby, try asking for a quiet room (S-150 zł, Sb-198 zł, D-200 zł, Db-248 zł, 10 percent cheaper Fri–Sun, slow-motion elevator, ulica Mazowiecka 10, tel. & fax 022-827-2365, www.mazowiecki.com.pl, recepcja .mazowiecki@hotelewam.pl).

Hostels

$ Oki Doki Hostel, on a pleasant square a few blocks in front of the Palace of Culture and Science, is colorful, creative, and easygoing. Each of its 37 rooms was designed by a different artist with a special theme—such as van Gogh, Celtic spirals, heads of state, or Lenin. It's well-run by Ernest—a Pole whose parents loved Hemingway—and his wife Łucja, who are energetic and welcoming (S-110–130 zł, D-140–170 zł, Db-180–210 zł, T-190 zł; dorm bed in 4-bed room-55–65 zł, in 5- to 6-bed room-45–55 zł, in 8-bed room-45 zł, prices flex with demand, includes breakfast except for dorm-dwellers—who pay 10 zł, slightly cheaper Oct–April, free Internet access and Wi-Fi, laundry service-10 zł, kitchen, lots of stairs with no elevator, plac Dąbrowskiego 3, tel. 022-826-5112, fax 022-826-8357, www.okidoki.pl, okidoki@okidoki.pl). Ask about their second location, Oki Doki Castle, with more private rooms right on Castle Square in the Old Town.

$ The IYHF **Szkolne Schronisko** hostel, with 110 beds and lots of school groups, is well run, bright, and clean. The downside: It's on the fifth floor, with no elevator (non-members welcome, all prices per person: dorm beds-36 zł, S-65 zł, twin D-60 zł, T-55 zł, Q-45 zł, includes sheets, 3 zł for towel, cash only, no breakfast but members' kitchen, 10 percent cheaper for hostel members, closed 10:00–16:00, curfew at 24:00, or 2:00 in the morning July–Aug; email or fax ahead in summer to reserve limited S, D, and T rooms; good location across the street from National Museum at ulica Smolna 30, tel. & fax 022-827-8952, www.hostelsmolna30 .pl, info@hostelsmolna30.pl).

$ Dom Przy Rynku is a small, friendly, charming, 40-bed hostel with two goals: housing kids from dysfunctional families, and raising money for its work by renting out beds to tourists (when it's not housing children). Located in the peaceful New Town, the cozy rooms are decorated for grade-schoolers. Beds are rented in July and August, and on Friday and Saturday nights all year (55 zł per bed in 2- to 5-bed rooms, rooms segregated by gender, bus #175 from station or airport to Franciszkańska stop, corner of Kościelna and Przyrynek streets at Rynek Nowego Miasta 4, tel. & fax 022-831-5033, www.cityhostel.net, info@cityhostel.net).

EATING

While the Old Town has a tourist-friendly atmosphere and traditional Polish food, Varsovians know that these days, the Nowy Świat area is where it's at—with trendy international restaurants and an enticing *al fresco* scene on balmy summer evenings. This is especially enticing since Warsaw offers your best break from traditional Polish food. Most restaurants are open until the "last guest," which usually means about 23:00 (sometimes later in summer).

In or near the Old Town

Rather than spending too much to eat on the Old Town Market Square, I prefer to venture a few blocks to find a place with good food and much lower prices. For locations, see the maps on pages 287 and 300.

At **Restauracja pod Samsonem** ("Under Samson"), dine on affordable Jewish and Polish comfort food with well-dressed locals. The ambience is pleasant, the service is playfully opinionated, and the low prices make up for the fact that you have to pay to check your coat and use the bathroom (most main dishes 15–35 zł, enjoyable outdoor seating in summer, daily 10:00–23:00, ulica Freta 3/5, tel. 022-831-1788).

Podwale Piwna Kompania, a lively, smoky place filled with Varsovians, feels closer to Prague than to Warsaw. You'll enjoy the large plates of stick-to-your-ribs beer-hall fare, the Pilsner Urquell beer on tap, and the Czech beer-hall or beer-garden ambience (most main dishes 20–40 zł, daily 11:00–1:00 in the morning, just outside Old Town walls near the Barbican at ulica Podwale 25, tel. 022-635-6314).

Pierogarnia na Bednarskiej brags, "only our grandmothers make better pierogi." In addition to the classic Polish dumplings, the menu includes soups and a fun variety of drinks (from unusual fruit juices to *kvas,* the non-alcoholic dark beer). Order at the counter and take a seat—they'll call you when your food's ready. With mellow country decor, wooden menus, and a loyal local crowd, this is a handy spot for a quick, cheap meal along the Royal Way (12-zł plates of pierogi, 14-zł combo-plate includes soup and salad, daily 11:00–21:00, hiding on a quiet street behind the statue of Adam Mickiewicz at ulica Bednarska 28/30, tel. 022-828-0392).

Siedem Grzechów ("Seven Sins") is an old-style Warsaw restaurant serving top-notch Polish, Russian, and international cuisine in a 1930s ivy, velvet, and burgundy ambience. The place fills a dressy cellar with jazz and photos of pre-war Warsaw (20–50-zł main dishes, daily 11:00–23:00, usually live music Sat 20:00–22:00, a few blocks before the Old Town on the Royal Way at Krakowskie Przedmieście 45, tel. 022-826-4770).

BrowArmia is a hit with beer-lovers. This sprawling brewpub makes four different types of beer (plus special seasonal beers) and serves decent pub grub. The dark, mod, long interior fills two levels (including a fun cellar), but in good weather I'd stake out a spot on the terrace—ideal for people-watching along the Royal Way (30–50-zł main dishes, daily 12:00–24:00, live music or DJ in cellar on weekends, right on Krakowskie Przedmieście near Piłsudski Square at ulica Królewska 1, tel. 022-826-5455).

On the Old Town Market Square: You'll pay triple to eat right on the Old Town Market Square, but some visitors figure it's worth the splurge (plan on 60–120 zł per main dish). If money's no object, these two places are tops: **U Fukiera,** at #27, offers traditional Polish and pan-European meals in a sophisticated setting with carefully designed pre-war atmosphere. In summer, sit at their tables out on the square, or find your way to the cozy courtyard garden in back (daily 12:00–24:00, tel. 022-831-1013). The slightly pricier option is **Gessler,** at #21. Its cellar, serving countryside Polish dishes, is furnished with tables, chairs, doors, beams, and entire walls imported from actual country inns (daily 10:00–24:00, tel. 022-887-0344). In Gessler's lobby hang photos of famous patrons. It's the only place you'll see Hillary Rodham Clinton, George H. W. Bush, and Henry Kissinger side by side— and smiling. (A sly Fidel Castro watches over the three of them.)

On or near Nowy Świat

While most Old Town eateries are traditional and cater to tourists, locals flock to the Nowy Świat neighborhood (near the National Museum and Central Train Station) for a fun night on the town.

Fancy Eateries on Foksal Street: Foksal—the first cross street as you go down Nowy Świat from aleja Jerozolimskie—has a thriving assortment of about a half-dozen cafés and restaurants: Mexican, Italian, Asian, international, and more. Most have inviting outdoor seating that's ideal on a balmy summer evening. The clientele is young and sophisticated, and there's not a pierogi in sight. Find the place with the cuisine and ambience you like best. **Papaya** has delicious pan-Asian fare (including good-for-Poland sushi) and trendy, minimalist, black-and-white decor (30–60-zł main dishes plus pricier splurges, daily 12:00–24:00, at #16, tel. 022-826-1199). **Living Room** features pricey, healthy international fare. The outdoor seating is tops, or dine in the tight, stylish dining room (50–80-zł main dishes, daily 12:00–2:00 in the morning, at #18, tel. 022-826-3928).

Cheaper Milk Bars: **Sandwicz,** a colorful milk bar, serves up Polish grub (with both vegetarian and meat options) and has a self-serve salad bar (help yourself, then take to cashier to weigh and pay). Strangely, sandwiches often aren't available (8–16-zł main dishes, Mon–Fri 7:30–20:30, Sat–Sun 10:00–20:30, Nowy Świat 28). For a more communist-style milk bar—with lower prices, dreary decor, and grumpier service—head to **Bar Mleczny Familijny,** about a block up Nowy Świat and across the street; or **Uniwersytecky Bar,** a few blocks farther up the Royal Way near the university (described on page 290). For more on milk bars, see page 199.

Uniquely Polish Treats

These two places are on or close to the busy Nowy Świat boulevard.

A. Blikle, Poland's most famous pastry shop, serves a wide variety of delicious pastries. This is where locals shop for cakes when they're having someone special over for coffee. The specialty: *pączki* (PONCH-kee), the quintessential Polish doughnut, filled with rose-flavored jam. You can get your goodies "to go" in the shop (2.50-zł *pączki*, Mon–Sat 9:00–19:00, Sun 10:00–18:00); or pay more to enjoy them with coffee in the swanky, classic café with indoor or outdoor seating (6-zł *pączki*, daily 10:00–22:00; both at Nowy Świat 35).

E. Wedel Pijalnia Czekolady thrills chocoholics. Emil Wedel made Poland's favorite chocolate, and today, his former residence houses this chocolate shop and café (Mon–Sat 8:00–22:00, Sun 11:00–20:00, between Palace of Culture and Science and Nowy Świat at ulica Szpitalna 1, tel. 022-827-2916). This is the spot for delicious pastries and a *real* hot chocolate, *czekolada do picia* (9-zł "drinking chocolate"—that means a cup of melted chocolate, not just hot chocolate milk). The menu describes it as, "True Wedel ecstasy for your mouth that will take you to a world of dreams and desires." Or, if you fancy chocolate mousse, try *pokusa* ("Wedel Temptation"). Wedel's was *the* Christmas treat for locals under communism. Cadbury bought the company when Poland privatized, but they kept the E. Wedel name, which is close to all Poles' hearts...and taste buds.

TRANSPORTATION CONNECTIONS

Virtually all trains into and out of Warsaw go through the hulking Central Train Station (see "Arrival in Warsaw," page 282.) If you're heading to Gdańsk, note that the red-brick Gothic city of Toruń and the impressive Malbork Castle are on the way (though on separate train lines, so you can't do both en route; see Gdańsk and Pomerania chapters).

From Warsaw by Train to: Kraków (hourly, 2.75 hrs), **Gdańsk** (nearly hourly, 4 hrs), **Toruń** (5/day, 3 hrs direct, longer with a transfer in Kutno), **Malbork** (nearly hourly, 3.5 hrs direct), **Prague** (2/day direct including 1 night train, more with changes, 8.5–9.5 hrs), **Berlin** (3/day direct, 5.75 hrs—eventually will be much shorter with construction of new high-speed rail line; plus 1 direct night train, 7.75 hrs), **Budapest** (2/day direct, including 1 night train, 10.5–11.5 hrs; or 1 each per day with transfer in Győr, Hungary, or Břeclav, Czech Republic, both 10 hrs), **Vienna** (2/day direct, including 1 night train, 7.75–8.5 hrs).

GDAŃSK and the TRI-CITY

Gdańsk (guh-DANSK) is a true find on the Baltic Coast of Poland. You may associate Gdańsk with the images of dreary dock-workers you saw on the nightly news in the 1980s—but there's so much more to this city than shipyards, Solidarity, and smog. It's surprisingly easy to look past the urban sprawl to find one of northern Europe's most historic and picturesque cities.

Gdańsk is second only to Kraków as Poland's most appealing destination. The gem of a Main Town boasts block after block of red-brick churches and narrow, colorful, ornately decorated Hanseatic burghers' mansions. Its history is also fascinating—from its medieval Golden Age to the headlines of our own generation, big things happen here. You might even see old Lech Wałęsa still wandering the streets.

And yet, Gdańsk is also looking to its future, finally repairing some of its World War II damage after a long communist hibernation. Its selection as one of the host cities for the 2012 Euro Cup soccer tournament will kick off a flurry of new construction in the coming years—including a futuristic new stadium shaped like a translucent glob of amber. Visit now, while the city still has some rough edges. (They won't last.)

Gdańsk is just the beginning. From here, the "Tri-City" continues north along the coast, offering several day-trip opportunities. The faded elegance of the seaside resort Sopot beckons to tourists, while the modern burg of Gdynia sets the pace for today's Poland. Beyond the Tri-City, the sandy Hel Peninsula is a popular spot for summer sunbathing.

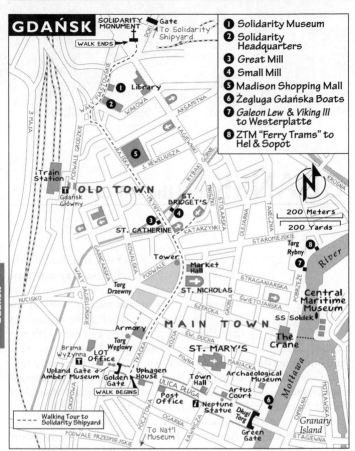

GDAŃSK

- ❶ Solidarity Museum
- ❷ Solidarity Headquarters
- ❸ Great Mill
- ❹ Small Mill
- ❺ Madison Shopping Mall
- ❻ Żegluga Gdańska Boats
- ❼ *Galeon Lew* & *Viking III* to Westerplatte
- ❽ ZTM "Ferry Trams" to Hel & Sopot

Planning Your Time

This region merits at least two days to make the trip here worthwhile. Gdańsk has more than enough sightseeing for a full day, but a second day allows you to see everything in town at a more relaxing pace, and take your pick from among several possible side-trips.

Gdańsk sightseeing has two major components: the "Royal Way" (historic main drag with small but good museums—described in my self-guided walk) and the modern shipyard where Solidarity was born (with a fascinating museum, also fully described in this chapter). With just one day, do one of these activities in the morning, and the other in the afternoon. With two days, do one each day, and round your time out with other attractions: art-lovers enjoy the National Museum (with a stunning painting by Hans Memling), history buffs make the pilgrimage to Westerplatte (where World

War II began), and church fans visit Oliwa Cathedral in Gdańsk's northern suburbs (on the way to Sopot).

With more time, consider the wide variety of side-trips. The most popular option is the full-day round-trip to Malbork Castle (40–50 min each way by train, plus at least 3 hours to tour the castle—see next chapter). Closer to Gdańsk, it only takes a few hours to get a feel for the resort town of Sopot (25 min each way by train); with more time, laze around longer on Sopot's beaches, or make a quick visit to Gdynia to round out your take on the Tri-City. If you have a full day and great weather, and you don't mind fighting the crowds for a patch of sandy beach, go to Hel.

Gdańsk gets busy in late June, when school holidays begin, and it's downright crowded with mostly German tourists from July to mid-September—especially during St. Dominic's Fair (Jarmark Św. Dominika, first three weeks of August), with market stalls, concerts, and other celebrations. The city is dead in the winter.

ORIENTATION

(area code: 058)

Gdańsk, with 460,000 residents, is part of a larger metropolitan area called the Tri-City (Trójmiasto, total population 750,000).

But the tourist's Gdańsk is compact, welcoming, and walkable—virtually anything you'll want to see is within a 20-minute stroll of everything else.

Focus on the "Main Town" (Główne Miasto), home to most of the sights described in this chapter, including the spectacular "Royal Way" main drag, ulica Długa. The "Old Town" (Stare Miasto) has a handful of old brick buildings and faded, tall, skinny houses—but the area is mostly drab and residential, and not worth much time. Just beyond the northern end of the Old Town (about a 20-min walk from the heart of the Main Town) is the entrance to the Gdańsk Shipyard, with the excellent Solidarity museum. From here, shipyards sprawl for miles.

The second language in this part of Poland is German, not English—and German tourists flock here in droves. (This was a predominantly German city until the end of World War II.) Scandinavian shoppers come across the Baltic Sea to take advantage of the low prices. Americans seem to be in short supply...for now.

You'll win no Polish friends calling the city by its more familiar German name, Danzig.

Gdańsk History

Visitors to Gdańsk are surprised at how "un-Polish" the city's history is. In this cultural melting pot of German, Dutch, and Flemish merchants (with a smattering of Italians and Scots), Poles were only a small part of the picture until the city became exclusively Polish after World War II. However, in Gdańsk, cultural backgrounds traditionally took a back seat to the bottom line. Wealthy Gdańsk was always known for its economic pragmatism—no matter who was in charge, Gdańsk merchants made money.

Gdańsk is Poland's gateway to the waters of Europe—where its main river (the Vistula) meets the Baltic Sea. The town was first mentioned in the 10th century, and was seized in 1308 by the Teutonic Knights (who called it "Danzig"; for more on the Teutonic Knights, see page 370). The Knights encouraged other Germans to come settle on the Baltic coast, and gradually turned Gdańsk into a wealthy city. In 1361, Gdańsk joined the Hanseatic League, a trade federation of mostly Germanic merchant towns that provided mutual security. By the 15th century, Gdańsk was a leading member of this mighty network, which virtually dominated trade in northern Europe (and also included Toruń, Kraków, Lübeck, Hamburg, Bremen, Bruges, Bergen, Tallinn, Novgorod, and nearly a hundred other cities).

In 1454, the people of Gdańsk rose up against the Teutonic Knights, burning down their castle and forcing them out of the city. Three years later, the Polish king borrowed money from wealthy Gdańsk families to hire Czech mercenaries to take the Teutonic Knights' main castle, Malbork (see page 364). In exchange, Gdańsk merchants were granted special privileges, including exclusive export rights. Gdańsk now acted as a middleman for all trade passing through the city, but paid only a modest annual tribute to the Polish king.

The 16th and 17th centuries were Gdańsk's Golden Age. Now a part of the Polish kingdom, the city had access to an enormous hinterland of natural resources to export—yet it maintained a privileged, semi-independent status. Like Amsterdam, Gdańsk

Tourist Information

Gdańsk's TI—the only one I've seen with a tip jar—is in a red, high-gabled building across **ulica Długa** from the Town Hall. Pick up the free map and brochure, and browse through the other brochures and guidebooks (May–Sept Mon–Fri 9:00–18:00, Sat–Sun 10:00–18:00, until 20:00 during fair in Aug; Oct–April Mon–Fri 9:00–17:00, Sat–Sun 9:00–15:00; ulica Długa 45, tel. 058-301-9151). There are also small TIs at the **Main Train Station** (in a small kiosk out front) and the **airport.**

became a tolerant, progressive, and booming merchant city. Its mostly Germanic and Dutch burghers imported Dutch, Flemish, and Italian architects to give their homes an appropriately Hanseatic flourish. At a time of religious upheaval in the rest of Europe, Gdańsk became known for its tolerance—a place that opened its doors to all visitors (many Mennonites and Scottish religious refugees emigrated here). It was also a haven for great thinkers, including philosopher Arthur Schopenhauer and scientist Daniel Fahrenheit (who invented the mercury thermometer).

Gdańsk declined, along with the rest of Poland, in the late 18th century, and became a part of Prussia (today's Germany) during the partitions. But the people of Gdańsk—even those of German heritage—had taken pride in their independence, and weren't enthusiastic about being ruled from Berlin. After World War I, Gdańsk once again became an independent city-state, the Free City of Danzig (populated by 400,000 Germans and only 15,000 Poles). The city, along with the so-called Polish Corridor connecting it to Polish lands, effectively cut off Germany from its northeastern territory. On September 1, 1939, Adolf Hitler started World War II when he invaded Gdańsk to bring it back into the German fold. Nearly 80 percent of the city was destroyed in the war.

After World War II, Gdańsk officially became part of Poland, and was painstakingly reconstructed (mostly replicating its Golden Age). In 1970, and again in 1980, the shipyard of Gdańsk witnessed strikes and demonstrations that would lead to the fall of European communism. Poland's great anti-communist hero and first post-communist president—Lech Wałęsa—is Gdańsk's most famous resident, and still lives here today.

A city with a recent past that's both tragic and uplifting, Gdańsk celebrated its 1,000th birthday in 1997. This came with a wave of renovation and refurbishment, which left the gables of the atmospheric Hanseatic quarter gleaming.

Arrival in Gdańsk

By Train: Gdańsk's Main Train Station (Gdańsk Główny) is a pretty brick palace on the western edge of the old center. Trains to other parts of Poland (marked *PKP*) use tracks 1–3; regional trains with connections to the Tri-City (marked *SKM*) use the shorter tracks 3–5 (for more on regional SKM trains, see page 359).

Inside the terminal building, you'll find ticket windows and a helpful TI (in the back corner of the main hall, look for *it* sign). Outside, the pedestrian underpass by the McDonald's takes you beneath the busy road (go down the stairs and turn right; first set of exits: tram stop; end of corridor: Old Town). To reach the heart of the Main Town, you can ride the **tram** (buy tickets—*bilety*—at the *RUCH* kiosk by track 5 or at any window marked *Bilety ZKM* in pedestrian underpass; access tram stop via underpass, then board tram #8, #13, or #14 going to the right with your back to the station; go just 1 stop to Brama Wyżynna, in front of the LOT airlines office). But by the time you buy your ticket and wait for the tram, you might as well **walk** the 15 minutes to the same place (go through underpass, exit to the right and follow the busy road until you reach LOT airlines office, then head left toward all the brick towers). Or even easier, take a **taxi** (shouldn't cost more than 15 zł to any of my recommended hotels).

By Plane: Gdańsk's small airport (recently named for Lech Wałęsa) is about five miles west of the city center (tel. 058-348-1163, www.airport.gdansk.pl). There's one main terminal hall for both check-in and arrivals, with a TI desk and ATMs. **Bus #B** connects the airport with downtown, stopping near the Main Train Station and at Brama Wyżynna, near the heart of the Main Town (4.20 zł, 2–3/hr on weekdays, 1–2/hr on weekends, 40 min, buy ticket at TI desk or on board, exit terminal and turn right to find bus stop). The 25-minute **taxi** ride into town will cost you about 50 zł (the City Plus Hallo taxi company is the only official one for the trip into town, but you can take any taxi *to* the airport).

Helpful Hints

Blue Monday: In the off-season, most of Gdańsk's museums are closed Monday. In the busy summertime, some of these museums are open—and free—limited hours on Monday. If museums are closed, Monday is a good day to visit churches or take a side-trip to Sopot (but not Malbork Castle, which is also closed Mon).

Last Entry: The "last entry" time for museums is 30 minutes before closing—and it's strictly enforced. Museum-goers who cut it close discover that ticket-sellers sometimes clock out a few minutes early.

Getting Around Gdańsk

If you're staying at one of my recommended hotels, everything is within easy walking distance. Public transportation is useful for residents, but not really for sightseers.

By Public Transportation: Gdańsk has a fine network of trams and buses. Buy tickets *(bilety)* at kiosks marked *RUCH* or *Bilety ZKM*. Prices depend on the time limit on the ticket (1.40 zł/10 min, 2.80 zł/30 min, 4.20 zł/1 hr, 9.10 zł/24 hrs). Tell the ticket seller where you're going when you buy your ticket, and they'll sell you the right one. Stops worth knowing about: Plac

Solidarnośći (near the shipyards), Gdańsk Główny (in front of the Main Train Station), and Brama Wyżynna (near the heart of the tourist zone, in front of LOT airlines office). When buying tickets, don't confuse *ZKM* (the company that runs Gdańsk city transit) with *SKM* (the company that runs regional trains to outlying destinations). To make things even more confusing, ZKM's parent company is ZTM.

To get beyond central Gdańsk to visit the Oliwa cathedral, see "Outer Gdańsk" (page 350). For directions to towns of Sopot and Gdynia, and the Hel Peninsula, see "Getting Around the Tri-City" (page 359).

By Taxi: They cost about 5 zł to start, then 2 zł per kilometer. Find a taxi stand, or call a cab (try Super Hallo Taxi, tel. 9191, or City Plus Hallo Taxi, tel. 9686).

TOURS

Walking Tours—In peak season, the TI sometimes offers a three-hour English walking tour (80 zł, offered with demand in July–Aug only, no set schedule—ask at TI).

Private Guide—Hiring your own local guide is an exceptional value. **Agnieszka Syroka** is bubbly and personable, and also does tours of Malbork Castle (300–400 zł for up to 4 hrs, more for all day, mobile 0502-554-584, www.tourguidegdansk.com, asyroka @interia.pl).

SELF-GUIDED WALKS

▲▲▲Gdańsk's Royal Way

In the 16th and 17th centuries, Gdańsk was Poland's wealthiest city, with gorgeous architecture (much of it in the Flemish Mannerist style) rivaling that in the two historic capitals, Kraków and Warsaw. During this Golden Age, Polish kings would visit this city of well-to-do Hanseatic League merchants, and gawk along the same route trod by tourists today. The following walk introduces you to the best of historic Gdańsk. It only takes about 30 minutes, not counting multiple worthwhile sightseeing stops. This stroll turns tourists into poets. On my last visit, a traveler gasped to me, "It's like stepping into a Fabergé egg."

Begin at the west end of the Main Town, between the big white gate and the big brick gate (near the LOT airlines office, the busy road, and the Brama Wyżynna tram stop).

City Gates: Medieval Gdańsk had an elaborate network of protection for the city, including several moats and gates—among them the white **Upland Gate** (Brama Wyżynna); the shorter, red-brick **Torture House** (Wieża Więzienna); and the taller, red-brick

326   Rick Steves' Eastern Europe

Prison Tower (Katownia). The three gates were all connected back then, and visitors had to pass through all of them to enter the city. These buildings, with walls up to 15 feet thick, have recently been turned into the fine Amber Museum (described on page 334).

Now walk around the left side of the Torture House and Prison Tower. Look to your left to see a long brick building with four gables (next to the modern theater building). This is the 16th-century **Armory** (Zbrojownia), one of the best examples of Dutch Renaissance architecture in Europe. Though this part of the building looks like four separate house facades, it's a kind of urban camouflage to hide its real purpose from potential attackers. But there's at least one clue to what it's for: Find the exploding cannonballs at the tops of the turrets. The round, pointy-topped tower next door is the **Straw Tower.** Gunpowder was stored here, and the roof was straw—so if it exploded, it would blow its top without destroying the walls.

• *Continue around the brick buildings until you're face-to-face with the...*

Golden Gate (Złota Brama): The other gates were defensive, but this one's purely ornamental. The four women up top

represent virtues that the people of Gdańsk should exhibit toward outsiders: Peace, Freedom, Prosperity, and Fame. The inscription, a psalm in medieval German, compares Gdańsk to Jerusalem: famous and important. In the middle is one of the coats of arms of Gdańsk—two white crosses under a crown on a red shield. You'll see this symbol many times today.

• *Now go through the gate, entering the "Long Street"...*

Ulica Długa: Look back at the gate you just came through. The women on top of this side represent virtues the people of Gdańsk should cultivate in themselves: Wisdom, Piety, Justice, and Concord (if an arrow's broken, let's take it out of the quiver and fix it).

Begin to wander this intoxicating promenade. Gdańsk was cosmopolitan and exceptionally tolerant in the Middle Ages, attracting a wide range of people (including many who were persecuted elsewhere): Jews, Scots, Dutch, Flemish, Italians, Germans, and more. Members of

each group brought with them strands of their culture, which they wove into the tapestry of this city—demonstrated by the eclectic homes along this street.

Today's generation is leaving its mark as well—each time I return, new cafés and restaurants have opened along this street. For example, the Rooster restaurant on the right is part of a chain that's sweeping Poland. What an innovative concept! Where these clever entrepreneurs get their creative ideas, I'll never know.

This lovely street wasn't always so lively and carefree. In fact, at the end of World War II, ulica Długa was in ruins. The city was damaged when the Germans first invaded, sparking the war. But the worst devastation came when the Soviets arrived. This was the first traditionally German city that the Red Army reached on their march toward Berlin—and the soldiers were set loose to level the place in retaliation for all of the pain the Nazis had caused. (Soviets didn't destroy nearby Gdynia—which they considered Polish, not German.) Soviet officers turned a blind eye as their soldiers raped and brutalized residents. An entire order of horrified nuns committed suicide by throwing themselves into the river. And upwards of 80 percent of this area was destroyed. It was only thanks to detailed drawings and photographs that these buildings could be so carefully reconstructed, mostly using the original brick.

During Gdańsk's Golden Age, these houses were taxed based on frontage (like the homes lining Amsterdam's canals)—so they were built skinny and deep. The widest houses belonged to the super-elite. Different as they are from the outside, each house had the same general plan inside. Each had three parts, starting with the front and moving back: First was a fancy drawing room, to show off for visitors. Then came a narrow corridor to the back rooms—often along the side of an inner courtyard. Because the houses had only a few windows facing the outer street, this courtyard provided much-needed sunlight to the rest of the house. The residential quarters were in the back, where the people actually lived: bedroom, kitchen, office. To see the interior of one of these homes, pay a visit to the very interesting **Uphagen House** (#12, on the right, about two blocks in front of the gate; described on page 334).

Across the street and a little farther down are some of the most striking **facades** along all of ulica Długa. The blue-and-white house with the three giant heads is from the 19th century, when eclecticism was hot—borrowing bits and pieces from various architectural eras. This was one of the few houses on the street that survived World War II.

At the next corner on the right is the huge, blocky, red **post office,** which doesn't quite fit with the skinny facades lining the rest of the street. But step inside. With doves fluttering under an

Gdańsk at a Gdlance

▲▲▲**Ulica Długa** Gdańsk's colorful showpiece main drag, cutting a picturesque swath through the heart of the wealthy burghers' neighborhood. **Hours:** Always open.

▲▲▲**Solidarity Sights and Gdańsk Shipyard** The shipyard that was home to the beginning of the end of European communism, housing a towering monument and an excellent museum. **Hours:** Memorial and shipyard gate—always open. "Roads to Freedom" exhibit—May–Sept Tue–Sun 10:00–17:00, Oct–April Tue–Sun 10:00–16:00, closed Mon year-round.

▲▲**Main Town Hall** Ornately decorated meeting rooms, exhibits of town artifacts, and climbable tower with sweeping views. **Hours:** Mid-June–mid-Sept Mon 11:00–15:00, Tue–Sat 10:00–18:00, Sun 11:00–18:00; mid-Sept–mid-June Tue 10:00–15:00, Wed–Sat 10:00–16:00, Sun 11:00–16:00, closed Mon.

▲▲**Artus Court** Grand meeting hall for guilds of Golden Age Gdańsk, boasting an over-the-top tiled stove. **Hours:** Mid-June–mid-Sept Mon 11:00–15:00, Tue–Sat 10:00–18:00, Sun 11:00–18:00; mid-Sept–mid-June Tue 10:00–15:00, Wed–Sat 10:00–16:00, Sun 11:00–16:00, closed Mon.

▲▲**St. Mary's Church** Giant red-brick church crammed full of Gdańsk history. **Hours:** Mon–Sat 9:00–17:30, Sun 13:00–17:30.

▲**Amber Museum** High-tech new exhibit of valuable golden globs of petrified tree sap. **Hours:** Mid-June–mid-Sept Mon 11:00–15:00, Tue–Sat 10:00–18:00, Sun 11:00–18:00; mid-Sept–mid-

airy glass atrium, the interior's a class act. (To mail postcards, take a number—category C—from the machine on the left.)

Across the street and a few doors down from the post office, notice the colorful **scenes** just overhead on the facade of the cocktail bar. These are slices of life from 17th-century Gdańsk: drinking, talking, buying, fighting, playing music. The ship is a *koga*, a typical symbol of Gdańsk.

A couple of doors down from the cocktail bar is **Neptun Cinema** (marked *KINO*). In the 1980s, this was the only movie theater in the city, and locals lined up all the way down the street to get in. Young adults remember coming here with their grandparents to see a full day of cartoons. Now, as with traditional main-street cinemas in the US, the rising popularity of multiplexes threatens to close this place down.

June Tue 10:00–15:00, Wed–Sat 10:00–16:00, Sun 11:00–16:00, closed Mon.

▲**Uphagen House** Tourable 18th-century interior, typical of the pretty houses that line ulica Długa. **Hours:** Mid-June–mid-Sept Mon 11:00–15:00, Tue–Sat 10:00–18:00, Sun 11:00–18:00; mid-Sept–mid-June Tue 10:00–15:00, Wed–Sat 10:00–16:00, Sun 11:00–16:00, closed Mon.

▲**Central Maritime Museum** Sprawling exhibit on all aspects of the nautical life, housed in several venues (including the land-mark medieval Crane and a permanently moored steamship) connected by a ferry boat. **Hours:** July–Aug daily 10:00–18:00; Sept–Oct and March–June Tue–Sun 10:00–16:00, closed Mon; Nov–Feb Tue–Sun 10:00–15:00, closed Mon.

Archaeological Museum Decent collection of artifacts from this region's past. **Hours:** July–Aug Tue–Sun 10:00–17:00, closed Mon; Sept–June Tue and Thu–Fri 9:00–16:00, Wed 10:00–17:00, Sat–Sun 10:00–16:00, closed Mon.

National Museum in Gdańsk Ho-hum art collection with a single blockbuster highlight: Hans Memling's remarkable *Last Judgment* altarpiece. **Hours:** Tue–Fri 9:00–16:00, Sat–Sun 10:00–16:00, closed Mon.

Oliwa Cathedral Suburban church with long, skinny nave and playful organ. **Hours:** Church open long hours daily; frequent organ concerts in summer.

Across the street from the theater are three houses belonging to the very influential medieval **Ferber family,** which produced many burghers, mayors, and even a bishop. On the house with the little dog over the door (#29), look for the heads in the circles. These are Caesars of Rome. At the top of the building is Mr. Ferber's answer to the constant question, "Why build such an elaborate house?"—*PRO INVIDIA,* "For the sake of envy."

Next door, notice the outdoor tables for Gdańsk's most popular milk bar, **Bar Mleczny Neptun** (see page 356 in "Eating"). Now you're just a few steps from the **Main Town Hall** (Ratusz Głównego Miasta). This building features a climbable observation tower and houses a superb museum with ornately decorated meeting rooms for the city council (see description on page 335).

• *Just beyond the Main Town Hall, ulica Długa widens and becomes...*

Długi Targ: The centerpiece of "Long Square" is one of Gdańsk's most important landmarks, the statue of **Neptune**—god of the sea. He's a fitting symbol for a city that dominates the maritime life of Poland. Behind him is another fine museum, the **Artus Court** (see page 337). This meeting hall for various Gdańsk brotherhoods is home to the most impressive stove you've ever seen.

As you continue down Długi targ, notice the **balconies** extending out into the square, with access to cellars underneath. These were a common feature on ulica Długa in Gdańsk's Golden Age, but were removed in the 19th century to make way for a new tram system. You'll find more balconies like these on Mariacka street, which runs parallel to this one (2 blocks to the left).

• *At the end of Długi targ is the...*

Green Gate (Zielona Brama): This huge gate was actually built as a residence for visiting kings...who usually preferred to stay back by Neptune instead (maybe because the river, just on the other side of this gate, stunk). It might not have been good enough for kings and queens, but it's plenty fine for a former president—Lech Wałęsa's office is upstairs (see the plaque, *Biuro Lecha Wałęsy*). Other parts of the building are used for temporary exhibitions.

Notice that these bricks are much smaller than the ones we've seen earlier on this walk. That's because those were locally made, but these are Dutch. Boats would come here empty, load up with goods, and take them back to Holland. For ballast, they brought bricks on the trip from Holland—which they left here to be turned into this gate.

• *Now go through the gate, and turn left along the...*

Riverfront Embankment: The Motława River—actually a side channel of the mighty Vistula—was the source of Gdańsk's phenomenal Golden Age wealth. This embankment was jam-packed in its heyday, the 14th and 15th centuries. It was so crowded with boats that you could hardly see the water, and boats had to pay a time-based tax for tying up to a post. Instead of an actual embankment (which was built later), there was a series of wooden piers to connect the boats directly to the gates of the city. Now it's a popular place to stroll and to buy amber.

Across the river is **Granary Island** (Spichrze), where grain was stored until it could be taken away by ships. Before World War II, there were some 400 granaries here; it's still in ruins. Three granaries have been reconstructed on the next island up, and house exhibits for the Central Maritime Museum (see page 339); another is now Hotel Królewski (see "Sleeping," page 351). A big international company has bought this island, and plans to develop the prime real estate into a new city-center zone of shops, restaurants, houses, and hotels.

Continue along the embankment until you see the five big, round stones on your left. These are the **five little ladies**—mysterious ancient sculptures. If you look closely, you can make out their features, especially the chubby one on the end. If you touch one, you'll come back to Gdańsk...or so the tour guides say.

The next huge red-brick fort houses the **Archaeological Museum** and a tower you can climb for a good view (see page 339). The gate in the middle leads to **Mariacka street,** a calm, atmospheric drag leading to St. Mary's Church (see page 338) and lined with old balconies, amber shops, and imaginative gargoyles (which locals call "pukers" when it rains).

• *Just up ahead on the embankment is Gdańsk's number-one symbol, and our last stop...*

The Crane (Żuraw): This monstrous 15th-century crane might be undergoing renovation during your visit. It was once used for loading ships, picking up small crafts for repairs, and uprighting masts...beginning a shipbuilding tradition that continued to the days of Lech Wałęsa. The crane mechanism was operated by several hardworking sailors scrambling around in giant hamster wheels up top (you can see the wheels if you look up). The Crane houses part of the Central Maritime Museum (described on page 339).

• *Our orientation tour is over. Now get out there and enjoy Gdańsk... do it for Lech!*

▲From the Main Town to the Solidarity Shipyard

This lightly guided walk links Gdańsk's two most important sightseeing areas. Along the way, you'll see some important historic landmarks, tour two of Gdańsk's more interesting red-brick churches, and wander through the city's best shopping district. The stroll takes about 20 minutes, not counting stops for sightseeing and shopping.

Begin at the top of ulica Długa, with your back to the Golden Gate. Head a few steps down the street and take a left on Tkacka. After one long block on the left, you'll see the back of the **Armory** building (described in the self-guided walk, above). This pearl of

Renaissance architecture recently had a striking facelift—examine the exquisite decorations.

After three short blocks, detour to the right down Świętojańska and use the side door to enter the brick **St. Nicholas Church** (Kościół Św. Mikołaja, with the ornate towers on the ends). Near the end of World War II, when the Soviet army reached Gdańsk on its march westward, they were given the order to burn all of the churches. Only this one—dedicated to Russia's patron saint—was spared. As the best-preserved church in town, today it has a more impressive interior than the others, with lavish black-and-gold Baroque altars.

Backtrack out to the main street and continue north. Immediately after the church (on the right), you'll see Gdańsk's newly renovated **Market Hall.** Look for the coat of arms of Gdańsk over each of its four doors (two white crosses on a red shield). Inside you'll find mostly local shoppers—browsing through produce, other foods, and clothing—as well as the graves of medieval Dominican monks that were discovered when the building was renovated (in the basement). Look up to appreciate the delicate iron-and-glass canopy.

Across the street from the Market Hall is a round red-brick **tower,** once part of the city's protective wall. This marks the end of the Main Town, and the beginning of the Old Town.

Another long block up the street is the huge **St. Catherine's Church** (Kościół Św. Katarzyny, on the right). "Katy," as locals call it, is the oldest church in Gdańsk. In May of 2006, a carelessly discarded cigarette caused the church roof to burst into flames. Local people ran into the church and pulled everything outside, so nothing valuable was damaged. Even the carillon bells were saved. But the roof and wooden frame were totally destroyed. The people of Gdańsk are determined to rebuild this important symbol of the city. Within days of the fire, fundraising concerts were held to scrape together most of the money needed to raise the roof once more. However, promised government funding hasn't come through, so rebuilding may take more time. Still, even during the reconstruction, some parts of the church may be open to visitors.

The church hiding behind Katy—named for Catherine's daughter Bridget—has important ties to Solidarity, and is worth a quick detour. To get there, walk along the side of St. Catherine's Church, past the monument to Pope John Paul II.

St. Bridget's Church (Kościół Św. Brygidy) was the home church of Lech Wałęsa during the tense days of the 1980s. This church and its priest, Henryk Jankowski, were particularly aggressive in supporting the ideals of Solidarity. Jankowski became a mouthpiece for the movement, and Wałęsa named his youngest daughter Brygida in gratitude for the church's support. In the back corner, under the wall of wooden crosses, find the tomb of Solidarity martyr Jerzy Popiełuszko, a famously outspoken Warsaw priest who was kidnapped, beaten, and murdered by the communist secret police. Here, notice that his hands and feet are tied. At the front of the church, check out the enormous, unfinished altar made entirely of amber, featuring the Black Madonna of Częstochowa and a royal Polish eagle. If and when it's finished, it'll be 36 feet high, 20 feet wide, and 10 feet deep. But some locals criticize this ambitious project as an example of Father Jankowski's recent missteps. Despite his fame and contributions to Solidarity, Jankowski has taken a nosedive in public opinion in the last few years—thanks to projects like this, as well as accusations of anti-Semitism and implications of pedophilia and corruption. Because of these issues, and because of his worsening health, Jankowski has been forced to "retire."

Backtrack out past St. Catherine's Church to the main street. Just across from St. Catherine's is a red-brick building with lots of little windows in the roof. This is the **Great Mill** (Wielki Młyn), which has been converted into a shopping mall (Mon–Fri 10:00–19:00, Sat 10:00–16:00, closed Sun). As you continue north and cross the stream, you'll also see the picturesque **Small Mill** (Mały Młyn) straddling the stream on your right.

After another block, on your right, is the modern **Madison shopping mall** (Mon–Sat 9:00–21:00, Sun 10:00–20:00). Two blocks to your left (up Heweliusza) are more shopping malls and the Main Train Station. But to get to the shipyard, keep heading straight up Rajska. After another long block, jog right (between the big, green-glass skyscraper and today's Solidarity headquarters) and head for the three tall crosses. On the way, you'll pass the low-profile entrance to the "Roads to Freedom" exhibit, which we'll return to after visiting the shipyard.

For a self-guided tour of the shipyard and Solidarity museum, see page 342.

SIGHTS

Main Town (Główne Miasto)

The following sights are all in the Main Town, listed roughly in the order you'll see them on the self-guided walk of the Royal Way.

Gdańsk Historical Museum

The Gdańsk Historical Museum has four excellent branches, and all have the same hours (which tend to change from year to year): mid-June–mid-Sept Mon 11:00–15:00, Tue–Sat 10:00–18:00, Sun 11:00–18:00; mid-Sept–mid-June Tue 10:00–15:00, Wed–Sat 10:00–16:00, Sun 11:00–16:00, closed Mon; last entry 30 min before closing. These museums are free on Mondays in summer, and on Tuesdays in winter (central tel. 058-767-9100, www.mhmg.gda.pl).

▲**Amber Museum (Muzeum Bursztynu)**—This new museum, housed in a pair of connected brick towers just outside the Main Town's Golden Gate, has two oddly contradictory parts. One shows off one of Gdańsk's favorite local resources, amber, while the other focuses on implements of torture (10 zł, free on Mon in summer, free on Tue in winter, see hours above; enter at end facing Golden Gate).

Partially explained in English, the Amber Museum offers a good introduction to the globby yellow stuff. As the museum fills an old guard tower, you'll have to walk up several flights of stairs to see it all. For a primer before you go, check out the "All About Amber" sidebar.

Climb up one flight of stairs, buy your ticket, then head up to the second floor for a scientific look at amber. View inclusions (items trapped in the resin) through a microscope, and see dozens of samples showing the full rainbow of amber shades. Interactive video screens explain the creation of amber. The third-floor exhibit explains the "Amber Road" (the ancient Celtic trade route connecting Gdańsk to Italy), outlines medicinal uses of the stuff, and displays a wide range of functional items made from amber—clocks, pipe stems, candlesticks, chandeliers, jewelry boxes, and much more. The fourth floor shows off more artistic items made of amber—sculptures, candelabras, beer steins, chessboards, and a model ship with delicate sails made of amber. At the top floor, you'll find a modern gallery showing more recent amber craftsmanship, and displays about amber's role in fashion today.

On your way back down, detour along the courtyard to find the museum's dark side (Torture Museum). First is a brief exhibit about the building's history—including its chapter as a prison tower. The rest of the exhibit, with sound effects and a few artifacts, describes medieval torture and imprisonment (but pales in comparison to other torture museums in Europe).

▲**Uphagen House (Dom Uphagena)**—This interesting place is your chance to glimpse what's behind the colorful facades lining ulica Długa (8 zł, free on Mon in summer, free on Tue in winter, see hours on page 329; ulica Długa 12). Check out the cut-away model just inside the entry to see the three parts you'll visit: dolled-up visitors' rooms in front, a corridor along the courtyard, and private rooms in the back. You'll begin upstairs, in the salon—used to show off for guests. Most of this furniture is original (saved from WWII bombs by locals who hid it in the countryside). Then you'll pass into the dining room, with knee-high paintings of hunting and celebrations. Along the passage to the back, each room has a

All About Amber

Poland's Baltic seaside is known as the Amber Coast. You'll see amber (bursztyn) in Gdańsk's new Amber Museum, in the collection at Malbork Castle (see page 364)—and in shop windows everywhere. This fossilized tree resin originated here on the north coast of Poland 40 million years ago. It comes in as many different colors as Eskimos have words for snow: 300 distinct shades, from yellowish-white to yellowish-black, from opaque to transparent. (I didn't believe it either, until I toured Gdańsk's museum.) Darker-colored amber is generally mixed with ash and sand—making it more fragile, and generally less desirable. Lighter amber is mixed with gasses and air bubbles.

Amber has been popular since long before there were souvenir stands. Archaeologists have found graves of Roman citizens (and their coins) who were buried with crosses made of amber. Almost 75 percent of the world's amber is mined in northern Poland, and it often simply washes up on the beaches after a winter storm. Some of the elaborate amber sculptures displayed at the museum are created by joining pieces of amber with "amber glue"—made of melted-down amber mixed with an adhesive agent. More recently, amber craftsmen are combining amber with silver to create artwork—a method dubbed the "Polish School."

In addition to being good for the economy, some Poles believe amber is good for their health. A traditional cure for arthritis pain is to pour strong vodka over amber, let it set, and then rub it on sore joints. Other remedies call for mixing amber dust with honey or rose oil. It sounds superstitious, but it works—amber contains a mineral that actually can help certain health problems.

theme: butterflies in the smoking room, then flowers, then birds in the music room. In the private rooms at the back, notice how much simpler the decor is. Back downstairs, you'll pass through the kitchen, the pantry, and a room with photos from the house before the war, which they used to reconstruct what you see today. The upper floors often house temporary exhibits.

▲▲**Main Town Hall (Ratusz Głównego Miasta)**—This landmark building, which may be closed for renovation, contains remarkable decorations from Gdańsk's Golden Age (8 zł, free on Mon in summer, free on Tue in winter, see hours on page 328; ulica Długa 47). You can also climb to the top of the **tower** for commanding views (4 zł extra, mid-June–mid-Sept only).

Buy your ticket down below (good gift shop), then head up the stairs and inside. In the entry room, examine the photo showing

this building at the end of World War II (you'll see more upstairs). The ornately carved wooden **door,** which you'll pass through in a minute, also deserves a close look. Above the door are two crosses under a crown. This seal of Gdańsk is being held—as it's often depicted—by a pair of lions. The felines are stubborn and independent, just like Gdańsk. Close the door partway to look at the carvings of crops. Around the frame of the door are mermen, reminding us that these crops, like so many other resources of Poland, are transported on the Vistula and out through Gdańsk.

Go through the door into the **Red Hall,** where the Gdańsk city council met in the summertime. (The lavish fireplace—with another pair of lions holding the coat of arms of Gdańsk—was just for show.) City council members would sit in the seats around the room, debating city policy. The shin-level paintings depict the earth; the exquisitely detailed inlaid wood just over the seats are animals; the paintings on the wall above represent the seven virtues the burghers meeting in this room should have; and the ceiling is all about theology. Examine that ceiling. You'll see 25 paintings total, with both Christian and pagan themes—meant to inspire the decision-makers in this room to make good choices. The smaller ones around the edges are scenes from mythology and the Bible. The one in the middle (from 1607) shows God's relationship to Gdańsk. In the foreground, the citizens of Gdańsk go about their daily lives. Above them, high atop the arch, God's hand reaches down (from within clouds of Hebrew characters) and grasps the city's steeple. The rainbow arching above also symbolizes God's connection to Gdańsk. Mirroring that is the Vistula River, which begins in the mountains of southern Poland (on the right), runs through the country, and exits at the sea in Gdańsk (on the left, where the rainbow ends).

Continue into the not-so-impressive Winter Hall, with another fireplace and coat of arms held by lions. Keep going through the next room, into a room with before-and-after photos of **WWII damage.** At the foot of the destroyed crucifix is a book with a bullet hole in it. The twist of wood is all that's left of the main support for the spiral staircase (today reconstructed in the room where you entered). Ponder the tragedy of war...and the inspiring ability of a city to be reborn.

Upstairs are some temporary exhibits, and several examples

of **Gdańsk-style furniture.** These pieces are characterized by three big, round feet along the front, lots of ornamentation, and usually a virtually-impossible-to-find lock (sometimes hidden behind a movable decoration). You'll also see a coin collection, from the days when Gdańsk had the elite privilege of minting its own currency.

▲▲**Artus Court (Dwór Artusa)**—In the Middle Ages, there were many brotherhoods and guilds (like businessmen's clubs) in Gdańsk. For their meetings, the city provided this elaborately decorated hall, named for King Arthur (a medieval symbol for prestige and power). Just as in King Arthur's Court, this was a place where powerful and important people came together. Such halls were once common in Baltic Europe, but this is the only original one that survives (8 zł, free on Mon in summer, free on Tue in winter, see hours on page 328; in tall, white, triple-arched building behind Neptune statue at Długi targ 43–44).

In the grand hall, you'll see various **cupboards** lining the walls. Each organization that met here had a place to keep its important documents and office supplies. Suspended from the ceiling are seven giant **model ships** that depict Baltic vessels, symbolic of the city's connection to the sea.

In the far back corner is the museum's highlight: a gigantic **stove** decorated with 520 colorful tiles featuring the faces of kings, queens, nobles, mayors, and burghers. Half of these people were Protestant, and half were Catholic, mixed together in no particular order—a reminder of the importance of religious tolerance. Virtually all of these tiles are original, having survived WWII bombs. Of the missing tiles, three were recently discovered by a bargain-hunter wandering through a flea market in the southern part of the country—and returned to their rightful home.

Notice the huge **paintings** on the walls above, with 3-D animals emerging from flat frames. Hunting is a popular theme in local artwork. Like minting coins, hunting was a privilege usually reserved for royalty, but extended in special circumstances to special towns...like Gdańsk. If you look closely, it's obvious that these "paintings" are digitally generated reproductions of the originals, which were damaged in World War II.

The next room—actually in the next-door building—is a typical front room of the burghers' homes lining ulica Długa. (Ogle the gorgeously carved wooden staircase.) Upstairs is a hall of knights—once again evoking Arthurian legend. As you exit to the back, you'll see a miniature reconstruction of the whole grand room, including paintings that have yet to be re-created. As you leave, you're just down the street from St. Mary's Church; to get back to the main drag, go back around the block, to the left.

Other Museums and Churches

▲▲St. Mary's Church (Kościół Mariacki)—Gdańsk has so many striking red-brick churches, it's hard to keep track of them. But if you visit only one, make it St. Mary's. This is the biggest brick church in the world, accommodating up to 25,000 people (standing room only). Built over 159 years in the 14th and 15th centuries, the church is an important symbol of Gdańsk (church free for individuals to enter but donation requested, open for tourists Mon–Sat 9:00–17:30, Sun 13:00–17:30).

As you enter the church, notice all of the white, empty space—unusual in a Catholic country, where frilly Baroque churches are the norm. In the Middle Ages, Gdańsk's tolerance attracted people who were suffering religious persecution. As the Protestant population grew, they needed a place to worship. St. Mary's, like most other Gdańsk churches, eventually became Protestant—leaving these churches with the blank walls you see now. Today you'll find only one Baroque church in central Gdańsk (the domed pink-and-green chapel behind St. Mary's).

Most Gothic stone churches are built in the basilica style—with a high nave in the middle, shorter naves on the side, and flying buttresses to support the weight. (Think of Paris' Notre-Dame.) But that design doesn't work with brick. So, like all Gdańsk churches, St. Mary's is a "hall church"—with three naves the same height, and no exterior buttresses.

Also like other Gdańsk churches, St. Mary's gave refuge to the Polish people after the communist government declared martial law in 1981. If a riot broke out and violence seemed imminent, people would flood into churches for protection. The ZOMO riot police wouldn't follow them inside.

Most of the church decorations are original. A few days before World War II broke out in Gdańsk, locals hid precious items in the countryside. Take some time now to see a few of the highlights.

Head up the right nave and find the opulent family marker to the right of the main altar. Look for the falling baby. This is Constantine Ferber. As a precocious child, Constantine leaned out his window on ulica Długa to see the king's processional come through town. He slipped and fell, but landed in a salesman's barrel of fish. Constantine grew up to become the mayor of Gdańsk.

Look on the side of the post for the coat of arms with the three pigs' heads. This story relates to another member of the illustrious Ferber clan. An enemy army was laying siege to the town, and tried to starve them out. A clever Ferber decided to load the cannons with pigs' heads to show the enemy that they had plenty of food—it worked, and the enemy left.

Circle around, past the front of the beautifully carved main altar. Behind it is the biggest stained-glass window in Poland,

and below the window is a huge, empty glass case. The case was designed to hold Hans Memling's *Final Judgment* painting, which used to be on display here, but is currently being held hostage by the National Museum. The museum claims the church isn't a good environment for such a precious work, but the priest had this display case built to convince the museum to give it back. You can see a smaller replica up by the main door of the church (in the little chapel on the right just before you exit), but true art fans will want to venture to the National Museum to see the much larger and far more masterful original (described on page 340).

Before you head back out to the mini-Memling (and the exit), venture to the far side of the altar and check out the elaborate astronomical clock. Below is the calendar showing the saint's day, and above are zodiac signs and the time (only one hand).

If you've got the energy, climb the 408 steps up the church's 270-foot-tall **tower.** You'll be rewarded with sweeping views of the entire city (tower climb-3 zł, entrance in back corner).

Archaeological Museum (Muzeum Archeologiczne)—This modest museum is worth a quick peek for those interested in archaeology. The ground floor has exhibits on excavated finds from Sudan, where the museum has a branch program. Upstairs, look for the distinctive urns with cute faces, dating from the Hallstatt Period and discovered in slate graves around Gdańsk. Also upstairs are some Bronze and Iron Age tools; before-and-after photos of WWII Gdańsk; and a reconstructed 12th-century Viking-like Slavonic longboat (5 zł; July–Aug Tue–Sun 10:00–17:00, closed Mon; Sept–June Tue and Thu–Fri 9:00–16:00, Wed 10:00–17:00, Sat–Sun 10:00–16:00, closed Mon; ulica Mariacka 25–26, tel. 058-322-2100). You can also pay 2 zł to climb the building's tower, with good views up Mariacka street toward St. Mary's Church.

▲Central Maritime Museum (Centralne Muzeum Morskie)—Gdańsk's history and livelihood are tied to the sea. This collec-

tion, spread out among several buildings on either side of the river, examines all aspects of this connection. While nautical types may get a thrill out of the creaky, sprawling museum, most visitors find it little more than a convenient way to pass some time and enjoy a cruise across the river.

There are four parts of the exhibit. Two of them are on the Main Town side of the river: The building next to the Crane (Żuraw), where you buy your ticket, houses different kinds of **boats from around the world,** mostly from non-European cultures. A Venetian gondola greets you at the entry. The medieval **Crane** itself—Gdańsk's most important symbol—houses an exhibit on living in the city during its Golden Age (16th–17th centuries). You'll see models of Baltic buildings (including the Crane you're inside), plus traditional tools and costumes. For more on the Crane, see page 331.

The other two parts of the museum are across the river on Ołowianka Island. You'll reach the island via the little **ferry** (*prom*, 1 zł 1-way, included in 15-zł ticket). The ferry runs about every 15 minutes in peak season (during museum hours only), but frequency declines sharply in the off-season (and it doesn't run if the river freezes). This also gives fine views back on the Crane.

Once on the island, you'll visit the three rebuilt **Old Granaries** (Spichlerze). These make up the heart of the exhibit, tracing the history of Gdańsk—particularly as it relates to the sea—from prehistoric days to the present. Models of the town and region help put things into perspective. You'll see exhibits on underwater exploration, navigational aids, artifacts of the Polish seafaring tradition, peek-a-boo cross-sections of multi-level ships, and models of the modern-day shipyard where Solidarity was born. This place is home to more miniature ships than you ever thought you'd see, and the Nautical Gallery upstairs features endless rooms with paintings of boats.

Finally, crawl through the holds and scramble across the deck of a decommissioned steamship docked permanently across from the Crane, called the *Sołdek.* Below decks, you'll see where they shoveled the coal; wander through a maze of pipes, gears, valves, gauges, and ladders; and visit the rooms where the sailors lived, slept, and ate. You can even play captain in the bridge. The place would be much improved with a smarter exhibit—which is planned for the future (ship sometimes closed in winter).

Cost, Hours, Location: Individually, each of the four parts of the museum costs 6 zł, but a 15-zł ticket gets you in everywhere and also covers the ferry across the river. It's open July–Aug daily 10:00–18:00; Sept–Oct and March–June Tue–Sun 10:00–16:00, closed Mon; Nov–Feb Tue–Sun 10:00–15:00, closed Mon (ulica Ołowianka 9–13, tel. 058-301-8611, www.cmm.pl). Throughout the museum, there's an irritating lack of English information, though some exhibits have descriptions you can borrow.

National Museum in Gdańsk (Muzeum Narodowe w Gdańsku)—This art collection, housed in what was a 15th-century Franciscan monastery, is worth ▲▲ to art-lovers for one reason: Hans Memling's glorious *Last Judgment* triptych altarpiece, one of the two most important pieces of art to be seen in Poland (the other is da Vinci's *Lady with an Ermine* in Kraków—see page 234). If you're not a purist, you can settle for seeing the much smaller replica in St. Mary's Church. But if medieval art is your bag, make the 10-minute walk here from the Main Town (10 zł, Tue–Fri 9:00–

16:00, Sat–Sun 10:00–16:00, last entry at 15:30, closed Mon; walk 10 min due south from ulica Długa's Golden Gate, take pedestrian underpass beneath the big cross-street, then continue down the busy street until you see signs for the museum; ulica Toruńska 1, tel. 058-301-7061, www.muzeum.narodowe.gda.pl).

From the entry, the altarpiece by Hans Memling (c. 1440–1494) is at the top of the stairs. The history of the painting is as interesting as the work itself. It was commissioned in the mid-15th century by the Medicis' banker in Florence, Angelo di Jacopo Tani. The ship delivering the painting from England to Florence was hijacked by a Gdańsk pirate, who brought the altarpiece to his hometown to be displayed in St. Mary's Church. For centuries, it was admired from afar by kings, emperors, and czars, until it was seized by Napoleon in the early 19th century and taken to Paris, where it hung in the Louvre. Gdańsk finally got the painting back, only to have it exiled again—this time into St. Petersburg's Hermitage Museum—after World War II. On its return to Gdańsk in 1956, it was claimed by this museum—though St. Mary's wants it back.

Have a close look at Memling's well-traveled work. It's the end of the world, and Christ rides in on a rainbow to judge humankind. Angels blow reveille, waking the dead, who rise from their graves. The winged archangel Michael—dressed for battle and wielding the cross like a weapon—weighs the grace in each person, sending them either to the fires of hell (right panel) or up the sparkling-crystal stairway to heaven (left).

It takes all 70 square feet of paneling to contain this awesome scene. Jam-packed with dozens of bodies, a Bible's worth of symbolism, and executed with astonishing detail, the painting can keep even a non-art-lover occupied. Notice the serene, happy expressions of the righteous, as they're greeted by St. Peter (with his giant key) and clothed by angels. And pity the condemned, their faces filled with terror and sorrow as they're tortured by grotesque devils more horrifying than anything Hollywood can devise.

Tune into the exquisite details: the angels' robes, the devils' genetic-mutant features, the portrait of the man in the scale (a Medici banker), Michael's peacock wings. Get as close as you can to the globe at Christ's feet and Michael's shining breastplate, and you'll even make out the whole scene in mirror reflection. Then back up and take it all in—three panels connected by a necklace of bodies that curves downward through hell, across the earth, then rising up to the towers of the New Jerusalem. On the back side of the triptych, you'll see reverent portraits of the painting's patron, Angelo Tani, and his new bride, Catarina.

Beyond the Memling, the rest of the collection isn't too

thrilling. The rest of the upstairs has more Flemish and Dutch art, as well as paintings from Gdańsk's Golden Age and various works by Polish artists (including canvases by Młoda Polska artists Jacek Malczewski and Olga Boznańska—explained on page 219). The ground floor features a cavernous, all-white cloister filled with Gothic altarpiece sculptures, gold- and silverware, majolica and Delft porcelain, and characteristic Gdańsk-style furniture.

▲▲▲Solidarity (Solidarność) and the Gdańsk Shipyard (Stocznia Gdańska)

Gdańsk's single best experience is exploring the shipyard that witnessed the beginning of the end of communism's stranglehold on Eastern Europe. Here in the industrial wasteland that Lech Wałęsa called the "cradle of freedom," you'll learn the story of the brave Polish shipyard workers who took on—and ultimately defeated—an Evil Empire.

A visit to the Solidarity sights has two main parts: the memorial and gate out in front of the shipyard, and the excellent "Roads to Freedom" exhibit nearby. Allow 90 minutes for the whole visit.

Cost, Hours, Information: Memorial and shipyard gate—free and always open; "Roads to Freedom" exhibit—6 zł, May–Sept Tue–Sun 10:00–17:00, Oct–April Tue–Sun 10:00–16:00, closed Mon year-round, Wały Piastowskie 24, tel. 058-769-2920, www .fcs.org.pl.

Getting to the Shipyard: The Solidarity monument and shipyard are at the north end of the Old Town, about a 20-minute walk from ulica Długa. For the most interesting approach, see my self-guided walk on page 331.

Background: After the communists took over Eastern Europe at the end of World War II, the oppressed people throughout the Soviet Bloc rose up in different ways. The most dramatic uprisings—Hungary's 1956 Uprising (see page 438) and Czechoslovakia's 1968 "Prague Spring" (see page 36)—were both brutally crushed under the treads of Soviet tanks. The formula for freedom that finally succeeded—and was lucky enough to coincide with the *perestroika* and *glasnost* policies of the Soviet premier Mikhail Gorbachev—was a patient, decade-long series of strikes spearheaded by Lech Wałęsa and his trade union, called Solidarność—"Solidarity." While some American politicians would like to take credit for defeating communism, Wałęsa and his fellow workers were the ones fighting on the front lines, armed with nothing more than guts.

➔ Self-Guided Tour: First we'll visit the memorial and peek into the shipyard, then we'll backtrack to the museum. Begin at the towering monument—with three anchor-adorned crosses—near the entrance gate to the shipyard.

Monument of the Fallen Shipyard Workers: The seeds of August 1980 were sown a decade before. Since becoming part of the Soviet Bloc, the Poles staged frequent strikes, protests, and uprisings to secure their rights, all of which were put down by the regime. But the bloodiest of these took place in December 1970—a tragic event memorialized by this monument.

The 1970 strike was prompted by price hikes. The communist government set the prices for all products. As Poland endured drastic food shortages in the 1960s and 1970s, the regime frequently announced what they called "regulation of prices"—increasing the cost of essential foodstuffs, while at the same time symbolically lowering prices of unimportant items that nobody could afford anyway (like elevators and TV sets). The regime was usually smart enough to raise prices on January 1—when the people were fat and happy after Christmas, and too hungover to complain. But on December 12, 1970, bolstered by an ego-stoking visit by West German Chancellor Willy Brandt, Polish premier Władysław Gomułka increased prices. The people of Poland—who cared more about the price of Christmas dinner than relations with Germany—struck back.

A wave of strikes and sit-ins spread along the heavily industrialized north coast of Poland, most notably in Gdańsk, Gdynia, and Szczecin. Thousands of angry demonstrators poured through the gate of this shipyard, marched into town, and set fire to the Communist Party Committee building. In an attempt to quell the riots, the government-run radio implored the people to go back to work. On the morning of December 17, workers showed up at shipyard gates across northern Poland—and were greeted by the army and police. Without provocation, the Polish army opened fire on the workers. While the official death toll for the massacre stands at 44, others say the true number is much higher. This monument, with a trio of 140-foot-tall crosses, honors those lost to the regime that December.

Go to the middle of the wall behind the crosses, to the monument of the worker wearing a flimsy plastic work helmet, attempting to shield himself from bullets. Behind him is a list—pockmarked with symbolic bullet holes—of workers murdered on that day. *Lat* means "years old"—many teenagers were among the dead. The quote at the top of the wall was from Pope John Paul II, who was elected eight years after this tragedy. The Pope was known for his clever way with words, and this very carefully

Lech Wałęsa

In 1980, the world was turned on its ear by a walrus-mustachioed shipyard electrician. Within three years, this seemingly run-of-the-mill Pole had precipitated the collapse of communism, led a massive 10 million-member trade union with enormous political impact, was named *Time* magazine's Man of the Year, and won a Nobel Peace Prize.

Lech Wałęsa was born in Popowo, Poland, in 1943. After working as a car mechanic and serving two years in the army, he became an electrician at the Gdańsk Shipyard in 1967. Like many Poles, Wałęsa felt stifled by the communist government, and was infuriated that a system that was supposed to be for the workers clearly wasn't serving them.

When the shipyard massacre took place in December 1970, Wałęsa was at the forefront of the protests. He was marked as a dissident, and in 1976, he was fired. He hopped from job to job and was occasionally unemployed—a rock-bottom status reserved for only the most despicable derelicts. But Wałęsa soldiered on, fighting for the creation of a trade union and building up quite a file with the secret police.

In August 1980, Wałęsa heard news of the beginnings of the Gdańsk strike, and raced to the shipyard. In an act that has since become the stuff of legends, Wałęsa scaled the shipyard wall to get inside.

Before long, Wałęsa's dynamic personality won him the unofficial role of the workers' leader and spokesman. He negotiated with the regime to hash out the August Agreements, becoming a rock star–type hero during the so-called "16 Months of Hope"...until martial law came crashing down in December of 1981. Wałęsa was arrested and interned for 11 months in a country house. After being released, Wałęsa continued to struggle under-

phrased quote—which served as an inspiration to the Poles during their darkest hours—skewers the regime in a way subtle enough to still be tolerated: "Let thy spirit descend, and renew the face of the earth—*this* earth" (that is, Poland). Below that is the dedication: "They gave their lives so you can live decently."

Stretching to the left of this center wall are plaques representing labor unions from around Poland—and around the world (look for the Chinese characters)—expressing solidarity with these workers. To the right is an enormous Bible verse: "May the Lord give strength to his people. May the Lord bless his people with the ground, becoming a symbol of anti-communist sentiment.

Finally, the dedication of Wałęsa and Solidarity paid off, and Polish communism dissolved—with Wałęsa rising from the ashes as the country's first post-communist president. But the skills that made Wałęsa a rousing success at leading an uprising did not translate to the president's office. Wałęsa proved to be a stubborn, headstrong politician, frequently clashing with the parliament. He squabbled with his own party, declaring a "war at the top" of Solidarity and rotating higher-ups to prevent corruption and keep the party fresh. He also didn't choose his advisors well, enlisting several staffers who wound up immersed in scandal. His overconfidence was his Achilles' heel, and his governing style verged on authoritarian.

Unrefined and none too interested in scripted speeches, Wałęsa was a simple man who preferred playing ping-pong with his buddies to attending formal state functions. Though lacking a formal education, Wałęsa had unsurpassed drive and charisma... but that's not enough to lead a country—especially during an impossibly complicated, fast-changing time, when even the savviest politician would certainly have stumbled.

Wałęsa was defeated at the polls (by the Poles) in 1995, and when he ran again in 2000, he received a humiliating 1 percent of the vote. Since leaving office, Wałęsa has kept a lower profile, but still delivers speeches worldwide. Many poor Poles grumble that Lech, who started life simple like them, has forgotten the little people. But his fans point out that he gives much of his income to charity. And he still always wears a pin featuring the Black Madonna of Częstochowa—the symbol of Polish Catholicism—on his lapel.

Poles say there are at least two Lech Wałęsas: the young, working-class idealist Lech, at the forefront of the Solidarity strikes, who will always have a special place in their hearts; and the failed President Wałęsa, who got in over his head and tarnished his legacy.

gift of peace" (Psalms 29:11).

More than a decade after the massacre, this monument was finally constructed. It marked the first time a communist regime ever allowed a monument built to honor its own victims. Wałęsa called it a harpoon in the heart of the communists. Inspired by the brave sacrifice of their true comrades, the shipyard workers rose up here in August of 1980, formulating the "21 Points" of a new union called Solidarity. The demands included the right to strike and form unions, the freeing of political prisoners, and an increase in wages. These 21 Points are listed in Polish on the panel at the far end of the right wall, marked *21 X TAK Solidarność* ("21 times yes Solidarity").

• *Now continue to the gate and peer through into the birthplace of Eastern European freedom.*

Gdańsk Shipyard (Stocznia Gdańska) Gate #2: When a Pole named Karol Wojtyła was elected Pope in 1978—and visited his homeland in 1979—he inspired his 40 million countrymen to believe that impossible dreams can come true. Prices continued to go up, and the workers continued to rise up. By the summer of 1980, it was clear that the dam was about to break.

In August, Anna Walentynowicz—a Gdańsk crane operator and known dissident—was fired unceremoniously just short of her retirement. This sparked a strike in the Gdańsk Shipyard (then called the Lenin Shipyard) on August 14, 1980. An electrician named Lech Wałęsa had been fired as an agitator years before, and wasn't allowed into the shipyard. But on hearing news of the strike, Wałęsa went to the shipyard and climbed over the wall to get inside. The strike had a leader.

Imagine being one of the 16,000 workers who stayed here for 18 days during the strike—hungry, cold, sleeping on sheets of Styrofoam, inspired by the new Polish pope, excited about finally standing up to the regime...and terrified that you might be gunned down at any moment, like your friends were a decade before. Because you're afraid to leave the shipyard, your only way to communicate with the outside world is through this gate—your wife or brother shows up here and asks for you, and those inside spread the word until you come talk to them. Occasionally, a truck pulls up to the gate, and Lech Wałęsa stands on its cab with a megaphone and faces the thousands of people assembled here—giving them progress reports of the negotiations, and pleading for supplies. The people of Gdańsk respond, bringing armfuls of bread and other food, keeping the workers going. This truly is Solidarity.

Two items hung on the fence. One of them (which still hangs there today) was a picture of Pope John Paul II—a reminder to believe in your dreams and have faith in God (for more on the pope and his role in Solidarity, see page 222). The other item was a makeshift list of the strikers' 21 Points—demands scrawled in red paint and black pencil on pieces of plywood.

• *You'll likely see construction in the area beyond the gate. This part of the shipyard—long abandoned—is gradually being redeveloped into a "new city center" for Gdańsk, with shopping, restaurants, and homes. The centerpiece will be the new European Center of Solidarity (still an active union in some countries). Due to the redevelopment, the following sights may be moved or inaccessible during your visit. If so, simply skip down to the next section.*

Go around the gate (to the right, past the souvenir stand) and enter the shipyard. As you walk, you may see giant photographs from the summer of 1980.

Shipyard Path: As you walk on the path, you'll pass through two huge symbolic gateways. The first resembles the rusted hull of a ship, representing the protest of the shipbuilders. Inside are two electronic strips: on the left, displaying communist slogans; on the right, the wisdom of Lech Wałęsa and Solidarity.

The next gateway—a futuristic, colorful tower—is a small-scale version of a 1,000-foot-tall monument planned by the prominent Soviet constructivist architect Vladimir Tatlin. This fanciful but unfulfilled design represents the misguided, failed optimism of the communist "utopia."

You likely won't be able to walk beyond these gateways. But on the other side of the gate, the low-profile, red-brick building is the BHP Conference Hall—the place where the communists actually sat down across the table from Lech Wałęsa and worked out a compromise. This building is being restored, and will be a centerpiece of the "Roads to Freedom" exhibit when it moves back here in several years.

• *The museum where we'll learn the rest of the story is about 100 yards back toward the Main Town. With the main shipyard gate to your back, walk straight ahead, passing the green-and-yellow building on your right-hand side. Cross the street and walk toward the green skyscraper. After about a block, you'll see stairs leading underground, into the...*

"Roads to Freedom" Exhibit: Walk downstairs and buy your ticket, which is designed to look like the communist ration coupons that all Poles had to carry and present before they could buy certain goods. Cashiers would stand with scissors at the ready, prepared to snip off a corner of your coupon after making the sale. Consider picking up a Solidarity book or other souvenir at the excellent gift shop here before moving on.

To the right of the ticket desk, you'll see some depressing reminders of the communist days. The phone booth is marked *Automat Nieczynny*—"Out of Order"—as virtually all phone booths were back then. In the humble, authentic commie WC, notice that instead of toilet paper, there's a wad of old newspapers. (Actual toilet paper was cause for celebration.)

Across from the ticket desk is a typical **Polish shop** (marked *spożyw*, a truncated version of *spożywczy*, or "grocery store") from the 1970s, at the worst of the food shortages. Great selection, eh? Often the only things in stock were vinegar and mustard. Milk and bread were generally available, but they were low quality—it wasn't unusual to find a cigarette butt in your loaf. The few blocks of cheese and other items in the case aren't real—they're props (marked *atrapy*—"fake"), so the shop wouldn't look completely empty. Sometimes they'd hang a few pitiful, phony salamis from the hooks—otherwise, people might think it was a tile shop. The only real meat in here was the flies on the flypaper. Shockingly, shoppers (mostly women) would sometimes have to wait in line literally all day long just to pick over these scant choices. People didn't necessarily buy what they needed; instead, they'd buy anything that could be bartered on the black market. On the counter, notice the little jar holding clipped-off ration coupons.

Continue into the exhibit. The first room explains the **roots** of the shipyard strikes, including the famous uprisings in Hungary and Czechoslovakia, and the December 1970 riots in Poland. (Interactive computer screens tell you more about these events.) The prison cell is a reminder of Stalin's strong-arm tactics for getting the people of Eastern Europe to sign on to his new system.

Then you move into the heart of the exhibit, **August 1980.** Past the plaster statue of Lenin are several tables. These were the actual tables used (in the red-brick building back in the shipyard) when the communists finally agreed to negotiate after 18 days of protests. On the afternoon of August 31, 1980, the Governmental Commission and the Inter-Factory Strike Committee (MKS) came together and signed the August Agreements, which legalized Solidarity—the first time any communist government permitted a workers' union. Photos and a video show the giddy day, as the Polish Bob Dylan laments the evils of the regime. Lech Wałęsa—sitting at the big table, with his characteristic walrus moustache—signed the agreement with a big, red, souvenir-type pen adorned with a picture of Pope John Paul II (displayed across the room). Other union reps, sitting at smaller tables, tape-recorded the proceedings, and played them later at their own factories to prove the unthinkable had happened. Near the end of this room are replicas of the plywood boards featuring the 21 Points, which hung on the front gate we just saw.

While the government didn't take the agreements very seriously, the Poles did...and before long, 10 million of them—one out of every four Poles—became members of Solidarity. So began the **16 Months of Hope**—the theme of the next room. Newly legal, Solidarity continued to stage strikes and made its opposition known. Slick Solidarity posters and children's art convey the childlike enthusiasm with which the Poles seized their hard-won kernels of freedom. The poster with a baby in a Solidarity T-shirt—one year old, just like the union itself—captures the sense of hope. The grasp of the communist authorities on the Polish people began to slip. The rest of the Soviet Bloc looked on nervously, and the Warsaw Pact army assembled at the Polish border and glared at the uprisers. The threat of invasion hung heavy in the air.

Head down the hallway to see Solidarity's progress come crashing down. On Sunday morning, December 13, 1981, the

Polish head of state, General Wojciech Jaruzelski, appeared on national TV and announced the introduction of **martial law.** Solidarity was outlawed, and its leaders were arrested. Frightened Poles heard the announcement and looked out their windows to see Polish Army tanks rumbling through the snowy streets. Jaruzelski claimed that he imposed martial law to prevent the Soviets from invading. Today, many historians question whether martial law was really necessary—though Jaruzelski remains remorseless. Martial law was a tragic, terrifying, and bleak time for the Polish people. But Solidarity moved underground and continued the fight for freedom. Notice that their martial law–era propaganda was produced with far more primitive printing equipment than their earlier posters.

In the next room, you see a clandestine print shop like those used to create that illegal propaganda. Surrounding the room are sobering displays of **ZOMO riot gear.** A film reveals the ugliness of martial law. Watch the footage of General Jaruzelski—wearing his trademark dark glasses—reading the announcement of martial law. Chilling scenes show riots, demonstrations, and crackdowns by the ZOMO police—including one demonstrator who's run over by a truck. Another old woman is stampeded by a pack of fleeing demonstrators.

The next room shows a film tracing the whole history of **communism in Poland** (with a copy of Lech Wałęsa's Nobel Peace Prize).

For a happy ending, head into the final room, with another, uplifting film about the **fall of the Iron Curtain** across Eastern Europe—right up through the 2004 "Orange Revolution" in Ukraine.

Here's how it happened in Poland: By the time the Pope visited his homeland again in 1983, martial law was lifted, and Solidarity—still technically illegal—had gained momentum, gradually pecking away at the communists. With the moral support of the Pope and the entire Western world, the brave Poles were the first European country to throw off the shackles of communism when, in the spring of 1989, the "Round Table Talks" led to the opening up of elections. The government arrogantly called for parliamentary elections, reserving 65 percent of seats for themselves. The plan backfired, as virtually every contested seat went to Solidarity. This success inspired people all over Eastern Europe, and by that winter, the Berlin Wall had crumbled and the Czechs and Slovaks had staged their Velvet Revolution. Lech Wałęsa—the shipyard electrician who started it all by jumping over a wall—became the first president of post-communist Poland. And a year later, in Poland's first true elections since World War II, 29 different parties won seats in the Sejm (Parliament). This celebration of democracy was brought to the Polish people by a brave electrician and the workers of Gdańsk.

Outer Gdańsk

These two sights—worthwhile only to those with a special interest—are each within the city limits of Gdańsk, but they take several hours to see round-trip.

Oliwa Cathedral (Katedra Oliwska)—The suburb of Oliwa, at the northern edge of Gdańsk, is home to this visually striking church. The quirky, elongated facade hides a surprisingly long and skinny nave. The ornately decorated 18th-century organ over the main entrance features angels and stars that move around when the organ is played. While locals are proud of this place, it's hard to justify the effort it takes to get out here. Skip it unless you just love Polish churches or you're going to a concert.

Concerts: Concerts of the animated organ occur frequently, especially in summer (June–Aug generally at the top of each hour Mon–Fri 10:00–16:00—except at 14:00—Sat 10:00–15:00, Sun 15:00–17:00; May and Sept Mon–Sat at the top of each hour 10:00–13:00, Sun at 15:00 and 16:00; 1–2/day off-season). Confirm the schedule at the TI before making the trip. Note that on Sundays and holidays, there are no concerts before 15:00.

Getting There: Oliwa is about six miles northwest of central Gdańsk, on the way to Sopot and Gdynia. To get to Oliwa, you have two options: Take **tram** #6 or #12 from Gdańsk's Main Train Station. These trams let you off right at the entrance to Oliwski Park. Go straight through to the back of the park; near the end, you'll see the copper roof and two skinny, pointy spires of the cathedral on your right. Exit through the back of the park, bear right, and go one block to find the entrance to the church. Your other option is to take a **commuter SKM train** from Gdańsk's Main Station 15 minutes to the "Gdańsk Oliwa" stop (see "Getting Around the Tri-City," page 359). From the Oliwa train station, it's a 15-minute walk or 10-zł taxi ride to the cathedral. Walk straight ahead out of the station and turn right when you get to the busy road. Cross the road at the light and enter the tree-filled Park Oliwski at the corner, then follow the directions above.

Westerplatte—World War II began on September 1, 1939, when Adolf Hitler sent the warship *Schleswig-Holstein* to attack this Polish munitions depot, which was guarding Gdańsk's harbor. Though it may interest WWII history buffs, there's little to see at this site aside from a modest museum and a towering monument. As it's surrounded by shipyard sprawl, it's not a particularly pleasant trip, either.

Getting There: It's quickest to take **bus** #106 from Brama Wyżynna (just outside the Main Town) to the end (about 30 min).

Or cruise there in 45 minutes on Żegluga Gdańska boats or the old-fashioned *Galeon Lew* (see "Transportation Connections," page 357).

SHOPPING

The big story in Gdańsk is amber *(bursztyn)*, a fossil resin available in all shades, shapes, and sizes (see "All About Amber," page 335). While you'll see amber sold all over town, the best place to browse and buy is along the atmospheric ulica Mariacka (between the Motława River and St. Mary's Church). This pretty street, with old-fashioned balconies and dozens of display cases, is fun to wander even if you're not a shopper. Other good places to buy amber are along the riverfront embankment and on ulica Długa. To avoid rip-offs—such as amber that's been melted and reshaped—always buy it from a shop, not from someone standing on the street. (But note that most shops also have a display case and salesperson out front, which are perfectly legit.) Prices everywhere are about the same, so rather than seeking out a specific place, just window-shop until you see what you want. Styles range from gaudy necklaces with huge globs of amber, to tasteful smaller pendants in a silver setting, to cheap trinkets. All shades of amber—from near-white to dark brown—cost about the same, but you'll pay more for inclusions (bugs or other objects stuck in the amber). You can get a basic amber pendant on a silver chain or a pair of small earrings for about 30 zł. If you want to pay more for bigger pieces or a more stylish setting, merchants will happily take your money.

Gdańsk also has several modern shopping malls, most of them in the Old Town or near the Main Train Station. The walk between the Main Town and the Solidarity shipyard goes past some of the best malls (see page 331).

SLEEPING

Gdańsk's accommodation scene, miserably sparse until recently, is steadily improving. Several new hotels have cropped up in the last few years—and lots more are planned for the future. To get the best deal, it's essential to book ahead for peak season (mid-June–mid-Sept), when prices increase.

Across the River

While these three places are a few minutes farther by foot from the action, they're all well priced.

$$$ Hotel Królewski, a classy hotel in a beautifully renovated red-brick granary, offers 30 stylish rooms, good rates, and a friendly staff. It's just beyond the three granaries of the Maritime Museum, across the river from the Crane (Sb-350 zł, Db-400 zł,

Sleep Code

(3 zł = about $1, country code: 48)
S = Single, **D** = Double/Twin, **T** = Triple, **Q** = Quad, **b** = bathroom,
s = shower only. Unless otherwise noted, breakfast is included,
credit cards are accepted, and English is spoken.

To help you sort easily through these listings, I've divided
the rooms into three categories, based on the price for a standard double room with bath:

  $$$ Higher Priced—Most rooms 400 zł or more.
   $$ Moderately Priced—Most rooms between
                      300–400 zł.
    $ Lower Priced—Most rooms 300 zł or less.

fancier suite-like Db "plus"-450 zł, pricier apartments, lower rates
Oct–April, request a view room—they cost the same as non-view
rooms, non-smoking rooms, elevator, free Wi-Fi, good restaurant,
ulica Ołowianka 1, tel. 058-326-1111, fax 058-326-1110, www
.hotelkrolewski.pl, office@hotelkrolewski.pl). You can commute
to your sightseeing by ferry (take the 1-zł boat trip across the river
offered by the Maritime Museum—see page 340). But the ferry
runs only during the museum's opening hours, and is sporadic off-
season. If the ferry isn't running, it's a scenic 10-minute walk along
the river and over the bridge into the Main Town.

$ *On Ulica Spichrzowa:* Several new hotels are on the back side
of a charmingly restored row of colorful houses on the island just
across the river from the main drag. While they overlook a dreary
vacant lot, these places (and others on the same street) offer a good
value in a convenient location: **$$ Willa Litarion** is run by the
eager Owsikowski family. Each of the 13 small rooms has a totally
different design, but all are artsy and mod (Sb-225 zł, Db-330 zł,
bigger "deluxe" Db-360 zł, 10–15 percent cheaper Oct–April, extra
bed-60 zł, no elevator, parking garage-20 zł, ulica Spichrzowa 18,
tel. 058-320-2553, fax 058-320-2563, www.litarion.pl, recepcja
@litarion.pl). **$ Willa Biała Lilia** ("Villa of the White Lily"), next
door, has 16 uninspired but modern and comfortable rooms (Sb-
230 zł, Db-265 zł, 15 zł more per person for bigger "deluxe" rooms,
extra bed-60 zł, slightly cheaper Oct–April, no elevator, parking
garage-20 zł, ulica Spichrzowa 16, tel. 058-301-7074, fax 058-320-
1473, www.bialalilia.pl, bialalilia@bialalilia.pl).

$ Dom Muzyka rents 87 simple, tidy rooms in a nondescript
residential neighborhood. The catch: It's very difficult to find, hid-
ing in the back of the big Academy of Music building (Akademia
Muzyczna). But the prices are worth the hunt, and once you're

GDAŃSK HOTELS & RESTAURANTS

1. Hotel Królewski
2. Willa Litarion & Willa Biała Lilia
3. To Dom Muzyka Hotel
4. Hotel Wolne Miasto
5. Hanza Hotel
6. Kamienica Goldwasser Hotel/Restaurant
7. Gotyk House
8. Dom Harcerza Hostel
9. Przy Targu Rybnym Hostel
10. Baltic Hostel
11. Bar pod Rybą Restaurant
12. Bar Mleczny Neptun
13. Targ Rybny/Fishmarkt Rest.
14. Czerwone Drzwi Rest.
15. Dom pod Łososiem Rest.
16. Pierogarnia u Dzika Rest.
17. Pi Kawa Café
18. Cukiernia Kaliszczak

Gate

SOLIDARITY MONUMENT

DOKI

WAŁY PIASTOWSKIE

Library

WAŁOWA

 AKASMITNA

3 MAJA

PODWALE GRODZKIE

RAJSKA

J. HEWELIUSZA

ŁAGIEWNIKI

RYBAKI GÓRNE

200 Meters

200 Yards

Gdańsk

Train Station

Gdańsk Główny

OLD TOWN

PŁYNY

GARNCARSKA

KOWALSKA

TKNISZKI

STOLARSKA

ST. BRIDGET'S

KROSNA

OLEJARNA

TACZNA

KATARZYNKI

ST. CATHERINE

STAROMIEJSKIE

Targ Rybny

River

WAŁY JAGIELLOŃSKIE

HUCISKO

Tower

Market Hall

Targ Drzewny

STRAGANIARSKA

ST. NICHOLAS

GROBLA

ŚWIĘTOJAŃSKA

POBRZEŻE

13

5

Central Maritime Museum

SS Sołdek

1

Armory

Targ Węglowy

Brama Wyżynna

LOT Office

MAIN TOWN

16 KOZIA

14

TKACKA

DUCHA

The Crane

15

TOKARSKA

Upland Gate & Amber Museum

Golden Gate

17

18

ST. MARY'S

PIWNA

Uphagen House

ULICA

Post Office

DŁUGA

12

Town Hall

Artus Court

7

Archaeological Museum

OKOPOWA

POCZTOWA

8

Neptune Statue

11

Granary Island

Green Gate

CHMIELNA

MOTŁAWA

OGARNA

ŁAWNICZA

Długi Targ

3

STAGIEWNA

PODWALE PRZEDMIEJSKIE

SPICHRZOWA

2

set up, it's an easy 10-minute walk to the sights. Their "deluxe" rooms are bigger and overlook the quiet courtyard, while most of the standard rooms face a busy street. Since the deluxe rooms are mostly twins, and the streetside standard rooms have air-conditioning and good soundproof windows, I'd go with standard (Sb-200 zł, standard Db-280 zł, deluxe Db-300 zł, apartment-420 zł, extra bed-80 zł, 10 zł less per person Oct–April, elevator, free Wi-Fi, popular with tour groups, good restaurant, ulica Łąkowa 1–2, tel. 058-326-0600, fax 058-326-0601, www.dom-muzyka.pl, biuro @dom-muzyka.pl). From the Main Town's Green Gate, cross the two bridges, then walk a long block along the modern commercial building and turn right just before the park (on Łąkowa, across from the big brick church). Walk to the end of this block; before the busy road, go through the gate just before the big, yellow-brick building on the right. Once inside the gate, the hotel is around the back of the yellow building, the farthest door down. If you get lost, just ask people, "Hotel?"

In the Main Town

You'll pay a premium to sleep in the Main Town itself, but many find it worth the extra expense.

$$$ Hotel Wolne Miasto ("Free City") offers rich, wood-carved public spaces and 43 elegant, well-priced rooms on the edge of the Main Town, just two blocks from the main drag. Since it's above a popular disco that gets noisy on weekends (Thu–Sat nights), request a quieter room when you reserve (Sb-360 zł, Db-410 zł, bigger "deluxe" Db-490 zł, cheaper Sept–June, air-con, elevator, ulica Świętego Ducha 2, tel. 058-322-2442, fax 058-322-2447, www.hotelwm.pl, rezerwacja@hotelwm.pl).

$$$ Hanza Hotel offers a fun, neo-Hanseatic exterior and 60 modern, uninspired, business-class rooms. It charges—and gets—top złoty for its ideal riverfront location, little character, and disinterested staff. Prices are outrageously high in the summer, but a bit more reasonable off-season (June–early Sept: Sb-695 zł, Db-745 zł; May and mid-Sept–Oct: Sb-665 zł, Db-695 zł; Nov–April: Sb-395 zł, Db-465 zł; request riverview room for no extra charge, air-con, elevator, Tokarska 6, tel. 058-305-3427, fax 058-305-3386, www.hanza-hotel.com.pl, hotel@hanza-hotel.com.pl).

$$ Kamienica Goldwasser, renting seven rooms over a good restaurant (see "Eating," below), is perfectly located, right on the river embankment next door to the Crane. Each room is different, but all are thoughtfully decorated, with windows facing both the river and the back. Three of the rooms are smaller and cheaper—similar to the bigger rooms, but with cramped bathrooms, and an especially good value (small Sb-275 zł, big Sb-375 zł, small Db-375 zł, big Db-475 zł, extra bed-100 zł, lots of stairs and no elevator,

Długie Pobrzeże 22, tel. & fax 058-301-8878, www.goldwasser.pl, kamienica@goldwasser.pl).

$ Gotyk House, Gdańsk's best deal, is run with warmth and pride by the Rybicki family. This we-try-harder guest house offers six modern, simple rooms with creative touches in what's supposedly the city's oldest house, next door to St. Mary's Church (Sb-250 zł, Db-280 zł, 30 zł less Oct–April, tight public spaces and tiny breakfast room, ulica Mariacka 1, tel. 058-301-8567, mobile 0602-844-535, www.gotykhouse.eu, reservation@gotykhouse.eu).

$ Dom Harcerza is a Polish-style budget hotel/hostel with 21 old, musty, but well-maintained rooms on the second floor of a dreary office building. This institutional-feeling place won't win any prizes for personality, and communication can be difficult, but it's cheap and nicely located in a corner of the Main Town just two blocks south of the Golden Gate (bunk in 4- to 12-bed dorm-30–40 zł depending on size, S-50 zł, D-120 zł, Db-220 zł, T-150 zł, Tb-260 zł, Q-160 zł, 25 percent cheaper Oct–April, includes sheets, breakfast-9 zł, cash only, fun ground-floor café, ulica Za Murami 2–10, tel. 058-301-3621, fax 058-301-2472, www .domharcerza.pl, rezerwacja@domharcerza.pl).

$ Przy Targu Rybnym, a three-minute walk from the Crane at the north end of the embankment, is Gdańsk's most central hostel. Waldemar runs this easygoing, low-key, slightly grungy place with a spirit of fun that permeates the chummy common room. Aside from dorm beds, it offers "private" rooms for two to four people, most with shared bathrooms down the hall (bunk in dorm or crowded basement slumbermill-50 zł, D-150 zł, Db-180 zł, T-210 zł, Q-240 zł, private rooms about 30 percent more in Aug, prices include sheets and breakfast, free Internet access, 15-zł laundry service, ulica Grodzka 21, tel. 058-301-5627, www .gdanskhostel.com.pl, gdanskhostel@hotmail.com). If they're booked up, Waldemar might send you to his **Baltic Hostel,** which is cheaper (dorm bunk-35 zł, private 2– to 4-person-100 zł, more in Aug) but in a much less convenient location (away from the center, north of the train station at 3 Maya #25; tel. 058-721-9657, www .baltichostel.com.pl, baltichostel@hotmail.com).

EATING

In addition to the traditional Polish fare, Gdańsk has some fine Baltic seafood. Herring *(śledź)* is popular here, as is cod *(dorsz)*. Natives brag that their salmon *(łosoś)* is better than Norway's. For a stiff drink, sample *Goldwasser* (similar to Goldschlager). This sweet and strong liqueur, flecked with gold, was supposedly invented here in Gdańsk. The following options are all in the Main Town, within three blocks of ulica Długa.

Budget Restaurants on the Main Drag

These two places are incredibly cheap, tasty, quick, and wonderfully convenient—right on ulica Długa. They're worth considering even if you're not on a tight budget.

Bar pod Rybą ("Under the Fish") is nirvana for fans of baked potatoes *(pieczony ziemniak)*. They offer more than 20 varieties, piled high with a wide variety of toppings and sauces, from Mexican beef to herring to Polish cheeses. They also offer fish dishes with salad and potatoes, making this a cheap place to sample local seafood. The tasteful decor—walls lined with old bottles, antique wooden hangers, and paintings by the owner—is squeezed into a single cozy room packed with happy eaters. In the summer, order inside, and they'll bring your food to you at an outdoor table (potatoes and fish dishes are each about 10–20 zł, daily 11:00–19:00, until 21:00 in summer, Długi Targ 35–38, tel. 058-305-1307).

Bar Mleczny Neptun is your best milk-bar option in the Main Town. A good meal, including a drink, runs about 10–15 zł. This popular place has more charm than your typical institutional milk bar, including outdoor seating along the most scenic stretch of the main drag. The items on the counter are for display—rather than take what's there, point to what you want and they'll dish it up fresh (Mon–Fri 7:00–18:00, until 19:00 in summer, Sat 10:00–17:00, open Sun only in summer 11:00–17:00, ulica Długa 33–34, tel. 058-301-4988). For more on milk bars, see page 199.

Other Restaurants with Polish Fare

Kamienica Goldwasser, which also rents rooms (see "Sleeping"), offers good Polish and international cuisine at fair prices. This is the best choice for dining along the riverfront embankment. Choose between cozy, romantic indoor seating on several levels, or scenic outdoor seating (most main dishes 25–65 zł, daily 10:00–24:00, occasional live music, near the Crane at Długie Pobrzeże 22, tel. 058-301-8878). They run another good restaurant a five-minute walk farther up the embankment: **Targ Rybny/Fishmarkt** ("The Fish Market"), with a warm, mellow Tuscan atmosphere, classy but not stuffy service, and an emphasis on fish (most main dishes 20–40 zł, plus pricier seafood splurges, daily 10:00–22:00, just behind the park and parking lot at ulica Targ Rybny 6C, tel. 058-320-9011).

Czerwone Drzwi ("The Red Door") serves up tasty Polish and international cuisine in a single-room, six-table restaurant. The decor is artsy, and there's jazz on the soundtrack (18–25-zł pierogi, big 20-zł salads, 30–40-zł main dishes, daily 11:00–24:00, ulica Piwna 52/53, tel. 058-301-5764).

Dom pod Łososiem ("House Under the Salmon"), with over-the-top formality, will make you feel like a rich burgher's family invited you over for dinner (right down to the greeting by a stiff, bow-tied maître d'). This elegant splurge restaurant has been serving guests for more than 400 years, racking up an impressive guest list (some pictured in the lobby)—and, somewhere in there, inventing *Goldwasser*. Reservations are smart for dinner (most main dishes 55–85 zł, emphasis on fish, daily 12:00–23:00, ulica Szeroka 52–54, tel. 058-301-7652).

Pierogarnia u Dzika ("By the Boar") offers more than a dozen varieties of pierogi (Polish ravioli)—plus meat and fish dishes—in a contemporary setting enhanced by all manner of stuffed and skinned boar. Locals swear by this place, where the pierogi is actually homemade (pierogi-15–25 zł, get the sampler *Królestwo Pierogów*—"King's Plate"—to try several different varieties, main dishes-30–40 zł, daily 11:00–21:30, ulica Piwna 59–60, tel. 058-305-2676). This same street (ulica Piwna, "Beer Street") is lined with several other fun, trendy eateries.

Coffee and Sweets

Gdańsk's Main Town is full of hip cafés that lure in young people with long menus of exotic coffee drinks and tasty cakes. Here are two good options—one new, one old.

Pi Kawa (as in 3.14, pronounced "pee" in Polish) is a trendy, atmospheric café with a wide variety of coffee drinks and herbal teas, best accompanied by the delicious *szarlotka* (Polish apple cake). The decor is cozy Old World, and the café is packed with socializing locals (6–15-zł cakes, daily 10:00–22:00, until 24:00 in summer, ulica Piwna 5–6).

Cukiernia Kaliszczak, a bakery right on ulica Długa, is a no-frills throwback to the communist days, with delicious 3-zł cakes and ice cream and delightfully grumpy service (daily 9:00–21:00, ulica Długa 74).

TRANSPORTATION CONNECTIONS

By Train

Gdańsk is well-connected to the Tri-City via the commuter SKM trains (see below). It also has frequent connections to Warsaw, and handy night trains to Berlin and Kraków.

From Gdańsk by Train to: Hel (town on Hel Peninsula, 3/day direct July–Aug only, 2.25–3.25 hrs; otherwise about hourly with transfer in Gdynia), **Malbork** (about 2/hr, 40–50 min), **Toruń** (4/day direct, 3 hrs; at least hourly with a transfer in Bydgoszcz, 3–4 hrs), **Warsaw** (nearly hourly, 4 hrs), **Kraków** (4/day direct, 7.25 hrs; plus 2 night trains, 11 hrs; more with transfer in Warsaw), **Berlin** (4/day, 8.25–9.25 hrs, transfer in Szczecin, Poznań, or Frankfurt an der Oder; plus 1 direct night train, 10 hrs).

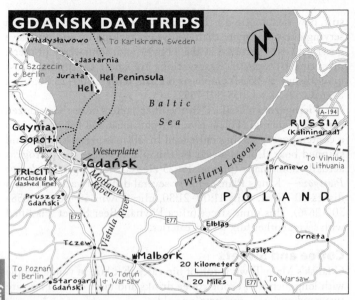

GDAŃSK DAY TRIPS

Władysławowo ·   To Karlskrona, Sweden

Jastarnia

To Szczecin & Berlin   Jurata·   ·Hel Peninsula

Hel·

Baltic

Sea

Gdynia·

Sopot·

Oliwa·   *Westerplatte*

TRI-CITY ·Gdańsk
(enclosed by
dashed line)   Motława River

A-194

RUSSIA
(Kaliningrad)

To Vilnius,
Braniewo Lithuania

Wiślany Lagoon

Pruszcz Gdański

E75   Vistula River   E77   Elbląg   P O L A N D

Orneta·

Tczew   ■Malbork   Paslęk

20 Kilometers

To Poznań & Berlin   ·Starogard Gdański   To Toruń & Warsaw   20 Miles   E77   To Warsaw

By Boat

Various boats depart from Gdańsk's embankment to nearby destinations, including **Westerplatte** (the monument marking where World War II started) and **Hel** (the beachy peninsula, described below). While boats also run sporadically to Sopot and Gdynia, the train is better for those trips (described under "Getting Around the Tri-City," below).

As these boat schedules tend to change from year to year, confirm your plans carefully at the TI. All boat trips are weather permitting, especially the faster hydrofoils.

To Westerplatte: To travel by boat to the monument at Westerplatte—where World War II began—you have two options. Żegluga Gdańska boats run from Gdańsk to Westerplatte daily April through October (29 zł one-way, 43 zł round-trip, 50 min each way, 6/day in each direction, fewer off-season). Or—more enjoyable—consider the short cruise through Gdańsk's outlying shipyards on one of two fun replica ships: the 17th-century *Galeon Lew* ("Lion Galleon"), or the Norse longboat-style *Viking III*. These ships do a lazy 90-minute circuit out to Westerplatte and back (if at least six people want to get off at Westerplatte and then take the bus or a different boat back, they'll stop there for you; otherwise, you'll stay on the boat for the full round-trip). It's not exactly pretty—you'll see more industry than scenery—but it's a good excuse to set sail (35 zł round-trip, 20 zł one-way, the two boats take turns departing at the top of each hour 9:00–19:00 in

July–Aug, fewer departures May–June and Sept, from the embankment near the Crane, mobile 0501-571-383, www.rejsyturystyczne .pl). In summer, the trip sometimes features live music. If you've ever wanted to hear "What Can You Do with a Drunken Sailor?" in Polish, here's your chance.

To Hel: Various boats—mostly the ZTM "ferry trams" *(tram-waj wodny)*—zip out to Hel in two hours three times a day in July and August, with a stop in Sopot (sometimes also runs on weekends in shoulder season; carefully confirm departure point, which can change but will likely be at the north end of the embankment, past the Crane).

In shoulder season (April–June and Sept–Oct), even though most boats stop running from Gdańsk, several routes still run between Sopot, Gdynia, and Hel. Boats generally don't run in winter (Nov–March).

Near Gdańsk: The Tri-City (Trójmiasto)

Gdańsk is the anchor of the three cities that make up the metropolitan region known as the Tri-City (Trójmiasto). The other two parts are as different as night and day: a once-swanky resort town (Sopot) and a practical, nose-to-the-grindstone business center (Gdynia). The Tri-City as a whole is home to bustling industry and a sprawling university, with several campuses and plenty of well-dressed, English-speaking students. Beyond the Tri-City, the long, skinny Hel Peninsula—a sparsely populated strip of fishing villages and fun-loving beaches—arches dramatically into the Baltic Sea.

Sopot—boasting sandy beaches, tons of tourists, and a certain elegance—is clearly the most appealing day-trip option. Gdynia offers a glimpse into workaday Poland, but leaves most visitors cold. Hel, which requires the better part of a day to visit, is worthwhile only if you've got perfect summer weather and a desire to lie on the beach.

Getting Around the Tri-City

Gdańsk, Sopot, and Gdynia are connected both by regional commuter trains (*kolejka*, operated by SKM) as well as trains of Poland's national railway (operated by PKP). Trains to Hel are always operated by PKP. Tickets for one system can't be used on the other. While the two different trains chug along the same tracks, they use different (but nearby) stations. For example, at Gdańsk's Main Station, national PKP trains use tracks 1–3, while regional SKM trains use tracks 3–5. And in Sopot, the SKM station is a few hundred feet before the PKP station.

Regional SKM trains are much more frequent—they go in each direction about every 10–15 minutes (less frequently after 19:30). In Gdańsk, buy tickets at any kiosk marked *SKM Bilety* (easiest at the kiosk on platform 4). Figure 2.80 zł and 25 minutes to Sopot, or 4 zł and 40 minutes to Gdynia. Before boarding, be sure to validate your ticket by punching it in the very easy-to-miss yellow or blue slots under the boards with SKM information. Each city has multiple stops. In Gdańsk, use "Gdańsk Główny" (the end of the line); for Sopot, use the stop called simply "Sopot" (only one word); and for Gdynia, it's "Gdynia Główna" (the main station).

The bigger PKP trains are faster, but less frequent—unless you notice one happens to be leaving at a convenient time, I'd skip them and stick with the easy SKM trains.

For a more romantic—and much slower—approach, consider the boat (see Gdańsk's "Transportation Connections" earlier in this chapter).

Sopot

Sopot (SOH-poht), dubbed the "Nice of the North," was a celebrated haunt of beautiful people during the 1920s and 1930s, and remains a popular beach getaway to this day.

Sopot was created in the late 19th century by Napoleon's doctor, Jean Georges Haffner, who believed Baltic Sea water to be therapeutic. By the 1890s, it had become a fashionable seaside resort. This gambling center boasted enough high-roller casinos to garner comparisons to Monte Carlo.

The casinos are gone, but the health resorts remain, and you'll still see more well-dressed people here per capita than just about anywhere in the country. While it's not quite Cannes, Sopot features a relative feeling of high class unusual in otherwise unpretentious Poland. But even so, a childlike spirit of summer-vacation fun pervades this St-Tropez-on-the-Baltic—making it an all-around enjoyable place.

Planning Your Time

You can get the gist of Sopot in just a couple of hours. Zip in on the train, follow the main drag to the sea, wander the pier, get your feet wet at the beach, then head back to Gdańsk.

Why not come here in the late afternoon, enjoy those last few rays of sunshine, stay for dinner, then take a twilight stroll on the pier?

ORIENTATION

The main pedestrian drag, Monte Cassino Heroes street (ulica Bohaterów Monte Cassino), leads to the Molo, the longest pleasure pier in Europe. From the Molo, a broad, sandy beach stretches in each direction. Running parallel to the surf is a tree-lined, people-filled path made for strolling.

Tourist Information

Sopot's helpful TI is directly in front of the PKP train station (look for blue *it* sign). Pick up the free map, info booklet, and events schedule. They also offer a free room-booking service (daily June–mid-Sept 9:00–20:00, mid-Sept–May 10:00–18:00, ulica Dworcowa 4, tel. 058-550-3783, www.sopot.pl).

Arrival in Sopot

From the SKM station, exit to the left and walk down the street. After a block, you'll see the PKP train station on your left—detour here to find the TI (described above). Then continue on to the can't-miss-it main drag, ulica Bohaterów Monte Cassino (marked by the big red-brick church steeple). Follow it to the right, down to the seaside.

SIGHTS

▲**Monte Cassino Heroes Street (Ulica Bohaterów Monte Cassino)**—This in-love-with-life promenade may well be Poland's most manicured street. Especially after all the suburban and industrial dreck you passed through to get here, you'll be charmed by this pretty drag. The street is lined with happy tourists, trendy cafés, al fresco restaurants, movie theaters, and late-19th-century facades (known for their wooden balconies).

The most popular building along here (on the left, about half-way down) is the so-called **Crooked House** (Krzywy Domek), a trippy, Gaudí-inspired building that looks like it's melting. Hard-partying locals prefer to call it the "Drunken House," and say that when it looks straight...it's time to stop drinking.

At the bottom of the boulevard, just before the Molo, pay 3 zł to climb to the top of the Art Nouveau lighthouse for a waterfront panorama.

Molo (Pier)—At more than 1,600 feet long, this is Europe's longest wooden entertainment pier. While you won't find any amusement-park rides, you will be surrounded by vendors, artists, and Poles having the time of their lives. Buy a *gofry* (Belgian waffle topped with whipped cream and fruit) or an oversized cloud of *wata cukrowa* (cotton candy), grab your partner's hand, and stroll with gusto (4 zł, free Oct–April, open long hours daily).

Scan the horizon for sailboats and tankers. Any pirate ships? For a jarring reality check, look over to Gdańsk. Barely visible from the Molo are two of the most important sites in 20th-century history: the towering monument at Westerplatte, where World War II started; and the cranes rising up from the Gdańsk Shipyard, where Solidarity was born and European communism began its long goodbye.

In season, the end of the Molo is sometimes home to an over-priced but fun wax museum, populated by famous Poles (Wałęsa, Copernicus, Chopin) and others (Kennedy, Beatles, Bush).

In spring and fall, the Molo is a favorite venue for pole vaulting—or is that Pole vaulting?

The Beach—Yes, Poland has beaches. Nice ones. When I heard Sopot compared to places like Nice, I'll admit that I scoffed. But when I saw those stretches of inviting sand as far as the eye can see, I wished I'd packed my swim trunks. (You could walk from Gdańsk to Gdynia on beaches like this.) The sand is finer than anything I've seen in Croatia...though the water's not exactly crystal-clear. Most of the beach is public, except for a small private stretch in front of the Grand Hotel Sopot (described below). Year-round, it's crammed with locals. At these northern latitudes, the season for bathing is brief and crowded.

Overlooking the beach next to the Molo is the **Grand Hotel Sopot.** It was renovated to top-class status just recently, but its history goes way back. They could charge admission for room #226, a multi-room suite that has hosted the likes of Adolf Hitler, Marlene Dietrich, and Fidel Castro (but not all at the same time). With all the trappings of Sopot's belle époque—dark wood, plush upholstery, antique furniture—this room had me imagining Hitler sitting at the desk, looking out to sea, and plotting the course of World War II.

Gdynia

Compared to its flashier sister cities, straightforward Gdynia (guh-DIN-yah) has retained a more working-class vibe, still in touch with its salty, fishing-village roots. Gdynia feels much less historic than Gdańsk or Sopot, as it was mostly built in the 1920s to be Poland's main harbor after Gdańsk became a free city. Although nowhere as attractive as Gdańsk or Sopot, Gdynia has an authentic feel and a fine waterfront promenade (www.gdynia.pl).

Gdynia is a major business center, and—thanks to its youthful, progressive city government—has edged ahead of the rest of Poland in transitioning from communism. It enjoys one of the highest income levels in the country. Many of the crumbling downtown buildings have been renovated, and Gdynia is becoming known for its top-tier shopping—all the big designers have boutiques here. If a local woman has been shopping on Świętojańska street in Gdynia, it means that she's got some serious złoty.

Because Gdańsk's port is relatively shallow, the biggest cruise ships must put in at Gdynia...leaving confused tourists to poke around town looking for some medieval quaintness, before coming to their senses and heading for Gdańsk. Gdynia is also home to a major military harbor, and an important NATO base.

To get a taste of Gdynia, take the SKM train to the "Gdynia Główna" station, follow signs to *wyjście do miasta*, cross the busy street, and walk 15 minutes down Starowiejska. When you come to the intersection with the broad Świętojańska street, turn right (in the direction the big statue is looking) and walk two blocks to the tree-lined park on the left. Head through the park to the Southern Pier (Molo Południowe). This concrete slab—nowhere near as charming as Sopot's wooden-boardwalk version—features a modern shopping mall and a smattering of sights, including an aquarium and a pair of permanently moored museum boats.

Hel Peninsula (Mierzeja Helska)

Out on the edge of things, this slender peninsula juts 20 miles into the ocean, providing a sunny retreat from the big cities—even as it shelters them from Baltic winds. Trees line the peninsula, and the northern edge is one long, sandy, ever-shifting beach.

On hot summer days, Hel is a great place to frolic in the sun with Poles. Sunbathing and windsurfing are practically a religion here. Small resort villages line Hel Peninsula: Władysławowo (at the base), Chałupy, Kuźnica, Jastarnia, Jurata, and—at the tip—a town also called Hel. Beaches right near the towns can be crowded in peak season, but you're never more than a short walk away from your own stretch of sand. There are few permanent residents, and the waterfront is shared by budget campgrounds and hotels hosting middle-class families, and mansions of Poland's rich and famous (former president Aleksander Kwaśniewski has a summer home here).

The easiest way to go to Hel—aside from coveting thy neighbor's wife—is by boat (see "Transportation Connections," page 357). Trains from Gdańsk also reach Hel (summer only), and from Gdynia, you can take a train, bus, or minibus. Hel is immensely popular in the summer, when it's notorious for its traffic jams.

POMERANIA

Malbork Castle • Toruń

The northwestern part of Poland—known as Pomerania (Pomorze)—has nothing to do with excitable little dogs, but it does offer plenty of attractions. Two in particular are worth singling out, both conveniently located between Gdańsk and Warsaw. Malbork, the biggest Gothic castle in Europe, is one of the most interesting castles in Eastern Europe. Farther south, the Gothic town of Toruń—the birthplace of Copernicus, and a favorite spot of every proud Pole—holds hundreds of red-brick buildings (and, it seems, even more varieties of tasty gingerbread).

Planning Your Time

Malbork works well as a side-trip from Gdańsk (frequent trains, 40–50 min), and it's also on the main train line from Gdańsk to Warsaw. While Toruń doesn't merit a long detour, it's worth a stroll or an overnight if you want to sample a smaller Polish city. Unfortunately, Toruń is on a different train line than Malbork—if you visit both in one day, it'll be a very long one. Ideally, if traveling round-trip from Warsaw, see one of these destinations coming to Gdańsk, and visit the other on the way back. Or do Malbork as a side-trip from Gdańsk, then visit Toruń on the way to Warsaw.

Malbork Castle

Malbork Castle is soaked in history. The biggest brick castle in the world, the largest castle of the Gothic period, and one of Europe's most imposing fortresses, it sits smugly on a marshy plain at the edge of the town of Malbork, 35 miles southeast of Gdańsk.

This was the headquarters of the notorious Teutonic Knights, a Germanic band of ex-Crusaders who dominated northern Poland in the Middle Ages.

When the Teutonic Knights were invited to Polish lands to convert neighboring pagans in the 13th century, they found the perfect site for their new capital here, on the bank of the Nogat River. Construction began in 1274. After the Teutonic Knights conquered Gdańsk in 1308, the order moved its official headquarters from Venice to Malbork, where they remained for nearly 150 years. They called the castle Marienburg, the "Castle of Mary," in honor of the order's patron saint.

At its peak in the early 1400s, Malbork was both the imposing home of a seemingly unstoppable army, and Europe's final bastion of chivalric ideals. Surrounded by swamplands, with only one gate in need of defense, it was a tough nut to crack. Malbork Castle was never taken by force in the Middle Ages, though it had to withstand various sieges by the Poles during the Thirteen Years' War (1454–1466)—including a campaign that lasted over three years. Finally, in 1457, the Polish king gained control of Malbork by buying off Czech mercenaries guarding the castle. Malbork became a Polish royal residence for 300 years. But when Poland was partitioned in the late 18th century, this region went back into German hands. The castle became a barracks, windows were sealed up, delicate vaulting was damaged, bricks were quarried for new buildings, and Malbork deteriorated.

In the late 19th century, Romantic German artists and poets rediscovered the place. An architect named Konrad Steinbrecht devoted 40 years of his life to Malbork, painstakingly restoring the palace to its medieval splendor. A half-century later, the Nazis used the castle to house POWs, and about half of it was destroyed by the Soviet army, who saw it as a symbol of longstanding German domination. But it was restored once again, and today Malbork has been returned to its Teutonic glory.

Getting There

Malbork is on the train line between Gdańsk and Warsaw. Coming by train from Gdańsk, you'll enjoy views of the castle on your right as you cross the Nogat River. The humble, dingy Malbork train station has handy lockers (4–8 zł depending on size of bag) and a less reliable baggage-check office (*przechowalnia bagażu,* by ticket windows; if it's closed, be insistent, and someone should eventually help you). To get from the station to the castle, consider taking a **taxi** (shouldn't cost more than 10 zł, though many corrupt cabbies charge twice that—keep asking until someone agrees to 10 zł). Or you can **walk** 15 minutes to the castle: Leave the station to the right, walk straight, and go through the pedestrian underpass beneath the busy road (by the red staircase). When you emerge on the other side, follow the busy road (noticing peek-a-boo views on your right of the castle's main tower) and take your first right turn (onto Kościuszki, the main shopping street). When you reach the fork at the end of the street, jog right onto Piastowska, which you'll follow to the big, red castle. Cross the two moats and turn right, following the castle wall to the end, where you'll find the ticket office (marked *kasa*).

ORIENTATION

Cost and Hours: Malbork has two seasons: high season (mid-April–mid-Sept) and low season (the rest of the year). In high season, entry costs 30 zł, and the castle exhibits are open Tue–Sun 9:00–19:00 (last entry 17:30, grounds open until 20:00). In low season, it costs 25 zł, and the exhibits are open Tue–Sun 10:00–15:00 (last entry 13:00, grounds open until 16:00; in early April and late Sept, it's open until 17:00 with last entry at 15:30). On Mondays throughout the year, most of the castle is closed, with only a few sparse exhibits remaining open. In summer, they also offer a family ticket for a small savings. The ticket office opens 30 minutes before the castle. You'll pay an extra 15 zł for a sticker allowing you to take photos inside the buildings (photographing the grounds is free). For details, see www.zamek.malbork.pl.

Tours: You are technically required to enter the castle with a three-hour tour (Polish tour included in your ticket), but most non-Polish speakers simply split off from their guide and tour the place on their own—simply enter with any tour, wander off, and explore the castle using my self-guided tour (see next page).

Getting an **English tour** can be frustrating. In July and August, English tours run three times a day (likely at 11:00, 13:30, and 15:30; 5 zł extra). Year-round, you can also pay 150 zł for a private English tour (English guides are easier to arrange—even on short notice—in summer, but more difficult in winter). Ideally, contact the castle a few days ahead to reserve a guide (tel. 055-647-0978, fax 055-647-0976, kasa@zamek.malbork.pl; better to reserve by email or fax), or hire your own guide in Gdańsk (such as Agnieszka Syroka—see page 325). Alternatively, if you show up and there's no English tour, ask if an English-speaking guide is available. Then take the initiative, play "tour guide," and get together a group of frustrated English-speakers by the cashier. On my last trip, it took me only a few minutes to gather together 10 strangers eager for some English information—bringing the per-person cost of the tour down to just 15 zł.

Best Views: The views of massive Malbork are stunning—especially at sunset, when the red brick glows. Be sure to walk out

across the bridge over the Nogat River. The most scenic part of the castle is probably the twin-turreted, riverside Bridge Gate, which used to be connected by a bridge to the opposite bank.

Sound-and-Light Show: Every night from May through mid-September, there's a sound-and-light show in the castle court-yard. Though the commentary is in Polish, the show gives you a different perspective on the mighty fortress (15 zł, buy tickets at castle drawbridge, begins after dark—which can be as late as 22:00 at these northern latitudes). Don't make a special trip (or stay late) just for this show—it really only makes sense if you're spending the night (see "Sleeping," page 377).

SELF-GUIDED TOUR

The official tour of Malbork lasts about three hours. And, while there's plenty to see, this self-guided tour allows you to see it at your own pace. (Remember, you can split off from your group at any time.) This tour also works if you're tagging along with a Polish group, since it corresponds more or less to the route most Malbork guides take. Still, every guide is a little different, exhibits tend to move around, and entrances can be unexpectedly closed. Use the map in this chapter to navigate and jump around as needed. The castle complex is a bit of a maze, with various entrances and exits for each room, often behind closed (but unlocked) doors. Don't be shy about grabbing a medieval doorknob and letting yourself in.

Lower Castle and Entrance Gate

Stand in front of the gate to one of Europe's most intimidating fortresses—home to the Grand Master, monks, and knights of the Teutonic Order. Across from the gate is the Lower Castle, which was an infirmary and hospital for injured knights and retirees. The end closest to you is the Chapel of St. Lawrence; farther away, the former farm buildings have been converted into hotel rooms and restaurants (see "Sleeping," page 377).

Go through the first gate and up the wooden bridge. Above the door to the second (brick) gate is a sculpture of St. Mary with the Baby Jesus...next to a shield and helmet. The two messages to visitors: This castle is protected by Mary, and the Teutonic Knights are here to convert pagans—by force, if necessary (or, as it turned out, even if not necessary).

Pass through the first gate, into the entry area. Imagine

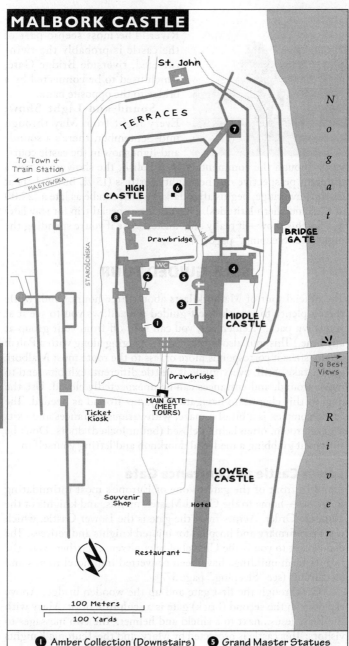

MALBORK CASTLE

St. John

TERRACES

To Town & Train Station

PIASTOWSKA

STAROŚCIŃSKA

HIGH CASTLE

6

7

BRIDGE GATE

8

Drawbridge

WC

2

5

4

3

MIDDLE CASTLE

1

To Best Views

Drawbridge

MAIN GATE (MEET TOURS)

Ticket Kiosk

Nogat

River

LOWER CASTLE

Souvenir Shop

Hotel

Restaurant

N

100 Meters

100 Yards

1 Amber Collection (Downstairs)
2 Armory (Upstairs)
3 "Boiler Room" (Downstairs)
4 Grand Master's Palace
5 Grand Master Statues
6 Well
7 Dansker Tower
8 St. Mary's Church

Malbork Castle

the gate behind you closing. You look up to see wooden chutes where archers are preparing to rain arrows down on you. Your last thought: Maybe we should have left the Teutonic Knights alone, after all.

Before you're pierced by arrows, read the castle's history into its walls: The foundation is made of huge stones, which are rare in these marshy lands—they were brought from Sweden. But most of the castle, like so many other buildings in northern Poland, was built with handmade red brick. Throughout the castle, the darker-colored, rougher brick is original, and the lighter-colored, smoother brick was used for restoration (in the 19th century, and again after World War II).

Venture through two more enclosed spaces, watching for the holes in the wall (for more guards and soldiers). The Teutonic Knights connected nearby lakes to create a system of canals, forming a moat around the castle that could be crossed only by this drawbridge. Ponder the fact that you have to go through five separate, well-defended gates to reach the...

Middle Castle (Zamek Średni)

This part of Malbork, built at an uphill incline to make it even more imposing, was designed to impress. Knights and monks lived here.

Let's get oriented: To your left is the east wing, where guests would sleep. Today this houses the Amber Collection (ground floor) and the Armory (upstairs). To the right (west) as you enter the main courtyard is the Grand Refectory (closer to the entrance) and the Grand Master's Palace (the taller, squarer building at the far end).

• *Before we move on, this is a good time to read up on the history of the Teutonic Knights (see sidebar). When you're ready to continue, enter the ground floor of the building on the left (remember, don't be shy about opening closed doors), and visit the...*

Amber Collection

This exhibit will make jewelry shoppers salivate. (Even as someone with zero interest in amber, I enjoyed it.) For a primer, read "All About Amber" on page 335.

View the displays clockwise (and chronologically) from the entrance. Begin at the huge chunks of raw amber, and the illuminated display of inclusions (bugs stuck in the amber, à la *Jurassic Park*). In the next cases are ancient amber artifacts, some of them

Malbork Castle

The Teutonic Knights

The Order of the Teutonic Knights began in the Holy Land in 1191, during the Third Crusade. Officially called the "Order of the Hospital of the Blessed Virgin Mary of the German House of Jerusalem," these German monks and knights took vows of poverty, chastity, and obedience. They also built hospitals and cared for injured knights. When the Crusades ended in the 12th century, the order found itself out of a job, and went back to Europe. They set up shop in Venice, and reorganized as a chivalric order of Christian mercenaries—pagan-killers for hire.

The Teutonic Knights were hired in 1226 for a gig in northern Poland, where the duke asked them to subdue a tribe of pagans who had been attacking his lands. The Teutonic Knights—claiming to be missionaries (and wearing white cloaks decorated with black crosses)—spent 60 years "saving" the pagans by turning them into serfs or brutally massacring them.

Like houseguests who didn't know when to leave, the Teutonic Knights decided they enjoyed northern Poland—and stuck around. The Knights made themselves at home, building one of Europe's biggest and most imposing fortresses: Malbork. Because they were fanatical Christians, they won the support of the pope and the Holy Roman Emperor. When the Teutonic Knights seized large parts of northern Poland in 1308, including Gdańsk—cutting off Polish access to the Baltic Sea—the Polish royals began to realize their mistake. The Teutonic Knights invited more Germans to come join them, building their numbers and tightening their grasp on the region. They grew rich from Hanseatic trade, specializing in amber, grain, and timber. The Knights conquered Estonia and Latvia, and began to threaten the Poles' pagan neighbor to the east, Lithuania. By the late 14th century, the Teutonic Knights were enjoying a Golden Age at the expense of the Poles and Lithuanians.

At about this time, Poland's long-lived Piast dynasty died out. Inspired by a mutual desire to fight back against the Teutonic

up to 3,000 years old. These were found in graves, put there by people who thought amber would help the deceased enter a better world. Along the rest of this wall are all manner of amber creations, from boxes and brooches to chess sets and pipes. Many of the finely decorated jewelry boxes and chests have ivory, silver, or shell inlays—better for contrast than gold. The portable religious shrines and altars could be used for travel, allowing people to remain reverent on the road and still pack light. At the end of the hall are two truly exquisite pieces: a small casket and an altar.

Working your way back up the other side of the room, you'll

Knights, the Poles and the Lithuanians decided to join their kingdoms. In 1386, Polish Princess Jadwiga married Lithuanian Prince Władysław Jagiełło (who converted to Christianity for the occasion), uniting Poland and Lithuania and kick-starting a grand new dynasty, the Jagiellonians.

Just as every American knows the date July 4, 1776, every Pole knows the date July 15, 1410—the Battle of Grunwald. King Władysław Jagiełło and Grand Duke Vytautas the Great led a ragtag army of some 40,000 soldiers—Lithuanians, Poles, other Slavs, and even speedy Tatar horsemen—against 27,000 Teutonic Knights. At the end of the day, some 18,000 Poles and Lithuanians were dead—but so were half of the Teutonic Knights (and the other half had been captured). Poland and Lithuania were victorious. Though the Teutonic Knights remained in Poland—extending their Germanic cultural influence on the region well into the 20th century—their political power waned, they pulled out of Lithuania, and they once again allowed free trade on the Vistula. A generation later, the Thirteen Years' War (1454–1466) finally put an end to the Teutonic Knights' domination of northern Poland. The order officially dissolved in 1575, when they converted to Protestantism...though some conspiracy theorists (and *Da Vinci Code* enthusiasts) claim the Teutonic Knights are still very much active.

The Knights' influence on Poland persists today—even beyond the striking red-brick churches and castles scattered around the northern part of the country. The Polish novelist Henryk Sienkiewicz's *The Teutonic Knights* is a cultural benchmark and a favorite work of many Poles. The 19th-century Romantics who fanned the flames of Polish patriotism turned the Teutonic Knights into a symbol of Germanic oppression. Even today, Poles—and all Slavs—think of the Teutonic Knights as murderous invaders...while the Germans see them as a mere footnote in their history.

see more modern uses for amber—necklaces and other jewelry, miniature ships, wine glasses, and belts for skinny-waisted, fashion-conscious women. Look for the amber crucifix. This is a small replica of a six-foot-tall amber and silver cross presented to Pope John Paul II by the people of Gdańsk. In the display case by the door, you can see the full range of amber colors, from opaque white at the top, to transparent yellow in the middle, to virtually black at the bottom.

• *Go back outside and turn left, to the wooden staircase above the café. Go up that staircase, and several more inside, to the top-floor...*

Armory

Browse your way through the impressive array of swords, armor, and other armaments (English descriptions). Look for the 600-year-old "hand-and-a-half" swords—too big to be held in one hand. At the end, in the display of cannons, pikes, and spears, look for the giant shield. These shields could be lined up to form a portable "wall" to protect the knights.

Head downstairs to the second room of the armory, displaying suits of armor (including for horses). Here you'll see some five-foot-long "two-hand swords" even bigger than the ones upstairs. On the left, find the suit of armor from the Hussars—Polish horseback knights who had wings on their armor, which created a terrifying sound when galloping.

• *Head back outside and across the main courtyard, entering the smaller courtyard through the passage next to the dark-wood-topped tower. Find the steep steps down into the...*

"Boiler Room"

The Teutonic Knights had a surprisingly sophisticated method for heating this huge complex. You see a furnace for fire down below, and a sort of a holding area for super-heated rocks up above. This method allowed the rocks to send heat through the vents without also filling them with smoke. This is one of 11 such "boiler rooms" in the castle complex. As you tour the rest of the castle, keep an eye out for little saucer-sized vents in the floor where the heat came through.

• *Head back out into the main courtyard and turn right, going uphill about 30 yards. At the upper part of this castle are two doors; take the one on the right, then climb up the stairs into the...*

Grand Master's Palace

This was one of the grandest royal residences in medieval Europe, used in later times by Polish kings and German Kaisers. (Today it's sometimes used for special exhibitions.)

• *From the top of the stairs, head down the hall to the right. Notice the troughs in the ground—anyone wanting an audience with the Grand Master had to wash both his hands and his feet.*

At the end of the hall, on the left, enter the elegant...

Summer Refectory: This was where the G. M. dined. With big stained-glass windows, and all of the delicate vaulting supported by a single pillar in the middle, this room was clearly not designed with defense in mind. In fact, medieval Polish armies focused their attacks on this room. On one legendary occasion, the attackers—tipped off by a spy—knew that an important meeting was going on here, and fired a cannonball into the room. It just barely missed the pillar. (You can see where the cannonball hit the wall, just above the fireplace.) The ceiling eventually did collapse during World War II.

As you continue into the **Winter Refectory,** notice that it has fewer windows (better insulation) and little manhole-like openings in the floor where the "central heating" came into the room.

• *Keep going, and you'll circle back around to where you came in. Go through the door just to the left of the stairs, into the...*

Private Rooms of the Grand Master: This residence of the Top Knight features show-off decor (including some 15th-century original frescoes of wine leaves and grapes). The Grand Master even had his own chapel, dedicated to St. Catherine. Though the Teutonic Order dictated that the monks sleep in dormitories, the Grand Master made an exception for himself—and you'll see his private bedroom (with rough original frescoes of four female martyrs).

• *You'll enter a small hall at the very end of these rooms. If it's open, go through the little door at the right end of this hall, and walk down to the...*

Grand Refectory: This enormous dining hall, damaged in World War II, recently completed a 10-year restoration project. With remarkable palm vaulting and grand frescoes, the Grand Refectory hosted feasts for up to 400 people to celebrate a military victory or to impress a visiting king.

• *Head outside. You're back by the boiler room. Go back out into the main courtyard and walk to the top. Look for the four...*

Grand Master Statues

These four statues came from a 19th-century Prussian monument that was mostly destroyed when the Soviets took Malbork at the end of World War II. Though this was a religious order, these powerful guys look more like kings than monks. From right to left, shake hands with Hermann von Salza (who was Grand Master when the Teutonic Knights came to Poland); Siegfried von Feuchtwangen (who actually moved the T. K. capital from Venice to Malbork, and who conquered Gdańsk for the Knights—oops, can't shake his hand, which was supposedly chopped off by Soviet troops); Winrich von Kniprode (who oversaw Malbork's Golden Age, and turned it into a castle fit for a king); and Markgraf Albrecht von Hohenzollern (the last Grand Master before the order dissolved and converted to Protestantism).

• *To the right of the statues, continue over the...*

Drawbridge

As you cross, notice the extensive system of fortifications and moats protecting the innermost part of the castle. Check out the cracks in the walls—an increasing threat to the ever-settling castle set on this marshy, unstable terrain. The passage is lined with holes (for surveillance), with chutes up above (to pour scalding water or pitch on unwanted visitors). It's not quite straight—so a cannon fired here would hit the side wall of the passage, rather than entering the High Castle. Which is what you're about to do now.

High Castle (Zamek Wysoki)

This is the beating heart of the castle, and its oldest section. As much a monastery as a fortress, the High Castle was off-limits to all but 60 monks of the Teutonic Order and their servants. (The knights stayed in the Middle Castle.) Here you'll find the monks' dormitories, chapels, church, and refectory. As this was the nerve center of the Teutonic Knights—the T. K. HQ—it was also their last line of defense. They stored enormous amounts of food here in case of a siege.

In the middle of the High Castle courtyard is a **well**—an essential part of any inner castle, especially one as prone to sieges as Malbork. At the top is a sculpture of a pelican. Because this noble bird was believed to kill itself to feed its young (notice that it's piercing its own chest with its beak), it was often used in the Middle Ages as a symbol for the self-sacrifice of Jesus.

• *Take some time to explore the...*

Ground Floor

Working clockwise around the courtyard from where you entered, you'll find the following: A door leads to the prison and torture chamber (with small "solitary confinement" cells near the entrance), and a long hall behind with a single tiny window. Along the back of the cloister is a WWII photo of Malbork. Beyond that, hiding in the far corner, is an exhibit on medieval stained-glass windows. Somewhere around here, you should see a demonstration of how medieval money was made. The Teutonic Knights minted their own coins—and you can buy your very own freshly minted replica today.

• *Continuing around the courtyard (to the right from where you entered), you'll find the most interesting exhibit on this floor, the...*

Kitchen: This exhibit really gives you a feel for medieval monastery life. The monks who lived here ate three meals a day, along with lots of beer (made here) and wine (imported from France, Italy, and Hungary). A cellar under the kitchen was used as a primitive refrigerator—big chunks of ice were cut from the frozen river in winter, stored in the basement, and used to keep food cool in summer. Behind the long table, see the big dumbwaiter (with shelves), which connects this kitchen with the refectory upstairs. Step into the giant stove and look up the biggest chimney in the castle.

• *Now go back out into the courtyard, and climb up the stairs near where you came in.*

Middle Floor
• *From the top of the stairs, the first door on the left (with the colorfully painted arch) leads to the most important room of the High Castle, the...*

Chapter Room: Monks gathered here after Mass, and it was also the site for meetings of Teutonic Knights from around the countryside. If a Grand Master was killed in battle, the new one would be elected right here. Each monk had his own seal and a name over his seat. The big chair belonged to the Grand Master. Above his chair, notice the little windows, connecting this room to St. Mary's Church next door (described below). Church music would come into this room through these windows...imagine the voices of 60 monks bouncing around with these acoustics.

While monks are usually thought to pursue simple lives, the elegant vaulting in this room is anything but plain. The 14th-century frescoes (restored in the 19th century) depict Grand Masters. In the floor are more vents for the central heating.

• *Leave the Chapter House and walk straight ahead, imagining the monk-filled corridors of Teutonic times. The first door on the right is the...*

Treasury: The first room has a small display of coins and amber (which helped make the Teutonic Knights rich). As you explore the rooms of the tax collector and the house administrator, notice the wide variety of safes and other lock boxes. Near the end, look for the small bed—for a small medieval person.

• *Continue around the cloister. At the end of the corridor, look for the little devil at the bottom of the vaulting (on the right, about eye level). He's pulling his beard and crossing his legs—pointing you down the long corridor to the...*

Dansker Tower: From the devil's grimace, you might have guessed that this tower houses the latrine. For obvious sanitary (and olfactory) reasons, it's set apart from the main part of the castle. The toilets dropped straight down into the moat. The bins above them are filled with cabbage leaves, used by the T. K. as TP. This tower could also serve as a final measure of defense—it's easer to defend than the entire castle. Food was stored above, just in case.

• *Head back toward the main part of the High Castle. On the right-hand side of the long passage, look for a door into the...*

Church Exhibition: These rooms used to be dormitories for the monks, and today they display a wide range of relics from the church (with English descriptions). The first room features an elaborate monstrance (vessel used to carry the Communion host) and various statues, including an evocative, hands-less 15th-century Christ praying in the Garden of Gethsemane. The next room displays pictures of various eras of Malbork Castle, as well as some fragments of statues rescued from the destroyed St. Mary's Church. The huge, mangled crucifix dates from the mid-14th century. At the end of this exhibition is a replica of a Gothic altarpiece, with graphic paintings of the murder and dismemberment of Poland's patron saint, Adalbert.

• *Go back out into the main cloister, turn right, and continue down to the end, arriving at the...*

Golden Gate: This elaborate doorway—covered in protective glass—marks the entrance to St. Mary's Church. Ringed with detailed carvings from the Old Testament, and symbolic messages about how monks of the Teutonic Order should live their lives, it's a marvelous example of late-13th-century art. On the left, find the five wise virgins who filled their lamps with oil, conserved it wisely, and are headed to heaven. On the right, the five foolish virgins who overslept and used up all their oil are damned, much to their dismay.

• *If the door's open, go ahead on into...*

St. Mary's Church: This holy site was destroyed in World War II and sat for decades with no roof. After so much neglect, it's finally being renovated...slowly. Pictures of the original church with English descriptions explain some of the fragments.

• *Go through the door on the left (as you exit St. Mary's Church) and take the narrow spiral staircase upstairs to the final set of exhibits.*

Top Floor

Walk through the long hallway of temporary exhibits. At the end, go down the stairs into the monks' common room (on the left). Over the fireplace is a relief depicting the Teutonic Knights fighting the pagans. To the left of that (see the stone windows) is a balcony where musicians could perform to entertain the monks after a meal. The next, very long room, with seven pillars, is the refectory, where the monks ate in silence. Along the right-hand wall are confessional-like, lockable storage boxes. At the end of this room, just beyond another decorated fireplace, notice the grated hole in the wall. This is where the dumbwaiter comes up from the kitchen (which we saw below). Beyond this room is an exhibit about the architectural renovation of the castle. On your way back out, you'll have the opportunity to pay 6 zł to climb the very tight and steep steps up to the top of the tower for a view over the castle complex.

• *Your Malbork tour ends here. When finished, you can head back the way you came. En route, you can walk around terraces lining the inner moat, between the castle walls (stairs lead down off of the drawbridge). It's hardly a must-see, but it's pleasant enough, with the Grand Master's garden, a cemetery for monks, and the remains of the small St. Anne's Chapel (with Grand Master tombs).*

Sleep Code

(3 zł = about $1, country code: 48)
S = Single, **D** = Double/Twin, **T** = Triple, **Q** = Quad, **b** = bathroom,
s = shower only. Unless otherwise noted, breakfast is included,
credit cards are accepted, and English is spoken.

To help you sort easily through these listings, I've divided
the rooms into two categories, based on the price for a standard double room with bath:

$$ Higher Priced—Most rooms 200 zł or more.
$ Lower Priced—Most rooms less than 200 zł.

SLEEPING

Malbork is so well-connected by rail to Gdańsk and Warsaw that
there's little sense in sleeping here. If you do stay, consider the
nighttime sound-and-light show in the castle courtyard.

$$ Hotel Zamek is housed in Malbork's Lower Castle, a red-
brick building that was once a hospital, just across from the main
part of the fortress. The 42 rooms are overpriced, dark, musty, old-
feeling, and a little creepy...but, hey—you're next door to one of
Europe's grandest Gothic castles (Sb-275 zł, Db-330 zł, Tb-430
zł, cheaper mid-Sept–mid-June, elevator, ulica Starościńska 14, tel.
& fax 055-272-3367).

TRANSPORTATION CONNECTIONS

From Malbork by Train to: Gdańsk (about 2/hr, 40–50 min),
Toruń (about every 2 hrs, 3 hrs, transfer in Tczew), **Warsaw**
(nearly hourly, 3.5 hrs direct).

Toruń

Toruń is a pretty, lazy Gothic town conveniently located about
halfway between Warsaw and Gdańsk. It's worth a couple of hours
to stroll the lively streets, ogle the huge red-brick buildings, and
savor the flavor of Poland's most livable city.

With about 210,000 residents and 30,000 students (at
Copernicus University), Toruń is a thriving burg. Locals brag
that their city is a "mini-Kraków." But that sells both cities short.
Toruń lacks Kraków's over-the-top romanticism, and its sights are
quickly exhausted. On the other hand, Toruń may well be Poland's
most user-friendly city: tidy streets with a sensible grid plan (and

English signposts to keep you on track), wide pedestrian boulevards crammed with locals who greet each other like they're long-lost friends, and an easygoing ambience that seems to say, "Hey—relax." And, while it has its share of tourists, Toruń feels more off-the-beaten-path than the other Polish destinations in this book.

Toruń clings fiercely to its two claims to fame: It's the proud birthplace of the astronomer Copernicus (Mikołaj Kopernik), and home to a dizzying variety of gingerbread treats (*piernika;* peer-NEE-kah).

ORIENTATION

(area code: 056)
Everything in Toruń worth seeing is in the walled Old Town, climbing up a gentle hill from the Vistula River. The broad, traffic-free main drag, ulica Szeroka (called Różana at the entrance of town) bisects the Old Town, running parallel to the river.

Arrival in Toruń

Toruń's main train station (called Toruń Główny) is about a mile away—and across the river—from the Old Town. The main hall has ticket windows, an ATM, and lockers (4–8 zł, depending on bag size).

To reach the Old Town, you have two options: If you go out the door from the main hall, you'll spot **taxis** waiting to take you into town (the trip should cost no more than 10 zł). To take the **bus,** buy a 2-zł ticket from the *RUCH* kiosk overlooking the tracks near the main hall. Then follow the pedestrian underpass beneath track 4 (entrance to underpass marked with low-profile *wyjście do miasta* sign and bus icon, outside main hall and to the left). When you emerge on the other side, the bus stop for bus #22 or #27 into the center is ahead and on your right. Take the bus to Plac Rapackiego, the first stop after the long bridge. To return to the station, catch bus #22 or #27 across the busy road from where you got off.

Tourist Information

The TI is on the main square, behind the Old Town Hall. Pick up the free map, and get information about hotels in town and city tours (Tue–Fri 9:00–18:00, Mon and Sat 9:00–16:00, closed Sun except May–Aug, when it's open 9:00–13:00, Rynek Staromiejski 25, tel. 056-621-0931, www.it.torun.pl).

SELF-GUIDED WALK

Welcome to Toruń

This very lightly guided introductory stroll takes you through the heart of Toruń. With no stops, you could do it in 10 minutes.

From the Plac Rapackiego bus stop, head into the town through the passageways under the colorful buildings. Within a block, you're at the bustling **Old Town Market Square** (Rynek Staromiejski), surrounded by huge brick buildings and outdoor restaurants buzzing with lively locals. The big building in the center is the **Old Town Hall** (Ratusz Staromiejski), with a boring museum and a climbable tower. The building with the pointy spires on the right (across from the Old Town Hall) is the **Artus Court,** where the medieval town council and merchants' guilds met (sadly, unlike the similar court in Gdańsk, it's not open to the public).

The guy playing his violin in front of the Old Town Hall is a **rafter** *(retman)*—one of the medieval lumberjacks who lashed tree trunks together and floated them down the Vistula to Gdańsk. This particular rafter came to Toruń when the town was infested with frogs. He wooed them with his violin and marched them out of town. (Hmm...sounds like a certain piper in another medieval Hanseatic city, Bremen....)

The bigger statue, at the other end of the Old Town Hall, depicts **Mikołaj Kopernik,** better known as Nicholas Copernicus (1473–1543). This Toruń-born son of aristocrats turned the world on its ear when he suggested that the sun, not the earth, is the center of the universe (an idea called the "heliocentric theory"). Toruń is serious about this local boy done good—he's the town mascot, as well as the namesake of the local university. Among its fields of study, Copernicus U. has a healthy astronomy program. There's a planetarium in the Old Town (just past the far corner of the square) and a giant radio telescope on the town outskirts. Despite all the local fuss over Copernicus, there's some dispute about his ethnicity; he was born in Toruń, all right, but at a time when it was a predominantly German town. So is he Polish or German? (For more on Copernicus, visit his birth house—now a modest museum on the astronomer—just two blocks away, and described under "Sights").

What's that sweet smell in the air? For Poles, Toruń is synonymous with **gingerbread** *(piernika)*. This Toruń treat can be topped with different kinds of jams or glazes, and/or dipped in chocolate. You'll see gingerbread shops all over town, mostly selling the same stuff. The shop in the Artus Court building on the Old Town Market Square is handy and atmospheric; more are around the corner on ulica Żeglarska (toward the river; the shop on the right near the end of the block has a handy bulk system—point to what looks good and get exactly the amount and types you want).

Having satisfied your ginger tooth, head back to the square and join the human stream down the appropriately named **ulica Szeroka** ("Wide Street"), an enjoyable pedestrian promenade through the heart of town. Just before the road forks at the white Empik building, look down Przedzamcze to the right to see fragments of the town wall. This marks the border between the Old Town and the New Town (chartered only about 30 years later—both in the 13th century). While these areas are both collectively known today as the unified "Old Town," they were quite different in the Middle Ages—each with its own market square, and separated by a wall. (If you're curious to see the New Town Square and Town Hall, continue up ulica Szeroka and bear left at the fork.)

To end our walk, follow the wall to the right, down Przedzamcze, to reach the **ruins** of a castle built by the Teutonic Knights who were so influential in northern Poland in the Middle Ages (see page 370). The castle was destroyed in the 15th century by the locals—who, aside from a heap of bricks, left only the tower that housed the Teutonic toilets.

Beyond the castle ruins is the **Vistula** riverbank. The road that runs along the river here is called Bulwar Filadelfijski—for Toruń's sister city in Pennsylvania.

SIGHTS

Toruń is more about strolling than it is about sightseeing—the town's museums are underwhelming. Aside from its half-dozen red-brick churches (any of which are worth dropping into), the following attractions are worth considering on a rainy day.

Gingerbread Museum (Muzeum Piernika)—This fun attraction—by far Toruń's liveliest—is an actual, working gingerbread bakery of yore. Barefoot, costumed medieval bakers greet you and walk you through the traditional process of rolling, cutting out, baking, and tasting your own batch of gingerbread cookies (30–40 min, start to finish). After aging for 12 weeks to achieve the proper consistency, the dough bakes only 12 minutes—or, according to the medieval bakers, about 50 Hail Marys (10 zł, may have to wait a few minutes for an English guide to help you, daily 9:00–18:00, 2 blocks toward the river from Old Town Market Square at Rabiańska 9, www.muzeumpiernika.pl).

Copernicus House (Dom Kopernika)—Filling a pair of beautiful, gabled brick buildings, this dull and overpriced little museum celebrates the hero of Toruń. As much about medieval Toruń as about the astronomer, and sprawling over several floors in the two buildings, the exhibits loosely explain the astronomer's life and achievements. While the displays—mostly copies of important documents and paintings, models of his instruments, and English descriptions—are pretty flat, it's mildly interesting to walk around the creaky interiors. The second part of the exhibit is an 18-minute "sound-and-light show" (slideshow with recorded commentary) about medieval Toruń, with a model of the city that lights up dramatically at appropriate moments (ask for English show when you enter; museum-10 zł, slideshow-12 zł, both-18 zł; May–Sept Tue–Sun 10:00–18:00, closed Mon; Oct–April Tue–Sun 10:00–16:00, closed Mon; Kopernika 15/17, www.muzeum.torun.pl). To get to the museum from the Old Town Market Square, head down Żeglarska and take the first right—on Kopernika, of course.

Ethnographic Park (Park Etnograficzny)—This open-air folk museum, while not ranking with Europe's best, is at least your most convenient opportunity to stroll through some traditional buildings from the region. It's in the middle of a pleasant park just outside the Old Town (8.50 zł; mid-April–Sept Mon, Wed, and Fri 9:00–16:00, Tue, Thu, and Sat–Sun 10:00–18:00; Oct–mid-April Tue–Fri 9:00–16:00, Sat–Sun 10:00–16:00, closed Mon; Wały Gen. Sikorskiego 19, www.met.torun.pl). To get there from the Old Town Market Square, walk up Chełmińska with the river at your back and the Old Town Hall on your left. Cross the busy road, and you're in the park. Even if you're not interested in the museum, the relaxing park surrounding it is a fine place to pass some time.

SLEEPING

Toruń's Old Town has more than its share of good-value hotels (Db-200–300 zł). The TI has a brochure listing the options, and can help you find a room for no extra charge.

$$Hotel Karczma "Spichrz" ("Granary") is a fresh, atmospheric hotel in a renovated old granary. Its 23 rooms and public spaces are a fun blend of old and new—with huge wooden beams around every corner, and the scent of the restaurant's wood-fired grill wafting through the halls. It's comfortable, central, well-priced, and a little kitschy (Sb-190 zł, Db-250 zł, tall people may not appreciate low ceilings and beams, elevator, a block off the main drag toward the river at ulica Mostowa 1, tel. 056-657-1140, fax 056-657-1144, www.spichrz.pl, hotel@spichrz.pl). The restaurant is also good (grilled meat dishes-20–30 zł, daily 12:00–23:00).

$ Hotel Retman ("Rafter") has 29 older but nicely appointed rooms over a restaurant just down the street from the Gingerbread

Museum (Sb-160 zł, Db-210 zł; Fri–Sun prices drop to Sb-130 zł, Db-170 zł; ulica Rabiańska 15, tel. 056-657-4460, fax 056-657-4461, www.hotelretman.pl, recepcja@hotelretman.pl).

TRANSPORTATION CONNECTIONS

Toruń is a handy stopover on the way between Warsaw and Gdańsk. It's on a different train line than Malbork—so visiting both Toruń and the mighty Teutonic castle in the same day is surprisingly time-consuming.

From Toruń by Train to: Warsaw (5/day, 3 hrs direct, longer with a transfer in Kutno), **Gdańsk** (4/day direct, 3 hrs; at least hourly with transfer in Bydgoszcz, 3–4 hrs), **Kraków** (1/day direct, 7.75 hrs; better to transfer at Warsaw's Zachodnia station: 4/day, 5.75–6.5 hrs).

HUNGARY

HUNGARY

Magyarország

Hungary is an island of Asian-descended Magyars in a sea of Slavs. Even though the Hungarians have thoroughly integrated with their Slavic and German neighbors in the millennium since they arrived, there's still something about the place that's distinctly Magyar (MUD-jar). Visiting quirky, idiosyncratic Hungary is not quite the same as touring the rest of Eastern Europe: Everything's a little different—in terms of history, language, culture, customs, and cuisine—but it's hard to put your finger on exactly how.

Just a century ago, Hungary controlled half of one of Europe's grandest empires. Today, perhaps clinging to their former greatness, Hungarians remain old-fashioned and nostalgic. With their dusty museums and bushy moustaches, they love to remember the good old days. Buildings all over the country are marked with plaques boasting *MŰEMLEK* ("historical monument").

Thanks to this focus on tradition, the Hungarians you'll encounter are generally polite, formal, and professional. Hungarians have class. Everything here is done with a proud flourish. You get the impression that people in the service industry wear their uniforms as a badge of honor rather than a burden. When a waiter comes to your table in a restaurant, he'll say, *"Tessék parancsolni"*—literally, "Please command, sir." The standard greeting, *"Jó napot kívánok,"* means "I wish you a good day." Women sometimes hear the even more formal greeting, *"Kezét csókolom"*—"I kiss your hand." And when your train or bus makes a stop, you won't be alerted by a mindless, blaring beep or hoot—but instead, peppy music. (You'll be humming these contagious little ditties all day.)

Hungarians are just as orderly and tidy as Germans...in their own sometimes unexpected ways. Yes, Hungary has as much litter and graffiti—and as many crumbling buildings—as any other Eastern European country, but you'll find great reason within the chaos. My favorite town name in Hungary: Hatvan. This means "Sixty" in Hungarian...and it's exactly 60 kilometers from Budapest. You can't argue with that kind of logic.

This tradition of left-brained thinking hasn't produced many

great Hungarian painters or poets. But it has made tremendous contributions to the field of science, technology, business, and industry. Hungarians of note include Edward Teller (instrumental in creating the A-bomb), John von Neumann (a pioneer of computer science), Andy Grove (who, as András Grof, immigrated to the US and founded Intel), and George Soros (who fled to the US under communism, became a billionaire through shrewd investment, and is loved by the Left and loathed by the Right as a major contributor to liberal causes). Perhaps the most famous Hungarian "scientist" created something you probably have in a box in your basement: Ernő Rubik, and his famous cube. Hungary's enjoyment of a good mind-bending puzzle is also evident in their fascination with chess, which you'll see played in cafés, parks, and baths.

Like their Austrian neighbors, Hungarians know how to enjoy the good life. Favorite activities include splashing and soaking in their many thermal baths (see sidebar on page 462). "Taking the waters," Hungarian-style, deserves to be your top priority while you're here. Though public baths can sound intimidating, they're a delight. I've recommended my two favorite baths in Budapest and a fine one in Eger, and given you careful instructions to help you enjoy the warm-water fun like a pro. (To allay your first fear: Yes, you can wear your swimsuit the entire time.)

Hungarians are also reviving an elegant, Vienna-style café culture that was dismantled by the communists. Classical music is revered, perhaps as nowhere else outside Austria. Aside from scientists and businessmen, the best-known Hungarians are composers: Béla Bartók, Zoltan Kodály (who popularized the famous solfège sight-singing method taught in music schools worldwide), and Franz Liszt (actually Austrian, but of Hungarian ancestry).

As you can guess from the many grandiose structures built in Budapest in the late 1800s, Hungarians are also romantic. Over-the-top, melodramatic Latin American soap operas are popular

Hungary Almanac

Official Name: Magyar Köztársaság, or simply Magyarország.

Snapshot History: Settled by the Central Asian Magyars in A.D. 896, Hungary became Catholic in the year 1000, and went on to become Christian Europe's front line in fighting against the Ottomans (Muslims from today's Turkey) in the 16th–17th centuries. After serving as co-capital of the vast Austro-Hungarian Empire and losing World Wars I and II, Hungary became a Soviet satellite until achieving independence in 1989.

Population: Hungary's 10 million people (similar to Michigan) are 92 percent ethnic Hungarians who speak Hungarian. One in 50 is Roma (Gypsy). Half the populace is Catholic, with 20 percent Protestant and 25 percent listed as "other" or unaffiliated. Of the world's approximately 12 million ethnic Hungarians, one in six lives outside Hungary (mostly in areas of Romania, Slovakia, Serbia, and Croatia that were once part of Hungary).

Latitude and Longitude: 47°N and 20°E; similar latitude to Seattle, Paris, and Vienna.

Area: 36,000 square miles, similar to Indiana or Maine.

Geography: Hungary is situated in the Carpathian Basin, bound on the north by the Carpathian Mountains and on the south by the Dinaric Mountains. Though it's surrounded by mountains, Hungary itself is relatively flat, with some gently rolling hills. The Great Hungarian Plain—which begins on the east bank of the Danube in Budapest—stretches all the way to Asia. Hungary's two main rivers—the Danube and Tisza—run north–south through the country, neatly dividing it into three regions.

Biggest Cities: Budapest (the capital on the Danube, 1.7 million), Debrecen (in the east, 205,000), and Miskolc (in the north, 180,000).

Economy: The Gross Domestic Product is $175 billion (a third of Poland's), but the GDP per capita is $17,500 (about 20 percent

here (dubbed into Hungarian, of course). When the European Union expanded on May 1, 2004, the biggest celebrations anywhere were here in Hungary—where people love an excuse to party.

While one in five Hungarians lives in Budapest, the countryside plays an important role in Hungary's economy—this has always been a highly agricultural region. You'll pass fields of wheat and corn, but the grains are secondary to Hungarians' (and tourists') true love: the wine. Hungarian winemaking standards plummeted under the communists, but many vintner families are now reclaiming their land, returning to their precise traditional more than Poland's). Thanks to its progressive "goulash communism," Hungary had a head start on many other former Soviet Bloc countries and is now thriving, privatized...and largely foreign-owned. In the 1990s, many communist-era workers lost their jobs (especially women). Today, the workforce is small (only 57 percent of eligible workers) but highly skilled. Grains, metals, and machinery are major products, and nearly a third of trade is with Germany.

Currency: 200 forints (Ft, or HUF) = about $1.

Government: The single-house National Assembly (386 seats) is the only ruling branch directly elected by popular vote. The legislators in turn select the figurehead President (currently the right-of-center László Sólyom) and the ruling Prime Minister (the very controversial Socialist Ferenc Gyurcsány—see page 394).

Flag: Three horizontal bands, top to bottom: red (representing strength), white (faithfulness), and green (hope). It's identical to the Italian flag—only flipped 90 degrees counterclockwise. It often includes the Hungarian coat of arms: horizontal red-and-white stripes (on the left); the patriarchal, or double-barred, cross (on the right); and the Hungarian crown (on top). In the communist era, a socialistic emblem was placed in the center of the flag. A memorable symbol of dissent in those times (especially during the 1956 Uprising) was a Hungarian flag with a hole cut in the middle.

The Average Hungarian: Eats a pound of lard a week (they cook with it). One in five Hungarians uses the Internet. The average family has three members, and they spend almost three-fourths of their income on (costly) housing. According to a recent condom-company survey, the average Hungarian has sex 131 times a year (behind only France and Greece), making them Europe's third-greatest liars.

methods, and making wines worth being proud of once more.

Somehow Hungary, at the crossroads of Europe, has managed to become cosmopolitan while remaining perfectly Hungarian. In the countryside, where less mixing has occurred, Magyar culture and occasional Central Asian facial features are more evident. But in the cities, the Hungarians—like Hungary itself—are a cross-section of Central European cultures: Magyars, Germans, Czechs, Slovaks, Poles, Serbs, Jews, Ottomans, Romanians, Roma (Gypsies), and many others. Still, no matter how many generations removed they are from Magyar stock, there's something different about a Hungarian—and not just the language. Look a Hungarian in the eye, and you'll see a glimmer of the marauding Magyar, stomping in from the Central Asian plains a thousand years ago.

Practicalities

First Name Last: In Hungary, a person's family name is listed first, and the given name is last—just as in many other Eastern cultures (think of Kim Jong Il). The composer known as "Franz Liszt" in German is "Liszt Ferenc" in his homeland. To help reduce confusion, many Hungarian business cards list the surname in capital letters.

Hello Goodbye: Hungarians have an endearing habit of using the English word "hello" for both "hi" and "bye," just like the Italians use *"ciao."* You'll often overhear a Hungarian end a telephone conversation with a cheery "Hello!"

Telephones: Like many things in Hungary, the telephone system is uniquely confusing. You must dial different codes whether you're calling locally, long distance within the country, or internationally to Hungary.

To dial a number in the same city, simply dial direct, with no area code.

To dial long-distance within Hungary, you have to add the prefix 06, followed by the area code (e.g., Budapest's area code is 1, so you dial 06-1, then the rest of the number).

To make an international call to Hungary, start with the international access code (00 if calling from Europe, 011 from the United States or Canada), then Hungary's country code (36), then the area code (but not the 06) and number.

To make an international call from Hungary, dial 00, the country code of the country you're calling (see chart in appendix), the area code if applicable (may need to drop initial zero), and the local number.

Hungarian phone numbers beginning with 0680 are toll-free; those beginning with 0620, 0630, or 0670 are mobile phones; and 0681 or 0690 are expensive toll lines. To call these numbers from within Hungary, simply dial direct. To dial them from outside Hungary, you need to drop the 06 at the beginning. So to call the Hungarian mobile phone number 0620-926-0557 from the United States, you dial 011 (the US international access code), then 36 (Hungary's country code), then 20 (omitting the 06), then 926-0557.

Telephone cards, which you insert into pay phones, are sold locally at tobacco shops and newsstands. Cheap international telephone cards (which aren't insertable but can be used from virtually any phone—see page 940) are just catching on in Hungary.

Hungarian History

Hungary has a colorful and illustrious history. In terms of political influence in Eastern Europe's past, the Hungarians rank with the Germans and the Russians.

Welcome to Europe

The Magyars, led by the mighty Árpád, thundered into the Carpathian Basin in A.D. 896. They were a rough-and-tumble nomadic people from Central Asia who didn't like to settle down in one place. They'd camp out in today's Hungary in the winters, and in the summers, they'd go on raids throughout Europe—terrorizing the Continent from Constantinople (modern-day Istanbul) to the Spanish Pyrénées. For half a century, they ranked with the Vikings as the most feared people in Europe.

After decades of running roughshod over Europe, the Hungarians were finally defeated by a German and Czech army at the Battle of Augsburg in 955. If they were to survive, the nomadic Magyars had to settle down. King Géza baptized his son, István (who was Árpád's great-great-grandson), and married him to a Bavarian princess at an early age.

Magyars Tamed

On Christmas Day in the year 1000, King István (Stephen) was symbolically crowned by the pope, and Hungary became a legitimate Christian nation (see page 428). The domestication of the nomadic Magyars was difficult, but Hungary eventually emerged as a major European power. The kingdom reached its peak in the late 15th century, when the enlightened King Mátyás Corvinus fostered the arts and sparked a mini-Renaissance (see page 424).

Ottoman Invasion

Soon after the reign of good king Mátyás, the Ottomans came slicing their way through the Balkan Peninsula towards Central Europe. In 1526, they entered Hungary. By 1541, they took Buda. During the Ottoman occupation, the Magyars moved the capital of the little that remained of their land—"rump Hungary"—to Bratislava (which they called "Pozsony"). During this era, the Ottomans built many of the baths that you'll still find throughout Hungary—and spiced up the food with paprika.

Christian-centric European historians have long viewed the Ottoman rule of southeastern Europe as an oppressive regime, but some experts have recently suggested otherwise. While it was advantageous for a European subject to adopt Islam (for lower taxes and other privileges), the Ottomans did not forcibly convert anyone—unlike the arguably more oppressive Catholics who controlled other parts of Europe at the time. (Remember the Spanish

Who Were the Magyars?

The ancestors of today's Hungarians, the Magyars, are a mysterious lot. Of all the Asian invaders of Europe, they were arguably the most successful—integrating more or less smoothly with the Europeans, and thriving well into the 21st century. Centuries after the Huns, Tatars, and Ottomans retreated east, leaving behind only fragments of their culture, the Hungarians remain a fixture in contemporary Europe.

The history of the Magyars before they arrived in Europe in A.D. 896 is hotly contested. Because their language is related only to Finnish and Estonian, it's presumed that these three peoples were once a single group, which likely originated east of the Ural Mountains (in the steppes of present-day Asian Russia).

After the Magyars' ancestors spent some time in Siberia, climatic change pushed them south and west, eventually (likely around the fifth century A.D.) crossing the Ural Mountains and officially entering Europe. They settled near the Don River (in today's southwestern Russia) before local warfare pushed them farther and farther west. The Magyars began raiding European lands, eventually setting up camp in the Carpathian Basin—today's Hungary—in A.D. 896.

After dominating Europe for many decades, the Hungarians were routed in battle and forced to adopt Christianity—a turning point that ultimately allowed them to flourish. Over the next several centuries, the Hungarians' Asian features and customs mostly faded away as they intermarried with Germans, Slavs, and

Inquisition and the expulsion of the Jews from Spain in 1492?) In later years, under Catholic Hapsburg rule, the Hungarians became notorious for their frequent and fierce uprisings. But under the Ottomans, no such record exists—leading many historians to believe that Hungarians preferred Ottoman (Muslim) rule to Hapsburg (Catholic) rule.

Crippled by the Ottomans and lacking power and options, Hungary came under control of the Austrian Hapsburg Empire, which finally wrested Buda from the Ottomans in 1686. The Hapsburgs repopulated Buda and Pest with Germans, while Magyars reclaimed the countryside.

The Hapsburgs

The Hungarians resisted Hapsburg rule, and three Magyars in particular are still noted for their rebellion against Vienna: Ferenc Rákóczi, who led Hungarians in the War of Independence (1703–1711); Lajos Kossuth, who was at the forefront of the 1848 Revolution; and Kossuth's contemporary, Count István Széchenyi, other European peoples. By the 16th century, the Hungarians became Europe's front line in fending off the invasion of another Asian group, the Ottomans. Hungarian integration with the other peoples of Europe continued over the next several centuries, and through to the present day. In fact, a recent genetic study found that Hungarians are the most ethnically diverse nationality on the planet.

But even though certain aspects of their Magyar heritage have been lost, the Hungarians have done a remarkable job of clinging on to their Asian roots. They still do things their own way, making Hungary subtly but unmistakably different from its neighboring countries. And people of German-Hungarian, Slavic-Hungarian, and Jewish-Hungarian descent still speak a language that's not too far removed from the Asian tongue spoken by those original Magyars.

Were the Hungarians (Magyars) descended from the Huns, a similarly violent nomadic tribe that lived in the same area centuries earlier? Until recently, legends and historians speculated a tie between these two groups. In fact, the word "Hungarian" is at least partly derived from "Hun." But, even though it's a popular romantic notion to link these two mysterious tribes, recent historians strongly doubt that the two ever had anything to do with each other. Even so, many Hungarians still take pride in the legendary link to the Huns...and "Attila" remains a popular name even today.

who fought the Hapsburgs with money—building structures like Budapest's iconic Chain Bridge. Countless streets, squares, and buildings throughout the country are named for these three Hungarian patriots.

But centuries of alliance with the Hapsburgs eventually paid off. After the 1848 Revolution in Hungary and an important military loss to the Prussians, Austria realized that it couldn't control its rebellious Slavic holdings all by itself. With the Compromise of 1867, Austria granted Budapest the authority over the eastern half of their lands, creating the so-called Dual Monarchy of the Austro-Hungarian Empire.

Hungary enjoyed a Golden Age and Budapest prospered, governing large parts of today's Slovakia, Croatia, and Transylvania (northwest Romania). Composers Franz Liszt (more Germanic than Magyar) and Béla Bartók incorporated the folk and Roma (Gypsy) songs of the Hungarian and Transylvanian countryside into their music.

Hungary

The Crisis of Trianon

Hungary, allied with Austria and Germany, came up on the losing end of World War I. As retribution, the 1920 Treaty of Trianon (named for the palace on the grounds of Versailles where it was signed) reassigned two-thirds of Hungary's former territory and half of its population to Romania, Czechoslovakia, Slovenia, Croatia, and Serbia. Not unlike the overnight construction of the Berlin Wall, towns along the new Hungarian borders were suddenly divided down the middle. Many Hungarians found themselves unable to visit relatives or commute to jobs that were in the same country the day before. This sent hundreds of thousands of Hungarian refugees—now "foreigners" in their own towns—into Budapest, sparking an enormous boom in the capital.

To this day, the Treaty of Trianon is regarded as one of the greatest tragedies of Hungarian history. More than two million ethnic Hungarians live outside Hungary (mostly in Romania)—and many Hungarians claim that these lands still belong to the Magyars. The sizeable Magyar minorities in neighboring countries have often been mistreated—particularly in Romania (under Ceauşescu), Yugoslavia (under Milošević), and Slovakia (under Mečiar). You'll see maps, posters, and bumper stickers with the distinctive shape of a much larger, pre-WWI Hungary...patriotically displayed by Magyars who feel as strongly about Trianon as if it happened yesterday. When the European Union expanded in 2004, some Hungarians saw it as a happy ending in the big-picture sense—they were once again united with Slovakia, part of the territory they had lost.

After World War I, the newly shrunken Kingdom of Hungary had to reinvent itself. The WWI hero Admiral Miklós Horthy had won many battles with the Austro-Hungarian navy. Though the new Hungary had no sea and no navy, Horthy retained his rank and ruled the country as a regent. A popular joke points out that during this time, Hungary was a "kingdom without a king" and a landlocked country ruled by a sea admiral. This sense of compounded deficiency pretty much sums up the morose attitude Hungarians have about those gloomy post-Trianon days.

World War II and the Arrow Cross

As Hitler rose to power, some countries that had felt unfairly treated in the aftermath of World War I—including Hungary and Croatia—saw Nazi Germany as a vehicle to greater independence. Admiral Horthy ceded power to the Nazis with the hope that they might help Hungary regain the crippling territorial losses of Trianon. Being an ally to the Nazis, rather than an occupied state, also allowed Hungary a certain degree of self-determination through the war—saving its sizeable Jewish population from

---

Top 10 Dates That Changed Hungary

A.D. 896—The nomadic Magyars (a tribe from Central Asia) arrive in the Carpathian Basin and begin to terrorize Europe.

1000—The pope crowns King István (Stephen), marking the domestication of the Magyars.

1541—Invading Ottomans take Buda and Pest...and cook with paprika.

1686—The Austrian Hapsburgs drive out the Ottomans, making Hungary part of their extensive empire (despite occasional rebellions from nationalistic Hungarians).

1848—A Golden Age begins, as Hungary gains semi-autonomy from Austria, rebuilds Budapest, rules surrounding territories, and inspires great artists.

1920—Losers in World War I, Hungary is stripped of two-thirds its territory and half its population in the Treaty of Trianon... and they're still angry about it.

1945—After World War II, the Soviet Union "liberates" the country and establishes a communist state.

1956—Hungarians bravely revolt. A massive invasion of Soviet tanks and soldiers brutally suppresses the rebellion, killing 25,000.

1989—Hungary is the first Soviet satellite to open its borders to the West, sparking similar reforms throughout Eastern Europe.

2004—Hungary joins the European Union.

---

immediate deportation to concentration camps. Winning back chunks of Slovakia, Transylvania, and Croatia in the early days of World War II also bolstered the Nazis' popularity in Hungary.

As Nazism took hold in Germany, the Hungarian fascist movement—spearheaded by the Arrow Cross Party (Nyilaskeresztes Párt)—gained popularity within Hungary. As Germany increased its demands for Hungarian soldiers and food, Admiral Horthy resisted...until Hitler's patience wore thin. In March of 1944, the Nazis invaded and installed the Arrow Cross in power. The Arrow Cross made up for lost time, immediately beginning a savage campaign of executing Hungary's Jews—not only sending them to concentration camps, but butchering them in the streets. Almost 600,000 Hungarian Jews were murdered. For more on this dark era of Hungarian history, see the "House of Terror" museum listing on page 446 of the Budapest chapter.

The Soviet Army eventually liberated Hungary—but at the expense of Budapest, where a months-long siege reduced the proud city to rubble.

Hungary

Communism...with a Pinch of Paprika

After World War II, the Soviets installed Mátyás Rákosi as head of state. In 1956, the Hungarians staged an uprising, led by Communist Party reformer Imre Nagy (see page 438). Moscow sent in troops, 25,000 Hungarians were killed, and 200,000 fled to the West. (If you know any Hungarians in the US, their families more than likely fled there in 1956.) János Kádár was installed to run a harder-line government, and though he cooperated with Moscow, he gradually allowed the people of Hungary more freedom than citizens of neighboring countries had.

Life here became better and livelier than elsewhere in the Soviet bloc—a system dubbed "goulash communism." With little fanfare, the Hungarian parliament—always skeptical of the Soviets—peacefully voted to end the communist regime in February of 1989. Later that year, Hungary was the first Eastern Bloc nation to open its borders to the West, a major advance in the fall of communist regimes across Eastern Europe. Hungary's first post-communist president, Árpád Göncz, was a protestor from the 1950s who was famous for translating *The Lord of the Rings* into Hungarian while he was in prison.

Hungary Today

In 2004, Hungary eagerly joined the EU, excited about its future in a united Europe. But as they've adjusted to life after communism, Hungary's leaders have struggled with how to afford the generous social-welfare network its people have come to expect. The Hungarian Socialist Party, which took control of parliament in 2002, impressed citizens by maintaining and even extending some social programs, but experts began to worry the mounting public debt would bankrupt the country.

Hungary made international headlines in the fall of 2006, when Prime Minister Ferenc Gyurcsány, a Socialist, was involved in an embarrassing gaffe that almost led to a minor revolution. After the Hungarian Socialist Party won re-election in April 2006, Gyurcsány gave a secret speech to his party. The intent of his shockingly frank remarks was to give his colleagues a wake-up call. But Gyurcsány's method—ranting on and on about how badly they'd fouled things up (and using very colorful language)—was ill-advised. Someone in the meeting recorded the whole thing, waited a few months, then turned the audio tape over to the press.

On September 17, 2006, Hungarians turned on their TVs to hear their Prime Minister detailing the ways he and his party had driven their country to the brink of ruin, and then shamelessly lied about it to stay in power: "We have screwed up. Not a little but a lot. No country in Europe has screwed up as much as we have... We did not actually do anything for four years. Nothing...We lied morning, noon, and night."

The following night, demonstrators (many of them members of fringe political groups—and even, according to local scuttlebutt, known gangs of soccer hooligans) showed up at two strategic squares in downtown Budapest, demanding Gyurcsány's resignation. Riot police were sent in to subdue the looters with water cannons and tear gas. The violence was quickly put down, but the unrest continued to simmer for several months. Gyurcsány refused to resign, but Hungary's politicians learned a valuable lesson about dealing with a fragile new democracy.

Hungary continues to struggle with rampant inflation, which has postponed its adoption of the euro currency. But regardless of its economic woes—and the sensationalistic coverage of the 2006 events on international news networks—Hungary remains an enjoyable, welcoming, and safe place to travel.

Hungarian Food

Hungary is known in Eastern Europe for its spicy food. Hungarian cuisine is as rich and complex as Polish and Czech food are simple. Everything is heavily seasoned: with paprika, tomatoes, and peppers of every shape, color, size, and flavor.

Hungarians dine at a *vendéglő* or *étterem* (restaurant). They gather with friends at a *kávéház* (café, literally, "coffeehouse"), which sometimes has light food, too. And for dessert, it's a *cukrászda* (pastry shop—*cukr* means "sugar").

Many American visitors to Hungary can't wait to taste goulash in its homeland—only to be disappointed that it isn't quite what they expected. The word "goulash" comes from the Hungarian *gulyás leves,* or "shepherd's soup." Here in its homeland, it's a clear, spicy broth with chunks of meat, potatoes, and other vegetables. Only outside of Hungary is the word used to describe a thick stew.

Aside from the obligatory *gulyás,* make a point of trying another unusual Hungarian specialty: cold fruit soup *(hideg gyümölcs leves).* This cream-based treat—generally eaten before the meal, even though it tastes more like a dessert—is usually made with *meggy* (sour cherries), but you'll also see versions with *alma* (apples) or *körte* (pears). Other Hungarian soups *(levesek)* include *bableves* (bean soup), *zöldségleves* (vegetable soup), *gombaleves* (mushroom soup), and *halászlé* (fish broth with paprika).

Hungarians adore all kinds of meat *(hús). Csirke* is chicken,

Paprika Primer

The quintessential ingredient in Hungarian cuisine is paprika. In Hungarian, the word *paprika* can mean both peppers (red or green) and the spice that's made with them. Peppers can be stewed, stuffed, sautéed, baked, grilled, or pickled. For seasoning, red shakers of dried paprika join the salt and pepper on tables.

There are more than 40 varieties of paprika spice, with two main types: hot (*csípős* or *erős*) and sweet (*édesnemes* or simply *édes*, often comes in a white can). A can of paprika is a handy and tasty souvenir of your trip (see "Shopping" in the Budapest chapter, page 468). On menus, anything cooked *paprikás* (PAH-pree-kash) will be a little spicy. To add even more kick to your food, ask for a jar of *erős pista* (EH-rewsh PEESH-tah)—a spicy paste that's best used sparingly.

borjú is veal, *kacsa* is duck, *liba* is goose, *libamáj* is goose liver (which shows up everywhere—for example, anything prepared "Budapest style" comes with goose liver), *sertés* is pork, *sonka* is ham, *kolbász* is sausage, *szelet* is schnitzel (*Bécsi szelet* means Wiener schnitzel)—and the list goes on. Lard is used quite a bit in cooking, making Hungarian cuisine very rich and filling. Meat goes well with *káposzta* (cabbage), which may be *töltött* (stuffed) with the meat.

Vegetarians have a tricky time in Hungary, with many restaurants offering only a plate of deep-fried vegetables. They haven't quite figured out how to do a good, healthy, leafy salad; a traditional restaurant will generally offer only marinated cucumbers (listed on menus as "cucumber salad"), a plate of sliced-up pickles ("pickled cucumbers"), marinated spicy peppers, or something with cabbage—using lettuce only as a garnish.

In Hungary, you sometimes pay for *köretek* (starches) separately from the meat course. You'll be asked to choose between *galuska* (noodles), *burgonya* (potatoes), *krumpli* (French fries), *krokett* (like Tater Tots), or *rizs* (rice). *Kenyér* (bread) often comes with the meal.

A popular snack, especially in Budapest, is *lángos*—a savory deep-fried doughnut spread with cheese, garlic, and sour cream. In restaurants, a fancier version (often with meat) can be served as an entrée.

Pastries are a big deal here. Hungary's streets are lined with *cukrászda* (pastry shops) where you can simply point to which treat you'd like. Try the *Dobos torta* (a layered chocolate-and-caramel cream cake), *somlói galuska* (a dumpling with vanilla, nuts, and chocolate), anything with *gesztenye* (chestnuts), and *rétes* (strudel with various fillings, including *túrós*, curds). On dessert menus at restaurants, you'll also see *palacsinta* (pancakes), usually served *diós* (with walnuts), *mákos* (with poppy seeds), or *gündel* (with nuts, chocolate, cream, and raisins). And many *cukrászda* also serve *fagylalt* (ice cream, *fagyi* for short), sold by the *gomboc* (ball).

To drink: *Sör* means "beer," and *bor* means "wine" (*vörös* is red and *fehér* is white). For more on Hungarian wines, see page 509 in the Eger chapter. *Kávé* and *tea* (pronounced TEY-ah) are coffee and tea, and *víz* (water) comes as *szódavíz* (soda water, sometimes just carbonated tap water) or *ásványvíz* (spring water, more expensive).

Unicum is a unique and beloved Hungarian liqueur made of 40 different herbs and aged in oak casks. The flavor is powerfully unforgettable—like Jägermeister, but harsher. A swig of Unicum is often gulped before the meal, but it's also used as a cure for an upset stomach (especially if you've eaten too much rich food—not an uncommon problem in Hungary). The liqueur has a history as unique and complicated as its flavor. Invented by a Doctor Zwack in the late 18th century, the drink impressed Hapsburg emperor Josef II, who supposedly declared: *"Das ist ein Unikum!"* ("This is a specialty!"). The Zwack company went on to thrive during Budapest's late-19th-century Golden Age (when Unicum was the subject of many whimsical Guinness-type ads). But when the communists took over after World War II, the Zwacks fled to America—taking their secret recipe for Unicum with them. The communists continued to market the drink with their own formula, which left Hungarians (literally and figuratively) with a bad taste in their mouths. In a landmark case, the Zwacks sued the communists for infringing on their copyright...and won. In 1991, Péter Zwack—who had been living in exile in Italy—triumphantly returned to Hungary and resurrected the original family recipe. To get your own taste of this family saga, look for the round bottle with the red cross on the label (www.zwack.hu).

If you're drinking with some new Magyar friends, impress them with the standard toast: *Egészségedre* (EH-gehs-sheh-geh-dreh; "to your health"). But don't clink your beer glasses with theirs. They still remember the 1848 Revolution against the Hapsburgs, which ended with the Hapsburg execution of 13 great Hungarian leaders. The Hapsburgs clinked their beer mugs to the victory. To this very day, clinking beer mugs is, for many Hungarians, just bad style. (While some say the taboo expired after 150 years, others still take it seriously.) Clinking wine glasses is perfectly fine, but always make meaningful eye contact as you clink.

When your waiter brings your food, he'll probably say, *"Jó étvágyat!"* (Bon appétit!). When you're ready for the bill, you can simply say, *"Fizetek"* (FEE-zeh-tehk—"I'll pay").

Hungarian Language

Even though Hungary is surrounded by Slavs, Hungarian is not at all related to Slavic languages. In fact, Hungarian isn't related to *any* European language (except for very distant relatives Finnish and Estonian). It isn't even an Indo-European language—which means that English is more closely related to Hindi, Russian, and French than it is to Hungarian.

Hungarian is agglutinative, which means that you start with a simple root word and then start tacking on suffixes to create meaning—sometimes resulting in a pileup of extra sounds at the end of a very long word. The emphasis always goes on the first syllable, and the following syllables are droned downhill in a kind of a monotone—giving the language a distinctive cadence that Hungary's Slavic neighbors love to tease about.

While the language is overwhelming for tourists, one easy word is *"Szia"* (SEE-yah), which means both hello and goodbye (like "ciao" or "aloha").

Hungarian pronunciation is straightforward, once you remember a few key rules. The trickiest: *s* alone is pronounced "sh," while *sz* is pronounced simply "s." This explains why you'll hear in-the-know travelers pronouncing Budapest as "BOO-dah-pesht." You might catch the *busz* up to Castle Hill—pronounced "boose." And "Franz Liszt" is easier to pronounce than it looks: It sounds just like "list." To review:

s sounds like "sh" as in "shirt"

sz sounds like "s" as in "saint"

Hungarian has a set of unusual palatal sounds that don't quite have a counterpart in English. To make these sounds, gently press the thick part of your tongue to the roof or your mouth (instead of using the tip of your tongue behind your teeth, as we do in English):

gy sounds like "dg" as in "hedge"

ny sounds like "ny" as in "canyon" (not "nee")

ty sounds like "tch" as in "itch"

cs sounds like "ch" as in "church"

As for vowels: The letter *a* almost sounds like o (aw, as in "hot"); but with an accent *(á)*, it brightens up to the more standard "ah." As with Czech, an accent *(á, é, í, ó, ú)* indicates that you linger on that vowel (but not necessarily that you stress that syllable). Like German, Hungarian has umlauts *(ö, ü)*, meaning you purse your lips when you say that vowel. A long umlaut *(ő, ű)* is the same sound, but you hold it a little longer.

Here are a few other letters than sound different in Hungarian than in English:

c and **cz** both sound like "ts" as in "cats"

zs sounds like "zh" as in "leisure"

j and **ly** both sound like "y" as in "yellow"

Key Hungarian Phrases

English	Hungarian	Pronounced
Hello. (formal)	Jó napot kívánok.	yoh NAH-pot KEE-vah-nohk
Hi. / Bye. (informal)	Szia.	SEE-yah
Do you speak English?	Beszél angolul?	BEH-sehl AHN-goh-lool
Yes. / No.	Igen. / Nem.	EE-gehn / nehm
Please.	Kérem.	KAY-rehm
You're welcome.	Szívesen.	SEE-veh-shehn
Can I help you?	Tessék.	TEHSH-shehk
Thank you.	Köszönöm.	KUR-sur-nurm
I'm sorry. / Excuse me.	Bocsánat.	BOH-chah-nawt
Good.	Jól.	yohl
Goodbye.	Viszontlátásra.	VEE-sohnt-lah-tahsh-rah
one / two	egy / kettő	edj / KEH-tur
three / four	három / négy	HAH-rohm / nedj
five / six	öt / hat	urt / hawt
seven / eight	hét / nyolc	heht / NEE-ohlts
nine / ten	kilenc / tíz	KEE-lehnts / teez
hundred	száz	sahz
thousand	ezer	EH-zehr
How much?	Mennyi?	MEHN-yee
local currency	forint (Ft)	FOH-reent
Where is...?	Hol van...?	hohl vawn
...the toilet	...a toalet	aw TOH-ah-leht
men	férfi	FEHR-fee
women	női	NUR-ee
water / coffee	víz / kávé	veez / KAH-veh
beer / wine	sör / bor	shewr / bohr
Cheers!	Egészségedre!	EH-gehs-sheh-geh-dreh
the bill (literally, "I'll pay")	fizetek	FEE-zeh-tehk

Okay, maybe it's not *so* simple. But you'll get the hang of it.

As you're tracking down addresses, these definitions will help: *tér* (square), *utca* (road), *út* (boulevard), *körút* (ring road), *fürdő* (bath), and *híd* (bridge). Words ending in *k* are often plural.

heart and soul of Eastern Europe. It's a rich cultural stew made up of Hungarians, Germans, Slavs, and Jews, with a dash of Turkish paprika—whether for oompuhoos in a thermal bath. Each group has left its mark, but through that paprika...Budapest.

BUDAPEST

Budapest is the capital of Eastern Europe. It's a city of nuance and paradox—cosmopolitan, complicated, and challenging for the first-timer to get a handle on. Novices are sometimes overwhelmed by Budapest...but seasoned travelers enjoy this grand city more with each return visit. Though Prague and Kraków have more romance (and crowds), travelers in the know find Budapest to be Eastern Europe's most fascinating and rewarding destination.

Budapest (locals say "BOO-dah-pesht") is hot—literally. The city sits on a thin layer of earth above thermal springs, which power its many baths. Even the word *Pest* comes from a Slavic word for "oven." Two thousand years ago, the Romans had a settlement (called Aquincum) on the north edge of today's Budapest. Several centuries later, in A.D. 896, the Magyars arrived from the steppes of Central Asia and took over the Carpathian Basin (roughly today's Hungary). In the 16th century, the Ottomans invaded—occupying the region for 145 years. When the Ottomans were forced out, Buda and Pest were in ruins. The Hapsburgs repopulated them, giving the cities a more Austrian style.

The Great Compromise of 1867 granted Hungary an equal stake in the Austro-Hungarian Empire. Six years later, the cities of Buda, Pest, and Óbuda united to form the capital city of Budapest, which governed a huge chunk of Eastern Europe. For the next few decades, Hungarian culture enjoyed a Golden Age, and Budapest was a boomtown. The expansion reached its peak with a flurry of construction surrounding the year 1896—Hungary's 1,000th birthday (see page 410).

During the Soviet era, Hungary's milder "goulash communism" meant that Budapest, though still oppressed, was a place where other Eastern Europeans felt they could let loose. Twenty years ago, a stroll down Váci utca was the closest Czechs and Poles could get to a day pass to the West—including a chance to taste a Big Mac at the first McDonald's behind the Iron Curtain.

Budapest was built as the head of a much larger empire than it currently governs. Like Vienna, the city today feels a bit too grandiose for the capital of a small country. But Budapest remains the heart and soul of Eastern Europe. It's a rich cultural stew made up of Hungarians, Germans, Slavs, and Jews, with a dash of Turkish paprika—simmered for centuries in a thermal bath. Each group has left its mark, but through it all, something has remained that is distinctly...Budapest.

Planning Your Time

Budapest demands at least three nights and two full days. The city has oodles of good museums, but none of them is strictly must-see; which ones you visit depends entirely on your interests. Skim my listings and figure out which sights sound good to you. I've suggested where you might fit them in below.

I like this efficient but ambitious two-day plan:

Day 1: Begin at the square called Vörösmarty tér, consider coffee at Gerbeaud, and stroll down Váci utca (see page 435). At the end of the street, explore the Great Market Hall.

From the Great Market Hall, you're a quick walk or tram ride (#47 or #49) from the Great Synagogue and the National Museum. If you'd prefer to tour the Parliament—farther to the north—do it this morning (tram #2 or #2A zips you right there from the Great Market Hall).

After lunch in Pest, stroll over the Chain Bridge and ride the funicular up to Castle Hill. Following my self-guided walk (page 421), visit Matthias Church, Fishermen's Bastion, and the Castle Hill museums of your choice.

After dinner, take a twilight sightseeing cruise, go to a concert (folk music nightly at 20:00) or the opera, or stroll the Danube embankments and bridges.

Day 2: Start at St. István's Basilica, then work your way up the lively boulevard called Andrássy út. Depending on your interests, you can stop at (in this order): the Museum of Trade and Tourism, the Postal Museum, the Opera House (duck in to see the lobby, or return later for a full-blown tour at 15:00 or 16:00), Franz Liszt Square (lots of cafés and restaurants), busy Oktogon square, and the House of Terror museum. To skip ahead (or backtrack quickly), hop on the M1 Metro line, which runs beneath Andrássy út from start to finish. At the end of Andrássy út, explore Heroes' Square and City Park.

Reward yourself with a nice, long soak in the Széchenyi Baths

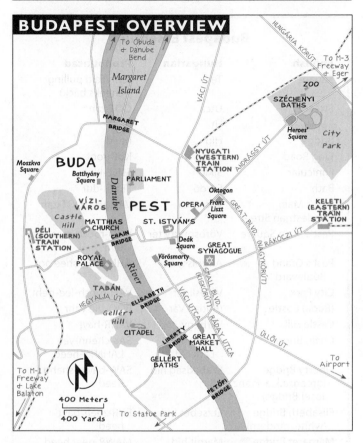

BUDAPEST OVERVIEW

(secure lockers, rental suits, open until 22:00, get there by 20:00 to have enough time). The ritzy Gundel Restaurant is across from the baths, and other, less-fancy dining options are nearby. For the evening, consider the same options as for Day 1.

To speed things up and fit in Statue Park, squeeze in the statues in the morning of Day 2 (bus departs Deák tér at 11:00), then do an accelerated ramble down Andrássy boulevard.

You'll have no trouble filling a third day—it gives you more time for Statue Park, more museums, and outlying areas (such as Óbuda and Szentendre). After many years, I still discover new joys each time I return.

Eger is the best day trip (2.25 hrs by train each way, even better if you spend the night—see Eger chapter). Szentendre, on the Danube Bend, is closer but very touristy (doable in a half-day or even just in the late afternoon/evening). With a car (or a hired driver—see "Drivers," page 413), you could spend a day seeing the entire Danube Bend—Szentendre, Visegrád, and Esztergom—

Budapest Essentials

English	Hungarian	Pronounced
Square	Tér	tehr (said pulling cheeks back)
Street	Utca	OOT-zah
Boulevard	Út	oot
Bridge	Híd	heed
Ring Road	Körút	KUR-root
Funicular	Sikló	SHEE-kloh
Bath	Fürdő	FEWR-dur
Pest's Main Pedestrian Street	Váci utca	VAH-tsee OOT-zah
Pest's Main Square	Vörösmarty tér	VOO-roosh-mar-tee tehr
Pest's Grand Boulevard	Andrássy út	AHN-drah-shee oot
City Park	Városliget	VAH-rohsh-lee-geht
(Buda) Castle	(Budai) Vár	BOO-die vahr
Castle Hill	Várhegy	VAHR-hayj
Chain Bridge	Széchenyi Lánchíd	SAY-chehn-yee LAHNTS-heed
Liberty Bridge (green, a.k.a. Franz Josef Bridge)	Szabadság híd	SAW-bawd-shahg heed
Elisabeth Bridge (white, modern)	Erzsébet híd	EHR-zheh-bayt heed
Margaret Bridge (crosses Margaret Island)	Margit híd	MAWR-geet heed
Danube River	Duna	DOO-naw
Eastern Train Station	Keleti pályaudvar	KEH-leh-tee PAH-yuh-uhd-vahr
Western Train Station	Nyugati pályaudvar	NYOO-gaw-tee PAH-yuh-uhd-vahr
Southern Train Station	Déli pályaudvar	DAY-lee PAH-yuh-uhd-vahr
Suburban Train System	HÉV	hayv

ideally on the way to Vienna or Bratislava (see Danube Bend chapter).

ORIENTATION

(area code: 1)

Budapest is huge—with nearly two million people, it's much larger than Prague. The city is split down the center by the Danube River. On the west side of the Danube is hilly **Buda,** dominated by Castle Hill (packed with tourists by day, dead at night). The pleasant Víziváros ("Water Town"; VEE-zee-vah-rohsh) neighborhood is between the castle and the river.

On the east is flat **Pest** (pronounced "pesht"), the commercial heart of the city, which bustles day and night. The red-domed, riverside Parliament, visible from any point along the Danube, marks the northern edge of the tourists' Pest. A few blocks to the south, the Váci utca pedestrian drag runs parallel to the Danube, ending at the steps of the Great Market Hall. From Deák Square in the center of Pest, Andrássy út (and the yellow M1 Metro line beneath it) runs out past the Opera House to the Oktogon, House of Terror museum, Heroes' Square, City Park, and Széchenyi Baths.

Buda and Pest are connected by a series of characteristic **bridges.** From north to south, there's the low-profile Margaret Bridge (Margit híd, crosses Margaret Island), the famous Chain Bridge (Széchenyi lánchíd), the white and modern Elisabeth Bridge (Erzsébet híd), and the green Liberty Bridge (Szabadság híd). The bridges are fun to cross by foot, but it's faster to go under the river (on the M2 Metro line), or to cross over it by tram (#47 and #49 over the Liberty Bridge) or by bus (#16 over the Chain Bridge and #78 across the Elisabeth Bridge are both handy).

Pest is surrounded by a series of **ring roads** (körút). The innermost ring road—called the Kiskörút, or "Small Boulevard"—surrounds central Pest. The outer ring road—Nagykörút, or "Great Boulevard"—is about halfway between the river and City Park. The ring roads change names every few blocks, but they are always called körút. Arterial **boulevards** called út (such as Andrássy út) stretch from central Pest into the suburbs, like spokes on a wheel. Almost everything a tourist wants to see in Pest is either inside the innermost ring—in the **Belváros** ("Inner City")—or along one of these main boulevards (and therefore well covered by public transit). Buda is also surrounded by a ring road, and the busy Hegyalja út rumbles through the middle of the tourists' Buda (between Castle and Gellért hills).

Budapest uses a **district** system (like Paris and Vienna), and addresses often start with the district number (as a Roman numeral). Districts are called kerület. Castle Hill is district I.

Budapest

Notice that the district number does not necessarily indicate how central a location is: Districts II and III are to the north of Buda, where few tourists go, while the heart of Pest is district V.

Tourist Information

Budapest has several TIs (www.budapestinfo.hu, tel. 1/438-8080). The main branch is a few steps from the M2 and M3 Metro station at **Deák tér** (daily 8:00–20:00, Sütő utca 2, near the McDonald's). Other locations include **Franz Liszt Square,** a block south of the Oktogon on Andrássy út (June–Sept daily 10:00–19:00; Oct–April Mon–Fri 10:00–18:00, closed Sat–Sun; May Mon–Fri 10:00–18:00, Sat 10:00–16:00, closed Sun; Liszt Ferenc tér 11, tel. 1/322-4098); **Castle Hill,** across from Matthias Church (daily May–Oct 9:00–20:00, Nov–April 9:00–18:00, Szentháromság tér, tel. 1/488-0475); and in both Terminals 1 and 2B at the **airport** (daily 9:00–22:00).

While Budapest's TIs typically aren't very helpful, they do produce some free, useful publications, including the good city map, the *Budapest Panorama* events guide, and the information-packed *Budapest Guide* booklet. At all of the TIs, you can also collect a pile of other free brochures (on sights, bus tours, and more) and buy a Budapest Card.

Budapest Card: Even though this sightseeing card has shot up in price in recent years, it can still sometimes be a good value for busy sightseers. You get free travel on public transportation and entry to virtually all of Budapest's museums (though you'll pay extra for special exhibits), plus minor discounts on other worthwhile attractions (including boat tours and thermal baths). With the Budapest Card, you have the freedom to hop the Metro for one stop to save 10 minutes of walking, or drop into semi-interesting sights for a peek. This is especially useful since Budapest has lots of "quickie" museums that don't really merit a long visit. The card costs 6,500 Ft for 48 hours, or 8,000 Ft for 72 hours (includes handy 112-page booklet with maps, updated hours, and brief museum descriptions). You can buy the card all over Budapest—at TIs, travel agencies, major Metro stations, sights, and many hotels. Be sure to sign and date your card before you use it.

Alternative Tourist Information Offices: Ben Frieday, an American in love with Budapest (and one of its women), runs **Discover Hungary.** This office specializes in answering questions Americans (especially backpackers) have about Budapest. They have two locations in central Budapest: at Deák tér (Sütő utca 2, in the courtyard between the McDonald's and TI, marked "Yellow Zebra") and near Andrássy út (behind the Opera House at Lázár utca 16; also has a small English bookstore). At either branch, you can use the Internet (200 Ft/15 min), rent a bike, and find out more

Sightseeing Modules

Budapest is a sprawling city, with sights scattered over a huge area. But if you organize your sightseeing efficiently and dive into the easy-to-master public transportation system, Budapest gets small. Break the city into manageable chunks, and digest them one at a time:

Buda
- **Castle Hill** (Royal Palace, Matthias Church, and various museums)
- **Gellért Hill** (Gellért Baths, Citadella, and Cave Church)

Pest
- **Central Pest, a.k.a. Belváros** (north to south: Parliament, Vörösmarty Square, Váci utca pedestrian drag, Danube embankment and cruises, Great Synagogue, National Museum, and Great Market Hall)
- **Andrássy út** (from center to outskirts: St. István's Basilica, Museum of Trade and Tourism, Opera House, Franz Liszt Square, Oktogon, House of Terror, Heroes' Square, City Park, and Széchenyi Baths)

Outer Budapest
- **Óbuda** (Vasarely Museum, Imre Varga Collection, and Aquincum Roman ruins)
- **Statue Park**
- **Danube Bend** (begins just north of Óbuda: Szentendre, Visegrád, and Esztergom; see Danube Bend chapter)

about Budapest (both offices open May–Oct daily 9:30–19:30, shorter hours off-season, tel. 1/266-8777, www.discoverhungary .com). Ben also runs Yellow Zebra bike tours, Absolute Walking Tours, and Segway Tours (see page 417 and page 420).

Arrival in Budapest
By Train
Budapest has three major train stations (*pályaudvar*, abbreviated *pu.*): Keleti (Eastern) Station, Nyugati (Western) Station, and Déli (Southern) Station. A century ago, the name of the station indicated which part of Europe it served. But these days, there's no correlation: Trains going to the east might leave from the Western Station, and vice-versa. Even more confusing, the station used by a particular train can change from year to year. Before departing from Budapest, it's essential to carefully confirm which station your train leaves from.

The Keleti (Eastern) Station and Nyugati (Western) Station—

both cavernous, slightly run-down, late-19th-century Erector-set masterpieces in Pest—are the ones you're most likely to use. Déli (Southern) Station, behind Castle Hill in Buda, is less useful for most tourists.

The taxi stands in front of each train station are notorious for ripping off tourists—it's better to call for a taxi (see "Getting Around Budapest—By Taxi," page 416).

Keleti (Eastern) Station: The Keleti Station (Keleti pu.) is just south of City Park, east of central Pest. On arrival, go to the front of long tracks 6–9 to reach the exits and services. Several travel agencies with *Tourist Information* signs cluster near the head of the tracks. None is official, but all have a few helpful fliers, and most can sell you a Budapest Card. Along track 6, you'll find a left-luggage desk, an ATM (at K&H Bank), money-exchange booths (avoid Interchange, which has bad rates), and international information and ticket windows (hiding down a hallway, look for *nemzetközi pénztár;* lockers nearby). Domestic ticket windows are across the tracks, near track 9.

The big staircase at the head of the tracks leads down to more domestic ticket windows, WCs, telephones, more ATMs, and (a few minutes' walk straight ahead, through the open-air court-yard) a passageway to the Metro station entrance (M2 line; see "Getting Around Budapest—By Metro," page 414). If you go out the front door, you'll stumble over a cluster of suspicious-looking, unmarked taxis. You can try to negotiate with these goons—the fair rate to downtown is about 1,500 Ft—but it's far more reliable and less hassle to phone for a taxi (buy phone card at newsstand, go to the phone bank downstairs, call 266-6666 or 211-111, tell the English-speaking dispatcher where you are, and go out front to meet your taxi).

Nyugati (Western) Station: The Nyugati train station (Nyugati pu.) is the most central of Budapest's stations, on the northeast edge of downtown Pest. Most international arrivals use tracks 1–9, which are set back from the main entrance. From the head of these tracks, exit straight ahead into a parking lot with taxis and buses, or use the stairs just inside the doors to reach an under-pass and the Metro (M3 line, see "Getting Around Budapest—by Metro," page 414). Note that the taxis here are often crooked—it's far better to call for your own cab (see instructions and phone numbers above). If you're homesick, leave through this door and go immediately to the right to discover the huge, American-style **WestEnd City Center mall** (complete with a T.G.I. Friday's, daily 8:00–23:00).

Ticket windows are through an easy-to-miss door across the tracks by platform 13 (marked *cassa* and *információ;* once you enter the ticket hall, international windows are in a second room at the far end—look for *nemzetközi*).

From the head of tracks 10–13, exit straight ahead and you'll be on Teréz körút, the very busy Great Boulevard ring road. (Váci utca, at the center of Pest, is dead ahead, about 20 min away by foot). In front of the building is access to handy trams #4 and #6 (zipping all the way around Pest's great ring); to the right you'll find stairs leading to an underpass (use it to avoid crossing this busy intersection, or to reach the Metro's M3 line); and to the left you'll see the classiest Art Nouveau McDonald's on the planet. (Seriously. Take a look inside.)

Déli (Southern) Station: The dreary, dark-granite Déli Station (Déli pu.) is smaller, more modern, and very communist-feeling. It's tucked behind Castle Hill on the Buda side. From the tracks, go straight ahead into the vast, empty-feeling main hall, with well-marked domestic and international ticket windows at opposite ends. A left-luggage desk is outside, beyond track 1. If you head downstairs, you'll find several shops and eateries, and access to the very convenient M2 Metro line, which connects you easily to several key points in town: Batthyány tér (on the Buda embankment, at the north end of the Víziváros neighborhood), Deák tér (the heart of Pest, with connections to other Metro lines), and the Keleti train station.

By Plane

Budapest Ferihegy Airport is 10 miles southeast of the center (airport code: BUD, tel. 1/296-7000, www.bud.hu). The airport has two terminals, connected by a shuttle bus. Terminal 1 is used by the low-cost airlines. Terminal 2 has two adjacent parts: 2A is for Malev, the Hungarian national airline, while all other carriers use 2B. (If you're flying out of Budapest, confirm which terminal your flight leaves from.) Both terminals have similar services, including ATMs and TI desks.

A handy new **train** links Terminal 1 with the Nyugati (Western) train station near downtown Pest (300–700 Ft, depending on train; about 3/hr on weekdays, 2/hr on weekends, 25 min). From terminals 2A and 2B, take the airport shuttle to Terminal 1 to catch this train.

The other options for getting into town are the same from either terminal. The fastest door-to-door option is to take a **taxi.** Zóna Taxi has a monopoly at the taxi stand out front, with a fixed off-meter price depending on where you're going (about 4,500 Ft to downtown, 1,000 Ft less from downtown to the airport, about 30 min, tel. 1/365-5555, www.zonataxi.eu). Going *to* the airport, you can call Zóna or any other taxi company (see "Getting Around Budapest—By Taxi," page 416).

The airport-shuttle **minibus** is cheaper for a solo traveler,

Budapest

Tonight We're Gonna Party Like It's 1896

Visitors to Budapest need only remember one date: 1896. For the millennial celebration of their ancestors' arrival in Europe, Hungarians threw a huge blowout party. In the thousand years between 896 and 1896, the Magyars had gone from being a nomadic Central Asian tribe that terrorized the Continent to sharing the throne of one of the most successful empires Europe had ever seen.

Much as the year 2000 saw a fit of new construction worldwide, Budapest used its millennial celebration as an excuse to build monuments and buildings appropriate for the co-capital of a huge empire, including:

- **Heroes' Square** and the **Millennium Monument**
- **Vajdahunyad Castle** (in City Park)
- The riverside **Parliament** building (96 meters tall, with 96 steps at the main entry)
- **St. István's Basilica** (also 96 meters tall)
- The M1 (yellow) Metro line, a.k.a. *Földalatti* ("Underground")—the first subway on the Continent
- The **Great Market Hall** (and four other market halls)
- **Andrássy út** and most of the fine buildings lining it
- The **Opera House**
- A complete rebuilding of **Matthias Church** (on Castle Hill)
- The **Fishermen's Bastion** decorative terrace (by Matthias Church)
- The green **Liberty Bridge** (then called Franz Josef Bridge, in honor of the ruling Hapsburg emperor)

Ninety-six is the key number in Hungary—even the national anthem (when sung in the proper tempo) takes 96 seconds. But after all this fuss, it's too bad that the date was wrong: A commission—convened to establish the exact year of the Magyars' debut—determined it happened in 895. But city leaders knew they'd never make an 1895 deadline, and requested the finding be changed to 896.

but two people might as well take a taxi (2,600 Ft per person for minibus ride to any hotel in the city center, 15 percent discount with Budapest Card—you can buy the card at the minibus desk when you buy your ticket, about 30–45 min depending on hotel location, tel. 1/296-8555; if arranging a minibus transfer *to* the airport, call at least 48 hours in advance). Because they prefer to take several people at once, you may have to wait a while for a quorum to show up (about 15 minutes in busy times, up to an hour when it's slow—they can give you an estimate).

Finally, the cheapest but most complicated option is to take **public bus** #200 to the Kőbánya-Kispest M3 Metro station, and then take the Metro into town (allow about an hour total for the trip to the center).

By Car

A car is unnecessary at best and a headache at worst. Unless you're heading to an out-of-town sight (such as Statue Park), park the car at your hotel and take public transportation. Public parking costs 150–450 Ft per hour (pay in advance at machine and put ticket on dashboard—watch locals and imitate; free parking Mon–Fri after 18:00 and all day Sat–Sun—but you'll have to pay all the time in touristy zones). Be careful to park within the lines—otherwise, your car is likely to get booted (I've seen more than one confused tourist puzzling over the giant red brace on their wheel). A guarded parking lot is safer, but more expensive (figure 3,000–4,000 Ft/day, ask your hotel or look for the blue *P*s on maps).

Helpful Hints

Rip-Offs: Budapest feels—and is—safe, especially for a city of its size. There's little risk of violent crime here. And, while people routinely try to rip me off in Prague, I've never had a problem in Budapest. Still, many of my readers report falling victim to scams and con artists in Budapest. As in any big city, it's especially important to beware of pickpockets in crowded and touristy places, particularly on the Metro and in trams. Wear a money belt and watch your valuables closely. Keep your wits about you and refuse to be bullied or distracted. Any deal that seems too good to be true...probably is.

Budapest restaurants—especially on the Váci utca shopping street—are notorious for overcharging tourists. Don't eat at a restaurant that doesn't list prices on the menu, and always check your bill carefully. It's best to steer clear of those overpriced Váci utca eateries entirely—even if they charge you what's listed, it's still a rip-off.

If you're a male in a touristy area and a gorgeous local girl (nicknamed a *konzumlány,* or "consumption girl") takes a liking to you, avoid her. The foreplay going on here will climax in your grand rip-off. (You'll wind up at her "favorite bar," with astronomical prices and a burly bouncer.) Another common scam involves a man stopping you on the street to "change money." A policeman arrests him—and you—and needs to see your wallet to find out if he's a con artist. They are a team and you are being robbed.

Budapest's biggest crooks? Unscrupulous cabbies (see "Getting Around Budapest—By Taxi," page 416). I've said it before, I'll say it again: Locals *always* call for a cab, rather than hail one on the street or at a taxi stand. If you're not comfortable making the call yourself, ask your hotel or restaurant to call for you.

Blue Monday: Virtually all of Budapest's museums are closed on Mondays. But never fear—you can still take advantage of these sights and activities: both major baths, Statue Park, Great Synagogue, Matthias Church and Budapest History Museum on Castle Hill, St. István's Basilica, Parliament tour, Opera House tour, City Park (and Zoo), Great Market Hall, Danube cruises, concerts, and bus, walking, and bike tours.

Internet Access: Internet cafés are everywhere—just look for signs or ask your hotel. In Pest, I like **Discover Hungary/Yellow Zebra,** with fast access and good prices (200 Ft/15 min; for locations, hours, and contact information, see "Discover Hungary" listing on page 406). In Buda's Víziváros neighborhood, try the **Soho Coffee Company** (on Fő utca—see page 484).

Post Offices: These are marked with a smart green *posta* logo (usually open Mon–Fri 8:00–18:00, Sat 8:00–12:00, closed Sun).

Laundry: Budapest doesn't have a handy coin-op, self-serve launderette, but a few places can do your laundry for a reasonable price.

In Pest, your best option is **Landromat-Mosómata,** just behind the Opera House (1,600 Ft to wash and dry a big load, generally takes about 3 hours, Mon–Fri 9:00–19:00, Sat–Sun 10:00–16:00; walk straight behind the Opera House and turn right on Ó utca, then look left for signs at #24–26; mobile 0620-392-5702). Another option—closer to Váci utca but with more difficult communication—is **Patyolat Gyorstisztító.** They say it's "self-service," but usually you can just drop off your clothes with the monolingual laundry ladies in the morning and pick them up in the afternoon (borrow the English information sheet, allow 2,500 Ft to wash and dry a load, Mon–Fri 7:00–19:00, closed Sat–Sun, just up from Váci utca at the corner of Vármegye utca and Városház utca).

In Buda's Víziváros neighborhood, on Batthyány tér, go upstairs in the big market hall to find **Topclean** (allow 1,200 Ft/kilogram, Mon–Fri 9:00–19:00, Sat 9:00–14:00, closed Sun; drop off before 10:00 and pick up that afternoon, or drop off after 10:00 and pick up the next day; above the Spar supermarket, tel. 1/487-0639).

English Newspapers: Newsstands sell two weekly English newspapers: the *Budapest Sun* (399 Ft, often free at hotels or TIs) and the *Budapest Times* (580 Ft, more business-oriented).

Local Guidebook: András Török's fun, idiosyncratic *Budapest: A Critical Guide* is the best book by a local writer. Its quirky walking tours do a nice job capturing the city's spirit (available in English at most souvenir stands).

English Bookstores: The **Central European University Bookshop** sells guidebooks and popular American magazines and paperbacks, and offers the best selection anywhere of scholarly books about this region (all in English; Mon–Fri 10:00–18:00, Sat 10:00–14:00, closed Sun, just down the street from the front of St. István's Basilica at Zrínyi utca 12, tel. 1/327-3096). This university—offering graduate study for Americans and students from all over Eastern Europe—is predominantly funded by George Soros, a Hungarian who emigrated to the US and became a billionaire and high-profile donor to left-wing causes. **Tree Hugger Dan,** which bills itself as a "local bookstore with a global conscience," has a wide variety of English books and other good expat resources, as well as its own café (Mon–Fri 10:00–19:00, Sat 10:00–17:00, Sun 10:00–16:00, just off Andrássy út between House of Terror and Oktagon square at Csengery utca 48, mobile 061-322-0774; second location inside Discover Hungary branch near Opera House—see page 445). **Red Bus Bookstore** has shelves of used books in English—and they buy books, too (Mon–Fri 11:00–18:00, Sat 10:00–14:00, closed Sun, Semmelweis utca 14, tel. 1/337-7453).

Bike Rental: Rent a bike at **Yellow Zebra,** part of Discover Hungary (500 Ft/hr, 2,000 Ft/half-day, 3,000 Ft/full day; for locations, hours, and contact information, see "Discover Hungary" listing on page 406).

Drivers: Friendly, English-speaking **Gábor Balázs** can drive you around the city or into the surrounding countryside (3,500 Ft/hr, 3-hr minimum in city, 4-hr minimum in countryside—good for a Danube Bend excursion, mobile 0620-936-4317, from the US call 011-36-20-936-4317, balazs.gabor@chello .hu). **József Király** runs a 10-car company, Artoli (17,500 Ft/4 hours within town, 35,000 Ft/8 hours to Danube Bend, 15,000 Ft extra for English-speaking guide, these prices for up to 4 people—more for bigger groups, tel. 1/240-4050, mobile 0620-369-8890, from the US call 011-36-20-369-8890, artoli@t-online.hu). Note that these are drivers, not tour guides. For tour guides, see page 417.

Courtyards: Behind most of Pest's once-grand, now-crumbling facades, you'll find cozy courtyards where residents carry out much of their lives. These courtyards, shared among neighbors and ringed by a common balcony, stay cool through the summer. Poking into some of these courtyards (which are generally open to the public, offering a handy shortcut through city blocks) is an essential Back Door experience for understanding the inner life of the city.

Best Views: Budapest is a city of marvelous vistas. Some of the best are from the Citadella (high on Gellért Hill), the promenade in front of Buda Castle, the embankments or many bridges spanning the Danube (especially the Chain Bridge), and tour boats on the Danube—lovely at night.

Getting Around Budapest

Budapest is huge. Connecting your sightseeing by foot is tedious and unnecessary; use the excellent public transportation system instead. The same tickets work for the Metro, trams, and buses. Buy them at kiosks, Metro ticket windows, or machines. The new machines are slick and easy, but the old orange ones are tricky: Put in the appropriate amount of money, then wait for your ticket or press the button. As it can be frustrating to find a ticket machine (especially when you see your tram or bus approaching), I generally invest in a multi-day ticket or Budapest Card so I have the freedom of hopping on at will.

Your options are:

• Single ticket (*vonaljegy,* for a ride of up to an hour with no transfers)—230 Ft;

• Short single Metro ride (*metroszakaszjegy,* 3 stops or fewer on the Metro)—180 Ft;

• Transfer ticket (*átszállójegy*—allowing up to 90 minutes, including 1 transfer)—380 Ft; or

• Unlimited multi-day tickets (1,350 Ft/1 day, 3,100 Ft/3 days, 3,600 Ft/7 days)—but if you're here more than a day and plan to do lots of sightseeing, consider a Budapest Card instead (see "Tourist Information," page 406).

Always validate single-ride tickets as you enter the bus, tram, or Metro station (stick it in the elbow-high box). On older buses and trams that have little red validation boxes, stick your ticket in the black slot, then pull the slot towards you to punch holes in your ticket. A transfer ticket must be validated a second time when you transfer. The stern-looking guys with blue-and-green armbands waiting as you exit the Metro want to see your validated ticket or signed and dated Budapest Card. Cheaters are fined 5,000 Ft on the spot, and you'll be surprised how often you're checked (inspectors are most commonly seen at train stations and along the touristy M1 line). All public transit runs from 4:30 in the morning until 23:10. A useful route-planning website is www.bkv.hu.

By Metro

Riding Budapest's Metro, you really feel like you're down in the efficient guts of the city. It's every bit as convenient and slick as Vienna's or Berlin's—but it has more character than those stodgy systems.

There are three lines:

• **M1 (yellow)**—The first Metro line on the Continent, this shallow line runs under Andrássy út from the center to City Park (see "The Millennium Underground of 1896," page 441).

• **M2 (red)**—Built during the communist days, it's 115 feet deep, doubles as a bomb shelter, and comes with a tornado ventilation system—notice the gale. The only line going under the Danube to Buda (for now), M2 connects the Déli train station, Moszkva tér (where you catch bus #10 to the top of Castle Hill), Batthyány tér (where you catch the HÉV train to Óbuda or Szentendre), and the Keleti train station.

• **M3 (blue)**—This line makes a broad, boomerang-shaped swoop north to south on the Pest side. Key stops include the Nyugati train station and Kálvin tér (near the Great Market Hall and many recommended hotels).

The three lines cross only once: at the **Deák tér** stop (often signed as *Deák Ferenc tér*) in the heart of Pest, where Andrássy út begins. Most M2 and M3 Metro stations are at intersections of ring roads and other major thoroughfares. You'll usually exit the Metro into a confusing underpass packed with kiosks, fast-food stands, and makeshift markets. Orange directional signs help you find the right exit.

The Metro stops themselves are usually very well marked, with a list of upcoming stops on the wall behind the tracks. Digital clocks either count down to the next train's arrival, or count up from the previous train's departure; either way, you'll rarely wait more than five minutes.

You'll ride very long, steep, fast-moving escalators to access the M2 and M3 lines. Hang on tight, enjoy the breeze as trains below shoot through the tunnels...and don't make yourself dizzy by trying to read the Burger King ads.

Note that Budapest is building a new Metro line **(M4, green)**, which will go from south Buda to the Gellért Baths, under the Danube to the Great Market Hall and Kálvin tér (where it will cross the M3 line), then up to Keleti Station (where it will cross the M2 line). As new stations on this line are finished, they'll open to the public, but the whole line won't be done for several years.

The city is also systematically upgrading many of its existing Metro stations (usually in July and August). If a particular stretch of Metro line is closed, buses run the same route instead. This can extend the length of your trip—allow plenty of time. For the latest on which stations are closed, ask your hotel or the TI, or check www.bkv.hu.

By Tram

Budapest's trams are handy and frequent, taking you virtually anywhere the Metro doesn't. Here are some trams you might use:

Trams **#2** and **#2A:** Run along Pest's Danube embankment parallel to Váci utca, between the Parliament and the Great Market Hall.

Trams **#19** and **#41:** Run along Buda's Danube embankment, stopping at Gellért Hotel, the bottom of the Castle Hill funicular (Adam Clark tér), several recommended Víziváros hotels, and Batthyány tér (end of the line, M2 Metro station, and HÉV trains to Óbuda and Szentendre).

Trams **#4** and **#6:** Zip around Pest's Great Boulevard ring road (Nagykörút), connecting the Nyugati train station and Oktogon with the tip of Margaret Island and Buda's Moszkva tér (M2 Metro station).

Trams **#47** and **#49:** Connect the Gellért Baths in Buda with Pest's Small Boulevard ring road (Kiskörút), with stops at the Great Market Hall, the National Museum, the Great Synagogue (Astoria stop), and Deák tér (end of the line).

By Bus

The tram and Metro network can get you nearly anywhere, so you're less likely to take a bus. One exception is getting to the top of Castle Hill: Take little bus **#10** (from Moszkva tér) or handy bus **#16** (Deák tér, Roosevelt tér, crosses Chain Bridge, Adam Clark tér, and up to Dísz tér atop Castle Hill near the Royal Palace). Bus **#78** provides a handy connection over the Elisabeth Bridge between Buda and Pest. And buses **#70** and **#78** offer a shortcut from near the Opera House (intersection of Andrássy út and Nagymező utca) to the Parliament (Kossuth tér).

By Taxi

Budapest's public transportation is good enough that you probably won't need to take many taxis. But if you do, you're likely to run into a dishonest driver. Arm yourself with knowledge: Cabbies are not allowed to charge more than a drop rate of 300 Ft, and then 240 Ft per kilometer (more expensive 22:00–6:00)—though the more reputable companies charge less. Prices are per ride, not per passenger. A 10 percent tip is expected. A typical ride within central Budapest shouldn't run more than 2,000 Ft. Despite what some slimy cabbies may tell you, there's no legitimate extra charge for crossing the river.

Instead of hailing a taxi on the street, do as the locals do and call a cab from a reputable company—it's cheaper and you're more likely to get an honest driver. Try **City Taxi** (tel. 1/211-111), **Taxi 6x6** (tel. 1/266-6666), or **Főtaxi** (1/222-2222). While most dispatchers speak English, if you're uncomfortable calling, you can ask your hotel or restaurant to call for you. (Request that they call a "City Taxi"—otherwise, they might call a pricier company to get a bigger kickback.)

Many cabs you'd hail on the streets are there only to prey on rich, green tourists. Avoid unmarked taxis and cabs waiting at tourist spots and train stations. If you do wave down a cab on the street, choose one that's marked with an official company logo and telephone number, and has a yellow license plate (if it's not yellow, it's not official). Ask for a rough estimate before you get in—if it doesn't sound reasonable, walk away. If you wind up being dramatically overcharged for a ride, simply pay what you think is fair and go inside. If the driver follows you (unlikely), your hotel receptionist will defend you.

On my last trip to Budapest, I arrived late at night at the Keleti train station. The lone, unmarked taxi out front wanted 4,000 Ft for the ride to my hotel. Following my own advice, I called a legitimate company and ordered a taxi from the English-speaking dispatcher. A few minutes later, an honest cabbie picked me up and took me to my hotel...for 1,500 Ft.

TOURS

Walking Tours—A youthful, backpacker-oriented company, **Absolute Walking Tours,** is run by Oregonian Ben Frieday. These tours are loose and informal, but informative. You can choose from a number of different itineraries, which include the following: The Absolute Walk gives you a good overview of Budapest (4,000 Ft, mid-May–Sept daily at 9:30 and 13:30, Oct–mid-May daily at 10:30, 3.5 hrs). The Hammer and Sickle Tour includes a guided visit to Statue Park (you take the regular direct bus to Statue Park with other passengers), then a quick visit to a mini-museum of communist artifacts (6,500 Ft, 4/week, 3 hrs). Absolute Hungro Gastro, focused on Hungarian cuisine, gives you information on traditional recipes and ingredients, and a chance to taste several specialties and wines at a local restaurant (8,000 Ft, 3/week, 1/week in winter, 3 hrs). In the evening, consider the Absolute Night Stroll, which includes a one-hour cruise on the Danube (5,000 Ft, mid-May–Sept only, 4/week, 2.5 hrs) or the rowdier Pub Crawl, which sometimes continues late into the night (4,500 Ft, departs 20:30, 4/week, at least 3 hrs). History buffs appreciate the 1956 Uprising Walk, which visits some of the sites of those bloody but inspirational events five decades ago (6,500 Ft, 2/week, 3 hrs).

All tours depart from blocky, green-domed church at Deák tér, near the Metro station (tel. 1/266-8777, www.absolutetours .com). Travelers with this book get a 500-Ft discount on any tour in 2008, as does anyone with a student card.

Budapest at a Glance

In Buda

▲▲**Matthias Church** Landmark Neo-Gothic church with gilded history-book interior and revered 16th-century statue of Mary and Jesus. **Hours:** Mon–Sat 9:00–17:00, Sun 13:00–17:00, sometimes closed Sat after 13:00 for weddings. See page 429.

▲▲**Gellért Baths** Touristy baths in elegant hotel. **Hours:** May–Sept daily 6:00–19:00; Oct–April Mon–Fri 6:00–19:00, Sat–Sun 6:00–17:00. See page 432.

▲▲**Statue Park** Larger-than-life communist big shots all collected in one park, on the outskirts of town. **Hours:** Daily 10:00–sunset. See page 456.

Royal Palace Reconstructed fortress on Castle Hill housing a pair of decent museums (Budapest History Museum and National Gallery). **Hours:** History Museum—mid-May–mid-Sept daily 10:00–18:00; March–mid-May and mid-Sept–Oct Wed–Mon 10:00–18:00, closed Tue; Nov–Feb Wed–Mon 10:00–16:00, closed Tue. National Gallery—Tue–Sun 10:00–18:00, closed Mon. See page 423.

In Pest

▲▲▲**Széchenyi Baths** Budapest's steamy soaking scene in City Park—the city's single best attraction. **Hours:** Daily 6:00–22:00, possibly until 19:00 or 17:00 in winter. See page 460.

▲▲**Great Market Hall** Colorful Old World mall with produce, cheap eateries, souvenirs, and great people-watching. **Hours:** Mon 6:00–17:00, Tue–Fri 6:00–18:00, Sat 6:00–14:00, closed Sun. See page 436.

▲▲**Hungarian State Opera House** Neo-Renaissance splendor and affordable opera. **Hours:** Lobby/box office open Mon–Sat from 11:00 until show time—generally 19:00; Sun open three hours before performance—generally 16:00–19:00, or 10:00–13:00 if there's a matinee; English tours nearly daily at 15:00 and 16:00. See page 445.

▲▲**House of Terror** Harrowing remembrance of Nazis and communist secret police in former headquarters/torture site. **Hours:** Tue–Fri 10:00–18:00, Sat–Sun 10:00–19:30, closed Mon. See page 446.

▲▲**Heroes' Square** Mammoth tribute to Hungary's historic figures, fringed by a couple of art museums. **Hours:** Square always open; Museum of Fine Arts—Tue–Sun 10:00–17:30, closed Mon; Palace of Art—Tue–Wed and Fri–Sun 10:00–18:00, Thu 12:00–20:00, closed Mon. See page 448.

▲▲**City Park** Budapest's backyard, with Art Nouveau zoo, Transylvanian castle replica, amusement park, and Széchenyi Baths. **Hours:** Park always open. See page 449.

▲**Váci utca** Hopping pedestrian boulevard and tourist magnet, featuring Eastern Europe's first McDonald's. **Hours:** Always open. See page 435.

▲**Hungarian Parliament** Vast, riverside Neo-Gothic government center. **Hours:** English tours usually daily at 10:00, 12:00, and 14:00. See page 439.

▲**Postal Museum** Funky tribute to old postal service objects in elegant old Andrássy út mansion. **Hours:** Tue–Sun 10:00–18:00, closed Mon. See page 444.

▲**Vajdahunyad Castle** Disney World–type complex in City Park with replicas of historic Hungarian architecture, anchored by a massive Transylvanian castle. **Hours:** Grounds always open. See page 450.

▲**Great Synagogue** The world's second-largest after New York's, with museum and garden memorial. **Hours:** April–Oct Mon–Thu 10:00–17:00, Fri 10:00–15:00, Sun 10:00–18:00; Nov–March Mon–Thu 10:00–15:00, Fri and Sun 10:00–14:00; always closed Sat and Jewish holidays. See page 451.

▲**Holocaust Memorial Center** Excellent memorial and museum honoring Hungarian victims of the Holocaust. **Hours:** Tue–Sun 10:00–18:00, closed Mon. See page 452.

Hungarian National Museum Extensive collection of fragments from Hungary's history. **Hours:** Tue–Sun 10:00–18:00, closed Mon. See page 437.

Hungarian Museum of Trade and Tourism Intriguing time-tunnel look at 19th-century businesses. **Hours:** Wed–Mon 11:00–19:00, closed Tue. See page 444.

Budapest

Private Guides—Budapest has plenty of enthusiastic, hardworking young guides who speak great English and enjoy showing off their exciting city. Given the reasonable fees and efficient use of your time, hiring your own personal expert is an excellent value. I have two favorites, either of whom can do half-day or full-day tours, and can also drive you into the countryside (such as to the Danube Bend). **Péter Pölczman** is an exceptional guide who really puts you in touch with the Budapest you came to see (18,000 Ft/4–5 hrs, 25,000 Ft/8 hrs, mobile 0620-926-0557, from the US call 011-36-20-926-0557, polczman@freestart.hu or peter.polczman@guideclub.net). **Andrea Makkay** is also good, with a professional and polished approach (23,000 Ft/4 hrs, 39,000 Ft/8 hrs; mobile 0620-962-9363, from the US call 011-36-20-962-9363, www.privateguidebudapest.com, amakkay@t-online.hu—arrange details by email).

Danube Boat Tours—Cruising the Danube, while touristy, is fun and convenient. The most established company, **Legenda,** runs new, glassed-in panoramic boats day and night. I've negotiated a special discount with Legenda for my readers (but you must book direct, and ask for the Rick Steves price). By **day,** the one-hour cruise costs 2,900 Ft for Rick Steves readers; most departures include an optional one-hour walking tour around Margaret Island, Budapest's playground (8/day May–Aug, 7/day April and Sept, 3/day March and Oct, 1/day Nov–Feb). By **night,** the one-hour cruise (with no Margaret Island visit) costs 3,700 Ft for Rick Steves readers (3/day March–Oct, 1/day Nov–Feb). All cruises include two drinks and headphone commentary. By night, TV monitors show the interior of the great buildings as you float by. The Legenda dock is in front of the Marriott on the Pest embankment (find pedestrian access under tram tracks just downriver from Vigadó tér, tel. 1/317-2203, www.legenda.hu).

Other companies (such as Mahart) also offer similar, cheaper Danube cruises, but Legenda is a class act worth paying a little extra for.

Bike Tours—A sister company of Absolute Walking Tours, **Yellow Zebra,** wheels by Budapest's major sights on a 3.5-hour tour (5,000 Ft, April–Oct daily at 11:00, also at 16:00 July–Aug, no tours Nov–March, meet at Deák tér, tel. 1/266-8777, www.yellowzebrabikes.com).

Segway Tours—In addition to walking and bike tours, Ben Frieday's Discover Hungary also offers tours of Budapest by Segway (stand-up electric scooter). Although expensive, it's a unique way to see the city while trying out a Segway (14,500 Ft, daily at 10:00, also daily at 18:30 April–Oct, 2.5–3 hrs with 30- to 45-min training beforehand, 6 people per group, must reserve and pre-pay at www.citysegwaytours.com or call the office when in Budapest—tel. 1/269-3843).

Bus Tours—Several companies run bus tours that glide past all the big sights. The different companies are essentially the same (figure 5,000 Ft/2-hr tour, 6,500 Ft/3-hr tour). A hop-on, hop-off bus tour by **City-Circle Sightseeing** makes 12 stops as it cruises around town (4,500 Ft for a 24-hr ticket). Most companies also offer a wide variety of other tours, including dinner boat cruises and trips to the Danube Bend. Pick up fliers about all these tours at the TI or in your hotel lobby.

SIGHTS

Buda

Castle Hill (Várhegy)

Buda's main sights are all on Castle Hill. Many visitors expect this high-profile district to be time-consuming. Don't make it more than it is. For most, it's enough to simply stroll through in a couple of hours. The major landmarks are the huge, green-domed Royal Palace at the south end of the hill (housing a pair of ho-hum museums) and the frilly-spired Matthias Church near the north end (which is the only sight that's really worth entering). In between are tourist-filled pedestrian streets and dull but historic buildings. A few other interesting but non-essential museums are scattered around the hill. I've listed the sights in order from south to north, and linked them together on a self-guided tour.

When to Visit: Castle Hill is packed with tour groups in the morning, but it's much less crowded in the afternoon. Since restaurants up here are expensive and low quality, Castle Hill is an ideal after-lunch activity. If you want a good, inexpensive meal on this side of the river, head to the Víziváros neighborhood between the castle and the river (see "Eating," page 482).

Getting to Castle Hill: The Metro and trams won't take you to the top of Castle Hill. You can hike, taxi, ride the funicular (described below), or catch a bus. From central Pest, your easiest bet is to hop on **bus #16** (departs from Deák, Roosevelt, and Adam Clark squares). **Bus #10** does a loop from Moszkva tér (Moscow Square) north of the castle (M2: Moszkva tér, bus stops just uphill from Metro station, look for small bus with the words *Dísz tér*). Castle Hill buses are specially designed to be lightweight, as the hill is honeycombed with limestone caves. The handiest stop for either of these buses is at Dísz tér, right in the middle of the hill (across from old Ministry of War building). If you arrive at Dísz tér, you can backtrack to the Royal Palace and *Turul* bird statue, or skip ahead to the Dísz tér listing in the walking tour (all of this is described below).

The **funicular** (*sikló*, SHEE-kloh), lifting visitors from the Chain Bridge to the top of Castle Hill, is a Budapest landmark.

BUDA'S CASTLE HILL

1 Budapest History Museum
2 Hungarian National Gallery
3 Turul Bird Statue
4 Sándor Palace
5 Former Ministry of War
6 Crafts Market
7 Entrance to Labyrinth of Buda Castle
8 Meeting Point for Underground Tours
9 Fishermen's Bastion
10 Matthias Church
11 Hilton Hotel
12 Remains of St. Mary Magdalene Church
13 Museum of Military History

Built in 1870 to provide cheap transportation to Castle Hill work-ers, today it's a pricey little tourist trip. Read the fun first-person history you'll see in glass cases at the top station (700 Ft one-way, 1,300 Ft round-trip, not covered by Budapest Card, daily 7:30–22:00, departs every 5 min, closed for maintenance every other Mon).

• *From the top of the funicular, enjoy the views of the Danube and go a few yards to the big bird at the top of the stairs.*

The *Turul*—This mythical bird of Magyar folktales watches over the palace. The Turul supposedly led the Hungarian migrations in the ninth century. He dropped his sword in the Carpathian Basin, indicating that this was to be the permanent home of the Magyar people. During a surge of nationalism in the 1920s, a movement named after this bird helped revive traditional Hungarian culture. Turul birds also top the towers of the green Liberty Bridge, just downriver.

• *Stretching to your right is the giant Royal Palace. This part of Castle*

Hill can easily be skipped (jump to "From the Funicular and Royal Palace to Matthias Church," page 426). But for an optional detour through the palace area, climb down the stairs and walk along the grand terrace toward the giant equestrian statue. As you walk, ponder the history of this site...

Royal Palace (Királyi Palota)—The imposing palace on Castle Hill is a dull contemporary construction, barely hinting at the colorful story of this hill since the day that the legendary Turul dropped his sword.

Originally, the main city of Hungary wasn't Buda or Pest, but Esztergom (just up the river, described in Danube Bend chapter). In the 13th century, Tatars swept through Eastern Europe, destroying much of Hungary. King Béla IV decided to rebuild a walled Buda here, a more protected location in the interior of the country. The city has dominated the region ever since, gradually becoming the Hungarian capital. Over the years, the original Romanesque fortress here was rebuilt and accentuated with a textbook's worth of architectural styles: Gothic, Renaissance, and Baroque. It was one of Europe's biggest palaces by the early 15th century, when King Mátyás Corvinus made the palace even more extravagant, putting Buda—and Hungary—on the map.

Just a few decades later, the invading Ottomans occupied Buda and turned the palace into a military garrison. When the Hapsburgs laid siege to the hill for 77 days in 1686, gunpowder stored in the cellar exploded, destroying the palace. The Hapsburgs took the hill, but Buda was deserted and in ruins. The town was resettled by Austrians, who built a new Baroque palace, hoping that the Hapsburg monarch would move in—but none ever did. The useless palace became a garrison, then a university, and later the viceroy's residence. It was damaged again during the 1848 Revolution, but was repaired and continued to grow right along with Budapest's prominence (for more on the 1848 Revolution, see page 438).

As World War II drew to a close, Buda became the front line between the Nazis and the approaching Soviets, who laid siege to the hill for about 100 days. The palace was again destroyed.

While grand and impressive from afar, the current version of the palace—a historically inaccurate, post-WWII reconstruction—feels dull and soulless, like a tuxedo on a mannequin. It's a loose rebuilding of previous versions, lacking the style and sense of history that this important site deserves. The most prominent feature of today's palace—the green dome—didn't even exist in earlier versions.

The big **equestrian statue** in front of the palace depicts Eugene of Savoy, a French general who had great success fighting the Hungarians' hated enemies, the Ottomans.

Budapest

Mátyás Corvinus: The Last Hungarian King

The Árpád dynasty—descendants of the original Magyar tribes—died out in 1301. For more than 600 years, Hungary would be ruled by foreigners...with one exception.

In the middle of the 15th century, Hungary had bad luck hanging on to its foreign kings: Two of them died unexpectedly within seven years. Meanwhile, homegrown military general János Hunyadi was enjoying great success on the battlefield against the Ottomans. When the five-year-old Ladislas V was elected king, Hunyadi was appointed regent and essentially ruled the country.

Hunyadi defeated the Ottomans in the crucial 1456 Battle of Belgrade, which kept them out of Hungary (at least for another 70 years) and made him an even greater hero to the Hungarian people. During this time, Hunyadi was briefly imprisoned by the Ottomans, and his family feared him dead. According to one legend, a raven appeared in the window of his cell, and Hunyadi gave the bird his ring. The raven flew it to Hunyadi's family to reassure them that he lived on. The raven (often with a ring in its beak) became part of the family crest, as well as the family name: Corvinus (Latin for "raven").

Tragically, soon after his escape from prison and great victory over the Ottomans, Hunyadi died of the plague. When King Ladislas also died (at the tender age of 16), the nobles looked for a new hero...and found one in Hunyadi's son, Mátyás (Matthias) Corvinus. He became the first Hungarian-descended king in more than 150 years.

• *Before heading on to Matthias Church (Castle Hill self-guided tour continues below), consider visiting the...*

Castle Museums—The palace houses two worthwhile (but not must-see) museums. The history museum is decent, but the art museum ranks pretty low on a European scale.

• *The main entrance to the National Gallery is just behind the big Savoy statue. To reach the history museum, go through the small passageway to the right of the National Gallery entrance. You'll pass an ornate fountain starring Mátyás Corvinus, then hook left into the palace courtyard (behind the dome). The museum entrance is at the far end of the courtyard.*

The **Budapest History Museum** (Budapesti Történeti Múzeum), a good but stodgy museum begging for a makeover, celebrates the earlier grandeur of Castle Hill. If Budapest really intrigues you, this is a fine place to explore its history. The core of the exhibit (on the first two floors) traces the history of the city. On the ground floor (back-right corner), stroll through the

Progressive and well-educated, Mátyás Corvinus (r. 1458–1490) was the quintessential Renaissance king—a benefactor of the poor and a true humanist. He patronized the arts and built palaces legendary for their beauty. He dressed up as a commoner and ventured into the streets to see firsthand how the nobles of his realm treated his people.

Mátyás was a strong, savvy leader. He created Central Europe's first standing army—30,000 mercenaries known as the Black Army. No longer reliant on the nobility for military support, Good King Mátyás was able to drain power from the nobles and make taxation of his subjects more equitable—earning him the nickname the "people's king."

King Mátyás was also a shrewd military tactician. Realizing that squabbling with the Ottomans would squander his resources, he made peace with the Ottoman sultan to stabilize Hungary's southern border. Then he swept north, invading Moravia, Bohemia, and even Austria. By 1485, Mátyás moved into his new palace in Vienna, and Hungary was enjoying a Golden Age.

Five years later, Mátyás died mysteriously at the age of 47, and his empire disintegrated. It is said that when Mátyás died, justice died with him. To this day, Hungarians consider him the greatest of all kings, and they sing of his siege of Vienna in their national anthem. They're proud that for a few decades in the middle of half a millennium of foreign oppression, they had a truly Hungarian king—and a great one at that.

good collection of 14th-century sculptures. Many have strong Magyar features—notice that they look Central Asian (similar to Mongolians). One floor up, the good "Budapest in the Modern Times" exhibit traces the rocky 18th and 19th centuries, with a focus on the gradual movement towards merging Buda and Pest. The top floor has artifacts of Budapest's prehistoric residents. The cellar illustrates just how much this hill has changed over the centuries—and how dull today's version is in comparison. You'll wander through a maze of old palace parts, including the remains of an original Gothic chapel, a knights' hall, and marble remnants (reliefs and fountains) of Mátyás Corvinus' lavish Renaissance palace (1,100 Ft, covered by Budapest Card, some good English descriptions posted, other descriptions are borrowable, mid-May–mid-Sept daily 10:00–18:00; March–mid-May and mid-Sept–Oct Wed–Mon 10:00–18:00, closed Tue; Nov–Feb Wed–Mon 10:00–16:00, closed Tue; last entry 1 hour before closing, tel. 1/487-8800).

Budapest

The huge **Hungarian National Gallery** (Magyar Nemzeti Galéria) has an excellent collection of 15th-century winged altars, plus halls and halls of paintings and sculptures by Hungarian artists you've never heard of—for good reason. As most of the paintings date from after Hungary's unsuccessful 1848 Revolution, they're dreary and pessimistic—a key theme here is epic failure. One artist worth looking for is Tivadar Csontváry-Kosztka, revered by Hungarians as their version of van Gogh. After suffering a psychotic break while sketching oxen, the well-traveled Csontváry-Kosztka took up painting. Recently his paintings have become the most in-demand and expensive of Hungarian artists. You'll find a giant canvas by Csontváry-Kosztka of the theater at Taormina, Sicily, on the second-floor landing, and a couple other, smaller canvases in the 20th-century section one more flight up (1,000 Ft, covered by Budapest Card, maybe more for special exhibitions, Tue–Sun 10:00–18:00, closed Mon, tel. 1/201-9082). Skip the 300-Ft elevator trip to the dome—the views are no better than from the terrace out front.

• *Ready to move on? The following walk connects the dots between the palace and Matthias Church.*

From the Funicular and Royal Palace to Matthias Church: From the Turul bird and the top of the funicular (with your back to the Royal Palace), walk along the non-river side of the big white building, **Sándor Palace.** This mansion underwent a very costly renovation under the previous Hungarian prime minister, who hoped to make it his residence. But in 2002, the same year it was finished, he lost his bid for reelection. The spunky new PM refused to move in. By way of compromise, now the president's office is here.

As you continue along the side of Sándor Palace, you'll notice the remains of a medieval monastery and church in the field to your left. Beyond that, past the flagpoles, is the ongoing excavation of the medieval Jewish quarter—more reminders that most of what you see on today's Castle Hill has been destroyed and rebuilt many times over.

After Sándor Palace, you'll pass the yellow National Dance Theater, where Beethoven once performed. The hulking, war-damaged building beyond that (on the left) used to house the **Ministry of War.** Most of the bullet holes are from World War II, while others were left by the Soviets who occupied this hill in response to the 1956 Uprising (see page 438). The building is a political hot potato—prime real estate, but nobody can decide what to do with it.

Just after the Ministry of War, at the cross street, you reach **Dísz tér** (Parade Square), which has a convenient bus stop for connecting to other parts of Budapest (the castle bus to Moszkva tér, or bus #16 to the Pest side of the Chain Bridge).

Across the street from the Ministry of War (on the right) is the entrance to a courtyard with an open-air Hungarian **crafts market.** While it's fun to browse, prices here are high (haggle away). The Great Market Hall has a better selection and generally lower prices (see page 436).

Continue uphill on **Tárnok utca.** This area often disappoints visitors. After being destroyed by Ottomans, it was rebuilt in sensible Baroque, lacking the romantic time-capsule charm of a medieval old town (like perfectly preserved Prague or Kraków). But if you poke your head into some courtyards, you'll almost always see some original Gothic arches and other medieval features.

• *A block to the left (detour through the little park at the fork), you'll find the entrance to a highly optional sight...*

Labyrinth of Buda Castle (Budavári Labirintus)—There are miles of caves burrowed under Castle Hill, carved out by water, expanded by the Ottomans, and used by locals during the siege of Buda at the end of World War II. Armchair spelunkers can explore these caverns and see a conceptual exhibit that traces human history (1,500 Ft, 20 percent discount with Budapest Card, daily 9:30–19:30, last entry 19:00, entrance between Royal Palace and Matthias Church at Úri utca 9, Budapest I, tel. 1/212-0207, www.labirintus.com). After 18:00, they turn the lights out and give everyone gas lanterns. The exhibit loses something in the dark, but it's nicely spooky and a fun chance to startle amorous Hungarian teens—or be startled by mischievous ones.

• *For something more serious than the hokey Labyrinth, consider the...*

Tours of Secret Military Hospital and Bunker (Titkos Katonai Kórház és Atombunker)—This new, alternative way to get into the caves below Castle Hill takes a more strictly historical focus, by leading visitors on an underground, chronological trip through history (with English commentary). Wax figures and an actual subterranean hospital bring the caves to life (2,500 Ft, Tue–Sun at 16:00, 17:00, and 18:00, no tours Mon, tours depart from the hospital entrance at Lovas utca 4C, reserve by calling mobile 0620-441-2052, www.sziklakorhaz.hu). To find the meeting point, stand with your back to Matthias Church and the Fishermen's Bastion (described next). Walk straight past the plague column and down the little street (Szentháromság), then go down the steps through the wall.

• *Back on Tárnok utca, continue up to the little park with the TI (on your right; pick up their handy* Castlewalk *map). Just beyond the park, a warty plague column marks the main square of old Buda (though the column may be missing for restoration). Across the square is the...*

Fishermen's Bastion (Halászbástya)—This Neo-Romanesque fantasy rampart offers beautiful views over the Danube to Pest. In

the Middle Ages, the fish market was just below here (in today's Víziváros, or Water Town), so this part of the rampart actually was guarded by fishermen. The current structure, though, is completely artificial—an example of Budapest sprucing itself up for 1896 (see page 410). Its seven towers represent the seven Magyar tribes. The cone-headed arcades are reminiscent of tents the nomadic Magyars called home before they moved west to Europe.

Survey Pest across the Danube from this viewpoint. The two domes are the Parliament and St. István's Basilica—both 96 meters high, built in...you guessed it...1896. The Chain Bridge cuts Pest in two: The left half is administrative, with government ministries, embassies, banks, and so on; the right half (stretching to the modern, white Elisabeth Bridge) is the commercial center of Pest, with the best riverside promenade.

Paying to climb up the bastion makes little sense (400 Ft, 10 percent discount with Budapest Card, buy ticket at automated machine by bastion entrance or at kiosk near TI in park, daily mid-March–mid-Oct 9:00–23:00; after closing time and off-season, no tickets are sold, but bastion is open and free to enter). Enjoy virtually the same view through the windows (left of café) for free. The café offers a scenic break if you don't mind the tour groups. Note that the grand staircase leading down from the bastion offers a handy shortcut to the Víziváros neighborhood and Batthyány tér (for affordable restaurants there, see "Eating" on page 482).

• Between the bastion and the big church stands a...

Statue of St. István (Stephen)—Hungary's first Christian king tamed the nomadic, pagan Magyars and established strict laws and the concept of private property. István's father, King Géza, lost a major battle against the forces of Christian Europe—and realized that he must raise his son as a Catholic and convert his people, or they would ultimately be forcefully driven out of Europe. The reliefs on this statue show the Pope crowning St. István (EESHT-vahn) in the year 1000, bringing Hungary into Christendom. This meant the rest of Europe was now inclined to help Hungary against the Ottomans and to bully the Slavs. Without this pivotal event, locals believe that the Magyar nation would have been lost. A passionate evangelist—more for the survival of his Magyar nation than for the salvation of his people—István beheaded those who wouldn't convert. To make his point perfectly clear, he quartered his reluctant uncle and sent him on four separate, simultaneous tours of the country to show Hungarians that Christianity was a smart choice. Gruesome as he was, István was sainted within 30 years of his death.

• *Next to St. István is the can't-miss-it...*

▲▲**Matthias Church (Mátyás-Templom)**—Budapest's best church has been destroyed and rebuilt several times in the 800

years since it was founded by King Béla IV. Today's version—renovated at great expense in the late 19th century, and restored after World War II—is an ornately decorated lesson in Hungarian history. While it's officially named the "Church of Our Lady," everyone calls it the Matthias Church, for the popular Renaissance king who got married here...twice.

Cost and Hours: 700 Ft, includes Museum of Ecclesiastical Art, covered by Budapest Card, 12-stop audioguide-400 Ft, Mon–Sat 9:00–17:00, Sun 13:00–17:00, may close Sat after 13:00 for weddings, Szentháromság tér 2, tel. 1/355-5657, www.matyas-templom.hu.

❷ **Self-Guided Tour:** Examine the **exterior.** While the nucleus of the church is Gothic, most of what you see outside—including the frilly, flamboyant steeple—was added for the 1896 celebrations. At the top of the spire facing the river, notice the raven—the ever-present symbol of King Mátyás Corvinus.

The sumptuous **interior** is wallpapered with gilded pages from a Hungarian history textbook. Different eras are represented by symbolic motifs. For example, the wall immediately to the left of the entry represents the Renaissance, with a giant coat of arms of the beloved King Mátyás Corvinus. (The tough guys in armor on either side are members of his mercenary Black Army, the source of his power.) Notice another raven, with a ring in its beak. Meanwhile, the wall across from the entry—with Oriental motifs—commemorates the Ottoman reign of Buda.

Work your way clockwise around the church from the entry. The first chapel (in the back corner, by the entry)—the **Loreto Chapel**—holds the church's prize possession. Peer through the black iron grill to see the 1515 statue of Mary and Jesus. Anticipating Ottoman plundering, locals walled over this precious statue. The occupying Ottomans used the church as their primary mosque—oblivious to the statue plastered over in the niche. Then, a century and a half later, during the siege of Buda in 1686, gunpowder stored in the castle up the street detonated, and the wall crumbled. Mary's triumphant face showed through, terrifying the Ottomans. Supposedly this was the only part of town taken from the Ottomans without a fight.

As you look down the **nave,** notice the banners. They've hung here since the Mass that celebrated Hapsburg monarch Franz Josef's coronation at this church on June 8, 1867. In a sly political compromise to curry favor in the Hungarian part of his territory, Franz Josef was "Emperor" of Austria, but only "King" of Hungary. (If you see the old German phrase "K + K"—still used today as a boast of royal quality—it refers to this *"König und Kaiser"* arrangement.) So, after F. J. was crowned emperor in Vienna, he came down the Danube and said to the Hungarians, "King me."

Continue circling around the church. On the left side of the church (toward the altar from the gift shop) is the altar of St. Imre, the son of the great King (and later Saint) István. This heir to the Hungarian throne was mysteriously killed by a boar while hunting when he was only 19 years old. Though he didn't live long enough to do anything important, he rode his father's coattails to sainthood. The next chapel is the tomb of Béla III, utterly insignificant except that this is one of only two tombs of Hungarian kings that still exist in the country. The rest—including all of the biggies—were defiled by the Ottomans. Up next to the main altar is the chapel of László—St. István's nephew, who stepped in as king of Hungary when the rightful heir, St. Imre, was killed.

Along the left aisle is the entrance to the upstairs gallery, which holds the **Museum of Ecclesiastical Art** (Egyházművészeti Gyűjteménye, same ticket and hours as church). The original Hungarian crown is under the Parliament's dome, and a hassle to visit (see page 439)—but a replica is up here, and worth a peek. The church also hosts concerts (Oct–Feb only, maybe a few in shoulder season, none in summer; ticket desk at church entry).

• *To continue your exploration of Buda, take a stroll along...*

North Castle Hill—The following walk takes you through Buda north of Matthias Church. As this was the site of a Nazi military headquarters, it was heavily bombed toward the end of World War II. (During a 100-day siege, 80 percent of the city's buildings were damaged or destroyed.)

Leave the courtyard beside the church and turn right—passing the 1713 Holy Trinity plague column on your left—so that you're walking along the front of the glassy, modern **Hilton Hotel.** To minimize the controversy of building upon so much history, architects thoughtfully incorporated the medieval ruins into its modern design. Built in 1976, the Hilton was the first plush Western hotel in town. Before 1989, it was a gleaming center of capitalism, offering a cushy refuge for Western travelers and a stark contrast to what was, at the time, a very gloomy city.

Halfway down the hotel's facade, you'll see fragments of a 13th-century wall, with a monument to King Mátyás Corvinus. After the wall, continue along the second half of the Hilton Hotel facade. Turn right into the gift-shop entry, and then go right again inside the second glass door. Through yet another glass door, stairs on the left lead down to a reconstructed 13th-century Dominican cloister; at the far end of the cloister are more stairs, to the Faust Wine Cellar (daily 16:00–23:00), a friendly place with fine wine by the glass. For an even better look at what was here back then, go back up the stairs and turn left. As you enter the lounge, look out the back windows to see fragments of the 13th-century Dominican church incorporated into the structure of the hotel. If you stood here eight centuries ago, you'd be looking straight down the church's nave. You can even see tomb markers in the floor.

Back out on the street, cross the little park and duck into the entryway of the **Fortuna Passage.** Along the passageway to the courtyard, you can see the original Gothic arches of the house that once stood here. In the Middle Ages, every homeowner had the right to sell wine without paying taxes—but only in the passage of his own home. He'd set up a table here, and his neighbors would come by to taste the latest vintage. These passageways evolved into very social places, like the corner pub.

Leaving the passage, turn left down Fortuna utca and walk to the end of the street, where you'll see the **Vienna Gate.** If you go through it and walk for about 10 days, you'll get to Vienna. (For now, settle for climbing up to the top for a view of some Buda residential neighborhoods.)

• *Now walk left along the hulking, mosaic-roofed National Archive building (with your back to the Danube) until you reach the...*

Remains of St. Mary Magdalene Church—This was once known as the Kapisztrán Templom, named after a hero of the Battle of Belgrade in 1456, an early success in the struggle to keep the Ottomans out of Europe. (King Mátyás' father, János Hunyadi, led the Hungarians in that battle.) The Pope was so tickled by the victory that he decreed that all church bells should toll at noon in memory of the battle—and, technically, they still do. Californians will recognize the Kapisztrán's Spanish name: San Juan de Capistrano. This church was destroyed by bombs in World War II, though no worse than Matthias Church. But, since this part of town was depopulated after the war, there was no longer a need for a second church. The remains of the church were torn down, the steeple was rebuilt as a memorial, and a carillon was added—so that every day at noon, the bells can still toll.

• *Across the square from the church is a monument to San Juan de Capistrano. Walking around the big building, you come to a viewpoint overlooking modern Buda, and on the green hill beyond that, you find the Beverly Hills of Budapest—where the local rich and famous live. To the right, near the flagpole, is the entry to the...*

Museum of Military History (Hadtörténeti Múzeum)—This fine museum explains various Hungarian military actions through history in painstaking detail. Watch military uniforms and weaponry evolve from the time of Árpád to today. With enough old uniforms and flags to keep an army-surplus store in stock for a decade, this place might interest military and history buffs (1,000 Ft, covered by the Budapest Card, maybe more for special exhibitions, April–Sept Tue–Sun 10:00–18:00, closed Mon; Oct–March Tue–Sun 10:00–16:00, closed Mon; closed mid-Dec–mid-Jan, Tóth Árpád sétány 40, Budapest I, tel. 1/325-1600).

• *Your tour is over. From here, you can backtrack to enjoy more time on Castle Hill. Or consider going back to the Vienna Gate and heading downhill. You'll run into bustling Moszkva tér, which has a handy Metro stop (M2 line) and a huge, modern, popular shopping complex (Mammut, or "Mammoth").*

Gellért Hill (Gellérthegy)

The hill rising from the Danube banks just downriver from the castle is Gellért Hill. When King István converted Hungary to Christianity in the year 1000, he brought in Bishop Gellért, a monk from Venice, to tutor his son. But some rebellious Magyars had other ideas. They put the bishop in a barrel, drove long nails in from the outside, and rolled him down this hill...tenderizing him to death. Gellért became the patron saint of Budapest and gave his name to the hill that killed him.

Gellért Hill's only real attraction is the **baths** at Gellért Hotel (see page 464 of "Budapest's Baths"). The hill is a fine place to commune with nature on a hike or jog.

Monument Hike—The north slope of Gellért Hill is good for a low-impact hike. You'll see many interesting monuments, most notably the memorial to Bishop Gellért himself (you can't miss it as you cross the Elisabeth Bridge on Hegyalja út). A bit farther up, seek out a newer monument to the world's great philosophers—Eastern, Western, and in between—from Gandhi to Plato to Jesus. Nearby is a scenic overlook with a king and a queen holding hands on either side of the Danube.

Citadella—This strategic, hill-capping fortress was built by the Hapsburgs after the 1848 Revolution to keep an eye on their Hungarian subjects. There's not much to do up here (no museum or exhibits, just a hotel), but it's a good destination for an uphill hike, and provides excellent views over all of Budapest.

The hill is crowned by the **Liberation Monument,** featuring a woman holding aloft a palm branch. The locals call it "the lady with the big fish" or "the great bottle opener." The heroic Soviet soldier—who once inspired the workers with a huge red star from the base of the monument—is now in Statue Park (see page 456).

Cave Church (Sziklatemplom)—Hidden in the hillside on the south end of the hill (across the street from Gellért Hotel) is Budapest's atmospheric cave church—literally burrowed into the rock face. The communists bricked up this church when they came to power, but now it's open for visitors once again (free entry, but closed to sightseers during frequent services).

Pest

Central Pest (Belváros), Along Váci utca

▲**Vörösmarty tér**—The prominent square called Vörösmarty tér (VOO-roosh-mar-tee tehr), at the north end of the Váci utca pedestrian boulevard, is named for a 19th-century Romantic poet (see his statue in the center) who stirred nationalistic spirit with his writing.

Find the landmark **Gerbeaud** pastry shop at the north end of the square. Between the World Wars, the well-to-do ladies of Budapest would meet here after shopping their way up Váci utca. Today it's still *the* meeting point in Budapest (described under "Cafés and Pastry Shops," page 483).

As you face Gerbeaud, the street to your left leads to the Danube embankment (ideal for a scenic stroll), and the street to your right leads past Erzsébet tér (once Pest's market square) to Andrássy út, lined with sights, restaurants, and hotels (see "Andrássy út and City Park," page 441). If you jog left around the Gerbeaud and then go straight, you'll reach the Parliament in about 10 minutes (see "Hungarian Parliament and Nearby," page 439).

The yellow M1 Metro stop in the middle of the square is the entrance to the shallow *Földalatti*, or "underground"—the first subway on the Continent (built for the millennial celebration in 1896). Today, it still carries passengers to Andrássy út sights (it runs under that street all the way to City Park).

Three hundred years ago, Vörösmarty tér was a rough-and-tumble, often-flooded quarter just outside the Pest city walls. People came here to enjoy brutal, staged fights between bloodhounds and bears (like cockfights, only bigger and angrier, with more fur and teeth). The Ottoman invaders had finally been forced out of Pest, and the city was nearly deserted. After a series of battles for Hungarian independence, the Hapsburgs moved into ruined Pest in the 1710s. They populated the city with Austrians. (While there was a small Hungarian minority, most Magyars lived in the countryside.) The Austrians of Pest began rebuilding the city, virtually from scratch—most of the buildings you'll see are no older than 300 years.

For more of the story, stroll down the street across the square from Gerbeaud: Váci utca.

PEST CENTER SIGHTS

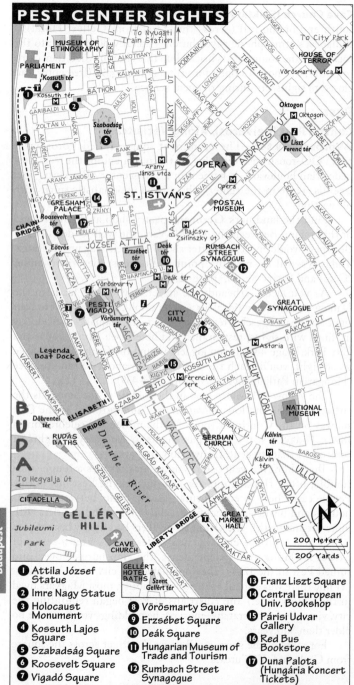

Budapest

1 Attila József Statue
2 Imre Nagy Statue
3 Holocaust Monument
4 Kossuth Lajos Square
5 Szabadság Square
6 Roosevelt Square
7 Vigadó Square

8 Vörösmarty Square
9 Erzsébet Square
10 Deák Square
11 Hungarian Museum of Trade and Tourism
12 Rumbach Street Synagogue

13 Franz Liszt Square
14 Central European Univ. Bookshop
15 Párisi Udvar Gallery
16 Red Bus Bookstore
17 Duna Palota (Hungária Koncert Tickets)

▲**Váci utca**—This pedestrian boulevard—Budapest's shopping and tourism artery—was dreamland for Eastern Europeans back in the 1980s. It was here that they fantasized about what it might be like to be free, while drooling over Nikes, Reeboks, and Big Macs before any of these Western evils were introduced elsewhere in the Warsaw Pact region.

Ironically, this street—once prized by Hungarians and other Eastern Europeans because it felt so Western—is what many Western tourists today mistakenly think is the "real Budapest." You could have a fun and fulfilling trip to this city without setting foot on Váci utca (VAH-tsee OOT-zah). But many visitors are mesmerized by this people-friendly stretch of souvenir stands, Internet cafés, and upscale boutiques—and a ramble along Váci utca does have stories to tell. The following commentary will help you uncover artifacts of authentic Pest between the postcard racks.

❍ **Self-Guided Walk:** "Váci utca" means "street to Vác"—a town 25 miles to the north. This has long been the street where the elite of Pest would go shopping, then strut their stuff for their neighbors on an evening promenade (*korzó* in Hungarian). Today, the tourists do the strutting here—and the Hungarians go to suburban shopping malls.

As you walk, be sure to look up. Along this street and throughout Pest, spectacular facades begin on the second floor, above a plain entryway (in the 1970s, ground-floor shop windows were made uniformly dull by the communist government). Pan up to see some of Pest's best architecture. These were the townhouses of the aristocracy whose mansions dotted the countryside.

At the end of the first block, next to the Tatuum store on the right, a **plaque** notes that Pest's medieval town wall was torn down in 1789. The no-longer-needed wall had been gradually crumbling for centuries, and as residents rebuilt from the Ottoman occupation, it was just getting in the way.

On the next block, find the quirky **Modernist facade** at #8 on the left (over the Clinique shop). Compare this one to the building marked *Douglas* (#11A, across the street a few doors up). The first is more traditional Modernism, but the second is a great example of the **Secession** style. Modernist architecture was rebellious: It rejected what came before—which is why it still looks weird to us today. But the Secession did one better and rejected Modernism.

At the end of the block, the unassuming **McDonald's** (on the right, down Régi Posta utca) was a landmark in Eastern Europe—the first McDonald's behind the Iron Curtain. Budapest has always been a little more rebellious, independent, and cosmopolitan than its Eastern European neighbors, who flocked here during the communist era. Since you had to wait in a long line—stretching around the block—to get a burger, it wasn't "fast food"...but at least it was "West food."

Continuing your stroll, you'll notice that some of the **facades** are plain (like the one above the tobacco shop on the right, just after the street leading to McDonald's). Many of these used to be more ornate, like the others, but they were destroyed by WWII bombs and rebuilt in a stripped-down style.

About halfway along the Váci utca stroll, you'll approach a busy cross-street (which goes over the white Elisabeth Bridge to Buda). Here we'll detour a bit off Váci utca to reach a sight few tourists find: Before the busy street, across from the Subway restaurant, turn left onto Kígyó utca. Partway up the block on the left, look for the entrance (at Lajos Kossuth út 11) to the **Párisi Udvar gallery.** This is perhaps the grandest of Pest's impressive hidden galleries, once used for elegant shopping, now faded and ignored. Enjoy the delicate woodwork and breathtaking stained-glass dome. While many of the storefronts inside are abandoned, a few are still alive and kicking (including a bookstore with English guidebooks). This place is a reminder that if you only experience what's on the main streets in Budapest, you'll miss a big part of the story. (Note that you can also access this gallery from the other end, around the corner at Petőfi Sándor utca 2.)

Now return to the main Váci utca thoroughfare and go under the busy road. The last stretch of Váci utca heads toward the huge market hall. This used to be a strongly Serbian neighborhood—look for Cyrillic writing on some of the buildings. In fact, near the end of this street, the side street (to the left) called Szerb utca still has a **Serbian Orthodox church,** heavy with incense and packed with icons. Traditionally, Hungary's territory included most of Slovakia and large parts of Romania, Croatia, and Serbia—and people from all of those places (along with Jews and Gypsies) flocked to Buda and Pest. And yet, most of the residents of this cosmopolitan city still speak Hungarian. Through centuries of foreign invasions and visitors, Budapest remains Magyar. (Remember that after the Ottomans left, Budapest was mostly Austrian. The Austrians didn't go anywhere...they "became" Hungarian, assimilated into the local culture.)

• *At the end of Váci utca, you'll come to the...*

▲▲**Great Market Hall (Nagyvásárcsarnok)**—This market hall (along with four others) was built—you know it—around the year 1896. The cavernous interior features three levels. The ground floor has produce stands, bakeries, butcher stalls, heaps of paprika, goose liver, and sausages. Upstairs are fun, super-cheap, stand-up, Hungarian-style fast-food joints and six-stool pubs, along with a great selection of souvenirs both traditional (paprika) and not-so-traditional (commie kitsch T-shirts; for all the details, see "Shopping" on page 468). Along the upstairs back wall are historic

photos of the market hall (and WCs). The basement is pungent with tanks of still-swimming carp, catfish, and perch, and piles of pickles.

The market was kept open during communism. Margaret Thatcher came to visit in 1989. She expected atrocious conditions compared to English markets, but was pleasantly surprised to find this place up to snuff. This was, after all, "goulash communism" (Hungary's pragmatic mix, which allowed a little private enterprise to keep people going). On the steps of this building, she delivered a historic speech about open society, heralding the impending arrival of the market economy.

The market hall is ideal for lunch, picnic shopping, and people-watching (Mon 6:00–17:00, Tue–Fri 6:00–18:00, Sat 6:00–14:00, closed Sun, Fővám körút 1–3, Budapest IX, M3: Kálvin tér). See "Eating," page 477, for ideas.

From the market, walk to the river. You'll pass (on the left) the **University of Economics,** which was called Karl Marx University two decades ago.

• *Near the Great Market Hall, you have several sightseeing options. The bridge leads straight to Gellért Hotel, with its famous hot-springs bath, at the foot of Gellért Hill (see "Gellért Baths," page 464). Trams #2 and #2A run from here along the Danube directly back to central Pest, the Chain Bridge, and the Parliament. Or you can walk about 10 minutes (or take tram #47 or #49) around the Small Boulevard away from the Danube to reach one more (optional) sight...*

Hungarian National Museum (Magyar Nemzeti Múzeum)— One of Budapest's biggest museums features all manner of Hungarian historic bric-a-brac, from the Paleolithic age to a more recent infestation of dinosaurs (the communists). The first floor focuses on the Carpathian Basin in the pre-Magyar days, with ancient artifacts and Roman remains. The basement features a lapidarium, with medieval tombstones and more Roman ruins. On the second floor, 20 rooms take you on a very fast overview trip from the arrival of the Magyars in 896 up to the 1989 revolution. Unless you've got a pretty good handle on Hungarian history, the exhibits are difficult to appreciate (with only a few big-picture English explanations). The most interesting part comes at the very end, with an exhibit on the communist era, featuring both pro- and anti-Party propaganda. The exhibit ends with video footage of the 1989 end of communism—demonstrations, monumental parliament votes, and a final farewell to the last Soviet troops leaving Hungarian soil. Another uprising—the 1848 Revolution

Budapest

Hungarian Revolutions

Foreign powers who have oppressed the Hungarians have found them difficult to suppress. In each case, the Hungarians initially encountered bloodshed and more oppression, but ultimately brought about positive change. The dates these revolutions began remain national holidays.

Lajos Kossuth and the 1848 Revolution

Of the many Hungarian uprisings against Hapsburg rule (1526–1918), the 1848 Revolution was the most dramatic. In 1848, a wave of nationalism spread across Europe. The spirit of change caught on in Hungary, where lawyer and parliamentarian Lajos Kossuth led an uprising sparked on March 15. Though the Austrians were initially overwhelmed by the revolt, they eventually brought in Russian troops to regain control. For a few years, the Hapsburgs cracked down on their Hungarian subjects—but within 20 years, they ceded half the authority of their empire to Budapest, creating the Dual Monarchy.

Imre Nagy and the 1956 Uprising

The Hungarian politician Imre Nagy (EEM-ray nodge, 1896–1958) was a lifelong communist. In the 1930s, he allegedly worked for the Soviet secret police. In the late 1940s, he quickly moved up the hierarchy of Hungary's communist government, becoming prime minister in 1953. But in the Moscow shuffle following Stalin's death, Nagy was quickly demoted.

When violence broke out in Budapest on October 23, 1956, Nagy reemerged as the leader of the reform movement. Nagy's new brand of communism strove to separate from the Soviets and create a less-stringent system that Hungarians could live with. For a few short days, it seemed as though Hungary's communism would moderate—until Soviet tanks rumbled into Budapest. In a Tiananmen Square–style crackdown, the Soviets brutally put down the uprising and occupied the city. By the time the Red Army left, 25,000 protesters were dead, and 200,000 Hungarians had fled to Austria. Nagy was arrested, given a sham trial, and executed in 1958. He was buried disgracefully, face-down in an unmarked grave, and his name was taboo in Hungary for 30 years.

Though the uprising met a tragic end, within a few years Hungary's harshness did soften, and the milder, so-called "goulash communism" emerged. As the Eastern Bloc thawed in 1989, Nagy became a martyr and a hero. His body was discovered and given a proper reburial in July of that exciting year—heralding the quickly approaching end of the communist era.

against Hapsburg rule—was declared from the steps of this impressive Neoclassical building (1,000 Ft, covered by Budapest Card, maybe extra for special exhibitions, Tue–Sun 10:00–18:00, closed Mon, last entry 30 min before closing, near Great Market Hall at Múzeum körút 14–16, Budapest VIII, tel. 1/327-7700, www.hnm.hu).

• *Note that from the National Museum, you can continue about another 10 minutes around the Small Boulevard to the Great Synagogue (see page 451).*

Hungarian Parliament and Nearby

The Parliament building, which dominates Pest's skyline, is the centerpiece of a banking and business district that bustles by day but is quiet on weeknights and weekends. This area—especially Kossuth Lajos tér behind the Parliament—also features some of the best of Budapest's many monuments.

▲**Hungarian Parliament (Országház)**—The Parliament building, like so much of Budapest, was built for the city's millennial

celebration in 1896. Its elegant Neo-Gothic design and riverside location were inspired by its counterpart in London. Architecture snobs shake their heads and wonder why this frilly Gothic monstrosity is topped with a Renaissance dome—typical of the kitchen-sink historicism popular at the time. (To make matters worse, there used to be a huge red communist star on top of the tallest spire.) But I think it's beautiful.

The best views of the building are from across the Danube—especially in the late-afternoon sunlight.

This enormous building—with literally miles of stairs—was appropriate for a time when Budapest ruled much of Eastern Europe. But today it's just plain too big—the legislature only occupies an eighth of the building. Like Britain's Parliament, this building used to be home to a House of Lords and a House of Commons. The Lords are long gone, and their vacated territory is what visitors tour. Guided tours of the Parliament's opulent interior include the elegant main entryway, a legislative chamber, and the Hungarian crown, under the ornate dome.

Cost, Hours, and Information: 2,600 Ft, not covered by Budapest Card, English tours usually daily at 10:00, 12:00, and 14:00—but schedule can change so confirm in advance; Kossuth tér 1–3, Budapest V, M2: Kossuth tér, tel. 1/441-4904, www.mkogy.hu.

Getting Tickets: The ticket office opens each day at 8:00

(tickets sold for same-day tours only). On busy days, tickets can sell out—so if your heart is set on getting in, buy your tickets early. Behind the Parliament, follow signs to entry *X* (slightly right of center as you face the back of the giant building), and find the line at the fence marked *for buying tickets*. Wait for the guard to let you enter the door marked *X,* pay the cashier, and return to the mob to wait for your tour.

Kossuth (Lajos) Tér—The square behind the Parliament building, named for the hero of the 1848 Revolution against the Hapsburgs (described on page 438), is sprinkled with several interesting monuments. Just behind the Parliament is a grassy park with statues of various important Hungarians. A newer monument features a Hungarian flag with a hole cut out of the middle. This commemorates the 1956 Uprising, when protesters removed the socialist-style seal the Soviets had added to their flag. In the early days of that uprising, communist police (ÁVH) on the rooftops above opened fire on demonstrators gathered in this square—massacring many and leaving no doubt that Moscow would not tolerate any form of dissent.

Now imagine this square in the fall of 2006, when it became the site of demonstrations—initially impromptu, then carefully choreographed—against Hungary's prime minister, Ferenc Gyurcsány. Using particularly colorful language in a speech intended only for his own party members, Gyurcsány admitted to lies, deceit, and deception in the way he'd run the government and the recent election. When the tape was leaked to the media, Hungarians showed up here to (unsuccessfully) demand Gyurcsány's resignation. While a few of the demonstrations turned violent, most remained peaceful...and lucrative (concessions stands appeared just a few days into the weeks-long demonstration). For more information on these recent events, see page 394.

Near the Parliament are three other interesting monuments. Just beyond the southeast corner of Kossuth tér, on Vértanúk tere, a contemplative statue of **Imre Nagy,** hero of the 1956 Uprising, stands on a bridge (see page 438). Down closer to the river, by the tram tracks on the end of the Parliament facing the Chain Bridge, look for a statue of the pensive **Attila József,** a popular modern poet who committed suicide at age 32. He's looking over the Danube, a common motif in his works. From this statue, walk to the river-view terrace and look along the river's edge toward the Chain Bridge. If you look carefully, you'll see in the distance a new **Holocaust Monument**—consisting of 50 pairs of bronze shoes—lining the embankment just before the tree-filled, riverfront park. The monument commemorates the Jews who were killed when the Nazis' puppet government, the Arrow Cross, came to power in Hungary in 1944. While many Jews were sent to concentration

---

The Millennium Underground of 1896

Built to get the masses of visitors conveniently out to Heroes' Square, this fun and extremely handy little Metro line follows Andrássy út from Vörösmarty Square (Pest's main square) to City Park. Just 20 steps below street level, it's so shallow that you must follow the signs on the street (listing end points) to gauge the right direction, because there's no underpass for switching platforms. The first underground on the Continent (London's is older), it originally had horse-drawn cars. Trains depart every couple of minutes. Recently renovated, the M1 line retains its 1896 atmosphere, along with fun black-and-white photos of the age.

---

camps, the Arrow Cross simply massacred some of them right here, shooting them and letting their bodies fall into the Danube. You can't get to the shoes directly from here (there's no safe cross-walk over the embankment road). For a slightly better view of the Holocaust Monument, you can walk along the tram tracks to another viewpoint just downriver; but to actually reach the shoes themselves, you'll have to access the embankment from near the Chain Bridge, then walk back up this way along the water.

At the top end of Kossuth tér is the...

Museum of Ethnography (Néprajzi Múzeum)—This museum, housed in one of Budapest's grandest venues (the former supreme court building), feels deserted. Its fine exhibit on Hungarian folk culture (mostly from the late-19th century) takes up only a small corner of the cavernous building. This permanent exhibit, with surprisingly good English explanations, shows off costumes, tools, wagons, boats, beehives, furniture, and ceramics of the many peoples who lived in pre-WWI Hungary (which also included much of today's Slovakia and Romania). The museum also has a collection of artifacts from other European and world cultures, which it cleverly assembles into good temporary exhibits (800 Ft, covered by Budapest Card, maybe more for special exhibitions, Tue–Sun 10:00–18:00, closed Mon, Kossuth tér 12, Budapest V, M2: Kossuth tér, tel. 1/473-2442).

Andrássy út and City Park

Connecting central Pest to City Park, Andrássy út is Budapest's main boulevard, lined with shops, theaters, cafés, and locals living well. Budapesters claim it's like the Champs-Elysées and Broadway rolled into one. While that's a stretch, it is a good place to stroll and get a feel for today's urban Pest. The best part to wander is between the boulevard's beginning at Deák tér and the Oktogon.

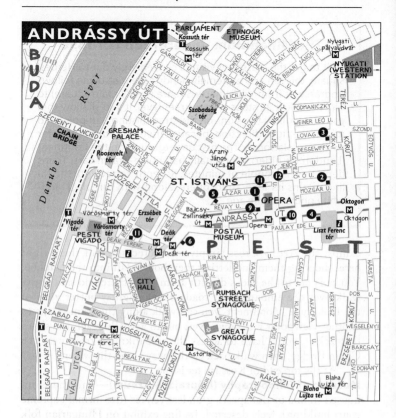

It was here that Steven Spielberg filmed much of *Munich*, since this part of Budapest has fine architecture that could stand in for many great European cities.

The following sights are listed in order, from Deák tér (in central Pest) to City Park. The M1 line runs every couple of minutes just under the street—so if you get tired of walking, it's easy to skip several blocks ahead (stops marked by yellow *Földalatti* signs; see "The Millennium Underground of 1896" sidebar, previous page).

St. István's Basilica (Szent István Bazilika)—Step into the dark, gloomy interior of Budapest's largest Catholic church and you'll see not Jesus, but St. István (Stephen), Hungary's first Christian king, glowing above the high altar. (See the "Statue of St. István" listing on page 428 for more on this important Hungarian.) The church is only about 100 years old—like most Budapest landmarks, it was built around 1896. Recently renovated, the interior is tidy and proud. Though it looks like a major landmark and is packed with tour groups, the church isn't that compelling (free, Mon–Fri 9:00–17:00, Sat 9:00–13:00—but often closed on summer Saturdays for weddings, Sun 13:00–17:00, Szent István tér,

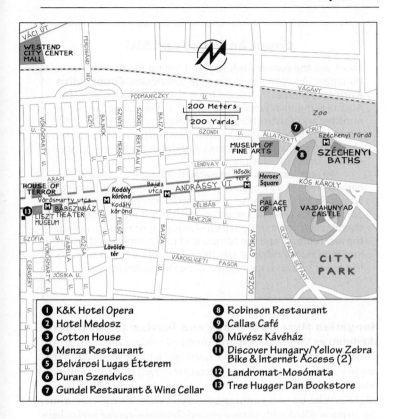

1 K&K Hotel Opera
2 Hotel Medosz
3 Cotton House
4 Menza Restaurant
5 Belvárosi Lugas Étterem
6 Duran Szendvics
7 Gundel Restaurant & Wine Cellar
8 Robinson Restaurant
9 Callas Café
10 Művész Kávéház
11 Discover Hungary/Yellow Zebra Bike & Internet Access (2)
12 Landromat-Mosómata
13 Tree Hugger Dan Bookstore

Budapest V, M1: Bajcsy-Zsilinszky út or M3: Arany János utca).

The church's primary claim to fame is the **"holy right hand" of St. István.** The sacred fist—a somewhat grotesque, 1,000-year-old withered stump—is in a jeweled box in the chapel to the left of the main altar (follow signs for *Szent Jobb Kápolna,* chapel often closed). Pop in a coin for two minutes of light. In the back corner of the church, you'll find a small exhibit about the building's history.

The church also has a measly treasury (400 Ft) and panoramic **observation deck,** with a decent view that gives a sense of the sprawl of Pest (500 Ft, 20 percent discount with Budapest Card, elevator to midlevel, then 137 stairs or smaller elevator, plus a few stairs to top of tower, daily April–May 10:00–16:30, June–Aug 9:30–18:00, Sept–Oct 10:00–17:30, closed Nov–March).

Count Andrássy and Sisi

You'll see the names Andrássy and Sisi (or Elisabeth) a lot in Budapest. A key player in the 1848 Revolution, **Count Julius Andrássy** ultimately helped forge the Dual Monarchy of the Austro-Hungarian Empire. He served as the Hungarian prime minister and Austro-Hungarian foreign minister (1871–1879), eventually being forced to step down after his unpopular campaign to appropriate Bosnia and Herzegovina (and consequently boost the Slav population).

Sisi was **Empress Elisabeth,** the Princess Diana of the early 20th-century Hapsburgs (see page 851). Her pet project was advancing the cause of Hungarian autonomy within the empire. While she was married to Emperor Franz Josef, she spent seven years in Budapest—enjoying horseback riding, the local cuisine, and the company of the charming and good-looking Count Andrássy. Her third daughter—believed to be the count's—was known as the Little Hungarian Princess.

Hungarian Museum of Trade and Tourism (Magyar Kereskedelmi és Vendéglátóipari Múzeum)—More interesting than it sounds, this museum takes a nostalgic look at workaday 19th-century Pest commerce. Since it recently moved into this new location—a stately former bank building—the museum's full collection might not be up and running when you visit. In the meantime, the space is filled with temporary exhibitions—recent topics have included champagne and the history of ice cream. You might also see fun old-fashioned posters, as well as other artifacts offering a peek into the fancy hotels, restaurants, and coffeehouses of the day (600 Ft, 20 percent discount with Budapest Card, Wed–Mon 11:00–19:00, closed Tue, hiding around the back of St. István's Basilica—to the left as you face the church—at Szent István tér 15; Budapest V, tel. 1/375-6249).

▲**Postal Museum (Postamúzeum)**—This quirky museum, in a fine old apartment from Budapest's Golden Age, features a delightful collection of postal artifacts. You'll see post office coats of arms, 100-year-old postal furniture, antique telephone boxes, historic mailman uniforms, and all manner of postal paraphernalia that was cutting-edge a century ago. It's displayed in an elegant old merchant's mansion with big Murano crystal chandeliers, all the original ornate woodwork, and creaky parquet floors. The apartment—decorated as it was when built in the 1880s—is as interesting as the museum's collection. If she's not too busy, English-speaking Nora, who's usually around, loves to explain the place and demonstrate the old telephone-operator switchboard (400 Ft, covered by

Budapest Card, Tue–Sun 10:00–18:00, closed Mon, loaner English information in each room—or buy the 500-Ft guidebook, just up the street from St. István's Basilica at Andrássy út 3, look for easy-to-miss sign and dial 10 to get upstairs, Budapest VI, M1: Bajcsy-Zsilinszky út, tel. 1/269-6838, www.postamuzeum.hu).

▲▲**Hungarian State Opera House (Magyar Állami Operaház)**— The Neo-Renaissance home of the Hungarian State Opera features performances almost daily (except July–Aug, during outdoor music season). Designed by Miklós Ybl, the building was constructed in the 1890s using almost entirely Hungarian materials. After being damaged in World War II, it was painstakingly restored in the early 1980s. Today, with lavish marble-and-frescoes decor, a gorgeous gilded interior, and high-quality performances at bargain prices, this is one of Europe's finest opera houses. To take in an opera here, see "Budapest Music Scene," page 466.

Even if you don't see a performance, you can slip in the front door and check out the sumptuous entryway when the box office is open (Mon–Sat from 11:00 until show time—generally 19:00; Sun open 3 hours before the performance—generally 16:00–19:00, or 10:00–13:00 if there's a matinee; Andrássy út 22, Budapest VI, M1: Opera). Better yet, take one of the excellent 45-minute **tours** in English (nearly daily at 15:00 and 16:00, reservations not necessary, but it's smart to call ahead and confirm schedule; 2,500 Ft, 10 percent discount with Budapest Card, 500 Ft to take photos, buy ticket in opera shop—enter the main lobby and go left, shop open Mon–Fri 10:30–12:45 & 13:30–17:00, Sat–Sun 13:30–17:00, open later during performances, tel. 1/332-8197).

Franz Liszt Square (Liszt Ferenc tér)—This leafy, trendy square on the right (south) side of Andrássy út is surrounded by hip, expensive cafés and restaurants. (The best is the kitschy communist themed restaurant Menza—see page 481.) This is *the* scene for Budapest's yuppies. At the far end of the square is the Music Academy also named for Liszt—a German composer with a Hungarian name, who loved his family's Magyar heritage (though he didn't speak Hungarian) and spent his last five years in Budapest.

The happening Liszt Square scene continues along two streets near the Opera House, **Hajós utca** and **Nagymező utca**—each with its own chic cluster of restaurants and bars. Loosely referred to as the "Broadway Quarter," this zone also has several theaters, and is an enjoyable place to stroll on a summer evening.

Oktogon—During the communist era, this square—at the intersection of Andrássy út and the Great Ring Road (Nagykörút)—was called "November 7 tér" in honor of the Bolshevik Revolution. (Andrássy út was renamed "Sztálin út"; later, after Stalin fell out of fashion, it was simply "People's Republic Boulevard.") Today kids have nicknamed it "American tér" for the fast-food joints littering the square and streets nearby. From this square, Andrássy út gradually becomes the dull diplomatic quarter—less colorful, with tame, embassy-lined streets and stately mansions. From the center of Andrássy út, you can see the column of Heroes' Square at the end of the boulevard.

▲▲**House of Terror (Terror Háza)**—The former headquarters of the darkest sides of two different regimes—the Arrow Cross (Nazi-occupied Hungary's version of the Gestapo) and the ÁVO/ÁVH (communist Hungary's secret police)—is now, fittingly, an excellent museum of that time of terror. This is a powerful experience, particularly for elderly Hungarians who knew both victims and perpetrators and have personal memories of the terrors that came with Hungary's "double occupation." While the high-tech, conceptual museum is designed for Hungarians, the English audioguide (1,300 Ft extra) and free handouts help foreign visitors appreciate the experience.

Cost, Hours, Location: 1,500 Ft, 20 percent discount with Budapest Card, more for special exhibitions, Tue–Fri 10:00–18:00, Sat–Sun 10:00–19:30, closed Mon, café, bookshop, Andrássy út 60, Budapest VI, M1: Vörösmarty utca—*not* the Vörösmarty tér stop, tel. 1/374-2600, www.terrorhaza.hu. Outside, an overhang casts the shadow of the word "TERROR" onto the building.

Audioguide and Information: The 1,300-Ft English audioguide is good but almost too thorough, and can be difficult to hear over the din of the Hungarian soundtracks in each room. You can't fast-forward through the very dense and sometimes long-winded commentary. As an alternative, my self-guided tour (below) covers the key points. A silver plaque in each room provides the basics (in English). For more in-depth information (very similar to what's covered by the audioguide), each room is stocked with good, free English fliers.

Background: Hungary initially allied with Hitler to retain a degree of self-determination, and to try to regain their huge territorial losses after World War I. But in March 1944, the country was taken over by the Nazi-affiliated Arrow Cross. The Arrow Cross immediately set to work exterminating Budapest's Jews (most of whom had survived until then). By May, trains were already heading for Auschwitz. As the end of the war neared, Arrow Cross members resorted to more desperate measures, lining Jews up along the Danube and shooting them into the river (now commemorated by a monument near the Parliament—see page 440). To save bullets, they'd sometimes tie several victims together, shoot one of them, and throw him into the freezing Danube—dragging the others in with him. They executed hundreds in the basement of this building. When the communists moved into Hungary, they took over the same building as headquarters for their secret police (the ÁVO, later renamed ÁVH). To keep dissent to a minimum, the secret police terrorized, tried, deported, or executed anyone suspected of being an enemy of the state.

➋ **Self-Guided Tour:** Buy your ticket (and rent an audio-guide, if you wish) and head into the museum. The atrium features a Soviet tank and a huge wall covered with portraits of the victims

of this building.

The one-way exhibit begins, two floors up, then spirals down to the cellar. To begin, you can either take the elevator (to floor 2), or walk up the red stairwell nearby, decorated with old sculptures from the communist days.

Once on the second floor, enter the exhibition and watch a video that sets the stage for Hungary's 20th century: its territorial losses after World War I; its alliance with, then invasion by, the Nazis; and its "liberation," then occupation, by the USSR.

Go through rooms with Arrow Cross (Nazi) propaganda and uniforms, and then enter a room about the much-feared gulags—hard-labor camps where potential and actual dissidents were sent to be punished, to remove their dangerous influence from society, and to make an example of those who would dare to defy the regime. While there were some camps in Hungary, most gulags were in the distant corners of the USSR (such as Siberia). On the carpet, a giant map of the USSR shows the locations of some of these camps, from which some 300,000 Hungarians never returned.

The locker room, with the theme "changing clothes," satirizes the readiness of many Hungarians to align with whoever was in power—Nazi or communist. The next room shows a distorted communist stage, the glossy facade of the Soviets. But behind the scenes, we see the real source of their power: propaganda and surveillance equipment to keep the "workers" under control. This floor concludes with an exhibit on resistance against the regime...and its consequences.

On the next floor down, the exhibit continues with the theme of resettlement and displacement, and a haunting torture cell. Then you'll walk through a labyrinth of pork-fat bricks, which remind old-timers of the harsh conditions of the 1950s (lard on bread for dinner). Look for the ration coupons, which people had to present before being allowed to buy even these measly staples.

The next section explains that the communist secret police imprisoned, abused, or murdered one person from every third Hungarian family. After the ÁVO leader's office, you'll see a mock courtroom with a video about "show trials"—high-profile, loudly publicized trials of people who had supposedly subverted the regime. (While these people were often innocent, it was handy to make an example of them.) From 1945 until the 1956 Uprising, more than 71,000 Hungarians were accused of political crimes, and 485 were executed.

Next you'll pass through another method for controlling the people: bright, cheery communist propaganda. A room with a giant cross hidden in the floor symbolizes the importance of religion, back when joining the Church was a way to express rebellion. There's a special focus on Cardinal József Mindszenty, who was arrested and beaten by the communists, and later sought refuge in the US embassy for 15 years (see sidebar on page 495).

At the end of this floor, you'll board an elevator that gradually creeps down into the cellar, while you watch a three-minute video of a guard explaining the execution process. When the door opens, you're in the cellar. In the early 1950s, this basement was the scene of torture; in 1956, it became a clubhouse of sorts for the local communist youth. It has now been reconstructed circa 1955. You'll wander through actual former cells—including a "standing cell" (where the prisoner was forced to stand 24 hours a day), a padded cell, and a dark cell—with photos of the people who once filled them. In one disturbing room, you'll actually see a gallows used for executions. The exhibit about the 1956 Uprising—with videos and a flag with a hole cut out of the middle—is followed by a wall of postcards, commemorating the more than 200,000 people who fled to the West after the communist crackdown. The Hall of Tears remembers all of the victims of the communists.

Near the end, the only color video clips show the festive and exhilarating days in 1991 when the Soviets departed, making way for freedom. Scenes also include the reburial of the Hungarian hero, Imre Nagy; the Pope's visit; and the dedication of this museum. The chilling finale: walls of photographs of the "victimizers"—members and supporters of the Arrow Cross and ÁVO, many of whom are still living, and who were never brought to justice.

▲▲**Heroes' Square (Hősök tere)**—Like much of Budapest, this Who's Who of Hungarian history at the end of Andrássy út was built to celebrate the city's 1,000th birthday in 1896 (M1: Hősök tere). More than just the hottest place in town for skateboarding, this is the site of several museums and the gateway to City Park (filled with diversions for sightseers).

Step right up to the **Millennium Monument** to meet the world's most historic Hungarians (who look to me like their language sounds). The granddaddy of all Magyars, Árpád, stands proudly at the bottom of the pillar, peering down Andrássy út.

The 118-foot-tall pillar supports the archangel Gabriel as he offers the crown to St. István (he accepted it and Christianized the Magyars). In front of the pillar is the Hungarian War Memorial (fenced in to keep skateboarders from enjoying its perfect slope). Behind the pillar, colonnades feature Hungarian VIPs. Look for names you recognize: István, Béla IV, Mátyás Corvinus. But hey... where are the Hapsburgs? At the time of the monument's construction, Budapest was part of the Austrian Empire, and Hapsburgs stood in the right-hand colonnade. When Hungary regained its independence in World War I, the people tore down the sculpture of the unpopular Franz Josef. (A statue of the less-hated Maria Theresa was left alone...but was ultimately destroyed by a WWII bomb.) After World War II, the Hapsburgs were replaced by Hungarians. In fact, the last two heroes—Ferenc Rákóczi and Lajos Kossuth—were revolutionaries who fought against Austria. The sculptures on the top corners of the two colonnades represent, in order from left to right: Work and Welfare, War, Peace, and the Importance of Packing Light.

As you face Árpád, the **Museum of Fine Arts** (Szépművészeti Múzeum), which has an especially good Spanish collection, is to your left (1,200 Ft, covered by Budapest Card, maybe more for special exhibitions, Tue–Sun 10:00–17:30, closed Mon, last entry 30 min before closing, tel. 1/469-7100). The **Palace of Art** (Műcsarnok), used for temporary contemporary art exhibits, is to your right (price depends on exhibitions—usually 1,000 Ft, 20 percent discount with Budapest Card, Tue–Wed and Fri–Sun 10:00–18:00, Thu 12:00–20:00, closed Mon, tel. 1/460-7000, www .mucsarnok.hu).

If you leave Heroes' Square between the two colonnades behind the main pillar, you'll cross a bridge into...

▲▲City Park (Városliget)—This is the city's not-so-central Central Park. The park was the site of the overblown 1896 Millennium Exhibition, celebrating Hungary's 1,000th birthday...and it's still packed with huge party decorations: a zoo with quirky Art Nouveau buildings, a replica of a Transylvanian castle, a massive bath/swimming complex, walking paths, and an amusement park. The park is also filled with unwinding locals.

If the sightseeing grind gets you down, spend the afternoon taking a mini-vacation from your busy vacation the way Budapesters do—stroll in the park and soak in the baths.

Orient yourself from the bridge behind Heroes' Square: The huge Vajdahunyad Castle is on your right (go straight and look for bridge to enter complex). Straight into the park and on the left are the big copper domes of the fun, relaxing Széchenyi Baths (see "Budapest's Baths" page 460). And the zoo is past the lake on the left. Three recommended restaurants are at the end of the lake near the zoo (see "Eating," page 481).

▲Vajdahunyad Castle (Vajdahunyad Vára)—The huge complex is a replica of a famous castle in Transylvania (part of Hungary for centuries), surrounded by other styles of traditionally Hungarian architecture (textbook Romanesque, Gothic, Renaissance, and Baroque). Some find it artificial in a Walt Disney World sort of way; others think it's pretty cool. You can enter the castle complex for free to poke around the grounds. (After crossing the bridge behind Heroes' Square, turn right.)

As you enter the complex through the castle facade, you'll see a replica of a 13th-century **Benedictine chapel** on the left—Budapest's most popular spot for weekend weddings in the summer. Farther ahead on the right, you'll see a big Baroque mansion—which houses, of all things, the **Museum of Hungarian Agriculture** (Magyar Mezőgazdasági Múzeum). The museum brags that it's Europe's biggest agriculture museum, but the lavish interior is more interesting than the exhibits (500 Ft, covered by Budapest Card, maybe more for special exhibitions; April–Oct Tue–Sun 10:00–17:00, closed Mon; Nov–March Tue–Fri 10:00–16:00, Sat–Sun 10:00–17:00, closed Mon; last entry 30 min before closing, tel. 1/363-2711).

Across the street from the museum entry, you'll see a monument to **Anonymous**—specifically, the Anonymous who penned the first Hungarian history in the Middle Ages.

▲▲▲Széchenyi Baths (Széchenyi Fürdő)—Just beyond Vajdahunyad Castle, in the middle of the park, are Budapest's best baths. For details, see "Experiences" on page 459.

Zoo (Állatkert)—Aside from animals, the zoo also has redeeming sightseeing value: Many of its structures are playful bits of turn-of-the-20th-century Art Nouveau. To reach the beautiful Art Nouveau elephant house, turn right inside the main entry, then right again at the fork, and look for the white-and-turquoise tower. The zoo is a perfect example of a sight that's not really worth the price of entry, but makes for a fun 15-minute walk-through with the Budapest Card (1,700 Ft, covered by Budapest Card; May–Aug Mon–Thu 9:00–17:30, Fri–Sun 9:00–18:00; April and Sept Mon–Thu 9:00–16:30, Fri–Sun 9:00–17:00; Oct and March Mon–Thu

9:00–16:00, Fri–Sun 9:00–16:30; Nov–Feb daily 9:00–15:00; these are last entry times—zoo stays open 1 hour later; Állatkerti körút 6–12, Budapest XIV, tel. 1/364-0109, www.zoobudapest.com).

Jewish Budapest

As the former co-capital of an empire that included millions of Jews, Budapest always had a high concentration of Jewish residents. Before World War II, 5 percent of Hungary's population and 25 percent of Budapest's was Jewish (the city was dubbed "Judapest" by its snide Viennese neighbors up the river). Hungary lost nearly 600,000 Jews to the Holocaust, at the hands of the brutal Nazi puppet government called the Arrow Cross. (For more about the Holocaust in Hungary, see the "House of Terror" listing on page 446.) Today, only half of one percent of Hungarians are Jewish—and most of them are in Budapest. In recent years, since the thawing of communism, Hungarian Jews have been taking a renewed interest in their heritage.

The first sight listed here is very central, close to Pest's Deák tér; the other is just outside central Pest, a Metro ride plus a five-minute walk away.

▲**Great Synagogue (Zsinagóga)**—This impressively restored synagogue is the second biggest in the world, after one in New York

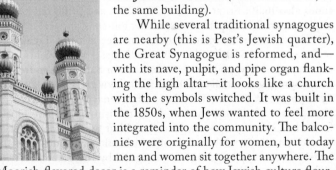

City. Your synagogue ticket also includes the **Jewish Museum** (Zsidó Múzeum, in the same building).

While several traditional synagogues are nearby (this is Pest's Jewish quarter), the Great Synagogue is reformed, and—with its nave, pulpit, and pipe organ flanking the high altar—it looks like a church with the symbols switched. It was built in the 1850s, when Jews wanted to feel more integrated into the community. The balconies were originally for women, but today men and women sit together anywhere. The Moorish-flavored decor is a reminder of how Jewish culture flourished in Iberia. After World War II, the synagogue was refurbished with financial support from Tony Curtis, an American actor of Hungarian-Jewish origin (he and his daughter Jamie Lee continue to support these causes today). Other people of Hungarian-Jewish descent include big names from every walk of life: Harry Houdini (born Erich Weisz), Elie Wiesel, Estée Lauder, Goldie Hawn, Peter Lorre, and Eva and Zsa Zsa Gabor.

Behind the synagogue, the *Tree of Life* sculpture was built on the site of mass graves of those killed by the Nazis. The willow makes an upside-down menorah, each individual leaf lists the

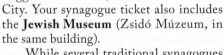

name of a victim, and pebbles represent prayers. You can visit the *Tree* even if you don't buy a ticket for the synagogue (enter through synagogue security gate and go straight ahead through doors and under arcade to the park behind the synagogue; if synagogue is closed, go around left side to view monument through a fence).

Cost and Hours: 1,400 Ft includes Great Synagogue and Jewish Museum, discount with Budapest Card; April–Oct Mon–Thu 10:00–17:00, Fri 10:00–15:00, Sun 10:00–18:00; Nov–March Mon–Thu 10:00–15:00, Fri and Sun 10:00–14:00; always closed Sat and Jewish holidays, last entry 30 minutes before closing, Dohány utca 2, Budapest VII, M2: Astoria plus a five-minute walk, tel. 01/344-5131, www.aviv.hu.

Tours: Two companies lead tours of the synagogue, museum, and related sights. For the best overview, try **Aviv Travel**'s quick 45-minute tour, which combines the Great Synagogue and the *Tree of Life* (1,700 Ft). A longer 80-minute tour covers the above, plus a guided visit to the synagogue's museum (2,000 Ft). And the 90-minute version covers the Great Synagogue, *Tree of Life*, and the nearby synagogue on Rumbach Street (explained next), but not the museum (2,400 Ft). Since these tours include admission, you're paying a small price for the guiding—making this a great, affordable way to really understand the place. Tickets are sold, and tours depart, from the kiosk next to the Great Synagogue entry (Mon–Thu and Sun hourly on the half-hour 10:30–5:30, sometimes also 16:30; Fri at 10:30, 11:30, 12:30, and 13:00 only; tours might depart 2/hr at peak times; no Sat tours).

For a longer and pricier tour, consider **Hidden Treasures'** walking tours (3,500 Ft/1 hr, 6,000 Ft/2 hrs, 8,000 Ft/3 hrs, each tour departs 2/day, no tours Fri afternoon or Sat, meets in front of Great Synagogue, mobile 0670-533-5696, www.greatsynagogue.hu).

Synagogue at Rumbach Street—This synagogue, deserted for years, has recently reopened its doors to visitors. Just two blocks from the Great Synagogue, its colorful but faded Moorish-style interior evokes the Golden Age of Jewish culture in Budapest. The late-19th-century building was designed by the great Viennese architect Otto Wagner. It may be closed for further renovation, but if it's open (ask at Great Synagogue) and you enjoyed the Great Synagogue, it's worth a look (500 Ft, Mon–Thu and Sun 10:00–16:30, Fri 10:00–14:30, closed Sat, 2 blocks down Rumbach street toward Andrássy út from the *Tree of Life*).

▲Holocaust Memorial Center (Holokauszt Emlékközpont)— This new center is making great strides in honoring the nearly 600,000 Hungarian victims of the Nazis (one in every 10 Holocaust victims was Hungarian). Located a short Metro ride outside of central Pest, the impressive modern complex (with a beautifully restored 1920s synagogue as its centerpiece) is intended to serve as a museum of the Hungarian Holocaust, a monument to its victims, a space for excellent temporary exhibits, and a research and documentation center of Nazi atrocities. A black marble wall in the courtyard is etched with the names of victims, and an information center downstairs helps teary-eyed Hungarians locate the names of their relatives.

The permanent exhibit, called "From Deprivation of Rights to Genocide," traces in English the gradual process of marginalization, then dehumanization, that befell Hungary's Jews as World War II wore on. The one-way route uses high-tech exhibits, including interactive touch screens and movies, to tell the story. By showing there was pervasive anti-Semitism long before World War II, the pointed commentary casts doubt on the widely held belief that Hungary allied itself with the Nazis partly to protect its Jews. While the exhibit occasionally acknowledges Roma (Gypsy) victims, its primary focus is on the fate of the Hungarian Jews. Occasionally the exhibit zooms in to tell the story of an individual or single family, following their personal story through those horrific years. The finale is the interior of the synagogue, now a touching memorial filled with glass seats, each one displaying the image of a Jewish worshipper who once filled it (1,000 Ft, 500-Ft English audioguide repeats posted English information, Tue–Sun 10:00–18:00, closed Mon, Páva utca 39, Budapest IX, M3: Ferenc körút, tel. 1/455-3333, www.hdke.hu). To reach the complex, take the M3 Metro line to Ferenc körút. Use the exit marked *Holokauszt Emlékközpont* and take the left fork at the exit. Walk straight ahead two long blocks, then turn right down Páva utca.

The Danube (Duna)

The mighty river coursing through the heart of the city defines Budapest. For many visitors, a highlight is taking a touristy but beautiful boat cruise up and down the Danube—especially at night (see "Tours," page 420). Here are some other river-related activities to consider.

▲**Danube Embankment (Dunakorzó)**—Pest's breezy riverfront promenade (from Elisabeth Bridge to the Chain Bridge) is a fine place for a stroll. Start on Vigadó tér, two blocks towards the river from Vörösmarty tér, and head south. Along the way, keep an eye out for the *Little Princess* statue leaning on the railing—one of Budapest's symbols, even though it's just over a decade old. When Prince Charles visited Budapest, he liked this statue so much that he had a replica made for himself. You'll pass a few souvenir stalls and big, fancy hotels (including Hyatt and InterContinental), and enjoy sweeping views of Buda, some of the international river-cruise ships, and the city's many bridges. While dining values aren't good here, Spoon—on the boat moored in front of the

InterContinental Hotel—is fun (see "Eating," page 479).

▲**Chain Bridge (Széchenyi Lánchíd)**—One of the world's great bridges connects Pest's Roosevelt tér and Buda's Adam Clark tér. This historic, iconic bridge, guarded by lions (symbolizing power), is Budapest's most enjoyable and convenient bridge to cross on foot. (This is especially handy for commuting to the top of Castle Hill, since both bus #16 and the funicular to the top depart from the Buda end of the bridge.)

Until the mid-19th century, only pontoon barges spanned the Danube between Buda and Pest. In the winter, the pontoons had to be pulled in, leaving locals to rely on ferries (in good weather) or a frozen river. People often walked across the frozen Danube, only to get stuck on the other side during a thaw, with nothing to do but wait for another cold snap.

Count István Széchenyi was stranded for a week trying to get to his father's funeral. After missing it, Széchenyi commissioned Budapest's first permanent bridge. The Chain Bridge was built by Scotsman Adam Clark between 1842 and 1849, and it immediately became an important symbol of Budapest. Széchenyi—a man of the Enlightenment—charged both commoners and nobles a toll for crossing his bridge, making it an emblem of equality in those tense times. Like all of the city's bridges, the Chain Bridge was destroyed by the Nazis at the end of World War II, but was quickly rebuilt.

Margaret Island (Margitsziget)—Budapesters come to play in this huge, leafy park, a wonderful spot for strolling, jogging, biking, and people-watching (accessible from Margaret Bridge— trams #4 and #6 stop at the gateway to the island). The island is also home to some of Budapest's many baths.

Outer Budapest

The following sights, while technically in Budapest, take a little more time to reach.

Óbuda

Budapest was originally three cities: Buda, Pest, and Óbuda. Óbuda (or "Old Buda") is the oldest of the three—the first known residents of the region (Celts) settled here, and today it's still littered with ruins from the next occupants (Romans). Despite all the history, the district is disappointing, worth a look only for those interested in Roman ruins or 20th-century Hungarian painting and sculpture. To reach the first three sights listed here, go to Batthyány tér in Buda (M2 Metro line) and catch the HÉV suburban train north to the Árpád híd stop. The Vasarely Museum is 50 yards from the station. The town square is 100 yards beyond that, and 200 yards later (turn left at the ladies with the umbrellas), you'll find the Imre Varga Collection. Aquincum is three stops farther north on the HÉV line.

Vasarely Museum—This museum features two floors of eye-popping, colorful paintings by the founder of Op Art, Victor Vasarely. The exhibition follows his artistic evolution from his youth as a graphic designer to the playful optical illusions he was most famous for. (If this art gets you pondering Rubik's Cube, it may come as no surprise that Ernő Rubik was a professor of mathematics right here in Budapest.) Vasarely, and the movement he pioneered—which was heavy on optical illusions—helped to inspire the trippy styles of the 1960s (600 Ft, covered by Budapest Card, Tue–Sun 10:00–7:30, closed Mon, Szentlélek tér 6, Budapest III, tel. 1/388-7551, www.vasarely.tvn.hu). This museum is immediately on the right as you leave the Árpád híd HÉV station.

Óbuda Main Square (Fő Tér)—If you keep going past the Vasarely Museum and turn right, you enter Óbuda's cute Main Square. The big, yellow building was the Óbuda Town Hall when this was its own city. Today it's still the office of the district mayor. To the right of the Town Hall, you'll see a whimsical, much-photographed statue of women with umbrellas. Replicas of this sculpture, by local artist Imre Varga, decorate the gardens of wealthy summer homes on Lake Balaton. Varga created many of Budapest's distinctive monuments. His museum is just down the street (turn left at the umbrella ladies).

▲Imre Varga Collection (Varga Imre Kiállítóház)—Imre Varga worked from the 1950s through the 1990s. His statues, while occasionally religious, mostly commented on life during communist times, when there were three types of artists: banned, tolerated, and supported. Varga was tolerated. His themes included forced marches and mass graves. One headless statue comes with medallions nailed into his chest. (These medallions were Varga's own, from his pre-communist military service. Anyone with such medallions was persecuted by communists in the 1950s...so Varga disposed of his this way.) Varga actually drops by each Saturday morning at 10:00 to chat with visitors. He speaks English, and, while now in his 80s, he enjoys explaining his art. Don't miss the garden, where you'll see three prostitutes illustrating "the passing of time" (500 Ft, covered by Budapest Card, Tue–Sun 10:00–18:00, closed Mon, Laktanya utca 7, Budapest III, tel. 1/250-0274).

Aquincum Museum—Long before Magyars laid eyes on the Danube, Óbuda was the Roman city of Aquincum. Here you can explore the remains of the 2,000-year-old Roman town and amphitheater. The museum is proud of its centerpiece, a water organ (850 Ft, covered by Budapest Card, May–Sept Tue–Sun 9:00–18:00, closed Mon; Oct and late April Tue–Sun 9:00–17:00, closed Mon; closed Nov–mid-April, Szentendrei út 139, Budapest III, HÉV north to Aquincum stop, tel. 1/250-1650). From the HÉV stop, cross the busy road and turn to the right. Go through the railway underpass, and you'll see the ruins ahead and on the left as you emerge.

▲▲Statue Park (Szoborpark, a.k.a. "Memento Park")

When regimes fall, so do their monuments. Just think of all those statues of Stalin and Lenin—or Saddam Hussein—crashing to the

ground. Throughout Eastern Europe, people couldn't wait to get rid of these reminders of their oppressors. But some clever entrepreneur hoarded Budapest's, and has collected them in a park just southwest of the city— where tourists flock to get a taste of the communist era. Though it can be time-consuming to visit, this collection is worth ▲▲▲ for those fascinated by the Red old days.

Cost, Hours, Location: 1,500 Ft, covered by Budapest Card, daily 10:00–sunset, six miles southwest of city center at the corner of Balatoni út and Szabadka út, Budapest XXII, tel. 1/424-7500, www.szoborpark.hu.

Getting There: The park runs a direct bus from Deák tér in downtown Budapest (where all three Metro lines converge, bus stop is at corner of busy Bajcsy-Zsilinszky út and Harmincad utca, year-round daily at 11:00, July–Aug also at 15:00; round-trip takes 1.75 hours total, including a 40-min visit to the park, 3,950 Ft round-trip, discount with Budapest Card, price includes park entry). The trip by public transportation (explained in ads and brochures you'll see everywhere) is too complicated—I'd skip the park unless you can catch this bus.

Background: Under the communists, creativity was discouraged. Art was acceptable only if it furthered the goals of the state. The only sanctioned art in communist Europe was Social Realism. Aside from a few important figureheads, individuals didn't matter. Everyone was a cog in the machine—strong, stoic, doing their job well and proudly for the good of the people. Individual characteristics and distinguishing features were unimportant; people are represented as automatons serving their nation. Artistic merit was virtually ignored. Most figures are trapped in stiff, unnatural poses that ignore the 3,000 years of artistic evolution since the Egyptians.

❷ **Self-Guided Tour:** As you approach the park, you're greeted by an imposing red-brick **entry facade** featuring three of the Communist All-Stars—Lenin, Marx, and Engels. (They couldn't save the biggest "star" of all, Stalin—he was destroyed in the 1956 Uprising.) Like the rest of the park, this gate is highly conceptual in its design: It looks impressive and monumental...but, like the rotted-out pomp of communism, there's nothing behind it. It's a glossy stage-set with no substance. If you try to go through the main, central part of the gate, you'll run into an always-locked door. Instead, as with the communist system, you have to find another way around (in this case, the smaller gate to the left).

Once inside and past the ticket-window building, notice that the main road takes you confidently toward...a dead end (the brick wall). Once again, as with life under the communists, you'll have to deviate from this main axis to actually accomplish anything. Even so, notice that the six cul-de-sacs branching off the main road all bring you right back to where you started—the futility of communism.

Work your way counterclockwise around the park. Dominating the first cluster of statues (to your right as you enter) is a **giant soldier** holding the Soviet flag. This statue once stood at the base of the Liberation Monument that still overlooks the Danube from Gellért Hill—in honor of the Red Army that saved Budapest from the Nazis. Typical of Social Realist art, this soldier has a clenched fist (symbolizing strength) and a face that shows no emotion. After the fall of communism, some critics wanted the entire monument torn down. As a compromise, they covered it with a sheet for a while to exorcise the communist mojo, then re-unveiled it. To the left of this soldier, see the **two comrades** stiffly shaking hands: the Hungarian worker thrilled to meet the Soviet soldier. Beyond them is a **long wall,** with a triumphant worker breaking through the left end—too busy doing his job to be very excited. (The three big blocks protruding from the wall are for hanging commemorative wreaths.)

In the next set of statues, you'll see a bust of the Bulgarian communist leader **Gregori Dimitrov**—one of communist Hungary's many Soviet Bloc comrades. After the 1956 Uprising, protestors put a noose around this bust's neck, and hanged it from a tree. Next is a full-size statue of Dimitrov, a gift from "the working people of Sofia." (Talk about a white elephant.) At the back of this loop are three blocky portraits. The middle figure is an important symbol of Hungarian communism: **Béla Kun** fought for the Austro-Hungarian Empire in World War I. He was captured by the Red Army, taken to the Soviet Union, and became mysteriously smitten with communism. After proving himself too far left even for Lenin, Kun returned to Hungary in 1918 and formed a Hungarian Communist Party at a time when communism was most definitely not in vogue. We'll see more of Kun later in the park. To the left is one of the park's best-loved, most-photographed, and most artistic statues: **Vladimir Lenin,** in his famous "hailing a cab" pose.

In the final circle of statues on this side, you'll see a rusty pair of **workers' hands** holding a sphere (which was once adorned with a red star). The sphere represents the hard-won ideals of communism, carefully protected by the hands—but also held out for others to appreciate. The **monument to Hungarian soldiers** honors those who fought against Francisco Franco in the Spanish Civil War. Dominating this group is a **communist worker** charging into the future, clutching the Soviet flag. (Budapesters of the time had a different interpretation: a thermal bath attendant running after a customer who'd forgotten his towel.) To the left is a monument to the communist version of the Boy Scouts: the elementary school–age **Little Drummers,** and the older **Pioneers.** While these organizations existed before the communists, they were slowly infiltrated and turned into propaganda machines by the regime. These kids—with their jaunty red and blue neckerchiefs—were sent to camp to be properly raised as good little communists; today, many of them have forgotten the brainwashing, but still have fond memories of the socializing.

Where the main path dead-ends at the wall, it's flanked by statues of two **Soviet officers** who negotiated with the Nazis to end the WWII siege of Budapest. One was killed by a Nazi land mine, while the other was shot under mysterious circumstances as he returned from a successful summit. Both became heroes for the communist cause. Were they killed by wayward Nazi soldiers, as the Soviets explained—or by their own Red Army, to create a pair of convenient martyrs?

Continuing counterclockwise to the back-left circle, you'll see a plundered monument (missing its figures and red star), then a **fallen hero** with arm outstretched, about to fall to the ground—mortally wounded, yet victorious. This monument to "the Martyrs of the Counter-Revolution" commemorates those who died attempting to put down the 1956 Uprising. The long, **white wall** at the back of this section tells quite a story (from left to right): The bullet holes lead up to a jumbled, frightful clutter (reminiscent of

Pablo Picasso's *Guernica*) representing World War II. Then comes the bright light of the Soviet system, and by the end everyone's looking boldly to the future (and enjoying a bountiful crop, to boot).

The next group—which includes a statue of an interior minister made a foot shorter at the bottom when the Iron Curtain fell—is dominated by a dramatic, unusually emotive sculpture by an actual artist, **Imre Varga** (described on page 455). Designed to commemorate the 100th anniversary of Béla Kun's birth, this clever statue accomplishes seemingly contradictory feats. On the one hand, it reinforces the communist message: Under the able leadership of Béla Kun (safely overlooking the fray from above), the crusty, bourgeois old regime of the Hapsburg Empire (on the left, with the umbrellas and fancy clothes) was converted into the workers' fighting force of the Red Army (on the right, with the bayonets). And yet, those silvery civilians in back seem more appealing than the lunging soldiers in front. And notice the lamppost next to Kun: In Hungarian literature, a lamppost is a metaphor for the gallows—reminding viewers that Kun was ultimately executed by the very communist system he espoused, during Stalin's purges of the late 1930s.

The final group of statues, up near the front, all commemorate the key communist holiday of **April 4, 1945,** when the Soviets forced the final Nazi soldier out of Hungary. At the back of the loop, the Hungarian worker and Soviet soldier (who appear to be doing calisthenics) are absurdly rigid even though they're trying to be dynamic. (Even the statues couldn't muster genuine enthusiasm for communist ideals.) The woman holding the palm leaf is reminiscent of the Liberation Monument back on the Danube—who, after all, celebrates the same glorious day. The tall panel nearest the entrance shows a Hungarian woman and a Soviet woman setting free the doves of peace. According to the inscription, "Our freedom and peace is based on the enduring Hungarian-Soviet friendship." (With friends like these....)

As you exit, peruse the gift shop's fun parade of communist kitsch; consider picking up the good English guidebook, the CD of *Communism's Greatest Hits,* and maybe a model of a Trabant (the classic two-stroke commie-mobile). A real Trabant is often parked just inside the gate.

EXPERIENCES

Perhaps more than anything else, Budapest is about enjoying the good life. Two experiences in particular are "must-dos" while in Budapest: soaking in a thermal bath and taking in a fine musical performance.

Budapest's Baths

Splashing and relaxing in Budapest's thermal baths is the city's only ▲▲▲ activity. Though it might sound daunting, bathing with the Magyars is far more accessible than you'd think. Before you go—or if you need more convincing—read the "Taking the Waters" sidebar. The short version: These baths are basically like your hometown swimming pool—except the water is 100 degrees, there are plenty of jets and bubbles to massage away your stress, and you're surrounded by Hungarians in bikinis and Speedos. Overcome your jitters, follow my instructions, and dive in...or miss out on *the* quintessential Budapest experience.

Budapest's two-dozen baths *(fürdő)* were taken over by the communist government, and they're all still owned by the city. The two baths listed here are the best-known, most representative, and most convenient for first-timers: Széchenyi Baths are more casual and popular with locals, while the Gellért Baths are touristy, famous, and genteel. To me, Széchenyi is second to none, but some travelers prefer the Gellért experience. For more information, see www.spasbudapest.com.

▲▲▲ Széchenyi Baths (Széchenyi Fürdő)

To soak with the locals, head for this bath complex—the big, yellow, copper-domed building in the middle of City Park. Széchenyi (SAY-chehn-yee) is the best of Budapest's many bath experiences—and, thanks to a recent renovation, it feels even classier than the famous Gellért Baths. Relax and enjoy some Hungarian good living. Magyars of all shapes and sizes stuff themselves into tiny swimsuits and strut their stuff. Housewives float blissfully  in the warm water. Intellectuals and Speedo-clad elder statesmen stand in chest-high water around chessboards and ponder their next moves. This is Budapest at its best.

Cost: 2,800 Ft for personal changing cabin, 2,400 Ft for locker in gender-segregated locker room, small discount with Budapest Card, cheaper if you arrive within three hours of closing time, price includes thermal baths, swimming pool, and sauna. Couples can share a changing cabin: One person pays the cabin rate, the other pays the locker rate, but both use the same cabin. There's also a wide array of massages and other special treatments—find the English menu in the lobby (make an appointment as you enter). Once inside the complex, you can rent a swimsuit or towel (about 300 Ft each with a 2,000–4,000-Ft deposit). Renting a small safe for your valuables costs 500 Ft.

Hours: Swimming pool (the best part, outdoors) generally open daily 6:00–22:00, thermal bath (less appealing, indoors) daily 6:00–19:00, last entry one hour before closing. The bath hours have changed frequently the last few years, and may unexpectedly revert to shorter hours—until 19:00 or 17:00—in winter.

Location and Entrances: Állatkerti körút 11, Budapest XIV, M1: Széchenyi fürdő. The huge bath complex has three entrances. The busiest one—technically the **"thermal bath entrance"**—is the grand main entry, facing south (roughly towards Vajdahunyad Castle). I avoid this entrance—there's often a line during peak times, and it's a bit more confusing to find your way once inside. Instead, I prefer the **"swimming pool entrance,"** facing the zoo on the other side of the complex—it's faster, has shorter lines, and is open later. A smaller third entrance, to the right as you face the zoo entry (near the Metro stops), provides access to either the thermal bath changing rooms or the swimming pool changing rooms, but can also have long lines.

Entry Procedure: Pay the cashier, and you'll be given a receipt (keep this for later) and a plastic card (red for a changing cabin, blue for a locker). Wave your plastic card over the turnstile to enter the complex. Once inside, rent a towel or swimsuit if needed (do this before you change, as you'll need money). To find the towel/suit rental desk from the swimming pool entrance, take the first staircase down on your right as you enter the hallway to the cabins.

Once you've got your towel/suit, show your plastic card to one of the attendants (who wear white smocks and occasionally speak a few words of English). They'll either direct you to a locker room (remember, men are *férfi* and women are *nöi*) or show you to a changing cabin (again, couples can share a cabin). After changing, find your attendant and have them lock your cabin for you. They'll tell you to remember your cabin number, and give you a little metal disc to put around your wrist to claim your cabin later.

Phew. Now let's have some fun.

Taking the Waters: The bath complex has two parts. Inside is the thermal bath section, a series of mixed-gender indoor pools. The water here is quite hot—most about 40 degrees Celsius, or 104 Fahrenheit—and some of the pools have very green water, supposedly caused by the many healthy minerals. Outside is the swimming pool area, with three pools. Orient yourself with your back to the main building: The pool to the right is for fun (cooler water—30 degrees Celsius, or 86 Fahrenheit, warmer in winter, lots of jets and bubbles, lively and often crowded, includes fun current pool); the pool on the left is for relaxation (warmer water—38 degrees Celsius, or 100 Fahrenheit, mellow atmosphere, a few massage jets, chess); and the main pool in the center is all business

Taking the Waters

American tourists often feel squeamish at the thought of bathing with Speedo-clad, pot-bellied Hungarians. Relax! If you choose the right bath (such as the ones
I've recommended), "taking the waters" is no more challenging than a trip to a water park. I was nervous on my first visit, too. But now I feel like a trip to Hungary just isn't complete without a splish-splash in the bath.

All this fun goes way back. Hungary's Carpathian Basin is a thin crust on top of a lot of hot water. The Romans named their settlement at present-day Budapest "Aquincum"—meaning "abundant waters"—and took advantage of those waters by building many baths. Centuries later, the occupying Ottomans revived the custom. Locals brag that if you poke a hole in the ground anywhere in Hungary, you'll find a hot-water spring. Judging from Budapest, they may be right: The city has 123 natural springs and some two-dozen thermal baths *(fürdő)*. While these spas have traditionally served a medicinal purpose, today Hungary is trying a new angle on its hot water: entertainment. Adventure water parks are springing up all over the country.

While Hungary has several mostly nude, segregated Turkish baths, the places I list are less intimidating: Men and women are usually together, and you can keep your swimsuit on the entire time. (Even at mixed baths, there generally are a few clothing-optional, gender-segregated areas, where locals are likely to be nude—or wearing a *kötény*, or loose-fitting loincloth.)

The baths I recommend have various types of pools. Big pools with cooler water are for serious swimming, while the smaller, hotter thermal baths *(gyógyfürdő, or simply gőz)* are for relaxing, enjoying the jets and current pools, and playing chess. Most pools are marked with the water temperature in Celsius (cooler pools are about 30°C/86°F; warmer pools are closer to 36°C/97°F or 38°C/100°F, about like the hot tub back home; and the hottest are 40°C/104°F...yowtch!). You'll also usually find a steam room, as well as sunbathing areas (which may be segregated and clothing-optional).

The most difficult part of visiting a Hungarian bath is the inevitably complicated entrance procedure. This is one of today's best time-travel experiences to communist Eastern Europe. Expect monolingual staff, a complex payment and locker-rental scheme, and lengthy menus of massages and other treatments. I've explained the specifics for each bath, but be forewarned that they can change from year to year, or even from day to day. Keep track of any receipt or slip of paper you're given, as you may be asked to show it later (for a refund or to get your deposit back). Hang in there, go where people direct you, and enjoy this unique cultural experience. Remember, they're used to tourists—so don't be afraid to act like one. If you can make it through those first few confusing minutes, you'll soon be relaxing like a pro.

While enjoying the baths, you can leave your clothing and other belongings in your locked cabin or locker. Although I've found these to be safe, and bath employees assure me that thefts are rare, it's at your own risk. Another option is to leave valuables in a safe (generally costs 500 Ft, ask when you buy ticket). People have been known to steal rental towels from around the pools to collect the deposit—keep an eye on your towels and any other belongings you bring to the poolside. Many locals bring plastic shopping bags to hold their essentials: towels, leisure reading, and sunscreen.

Note that the jets, bubbles, waves, waterfalls, and whirlpools sometimes take turns running. For example, a current pool runs for 10 minutes, then a series of jets starts up and the current pool stops for 10 minutes, then the current pool starts up again, and so on. If a particularly fun feature of the pool doesn't seem to be working, just give it a few minutes.

If you stay less than a designated time (usually three hours), you will usually get a refund when you leave—if you get a receipt, take it to the ticket window and see if they'll give you anything back.

Here are some useful phrases:

English	Hungarian	Pronounced
Bath	*Fürdő*	FEWR-dur
Men	*Férfi*	FEHR-fee
Women	*Női*	NUR-ee
Changing Cabin	*Kabin*	KAH-been
Locker	*Szekrény*	SEHK-rayn
Ticket Office	*Pénztár*	PAYNZ-tar
Thermal Bath	*Gyógyfürdő, Gőz*	JODGE-fewr-dur, gorz

Please trust me, and take the plunge. If you go into it with an easygoing attitude and a sense of humor, I promise you'll have a blast.

Budapest

(the coolest water, doing laps, swimming cap required). Stairs to saunas are below the doors to the inside pools. You get extra credit for joining the gang in a chess match.

Exit Procedure: If you rented a towel or swimsuit, return it to the desk where you got it, and present your receipt to get your deposit back. Then, as you exit the complex, insert your card into the turnstile and another receipt will print out. If you stayed less than three hours, the receipt will indicate the amount of your refund *(Visszatérítés: Jár* {amount} *Ft)*. Present this and your original receipt at the cashier as you exit to claim your "time-proportional repayment." (If you arrived within three hours of closing time, you already got a discount and won't get a refund.) Then continue your sightseeing...soggy, but relaxed.

▲▲Gellért Baths (Gellért Fürdő)

Using the baths at Gellért Hotel costs more than the Széchenyi Baths, and you won't run into nearly as many locals—this is definitely a more upscale, touristy, spa-like scene. Because most of the hottest pools are in gender-segregated areas, it's not ideal for opposite-sex couples or families who want to spend time together. But if you want a soothing, luxurious bath experience in an elegant setting, this is the place. And if it's fun you're looking for, the Gellért Baths have something Széchenyi doesn't: a huge, deliriously enjoyable wave pool that'll toss you around like a queasy surfer (summer only).

Note that this bath complex is undergoing an extensive renovation, so some pools or locker-room areas will likely be closed over the next few years. This means the entry procedure described below is subject to change (for example, men and women might share one thermal bath—and, of course, stay clothed the whole time).

Cost: 3,100 Ft for personal changing cabin, 2,800 Ft for locker in gender-segregated locker room, cheaper after 16:00, 10 percent discount with Budapest Card. When you buy your ticket, tell them if you want to buy a massage or rent a towel or a swimsuit (600 Ft each with a 4,000-Ft deposit). The 1,000-Ft visitor ticket to see—but not use—the baths is pointless, as you'll see virtually nothing more than what's visible from the ticket window.

Hours and Location: May–Sept daily 6:00–19:00; Oct–April Mon–Fri 6:00–19:00, Sat–Sun 6:00–17:00; last entry 1 hour before closing. It's on the Buda side of the green Liberty Bridge (trams #47 and #49 from Deák tér in Pest, or trams #19 and #41 along the Buda embankment from Víziváros below the castle). The entrance to the baths is under the white dome opposite the bridge (Kelenhegyi út 4–6, Budapest XI, tel. 1/466-6166, ext. 165).

Entry Procedure: As you enter, a generally English-speaking information desk is dead ahead, with cashiers on either side. Beyond the cashier on the left is a window where you can deposit valuables in the safe (500 Ft).

This is the normal procedure (likely to change during the period of renovation): In the summer they sell two different tickets based on which changing area you'll use. With a **thermal bath ticket,** you'll change in a large, gender-segregated area that connects directly to the also-segregated thermal baths (so some people walk nude directly from their cabins to the bath); this means that opposite-sex couples can't share a changing cabin. With a **swimming pool ticket,** you'll go to a mixed area where opposite-sex couples can share a cabin (this area also has gender-segregated locker rooms). Both tickets allow you to move freely between the thermal baths and swimming pool areas once you're inside.

Your entry ticket consists of two parts: a receipt-like slip of paper (which you'll surrender to get into the changing area); and a plastic card used to keep track of how long you're inside (which you'll insert in the turnstile to exit). Keep track of both of these items until you're asked for them.

A dizzying array of **massages** and **treatment options** are also sold at the ticket window. Most are available only with a doctor's note, but anyone can get a "medical massage" (with oil, 2,800 Ft/15 min, 3,800 Ft/30 min) or a "refreshing massage" (with cold soapy water, 2,500 Ft/15 min, 3,500 Ft/30 min). In a different area of the complex, you can also get a "Thai massage"—but you have to arrange that separately.

Pay for everything you want (including massages or towel rentals), enter, and glide through the swanky lobby. Look for the indoor swimming pool on your right, about halfway down the main hall. Just under the window into the pool are stairs leading down to a maze of corridors that take you to the changing rooms (for swimming pool tickets). If you have a thermal bath ticket, the entrances are to the right (women/*női*, closer to the entrance) and the left (men/*férfi*, at the end of the hall) of the swimming pool entrance. If you paid to rent a towel or swimsuit, pick it up from the attendant on your way.

Taking the Waters: Once you've changed, you can spend your time either indoors or out. Outside are several sunbathing areas and a warm thermal pool (up the stairs). But the main attraction out here is the big, unheated wave pool in the center (generally closed Oct–April, weather-dependent). Not for the squeamish, this pool thrashes fun-loving swimmers around like driftwood.

The swells in the deeper area are fun and easy to float on, but the crashing waves at the shallow end are vigorous, if not dangerous. If there are no waves, just wait around a while (you'll hear a garbled message on the loudspeaker five minutes before the tide comes in).

Inside, the central, genteel-feeling hall is home to a cool-water swimming pool (swimming cap required—free loaners available) and a crowded hot-water pool. Off of that pool are doors to the gender-segregated, clothing-optional massage rooms and thermal baths, with nude or loin-clothed bathers stewing in pools at 36 and 38 degrees Celsius (97 and 100 degrees Fahrenheit), as well as cold plunge pools and eucalyptus-scented steam rooms. If you paid for a massage, report to the massage room in this section when you're ready (no appointments—first-come, first-served; you may wait 30 min or more).

Exit Procedure: When you're finished, return your towel and swimsuit to get the slip to reclaim your deposit money (at cashier as you leave). If you were at the bath for less than four hours, you'll also get money back when you leave (if the change isn't automatically dispensed when you go through the exit turnstile, take your plastic card to the cashier).

Budapest Music Scene

Budapest is a great place to catch a good—and inexpensive—concert. In fact, Viennese music lovers often make the three-hour trip here just to take in a fine, cheap opera in a luxurious setting. Options range from a performance at one of the world's great opera houses to light, touristy Hungarian folk concerts. The tourist concerts are the simplest option—you'll see the fliers everywhere—but you owe it to yourself to do a little homework and find something more authentic. The monthly *Budapest Panorama* brochure makes it easy (free, available at the TI)—listing performances with dates, venues, performers, and contact information for getting tickets. Or check schedules online (try www.wherebudapest.hu).

▲▲A Night at the Opera—Consider taking in an opera by one of the best companies in Europe, in one of Europe's loveliest opera houses, for bargain prices. The Hungarian State Opera performs almost nightly, both at the main Opera House (Andrássy út 22, Budapest VI, M1: Opera, see page 445) and in the Erkel Színház theater (not nearly as impressive, near the Keleti train station at Köztársaság tér 30, Budapest VIII, tel. 1/333-0540). Be careful to get a performance in the Opera House—not the Erkel Színház. Note that there are

generally no performances in July and August, when Budapest's outdoor music season is in full swing.

Ticket prices range from 1,000 to 17,000 Ft, but the best music deal in Europe may be the 400-Ft, obstructed-view tickets (easy to get, as they rarely run out—even when other tickets are sold out). If you buy one of these opera-tickets-for-two-bucks, you'll get a seat in one of two places: If you're sitting at the back of one of the boxes along the side of the theater, you can either sit comfortably, and see nothing; or stand and crane your neck to see about half the stage. If you sit on the top of the side balcony, you can stand near the door for a view of the stage. If the seats in front of you don't fill up, scooting up to an empty seat when the show starts is less than a capital offense. Either way, you'll hear every note along with the big spenders. If a full evening of opera is too much for you, you can leave early or come late (but buy your ticket ahead of time, as the box office closes when the performance starts).

To get tickets, your best option is to order online (www.opera .hu or www.jegymester.hu), then print your voucher and pick up the tickets just before the show. Alternatively, you can call or fax the box office at the main Opera House (tel. 1/353-0170, fax 1/311-9017), but then you have to pick up your tickets in person the day before. The easiest option is just to drop by in person and see what's available during your visit (box office open and phone answered Mon–Sat from 11:00 until show time—generally 19:00; Sun open 3 hours before the performance—generally 16:00–19:00, or 10:00–13:00 if there's a matinee). There are often a few tickets available at the door (even if it's supposedly "sold out").

Tourist Concerts—Hungária Koncert offers a wide range of made-for-tourist concerts. These concerts take place in one of two historic venues: the **Budai Vigadó** ("Buda Concert Hall"—on Corvin tér in Víziváros, between Castle Hill and the Danube); or a former casino called the **Duna Palota** ("Danube Palace"—3 long blocks north of Vörösmarty tér in Pest, behind Roosevelt tér and the Chain Bridge at Zrínyi utca 5). The most popular options are Hungarian folk music-and-dance shows by various interchangeable troupes (3,300–5,600 Ft, June–Oct Sun–Fri at 20:00, can be at either theater) and classical "greatest hits" by the Danube Symphony Orchestra (the best group, 6,400–8,900 Ft, discount with Budapest Card, June–Oct Sat at 20:00, always at Duna Palota). Or you can take in an organ concert in the Baroque St. Anne's Church (3,600 Ft, discount with Budapest Card, June–Sept Fri and Sun at 20:00, May Fri only at 20:00, on Batthyány tér at the north end of Víziváros). They also offer dinner cruises on the Danube and in-depth tours of the Jewish Quarter.

While highbrow classical music buffs will want a more serious concert, these shows are crowd-pleasers. If you book direct, you'll get a 10 percent Rick Steves discount on anything they offer (must book in person, by phone, or by email—not valid if you buy your tickets on their website or through your hotel). The main office is in the Danube Palace at Zrínyi utca 5 (daily April–Dec 8:00–21:00, Jan–March 8:00–18:00, open later during concerts, tel. 1/317-2754 or 1/317-1377, http://ticket.info.hu, hunkonc@ticket.info.hu).

SHOPPING

Budapest's single best shopping venue is the Great Market Hall (see page 436). Aside from all the colorful produce downstairs, the upstairs gallery is full of fiercely competitive souvenir vendors (bargaining is the norm). There's also a folk-art market on Castle Hill (near the bus stop at Dísz tér), but it's generally more touristy and a little more expensive. And, while Váci utca has been Budapest's main shopping thoroughfare for generations, today it features the city's highest prices and worst values. At any outdoor market, you're welcome to haggle, but not inside shops.

The most popular souvenir is the quintessential Hungarian spice: **paprika.** Sold in metal cans, linen bags, or porcelain vases— and often accompanied by a tiny wooden scoop—it's a nice way to spice up your cooking with memories of your trip. (But remember that only sealed containers will make it through Customs on your way back home.) For more on paprika, see page 396.

Another popular local item is a hand-embroidered **linen tablecloth.** The colors are often red and green—the national colors of Hungary, of course—but white-on-white designs are also available (and classy). If the stitching is too regular and perfect, it's done by machine, and therefore less valuable.

You'll see **crystal** sold in some shops; it's mostly of Czech origin, but cut in Hungary. Other handicrafts to look for include **chess sets** (most from Transylvania) and **nesting dolls.** While these dolls have more to do with Russia than with Hungary, you'll see just about every modern combination available: from *South Park* characters, to Russian heads of state, to infamous terrorists, to American residents. Tacky...but fun. Fans of communist kitsch can look for cool **T-shirts** that poke fun at that bygone era (but the very best selection is at the Statue Park gift shop—see page 456).

If you're looking for a modern, American-style shopping mall, look no farther than **WestEnd City Center** (daily 8:00–23:00, next door to Nyugati train station at Váci út 1–3, M3: Nyugati pu., www.westend.hu) or **Mammut** ("Mammoth"; Mon–Sat 10:00–21:00, Sun 10:00–18:00, next to Moszkva Square at Lövőház utca 2–6, M2: Moszkva tér, www.mammut.hu).

SLEEPING

Hotels in Budapest are expensive, and generally you get what you pay for. Since my €100 listings are substantially nicer than my €85 listings, I'd spring for the extra expense to have a comfortable home base here. (But if you're on a tight budget, don't overlook the good-value Bellevue B&B and Mária and István.)

The Formula 1 races (one weekend in early Aug) send rates through the roof. September is extremely tight (because of conferences), with October close behind—book as far ahead as possible for those times. Most rates drop 10–25 percent in the off-season (generally Nov–March). Most hotels don't include the 3 percent tourist tax in their rates. Be warned that some big chains—both cheap (Ibis) and expensive (Four Seasons)—also don't include the whopping 20 percent sales tax, which can make your hotel cost nearly a quarter more than you expected. (Independent hotel rates typically do include sales tax.)

If your hotel does not serve (or charges extra for) breakfast, consider eating instead at one of three good cafés I've recommended: Gerlóczy Café (see page 478), Centrál Kávéház (page 478), or Callas (page 484).

Pest

Most travelers find staying in Pest more convenient than sleeping in Buda. Most sights worth seeing are in Pest, which also has a much higher concentration of Metro and tram stops, making it a snap to get around. Pest feels more lively and local than stodgy, touristy Buda, but it's also much more urban—if you don't enjoy big cities,

---

Sleep Code

(€1 = $1.40, 200 Ft = about $1, country code: 36, area code: 1)

S = Single, **D** = Double/Twin, **T** = Triple, **Q** = Quad, **b** = bathroom, **s** = shower only. Unless otherwise noted, breakfast is included and credit cards are accepted. Everyone speaks English, and prices are quoted in euros.

To help you sort easily through these listings, I've divided the rooms into three categories, based on the price for a standard double room with bath:

$$$ **Higher Priced**—Most rooms €100 or more.
$$ **Moderately Priced**—Most rooms between €70–100.
$ **Lower Priced**—Most rooms €70 or less.

sleep in Buda instead. I've arranged my listings by neighborhood, clustered around the most important sightseeing sectors.

Central Pest (Belváros), near Váci utca

Sleeping on the very central and convenient Váci utca comes with overly inflated prices. But these less expensive options—just a block or two off Váci utca—offer some of the best values in Budapest.

$$$ Peregrinus Hotel, overpriced despite its ideal location, has 25 high-ceilinged, spacious, outdated rooms (most of which lack air-conditioning—unusual for this price range). Because it's run by the big ELTE university, many of its guests are visiting professors and lecturers (Sb-€78, Db-€110, extra bed-€30, 20 percent cheaper Nov–March, elevator, free Internet access in lobby and cable Internet in rooms, just off Váci utca at Szerb utca 3, Budapest V; 5-min walk to M3: Kálvin tér, or tram #47 or #49 to Fővám tér; tel. 1/266-4911, fax 1/266-4913, www.peregrinushotel .hu, peregrinushotel@elte.hu).

$$ Gerlóczy Café & Rooms, which also serves good meals (see "Eating," page 478), is the best spot in central Budapest for affordable elegance. The 18 rooms, around a classy old spiral-staircase atrium, recently underwent a thoughtful and stylish renovation. Since this is a brand-new place, prices are likely to increase—but even then, it'll remain a good value for the quality and location (Sb/Db-€80–90, plus €10 per person for required breakfast in the café—which is fine since they serve excellent breakfasts; some restaurant noise on lower floors until 23:00, air-con, elevator, free Wi-Fi, 2 blocks from Váci utca, just off Városház utca at Gerlóczy utca 1, M3: Ferenciek tere, tel. 1/235-0953, www .gerloczy.hu, info@gerloczy.hu).

$$ Leo Panzió is a peaceful oasis with 14 modern rooms in a hulking building that's seen better days. The location is central, the antique elevator is wonderfully rickety, the staff is polite and professional, and the double-paned windows keep out most of the noise from the busy street below (Sb-€73, Db-€89, Tb-€118, extra bed-€29, 15 percent cheaper Nov–March, all rooms have a strange but well-marked little step down in the middle of the room, entirely non-smoking, air-con, free Wi-Fi, Kossuth Lajos utca 2A—dial 58 at the door to call reception, Budapest V, M3: Ferenciek tere, tel. 1/266-9041, tel. & fax 1/266-9042, www.leopanzio.hu, leo @leopanzio.hu).

$$ Kálvin-Ház, a long block up from the Great Market Hall, offers 38 big rooms with old-fashioned furnishings and squeaky parquet floors. The new top-floor rooms have a bit less classic character, but are air-conditioned and tidier than the older rooms (all rooms cost the same: Sb-€70, Db-€95, apartment-€120, extra bed-€20, 15 percent cheaper Nov–March, elevator, free Internet

PEST HOTELS AND RESTAURANTS

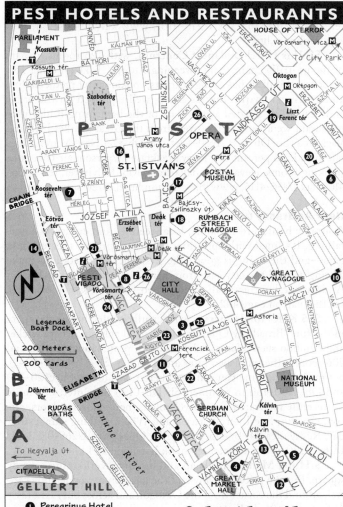

1. Peregrinus Hotel
2. Gerlóczy Café & Rooms
3. Leo Panzió Hotel
4. Kálvin-Ház Hotel
5. Ibis Hotel Budapest Centrum
6. Hotel Queen Mary
7. Four Seasons Gresham Palace
8. Mellow Mood Central Hostel
9. Domino Hostel
10. Marco Polo Hostel
11. Bor La Bor Restaurant
12. Vörös Postakocsi Étterem
13. Café Intenzo
14. Spoon Restaurant
15. Trattoria Toscana & Taverna Dionysos
16. Café Kör
17. Belvárosi Lugas Étterem
18. Duran Szendvics
19. Menza Restaurant
20. Shalimar Restaurant
21. Gerbeaud Café
22. Centrál Kávéház
23. Jégbüfé Snack Bar
24. Historic McDonald's
25. Patyolat G. Laundry
26. Discover Hungary/Yellow Zebra Bike & Internet Access (2)

Budapest

access and Wi-Fi, Gönczy Pál utca 6, Budapest IX, M3: Kálvin tér, tel. 1/216-4365, fax 1/216-4161, www.kalvinhouse.hu, info @kalvinhouse.hu).

$$ Ibis Hotel Budapest Centrum, with 126 rooms, is part of the no-frills chain that's sweeping Europe. Like all other Ibis branches, this place has spongy carpets, cookie-cutter predictability, and utterly no charm. But it's cheap, well-equipped for the price, and beautifully located at the start of the happening Ráday utca restaurant scene, just up the street from the Great Market Hall and Váci utca (Sb/Db-€79 April–Oct, Sb/Db-€65 Nov–March, does not include 23 percent tax, lousy breakfast-€9/person, air-con, non-smoking rooms, elevator, Ráday utca 6, M3: Kálvin tér, tel. 1/456-4100, fax 1/456-4116, www.ibis-centrum.hu, h2078@accor.com).

Near Andrássy út

Andrássy boulevard is handy, local-feeling, and endlessly entertaining. It's lined with appealing cafés, restaurants, theaters, and bars—and the living is good. The frequent Metro stations make getting around the city easy from here. None of these hotels is on Andrássy út, but they're all within a two-block walk. For locations, see the map on page 442.

$$$ K+K Hotel Opera is wonderfully located beside the opera in the fun "Broadway Quarter." It's a regal splurge, where wicker and bamboo seem classy. It has helpful, professional service and 206 rooms. The published rates are sky-high (Sb-€194, Db-€242), but most of the time you can get a better deal (often Sb-€120–140 and Db-€140–160 in summer, Sb/Db-€120 in winter, €25 more for recently renovated "executive" rooms, non-smoking floors, air-con, elevator, free Internet access and Wi-Fi, parking garage-€15/day, Révay utca 24, Budapest VI, M1: Opera, tel. 1/269-0222, fax 1/269-0230, www.kkhotels.com, kk.hotel.opera@kkhotels.hu).

$ Hotel Medosz is cheap and dumpy, overlooking a seedy square. But the prices are low and the location is wonderfully central, around the corner from the Oktogon and across busy Andrássy út from the trendy Franz Liszt Square. Beyond the chilling concrete communist facade and gloomy lobby are 67 rooms—old and uninspired but perfectly adequate, comrade (Sb-€49, Db-€59, €10 cheaper Nov–March, elevator, pay Internet access and Wi-Fi, nearby nightclubs can be noisy—ask for a quieter courtyard room, Jókai tér 9, Budapest VI, M1: Oktogon, tel. 1/374-3000, fax 1/332-4316, www.medoszhotel.hu, info@medoszhotel.hu).

Elsewhere in Pest

These fine values are scattered around central Pest.

$$$ Cotton House is a fun, blast-from-the-past theme hotel. Its 23 retro rooms are fresh and comfy, with 1930s themes; each room is devoted to a different mobster (Al Capone) or old-time performer (Ella Fitzgerald, Elvis Presley, Frank Sinatra). The stylish furnishings are a clever mix of actual old and neo-old (Sb/Db-€100 with shower, €110 with bathtub, €120 with Jacuzzi, 15 percent less Jan–March, air-con, non-smoking rooms, elevator, free Internet access, pay Wi-Fi, some street noise on weekends, close to the Nyugati train station and a few blocks from the Oktogon at Jókai utca 26, Budapest V, M3: Nyugati pu., tel. 1/354-2600, fax 1/354-1341, www.cottonhouse.hu, info@cottonhouse.hu). In the basement is an elaborate jazz club, with a restaurant, cigar room (with a wall of rentable humidor lockers), and oodles of atmosphere. Live ragtime music fills the lower floors almost nightly until 23:00—request a quieter upstairs room if you turn in early.

$$ Hotel Queen Mary (named not for the British monarch, but for the owner's wife) is simple and affordable, with 26 unimaginative but new-feeling rooms. The price is right, but the neighborhood—a block south of the Great Boulevard ring road and two blocks beyond the end of Franz Liszt Square—is dingy and gloomy (though it is central and safe). This place is likely to have rooms when others are full (Sb-€75, Db-€85, Tb-€105, prices soft—ask for discount in slow times, 30 percent cheaper Nov–March, air-con, elevator, free cable Internet, Kertész utca 34, between M1: Oktogon and M2: Blaha Lujza tér, tel. 1/413-3510, fax 1/413-3511, www.hotelqueenmary.hu, info@hotelqueenmary.hu).

$ Mária and István, your chatty Hungarian aunt and uncle, are saving a room for you in their Old World apartment. For warmth and hospitality at youth-hostel prices, consider bunking in one of their two simple, old-fashioned rooms, which share a bathroom. The smaller room is cheaper and quieter; the bigger room gets some street noise on weekends (S-€20–24, D-€30–36, T-€42–48, price depends on size of room and length of stay—longer is cheaper, no breakfast but guests' kitchen, cash only, elevator, Ferenc körút 39, Budapest IX, M3: Ferenc körút, tel. & fax 1/216-0768, www.mariaistvan.hu, mariaistvan@t-online.hu). From the Ferenc körút Metro stop, follow signs for the *Ferenc körút 41–45* exit, bear right up the stairs, and walk straight about a block and a half, looking for #39 (on the left, after the post office). Mária and István also rent two apartments that are two Metro stops farther from the center (Db-€50–56, Tb-€60–66, Qb-€68–80, family apartment, both near M3: Nagyvarad tér).

In Opulence, Facing the Chain Bridge

$$$ Four Seasons Gresham Palace is Budapest's top hotel—and one of its most expensive. Stay here only if money is truly no object. You'll sleep in arguably Budapest's finest Art Nouveau building. Damaged in World War II, the Gresham Palace sat in disrepair for decades. Today it's sparkling from a recent head-to-toe renovation, and every detail in its lavish public spaces and 179 rooms is perfectly in place. Even if you're not sleeping here, dip into the lobby and café to soak in the elegance (non-view Db-€320–450, Danube-view Db-€520–860, prices don't include 23 percent tax—not a typo, air-con, non-smoking rooms, elevator, top-floor spa, Roosevelt tér 5–6, tel. 1/268-6000, fax 1/268-5000, www.fourseasons .com/budapest, budapest.reservations@fourseasons.com).

Mellow Mood Hostels

Budapest's biggest and best-run hostel chain has several good outlets around town. All have slippery rates that depend on the season; you'll get the best deal (save 20–30 percent) if you book in advance online (all are cash only). Mellow Mood also runs several budget hotels around the city, but they're not a good value.

$ Mellow Mood Central Hostel is the main branch, but might close in the future; if it's open, it has 176 beds in 33 bright, cheery, clean rooms, including five twins (prices per person: twin Db-€24–32, T-€17–28, Q-€15–25, bunk in 6-bed dorm-€14–23, in 8-bed dorm-€11–22, includes sheets, towel-500 Ft, no breakfast, pay laundry and Internet access, a block north of Váci utca at Bécsi utca 2, tel. 1/411-1310, fax 1/411-1494, www.mellowmoodhostel .com, sales@mellowmoodhostel.com).

$ Domino Hostel has 146 beds in the best location, on Váci utca near the Great Market Hall (same rates as Mellow Mood, elevator, pay laundry and Internet access, Váci utca 77, enter at Havas utca 6, tel. 1/235-0492, www.dominohostel.com, info @dominohostel.com).

$ Marco Polo Hostel has a few dorm beds and 36 more twin rooms in a less convenient location (slightly higher rates than Mellow Mood, Nyár utca 6, M2: Blaha Lujza tér, tel. 1/413-2555, fax 1/413-6058, www.marcopolohostel.com, sales@marcopolohostel .com).

Buda

Víziváros

The Víziváros neighborhood—or "Water Town"—is the lively part of Buda, squeezed between Castle Hill and the Danube, where fishermen and tanners used to live. Across the river from the Parliament building, it comes with fine views. Víziváros is the most pleasant central area to stay on the Buda side of the Danube. It's expensive and a little less convenient than Pest, but also less urban-feeling.

The following hotels (except the last one) are between the Chain Bridge and Buda's busy Margit körút ring road. Trams #19 and #41 zip along the embankment in either direction. Battyány tér, a few minutes' walk away, is a handy center with lots of res-taurants (see "Eating," page 483), a place to drop off your laundry (Topclean—see "Laundry," page 412), and a Metro stop (M2 line). For a good hangout with Internet access near these hotels, try Soho Coffee Company (see page 484). Each of these places comes with professional, helpful staff.

$$$ Hotel Victoria, with 27 business-class rooms—each with a grand river view—is a fine value. This tall, narrow place (three rooms on each of nine floors) is run with pride and attention to detail. With a friendly staff, it's a winner (Sb-€117, Db-€123, extra bed-€46, 30 percent less Nov–March, air-con, elevator, free sauna, free Internet access and Wi-Fi, reserve €13/day parking garage ahead or park free on street, Bem rakpart 11, Budapest I, tel. 1/457-8080, fax 1/457-8088, www.victoria.hu, victoria@victoria.hu).

$$$ art'otel impresses New York City sophisticates. Every detail of the 165-room art'otel—from the breakfast dishes to the carpets to the good-luck blackbird perched in each room—was designed by American artist Donald Sultan. This big, stylish hotel is a fun, classy splurge (high rack rates, but usually Sb/Db-€109–165 depending on season, figure Sb/Db-€129 in summer, breakfast-€12/person, Danube view-€20 more, bigger "executive" rooms-€30 more, deluxe "art suites"-€60 more, air-con, non-smoking rooms, elevator, free Internet access in business lounge, free sauna and mini-exercise room, Bem rakpart 16–19, Budapest I, tel. 1/487-9487, fax 1/487-9488, www.artotel.hu, budapest@artotel.hu).

$$$ Hotel Astra is quiet, old-fashioned, and well maintained. Its 12 rooms—surrounding a peaceful courtyard—are woody, elegant, and spacious (Sb-€97, Db-€112, sumptuous Sb or Db suite-€139, extra bed-€20, 10 percent less Nov–March, cash only, air-con, pay Wi-Fi, Vám utca 6, Budapest I, tel. 1/214-1906, fax 1/214-1907, www.hotelastra.hu, hotelastra@euroweb.hu).

$$$ Carlton Hotel, with 95 smallish rooms, is all business and no personality. But the location—where the Castle Hill funic-ular meets the Chain Bridge—is handy for getting to both Buda and Pest (Sb-€95, Db-€110, extra bed-€21, prices 20 percent lower Nov–March, non-smoking rooms, elevator, pay Internet access and Wi-Fi, parking garage-€12/day, Apor Péter utca 3, Budapest I, tel. 1/224-0999, fax 1/224-0990, www.carltonhotel.hu, carltonhotel@t-online.hu).

$ Bellevue B&B, hiding in a quiet residential area on the Víziváros hillside just below the Fishermen's Bastion staircase, is easily Budapest's best deal. This gem is run by welcoming retired economists Judit and Lajos Szuhay, who lived in Canada for four years and speak flawless English. The breakfast room and some of the five straightforward, comfortable rooms have views across

Budapest

BUDA HOTELS AND RESTAURANTS

To Moszkva Square, Bus #10 & M VÁRFOK UT.
SZABÓ ILONKA
To 6 MKT. HALL B M Batthyány tér
OSTROM
VÁRFOK UT.
TOLDY FERENC
DONÁTI U.
ISKOLA
VÁM
ST. ANNE'S
VIENNA GATE
MÁTRAY UT.
LOYAS UT.
TÁNCSICS
FRANK
BUDAI VIGADÓ CONCERT HALL
CALVINIST CHURCH
FORTUNA
FISHERMEN'S BASTION
3
ORSZÁGHÁZ
ÚRI
Hess tér 8
5 VÍZI-VÁROS
Corvin tér 2
BEM
12
Danube River
LOGODI U.
9
Szentháromság tér
MATTHIAS CHURCH
HUNYADI JÁNOS
14
1
SZENTHÁR.
7
i
FŐ
ATTILA U.
LOVAS U.
TÁRNOK U.
HUNYADI JÁNOS U.
PONTY
FŐ UTCA
11
Vérmező Park
Bus #10 B
Post
Dísz tér
Bus #16
4
RÁKPART
CHAIN BRIDGE
100 Meters
N
PALOTA
SZ. GYÖRGY
SZINHÁZ U.
Ádám
Clark tér
T
100 Yards
LOGODI U.
Funicular "Sikló"
Tram 19 & 41
ALAGÚT UT.
ATTILA UT.
GELLÉRTHEGY U.
ROYAL PALACE
entrance
LÁNCHID UTCA

❶ Hotel Victoria
❷ art'otel
❸ Hotel Astra
❹ Carlton Hotel
❺ Bellevue B&B
❻ To Hotel Papillon
❼ Burg Hotel
❽ Hilton Budapest
❾ Hotel Kulturinnov

❿ Tabáni Terasz Restaurant
⓫ Brasserie Alexandre Dumas
⓬ Horgásztanya Restaurant
⓭ Batthyány tér Eateries & Topclean Laundry
⓮ Soho Coffee Co. & Internet

VARALJA
TABÁN ❿
To Gellért Hill & Gellért Baths
ATTILA U.

the Danube to the Parliament and Pest. Judit (YOO-deet) and Lajos (LIE-yosh) are generous with travel tips, and will send you detailed directions on how to find their place (let them know what time you're arriving). As this B&B is understandably popular, book ahead (Sb-€48–65, Db-€58–75, price depends on room size and view, 20–30 percent cheaper mid-Oct–mid-April, cash only, non-smoking, air-con, free Internet access and Wi-Fi, Szabó Ilonka utca 15/B, mobile 0630-951-5494 or 0630-370-8678; from the US dial 011-36-30-951-5494 or 011-36-30-370-8678; www.bellevuebudapest.com, judit@bellevuebudapest.com).

$ **Hotel Papillon** is farther north, in a forgettable residential area a 10-minute walk past Moszkva tér. It's a cheery little place with 30 homey, pastel rooms, a garden with a tiny pool, and great prices (Sb-€44, Db-€55, 20 percent more for "superior" room with air-con, 25 percent less Nov–March, tram #4 or #6 from Moszkva tér to Mechwart stop, Rózsahegy utca 3B, tel. 1/212-4750, fax 1/212-4003, www.hotelpapillon.hu, rozsahegy@t-online.hu).

Castle Hill

Romantics often like calling Castle Hill home. The next three hotels share Holy Trinity Square (Szentháromság tér) with Matthias Church. They couldn't be closer to the Castle Hill sights, but they're in a tourist zone—dead at night, and less convenient to Pest than other listings.

$$$ Burg Hotel, with 26 rooms, is simply efficient: concrete, spacious, and comfy, with a professional staff. You'll find more conveniently located hotels for less money elsewhere, but if you simply *must* stay in a modern hotel across the street from Matthias Church, this is it (Sb-€105, Db-€115, Db apartment-€134, extra bed-€39, 10 percent discount with this book unless they're very busy, 35 percent cheaper for 3-night stays, prices 15 percent less Nov–March, no elevator, entirely non-smoking, top-floor rooms are extremely long, pay Internet access, Szentháromság tér 7–8, Budapest I, tel. 1/212-0269, fax 1/212-3970, www.burghotelbudapest .com, hotel.burg@mail.datanet.hu, Lajos).

$$$ Hilton Budapest is a 322-room landmark—the first big Western hotel in town, back in the gloomy days of communism. Today it still offers a complete escape from Hungary and a chance to be surrounded by rich tourists mostly from Japan, Germany, and the United States (rack rates: Sb/Db-€220, you'll usually pay closer to Db-€120 in slower times—a great deal, check for better prices online, best rates are for 3-week advance booking with full nonrefundable prepayment, €30 more for Danube-view rooms, breakfast-€27/person, non-smoking floors, elevator, pay Wi-Fi, Hess András tér 1–3 on Castle Hill next to Matthias Church, tel. 1/889-6600, fax 1/889-6644, www.budapest.hilton.com, reservations.budapest@hilton.com).

$$ Hotel Kulturinnov, run by the Hungarian Culture Foundation and sweetly staffed by Judit, is tucked away in the upper floor of a big building that feels more like a museum than a hotel. The 16 rooms are basic and old-feeling, but it's still a great value for the location (Sb-€64, Db-€80, Tb-€100, extra bed-€20, 25 percent less Nov–March, elevator, free Wi-Fi, through the lobby and upstairs at Szentháromság tér 6, Budapest I, tel. 1/224-8102, fax 1/375-1886, www.mka.hu, hotel@mka.hu).

EATING

Dining in Budapest is surprisingly expensive (by Eastern European standards). With the recent influx of tourists, and the resulting increase in prices, most Budapesters can't afford to eat out in the areas where you'll be spending your time. If you really want to eat local-style, head for the big shopping malls (like the WestEnd City Center near Nyugati train station, or Mammut near Moszkva tér).

Budapest

There, you can truly dine with the Budapesters...at T.G.I. Friday's and McDonald's, just like back home.

In lieu of actual "local" restaurants, I've sniffed out a few good options with an at least partly local clientele—as well as a few memorable, decidedly touristy places that are just plain fun. I've focused on eateries serving traditional Hungarian fare (see page 395), but also included a few international and ethnic alternatives.

Note that some Budapest restaurants add a 10 percent service charge to the bill. This is generally noted on the menu, and appears as a line item after the subtotal on the bill (look for "service," *borravaló*, or *felszolgálási díj*). In these cases, an additional tip is not necessary.

Pest

I've listed these options by neighborhood, for easy reference with your sightseeing.

In Central Pest (Belváros), near Váci utca

When you ask natives about good places to eat on Váci utca, they just roll their eyes. Budapesters know that only rich tourists who don't know better would throw their money away on the relatively bad food and service along this high-profile pedestrian drag. But wander a few blocks off the tourist route, and you'll discover alternatives with fair prices and better food.

Centrál Kávéház, while famous as a grand, old-fashioned café, is also one of Budapest's best spots for a central, characteristic meal. Since it's across the street from the university library, it's popular with students and professors. Choose between the lively, vast downstairs, or the more refined upstairs dining room—both featuring elegant, early-1900s ambience (small but filling 1,500-Ft "Zóna" plates, larger 2,500–3,500-Ft main dishes, read the fun history in the menu, daily 8:00–24:00, Károlyi Mihály utca 9, Budapest V, tel. 1/266-2110).

Gerlóczy Café is more stylish, intimate, and upscale than Centrál Kávéház. Tucked on a peaceful little square next to the giant City Hall, and flanked by gourmet salami and cheese shops, this classy café features international cuisine with several seating options (out on the square, in the coffee-house interior, upstairs in the non-smoking section, or down in the wine cellar). There's a good permanent menu, special themed menus that change every few months, and new specials that they try out each weekend. The clientele is a mix of tourists and upscale-urban Budapesters, including local politicians and actors from several nearby theaters (1,500–2,000-Ft pastas, 1,700–4,000-Ft main dishes, good breakfasts with egg dishes for under 1,000 Ft, excellent fresh-baked pastries and bread, daily 7:00–23:00, 2 blocks from Váci utca, just off Városház utca at Gerlóczy utca 1, tel. 1/235-0953). They rent good rooms, too (see "Sleeping," page 470).

Bor La Bor features traditional, regional, updated Hungarian specialties at reasonable prices in a modern cellar atmosphere (2,000–3,000-Ft main dishes, daily 12:00–24:00, a block north of Váci utca at Veres Pálné utca 7, tel. 1/328-0382).

Great Market Hall: At the far south end of Váci utca, you can eat a quick lunch on the upper floor of the Great Market Hall (Nagyvásárcsarnok). The stalls along the right side of the building offer the lowest prices, lots of choices, a sense of adventure, and the most local atmosphere. Grab a bar stool or you'll stand while you munch. Fakanál Étterem—the glassed-in, sit-down cafeteria above the main entrance—is overpriced and touristy, but decent. Produce and butcher stands line the main floor, and it's easy to miss the big, modern grocery store in the basement (the end nearest Váci utca).

Ráday Utca

Ráday utca is Budapest's "restaurant row." While tourists foolishly blow their budgets a few blocks away on Váci utca, Budapesters hang out at this street's trendy, inventive eateries and pubs (many places serve only drinks). The outdoor seating along here is inviting on a balmy evening. And, while the similar scene at Franz Liszt Square (described on page 481) is becoming more touristy and snooty-upscale, locals still outnumber visitors on Ráday utca. It's worth going out of your way to come here and simply wander, choosing the place that looks best. Just take the M3 Metro line to Kálvin tér Metro stop—a three-minute walk from the Great Market Hall—and stroll south.

While the eateries along here are mostly interchangeable, the most established and respected is **Vörös Postakocsi Étterem** ("Red Mail Coach Restaurant"), serving traditional Hungarian food outside and in the 1930s-nostalgic dining room (2,000–4,000-Ft main dishes, daily 11:30–24:00, Ráday utca 15, tel. 1/217-6756). At the start of Ráday utca, where it meets the busy ring road, you'll find the low-key and also good **Café Intenzo** (daily 10:00–1:00 in the morning, Kálvin tér 9, tel. 1/219-5243).

Danube Promenade

The riverbank facing the castle is lined with hotel restaurants and permanently moored restaurant boats. You'll find bad service, mediocre food, mostly tourists, and sky-high prices...but the atmosphere and people-watching are marvelous.

Spoon, a boat in front of the InterContinental Hotel next to the Chain Bridge, is your best Danube dining option. This hip, upscale place offers pricey, elaborately prepared European and

Asian cuisine (3,000–6,000-Ft main dishes). Choose between a dressy candlelit dining room or outdoor tables above decks. The bathrooms—Budapest's most scenic—are a must, even if you don't have to go. If you're going to pay too much to eat along the river, you might as well do it here (daily 12:00–24:00, often booked for special events—call ahead to be sure it's open and to reserve a riverside table, Vigadó tér, dock #3, tel. 1/411-0933, www.spooncafe.hu).

For a more affordable and more local experience, head a bit farther south, near the green Liberty Bridge. Along the embankment road called Belgrád Rakpart, you'll find a cluster of fun and lively ethnic restaurants (including good Italian at **Trattoria Toscana**, #13, and a mini-Santorini with Greek fare at **Taverna Dionysos**, #16).

Near St. István's Basilica

The area near St. István's Basilica—a few steps from the start of Andrássy út—has been neatly pedestrianized, and several appealing eateries have popped up here recently.

On Sas Utca, in Front of St. István's Basilica: The street called Sas utca, running along the bottom of the grand plaza in front of St. István's, is lined with a handful of trendy, pricey, well-regarded, and somewhat snobby restaurants (such as Mokka and Dio). For something a bit cheaper and better than the others, head for **Café Kör** ("Circle"). This stylish but unpretentious eatery serves up Hungarian and international fare in a tasteful one-room interior and at a few sidewalk tables. Because it's beloved by local foodies, reservations are essential on weekends (2,000–4,000-Ft main dishes, good lunch specials, Mon–Sat 10:00–23:00, closed Sun, Sas utca 17, tel. 1/311-0053).

Behind St. István's Basilica: **Belvárosi Lugas Étterem** is your cheap-and-central, no-frills option. *Lugas* is a Hungarian word for a welcoming garden strewn with grape vines, and the cozy dining room—with a dozen tables of happy eaters—captures that spirit. Or sit at the sidewalk tables outside on busy Bajcsy-Zsilinszky boulevard. The food is typically Hungarian—simple and good (1,000–2,500-Ft main dishes, order starches separately, daily 12:00–23:30, directly behind and across the street from St. István's Basilica at Bajcsy-Zsilinszky út 15, tel. 1/302-5393).

Cheap Sandwiches: **Duran Szendvics**, a cheery little eatery, is reminiscent of Scandinavian open-faced sandwich shops, where a dozen or so tempting little treats are displayed. Two sandwiches and a drink make a quick and healthy meal for about $3 (they'll also box things to go for a classy picnic). Look at the window outside before ordering. This is your chance to try caviar cheaply (sandwiches less than 200 Ft, Mon–Fri 8:00–18:00, Sat 9:00–13:00,

Sun 8:00–12:00; near Postal Museum at the start of Andrássy út; Bajcsy-Zsilinszky út 7, tel. 1/267-9624). Similar places are popping up all over the city.

Franz Liszt Square (Liszt Ferenc Tér)

Franz Liszt Square, a leafy park on the most interesting stretch of Andrássy út, boasts a stylish cluster of pricey, pretentious yuppie restaurants, many with outdoor seating (lively on a summer evening). This is *the* place for Budapesters to see and be seen... but only for the ones who can afford it (most main dishes hover around 2,500–4,000 Ft). Take the Metro to Oktogon and follow your nose.

My favorite Liszt Square eatery, **Menza** (the old communist word for "School Cafeteria"), wins the "Best Design" award. Recycling 1970s furniture and an orange-and-brown color scheme, it's a postmodern parody of an old communist café—half kitschy-retro, half brand-new-feeling. When locals come in here, they can only chuckle and say, "Yep. This is how it was." With tasty and well-priced updated Hungarian cuisine, embroidered leather-bound menus, brisk but efficient service, breezy jazz on the soundtrack, and indoor or outdoor seating, it's a memorable spot (1,400–2,900-Ft main dishes, daily 10:00–24:00, halfway up Andrássy út at Liszt Ferenc tér 2, tel. 1/413-1482, www.menza.co.hu). If you like the Franz Liszt Square scene, you'll find more on Kertész utca beyond the end of the square, and in the "Broadway Quarter" near the Opera House (on Hajós utca and Nagymező utca).

Indian: **Shalimar** hides in a stuffy cellar in a dreary neighborhood two blocks beyond the end of Franz Liszt Square. Everything about this place is unexceptional...except the food. The restaurant—packed with young locals who know they're on to something good—is my number-one place in Eastern Europe for a break from pork and kraut (1,700–2,500-Ft main dishes, daily 12:00–16:00 & 18:00–24:00, reservations smart for dinner, Dob utca 50, tel. 1/352-0297).

Near City Park

These three touristy eateries cluster around the end of the lake behind the Millennium Monument in City Park. All are open for both lunch and dinner. The first one is Budapest's best-known, fanciest splurge; the other two are more reasonable and casual, but still pretty pricey.

Gundel Restaurant has been *the* dining spot for VIPs and celebrities since 1894. The pricey place is an institution—President Bill Clinton ate here. Pope John Paul II didn't, but when his people called out for dinner, they called Gundel. The elegant main room is decorated with fine 19th-century Hungarian paintings and an

Art Deco flair, while the more casual outdoor garden terrace is leafy and delightful. The Hungarian cuisine flirts with sophisticated international influences (4,000–11,000-Ft main courses, 20,000–40,000-Ft fixed-price meals). At lunch, choose from the same pricey à la carte items, or opt for a more affordable fixed-price meal (4,000–5,000 Ft). Sunday brunch, with a different theme each week, is popular here (6,000 Ft, served 11:30–15:00). Reserve ahead for dinner, and request near or far from the live "Gypsy" music (12 percent service charge automatically added to bill, open daily 12:00–15:00 & 18:30–24:00, music nightly, Állatkerti út 2, tel. 1/889-8192, www.gundel.hu). The dress code is formal: Jackets are required for men having dinner in the dining room, but not for lunch, for Sunday brunch, or if you sit outside. (You can borrow a free jacket at the door if you travel like me. Ties and dresses are not required.)

Gundel's **Borvendéglő** ("Wine Cellar") offers similar food in a more casual atmosphere at half the price. With an even more extensive wine list than the main restaurant upstairs, this option is ideal for wine-lovers. In addition to full dinners, including some "home-style" dishes (2,000–5,000 Ft, pricier 7,000–10,000-Ft tasting *menus* with wine pairings), they offer wine-and-cheese-tastings (4 wines-3,000 Ft, 7 wines-4,500 Ft; Mon–Sat 18:00–23:00, closed Sun, downstairs from Gundel at Állatkerti út 2, tel. 1/889-8100).

Robinson, stranded on an island in City Park's lake, is a hip, playful, mellow theme restaurant. With island-castaway ambience and more outdoor seating than indoor, it's made to order for lazing away a sunny afternoon at the park. The upstairs café terrace has a long menu of 1,000-Ft desserts and ice-cream treats, coffee drinks, and light 2,000–2,500-Ft salads and sandwiches (daily in summer 11:00–23:00, terrace closed Oct–April). The downstairs terrace and elegant, glassed-in dining room feature pricey international and Hungarian cuisine (3,000–6,000-Ft main dishes, daily 12:00–16:00 & 18:00–24:00, reserve ahead and ask for lakefront seating, Városligeti tó, tel. 1/422-0222, www.robinsonrestaurant.hu).

Buda

Eateries on Castle Hill are generally overpriced and touristy—as with Váci utca, locals never eat here. Instead, they head down the hill into the Víziváros (Water Town) neighborhood.

Víziváros

My first listing is just beyond the southern tip of Castle Hill, near the Elisabeth Bridge. The rest are in the heart of Víziváros, right between Castle Hill and the river. For specific locations, see the map on page 476.

Tabáni Terasz offers delicious Hungarian food between the castle and the big, white Elisabeth Bridge. The historic 250-year-old building has several seating options: in a cozy, classy drawing-room interior; on a terrace out front; or in the inner courtyard (2,000–4,000-Ft main dishes, daily 12:00–23:00, by the single-spired yellow church at Apród utca 10, tel. 1/201-1086).

Brasserie Alexandre Dumas is an airy, modern, glassy eatery on the ground floor of the French Institute. Since the chef is French and many of its clients are French consulate workers, you know the cuisine is good. At lunch, you can get online for free while you munch on a 1,000–1,500-Ft salad or sandwich, or a 1,500–2,000-Ft fixed-price lunch. At dinner, enjoy 2,000–3,000-Ft French dishes. On a sunny day, sit on their outdoor terrace, with fine river views (Mon–Sat 9:00–23:00, closed Sun, Fő utca 17).

Horgásztanya ("Fishermen's Pub"), with a confused fisherman suspended from the ceiling, is cheaper and more local than most of my listings. Natives go here for reliable, unpretentious Hungarian food (1,500–2,500-Ft main dishes, daily 12:00–23:00, lots of fish on the menu, a block up from Danube at corner of Halász utca and Fő utca, Fő utca 27, Budapest I, tel. 1/212-3780).

Batthyány Tér: This bustling square—the transportation hub for Víziváros—is overlooked by a recently renovated, late-19th-century market hall (today housing a supermarket downstairs and a handy laundry upstairs—see page 412). Several worthwhile, affordable eateries cluster around this square (all open long hours daily). Survey your options before settling in. **Nagyi Palacsintázója** ("Granny's Pancakes")—just to the right of the market hall entrance—serves up cheap and tasty crêpes *(palacsinta)* to a local crowd (300–800-Ft sweet or savory crêpes, convenient 800–1,000-Ft combo-meals, communication can be challenging—ask for English menu, Batthyány tér 5). As you face the market hall, go up the street that runs along its left side (Markovits Iván utca) to reach more good eateries: At the end of the block on the right is **Éden Vegetarian Restaurant,** a self-service, point-and-shoot place (main dishes for less than 1,000 Ft, Mon–Sat 7:00–18:00, closed Sun, tel. 1/375-7575). And around the back side of the market hall is **Bratwursthäusle/Kolbászda,** a fun little beer hall/beer garden with specialties and blue-and-white checkerboard decor from Bavaria. Sit outside, or in the woody interior (1,000-Ft sausages, daily 11:00–23:00, Gyorskocsi utca 6, tel. 1/225-3674).

Cafés and Pastry Shops (Kávéház and Cukrászda)

Budapest once had a thriving café culture, like Vienna's. But realizing that these neighborhood living rooms were breeding grounds for dissidents, the communists closed the cafés or converted them into *eszpresszós* (with uncomfortable stools instead of easy chairs) or *bisztró*s (stand-up fast-food joints with no chairs at all). Today Budapest's café scene is slowly coming back to life. Unless otherwise noted, these places serve only coffee and cakes—not meals.

On Vörösmarty Square: Gerbeaud (zhehr-BOH) isn't just a café—it's a landmark, the most famous restaurant in Budapest. Aside from coffee and pastries, you can also get a sandwich, salad, or other light meals. It's touristy, but central, historic, and great for people-watching (700-Ft coffee drinks, 600–1,000-Ft cakes, 1,500–3,000-Ft salads and sandwiches, daily 9:00–21:00, on Vörösmarty tér, tel. 1/429-9000).

Two Blocks up from Váci utca: Centrál Kávéház and **Gerlóczy Café,** both listed as restaurants under "Eating" (see page 478), nicely recapture Budapest's early-1900s ambience, with elegant cakes and coffees, loaner newspapers, and a management that encourages loitering.

Near Ferenciek tere: Jégbüfé is where Pest urbanites get their quick, cheap, stand-at-a-counter fix of coffee and cakes. And for those feeling nostalgic for the communist days, little has changed here. First, choose what you want at the counter. Then try to explain it to the cashier across the aisle. Finally, take your receipt back to the appropriate part of the counter (figure out the four different zones: coffee, soft drinks, ice cream, cakes), trade your receipt for your goodie, go to the bar, and enjoy it standing up (Mon–Sat 7:00–21:30, Wed until 20:30, Sun 8:00–21:30, Ferenciek tere 10). Now...back to work.

Near the Opera House: The new **Callas** features ideal outdoor seating facing the Opera House, and one of the finest Art Nouveau interiors in town, with gorgeous Jugendstil chandeliers. While their full meals are pricey (2,500–6,000 Ft), this is a wonderful spot on Andrássy út for a coffee break, a tasty dessert, or a surprisingly affordable breakfast (ham and eggs plus coffee for 1,500 Ft, 400–600-Ft pastries, daily 8:00–24:00, Andrássy út 20, tel. 1/354-0954). Across the street and a block toward the Oktogon, **Művész Kávéház** is a classic coffeehouse with 19th-century elegance, a hoity-toity high-ceilinged interior, outdoor seating on Andrássy út, and a wide variety of cakes (200–500-Ft cakes, daily 9:00–23:45, Andrássy út 29, tel. 1/352-1337).

In Buda's Víziváros Neighborhood: Soho Coffee Company is a taste of Seattle with a Hungarian accent, combining good American-style lattes, cozy stay-awhile atmosphere, Internet access (500 Ft/hr), and a jazz soundtrack (Mon–Fri 8:00–21:00, Sat–Sun 9:00–21:00, Fő utca 23).

TRANSPORTATION CONNECTIONS

Budapest has three main stations (*pályaudvar,* or *pu.* for short): Keleti (Eastern), Nyugati (Western), and Déli (Southern). There's no telling which station each train will use, especially since it can change from year to year—always confirm carefully which station your train leaves from. For general rail information in Hungary, call 1/461-5400; for information about international trains, call 1/461-5500.

From Budapest by Train to: Vienna (that's *Bécs* in Hungarian, 6/day direct, 3 hrs), **Bratislava** (that's *Pozsony* in Hungarian, 4/day direct, more with transfers, 2.25–4 hrs), **Prague** (every 2 hours, 7–8.5 hrs, 1 direct night train, 9 hrs), **Kraków** (1 direct night train/day with early arrival in Kraków, 11 hrs—for details, see page 407; otherwise transfer in Katowice, Poland, or Břeclav, Czech Republic; 9–10 hrs), **Ljubljana** (2/day direct, 8–9 hrs, no convenient night train), **Munich** (1/day direct, 7.5 hrs; plus 1 direct night train/day, 10 hrs; otherwise transfer in Regensburg, Germany, or Vienna), **Berlin** (3/day direct, 13 hrs; plus 1 direct night train/day, 14 hrs), **Zagreb** (2/day direct, 5 or 7 hrs), **Eger** (5/day direct, 2.5 hrs, more with transfer in Füzesabony), **Szentendre** (4–7/hr, 40 min on suburban HÉV train, leaves from Batthyány tér), **Visegrád** (trains arrive at Nagymaros-Visegrád station, across the river—take shuttle boat to Visegrád; hourly, 1 hr), and **Esztergom** (hourly, 1.5 hrs). Note that Nagymaros (the Visegrád station) and Esztergom are on opposite sides of the river—and on different train lines.

By Boat: In the summer, Mahart runs daily high-speed hydrofoils up the Danube to Vienna. While this is not particularly scenic, and slower than the train, it's a fun alternative for nautical types. The boat leaves Budapest mid-April–Oct daily at 9:00 and arrives in Vienna at 15:20 (Vienna to Budapest: 9:00–14:30). The trip costs €79 one-way. On any of these boats, you can also stop in the Slovak capital, Bratislava. To confirm times and prices, and to buy tickets, contact Mahart (Budapest tel. 1/484-4010, www.mahartpassnave.hu).

Budapest

THE DANUBE BEND

Dunakanyar

The Danube, which begins as a trickle in Germany's Black Forest, becomes the Mississippi River of Central Europe as it flows east through Vienna, then makes a sweeping right turn—called the Danube Bend—south towards Budapest, Belgrade, and the Black Sea. Three river towns north of Budapest on the Danube Bend offer a convenient day-trip getaway for urbanites who want to commune with nature.

Hungarians sunbathe and swim along the banks of the Danube, or hike in the rugged hills that rise up from the river. This is also one of Hungary's most historic stretches—for centuries, Hungarian kings ruled not from Buda or Pest, but from Visegrád and Esztergom. Closest to Budapest is Szentendre, whose colorful, storybook-cute Baroque center is packed with tourists. The ruins of a mighty castle high on a hill watch over the town of Visegrád. Esztergom, birthplace of Hungary's first Christian king, has the country's biggest and most important church. All of this is within a one-hour drive of the capital, and also reachable (up to a point) by public transportation.

Planning Your Time

Budapest itself has several days' worth of sightseeing, and Eger is the most satisfying side-trip (see next chapter). But with plenty of time and a desire to see more of Hungary, the Danube Bend deserves a day. Szentendre is the easiest Danube Bend destination—just a quick suburban-train (HÉV) ride away, it can be done in just a few hours. Visegrád and Esztergom are more difficult to reach by public transportation; both require a substantial walk from the train or bus stop to the town's major sight.

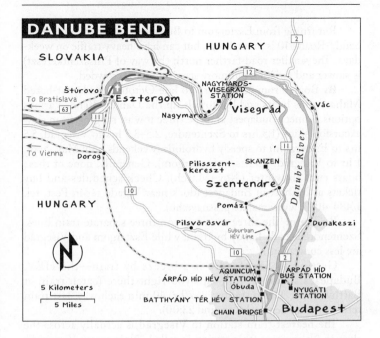

Don't try to see all three towns in one day by public trans-portation—focus on one or two. Take a tour, rent a car, or hire a driver to see all three (for recommended drivers, see "Drivers" on page 413 of the Budapest chapter). With a car, try this one-day plan: 9:00–Leave Budapest; 9:30–Arrive at Szentendre and see the town; 12:00–Leave Szentendre; 12:30–Lunch in Visegrád; 13:30–Tour Visegrád Royal Palace and Citadel; 15:30–Leave Visegrád, 16:00–Visit Esztergom Basilica, 17:00–Head back to Budapest. With extra time, add a visit to the Hungarian Open-Air Folk Museum ("Skanzen") near Szentendre.

If you're driving between Budapest and Vienna (or Bratislava), the Danube Bend towns are a fine way to break up the journey, but seeing all three en route makes for a very long day. Again, choose one or two.

Getting Around the Danube Bend

Going north from Budapest, the three towns line up along the same road on the west side of the Danube—Szentendre, Visegrád, Esztergom—each spaced about 15 miles apart.

By Car: It couldn't be easier. Get on road #11 going north out of Buda, which will take you through each of the three towns—the road bends with the Danube. As you approach Szentendre, watch for signs for *Centrum Szentendre* to branch off to the right, toward the old center and the river promenade.

Returning from Esztergom to Budapest, consider "cutting the bend." Road #10 is most direct, but can have heavy traffic on weekdays. The smaller road farther north (by way of Pilisszentkereszt) is slower and twistier, but more scenic and less crowded.

By Boat: From early April to late October, Budapest-based Mahart runs boats and hydrofoils up the Danube Bend. Various options connect Budapest and the three towns, ranging from slow excursion ships (1.5 hrs to Szentendre, 2.5–3.5 hrs to Visegrád, 5.5 hrs to Esztergom) to speedy hydrofoils (weekends only May–Sept, 1 hr to Visegrád, 1.5 hrs to Esztergom). Generally, none of these boats runs in winter (Nov–March). Check schedules and buy tickets at Mahart in Budapest (dock near Vigadó tér in Pest, tel. 1/484-4010, www.mahartpassnave.hu).

By Train: The three towns are on three separate train lines. Szentendre is truly handy by train, while Esztergom and Visegrád are less convenient.

Getting to **Szentendre** is a breeze by train—the HÉV, Budapest's suburban rail, zips you right there (catch train at Batthyány tér Metro station, 4–7/hr, 40 min each way, last train returns from Szentendre around 23:00).

The nearest train station to **Visegrád** is actually across the river in Nagymaros (this station is called "Nagymaros-Visegrád"; don't get off at the station called simply "Nagymaros"). From the station, you'll walk five minutes to the river and take a ferry across to Visegrád (see "Arrival in Visegrád," page 492). Trains run hourly between Nagymaros-Visegrád and Nyugati Station in Budapest (1 hr).

To **Esztergom,** trains run hourly from Budapest's Nyugati Station (1.5 hrs), but the Esztergom train station is a 45-minute walk from the basilica.

By Bus: Buses are the best way to hop between the three towns. They're as quick as the train if you're coming from Budapest, but can be standing-room only. All buses to the Danube Bend leave from Budapest's Árpád híd bus station (near the M3 Metro station of the same name). There are two main routes. The river route (roughly hourly, more frequent during weekday rush hours) runs from Budapest along the Danube through Szentendre (30 min) and Visegrád (80 min), then past Esztergom Basilica to the Esztergom bus station (2 hrs). The inland route goes over the hills and through the town of Piliscsaba on the way to the Esztergom bus station (every 15–30 min, 80 min, last bus back leaves Esztergom 22:00). Buses make many stops en route, so you'll need to pay attention for your stop (ask driver or other passengers for help).

By Tour from Budapest: If you want to see all three towns in one day, don't have a car, and don't want to shell out for a private driver, a bus tour is the most convenient way to go. All of the companies are about the same (all three towns in 9–10 hrs, including lunch and shopping stops, plus return by boat, for around 18,000 Ft); look for fliers at the TI or in your hotel's lobby.

Szentendre

The old town of Szentendre (SEHN-tehn-dreh, "St. Andrew" in English, pop. 23,000) rises gently from the Danube, a postcard-pretty village with a twisty Mediterranean street plan filled with Austrian Baroque houses. Szentendre's old center rivals Budapest's Castle Hill as the most touristy spot in Hungary. It promises a taste of Hungarian village life without having to stray far from Budapest...but it sometimes feels like too many people had the same idea.

In addition to attracting tourists, Szentendre is also where Budapesters bring their wives or girlfriends for that special weekend lunch. The town has a long tradition as an artists' colony, and it still has more than its share of museums and galleries. Venture off the souvenir-choked, tourist-clogged main streets and you'll soon have quiet back lanes under colorful Baroque steeples all to yourself.

Tourist Information

The TI is along the tourist route between the station and the main square (Dumtsa Jenő utca 22, just by the stream, tel. 26/317-965, www.szentendre.hu).

Arrival in Szentendre

The combined **train/HÉV and bus station** is at the southern edge of town. To reach the town center from the station, go through the pedestrian underpass at the head of the train tracks. This funnels you onto the small Kossuth Lajos utca, which leads in 10 minutes to the main square. (A handy map of town is posted by the head of the tracks.) Some **boats** arrive right near the main square (including a convenient summer express boat from Budapest), but most come to a pier about a 15-minute walk north of the center. After you get off the boat, take the first path to your left; stay on this, and it'll lead you straight into town.

SIGHTS

▲**Main Square (Fő Tér)**—Szentendre's top sight is the town itself. Start at the main square, Fő tér. Take a close look at the cross, erected in 1763 to give thanks for surviving the plague. Notice the Cyrillic lettering. After the Ottomans were forced out of Hungary, this town was rebuilt primarily by Serbs who had fled those same Ottomans down south. Look at the very narrow alleyways around the square. Mediterranean towns often have walls close together to create shade in the hot sun. Even though Hungary has a milder climate, old habits die hard: The Serbs built the town in that style anyway.

Various minor sights and museums line the lanes that branch off this square:

Just up Alkotmány utca from the square, the tallest of Szentendre's church spires belongs to the red-painted **Serbian Orthodox cathedral,** with a fine iconostasis (partition with icons) inside, and an icon collection in the attached museum (500 Ft, May–Sept Tue–Sun 10:00–18:00, closed Mon and Oct–April).

Leave the square on Görög utca and take your first right to find the **Margaret Kovács Museum** (Kovács Margit Múzeum), dedicated to a local artist (1902–1977) famous for whimsical, wide-eyed pottery sculptures based on Hungarian folktales and biblical themes (700 Ft, Tue–Sun 9:00–17:00, later in peak season, closed Mon, Vastagh György utca 1).

Between the square and the TI, you'll find the **Marzipan Museum**—a candy and ice-cream store whose upper floor displays marzipan models of the Hungarian Parliament, the Turul bird, the Muppets, and much more. It's fun for kids, but skippable for adults (shop free, upper floor 400 Ft, daily April–Oct 9:00–19:00, Nov–March 10:00–18:00, Dumtsa Jenő utca 12, tel. 26/311-931).

Enjoy a stroll through town. Head off to the back streets (try the hill behind the square) and you'll be surprised at how quickly you find yourself alone with Szentendre.

▲**Hungarian Open-Air Folk Museum (Szabadtéri Néprajzi Múzeum, a.k.a. Skanzen)**—Three miles northwest of Szentendre is an open-air museum featuring examples of traditional Hungarian architecture from all over the country. As with similar museums throughout Europe, these aren't replicas—each building was taken apart at its original location, transported piece by piece, and reassembled here. The museum is huge and spread out, so a thorough visit could take several hours. The admission price includes a map in English, and the museum shop sells a more comprehensive English guidebook (1,000–1,200 Ft depending on special exhibits, April–Oct Tue–Sun 9:00–17:00, closed Mon and Nov–March, last entry 30 min before closing, Sztaravodai út, tel. 26/502-500, www.skanzen.hu).

Buses from the Szentendre station leave for Skanzen every 60–90 minutes (departs from platform 7, 12-min trip, no buses 12:00–14:00 on weekends). A **taxi** to the museum should cost no more than 2,000 Ft; the TI can call one for you.

SLEEPING

(€1 = $1.40, 200 Ft = about $1, country code: 36, area code: 26)
In recent years, the delightful little burg of Szentendre has become a bedroom community for nearby Budapest. I don't advise staying here if Budapest is your main interest—it takes too long to get into the city. But if you must stay here, these two places rent acceptable second-story rooms along the Danube embankment just north of the center.

Corner Panzió has six cozy, woody rooms. Prices rise in the summer, when they turn on the air-conditioning (June–Sept: Sb/Db-€40, breakfast-€4; Oct–May: Sb/Db-€30, breakfast-€2; cash only, Dunakorzó 4, tel. & fax 26/301-524, www.radoczy.hu, nikov@freemail.hu).

Centrum Panzió has eight pleasant-enough rooms with a dark red color scheme (Sb-€45, Db-€50–55, includes breakfast, cash only, air-con, Bogdányi utca 15, at corner of Dunakorzó, tel. & fax 26/302-500, mobile 0620-482-1575, www.hotelcentrum.hu, hotel.centrum@t-online.hu).

Visegrád

Visegrád (VEE-sheh-grahd, Slavic for "High Castle," pop. 1,600) is a small village next to the remains of two major-league castles: a hilltop citadel and a royal riverside palace.

The Romans were the first to fortify the steep hill overlooking the river. Later, when Károly Róbert (Charles Robert), from the French Anjou dynasty, became Hungary's first non-Magyar king in 1323, he was so unpopular with the nobles in Buda that he had to set up court in Visegrád, where he built a new residential palace down closer to the Danube. Later, King Mátyás Corvinus— notorious for his penchant for Renaissance excess—ruled from Buda but made Visegrád his summer home, and turned the riverside palace into what some called a "paradise on earth." Mátyás knew how to party; during his time here, red marble fountains flowed with wine.

In memory of these grand times, **Hotel Visegrád** today runs a Renaissance-themed restaurant, with period cookware, food, costumed waitstaff, and live lute music—just the spot for Danube Bend tour groups (can't miss it, by the palace).

Today, both citadel and palace are but a shadow of their former splendor. The citadel was left to crumble after the Hapsburg reoccupation of Hungary in 1686, while the palace was covered by a mudslide during the Ottoman occupation, and is still being excavated. The citadel is more interesting, but difficult to reach by public transport. Non-drivers who don't want to make the steep hike to the citadel, and are in too much of a hurry to sort through the taxi and bus options, should skip this town.

ORIENTATION

The town of Visegrád is basically a wide spot in the riverside road, squeezed between the hills and the riverbank. At Visegrád's main intersection (coming from Szentendre/Budapest), the cross road leads to the left through the heart of the village, then hairpins up the hills to the citadel. To the right is the dock for the ferry to Nagymaros (home to the closest train station, called Nagymaros-Visegrád—see "Arrival in Visegrád").

The town has two sights. The less interesting riverside Royal Palace is a 15-minute walk downriver (towards Szentendre/Budapest) from the village center. The hilltop citadel, high above the village, is the focal point of a larger recreational area best explored by car.

Tourist Information

The **Visegrád Tours** travel agency at the village crossroads is not an official TI, but does have transport schedules posted in the window, sells maps, and hands out a few free leaflets (daily April–Oct 8:00–17:30, Nov–March 10:00–16:00, Rév utca 15, tel. 26/398-160). For more information on Visegrád, see www.visegrad.hu.

Arrival in Visegrád

Train travelers arrive across the river at the Nagymaros-Visegrád station (don't get off at the station called simply "Nagymaros"). Walk five minutes to the river and catch the ferry to Visegrád, which lands near the village's main crossroads (hourly, usually in sync with the train, last ferry around 20:30). Visegrád's most convenient **bus stop** is at the main crossroads, but there's also a stop a little downstream, by the river boat dock. This **dock,** near the Royal Palace and Hotel Visegrád, is where boats from Budapest stop. To reach the village center from the dock, follow the paved riverside footpath 15 minutes upriver (toward Esztergom).

SIGHTS

▲**Visegrád Citadel (Fellegvár)**—The remains of Visegrád's hilltop citadel are fun to explore. Scramble across the ramparts, try your hand with a bow and arrow, or pose with a bird of prey perched on your arm. See fun wax sculptures enjoying a medieval feast—and demonstrating the collection of torture devices. Only a few exhibits have English labels, but you can borrow the English

audioguide. At the top, you have commanding views over the Danube Bend—which, of course, is exactly why they built it here (1,000 Ft, mid-March–mid-Oct daily 10:00–18:00; mid-Oct–mid-March Sat–Sun 10:00–16:00 in good weather only, usually closed Mon–Fri; last entry 30 min before closing, tel. 26/398-101).

Around the citadel is a **recreational area** that includes three restaurants, a picnic area, a luge and toboggan run, a network of hiking paths, a Waldorf school, and a children's nature education center and campground. By the luge run and walkable from the citadel, the **Nagyvillám restaurant** is elegant, with breathtaking views from the best tables (April–Oct daily 12:00–22:00, closed Nov–March, tel. 26/398-070). A bit farther away, the simpler **Mogyoróhegy restaurant** is in an early building by Organic architecture pioneer Imre Makovecz, who also designed the striking school gymnasium in Visegrád village—white and brown, with a row of 12 spikes on the roof (restaurant open mid-April–Sept daily 9:00–20:00, closed Oct–mid-April, tel. 26/398-237; for more on Makovecz, see page 509). Only drivers can reach the **picnic area** (called Telgárthy-rét), in a shady valley with paths and waterfalls.

Getting There: To **drive** to the citadel, simply follow *Fellegvár* signs down the village's main street and up into the hills. To get to the citadel from the town center without a car, you have three options:

1. **Hike.** Buy a map at the Visegrád Tours office and figure on 40 steep minutes from the village center.

2. Take the **taxi service** called "City Bus." The minivan trip up and back costs 2,000 Ft total, no matter how many people ride along (ask at Visegrád Tours or call 26/397-372).

3. Take the **public bus** (200 Ft, April–Sept only, 2/day, catch from bus stop on Danube side of main road at the crossroads, generally departs around 12:28 and 15:28 or 1 min earlier at Royal Palace, reconfirm schedules in advance; this bus comes from Szentendre, where it departs about 45 min earlier).

Royal Palace (Király Palota)—Under King Mátyás Corvinus, this riverside ruin was one of Europe's most elaborate Renaissance palaces. During the Ottoman occupation, it was deserted and eventually buried by a mudslide. For generations, the palace's existence faded into legend, so its rediscovery in 1934 was a surprise. Today, the partially excavated remains are tourable; unfortunately, there's no English-language guidebook. Keep your eye out for the red marble fountain, which spouted wine for parties (500 Ft; mid-April–mid-Oct Tue–Sun 9:00–18:00, closed Mon; mid-Oct–mid-April Tue–Sun 9:00–16:00, closed Mon; tel. 26/398-026, www.visegradmuzeum.hu).

Esztergom

Esztergom (EHS-tehr-gohm, pop. 29,000) is an unassuming town with a big Suzuki factory. You'd never guess it was the first capital of Hungary—until you see the towering 19th-century Esztergom Basilica, built on the site where István (Stephen) I, Hungary's first Christian king, was crowned in A.D. 1000.

Arrival in Esztergom

Esztergom's **boat dock** is more convenient to the basilica than the bus or train stations are (can't miss the basilica as you disembark—hike on up). If arriving by **bus** from Visegrád, get off by the basilica, not at the bus station. (Buses taking the inland route from Budapest via Piliscsaba do not pass the basilica.) To reach the basilica on foot from the **train station,** allow at least 45 minutes. Continue in the same direction as the train tracks, and when the street forks, go straight along the residential Ady Endre utca. After a few minutes, you'll pass the bus station, from which it's 30 minutes farther to the basilica. Local buses run between the train station and the basilica roughly hourly. On Wednesdays and Fridays, an open-air market livens up the street between the bus station and the center.

If you happen to be on your way to Bratislava, there is also a handy train station across the river in **Štúrovo, Slovakia** (cross the border on foot as you cross the bridge).

SIGHTS

▲▲Esztergom Basilica (Esztergomi Bazilika)

This basilica commemorates Hungary's entry into the fold of Western Christendom. It tops a hill a steep hike up from the center of town and the boat dock. The hill was once strongly fortified, and some ruins of its castle survive (housing a mediocre museum). The Neoclassical basilica, completed in 1869, was built on top of these remains. With a 330-foot-tall dome, this is the biggest church in Hungary. St. István was born in Esztergom, and on Christmas Day

Cardinal József Mindszenty
(1892–1975)

Mindszenty was a Catholic Church leader who spoke out aggressively against the communist government. In 1948, the communists arrested him and tortured him for 39 days. He was imprisoned in Budapest until the 1956 Uprising, when he was freed and took refuge in the US Embassy. There he stayed for 15 years, unable to leave for fear of being captured. (Many Catholic Americans remember praying for Cardinal Mindszenty every day when they were kids.) In 1971, he agreed to step down from his position, then fled to Austria.

On his deathbed in 1975, Mindszenty said that he did not want his body returned to Hungary as long as there was a single Russian soldier still stationed there. As the Iron Curtain was falling in 1989, Mindszenty emerged as an important hero to post-communist Hungarians, who wanted to bring his remains back to his homeland. But Mindszenty's secretary, in accordance with the Cardinal's final wishes, literally locked himself to the coffin—refusing to let the body be transported as long as any Soviet soldier remained in Hungary. In May 1991, when only a few Russians were still in Hungary, Mindszenty's remains were finally brought to the crypt in the Esztergom Basilica.

in the year 1000—shortly after marrying the daughter of the king of Bavaria and accepting Christianity—he was crowned here by a representative of the Pope (for more on St. István, see page 428).

Enter through the side door, which is on the left as you face the front of the basilica (free, daily 6:00–18:00). In the foyer, the stairway leading down to the right takes you to the crypt housing the remains of Cardinal József Mindszenty, revered for standing up to the communist government (300 Ft, daily 9:00–16:30, last entry 15 min before closing). The stairway leading up goes to the church tower (500 Ft).

Enter the cavernous **nave.** There are plenty of fancy tour-guide stats about this church—for example, the altarpiece supposedly has the biggest single-canvas painting in the world. But mostly, the sheer size of the church is what impresses visitors.

As you face the altar, find the chapel on the left before the transept. This Renaissance **Bakócz Chapel** actually predates the basilica by 350 years. When the basilica was built, they disassembled the chapel into 1,600 pieces and rebuilt it inside the new structure. The heads around the chapel's altar were defaced by the Muslim Ottomans, who believed that only God—not sculptors—can create man.

Esztergom

The **treasury** is to the right of the main altar (600 Ft, daily 9:00–16:30). Though the collection is standard ecclesiastical stuff, there are some interesting models inside the entry: a big one showing off the even more ambitious original plans for the basilica complex; smaller ones of the frames of the basilica's wooden nave and metal dome; and yet another showing what Esztergom looked like in the early 16th century (notice the more modest church that stood where this basilica is today).

When you're finished in the basilica, head around to the back for a **Danube overview.** That's Štúrovo, Slovakia, across the river. The bridge connecting them was destroyed in World War II and rebuilt only recently. Before its reconstruction, no bridges spanned the Danube between Budapest and Bratislava.

Eating: A huge restaurant catering to tour groups is built into the fortifications underneath the basilica (enter from bus parking lot). On Batthyány Lajos utca, a block into the residential neighborhood across the street, are two smaller restaurants with garden seating: the **Szent Tamás-hegyi Vendeglő** and the more expensive **Csülök Csárda.**

EGER

You've probably never heard of the enchanting Back Door town of Eger (EH-gehr). It's a mid-sized city (pop. 70,000) in northern Hungary, the seat of a bishop and home to a small teacher-training college. Hungarians think proudly of Eger as the town that, against all odds, successfully held off the Ottoman advance into Europe in 1552. This stirring history makes Eger the mecca of Hungarian school field trips. If the town is known internationally for anything, it's for the surrounding wine region (its best-known red wine is Bull's Blood, or Egri Bikavér).

But don't let its lack of fame keep you away—in fact, that's part of Eger's charm. Rather than growing jaded from floods of American tourists, Egerites go about their daily routines amidst lovely Baroque buildings, watched over by one of Hungary's most important castles. Everything in Eger is painted with vibrant colors, and even the communist apartment blocks seem quaint. It all comes together to make Eger an ideal introduction to small-town Hungary.

Planning Your Time

Mellow Eger is just the spot to catch your breath in the middle of an intense itinerary. The town is worth a relaxing day on a trip between Kraków and Budapest, or as a side-trip from Budapest (possible in a day, but better as an overnight). The sights are few but fun, the ambience is great, and strolling is a must.

A perfect day in Eger begins with a browse through the colorful market and a low-key ramble on the castle ramparts. Then head to the college building called the Lyceum to visit the library and astronomy museum, and climb up to the thrillingly low-tech camera obscura. Take in the 11:30 organ concert in the cathedral across the street from the Lyceum (mid-May–mid-Oct only). In the afternoon, unwind on the square or, better yet, at the thermal bath. If you need more to do, consider a drive into the countryside (including visits to local vintners—get details at TI). Round out your day with dinner on Little Dobó Square, or a visit to Eger's touristy wine caves in the Sirens' Valley.

ORIENTATION

(area code: 36)
Eger Castle sits at the top of the town, hovering over Dobó Square (Dobó István tér). This main square is divided in half by the Eger Creek, which bisects the town. Two blocks west of Dobó Square is the main pedestrian drag, Széchenyi utca, where you'll find the Lyceum and the cathedral. A few blocks due south from the castle (follow Eger Creek) are Eger's various spas and baths.

Tourist Information

Eger's on-the-ball, eager-to-please TI (TourInform) is the most efficient place to get any Eger question answered. They give out a free brochure and town map, as well as piles of other brochures about the city and region. They can't book rooms, but they can help you find one—or anything else you're looking for (mid-June–mid-Sept Mon–Fri 9:00–18:00, Sat–Sun 9:00–13:00; mid-Sept–mid-June Mon–Fri 9:00–17:00, Sat 9:00–13:00, closed Sun; Bajcsy-Zsilinszky utca 9, tel. 36/517-715, www.eger.hu). You can also get online here (30 min/200 Ft).

Arrival in Eger

By Train: Eger's tiny train station is a 20-minute walk south of the center. The closest ATM is at the Spar grocery store just up the street (turn left out of station, walk about 100 yards, and look for red-and-white supermarket on your right; ATM is around front). There's no official baggage storage, but sometimes workers at the train station might be able to hold a bag for you if you ask sweetly.

A **taxi** into the center will cost you 1,000–1,400 Ft. Even in little Eger, it's always best to take a taxi with a company name and number posted.

To catch the **bus** toward the center, go straight out of the station, and when the road you're on veers right, cross it to get to the bus stop (to the left) on the busier road above it. Bus #11, #12, or #14 cut about 10 minutes off the walk into town (200 Ft, buy ticket from driver; or 130 Ft if you buy it inside train station—ask for *helyijárat buszjegy*). Get off the bus when you see the big, yellow cathedral.

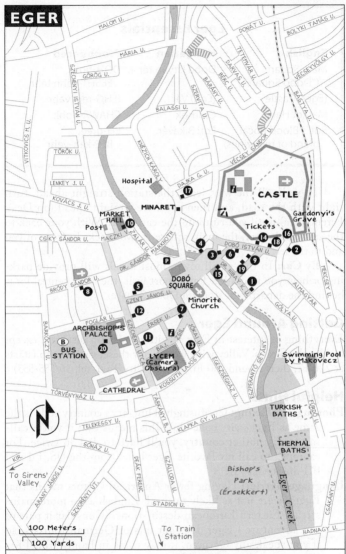

Eger Essentials

English	Hungarian	Pronounced
Main Square ("Dobó Square")	Dobó István tér	DOH-boh EESHT-vahn tehr
(Eger) Castle	(Egri) Vár	(EHG-ree) vahr
Market Hall	Csarnok	CHAWR-nohk
Bull's Blood (local blend of red wines)	Egri Bikavér	EH-gree BEE-kah-vehr

To **walk** all the way, leave the station straight ahead, turn right with the road, and then continue straight ahead (on Deák Ferenc utca) until you run into the cathedral. With your back to the cathedral entry, the main square is two blocks in front of you and to the left.

By Car: In this small town, most hotels will provide parking or help you find a lot. For a short visit, the most central lot is behind the department store on Dobó Square.

Getting Around Eger

Everything of interest in Eger is within walking distance, except maybe the Sirens' Valley wine caves—for these, catch a cab (starts at 220 Ft, then around 250 Ft/km; try City Taxi, tel. 36/555-555).

Helpful Hints

Phoning and Faxing: Confusingly, Hungary's country code is the same as Eger's city code (36). This means that if you're calling from another country, you'll have to dial 36 twice. For example, to call my favorite Eger hotel from the US, I'd dial 011-36-36-411-711.

Language Barrier: Having fewer American visitors means that Egerites are not as likely to speak English as in more mainstream Eastern European destinations. (Consider it part of the adventure.) Eger does get lots of German tourists, so if you speak any German, it may come in handy. The TI is happy to act as a go-between with a Hungarian-only sight or business.

Blue Monday: Note that the castle museums and the Lyceum are closed on Mondays. But you can still visit the cathedral (and enjoy its organ concert—see next), swim in the thermal bath, explore the market, see the castle grounds, and enjoy the local wine.

Organ Concert: Daily from mid-May to mid-October, Hungary's second-biggest organ booms out a glorious 30-minute concert in the cathedral (500 Ft, Mon–Sat at 11:30, Sun at 12:45).

Internet Access: The TI has one terminal (30 min/200 Ft; see "Tourist Information," above). The town generally has other Internet cafés, but as these are prone to go out of business, ask the TI or your hotelier for viable options.

Walking Tours: The TI offers a town walking tour in English once weekly in summer (1,000 Ft, likely July–Sept Tue at 17:00—but confirm details at TI).

Tourist Train: A hokey little tourist train leaves the main square at the top of each hour. It does a circuit around town, then heads out to the Sirens' Valley wine caves (500 Ft, 50-min trip).

SIGHTS

▲▲**Dobó Square (Dobó István tér)**—Dobó Square is the heart of Eger. In most towns this striking, the main square is packed

with postcard stalls and other tourist traps. Refreshingly, Eger's square seems mostly packed with Egerites. Ringed by breathtaking Baroque buildings, decorated with vivid sculptures depicting the city's noble past, and watched over by Eger's historic castle, this square is one of the most pleasant spots in Hungary.

The statue in the middle is **István Dobó,** the square's namesake and Eger's greatest hero, who defended the city—and all of Hungary—from an Ottoman invasion in 1552 (see his story in the sidebar). Next to Dobó is his co-commander, István Mekcsey. And right at their side is one of the brave women of Eger—depicted here throwing a pot down onto the attackers.

Use the square to orient yourself to the town. Behind the statue of Dobó is a bridge over the stream that bisects the city, and on the other side of the bridge is the charming **Little Dobó Square,** home to the town's best hotels (see "Sleeping," page 511). As you cross the bridge toward Little Dobó Square, look to the left and you'll see the northernmost Ottoman minaret in Europe— once part of a mosque (see page 506). Hovering above Little Dobó Square is Eger Castle.

Now face in the opposite direction, with the castle at your back. On your right is a handy department store (with an ATM by the door). On your left, dominating the square, is the picturesque pink **Minorite Church**—often said to be the most beautiful Baroque church in Hungary. It's exquisitely photogenic outside, but the shabby interior is less interesting, aside from the hand-carved pews, each of which is a little different.

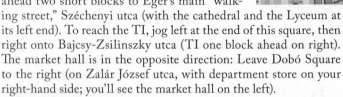

Next to the Minorite Church is the town hall. The **monument** in front of the town hall also commemorates the 1552 defense of Eger: one Egerite against two Ottoman soldiers, reminding us of the townspeople's bravery despite the odds.

Now let's get oriented to Eger's other attractions. At the bottom end of this square, various pedestrian shopping lanes lead straight ahead two short blocks to Eger's main "walk-ing street," Széchenyi utca (with the cathedral and the Lyceum at its left end). To reach the TI, jog left at the end of this square, then right onto Bajcsy-Zsilinszky utca (TI one block ahead on right). The market hall is in the opposite direction: Leave Dobó Square to the right (on Zalár József utca, with department store on your right-hand side; you'll see the market hall on the left).

▲**Eger Castle (Egri Vár)**—This castle is Hungary's Alamo, where István Dobó defended Eger from the Ottomans in 1552. These days, it's usually crawling with school-age kids on field trips from all over the country.

The great St. István—Hungary's first Christian king—founded a church on this hill a thousand years ago. The church was destroyed by Tatars in the 13th century, and this fortress was built to repel another attack.

The castle grounds feature several small museums, including a history museum, picture gallery, dungeon, underground casements (tunnels through the castle walls), Heroes' Hall (with the grave of István Dobó), and temporary exhibits. For those of us who didn't grow up hearing the legend of István Dobó, the whole complex is hard to appreciate. Most visitors find that the most rewarding plan is to stroll up, wander around the grounds, enjoy the view over-looking the town (find the minaret and other landmarks), maybe pay a visit to the waxworks (see "Other Castle Sights"), and then head back down past a gaggle of colorful shops.

Cost and Hours: A 500-Ft ticket gets you into the castle grounds only (free Nov–March). To go inside all the museums (except the privately run "Other Castle Sights," described in next paragraph), buy the 1,200-Ft ticket. The underground casements, Heroes' Hall, and St. István's ruined church are only accessible by one-hour Hungarian tour, with some posted information in English (tours depart frequently in summer, sporadically off-sea-son). Sometimes it's possible to join an English tour for 800 Ft extra (ask at information window when you arrive; most likely

István Dobó and the Siege of Eger

In the 16th century, Ottoman invaders swept into Hungary. They easily defeated a Hungarian army—in just two hours—at the notorious Battle of Mohács in 1526. When Buda and Pest fell to the Ottomans in 1541, all of Europe looked to Eger as the last line of defense. István Dobó and his second-in-command, István Mekcsey, were put in charge of Eger's forces. They prepared the castle (which still overlooks the square) for a siege and waited.

On September 11, 1552—after a summer spent conquering more than 30 other Hungarian fortresses on their march northward—40,000 Ottomans arrived in Eger. Only about 2,000 Egerites (soldiers, their wives, and their children) remained to protect their town. The Ottomans expected an easy victory, but the siege dragged on for 39 days. Eger's soldiers fought valiantly, and the women of Eger also joined the fray, pouring hot tar down on the Ottomans...everyone pitched in. A Hungarian officer named Gergely Bornemissza, sent to reinforce the people of Eger, startled the Ottomans with all manner of clever and deadly explosives. Finally, the Ottomans left in shame, Eger was saved, and Dobó was a national hero.

The unfortunate epilogue: The Ottomans came back in 1596 and, this time, succeeded in conquering an Eger Castle guarded by unmotivated mercenaries. The Ottomans sacked the town and controlled the region for close to a century.

In 1897, a castle archaeologist named Géza Gárdonyi moved from Budapest to Eger, and tales of the siege captured his imagination. Gárdonyi wrote a book about István Dobó and the 1552 Siege of Eger called *Egri Csillagok* ("Stars of Eger," translated into English as *Eclipse of the Crescent Moon,* available at local bookstores and souvenir stands). The book—a favorite of many Hungarians—is taught in schools, keeping the legend of Eger's heroes alive today.

in July–Aug, but there's no set schedule). The castle grounds are open April–Aug daily 8:00–20:00, Sept until 19:00, March and Oct until 18:00, Nov–Feb until 17:00. The castle museums are open March–Oct Tue–Sun 9:00–17:00 (last entry 40 min before closing). On Monday in March–Oct, and every day in Nov–Feb, all of the official castle museums are closed except the casements, which—as usual—you can visit only with a guided tour (since most sights are closed, you'll pay a reduced price of 1,000 Ft; some of the "Other Castle Sights" described next are open Mon). General castle info: tel. 36/312-744, www.div.iif.hu.

Other Castle Sights: In addition to the official castle

museums, there are four privately run exhibits, each with its own sporadic hours and prices: an **archery** exhibit (pay to use old-fashioned bows and crossbows—150 Ft/1 arrow, 300 Ft/3 arrows, downstairs in "dungeon" just across from information window); the **mint,** with a display of former currencies and a chance to make your own souvenir (entry-350 Ft, souvenirs extra, in cellar of Gothic palace); a new exhibit on the **Etruscans;** and the **waxworks,** or "Panoptikum" (400 Ft, daily April–Oct 9:00–18:00, Nov–March 9:00–16:00). Of these, the waxworks is by far the best—in fact, it's the most enjoyable part of the whole castle complex. You'll see a handful of eerily realistic heroes and villains from the siege of Eger (including István Dobó himself and the leader of the Ottomans sitting in his colorful tent). Notice the exaggerated Central Asian features of the Egerites—a reminder that the Magyars were more Asian than European. Sound effects add to the fun...think of it as a very low-tech, walk-through *Ottomans of the Caribbean*. You'll also have the chance to scramble through a segment of the casements that run inside the castle walls.

Getting There: To reach the castle from Dobó Square, cross the bridge toward Senator Ház Hotel (listed on page 512), then jog right around the hotel, turning right onto Dobó István utca. Take this street a few blocks until it swings down to the right; the ramp up to the castle is across the little park to your left.

▲▲**Lyceum (Líceum)**—In the mid-18th century, Bishop Károly Eszterházy wanted a university in Eger, but Hapsburg Emperor Josef II refused to allow it. So instead, Eszterházy built the most impressive teacher-training college on the planet, and stocked it with the best books and astronomical equipment money could buy. The Lyceum still trains local teachers (enrollment: about 2,000). Since Eger is expensive by Hungarian standards, many families live in the surrounding countryside. The kids all come into Eger for school—and lots of teachers are needed. But the halls of the Lyceum are also roamed by tourists who have come to visit its classic old library (700 Ft), and its astronomy museum, with a fascinating camera obscura (covered by a separate 700-Ft ticket; both library and museum open March–mid-Oct Tue–Sun 9:30–15:30, closed Mon; mid-Oct–Feb Sat–Sun only 9:30–13:30, closed Mon–Fri; last entry 30 min before closing, Eszterházy tér 1, at south end of Széchenyi utca at intersection with Kossuth utca, enter through main door across from cathedral and buy tickets just inside and to the left).

Library: First, visit the old-fashioned library one floor up (from main entry hall, cut through the middle of the courtyard, climb up a flight of stairs, and look for room 223, marked *Bibliothek*). The library houses 50,000 books (here and in the two adjoining rooms, with several stacked two deep; plus another 100,000 elsewhere in the building). Dr. Imre Surányi and his staff have spent the last decade cataloging these books. This is no easy task, since they're in over 100 languages—from Thai to Tagalog—and are shelved according to size, rather than topic. You'll likely meet Dr. Surányi's assistant, Dénes Szabó (if he's not away for a choral contest), or the resident tour guide, Katalin Bódi. Either of them will happily show you a copy of the library's pride and joy: a letter from Mozart. The shelves are adorned with golden seals depicting great minds of science, philosophy, and religion. Take some time to marvel at the gorgeous ceiling fresco, dating from 1778. If you want to thank the patron of this museum, say *köszönöm* to the guy in the second row up, to the right of the podium (second from left, not wearing a hat)—that's Bishop Károly Eszterházy. While the Lyceum now belongs to Eger, his library is still the property of the archbishop.

Astronomical Museum: Several flights above (leave library to the right, go to end of hall to reach stairs) is the **Astronomical Tower,** with some dusty old stargazing instruments, as well as a meridian line in the floor (the dot of sunlight dances along this line each day around noon). Across the hall is a fun interactive exhibit where you can try out scientific experiments—such as using air pressure to make a ball levitate or sending a mini "hot-air balloon" up to the ceiling. Yet a few more flights up is the Lyceum's treasured **camera obscura.** You'll enter a dark room around a big, bowl-like canvas, and the guide will fly you around the streets of Eger (presentations about 2/hr, maybe more when busy). Fun as it is today, this camera must have seemed like magic when it was built in 1776—well before anyone had seen "moving pictures." It's a bit of a huff to get up here (nine flights of stairs, 302 steps all together)—but the camera obscura and the view of Eger from the outdoor terrace are worth it.

▲▲Eger Cathedral—Eger's 19th-century bishops peppered the city with beautiful buildings, including the second biggest church in Hungary (after Esztergom's—see Danube Bend chapter). With a quirky, sumptuous, Baroque-feeling interior, Eger's cathedral is well worth a visit (free entry, cathedral is the big, can't-miss-it yellow building at Pyrker János tér 1, just off Széchenyi utca).

Eger Cathedral was built in the 1830s by an Austrian archbishop who had previously served in Venice, and who thought Eger could use a little more class. The colonnaded Neoclassical facade, painted a pretty Hapsburg yellow, boasts some fine Italian sculpture. As you walk up the main stairs, you'll pass saints István and László—Hungary's first two Christian kings—and then the apostles Peter and Paul.

Enter the cathedral and walk to the first collection box, partway down the nave. Then, facing the door, look up at the ornate **ceiling fresco:** On the left, it shows Hungarians in traditional dress, and on the right, the country's most important historical figures. At the bottom, you see this cathedral, celestially connected with St. Peter's in Rome (at the top). This symbol of devotion to the Vatican was a brave statement when it was painted in 1950. The communists were closing churches in other small Hungarian towns, but the Eger archbishop had enough clout to keep this one open.

Continue to the transept. A few years ago, the **stained-glass windows** at either end were donated to the cathedral by a rich Austrian couple to commemorate the 1,000th anniversary of Hungary's conversion to Christianity—notice the dates 1000 (when King István was crowned by the Pope) and 2000.

As you leave, notice the enormous **organ**—Hungary's second-largest—above the door. In the summer, try to catch one of the cathedral's daily half-hour organ concerts (500 Ft, mid-May–mid-Oct Mon–Sat at 11:30, Sun at 12:45, no concerts off-season).

If you walk up Széchenyi utca from here, you'll see the fancy Archbishop's Palace on your left—still home to Eger's archbishop.

▲Market Hall (Piaccsarnok)—Wandering Eger's big indoor market will give you a taste of local life—and maybe some local food, too. It's packed with Egerites choosing the very best of the fresh produce. Tomatoes plus peppers of all colors and sizes are abundant—magic ingredients that give Hungarian food its kick (and that won't grow in colder Poland or the Czech Republic, which have tamer cuisine). To reach the market, leave Dobó Square with the castle to your back; turn right on Zalár József utca, and you'll see the market on your left in two blocks, at the intersection with Dr. Sándor utca (June–Sept Mon–Fri 6:00–18:00, Sat 6:00–13:00, Sun 6:00–10:00; Oct–May Mon–Fri 6:00–17:00, Sat 6:00–13:00, Sun 6:00–10:00).

Minaret—Once part of a mosque, this slender, 130-foot-tall minaret represents the century of Ottoman rule that left its mark on Eger and all of Hungary. The little cross at the top symbolizes the eventual Christian victory over Hungary's Ottoman invaders. You can climb the minaret's 97 steps for fine views of Eger, but it's not for those scared of heights or tight spaces (200 Ft, April–Oct daily 10:00–18:00, closed Nov–March; if it's locked, ask for the key at nearby Hotel Minaret).

▲Kopcsik Marzipan Museum (Kopcsik Marcipánia)—Lajos Kopcsik is a master sculptor who's found his medium: marzipan. Kopcsik can make this delicate mixture of sugar and ground almonds take virtually any form. In this surprisingly engaging little museum, you'll see several remarkable, colorful examples of Kopcsik's skill: sword, minaret, gigantic wine bottle, suitcase, Russian stacking dolls, old-timey phonograph, grandfather clock, giant bell...and paintings galore (including van Gogh's sunflowers and Picasso's musicians). The list literally goes on for four pages. Who'd have thought you could do so much with candy? (400 Ft, ask for printed English information; Easter–Oct daily 9:00–18:00; Nov–Easter Tue–Sun 9:00–17:00, closed Mon; Harangöntő utca 4, tel. 36/516-449.)

Other Museums—Two small museums lie between Little Dobó Square and the entrance to the castle; neither is worth a visit, unless you have a special interest in the subject matter. The **Palóc Folklore Museum** is a measly little place with a handful of traditional tools, textiles, ceramics, costumes, and pieces of furniture (200 Ft, borrow the skimpy English information, Easter–Sept Tue–Sun 9:00–17:00, closed Mon and Oct–Easter, Dobó utca 12). The **Historical Exhibition of Weapons** (Történeti Tárház) is just that, featuring centuries of Eger armaments: clubs, rifles, and everything in between (300 Ft, Tue–Sun 10:00–17:00, closed Mon, 450-Ft booklet labels weapons in English, 1,600-Ft English book gives more info, Dobó utca 9, actually just down Fazola Henrik utca).

Another attraction is hiding just off the main walking street, Széchenyi utca. The **Town Under the Town** (Város a Város Alatt) exhibit offers guided tours of the archbishop's former wine cellar network, which honeycombs the land behind the Archbishop's Palace (800 Ft, departs as the top of each hour, daily April–Sept 10:00–21:00, Oct–March 10:00–17:00, last tour departs 1 hour before closing, www.varosavarosalatt.hu). To find it, walk up the wide, pedestrianized Széchenyi utca from the cathedral and Lyceum. Look for the passage in the yellow palace just after the cathedral (on the left). Walk through this courtyard, then bear left as you emerge to find the cellar entrance.

EXPERIENCES

Aqua Eger
Swimming and water sports are as important to Egerites as good wine. They're proud that many of Hungary's Olympic medalists in aquatic events have come from this county.

To test the waters of this part of Eger, you can join the locals lounging and laughing around in the city bath (see "Taking the Waters" on page 462). Or you can take a more serious approach— doing laps (and appreciating the unique architecture) at the city swimming pool.

▲Thermal Bath Complex (Eger Thermálfürdő)—For a refreshing break from the sightseeing grind, consider a splash in the spa. This is a fine opportunity to try a Hungarian bath: modern enough to feel accessible (men and women are clothed and together most of the time), but frequented mostly by locals. While Budapest has many great baths (see page 460), you may want to take a dip in low-key Eger and save your Budapest time for big-city sights.

You'll enter and be given a little barcode to swipe across the turnstile scanner. Trade this in for a key to a locker (1,000-Ft deposit per key, which will be refunded). Change (private changing cabins available in the locker room for no extra charge), stow your stuff in a locker, put the key around your wrist, then join the fun. The heart of the complex is the new, green-domed, indoor-outdoor "adventure bath." Its cascades, jets, bubbles, geysers, and powerful current pool will make you feel like a kid again. For some warmer water, follow your nose to the old-fashioned sulfur pool—where Egerites sit peacefully, ignore the slight stink, and (supposedly) feel their arthritis ebb away. There's also a big outdoor lap pool (closed off-season).

Note that you can't rent a swimsuit or a towel; bring both with you, along with shower sandals for the locker room (if you've got them).

Cost, Hours, Location: 1,100 Ft, adventure bath included Oct–April but 700 Ft extra May–Sept. Open May–Sept Mon–Fri 6:00–19:30, Sat–Sun 8:00–19:00; Oct–April daily 9:00–18:30. It's at Petőfi tér 2 (tel. 36/314-142, www.egertermal.hu). It's easy to reach, within a 10-minute walk of most hotels. From Dobó Square, follow the stream four blocks south (signs for *Strand*), past the big, unusual Bitskey Aladár swimming pool building. Continue following the stream into the park; you'll see the main entrance to the bath on your left over a bridge.

Bitskey Aladár Pool—This striking new swimming pool was designed by Imre Makovecz, the father of Hungary's trendy Organic architectural style. Some Eger taxpayers resented the pool's big price tag, but it left the city with a truly distinctive building. You don't need to be an architecture student to know

that the pool is special. It's worth the five-minute walk from Dobó Square just to take a look. Oh, and you can swim in it, too (750 Ft; Mon–Fri 6:00–20:00; until 21:00 on Mon, Wed, and Fri; Sat 8:00–20:00, Sun 8:00–18:00; follow Eger Creek south from Dobó

Hungary's Organic Architecture

In recent years, a uniquely Hungarian style of architecture has caught on: Organic. The Hungarian brand of Organic was developed and championed by Imre Makovecz. After being blackballed by the communists for his nationalistic politics, Makovecz was denied access to building materials, so he taught himself to make impressive structures with nothing more than sticks and rocks.

Now that the regime is dead and Makovecz is Hungary's premier architect, he still keeps things simple. He believes that a building should be a product of its environment, rather than a cookie-cutter copy. Organic buildings use indigenous materials (especially wood) and take on untraditional forms—often inspired by animals or plants—that blend in with the landscape. Organic buildings look like they're rising up out of the ground, rather than plopped down on top of it. You generally won't find this back-to-nature style in big cities like Budapest; Makovecz prefers to work in small communities such as Eger (see photo on page 508), instead of working for corporations.

Organic architecture has caught on throughout Hungary, becoming *the* post-communist style. Even big supermarket chains are now imitating Makovecz. If you see a building with white walls and a big, overhanging roof (resembling a big mushroom)...that's Organic architecture.

Square to Frank Tivadar utca, tel. 36/511-810). Like the thermal bath complex, this place does not rent out swimsuits—B.Y.O.S.S.

Eger Wine

Eger is at the heart of one of Hungary's best-known wine regions, internationally famous for its **Bull's Blood** (Egri Bikavér). You'll likely hear various stories as to how Bull's Blood got its name during the Ottoman siege of Eger. My favorite version: The Ottomans were amazed at the ferocity displayed by the Egerites, and wondered what they were drinking that boiled their blood and stained their beards so red...it must be potent stuff. Local merchants, knowing that the Ottomans were Muslim and couldn't drink alcohol, told them it was bull's blood. The merchants made a buck, and the name stuck.

Creative as these stories are, they're all bunk—the term dates only from 1851. Egri Bikavér is a blend—everyone has their own recipe—so you generally won't find it at small producers. Cabernet Sauvignon, Merlot, Kékfránkos, and Kékoportó are the most commonly used grapes.

Try Egri Bikavér, but don't stop there. Other local wines

Eger

worth trying include Leányka ("Little Girl"), Kékfránkos ("Blue Frankish"), Furmint, Hárslevélű, and Kéknyelű. You also might have heard of Tokaji Aszú wine (a sweet white made from a grape of Hungarian origin, also grown in the Alsace region of France—where it's known as *tokay*). Tokaj is a town (not too far from Eger), and Aszú is a "noble rot" grape. These grapes are harvested immediately after the first frost, when they burst and wither on the vine like raisins.

While it would be enjoyable to drive around the Hungarian countryside visiting wineries, the most accessible way for most visitors to get a taste of local wine is at the **Bikavér Borház** wine shop right on Little Dobó Square (across from Offi Ház). In addition to a well-stocked (if slightly overpriced) wine shop, they have a wine bar (six tastings and two cheeses for under 2,000 Ft, or wine by the glass; daily 10:00–22:00, Kis-Dobó tér 10, tel. 36/413-262).

Sirens' Valley (Szépasszony-völgy)—When the Ottoman invaders first occupied Eger, residents moved into the valley next door, living in caves dug into the hillside. Eventually the Ottomans were driven out, the Egerites moved back to town, and the caves became wine cellars. (Most Eger families who can afford it have at least a modest vineyard in the countryside.) There are more than 300 such caves in the valley to the southwest of Eger, several of which are open for visitors.

The best selection of these caves (about 50) is in the Sirens' Valley (sometimes also translated as "Valley of the Beautiful Women"—or, on local directional signs, the less poetic "Nice Woman Valley"). It's a fun scene—locals showing off their latest vintage, with picnic tables and tipsy tourists spilling out into the street. At some places, you'll be offered free samples; others have a menu for tastes or glasses of wine. While you're not expected to buy a bottle, it's a nice gesture to buy one if you've spent a while at one cave (and it's usually very cheap). Most caves offer something light to eat with the wine, and you'll also see lots of non-cave, full-service restaurants. Some of the caves are fancy and finished, staffed by multilingual waiters in period costume. Others feel like a dank basement, with grandpa leaning on his moped out front and a monolingual granny pouring the wine inside. (The really local places—where the decor is cement, bottles don't have labels, and food consists of potato chips and buttered Wonder Bread—can be the most fun.) This experience is a strange mix of touristy and local, but not entirely accessible to non-Hungarian-speakers—it works best with a bunch of friends and an easygoing, social attitude. Hopping from cave to musky cave can make for an enjoyable evening, but be sure to wander around a bit to see the options before you dive in. Caves #2 (Bíró Borozó), #34, #43, and the one called "Kiss" have a particularly good reputation (cellars generally open 10:00–22:00 in summer, best June–Aug after

Eger

19:00 and good-weather weekends in the shoulder season; it's much quieter off-season, when only a handful of cellars remain open for shorter hours).

Getting to the Sirens' Valley: The valley is a 25-minute walk southwest of Eger. Figure no more than 1,000 Ft for a **taxi** between your hotel and the caves. During the summer, you can catch the 500-Ft **tourist train** from Eger's main square to the caves (see "Helpful Hints," page 501), then take a later train back. To **walk,** leave the pedestrian zone on the street next to the cathedral (Törvényház utca), with the cathedral on your right-hand side. Take the first left just after the back end of the cathedral (onto Trinitárius utca), go one long block, then take the first right (onto Király utca). At the fork, bear to the left. You'll stay straight on this road—crossing busy Koháry István utca—for several blocks, through some nondescript residential areas (on Szépasszony-völgy utca). When you crest the hill and emerge from the houses, you'll see the caves (and tour buses) below you on the left—go left (downhill) at the fork to get there. First you'll come to a stretch of touristy non-cave restaurants; keep going past these, and eventually you'll see a big loop of caves on your left.

SLEEPING

Eger is a good overnight stop, and a couple of quaint, well-located hotels in particular—Senator Ház and Offi Ház—are well worth booking in advance. The TI can help you find a room; if you're stumped, the area behind the castle has a sprinkling of guesthouses

Sleep Code

(200 Ft = about $1, country code: 36, area code: 36)
S = Single, **D** = Double/Twin, **T** = Triple, **Q** = Quad, **b** = bathroom, **s** = shower only. Unless otherwise noted, English is spoken, breakfast is included, and credit cards are accepted.

To help you sort easily through these listings, I've divided the rooms into three categories, based on the price for a standard double room with bath:

$$$ Higher Priced—Most rooms 20,000 Ft or more.
$$ Moderately Priced—Most rooms between 15,000–20,000 Ft.
$ Lower Priced—Most rooms 15,000 Ft or less.

Phone Tip: Remember, if calling or faxing Eger internationally, you'll have to dial 36 twice (once for the country code, again for the area code).

(vendégház). Elevators are rare (except at Panoráma)—expect to climb one or two flights of stairs to reach your room. A tax of 310 Ft per person will be added to your bill (not included in the prices listed here).

$$$ Panoráma Hotel is a good big-hotel option, still close to Dobó Square. You'll miss the quaintness of some of the other listings—its 38 faded, overpriced rooms are all business—but you get free access to its "Unicornis Thermarium" spa facility (Sb-20,000 Ft, Db-24,000 Ft, Tb-29,000 Ft, 15 percent cheaper Nov–March, apartments also available, air-con, elevator, free parking, Dr. Hibay K. utca 2, tel. 36/412-886, fax 36/410-136, www.panoramahotels .hu, hoteleger@panoramahotels.hu).

$$$ Imola Udvarház rents six spacious apartments—with kitchen, living room, bedroom, and bathroom—all decorated in modern Scandinavian style (read: Ikea). They're pricey, but roomy and well-maintained, with a great location near the castle entrance (July–Aug: Sb-19,000 Ft, Db-22,000 Ft, Tb-24,000 Ft, Qb-26,000 Ft; each room 2,000 Ft less April–June and Sept–Oct and 4,000 Ft less Nov–March; air-con, free Wi-Fi, enter through restaurant courtyard at Dózsa György tér 4, tel. & fax 36/516-180, udvarhaz@imolanet.hu).

$$ Senator Ház Hotel is one of my favorite small, family-run hotels in all of Eastern Europe. Though the 11 rooms are a bit worn, this place is cozy and well-run by András Cseh and his right-hand man, Viktor. With oodles of character, all the right quirks, and a picture-perfect location just under the castle on Little Dobó Square, it's a winner (Sb-13,800 Ft, Db-19,800 Ft, extra bed-5,400 Ft, 15–30 percent cheaper mid-Oct–May, air-con, Internet access for guests-300 Ft/30 min, Dobó István tér 11, tel. & fax 36/411-711, www.senatorhaz.hu, senator@enternet.hu). The Cseh family also runs **Pátria Vendégház**—two doubles (19,800 Ft) and four apartments (22,000 Ft) with luxurious decor around a courtyard in a nearby building (same contact info as Senator Ház Hotel).

$$ Offi Ház Hotel shares Little Dobó Square with Senator Ház. Its five rooms are classy and romantic (Sb-13,500 Ft, Db-15,500 Ft, Db suite-18,500 Ft, Tb suite-23,000 Ft, extra bed-4,500 Ft, 15 percent cheaper Nov–March, non-smoking, air-con, free cable Internet, Dobó István tér 5, tel. & fax 36/518-210, www .offihaz.hu, offihaz@t-online.hu, Offenbächer family).

$$ Szent János Hotel, less charming and more businesslike than the Senator Ház and Offi Ház, offers a good but less atmospheric location, 11 straitlaced rooms, and a pleasant winter garden to relax in (Sb-12,000 Ft, Db-17,000 Ft, extra bed-4,000 Ft, 15 percent cheaper Nov–April, non-smoking rooms, air-con, free cable Internet, McDonald's walk-up window across the street can be noisy at night—especially weekends—so request a quiet back room,

Eger

a long block off Dobó Square at Szent János utca 3, tel. 36/510-350, fax 36/517-101, www.hotelszentjanos.hu, hotelszentjanos @hotelszentjanos.hu).

$ Dobó Vendégház, run by friendly Mariann Kleszo, has seven basic but colorful rooms just off Dobó Square. Mariann speaks nothing but Hungarian, but gets simple reservation emails and faxes translated by a friend (Sb-7,500 Ft, Db-11,000 Ft, Tb-13,000 Ft, Qb-17,000 Ft, cash only, some rooms have air-con, free Wi-Fi, Dobó utca 19, tel. 36/421-407, fax 36/515-715, www.hotels .hu/dobo_vendeghaz, dobovh@t-online.hu).

EATING

Bajor Sörház (known to locals as "HBH" for the brand of beer on tap) is favored by tourists and locals alike for its excellent Hungarian cuisine. Everything's good here. You could make a meal of the giant 700-Ft bowl of their spicy *gulyás leves* soup (that's *real* Hungarian goulash, described on page 395)—but it's fun to supplement it with some other well-prepared Hungarian dishes. This is a good place for two or more people to split several dishes. They also feature some Bavarian specialties...but with a Hungarian accent (most main dishes 1,500–3,000 Ft, daily 11:30–22:00, outdoor tables in summer, right at the bottom of Dobó Square at Bajcsy-Zsilinszky utca 19, tel. 36/515-516). If you're lucky, you may get to meet animated István "Call Me Steve Miller" Molnár, one of my favorite Hungarians.

The recommended hotels **Senator Ház** and **Offi Ház** both have restaurants at the top end of Dobó Square that are open long hours daily (both are listed under "Sleeping"). These places have fine Hungarian and international food (most main dishes 1,500–2,500 Ft) and postcard-perfect outdoor seating that shares Little Dobó Square with a gazebo featuring cheesy live music in summer. This is *the* place to see and be seen in Eger.

Szantofer Vendéglő serves traditional Hungarian food at local prices to both Egerites and tourists. The good, unpretentious, fill-the-tank food is presented with an artistic flourish, and the creatively translated menu is good for a laugh (most main dishes 1,200–2,000 Ft, daily 11:30–22:00, Bródy Sándor utca 3, tel. 36/517-298).

Palacsintavár ("Pancake Castle"), near the ramp leading up to the castle, isn't your hometown IHOP. This cellar bar serves up inventive, artfully presented crêpe-wrapped main courses to a mostly-students clientele. It's decorated with old cigarette boxes, and cutting-edge rock music plays on the soundtrack (most main dishes 1,300–1,500 Ft, daily 12:00–22:30, Dobó utca 9).

Elefanto, above the market hall, offers good pizzas and pastas

(800–1,300 Ft) and international dishes (1,600–2,500 Ft) in a pleasant treehouse ambience. In warm weather, enjoy the covered terrace seating (daily 12:00–23:00, Katona István tér 2, tel. 36/412-452).

Fast and Cheap: **Rádi Bisztró** is a popular student hangout and a convenient spot for 200-Ft pastries and inexpensive, premade 400-Ft sandwiches (Mon–Fri 7:00–18:00, Sat 7:00–14:00, closed Sun, just down the street from the Lyceum at Széchenyi utca 2).

Dessert: *Cukrászda* (pastry shops) line the streets of Eger. For deluxe, super-decadent pastries of every kind imaginable—most for less than 400 Ft—drop by **Dobós Cukrászda** (daily 9:30–21:00, point to what you want inside and they'll bring it out to your table, Széchenyi utca 6, tel. 36/413-335). For a more local scene, find the tiny **Sárvári Cukrászda,** behind the Lyceum. Their pastries are good, but Egerites line up here after a big Sunday lunch for their homemade gelato (130 Ft/scoop, Mon–Fri 7:00–19:00, Sat–Sun 10:00–19:00, Kossuth utca 1, between Jókai utca and Fellner utca). On Dobó utca between the main square and the castle, look for **Sisi Rétesbolt,** which serves up delicious strudel that you can watch them make right there (300 Ft, daily 10:00–17:00, Dobó utca 10).

TRANSPORTATION CONNECTIONS

From Eger by Train: The only major destination you'll get to directly from Eger's train station is **Budapest** (5/day direct to Budapest's Keleti Station, 2.5 hrs). For most other destinations, you'll connect through Füzesabony (see next) or Budapest.

Note that Eger is not as well-connected as the smaller, nearby junction town of **Füzesabony** (FOO-zesh-ah-boyn). Eger is connected to Füzesabony by frequent trains (13/day, 17 min). The very rustic Füzesabony station does not have lockers, but—oddly enough—does have a modest museum of local artifacts. There is no ATM at the station—exit straight from the station and walk about two blocks, and you'll find an ATM on your right.

In Füzesabony, you can transfer to Budapest (including some speedy InterCity trains—with a 900-Ft supplement—that get you to Budapest in 2 hours total). Füzesabony is also the transfer point for the night train between Budapest and Kraków (explained below).

From Eger to Budapest by Bus: Since Eger's bus station is more central than its train station, some travelers prefer the bus to Budapest (about hourly direct, 2.25 hrs). The bus station is a five-minute uphill walk behind Eger's cathedral and Archbishop's Palace: Go behind the cathedral and through the park, and look for the modern, green, circular building. Blue electronic boards in the center of the bus-station complex show upcoming departures. This bus leaves you near Budapest's Stadionok Metro stop (on the red/M2 line).

Night Train Between Eger and Kraków

To do this trip in either direction, you'll transfer in Füzesabony (which is on the main Budapest–Kraków line). Be warned that this is a pretty dreary trip, with old three-bunk sleeper cars, gross WCs, and lots of noise and bumps. But, short of flying, this is the most efficient way to get between Hungary and Kraków.

From Kraków to Eger: Note that your train actually continues on to Budapest—so you'll have to be on your toes to get off at Füzesabony (usually around 7:30; confirm specific time before you travel). When you board the night train, make sure the conductor knows where you're getting off; he should wake you up about 20 minutes before reaching Füzesabony (set an alarm just in case), and he'll have to unlock the door to let you off the train. Once in Füzesabony, you'll have about a half-hour before the next Eger-bound train leaves. That's plenty of time to get some local cash (see above), buy your ticket to Eger (about 300 Ft), and hop on the train.

From Eger to Kraków: First you'll have to transfer in Füzesabony. You can either take the 20-minute train trip from Eger to Füzesabony (about 300 Ft), or—if you've got more money than time—skip the walk to the Eger station and take a 20-minute taxi ride (about 7,000 Ft) directly to Füzesabony to catch the train on to Kraków.

SLOVENIA

SLOVENIA

Slovenija

Tiny, overlooked Slovenia is one of Europe's most unexpectedly charming destinations. At the intersection of the Slavic, German, and Italian worlds, Slovenia is an exciting mix of the best of each culture. Though it's just a quick trip away from the tourist throngs in Venice, Munich, Salzburg, and Vienna, Slovenia has stayed off the tourist track—a handy detour for in-the-know Back Door travelers.

Today, it seems strange to think that Slovenia was ever part of Yugoslavia. Both in the personality of its people and in its landscape, Slovenia feels more like Austria. Slovenes are more industrious, organized, and punctual than their fellow former Yugoslavs... yet still friendly, relaxed, and Mediterranean. Locals like the balance. Visitors expecting minefields and rusting Yugo factories are pleasantly surprised to find Slovenia's rolling countryside dotted instead with quaint alpine villages and the spires of miniature Baroque churches, with breathtaking, snowcapped peaks in the distance.

Only half as big as Switzerland, but remarkably diverse for its size, Slovenia can be easily appreciated on a brief visit. Travelers can hike on alpine trails in the morning and explore some of the world's best caves in the afternoon, before relaxing with a seafood dinner on the Adriatic.

Slovenia enjoys a powerhouse economy—the healthiest in Eastern Europe. The Austro-Hungarian Empire left it with a strong industrial infrastructure, which the Yugoslav government expanded. By 1980, 60 percent of all Yugoslav industry was in little Slovenia (which had only 8 percent of Yugoslavia's population and 8 percent of its territory). With independence, Slovenia continued this trend, pushing their mighty little economy into the future. Of the 10 new nations that joined the European Union in 2004, Slovenia was the only one rich enough to be a net donor (with a higher per-capita income than the average), and the only one already qualified to join the euro currency zone (it adopted the euro in January of 2007). Thanks to its longstanding ties to the West and can-do spirit, Slovenia already feels more Western than

SLOVENIA

AUSTRIA

HUNGARY

Klagenfurt

Villach

Jesenice

Mt. Triglav

Bled

JULIAN ALPS

Kobarid

Lake Bled

Lake Bohinj

Kranj

Soča R

ITALY

LOGARSKA DOLINA

Velenje

Celje

Drava

Maribor

Ptuj

River

CROATIA

Ljubljana

SLOVENIA

Sava

Zagreb

River

PREDJAMA CASTLE

Novo Mesto

Samobor

KARST

POSTOJNA CAVES

Lipica

SKOCJAN CAVES

Trieste

Piran

Koper

Adriatic Sea

ISTRIA

Opatija

Rijeka

50 Kilometers

50 Miles

any other destination in this book.

The country has a funny way of making people fall in love with it. Slovenes are laid-back, easygoing, stylish, and fun. They won't win any world wars (they're too well-adjusted to even try)... but they're exactly the type of people you'd love to chat with over a cup of coffee. Many of today's American visitors are soldiers who participated in the conflict in nearby Bosnia and have good memories of their vacations here in Slovenia. Now they're bringing their families back with them.

The Slovene language is as mellow as the people. While Slovenes use Serb and German curses in abundance, the worst they can say in their native tongue is, "May you be kicked by a horse." For "Darn it!" they say, "Three hundred hairy bears!"

Coming from such a small country, locals are proud of the few things that are distinctly Slovenian, such as the roofed hayrack.

Foreigners think that Slovenes' fascination with these hayracks is strange...until they visit, and see them absolutely everywhere (especially in the northwest part of the country). Because of the frequent rainfall, the hayracks are covered by a roof that allows the hay to dry thoroughly. The most traditional kind is the *toplar*, consisting of two hayracks connected by one big roof. It looks like a skinny barn with open, fenced sides. Hay

Slovenia Almanac

Official Name: Republika Slovenija, or simply Slovenija.

Snapshot History: After being dominated by Germans for centuries, Slovenian culture proudly emerged in the 19th century. After World War I, Slovenia merged with its neighbors to become Yugoslavia, then broke away and achieved independence for the first time ever in 1991.

Population: Slovenia's two million people (similar to Nevada) are 83 percent ethnic Slovenes who speak Slovene, plus a smattering of Serbs, Croats, and Muslim Bosniaks. The majority of the country is Catholic.

Latitude and Longitude: 46° N and 14° E (latitude similar to Lyon, France; Quebec, Canada; or Bismarck, North Dakota).

Area: At 7,800 square miles, it's about the size of New Jersey, but with a fourth the population.

Geography: Tiny Slovenia has three extremely different terrains and climates: the warm Mediterranean coastline (just 29 miles long—about one inch per inhabitant); the snow-capped, forested alpine mountains in the northwest (including 9,400-foot Mount Triglav); and the moderate-climate, central limestone plateau that includes Ljubljana and the cave-filled Karst region. If you look at a map of Slovenia and squint your eyes a bit, it really begins to look like a chicken running towards the east.

Biggest Cities: Nearly one in five Slovenes lives in the two biggest cities: Ljubljana (the capital, pop. 265,000) and Maribor (in the east, pop. 115,000). Half the country lives in rural villages.

Economy: With a Gross Domestic Product of $47 billion and a GDP per capita of $23,400, Slovenia's economy is much stronger than the average Eastern European country. Slovenia's wealth comes largely from manufactured metal products (trucks and machinery) traded with a diverse group of partners.

Currency: Slovenia adopted the euro currency in January of 2007. €1 = about $1.40. For more, see "Euro Conversion" under "Practicalities" on page 522.

Government: The country is headed by the prime minister (Janez Janša through at least 2008), who heads up the leading vote-getting party in legislative elections. He governs along with the figurehead president Danilo Türk. Janša and the recently deceased Jože Pučnik (for whom Ljubljana's airport was recently renamed) represent the right wing of Slovenian politics, while Milan Kučan and Janez Drnovšek—each of whom is now retired, after serving as both president and prime minister—and the new President Türk represent the left. (Slovenia's relatively peaceful succession is credited largely to former Prime Minister Kučan, who remains a popular figure.) The National Assembly consists of about 90 elected legislators; there's also a second house of parliament, which has much less power. Despite the country's small size, it is divided into some 200 municipalities.

Flag: Three horizontal bands of white (top), blue, and red. A shield in the upper left shows Mount Triglav, with a wavy-line sea below and three stars above.

The Average Slovene: The average Slovene skis, in this largely alpine country, and is an avid fan of the oddly popular sport of team handball. He or she lives in a 250-square-foot apartment, earns $1,400 a month, watches 16 hours of TV a week (much of it in English with Slovene subtitles), and enjoys a drink-and-a-half of alcohol every day.

Notable Slovenes: A pair of prominent Ohio politicians—perennial presidential candidate Dennis Kucinich and Senator George Voinovich, both from the Cleveland area—are each half-Slovene. (In fact, in 1910, Cleveland had the biggest Slovenian population of any city in the world—just ahead of Trieste and Ljubljana.) Classical musicians might know composers Giuseppe Tartini and Hugo Wolf. Even if you haven't heard of architect Jože Plečnik yet, you'll hear his name a hundred times while you're in Slovenia—especially in Ljubljana (see page 530). Most famous of all is the illustrious Melania Knauss—a *GQ* cover girl who's also Mrs. Donald Trump.

Sporty Slovenes: If you follow alpine sports or team handball, you'll surely know some world-class athletes from Slovenia. NBA fans might recognize basketball players Primož Brezec and Bostjan Nachbar, as well as some lesser players. The athletic Slovenes—perhaps trying to compensate for the miniscule size of their country—have accomplished astonishing feats: Davo Karničar has skied down from the summits of some of the world's tallest mountains (including Everest, Kilimanjaro, and McKinley; www.davokarnicar.com). Benka Pulko became the first person ever to drive a motorcycle around the world (that is, all seven continents, including Antarctica; total trip: 118,000 miles in 2,000 days—also the longest solo motorcycle journey by a woman; www.benkapulko.com). Dušan Mravlje ran across all the continents (www.dusanmravlje.si). And ultra-marathon swimmer Martin Strel has swum the entire length of several major rivers, including the Danube (1,775 miles), the Mississippi (2,415 miles), the Yangtze (3,915 miles), and the Amazon (3,393 miles; for more, see www.martinstrel.com).

hangs on the sides to dry; firewood, carts, tractors, and other farm implements sit on the ground inside; and dried hay is stored in the loft up above. But these wooden *toplarji* are firetraps, and a stray bolt of lighting can burn one down in a flash. So in recent years, more farmers are moving to single hayracks *(enojni);* these are still roofed, but have posts made of concrete, rather than wood. You'll find postcards and miniature wooden models of both kinds of hayracks (a fun souvenir).

Another good (and uniquely Slovenian) memento is a creatively decorated front panel from a beehive *(panjske končnice)*. Slovenia has a strong beekeeping tradition, and beekeepers once believed that painting the fronts of the hives made it easier for bees to find their way home. Replicas of these panels are available at gift shops all over the country. (For more on the panels and Slovenia's beekeeping heritage, see page 586.)

Slovenia is also the land of polka. Slovenes claim it was invented here, and singer/accordionist Slavko Avsenik—from the village of Begunje near Bled—cranks out popular oompah songs that make him bigger than the Beatles (and therefore, presumably, Jesus) in Germany. You'll see the Avsenik ensemble and other oompah bands on Slovenian TV, where hokey Lawrence Welk–style shows are a local institution.

To really stretch your euros, try one of Slovenia's more than 200 farmhouse bed-and-breakfasts, called "tourist farms" *(turistične kmetije)*. These are actual, working farms (often organic) that sell meals and/or rent out rooms to tourists to help make ends meet. You can use a tourist farm as a home base to explore the entire country—remember, the farthest reaches of Slovenia are only a day trip away. A comfortable, hotelesque double with a private bathroom—plus a traditional Slovenian dinner and a hearty breakfast—costs as little as $50. Request a listing from the Slovenian Tourist Board (see page 930), or find information at www.slovenia-tourism.si (select "Accommodations," then "Holiday Farm House").

Slovenia is poised to become one of Eastern Europe's top destinations in the next few years. Locals are reporting a sharp increase in visitors. Now is the time for *you* to visit, while the locals are still friendly, the prices still reasonable, and the lanes and trails yours alone.

Practicalities

Euro Conversion: Even though Slovenia has used the euro currency since January of 2007, some locals still think in terms of the previous currency, the *tolar* (which you might see on menus or price lists). There were about 190 tolars in one dollar, and about 240 tolars in one euro.

Smoking Ban: Smoking is prohibited in public places, unless it's a specially designated (and well-ventilated) smoking room. Larger hotels still have some "smoking" rooms, but smoking isn't allowed in public spaces.

Sunday Closures: Slovenia can be extremely sleepy on Sundays, even in the larger towns and cities, where virtually all shops are closed. Plan ahead. Fortunately, many restaurants remain open, plus a select few grocery stores.

Telephones: Insertable phone cards, sold at newsstands and kiosks everywhere, get you access to the modern public phones.

When calling locally, dial the seven-digit number. To make a long-distance call within the country, start with the area code (which begins with 0). To call a Slovenian number from abroad, dial the international access number (00 if calling from Europe, 011 from the US or Canada) followed by 386 (Slovenia's country code), then the area code (without the initial 0) and the seven-digit number. To call out of Slovenia, dial 00, the country code of the country you're calling (see chart in appendix), the area code if applicable (may need to drop initial zero), and the local number.

Slovenian phone numbers beginning with 080 are toll-free; 090 and 089 denote expensive toll lines. Mobile phone numbers usually begin with 031, 041, 051, 040, or 070.

Slovenian History

Slovenia has a long and not very interesting history as part of various larger empires. Charlemagne's Franks conquered the tiny land in the eighth century, and, ever since, Slovenia has been a backwater of the Germanic world—first as a holding of the Holy Roman Empire, and later, the Hapsburg Empire. Slovenia seems as much German as Slavic. But even as the capital, Ljubljana, was populated by Austrians (and called Laibach by its German-speaking residents), the Slovenian language and cultural traditions survived in the countryside.

Ljubljana rose to international prominence for half a decade (1809–1813) when Napoleon named it the capital of his "Illyrian Provinces," stretching from Austria's Tirol to Croatia's Dalmatian Coast. During this time, the long-suppressed Slovene language was used for the first time in schools and the government. Inspired by the patriotic poetry of France Prešeren, national pride surged.

The most interesting chapter in Slovenian history took place in the last century. Some of World War I's fiercest fighting occurred at the Soča (Isonzo) Front in northwest Slovenia—witnessed by young Ernest Hemingway, who drove an ambulance (see sidebars on page 598 and 604). After the war, from 1918 to 1991, Slovenia was Yugoslavia's smallest, northernmost, and most affluent republic. Concerned about Serbian strongman Slobodan Milošević's

Slo-what?-ia

"The only thing I know about Slovakia is what I learned firsthand from your foreign minister, who came to Texas."

— George W. Bush, to a Slovak journalist (Bush had actually met with Dr. Janez Drnovšek, who was then Slovenia's prime minister)

Maybe it's understandable that many Americans confuse Slovenia with Slovakia. Both are small, mountainous countries that not too long ago were parts of bigger, better known, now defunct nations. But anyone who has visited Slovenia and Slovakia will set you straight—they feel worlds apart.

Slovenia, wedged between the Alps and the Adriatic, is a tidy, prosperous country with a strong economy. Until 1991, Slovenia was one of the six republics that made up Yugoslavia. Historically, Slovenia has had very strong ties with Germanic culture—so it feels German.

Slovakia—two countries away, to the northeast—is slightly bigger. Much of its territory is covered by the Carpathian Mountains, most notably the dramatic, jagged peaks of the High Tatras. In 1993, the Czechs and Slovaks peacefully chose to go their separate ways, so the nation of Czechoslovakia dissolved into the Czech Republic and the Slovak Republic (a.k.a. Slovakia). Slovakia was hit hard by the communists, and still suffers from a weak economy and high poverty levels. Slovakia was part of Hungary until the end of World War I, and feels Hungarian (especially the southern half of the country, where many Hungarians still live).

To make things even more confusing, there's also **Slavonia.** This is the thick, inland "panhandle" that makes up the northeast half of Croatia, along Slovenia's southeast border. Much of the warfare in Croatia's 1991–1995 war took place in Slavonia (including Vukovar; see Understanding Yugoslavia chapter).

I won't tell on you if you mix them up. But if you want to feel smarter than a president, do a little homework and get it right.

politics, Slovenia seceded in 1991. Because more than 90 percent of the people here were ethnic Slovenes, the break with Yugoslavia was simple and virtually uncontested. Its war for independence lasted just 10 days and claimed only a few dozen lives. (For more details, see the Understanding Yugoslavia chapter, page 915.)

After centuries of looking to the West, Slovenia became the first of the former Yugoslav republics to join the European Union

Slovenia

Pršut

In Slovenia and Croatia, *pršut* (purr-SHOOT) is one of the essential food groups. This air-cured ham (like Italian prosciutto) is soaked in salt and sometimes also smoked. Then it hangs in open-ended barns for up to a year and a half, to be dried and seasoned by the howling Bora wind. Each region produces a slightly different *pršut*. In Dalmatia, a layer of fat keeps the ham moist; in Istria, the fat is trimmed, and the *pršut* is dryer.

Since Slovenia joined the European Union, strict new standards have swept the land. Separate rooms must be used for the slaughter, preparation, and curing of the ham. While this seems fair enough for large producers, small family farms that want to produce just enough *pršut* for their own use—and maybe sell one or two ham hocks to neighbors—find they have to invest thousands of euros to be compliant.

in May 2004. The Slovenes have been practical about this move, realizing it's essential for their survival as a tiny nation in a modern world. But there are trade-offs, and "Euroskeptics" are down on EU bureaucracy. As borders disappear, Slovenes are experiencing more crime. Local farming is threatened by EU standards. There are no more cheap bananas (because brown ones must be trashed), and "you can't sell a cucumber with more than a three-degree curve." Slovenian businesses are having difficulty competing with big German and Western firms. Before EU membership, only Slovenes could own Slovenian land. But now wealthy foreigners are buying property, driving up the cost of real estate.

As Slovenia became the first post-communist country to adopt the euro currency in January 2007, locals worried about a potential increase in prices...even as they felt proud of their economic achievements. It seems that throughout all of the changes in the last two decades, Slovenes have maintained their sense of humor and easygoing attitude.

Slovenian Food

Slovenian cuisine has enjoyed influence from a wide variety of sources. Slovenes brag that their cuisine melds the best of Italian and German cooking—but they also embrace other international influences, especially French. Like Croatian food, Slovenian cuisine also features some pan-Balkan elements. The eggplant-and-red-bell-pepper condiment *ajvar* is popular here. For fast food, you'll find *burek*, *čevapčići*, and *ražnjići* (see "Balkan Flavors," page 627). Slovenia enjoys Italian-style fare, with a pizza or pasta restaurant on seemingly every corner. Hungarian food simmers in the northeast corner of the country (where many Magyars reside). But most of all, Slovenian food has a distinctly German vibe—including the "four S's": sausages, schnitzels, strudels, and sauerkraut.

Traditional Slovenian dishes are prepared with groats—a grainy mush made with buckwheat, barley, or corn. Buckwheat, which thrives in this climate, often appears on Slovenian menus. You'll also see plenty of *štruklji* (dumplings), which can be stuffed with cheese, meat, or vegetables. *Repa* is turnip prepared like sauerkraut. Among the hearty soups in Slovenia is *jota*—a staple for Karst peasants, made from *repa*, beans, and vegetables.

The cuisine of Slovenia's Karst region (the arid limestone plain south of Ljubljana) is notable. The small farms and wineries of this region have been inspired by Italy's "Slow Food" movement, and believe that cuisine is meant to be gradually appreciated, not rushed—making the Karst a destination for gourmet tours. Karstic cuisine is similar to France's nouvelle cuisine—several courses in small portions, with a focus on unusual combinations and preparations—but with a Tuscan flair. The Karst's tasty air-dried ham *(pršut)*, available throughout the country, is worth seeking out (see sidebar previous page). Istria (the peninsula just to the south of the Karst, in southern Slovenia and Croatia) produces truffles that, locals boast, are as good as those from Italy's Piedmont.

Voda is water, and *kava* is coffee. Radenska, in the bottle with the three little hearts, is Slovenia's best-known brand of mineral water—good enough that the word *Radenska* is synonymous with bottled water all over Slovenia and throughout the former Yugoslavia.

Adventurous teetotalers should forego the Coke and sample Cockta, a Slovenian cola with an unusual flavor (which sup-

posedly comes from berry, lemon, orange, and 11 herbs). Originally called "Cockta-Cockta," the drink was introduced during the communist period, as an alternative to the difficult-to-get Coke. This local variation developed a loyal following...until the Iron Curtain fell, and the real Coke became readily available. Cockta sales plummeted. But in recent years—prodded by the slogan "The Taste of Your Youth"—nostalgic Slovenes are drinking Cockta once more. Aside from having happy childhood memories of sipping Cockta, Slovenes figure they can be proud that their small country produced a soft drink that rivals Coca-Cola.

To toast, say, *"Na ZDROW-yeh!"*—if you can't remember it, think of "Nice driving!" The premier Slovenian brand of *pivo* (beer) is Union (OO-nee-ohn), but you'll also see a lot of Laško (LASH-koh), whose mascot is the Zlatorog (or "Golden Horn," a mythical chamois-like animal).

Slovenia produces some fine *vino* (wine). The Celts first made wine in Slovenia; the Romans improved the process and spread it throughout the country. Slovenia has three primary wine regions. Podravje, in the northeast, is dominated by *laški* and *renski riesling* and other top-quality wines. Posavje, in the southeast, produces both white and red wines, but is famous for the light, russet-colored *cviček* wine. Primorska, in the southwest, has a Mediterranean climate and produces mostly reds. One of the most popular is *teran*, made from *refošk* grapes, which grow in iron-rich red soil (*terra rossa*)—infusing them with a high lactic acid content that supposedly gives the wine healing properties.

Slovenia's national dessert is *potica*, a rolled pastry with walnuts and sometimes also raisins. For more tasty treats, see the "Bled Desserts" sidebar on page 584. Locals claim that Ljubljana has the finest gelato outside of Italy—which, after all, is just an hour down the road.

Slovenian Language

Slovene is surprisingly different from languages spoken in the other former Yugoslav republics. While Serbian and Croatian are mutually intelligible, Slovene is gibberish to Serbs and Croats. Most Slovenes, on the other hand, know Serbo-Croatian—because, a generation ago, everybody in Yugoslavia had to learn it. Linguists have identified some 250 dialects of Slovene. Locals can tell which city—or sometimes even which remote mountain valley—someone comes from by their accent.

The tiny country of Slovenia borders Italy and Austria, with important historical and linguistic ties to both. For self-preservation, the Slovene population has always been forced to function in many different languages. All of these factors make Slovenes excellent linguists. Most young Slovenes speak effortless, flawless English—then admit that they've never set foot in the US or Britain, but love watching American movies and TV shows (which are always subtitled, never dubbed).

As with other Slavic languages, *c* is pronounced "ts" (like "cats"). The letter *j* is pronounced as "y"—making "Ljubljana" easier to say than it looks (lyoob-lyee-AH-nah). Slovene only has one diacritical mark: the *strešica*, or "little roof." This makes *č* sound like "ch," *š* sound like "sh," and *ž* sound like "zh" (as in "measure"). The only trick: As in English, which syllable gets the emphasis

Slovenia

Key Slovene Phrases

English	Slovene	Pronounced
Hello. (formal)	*Dober dan.*	DOH-behr dahn
Hi. / Bye. (informal)	*Živjo.*	ZHEEV-yoh
Do you speak English?	*Ali govorite angleško?*	AH-lee goh-voh-REE-teh ahng-LEHSH-koh
yes / no	*ja / ne*	yah / neh
Please. / You're welcome.	*Prosim.*	PROH-seem
Can I help you?	*Izvolite?*	eez-VOH-lee-teh
Thank you.	*Hvala.*	HVAH-lah
I'm sorry. / Excuse me.	*Oprostite.*	oh-proh-STEE-teh
Good.	*Dobro.*	DOH-broh
Goodbye.	*Nasvidenje.*	nahs-VEE-dehn-yeh
one / two	*ena / dve*	EH-nah / dveh
three / four	*tri / štiri*	tree / SHTEE-ree
five / six	*pet / šest*	peht / shehst
seven / eight	*sedem / osem*	SEH-dehm / OH-sehm
nine / ten	*devet / deset*	deh-VEHT / deh-SEHT
hundred	*sto*	stoh
thousand	*tisoč*	TEE-sohch
How much?	*Koliko?*	KOH-lee-koh
local currency	*euro (€)*	EE-oo-roh
Where is...?	*Kje je...?*	kyeh yeh
...the toilet	*...vece*	VEHT-seh
men	*moški*	MOHSH-kee
women	*ženski*	ZHEHN-skee
water / coffee	*voda / kava*	VOH-dah / KAH-vah
beer / wine	*pivo / vino*	PEE-voh / VEE-noh
Cheers!	*Na zdravje!*	nah ZDROW-yeh
the bill	*račun*	rah-CHOON

is unpredictable. Slovenes use many of the same words as Croatians, but put the stress on an entirely different place.

As you're tracking down addresses, these definitions will help: *trg* (square), *ulica* (street), *cesta* (avenue), *avtocesta* (expressway), and *most* (bridge).

LJUBLJANA

Slovenia's capital, Ljubljana (lyoob-lyee-AH-nah), with a lazy Old Town clustered around a castle-topped mountain, is often likened to Salzburg. It's an apt comparison—but only if you inject a healthy dose of breezy Adriatic culture, add a Slavic accent, and replace Mozart with local architect Jože Plečnik.

Ljubljana feels much smaller than its population of 265,000. While big-league museums are in short supply, the town itself is an idyllic place that sometimes feels too good to be true. Festivals fill the summer, and people enjoy a Sunday stroll any day of the week. Fashion boutiques and cafés jockey for control of the Old Town, while the leafy riverside promenade crawls with stylishly dressed students sipping *kava* and polishing their near-perfect English. Laid-back Ljubljana is the kind of place where graffiti and crumbling buildings seem elegantly atmospheric instead of shoddy.

Batted around by history, Ljubljana has seen cultural influences from all sides—most notably Prague, Vienna, and Venice. This has left the city a happy hodgepodge of cultures. Being the midpoint between the Slavic, Germanic, and Italian worlds gives Ljubljana a special spice. And now Ljubljana is proud to be a trendsetter in the "New Europe"—most notably as Slovenia holds the rotating EU presidency for the first six months of 2008.

People often ask me: What's the "next Prague"? And I have to answer Kraków. But Ljubljana is the *next* "next Prague."

Planning Your Time

Ljubljana deserves a full day. While there are few must-see sights, the city's biggest attraction is its ambience. You'll spend much of

Ljubljana's Two Big Ps

Mind your Ps, and your visit to Ljubljana becomes more meaningful:

Jože Plečnik (YOH-zheh PLAYCH-neek, 1872–1957) is the architect who shaped Ljubljana, designing virtually all of the city's most important landmarks. For more information, see page 552.

France Prešeren (FRAHN-tseh preh-SHAY-rehn, 1800–1849) is Slovenia's greatest poet and the namesake of Ljubljana's main square. Some civic-minded candy shops—trying to imitate the success of Austria's "Mozart Ball" chocolates—have started marketing chocolate "Prešeren Balls."

your time strolling the pleasant town center, exploring the many interesting squares and architectural gems, shopping the boutiques, and sipping coffee at sidewalk cafés along the river.

Here's the best plan for a low-impact sightseeing day: Begin on Prešeren Square, the heart of the city. Cross the Triple Bridge and wander through the riverside produce market before joining the town walking tour at 10:00 (daily May–Sept; less frequent off-season). After the tour, wander along the Ljubljanica River to Jože Plečnik's National and University Library, French Revolution Square, and on to my favorite Ljubljana museum, the Jože Plečnik House (note this sight's limited hours, and plan accordingly: Tue–Thu 10:00–18:00, Sat 9:00–15:00, closed Sun–Mon and Fri). With more time, or if the Plečnik House is closed, stroll through the museum zone (west of Prešeren Square) and through Tivoli Park, dropping into various museums along the way (the Contemporary History Museum in Tivoli Park is best, open daily until 18:00).

Ljubljana is dead and disappointing on Sundays (virtually all shops are closed and the produce market is quiet, but museums are generally open, a modest flea market stretches along the riverfront, and the TI's walking tour still runs). The city is also relatively quiet in August, when the students are on break and many locals head to beach resorts. They say that in August, even homeless people go to the coast.

ORIENTATION

(area code: 01)

Ljubljana—with narrow lanes, architecture that mingles the Old World and contemporary Europe, and cobbles upon cobbles of wonderful distractions—can be disorienting for a first-timer. But the charming central zone is compact, and with a little wandering,

The Story of Ljubljana

In ancient times, Ljubljana was on the trade route connecting the Mediterranean (just 60 miles away) to the Black Sea (toss a bottle off the bridge here, and it can float to the Danube and, eventually, all the way to Russia). Legend has it that Jason and his Argonauts founded Ljubljana when they stopped here for the winter on their way home with the Golden Fleece. The town was Romanized (and called Emona) before being overrun by Huns, only to be resettled later by Slavs.

In 1335, Ljubljana fell under the jurisdiction of the Hapsburg Emperors (who called it Laibach). After six centuries of Hapsburg rule, Ljubljana still feels Austrian—especially the abundant Austrian Baroque and Viennese Art Nouveau architecture—but with a Mediterranean flair.

Napoleon put Ljubljana on the map when he made it the capital of his Illyrian Provinces, a realm that stretched from the Danube to Dubrovnik, from Austria to Albania (for only four years, 1809–1813). For the first time, the Slovene language was taught in schools, awakening a newfound pride in Slovenian cultural heritage. People still look back fondly on this very brief era, which was the first (and probably only) time when Ljubljana rose to prominence on the world stage. After more than 600 years of being part of the Hapsburg Empire, Ljubljana has no "Hapsburg Square"...but they do have a "French Revolution Square."

you'll quickly get the hang of it.

The Ljubljanica River—lined with cafés, restaurants, and a buzzing outdoor market—bisects the city, making a 90-degree turn around the base of a castle-topped mountain. Most sights are either on or just a short walk from the river. Visitors enjoy the distinctive bridges that span the Ljubljanica, including the landmark Triple Bridge (Tromostovje) and pillared Cobblers' Bridge (Čevljarski Most)—both designed by Jože Plečnik. Between them is a very plain wooden bridge dubbed "the Ugly Duckling." The center of Ljubljana is Prešeren Square, watched over by a big statue of Slovenia's national poet, France Prešeren.

I've organized the sights in this chapter based on which side of the river they're on: the east (castle) side of the river, where Ljubljana began, with more medieval charm; and the west (Prešeren Square) side of the river, which has a more Baroque/Art Nouveau feel and most of the urban sprawl. At the northern edge of the tourist's Ljubljana is the train station; at the southern edge is the garden district of Krakovo and the Jože Plečnik House.

In the mid-19th century, the railway connecting Vienna to the Adriatic (Trieste) was built through town—and Ljubljana boomed. But much of the city was destroyed by an earthquake in 1895. It was rebuilt in the Art Nouveau style so popular in Vienna, its capital at the time. A generation later, architect Jože Plečnik bathed the city in his distinctive, artsy-but-sensible, classical-meets-modern style.

In World War II, Slovenia was occupied first by the Italians, then by the Nazis. Ljubljana had a thriving resistance movement that the Nazis couldn't suppress—so they simply fenced off the entire city and made it a giant prison for three years, allowing only shipments of basic food supplies to get in. But the Slovenes—who knew their land far better than their oppressors did—continued to slip in and out of town undetected, allowing them to agitate through the end of the war.

In 1991, Ljubljana became the capital of one of Europe's youngest nations. Today the city is filled with university students, making it a very youthful-feeling town. Ljubljana has always felt free to be creative, and recent years—with unprecedented freedoms—have been no exception. This city is on the cutting edge when it comes to architecture, public art, fashion, and trendy pubs. But the scintillating avant-garde culture has soft edges—hip, but also non-threatening and user-friendly.

Tourist Information

Ljubljana's helpful, businesslike TI has a website (www.ljubljana -tourism.si) and four branches: at the **Triple Bridge,** across from Prešeren Square (daily June–Sept 8:00–21:00, Oct–May 8:00–19:00, Stritarjeva ulica 1, tel. 01/306-1215); at the upper corner of the **market** (Internet access for a fee, bike rental, and information about the rest of Slovenia; daily June–Sept 8:00–21:00, Oct–May 8:00–19:00, Krekov trg 10, tel. 01/306-4575); at the **train station** (daily June–Sept 8:00–22:00, Oct–May 10:00–19:00, Trg O.F. 6, tel. 01/433-9475); and at the **airport** (hours depend on flight schedule, generally daily 11:00–19:00).

At any TI, pick up a pile of free resources: the big city map, the Tourist Guide, the monthly *Where to?* events guide, *Ljubljana Life* magazine (with restaurant reviews), and a wide range of informative brochures. The TI also offers a free room-finding service. Skip the **Ljubljana City Card,** which includes access to public transportation and free entry or discounts at some city museums (€13/72 hrs).

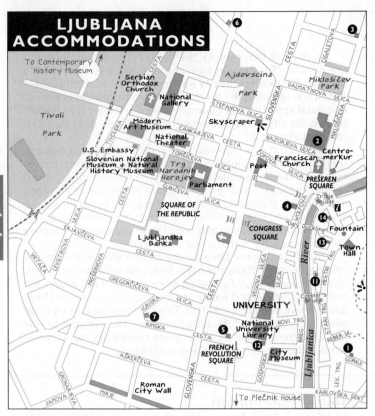

LJUBLJANA ACCOMMODATIONS

Ljubljana

Arrival in Ljubljana

By Train: Ljubljana's modern, user-friendly train station (Želez-niška Postaja) is on the north edge of the city center. Emerging from the passage up to track 1a, turn right and walk under the long canopy along the train tracks to find the yellow arrivals hall. Everything is well-signed in English, including a **TI** (see above), handy train-information office (with useful handouts outlining trips to several domestic and international destinations, daily 5:30–21:30), and ticket office with **ATM** (office open daily 5:00–22:00). Arrivals are *prihodi*, departures are *odhodi*, and track is *tir*.

The main square—and all of my recommended hotels—are within easy **walking** distance. It's a 10-minute stroll to get to the city center: Leave the arrivals hall to the right and walk a long block along the busy Trg Osvobodilne Fronte (or "Trg O.F." for short). At the post office (yellow *pošta-PBS* sign), cross Trg O.F., head straight down Miklošičeva, and you'll reach Prešeren Square.

Unscrupulous **taxis** wait for you in front of the station. These crooks are accustomed to charging you whatever they want with-

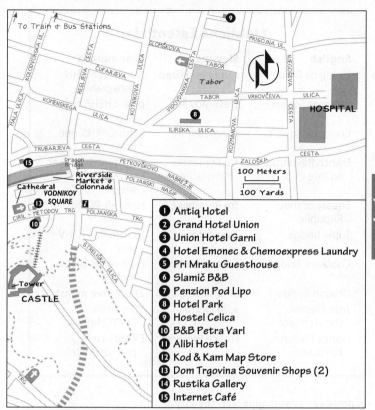

To Train & Bus Stations

HOSPITAL

100 Meters
100 Yards

Tabor

Dragon Bridge
Riverside Market & Colonnade
Cathedral
VODNIKOV SQUARE
Tower
CASTLE

1 Antiq Hotel
2 Grand Hotel Union
3 Union Hotel Garni
4 Hotel Emonec & Chemoexpress Laundry
5 Pri Mraku Guesthouse
6 Slamič B&B
7 Penzion Pod Lipo
8 Hotel Park
9 Hostel Celica
10 B&B Petra Varl
11 Alibi Hostel
12 Kod & Kam Map Store
13 Dom Trgovina Souvenir Shops (2)
14 Rustika Gallery
15 Internet Café

Ljubljana

out using the meter. The most likely scenario is that you'll pay a euro or two too much for the convenience of taking a taxi to your hotel—but *never* pay more than €5 total to any of my recommended hotels. For more on taxis—and how to avoid rip-off cabbies—see "Getting Around Ljubljana—By Taxi," page 538.

By Bus: Ljubljana's bus station (Autobusna Postaja) is a low-profile building (with ticket windows, Internet access, a bakery, and newsstands) in the middle of Trg O.F., right in front of the train station. To get into the center, see "By Train," above.

By Car: As you approach Ljubljana on the expressway, the toll road ends. Once you're on the ring road, simply follow signs for *Center*. Once you get into the city center, you'll begin to see directional signs to individual hotels. Ask your hotel about parking—most have some available, usually for a price. If you need to gas up your rental car before returning it, you'll find a huge gas station on Tivolska Cesta (just west of the train station, near the big Union brewery). Otherwise, your options in the center are limited—it's better to look for a gas station on the

Ljubljana Essentials

English	Slovene	Pronounced
Ljubljana Castle	Ljubljanski Grad	lyoob-lyee-AHN-skee grahd
Prešeren Square	Prešernov Trg	preh-SHEHR-nohv turg
Congress Square	Kongresni Trg	kohn-GREHS-nee turg
French Revolution Square	Trg Francoske Revolucije	turg frant-SOH-skeh reh-voh-LOOT-see-yeh
Square of the Republic	Trg Republike	turg reh-POOB-lee-keh
Triple Bridge	Tromostovje	troh-moh-STOHV-yeh
Cobblers' Bridge	Čevljarski Most	chehv-LAR-skee mohst
Dragon Bridge	Zmajski Most	ZMAY-skee mohst
Jože Plečnik, the architect	Jože Plečnik	YOH-zheh PLAYCH-neek
France Prešeren, the poet	France Prešeren	FRAHN-tseh preh-SHAY-rehn

expressway as you approach the city.

By Plane: See "Transportation Connections," page 566.

Helpful Hints

Pedestrian Safety: Many Ljubljana residents prefer to commute by bike. As a pedestrian, I've had many close calls with bikes whizzing by. Keep your eyes open and stay out of the designated bike lanes on the sidewalks (often marked in red).

Closed Days: Most Ljubljana museums (except the castle and a few less-important museums) are closed on Mondays. Remember that the highly recommended Jože Plečnik House is closed Sundays, Mondays, and Fridays—time your visit here carefully to coincide with a scheduled English tour (see page 555).

Markets: In addition to the regular **market** that sprawls along the riverfront (described under "Sights," page 543), a colorful **flea market** hops along the castle side of the Ljubljanica River (south of the TI) every Sunday from 8:00–14:00.

Money: Most banks are open Mon–Fri 8:00–12:00 & 15:00–17:00, a few also open Sat 9:00–12:00, closed Sun.

Internet Access: Most hotel lobbies have Internet access for guests.

The TI at the upper end of the market has several terminals (€1/30 min, see "Tourist Information," above). **Cyber Café Xplorer** is twice as expensive but has longer hours (Mon–Fri 10:00–22:00, Sat–Sun 14:00–22:00, across the river from the market at Petkovškovo nabrežje 23).

Post Office: The main post office *(pošta)* is in a beautiful yellow Art Nouveau building a block up Čopova from Prešeren Square, at the intersection with the busy Slovenska cesta (Mon–Fri 7:00–20:00, Sat 7:00–13:00, closed Sun).

Map Store: Kod & Kam has a huge selection of maps, English guidebooks, and other books about Slovenia (Mon–Fri 9:00–19:00, until 20:00 May–Aug, Sat 8:00–13:00, closed Sun, hiding at the bottom of French Revolution Square by the City Museum at Trg Francoske Revolucije 7, tel. 01/200-2732).

Architecture Guidebooks: Ljubljana is a turn-on for architecture buffs. If you want to learn more about this city's quirky buildings, consider the excellent €13.50 architecture guidebook, or the €17 book about Jože Plečnik's work (sold at TIs and many bookstores).

Laundry: Most hotels can do your laundry, but it's pricey. **Hostel Celica** serves as the town's self-serve launderette (€5/load, not very central at Metelkova 8, see page 559). Or try **Chemoexpress,** where you can drop your laundry off in the morning and pick it up in the afternoon (about €20 for a load, Mon–Fri 7:00–18:00, closed Sat–Sun, hiding in a courtyard at Wolfova 12, tel. 01/231-0782).

Car Rental: Figure about €60 per day (includes tax and insurance, no extra charge for drop-off elsewhere in Slovenia). Handy options include **Europcar** (in City Hotel at Dalmatinova 15, mobile 031-382-052, www.europcar.si) and **Avis** (Čufarjeva 2, tel. 01/430-8010, www.avis.si).

Best Views: When the café at the top of The Skyscraper is open, it offers the best views in town (see page 551). Views from the castle (see page 546) are nearly as good. My favorite views are from the wooden bridge called the "Ugly Duckling" (between the Triple and Cobblers' bridges), especially at night. On sunny, blue-sky days, the colorful architecture on and near Prešeren Square pops, and you'll take photos like crazy along the river promenade.

Getting Around Ljubljana

By Bus: Virtually all of Ljubljana's sights are easily accessible by foot, so public transportation probably isn't necessary. But just in case: A token, or *žeton,* for a bus trip costs €0.80 (buy at kiosk, bus station, or TI). If you pay on board, it's €1 and you need exact change. An all-day ticket costs €4 (sold only at bus station, TI, or LPP transit office).

By Taxi: There are several companies with different rates, but taxis usually start at about €1, and then charge €1 per kilometer. Additional "surcharges" (such as for luggage) are bogus—and are often tacked on as a surprise after you reach your destination. Crooked cabbies are a big problem in Ljubljana (especially those hanging out at the train station). A ride within the city center (such as from the station to a hotel) shouldn't cost more than €5. Your best strategy is to ask for an estimate up front. The cabbie will probably want to just take you for a flat price without using the meter. This is the easiest solution, but realize you'll probably wind up paying a euro or two more than you would if he used the meter. (If you're feeling stingy and feisty, try insisting on the meter.) Another common trick is to charge you the "Sunday and holidays" *(nedelja in počitnice)* rate even on weekdays. If you're suspicious, ask your cabbie to explain why he's chosen the tariff. You'll likely (but not definitely) avoid crooked cabbies if you call for a taxi, and it's always cheaper than hailing one on the street. While this might sound intimidating, dispatchers generally speak some English. Your hotel, restaurant, or maybe the TI (if they're not too busy) can call a cab for you. **Yellow Taxi** is more reputable than the norm (mobile 041-731-831); **Metro Taxi** is known for being inexpensive (mobile 041-240-200).

By Bike: Ljubljana is a cyclist's delight, with lots of well-marked bike lanes. A few hotels have rental or loaner bikes, or you can rent bikes at the market square TI (€1/2 hrs, €5/day; see "Tourist Information," earlier in this chapter).

TOURS

Most of Ljubljana's museums are disappointing; the town's ambience, architecture, and public art are its best attraction. To help you appreciate it all, taking a walking tour—either through the TI or by hiring your own local guide—is worth ▲▲.

Walking Tour—The TI organizes excellent two-hour guided town walks of Ljubljana in English, led by knowledgeable guides. In summer, the walk also includes a trip up to the castle (by funicular in the morning, and by tourist train in the afternoon). From April through September, there are two tours daily: at 10:00 and 18:00. From October through March, the walking tour (no castle) goes only on Fridays, Saturdays, and Sundays at 11:00 (€7.50/tour, meet at Town Hall around corner from Triple Bridge TI).

Local Guides—Having an expert show you around his or her hometown for two hours for €50 has to be the best value in town. Ljubljana's hardworking guides lead tours on a wide variety of topics and can tailor their tour to your interests (figure €50/2 hrs,

Ljubljana at a Glance

▲▲▲People-Watching Ljubljana's single best activity is sitting at an outdoor café along the river and watching the vivacious, stylish, fun-loving Slovenes strut their stuff. **Hours:** Anytime.

▲▲▲Jože Plečnik House Final digs of the famed home-town architect who shaped so much of Ljubljana, explained by an enthusiastic guide. **Hours:** English tours begin at the top of each hour Tue–Thu 10:00–18:00, Sat 9:00–15:00, last tour departs 1 hour before closing, closed Sun–Mon and Fri.

▲▲Riverside Market Lively market area in the Old Town with produce, clothing, souvenirs—even wild-boar salami. **Hours:** Best in the morning, especially Sat; market hall open Mon–Fri 7:00–16:00, Sat 7:00–14:00, closed Sun.

▲▲Serbian Orthodox Church of Sts. Cyril and Method Beautifully decorated house of worship giving insight into the Orthodox faith. **Hours:** Tue–Sun 9:00–12:00 & 14:00–18:00, closed Mon.

▲▲National and University Library Plečnik's pièce de résistance, with an intriguing facade, piles of books, and a bright reading room. **Hours:** Main stairwell open Mon–Fri 9:00–20:00, Sat 9:00–14:00, closed Sun; student reading room open to the public mid-July–mid-Aug Mon–Fri 14:00–20:00.

▲Dragon Bridge Distinctive Art Nouveau bridge adorned with the city's mascot. **Hours:** Always roaring.

▲Ljubljana Castle Tower with good views and so-so 3-D film. **Hours:** Grounds open daily May–Sept 9:00–22:00, Oct–April 10:00–21:00; castle open daily May–Sept 9:00–21:00, Oct–April 10:00–18:00, film plays all day on the half-hour.

▲Contemporary History Museum Baroque mansion in Tivoli Park, with exhibit highlighting Slovenia's last 100 years. **Hours:** Daily 10:00–18:00.

▲City Museum of Ljubljana Modern, high-tech exhibit on the city's history. **Hours:** Tue–Sun 10:00–18:00, closed Mon.

▲Architectural Museum of Ljubljana Castle with Plečnik exhibit on the edge of town. **Hours:** Mon–Fri 9:00–15:00, Sat 10:00–18:00, Sun 10:00–15:00.

50 percent more for same-day booking, contact TI for details, arrange at least 24 hours before). **Marijan Krišković,** who leads tours for me throughout Europe, is an outstanding guide (mobile 040-222-739, kriskovic@yahoo.com). **Barbara Jakopič,** soft-spoken but extremely knowledgeable, is also good (mobile 040-530-870, b_lucky2@yahoo.com). **Minka Kahrič,** who's traveled solo to the North Pole, also leads tours closer to home—including walks around Ljubljana and excursions into the countryside (€50/2-hour walking tour; driving: €80/up to 4 hours, €120/up to 8 hours; mobile 059-016-116 or 041-805-962, www.minkakahric.si).

Boat Cruise—Consider seeing the town from the Ljubljanica River, with English commentary from a live guide (€7.50; June–Sept daily at 18:30, Sat–Sun also at 10:30; April–May and Oct daily at 17:30, Sat–Sun also at 10:30; weather permitting, few or no cruises Nov–March, confirm schedule at TI, departs from near the Triple Bridge—about one block along the embankment away from the market). Because Ljubljana is a small town that's easily seen by foot, this trip is more romantic than informative.

Bike Tour—The TI offers a bike tour of the city by request (€12.50, 2 hours, 3-person minimum, arrange at least 24 hours ahead, get details at TI).

SELF-GUIDED SPIN-TOUR

▲▲Prešeren Square

The heart of Ljubljana is lively Prešeren Square (Prešernov trg). It's always been bustling, but now it's more people-friendly than ever, since a recent mayor outlawed buses and taxis here.

The city's meeting point is the large **statue of France Prešeren,** Slovenia's greatest poet, whose works include the lyrics

to the Slovenian national anthem (and whose silhouette adorns Slovenia's €2 coin). The statue shows Prešeren, an important catalyst of 19th-century Slovenian nationalism, being inspired from overhead by the Muse. This statue provoked a scandal and out-raged the bishop when it went up a hundred years ago—a naked woman sharing the square with a church! To ensure that nobody could be confused about the woman's intentions, she's conspicuously depicted with typi-cal muse accessories: a laurel branch and a cloak. Even so, for the first few years they covered the scandalous statue with a tarp each night. And the model who posed for the Muse was so disgraced that no one in Slovenia would hire her—so she emigrated to the US and never returned.

Stand at the base of the statue to get oriented. The bridge crossing the Ljubljanica River is one of Ljubljana's most important landmarks, Jože Plečnik's **Triple Bridge** (Tromostovje). The middle (widest) part of this bridge already existed, but Plečnik added the two side spans to more efficiently funnel the six streets of traffic on this side of the bridge to the one street on the other side. The bridge's Venetian vibe is intentional: Plečnik recognized that Ljubljana, located midway between Venice and then-capital Vienna, is itself a bridge between the Italian and Germanic worlds. Across the bridge is the TI, WCs, ATMs, market and cathedral (to the left), and the Town Hall (straight ahead).

Now turn 90 degrees to the right, and look down the first street after the riverbank. Find the pale woman in the picture frame on the second floor of the first yellow house. This is **Julija,** the unrequited love of Prešeren's life. Tour guides spin romantic tales about how the couple met. But the truth is far less exciting: He was a teacher in her father's house when he was in his 30s and she was four. Later in life, she inspired him from afar—as she does now, from across the square—but they never got together. She may have been his muse, but when it came to marriage, she opted for wealth and status.

In 1895, a devastating earthquake destroyed half the city. While tragic, it allowed Ljubljana to rebuild in style. Today

Ljubljana—especially the streets around this square—is an architecture-lover's paradise. The **Hauptmann House,** to the right of Julija, was the only building on the square to survive the quake. A few years later, the owner redecorated it in the then-trendy Viennese Art Nouveau style you see today, using bright colors (since his family sold dyes). All that remains of the original is the little Baroque balcony above the entrance.

Just to the right of the Hauptmann House is a car-sized **model** of the city center—helpful for orientation. The street next to it (with the McDonald's) is **Čopova,** once the route of Ljubljana's Sunday promenade. A century ago, locals would put on their Sunday best and stroll from here to Tivoli Park, listening to musicians and dropping into cafés along the way. Plečnik called it the "lifeline of the city," connecting the green lungs of the park to this urban center. Today, busy Slovenska avenue and railroad tracks cross the route, making the promenade less inviting. But in the last decade, Ljubljana has been trying to recapture its golden age, and some downtown streets are pedestrian-only on weekends once again. The new evening *paseo* thrives along the river between the Triple Bridge and Cobblers' Bridge.

Continue looking to the right, past the big, pink landmark Franciscan Church of St. Mary. The characteristic glass awning marks **Centromerkur**—the first big post-quake department store, today government-protected. At the top of the building is Mercury, god of commerce, watching over the square that has been Ljubljana's commercial heart since the city began. (If you look carefully, you can see the mustachioed face of the building's owner hiding in the folds of cloth by Mercury's left foot.) Since this area was across the river from medieval Ljubljana (beyond the town's limits...and the long arm of its tax collector), it was the best place to sell and buy goods. Today it's the heart of Ljubljana's boutique culture. Step into the Centromerkur store to admire the interior, which is exactly the same as when it was built. The old-fashioned layout isn't convenient for modern shoppers—no elevator, tight aisles—but no matter how much anyone complains, the management isn't allowed to change a thing.

The street between Centromerkur and the pink church is **Miklošičeva cesta,** which connects Prešeren Square to the train station. When Ljubljana was rebuilding after the 1895 earthquake, town architects and designers envisioned this street as a showcase of its new, Vienna-inspired Art Nouveau image.

Up Miklošičeva street and on the left is the prominent **Grand Hotel Union,** with a stately domed spire on the corner. When these buildings were designed, Prague was the cultural capital of the Slavic world. The new look of Ljubljana paid homage to "the golden city of a hundred spires" (and copied Prague's romantic image). There was actually a law for several years that new corner buildings had to have these spires. Even the trees you'll see around town were part of the vision. When the architect Plečnik designed the Ljubljanica River embankments a generation later, he planted tall, pointy poplar trees and squat, rounded willows—imitating the spires and domes of Prague.

Detour a block up Miklošičeva cesta to see two more architectural gems of that era (across from the Grand Hotel Union): First is a Secessionist building—marked **Zadružna Zveza**—with classic red, blue, and white colors (for the Slovenian flag). Next is the noisy, pink, zigzagged **Cooperative Bank.** The bank was designed by Ivan Vurnik, an ambitious Slovenian architect who wanted to invent a distinctive national style after World War I, when the Hapsburg Empire broke up and Eastern Europe's nations were proudly emerging for the first time.

Prešeren Square is the perfect springboard to explore the rest of Ljubljana. Now that you're oriented, visit some of the areas listed next.

SIGHTS

East of the River, Under the Castle: The Market and Old Town

The castle side of the river is the city's most colorful and historic quarter, packed with Old World ambience.

▲▲**Riverside Market**—In Ljubljana's thriving Old Town market, big-city Slovenes enjoy buying directly from the producer. Prices go down as the day gets late and as the week goes on. The market, worth an amble anytime, is best on Saturday mornings, when the townspeople take their time wandering the stalls. In this tiny capital of a tiny country, you may even see the president searching for the perfect melon.

Begin your walk through the market at the Triple Bridge (and TI). The riverside **colonnade,** which echoes the long-gone medieval city wall, was designed by (who else?) Jože Plečnik. This first stretch—nearest the Triple Bridge—is good for souvenirs: wood-carvings, miniature painted frontboards from beehives, honey products (including honey brandy), and lots of colorful candles (bubbly Marta will gladly paint a special message on your candle for no extra charge).

Farther in, the market is almost all local, and the colonnade is populated by butchers, bakers, fishermen, and lazy cafés. Peek down at the actual river and see how the architect wanted the town and river to connect. The lower arcade is a people zone, with easy access from the bridge, public WCs, inviting cafés, and a stinky fish market *(ribarnice)* offering a wide variety. The restaurant just below, **Ribca,** serves fun fishy plates, beer, and coffee with great riverside seating (open Mon–Sat only until 16:00; see "Eating," page 561).

Across from the stairs down into the fish market, about where the souvenir stands end, you reach the first small market square. On your right, notice the 10-foot-tall concrete **cone.** Plečnik wanted to make Ljubljana the "Athens of the North," and imagined a huge hilltop cone crowning the center of a national acropolis—a complex for government, museums, and culture. This ambitious plan didn't make it off the drawing board, but part of Plečnik's Greek idea came true: this marketplace, based on an ancient Greek *agora.* Plečnik's cone still captures the Slovenes' imaginations...and adorns Slovenia's €0.10 coin.

At the top of this square, you'll find the 18th-century **cathedral** *(stolnica)* standing on the site of a 13th-century Romanesque church. The cathedral is dedicated to St. Nicholas, protector against floods and patron saint of the fishermen and boatmen who have long come to sell their catch at the market. Go under the high arch, then take a close look at the intricately decorated side door on the left. This remarkable door was created for Pope John Paul II's visit here in 1996. Buried deeply in the fecund soil of their ancient and pagan history, the nation's linden tree of life sprouts with the story of the Slovenes. The ceramic pots represent the original Roman settlement here. Just to the left, above the tree, are the Byzantine missionaries Cyril and Method, who came here to convert the Slavs to Christianity in the ninth century. Just above, Crusaders and Ottomans do battle. Near the top, see the Slovenes going into the cave—entering the dark 20th century (World War I, World War II, and communism). At the top is Pope John Paul II (the first Slavic pontiff, who also oversaw the fall of communism). Directly below him is Slovenia's first saint; and to the right is Frederic Baraga, a 19th-century bishop who became a missionary in Michigan and codified Chippewa grammar (notice the Native American relief on the book he's holding). In the upper right-hand corner is a sun, which has been shining since Slovenia gained its independence in 1991.

The interior is stunning Italian Baroque (free, open long hours daily). The transept is surrounded by sculptures of four bishops of Roman Ljubljana (when it was called Emona, or Aemon). The bust on the right depicts Anton Vovk, a 20th-century bishop who's one miracle shy of sainthood. Left of the main altar, notice the distinctive chair. This was designed by the very religious Jože Plečnik, whose brother was a priest here. Look up over the nave to enjoy the recently restored, gorgeous ceiling fresco.

Around back is a similar door, carved with images of the six 20th-century bishops of Ljubljana.

The building at the end of this first market square is the seminary palace. In the basement is a **market hall,** with vendors selling cheeses, meats, baked goods, dried fruits, and other goodies (Mon–Fri 7:00–16:00, Sat 7:00–14:00, closed Sun). This place is worth a graze. Most merchants are happy to give you a free sample (point to what you want, and say *probat, prosim*—"a taste, please").

When you leave the market hall, continue downstream into the big **main market square,** packed with produce and clothing stands. (The colorful flower market hides behind the market hall.) The row of vendors nearest the colonnade sell fruit from all over, but the ones located deeper in the market sell only locally grown produce. These producers go out of their way to be old-fashioned— many of them still follow the tradition of pushing their veggies on wooden carts (called *cizas*) to the market from their garden patches in the suburbs. Once at the market, they simply display their goods on top of their cart, turning it into a sales kiosk. Notice that vendors handle their produce wearing special gloves—it's considered rude for customers to touch the fruits and vegetables before they're bought. Over time, shoppers develop friendships with their favorite producers. On busy days, you'll see a long line at one stand, while the other merchants stand bored. Your choice is simple: Get in line, or eat sub-par produce.

Near the market hall, look for the little **scales** in the wooden kiosks marked *Kontrola Tehtnica*—allowing buyers to immediately check whether the producer cheated them (not a common problem, but just in case). The Hapsburg days left locals with the old German saying, "Trust is good; control is better."

At the corner of this market square (toward Prešeren Square), you'll notice a big gap along the riverfront colonnade. This was to be the site of a huge, roofed **Butchers' Bridge** designed by Jože Plečnik, but the plans never materialized. Aware of Plečnik's newfound touristic currency, some town politicians have recently dusted off the old plans and proposed building the bridge after all these years. (If you look across the river, you'll see that the cornerstone was already put in place by an overzealous politician.) It's a controversial project, and every time a new mayor is elected, the decision is reversed.

If you want a unique taste as you finish exploring the market, enter the colonnade near the very end and find the **Divjač'na Hubert** stand at #22, specializing in game. Ask for a *probat* (taste) of *divji prašič salama*—wild-boar salami.

Just beyond the end of the market colonnade is the...

▲**Dragon Bridge (Zmajski Most)**—The dragon has been the symbol of Ljubljana for centuries, ever since Jason (of Argonauts

and Golden Fleece fame) supposedly slew one in a nearby swamp. This is one of the few notable bits of Ljubljana architecture not by Plečnik (but by Jurij Zaninović, a fellow student of Vienna architect Otto Wagner). While the dragon is the star of this very photogenic Art Nouveau bridge, the bridge itself was officially dedicated to the 40th anniversary of Hapsburg Emperor Franz Josef's reign (see the dates on the side: 1848–1888). Tapping into the emp's vanity got new projects funded—vital as the city rebuilt after its devastating earthquake of 1895. But the Franz Josef name never stuck; those dragons are just too darn memorable.

▲**Town Square (Mestni Trg) and the Old Town**—Ljubljana's Town Square, just across the Triple Bridge and up the street from Prešeren Square, is home to the **Town Hall** (Rotovž), highlighted by its clock tower and pillared loggia. Step inside the Renaissance courtyard to see artifacts and a map of late-17th-century Ljubljana. Studying this map, notice how the river, hill, and wall worked together to fortify the town. Courtyards like this (but humbler) are hidden through the city. As rent in these old places is cheap, many such courtyards host funky and characteristic little businesses. Be sure to get off the main drag and poke into Ljubljana's nooks and crannies.

In the square is a recent replica of the **Fountain of Three Carolinian Rivers,** inspired in style and theme by Rome's many fountains. (The original is in a museum.) The figures with vases represent this region's three main rivers: Ljubljanica, Sava, and Krka. This is one of many works in town by Francesco Robba, an Italian who came to Ljubljana for one job, fell in love with a Slovene, and stayed here the rest of his life—decorating the city's churches with beautiful Baroque altars.

In the early 19th century, Ljubljana consisted mainly of this single street, running along the base of Castle Hill (plus a small "New Town" across the river). Stretching south from here are two other "squares"—Stari trg (Old Square) and Gornji trg (Upper Square)—that have long since grown together into one big, atmospheric promenade lined with quaint boutiques, restaurants, and cafés (perfect for a stroll). Virtually every house along this drag has a story to tell, of a famous resident or infamous incident. As you walk, keep your eyes open for Ljubljana's mascot dragon—it's everywhere. At the end of the pedestrian zone (at Gornji trg), look uphill and notice the village charms of some of the oldest buildings in town (four medieval houses with rooflines slanted at the ends, different from the others on this street).

▲**Ljubljana Castle (Ljubljanski Grad)**—The castle above town offers enjoyable views of Ljubljana and the surrounding coun-

tryside. There probably has been a settlement on this site since prehistoric times, though the first castle here was Roman. The 12th-century version was gradually added on to over the centuries, until it fell into disrepair in the 17th century. Today's castle was rebuilt in the 1940s, renovated in the 1970s, and is still technically unfinished (subject to ongoing additions). The castle houses a restaurant, a gift shop, temporary exhibition halls, and a Gothic chapel with Baroque paintings of the coat of arms of St. George (Ljubljana's patron saint, the dragon-slayer). Above the restaurant are two wedding halls—Ljubljana's most popular places to get married (free for locals). While the castle and its attractions are ho-hum, the views are worth the trip.

It's free to enter the castle grounds (daily May–Sept 9:00–22:00, Oct–April 10:00–21:00, tel. 01/232-9994). Inside are two optional activities you have to pay for (€3.30 covers both, daily May–Sept 9:00–21:00, Oct–April 10:00–18:00): the **castle tower,** with 92 steps leading to one of the best views in town; and a 20-minute **3-D film** about the history of Ljubljana (touted as a "virtual museum," but barely worth your time; plays all day on the half-hour).

Tours of the castle in Slovene and English leave from the entry bridge daily June through mid–September at 10:00 and 16:00 (€4.60, tour lasts 60–90 min). The castle is also home to the Ljubljana Summer Festival, with **concerts** throughout the summer (tel. 01/426-4340, www.festival-lj.si).

Getting to the Castle: A new **funicular** whisks visitors to the top in a jiff (€2, daily May–Sept 10:00–23:00, Oct–April 10:00–21:00, catch it at Krekov trg, across the busy street from the market square TI). Another sweat-free route to the top is via the **tourist train** that leaves at the top of each hour (or more frequently, with demand) from in front of the Triple Bridge TI (€3 round-trip, daily in summer 9:00–21:00, shorter hours off-season, doesn't run in snow or other bad weather). There are also two handy **trails** to the castle. The steeper-but-faster route begins near the Dragon Bridge (find Študentovska lane, just past the statue of Vodnik in the market). Slower but easier is Reber, just off Stari trg (Old Square), a few blocks south of the Town Hall (once on the trail, always bear left, then go right when you're just under the castle—follow signs).

West of the River, Beyond Prešeren Square: The Museum Zone and Tivoli Park

The Prešeren Square (west) side of the river is the heart of modern Ljubljana, and home to several prominent squares and fine museums. These sights are listed roughly in order from Prešeren Square, and can be linked to make an interesting walk.

• *Leave Prešeren Square in the direction the poet is looking, bear to your left (up Wolfova, by the picture of Julija), and walk a block to...*

Congress Square (Kongresni Trg)—This grassy, tree-lined square is ringed by some of Ljubljana's most important buildings: the University headquarters, the Baroque Ursuline Church of the Holy Trinity, a classical mansion called the Kažina, and the Philharmonic Hall. At the top end of the square, by the entry to a pedestrian underpass, a Roman sarcophagus sits under a gilded statue of a **Roman citizen**—a replica of an artifact from 1,700 years ago, when this town was called Emona. The busy street above you has been the main trading route through town since ancient Roman times. This square hosts the big town events. Locals remember how, when President Clinton visited, tens of thousands packed the square. (When President George W. Bush came, almost nobody showed up.)

• *Take the underpass beneath busy Slovenska avenue (the town's main traffic thoroughfare), then continue straight through the shopping mall into the...*

▲**Square of the Republic (Trg Republike)**—This unusual square is essentially a parking lot ringed by an odd collection of buildings. While hardly quaint, the Square of the Republic gives you a good taste of a modern corner of Ljubljana. And it's historic—this is where Slovenia declared its independence in 1991.

The **twin office towers** (with the world's biggest digital watch, flashing the date, time, and temperature) were designed by Plečnik's protégé, Edvard Ravnikar. As harrowing as these seem, imagine if they had followed the original plans—twice as tall as they are now, and connected by a bridge, representing the gateway to Ljubljana. These buildings were originally designed as the Slovenian parliament—but they were scaled back when Tito didn't approve (since it would have made Slovenia's parliament bigger than the Yugoslav parliament in Belgrade). Instead, the **Slovenian Parliament** is across the square, in the strangely low-profile office building with the sculpted entryway. The carvings are in the Social Realist style, celebrating the noble Slovenian people conforming to communist ideals for the good of the entire society. Completing the square are a huge conference center (Cankarjev Dom, the white building behind the skyscrapers), a shopping mall, and some public art.

• *Just a block north, through the grassy park (Trg Narodni Herojev), you'll find the...*

Slovenian National Museum (Narodni Muzej Slovenije) and Slovenian Museum of Natural History (Prirodoslovni Muzej Slovenije)—These two museums share a single historic building facing a park behind the Parliament. While neither collection is particularly good, they're both worth considering if you have a special interest or if it's a rainy day (€3 for each museum, or €5 for both, some English descriptions, daily 10:00–18:00, Thu until 20:00, Muzejska 1, tel. 01/241-0940, www.narmuz-lj.si and www2.pms-lj.si).

The **National Museum** occupies the ground floor, featuring a lapidarium with carved-stone Roman monuments and exhibits on Egyptian mummies. (Temporary exhibits are also on this level.) Upstairs and to the right are more exhibits of the National Museum, with archaeological findings ranging from old armor and pottery to the museum's pride and joy, a fragment of a 45,000-year-old Neanderthal flute.

Upstairs and to the left is the **Natural History** exhibit, featuring the flora and fauna of Slovenia. You'll see partial skeletons of a mammoth and a cave bear, plenty of stuffed reptiles, fish, and birds, and an exhibit on "human fish" (*Proteus anguinus*—long, skinny, pale-pink salamanders).

• *At the far end of the building is a glassed-in annex displaying Roman stone monuments (free). Turning left around the museum building and walking one block, you'll see the...*

US Embassy—This pretty yellow chalet (with brown trim and a red roof, at Prešernova cesta 31) wins my vote for quaintest embassy building in the world. Resist the urge to snap a photo... those guards are all business.

• *Just up Prešernova street from the embassy are two decent but skippable art museums:*

National Gallery (Narodna Galerija)—This museum has three parts: European artists, Slovenian artists, and temporary exhibits. Find the work of Ivana Kobilca, a late-19th-century Slovenian Impressionist. Art-lovers enjoy her self-portrait in *Summer*. If you're going to Bled, you can get a sneak preview with Marko Pernhart's huge panorama of the Julian Alps (€5, free on Sat after 14:00, open Tue–Sun 10:00–18:00, closed Mon, enter through big glass box between two older buildings at Prešernova 24, tel. 01/241-5435, www.ng-slo.si).

Museum of Modern Art (Moderna Galerija Ljubljana)—This museum, which might be closed for renovation, has a ho-hum permanent collection of modern and contemporary Slovenian artists, as well as temporary exhibits by both Slovenes and international artists (if open, likely €4, Tue–Sat 10:00–18:00, closed Mon, Tomšičeva 14, tel. 01/241-6800, www.mg-lj.si).

• *By the busy road near the art museums, look for the distinctive Neo-Byzantine design (tall domes with narrow slits) of the...*

▲▲Serbian Orthodox Church of Sts. Cyril and Method—Ljubljana's most striking church interior isn't Catholic, but Orthodox. This church was built in 1936, soon after the Slovenes joined a political union with the Serbs. Wealthy Slovenia attracted its poorer neighbors from the south—so it built this church for

that community. Since 1991, the Serb population continues to rise, as people from the poorer parts of the former Yugoslavia flock to prosperous Slovenia.

Step inside for the best glimpse of the Orthodox faith this side of Dubrovnik (free, Tue–Sun 9:00–12:00 & 14:00–18:00, closed Mon). The church is colorfully decorated without a hint of the 20th century, mirroring a very conservative religion. You'll see Cyrillic script in this building, which feels closer to Moscow than to Rome. Notice that there are no pews, because worshippers stand throughout the service. On the left, find the small room with tubs of water, where the faithful light tall, skinny beeswax candles (purchased at the little window in the back corner). The painted screen, or iconostasis, is believed to separate our material world from the spiritual realm behind it. Ponder the fact that several centuries ago, before the Catholic Church began to adapt to a changing world, all Christians worshipped this way. For more on the Orthodox faith, see the sidebar on page 659.

• *On the other side of the busy street is...*

Tivoli Park (Park Tivoli)—This huge park, just west of the center, is where Slovenes relax on summer weekends. The easiest access is through the graffiti-covered underpass from Cankarjeva cesta (between the Serbian Orthodox Church and the Museum of Modern Art). As you emerge, the Neoclassical pillars leading down the promenade clue you in that this part of the park was designed by Jože Plečnik.

• *Aside from taking a leisurely stroll, the best thing to do in the park is visit the...*

▲Contemporary History Museum (Muzej Novejše Zgodovine)—In a Baroque mansion (Cekinov Grad) in Tivoli Park, a well-done exhibit called "Slovenians in the 20th Century" traces the last hundred years of Slovenia. Downstairs are temporary exhibits, and upstairs are several rooms using models, dioramas, and light-and-sound effects to creatively tell the story of one of Europe's youngest nations. It's a little difficult to fully appreciate, even with the English descriptions. But the creativity and the spunky spirit of the place are truly enjoyable. The "Slovenia 1945–1960" exhibit outlines both the good and the bad of the early Tito years (including a photo album with Tito's visits to Slovenia). But the most moving room has artifacts from the Slovenes' brave declaration of independence from a hostile Yugoslavia in 1991. The well-organized Slovenes had only to weather a 10-day skirmish to gain their autonomy. (It's chilling to think that bombers were en route to leveling this gorgeous city. The planes were called back at the last minute, by a Yugoslav National Army officer with allegiances to Slovenia.) The free English brochure explains everything (€3.50, permanent exhibit free first Sun of the month, open daily 10:00–18:00, in Tivoli Park at Celovška cesta 23, tel. 01/300-9610, www.muzej-nz.si).

Getting There: The museum is a 20-minute walk from the center, best combined with a wander through Tivoli Park. The fastest approach: As you emerge from the Cankarjeva cesta underpass into the park, turn right and go straight ahead for five minutes, continue straight up the ramp, then turn left after the tennis courts and look for the big pink-and-white mansion.

• *Hungry? Near the museum, look for the "Hot Horse" food kiosk, selling €3.50 horseburgers (no joke). A local institution, this is a popular place to get together with friends and neigh-bors. The giant, modern, blocky, light-blue building across the busy road is the Union Pivovar—the brewery for Slovenia's favorite brew.*

On your way back to the center, consider stopping by...

The Skyscraper (Nebotičnik)—This 1933 Art Deco building was the first skyscraper in Slovenia, for a time the tallest building in Central Europe, and one of the earliest European buildings that was clearly influenced by American architecture. When it's open, The Skyscraper's observation deck offers the best view of Ljubljana's skyline.

The Skyscraper has weathered an often-unlucky history. At the time it was constructed, Jože Plečnik was calling the shots when it came to Ljubljana architecture, so this building's designer had to get Plečnik's approval before he could build. Plečnik agreed, but didn't like the plan for 12 stories—so he asked to make it nine instead. After agreeing, the building's architect went ahead and built the last three stories anyway.

Ever since, say the locals, The Skyscraper has been cursed. The 12th-story observation deck had to close a few years back because it had become the most popular spot in the country for suicide attempts. Now it has been (ineffectively) retrofitted to try to prevent people from diving off. Two different restaurants on the top floor have come and gone over the last five years, and plans for a new one are constantly on-again, off-again (if you want to see whether it's open, The Skyscraper is 2 blocks from Prešeren Square at Štefanova ulica 1).

• *A few blocks south, near several Jože Plečnik sights (see below) at the river end of French Revolution Square, you'll find the...*

▲City Museum of Ljubljana (Mestni Muzej Ljubljana)—This new, thoughtfully presented museum, located in the recently restored Auersperg Palace, offers a high-tech, in-depth look at the "Faces of Ljubljana." You'll begin your visit in the cellar, with Roman ruins (including remains of the original Roman road and sewer system, found right here and displayed in situ) and layers of medieval artifacts.

Then you'll head up to the first floor, which traces the social history of Ljubljana through the eyes of its participants: men (displaying shooting targets, from the "country clubs" of the late-18th-cenutry aristocracy); women (with stories and artifacts of six women who've had an impact on the city); children (who were hidden from the authorities during the Nazi occupation); and youth (specifically in the 1960s and 1970s, when Ljubljana's Šumi bar was

Jože Plečnik
(1872–1957)

There is probably no other single architect who has shaped one city as Jože Plečnik (YOH-zheh PLAYCH-neek) shaped Ljubljana. From libraries, office buildings, cemeteries, and stadiums to landscaping, riverside embankments, and market halls, Plečnik left his mark everywhere. While he may not yet register very high on the international Richter scale of important architects, the Slovenes' pride in this man's work is understandable.

Plečnik was born in Ljubljana and trained as a furniture designer, before his interest turned to architecture. He studied in Vienna under the Secessionist architect Otto Wagner. His first commissions, done around the turn of the 20th century in Vienna, were pretty standard Art Nouveau stuff. Then Tomáš Masaryk, president of the new nation of Czechoslovakia, decided that the dull Hapsburg design of Prague Castle could use a new look to go with its new independence. But he didn't want an Austrian architect; it had to be a Slav. In 1921, Masaryk chose Jože Plečnik, who sprinkled the castle grounds with his distinctive touches. By now, Plečnik had perfected his simple, eye-pleasing style, which mixes modern

Yugoslavia's answer to Haight-Ashbury).

Of the various themed exhibits on the second floor, the most interesting ("From State to State") explains how Ljubljana has belonged to 10 different states over the last 200 years, ranging from the genteel Hapsburg Empire to the oppressive Nazi regime to the benevolent EU. Another exhibit examines the modern woes of traffic, including noise and air pollution, and gives you the opportunity to sit in a mustard-yellow, communist-era Fiat Fičko car.

Rounding out the collection is a relaxing 15-minute movie and a range of special exhibits on the ground floor. While everything is well-described in English, a tour guide on the museum's staff might be able to show you around if it's not too busy—ask (entry-€4, Tue–Sun 10:00–18:00, closed Mon, kid-friendly, Gosposka 15, tel. 01/241-2500, www.mm-lj.si).

• *If visiting the museum, don't miss the nearby National University Library and French Revolution Square—both described under "Jože Plečnik's Architecture," next.*

and classical influences, with lots of columns and pyramids—simultaneously austere and playful.

By the time Plečnik finished in Prague, he had made a name for himself. His prime years were spent creating for the Kingdom of Yugoslavia (before the ideology-driven era of Tito). Plečnik returned home to Ljubljana and set to work redesigning the city, both as an architect and as an urban planner. He lived in a humble house behind the Trnovo Church (now a tourable museum—see page 555), and on his walk to work every day, he pondered ways to make the city even more livable. Wandering through town, notice how thoughtfully he incorporated people, nature, the Slovenian heritage, town vistas, and symbolism into his works—it's feng shui on a grand urban scale.

For all of Plečnik's ideas that became reality, even more did not. After World War II, the very religious Plečnik fell out of favor with the new communist government, and found it more difficult to get his projects completed. (It's fun to imagine how this city might look if Plečnik had always gotten his way.) After his death in 1957, Plečnik was virtually forgotten by Slovenes and scholars alike. His many works in Ljubljana were taken for granted.

But in 1986, an exposition about Plečnik at Paris' Pompidou Center jump-started interest in the architect. Within a few years Plečnik was back in vogue. Today, scholars laud him as a genius who was ahead of his time...while locals and tourists enjoy the elegant simplicity of his works.

South of Prešeren Square: Jože Plečnik's Architecture

Jože Plečnik is to Ljubljana what Antoni Gaudí is to Barcelona: a homegrown and amazingly prolific genius who shaped his town with a uniquely beautiful vision. And, as in Barcelona, Ljubljana has a way of turning people who couldn't care less about architecture into huge Plečnik fans. There's plenty to see. In addition to the Triple Bridge (described on page 541), the riverside market (page 543), and the sights listed here, Plečnik designed the embankments along the Ljubljanica and Gradaščica Rivers in the Trnovo neighborhood; the rebuilt Roman wall along Mirje street, south of the center; the Church of St. Francis, with its classicist bell tower; St. Michael's Church on the Marsh; Orel Stadium; Žale Cemetery; and many more buildings throughout Slovenia.

Some of the best Plečnik sights are near the river, just south of Congress and Prešeren squares. I've linked them up in the order of handy self-guided walk.

• *From Prešeren Square, stroll south along the river. After the plain wooden bridge called the "Ugly Duckling," you'll come to the...*

▲▲**Cobblers' Bridge (Čevljarski Most)**—Named for the actual cobblers (shoemakers) who set up shop along the river in olden

times, the bridge encapsulates Plečnik's style perhaps better than any other structure: simple, clean lines adorned with classical columns. Ideal for people-watching (with the castle hovering scenically overhead), this is one of Ljubljana's most appealing spots.

• *Continue past the Cobblers' Bridge on the right side of the river. After about a block, turn right up the parked-up street called Novi trg. At the top of this street, on the left, is a red-brick building embedded with gray granite blocks in an irregular checkerboard pattern. This is the...*

▲▲**National and University Library (Narodna in Univerzitetna Knjižnica, or NUK)**—Widely regarded as Plečnik's masterpiece, this building is a bit underwhelming...until an understanding of

its symbolism brings it to life. On the surface, the red-and-gray color scheme evokes the red soil and chunks of granite of Plečnik's home region, the Karst. But on a deeper level, the library's design conveys the message of overcoming obstacles to attain knowledge. The odd-sized and -shaped blocks in the facade actually represent

a complex numerological pattern that suggests barriers on the path to enlightenment. The sculpture on the river side is Moses—known for leading his people through 40 years of hardship to the Promised Land. On the right side of the building, find the horse-head doorknobs—representing the winged horse Pegasus (grab hold, and he'll whisk you away to new levels of enlightenment). Step inside. The main staircase is dark and gloomy—modeled after an Egyptian tomb. But at the top, through the door marked *Velika Čitalnica*, is the bright, airy main reading room: the ultimate goal, a place of learning.

Aside from being a great work of architecture, the building also houses the most important library in Slovenia, with more than two million books (about one per Slovene). The library is supposed to receive a copy of each new book printed in the country. In a freaky bit of bad luck, this was the only building in town damaged in World War II, when a plane crashed into it. But the people didn't want to see their books go up in flames—so hundreds of locals formed a human chain, risking life and limb to get the books out of the burning building.

You can easily duck into the main stairwell (free, Mon–Fri 9:00–20:00, Sat 9:00–14:00, closed Sun). The quiet student reading room is officially open for visitors during very limited hours, when it's technically closed to students (mid-July–mid-Aug Mon–Fri 14:00–20:00). If you're not here during that one-month span, and you're really determined to see the room, you can stick close to a student going inside. To get out, follow another student—or push gently on the door (it usually opens easily).

• *Directly behind the library is a mellow square with an obelisk in the middle. This is...*

▲French Revolution Square (Trg Francoske Revolucije)— Plečnik designed the **obelisk** in the middle of the square to commemorate Napoleon's short-lived decision to make Ljubljana the capital of his Illyrian Provinces. It's rare to find anything honoring Napoleon outside of Paris, but he was good to Ljubljana. Under his rule, Slovenian culture flourished, schools were established, and roads and infrastructure were improved. The monument contains ashes of the unknown French soldiers who died in 1813, when the region went from French to Austrian control.

The Teutonic Knights of the Cross established the nearby **monastery** (Križanke, ivy-capped wall and gate, free entry) in 1230. The adaptation of these monastery buildings into the Ljubljana Summer Theatre was Plečnik's last major work (1950–1956).

• *From here, it's a scenic 10-minute walk to the next sight. From the obelisk, walk down Emonska toward the twin-spired church. You'll pass (on the left) the delightful Krakovo district—a patch of green countryside in downtown Ljubljana. Many of the veggies you see in the riverside market come from these carefully tended gardens. (This mellow residential zone also has a pair of good restaurants—see "Eating," later in this chapter) When you reach the Gradaščica stream, head over the bridge (also designed by Plečnik) and go around the left side of the church to find the house.*

▲▲▲Jože Plečnik House (Plečnikova Zbirka)—Ljubljana's favorite son lived here from 1921 until his death in 1957. He added on to an existing house, building a circular bedroom for himself and filling the place with bric-a-brac he designed, as well as artifacts, photos, and gifts from around the world that inspired him as he shaped Ljubljana. Living a simple, almost monastic lifestyle, Plečnik knew what he liked—and these tastes are mirrored in his house. As a visitor to his home, you're in good company. He invited only his closest friends here—except during World War II, when Ljubljana was occupied by Nazis, the university was closed, and Plečnik allowed his students to work with him here as well.

Today the house is decorated exactly as it was the day Plečnik died, containing much of his equipment, models, and plans. There are very few barriers, so you are in direct contact with the world of the architect. Perhaps no other museum in Europe gives such an intimate portrait of an artist; you'll feel like Plečnik invited you over for dinner. It's still furnished with unique, Plečnik-designed furniture and ingenious, one-of-a-kind inventions. Whether or not you care about Plečnik, architecture, or design, you can't help but be tickled by this man's sheer creativity, and by the world he forged for himself to live in.

The house can be toured only with a guide, whose enthusiasm brings the place to life. Thirty-minute English tours begin at the top of each hour (€5, €2 guidebook, Tue–Thu 10:00–18:00, Sat 9:00–15:00, last tour departs 1 hour before closing, closed Sun–Mon and Fri, Karunova ulica 4, tel. 01/280-1600, www.aml .si, well-run by Ana and Natalija). The 15-minute stroll from the center—the same one Plečnik took to work each day—is nearly as enjoyable as the house itself.

• *The final sight is on the outskirts of town.*

▲**Architectural Museum of Ljubljana (Arhitekturni Muzej Ljubljana)**—If your visit to Ljubljana has infected you with Plečnik fever, you can trek out to this interesting museum, located in Fužine Castle on the outskirts of Ljubljana. The permanent exhibit features parts of the 1986 Paris exhibition that made Plečnik famous all over again. Downstairs is a display of plans and photos from Plečnik's earlier works in Vienna and Prague, and upstairs, you'll find an exhibit on his works in Slovenia, including some detailed plans and models for ambitious projects he never completed (like the huge, cone-shaped parliament building atop Castle Hill). It's worthwhile, but a bit of a hassle to reach—only true enthusiasts should pay a visit (€3, Mon–Fri 9:00–15:00, Sat 10:00–18:00, Sun 10:00–15:00, last entry 30 min before closing, Pot na Fužine 2, tel. 01/540-9798, www.aml.si). Take bus #20 or #22 from Congress Square (direction: Fužine) to the end of the line (about 20 min).

SHOPPING

Ljubljana, with its easygoing ambience and countless boutiques, is made to order for whiling away an afternoon shopping. It's also a fun place to stock up on souvenirs and gifts for the folks back home. Popular items include wood carvings and models (especially of the characteristic hayracks that dot the countryside), different flavors of schnapps (the kind with a whole pear inside—cultivated to actually grow right into the bottle—is the classiest), honey mead brandy (*medica*—sweet and smooth), and those adorable painted frontboard panels from beehives (see page 586).

The most atmospheric trinket-shopping is in the first stretch of the **market colonnade,** along the riverfront next to the Triple Bridge (see page 543). The best souvenir shop in town is **Dom Trgovina,** just a block across the Triple Bridge from Prešeren Square and facing the Town Hall (Mon–Fri 9:00–19:00, Sat 9:00–13:00, closed Sun, Mestni trg 24, tel. 01/241-8300). Another location is across from the TI on the main market square (Mon–Fri 8:00–19:00, Sat 8:00–15:00, closed Sun, Ciril-Metodov trg 5). If you're looking for serious handicrafts rather than trinkets, drop by the **Rustika** gallery, just over the Triple Bridge (on the castle side). In addition to beehive panels, they also have lace, painted chests and boxes, and other tasteful local-style mementos (Mon–Fri 9:00–20:00, Sat 10:00–15:00 & 16:00–20:00, Sun 10:00–14:00, Stritarjeva ulica 9). There's another location up at the castle courtyard.

Another item you'll see sold all over the country are **Peko shoes.** Made in a town north of Ljubljana called Tržič, Pekos are similar to high-fashion Italian models, but much cheaper. The name is an abbreviation of its founder's name: Peter Kozina (www .peko.si).

SLEEPING

Ljubljana offers good but relatively expensive accommodations. I've focused my listings in or within easy walking distance of the city center. Because good values are scarce, it's important to book ahead. The most expensive hotels raise their prices even more during conventions (Sept–Oct, and sometimes also June). Expect packed hotels and even higher rates through most of 2008, when Slovenia holds the rotating EU presidency (and many special events are planned here). The TI can give you a list of cheap private rooms *(sobe).* To locate the following accommodations, see the map on page 534.

$$$ Antiq Hotel is a family-run boutique hotel idyllically situated on a cobbled square in Ljubljana's Old Town. Its 16 idiosyncratically decorated rooms sprawl through two buildings with lots of stairs and a mazelike floor plan (Sb-€123–133, Db-€144–168, prices include taxes, air-con, free Wi-Fi, some rooms have low beams and doors, Gornji trg 3, tel. 01/421-3560, fax 01/421-3565, www.antiqhotel.si, info@antiqhotel.si).

$$$ Grand Hotel Union is Ljubljana's top address, as much an Art Nouveau landmark as a hotel. You'll pay dearly for its Old World elegance, hundred years of history, professional staff, big pool, and perfect location (right on Prešeren Square). While their rack rates are outrageously high, you can often snare a great deal in the summer (July–Aug), winter, and on many weekends. The

Ljubljana

Sleep Code

(€1 = about $1.40, country code: 386, area code: 01)
S = Single, **D** = Double/Twin, **T** = Triple, **Q** = Quad, **b** = bathroom.
Unless otherwise noted, credit cards are accepted, breakfast is included, and the modest tourist tax (€1 per person, per night) is not. Everyone speaks English.

To help you easily sort through these listings, I've divided the rooms into three categories based on the price for a standard double room with bath:

$$$ Higher Priced—Most rooms €110 or more.
$$ Moderately Priced—Most rooms between €55–110.
$ Lower Priced—Most rooms €55 or less.

---

194 plush "Executive" rooms are in the main building (rack rates: Sb-€233, Db-€276; may be as low as Db-€100 in slow times, non-smoking floors, elevator, free Internet access, free cable Internet in rooms, parking-€17/day, Miklošičeva cesta 1, tel. 01/308-1270, fax 01/308-1015, www.gh-union.si, hotel.union@gh-union.si). Its 133 "Business" rooms next door are less luxurious, almost as expensive, and a lesser value (rack rates: Sb-€212, Db-€266; same potential deals as "Executive" rooms, non-smoking floors, elevator, parking and Internet access at main hotel, free cable Internet, Miklošičeva cesta 3, tel. 01/308-1170, fax 01/308-1914, www.gh-union.si, hotel .business@gh-union.si). Because of a noisy nearby disco, request a quieter room at either building if you're here on a weekend.

$$$ Union Hotel Garni, technically part of the Grand Hotel Union up the street, has been threatening to change its name for years. Whatever it's called, the hotel has 74 rooms similar to (but slightly smaller than) the "Business" rooms at the main hotel, but cheaper and in a friendlier, less-pretentious package. The hotel is nicely situated between Prešeren Square and the train station (rack rates: Sb-€167, Db-€217; much lower prices likely July–Aug, in winter, and on weekends; extra bed-€27, non-smoking rooms, elevator, free cable Internet in rooms, parking garage-€19/day, Miklošičeva cesta 9, tel. 01/308-4300, fax 01/230-1181, www .astralhotel.net, hotel.garni@gh-union.si).

$$ Hotel Emonec (eh-MOH-nets), an excellent value with some of the best-located rooms in Ljubljana, hides just off of Wolfova lane between Prešeren and Congress squares. Its 39 rooms—in two buildings across a courtyard from each other—are simple, sleek, and a bit institutional, but the price is right. The catch: It's near a noisy disco, so light sleepers should request a quiet room (Sb-€57, small Db-€64, bigger "standard" Db-€74, Tb-

€87, Qb-€100, pay Internet access, free Wi-Fi, free loaner bikes for guests, Wolfova 12, tel. 01/200-1520, fax 01/200-1521, www .hotel-emonec.com, hotelemonec@siol.net).

$$ Pri Mraku Guesthouse has 36 comfortable-but-overpriced rooms in a very pleasant neighborhood near French Revolution Square. Despite its quirks (a so-so breakfast and lots of stairs with no elevator), it's my sentimental favorite in Ljubljana (Sb-€69–73, Db-€102, extra bed-€20, ground-floor and top-floor rooms have air-con and cost about €15 more, same prices year-round, non-smoking floor, free Internet access, Rimska 4, tel. 01/421-9650, fax 01/421-9655, www.daj-dam.si, mrak@daj-dam.si).

$$ Slamič B&B has seven new, nicely appointed, modern rooms over an upscale café in a nondescript neighborhood about a seven-minute walk from Prešeren Square (Sb-€65–80, Db-€95–107, price depends on size, 15 percent cheaper Fri–Sun, lots of stairs with no elevator, Kersnikova 1, tel. 01/433-8233, fax 01/433-8022, www.slamic.si, info@slamic.si).

$$ Penzion Pod Lipo has 10 rooms above a restaurant in a pleasant, mostly residential area about a 10-minute walk from Prešeren Square. While the rooms are simple, this is a good budget option (Db-€59, Tb-€72, Qb-€96, breakfast in restaurant-€3 extra, cash only, reception open 8:00–24:00, non-smoking, free Internet access, free cable Internet in rooms, tel. 01/251-1683, mobile 031-809-893, www.penzion-podlipo.com, ko.mar2@siol .net, Marjan).

$$ Hotel Park, for years a dreary communist dinosaur, has found new life as a bright, newly renovated budget hotel with 159 basic, Ikea-and-linoleum rooms and 42 cheaper "hostel" rooms. The 12-story building, in a nondescript residential neighborhood, is about halfway between Prešeren Square and the train station (a dull 10-min walk to either). Because renovations are ongoing, check with the hotel for the latest (likely rates: "hostel" rooms—S/D-€46, or €20 per person in a bathless quad, "superior" Sb/Db virtually the same as the hotel rooms and a great deal at €52; "hotel" rooms—Sb-€59, Db-€81; elevator, Internet access, Tabor 9, tel. 01/300-2500, fax 01/433-0546, www.hotelpark.si, info@hotelpark.si).

$$ B&B Petra Varl offers comfortable, affordable, nicely appointed rooms just above the bustling riverside market. Petra, who's an artist and speaks great English, will help you feel at home. This place is a great budget option for non-hostelers, so book early (Db-€60, €5 less Nov–Feb, extra bed-€10, includes kitchenette with do-it-yourself breakfast, cash only, air-con, free cable Internet in rooms, go into courtyard at Vodnikov trg 5 and look for *B&B* sign at 5A, mobile 041-389-470, petra@varl.si).

$ Hostel Celica, a proud, innovative, and lively place, is funded by the city and run by a nonprofit student organization.

This former military prison's 20 cells *(celica)* have been converted into hostel rooms—each one unique, decorated by a different designer (tours of the hostel daily at 14:00). The top floor features more-typical hostel rooms (each with its own bathroom, for 3–12 people). The building also houses an art gallery, tourist information, Internet access, self-serve laundry, restaurant, and shoes-off "Oriental café" (all prices listed are per person—cell rooms: S-€45, D-€25, T-€20; bed in top-floor rooms with bathrooms: 3- to 5-bed room-€23, 6- to 7-bed dorm-€20, 12-bed dorm-€18; includes breakfast and sheets, no curfew, non-smoking, bike and car rental, active excursions around Slovenia, Metelkova 8, a dull 15-min walk to Prešeren Square, 8 min to the train station, tel. 01/230-9700, fax 01/230-9714, www.hostelcelica.si, info@souhostel.si). Light sleepers take note: The hostel hosts live music events about two nights per week until around 24:00, but otherwise maintains "quiet time" after 23:00. However, the surrounding neighborhood—a bit run-down and remote, but safe—is a happening nightlife zone, which can make for noisy weekends.

$ **Alibi Hostel,** an official IYHF hostel creatively run by Gorazd, offers 100 beds and a funkier, more laid-back scene than Celica. The rooms are colorful and scruffy, and it's ideally located right on Ljubljana's main riverfront-café drag. The imaginative graffiti murals—featuring a stripper with memorable piercings, and a certain cowboy president—are guaranteed to offend just about anyone over 30 (dorm bed-€22, D-€55, includes sheets and tax, 10 percent cheaper for members, cheaper Nov–May, no breakfast, €20 key deposit, free Internet access, Cankarjevo nabrežje 27, tel. 01/251-1244, www.alibi.si).

EATING

Though heavy, meat-and-starch Slovenian food is available, Ljubljana also offers an abundance of pizza and other Italian fare—not to mention plenty of other international options (French, Thai, Indian, Chinese, even Mexican). The main drag through the Old Town is lined with inviting eateries, their tables spilling out into the cobbled pedestrian street. Prešeren Square thrives in the evenings, often with live bands leading a celebration of life and youth. To locate these restaurants, see the map on page 534.

Mid-Range, Local-Style Cuisine

Very few places serve strictly Slovenian food; at this crossroads of cultures (and cuisines), Italian and French flavors are just as "local" as anything else. But the following eateries are as close to "real Slovenian cuisine" as you'll get.

Sokol, with brisk, traditionally clad waiters serving typical

Slovenian food, is a reliable option (soup in a bread bowl is a favorite starter). The sprawling Slovenian-village interior is fun and woody, jaunty polka plays on the soundtrack, and the location is very central. If you want honest-to-goodness Slovenian food in the center, this is your only real option. All of this means it's deluged by tourists, so don't expect top quality or a good value (€7–20 main dishes, salads, veggie options, Mon–Sat 7:00–23:00, Sun 10:00–23:00, on castle side of Triple Bridge at Ciril-Metodov trg 18, tel. 01/439-6855).

As Lounge ("Ace"), a cheaper side-restaurant of the fancy Gostilna As (described under "Upscale International" on page 563), features drinks, €5–8 salads and sandwiches, €7–10 pastas, and €10–15 main dishes. You'll sit in the lively, leafy courtyard or the glassed-in winter garden (food served daily 12:00–23:00, longer hours for drinks, Čopova ulica 5A, or enter courtyard with *As* sign near image of Julija on Wolfova ulica, tel. 01/425-8822). The courtyard also has several other fun eateries—and, in the summer only, live music and a much-loved gelato stand.

Ribca ("Fish"), under the first stretch of market colonnade near the Triple Bridge, is your best bet for a relatively quick and cheap riverside lunch. Choose between the two straightforward menus: grilled fillets or fried small fish (€3–8 dishes, plus salads sold by the 100-gram unit). With the fragrant fish market right next door, you know it's fresh. If you just want to enjoy sitting along the river below the bustling market, this is also a fine spot for a coffee or beer (open Mon–Sat 8:00–16:00, closed Sun).

Zlata Ribica ("Golden Fish")—not to be confused with plain old Ribca, described above—is along the castle side of the embankment, with the best riverfront view in town. But the food lives up to the location: modern Slovenian cuisine (with an emphasis on fish, of course) and delicious pastas, especially gnocchi (€8–10 pastas, €10–20 main dishes, daily 10:00–24:00, between the Triple and Cobblers' bridges at Cankarjevo nabrežje 5–7, tel. 01/241-2680).

Pizzerias

Ljubljana has lots of great sit-down pizza places. Expect to pay €5–10 for an average-sized pie (wide variety of toppings).

Pizzeria Foculus, tucked in a boring alleyway a few blocks up from the river, has a loyal local following, a happening atmosphere, an innovative leafy interior, a few outdoor tables, and Ljubljana's best pizza (over 50 types for €5–8, €4–6 salads, Mon–Fri 10:00–24:00, Sat–Sun 12:00–24:00, just off French Revolution Square across the street from Plečnik's National and University Library at Gregorčičeva 3, tel. 01/251-5643).

Ljubljanski Dvor enjoys the most convenient and scenic location...even if the pizza isn't quite as good. On a sunny summer

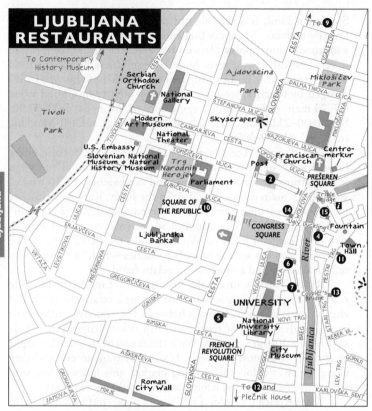

day, the outdoor riverside terrace is unbeatable. The interior has a simple pizza parlor downstairs, with a more refined dining room upstairs (selling the same €5–10 pizzas, plus €10–15 Italian main dishes; pizza parlor open daily 12:00–23:00, upstairs restaurant closed Sun in winter, just 50 yards from Cobblers' Bridge at Dvorni trg 1, tel. 01/251-6555). For cheap take-away, go around back to the walk-up window on Congress Square (€2 slices to go, along with other light food, picnic in the park or down on the river—plenty of welcoming benches, Mon–Sat 9:00–24:00, closed Sun).

Fast and Cheap

Paninoteka serves tasty €3 grilled sandwiches, €4–6 wraps, and €6 salads right along the river. The outdoor seating—a prime people-watching vantage point, with the Cobblers' Bridge and the castle above—is particularly inviting on a sunny day (order at the display case for take-away, or sit at a table to be waited on; great vegetarian options, casual service, Mon–Sat 8:00–1:00 in the morning, Sun 9:00–23:00, fine outdoor seating, Jurčičev trg 3,

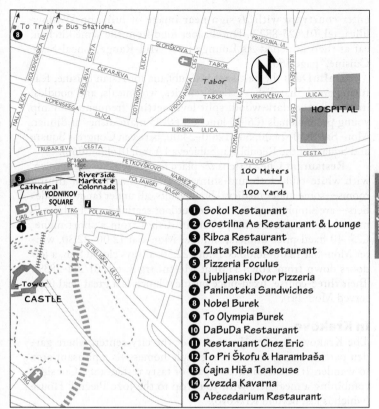

To Train & Bus Stations

HOSPITAL

Tabor

Dragon
Bridge

Riverside
Market &
Colonnade

Cathedral

VODNIKOV
SQUARE

CIRIL - METODOV TRG

POLJANSKA TRG

Tower

CASTLE

100 Meters

100 Yards

1. Sokol Restaurant
2. Gostilna As Restaurant & Lounge
3. Ribca Restaurant
4. Zlata Ribica Restaurant
5. Pizzeria Foculus
6. Ljubljanski Dvor Pizzeria
7. Paninoteka Sandwiches
8. Nobel Burek
9. To Olympia Burek
10. DaBuDa Restaurant
11. Restaurant Chez Eric
12. To Pri Škofu & Harambaša
13. Čajna Hiša Teahouse
14. Zvezda Kavarna
15. Abecedarium Restaurant

Ljubljana

mobile 059-018-445).

Burek, the typical Balkan snack (see "Balkan Flavors" sidebar on page 627), can be picked up at street stands around town. Most are open 24 hours and charge about €2 for a hearty portion. Try **Nobel Burek,** next to Miklošičeva cesta 30, or **Olympia Burek,** around the corner on Pražakova ulica (across the street from #1).

Upscale International

These fine restaurants are good for a splurge. At any of these, it's important to make a dinner reservation.

Gostilna As ("Ace"), tucked into a courtyard just off Prešeren Square, offers fish-lovers the best blow-out in town. It's dressy, pricey, and pretentious (waiters ignore the menu and recommend what's fresh). Everything is specially prepared each day and beautifully presented. It's loosely based on the "slow food" model: Servings are small, so you're expected to take your time and order two or three courses (mostly fish and Italian, €10–18 starters, €20–35 main dishes, daily 12:00–24:00, Čopova ulica 5A,

enter courtyard with *As* sign near image of Julija on Wolfova ulica, tel. 01/425-8822). For cheaper food from the same kitchen, eat at their attached As Lounge (see "Mid-Range, Local-Style Cuisine," page 560).

DaBuDa is the best spot in Ljubljana for Asian cuisine, featuring good Thai dishes (salads, curries, wok meals, and noodles) in a very mod dark-wood, split-level setting frequented by hip young professionals (€6–10 lunches, €9–15 main dishes at dinner, Mon–Sat 11:30–24:00, Sun 12:00–24:00, between Congress Square and Square of the Republic at Šubičeva 1A, tel. 01/425-3060).

Restaurant Chez Eric is *the* place for French cuisine in town, with white-tablecloth-and-shiny-crystal formality. The dining rooms—some under medieval brick vaults, all under fancy chandeliers—are simply elegant, and the outdoor seating is on Ljubljana's most historic square (€15–20 main dishes from a short menu, €25–40 fixed-price dinners, summer Mon–Sat 12:00–22:30, winter Mon–Sat 12:00–16:00 & 19:00–22:30, always closed Sun, a few doors down from Town Hall at Mestni trg 3, tel. 01/251-2839). Their three-course, fixed-price business lunch is a great deal (€10, served Mon–Fri).

In Krakovo

The Krakovo district—just south of the city center, where garden patches nearly outnumber simple homes—is a pleasant area to wander. It's also home to a pair of tasty restaurants. Consider combining a meal here with your trip to the Jože Plečnik House (which is just beyond Krakovo).

Pri Škofu ("By the Bishop") is a laid-back, informal place with mostly outdoor seating and a focus on freshness and traditional Slovenian cuisine. There's no menu—the waiter tells you what's good today...and it is. This hidden gem is a bit pricey, but deliciously memorable. Reservations are essential (€7 lunches, €10–15 main dishes at dinner, Mon–Fri 8:00–24:00, Sat–Sun 12:00–24:00, Rečna 8, tel. 01/426-4508).

Harambaša is the closest thing to a ticket to Sarajevo. Serving Balkan grilled meats, this popular-with-students eatery has Turkish-flavored decor, old pictures, and cuisine reminiscent of the Bosnian capital. For a refresher on the meat dishes, see "Balkan Flavors" on page 627. The menu is limited, which makes ordering easy. Their handy €6 *pola-pola* combo-plate—with lotsa meat combined with chopped onions, *kajmak* (a buttery spread), and *lepinja* (bread)—makes for a simple but filling lunch. Also consider the Turkish coffee (a high-octane brew with "mud" at the bottom) and baklava. Vegetarians need not apply (€4–6 main dishes, Mon–Fri 10:00–22:00, Sat 12:00–22:00, Sun 12:00–18:00, Vrtna ulica 8, mobile 041-843-106).

Coffee, Tea, and Treats

Riverfront Cafés: Enjoying a coffee, beer, or ice-cream cone along the Ljubljanica River embankment (between the Triple and Cobblers' bridges) is Ljubljana's single best experience. Tables spill out into the street, and some of the best-dressed, best-looking students on the planet happily fill them day and night. (A common question from first-time visitors to Ljubljana: "Doesn't anybody

here have a job?") This is simply some of the top people-watching in Europe. Rather than recommend a particular place (they're all about the same), I'll leave you to explore and find the spot with the breezy ambience you like best. When ordering, the easiest choice is a *bela kava*—"white coffee," basically a latte.

Tea House: If coffee's not your cup of tea, go a block inland to the teahouse **Čajna Hiša**. They have a shop (called Cha) with over 100 varieties of tea, plus porcelain teapots and cups from all over (Mon–Fri 9:00–20:00, Sat 9:00–13:30, closed Sun). The café serves about 50 different types of tea, light food, and desserts (€3 cakes and sandwiches, €5–7 salads, Mon–Fri 9:00–23:00, Sat 9:00–15:00 & 18:00–23:00, closed Sun, on the main drag in the Old Town a few steps from Cobblers' Bridge at Stari trg 3, tel. 01/252-7010).

Treats: **Zvezda Kavarna,** a trendy, central place at the bottom of Congress Square, is a local favorite for cakes, pastries, and ice cream (decadent €3 cakes, Mon–Sat 7:00–23:00, Sun 10:00–20:00, a block up from Prešeren Square at Wolfova 14, tel. 01/421-9090). **Abecedarium** (ah-beh-tseh-dah-ree-oom, like the alphabet) serves up delicious Nutella-banana cake (and other food) with indoor or outdoor seating near the Triple Bridge. It's located in the oldest house in town, named for a work by one of Slovenia's greatest writers—who also lived in the house (daily 8:00–1:00 in the morning, Ribji trg 2, tel. 01/426-9514).

Ice Cream: Ljubljana is known for its Italian gelato–style ice cream. You'll see fine options all along the Ljubljanica River embankment. Favorites include the courtyard garden at **Gostilna As** (page 563, summer only) and **Zvezda Kavarna** (above).

TRANSPORTATION CONNECTIONS

Note that in Slovene, Vienna is "Dunaj" and Budapest is "Budimpešta."

Getting to the Dalmatian Coast: If connecting directly to Croatia's Dalmatian Coast, you have three options: Train to

Zagreb (2.5 hrs), where you'll catch a cheap Croatia Air flight or a bus; take the long, once-daily train connection from Ljubljana to Split (8 hrs, requires a change in Zagreb); or, much slower, take the train to Rijeka, then cruise on a boat down the coast from there. (For specifics on flights, buses, and boats, see "Getting to the Dalmatian Coast," page 617.)

From Ljubljana by Train to: Lesce-Bled (roughly hourly, 1 hr—but bus is better), **Postojna** (nearly hourly, 1 hr), **Divača** (close to Škocjan caves and Lipica, nearly hourly, 1.75 hrs), **Piran** (direct bus is better—see below; otherwise allow 4 hours, train to Koper, 5/day, 2.5 hrs; then bus to Piran, 7/day, 30 min), **Maribor** (hourly, 2–3 hrs, more with a transfer in Zidani Most), **Ptuj** (3/day, 2.5 hrs, more with transfer in Pragersko), **Zagreb** (8/day, 2.5 hrs), **Rijeka** (2–3/day direct, 2.5 hrs), **Split** (1/day, 9 hrs, transfer in Zagreb), **Vienna** (that's **Dunaj** in Slovene, 1/day direct, 6 hrs; otherwise 6/ day with transfer in Villach, Maribor, or Graz, 6–7 hrs), **Budapest** (that's **Budimpešta** in Slovene; 2/day direct, 8–9 hrs, night train departs Ljubljana around 2:00 in the morning), **Venice** (2/day direct, 4 hrs), **Salzburg** (4/day direct, 5 hrs), **Munich** (3/day direct, 6 hrs, including 1 night train; otherwise transfer in Salzburg). Train info: tel. 01/291-3332, www.slo-zeleznice.si.

By Bus to: Bled (Mon–Sat hourly—usually at the top of each hour, fewer on Sun, 1.25 hrs, €6.30), **Postojna** (at least hourly, 1 hr, €6), **Divača** (close to Škocjan caves and Lipica, every 2 hrs, 1.5 hrs, €8), **Piran** (7/day, 2.5 hrs, €12), **Rijeka** (1/day in season, 5.5 hrs), **Rovinj** (1/day late June–late Sept, generally departs Ljubljana around 13:45, 5.5 hrs, €22, no buses off-season). For any bus, you have to buy tickets at the bus station ticket windows—not from the driver. Bus info: tel. 090-4230 (toll number—about €0.75/min), www.ap-ljubljana.si. If you pick up the blue phone in the bus station, you'll be connected to a free information line.

Ljubljana's Airports

Slovenia's only **airport** (airport code: LJU) is 14 miles north of Ljubljana, about halfway to Bled. The airport goes by three names: Ljubljana Airport (the international version); Brnik (for the town that it's near); and Jože Pučnik Airport (a politician for whom it was controversially renamed in 2007). Almost every flight is operated by Adria Airways (www.adria-airways.com), but recently, EasyJet (www.easyjet.com), Wizz Air (www.wizzair.com), and Czech Airlines (www.csa.cz) have also entered the fray. Airport info: tel. 04/206-1000, www.lju-airport.si. There's a TI in the airport's arrivals hall (see "Tourist Information," page 533).

Getting Between Ljubljana and Ljubljana Airport: Two different **buses** connect Brnik with Ljubljana's bus station: a public bus (€4.10, 45 min, hourly, generally departs bus station at :10 past each hour), and an airport bus operated by Adria Airways (€5, 30 min, 10/day, departs down the block from the bus station—past the post office). There's also a private shuttle that runs between the airport and any hotel in town (€8, arrange in advance for hotel pick-up, mobile 040-771-771). Figure about €25 for a taxi to the airport, but more like €40 *from* the airport (since you have to use a pricey taxi in the stand out front).

The Austrian Option: Since Ljubljana's airport is the only one in the country and thus charges extremely high taxes and airport fees, many Slovenes prefer to fly out of Austria. The airport in **Klagenfurt** (airport code: KLU, also known as Alpe-Adria Airport), just over the Austrian border to the north, is subsidized by the local government to keep prices low and compete with Ljubljana's airport. Especially if you're connecting to Bled, it's somewhat handy to reach (from Ljubljana or Bled, take the train to Villach, then to Klagenfurt's Annabichl station, which is a 5-min walk from the airport; total trip 3 hrs from Ljubljana, or 2 hrs from Bled; www.klagenfurt-airport.com). A taxi transfer to Bled runs a hefty €120 and takes about an hour (see "By Taxi" on page 573, in the "Getting Around Lake Bled (Literally)" section of the Lake Bled chapter). Austrian Airlines (www.aua.com) flies from Klagenfurt, as do low-cost carriers such as Ryanair (www.ryanair.com) and TUIfly (www.tuifly.com).

All this competition is keeping Slovenia's national airline, Adria, on its toes. While it's generally pretty pricey to fly Adria, the airline often posts a few heavily discounted fares for each flight on its website (such as less than €100 one-way from Ljubljana to London or Paris; first come, first served, www.adria-airways.com).

LAKE BLED

Lake Bled—Slovenia's leading mountain resort—comes complete with a sweeping alpine panorama, a fairy-tale island, a cliff-hanging medieval castle, a lazy lakeside promenade, and the country's most sought-after desserts. While Bled has all the modern resort-town amenities, its most endearing qualities are its stunning setting, its natural romanticism, and its fun-loving wedding parties.

Since the Hapsburg days, Lake Bled (pronounced like it looks) has been *the* place where Slovenes wow visiting diplomats. Tito had one of his vacation homes here (today's Hotel Vila Bled), and more recent visitors have included Prince Charles, Madeleine Albright, and Laura Bush.

The lake's main town, also called Bled, has plenty of ways to idle away an afternoon. While the town itself is more functional than quaint, it offers postcard views of the lake and handy access to the region. Hike up to Bled Castle for intoxicating vistas. Make a wish and ring the bell at the island church. Wander the dreamy path around the lake. Then relax with some of Bled's famous desserts while you take in the view of Triglav, Slovenia's favorite mountain (see "Mount Triglav" sidebar on page 596). Bled quiets down at night—no nightlife beyond a handful of pubs—giving hikers and other holiday-makers a chance to recharge. Bled is also a great jumping-off point for a car trip through the Julian Alps (see next chapter).

Planning Your Time

Bled and its neighboring mountains deserve two days. With one day, spend it in and around Bled (or, to rush things, spend the morning in Bled and the afternoon day-tripping). With a second day and a car, drive through the Julian Alps using the self-guided tour in the next chapter. The circular route takes you up and over the stunning Vršič Pass, then down the scenic and historic Soča River Valley. Without a car, skip the second day, or spend it doing nearby day trips: Bus or bike to Radovljica to see the bee museum, hike to Vintgar Gorge, or visit the more rustic Lake Bohinj (all described under "Near Lake Bled," at the end of this chapter).

ORIENTATION

(area code: 04)

The town of Bled is on the east end of 1.5-mile-long Lake Bled. The lakefront is lined with cafés and resort hotels. A 3.5-mile path meanders around the lake. Lake Bled is particularly peaceful, as no motorized boats are allowed.

The tourists' center of Bled is a cluster of big resort hotels, dominated by the giant, red Hotel Park (dubbed the "red can"). The busy street called **Ljubljanska cesta** leads out of Bled town towards Ljubljana and most other destinations. Just up from the lakefront, across Ljubljanska cesta from Hotel Park, is the modern **commercial center** (Trgovski Center Bled), with a travel agency, grocery store, ATM, shops, and a smattering of lively cafés. Nicknamed "Gadhafi" by the people of Bled, the commercial center was designed for a Libyan city, but the deal fell through—so the frugal Slovenes built it here instead. Just up the road from the commercial center, you'll find the post office and library (with Internet access).

Bled's less-touristy Old Town is under the castle, surrounding the pointy spire of St. Martin's Church. There you'll find the bus station, several good restaurants, a few hostels, and more locals than tourists.

The mountains poking above the ridge at the far end of the lake are the Julian Alps, crowned by the three peaks of Mount Triglav. The big mountain behind the town of Bled is Stol ("Chair"), part of the Karavanke range that defines the Austrian border.

Tourist Information

Bled's helpful TI is in the long, lakefront casino building across the street from the big, red Hotel Park (as you face the lake, the TI is hiding around the front at the far left end, overlooking the lake). Pick up the good map (with the lake on one side, and the whole region on the other) and the free Bled information booklet. Get advice on hikes and day trips, and if you're doing any serious hiking, spring for a good regional map (July–Aug Mon–Sat 8:00–21:00, Sun 9:00–18:00; May–June and Sept Mon–Sat

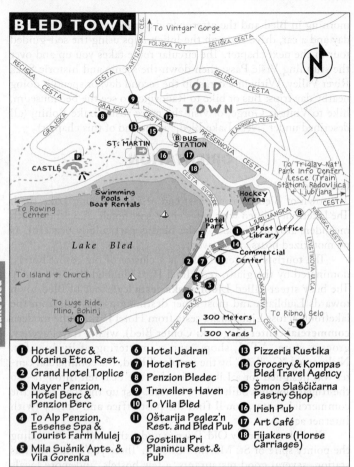

BLED TOWN

To Vintgar Gorge

OLD TOWN

POLJSKA POT
SELIŠKA CESTA
PARTIZANSKA CES.
PRILANIŠKA CES.
REČIŠKA CESTA
CESTA
GRAJSKA
GRAJSKA CESTA
SELIŠKA CESTA
VLADINSKA CESTA
PREŠERNOVA CESTA

ST. MARTIN
BUS STATION

CASTLE
P

Swimming Pools & Boat Rentals

To Rowing Center

Lake Bled

To Island & Church

To Luge Ride, Mlino, Bohinj

Hockey Arena

LJUBLJANSKA CESTA

To Triglav Nat'l Park Info Center, Lesce (Train Station), Radovljica & Ljubljana

RIBENSKA CESTA
LEVSTIKOVA ULICA

Hotel Park
Post Office
Library
Commercial Center

CANKARJEVA CESTA

POD STRAŽO

CESTA SVOBODE

To Ribno, Selo

300 Meters
300 Yards

① Hotel Lovec & Okarina Etno Rest.
② Grand Hotel Toplice
③ Mayer Penzion, Hotel Berc & Penzion Berc
④ To Alp Penzion, Essense Spa & Tourist Farm Mulej
⑤ Mila Sušnik Apts. & Vila Gorenka
⑥ Hotel Jadran
⑦ Hotel Trst
⑧ Penzion Bledec
⑨ Travellers Haven
⑩ To Vila Bled
⑪ Oštarija Peglez'n Rest. and Bled Pub
⑫ Gostilna Pri Planincu Rest. & Pub
⑬ Pizzeria Rustika
⑭ Grocery & Kompas Bled Travel Agency
⑮ Šmon Slaščičarna Pastry Shop
⑯ Irish Pub
⑰ Art Café
⑱ Fijakers (Horse Carriages)

8:00–19:00, Sun 11:00–17:00; Oct–April Mon–Sat 9:00–18:00, Sun 12:00–16:00; Cesta Svobode 10, tel. 04/574-1122, www.bled .si). The TI can give you a list of accommodations, but they can't find you a room (instead, book direct or go to Kompas Bled Travel Agency—see page 572).

For more details on hiking in Triglav National Park, pay a visit to the new **Triglav National Park Information Center,** on the main road out of town (free information, maps and guidebooks for sale, possible charge for exhibition, Tue–Sun 10:00–18:00, closed Mon, Ljubljanska cesta 27, tel. 04/578-0200, www.tnp.si).

Arrival in Bled

By Train: Two train stations have the name "Bled." The **Bled Jezero** ("Bled Lake") station is across the lake from Bled town,

Bled and the Julian Alps Essentials

English	Slovene	Pronounced
Slovenia's Biggest Mountain	Triglav	TREE-glahv
Lake Bled	Blejsko Jezero	BLAY-skoh YAY-zay-roh
The Island	Otok	OH-tohk
Bled Castle	Blejski Grad	BLAY-skee grahd
Town near Bled with Train Station	Lesce	lest-SEH
Town with Bee Museum	Radovljica	rah-DOH-vleet-suh
Gorge near Bled	Vintgar	VEENT-gar
Rustic Lake near Bled	Bohinj	BOH-heen
Scenic High-Mountain Pass	Vršič	vur-SHEECH
Historic River Valley	Soča	SOH-chah

Lake Bled

and is used only by infrequent, slow, tourist-oriented trains into the mountains. You're much more likely to use the **Lesce-Bled** station in the nearby village of Lesce. The Lesce-Bled station is on the main line and has much better connections to Ljubljana and international destinations. So if you're buying a train ticket or checking schedules, request "Lesce-Bled" rather than just "Bled." (This is so important, I'll remind you again later.)

The small **Lesce-Bled station** is in the village of Lesce, about 2.5 miles from Bled. As you leave the station, the nearest ATM is upstairs in the shopping center across the street. A taxi to Bled should run about €10, or you can take the bus (2/hr, 10 min, €1.30). If taking the train out of Lesce-Bled, you can buy tickets at the station or on the train—nobody in Bled town sells tickets.

By Bus: Bled's bus station is just up from the lake in the Old Town. To reach the lake, walk straight downhill on Cesta Svobode. To get from the bus station to the commercial center, jog uphill and turn right on Prešernova cesta, which runs into Ljubljanska cesta just above the commercial center.

By Car: Coming from Ljubljana, you'll wind your way into Bled on Ljubljanska cesta, which rumbles through the middle of town before swinging left at the lake. Ask your hotel about parking. Also see "Route Tips for Drivers," on page 585.

Helpful Hints

Travel Agency: Kompas Bled Travel Agency, in the commercial center, rents bikes, sells books and maps, offers a room-booking service (including many cheap rooms in private homes—though most are away from the lake), and sells various tours around the region (Mon–Sat 8:00–19:00, Sun 8:00–12:00 & 16:00–19:00, June–Sept until 20:00, Ljubljanska cesta 4, tel. 04/572-7500, www.kompas-bled.si, kompas.bled@siol.net).

Money: Bled town's handiest ATMs are at **SKB Banka** (upstairs in round building at commercial center) and **Gorenjska Banka** (at far end of Hotel Park).

Internet Access: Most of the bigger hotels have access for guests in the lobby. The public library has fast access (free up to 1 hour per day, erratic hours but usually Mon–Fri 10:00–19:00, Sat 8:00–12:00, closed Sun, next to the post office on Ljubljanska cesta).

Post Office: If you're coming up from the lake on Ljubljanska cesta, it's just past the commercial center and library (Mon–Fri 8:00–19:00, Sat 8:00–12:00, closed Sun, slightly longer hours July–Aug, tel. 04/575-0200).

Laundry: Most hotels can do laundry for you, but it's expensive (priced by the piece). You'll get a better deal from a pair of can-do locals who'll pick up your laundry at your hotel and return it clean (€15/load for 24-hour service, €5 more for same-day express service, Anže Štalc and Maja Tarman, mobile 041-575-522).

Car Rental: The Julian Alps are ideal by car. Several big chains rent cars in Bled—figure €60 per day, including tax, insurance, and unlimited mileage (no extra charge for drop-off elsewhere in Slovenia). **Europcar** (in Hotel Krim, tel. 04/574-1155) usually has better rates than **Avis** (in the commercial center, tel. 04/576-8700).

Massage: If you're here to relax, consider a massage at the **Essense** wellness center at Alp Penzion (recommended in "Sleeping," page 581). This new, modern facility, about a 15-minute walk or five-minute taxi ride above the lake, offers a wide range of spa treatments, including pedicure, Thai massage, and Indian ayurveda massage (with warm oils). A standard 50-minute massage will run you about €30 (call first to arrange, Cankarjeva cesta 20A, tel. 04/576-7450, www.alp-penzion .com).

Getting Around Lake Bled (Literally)

By Bike: You can rent a mountain bike at the TI or at Kompas Bled Travel Agency (both listed above) for the same rates (€3.50/hr, €6/3 hrs, €8/half-day, €11/day). While walking around the lake is slo-mo bliss, biking it is also enjoyable. For a longer pedal, the new bike path to the nearby town of Radovljica (and its bee museum—see page 586) is about four miles one-way (get details at the TI or Kompas).

By Horse and Buggy: Buggies called *fijakers* are the romantic, expensive, and easy way to get around the lake. You'll see them along the lakefront between Hotel Park and the castle (around the lake-€30, one-way up to castle-€30, round-trip to castle with 30-min wait time-€40, mobile 041-710-970).

By Tourist Train: A touristy little train makes a circuit around the lake every 40 minutes in summer (€3, daily 9:00–21:00 in peak season, shorter hours off-season, weather-dependent, tel. 041-608-689).

By Tourist Bus: A handy shuttle bus passes through Bled once daily in summer. It leaves the bus station at 10:00, stops at a few hotels (including Grand Hotel Toplice), then goes up to the castle and on to the Vintgar Gorge entrance (€3, mid-June–Sept only, confirm schedule at TI or bus station).

By Taxi: Bled Tours, run by friendly, English-speaking Sandi Demšar, can take you to various destinations near Bled (€10 to the castle or to Lesce-Bled train station, €11 to Radovljica, €45 to Ljubljana airport, €120 to Klagenfurt airport in Austria, mobile 031-205-611, info@bledtours.si). Your hotel can also call a taxi for you.

By Boat: For information on renting your own boat, see "Boating," page 578. For details on the characteristic *pletna* boats, see "Getting to the Island," page 576.

By Plane: If you have perfect weather and deep pockets, there's no more thrilling way to experience Slovenia's high-mountain scenery than from a small propeller plane soaring over the peaks. Flights depart from a grass airstrip near the village of Lesce, a 10-minute drive or taxi ride from Bled. Expensive...but unforgettable (€70 for 15-min hop over Lake Bled only, €120 for 30-min flight that also buzzes Lake Bohinj, €170 for deluxe 45-min version around the summit of Triglav, arrange at least a day in advance, tel. 04/532-0100, www.alc-lesce.si, info@alc-lesce.si).

TOURS

Local Guides—Tina Hiti and **Sašo Golub** are fine guides who enjoy sharing the town and region they love with American visitors. Hiring one of them can add immeasurably to your enjoyment and understanding of Bled (€30/2 hrs, arrange several days in advance; Tina: mobile 040-166-554, tinahiti@gmail.com; Sašo: mobile 040-524-774, sasogolub@gmail.com). Either one can drive you in their car on a long day tour into the Julian Alps—or anywhere in Slovenia—for €120. (This price is for two people; it's more expensive for three or more people, since they have to rent a van.) I've spent great days with both Tina and Sašo, and was thankful they were behind the wheel. If these two are busy, they might send Tina's sister, Eva, or her father, Gorazd—a former Yugoslav Olympian (in ice hockey) who brings the older generation's perspective to the trip (both speak fine English).

Excursions—To hit several far-flung day-trip destinations in one go, you could take a package tour from Bled. Destinations range from Ljubljana and the Karst region to the Austrian Lakes to Venice (yes, Venice—it's doable as a long day trip from here). An all-day Julian Alps trip to the Vršič Pass and Soča Valley runs about €35 (sold by various agencies, including Kompas Bled—see page 572). This tour is handy, but two people can rent a car for the day for about the same price and do it at their own pace using the self-guided driving tour in the next chapter.

SIGHTS AND ACTIVITIES

Lake Bled

Bled doesn't have many "sights," but there are plenty of rewarding and pleasant activities.

▲▲The Island (Otok)—Bled's little island—capped by a super-cute church—nudges the lake's quaintness level over the top.

Locals call it simply "The Island" *(Otok)*. While it's pretty to look at from afar, it's also fun to visit.

The island has long been a sacred site with a romantic twist. On summer Saturdays, a steady procession of brides and grooms, cheered on by their entourages, head for the island. Ninety-eight steps lead from the island's dock up to the Church of the Assumption on top. It's tradition for the groom to carry—or try to carry—his bride up these steps. About four out of five are successful (proving themselves "fit for marriage"). During the communist era, the church was closed, and weddings were outlawed here. But the tradition reemerged—illegally—even before the regime ended, with a clandestine ceremony in 1989.

An eighth-century Slavic pagan temple dedicated to the goddess of love and fertility once stood here; the current Baroque version (with Venetian flair—the bell tower separate from the main church) is the fifth to occupy this spot. As you enter the church (€3), look straight ahead to the painting of Mary on the wall. She

Pletna Boats

The *pletna* is an important symbol of Lake Bled. These boats provide a pleasant way to reach the island and carry on an

important tradition dating back for generations. In the 17th century, Hapsburg Empress Maria Theresa granted the villagers from Mlino—the little town along the lakefront just beyond Bled—special permission to ferry visitors to the island. (Since Mlino had very limited access to farmland, they needed another source of income.) Mlino residents built their *pletnas* by hand, using a special design passed down from father to son for centuries—like the equally iconic gondolas of Venice. Eventually, this imperial decree and family tradition evolved into a modern union of *pletna* oarsmen, which continues to this day.

Today *pletna* boats are still hand-built according to that same centuries-old design. There's no keel, so the skilled oarsmen work hard to steer the flat-bottomed boat with each stroke—boats piloted by an inexperienced oarsman can slide around on very windy days. There are 21 official *pletnas* on Lake Bled, all belonging to the same union. The gondoliers dump all of their earnings into one fund, give a cut to the tourist board, and divide the rest evenly among themselves. Occasionally a new family tries to break into the cartel, underselling his competitors with a "black market" boat that looks the same as the official ones. While some see this as a violation of a centuries-old tradition, others view it as good old capitalism. Either way, competition is fierce.

Lake Bled

doesn't quite look like other Madonnas, because she has the ruddy features of Maria Theresa—the Hapsburg empress who controlled Slovenia at the time. The Madonna at the altar in front of the church is similarly pudgy...er, imperial.

Find the rope for the church bell, hanging in the middle of the aisle just before the altar. A local superstition claims that if you ring this bell three times, your dreams will come true. Worth a try.

If you're waiting for a herd of tourists to ring out their wishes, pass the time looking around the front of the church. When the church was being renovated in the 1970s, workers dug up several medieval graves (you can see one through the glass under the bell rope). They also discovered Gothic frescoes on either side of the altar, including, above the door on the right, an unusual ecclesiastical theme: the *bris* (Jewish circumcision ritual) of Christ.

A café (with a WC) and souvenir shop (with an exhibit of nativity scenes) are near the church at the top of the steps.

To descend by a different route, walk down the trail behind the church, then follow the path around the island's perimeter back to where your *pletna* boat awaits.

Getting to the Island: The most romantic route to the island is to cruise on one of the distinctive ***pletna*** boats (€10 per person round-trip, includes 30-min wait time at the island; catch one at several spots around the lake—most convenient from in front of Grand Hotel Toplice or just below Hotel Park, might have to wait for more passengers to fill the boat, generally run from dawn until around 20:00 in summer, stop earlier off-season, replaced by enclosed electric boats in winter—unless the lake freezes, mobile 031-316-575). For more on these characteristic little vessels, see the "*Pletna* Boats" sidebar. You can also **rent your own boat** to row to the island (see "Boating"). It's even possible to **swim** to the island, especially from the end of the lake nearest the island (see "Swimming," later in this chapter)—but you're not allowed into the church in your swimsuit.

▲▲**Walk Around the Lake**—Strolling the 3.5 miles around the lake is enjoyable, peaceful, and scenic. At a leisurely pace, it takes about an hour and a half...not counting stops to snap photos of the ever-changing view. On the way, you'll pass some great villas, mostly from the beginning of the 19th century. The most significant one was a former residence of Marshal Tito—today the Hotel Vila Bled, a great place to stop for a coffee and pretend Tito invited you over for a visit (see "Tito's Vila Bled," next). For the more adventurous, hiking paths lead up into the hills surrounding the lake (ask TI for details and maps; or hike to Vintgar Gorge, described on page 588).

Tito's Vila Bled—Before World War II, this villa on Lake Bled was the summer residence for the Yugoslav royal family. When Tito ran Yugoslavia, he entertained international guests here (big shots from the communist and non-aligned world, from Indira Gandhi to Khrushchev to Kim Il Sung). Since 1984, it's been a classy hotel and restaurant, offering guests grand Lake Bled views and James Bond ambience. For some, this is a nostalgic opportunity to send an email from Tito's desk, sip tea in his lounge, and gawk at his Social Realist wall murals. The garden surrounding the villa is filled with exotic trees, brought here by Tito's guests from distant lands.

The villa is a 20-minute lakeside walk from the town of Bled at Cesta Svobode 26 (it's the big, white villa with the long staircase at the southern end of lake, just beyond the village of Mlino). You can also ask your *pletna* gondolier to drop you off here after visiting the island. Those hiking around the lake will pass the gate leading through Tito's garden to the restaurant, where they are welcome to drop in for a meal, the salad bar, or just a cup of coffee. Tito fans might want to splurge for an overnight here (basic Db-€210, tel. 04/579-1500, www.vila-bled.com).

▲**Bled Castle (Blejski Grad)**—Bled's cliff-hanging castle, dating in one form or another from a thousand years ago, was the seat of the Austrian Bishops of Brixen, who controlled Bled in the Middle Ages. Your castle admission includes a modest castle museum (with a couple of interesting videos, creaky rooms, and good English descriptions); a small theater continuously showing a fun 20-minute movie about Bled (under the restaurant); a tiny chapel with 3-D frescoes that make it seem much bigger than it is; and a rampart walk with an "herbal gallery" (gift shop of traditional-meets-modern herbal brandies, cosmetics, and perfumes). These attractions are less than thrilling, but the sweeping views over Lake Bled and the surrounding mountainscapes justify the trip (€6, daily May–Oct 8:00–20:00, Nov–April 9:00–17:00, tel. 04/578-0525).

In addition, the castle is home to a pair of interesting, old-fashioned shops: You can visit a working replica of a **printing press** *(grajska tiskarna)* from Gutenberg's time, and press your own custom-made souvenir certificate for €5–10 (in the castle's oldest tower—from the 11th century). Or, at the **wine cellar** *(grajska klet de Adami),* bottle and cork your own bottle of wine (€10–15). These attractions are manned by a pair of gregarious guys, one dressed as a medieval printer and the other as a monk. Both men happen to be named Andrej (they switch costumes sometimes for a change of pace). Both shops are generally open daily in summer 10:00–18:00 (less off-season; if one of the shops is closed, the other should be open).

Eating at the Castle: The **restaurant** at the castle is fairly expensive, but your restaurant reservation gets you into the castle grounds for free (international cuisine and some local specialties, €10–20 main dishes, tel. 04/579-4424). Better yet, there's a scenic little **picnic spot** in the castle courtyard, with fine tables and views (buy sandwiches at the Mercator grocery store in the commercial center before you ascend—see listing under "Eating").

Getting to the Castle: Most people **hike** up the steep hill (20 min). The handiest trails are behind big St. Martin's Church: Walk past the front door of the church with the lake at your back, and look left after the first set of houses for the *Grad* signs marking the steepest route up (on this trail, bear uphill—or right—at the benches); or, for a longer but less steep route, continue past the church on the same street about five minutes, bearing uphill (left) at the fork, and find the *Grad* sign just after the Pension Bledec hostel on the left. Once you're on this second trail, don't take the sharp-left uphill turn at the fork (instead, continue straight up, around the back of the hill). Instead of hiking, you can take the 10:00 **tourist bus** (see "Getting Around Lake Bled (Literally)," page 572), your **rental car,** a **taxi** (around €10), or—if you're wealthy and romantic—a **horse and buggy** (€30, €10 extra to wait 30 min and bring you back down, see "Getting Around Lake Bled (Literally)"). However, these options take you only to the parking lot, from which it's a steep and slippery-when-wet five-minute hike up to the castle itself.

Boating—Bled is the rowing center of Slovenia. Town officials even lengthened the lake a bit so it would perfectly fit the standard two-kilometer laps, with 100 meters more for the turn. Three world championships have been held here. The town has produced many Olympic medalists, winning gold in Sydney and silver in Athens. You'll notice that local crew team members are characters—with a tradition of wild and colorful haircuts. You'll likely see them running or rowing. This dedication to rowing adds to Bled's tranquility, since no motorized boats are allowed on the lake.

If you want to get into the action, you'll find **rental rowboats** at the swimming pool under the castle (small 3-person boat: first hour-€12, additional hours-€6.50 each; bigger 5-person boat: first hour-€14, additional hours-€7.50 each; daily in summer 10:00–18:00) or at the campground on the far side of the lake (4-person boat-€10/hr, closed in bad weather and off-season).

Swimming—Lake Bled has several suitable spots for a swim. The swimming pools under the castle are filled with lake water and routinely earn the "blue flag," meaning the water is top-quality (swim all day-€6, less for afternoon only, June–Sept daily 8:00–19:00, closed Oct–May and in bad weather, tel. 04/578-0528). Bled's two beaches are at the far end of the lake. Both are free; the one at the campground (southwest corner) has lots of tourists, while locals prefer the one at the rowing center (northwest corner). If you swim to the island, remember that you can't get into the church in your swimsuit.

Luge Ride (Polento Sankanje)—Bled's "summer toboggan" luge ride, atop Mount Straža overlooking the lake, allows you to scream down a steep, curvy metal-rail track on a little plastic sled. A chairlift takes you to the top of the track, where you'll sit on your sled, take a deep breath, and remind yourself: Pull back on the stick to slow down, push forward on the stick to go faster. You'll drop 480 feet in altitude on the 570-yard-long track, speeding up to about 25 miles per hour as you race toward the lake. You'll see the track on the hillside just south of town, beyond the Grand Hotel Toplice (€5/ride, cheaper for multiple rides, chairlift only-€2.50, weather-dependent—if it rains, you can't go; mid-June–Aug daily

11:00–18:00; May–mid–June Sat–Sun only 11:00–19:00, closed Mon–Fri; Sept–Oct Sat–Sun only 11:00–17:00, closed Mon–Fri; closed Nov–April).

Day Trips—For details on some easy and enjoyable nearby side-trips—including a quirky bee museum, a scenic gorge hike, and a more remote lake experience—see "Near Lake Bled" at the end of this chapter.

NIGHTLIFE

Bled Pub Crawl

Bled is quiet after hours. However, the town does have a few fun bars that are lively with a young crowd (all open nightly until 2:00 in the morning). Since many young people in Bled are students at the local tourism school, they're likely to speak English...and eager to practice with a native speaker. Try a Smile, a Corona-type Slovenian lager. *Šnops* (schnapps) is a local specialty—popular flavors are plum *(slivovka),* honey *(medica),* blueberry *(borovničevec),* and pear *(hruškovec).*

Kick things off with the fun-loving local gang at **Gostilna Pri Planincu** near the bus station (described under "Eating"). Then head down Cesta Svobode toward the lake; just below Hotel Jelovica, you'll find the rollicking **Irish Pub** (a.k.a. "The Pub"), with Guinness and indoor or outdoor seating. For a more genteel atmosphere, duck across the street and wander a few more steps down toward the lake to find the **Art Café,** with a mellow ambience reminiscent of a van Gogh painting. Around the lake near the commercial center, **Bled Pub** (a.k.a. "The Cocktail Bar" or "Troha"—for the family that owns it) is a trendy late-night spot where bartenders sling a dizzying array of mixed drinks to an appreciative crowd (between the commercial center and the lake, above the recommended Oštarija Peglez'n restaurant). If you're still standing, several other, more low-key bars and cafés percolate the commercial center.

SLEEPING

Bled is packed with gradually decaying, communist-era convention hotels. A few have been nicely renovated, but most are stale, outmoded, and overpriced. It's a strange, incestuous little circle—the majority of the town's big hotels and restaurants are owned by the same company. Instead, I prefer staying in smaller, countryside, pension-type accommodations—many of them just a short walk above the lake. These quaint little family-run pensions book up early with Germans and Brits; reserve as far ahead as possible. I've listed the high-season prices (May–Oct). Off-season, prices

---

Sleep Code

(€1 = about $1.40, country code: 386, area code: 04)
S = Single, **D** = Double/Twin, **T** = Triple, **Q** = Quad, **b** = bathroom.
Unless otherwise noted, credit cards are accepted. Everyone
speaks English, and all of these accommodations include
breakfast. Bled levies a €1 tourist tax per person, per night (not
included in below prices unless noted).

To help you sort easily through these listings, I've divided
the rooms into three categories based on the price for a standard double room with bath:

$$$ Higher Priced—Most rooms €100 or more.
$$ Moderately Priced—Most rooms between €50–100.
$ Lower Priced—Most rooms €50 or less.

---

are typically 10–20 percent lower. For even cheaper beds, consider
one of the many *sobe* (rooms in private homes) scattered around
the lake (about €25 per person in peak season, often with a hefty
30 percent surcharge for stays shorter than three nights). Kompas
Bled Travel Agency can help you find a *soba* (see page 572)—but be
sure the location is convenient before you accept.

$$$ Hotel Lovec, a Best Western Premier, sits in a con-
venient (but non-lakefront) location just above the commercial
center. Gorgeously renovated inside and out, and run by a help-
ful and friendly staff, it's a welcoming, cheery, well-run alterna-
tive to Bled's many old, dreary communist hotels. Its 60 plush
rooms come with all the comforts (Sb-€145, Db-€160, €20 more
for a lake-view balcony, €24 less per room Nov–Feb, family and
"executive" suites available, delicious breakfast, elevator, free
Internet access in lobby and rooms, indoor pool, parking garage-
€10/day, Ljubljanska cesta 6, tel. 04/576-8615, fax 04/576-8625,
www.lovechotel.com, booking@kompas-lovec.eu).

$$$ Grand Hotel Toplice is the grande dame of Bled, with 87
high-ceilinged rooms, parquet floors, an elegant view lounge, posh
decor, all the amenities, and a long list of high-profile guests—
from Madeleine Albright to Jordan's King Hussein. Rooms in
the back are cheaper, but have no lake views and overlook a noisy
street—try to get one as high up as possible (non-view: Sb-€150,
Db-€170; lake view: Sb-€180, Db-€220; suites mostly with lake
views-€270; 15–20 percent less Nov–April, elevator, air-con, free 1-
hour boat rental for guests, free cable Internet, free parking, Cesta
Svobode 12, tel. 04/579-1000, fax 04/574-1841, www.hotel-toplice
.com, info@hotel-toplice.com). The hotel's name—*toplice*—means
"spa"; guests are free to use the hotel's natural spring–fed indoor

swimming pool (a chilly 72 degrees Fahrenheit).

$$ Mayer Penzion, perched on a bluff above Grand Hotel Toplice, is a steep five-minute uphill walk from lake. Wonderfully run by the Trseglav family, this place comes with 13 great-value rooms, a friendly and professional staff, an excellent restaurant, and an atmospheric wine-tasting cellar. They book up fast in summer with return clients, so reserve early (Sb-€50, Db-€75-80 depending on size and balcony, extra bed-€20, family deals, no extra charge for 1-night stays, elevator, Želeška cesta 7, tel. 04/576-5740, fax 04/576-5741, www.mayer-sp.si, penzion@mayer-sp.si). They also rent a cute little two-story Slovenian farm cottage next door (Db-€100, Tb/Qb-€120).

$$ Hotel Berc and **Penzion Berc,** run by the Berc brothers, are next door to Mayer Penzion. Both have cozy public spaces, free Internet access, and free loaner bikes, and are worth reserving ahead (both cash only and non-smoking, www.berc-sp.si). The new hotel building has 15 rooms with pleasantly woody decor (Sb-€40–45, Db-€65–75; price depends on size, season, and length of stay; all rooms have balconies, Pod Stražo 13, tel. 04/576-5658, fax 04/576-5659, hotel@berc-sp.si, run by Luka). The older, adjacent *penzion* offers 11 cheaper, almost-as-nice rooms (Sb-€35, Db-€60, €5 more for 1-night stays, 10 percent cheaper off-season, most rooms have balconies, Želeška cesta 15, tel. 04/574-1838, fax 04/576-7320, penzion@berc-sp.si, run by Miha).

$$ Alp Penzion is in a tranquil countryside setting amid cornfields, but still within a 15-minute walk of the lake. Its 11 rooms are small and straightforward, but comfortable. The place is enthusiastically run by the Sršen family, who offer lots of fun activities: tennis court, summer barbecue grill, and wine-tastings (Sb-€40, Db-€55–60—higher price is for balcony, Tb-€80, 10 percent more for 1-night stays, 5 percent cheaper if you pay cash, cheaper Nov–March, family rooms, free Internet access and loaner bikes, Cankarjeva cesta 20A, tel. 04/574-1614, fax 04/574-4590, www.alp-penzion.com, bled@alp-penzion.com). This place also runs the relaxing Essense spa (described on page 572).

$$ Mila Sušnik, who is friendly and speaks English, rents out two comfortable apartments a five-minute walk above town, near the Mayer and Berc pensions (listed above). Modern, tidy, and equipped with kitchens, these are a good budget choice for families (Db-€57, 20 percent extra for fewer than 3 nights, no breakfast, Želeška cesta 3, tel. 04/574-1731, fax 04/574-2719, www.bled-holiday.com, susnik@bled-holiday.com). It's just toward the lake from the bigger pensions, with a big crucifix out front.

Grand Hotel Toplice (listed earlier) runs two nearby annexes with much lower prices: **$$ Hotel Jadran,** on a hill behind the Toplice, has 45 tired, old rooms (reception tel. 04/579-1365).

$$ Hotel Trst is less homey, but its 31 rooms are a little bigger and have been lightly renovated (breakfast at the Toplice, reception tel. 04/579-1186, if nobody is at reception check in at Toplice, often closed in winter). Both have the same prices and can be reserved through Grand Hotel Toplice (non-view: Sb-€56, Db-€72; lake view: Sb-€81, Db-€96; extra bed-€21, all rooms €10 less Nov–April, Cesta Svobode 12; reservations for either hotel: tel. 04/579-1000, fax 04/574-1841, www.hotel-toplice.com, info @hotel-toplice.com). In the near future, the Jadran might be renovated—and increase its rates. At either place, ask for a room on the higher floors to avoid road noise (both have elevators).

$ Tourist Farm Mulej, farther out of town than my other listings and better for drivers, is a new but traditional farmhouse in a tranquil valley about a half-mile from the lake (1.5 miles from Bled town). Damjana and Jože, who run a working farm, rent out eight modern rooms—most with balconies—and serve breakfasts and dinners made with food they produce (Db-€50, or €66 with dinner, no extra charge for 1-night stays, cash only, family rooms, free cable Internet, Selo pri Bledu 20, tel. & fax 04/574-4617, www.mulej-bled.com, info@mulej-bled.com). It's in the farm village of Selo—drive along the lakeside road south from Bled, then turn off in Mlino towards Selo, and look for the signs (to the right) once in the village.

$ Penzion Bledec, an official IYHF hostel, is just below the castle at the top of the Old Town. Each of the 13 rooms has its own bathroom, and some can be rented as doubles (though "doubles" are actually underutilized triples and quads, with separate beds pushed together—so they're not reservable July–Aug or at other busy times). The friendly staff is justifiably proud of the bargain they offer (bed in 4– to 7-bed dorm-€19, Db-€50, Tb-€63, cheaper Nov–April, members pay 10 percent less, includes sheets and breakfast, entirely non-smoking, great family rooms, Internet access, full-service laundry for guests-€9/load, restaurant, Grajska 17, tel. 04/574-5250, fax 04/574-5251, www.mlino.si, bledec@mlino.si).

$ Travellers Haven is a new, low-key hostel loosely run by Gašper and Katja. The 27 beds fill six rooms in a nicely renovated hundred-year-old villa in the Old Town (€19 bunks, 2- to 6-beds per room, no breakfast but guest kitchen, tight bathrooms offer little privacy, reception open 8:00–22:00, free Internet and laundry machines, cellar bar, bike rental, Riklijeva cesta 1, mobile 031-704-455 or 041-396-545, www.travellers-haven.com, travellers-haven @t-2.net).

$ Vila Gorenka is your non-hostel, low-budget option. The Žerovec family's old-fashioned house has 10 basic, faded, musty rooms sharing two bathrooms upstairs from their home (S-€20, D-€36, cash only, no extra charge for 1-night stays, just below the

Mayer and Berc pensions at Želeška cesta 9, mobile 051-369-070, http://freeweb.siol.net/mz2, vila.gorenka@siol.net).

EATING

Okarina Etno, run by charming, well-traveled Leo Ličof, serves a diverse array of cuisines, all of them well-executed: international fare, traditional Slovenian specialties, and Indian (Himalayan) dishes. Leo has a respect for salads and vegetables and a passion for fish. Creative cooking, fine presentation, friendly service, and an atmosphere as tastefully eclectic as the food make this place a great splurge (€10–15 pastas, €11–28 main dishes, Mon–Fri 18:00–24:00, Sat–Sun 12:00–24:00, next to Hotel Lovec at Ljubljanska cesta 8, tel. 04/574-1458). Skim the guest book to find the page with Paul McCartney's visit from May 2005.

Oštarija Peglez'n ("The Old Iron"), conveniently located on the main road between the commercial center and the lake, cooks up tasty meals with an emphasis on fish. Choose between the delightful Slovenian cottage interior or the shady streetside terrace. Reservations are smart in summer (€5–8 salads and pastas, €8–20 main dishes, daily 12:00–24:00, fun family-style shareable plates, Cesta Svobode 7A, tel. 04/574-4218).

Mayer Penzion, just up the hill from the lakefront, has a dressy restaurant with good traditional cooking that's worth the short hike. This is where a Babel of international tourists come to swap hiking tips and day-trip tales. It's best to reserve ahead in summer (main dishes €8–20, Tue–Fri 17:00–24:00, Sat–Sun 12:00–24:00, closed Mon, indoor or outdoor seating, above Hotel Jadran at Želeška cesta 7, tel. 04/576-5740).

Gostilna Pri Planincu ("By the Mountaineers") is a homey, informal bar coated with license plates and packed with fun-loving and sometimes rowdy natives. A larger dining area sprawls behind the small, local-feeling pub, and there's outdoor seating out front and on the side patio. The menu features huge portions of stick-to-your-ribs Slovenian pub grub, plus Balkan grilled-meat specialties (€6–12 main dishes, fish splurges up to €20). Upstairs is a timbered pizzeria selling €3–8 wood-fired pies (pub and pizzeria both open daily 9:00–23:00, Grajska cesta 8, tel. 04/574-1613). The playful cartoon mural along the outside of the restaurant shows different types of mountaineers (from left to right): thief, normal, mooch ("gopher"), climber, and naked (...well, almost).

Pizzeria Rustika, in the Old Town, offers good wood-fired pizzas and salads. Its upstairs terrace is relaxing on a balmy evening (€5–8 pizzas, Tue–Sun 12:00–23:00, Mon 15:00–23:00—but opens at 12:00 in peak season, service can be slow when it's busy, Riklijeva cesta 13, tel. 04/576-8900).

Bled Desserts

While you're in Bled, be sure to enjoy the town's specialty, a cream cake called **kremna rezina** (KRAYM-nah ray-ZEE-nah; often referred to by its German-derived name, **kremšnita,** KRAYM-shnee-tah). It's a layer of cream and a thick layer of vanilla custard artfully sandwiched between sheets of delicate, crispy crust. Heavenly. Slovenes travel from all over the country to sample this famous dessert.

Slightly less renowned—but just as tasty—is **grmada** (gur-MAH-dah, "bonfire"). This dessert was developed by Hotel Jelovica as a way to get rid of their day-old leftovers. They take yesterday's cake, add rum, milk, custard, and raisins, and top it off with whipped cream and chocolate syrup.

Finally, there's *prekmurska gibanica*—or just **gibanica** (gee-bah-NEET-seh) for short. Originating in the Hungarian corner of the country, *gibanica* is an earthy pastry filled with poppy seeds, walnuts, apple, and cheese, and drizzled with rum.

These desserts are typically enjoyed with a lake-and-mountains view—the best spots are the Panorama restaurant by Grand Hotel Toplice and the terrace across from the Hotel Park (figure around €5 for cake and coffee at any of these places). For a more local (but non-lake view) setting, consider Šmon Slaščičarna (only slightly cheaper; see below).

The **Mercator** grocery store, in the commercial center, has the makings for a bang-up picnic. They sell pre-made sandwiches for about €3, or will make you one to order (point to what you want). This is a great option for hikers and budget travelers (Mon–Fri 7:00–19:00, Sat 7:00–15:00, Sun 8:00–12:00).

Dessert: While tourists generally gulp down their cream cakes on a hotel restaurant's lakefront terrace, local residents know the best desserts are at **Šmon Slaščičarna** (a.k.a. the "Brown Bear," for the bear on the sign). It's nicely untouristy, but lacks the atmosphere of the lakeside spots (€2–3 cakes, daily 7:30–21:00, near bus station at Grajska cesta 3, tel. 04/574-1616).

TRANSPORTATION CONNECTIONS

The most convenient train connections to Bled leave from the Lesce-Bled station, about 2.5 miles away (see details under "Arrival in Bled" on page 570). Remember, when buying a train ticket to Lake Bled, make it clear that you want to go to the Lesce-Bled station (not the Bled Jezero station, which is poorly connected to the main line). No one in the town of Bled sells train tickets; buy them at the station just before your train departs. If the ticket window there is closed, buy your ticket on board from the conductor (who will likely waive the €2.50 additional fee).

Note that if you're going to **Ljubljana,** the bus (which leaves from Bled town itself) is better than the train (which leaves from the Lesce-Bled train station).

From Lesce-Bled by Train to: Ljubljana (roughly hourly, 1 hr—but bus is better), **Salzburg** (5/day, 4 hrs), **Munich** (3/day, 6 hrs), **Vienna** (that's **Dunaj** in Slovene, 5/day, 6 hrs, transfer in Villach, Austria), **Venice** (3/day with transfer in Ljubljana or Villach, 6 hrs), **Zagreb** (5/day, 3.5 hrs).

By Bus to: Ljubljana (Mon–Sat hourly—usually at :30 past the hour, fewer on Sun, 1.25 hrs, €6.30), **Radovljica** (Mon–Fri at least 2/hr, Sat hourly, Sun almost hourly, 15 min, €1.60), **Lesce-Bled train station** (2/hr, 10 min, €1.30), **Lake Bohinj** (hourly, 40 min and €3.60 to Bohinj Jezero stop, 50 min and €4.10 to Bohinj Vogel or Bohinj Zlatorog stop), **Podhom** (15-min hike away from Vintgar Gorge, Mon–Fri 5/day in the morning, 1/day Sat, none Sun, 15 min, €1.30), **Spodnje Gorje** (also 15-min hike from Vintgar Gorge, take bus in direction of Krnica, hourly, 15 min, €1.30). Confirm times at the Bled bus station.

By Plane: The Ljubljana-Brnik Airport is between Lake Bled and Ljubljana, about a 45-minute drive from Bled. Connecting by taxi costs around €45 (set price up front—since it's outside of town, they don't use the meter). The bus connection from Bled to the airport is cheap (total cost: about €5), but complicated and time-consuming: First, go to Kranj (Mon–Fri 12/day, Sat–Sun 8/day, 35 min), then transfer to a Brnik-bound bus (at least hourly, 20 min). Many Bled residents prefer to fly from Klagenfurt, Austria. For details on both the Ljubljana and Klagenfurt airports, see page 566.

Route Tips for Drivers: Bled is less than an hour north of Ljubljana. The final link in the A-2 expressway will zip you right there—once construction wraps up. (The project is due to be completed in the near future). If it's not finished yet, you'll be diverted onto a smaller two-lane road. Watch for signs to *Bled*. Whether or not the expressway is done, the Bled exit will take you directly to the lake (where it's called Ljubljanska cesta).

To reach Radovljica (bee museum) or Lesce (train station), drive out of Bled on Ljubljanska cesta toward the expressway. Watch for the turnoff to those two towns on the right. They're on the same road: Lesce first (to reach train station, divert right when entering town), then Radovljica (for arrival and parking tips, see page 588).

Near Lake Bled

The countryside around Bled offers several day trips that can be done easily without a car (bus connection information is described in each section). The three listed here are the best (one small-town/museum experience, two hiking/back-to-nature options). They're more convenient than can't-miss, but each is worthwhile on a longer visit, and all give a good taste of the Julian Alps. For a self-guided driving tour through farther-flung (and even more striking) parts of the Julian Alps, see the next chapter.

Radovljica

The town of Radovljica (rah-DOH-vleet-suh) is larger than Bled, perched on a plateau above the Sava River. The town itself is nothing exciting, though its old-center pedestrian zone, Linhartov trg, makes for a pleasant stroll. But the town is home to a fascinating and offbeat beekeeping museum—which, with only a few rooms, still ranks as one of Europe's biggest on the topic.

Radovljica's **Apicultural Museum** (Čebelarski Muzej)—worth ▲—celebrates Slovenia's long beekeeping heritage. Since the days before Europeans had sugar, Slovenia has been a big honey producer. Slovenian farmer Anton Janša is considered the father of modern beekeeping, and was Europe's first official teacher of beekeeping (in Hapsburg, Vienna).

The first two rooms of the museum trace the history of beekeeping, from the time when bees were kept in hollowed-out trees to the present day. Notice the old-fashioned **tools** in the second room. When a new queen bee is born, the old queen takes half the hive's bees to a new location. Experienced beekeepers used the long, skinny instrument (a beehive stethoscope) to figure out when the swarm would fly the coop. Then, once the bees had moved to a nearby tree, the beekeeper used the big spoons to retrieve the queen—surrounded by an angry ball of her subjects—from her new home before she could get settled in. The beekeeper transported the furious gang into a manmade hive designed for easier, more sanitary collection of the honey. You can also see the tools beekeepers used to create smoke, which makes bees less aggressive. Even today, some of Slovenia's old-fashioned beekeepers simply light up a cigarette and blow smoke on any bees that get ornery.

The third room features the museum's highlight: whimsically painted beehive **frontboards** (called *panjske končnice*). Nineteenth-century farmers, believing these paintings would help the bees find their way home, developed a tradition of decorating their hives with religious, historical, and satirical folk themes (look for the devil sharpening a woman's tongue on a wheel). The depiction of

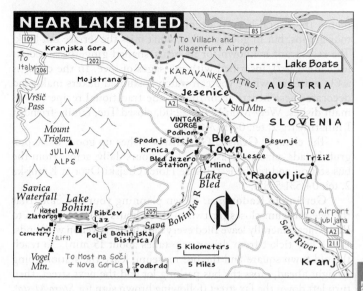

a hunter's funeral shows all the animals happy...except his dog. There's everything from portraits of Hapsburg emperors, to a "true crime" sequence of a man murdering his family as they sleep, to proto-"Lockhorns" cartoons of marital strife, to 18th-century erotica (one with a woman showing some leg, and another with a flip-up, peek-a-boo panel).

The life-size wooden statues were used to "guard" the beehives—and designed to look like fearsome Ottoman and Napoleonic soldiers.

You'll also find an interactive multimedia exhibit, a good video in English, temporary exhibitions, and—in the summer only—an actual, functioning beehive (try to find the queen). A new exhibit about favorite son Anton Tomaž Linhart, a beloved Slovenian playwright from Radovljica, is in the works. The gift shop is a good place for souvenirs, with hand-painted replicas of frontboards, honey brandy, candles, ornaments, and other bee products (museum entry-€2.50, good English descriptions, free sheet of English info, €1.60 English guidebook is a nice souvenir; May–Oct Tue–Sun 10:00–13:00 & 15:00–18:00, closed Mon; March–April and Nov–Dec Wed and Sat–Sun 10:00–12:00 & 15:00–17:00, closed Mon–Tue and Thu–Fri; closed Jan–Feb; upstairs at Linhartov trg 1, tel. 04/532-0520, www.muzeji -radovljica.si).

Eating in Radovljica: Several Radovljica restaurants near the bee museum have view terraces overlooking the surrounding mountains and valleys. **Lectar** offers pricey, hearty Slovenian fare in a rural-feeling setting with a user-friendly, super-traditional menu. Its several heavily decorated rooms are often filled with tour groups, but in good weather, don't miss the terrace out back. The restaurant is known for its heart-shaped gingerbread cookies (called *lect*), inscribed with messages of love. In the cellar is a €1 "museum" where you can watch costumed bakers make and decorate these hearts according to the traditional recipe (€9–18 main dishes, Wed–Mon 12:00–22:00, closed Tue, family-friendly, Linhartov trg 2, tel. 04/537-4800).

The cheaper **Grajska Gostilnica** dishes up good, basic pub grub (salads, pizza, pastas, open long hours daily, across from the bus station and to the left, inside Hotel Grajski Dvor at Kranjska 2, tel. 04/531-5585).

Getting to Radovljica: When planning your day, note that the bee museum closes for two to three hours at lunch. **Buses** to Radovljica generally leave Bled every half-hour (fewer on weekends, €1.60, buy ticket from driver, trip takes about 15 min). To reach the old town square and the bee museum, leave the station going straight ahead, cross the bus parking lot and the next street, then turn left down the far street (following brown sign for *Staro Mesto*). In five minutes, you'll get to the pedestrianized Linhartov trg (TI on right just before you enter pedestrian zone, tel. 04/531-5300). At the end of this square on the left is the big, yellow Baroque mansion that houses the bee museum (upstairs). **Drivers** leave Bled on Ljubljanska cesta, then turn right at the sign for *Radovljica* and go through the village of Lesce; the road dead-ends at Radovljica's pedestrian zone, where you'll find a parking lot and rustic garage. From here, it's a short walk to the bee museum (see directions for bus, above). A new **bike** path scenically and peacefully connects Bled with Radovljica (about 4 miles, get details at TI).

▲Vintgar Gorge

Just north of Bled, the river Radovna has carved this mile-long, picturesque gorge into the mountainside. Boardwalks and bridges put you right in the middle of the action of this "poor man's Plitvice." You'll cross over several waterfalls and marvel at the clarity of the water. The easy hike is on a boardwalk trail with handrails (sometimes narrow and a bit slippery). At the end of the gorge, you'll find a restaurant, WCs, and a bridge with a fine view. Go back the way you came, or take a prettier return to Bled (see "Scenic Hike Back to Bled"). The gorge is easily reachable from Bled by bus or foot, and is the best option for those who are itching for a hike but don't have a car (€3, daily May–late Oct 8:00–19:00 or until dusk, June–Aug until 20:00, closed late Oct–April, tel. 04/572-5266).

Getting to Vintgar Gorge: The gorge is 2.5 miles north of Bled. You can walk (1 hour) or bus (15-min ride plus 15-min walk, or 30-min ride on summer tourist bus) to the gorge entrance.

Walkers leave Bled on the road between the castle and St. Martin's Church and take the uphill (left) road at the fork. Just after the little yellow chapel, turn right on the road with the big tree, then immediately left at the Mercator grocery store. When the road swings left, continue straight onto Partizanska (marked for *Podhom* and a walking sign for *Vintgar;* ignore the bus sign for *Vintgar* pointing left). At the fork just after the little bridge, go left for Podhom, then simply follow signs for *Vintgar.*

In summer, the easy **tourist bus** takes you right to the gorge entrance in 30 minutes (see "Getting Around Lake Bled (Literally)," page 572). Otherwise, you can take a **local bus** to one of two stops: Podhom (Mon–Fri 5/day in the morning, 1/day Sat, none Sun, 15 min, €1.30) or Spodnje Gorje (take bus in direction of Krnica, hourly, 15 min, €1.30). From either the Podhom or the Spodnje Gorje bus stop, it's a 15-minute walk to the gorge (follow signs for *Vintgar*).

Drivers follow signs to *Podhom*, then *Vintgar* (see walking instructions, above).

Scenic Hike Back to Bled: If you still have energy once you reach the end of the gorge, consider this longer hike back with panoramic views. Behind the restaurant, find the trail marked *Katarina Bled.* You'll go uphill for 25 strenuous minutes (following the red-and-white circles and arrows) before cresting the hill and enjoying beautiful views over Bled town and the region. Continue straight down the road 15 minutes to the typical, narrow, old village of Zasip, then walk (about 30 min) or take the bus back to Bled.

Lake Bohinj

The pristine alpine Lake Bohinj (BOH-heen), 16 miles southwest of Bled, enjoys a quieter scene and (in clear weather) even better vistas of Triglav and the surrounding mountains. This is a real

back-to-nature experience, with just a smattering of hotels and campgrounds, rather than the well-oiled resort machine of Bled. Some people adore Bohinj; others are bored by it. If you think Bled is too touristy to allow you to really enjoy the nature, go to Bohinj.

Getting to Lake Bohinj: From Bled, hourly **buses** head for Bohinj, stopping at three different destinations: Bohinj Jezero (the village of Ribčev Laz, 40 min, €3.60), then Bohinj Vogel (a 10-minute walk from the base of the Vogel Mountain cable car, 50 min, €4.10), and finally a few hundred yards more to Bohinj Zlatorog (Hotel Zlatorog and the one-hour hike to the Savica

Lake Bled

waterfall trailhead, 50 min, €4.10). Off-season, there are fewer buses—confirm times before you depart. **Drivers** leave Bled going south along the lakefront road, Cesta Svobode; in the village of Mlino, you'll peel off from the lake and follow signs to *Boh Bistrica* (a midsize town near Lake Bohinj). Once in the town of Bohinjska Bistrica, turn right, following *Bohinj Jezero* signs. The road takes you to the village of Ribčev Laz and along the lakefront road with all the attractions.

Sights and Activities: A visit to Bohinj has three parts: a village, a cable car (and nearby cemetery), and a waterfall hike.

Coming from Bled, your first views of Bohinj will be from the little **village** called Ribčev Laz (loosely translated as "Good Fishin' Hole") at the southeast corner of the lake. Here you'll find a TI, a handful of hotels and ice-cream stands, and the Bohinj Jezero bus stop. The town's main landmark is its church, St. John the Baptist (to your right as you face the lake, past the distinctive stone bridge; not open to visitors). In the other direction, a five-minute stroll down the lakefront road, is a dock where you can catch an electric tourist boat to make a silent circuit around the lake (€8.50 round-trip, €6 one-way, daily 10:00–18:00, 2/hr, less off-season). The boat stops at the far end of the lake, at Camp Zlatorog—a 10-minute walk from the Vogel cable car (see below). Across from the Ribčev Laz dock is a fun concrete 3-D model of Triglav (compare to the real thing, hovering across the lake). Finally, a few more steps down the road, just beyond a boat rental dock, you'll see a statue of Zlatorog, the "Golden Horn"—a mythical chamois-like creature native to the Julian Alps.

The remaining sights are along this same road, which follows the lake to its end.

For a mountain perch without the sweat, take the **cable car** up to Vogel Mountain, offering impressive panoramic views of Mount Triglav and the Julian Alps (€10 round-trip, runs every 30 min, daily 7:00–19:00 in summer, 8:00–18:00 in winter, shorter hours and less frequent departures in spring and fall—confirm schedule before you make the trip, closed Nov, www.vogel.si). The top is a ski-in-winter, hike-in-summer area with fine views and a chairlift experience. The alpine hut Merjasec ("Wild Boar") offers tasty strudel and a wide variety of local brandies (including the notorious "Boar's Blood"—a concoction of several different flavors guaranteed to get you snorting). To reach the cable-car station, drivers follow signs to *Vogel* (to the left off the main lakefront road); by bus, get off at the Bohinj Vogel stop (request this stop from driver) and hike about 10 minutes up the steep road on the left (away from the lake).

Just beyond the cable-car station and Bohinj Vogel bus stop, look for the metal gate on the left marking a WWI **cemetery**—the final resting place for some Soča Front soldiers (see sidebar on page 604). While no fighting occurred here (it was mostly on the other side of these mountains), injured soldiers were brought to a nearby hospital. Those who didn't recover ended up here. Notice that many of the names are not Slovene, but Hungarian, Polish, Czech, and so on—a reminder that the entire multiethnic Austro-Hungarian Empire was involved in the fighting. If you're walking down from the cable-car station, the cemetery makes for a poignant detour on your way to the main road (look for it through the trees).

Up the valley beyond the end of the lake is Bohinj's final treat, a **waterfall** called Slap Savica (sah-VEET-seh). Hardy hikers enjoy following the moderate-to-strenuous uphill trail (including 553 stairs) to see the cascade, which dumps into a remarkably pure pool of aquamarine snowmelt (€2, daily in summer from 8:00 until dusk, allow about 90 min for the round-trip hike). Drivers follow the lakefront road to where it ends, right at the trailhead. Without a car, getting to the trailhead is a hassle. If you take the public bus from Bled, or the boats on the lake, they'll get you only as far as the Bohinj Zlatorog stop—the end of the line, and still a one-hour hike from the trailhead (from the bus stop, follow signs to *Slap Savica*). In summer, a sporadic shuttle bus takes you right to the trailhead. But frankly, it's not worth it if you don't have a car.

Sleeping near Lake Bohinj: Like most people who live in these parts, **$ Bojan and Ksenija Kočar** (BOH-yawn and kuh-SAYN-yah KOH-char) have spent years building their alpine home. In addition to housing the Kočars and their two teenagers, this delightful chalet also has several affordable rooms for tourists, as well as a beautifully hand-carved lounge/breakfast room. If you have a car and want to really get away from it all, consider sleeping here, in the countryside less than a mile from Lake Bohinj (about a 30-min drive from Lake Bled). Friendly, English-speaking Bojan—who's a bus driver—is often out of town, but Ksenija (who speaks less English) will take good care of you (Db-€34, or €44 for 1-night stays, includes breakfast, closed Jan–March, tel. 04/574-6660—best to call after 21:00, mobile 041-478-490, kocar.bojan@siol.net). Driving from Lake Bled, you'll go through the town of Bohinjska Bistrica, then the village of Polje; they're just beyond Polje, but before Lake Bohinj itself (the first farmhouse on the left after Polje, #49, look for *Rooms* sign).

Lake Bled

THE JULIAN ALPS

The Vršič Pass and the Soča River Valley

The countryside around Lake Bled has its own distinctive beauty. But to get the full Slovenian mountain experience, head for the hills. The northwestern corner of Slovenia—within yodeling distance of Austria and Italy—is crowned by the Julian Alps (named for Julius Caesar). Here, mountain culture has a Slavic flavor.

The Slovenian mountainsides are laced with hiking paths, blanketed in a deep forest, and speckled with ski resorts and vacation chalets. Beyond every ridge is a peaceful alpine village nestled around a quaint Baroque steeple. And in the center of it all is Mount Triglav—ol' "Three Heads"—Slovenia's symbol and tallest mountain (see page 596).

The single best day in the Julian Alps is spent driving up and over the 50 hairpin turns of the breathtaking Vršič Pass (vur-SHEECH, open May–Oct), and back down via the Soča (SOH-chah) River Valley, lined with offbeat nooks and Hemingway-haunted crannies. As you curl on twisty roads between the cut-glass peaks, you'll enjoy stunning high-mountain scenery, white-water rivers with superb fishing, rustic rest stops, thought-provoking WWI sights, and charming hamlets.

A pair of Soča Valley towns holds watch over the region. Bovec is all about good times (it's the white-water adventure-sports hub), while Kobarid attends to more serious matters (WWI history). While neither is a destination in itself, both Bovec and Kobarid are pleasant, functional, and convenient home bases for exploring this gloriously beautiful region.

Getting Around the Julian Alps

The Julian Alps are best by **car**. Even if you're doing the rest of your trip by train, consider renting a car here for maximum mountain day-trip flexibility. I've included a self-guided driving tour incorporating the best of the Julian Alps (Vršič Pass and Soča Valley).

It's difficult to do the Vršič Pass and Soča Valley without your own wheels. Hiring a **local guide** with a car can be a great value, making your time not only fun, but also informative. Cheaper but less personal, you could join a day-trip **excursion** from Bled. (Both options are explained in the "Tours" section of the previous chapter, page 574.) Or stay closer to Bled, and get a taste of the Julian Alps by taking advantage of easy and frequent **bus** connections to more convenient day-trip destinations (Radovljica, the Vintgar Gorge, and Lake Bohinj—all described under "Near Lake Bled" in the previous chapter).

Julian Alps Self-Guided Driving Tour

This all-day, self-guided driving tour, rated ▲▲▲, takes you over the highest mountain pass in Slovenia, with stunning scenery and a few quirky sights along the way. From waterfalls to hiking trails, WWI history to queasy suspension bridges, this trip has it all.

ORIENTATION

Most of the Julian Alps are encompassed by the Triglav National Park (Triglavski Narodni Park). (Some sights near Lake Bled—such as Lake Bohinj and the Vintgar Gorge—are also part of this park, but are covered in the previous chapter.) This drive is divided into two parts: the Vršič Pass and the Soča River Valley. While this drive is not for stick-shift novices, all but the most timid drivers will agree the scenery is worth the many hairpin turns. Frequent pull-outs offer plenty of opportunity to relax, stretch your legs, and enjoy the vistas.

Planning Your Time: Although this drive can be done in a day, consider spending the night along the way for a more leisurely pace. You can start and end in Bled or Ljubljana. For efficient sightseeing, I prefer to begin in Bled (after appreciating the mountains from afar for a day or two) and end in the capital.

Length of This Tour: These rough estimates do not include stops: Bled to the top of Vršič Pass—1 hour; Vršič Pass to Trenta (start of Soča Valley)—30 min; Trenta to Bovec—30 min; Bovec to Kobarid—30 min; Kobarid to Ljubljana or Bled—2 hours (remember, it's an hour between Ljubljana and Bled). In other words, if you started and ended in Bled and drove the entire route without stopping, you'd make it home in less than five hours...but you'd miss so much. It takes at least a full day to really do the region justice.

Tourist Information: The best sources of information are the Bled TI (see page 569), the Triglav National Park Information Centers in Trenta (page 598) and Bled (page 570), and the TIs in Bovec and Kobarid (pages 601 and 606).

Maps: Pick up a good map before you begin (available at local TIs, travel agencies, and gas stations). The all-Slovenia *Autokarta Slovenija* or the TI's "Next Exit: Goldenhorn Route" map both include all the essential roads, but several more detailed options are also available. The 1:50,000 Kod & Kam *Posoče* map covers the entire Vršič Pass and Soča Valley (but doesn't include the parts of the drive near Bled and Ljubljana).

OK...let's ride.

Part 1: Vršič Pass

From Bled or Ljubljana, take the A-2 expressway north, enjoying views of **Mount Triglav** on the left as you drive. About 10 minutes past Bled, you'll approach the industrial city of **Jesenice,** whose iron- and steelworks are now mostly closed. The nearby village of **Kurja Vas** ("Chicken Village") is famous for producing hockey players (18 of the 20 players on the 1971 Yugoslav hockey team—which went to the World Championships—were from this tiny hamlet).

As you zip past Jesenice, keep your eye out for the Hrušica exit (also marked for Jesenice, Kranjska Gora, and the Italian border; it's after the gas station, just before the tunnel to Austria). When you exit, turn left towards Kranjska Gora (yellow sign) and the Italian border.

Slovenes brag that their country—"with 56 percent of the land covered in forest"—is Europe's second-greenest. As you drive towards Kranjska Gora, take in all this greenery...and the characteristic Slovenian hayracks (recognized as part of the national heritage and now preserved; see page 519). The Vrata Valley (on the left) is a popular starting point for climbing Mount Triglav. On the right, watch for the statue of Jakob Aljaž, who actually bought Triglav back when such a thing was possible (he's pointing at his purchase). Ten minutes later, you'll cross a bridge and enjoy a great head-on view of Špik Mountain.

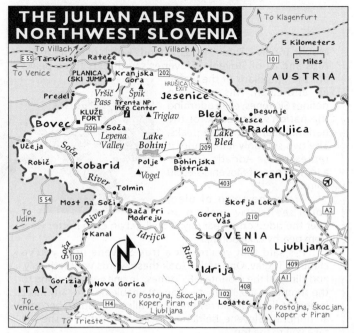

THE JULIAN ALPS AND NORTHWEST SLOVENIA

Entering Kranjska Gora (once Yugoslavia's leading winter resort, and still popular with Croatian skiers), you'll see a turnoff to the left marked for *Vršič*. But winter sports fanatics may want to take a 15-minute detour to see the biggest ski jump in the world, a few miles ahead (stay straight through Kranjska Gora, then turn left at signs for **Planica,** the last stop before the Italian border). Every year, tens of thousands of sports fans flock here to watch the ski-flying world championships. This is where a local boy was the first human to fly more than 100 meters (328 feet) on skis. Today's competitors routinely set new world records (currently 784 feet—that's 17 seconds in the air). From the ski jump, you're a few minutes' walk from Italy or Austria. This region—spanning three nations—lobbied unsuccessfully under the name Senza Confini (Italian for "without borders") to host the 2006 Winter Olympics. Despite the failed Olympic bid, this philosophy is in tune with the European Union's vision for a Europe of regions, rather than nations.

Back in Kranjska Gora, follow the signs for *Vršič*. Before long, you'll officially enter **Triglav National Park** and come to the first of this road's 50 hairpin turns (24 up, then 26 down)—each one numbered and labeled with the altitude in meters. Notice that they're cobbled to provide better traction. If the drive seems daunting, remember that 50-seat tour buses routinely conquer this

Mount Triglav

Mount Triglav ("Three Heads") stands watch over the Julian Alps and all of Slovenia. Slovenes say that its three peaks are the guardians of the water, air, and earth. This mountain defines Slovenes, even adorning the nation's flag: Look for the national seal, with three peaks. The two squiggly lines under it represent the Adriatic. Or take a look at one of Slovenia's €0.50 coins.

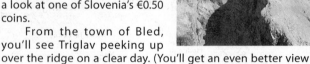

From the town of Bled, you'll see Triglav peeking up over the ridge on a clear day. (You'll get an even better view from nearby Lake Bohinj.)

It's said that you're not a true Slovene until you've climbed Triglav. One native took these words very seriously, and climbed the mountain 853 times...in one year. Climbing to the summit—at 9,396 feet—is an attainable goal for any hiker in decent shape. If you're here for a while and want to become an honorary Slovene, befriend a local and ask if he or she will take you to the top.

If mountain climbing isn't your style, relax at an outdoor café with a piece of cream cake and a view of Triglav. It won't make you a Slovene...but it's close enough on a quick visit.

pass...if they can do it, so can you. (Better yet, imagine the bikers who routinely pedal to the top. The best can do it in less than 30 minutes—faster than driving.)

After switchback #8, with the cute waterfall, park your car on the right and hike up the stairs to the little **Russian chapel** (recently renovated, so it looks shiny and new). This road was

built during World War I by at least 10,000 Russian POWs of the Austro-Hungarian Empire to supply the front lines of the Soča Front. The POWs lived and worked in terrible conditions, and several hundred died of illness and exposure. On March 8, 1916, an avalanche thundered down the mountains, killing hundreds more workers. This chapel was built where the final casualty was found.

The Julian Alps

Take a minute to pay your respects to the men who built the road you're enjoying today. Because it's a Russian Orthodox chapel, notice that the crosses topping the steeples have three crossbars. (For more on the Orthodox faith, see page 659.)

After #17, look as high as you can on the cliff face to see sunlight poking through a **"window"** in the rock. This natural formation, a popular destination for intrepid hikers, is big enough for the Statue of Liberty to crawl through.

After #22, at the pullout for Erjavčeva Koča restaurant, you may see tour-bus groups making a fuss about the mountain vista. They're looking for a ghostly face in the cliff wall, supposedly belonging to the mythical figure **Ajda.** This village girl was cursed by the townspeople after correctly predicting the death of the Zlatorog (Golden Horn), a magical, beloved, chamois-like animal. Her tiny image (with a Picasso nose) is just above the tree line, a little to the right—try to get someone to point her out to you (you can see her best if you stand at the signpost near the road).

After #24, you reach the **summit** (5,285 feet). On the right, a long gravel chute gives hikers a thrilling glissade down. (From the pullout just beyond #26, it's easy to view hikers "skiing" down.) As you begin the descent, keep an eye out for old WWI debris. A lonely guard tunnel stands after #28, followed by a tunnel marked *1916* (on the left) that was part of the road's original path. Then you'll see abandoned checkpoints from when this was the border between Italy and the Austro-Hungarian Empire. At #48 is a statue of **Julius Kugy,** an Italian botanist who wrote books about alpine flora.

At #49, the road to the right (marked *Izvir Soče*) leads to the **source of the Soča River.** If you feel like stretching your legs after all that shifting, drive about five minutes down this road to a restaurant parking lot. From here, you can take a challenging 20-minute uphill hike to the Soča source. This is also the starting point for a new, well-explained Soča Trail (Soška Pot) that leads all the way to the town of Bovec, mostly following the road we're driving on today. With plenty of time and a hankering to hike rather than drive, consider taking this trail (about 12 miles one-way).

Nearing the end of the switchbacks, follow signs for Bovec. Crossing the Soča River, you begin the second half of this trip.

Part 2: Soča River Valley

During World War I, the terrain between here and the Adriatic made up the Soča (Isonzo) Front. As you follow the Soča River south, down what's nicknamed the "Valley of the Cemeteries," the scenic mountainsides around you tell the tale of this terrible warfare. Imagine a young Ernest Hemingway driving his ambulance

Hemingway in Slovenia

It was against the scenic backdrop of the Slovenian Alps that a young man from Oak Park, Illinois, first came to Europe—the continent with which he would forever be identified. After graduating high school in 1917 and working briefly as a newspaper reporter, young Ernest Hemingway wanted to join the war effort in Europe. Bad vision kept him out of the army, but he craved combat experience—so he joined the Red Cross Ambulance Corps instead.

After a short detour through Paris, Hemingway was sent to the Italian Front. On his first day, he was given the job of retrieving human remains—gruesomely disfigured body parts—after the explosion of a munitions factory. Later he came to the Soča Front and spent time in Kobarid (which he called by its Italian name, Caporetto). In fact, he was here for the epic Battle of Kobarid, when the Italians had to retreat. In July of 1918, his ambulance was hit by a mortar shell. Despite his injuries, he saved an Italian soldier who was also wounded. According to legend, he packed his own wound with cigarette butts to stop the flow of blood.

Sent to Milan to recuperate, Hemingway fell in love with a nurse, but she later left him for an Italian military officer. A decade later, Hemingway wrote about Kobarid, the war, and his case of youthful heartbreak in the novel *A Farewell to Arms*.

The Julian Alps

through these same hills (see the sidebar).

But it's not all so gloomy. There are plenty of other diversions—interesting villages and churches, waterfalls and suspension bridges, and lots more. Perhaps most impressive is the remarkable clarity and milky-blue color of the Soča itself, which Slovenes proudly call their "emerald river."

The last Vršič switchback (#50) sends you into the village of **Trenta.** You'll pass a church and a botanical garden of alpine plants (Alpinum Juliana), then go over a bridge. Immediately after the bridge on the right is the parking lot for the Mlinarica Gorge. While the gorge is interesting, the bridge leading to it was damaged in a severe storm and hasn't yet been rebuilt—so it's best left to hardy hikers.

As you get to the cluster of buildings in Trenta's "downtown," look on the left for the **Triglav National Park Information Center,** which also serves as a regional TI (daily May–Oct 10:00–

18:00, Dec–April 10:00–14:00, closed Nov, tel. 05/388-9330, www
.tnp.si). The humble €4 museum here provides a look (with English
explanations) at the park's flora, fauna, traditional culture, and
mountaineering history. A poetic 15-minute slideshow explains
the wonders and fragility of the park (included in museum entry,
ask for English version as you enter).

About five miles after Trenta, in the town of Soča, visit the
Church of St. Joseph (with red onion dome, hiding behind the
big tree on the right). The church was damaged in the earthquakes
of 1998 and 2004, so the interior will likely be covered with scaffolding. But if it's not covered, you'll see some fascinating art.
During World War II, an artist hiding out in the mountains
filled this church with patriotic symbolism. The interior is bathed
in Yugoslav red, white, and blue—a brave statement made when
such nationalistic sentiments were dangerous. On the ceiling is St.
Michael (clad in Yugoslav colors) with Yugoslavia's three WWII
enemies at his feet: the eagle (Germany), the wolf (Italy), and the
serpent (Japan). The tops of the walls along the nave are lined with
saints—but these are Slavic, not Catholic. Finally, look carefully
at the Stations of the Cross and find the faces of hated Yugoslav
enemies: Hitler (fourth from altar on left) and Mussolini (first
from altar on right). Behind the church is a typical cemetery, with
civilian and (on the hillside) military sections.

For a good example of how the Soča River cuts like God's
bandsaw into the land, stop about two minutes past the church
at the small gravel lot (on the left) marked *Velika Korita Soče*
("Grand Canyon of Soča"). Venture out onto the suspension
bridge over the gorge...and bounce if you dare. Just beyond this
bridge is the turnoff (on the left) to the Lepena Valley, home of
the recommended Pristava Lepena pension—and their Lipizzaner
horses.

Roughly five miles after the town of Soča, you exit the
National Park, pass a WWI graveyard (on the left), and come to a
fork in the road. The main route leads to the left, through Bovec.
But first, take a two-mile detour to the right (marked *Predel*), where
the WWI **Kluže Fort** keeps a close watch over the narrowest part
of a valley leading to Italy (€3; July–Aug daily 9:00–21:00; June
and Sept Sun–Fri 9:00–17:00, Sat 9:00–18:00; closed Oct–May).
In the 15th century, the Italians had a fort here to defend against
the Ottomans. Half a millennium later, during World War I, it
was used by Austrians to keep Italians out of their territory. Notice
the ladder rungs fixed to the cliff face across the road from the
fort—allowing soldiers to quickly get up to the mountaintop.

Back on the main road, continue to **Bovec.** This town, which
saw some of the most vicious fighting of the Soča Front, was hit
hard by earthquakes in 1994 and 1998 (and another tremor in

2004). Today, it's been beautifully rebuilt and remains the adventure-sports capital of the Soča River Valley—also known as the "Adrenaline Valley," famous for its white-water activities. For a good lunch stop in Bovec, see my suggestions on page 603. But if you're not eating or spending the night here, feel free to skip it (continue along the main road to bypass the town center).

Heading south along the river—with water somehow both perfectly clear and spectacularly turquoise—watch for happy kayakers. When you pass the intersection at Žaga, you're just four miles from Italy. Along the way, you'll also pass a pair of waterfalls: The well-known Boka ("Slovenia's second-longest waterfall," on the right just before Žaga) and the hidden gem Veliki Kozjak (unmarked, on the left just before Kobarid). For either, you'll have to park your car and hike uphill to see the falls.

Signs lead to the town of **Kobarid,** home to a bustling square and some fascinating WWI sights. Even if you don't think you're interested in the Soča Front, consider dropping in at the Kobarid Museum. Driving up to the Italian Mausoleum hovering over the town is a must. (These sights are described on pages 606 and 607.)

Leaving Kobarid, continue south along the Soča to **Tolmin.** Before you reach Tolmin, decide on your route back to civilization...

Finishing the Drive

To Ljubljana: From Tolmin, you have two possible driving routes to the capital. Either option brings you back to the A-1 expressway south of Ljubljana, and will get you to the city in about two hours (though the second route has fewer miles).

The option you'll encounter first (turnoff to the right before Tolmin) is the smoother, longer route southwest to **Nova Gorica** (a city divided in half by the Italian border, and packed with casinos catering to Italian gamblers). From Nova Gorica, you can hop on the expressway.

I prefer the more rural second option: Continue through Tolmin, then head southeast through the hills back towards Ljubljana. Along the way, you could stop for a bite and some sightseeing at the town of **Idrija** (EE-dree-yah), known to all Slovenes for three things: its tourable mercury mine, fine delicate lace, and tasty *žlikrofi* (like ravioli). Back at the expressway (at Logatec), head north to Ljubljana or on to Bled.

To Bled: The fastest option is to load your car onto a **"Car Train"** (Autovlak) that cuts directly through the mountains. The train departs at 18:05 from Most na Soči (just south of Tolmin, along the Idrija route described above) and arrives at Bohinjska Bistrica, near Lake Bohinj, at 18:50 (about €11 for the car; also stops at Podbrdo en route, confirm schedule at the Bled TI before making the trip). From Bohinjska Bistrica, it's just a half-hour drive back to Bled. No reservations are necessary, but arrive at the train station about 30 minutes before the scheduled departure to allow time to load the car.

To **drive** all the way back, the fastest route (about 2 hours) is partially on a twisty, rough, very poor-quality road (go through Tolmin, turn off at Bača pri Modreju to Podbrdo, then from Petrovo Brdo take a very curvy road through the mountains into Bohinjska Bistrica and on to Bled). For more timid drivers, it's more sane and not too much longer to start out on the Idrija route toward Ljubljana (described above), but turn off in Želin (before Idrija) towards Skofja Loka and Kranj, then on to Bled. Or take one of the two routes described above for Ljubljana, then continue on the expressway past Ljubljana and back up to Bled (allow 3 hours).

Bovec

The biggest town in the area, Bovec has a happening main square and all the tourist amenities. It's best known as a hub for white-water adventure sports. While not exactly quaint, Bovec is charming enough to qualify as a good lunch stop or overnight home base. If nothing else, it's a nice jolt of civilization wedged between the alpine cliffs.

ORIENTATION

(area code: 05)

Tourist Information
The helpful TI on the main square offers fliers on mountain biking and water sports (flexible hours, generally June–Sept daily 8:30–20:30, shorter hours off-season, Trg Golobarskih Žrtev 8, tel. 05/389-6444, www.bovec.si).

Arrival in Bovec
The main road skirts Bovec (BOH-vets), but you can turn off (watch for signs on the right) to take the road that goes through the heart of town, then rejoins the main road farther along. As you approach the city center, you can't miss the main square, Trg Golobarskih Žrtev, with the TI and a pair of good restaurants (described in "Eating").

SLEEPING

In Bovec

$$$ Dobra Vila is a gorgeous new hotel with classy traditional-meets-contemporary decor that feels out of place in little, remote Bovec. Not that I'm complaining. Its 12 rooms are swanky, and the public spaces (including a sitting room/library, breakfast room/restaurant, wine cellar, small "movie theater," winter garden porch, and terrace with cozy mountain-view chairs) are welcoming. Enthusiastically run by Andreja and Sebastian Kovačič, it's a winner (Sb-€93, Db-€100, Db with balcony-€120, same prices year-round, fun old-fashioned elevator, on the left just as you enter town on the main road from the Vršič Pass at Mala Vas 112, tel. 05/389-6400, fax 05/389-6404, www.dobra-vila-bovec.com, welcome @dobra-vila-bovec.com).

$$ Martinov Hram has 11 nondescript modern rooms over a popular restaurant a few steps from Bovec's main square. While the rooms are an afterthought to the busy restaurant (reception at the bar), they're comfortable (very flexible rates, in peak season figure Sb-€40, Db-€70, a few euros less off-season, no extra charge for 1-night stays, Trg Golobarskih Žrtev 27, tel. 05/388-6214, sara .berginc@volja.net).

Near Bovec

$$$ Pristava Lepena is a relaxing oasis hiding out in the Lepena Valley just north of Bovec. Well-run by Milan and Silvia Dolenc, this place is its own little village: a series of rustic-looking cabins, a restaurant, and a sauna/outdoor swimming pool. Hiding behind the humble split-wood shingle exteriors is surprising comfort: 13

Sleep Code

(€1 = about $1.40, country code: 386, area code: 05)
S = Single, **D** = Double/Twin, **T** = Triple, **Q** = Quad, **b** = bathroom. Unless otherwise noted, breakfast is included and credit cards are accepted. Everyone speaks English and all of these accommodations include breakfast. These prices don't include the €1 tourist tax per person, per night.

To help you sort easily through these listings, I've divided the rooms into three categories based on the price for a standard double room with bath:

  $$$ Higher Priced—Most rooms €100 or more.
   $$ Moderately Priced—Most rooms between €50–100.
    $ Lower Priced—Most rooms €50 or less.

The Julian Alps

cozy apartments (with wood-burning stoves, TV, telephone, and all the amenities) that make you feel like relaxing. This place whispers "second honeymoon" (Db rates: July–Aug-€132, May–June and Sept-€116, early Oct and late April-€100, closed in winter, multi-night stays preferred, 1-night stays may be possible for 20 percent extra, dinner-€18, lunch and dinner-€30, nonrefundable 30 percent advance payment when you reserve; just before Bovec, turn left off the main road toward Lepena, and follow the white horses to Lepena 2; tel. 05/388-9900, fax 05/388-9901, www .pristava-lepena.com, pristava.lepena@siol.net). The Dolences also have three Welsh ponies and four purebred Lipizzaner horses (two mares, two geldings) that guests can ride (in riding ring-€15/hr, on trail-€20/hr, riding lesson-€25; non-guests may be able to ride for a few euros more—call ahead and ask).

$ **Tourist Farm Pri Plajerju,** on a picturesque plateau at the edge of Trenta (the first town at the bottom of the Vršič Pass road), is your budget option. Run by the Pretner family, this organic farm raises sheep and goats, and rents four apartments and one room in three buildings separate from the main house. While not quite as tidy as other tourist farms I recommend, it's the best one I found in the Soča Valley (July–Aug: Db-€32–36; March–June and Sept–Dec: Db-€28–34; price depends on size of room or apartment, closed Jan–Feb, breakfast-€5, dinner-€8, watch for signs to the left after passing through the village of Trenta, Trenta 16a, tel. & fax 05/388-9209, www.eko-plajer.com, info@eko-plajer.com).

EATING

In Bovec

Letni Vrt Pizzeria, dominating the main square, is the busiest place in town—with pizzas, pastas, salads, and more (closed Sun, Trg Golobarskih Žrtev 12, tel. 05/388-6335).

Martinov Hram, run by the Berginc family, is also good. The nicely traditional decor goes well with Slovenian specialties focused on sheep (good homemade bread, closed Mon, on the main road through Bovec, just before the main square on the right at Trg Golobarskih Žrtev 27, tel. 05/388-6214).

Kobarid

Kobarid feels older, and therefore a bit more appealing, than its big brother Bovec. This humble settlement was immortalized by a literary giant, Ernest Hemingway, who drove an ambulance on the Soča Front in World War I (see sidebar, page 598). He described Kobarid as "a little white town with a campanile in a valley. It was

The Soča (Isonzo) Front

The valley in Slovenia's northwest corner—called Soča in Slovene, and Isonzo in Italian—saw some of World War I's fiercest fighting. While the Western Front gets more press, this eastern border between the Central Powers and the Allies was just as significant. In a series of 13 battles involving 22 different nationalities along a 60-mile-long front, 300,000 soldiers died, 700,000 were wounded, and 100,000 were declared MIA. In addition, tens of thousands of civilians died. Eyewitness to these events was a young Ernest Hemingway, who drove an ambulance for the Italian army. (Later in life, he would write the novel *A Farewell to Arms* about his experiences—see "Hemingway in Slovenia" sidebar on page 598.)

On April 26, 1915, Italy joined the Allies. A month later, they declared war on the Austro-Hungarian Empire (which included Slovenia). Italy unexpectedly invaded the Soča Valley, quickly taking the tiny town of Kobarid, which they planned to use as a home base for attacks deeper into Austro-Hungarian territory. For the next 29 months, Italy launched 10 more offensives against the Austro-Hungarian army on the mountaintops. All of these Italian offensives were unsuccessful, even though the Italians outnumbered their opponents ten to one. This was unimaginably difficult warfare—Italy had to attack uphill, waging war high in the mountains, in the harshest of conditions. Trenches were carved into rock instead of mud, and many unprepared conscripts—brought here from faraway lands, and unaccustomed to the harsh winter conditions atop the Alps—froze to death. During one winter alone, some 60,000 soldiers were killed by avalanches.

Visitors take a look at this tight valley, hemmed in by seemingly impassible mountains, and wonder: Why would people fight so fiercely over such an inhospitable terrain? At the time, Slovenia was the natural route from Italy to the Austro-Hungarian capital at Vienna. The Italians believed that if they could hold this valley and push over the mountains, Vienna—and victory—would be theirs. Once committed, they couldn't turn back, and the war devolved into one of exhaustion—who would fall first?

a clean little town and there was a fine fountain in the square." Sounds about right.

Aside from its brush with literary greatness, Kobarid is known as a hub of Soča Front information (with an excellent WWI museum, a hilltop Italian mausoleum, and walks that connect the nearby sights), and for its surprisingly good restaurants. You won't find the fountain Hemingway wrote about—it's since been covered up by houses (though the town government hopes to excavate it as a tourist attraction). You will find a modern statue of

In the fall of 1917, Austro-Hungarian Emperor Karl appealed to his ally Germany, who agreed to assemble an army for a new attack to re-take Kobarid and the Soča Valley. In an incredible logistical puzzle, they spent just six weeks building and supplying this new army by transporting troops and equipment high across the mountaintops under cover of darkness...over the heads of their oblivious Italian foes dozing in the valley.

On October 24, Austria-Hungary and Germany launched a downhill attack of 600,000 soldiers into the town of Kobarid. This crucial 12th battle of the Soča Front, better known as the Battle of Kobarid, was the turning point—and saw the introduction of battlefield innovations that are commonplace in the military today. German field commanders were empowered to act independently on the battlefield, reacting immediately to situations rather than waiting for approval. Also, for the first time ever, the Austrian-German army used a new surprise-attack technique called *Blitzkrieg,* in which cavalry and infantry attacked simultaneously and quickly. (One German officer, Erwin Rommel, defied his superior and was demoted for his insolence, but later climbed the ranks again to become famous as Hitler's "Desert Fox" in North Africa.)

The *Blitzkrieg* attack caught the Italian forces off-guard, quickly breaking through three lines of defense. Within three days, the Italians were forced to retreat. (Because the Italian military worked from the top down, the soldiers were sitting ducks once they were cut off from their commanders.) The Austrians called their victory the "Miracle at Kobarid." But Italy felt differently. The Italians see the battle of Caporetto (the Italian name for Kobarid) as their Alamo. To this day, when an Italian finds himself in a mess, he says, "At least it's not a *Caporetto.*"

A year later, Italy came back—this time with the aid of British, French, and US forces—and easily retook this area. On November 4, 1918, Austria-Hungary conceded defeat. After more than a million casualties, the fighting at Soča was finally over.

Simon Gregorčič (overlooking the main intersection), the beloved Slovenian priest and poet who came from, and wrote about, the Soča Valley.

ORIENTATION

(area code: 05)

The main road cuts right through the heart of little Kobarid, bisecting its main square (Trg Svobode). The Kobarid Museum is along this road, on the left before the square. To reach the museum from the main square, simply walk five minutes back toward Bovec.

Tourist Information

The TI has good information on the area and Internet access (daily July–Sept 9:00–19:00; Oct–April 10:00–12:30 & 13:30–15:00, May–June 9:00–12:30 & 13:30–18:00, tel. 05/380-0490, on the main square at Trg Svobode 16, www.lto-sotocje.si and www.kobarid.si).

SIGHTS

▲▲▲**Kobarid Museum (Kobariški Muzej)**—This modest but world-class museum, offering a haunting look at the tragedy of the Soča Front, was voted Europe's best museum in 1993. The tasteful exhibits, with fine English descriptions and a pacifist tone, focus not on the guns and heroes, but on the big picture of the front and on the stories of the common people who fought and died here.

Cost, Hours, Location: €4, good €8 *Soča Front* book; April–Sept Mon–Fri 9:00–18:00, Sat–Sun 9:00–19:00; Oct–March Mon–Fri 10:00–17:00, Sat–Sun 9:00–18:00; Gregorčičeva 10, tel. 05/389-0000, www.kobariski-muzej.si.

➋ **Self-Guided Tour:** The entry is lined with hastily made cement and barbed-wire gravestones, flags representing all the nationalities involved in the fighting, and pictures of soldiers and nurses from diverse backgrounds who were brought together here (for example, the men wearing fezzes were from Bosnia-Herzegovina, annexed by the Austro-Hungarian Empire shortly before the war).

Buy your ticket and ask to watch the English version of the 19-minute film on the history of the Soča Front (informative but dry, plays on top floor).

The first floor up is divided into several rooms. The White Room, filled with rusty crampons, wire-cutters, pickaxes, and shovels, explains wintertime conditions at the front. The Room of the Rear shows the day-to-day activities away from the front line, from supplying troops to more mundane activities (milking cows, washing clothes, getting a shave, playing with a dog). The Black Room is the museum's most somber, commemorating the more than one million casualties of the Soča Front. These heart-breaking exhibits honor the common people whose bodies fertilized the battlefields of Europe. Horrific images of war injuries are juxtaposed with a display of medals earned by soldiers such as these—begging the question, was it worth it? The little altar was purchased by schoolchildren, who sent it to the front to offer the troops some solace.

Through the door marked *Room of the Krn Range* (also on the first floor up), find your way to the Kobarid Rooms, which trace the history of this region from antiquity to today. High on the wall, look for the timelines explaining the area's turbulent history. The one in the second room shows wave after wave of invaders (including Ottomans, Hapsburgs, and Napoleon). In the next room, above a display case with military uniforms, another timeline shows the various flags that flew over Kobarid's main square in the 20th century.

On the top floor, across from the room where the film plays (described above), you'll see a giant model of the surrounding mountains, painstakingly tracing the successful Austrian-German *Blitzkrieg* attack during the Battle of Kobarid.

▲▲**Italian Mausoleum (Kostnica)**—The 55 miles between here and the Adriatic are dotted with more than 75 cemeteries, reminders of the countless casualties of the Soča Front. One of the most dramatic is this mausoleum, overlooking Kobarid. The access road, across Kobarid's main square from the side of the church, is marked by stone gate towers (with the word *Kostnica*—one tower

is topped with a cross, and the other with a star for the Italian army).

Take the road up Gradič Hill—passing Stations of the Cross—to the mausoleum. Built in 1938 (when this was still part of Italy) around the existing Church of St. Anthony, this octagonal pyramid holds the remains of 7,014 Italian soldiers. The stark, cold, Neoclassical architecture is pure Mussolini. Names are listed alphabetically, along with mass graves for more than 1,700 unknown soldiers *(militi ignoti)*.

Walk behind the church and enjoy the **view.** Find the WWI battlements high on the mountain's rock face (with your back to church, they're at 10 o'clock). Incredibly, the fighting was done on these treacherous ridges; civilians in the valleys only heard the distant battles. Looking up and down the valley, notice the "signal churches" evenly spaced on hilltops, each barely within view of the next—an ancient method for spreading messages or warnings across long distances quickly.

If the **church** is open, go inside and look above the door to see a brave soldier standing over the body of a fallen comrade, fending off enemies with nothing but rocks.

When Mussolini came to dedicate the mausoleum, local

revolutionaries plotted an assassination attempt that couldn't fail. A young man planned to suicide-bomb Mussolini as he came back into town from this hilltop. But as Mussolini's car drove past, the would-be assassin looked at his fellow townspeople around him, realized the innocent blood he would also spill, and had a last-minute change of heart. Mussolini's trip was uneventful, and fascism continued to thrive in Italy.

World War I Walks—At the Kobarid Museum (and local TIs), you can pick up a free brochure outlining the **"Kobarid Historical Walk"** tracing WWI sites in town and the surrounding country-side (3 miles, mostly uphill, allow 3–5 hours). A newer **"Walk of Peace"** links several WWI sights all along the Soča Valley (details and map at TI). History buffs can also call ahead to arrange a private guide (€15/hr, tel. 05/389-0000).

SLEEPING

(€1 = about $1.40, country code: 386, area code: 05)
My first listing is right on the main square. The other two hide on side streets about a block off the main road through town, between the museum and the main square (about a 3-min walk to either).

$$$ Hotel Hvala is the only real hotel in town. Run by the Hvala family, its 31 contemporary rooms are comfortable, and the location can't be beat. The mural on the wall in the elevator shaft tells the story of the Soča Valley as you go up toward the top floor (mid-July–Aug: Sb-€72, Db-€108; April–mid-July and Sept–mid-Nov: Sb-€66, Db-€96; off-season: Sb-€59, Db-€82; pricier superior Db with air-con and sleek new decor-€160–200, hotel closed Feb and most of Nov, elevator, Trg Svobode 1, tel. 05/389-9300, fax 05/388-5322, www.hotelhvala.si, topli.val@siol.net).

$ Picerija Fedrig is a pizzeria that rents five simple but fine rooms upstairs (Db-€40, less for more than 1 night, 10 percent more in Aug, Volaričeva 11, tel. 05/389-0115, jernej.grahli@volja.net).

$ Apartma-Ra has four rooms and three apartments in a cozy, family-friendly house (D-€30, Db-€45, apartment-€90–110, cash only, Gregorčičeva 6C, tel. 05/389-1007, apartma-ra@siol.net).

EATING

Topli Val ("Heat Wave"), Hotel Hvala's restaurant, is pricey but good, with a menu that emphasizes fish (€9–15 pastas, €10–30 main dishes, lengthy list of Slovenian wines, daily 12:00–15:00 & 19:00–24:00, Trg Svobode 1, tel. 05/389-9300).

Kotlar Restaurant, across the square from Hotel Hvala, is similarly priced and well regarded (Wed–Sun 12:00–23:00, closed

Mon–Tue, Trg Svobode 11). Kotlar also rents rooms if you're in a pinch.

Picerija Fedrig (also listed under "Sleeping," previous page) serves up good €5–7 pizzas (Tue–Sun 12:00–22:00, closed Mon, Volaričeva 11, tel. 05/389-0115).

CROATIA

CROATIA

Hrvatska

Sunny beaches, succulent seafood, and a taste of *la dolce vita*...in Eastern Europe?

Croatia is known for two very different reasons: as a top fun-in-the-sun tourist destination, and as the site, just over a decade and a half ago, of one of the most violent European wars in generations. Thankfully, the bloodshed is in the past. While a trip to Croatia offers curious travelers the opportunity to understand a complicated chapter of recent history, most visitors focus instead on its substantial natural wonders: mountains, waterfalls, sun, sand, and sea.

With thousands of miles of seafront and more than a thousand islands, Croatia's coastline is Eastern Europe's Riviera. Holiday-makers love its pebbly beaches, predictably balmy summer weather, and melt-in-your-mouth seafood. Croatia is also historic. From ruined Roman arenas and Byzantine mosaics to Venetian bell towers, Hapsburg villas, and even communist concrete, past rulers have left their mark.

Croatia's main attraction is the Dalmatian Coast—the southern third of the country's coastline, stretching from Zadar to Dubrovnik. With an atmospheric Old Town and an epic history, Dubrovnik—Croatia's single best attraction—is like Venice without the canals. A day's sail to the north, bustling Split is the capital of the coast, boasting a vibrant seaside promenade and a lived-in warren of twisting lanes sprouting out of a massive Roman palace. Between Dubrovnik and Split are a half-dozen inviting island getaways, most notably the charming village of Korčula.

Croatia's idyllic coastline extends to the north, to the picture-prefect and ultra-romantic town of Rovinj, on the peninsula of Istria. But one of Croatia's most beautiful sights is actually inland: the waterfall wonderland of the Plitvice Lakes, one of Europe's best back-to-nature experiences. And to round things out, I've also included the underrated capital, Zagreb—with good museums, colorful street life, and a thriving café culture.

Croatia feels more Mediterranean than "Eastern European." Historically, Croatia has more in common with Venice and Rome than Vienna or Budapest. Especially on the coast, it's sometimes difficult to distinguish this lively, chaotic place from Italy. If you've become accustomed to the Germanic efficiency of Slovenia, Croatia's relaxed and unpredictable style can come as a shock.

Throughout the country, but especially on the tourist-thronged Dalmatian Coast, the standards for service (at restaurants, hotels, and so on) are lower than you might expect. While you'll meet plenty of wonderfully big-hearted Croatians, a few of my readers have characterized Croatian waiters or hotel desk clerks as "rude." I prefer to think of them as "efficient and direct." Either way, be prepared to fall victim to the "Croatian Shrug"—a simple gesture meaning, "Don't know, don't care." But most visitors happily put up with Croatia's minor frustrations to take advantage of its post-card beauty and laid-back rhythm. After all, you're on vacation.

If you want to blow through a lot of money here, you can. Croatian hotels, especially on the coast, are a terrible value, and there are plenty of touristy restaurants happy to overcharge you. But if you know where to look, there are also wonderful budget alternatives—foremost among them *sobe* (rooms in private homes). *Sobe* are a comfortable compromise: new-feeling, fresh, hotelesque doubles with a private bathroom and TV, for half the cost of a moldy room in a crumbling resort hotel just down the beach (for details, see page 616).

Europeans are reverent sun-worshippers, and on sunny days, virtually every square inch of coastal Croatia is occupied by a sun-bather on a beach towel. Nude beaches are a big deal, especially for vacationing Germans and Austrians. If you want to work on an all-around tan, seek out a beach marked *FKK* (from the German *Freikörper Kultur,* or "free body culture"). First-timers get comfortable in a hurry, finding they're not the only pink novices on the rocks. But don't get too excited—these beaches are most beloved by people you'd rather see with their clothes on.

Perhaps because sunshine is so important to the economy, Croatians often seem particularly affected by weather. They complain that the once-predictable climate has become erratic, with surprise rainy spells or heat waves in the once perfectly consistent, balmy summer months. (I dare you to tell a Croatian that global warming doesn't exist.) The weather report even includes a *biometeorološka prognoza* that indicates how the day's weather will affect your mood. Weather maps come with smiley or frowny faces, and forecasts predict, "People will be tired in the afternoon and not feel like working." Hmm...good excuse.

Every Croatian coastal town has two parts: The time-warp

old town, and the obnoxious resort sprawl. Main drags are clogged with gift shops selling shell sculptures and tasteless T-shirts. While European visitors enjoy this tacky-trinket tourism, Americans are generally more interested in Old World charm. Fortunately, it's generally easy to ignore this scene and instead poke your way into twisty old medieval lanes, draped with drying laundry and populated by gossiping housewives, humble fishermen's taverns, and soccer-playing kids.

Croatian popular music, the mariachi music of Europe, is the ever-present soundtrack of a Dalmatian vacation. Oliver Dragojević—singing soulful Mediterranean ballads with his gravelly, passionate voice—is the Croatian Tom Jones. Known simply as "Oliver," this beloved crooner gets airplay across Europe, and has spawned many imitators (such as the almost-as-popular Gibonni).

More traditional is the hauntingly beautiful *klapa* music—men's voices harmonizing a cappella, like barbershop with a soothing Adriatic flavor. Typically the leader begins the song, and the rest of the group (usually three to twelve singers) follow behind him with a slight delay. You'll see mariachi-style *klapa* groups performing in touristy areas; a CD of one of these performances (or of a professional group—Cambi is great) is a fun souvenir.

Croatia may be Europe's second most ardently Catholic country (after Poland). Under communism, religion was downplayed and many people gave up the habit of attending Mass (or mosque) regularly. But as the wars raged in the early 1990s, many Croatians rediscovered their religion. In Croatia's churches today, you may be surprised by how many people you see worshipping.

In the Yugoslav era, Croatia was flooded with tourists—both European and American—who fell in love with its achingly beautiful beaches and coves. In its heyday, Croatia hosted about 10 million visitors a year, who provided the country with about a third of its income. But then, for several years after the war, Croatia floundered. Just a decade ago, the streets of Dubrovnik were empty, lined with souvenir shops manned by desperate-looking vendors. But in the last few years, locals are breathing a sigh of relief as the number of visitors returns to pre-war highs. With astonishing speed, Croatia is becoming one of Europe's top destinations.

Today's Croatia is crawling with a Babel of international guests, speaking German, French, Italian, every accent of English...and a smattering of Croatian. And yet, despite the tourists, this place remains distinctly and stubbornly Croatian. You'd have to search pretty hard to find a McDonald's.

Helpful Hints

Stow Your Euros: Tourists are notorious for confusing euro bills with Croatian kuna bills (both modeled after the old German *Deutschmark,* and therefore similar). Make a point of deep-storing all euros while outside the euro zone, or you'll pay about seven times more than you should to enjoy Croatia. While some merchants accept euros in payment, most prefer to be paid in kunas (even if they list prices in euros).

Seasonality: Croatia is the most seasonal destination in this book. In a little coastal resort village, a few weeks can mean the difference between being a ghost town or being deluged with crowds. Peak season is July and August, though late June and all of September are becoming nearly as popular. Visiting Croatia in July or August is like spending spring break in Florida—fun, but miserably crowded. Shoulder season is late May through mid-June, and early October. During the off-season—mid-October through mid-May—many small towns close down entirely, with only one hotel and one restaurant remaining open during the lean winter months, and most of the town's residents moving to the interior to hibernate.

Be aware that even in peak season, schedules are made to be broken, and opening times can change suddenly based on demand. The hours I've listed *should* be right...but if you have your heart set on a certain sight, confirm times with the TI on your arrival.

Telephones: Croatia's phone system uses area codes. To make a long-distance call within the country, start with the area code. To call Croatia from another country, first dial the international access code (00 if calling from Europe, 011 from US or Canada), 385 (Croatia's country code), the area code (without the initial zero), and the local number. To call out of Croatia, dial 00, the country code of the country you're calling (see chart in appendix), the area code if applicable (may need to drop initial zero), and the local number.

Croatia's pay phones work on insertable phone cards (buy at newsstands or kiosks). Mobile phone numbers begin with 091, 098, or 099. Numbers beginning with 060 are pricey toll lines.

Free Tourist Help by Phone: The "Croatian Angels" service gives free information over a toll-free line in English (tel. 062-999-999, mid-June–Sept daily 8:00–24:00).

Addresses: Addresses listed with a street name and followed by "b.b." have no street number. In most small towns, locals ignore not only street numbers but also street names—navigate with a map or by asking for directions.

Slick Pavement: Old towns, with their well-polished pavement stones and many slick stairs, can be quite treacherous, especially after a rainstorm. (On a recent trip, one of this book's co-authors almost broke his arm slipping down a flight of stairs.) Tread with care.

Dalmatian Accommodation

Even under communism, Yugoslavs were savvy businesspeople. To maximize beach-tourism occupancy in the 1960s and 1970s, they razed quaint Old World buildings to make way for new, big resort hotels. Today, many of these coastal hotels have been refurbished to four- or five-star status and are charging exorbitant rates; others haven't been renovated in decades, and come with dingy old communist-era dark-wood furnishings and moldy-college-dorm ambience. Both types of hotels are ridiculously overpriced.

Fortunately, the void of mid-range sleeps is filled perfectly by what locals call "private accommodations": a rented apartment *(apartman)* or a room in a private home (*soba*, pronounced SOH-bah; plural *sobe*, SOH-bay). Private accommodations offer travelers a characteristic and money-saving alternative for a fraction of the price of a hotel.

Often run by empty-nesters, private accommodations are similar to British bed-and-breakfasts...minus the breakfast (ask your host about the best nearby breakfast spot). Generally the more you pay, the more privacy and amenities (private bathroom, TV, air-conditioning, kitchenette) you get. The simplest *soba* allow you to experience Croatia on the cheap, at nearly youth-hostel prices, while giving you a great opportunity to connect with a local family. The fanciest *sobe* are downright swanky, allowing for near-hotel anonymity. Apartments are bigger and cost more than *sobe,* but they're still far cheaper than hotels.

Registered *sobe* have been rated by the government using a system that assigns stars based on amenities. Three or more stars means that you'll have your own bathroom, two stars means that the bathroom's down the hall, and one star is rock-bottom basic. If you don't like the idea of sharing a toilet with strangers, look for three stars and you'll do fine. (Apartments always have private bathrooms, plus some modest kitchen facilities.) Many, but not all, three-star *sobe* also have TV and air-conditioning (but usually no telephone). The prices for private accommodations generally

Siesta: Croatians eat their big meal at lunch, then take a traditional Mediterranean siesta. This means that many stores, museums, and churches close in the mid-afternoon. It can make for frustrating sightseeing...but you're on vacation. If you can't beat 'em...join 'em.

Dalmatian Coast Practicalities

Although it's a long haul from the other destinations in this book, the Dalmatian Coast is well worth it: It's the cherry on top of your grand Eastern European adventure. The following tips are useful fluctuate with the seasons, and stays of fewer than three nights almost usually come with a 20–50 percent surcharge.

You can reserve most *sobe* in advance (usually by email). This represents a major financial risk for your host, who loses money if you don't show up. For this reason, some hosts may ask you to send a check as a deposit. *Sobe* hucksters who accost you on the street can be very aggressive about luring travelers away from their reserved rooms. But if you've booked a room at a particular place, you owe it to them to show up.

If you like to travel spontaneously, you'll have no problem finding *sobe* as you go. Locals hawking rooms meet each arriving boat, bus, and train. Many of these *sobe* have not been classified by the government, but they can sometimes turn out to be a good deal. The person generally shows photos of her place, you haggle for a price, then she escorts you to your new home. Be sure you understand exactly where it's located (i.e., within easy walking distance of the attractions) before you accept—ask to see the location on a map, and find out how long it takes to walk into town.

You can also keep an eye out for rooms as you walk or drive through town—you'll see blue *sobe* and *apartman* signs everywhere. It's actually fun to visit a few homes and make a deal. While it takes nerve to just show up without a room, this is standard operating procedure for backpackers.

As a last resort, you can enlist the help of a travel agency to find you a room—but you'll pay 10–30 percent extra (various agencies are listed in this book; to search from home, try www.dubrovnikapartmentsource.com for Dubrovnik, or www.adriatica.net for all of Croatia).

I'm accustomed to staying in hotels. But a few years ago, I found all of the hotels in Dubrovnik booked up. With some trepidation, I stayed in a *soba*...and I'll never go back to a Croatian resort hotel again. I've made it my mission to convince you to sleep in *sobe,* too.

Croatia

for those traveling to Dubrovnik, Split, and Korčula—cities covered in the next three chapters.

Getting to the Dalmatian Coast

It's a long way down to Dalmatia. But three recent developments help make the trip nearly painless: an expressway, a high-speed train line, and budget flights.

By Car or Bus: Thanks to Croatia's new A-1 super-expressway, the road trip from Zagreb to Split—which used to take seven hours—now takes less than five. Travelers who used to opt for an all-day journey or a bleary-eyed night bus now leave Zagreb after an early dinner, and arrive in Split before bedtime. In the coming years, the expressway will be extended south to Dubrovnik, making that trip even quicker. For the latest, see www.hac.hr.

By Train: Croatian Railways' new "tilting train" line connects Zagreb to Split three times a day. Because the trains can tilt slightly, and the tracks are banked, the new line is able to shave significant time off the trip—making it from the capital to the Dalmatian Coast in just five and a half hours.

By Plane: Several low-cost airlines (including SkyEurope— www.skyeurope.com) connect Dalmatia to northern Croatia and the rest of Europe. Even the national carrier, Croatia Airlines, often has surprisingly inexpensive tickets between Zagreb and Dubrovnik or Split. These cheap seats sell fast, so try to book several weeks ahead. You can find these deals online (www.croatiaairlines.hr), or contact a Croatia Airlines office (Croatian tel. 01/487-2727). If the cheapest seats are already sold out for the flight you need, American-based Europe by Air sells one-way tickets on Croatia Airlines flights for $99, though taxes and other fees bring the price closer to $160 (tickets can be purchased only in the US, US tel. 888-321-4737, www.europebyair.com).

By Boat: Overnight boats sail in each direction between Rijeka (on the northern Croatian coast—4 hours by train from Zagreb and 2.5 hours by train from Ljubljana) and Split. But this option is much slower than the three alternatives mentioned above.

Getting Around the Dalmatian Coast

There are no trains along the Dalmatian Coast (the southernmost station is in Split, with four daily connections to Zagreb). Once here, you'll rely on ferries, buses, or a rental car. I've listed the most useful boat schedules and bus departures in the "Transportation Connections" section for each destination.

By Boat: Ferries and speedy hydrofoils inexpensively shuttle tourists between major coastal cities and quiet island towns. Most of the ferries are run by Jadrolinija, which conveniently connects the three destinations in this book plus a lot more. Advance reservations are not necessary for deck passengers; you can almost always find a seat on the deck or in the on-board café. In peak season, drivers will want to arrive at the boat early (ask the local TI what time you should arrive). For schedules, see www.jadrolinija .hr. Recently, some new high-speed catamarans run by other companies are filling in the gaps in Jadrolinija's schedules, such as the *Krilo* between Split, Hvar, and Korčula (www.krilo.hr); and the *Nona Ana* between Dubrovnik and Korčula (www.gv-line.hr).

By Bus: South of Split, the new super-expressway is still under construction—which means it's a long drive along twisty two-lane roads to connect Dalmatian destinations (for example, Dubrovnik–Split takes about five hours). But buses can still be a good way to connect destinations when there are gaps in the boat schedule, even for islands. I've listed the options in each "Transportation Connections" section. If you're headed south along the coast, sitting on the right side comes with substantially better scenery (sit on the left for northbound buses).

By Car: Considering the long distances, cheap and frequent buses, long ferry lines for cars (as opposed to quick and fun connections for walk-ons), and worthlessness of a car in Dubrovnik or Split, those simply lacing together the major sights are better off without a car. Drivers should be prepared for twisty seaside roads, wonderful views, and plenty of tempting stopovers. As you approach any town, follow the signs to *Centar* (usually also signed with a bull's-eye symbol). Get parking advice from your hotel, or look for the blue-and-white *P* signs. Notice that between Split and Dubrovnik, you'll actually pass through Bosnia-Herzegovina for a

Croatia Almanac

Official Name: Republika Hrvatska, or just Hrvatska for short.

Snapshot History: After losing its independence to Hungary in A.D. 1102, Croatia watched as most of its coastline became Venetian and its interior was conquered by Ottomans. Croatia was "rescued" by the Hapsburgs, but after World War I it became part of Yugoslavia—a decision most Croats regretted until they finally gained independence in 1991 through a bitter war with their Serbian neighbors.

Population: Of the country's 4.5 million people, 90 percent are ethnic Croats (Catholic) and 4 percent are Serbs (Orthodox). (The Serb population was more than double that before the ethnic cleansing of the 1991–1995 war.) About 1 percent of Croatians are Bosniak (Muslim). "Croatians" are citizens of Croatia; "Croats" are a distinct ethnic group made up of Catholic South Slavs. So Orthodox Serbs living in Croatia can be Croatians, but they can't be Croats (since they're not Catholic).

Latitude and Longitude: 45°N and 15°E (similar latitude to Venice, Italy; Ottawa, Canada; or Portland, Oregon).

Area: 22,000 square miles, similar to West Virginia.

Geography: This boomerang-shaped country has two terrains: Stretching north to south is the long, rugged Mediterranean coastline (3,600 miles of beach, including more than 1,100 off-shore islands), which is warm and dry. Rising up from the sea are the Dinaric Mountains (which also cover virtually all of neighboring Bosnia-Herzegovina). To the northeast, beginning at about Zagreb, Croatia's flat, inland "panhandle" (called Slavonia) has hot summers and cold winters.

Biggest Cities: The capital, Zagreb (in the northern interior), has 780,000; Split (along the Dalmatian Coast) has 189,000; and Rijeka (on the northern coast) has 150,000.

Economy: Much of the country's wealth ($60 billion GDP, $13,500 GDP per capita) comes from tourism, banking, and trade with Italy. The country is still recovering from the turmoil of the 1990s: Unemployment is a stiff 14 percent, corruption is deeply rooted, and Croatia remains a European Union outsider.

few miles (the town of Neum; the borders are a breezy formality, but you may need to flash your passport).

Croatian History

For nearly a millennium, bits and pieces of what we today call "Croatia" were batted back and forth between foreign powers: Hungarians, Venetians, Ottomans, Hapsburgs, and Yugoslavs. Only in 1991 did Croatia (violently) regain its independence.

Currency: 1 kuna (kn, or HRK) = about 20 cents, and 5 kunas = about $1. *Kuna* is Croatian for "marten" (a fox-like animal), recalling the long-ago era when fur pelts were used as currency.

Government: The country's prime minister (currently Ivo Sanader, head of the majority party in parliament) is conservative, while the directly elected (but more figurehead) president, Stipe Mesić, is left-of-center. The single-house assembly (Sabor) of 152 legislators is elected by popular vote.

Flag: The flag has three horizontal bands (red on top, white, and blue) with a traditional red-and-white checkerboard shield in the center.

The Average Croatian: The average Croatian will live to age 74 and have 1.4 children. One in four uses the Internet. The average Croatian absolutely adores the soccer team Dinamo Zagreb and absolutely despises Hajduk Split...or vice versa.

Notable Croatians: A pair of big-league historical figures were born in Croatia: Roman Emperor Diocletian (A.D. 245–313) and explorer Marco Polo (1254?–1324). More recently, many Americans whose name ends in "-ich" have Croatian roots, including actor John Malkovich and Ohio politicians Dennis Kucinich and John Kasich, not to mention baseball legend Roger Marich...I mean, Maris. More Croatian athletes abound: NBA fans might recognize Toni Kukoč or Gordan Giricek, and at the 2002 and 2006 Winter Olympic Games, the women's downhill skiing events were dominated by Janica Kostelić. Actor Goran Višnjić (from TV's *ER*) was born and raised in Croatia, and served in the army as a paratrooper. You've likely never heard of the beloved Croatian sculptor Ivan Meštrović, but you'll see his expressive works all over the country. Inventor Nikola Tesla (1856–1943)—who, as a rival of Thomas Edison's, invented alternating current (AC)—was a Croatian-born Serb. And a band of well-dressed 17th-century Croatian soldiers stationed in France gave the Western world a new fashion accessory—the *cravate*, or necktie (for the full story, see page 693).

Croatia

Early History

Croatia's first inhabitants were the Illyrians (ancestors of today's Albanians). During antiquity, the Greeks and Romans both sailed ships up and down the strategic Dalmatian Coast, founding many towns that still exist today, and littering the Adriatic seabed with shipwrecks. Romans built larger settlements on the Dalmatian Coast as early as 229 B.C., and in the fourth century A.D., Emperor Diocletian built his retirement palace in the coastal town of Split.

As Rome fell in the fifth century, Slavs (the ancestors of today's Croatians) and barbarians flooded Europe. The northern part of Croatia's coast fell briefly under the Byzantines, who slathered churches with shimmering mosaics (the best are in the Euphrasian Basilica in Poreč, Istria).

Beginning in the seventh century, Slavic Croats began to control most of the land that is today's Croatia. In A.D. 925, the Dalmatian duke Tomislav united the disparate Croat tribes into a single kingdom. By consolidating and extending Croat-held territory and centralizing power, Tomislav created the first "Croatia."

Loss of Independence

By the early 12th century, the Croatian kings had died out, and neighboring powers (Hungary, Venice, and Byzantium) threatened the Croats. For the sake of self-preservation, Croatia entered into an alliance with the Hungarians in 1102—and for the next 900 years, Croatia was ruled by foreign states. The Hungarians gradually took more and more power from the Croats, exerting control over the majority of inland Croatia. Meanwhile, the Venetian Republic conquered most of the coast and peppered the Croatian Adriatic with bell towers and statues of St. Mark. Through it all, the tiny Republic of Dubrovnik flourished—paying off whomever necessary to maintain its independence, and becoming one of Europe's most important shipbuilding and maritime powers.

The Ottomans conquered most of inland Croatia in the 15th century, and challenged the Venetians—unsuccessfully—for control of the coastline. Most of the stout walls, fortresses, and other fortifications you'll see all along the Croatian coast date from this time, built by the Venetians to defend against Ottoman attack. In the 17th century, the Hapsburgs forced the Ottomans out of inland Croatia. Then, after Venice and Dubrovnik fell to Napoleon in the early 19th century, the coast also went to the Hapsburgs—beginning a long tradition of Austrians basking on Croatian beaches.

The Yugoslav Era, World War II, and the Ustaše

When the Austro-Hungarian Empire broke up at the end of World War I, Croats banded together with the Serbs, Bosniaks, and Slovenes in the union that would become Yugoslavia. But virtually as soon as Yugoslavia was formed, many Croats began to fear that the Serbs would steer Yugoslavia to their own purposes. So when the Nazis invaded and installed a puppet government—called the Ustaše—many Croats supported them, believing that fascism could provide them with greater independence from Serbia. Ustaše concentration camps were used to murder not only Jews and Roma (Gypsies), but also Serbs. Hot-tempered debate rages even today about how many Serbs died at the hands of the Ustaše—estimates

After the War

Some Americans shy away from Croatia, clinging to out-dated memories of wartime images on the nightly news. But those who venture here are, without exception, amazed by how peaceful and stable today's Croatia feels. Croatia's primary tourist region—the coast—was barely touched by the war (except Dubrovnik, which has been painstakingly restored). The interior is sprinkled with destroyed homes and churches—some standing gutted, skeletons of their original structures—but these villages are gradually being refurbished.

The only actual danger is that much of the Croatian interior was once full of landmines. Most of these mines have been removed, and fields that may be dangerous are usually clearly marked. As a precaution, stay on roads and paths, and don't go wandering through overgrown fields and deserted villages.

The biggest impact from the war has been on the people. Throughout the country, but especially in the war-torn interior, sadness and resentment hang heavy in the air. Though the country is repairing itself admirably, the Croatians' souls will take the longest to heal. They're still cheerful and welcoming—but a little less enthusiastically than before.

For more on Croatia during and after the war, see the Understanding Yugoslavia chapter, page 915.

vary wildly, from 25,000 to over a million, but most legitimate historians put the number in the hundreds of thousands.

Cardinal Alojzije Stepinac was one Croat who made the mistake of backing the Ustaše. By most accounts, Stepinac was a mild-mannered, extremely devout man who didn't agree with the extremism of the Ustaše...but also did little to fight it. When Tito came to power, he arrested, tried, and imprisoned Stepinac, who died under house arrest in 1960. In the years since, Stepinac has become a martyr for Catholics and Croat nationalists. But even though he's the single most revered figure of Croatian Catholicism, Stepinac remains highly controversial and unpopular among Serbs.

At the end of World War II, the Ustaše were forced out by Yugoslavia's homegrown Partisan Army, led by a charismatic war hero named Josip Broz, who went by his nickname, "Tito." Tito became "president for life," and Croatia once again became part of a united Yugoslavia. The union would hold together for more than 40 years, until it broke apart under Serbian President Slobodan Milošević and Croatian President Franjo Tuđman.

Franjo Tuđman
(1922–1999)

Independent Croatia's first president was the controversial Franjo Tuđman (FRAHN-yoh TOOJ-mahn). Tuđman began his career fighting for Tito on the left, but later had a dramatic ideological swing to the far right. His anti-communist, highly nationalistic HDZ party was the driving force for Croatian statehood, making him the young nation's first hero. But even as he fought for independence from Yugoslavia, his own ruling style grew more and more authoritarian. Today Tuđman remains a polemical figure.

Before entering politics, Tuđman was a historian. He revered the Ustaše, Croatia's Nazi-affiliated government during World War II, who murdered hundreds of thousands of Serbs and Jews in concentration camps. (Because the Ustaše governed the first "independent" Croatian state since the 12th century, Tuđman figured that these quasi-Nazis were the original Croatian "freedom fighters.") When Croatia voted for independence and Tuđman was elected president in 1990, he immediately reintroduced many Ustaše symbols, including their currency (the kuna, still used today). His actions raised eyebrows worldwide, and raised alarms in Croatia's Serb communities.

Tuđman espoused many of the same single-minded attitudes about ethnic divisions as the ruthless Serbian leader Slobodan Milošević. In fact, Tuđman and Milošević had secret, Hitler-and-Stalin-esque negotiations even as they were ripping into each other rhetorically. According to some reports, at one meeting they drew a map of Bosnia-Herzegovina on a cocktail napkin, then drew lines divvying up the country between themselves. When Tuđman's successor moved into the president's

For all the details on Yugoslavia and its breakup, see the Understanding Yugoslavia chapter, page 915.

Independence Regained

Croatia's declaration of independence from Yugoslavia in 1991 was met with fear and anger on the part of its Serb residents. Even before independence, the first volleys of a bloody war had been fired. The war had two phases: First, in 1991, Croatian Serbs declared independence from the new nation of Croatia, forming their own state and forcing out or murdering any Croats in "their" territory (with the thinly disguised support of Slobodan Milošević). Then a tense cease-fire fell over the region until 1995, when the second phase of the war ignited: Croatia pushed back through the Serb-dominated territory, reclaiming it for Croatia and forcing out or murdering Serbs living there. For details on this office, he discovered a top-secret hotline to Milošević's desk. Even today, Croatian newspapers routinely turn up decade-old photos of clandestine summits between the two leaders in Vienna.

To ensure that he stayed in power, Tuđman played fast and loose with his new nation's laws. He was notorious for changing the constitution as it suited him. By the late 1990s, when his popularity was slipping, Tuđman extended Croatian citizenship to anyone in the world who had Croatian heritage—a ploy aimed at getting votes from Croats living in Bosnia-Herzegovina, who were sure to line up with him on the far right.

Through it all, Tuđman kept a tight grip on the media, making it illegal to report anything that would disturb the public—even if true. When Croatians turned on their TV sets and saw the flag flapping in the breeze to the strains of the national anthem, they knew something was up...and switched to CNN to get the real story. In this oppressive environment, many bright, young Croatians fled the country, causing a "brain drain" that hampered the post-war recovery.

Tuđman died of cancer at the end of 1999. While history will probably judge him harshly, the opinion in today's Croatia is qualified. Most agree that Tuđman was an important and even admirable figure in the struggle for Croatian statehood, but he ultimately went too far and got too greedy. Tuđman's political party is still active, frequently naming streets, squares, and bridges for this "hero" of Croatian nationalism. But if he were alive, Tuđman would be standing trial before the International Criminal Tribunal in The Hague.

Croatia

bloody war, see the Understanding Yugoslavia chapter.

Imagine becoming an independent nation after nine centuries of foreign domination. The Croatians seized their hard-earned freedom with a nationalist fervor that bordered on fascism. This was a heady and absurd time, which today's Croatians recall with disbelief, sadness...and maybe a tinge of nostalgia.

In the Croatia of the early 1990s, even the most bizarre notions seemed possible. Croatia's first post-Yugoslav president, the extreme nationalist Franjo Tuđman (see sidebar), proposed implausible directives for the new nation—such as privatizing all of the nation's resources and handing them over to 200 super-elite families (which, thankfully for everyone else, never happened). The government began calling the language "Croatian" rather than "Serbo-Croatian," and creating new words from specifically Croat roots (see "Croatian Language," on page 631). The Croats even briefly considered replacing the Roman alphabet with the ninth-century Glagolitic script to invoke Croat culture and further differentiate Croatian from Serbia's Cyrillic alphabet. Fortunately for tourists, this plan didn't take off.

After Tuđman's death in 1999, Croatia began the new millennium with a more truly democratic leader, Stipe Mesić. The popular Mesić, who was once aligned with Tuđman, had split off and formed his own political party when Tuđman's politics grew too extreme. Tuđman spent years tampering with the constitution to give himself more and more power, but when Mesić took over, he reversed those changes and handed more authority back to the parliament.

Croatia Today

In 2003, Croatia applied for membership in the European Union. It's officially an EU candidate country, but several roadblocks have slowed its progress.

At first, Croatia's biggest hurdle to EU membership was its human-rights record during the recent war. Several Croatian officers were indicted for war crimes by the International Criminal Tribunal for the Former Yugoslavia (ICTY) in The Hague, Netherlands. But many Croatians feel that the soldiers branded as "war criminals" by The Hague are instead heroes of their war

GENERAL
ANTE GOTOVINA

of independence. The highest-profile Croatian figure to be arrested was Ante Gotovina, a lieutenant general accused of atrocities against Serb civilians. After four years in hiding, Gotovina was found and arrested in Spain in December of 2005, and sent to stand trial in The Hague. As a sign of support, photos of Gotovina appeared in towns throughout Croatia. Gotovina's name means "cash." Many Croatians grouse, "To get into the EU, we have to pay cash *(gotovina)*!"

Some Croatians remain skeptical about joining the EU for other reasons. One Croatian said to me, "We were just badly divorced. We're not ready to be married again." For the other countries that recently joined the EU, a concern with EU membership was that the new members' citizens would flood to the West. Some Croatians are worried about the opposite: Westerners buying up Adriatic beachfront property.

Despite the controversy, pro-EU President Stipe Mesić's re-election in 2005 is a clear signal that most Croatians are optimistic about becoming a part of a united Europe. Mesić is viewed both by

Balkan Flavors

All of the countries of the Balkan Peninsula—basically from Slovenia to Greece—have several foods in common. The Ottomans from today's Turkey, who controlled much of this territory for centuries, imported some goodies that remained standard fare here long after they left town. Whether you're in Slovenia, Croatia, Bosnia-Herzegovina, Montenegro, Serbia, or Albania, here are some local tastes worth seeking out.

A popular fast food you'll see everywhere is **burek** (BOO-rehk)—phyllo dough filled with meat, cheese, spinach, or apples. The more familiar **baklava** is phyllo dough layered with honey and nuts.

Grilled meats are a staple of Balkan cuisine. You'll most often see **ražnjići** (RAZH-nyee-chee—small pieces of steak on a skewer, like a shish kebab) and **čevapčići** (cheh-VAHP-chee-chee—minced meat formed into a sausage-link shape, then grilled). Sometimes you'll come across **pljeskavica** (plehs-kah-VEET-suh—similar to *čevapčići*, except the meat is in the form of a hamburger-like patty).

While Balkan cuisine favors meat, a nice veggie comple-ment is **đuveđ** (JOO-vedge)—a spicy mix of stewed vegeta-bles, flavored with tomatoes and peppers.

And you just can't eat any of this stuff without the ever-present condiment **ajvar** (EYE-var). Made from red bell pepper and eggplant, *ajvar* is like ketchup with a kick. Many Americans pack a jar of this distinctive, flavorful sauce to remember the flavors of the Balkans when they get back home. And these days, you can often find it at specialty grocery stores in the US (look for "eggplant/red pepper spread")

most Croatians and by international observers as precisely the kind of moderate, modern, European-minded leader a fledgling country needs to lead it into the 21st century.

Croatian Food

Like its people, the food in Croatia's different regions has been shaped by various influences—predominantly Italian, Turkish, and Hungarian. (Choosing between stru-

del and baklava on the same menu, you're constantly reminded that this is a land where East meets West.) And yet, the cuisine here is surpris-ingly uniform: 90 percent of coastal restaurants have a similar menu of seafood, pasta, and pizza. Olives and *pršut* (prosciutto—see sidebar on page 525) round out the Croatian staples. Because it's so easy to get into a culinary rut here, I've also recommended some more exotic alternatives.

On the coast, seafood is a specialty, and the Italian influence is obvious. According to Dalmatians, "Eating meat is food; eating fish is pleasure." They also say that a fish should swim three times: first in the sea, then in olive oil, and finally in wine—when you eat it.

You can get all kinds of seafood: fish, scampi, mussels, squid, octopus, you name it. Remember that prices for seafood dishes are listed either by the kilogram (1,000 grams) or by the 100-gram unit (figure about a half-kilo, or 500 grams—that's about one pound—for a large portion). Note that *škampi* (shrimp) often come still in their shells (sometimes with crayfish-like claws), which can be messy and time-consuming to eat. Before you order shrimp, ask if it's shelled. Even those not accustomed to eating octopus might want to try octopus salad—a flavorful mix of octopus, tomatoes, onions, and spices. In the interior, trout is popular.

If you're not a seafood-eater, there are plenty of meat options. A Dalmatian specialty is *pašticada*—braised beef in a slightly sweet wine-and-herb sauce, usually served with gnocchi. Dalmatia is also known for its mutton. Since the lambs graze on salty seaside herbs, the meat—often served on a spit—has a distinctive flavor. The most widely available meat dish is the "mixed grill"—a combination of various Balkan grilled meats, best accompanied by the eggplant-and-red-pepper condiment *ajvar* (see "Balkan Flavors" on page 627). The best meat dish in Croatia is veal or lamb prepared under a *peka*—a metal baking lid that's covered with red-hot coals, to allow the meat to gradually cook to tender perfection. Available only in traditional restaurants, this dish typically must be ordered in advance and for multiple people. You'll also find a break from seafood in the north (Zagreb) and east (Slavonia), where the food has more of a Hungarian flavor—heavy on meat served with cabbage, noodles, or potatoes.

Many tourists reserve meat and fish for splurge dinners, and mostly dine on cheaper and faster pastas and pizzas. You'll see familiar dishes, such as spaghetti Bolognese (with meat sauce) and spaghetti carbonara (with an egg, parmesan, and bacon sauce), gnocchi (*njoki*, potato dumplings), and lasagna. Risotto (a rice dish) is popular here, often mixed with squid ink and various kinds of seafood.

There are many good local varieties of cheese made with sheep's or goat's milk. Pag, an island in the Kvarner Gulf, produces a famous, very salty, fairly dry sheep's-milk cheese *(paški sir)*, which is also said to be flavored by the herbs the sheep eat.

A common side-dish is mangold *(blitva)*, similar to Swiss

Croatian Wine

The quality of Croatia's wine declined under the communists, as much of the industry was state-run and focused on mass production. Now that the communists are gone, vintner families are returning to their roots—literally—and bringing quality back to Croatian wine.

The northern part of the country primarily produces whites *(bijelo vino)*, usually dry *(suho)* but sometimes semi-dry *(polusuho)* or sweet *(slatko)*. The sunny mountains just north of Zagreb are covered with vineyards producing whites. From Slavonia (Croatia's inland panhandle), you'll find *graševina*—crisp, dry, and acidic (like Welsh Riesling); Krauthaker and Enjingi are well-respected brands. The Istrian Peninsula corks up some good whites, including *malvazija,* a very popular, light, mid-range wine (Muscat is also popular).

As you move south, along the Dalmatian Coast, the wines turn red—which Croatians actually call "black wine" *(crno vino)*. The most common grape here is *plavac mali* ("little blue")—a distant cousin of Californian Zinfandel grapes. Generally speaking, the best coastal reds are produced on the long Pelješac Peninsula, across from Korčula (the most well-respected regions are Dingač—literally, "Donkey"—and Postup). But each island also produces its own good wines. Korčula makes *pošip* (near the town of Čara), *grk,* and *korčulanka,* and Hvar has *bogdanuša.*

Miljenko Grgić (a.k.a. "Mike Grgich"), a Croatian-American who has started a Croatian branch of his California wine empire, is putting Croatian wines on the map. Grgić grows his red wines (*plavac mali* grapes) at Postup and Dingač on the Pelješac Peninsula, and his white wines on Korčula Island.

chard. When ordering salad, choose between mixed (typically shredded cabbage, tomatoes, and maybe some beets and a little lettuce) or green (mostly lettuce). Throughout Croatia, salad is typically served with the main dish unless you request that it be brought beforehand.

For dessert, look no further than the mountains of delicious, homemade ice cream *(sladoled)* that line every street in Dalmatia. I've worked hard to sample and recommend the best ice-cream parlors in each town. (Poor me.) Dalmatia's typical dessert is flan (crème caramel), which they call *rozata. Prošek* is a sweet dessert wine.

When you're ordering a drink, *voda* gets you water, *kava* is coffee, *pivo* is beer, and *vino* gets you wine. Mineral water is *mineralna voda.* Jamnica is the main Croatian brand of bottled water, but you'll also see Bistra and Studenac. The most popular Croatian

Key Croatian Phrases

English	Croatian	Pronounced
Hello. (formal)	*Dobar dan.*	DOH-bahr dahn
Ciao. (both "Hi" and "Bye"—informal)	*Bog.*	bohg
Do you speak English?	*Govorite li engleski?*	GOH-voh-ree-teh lee eng-LEHS-kee
yes / no	*da / ne*	dah / neh
Please. / You're welcome.	*Molim.*	MOH-leem
Can I help you?	*Izvolite?*	EEZ-voh-lee-teh
Thank you.	*Hvala.*	HVAH-lah
I'm sorry. / Excuse me.	*Oprostite.*	oh-PROH-stee-teh
Good.	*Dobro.*	DOH-broh
Goodbye.	*Do viđenija.*	doh-veed-JAY-neeah
one / two	*jedan / dva*	YEH-dahn / dvah
three / four	*tri / četiri*	tree / cheh-TEE-ree
five / six	*pet / šest*	peht / shehst
seven / eight	*sedam / osam*	SEH-dahm / OH-sahm
nine / ten	*devet / deset*	DEH-veht / DEH-seht
hundred	*sto*	stoh
thousand	*tisuća*	TEE-soo-chah
How much?	*Koliko?*	KOH-lee-koh
local currency	*kuna*	KOO-nah
Where is...?	*Gdje je...?*	guh-DYEH yeh
...the toilet	*...vece*	VEHT-seh
men	*muški*	MOOSH-kee
women	*ženski*	ZHEHN-skee
water / coffee	*voda / kava*	VOH-dah / KAH-vah
beer / wine	*pivo / vino*	PEE-voh / VEE-noh
Cheers!	*Živjeli!*	ZHEE-vyeh-lee
the bill	*račun*	RAH-choon

beers are Ožujsko and Karlovačko, but Slovene-produced Laško is also common. Even more beloved in Croatia is wine (see "Croatian Wine" sidebar). Along the coast, locals find it refreshing to drink wine mixed with mineral water (called, as in English, *špricer*). When toasting with some new Croatian friends, raise your glass with a hearty *"Živjeli!"* (ZHEE-vyeh-lee).

To request a menu, say, *"Meni, molim"* (MEH-nee, MOH-leem; "Menu, please"). To get the attention of your waiter, say *"Konobar"* (KOH-noh-bahr; "Waiter"). When he brings your food, he'll likely say, *"Dobar tek!"* ("Enjoy your meal!"). When you're ready for the bill, ask for the *račun* (RAH-choon).

Croatian Language

Croatian was once known as "Serbo-Croatian," the official language of Yugoslavia. Most Yugoslav republics—including Croatia, Serbia, and Bosnia-Herzegovina—spoke this same language (though Slovene is quite different). And while each of these countries has tried to distance its language from that of its neighbors since the war, the languages spoken in all of these places are still very similar. The biggest difference is in the writing: Croatians and Bosniaks use our Roman alphabet, while Serbs use Cyrillic letters.

In recent years, Croatia has attempted to artificially make its vocabulary different from Serbian. A decade ago, you'd catch a plane at the *aerodrom*. Today, you'll catch that same flight at the *zračna luka*—a new coinage that combines the old Croatian words for "air" and "port." These new words, once created, are artificially injected into the lexicon. Croatians watching their favorite TV show will suddenly hear a character use a word they've never heard before...and think, "Oh, we have another new word."

As with other Slavic languages, *c* is pronounced "ts" (as in "cats"). The letter *j* is pronounced as "y." The letters *č* and *ć* are slightly different, but they both sound more or less like "ch"; *š* sounds like "sh" and *ž* sounds like "zh" (as in "leisure"). One Croatian letter that you won't see in other languages is *đ*, which sounds like the "dj" sound in "jeans." In fact, this letter is often replaced with "dj" in English.

As you're navigating the roads, these definitions will help: *trg* (square), *ulica* (road), *most* (bridge), *otok* (island), *trajekt* (ferry), and *Jadran* (Adriatic). When attempting to pronounce an unfamiliar word, the accent is usually on the first syllable (and never on the last). Confusingly, Croatian pronunciation—even of the same word—can vary in different parts of the country. This is because modern Croatian has three distinct dialects, called Kajkavian, Shtokavian, and Chakavian—based on how you say "what?" (*kaj?*, *što?*, and *ča?*, respectively). That's a lot of variety for a language with only five million speakers.

DUBROVNIK

Dubrovnik is a living fairy tale that shouldn't be missed. It feels like a small town today, but 500 years ago, Dubrovnik was a major maritime power, with the third-biggest navy in the Mediterranean. Still jutting confidently into the sea and ringed by thick medieval walls, Dubrovnik deserves its nickname: the Pearl of the Adriatic. Within the ramparts, the traffic-free Old Town is a fun jumble of quiet, cobbled back lanes; tasty seafood restaurants; low-impact museums; narrow, steep alleys; and kid-friendly squares. After all these centuries, the buildings still hint at old-time wealth, and the central promenade (Stradun) remains the place to see and be seen. If I had to pick just one place to visit in Croatia, this would be it.

The city's charm is the sleepy result of its no-nonsense past. Busy merchants, the salt trade, and shipbuilding made Dubrovnik rich. But the city's most valued commodity was always its freedom—even today, you'll see the proud motto *Libertas* displayed all over town (see *"Libertas"* sidebar on page 634).

Dubrovnik flourished in the 15th and 16th centuries, but an earthquake destroyed nearly everything in 1667. Most of today's buildings in the Old Town are post-quake Baroque, although a few palaces, monasteries, and convents displaying a rich Gothic-Renaissance mix survive from Dubrovnik's earlier Golden Age.

Dubrovnik remained a big tourist draw through the Tito years, bringing in much-needed hard currency from Western visitors. Consequently, the city was never given the hard socialist patina of other Yugoslav cities (such as the nearby Montenegrin capital Podgorica, then known as "Titograd").

As Croatia violently separated from Yugoslavia in 1991,

Dubrovnik became the only coastal city to be pulled into the fighting (see "The Siege of Dubrovnik" sidebar, page 648). Imagine having your youthful memories of good times spent romping in the surrounding hills replaced by visions of tanks and warships shelling your hometown. The city was devastated, but Dubrovnik has been repaired with amazing speed. The only physical reminders of the war are lots of new, orange roof tiles. Locals, relieved the fighting is over but forever hardened, are often willing to talk openly about the experience with visitors—offering a rare opportunity to grasp the harsh realities of war from an eyewitness perspective.

While the war killed tourism in the 1990s, today the crowds are most decidedly back. In fact, the midday crush of multinational tourists in the Old Town when the cruise ships dock is Dubrovnik's biggest downside. But locals—relieved that all these visitors are finally getting their economy back on track—appreciate that the numbers are about back to pre-war levels. While Europeans and Australians have been flocking here for years, Americans have only just begun to re-discover Dubrovnik.

Planning Your Time

Although Dubrovnik's museums are nothing special, the town is one of those places that you never want to leave. The real attraction here is the Old Town and its relaxing, breezy ambience. Dubrovnik could easily be "seen" in a day, but a second or third day to unwind (or even more time, for side-trips) makes the long trip here more worthwhile.

To hit all the key sights in a single day, start at the Pile Gate, just outside the Old Town. Walk around the city's walls to get your bearings (before it gets too hot and crowded), then work your way down the main drag (following my "Welcome to Dubrovnik" self-guided walk). As you explore, drop in at any museums or churches that appeal to you. To squeeze the most into a single day (or with a second day), consider a boat excursion from the Old Port (Lokrum Island, just offshore, requires the least brainpower).

ORIENTATION

(area code: 020)
All of the sights worth seeing are in Dubrovnik's traffic-free, walled **Old Town** (Stari Grad) peninsula. The main pedestrian promenade through the middle of town is called the Stradun; from this artery, the Old Town climbs steeply uphill in both directions to the walls. The Old Town connects to the mainland through three gates (Pile Gate, to the west; Ploče Gate, to the east; and the smaller Buža Gate, at the top of the stepped lane called Boškovićeva). The Old Port (Gradska Luka), with leisure boats to nearby destinations, is

Libertas

Libertas—liberty—has always been close to the heart of every Dubrovnik citizen. Dubrovnik was a proudly independent republic for centuries, even as most of Croatia became Venetian and Hungarian. Dubrovnik believed so strongly in *libertas* that it was the first foreign state in 1776 to officially recognize an upstart, experimental republic called the United States of America.

In the Middle Ages, the city-state of Dubrovnik (then called Ragusa) bought its independence from whoever was strongest—Byzantium, Venice, Hungary, the Ottomans—sometimes paying off more than one at a time. Dubrovnik's ships flew whichever flags were necessary to stay free, earning the nickname "Town of Seven Flags." As time went on, Europe's big-league nations were glad to have a second major seafaring power in the Adriatic to balance the Venetian threat. A free Dubrovnik was more valuable than a pillaged, plundered Dubrovnik.

In 1808, Napoleon conquered the Adriatic and abolished the Republic of Dubrovnik. After Napoleon was defeated, the fate of the continent was decided at the Congress of Vienna. But Dubrovnik's delegate was denied a seat at the table. The more powerful nations, no longer concerned about Venice and fed up after years of being sweet-talked by Dubrovnik, were afraid that the delegate would play old alliances off of each other to reestablish an independent Republic of Dubrovnik. Instead, the city became a part of the Hapsburg Empire, and entered a long period of decline.

Libertas still hasn't died in Dubrovnik. In the surreal days of the early 1990s, when Yugoslavia was reshuffling itself, a movement for the creation of a new Republic of Dubrovnik gained some momentum (led by a judge who, in earlier times, had convicted others for the same ideas). Another movement pushed for Dalmatia to secede as its own nation. But now that the dust has settled, today's locals are content and proud to be part of an independent Republic of Croatia.

at the east end of town. While greater Dubrovnik has about 50,000 people, the local population within the Old Town is just 5,000 in the winter—and even less in summer, when many residents move out to rent their apartments to tourists.

The **Pile** (PEE-leh) neighborhood, a pincushion of tourist services, is just outside the western end of the Old Town (through the Pile Gate). Right in front of the gate, you'll find a TI and Internet café (sharing an office), ATMs, a post office, a Croatia Airlines office, taxis, buses (fanning out to all the outlying neighborhoods),

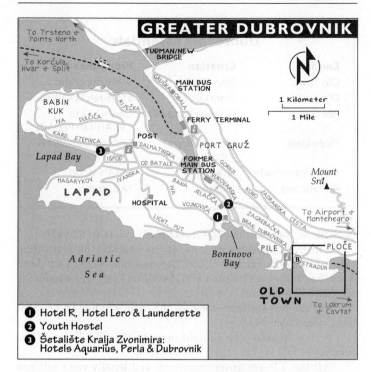

GREATER DUBROVNIK

To Trsteno & Points North
To Korčula, Hvar & Split
TUĐMAN/NEW BRIDGE
MAIN BUS STATION
GRUŠKA OBALA
BABIN KUK
RIJEČKA
IVA
DULČIĆA
KARD. STEPINCA
FERRY TERMINAL
POST
PALMATINSKA
PORT GRUŽ
Lapad Bay
ISPOD
OD BATALE
FORMER MAIN BUS STATION
GORNJI
VUKOVARSKA
Mount Srđ
MASARYKOV
IVANSKA
BANA
JELAČIĆA
KONO
JADRANSKA CESTA
LAPAD
IVA
VOJNOVIĆA
To Airport & Montenegro
HOSPITAL
LIGHT... PUT
ZAGREBAČKA
BRAN. DUBROVNIKA
PILE
PLOČE
Adriatic Sea
Boninovo Bay
STRADUN
OLD TOWN
To Lokrum & Cavtat

1 Kilometer
1 Mile

❶ Hotel R, Hotel Lero & Launderette
❷ Youth Hostel
❸ Šetalište Kralja Zvonimira: Hotels Aquarius, Perla & Dubrovnik

a cheap Konzum grocery store, and the Atlas Travel Agency (which books private rooms, excursions, and more—see "Helpful Hints," page 640). Just off this strip are some of Dubrovnik's best *sobe* (rooms in private homes—see "Sleeping," page 663). This is also the starting point for my self-guided "Welcome to Dubrovnik" walk (see page 643).

A mile or two away from the Old Town are beaches peppered with expensive resort hotels. My favorites are around **Boninovo Bay** (a 20-min walk or 5-min bus trip from the Old Town—see page 668), but most cluster on the lush **Lapad Peninsula** to the west (a 15-min bus trip from the Old Town). Across the bay from Lapad Peninsula is **Port Gruž,** with the main bus station and ferry terminal.

Tourist Information

Dubrovnik's TI has four branches (hours can fluctuate with demand, www.tzdubrovnik.hr):

• in the **Pile** neighborhood just outside the Old Town, 100 yards up the street from the Pile Gate (May–Sept daily 8:00–21:00; Oct–April Mon–Fri 8:00–20:00, Sat–Sun 8:00–16:00; Branitelja Dubrovnika 7, tel. 020/427-591; Internet access in the same office);

• at **Port Gruž,** across the street from the Jadrolinija ferry

Dubrovnik Essentials

English	Croatian	Pronounced
Old Town	Stari Grad	STAH-ree grahd
Old Port	Stara Luka	STAH-rah LOO-kah
Pile Gate	Gradska Vrata Pile	GRAHD-skah VRAH-tah PEE-leh
Ploče Gate	Gradska Vrata Ploče	GRAHD-skah VRAH-tah PLOH-cheh
Main Promenade	Stradun	STRAH-doon
Adriatic Sea	Jadran	YAH-drahn

dock (same hours as Pile TI, Gruška obala, tel. 020/417-983);
   • in the **Lapad** resort area, at the head of the main drag
(May–Sept Mon–Fri 8:00–20:00, Sat–Sun 8:00–16:00; Oct–April
Mon–Sat 9:00–16:00, closed Sun; Šetalište Kralja Zvonimira 25,
tel. 020/437-460); and
   • at the **bus station**—look for the little window (June–Sept
only, closed Oct–May).
   A new branch office might open in the Old Town in the
future.
   All the TIs are government-run and legally can't sell you
anything—but they can answer questions and give you a copy of
the free town map and monthly information booklet *Dubrovnik
Riviera*, which contains helpful maps, bus and ferry schedules,
museum prices and hours, a current schedule of events and performances, specifics on side-trip destinations, and more. If you need a
room and the TI isn't busy, they might be willing to call around to
find a place for you.

Arrival in Dubrovnik

For details on getting to the Dalmatian Coast, see page 617. As
throughout Croatia, you'll be met at the boat dock or bus station
by locals trying to get you to rent a room *(soba)* at their house. If
you've already reserved elsewhere, honor your reservation; if not,
consider the offer (but be very clear on the location before you
accept—many are nowhere near the Old Town).
   By Boat: The big boats arrive at Port Gruž, two miles northwest of the Old Town. On the road in front of the ferry terminal,
you'll find a bus stop (#1, #1a, #1b, and #3 go to Old Town's Pile
Gate; wait on the embankment side of the street) and a taxi stand
(figure 70 kn to the Old Town and most accommodations). Across
the street is the Jadrolinija office (with an ATM out front) and
a TI. You can book a private room *(soba)* at Atlas Travel Agency

(room-booking desk in boat terminal building) or at Gulliver Travel Agency (behind TI).

By Bus: Dubrovnik's main bus station (Autobusni Kolodvor) is just beyond the ferry terminal along the Port Gruž embankment (about 2.5 miles northwest of the Old Town). It's straightforward and user-friendly: pay toilets, baggage storage, a little TI window (summer only), and a helpful bus information window. To reach the Old Town's Pile Gate, walk straight ahead through the bus stalls, then bear right at the main road to the city bus stop (#1, #1a, #1b, or #3 to Pile). A taxi to the Old Town and most accommodations runs about 75 kn. While it's easiest simply to stay on your bus right to the main bus station, be aware that some buses might make other stops closer to the Old Town (for example, at the "fire station" bus stop just above the Old Town, or the so-called "former main bus station" about halfway between the main bus station and the Old Town—connected to the Pile Gate by local bus #1, #6, or #8). Ask your bus driver which stop is best for your destination.

By Plane: Dubrovnik's small airport (Zračna Luka) is in a place called Ćilipi, 13 miles south of the city. A Croatia Airlines bus meets most arriving flights at the airport (35 kn, 40 min; for Old Town accommodations, get off at "fire station" bus stop described below). Legitimate cabbies charge around 220 kn for the ride between the airport and the center (though some cabbies are charging as much as 300 kn; consider arranging your transfer in advance with one of the drivers listed on page 643, or through your *soba* host). Airport info: tel. 020/773-333, www.airport -dubrovnik.hr.

To get *to* the airport, you can take the same Croatia Airlines bus, which leaves from Dubrovnik's bus station 90 minutes before most flights (confirm schedule at TI). If you're staying in or near the Old Town, you'll find it more convenient to catch the airport bus at a stop that's just above the Old Town, nicknamed the "fire station" stop by locals. From the Old Town's main drag, hike up steep Boškovićeva lane and go through the wall at the Buža Gate. Once outside, continue straight under the arch and up the stairs, then swing right at the fire station onto the busy Krešimira street; the bus stop is a few steps up the road, by the deserted old cable-car station. The airport bus reaches this stop a few minutes after leaving the main bus station—wave it down or it might pass you by.

By Car: Coming from the north, you'll drive over the super-modern Tuđman Bridge (which most locals, mindful of their former president's tarnished legacy, call simply "the New Bridge"). Immediately after crossing the bridge, you have two options: To get to the bus station, ferry terminal (with some car-rental drop-off offices nearby), and Lapad Peninsula, take the left turn just after the bridge, wind down to the waterfront, then turn left and follow

Dubrovnik at a Glance

▲▲▲**Stradun Stroll** Charming walk through Dubrovnik's vibrant Old Town, ideal for coffee, ice cream, and people-watching. **Hours:** Always open. See page 643.

▲▲▲**Town Walls** Scenic mile-long walk along top of 15th-century fortifications encircling the city. **Hours:** July–Aug daily 8:00–19:30, progressively shorter hours off-season until 10:00–15:00 in mid-Nov–mid-March. See page 648.

▲**Franciscan Monastery Museum** Tranquil cloister, medieval pharmacy-turned-museum, and a century-old pharmacy still serving residents today. **Hours:** Daily April–Oct 9:00–18:00, Nov–March 9:00–17:00. See page 652.

▲**Cathedral** Eighteenth-century Roman Baroque cathedral and treasury filled with unusual relics such as a swatch of Jesus' swaddling clothes. **Hours:** Mon–Sat 9:00–20:00, Sun 11:00–17:30, shorter hours off-season. See page 654.

▲**Dominican Monastery Museum** Another relaxing cloister with precious paintings, altarpieces, and manuscripts. **Hours:** Daily May–Sept 9:00–18:00, Oct–April 9:00–17:00. See page 655.

▲**Synagogue Museum** Europe's second-oldest synagogue and Croatia's only Jewish museum, with 13th-century Torahs and Holocaust-era artifacts. **Hours:** May–mid-Nov daily 10:00–20:00; mid-Nov–April Mon–Fri 10:00–13:00, closed Sat–Sun. See page 656.

▲**Institute for the Restoration of Dubrovnik** Photos and videos of the recent war and an exhibit on restoration work. **Hours:** June–Sept Mon–Fri 9:00–13:00, closed Sat–Sun; rotating exhibits Oct–May. See page 657.

this road along the Port Gruž embankment. Or, to head for the Old Town, continue straight after the bridge. You'll pass above the Port Gruž area, then take the right turn-off marked *Dubrovnik* (with the little bull's-eye). You'll go through a tunnel, then turn left for *Centar,* and begin following the brown signs for *Grad* (Old Town); individual big hotels are also signed from here. You'll wind up just above the Old Town walls. Follow *Centar* and blue *P* signs to parking (there's a handy but expensive lot—nicknamed "the tennis court" by locals—just behind the wall); you can also drive around the right side of the wall to the bustling Pile neighbor-

▲**Serbian Orthodox Church and Icon Museum** Active church serving Dubrovnik's Serbian Orthodox community, and museum with traditional religious icons. **Hours:** Church—daily May–Sept 8:00–20:00, Oct–April 8:00–15:00, short services daily at 8:30 and 19:00, longer liturgy Sun at 9:00; museum—May–Oct Mon–Sat 9:00–14:00, closed Sun; Nov–April Mon–Fri 9:00–14:00, closed Sat–Sun. See page 658.

▲**Rupe Granary and Ethnographic Museum** Good folk museum with tools, jewelry, clothing, and painted eggs above immense underground grain stores. **Hours:** June–Oct daily 9:00–18:00; Nov–May Mon–Sat 9:00–14:00, closed Sun. See page 658.

Rector's Palace Antique furniture, guns, coins, and old prison cells in the former home of Venetian rectors who ruled Dubrovnik in the Middle Ages. **Hours:** Daily May–Oct 9:00–18:00, Nov–April 9:00–14:00. See page 653.

Maritime Museum Contracts, maps, paintings, and models from Dubrovnik's days as a maritime power and shipbuilding center. **Hours:** Vary with demand, usually March–Oct daily 9:00–18:00, Nov–Feb shorter hours and closed Sun. See page 656.

Aquarium Tanks of local sea life housed in huge, shady old fort. **Hours:** Daily July–Aug 9:00–21:00, progressively shorter hours off-season until 9:00–13:00 Nov–March. See page 656.

War Photo Limited Thought-provoking photographic look at contemporary warfare. **Hours:** June–Sept daily 9:00–21:00; May and Oct Tue–Sat 10:00–16:00, Sun 10:00–14:00, closed Mon; closed Nov–April. See page 657.

hood (described under "Orientation"). Your *soba* host or hotel can suggest the nearest parking lot (which might be far away in this designed-for-pedestrians town).

Helpful Hints

Festivals: Dubrovnik is most crowded during its Summer Festival, a month and a half of theater and musical performances held annually from July 10 to August 25 (www.dubrovnik-festival .hr). This is quickly followed by the Rachlin & Friends classical music festival in September (www.julianrachlin.com). For other options, see "Entertainment" on page 661.

Crowd-Beating Tips: Dubrovnik has been discovered—especially by cruise ships (700 of which visit each year). Cruise-ship crowds descend on the Old Town on most summer days, roughly between 10:00 and 16:00. In summer, try to do the big sights—especially walking around the wall—early or late, and hit the beach or take a siesta in the early afternoon, when the town is hottest and most crowded. On very busy days, as many as 30,000 cruise-ship day-trippers deluge Dubrovnik (seven ships' worth). If you're caught off-guard, it can be miserable. For others, it's entertaining to count the dozens of tour guides toting numbered paddles through the Old Town, and to watch the blocky orange transfer boats going back and forth to the ships moored offshore.

Travel Agency: You'll see travel agencies all over town. At any of them, you can buy seats on an excursion, rent a car, book a room, and pick up a pile of brochures. The most established company is **Atlas,** with an office just outside the Pile Gate from the Old Town—though the location is likely to change in the near future (June–Oct Mon–Sat 8:00–20:00, Sun 8:00–13:00; Nov–May Mon–Fri 8:00–19:00, Sat 8:00–15:00, closed Sun; possibly down the little alley at Sv. Đurđa 4, otherwise look for signs around the bus-stop area, tel. 020/442-574, fax 020/323-609, www.atlas-croatia.com, atlas.pile@atlas.hr). They also have an office at the ferry terminal building at Port Gruž.

Internet Access: You'll see signs all over town for Internet cafés with similar rates (around 5 kn/10 min). In the Old Town, my favorite is the modern **Netcafé,** with several speedy terminals right on Prijeko street, the "restaurant row" (daily 9:00–23:00, until 1:00 in the morning in summer, Prijeko 21, tel. 020/321-025, www.netcafe.hr). When staying in the Pile neighborhood, I use the **Dubrovnik Internet Centar** inside the Pile TI (May–Sept daily 8:00–24:00; Oct–April Mon–Sat 8:00–21:00, closed Sun; Branitelja Dubrovnika 7). If you have your own laptop, Dubrovnik Internet Centar sells vouchers to get online at hotspots around the Old Town (including the Stradun and Old Port; 50 kn/1 day, 100 kn/3 days).

Laundry: Hotels charge a mint to wash your clothes; *soba* hosts are cheaper, but often don't have the time (ask). The best affordable option is the full-service **launderette** near the hotels at Boninovo Bay, a 20-minute uphill walk or five-minute bus trip from the Pile Gate (90 kn for wash and dry in about 3 hours, no self-service, Mon–Fri 9:00–19:00, Sat 10:00–16:00, closed Sun, across from the big seafront Hotel Bellevue at Pera Čingrije 8, tel. 020/333-347).

English Bookstore: The **Algoritam** shop, right on the Stradun, has a wide variety of guidebooks, nonfiction books about Croatia and the former Yugoslavia, novels, and magazines— all in English (Mon–Fri 9:00–20:30, Sat 9:00–15:00, Sun 9:00–13:00, Placa 8).

Wine Shop: Vinoteka Miličić offers a nice selection of local wines and helpful advice for choosing one—though they do tend to push their own wines (daily 9:00–23:00 in peak season, shorter hours off-season, near the Pile end of the Stradun, tel. 020/321-777).

Car Rental: The big international chains such as **Avis** (tel. 020/313-634), **Europcar** (mobile 091-430-3031), and **Hertz** (tel. 020/425-000) have offices both at the airport and near the Port Gruž embankment where the big boats come in. In addition, the many travel agencies closer to the Old Town also have a line on rental cars. Figure €50–60 per day, including taxes, insurance, and unlimited mileage (at the bigger chains, there's usually no extra charge for drop-off elsewhere in Croatia). Be sure the agency knows if you're crossing a border (such as Montenegro or Bosnia-Herzegovina) to ensure you have the proper paperwork.

Best Views: Walking the **Old Town walls** late in the day, when the city is bathed in rich light, is a treat. The **Fort of St. Lawrence,** perched above the Pile neighborhood cove, has great views over the Old Town. A stroll east of the city walls offers nice views back on the Old Town (best light early in the day).

Better yet, if you have a car, head south of the city in the morning for gorgeously lit Old Town views over your right shoulder; various turn-offs along this road are ideal photo stops. The best one, known locally as the **"panorama point,"** is where the road leading up and out of Dubrovnik meets the main road that passes above the town (look for the pull-out on the right, with tour buses). Even if you're heading north, in good weather it's worth a quick detour south for this view.

For an even more adventurous view, consider driving (or better, hiring a driver to take you) up to the top of **Mount Srđ** over the Old Town (marked by the cross, TV tower, and old fortress). While this was once accessible by cable-car from near the Old Town, now you can reach it only via a very twisty and rugged road (it branches off the main road just south of the Old Town; the sunlight is best in the morning). Once up top, you'll enjoy impressive views down onto the Old Town, and superb scenery all around—including Bosnia-Herzegovina, Montenegro, and nearby islands (the Elaphite Islands and Mljet). Because this is a bit off the beaten path, it's best to

Dubrovnik

have a driver bring you up here (see "Hire Your Own Driver" under "Tours," below).

Getting Around Dubrovnik

If you're staying in or near the Old Town, everything is easily walkable. But those sleeping on Boninovo Bay or the Lapad Peninsula will want to get comfortable using the buses. Once you understand the system, commuting to the Old Town is a breeze.

By Bus: Libertas runs Dubrovnik's public buses. Tickets, which are good for an hour, are cheaper if you buy them in advance from a newsstand or your hotel (8 kn, ask for *autobusna karta*, ow-toh-BOOS-nah KAR-tah) than if you buy them from the bus driver (10 kn). A 24-hour ticket costs 25 kn (only sold at special bus-ticket kiosks, such as the one near the Pile Gate bus stop).

When you enter the bus, validate your ticket in the machine next to the driver (orange arrow in, white side up). Because most tourists can't figure out how to validate their tickets, it can take a long time to load the bus (which means drivers are understandably grumpy, and locals aren't shy about cutting in line).

All buses stop near the Old Town, just in front of the Pile Gate (buy tickets at the newsstand or bus-ticket kiosk right by the stop). From here, they fan out to just about anywhere you'd want to go (hotels on Boninovo Bay, Lapad Peninsula, and the ferry terminal and long-distance bus station). You'll find bus schedules and a map in the TI booklet.

By Taxi: Taxis start at 25 kn, then charge 8 kn per kilometer. The handiest taxi stand for the Old Town is just outside the Pile Gate. The biggest operation is Radio Taxi (tel. 020/970).

TOURS

In Dubrovnik

Walking Tours—Two companies—**Dubrovnik Walking Tours** and **Dubrovnik Walks**—offer similar one-hour walking tours of the Old Town daily at 10:00 (100 kn, also other departures and topics—look for fliers at TI). These tours are pricey and brief, touching lightly on the same basic information explained in this chapter.

Local Guide—For an in-depth look at the city, consider hiring your own local guide. **Štefica Curić** really knows her stuff and can give you an insider's look at the city (480 kn/2 hrs, mobile 091-345-0133, dugacarapa@yahoo.com). If Štefica is busy, she can refer you to another good guide for the same price. The TI can also suggest guides.

Bus-Plus-Walking Tours—Two big companies (**Atlas** and **Elite**) offer expensive tours of Dubrovnik (about 200 kn, 2 hrs).

From Dubrovnik

Package Excursions—The two big, competing travel agencies in Dubrovnik—Atlas and Elite—offer €45–65 **guided excursions** (by bus and/or boat) to nearby destinations, including Mostar, Montenegro, islands and villages near Dubrovnik, Korčula, and others. Atlas and Elite are basically interchangeable, and you can buy tickets at most travel agencies and hotel lobbies (schedules and prices change frequently—look for fliers or inquire locally). If one of the two big companies isn't running a tour to your preferred destination when you're in town, check with the other one (Atlas: tel. 020/442-574, www.atlas-croatia.com; Elite: tel. 020/358-200, www.elite.hr).

Hire Your Own Driver—I enjoy renting my own car to see the sights around Dubrovnik (see "Helpful Hints," above). But if you're more comfortable having someone else do the driving, consider hiring a driver. While the drivers listed here are not official tour guides, they both speak great English and offer ample commentary as you roll, and can help you craft a good day-long itinerary to Mostar, Montenegro, Korčula, or anywhere else near Dubrovnik (typically departing around 8:00 and returning in the early evening). Friendly **Pepo Klaić,** a veteran of the 1991 war, enjoys surprising my readers with worthwhile detours—go along with his suggestions (€250/day, €125 for half-day trip to nearer destinations, airport transfer for about 200 kn—cheaper than a taxi, these prices for up to 4 people—more expensive for bigger group, mobile 098-427-301, pepoklaic@yahoo.com). For €70, Pepo can drive you to the fortress at Mount Srđ up above the Old Town, with sweeping views of the entire area (about 1–1.5 hrs round-trip). **Petar Vlašić** can do similar tours for similar prices, and specializes in wine tours to the Pelješac Peninsula, with stops at various wineries along the way (220-kn airport transfers, mobile 091-580-8721, meritum@du.t-com.hr).

SELF-GUIDED WALK

▲▲▲Welcome to Dubrovnik: Strolling the Stradun

Running through the heart of Dubrovnik's Old Town is the 200-yard-long Stradun promenade—packed with people and lined with sights. This walk offers an ideal introduction to Dubrovnik's charms. It takes about a half-hour, not counting sightseeing stops.

• Begin at the busy square in front of the west entrance to the Old Town, the Pile (PEE-leh) Gate.

Pile Neighborhood

This bustling area is the nerve center of Dubrovnik's tourist industry—it's where the real world meets the fantasy of Dubrovnik (for details, see "Orientation," page 633). Near the new, modern, mirrors-and-TV-screens monument is a leafy café terrace. Wander over to the edge of the terrace and take in the imposing walls of the Pearl of the Adriatic. The huge, fortified peninsula just outside the city walls is the **Fort of St. Lawrence** (Tvrđava Lovrijenac), Dubrovnik's oldest fortress and one of the top venues for the Dubrovnik Summer Festival. Shakespearean plays are often performed here, occasionally starring Goran Višnjić, the Croatian actor who has become an American star on the TV show *ER*. You can climb this fortress for great views over the Old Town (20 kn, or covered by same ticket as Old Town walls on the same day).

• *Cross over the moat (now a shady park) to the round entrance tower in the Old Town Wall. This is the...*

Pile Gate (Gradska Vrata Pile)

Just before you enter the gate, notice the image above the entrance of **St. Blaise** (Sveti Vlaho in Croatian) cradling Dubrovnik in his arm. You'll see a lot more of Blaise during your time here—we'll find out why later on this walk.

Inside the outer wall of the Pile Gate and to the left, a white sign shows where each bomb dropped on the Old Town in the recent war. Once inside town, you'll see virtually no signs of the war—demonstrating the townspeople's impressive resilience in rebuilding so well and so quickly.

Passing the rest of the way through the gate, you'll find a lively little square surrounded by landmarks. To the left, a steep stairway leads up to the imposing **Minčeta Tower.** This is a good starting point for Dubrovnik's best activity, walking around the top of the wall (see page 648).

Next to the stairway is the small **Church of St. Savior** (Crkva Svetog Spasa). Appreciative locals built this votive church to thank God after Dubrovnik made it through a 1520 earthquake. When the massive 1667 quake destroyed the city, this church was one of the only buildings left intact. And during the recent war, the church survived another close call when a shell exploded on the ground right in front of it (you can still see faint pockmarks from the shrapnel).

The big, round structure in the middle of the square is **Onofrio's Big Fountain** (Velika Onofrijea Fontana). In the Middle Ages, Dubrovnik had a complicated aqueduct system that brought water from the mountains seven miles away. The water ended up here, at the town's biggest fountain, before continuing through the city. This plentiful supply of water, large reserves of salt (a key source of Dubrovnik's wealth, from the town of Ston), and a massive granary (now the Rupe Ethnographic Museum, described on page 658) made little, independent Dubrovnik very siege-resistant.

The big building on the left just beyond the small Church of St. Savior is the **Franciscan Monastery Museum.** This building, with a delightful cloister and one of Europe's oldest pharmacies, is worth touring (described on page 652).

• *When you're finished taking in the sights on this square, continue along...*

The Stradun

Dubrovnik's main promenade—officially called Placa, but better known as the Stradun—is alive with locals and tourists alike.

This is the heartbeat of the city: an Old World shopping mall by day and sprawling cocktail party after dark, when everybody seems to be doing the traditional evening stroll—flirting, ice-cream-licking, flaunting, and gawking. A coffee and some of Europe's best people-watching in a prime Stradun café is one of travel's great $3 bargains.

When Dubrovnik was just getting its start in the seventh century, this street was a canal. Romans fleeing from the invading Slavs lived on the island of Ragusa (on your right), and the Slavs settled on the shore. In the 11th century, the canal separating Ragusa from the mainland was filled in, the towns merged, and a unique Slavic-Roman culture and language blossomed. While originally much more higgledy-piggledy, this street was rebuilt in the current, more straightforward style after the 1667 earthquake.

During your time in Dubrovnik, you'll periodically hear the rat-a-tat-tat of a drum echoing through the streets from the Stradun. This means it's time to head for this main drag to get a glimpse of the colorfully costumed "town guards" parading through town (and a cavalcade of tourists running alongside them, trying to snap a clear picture). You may also see some of these characters standing guard outside the town gates. It's all part of the local tourist board's recent efforts to make their town even more atmospheric.

• *Branching off from this promenade are several museums and other attractions, described under "Sights" later in this chapter. At the end of the Stradun is a passageway leading to the Ploče Gate. Just before this passage is the lively Luža Square. Its centerpiece is...*

Dubrovnik

Orlando's Column (Orlandov Stup)

Columns like this were typical of towns in northern Germany. Dubrovnik erected the column in 1417, soon after it had shifted allegiances from the oppressive Venetians to the Hungarians. By putting a northern European symbol in the middle of its most prominent square, Dubrovnik decisively distanced itself from Venice. Anytime a decision was made by the Republic, the town crier came to Orlando's Column and announced the news. The step he stood on indicated the importance of his message— the higher up, the more important the news. It was also used as the pillory, where people were publicly punished. The thin line on the top step in front of Orlando is exactly as long as the statue's forearm. This mark was Dubrovnik's standard measurement—not for a foot, but for an "elbow."

• *Now stand in front of Orlando's Column and orient yourself with a...*

Luža Square Spin-Tour

Orlando is looking toward the **Sponza Palace** (Sponza-Povijesni Arhiv). This building, from 1522, is the finest surviving example of Dubrovnik's Golden Age in the 15th and 16th centuries. It's a combination of Renaissance (ground-floor arches) and Venetian Gothic (upstairs windows). Houses up and down the main promenade used to look like this, but after the 1667 earthquake, they were replaced with boring uniformity. This used to be the customs office *(dogana)*, but now it's an exhaustive archive of the city's history, with temporary art exhibits and a war memorial. The poignant **Memorial Room of Dubrovnik Defenders** (on the left as you enter) has photos of dozens of people from Dubrovnik who were killed fighting the Serbs in 1991. A TV screen and images near the ceiling show the devastation of the city. Though the English descriptions are (perhaps unavoidably) slanted to the Croat perspective, it's compelling to look in the eyes of the brave young men who didn't start this war...but were willing to finish it (free, long hours daily in peak season, shorter hours off-season).

To the right of Sponza Palace is the town's **Bell Tower** (Gradski Zvonik). The original dated from 1444, but it was rebuilt when it started to lean in the 1920s. The big clock may be an octopus, but only one of its hands tells time. Below that, the circle shows the phase of the moon. At the bottom, the old-fashioned digital readout tells the hour (in Roman numerals) and the minutes (in five-minute increments). At the top of each hour (and again three minutes later), the time is clanged out on the bell up top by two bronze bell ringers, Maro and Baro. (If this all seems like a copy of the very similar clock on St. Mark's Square in Venice, locals are quick to point out that this clock predates that one by several decades.) The clock still has to be wound every two days. Notice the little window between the moon phase and the "digital" readout: The clock-winder opens this window to get some light. During the recent war, the clock-winder's house was destroyed—with the winding keys inside. For days, the clock bell didn't run. But then, miraculously, the keys were discovered lying in the street. The excited Dubrovnik citizens came together in this square and cheered as the clock was wound and the bell chimed, signaling to the soldiers surrounding the city that they hadn't won yet.

The big building to the right of the Bell Tower is the **City Hall** (Vijećnica). Next to it is **Onofrio's Little Fountain** (Mala Onofrijea Fontana), the little brother of the one at the other end of the Stradun. Beyond that is the **Gradska Kavana,** or "Town Café." This hangout—historically Dubrovnik's favorite spot for gossiping and people-watching—was recently renovated, with seating all the way through the wall to the Old Port. Just down the street from the Town Café is the Rector's Palace, and then the cathedral (for more on each, see "Sights").

Behind Orlando is **St. Blaise's Church** (Crkva Sv. Vlaha), dedicated to the patron saint of Dubrovnik. You'll see statues and paintings of St. Blaise all over town, always holding a model of the city in his left hand. According to legend, a millennium ago St. Blaise came to a local priest in a dream and warned him that the up-and-coming Venetians would soon attack the city. The priest alerted the authorities, who prepared for war. Of course, the prediction came true. St. Blaise has been a Dubrovnik symbol—and locals have resented Venice—ever since.

• *Your tour is finished. From here, you've got plenty of sightseeing options (all described under "Sights"). As you face the Bell Tower, you can go up the street to the right to reach the Rector's Palace and cathedral; you can walk through the gate straight ahead to reach the Old Port; or you can head through the gate and jog left to find the Dominican Monastery Museum. Even more sights—including an old synagogue, an Orthodox church, two different exhibits of war photography, and the medieval granary—are in the steep streets between the Stradun and the walls.*

SIGHTS

All of Dubrovnik's sights are inside the Old Town's walls.

Combo-Tickets: Note that the Rector's Palace, Maritime Museum, and Rupe Granary and Ethnographic Museum—plus an uninteresting 16th-century Croatian writer's house—are covered by a single combo-ticket (40 kn to visit any two, 50 kn to visit all

Dubrovnik

The Siege of Dubrovnik

In June of 1991, Croatia declared independence from Yugoslavia. Within weeks, the nations were at war (for more on the war, see the Understanding Yugoslavia chapter, page 915). Though warfare raged in the Croatian interior, nobody expected that the bloodshed would reach Dubrovnik.

As refugees from Vukovar (in northeastern Croatia) arrived in Dubrovnik that fall, and told horrific stories of the warfare there, local residents began fearing the worst. Warplanes from the Serb-dominated Yugoslav National Army buzzed threateningly low over the town, as if to signal an impending attack.

Then, at 6:00 in the morning on October 1, 1991, Dubrovnik residents awoke to explosions on nearby hillsides. The first attacks were focused on Mount Srđ, high above the Old Town. First the giant cross was destroyed, then a communications tower (both have been rebuilt and are visible today). This first wave of attacks cleared the way for Serbian land troops, who quickly surrounded the city. The ragtag, newly formed Croatian Army quickly dug in at the old Napoleonic-era fortress at the top of Mount Srđ, where just 25 or 30 soldiers fended off a Serb takeover of this highly strategic position.

At first, shelling was focused on military positions on the outskirts of town. But soon, the Serbs began bombing residential neighborhoods, then the Pearl of the Adriatic itself: Dubrovnik's Old Town. Defenseless townspeople took shelter in their cellars, and sometimes even huddled together in the city wall's 15th-century forts. It was the first time in Dubrovnik's long history that the walls were actually used to defend against an attack.

Dubrovnik resisted the siege better than anyone expected. The Serbs were hoping that residents would flee the town, but the people of Dubrovnik stayed. Though severely outgunned and outnumbered, Dubrovnik's defenders managed to hold the fort atop Mount Srđ (just above the Old Town), while the Serbs controlled the nearby mountaintops. All supplies had to be carried up to the fort by foot or by donkey. Dubrovnik wasn't prepared for war, so they had to improvise their defense. Many brave young locals lost their lives when they slung old hunting rifles over their shoulders and, under cover of darkness, climbed the hills above Dubrovnik to meet the Serbs face-to-face.

four, tickets available at any participating sight). These tickets are a good deal if you plan to visit more than one of these sights.

▲▲▲Town Walls (Gradske Zidine)

Dubrovnik's single best attraction is strolling the scenic mile-and-a-quarter around the city walls. As you meander along this lofty perch—with a sea of orange roofs on one side, and the actual sea

After eight months of bombing, Dubrovnik was liberated by the Croatian Army, which attacked Serb positions from the north. By the end of the siege, 100 civilians were dead, as well as more than 200 Dubrovnik citizens who lost their lives actively fighting for their hometown (much revered today as "Dubrovnik Defenders"). More than two-thirds of Dubrovnik's buildings had been damaged, and more than 30,000 people had to flee their homes—but the failed siege was finally over.

Why was Dubrovnik—so far from the rest of the fighting—dragged into the conflict? The Serbs wanted to catch the city and surrounding region off-guard, gaining a toehold on the southern Dalmatian Coast so they could push north to Split. They also hoped to ignite pro-Serb passions in the nearby Serb-dominated areas of Bosnia-Herzegovina and Montenegro. But perhaps most of all, Yugoslavia wanted to hit Croatia where it hurt—its proudest, most historic, and most beautiful city, the tourist capital of a nation dependent on tourism. (It seems their plan backfired. Locals now say, "When Serbia attacked Dubrovnik, they lost the war"—because images of the historic city under siege swayed international public opinion *against* the Serbs.)

The war initially devastated the tourist industry. Now, to the casual observer, Dubrovnik seems virtually back to normal. Aside from a few pockmarks and bright, new roof tiles, there are scant reminders of what happened here just a decade and a half ago. But even though the city itself has been repaired, the people of Dubrovnik are forever changed. Imagine living in an idyllic paradise, a place that attracted and awed visitors from around the world...and then watching it gradually blown to bits. It's understandable if Dubrovnik citizens are a little less in love with life than they once were.

Dubrovnik has no real museum about its recent war, but two small sights can help you piece together the story: the Memorial Room of Dubrovnik Defenders in the Sponza Palace on Luža Square (page 646); and, a few blocks away across the Stradun, the Institute for the Restoration of Dubrovnik (page 657). Another sight, War Photo Limited, expands the scope to war photography from around the world (page 657).

Dubrovnik

on the other—you'll get your bearings and snap pictures like mad of the ever-changing views. Bring your map, which you can use to pick out landmarks and get the lay of the land.

There have been walls here almost as long as there's been a Dubrovnik. As with virtually all fortifications on the Croatian coast, these walls were beefed up in the 15th century, when the Ottoman navy became a threat. Around the perimeter are several

DUBROVNIK'S OLD TOWN

1. Villa Ragusa & Apts. Paviša
2. Lidija Matić Apts.
3. Karmen Apartments
4. Apartments Amoret (2)
5. Renata Zijadić Rooms
6. To Jadranka & Milan Benussi Rooms
7. Villa San Apartments
8. Paulina Čumbelić Rooms
9. Rest. Orhan Guest House
10. Nedjeljka Benussi Rooms
11. Villa Adriatica
12. Hotel Stari Grad
13. Atlas Travel Agency
14. Institute for the Restoration of Dubrovnik
15. War Photo Limited Gallery
16. Serbian Orthodox Church
17. Icon Museum
18. Algoritam Bookshop
19. Sloboda Cinema
20. Jadran Cinema
21. Market Square

To Ferry Terminal, Bus Station & Lapad Hotels

HILTON

PILE

PILE GATE

BIG FOUNTAIN

ST. SAVIOR

RUPE MUSEUM

BOKAR FORTRESS

FORT OF ST. LAWRENCE

Adriatic Sea

100 Meters
100 Yards

Ⓐ Wall Access

substantial forts, with walls rounded so that cannonballs would glance off harmlessly. These stout forts intimidated would-be invaders during the Republic of Dubrovnik's Golden Age, and protected local residents during the recent war.

Walking the walls also offers the best illustration of the damage Dubrovnik sustained during the recent war. It's easy to see that nearly two-thirds of Dubrovnik's roofs were replaced after the bombings (notice the new, bright-orange tiles—and how some buildings salvaged the old tiles, but have 20th-century ones underneath). Looking over this gorgeous panorama, ponder that the pristine-seeming Old Town was rebuilt using exactly the same materials and methods with which it was originally constructed.

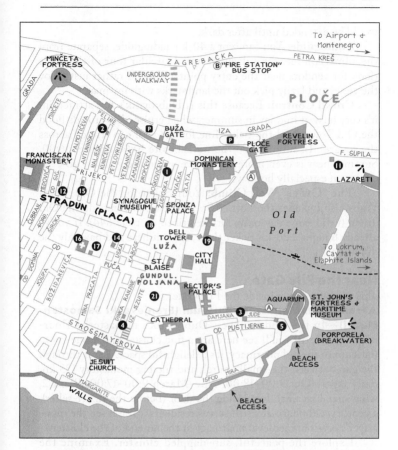

You can enter the walls at three points: just inside the Pile Gate, near the Dominican Monastery north of the Ploče Gate, and by the Maritime Museum south of the Old Port. The highest point is the empty Minčeta Tower, above the Pile Gate at the west end of town. The tower rewards those who climb it with a fine view. If you climb here first from the Pile Gate and then proceed clockwise, it's mostly downhill all the way around. (Posted signs suggest you go counterclockwise, so if it's crowded, you may find it's easier to go with the flow of other wall-walkers.) Speed demons with no cameras can walk the walls in less than an hour; strollers and shutterbugs should plan on longer.

Cost and Hours: 50 kn to enter walls, July–Aug daily 8:00–19:30, progressively shorter hours off-season until 10:00–15:00 in mid-Nov–mid-March. Note that posted opening times indicate when the walls close, *not* the last entry—ascend at least an hour before this time if you want to make it all the way around. There's talk of illuminating the walls in the future, in which case the hours would be extended until after dark.

Audioguide: You can rent a 40-kn audioguide, separate from the admission fee, for a dryly narrated circular tour of the walls (look for vendors near the entry points). But I'd rather just enjoy the views and lazily pick out the landmarks with my map.

Crowd Control: Because this is Dubrovnik's top attraction, it's very busy at midday in summer, when cruise-ship crowds flood the Old Town (and the ticket line for the wall can stretch across the square). In summer, do the walls before 10:00 or after 16:00. Summer heat is even more oppressive up on the wall, so go even earlier on especially hot days.

The "Other" Wall Climb: Your ticket for the Old Town Walls also includes the Fort of St. Lawrence just outside the Old Town (valid same day only; fort described on page 644). If you've already bought a 20-kn ticket there, show it here and pay only the difference.

Near the Pile Gate

This museum is just inside the Pile Gate.

▲**Franciscan Monastery Museum (Franjevački Samostan-Muzej)**—In the Middle Ages, Dubrovnik's monasteries flourished. While all you'll see here are a fine cloister and a one-room museum in the old pharmacy, it's a delightful space. Enter through the gap between the small church and the big monastery (25 kn, daily April–Oct 9:00–18:00, Nov–March 9:00–17:00, Placa 2, www.malabraca.hr). Just inside the door (before the ticket-seller), a century-old pharmacy still serves residents. (You'll see the monastery's original medieval pharmacy at the far end of the cloister.)

Explore the peaceful, sun-dappled **cloister.** Examine the capitals at the tops of the 60 Romanesque-Gothic double pillars. Each one is different. Notice that some of the portals inside the courtyard are made with a lighter-colored stone—these had to be repaired after being damaged in the recent war.

In the far corner stands the medieval **pharmacy.** Part of the Franciscans' mission was to contribute to the good health of the citizens, so they opened this pharmacy in 1317. The monastery has had a pharmacy in continual operation ever since. On display are jars, pots, and other medieval pharmacists' tools. The sick would come to get their medicine at the little window (on left side), which limited contact with the pharmacist and reduced the risk of passing on disease. Around the room, you'll also find some relics, old manuscripts, and a detailed painting of early 17th-century Dubrovnik.

Near Luža Square

These sights are at the far end of the Stradun (nearest the Old Port). As you stand on Luža Square facing the Bell Tower, the Rector's Palace and Cathedral are up the street called Pred Dvorom to the right, and the Dominican Monastery Museum is through the gate by the Bell Tower and to the left.

Rector's Palace (Knežev Dvor)—In the Middle Ages, the Republic of Dubrovnik was ruled by a rector (similar to a Venetian doge), who was elected by the nobility. To prevent any one person from becoming too powerful, the rector's term was limited to one month. Most rectors were in their 50s—near the end of the average lifespan, and less likely to shake things up. During his term, a rector lived upstairs in this palace. Because it's been plundered twice, this empty-feeling museum isn't as interesting as most other European palaces—but it does offer a glimpse of Dubrovnik in its glory days (35 kn, covered by 40-kn or 50-kn combo-ticket, daily May–Oct 9:00–18:00, Nov–April 9:00–14:00, some posted English information, skip the 30-kn audioguide, 6-kn English booklet is helpful, Pred Dvorom 3).

The exterior is decorated in the Gothic-Renaissance mix (with particularly finely carved capitals) that was so common in Dubrovnik before the 1667 earthquake. The courtyard is a venue for the Summer Festival, hosting music groups ranging from the local symphony to the Vienna Boys' Choir.

In the courtyard is the only secular statue created during the centuries-long Republic. Dubrovnik republicans, mindful of the dangers of hero-worship, didn't believe that any one citizen should be singled out. They made only one exception—for Miho Pracat (a.k.a. Michaeli Prazatto), a rich citizen who donated vast sums to charity and willed a fleet of ships to the city. But notice that Pracat's statue is displayed in here, behind closed doors, not out in public. The ground floor has some other exhibits, including some old prison cells. Supposedly these were placed within earshot of the rector's quarters, so he would hear the moans of the prisoners... and stay honest.

On the mezzanine level (stairs on right as you enter), you'll find an impressive collection of antique pharmacy jars, a decent display of furniture, a wimpy gun exhibit, and a ho-hum coin collection. On the upper floor (stairs on left as you enter, across from mezzanine stairs) are old apartments that serve as a painting gallery. The only vaguely authentic room is the red room in the corner, decorated more or less as it was in 1500, when it was the rector's office. Mihajlo Hamzić's exquisite *Baptism of Christ* painting, inspired by Italian painter Andrea Mantegna, is an early Renaissance work from the "Dubrovnik School" (see "Dominican Monastery Museum" listing, on page 655).

▲**Cathedral (Katedrala)**—Dubrovnik's original 12th-century cathedral was funded largely by the English king Richard the Lionhearted. On his way back from the Third Crusade, Richard was shipwrecked nearby. He promised God that if he survived, he'd build a church on the spot where he landed—which happened to be on Lokrum Island, just offshore. At Dubrovnik's request, Richard agreed to build his token of thanks inside the city instead. It was the finest Romanesque church on the Adriatic...before it was destroyed by the 1667 earthquake. This version is 18th-century Roman Baroque. Inside, you'll find a painting from the

school of Titian *(Assumption of the Virgin)* over the stark contemporary altar, and a quirky treasury *(riznica)* packed with 138 relics (church entry free, treasury entry-10 kn, both open Mon–Sat 9:00–20:00, Sun 11:00–17:30, shorter hours off-season).

Examining the **treasury** collection, notice that there are three locks on the treasury door—the stuff in here was so valuable, three different VIPs (the rector, the bishop, and a local aristocrat) had to agree before it could be opened. On the table near the door are several of St. Blaise's body parts (pieces of his arm, skull, and leg—all encased in gold and silver). In the middle of the wall directly opposite the door, look for the crucifix with a piece of the "true cross." On a dig in Jerusalem, St. Helen (Emperor Constantine's mother) discovered what she believed to be the cross that Jesus was crucified on. It was brought to Constantinople, and the Byzantine czars doled out pieces of it to Balkan kings. Note the folding three-paneled altar painting (underneath the cross). Dubrovnik ambassadors packed this on road trips (such as their annual trip to pay off the Ottomans) so they could worship wherever they traveled. On the right side of the room, the silver casket supposedly holds the actual swaddling clothes of the Baby Jesus (or, as some locals call it somewhat less reverently, "Jesus' nappy"). Dubrovnik bishops secretly passed these clothes down from generation to generation...until a nun got wind of it, and told the whole town. Pieces of the cloth were cut off to miraculously heal the sick, especially new mothers recovering from a difficult birth. No matter how often it was cut, the cloth always went back to its original form. Then someone tried to use it on the wife of a Bosnian king. Since she was Muslim, it couldn't help her, and it never worked again. Whether or not it's true, this legend hints at the prickly relationships between faiths (not to mention male chauvinism) here in the Balkans.

▲Dominican Monastery Museum (Dominikanski Samostan-Muzej)—You'll find many of Dubrovnik's art treasures—paintings, altarpieces, and manuscripts—gathered around the peaceful

Dominican Monastery cloister inside the Ploče Gate (20 kn, art buffs enjoy the 60-kn English book, daily May–Sept 9:00–18:00, Oct–April 9:00–17:00). Historically, this was the church for wealthy people, while the Franciscan Church (down at the far end of the Stradun) was for poor people. Services were staggered by 15 minutes to allow servants to drop off their masters here, then rush down the Stradun for their own service.

Work your way clockwise around the cloister. The room in the far corner from the entry contains paintings from the **"Dubrovnik School,"** the Republic's circa-1500 answer to the art boom in Florence and Venice. While the 1667 earthquake destroyed most of these paintings, about a dozen survive, and five of those are in this room. Don't miss the triptych by Nikola Božidarović with St. Blaise holding a detailed model of 16th-century Dubrovnik (left panel)—the most famous depiction of Dubrovnik's favorite saint. You'll also see reliquaries shaped like the hands and feet that they hold.

In the next room, you'll see a painting by **Titian** depicting St. Blaise, Mary Magdalene, and the donor.

The striking **church** is decorated with modern stained glass, a fine 13th-century stone pulpit that survived the earthquake (reminding visitors of the intellectual approach to scripture that characterized the Dominicans), and a precious 14th-century Paolo Veneziano crucifix hanging above the high altar. The most memorable piece of art in the church is the *Miracle of St. Dominic,* showing the founder of the order bringing a child back to life (over the altar to the right, as you enter). It was painted in the Realist style (late 19th century) by Vlaho Bukovac.

Near the Old Port (Stara Luka)

The picturesque Old Port, carefully nestled behind St. John's Fort, faces away from what was Dubrovnik's biggest threat, the Venetians. Spend a few minutes watching cruise-ship passengers coming and going on their goofy little transfer boats. The long seaside building

across the bay on the left is the Lazareti, once the medieval quarantine house. In those days, all visitors were locked in here for 40 days before entering town. (Today it hosts folk-dancing shows—see "Entertainment" on page 661.) A bench-lined harborside walk leads around the fort to a breakwater, providing a peaceful perch. From the breakwater, rocky beaches curl around the outside of the wall.

Excursions—At the port, you can haggle with captains selling excursions. The most popular are to **Lokrum Island,** just offshore (35 kn round-trip, 5 kn for a map, 2/hr in summer 9:00–17:00, mid-June–Aug until 19:00, none Oct–March); and to the archipelago called the **Elaphite Islands,** with visits to three different islands (about 250 kn with lunch, 180 kn without, several boats depart daily around 10:30–11:00, return around 18:00–18:30; so they can buy enough food, companies prefer you to reserve and pay a 50-kn deposit the day before).

Maritime Museum (Pomorski Muzej)—By the 15th century, when Venice's nautical dominance was on the wane, Dubrovnik emerged as a maritime power and the Mediterranean's leading shipbuilding center. The Dubrovnik-built "argosy" boat (from "Ragusa," an early name for the city) was the Cadillac of ships, frequently mentioned by Shakespeare. This small museum traces the history of Dubrovnik's most important industry with contracts, maps, paintings, and models—all well-described in English. The main floor takes you through the 18th century, and the easy-to-miss upstairs covers the 19th and 20th centuries. Boaters will find the museum particularly interesting (35 kn, covered by 40-kn or 50-kn combo-ticket, 5-kn English booklet, hours depend on demand, usually March–Oct daily 9:00–18:00, Nov–Feb shorter hours and closed Sun, upstairs in St. John's Fort, at far—or south—end of Old Port, tel. 020/323-904).

Aquarium (Akvarij)—Dubrovnik's aquarium, housed in the cavernous St. John's Fort, is an old-school place, with 27 tanks on one floor. A visit here allows you a close look at the local marine life, and provides a cool refuge from the midday heat (30 kn, kids-10 kn, English descriptions, daily July–Aug 9:00–21:00, progressively shorter hours off-season until 9:00–13:00 Nov–March, ground floor of St. John's Fort, enter from Old Port).

Between the Stradun and the Mainland

These two museums are a few steps off the main promenade toward the mainland.

▲**Synagogue Museum (Sinagoga-Muzej)**—When Jews were forced out of Spain in 1492, a steady stream of them passed through here en route to today's Turkey. Finding Dubrovnik to be a flourishing and relatively tolerant city, many stayed. Žudioska ulica ("Jewish Street"), just inside Ploče Gate, became the ghetto in 1546. It was walled at one end, and had a gate (which would be locked at night) at the other end. Today, the same street is home to the second-oldest continuously functioning synagogue in Europe (after Prague's—see page 76), which contains Croatia's only Jewish museum. The top floor houses the synagogue itself. Notice the lattice windows that separated the women from the men (according to Orthodox Jewish tradition). Below that, a small museum with good English descriptions gives meaning to the various Torahs (including a 14th-century one from Spain) and other items—such as the written orders *(naredba)* that Jews in Nazi-era Yugoslavia had to identify their shops as Jewish-owned and wear armbands. (The Ustaše—the Nazi puppet government in Croatia—interned and executed not only Jews and Roma/Gypsies, but also Serbs and other people they considered undesirable; see page 622.) Of Croatia's 24,000 Jews, only 4,000 survived the Holocaust. Today Croatia has about 2,000 Jews, including 12 Jewish families who call Dubrovnik home. A rabbi visits this synagogue a few times each year from Zagreb. Denis, who's usually here, can tell you more about Dubrovnik's Jewish history (15 kn, 10-kn English booklet; May–mid-Nov daily 10:00–20:00; mid-Nov–April Mon–Fri 10:00–13:00, closed Sat–Sun; Žudioska ulica 5, tel. 020/321-028).

War Photo Limited—If the tragic story of wartime Dubrovnik has you in a pensive mood, drop by this gallery with images of warfare from around the world. The brainchild of photojournalist Wade Goddard, this thought-provoking museum attempts to show the ugly reality of war through raw, often disturbing photographs taken in the field. Each summer, there are two different temporary exhibits (no permanent collection), always well-displayed on two floors. Note that the focus is not on Dubrovnik, but on war anywhere and everywhere (30 kn; June–Sept daily 9:00–21:00; May and Oct Tue–Sat 10:00–16:00, Sun 10:00–14:00, closed Mon; closed Nov–April; Antuninska 6, tel. 020/322-166, www .warphotoltd.com).

Between the Stradun and the Sea

▲**Institute for the Restoration of Dubrovnik (Zavod za Obnovu Dubrovnika)**—This small photo gallery is the closest thing Dubrovnik has to a museum about its recent war. The front two rooms display images of bombed-out Dubrovnik, each one juxtaposed with an image of the same building after being restored. The back room offers rotating exhibits about efforts to restore Dubrovnik to its pre-siege glory. The photos are too few, but still illuminating. The highlight of the exhibit is a video showing a series of breathless news reports from a British journalist stationed here during the siege. As you watch shells devastating this glorious city, and look in the eyes of its desperate citizens at their darkest hour, you might just begin to grasp what went on here not so long ago (free; June–Sept Mon–Fri 9:00–13:00, closed Sat–Sun; Oct–May the same space is used for rotating exhibits on other topics; Zuzorić 6, tel. 020/324-060).

▲**Serbian Orthodox Church and Icon Museum (Srpska Pravoslavna Crkva i Muzej Ikona)**—Round out your look at Dubrovnik's faiths (Catholic, Jewish, and Orthodox) with a visit to this house of worship—one of the most convenient places in Croatia to learn about Orthodox Christianity. Remember that people from the former Yugoslavia who follow the Orthodox faith are, by definition, ethnic Serbs. With all the (perhaps understandably) hard feelings about the recent war, this church serves as an important reminder that all Serbs aren't bloodthirsty killers.

Dubrovnik never had a very large Serb population (an Orthodox church wasn't even allowed inside the town walls until the mid-19th century). During the recent war, most Serbs fled, created new lives for themselves elsewhere, and see little reason to return. But some old-timers remain, and Dubrovnik's dwindling, aging Orthodox population is still served by this church. The candles stuck in the sand and water (to prevent fire outbreaks) represent prayers: The ones at floor level are for the deceased, while the ones higher up are for the living. The gentleman selling candles encourages you to buy and light one, regardless of your faith, so long as you do so with the proper intentions and reverence (free entry, good 20-kn English book explains the church and the museum, daily May–Sept 8:00–20:00, Oct–April 8:00–15:00, short services daily at 8:30 and 19:00, longer liturgy Sundays at 9:00, Od Puča 8). For a primer on the Orthodox faith, see the sidebar.

A few doors down, you'll find the **Icon Museum** (10 kn; May–Oct Mon–Sat 9:00–14:00, closed Sun; Nov–April Mon–Fri 9:00–14:00, closed Sat–Sun). This small collection features 78 different icons (stylized paintings of saints, generally on a golden background—a common feature of Orthodox churches) from the 15th through the 19th centuries, all identified in English. In the library—crammed with old shelves holding some 12,000 books—look for the astonishingly detailed calendar, with portraits of hundreds of saints. The gallery on the ground floor, run by Michael, sells original icons and reproductions (open longer hours than museum).

▲**Rupe Granary and Ethnographic Museum (Etnografski Muzej Rupe)**—This huge, 16th-century building was Dubrovnik's biggest granary. *Rupe* means "holes"—and it's worth the price of entry just to peer down into these cavernous underground grain stores, designed to maintain the perfect temperature to preserve

The Serbian Orthodox Church

The emphasis of this book is on the Catholic areas of the former Yugoslavia, but don't overlook the rich diversity of faiths in this region. Dubrovnik's Serbian Orthodox Church—as well as the one in Ljubljana (page 549)—offer an invaluable opportunity to learn about a faith that's often unfamiliar to visitors.

As you explore an Orthodox church, keep in mind that these churches carry on the earliest traditions of the Christian faith. Orthodox and Catholic Christianity came from the same roots, so the oldest surviving early-Christian churches (such as the stave churches of Norway) have many of the same features as today's Orthodox churches.

Notice that there are no pews. Worshippers stand through the service, as a sign of respect (though some older parishioners sit on the seats along the walls). Women stand on the left side, men on the right (equal distance from the altar—to represent that all are equal before God). The Orthodox Church uses essentially the same Bible as Catholics, but it's written in the Cyrillic alphabet, which you'll see displayed around any Orthodox church. Following Old Testament Judeo-Christian tradition, the Bible is kept on the altar behind the iconostasis, the big screen in the middle of the room covered with curtains and icons (golden paintings of saints), which separates the material world from the spiritual one. At certain times during the service, the curtains or doors are opened so the congregation can see the Holy Book.

Unlike many Catholic church decorations, Orthodox icons are not intended to be lifelike. Packed with intricate symbolism, and cast against a shimmering golden background, they're meant to remind viewers of the metaphysical nature of Jesus and the saints rather than their physical form, which is considered irrelevant. You'll almost never see a statue, which is thought to overemphasize the physical world...and, to Orthodox people, feels a little too close to violating the commandment, "Thou shalt not worship graven images." Orthodox services generally involve chanting (a dialogue that goes back and forth between the priest and the congregation), and the church is filled with the evocative aroma of incense.

The incense, chanting, icons, and standing up are all intended to heighten the experience of worship. While many Catholic and Protestant services tend to be more of a theoretical and rote consideration of religious issues (come on—don't tell me you've never dozed through the sermon), Orthodox services are about creating a religious experience. Each of these elements does its part to help the worshipper transcend the physical world and enter into communion with the spiritual one.

the seeds (63 degrees Fahrenheit). When the grain had to be dried, it was moved upstairs—where today you'll find a surprisingly well-presented Ethnographic Museum, with tools, jewelry, clothing, instruments, painted eggs, and other folk artifacts from Dubrovnik's colorful history (35 kn, covered by 40-kn or 50-kn combo-ticket; June–Oct daily 9:00–18:00; Nov–May Mon–Sat 9:00–14:00, closed Sun). The museum hides several blocks uphill from the main promenade, toward the sea (climb up Široka—the widest side street from the Stradun—which becomes Od Domina on the way to the museum).

ACTIVITIES

Swimming and Sunbathing—If the weather's good and you've had enough of museums, spend a sunny afternoon at the beach. There are no sandy beaches on the mainland near Dubrovnik, but there are lots of suitable pebbly options, plus several concrete perches. The easiest and most atmospheric place to take a dip is right off the Old Town. From the Old Port and its breakwater, uneven steps clinging to the outside of the wall lead to a series of great sunbathing and swimming coves (and even a showerhead sticking out of the town wall). Another delightful rocky beach hangs onto the outside of the Old Town's wall (with a smaller branch of Cold Drinks "Buža," described on page 674): Climb the steep steps behind the cathedral, and look for the door in the wall with the

No Toples No Nudist sign. Locals prefer to swim on Lokrum Island (where Toples and Nudist are most certainly permitted), because there are fewer tourists there. Other convenient public beaches are Banje (just outside Ploče Gate, east of Old Town) and the beach in the middle of Lapad Bay (near Hotel Kompas).

SHOPPING

Most souvenirs sold in Dubrovnik—from lavender sachets to plaster models of the Old Town—are pretty tacky. Whatever you buy, prices are much higher along the Stradun than on the side streets.

A classy alternative to the knickknacks is a typical local jewelry called *Konavoske puče* ("Konavle buttons"). Sold as earrings, pendants, and rings, these distinctive and fashionable filigree-style pieces consist of a sphere with several small posts. While they're sold around town, it's least expensive to buy them on the street called Od Puča, which runs parallel to the Stradun two blocks

toward the sea (near the Serbian Orthodox Church). The high concentration of jewelers along this lane keeps prices reasonable. You'll find the "buttons" in various sizes, in both silver (affordable) and gold (pricey).

You'll also see lots of jewelry made from red coral, which can only be gathered in small amounts from two small islands in northern Dalmatia. This means that particularly large chunks of coral are likely imported. To know what you're getting, shop at an actual jeweler instead of a souvenir shop.

ENTERTAINMENT

Musical Events

Dubrovnik annually hosts a full schedule of events for its Summer Festival (July 10–Aug 25, www.dubrovnik-festival.hr). Lovers of classical music enjoy the Rachlin & Friends festival in September (www.julianrachlin.com). But the town also works hard to offer traditional music outside of festival time. From April through October, free open-air folk music shows take place each Saturday or Sunday around 11:00 in the area near St. Blaise's Church. For something a little more formal, spirited folk-music concerts are performed for tourists twice weekly in the Lazareti (old quarantine building) just outside the Old Town's Ploče Gate (80 kn, usually at 21:30). About one night per week through the winter, you can watch the Dubrovnik Symphony Orchestra (usually at the Rector's Palace in good weather, or Dominican Monastery in bad weather). And since Dubrovnik is trying to become a year-round destination, the city also offers tourist-oriented musical events somewhere in town (often at a hotel) most nights throughout the winter. For the latest on any of these events, check the events listings in the *Dubrovnik Riviera* brochure, or ask the TI.

Nightlife

Dubrovnik's Old Town is one big, romantic parade of relaxed and happy people out strolling. The main drag is brightly lit and packed with shops, cafés, and bars, all open late. This is a fun scene. And if you walk away from the crowds, out on the port, or even up on the city walls, you'll be alone with the magic of the Pearl of the Adriatic. Everything feels—and is—very safe after dark.

If you're looking for a memorable bar after dark, consider these:

Cold Drinks "Buža," clinging scenically to Dubrovnik's outer wall, is an ideal place for a drink day or night (see listing on page 674).

Jazz Caffè Troubadour is cool, owned by a former member of the Dubrovnik Troubadours—Croatia's answer to the Beatles (or, perhaps more accurately, the Turtles). On balmy evenings, 50 chairs with tiny tables are set up theater-style in the dreamy alley facing the musicians. Step inside to see old 1970s photos of the band (40–60-kn drinks, daily 9:00–24:00, live jazz nightly from about 22:00 or whenever the boss shows up, often live piano at other times, next to cathedral at Bunićeva Poljana 2, tel. 020/323-476).

Hemingway's Cocktail Bar, a few steps from the cathedral on Pred Dvorom, is an outdoor lounge with big overstuffed chairs at a fine vantage point for people-watching (50–60-kn cocktails, daily 9:00–2:00 in the morning, shorter hours off-season, across from Rector's Palace).

For a younger scene, head to **Fresh,** just off the Stradun (see listing on page 673). The nearby **Africa** nightclub (just up the street) keeps the volume pumping into the wee hours.

Movies

The Old Town has a pair of movie theaters which show American blockbusters (usually in English with Croatian subtitles, unless the film's animated or for kids). The **Sloboda** cinema, right under the Bell Tower on Luža Square, is nothing special. But in good weather, head for the fun outdoor **Jadran** cinema, where you can lick ice cream (B.Y.O.) while you watch a movie with a Dubrovnik-mountaintop backdrop. This is a cheap, casual, and very Croatian scene, where people smoke and chat, and the neighbors sit in their windowsills to watch the movie (most nights in summer only, shows begin shortly after sundown; in the Old Town near the Pile Gate). To find out what's playing, look for posters around town.

SLEEPING

You basically have two options in Dubrovnik: a centrally located room in a private home *(soba);* or a resort hotel on a distant beach, a bus ride away from the Old Town. Since Dubrovnik hotels are generally a poor value, I highly recommend giving the *sobe* a careful look. For locations, see the map on page 650.

Be warned that the Old Town is home to many popular discos. My listings are quieter than the norm, but if you're finding a place on your own, you may discover you have a late-night soundtrack—particularly if you're staying near the Stradun.

No matter where you stay, prices are much higher mid-June through mid-September, and highest in July and August. Reserve

---

Sleep Code

(€1 = about $1.40, 5 kn = about $1, country code: 385, area code: 020)

S = Single, **D** = Double/Twin, **T** = Triple, **Q** = Quad, **b** = bathroom. The modest tourist tax (7 kn or €1 per person, per night, lower off-season) is not included in these rates. Hotels generally accept credit cards and include breakfast in their rates, while most *sobe* accept only cash and don't offer breakfast. Everyone listed here speaks English.

To help you sort easily through these listings, I've divided the rooms into three categories based on the price for a standard double room with bath in peak season:

$$$ **Higher Priced**—Most rooms 700 kn (€97) or more.
  $$ **Moderately Priced**—Most rooms between
                     400–700 kn (€55–97).
   $ **Lower Priced**—Most rooms 400 kn (€55) or less.

---

ahead in these peak times, especially during the Summer Festival (July 10–Aug 25 every year). Some accommodations prefer to list their rates in euros (and I've followed suit), but you'll pay in kunas.

Sobe (Private Rooms): A Dubrovnik Specialty

In Dubrovnik, you'll almost always do better with a *soba* than with a hotel. Before you choose, carefully read the information on page 616. All of my favorite *sobe* are run by friendly English-speaking Croatians, and are inside or within easy walking distance of the Old Town. There's a range of places, from simple and cheap rooms where you'll share a bathroom, to downright fancy places with private facilities and satellite TV, where you can be as anonymous as you like. Most *sobe* don't include breakfast, so I've listed some suggestions on page 674.

Book direct—middleman agencies tack on fees, making it more expensive for both you and your host. Note that many Dubrovnik *sobe* hosts might ask you to send them a deposit to secure your reservation. Sometimes they'll accept your credit-card number; others might want you to mail them a check or traveler's check (the better option) or wire them the money (which can be expensive). While it's a bit of a hassle, this request is reasonable and part of the experience of sleeping at a *soba*. Remember that you'll usually need to pay your bill in cash, not with a credit card.

In the Old Town, Above the Stradun Promenade

These excellent values are all a steep hike up from the Stradun.

$$$ **Apartments Paviša,** next door to Villa Ragusa (described next) and run by Pero and Davorka Paviša, has three good rooms at the top of the Old Town (July–Aug: Db-€100, May–June and Sept–Oct: Db-€70, Nov–April Db-€50, 10 percent discount if you book direct with this book, 20 percent more for 1- or 2-night stays, no breakfast, cash only, air-con, lots of stairs, Žudioska ulica 19, mobile 098-427-399 or 098-175-2342, www.apartmentspavisa.com, davorka.pavisa@du.t-com.hr). They also have two more rooms in the Viktorija neighborhood, about a 20-minute mostly uphill walk beyond the Ploče Gate east of the Old Town. While it's a long-but-scenic walk into town, the views from these apartments are spectacular (same prices as in-town rooms, Frana Supila 59, bus stop nearby).

$$ **Villa Ragusa** offers the nicest rooms for the price in the Old Town. Pero and Valerija Carević have renovated a 600-year-old house at the top of town that was damaged during the war. The five comfortable, modern rooms come with atmospheric old wooden beams, antique furniture, and thoughtful touches. There are three doubles with bathrooms (including a top-floor room with breathtaking Old Town views for no extra charge—request when you reserve), and two singles that share a bathroom. Because the Carevićs live off-site, be sure to let them know when you'll arrive so they can let you in (July–Aug: S-€40, Db-€80; May–June and Sept–Oct: S-€30, Db-€70; Nov–April: S-€25, Db-€50; 30 percent more for 1- or 2-night stays, €8 breakfast can be eaten here or at nearby Stradun café, cash only, air-con, lots of stairs with no elevator, Žudioska ulica 15, tel. 020/453-834, mobile 098-765-634, http://villaragusa.netfirms.com, villa .ragusa@du.t-com.hr). Pero offers his guests airport transfers for a very reasonable €20.

$$ **Lidija Matić** rents two clean, well-appointed apartments on a plant-filled lane—the steepest and most appealing stretch of stairs leading up from the Stradun. Lidija's sweet personality is reflected in the cheerful rooms, which are a great value if you don't mind the hike (July–Aug: Db-€70, May–June and Sept: Db-€55, Oct: Db-€50, Nov–April: Db-€40, these special prices for Rick Steves readers, 20 percent more for 1- or 2-night stays, no breakfast, cash only, air-con, climb the stairs past Dolce Vita gelato shop to Nalješkovićeva 22, tel. 020/321-493, mobile 091-517-7048, maroje.matic1@du.t-com.hr).

In the Old Town, near St. John's Fort
These three places are near St. John's Fort, at the end of the Old Port. To find the Karmen and Zijadić apartments from the cathedral, walk toward the big fort tower along the inside of the wall (follow signs for *akvarji*).

\$\$\$ Karmen Apartments, well-run by a Brit named Marc and his Croatian wife Silva, offers four apartments just inside the big fort. The prices are too high, and they're in all the guidebooks, but the apartments are big, well-equipped, and homey-feeling, each with a bathroom and kitchen. The decor is eclectic but tasteful, and Marc and Silva are good hosts (June–Sept: Db-€145, April–May and Oct–Nov: Db-€110, less Dec–March, smaller apartment-30 percent less, 20 percent more for 1- or 2-night stays, no breakfast, cash only, air-con, free Wi-Fi, near the aquarium at Bandureva 1, tel. 020/323-433, www.karmendu.com, apartments @karmendu.tk).

\$\$\$ Apartments Amoret has pricey but good apartments in two different buildings: Two over Amoret Restaurant in front of the cathedral (at Restićeva 2), and seven more sharing an inviting terrace on a quiet, untouristy lane a few blocks east (at Dinka Ranjine 5). The furnishings are a tasteful mix of traditional and modern, and it's run with class by the Dabrović family. Since they don't live on-site, arrange a meeting time and place when you reserve (July–Aug: Db-€90–110, June and Sept: Db-€80–100, May and Oct: Db-€60–80, Nov–April: Db-€50–70, price depends on size, 30 percent more for 1-night stays, 20 percent more for 2-night stays, 10 percent more for 3-night stays, cash only, air-con, tel. & fax 020/324-005, mobile 091-530-4910, www.dubrovnik-amoret .com, dubrovnik@post.t-com.hr).

\$\$ Renata Zijadić, a friendly mom who speaks good English, offers four well-located rooms with slanting floors, funky colors, and over-the-top antique furniture. A single and a double (both with great views) share one bathroom; another double features an ornate old cabinet, air-conditioning, and its own bathroom; and the top-floor apartment comes with low ceilings, air-conditioning, and fine vistas (July–Aug: S-220 kn, D-330 kn, Db-440 kn, apartment-650 kn; June and Sept: S-200 kn, D-300 kn, Db-365 kn, apartment-550 kn; cheaper Oct–May; no extra charge for 1- or 2-night stays, no breakfast, cash only, follow signs for wall access and walk up the steps marked *ulica Stajeva* going over the street to find Stajeva 1; tel. 020/323-623, www.dubrovnik-online.com /house_renata, renatadubrovnik@yahoo.com).

In the Pile Neighborhood, Just Outside the Old Town

There's a concentration of good *sobe* just outside the Old Town's Pile Gate. The Pile (PEE-leh) neighborhood offers all the conveniences of the modern world (grocery store, bus stop, post office, travel agency, etc.), just steps from Dubrovnik's magical Old Town. The first two places are uphill (away from the water) from the Pile Gate's bus stop; the rest cluster around a quiet, no-name cove near Restaurant Orhan. To reach this cove, leave the Pile Gate TI to

the right (on ulica u Pilama), then
go down the first flight of stairs on
your right; wind down the lanes to
the little bay and the lane called
Od Tabakarije.

**$$ Jadranka and Milan
Benussi,** a middle-aged profes-
sional couple, rent four rooms in
a quiet, traffic-free neighborhood. Their stony-chic home, com-
plete with a leafy terrace, is a steep 10-minute hike above the Old
Town—close enough to be convenient, but far enough to take you
away from the bustle and into a calm residential zone. Jadranka
speaks good English, enjoys visiting with her guests, and gives
her place a modern Croatian class unusual for *sobe* (July–Aug:
small Db-440 kn, big Db-520 kn, small apartment-680 kn, big
apartment with balcony-740 kn; June and Sept: small Db-400 kn,
big Db-480 kn, small apartment-630 kn, big apartment-700 kn;
cheaper Oct–May; 20 percent more for stays less than 4 nights,
no breakfast, cash only, all rooms have air-con and kitchenettes,
Miha Klaića 10, tel. 020/429-339, mobile 098-928-1300, www
.dubrovnik-online.com/apartments_benussi, mbenussi@inet.hr).
To find the Benussis, go to the big Hilton hotel just outside the Pile
Gate (across from the TI). Walk up the little stepped lane called
Marijana Blažića at the upper-left corner of the Hilton cul-de-sac.
When that lane dead-ends, go left up ulica Don Iva Bjelokosića
(more steps) until you see a little church on the left. The Benussi's
house is just before this church.

$$ Villa San, a lesser value run by the Ahmić family, offers
four apartments and one tiny bunk-bed room overlooking the bus
stop directly in front of the Pile Gate (July–Aug: Db-€70–90,
May–June and Sept–Oct: Db-€60–80, Nov–April: Db-€50–70,
price depends on room size, 20 percent more for 1- or 2-night stays,
pricier giant "penthouse" apartment, singles discouraged, no breakfast, cash only, air-con, above the bank behind the bus stop—go
around left side to find entrance at Tiha 2, tel. 020/411-884, mobile
098-178-5620, www.villa-san.com, info@villa-san.com).

$$ Nedjeljka Benussi, Jadranka Benussi's sister-in-law (see
above), rents three modern, straightforward rooms sharing two
bathrooms and a pretty view (May–Oct: D-400–500 kn, T-550
kn; Nov–April: D-300–400 kn, T-450 kn; price depends on room
size, no extra charge for 1-night stays, no breakfast, cash only, Sv.
Đurđa 4, tel. 020/423-062, mobile 098-170-5699).

$ Paulina Čumbelić is a kind, gentle woman renting four
old-fashioned rooms in her homey, clean, and peaceful house
(July–Aug: S-200 kn, D-300 kn, T-450 kn; other times: S-170
kn, D-260 kn, T-350 kn; 20 percent more for 1- or 2-night stays,

no breakfast, cash only, closed in winter, Od Tabakarije 2, tel. 020/421-327, mobile 091-530-7985).

$ Restaurant Orhan Guest House allows hotel anonymity at *sobe* prices. Its 11 simple rooms—in a couple of different buildings around the corner from the restaurant—are well located and quiet, with modern bathrooms (some also have air-con). As the rooms are an afterthought to the restaurant, don't expect a warm welcome (April–Sept: Sb or Db-400 kn, Oct–March: Sb or Db-300 kn, 100 kn more for 1-night stays, breakfast-50 kn, cash only, Od Tabakarije 1, tel. & fax 020/414-183, www.restaurant-orhan.com, restoran.orhan@yahoo.com). The restaurant is also a good spot for a scenic meal—see the listing on page 672.

Beyond the Ploče Gate, East of the Old Town

To reach these options, you'll go through the Ploče Gate and walk along the road stretching east from the Old Town (with fine views back on the Old Port). This area is shared by giant waterfront luxury hotels and residential areas, so it has a bit less character than the Pile and Old Town listings (which I prefer).

$$ Apartments Paviša, described on page 664, has two fine apartments in the Viktorija neighborhood about a 20-minute walk or short bus ride from town.

$$ Villa Adriatica has four very old-fashioned rooms just outside the Ploče Gate, a few steps from the Old Town. The rooms share a terrace with sweeping Old Port views and a common living room and kitchen furnished with museum-piece antiques. Check in at the Perla Adriatic travel agency, just outside the Ploče Gate (July–Aug: Db-€85–95, June and Sept: Db-€80–90, May and Oct: Db-€75–85, Nov–April: Db-€55–60, price depends on size and view, some rowdy street noise in cheaper rooms—especially on weekends, 20 percent more for 1- or 2-night stays, no breakfast, cash only, air-con, Frana Supila 4, tel. 020/411-962, fax 020/422-766, mobile 098-812-451, www.dubrovnik-online.com/villa _adriatica, miroslav.tomsic@du.t-com.hr, Tomšić family—son Teo speaks the best English).

Sobe-Booking Websites and Agencies

Several websites put you in touch with Dubrovnik's *sobe* and apartments. Of course, you'll save yourself and your host money if you book direct, but these sites are convenient. For example, www .dubrovnikapartmentsource.com, run by an American couple, offers a range of carefully selected, well-described accommodations. You can browse a variety of options, then reserve your choice and pay a non-refundable deposit by credit card. Another, bigger operation—with a wider selection but less personal attention—is www.adriatica.net.

If you arrive without a reservation and the TI isn't too busy, they might be able to call around and find you a *soba* for no charge. Otherwise, just about any travel agency in town can help you, on the spot or in advance...for a fee. **Atlas** is the biggest company (figure Db-€50 and apartment-€60–80 in June–Sept, €10 less in shoulder season; for more on Atlas, see page 640).

Hotels

If you must stay in a hotel, you have only a few good options. There are just two hotels inside the Old Town walls—and one of them charges $500 a night (Pucić Palace, www.thepucicpalace.com). Any big, resort-style hotel within walking distance of the Old Town will run you at least €200. These inflated prices drive most visitors to Boninovo Bay or the Lapad Peninsula, a bus ride west of the Old Town. In the mass-tourism tradition, most European visitors choose to take the half-board option at their hotel (i.e., dinner in the hotel restaurant). This can be convenient and a good value, but I'd rather not be tied down to eating at my hotel—the Old Town is full of well-priced little eateries worth going out of your way for (see "Eating" on page 671).

In the Old Town

$$$ Hotel Stari Grad knows it's the only real hotel option in the Old Town—and charges accordingly. It has eight modern yet nicely old-fashioned rooms a half-block off the Old Town's main drag. The rooftop breakfast terrace (summer only) enjoys a spectacular view over orange tiles. This place books up fast, so reserve early (July–Sept: Sb-1,200 kn, Db-1,600 kn; April–June and Oct: Sb-900 kn, Db-1,300 kn; Nov–March: Sb-650 kn, Db-950 kn; plus silly "insurance" charge of 8 kn per person per night, 10 percent more for 1- or 2-night stays, air-con, lots of stairs with no elevator, Od Sigurate 4, tel. 020/322-244, fax 020/321-256, www .hotelstarigrad.com, info@hotelstarigrad.com).

Near Boninovo Bay

Boninovo Bay is your best bet for an affordable and well-located hotel. Above this bay are Dubrovnik's only three-star hotels within walking distance of the Old Town (not to mention the city's only official youth hostel). These places offer slightly better prices and closer proximity to the Old Town than the farther-out Lapad Bay resorts. Boninovo Bay is an uphill 20-minute walk or five-minute bus ride from the Old Town (straight up Branitelja Dubrovnika). Once you're comfortable with the buses, the location is great: From Pile Gate, take bus #1a, #3, #4, #5, #6, #6a, #8, or #9; you'll see the bay on your left as you climb the hill, then get off at the stop after the traffic light (or stay on buses #4 and #6a, which stop even closer to the Hotel R and Hotel Lero). To reach the hotels from the Boninovo bus stop, go up Pera Čingrije (the busy road running along the top of the cliff overlooking the sea). There's a super little 24-hour bakery, Pekarnica Klas, on the right (across the street from the cliff-hanging Hotel Bellevue).

$$$ Hotel R, with just 10 rooms, feels friendlier and less greedy than all the big resort hotels (July–mid-Sept: Sb-€79, Db-€123; June and late Sept: Sb-€66, Db-€102; May and Oct: Sb-€53, Db-€80; April: Sb-€46, Db-€70; closed Nov–March, 20 percent more for 1- or 2-night stays, 10 percent more for balcony, half-board-€10, air-con, free Wi-Fi, just beyond the big Hotel Lero at Iva Vojnovića 32, tel. 020/333-200, fax 020/333-208, www.hotel-r.hr, helpdesk@hotel-r.hr).

$$$ Hotel Lero, 250 yards up the street from the bus stop, has 140 recently renovated rooms. Choose between sea views with some road noise, or quieter back rooms (early July–late Sept: Sb-€110, Db-€140; May–early July and late Sept–mid-Oct: Sb-€85, Db-€106; even less in winter; in busy times, you may be quoted more than these rates—try asking for a better deal; air-con, elevator, pay Internet access, free Wi-Fi in lobby, €5 for dinner, Iva Vojnovića 14, tel. 020/341-333, fax 020/332-123, www.hotel-lero.hr, sales@hotel-lero.hr).

$ Dubrovnik's fine **Youth Hostel** is quiet, modern, and well run by proud manager Laura. It's institutional, with 82 beds in 19 fresh, woody dorms and few extra hostel amenities (bed in 4- to 6-bed dorm: 115 kn July–Aug, 100 kn June and Sept, 90 kn May and Oct, 80 kn Nov–April; 10 kn more for non-members, includes sheets, breakfast-5 kn; open daily June–Oct 7:00–2:00 in the morning, Nov–May 8:00–14:00 & 18:00–20:00; up the steps at ulica bana Jelačića 15–17, tel. 020/423-241, fax 020/412-592, www.hfhs.hr, dubrovnik@hfhs.hr). From the Boninovo bus stop, go down Pera Čingrije toward Hotel Bellevue, but take the first right uphill onto ulica bana Jelačića and look for signs up to the hostel on your left, on ulica Vinka Sagrestana. Several houses nearby rent rooms to those who prefer a double...and pick off hostelers as they approach.

In Lapad

For a real resort-style vacation (at premium prices), many travelers call the touristy area around Lapad Bay home. The main street running through the middle of this scene, called Šetalište Kralja Zvonimira, is a nicely pedestrianized people-zone buzzing with tourists, restaurants, cafés, and mild diversions. From the bus stop, the main drag leads to a pleasant pebble beach good for swimming and a romantic bayside path. While I much prefer sleeping near the Old Town, this is an appealing place to be on vacation (even if

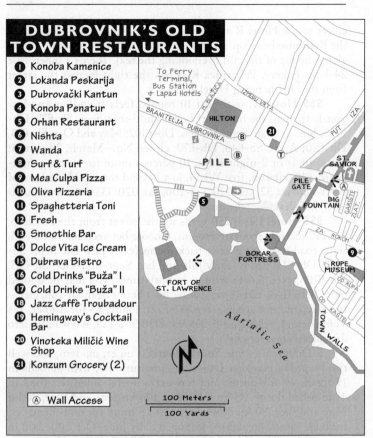

DUBROVNIK'S OLD TOWN RESTAURANTS

1. Konoba Kamenice
2. Lokanda Peskarija
3. Dubrovački Kantun
4. Konoba Penatur
5. Orhan Restaurant
6. Nishta
7. Wanda
8. Surf & Turf
9. Mea Culpa Pizza
10. Oliva Pizzeria
11. Spaghetteria Toni
12. Fresh
13. Smoothie Bar
14. Dolce Vita Ice Cream
15. Dubrava Bistro
16. Cold Drinks "Buža" I
17. Cold Drinks "Buža" II
18. Jazz Caffè Troubadour
19. Hemingway's Cocktail Bar
20. Vinoteka Miličić Wine Shop
21. Konzum Grocery (2)

Ⓐ Wall Access

100 Meters

100 Yards

the Old Town weren't just a short bus ride away). To get here from the Old Town's Pile gate, pile onto bus #6 with all the other tourists and get off at the Pošta Lapad stop (poorly marked—after bus turns left away from the big harbor, watch for low-profile yellow *pošta* sign on left; runs 4–6/hr until 24:30, trip takes 15 min). A taxi costs about 60 kn.

$$$ Small Hotels in Lapad: In this area, I like three new-ish, interchangeable small hotels. While not affiliated with each other, each one has similar amenities—air-con, elevator (except in Hotel Dubrovnik), Internet access either in lobby or in room—and similar prices (around Db-1,000–1,400 kn in July–Sept, but prices are very soft and can flex with demand, season, and length of stay; check online for the latest, and ask for a deal when you reserve). **Hotel Aquarius,** hiding a block off the main drag, has 24 comfortable, plush-feeling rooms and an inviting terrace out front (Mata Vodopića 8, tel. 020/456-111, fax 020/456-100, www.hotel-aquarius.net, stjepanka@hotel-aquarius.net). **Hotel**

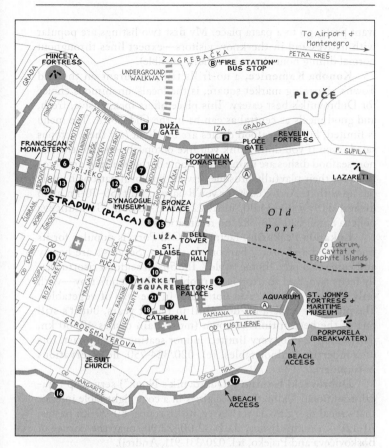

To Airport &
Montenegro

Perla, right on the main drag, has 25 modern rooms (tel. 020/438-244, fax 020/438-245, www.perla-dubrovnik.com, info@perla-dubrovnik.com). **Hotel Dubrovnik,** two doors up from the Perla, has 25 simpler rooms (tel. 020/435-030, fax 020/435-999, www.hoteldubrovnik.hr, info@hoteldubrovnik.com).

EATING

In the Old Town

Actual "local" restaurants don't exist in the very touristy Old Town, so I've selected eateries that provide better quality, value, or variety than the typical crank-'em-out fish joints and pizzerias. Anywhere you eat, breezy outdoor seating is a no-brainer, and scrawny, adorable kittens beg for table scraps.

Traditional Seafood Restaurants

In general, seafood restaurants are good only at seafood; if you

Dubrovnik

want pasta, go to a pasta place. My first two listings are popular with natives and in-the-know visitors—expect lines throughout normal dining hours (no reservations possible).

Konoba Kamenice, a no-frills fish restaurant on the Old Town's charming market square, is the locals' unanimous choice for Dubrovnik's best eatery. This place offers inexpensive, fresh, and good meals as central as can be in the Old Town. The menu is limited, but the seafood dishes are excellent (try their octopus salad, even if you don't think you like octopus)—though the few non-seafood dishes are uninspired. Some of the waitstaff are notorious for their playfully brusque service, but loyal patrons happily put up with it. Arrive early, or you'll have to wait (50–70-kn main dishes, daily 7:00–24:00, until 22:00 off-season, Gundulićeva poljana 8, tel. 020/323-682, no reservations).

Lokanda Peskarija, facing the Old Port, is popular for its fine seafood and pretty harborside setting. Servings are hearty and come in a pot, "home-style." The 50-kn seafood risotto easily feeds two, and sharing is no problem. The menu's tiny—with only seafood options, and not much in the way of vegetables. The place has gone a bit downhill in recent years, but it's still one of the best options in town (most main dishes 40–60 kn, daily 12:00–24:00, very limited indoor seating fills up fast, lots of wonderful outdoor tables, tel. 020/324-750, no reservations in summer).

Dubrovački Kantun ("Dubrovnik's Nook") serves up typical, traditional Dalmatian specialties in a cozy eight-table interior that's ideal on rainy days (hearty 30-kn soups, 60–70-kn pastas, 70–120-kn main dishes, daily 12:00–23:00, near the corner of Boškovićeva and Prijeko, tel. 020/331-911, Andrej).

Konoba Penatur hides along the side of St. Blaise's Church. This family-run eatery serves good, unpretentious food with shaded outdoor seating (60–110-kn main dishes, daily 11:00–24:00, Lučarica 2, tel. 020/323-700, Obrvan and Radić families).

Orhan Restaurant, overlooking the tranquil cove at the Pile neighborhood outside the Old Town, feels just beyond the tourist crush. It features disinterested service and forgettable food, but great views on a large terrace (reserve a seat here in advance). Watch the people walk the Old Town walls across the cove (50–100-kn pastas, 85–150-kn main dishes, daily 8:00–23:00, cash only, Od Tabakarije 1, tel. 020/414-183).

The Old Town's "Restaurant Row": Prijeko Street

The street called Prijeko, a block toward the mainland from the Stradun promenade, is lined with outdoor, tourist-oriented eateries—each one with a huckster out front trying to lure in diners. (Many of them aggressively try to snare passersby down on the

Stradun, as well.) This is hardly a local scene, but a stroll along here is fun, the atmosphere is lively, the sales pitches are entertainingly desperate, and the food is generally acceptable (if overpriced). While most places are interchangeably mediocre, the following places are out of the ordinary.

Nishta, featuring a short menu of delicious vegetarian fusion cuisine with Asian flair, offers a welcome change of pace from the Dalmatian seafood-pasta-pizza rut. Even if you're not a vegetarian, busy Swiss owner/chef Gildas' place is worth a visit (50–80-kn main dishes, daily 11:00–23:00, Prijeko 30, mobile 098-186-7440).

Wanda, run by Croatian-American-Swedish couple Goran and Katarina, works hard to offer inventive variations on the same old dishes. The menu, with fresh seasonal specials, satisfies food snobs (60–90-kn pastas, 120–200-kn main dishes, daily 12:00–15:00 & 18:00–23:00, Prijeko 8, mobile 098-944-9318). They have a second, simpler, more affordable restaurant called **Surf & Turf** two blocks away (just off the Stradun) serving burgers, salads, and grilled meat and fish (40–70-kn burgers and salads, 50–100-kn lunches, 90–160-kn dinners, Žudioska ulica 4).

Pizza and Pasta

Pizza: **Mea Culpa** is popular for its cheap and tasty pizzas and salad bar; take-out is also available (huge, splittable 40–60-kn pizzas, daily 8:00–24:00, until 23:00 in winter, 2 blocks off the main drag at Za Rokom 3, tel. 020/323-430). I've also eaten well at **Oliva Pizzeria,** serving up fresh pizzas just behind St. Blaise's Church (35–60-kn pizzas, Lučarica 5, Mon–Sat 10:00–24:30, Sun 11:00–24:30, tel. 020/324-594).

Pasta: **Spaghetteria Toni** is a cozy 10-table place popular with natives and tourists. While nothing fancy, they offer good pastas at reasonable prices (also has ample outdoor seating, 40–60-kn pastas, 35–50-kn salads, daily in summer 11:00–23:00, closed Sun in winter, closed Jan, Nikole Božidarevića 14, tel. 020/323-134).

Budget Options

Wraps and Smoothies: For a break from the grilled fish and pizza, sink your teeth into an American-style wrap. **Fresh,** a lively, popular hangout with a young backpacker following, features tasty 30-kn wraps, 20-kn smoothies, and patented "beer towers" for a powerful buzz (take-away available, daily 9:00–2:00 in the morning, Vetranićeva 4, mobile 091-896-7509). Fresh's "smoothies," while tasty, are basically party drinks. For a serious smoothie operation—where they custom-make your smoothie using fresh fruit—head a few blocks down the Stradun to **Smoothie Bar** (20–25-kn smoothies, also a low-key bar with 30-kn mixed drinks such as margaritas and mojitos, June–Sept daily 10:00–24:00, shorter hours off-season, closed Dec–Feb, Palmotićeva 5, mobile 098-186-7440; run by the Nishta people—see above).

Picnic in the Old Town: You can shop for fresh fruits and veggies at the open-air produce market (each morning near the cathedral, on the square called Gundulićeva Poljana). Supplement your picnic with grub from the cheap Konzum grocery store (one location just outside Pile Gate: Mon–Sat 7:00–21:00, Sun 8:00–20:00; another on the market square near the produce-vendors: Mon–Sat 7:00–20:00, Sun 7:00–19:00). Good picnic spots include the shaded benches overlooking the Old Port; the Porporela breakwater (beyond the Old Port and fort—comes with a swimming area, sunny no-shade benches, and views of Lokrum Island); and the green, welcoming park in what was the moat just under the Pile Gate entry to the Old Town.

Ice Cream: Dubrovnik has lots of great *sladoled*, but locals swear by the stuff at **Dolce Vita** (daily 9:00–24:00, a half-block off the Stradun at Nalješkovićeva 1A, tel. 020/321-666).

Breakfast
If you're sleeping in a *soba*, you'll likely be on your own for breakfast. Fortunately, you have plenty of cafés and pastry shops to choose from, and your host probably has a favorite she can recommend. In the Pile neighborhood, I like **Restaurant Orhan,** right on the cove (see listing above; 50 kn for omelet or continental breakfast, served daily 8:00–11:00). In the Old Town, **Dubrava Bistro**—nicknamed "Snack Bar" by locals—has great views and fine outdoor seating at the most colorful end of the Stradun (basic 35–45-kn egg dishes, daily 8:00–24:00, Placa 6, tel. 020/321-229). Some of the other restaurants listed in this "Eating" section (including Kamenice) also serve breakfast.

Drinks with a View
Cold Drinks "Buža" offers, without a doubt, the most scenic spot for a drink. Perched on a cliff above the sea, clinging like a barnacle to the outside of the city walls, this is a peaceful, shaded getaway from the bustle of the Old Town... the perfect place to watch cruise ships sail into the horizon. *Buža* means "hole in the wall"—and that's exactly what you'll have to go through to reach this place. Filled with mellow tourists and bartenders pouring wine from tiny screw-top bottles into plastic cups, it comes with castaway views and Frank Sinatra ambience. This is supposedly where Bill Gates hangs out when

he visits Dubrovnik (20–40-kn drinks, summer daily 9:00–into the wee hours, closed mid-Nov–Jan). To get here from the cathedral area, hike up the grand staircase to St. Ignatius' Church, then go left to find the lane that runs along the inside of the wall. From here, you can head right along the lane to the main Buža (look for the *Cold Drinks* sign pointing to a literal hole in the wall); or, for the lesser-known Buža II—smaller and with steep concrete steps leading down into the sea, good for swimmers or when the main Buža is full—go left along the same lane.

On Lapad Bay

If you want a break from the Old Town, consider venturing to Lapad Bay. The ambience is pleasant and Lapad is worth an evening stroll (for details on getting here, see page 669 in "Sleeping"). This area's main drag, **Šetalište Kralja Zvonimira,** is an amazingly laid-back pedestrian lane where bars have hammocks, Internet terminals are scattered through a forested park, and a folksy Croatian family ambience holds its own against the better-funded force of international tourism. Stroll from near Hotel Zagreb to the bay, marked by Hotel Kompas. From Hotel Kompas, a romantic walk—softly lit at night—leads past some splurge restaurants along the bay through the woods, with plenty of private little stone coves for lingering.

TRANSPORTATION CONNECTIONS

Note that the boats listed here leave from Dubrovnik's Port Gruž, a bus ride away from the Old Town (see "Arrival in Dubrovnik— By Boat," page 636).

From Dubrovnik by Big Jadrolinija Car Ferry: The big boats leave Dubrovnik in the morning and go to **Korčula** (5/ week July–Sept, 4/week June, 2/week Oct–May, 3–4 hrs), **Stari Grad** on Hvar Island (2/week year-round, 6.5 hrs), **Split** (2/week year-round, 8.25–9.25 hrs), and **Rijeka** (2/week year-round, 21 hrs including overnight from Split to Rijeka). Boat schedules are subject to change—confirm your plans at a local TI, or see www .jadrolinija.hr.

From Dubrovnik by Speedy *Nona Ana* Catamaran: This handy service connects Dubrovnik to popular islands to the north (Mljet, Korčula, and Lastovo). In the summer (June–Sept), it departs Dubrovnik each morning and heads for **Sobra** and **Polače** (1.75 hrs, 50 kn one-way) on Mljet Island. Four days per week, it continues to **Korčula** (2.75 hrs, 55 kn), and two days per week, it also reaches **Lastovo Island** (4 hrs, 60 kn). In the winter (Oct– May), the boat goes daily to **Sobra** on Mljet, and twice weekly to the more convenient **Polače** (though not to Korčula or Lastovo).

The catamaran leaves from Dubrovnik's Port Gruž (buy tickets at the kiosk next to the boat, ticket window opens 1 hour before departure; in peak season, it's smart to show up about an hour ahead to be sure you get on the boat). As this is a relatively new service and subject to change, confirm schedules at the Dubrovnik TI (or check www.gv-line.hr).

By Bus to: Split (almost hourly, generally at the top of each hour, less off-season, 5 hrs), **Korčula** (peak season: 2/day, 3.5 hrs; off-season: Mon–Sat 1/day, Sun 2/day; also consider the shuttle-bus service described on page 725), **Zagreb** (6/day, 10 hrs), **Mostar** in Bosnia-Herzegovina (3–4/day, less off-season, 4 hrs), **Kotor** in Montenegro (likely 2/day, 2.5 hrs), **Pula** and **Rovinj** (nightly, 14 hrs to Pula, 15 hrs to Rovinj). For bus information, call 060-305-070 (a pricey toll line, but worth it).

By Plane: To quickly connect remote Dubrovnik with the rest of your trip, consider a cheap flight (see "Getting to the Dalmatian Coast," page 617.) For information on Dubrovnik's airport, see page 637.

Can I Get to Greece from Dubrovnik? Not easily. Your best bet is to fly (though there are no direct flights, so you'll transfer elsewhere in Europe). Even though Croatia and Greece are nearly neighbors, no direct boats connect them, and the overland connection is extremely long and rugged.

What About Italy? Flying is the easiest option, though the only direct flight goes from Dubrovnik to Rome. You can take a direct night boat from Dubrovnik to Bari, or head to Split for more boat connections (for more on all of these boats, see page 706). The overland connection is overly long (figure 5 hrs to Split, then 5 hrs to Zagreb, then 7 hrs to Venice).

SPLIT

Dubrovnik is the darling of the Dalmatian Coast, but Split (pronounced as it's spelled) is Croatia's "second city" (after Zagreb), bustling with 189,000 people. If you've been hopping along the coast, landing in urban Split feels like a return to civilization. While most Dalmatian coastal towns seem made for tourists, Split is real and vibrant—a shipbuilding city with ugly sprawl surrounding an atmospheric Old Town, which teems with Croatians living life to the fullest.

Though today's Split throbs to a modern, young beat, its history goes way back—all the way to the Roman Empire. Along with all the trappings of a modern city, Split has some of the best Roman ruins this side of Italy. In the fourth century A.D., the Roman Emperor Diocletian (245–313) wanted to retire in his native Dalmatia, so he built a huge palace here. Eventually, the palace was abandoned. Then locals, fleeing seventh-century Slavic invaders, moved in and made themselves at home, and a medieval town sprouted from the rubble of the old palace. In the 15th century, the Venetians took over the Dalmatian Coast. They developed and fortified Split, slathering the city with a new layer of Gothic-Renaissance architecture.

But even as Split grew, the nucleus remained the ruins of Diocletian's Palace. To this day, 2,000 people live or work inside the former palace walls. A maze of narrow alleys is home to fashionable boutiques and galleries, wonderfully atmospheric cafés, and Roman artifacts around every corner.

Today's Split is struggling to decide how it fits into Croatia's new tourist-mecca image: Is it a big, drab metropolis; a

SPLIT OVERVIEW ↑ To Airport & Trogir

HRVATSKE MORNARICE

DOMOVINSKOG RATA

KAŠTELANSKA

Archaeological Museum

ZRINSKO FRANKOPANSKA

Suburban Bus Station

LOVREBEK

MAŽURANIĆEVO ŠET.

MATOŠEVA

MANDALINSKA PUT.

VUKOVARSKA

MARJAN PENINSULA

KRIŽEVA

MARMON.

OLD TOWN

SENJSKA

RIVA

ZVONIMIRA

MARASOVIĆEVA

MIHANOVIĆEVA

MEŠTROVIĆ GALLERY

PASSENGER BOAT LANDING

TRAIN STATION

MUS. OF CRO. ARCH. MONUMENTS

OBALA BRANIMIRA

OBALA KN. DOMAGOJA

BUS STATION

ŠET. IVANA MEŠTROVIĆA

City Harbor

To Kaštelet Ježinac

Bačvice Beach

N

CAR FERRY TERMINAL

Adriatic Sea

500 Meters

500 Yards   To Zadar & Rijeka   To Hvar, Korčula & Dubrovnik

no-nonsense transit point; an impressive destination in its own right, with sights to rival Dubrovnik's...or all three?

Planning Your Time

Split is Croatia's transit point—a hub for bus, boat, train, and flight connections to other destinations in the country and abroad. This means that many visitors to Dalmatia only change boats in Split. But the city is the perfect real-life contrast to the lazy, prettified Dalmatian beach resorts—it deserves a full day. Begin by strolling the remains of Diocletian's Palace, then have lunch or a coffee break along the Riva promenade. After lunch, browse the shops or visit a couple of Split's museums (the Meštrović Gallery, which is a long walk or short bus ride from the Old Town, is tops). Promenading along the Riva with the natives is *the* evening activity.

ORIENTATION

(area code: 021)

Split sprawls, but almost everything of interest to travelers is around the City Harbor (Gradska Luka). At the top of this harbor is the Old Town (Stari Grad). Between the Old Town and the sea is the Riva, a waterfront pedestrian promenade lined with cafés

and shaded by palm trees. The main ferry terminal (Trajektni Terminal) juts out into the harbor from the east side. Along the harborfront embankment between the ferry terminal and the Old Town are the long-distance bus station (Autobusni Kolodvor) and the forlorn little train station (Željeznička Stanica). West of the Old Town, poking into the Adriatic, is the lush and hilly Marjan peninsula.

Split's domino-shaped Old Town is made up of two square sections. The east half was once Diocletian's Palace, and the west half is the medieval town that sprang up next door. The shell of Diocletian's ruined palace provides a checkerboard street plan, with a gate at each end. But the streets built since are anything but straight, making the Old Town a delightfully convoluted maze (double-decker in some places). At the center of the former palace is the Peristyle square (Peristil), where you'll find the TI, cathedral, and highest concentration of Roman ruins.

Tourist Information

Split's TI is on the Peristyle square, in the very center of Diocletian's Palace (Easter–mid-Oct Mon–Sat 8:00–21:00, Sun 8:00–13:00; mid-Oct–Easter Mon–Fri 8:00–20:00, Sat 8:00–13:00, closed Sun; tel. 021/345-606, www.visitsplit.com). Pick up the free town map, monthly events guide, and other materials. The TI also sells books, maps, and the Splitcard (museum discount card—not worth considering for most visits).

Arrival in Split

For all the details on getting to the Dalmatian Coast, see page 617.

By Boat, Bus, or Train: Passenger boats (such as the speedy catamarans to Hvar and Korčula) dock at the Obala Lazareta embankment right in front of the Old Town. Bigger **car ferries** use various docks along the east side of the harbor (the main terminal, Trajektni Terminal, is at the far end). If you arrive at this ferry terminal, wade through the *sobe* hawkers to the main terminal building, where you'll find ATMs, WCs, a grocery store, and offices for all of the main ferry companies, including Jadrolinija (open long hours daily).

Split's **car ferry** terminal, **bus station** (Autobusni Kolodvor), and **train station** (Željeznička Stanica) all share a busy and very practical strip of land called Obala Kneza Domagoja, on the east

Split Essentials

English	Croatian	Pronounced
Old Town	Stari Grad	STAH-ree grahd
City Harbor	Gradska Luka	GRAHD-skah LOO-kah
Harborfront Promenade	Riva	REE-vah
Peristyle (old Roman square)	Peristil	PEH-ree-steel
Soccer Team	Hajduk	HIGH-dook
Local Sculptor	Ivan Meštrović	EE-vahn MESH-troh-veech
Adriatic Sea	Jadran	YAH-drahn

side of the City Harbor. From any of them, you can see the Old Town and Riva; just walk around the harbor toward the big bell tower (about a 10-min walk). Along the way, you'll pass travel agencies, left-luggage offices, locals trying to rent rooms, a post office, and Internet cafés. Arriving or leaving from this central location, you never need to deal with the concrete, exhaust-stained sprawl of outer Split.

By Plane: Split's airport (Zračna Luka Split-Kaštela) is across the big bay (Kaštelanski Zaljev), 15 miles northwest of the center, near the town of Trogir. A bus leaves Split 90 minutes before each Croatia Airlines flight (and some other companies' flights) from the small Air Terminal near the southeast corner of Diocletian's Palace, and meets each arriving flight at the airport (30 kn, 40 min). Cheaper public buses also leave regularly from the main bus station along the east side of the harbor (15 kn, 7/day Mon–Fri, fewer Sat–Sun, 40 min). Figure on paying a hefty 250 kn for a taxi to the center. Airport info: tel. 021/203-506, www.split-airport.hr.

By Car: Drivers are treated to the ugly side of Split as they approach (don't worry—it gets better). Coming into town, begin by following *Centar* signs. The road forks while you're still outside of downtown: One way is simply marked *Centar* (west end of Old Town), while the other directs you to the bus and train stations and the ferry terminal (east end of Old Town). Ask your hotel which is more convenient (many hotels are individually signposted at the fork). If you follow the signs for the ferry terminal, you'll pop out right at the southeast corner of Diocletian's Palace (by the Green Market). For handy (but expensive) parking, continue straight when the road swings left to the ferry terminal, and you'll drive right into a parking lot just outside the palace walls (10 kn/hr).

Driving around the city center can be tricky—Split is split by its Old Town, which is welded to the harbor by the pedestrian-only Riva promenade. This means drivers needing to get 300 yards from one side of the Old Town to the other must drive about 15 minutes entirely around the center, which can be miserably clogged with traffic. A semicircular ring road makes this better than it might be. To get to the west end, you'll go through a tunnel under the Marjan peninsula. To reach the car-ferry terminal (east side), follow *Trajektni* signs (look for the tiny ferry icon).

Helpful Hints

Internet Access: Internet cafés are plentiful in the Old Town; look for signs, especially around the Peristyle square. Closer to the stations and ferry terminal is **Backpacker C@fé,** run by Australian Steve Potter. This place has Internet access, coffee and drinks with outdoor eating, and used paperbacks for sale (30 kn/hr, daily July–Aug 6:00–23:00, shoulder season 6:30–22:00, even shorter hours off-season, near the beginning of Obala Kneza Domagoja, tel. 021/338-548). Modrulj Launderette (below) also has Internet access.

Post Office: A modern little post office is next to the bus station (Mon–Sat 7:00–19:00, closed Sun, on Obala Kneza Domagoja).

Laundry: Modrulj Launderette, a rare coin-operated launderette, is well run by an Australian couple, Shane and Julie (self-service-50 kn/load, full-service-75 kn/load, air-con, Internet access, left-luggage service; April–Oct daily 8:00–20:00; Nov–March Mon–Sat 9:00–17:00, closed Sun; Šperun 1, tel. 021/315-888). It's conveniently located just off the harbor at the west end of the Old Town, near the recommended Šperun and Konoba Varoš restaurants—handy if multitasking is your style.

Travel Agency: Turistički Biro, between the two halves of the Old Town on the Riva, books *sobe* and hotels, sells guidebooks and maps, and sells tickets for excursions (mid-June–Sept Mon–Fri 8:00–21:00, Sat 8:00–20:00, open Sun 9:00–14:00 mid-July–mid-Sept only, otherwise closed Sun; Oct–mid-June Mon–Fri 8:00–20:00, Sat 8:00–13:00, closed Sun; Riva 12, tel. & fax 021/347-100, www.turistbiro-split.hr, turist .biro.split@st.t-com.hr).

Luggage Storage: The neighboring train and bus stations both have safe and efficient left-luggage services *(garderoba)*. If one is very crowded, the other may be empty—check both before waiting in a long line. At the opposite (west) end of the Old Town, Modrulj Launderette also has a left-luggage service (see above).

Wine Shop: At **Vinoteka Bouquet,** at the west end of the Riva (near the restaurants and launderette on Šperun street), knowledgeable Denis can help you pick out a bottle of Croatian wine to suit your tastes (Mon–Fri 8:30–12:30 & 17:00–20:30, Sat 9:00–13:30, closed Sun, Obala Hrvatskog Narodnog Preporoda 3, tel. 021/348-031). For a wine primer before you visit, see page 629.

Who's Hajduk?: You'll see the word *Hajduk* (HIGH-dook), and a distinctive red-and-white checkerboard circle design (or red-and-blue stripes), all over town and throughout northern Dalmatia. Hajduk Split is the fervently supported local soccer team, named for a band of highwaymen bandits who rebelled against Ottoman rule in the 17th–19th centuries. Most locals adore Hajduk as much as they loathe their bitter rivals, Dinamo Zagreb.

G'day, *Gospod*: You may notice a surprising concentration of Australians in Split. Many of them are actually Australian-born Croats, returning to the cosmopolitan capital city of their parents' Dalmatian homeland.

Getting Around Split

Most of what you'll want to see is within walking distance, but some sights (such as the Meštrović Gallery) are more easily reached by bus or taxi.

By Bus: Local buses, run by Promet, cost 9 kn per ride (or 8 kn if you buy ticket from a newsstand or Promet kiosk, ask for a *putna karta;* zone I is fine for any ride within Split, but you need the 19-kn zone IV ticket for the ride to Trogir). For a round-trip, buy a 14-kn transfer ticket, which works like two individual tickets (must buy at Promet kiosk). Validate your ticket in the machine as you board the bus. Suburban buses to towns near Split (such as Trogir) generally use the suburban bus station (Prigradski Autobusni Kolodvor), a 10-minute walk due north of the Old Town on Domovinskog rata. Bus information: www.promet-split.hr.

By Taxi: Taxis start at 20 kn, then cost around 10 kn per kilometer. Figure 50 kn for most rides within the city (for example, from the ferry terminal to most hotels)—but if going from one end of the Old Town to the other, it can be faster to walk. To call for a taxi, try Radio Taxi (tel. 021/970).

TOURS
Of Split

Walking Tours—Various new, upstart companies offer similar walking tours of Split's Old Town. Look for fliers locally. The most established is **Lifejacket Adventures,** based at Modrulj

Launderette (90 kn, April–Nov nearly nightly at 20:00—call ahead to confirm; tours depart from in front of launderette, last about 2 hours, and include a drink at the end; mobile 098-931-6400).

Local Guides—Consider hiring an insider to show you around. **Maja Benzon** does walking tours through the Old Town (500 kn/up to 2 hrs, 600 kn/3 hrs, mobile 098-852-869, maja.benzon @gmail.com). You can also hire a guide through the **guide association,** which has an office on the Old Town's Peristyle square (330 kn for 2 people on a 2-hour tour, about 50 kn per person after that, up to 575 kn maximum for the group; June–Aug Mon–Fri 9:00–13:00 & 15:00–19:00, Sat 9:00–14:00, closed Sun; May and Sept Mon–Fri 9:00–17:00, Sat 9:00–15:00, closed Sun; Oct–April generally open mornings only but closed Sun; tel. 021/360-058, tel. & fax 021/346-267, mobile 098-361-936).

From Split

Lifejacket Adventures, run by Australian couple Shane and Julie, works hard to come up with culturally meaningful excursions that connect travelers to the Croatia they came to see. Many of their trips involve a cruise on an authentic, old-fashioned *falkuša* and *leut* fishing boats. Options include a sunset cruise, or a swim and a picnic on a nearby island. They also arrange custom excursions, with a focus on kayaking, hiking, wine, history, and archaeological sites. Because their schedule is always evolving, get the latest by checking their website (www.lifejacketadventures.com), calling 098-931-6400, or stopping by Split's launderette (which Shane and Julie also run—see "Helpful Hints," earlier in this chapter).

　　Elite Travel and **Atlas Travel** offer a variety of excursions from Split (mostly full-day, about 250–600 kn). Itineraries include a tour of Split and Trogir, white-water rafting on the nearby Cetina River, the island of Brač, the island of Hvar, Brač and Hvar together, the island of Korčula, Dubrovnik, and Plitvice Lakes National Park. This can be a quick, convenient way to get to places that are time-consuming to reach by public transportation. Get information and tickets at any travel agency, such as the Turistički Biro on the Riva (see "Helpful Hints").

SELF-GUIDED WALK

▲▲▲ Diocletian's Palace (Dioklecijanova Palača)

Split's top activity is visiting the remains of Roman Emperor Diocletian's enormous retirement palace, sitting on the harbor in the heart of the city. Since the ruins themselves are now integrated into the city's street plan, exploring them is free (though you'll pay to enter a few parts—such as the cellars and the cathedral/mausoleum). Fragments of the palace are poorly marked, and there are not any good guidebooks or audioguides for tracking down the remains, making Split a good place to take a walking tour or hire a local guide (see "Tours," earlier in this chapter). This self-guided tour explains the basics. To begin the tour, stand in front of the palace (at the east end of the Riva) to get oriented.

Background: Diocletian grew up just inland from Split, in the town of Salona (Solin in Croatian)—which was then the capital of the Roman province of Dalmatia. He worked his way up the Roman hierarchy and ruled as emperor for the unusually long tenure of 20 years (A.D. 284–305). Despite all of his achievements, Diocletian is best remembered for two questionable legacies: dividing the huge empire among four emperors (which helped administer it more efficiently, but began a splintering effect that arguably led to the empire's decline); and torturing and executing Christians, including thousands right here on the Dalmatian Coast.

As Diocletian grew older, he decided to return to his homeland for retirement. (Since he was in poor health, the medicinal sulfur spring here was another plus.) His massive palace took only 11 years to build—and this fast pace required a big push (more than 2,000 slaves died during construction). Huge sections of his palace still exist, modified by medieval and modern developers alike. To get a sense of the original palace, check out the big illustration posted across from the palace entry. (Across the street at the end of the Riva, notice the big car-size model of today's Old Town, which is helpful for orientation.)

Palace Facade

The "front" of today's Split—facing the harbor—was actually the back door of Diocletian's Palace. There was no embankment in front of the palace back then, so the water came right up to this door—sort of an emergency exit by boat.

Visually trace the outline of the gigantic palace, which was more than 600 feet long on each side. On the corner to the right stands a big, rectangular guard tower (one of the original 16). To the left, the tower is gone and the corner is harder to pick out (look for the beginning of the newer-looking buildings). Erase in your mind the ramshackle two-story buildings added 200 years ago, which obscure the grandness of the palace wall.

Halfway up the facade, notice the row of 42 arched window frames (mostly filled in today). Diocletian and his family lived in the seaside half of the palace. Imagine him strolling back and forth along this fine arcade, enjoying the views of his Adriatic homeland. The inland, non-view half of the palace was home to 700 servants, bodyguards, and soldiers.

• *Now go through the door in the middle of the palace (known as the*

"Brass Gate"; under the Substructure of Diocletian's Palace *banner).
Just inside the door is the entrance to...*

Diocletian's Cellars (Podromi)

Since the palace was built on land that sloped down to the sea,
these chambers were built to level out the main floor (like a modern "daylight basement"). These cel-
lars were filled with water from three
different sources: a freshwater spring,
a sulfur spring, and the sea. Later,
medieval residents used them as a
dump. Rediscovered only in the last
century, the cellars enabled archaeologists to derive the floor plan of
some of the palace's long-gone upper
sections. Today, these underground
chambers are used for art exhibits
and a little strip of souvenir stands.
But before you go shopping, explore

the cellars at this end (15 kn, short and dry 10-kn guidebook,
some posters inside explain the site; opens daily at 9:00 and closes
June–Aug at 21:00, Sept at 20:00, May and Oct at 18:00, April at
17:00; Nov–March Mon–Sat 9:00–14:00, closed Sun).

○ **Self-Guided Tour:** First visit the **western cellars** (to the left
as you enter). Near the ticket-seller, notice the big **topographical
map** of the Split area, clearly showing the city's strategic location—with a natural harbor sheltered by tall mountains. You'll
see the former Roman city of Salona, Diocletian's birthplace, just
inland.

Then head into the labyrinthine cellars. Start by going
through the door on the right just past the ticket-seller. This takes
you into the complex's vast, vaulted **main hall**—the biggest space
in the cellars, with stout pillars to support everything upstairs.
When those first villagers took refuge in the abandoned palace
from the rampaging Slavs in 641, the elite lived upstairs, grabbing what was once the emperor's wing. They carved the rough
holes you see in the ceiling to dump their garbage and sewage.
Over the generations, the basement (where you're standing) filled
up with waste and solidified, ultimately becoming a once-stinky,
then-precious bonanza for 19th- and 20th-century archaeologists.
Today this hall is used for everything from flower and book shows
to fashion catwalks.

Exit the main hall through either of the doors on the left, turn
right down the narrow corridor, then turn left at the end of the
corridor. In this room you'll see a stone olive oil press. Continue
through a small room and into a round room, which has a headless,

DIOCLETIAN'S PALACE

1. Palace Facade View
2. Cellar Entrance (Below)
3. Passage to Peristyle (Below) & Ethnographic Museum (Above)
4. Peristyle Square
5. Entry Vestibule
6. Cathedral of St. Dominus
7. Jupiter's Temple/St. John's Baptistery
8. View up Cardo Street
9. Bishop Gregory of Nin Statue
10. Split City Museum
11. Peristil Hotel
12. Hotel Vestibul Palace (Above)
13. Hotel Slavija
14. Hotel Kaštel
15. Sobe "Base"
16. Hostel Split
17. Zlagogajnica None Pizza
18. Zlatna Vrata Pizza & Pasta
19. Ivona Ice Cream
20. Turisticki Biro Travel Agency
21. Croata Tie Shop
22. Air Terminal Bus Stop

pawless black granite sphinx—one of 13 that Diocletian brought home from Egypt (only four survive, including an intact one we'll see soon on the Peristyle square). Look up to admire the circular brickwork. Then continue straight ahead into the long room, displaying two petrified beams. Looking just overhead, you'll see holes that once held these beams to support floorboards, making this a two-story cellar.

Exit through the door at the far-right corner (near the mound of ancient garbage) to another round room, featuring a bust of

Diocletian (or is it Sean Connery?). Continue straight ahead (near the public WCs), then turn left, left, and right into the second grand hall, with more beam holes and a giant replica of a golden Diocletian coin at the far end. Exiting this hall at the end opposite the coin, you'll find an unexcavated wing—a compost pile of ancient lifestyles, awaiting the tiny shovels and toothbrushes of future archaeologists. Here you'll also see original Roman sewer pipes—square outside and round inside—designed to fit into each other to create long pipes.

From here, head back out to the exit, and cross over into the **eastern cellars** (same ticket). While this section is less organized than the western part, be sure to find the semicircular marble table used by the Romans, who—as shown in Hollywood movies—ate lying down (three would lounge and feast, while servants dished things up from the straight side). This table was found in shards around this site, and painstakingly reassembled like a giant jigsaw puzzle over four years by archaeologists who didn't even know what they were building until it was nearly done.

• *When you're finished, head back to the main gallery. Ignore the tacky made-in-Malaysia trinket shops as you head down the passage and up the stairs into the...*

Peristyle (Peristil)

This square was the centerpiece of Diocletian's Palace. As you walk up the stairs, the entry vestibule into the residence is above

your head, Diocletian's mausoleum (today's Cathedral of St. Dominus) is to your right, and the street to Jupiter's Temple is on your left. The little chapel straight ahead houses the TI, and beyond that is the narrow street to the former main entrance to the palace, the Golden Gate.

Go to the middle of the square and take it all in. The red granite pillars—which you'll see all over Diocletian's Palace—are from Egypt, where Diocletian spent many of his pre-retirement years. Imagine the pillars defining fine arcades—now obscured by medieval houses. (As the Peristyle is undergoing a lengthy restoration, you may notice some of the ruins are lighter-colored than others.) The black sphinx is the only one of Diocletian's collection of 13 that's still (mostly) intact.

• *Climb the stairs (above where you came in) into the domed, open-ceilinged...*

Entry Vestibule: Impressed? That's the idea. This was the grand entry to Diocletian's living quarters, meant to wow visitors.

Emperors were believed to be gods. Diocletian called himself "Jovius"—the son of Jupiter, the most powerful of all gods. Four times a year (at the change of the seasons), Diocletian would stand here and overlook the Peristyle. His subjects would lie on the ground in worship, praising his name and kissing his scarlet robe. Notice the four big niches at floor level, which once held statues of the four tetrarchs who ruled the unwieldy empire after Diocletian retired. The empty hole in the ceiling was once capped by a dome (long since collapsed), and the ceiling itself was covered with frescoes and mosaics.

In this grand acoustical space—and elsewhere in the Old Town—you're likely to run into a roving band of CD-selling *klapa* singers, performing traditional a cappella harmonies.

Wander out back to the harbor side through medieval buildings (some with seventh-century foundations), which evoke the way local villagers came in and took over the once-spacious and elegant palace. Back in this area, you'll find the beautifully restored new home of the **Ethnographic Museum** (described under "Sights," later in this chapter).

• *Now go back into the Peristyle square and turn right, climbing the steps to the...*

Cathedral of St. Dominus (Katedrala Sv. Duje)

The original octagonal structure was Diocletian's elaborate mausoleum, built in the fourth century. But after the fall of Rome, it was

converted into the town's cathedral. Construction on the bell tower began in the 13th century and took 300 years to complete. Before you go inside, notice the sarcophagi ringing the cathedral. In the late Middle Ages, this was prime post-mortem real estate, since being buried closer to a cathedral improved your chances of getting to heaven. On the 13th-century main doors, notice the 14 panels on each of the two wings—showing 28 scenes from the life of Christ.

Various parts of the cathedral are covered by separate tickets: 10 kn for the "treasury" (actually the fee to enter the cathedral), another 10 kn to climb the tower, and yet another 5 kn for the crypt down below. All the sights are open similar hours, but can be closed unexpectedly for services (generally open daily in summer 7:00–19:00, often closed Sat afternoons for weddings and Sun mornings for Mass; in winter daily 7:00–12:00, maybe later on request; Kraj Sv. Duje 5, tel. 021/344-121).

Buy your treasury/cathedral ticket and step inside the oldest—and likely smallest—building used as a cathedral anywhere in Christendom. Imagine the place in pre-Christian times, with Diocletian's tomb in the center. The only surviving decor from those days are the granite columns and the relief circling the base of the dome (about 50 feet up)—a ring of carvings heralding the greatness of the emperor. The small, multicolored marble pillars around the top of the pulpit (near the entry) were scavenged from Diocletian's sarcophagus. These pillars are all that remain of Diocletian's remains.

Diocletian brutally persecuted his Christian subjects. To kick off his retirement upon his arrival on the Dalmatian Coast, he had Bishop Dominus of Salona killed, along with several thousand Christians. When Diocletian died, there were riots of happiness. In the seventh century, his mausoleum became a cathedral dedicated to the martyred bishop. The extension behind the altar was added in the ninth century. The sarcophagus of St. Dominus (to the right of the altar, with early-Christian carvings) was once the cathedral's high altar. To the left of today's main altar is the impressively detailed Renaissance altar of St. Anastasius—lying on a millstone, which is tied to his neck. On Diocletian's orders, this Christian martyr was drowned in the Adriatic. Posthumous poetic justice: Now Christian saints are entombed in Diocletian's mausoleum...and Diocletian is nowhere to be found.

For another 10 kn, you can climb 183 steep steps to the top of the 200-foot-tall **bell tower.** You'll be rewarded with sweeping views of Split, but it's not for claustrophobes or those scared of heights.

If you circle down and around the right side of the cathedral, you'll find the entrance to the **crypt** (separate 5-kn ticket). This musty, domed cellar (with eerie acoustics) was originally used to level out the foundation of Diocletian's mausoleum. Later Christians turned it into another chapel. The legend you'll likely hear about Diocletian torturing and murdering Christians in this very crypt, which began about the same time this became a church, is probably false.

Jupiter's Temple/St. John's Baptistery

Remember that Diocletian believed himself to be Jovius (that's Jupiter Jr.). On exiting the mausoleum of Jovius, worshippers would look straight ahead to the temple of Jupiter. (Back then, all of these medieval buildings weren't cluttering up the view.) Make your way through the narrow alley (directly across from the cathedral entry), past another headless, pawless sphinx, to explore the small temple (5 kn, same hours as cathedral; if it's locked, go ask the guy at the cathedral to let you in).

Split

About the time the mausoleum became a cathedral, this temple was converted into a baptistery. The big 12th-century baptismal font—large enough to immerse someone (as was the tradition in those days)—is decorated with the intricate, traditional *pleter* design also used around the border of Croatia's current passport stamp. Standing above the font is a statue of St. John the Baptist counting to four by the great Croatian sculptor Ivan Meštrović (see page 695). The half-barrel vaulted ceiling, completed later, is considered the best-preserved of its kind anywhere. Every face and each patterned box is different.

• *Back at the Peristyle square, stand in front of the TI with your back to the entry vestibule. The little street just beyond the TI (going left to right) connects the east and west gates. If you've had enough Roman history, head right (east) to go through the "Silver Gate" and find Split's busy, open-air Green Market. Or, head to the left (west), which takes you to the "Iron Gate" and People's Square (see below), and, beyond that, the fresh-and-smelly fish market. But if you want to see one last bit of Roman history, continue straight ahead up the...*

Cardo

A traditional Roman street plan has two roads: Cardo (the north–south axis) and Decumanus (the east–west axis). Split's Cardo street was the most important in Diocletian's Palace, connecting the main entry with the heart of the complex. As you walk, you'll pass a bank with modern computer gear all around its exposed Roman ruins (first building on the right, look through window), a Venetian merchant's palace (a reminder that Split was dominated by Venice from the 15th century on—step into his courtyard, first gate on left), an alley to the **City Museum** (on the right—see "Sights," next page), and a fan shop for Hajduk Split, the city's extremely popular soccer team (on left).

• *Before long, you'll pass through the...*

Golden Gate (Zlatna Vrata)

This great gate was the main entry of Diocletian's Palace. Its name wasn't literal—the "gold" instead suggests the importance of this gateway to Salona, the capital at the time. Standing inside the gate itself, you can appreciate the double-door design that kept the palace safe. Also notice how this ancient building is now being used in very different ways from its original purpose. Up above on the outer wall, you can see the bricked-in windows that contain part of a Dominican convent. At the top of the inner wall, notice somebody's garden terrace.

Go outside the gate, where you'll get a much clearer feel for the way the palace looked before so many other buildings were grafted on. Straight ahead from here is Salona (Solin), which was a major city of 60,000 (and Diocletian's hometown) before there was a Split. The big statue by Ivan Meštrović is **Bishop Gregory of Nin,** a 10th-century Croatian priest who tried to convince the Vatican to allow sermons during Mass to be said in Croatian, rather than Latin. People rub his toe for good luck (though only non-material wishes are given serious consideration).

• *Your tour is finished. Now enjoy the rest of Split.*

SIGHTS

In or near the Old Town

In addition to the palace, cellars, and cathedral described on my self-guided walk, you can also enjoy these attractions.

▲▲**People's Square (Narodni Trg)**—The lively square at the center of the Old Town is called by locals simply *Pjaca,* pronounced

the same as the Italian *piazza.* Stand in the center and enjoy the bustle. Look around for a quick lesson in Dalmatian history. When Diocletian lived in his palace, a Roman village popped up here, just outside the wall. Face the former wall of Diocletian's Palace (behind and to the right of the 24-hour clock tower). This was the western entrance, or so-called "Iron Gate." By the 14th century, a medieval town had developed, making this the main square of Split.

On the wall just to the right of the lane leading to the Peristyle, look for the life-size relief of **St. Anthony.** Notice the creepy "mini-me" clutching the saint's left leg—depicting the sculptor's donor, who didn't want his gift to be forgotten. Above this strange statue, notice the smaller, faded relief of a man and a woman arguing.

Turn around and face the square. On your left is the city's grand old café, **Gradska Kavana,** which has been the Old Town's venerable meeting point for generations. Today it's both a café and a restaurant with mediocre food but the best outdoor ambience in town (25-kn breakfasts, 50–70-kn pastas, 60–100-kn main dishes, daily 7:00–24:00, Narodni trg 1, tel. 021/317-835). The upstairs was once a fancy hotel, but when it fell on hard times and closed, its former employees (who hadn't been paid in a while) moved in and lived here for years. Now it's been bought by a different company and will likely be turned into a swanky hotel once again.

Across the square, the white building jutting out into the square was once the **City Hall,** and now houses temporary exhibitions. The loggia is all that remains of the original Gothic building.

At the far end of the square is the out-of-place **Nakić House,** built in the early-20th-century Viennese Secession style—a reminder that Dalmatia was part of the Hapsburg Empire, ruled by Vienna, from Napoleon's downfall through World War I.

The lane on the right side of the Nakić House leads to Split's **fish market** (Ribarnica), where you can see piles of still-wriggling catch of the day. No flies? It's thanks to the sulfur spring in the nearby spa building (with the gray statues, on the corner). Just beyond the fish market is the pedestrian boulevard Marmontova.

Ethnographic Museum (Etnografski Muzej)—This museum uses temporary exhibits to show off the culture, costumes, and customs of Dalmatia. The collection was recently transplanted to this gorgeously renovated early-medieval palace, hiding on the upper level of the Old Town behind Diocletian's entry vestibule. Check out the artsy "golden fleece" entry door. On the ground floor, you'll find the remains of a seventh-century church. The upstairs exhibit often includes a look at traditional folk dress (10 kn, some English explanations; June–mid-Sept Mon–Fri 9:00–21:00, Sat 9:00–13:00, closed Sun; mid-Sept–May Mon–Fri 9:00–14:00, Sat 9:00–13:00, closed Sun; Severova 7, tel. 021/344-164).

Split City Museum (Muzej Grada Splita)—This museum traces how the city grew over the centuries. It's a bit dull, but it can help you appreciate a little better the layers of history you're seeing in the streets. The ground floor displays Roman fragments (including coins from the days of Diocletian) and temporary exhibits. The upstairs focuses on the Middle Ages (find the terrace displaying carved stone monuments), and the top floor goes from the 16th century to the present (10 kn, some English descriptions, 75-kn guidebook is overkill; May–Sept Tue–Fri 9:00–21:00, Sat–Mon 9:00–16:00; Oct–April Tue–Fri 9:00–16:00, Sat–Sun 10:00–13:00, closed Mon; Papalićeva 1, tel. 021/360-171, www.mgst.net).

The 15th-century Papalić Palace, which houses the City Museum, is a sight all its own. At the end of the palace, near Cardo street, look up to see several typical Venetian-style Gothic-Renaissance windows. The stone posts sticking out of the wall next to them were used to hang curtains.

Radić Brothers Square (Trg Braće Radića)—Also known as Voćni Trg ("Fruit Square") for the produce that was once sold here, this little piazza is just off the Riva between the two halves of the Old Town. Overhead is a **Venetian citadel.** After Split became part of the Venetian Republic, there was a serious danger of attack by the Ottomans, so octagonal towers like this were built all along the coast. But this imposing tower had a second purpose: to encourage citizens of Split to forget about any plans of rebellion.

In the middle of the square is a studious sculpture by Ivan Meštrović of the 16th-century poet **Marko Marulić,** who is considered the father of the Croatian language. Marulić was the first to write literature in the Croatian vernacular, which before then had generally been considered a backward peasants' tongue.

On the downhill (harbor) side of the square is **Croata,** a necktie boutique that loves to explain how Croatian soldiers who fought with the French in the Thirty Years' War (1618–1648) had a distinctive way of tying their scarves. The French found it stylish, adopted it, and called it *à la Croate*—or eventually, *cravate*—thus creating the modern tie that many people wear to work every day throughout the world. Croata's selection includes ties with traditional Croatian motifs, such as the checkerboard pattern from the flag or writing in the ninth-century Glagolitic alphabet. Though pricey, these ties are good souvenirs (250–400 kn, Mon–Fri 8:00–20:00, Sat 8:00–13:00, closed Sun). You might also find a new, bigger second location of this shop on the Peristyle square.

Green Market—This lively open-air market bustles at the east end of Diocletian's Palace. Locals shop for produce and clothes here, and there are plenty of tourist souvenirs as well. Browse the wide selection of T-shirts, and ignore the creepy black-market tobacco salesmen who mutter at you: *"Cigaretta?"*

Archaeological Museum (Arheloški Muzej)—If you're intrigued by all the "big stuff" from Split's past (buildings and ruins), consider paying a visit to this collection of its "little stuff." A good exhibit of artifacts (mostly everyday domestic items) traces this region's history from its Illyrian beginnings chronologically through its notable Roman period (items from Split and Salona) to the Middle Ages. About a 10-minute walk north of the Old Town, it's worth the trip for archaeology fans (15 kn, Mon–Sat 9:00–14:00 & 16:00–20:00, closed Sun, Zrinsko Frankopanska 25, tel. 021/318-721). Don't confuse this with the less-interesting Museum of Croatian Archaeological Monuments, on the way to the Ivan Meštrović Gallery.

Ivan Meštrović Sights, West of the Old Town

The excellent Meštrović Gallery and adjacent Kaštelet Chapel just outside the Old Town can be reached by foot, bus, or taxi. Consider visiting the chapel first in summer, when it has shorter hours than the gallery.

▲▲**Meštrović Gallery (Galerija Meštrović)**—Split's best art museum is dedicated to the sculptor Ivan Meštrović, the most important of all Croatian artists (see sidebar on page 695). Many of Meštrović's finest works are housed in this palace, designed by the sculptor himself to serve as his residence, studio, and exhibition space. If you have time, it's worth the 20-minute walk or short bus or taxi ride from the Old Town.

Cost, Hours, Location: 30 kn, free guide booklet, 80-kn guidebook is overkill for most visitors, pricey mobile-phone audio-guides available; May–Sept Tue–Sat 9:00–21:00, Sun 9:00–18:00, closed Mon; Oct–April Tue–Sat 9:00–16:00, Sun 10:00–15:00, closed Mon; hours can be sporadic—call to confirm it's open before making the trip, Šetalište Ivana Meštrovića 46, tel. 021/340-800, www.mdc.hr/mestrovic.

Getting There: To get to the gallery, you can take **bus #12** from the little cul-de-sac at the west end of the Riva (departs 1/hr, detours into a residential area before returning to the park/sea-front road, then get off at the stop after the well-marked Muzej Hrvatskih Arheoloških Spomenika museum). Or you can **walk** about 20 minutes: Follow the harbor west of town toward the big marina, swing right with the road, and follow the park until you see the gallery on your right. A **taxi** between the Old Town and the gallery costs about 50 kn.

⊙Self-Guided Tour: After buying your ticket (and asking about the time for your return bus to the Old Town), climb the stairs toward Meštrović's house, pausing in the **garden** to admire a smattering of sculptures (including several female nudes, Cyclops hurling a giant shot-put, and an eagle).

Climbing another set of stairs, you reach the **Entrance Hall**, displaying sculptures mostly of Carrara marble, which was Michelangelo's favorite medium. Notice the black sculptures by the two staircases: on the left, representing birth, and on the right, representing death—Meštrović's works strove to capture the full range of human experience.

Go to the left, and enter the **Dining Room** at the end of the main floor. It's decorated with portraits of Meštrović's wife, mother, and children. Meštrović often used his mother as a model for older women, and his second wife Olga as a model for younger women. Also look for the self-portrait and two painted portraits of Meštrović (one as a young man, another shortly before his death). A painting of the *Last Supper* hangs in virtually every Dalmatian dining room. Meštrović's is no exception—he painted this version himself. At the end of the room are two giant caryatids carved from Dalmatian stone (embedded with fragments of seashells).

Now climb the stairs and go to the right, into the **Secession Room.** Some of these works—including the girl singing and the intimate portrait of a family—show the influence of Meštrović's contemporary, Rodin.

Pass through the room of drawings into the **Long Hall**, lined with life-size figures and a view terrace. The woman sitting with her knees apart and feet together is a favorite pose of Meštrović's.

Ivan Meštrović
(1883–1962)

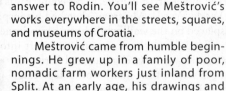

Ivan Meštrović (EE-vahn MESH-troh-veech), who achieved international fame for his talents as a sculptor, was Croatia's answer to Rodin. You'll see Meštrović's works everywhere in the streets, squares, and museums of Croatia.

Meštrović came from humble beginnings. He grew up in a family of poor, nomadic farm workers just inland from Split. At an early age, his drawings and wooden carvings showed promise, and a rich family took him in and made sure he was properly trained. He eventually went off to school in Vienna, where he fell in with the Secession movement and found fame and fortune. He lived in Prague, Paris, and Switzerland, fully engaged in the flourishing of European artistic culture at the turn of the 20th century (he counted Rodin among his friends). After World War I, Meštrović moved back to Croatia, where he had an atelier, or workshop, in Zagreb (now a museum).

Later in life—like Diocletian before him—Meštrović returned to Split and built a huge seaside mansion (today's Meštrović Gallery). The years between the World Wars were Meštrović's happiest and most productive. It was during this time that he sculpted his most internationally famous works, a pair of giant Native American warriors on horseback in Chicago's Grant Park. But when World War II broke out, Meštrović—an outspoken supporter of the ideals of a united Yugoslavia—was briefly imprisoned by the anti-Yugoslav Ustaše (Croatia's Nazi puppet government). After his release, Meštrović fled to Italy, then the US, where he lectured at prominent universities such as Notre Dame and Syracuse. After the war, the Yugoslav dictator Tito invited Meštrović to return, but the very religious artist refused to cooperate with an atheist regime. (Meštrović was friends with the Archbishop Alojzije Stepinac, who was imprisoned by Tito.) Meštrović died in South Bend, Indiana.

Meštrović worked in wood, plaster, marble, and bronze, and dabbled in painting. His sculptures depict biblical, mythological, political, and everyday themes. Meštrović's figures typically have long, angular fingers, arms, and legs. Whether whimsical or emotional, Meštrović's expressive, elongated faces—often with a strong-profile nose—powerfully connect with the viewer.

At the end of the hall is the **Study Room,** filled with minia-ture sculptures Meštrović created to prepare for larger-scale works. Notice the small study of *Job,* then go into the small side-room to see the much larger final version. One of Meštrović's most power-ful works, *Job*—howling with an agony verging on insanity—was carved by the artist in exile, as his country was turned upside-down by World War II. Meštrović sketched his inspiration for this piece (displayed on the wall) while he was imprisoned by the Ustaše.

Head down the stairs and turn left into the **Sacral Room.**
Meštrović was very religious, and here you can see some of his many works depicting biblical figures. The giant, wood-carved *Adam* and *Eve* dominate the room, but don't miss the smaller side-room, with another of the gallery's highlights: the quietly poignant *Roman Pietà.* Meštrović follows the classical pyramid form, with Joseph of Arimathea (top), Mary (left), and Mary Magdalene (right) surrounding the limp body of Christ. But the harmony is broken by the painful angles of the mourn-ing faces. While this sculpture is plaster,

Meštrović also completed a marble version for the campus of Notre Dame in the US.

▲**Kaštelet Chapel**—If you enjoy the gallery, don't miss the nearby Kaštelet Chapel ("Chapel of the Holy Cross"). Meštrović bought this 16th-century fortified palace to display his 28 wood reliefs of Jesus' life. Because he carved these over a nearly 30-year span (completing the last 12 when he was in the US), you can watch Meštrović's style change over time. (However, note that he didn't carve the reliefs in chronological order—ask for a booklet iden-tifying the topic and year for each one.) While the earlier pieces are well composed and powerful, the later ones seem more hastily done, as Meštrović rushed to complete his opus. Work clockwise around the room, tracing the life of Christ. Notice that some of the Passion scenes are out of order (a side effect of Meštrović's non-linear schedule). The beautiful *pietà* near the end still shows some of the original surface of the wood, demonstrating the skill required to create depth and emotion in just a few inches of medium. Dominating the chapel is an extremely powerful wooden crucifix, with Christ's arms, legs, fingers, and toes bent at unnatu-ral angles—a typically expressionistic flair Meštrović used to exag-gerate suffering.

Cost and Hours: The chapel is covered by the same 30-kn ticket as the gallery, but open shorter hours than the gallery in the summer (open year-round Tue–Sat 9:00–16:00, Sun 10:00–15:00, closed Mon)—so consider visiting the chapel first.

Getting There: It's a five-minute walk past the gallery down Šetalište Ivana Meštrovića (on the left, in an olive grove).

ACTIVITIES

▲▲Strolling the Riva (Obala Hrvatskog Narodnog Preporoda)—The official name for this seaside pedestrian drag is the "Croatian National Revival Embankment," but locals just call

it "Riva" (Italian for "harbor"). This is the town's promenade, an integral part of Mediterranean culture. After dinner, Split residents collect their families and friends for a stroll on the Riva. It offers some of the best people-watching in Croatia; make it a point to be here for an hour or

two after dinner. At the west end of the Riva, the people-parade of Croatian culture turns right and heads away from the water, up Marmontova. The stinky smell that sometimes accompanies the stroll isn't a sewer. It's sulfur—a reminder that the town's medicinal sulfur spas have attracted people here since the days of Diocletian.

The Riva recently underwent an extensive, costly, and controversial renovation. The old potholed pavement and scrubby gardens were torn up and replaced with a broad, sleek, carefully landscaped people zone. A clean, synchronized line of modern white lampposts and sun screens sashays down the promenade. But many locals miss the colorful quirks of the old version. For example, each café used to have its own tables and umbrellas; now they're forced to buy identical tables and chairs to make everything match. (In protest, some cafés have chosen to offer no outdoor seating at all.) Some locals think that the starkly modern strip is at odds with the rest of the higgledy-piggledy Old Town, while others see this as simply the early 21st century's contribution to the architectural hodgepodge that is Split. Gossip suggests that this strip will undergo another round of renovation to tone down the uniformity.

Hiking and Swimming on Marjan Peninsula—This long, hilly peninsula extends west from the center of Split. This is where Split goes to relax, with out-of-the-way beaches and lots of hiking trails (great views and a zoo on top).

Hit the Beach—Since it's more of a big city than a resort, Split's beaches aren't as scenic (and the water not as clear) as small towns elsewhere along the coast. The beach that's most popular—and crowded—is Bačvice, in a sandy cove just a short walk east of the main ferry terminal. You'll find less crowded beaches just to the east of Bačvice. Locals like to hike around Marjan, the peninsular city park (see above), ringed with several sunbathing beaches.

NIGHTLIFE

The Riva—Every night in Split, the sea of Croatian humanity laps at the walls of Diocletian's Palace along the town's pedestrian promenade. Choose a bench and watch life go by, or enjoy a drink at one of the many outdoor cafés.

Old Town Pubs—Wander the labyrinthine lanes of the Old Town to find the pub of your choice. The **Luxor** bar, right on the Peristyle square, often features live music in the evening, with cushions filling the steps surrounding Diocletian's entry hall (if you sit on a cushion, you're expected to order a drink, but you can sit or stand elsewhere for free). Several atmospheric bars cluster along Majstora Jurja (just inside the Golden Gate and—facing outside—to the left about a block) and near Radić Brothers Square (Trg Braće Radića; from the square's statue of Marulić, enter the Old Town and bear right, following the beat).

Bačvice Beach—This family-friendly beach by day becomes a throbbing party area for young locals late at night. Since all Old Town bars have to close by 1:00 in the morning, night owls hike on over to the Bačvice crescent of clubs. The three-floor club complex is a cacophony of music, with the beat of each club melting into the next—all with breezy terraces overlooking the harbor.

SLEEPING

Split's sleeps are expensive. Since there aren't enough beds in peak season, many hoteliers are shameless about gouging their customers. Lower your expectations.

Near the Old Town

These good values—the best options in Split—are within a five-minute walk of the Old Town. They're nearly as convenient as the Old Town options, but cheaper. Villa Diana, Villa Ana, and Dioclecijan Apartments are east of the Old Town, and Villa Varoš is west.

$$$ Villa Diana is a lesser value than the others listed here. It's right next door to Villa Ana (see below), with six small rooms over a cocktail bar. Because it's often unstaffed, you're basically on your own—clearly communicate your arrival time to be sure someone can check you in (July–Aug: Sb-690 kn, Db-840 kn; April–June and Sept–Oct: Sb-660 kn, Db-800 kn; Nov–March: Sb-590 kn, Db-730 kn; pricier apartments also available, air-con,

Sleep Code

(5 kn = about $1, country code: 385, area code: 021)
S = Single, **D** = Double/Twin, **T** = Triple, **Q** = Quad, **b** = bathroom.
The modest tourist tax (7 kn or €1 per person, per night, lower off-season) is not included in these rates. Hotels generally accept credit cards and include breakfast in their rates, while most *sobe* accept only cash and don't offer breakfast. All my recommended accommodations speak English.

To help you sort easily through these listings, I've divided the rooms into three categories based on the price for a standard double room with bath in peak season:

$$$ Higher Priced—Most rooms 800 kn or more.
$$ Moderately Priced—Most rooms between 500–800 kn.
$ Lower Priced—Most rooms 500 kn or less.

Kuzmanića 3, follow walking directions for Villa Ana, tel. & fax 021/482-460, www.villadiana.hr, info@villadiana.hr).

$$ Villa Ana, my favorite hotel in Split, has five modern, comfortable rooms in a smart little freestanding stone house a short walk from the Old Town. Though it's in a boring urban neighborhood, it's welcoming, well maintained, and well run by Danijel Bilobrk (Sb-600 kn, Db-750 kn, Tb-850 kn, roughly 150 kn less Nov–March, includes modest but good breakfast, air-con, reception open 7:00–23:00, may be closed mid-Dec–mid-Jan, a few tight free parking spots out front, 2 long blocks east of Old Town up busy Kralja Zvonimira, follow the driveway-like lane opposite Koteks skyscraper to Vrh Lučac 16, tel. 021/482-715, fax 021/482-721, www.villaana-split.hr, info@villaana-split.hr).

$$ Villa Varoš, run with class by Croatian-American Joanne Đonlić, has eight rooms and an apartment (with its own terrace) on a quiet residential lane just beyond the appealing, restaurant-lined Šperun street (April–Sept: Db-500 kn, Tb-550 kn, apartment-800 kn; Oct–March: Db-400 kn, Tb-450 kn, apartment-600 kn; optional 20-kn breakfast at nearby restaurant, air-con, stairs with no elevator, free Wi-Fi, Miljenka Smoje 1, tel. 021/483-469, mobile 098-469-681, www.villavaros.hr, joanne.d.o.o@st.t-com.hr).

$ Dioclecijan Apartments, run by Tomislav Skalic, has two small rooms and one apartment in a pleasant local neighborhood a five-minute walk from the Old Town. The decor is a tasteful mix of new and traditional (April–Sept: Db-400 kn, apartment-600 kn; Oct–March: Db-300 kn, apartment-450 kn; 1-night stays cost 75 kn more in apartment or 40 kn more in rooms, prices soft,

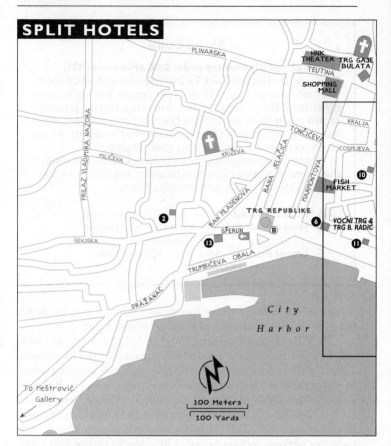

SPLIT HOTELS

cash only, no breakfast, air-con, Petrova 19, mobile 091-537-1826, tskalic@globalnet.hr). From near the Green Market, head up Kralja Zvonimira, and turn right down Petrova. The apartments are on your left as the road bends.

Inside the Old Town

While the Old Town is convenient, it's also a happening nightlife zone, so you're likely to encounter some noise (especially on weekends). Bring earplugs and request a quiet room, if one is available. Old Town bars are required to close by 1:00 in the morning, so at least things will quiet down before the birds start chirping. To locate these accommodations, see the maps on page 686 and above.

$$$ Peristil Hotel has 12 classy rooms over a restaurant just steps from the couldn't-be-more-central square of the same name. Run by the Caktaš family, it's homey and convenient, if pricey (July–Aug: Sb-1,000 kn, Db-1,200 kn; April–June and Sept–Oct: Sb-800 kn, Db-1,000 kn; Nov–March: Sb-700 kn, Db-

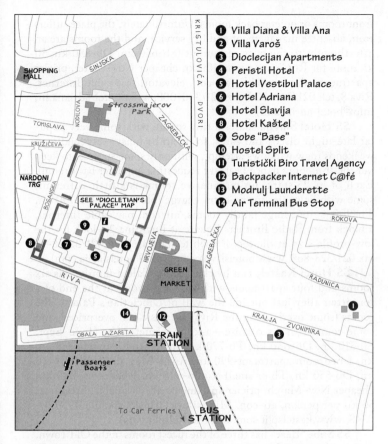

1. Villa Diana & Villa Ana
2. Villa Varoš
3. Dioclecijan Apartments
4. Peristil Hotel
5. Hotel Vestibul Palace
6. Hotel Adriana
7. Hotel Slavija
8. Hotel Kaštel
9. Sobe "Base"
10. Hostel Split
11. Turistički Biro Travel Agency
12. Backpacker Internet C@fé
13. Modrulj Launderette
14. Air Terminal Bus Stop

900 kn; air-con, stairs with no elevator, free cable Internet, some noise from nearby bars, just behind TI and inside Silver Gate at Poljana Kraljice Jelene 5, tel. 021/329-070, fax 021/329-088, www.hotelperistil.com, hotel.peristil@email.t-com.hr).

$$$ Hotel Vestibul Palace is the swankiest splurge in Split's Old Town, with starkly modern decor in an old shell. Tucked in a corner just behind the entry vestibule on the upper level of Diocletian's Palace, this plush place offers seven rooms with maximum comfort and style for maximum prices (July–Sept: Sb-1,200–1,420 kn, Db-1,420–1,950 kn; April–June: Sb-1,050–1,250 kn, Db-1,250–1,800 kn; cheaper Oct–March, prices depend on size and amenities of room, pricier suites also available, air-con, free Wi-Fi, Iza Vestibula 4, tel. 021/329-329, fax 021/329-333, www.vestibulpalace.com, info@vestibulpalace.com). They also have four more rooms in a nearby annex, called Villa Dobrić.

$$$ Hotel Adriana has 15 nice rooms perched right above the people-packed Riva promenade. Choose between harborview front rooms or quieter back rooms. Unfortunately, the place suffers from absentee management and iffy service, and the rooms are an afterthought to the busy restaurant (Sb-650 kn, Db-850 kn, 50 kn more for Riva-view room, 100 kn cheaper Nov–Easter, pricier apartments also available, air-con, elevator, free cable Internet, Riva 8, tel. 021/340-000, fax 021/340-008, www.hotel-adriana.hr, info@hotel-adriana.hr).

\$\$ Hotel Slavija shares a tiny square with some very popular late-night discos and cafés, so it can be noisy—especially on weekends (new windows attempt, with only some success, to keep out the throbbing dance beat; try requesting a quieter back room). Each of its 25 stark, unimaginative rooms is a little different, some with balconies for no extra charge (Sb-650 kn, Db-790 kn, Tb-900, suites, huge family rooms, air-con, pay cable Internet, a block from Radić Brothers Square at Buvinina 2—look for the low-profile sign at the top of a white staircase, tel. 021/323-840, fax 021/323-868, www.hotelslavija.com, info@hotelslavija.com).

\$\$ Hotel Kaštel, run by the quirky Čaleta family, has six rooms and four apartments with tiny bathrooms at the end of a forgotten alley just outside the wall of Diocletian's Palace. The rooms (some overlooking the Riva) are basic and overpriced, and some come with disco noise—ask for a quieter one (June–Sept: Sb-510 kn, Db-660 kn, Tb-770 kn, small studio apartment-770 kn, 1-bedroom apartment-990 kn; April–May and Oct: Sb-440 kn, Db-550 kn, Tb or small studio-620 kn, 1-bedroom-840 kn; cheaper Nov–March, pricier apartments also available, breakfast-50 kn per person, air-con, Mihovilova širina 5, mobile 091-120-0348, www.kastelsplit.com, info@kastelsplit.com).

\$\$ Sobe "Base" has three of the nicest rooms in the Old Town, each with most of the big hotel amenities (including free Wi-Fi and Internet terminals). You can't be more central: All of the colorful rooms—over an artsy gallery—overlook the front steps of the Jupiter's Temple (July–Aug: Db-510 kn, Sept–June: Db-450 kn, no extra charge for 1- or 2-night stays, cash only, no breakfast, air-con, Kraj Svetog Ivana 3, tel. 021/317-375, mobile 098-234-855 or 098-735-137, www.base-rooms.com, mail@base-rooms.com, Tina). Because some bustling bars are just around the corner, expect some nighttime noise (even though the double-paned windows do their darnedest to provide silence).

\$ Other *Sobe:* Though there are very few *sobe* inside Split's Old Town, there are plenty within a 10-minute walk. As in any coastal town, you can simply show up at the boat dock or bus station, be met by locals trying to persuade you into their rooms, and check out the best offer (about 250 kn for a double). Or you can try the **Turistički Biro,** a booking agency. You can generally make a reservation in advance, then drop by their office, pay, pick up your welcome packet, and head off to your awaiting landlady (mid-July–mid-Aug: S-250 kn, Sb-300 kn, D-380 kn, Db-430 kn; June–mid-July and mid-Aug–Sept: S-200 kn, Sb-235 kn, D-310 kn, Db-360 kn; Oct–May: S-175 kn, Sb-200 kn, D-260 kn, Db-310 kn; plus 7 kn per person, per night for tourist tax, no breakfast, 20 percent less for stays of 4 nights or more; office open mid-June–Sept Mon–Fri 8:00–21:00, Sat 8:00–20:00, open Sun 9:00–14:00 mid-July–mid-Sept only, otherwise closed Sun; Oct–mid-June Mon–Fri 8:00–20:00, Sat 8:00–13:00, closed Sun; Riva 12, tel. & fax 021/347-100, www.turistbiro-split.hr, turist.biro.split@st.t-com.hr).

$ Hostel Split is centrally located just off of Narodni Trg in the very heart of town. This small, youthful hostel has 23 beds in four cramped rooms, and a shared outdoor terrace to give everyone some much-needed breathing room. Run by a pair of Croat-Aussie women with the simple slogan "booze & snooze," it's Split's most central hostel option (price per bunk in 6-bed room: 150 kn in June–Sept, 125 kn mid-April–May, 110 kn Oct–mid-April, cash only, no breakfast, laundry service, free Internet access, 8 Narodni Trg, tel. 021/342-787, www.splithostel.com, info@splithostel.com).

EATING

Split's Old Town has oodles of atmosphere, but the street called Šperun, just a couple of blocks west of the Old Town, has several characteristic *konoba*s (traditional restaurants) with good prices (including my first two listings, below). Service in Split's restaurants tends to be a bit grouchy, and you may be unceremoniously turned away if they're very busy (reservations are wise, especially for dinner). To locate most of these eateries, see the map on page 704; for None and Zlatna Vrata, see the map on page 686.

Šperun Restaurant has a classy, cozy Old World ambience and a passion for good Dalmatian food. Animated owner Zdravko Banović and his son Damir serve a mix of Croatian and "eclectic Mediterranean," specializing in seafood. A "buffet" table of antipasti (starters) in the lower dining room shows you what you're getting, so you can select your ideal meal (not self-service—order from the waiter). This place distinguishes itself by offering a warm welcome and good food for reasonable prices (50–70-kn pastas, 50–110-kn meat and seafood, air-con interior, a few sidewalk tables, reservations wise in summer, daily 9:00–23:00, Šperun 3, tel. 021/346-999). Their annex across the street, **Bistrot Šperun Deva,** has a simpler and cheaper menu, lots of outdoor seating, and a handy breakfast for *sobe*-dwellers (30–40-kn salads, 60-kn plates, daily 8:00–23:00, Šperun 2).

Split

704 Rick Steves' Eastern Europe

SPLIT RESTAURANTS

❶ Šperun Restaurant &
   Bistrot Sperun Deva
❷ Konoba Varoš
❸ Black Cat Bistro
❹ Maslina Rest.
❺ Zlagogajnica None Pizza
❻ Ristorante Pizzeria Galija
❼ Zlatna Vrata Pizza & Pasta
❽ Karmen Ice Cream
❾ Hajduk Ice Cream
❿ Ivona Ice Cream
⓫ Tonik Juice Bar
⓬ Vinoteka Bouquet Wine Shop

City Harbor

100 Meters
100 Yards

Konoba Varoš, though bigger and more impersonal than Šperun, is beloved by natives and tourists alike for its great food. Serious waiters serve a wide range of Croatian cooking (including pastas, seafood, and meat dishes) under droopy fishnets in a slightly gloomy throwback interior (50–70-kn pastas, 60–100-kn main dishes, lots of groups, reservations smart—busiest 20:00–22:00, open daily 9:00–24:00, Ban Mladenova 7, tel. 021/396-138).

Black Cat Bistro, popular with expats, is your break from seafood, pizza, and pasta. This innovative eatery offers a simple menu of eclectic flavors, including Tex-Mex, Indian, and Asian—and all are reasonably well executed. The menu also features several hearty salads that go beyond the cabbage-and-lettuce rut. Sit inside, or out on the terrace (40–60 kn, daily 8:00–24:00, corner of Petrova and Šegvića, tel. 021/490-284). It's about a five-minute walk beyond the Old Town: From the Green Market, walk up Kralja Zvonimira and take the first right down Petrova (just past the big, white building); you'll see the restaurant on your right just

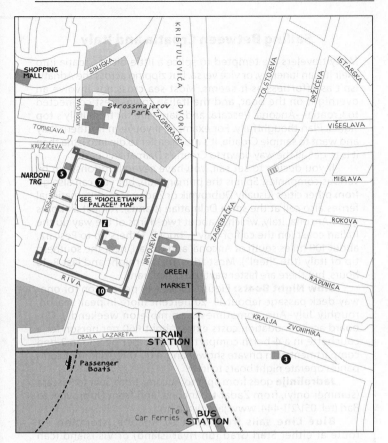

after the road curves to the left.

Maslina ("Olive"), an unpretentious family-run spot filled with locals, hides behind a shopping mall on the busy Marmontova pedestrian street. They serve a wide range of 30–60-kn pizzas and pastas, plus 60–100-kn meat and fish dishes (Mon–Sat 10:00–24:00, Sun 12:00–24:00, Teutina 1A, tel. 021/314-988, Pezo family). From near the top of Marmontova, look for the low-profile wooden archway on the left beyond the café tables (just before the big mall building with the McDonald's).

Take-Away Pizza: **Zlagogajnica None** ("Grandma's") is a stand-up or take-away pizza joint handy for a quick bite in the Old Town. In addition to pizzas, sandwiches, and bruschettas with various toppings, they serve up a pair of traditional pizza-like specialties (with crust on bottom and top, like a filled pizza): *viška pogača*, with tomatoes, onion, and anchovy; and *soparnik*, with a thin layer of spinach, onion, and olive oil (10–20 kn, Mon–Sat 7:00–23:00, closed Sun, just outside Diocletian's Palace

Split

Sailing Between Croatia and Italy

Many travelers are tempted to splice a little bit of Croatia into their Italian itinerary, or vice versa. But zipping across the Adriatic isn't as effortless as it seems. Most sea crossings involve an overnight on the boat, and the Italian towns best connected to Croatia—Ancona, Pescara, and Bari—are far from Italy's top sights. Plan thoughtfully. For example, if you're in northern Italy and want to sample Croatia, it's much easier to dip into Istria than it is to get all the way down to Croatia's Dalmatian Coast.

If you decide to set sail, you have several options, run by various companies. Split is the primary hub, but you can also go from other cities (usually Dubrovnik or Zadar; some international ferries also call at the small Dalmatian islands). Almost all boats go to Ancona, Italy, which is about two-thirds of the way up the Italian coast (on the calf of Italy's "boot"). Others go to Pescara, about 100 miles south of Ancona; and to Bari, near the southern tip of Italy (the "heel"). Most trips are overnight and last 8–10 hours, but there are faster daytime catamarans.

Slow Night Boats: Figure about €40 per person for one-way deck passage (about 10–20 percent more in peak season, roughly July–Aug; sometimes even more on weekends). On-board accommodation costs extra (about €60 per person for a couchette in a 4-berth compartment, €75 per person in 2-bed compartment with private shower and WC). Three different companies operate night boats to Italy:

Jadrolinija goes from Split to Ancona, from Split to Pescara (summer only), from Zadar to Ancona, and from Dubrovnik to Bari (tel. 051/211-444, www.jadrolinija.hr).

Blue Line sails from Split to Ancona, stopping en route at either Stari Grad (on Hvar Island) or Vis Island (can book at Split Tours travel agency in Split, tel. 021/352-533, www.blueline-ferries.com).

on the skinny street that runs along the wall at Bosanska 4, tel. 021/347-252).

Pizzerias: **Ristorante Pizzeria Galija,** at the west end of the Old Town, has a boisterous local following and good wood-fired pizza, pasta, and salads (30–50 kn, air-con, Mon–Sat 9:00–24:00, Sun 12:00–24:00, just a block off of the pedestrian drag Marmontova at Tončićeva 12, tel. 021/347-932; the recommended Hajduk ice-cream shop is nearby—see below). **Zlatna Vrata** ("Golden Gate"), right in the Old Town, offers wood-fired pizzas and pasta dishes. The food and interior are nothing special, but there's wonderful outdoor seating in a tingle-worthy Gothic court-yard with pointy arches and lots of pillars (30–50 kn, Mon–Sat 7:00–24:00, closed Sun, just inside the Golden Gate and—as you

Azzurraline goes between Bari and Dubrovnik, and between Bari and Kotor, Montenegro (Croatian tel. 020/313-178, Montenegrin tel. 085/313-617, Italian tel. 080-592-8400, www .azzurraline.com).

Most nights in summer, at least one of these companies runs a night boat. Other companies serving these routes come and go each year—ask the Split TI or poke around Split's main terminal building to discover the latest.

Fast Daytime Boats: Some speedier crossings are available. But because these boats are faster and smaller, they're also weather-dependent—so they don't run off-season. **Aliscafi SNAV** connects Split and Ancona in just 4.5 hours (€65 one-way, or €85 in peak season—late July–early Sept). They also zip from Split to Stari Grad (on Hvar Island), then on to the Italian town of Pescara (5 hours total, €70 one-way, or €90 in peak season; all boats sail daily mid-June–mid-Sept, Croatian tel. 021/322-252, Italian tel. 081-428-5555, www.snav.it). **La Riviera Lines** sometimes runs a similar fast boat between Termoli, Italy, and Korčula or Hvar (Italian tel. 0875-82248, www.lariveralines.com).

Trains Within Italy: From **Ancona,** you can catch a train to Venice (almost hourly, 4.25–5.25 hrs, most transfer in Bologna), Florence (almost hourly, 3–4.25 hrs, most transfer in Bologna), or Rome (8/day direct, 3–4.5 hrs). From **Pescara,** trains head to Rome (6/day direct, 3.75–4.25 hrs) and Florence (almost hourly, 4.5–5.25 hrs, transfer in Bologna). From **Bari,** you can hop a train to Naples (6/day, 3.75–6 hrs, most transfer in Caserta), Rome (3/day direct, 4.75 hrs), or Florence (8/day, 6.75–8.5 hrs, transfer in Rome or Bologna).

Note that in Italian, Split is called "Spalato" (which is also the sound you hear if seasickness gets the best of you).

face outside—up the skinny alley to the left, on Majstora Jurja, tel. 021/345-015).

Gelato: Split has several spots for delicious ice cream *(sladoled).* Most ice-cream parlors *(kuća sladoleda)* are open daily 8:00–24:00. To my taste buds, these three spots are much better than the other options in town: Locals swarm to a pair of places near Trg Gaje Bulata (the modern shopping square—with a McDonald's, big Prima mall, and modern-looking church—at the end of the Marmontova pedestrian drag just beyond the northwest corner of the Old Town): **Karmen** (hides behind the building in the middle of the square, facing the modern church on Kačićeva) and **Hajduk** (named for Split's soccer team; a block west from the top of Marmontova and around the corner from Galija pizzeria at Matošićeva 4). At the east end of the Riva, look for the more-central **Ivona** (near entrance to Diocletian's cellars at Kaštelanska cesta 65).

Smoothies and Fruit Juices: For a healthier energy boost, head for **Tonik Juice Bar,** run by Croat-Aussie Stefanie. You can select from the diverse menu, or they'll custom-make a smoothie to your liking (20–30 kn, June–Sept daily 7:00–23:00, shoulder season 8:00–21:00, less in winter, near the launderette and Šperun street restaurants at Ban Mladenova 5, mobile 098-641-376).

TRANSPORTATION CONNECTIONS

Split Boat Connections

As the transport hub for the Dalmatian Coast, Split has good boat connections to most anywhere you want to go. Big car ferries use the main ferry terminal at the end of the harbor, while passenger boats (including fast catamarans) depart from the handy Obala Lazareta embankment just in front of the Old Town. Be warned that the following boat information is highly subject to change—always confirm before you make your plans. To check Jadrolinija schedules, see www.jadrolinija.hr; for *Krilo* catamaran schedules, see www.krilo.hr. Split's Jadrolinija boat ticket office is in the main ferry terminal (see "Arrival in Split," page 679), with several smaller branch offices between there and the Old Town (tel. 021/338-333). You can buy *Krilo* tickets at the small Jadrolinija kiosk halfway along the harbor.

Big Jadrolinija Car Ferries: These hulking boats generally leave Split early in the morning (at 6:30 or 7:00) and head south, stopping at **Stari Grad** on Hvar Island (20-min bus ride from Hvar town; 2/week year-round, 1.75 hrs; the catamarans described below are faster and take you right to Hvar town), **Korčula town** (3/week July–mid-Sept, 2/week mid-Sept–June, 3.5–6 hrs), and **Dubrovnik** (2/week year-round, 8.25–9.25 hrs, more with transfer in Korčula). You can also sleep on the boat as it heads north to **Rijeka** (2/week, 11 hrs overnight).

Other Boats to Hvar Island: Ideally, catch a boat heading to Hvar town, the most interesting part of the island. Speedy **Jadrolinija catamarans** run daily year-round from Split to Hvar (June–Sept: 2/day, departing Split at 11:30 and 15:00; Oct–May: 1/day, departing Split at 14:00; 50 min to Hvar town, occasionally stops at Milna on Brač Island). A different company runs the similar *Krilo* **catamaran** directly from Split to Hvar town (June–Sept: departs Split daily at 17:00; Oct–May: departs Split daily except Sun at 16:00; 1 hr to Hvar town). Twice weekly in the winter (Oct–May only), a much **slower car ferry** putters from Split to Hvar town in two hours (even though this is a car ferry, only foot

passengers can get on and off at Hvar). Finally, you can also reach
Hvar Island on the **slow car ferries** from Split; these are frequent
but less convenient, since they take you to the town of Stari Grad,
across the island from Hvar town (at least 3/day, more in summer;
from Stari Grad, it's an easy 20-minute bus trip into Hvar town).

Other Boats to Korčula Island: Many of the same boats
that go to Hvar town (described above) continue on to Korčula
Island. The most convenient is the *Krilo* **catamaran,** which takes
you right to Korčula town (June–Sept: departs Split daily at
17:00; Oct–May: departs Split daily except Sun at 16:00; 3 hrs to
Korčula). The other boats leave you at Vela Luka, at the far end
of Korčula Island from Korčula town (buses meet arriving boats
to take passengers on the one-hour trip into Korčula town). The
Jadrolinija catamaran goes from Split to Hvar town, then to Vela
Luka (departs Split at 15:00 June–Sept, at 14:00 Oct–May, 2 hrs to
Vela Luka, occasionally stops at Mlina on Brač Island). Slower **car
ferries** also go from Split to Vela Luka (2/day late June–early Sept,
1–2/day late Sept–early June, 2.75 hrs).

Sailing to Italy: See the sidebar on page 706.

Split Overland Connections

By Bus to: Zagreb (at least hourly, 5–8 hrs, depending on route,
about 150 kn), **Dubrovnik** (almost hourly, less off-season, 5 hrs,
100–150 kn), **Korčula** (1 night bus leaves at 1:00 in the morning
and arrives 6:00, 105 kn), **Trogir** (at least hourly, 30 min, about 20
kn), **Zadar** (at least hourly, 3 hrs, about 75 kn), **Mostar** in Bosnia-
Herzegovina (7/day, 4–4.5 hrs), **Međugorje** in Bosnia-Herzegovina
(4/day, 3 hrs), **Rijeka** (10/day including some night buses, 8.5 hrs).
Zagreb-bound buses sometimes also stop at **Plitvice** (confirm with
driver and ask him to stop; about 5/day, 4–6 hrs, 100 kn). Each
of these routes is served by multiple companies, which charge
slightly different rates, so the prices listed here are rough estimates.
Reservations for buses are generally not necessary, but always ask
about the fastest option—which can save hours of bus time. Bus
info: www.ak-split.hr, tel. 021/338-483 or toll tel. 060-327-777.

By Train to: Zagreb (3/day, 5.5 hrs, plus 1 direct night train,
8 hrs). Train info: tel. 021/338-525 or toll tel. 060-333-444.

Split

KORČULA

The island town of Korčula (KOHR-choo-lah) boasts an atmospheric Old Town, some surprisingly engaging museums, and a dramatic, fjord-like mountain backdrop. Korčula—while certainly on the tourist trail—has an often-appealing, occasionally frustrating backwater charm. All things considered, Korčula is the most enjoyable Back Door stopover on the Dalmatian Coast.

Like so many other small Croatian coastal towns, Korčula was founded by the ancient Greeks. It became part of the Roman Empire, and was eventually a key southern outpost of the Venetian Republic. Four centuries of Venetian rule left Korčula with a quirky Gothic-Renaissance mix and a strong siesta tradition. Korčulans take great pride in the fact that Marco Polo was born here in 1254—the explorer remains the town's poster boy. Korčula is also known for its traditional *Moreška* sword dance.

You'll discover that there are two Korčulas: the tacky seaside resort and the historic Old Town. Savvy visitors ignore the tourist sprawl and focus on Korčula's medieval quarter, a mini-Dubrovnik poking out into the sea on a picture-perfect peninsula. Tiny lanes branch off the humble main drag like ribs on a fishbone. This street plan is designed to catch both the breeze and the shade. All in all, this laid-back island village is an ideal place to take a vacation from your busy vacation.

Planning Your Time

Korčula deserves the better part of a day, but you'll quickly exhaust the town's sightseeing options. If you're in a rush, you can spend one night on Korčula, see the town in the morning, then zip out on the evening *Nona Ana* boat to Dubrovnik (June–Sept

4/week)—but it's much more sane and relaxing to hang out here for two nights. With a single day, spend the morning wandering the medieval Old Town and exploring the handful of tiny museums (many close for siesta in the early afternoon, especially outside of peak season). In the afternoon, kick back at a café or restaurant and bask on the beach. If you're here on a Thursday, be sure to catch the performance of the *Moreška* dance (also Mon July–Aug). With a second day, unwind more, or consider a one-day package excursion to Mljet Island and its national park.

ORIENTATION

(area code: 020)

The long, skinny island of Korčula runs alongside the even longer, skinnier Pelješac Peninsula (famous for its wine). The main town and best destination on the island—just across a narrow strait from

Pelješac—is also called Korčula.

Korčula town is centered on its compact **Old Town** (Stari Grad) peninsula, which is connected to the mainland at a big staircase leading to the Great Land Gate. In the area in front of this staircase, you'll find ATMs, travel agencies, the Jadrolinija ferry office, several Internet cafés, the Konzum supermarket, a colorful outdoor produce market, and other handy tourist services.

Stretching to the south and east of the Old Town is **"Shell Bay,"** surrounded by a strip of tacky tourist shops and resort hotels. This seamier side of Korčula—best avoided—caters mostly to Brits and Germans here to worship the sun for a week or two.

To the west of Old Town is the serene waterfront street **Put Sv. Nikola,** where you'll find several *sobe* (including Rezi Depolo's—see "Sleeping," page 719), some inviting swimming areas, great views back on the Old Town, and more locals than tourists.

Tourist Information

Korčula's TI, run by Stanka Kraljević, is next to Hotel Korčula on the west side of the Old Town waterfront. Ask about the Korčula brochure and map (mid-June–Sept Mon–Sat 8:00–15:00 & 16:00–22:00, Sun 9:00–14:00; Oct–mid-June Mon–Sat 8:00–14:00, closed Sun, may be open Sun in shoulder season; tel. 020/715-701, www.korcula.net).

Arrival in Korčula

For all the details on getting to the Dalmatian Coast, see page 617.

By Boat: The big Jadrolinija ferries can arrive on either side of the Old Town peninsula, depending on the wind. (The Orebić passenger ferry and the fast catamarans generally dock at the west side of town.) From either side of the peninsula, it's just a two-minute walk to where it meets the mainland and all of the services described in "Orientation," previous page.

A few boats (car ferries from Orebić and Drvenik) use the Dominče dock two peninsulas east of Korčula, about a five-minute drive from town. Regular buses connect this dock with Korčula.

Some boats from Split and Hvar town arrive at Vela Luka, at the far end of Korčula Island. Each boat arriving at Vela Luka is met by a bus waiting to bring arriving travelers to Korčula town (about 1 hour).

By Bus: The bus station is at the southeast corner of Korčula's Shell Bay. If you leave the station with the bay on your right, you'll reach the Old Town. If you leave with the bay on your left, you'll get to hotels Liburna, Park, and Marko Polo.

By Car: See "Route Tips for Drivers" at the end of this chapter. Once in Korčula town, there's free parking at the bus station along the marina.

Helpful Hints

Jadrolinija Office: This office, essential for sorting through and confirming boat schedules, is located where the Old Town meets the mainland (June–Sept Mon–Fri 8:00–20:00, Sat 8:00–13:30 & 18:00–22:00, Sun 6:00–13:30; Oct–May generally Mon–Fri 8:00–14:00, Sat 8:00–13:00, Sun 9:00–13:00; tel. 020/715-410, www.jadrolinija.hr). But note that they don't sell tickets for the convenient *Krilo* catamaran to Hvar town and Split (buy *Krilo* tickets at Marko Polo Tours—see next). For a run-down of the confusing boat options to and from Korčula, see the end of this chapter.

Travel Agencies: Korčula has two major travel agencies. At either one, you can book an excursion, browse shelves of books and souvenirs, and get information about car rental and other activities: **Marko Polo Tours** (also sells tickets for *Krilo* catamaran; located near eastern ferry dock at Biline 5, tel. 020/715-400, fax 020/715-800) and **Atlas Travel** (a few steps down from Great Land Gate at Trg 19 Travnja, tel. 020/711-231, fax 020/715-580; main office closed in winter, but second office around the corner stays open). Both agencies are open similar hours (long hours daily in summer, closed for mid-afternoon break and sometimes closed Sun in shoulder season,

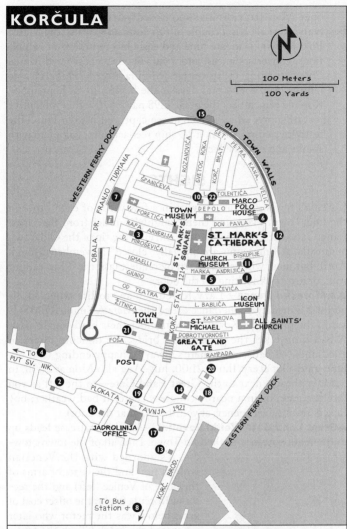

KORČULA

100 Meters
100 Yards

OLD TOWN WALLS

WESTERN FERRY DOCK

OBALA DR. FRANJO TUĐMANA

ŠPANIĆEVA

A. ROZANOVIĆA

SVETOG ROKA

SET. PETRA KANAVELIĆA VELIKA

KORČ. BRAT.

V. FORETIĆA

RAFA ARNERIJA

D. MIROŠEVIĆA

ISMAELLI

GIUNIO

OD TEATRA

ŽITNICA

KORČ. STAT. 1214

ST. MARK'S SQUARE

TOWN MUSEUM

DEPOLO

TOLENTIČA

MARCO POLO HOUSE

DON PAVLA

ST. MARK'S CATHEDRAL

CHURCH MUSEUM

BISKUPIJE

MARKA ANDRIJIĆA

J. BANIĆEVIĆA

L. BABLIĆA

ICON MUSEUM

TOWN HALL

KAPOROVA

ST. MICHAEL

ALL SAINTS' CHURCH

DOBROTVORNOSTI

GREAT LAND GATE

RAMPADA

FOŠA

POST

EASTERN FERRY DOCK

To ➝
PUT SV. NIK.

PLOKATA 19 TAVNJA 1921

JADROLINIJA OFFICE

KORČ. BROD.

To Bus Station &

❶ Apartments Lenni
❷ Royal Apartments
❸ Vitaić Family Rooms
❹ To Depolo Rooms
❺ Marco Polo Apartments
❻ Anka Portolan Rooms
❼ Hotel Korčula
❽ To Hotels Marko Polo, Liburna, Park & Bon Repos
❾ Pizzeria Amfora
❿ Adio Mare Restaurant
⓫ Konoba Marinero Restaurant
⓬ Konoba Morski Konjic Rest.
⓭ Fresh Eatery
⓮ Konzum Supermarket
⓯ Buffet "Massimo"
⓰ Cukarin Sweet Shop
⓱ Kiwi Ice Cream
⓲ Marko Polo Tours
⓳ Atlas Travel
⓴ Korkyra Travel Agency
㉑ *Moreška* Outdoor Theater
㉒ Marco Polo Gift Shop

Korčula

open Mon–Sat mornings and closed Sun in winter).

Festivals: Korčula has a couple of fun annual festivals. The Marco Polo Festival is in late June and early July, with lots of exhibitions, concerts, dances, and a parade with a costumed Marco Polo returning to his native Korčula after his long visit to China. And for several days at the beginning of September, Korčula remembers the great 1298 naval battle that took place just offshore, when the Genoese captured Marco Polo. The festivities culminate in a 14-ship reenactment, complete with smoke and sound effects.

SIGHTS

Korčula's few sights cluster within a few yards of each other in the Old Town. I've listed them roughly in order from the Great Land Gate (the Old Town's main entry) to the tip of the Old Town peninsula. All museums are officially "closed" November through April, but most will usually open by request (ask the TI to call for you...or just try knocking on the door).

▲▲*Moreška* **Dance**—Lazy Korčula snaps to life when locals perform a medieval folk dance called the *Moreška* (moh-REHSH-kah). The plot helps Korčulans remember their hard-fought past: A bad king takes the good king's bride, the dancing forces of good and evil battle, and there's always a happy ending (100 kn, June–mid-Oct every Thu at 21:00, July–Aug also Mon at 21:00, in outdoor theater next to the Great Land Gate—to the left as you face the gate, or in a nearby congress center if bad weather; buy tickets from travel agency, at your hotel, or at the door).

▲**Great Land Gate (Veliki Revelin)**—A noble staircase leads up to the main entrance to the Old Town. Like all of the town's tow-

ers, it's adorned with the Venetian winged lion and the coats of arms of the doge of Venice (left) and the rector of Korčula (right; the offset coat of arms below was the rector who later renovated the gate). Climb the tower to visit a small exhibit with costumes and photos from the *Moreška* dance, then head up to the top level to enjoy panoramic town views (15 kn, daily 10:00–16:00, until 19:00 in summer, generally closed Nov–May, English descriptions).

Just inside the gate is **Franjo Tuđman Square**, renamed in 2001 for the first president of an independent Croatia (see page 624). During the war, Tuđman was considered a hero. In later years, it was revealed that he had held secret negotiations with the Serbian leader Slobodan Milošević. As the key figure of a recent-but-bygone era that combined both joy and terror, Tuđman remains controversial in today's Croatia. But members of his party are still in power and hold local offices throughout the country, and sometimes adorn a square or street with his name.

On the left inside the gate is the 16th-century **Town Hall and Rector's Palace.** The seal of Korčula (over the center arch) symbolizes the town's importance as the southernmost bastion of the Venetian Republic: St. Mark standing below three defensive towers. The little church on the other side of the square is dedicated to **St. Michael** (Crkva Sv. Mihovila). Throughout Croatia, you'll often find churches to St. Michael just inside the town gates, as he is believed to offer saintly protection from enemies. Notice that a passageway connects the church to the building across the street—home to the Brotherhood of St. Michael, one of Korčula's many religious fraternal organizations (see "Icon Museum," page 717).

• *Now begin walking up the...*

Street of the Korčulan Statute of 1214 (Ulica Korčulanskog Statuta 1214)—This street is Korčula's backbone—in more ways than one (the street plan is designed as a fish skeleton). While most medieval towns slowly evolved with twisty, mazelike lanes, Korčula was carefully planned. The streets to the west (left) of this one are straight, to allow the refreshing northwesterly Maestral winds into town. To the east (right), they're curved (notice you can't see the sea) to keep out the bad-vibe southeasterly Jugo winds.

The street's complicated name honors a 1214 statute—the oldest known written law in Central Europe—with regulations about everyday life and instructions on maintaining the walls, protecting nature, keeping animals, building a house, and so on. As you head up the street, look up to notice some interesting decorations on the houses' upper floors.

• *If you continue up the street, you'll reach St. Mark's Square (Trg Sv. Marka). From here, you're a few steps from the next four sights.*

▲**St. Mark's Cathedral (Katedrala Sv. Marka)**—Korčula became a bishopric in the 14th century. In the 19th century—36 bishops

later—the Hapsburgs decided to centralize ecclesiastical power in their empire, and removed Korčula's bishop. The town still has this beautiful "cathedral"—but no bishop. On the ornately decorated tympanum above the main door, you'll see another Venetian statue of St. Mark (flanked by Adam and

Eve). Inside, above the main altar, is an original Tintoretto painting (recently restored in Zagreb). At the altar to the left, find the statue of St. Rok (better known by his Italian name, San Rocco) pointing to a wound on his leg. This popular-in-Croatia French saint is believed to help cure disease. As you leave, notice the weapons on the back wall, used in some of the pivotal battles that have taken place near strategically situated Korčula (free, May–Oct daily 9:00–14:00 & 17:00–19:00, may be open all day long in peak season, closed during church services, generally closed Nov–April but may be open Mon–Fri 9:00–12:00 after Easter).

▲**Church Museum (Opatska Riznica)**—This small museum has an eclectic and fascinating collection. Go on a scavenger hunt for the following items: a ceremonial necklace from Mother Teresa (who came from Macedonia, not far from here—she gave this necklace to a friend from Korčula), some old 12th-century hymnals, two tiny drawings by Leonardo da Vinci, a coin collection (including a 2,400-year-old Greek coin minted here in Korčula), some Croatian modern paintings, three amphora jugs, and two framed reliquaries with dozens of miniscule relics (15 kn; July–Aug daily 9:00–19:00, sometimes later; May–June and Sept–Oct Mon–Sat 9:00–14:00 & 17:00–20:00, closed Sun except sometimes open in the morning; generally closed Nov–April but may be open Mon–Fri 9:00–12:00 after Easter).

▲**Town Museum (Gradski Muzej)**—Housed in an old mansion, this museum does a fine job of bringing together Korčula's various claims to fame. It's arranged like a traditional Dalmatian home: shop on the ground floor, living quarters in the middle floors, kitchen on top. Notice that some of the walls near the entry have holes in them. Archaeologists are continually doing "digs" into these walls to learn how medieval houses here were built.

On the ground floor is a lapidarium, featuring fragments of Korčula's stone past (see the first-century Roman amphora jugs). Upstairs is a display on Korčula's long-standing shipbuilding industry, including models of two modern steel ships built here (the town still builds ship parts today). There's also a furnished living room and, in the attic, a kitchen. This was a smart place for the kitchen—if it caught fire, it was less likely to destroy the whole building. Notice the little WC in the corner. A network of pipes took kitchen and other waste through town and out to sea (15 kn, limited posted English information—pick up the free English guide brochure at entry; mid-June–Aug Mon–Sat 9:30–21:00, closed Sun; Sept–mid-June Mon–Fri 8:00–15:00—if it's locked, try knocking, closed Sat–Sun; tel. 020/711-420).

Marco Polo's House (Kuća Marka Pola)—Korčula's favorite son is the great 13th-century explorer Marco Polo. Though Polo sailed under the auspices of the Venetian Republic, and technically was a Venetian (since the Republic controlled this region), Korčulans proudly claim him as their own. Marco Polo was the first Westerner to sail to China, bringing back amazing stories and exotic goods (like silk) that Europeans had never seen before. After his trip, Marco Polo fought in an important naval battle against the Genoese near Korčula. He was captured, taken to Genoa, and imprisoned. He told his story to a cellmate, who wrote it down, published it, and made the explorer a world-class and much-in-demand celebrity. To this day, kids in swimming pools around the world try to find him with their eyes closed.

Today, Korčula is the proud home to "Marco Polo's House"— actually a more recent building on the site of what may or may not have been his family's property. The house is in poor repair, but most of the building has been purchased by the city to open to visitors. Currently you can just climb the stubby tower (for an uninspiring view), but in the future, the town hopes to turn the complex into a world-class museum about the explorer (15 kn, daily July–Aug 9:00–21:00, Easter–June and Sept–Oct 9:00–13:30 & 15:30–19:00, closed Nov–Easter, just north of cathedral on—where else?—ulica Depolo).

Across the street from the house's entrance, you'll find a clever **Marco Polo gift shop** selling various relatively classy items relating to the explorer—herbs, brandies, honey, ice cream, and so on. Each one comes with a little tag telling a tale of M.P.—for example, how the word "million" was based on his middle name, Emilio (because no existing word was superlative enough for his discoveries). There's even a life-size Marco Polo and Kublai Khan keeping an eye on the cash register (daily in summer 9:00–24:00, progressively shorter hours and closed for mid-afternoon break off-season, closed in winter, ulica Depolo 1A, mobile 091-189-8048).

▲**Icon Museum (Zbirka Ikona)**—Korčula is known for its many brotherhoods—centuries-old fraternal organizations that have sprung up around churches. The Brotherhood of All Saints has been meeting every Sunday after Mass since the 14th century, and they run a small but interesting museum of icons. Maja, who lives upstairs, speaks no English but will point out what's worth seeing. These golden religious images were brought back from Greece in the 17th century by Korčulans who had been fighting the Ottomans on a Venetian warship (10 kn, hours depend on demand, but generally May–Oct daily 10:00–14:00 & 17:00–20:00, may be open all day long in peak season, closed Nov–April—but try ringing the bell, on Kaprova ulica at the Old Town's southeast tip).

Brotherhoods' meeting halls are often connected to their church by a second-story walkway. Use this one to step into the Venetian-style **All Saints' Church** (Crkva Svih Svetih). Under the loft in the back of the church, notice the models of boats and

Korčula

tools—donated by Korčula's shipbuilders. Look closely at the painting to the right of the altar. See the guys in the white robes kneeling under Jesus? That's the Brotherhood, who commissioned this painting.

▲Old Town Walls—For several centuries, Korčula held a crucial strategic position as one of the most important southern outposts of the Venetian Republic (the Republic of Dubrovnik started at the Pelješac Peninsula, just across the channel). The original town walls around Korčula date from at least the 13th century, but the fortifications were extended (and new towers built) over several centuries to defend against various foes of Venice—mostly Ottomans and pirates.

The most recent tower dates from the 16th century, when the Ottomans attacked Korčula. The rector and other VIPs fled to the mainland, but a brave priest remained on the island and came up with a plan. All of the women of Korčula dressed up as men, and then everybody in town peeked over the wall—making the Ottomans think they were up against a huge army. The priest prayed for help, and the strong northerly Bora wind blew. Not wanting to take their chances with the many defenders and the weather, the Ottomans sailed away, and Korčula was saved.

By the late 19th century, Korčula was an unimportant Hapsburg beach town, and the walls had no strategic value. The town decided to quarry the top half of its old walls to build new homes (and to improve air circulation inside the city). While today's walls are half as high as they used to be, the town has restored many of the towers, giving Korčula its fortified feel. Each one has a winged lion—a symbol of Venice—and the seal of the rector of Korčula when the tower was built.

ACTIVITIES

Swimming—The water around Korčula is clean and suitable for swimming. You'll find pebbly beaches strewn with holiday-goers all along Put Sv. Nikola, the street that runs west from the Old Town. Another good swimming spot is at the very end of the Old Town peninsula. Or trek to the beaches near Lumbarda.

Lumbarda—For a break from Korčula town, venture about three miles southeast to Lumbarda, a tranquil end-of-the-road village. Lumbarda is known for its wine (the sweet *grk* dessert wine) and for its beaches: the pebbly Bilin Žal, just east of town; and the sandy Vela Pržina, about a 20-minute walk through vineyards to the south. While not worth going out of your way for, Lumbarda and its beaches are fun to explore on a lazy vacation day. From Korčula town, you can get to Lumbarda by water taxi (50 kn) or by bus (hourly Mon–Sat, fewer buses Sun, 10 kn, 15 min).

Excursions—Various companies offer day-long excursions to nearby destinations (generally available June–Oct, each itinerary offered 2–4 times per week). The most popular options are Dubrovnik (450 kn) and the national park on Mljet Island (350 kn, includes park entry fee). Korčula's two big travel agencies—Marko Polo and Atlas—sell tickets for different companies. If one isn't running a tour to the destination you want, the other might be (both agencies are listed under "Helpful Hints" earlier in this chapter). Several new, more active tour companies have popped up recently, offering canoe trips, snorkeling, kayaking, and other "adventures"—look for flyers around town (Sokol is well regarded, www.korcula-adventures.com).

Other Activities—You'll see travel agencies all over town where you can rent a car, bike, scooter, boat, sea kayak, or anything else

 you want for some vacation fun. Local captains take tourists on cruises to nearby bays and islands to get out on the water, swim, and enjoy a local-style "fish picnic." Inquire at any travel agency, or simply talk to a captain at the harbor (near the eastern ferry dock, at Shell Bay; figure about

200 kn per hour regardless of number of people). If you're a wine-lover, you can hire a driver to take you on a tour of Korčula Island, including stops at some wineries (ask at TI or travel agency).

SLEEPING

Korčula has only five hotels—all owned by the same company (which is, in turn, government-run). The lack of competition keeps quality low and prices ridiculously high—which makes *sobe* a particularly good alternative.

Sobe

My favorite *sobe* in Korčula offer similar comfort to the hotels at far lower prices—most of them with TVs and air-conditioning, to boot. These are your best *sobe* options, and worth reserving ahead.

$$ Apartments Lenni is run by Lenni and Periša (Peter) Modrinić, both of whom are outgoing and speak good English. They rent three tight, modern, comfortable rooms (one with a private bathroom across the hall) and three apartments in a nicely renovated house right in the heart of the Old Town. Since they live off-site, confirm your reservation the day before and let them know your arrival time (Db-€45, or €60 July–Aug; apartment-€55, or €70 July–Aug; cheaper off-season, 2-night minimum unless it's

Korčula

Sleep Code

(€1 = about $1.40, 5 kn = about $1, country code: 385, area code: 020)

S = Single, **D** = Double/Twin, **T** = Triple, **Q** = Quad, **b** = bathroom. The modest tourist tax (7 kn or €1 per person, per night, lower off-season) is not included in these rates. The hotels accept credit cards and include breakfast in their rates, while most *sobe* accept only cash and don't offer breakfast. While the accommodations quote their prices in euros, you'll pay in kunas. Everyone listed here speaks at least enough English to make a reservation (or knows someone nearby who can translate).

To help you sort easily through these listings, I've divided the rooms into three categories based on the price for a standard double room with bath in peak season:

$$$ Higher Priced—Most rooms €100 or more.
  $$ Moderately Priced—Most rooms between €55–100.
    $ Lower Priced—Most rooms €55 or less.

not too busy, no breakfast, cash only, air-con, near Konoba Marko Polo restaurant at Jakova Baničevića 13, tel. 020/711-400, mobile 091-551-6592, www.ikorcula.net/lenni, perisa.modrinic@du.t -com.hr).

$$ Royal Apartments are some of the most hotelesque (and most expensive) rooms in town. The five apartments are classy and new, making the place feel more like a small hotel with no real reception desk—arrange your arrival time carefully (July–Aug: small apartment-€80, big apartment-€90; June and Sept: small apartment-€70, big apartment-€80; closed Oct–May, no extra charge for 1- or 2-night stays, no breakfast, cash only, air-con, well-marked with green awning just west of Old Town at Trg Petra Šegedina 4, mobile 098-184-0444, royalapt@ica.net, Jelavić family—Anamarija speaks English, but Marko doesn't).

$$ The Vitaić family is a father-and-sons operation renting three rooms in the Old Town (July–Aug: Db-€65; May–June and Sept–Oct: Db-€45; closed Nov–April, no extra charge for 1- or 2-night stays, no breakfast, cash only, Dinko Mirošević 8, tel. 020/715-312, mobile 098-932-7670, vitaicfamily@net.hr).

$ Rezi and Andro Depolo, probably distant relatives of Marco, rent four comfy rooms on the bay west of the Old Town. Three of the rooms offer beautiful views to the Old Town, and the five-minute stroll into town is pleasant and scenic. English-speaking Rezi is very friendly and works to make her guests feel welcome (Db-€35, or €40 July–Aug, room with kitchen-€5 more, 30 percent more for 1-night stays, continental breakfast-€4, big breakfast-€5, cash only, air-con, Put Sv. Nikola 43; walk along waterfront from Old Town with bay on your right, look for *Apartments Depolo* sign at the yellow house set back from the street, just before the two monasteries; tel. 020/711-621, mobile 098-964-3687, viladepolo@hotmail.com).

$ Marco Polo Apartments has four bright and clean apartments in the Old Town (Db-€40, or €50 July–Aug, cash only or pay online through PayPal, air-con, ulica Marka Andrijica, mobile 099-686-3717, British tel. +44-794-620-8177, www.marcopolo -apartments.com, info@korculainfo.com).

$ Anka Portolan, with her helpful English-speaking grand-daughter Vesna, rents four fine, older-feeling rooms perfectly located near the wall in the Old Town (July–Aug: Db-€45, apartment-€50, progressively less off-season, no extra charge for 1- or 2-night stays, no breakfast, cash only, ulica Don Pavla Poše 7, tel. 020/711-711, vitomir.stankovic@du.t-com.hr).

$ *Booking* **Sobe** *Through an Agency:* While you can walk along Put Sv. Nikola and generally find a fine deal on a private room, you can also book one through one of Korčula's travel agencies for an additional 20 percent (figure Db-€35–50 in high season, €20–35 off-season, 30 percent more for 1- or 2-night stays). For information on the two main agencies—Marko Polo Tours and Atlas Travel—see "Helpful Hints," earlier in this chapter.

Hotels

All five of Korčula's hotels are owned by HTP Korčula. If you don't want to stay in a *soba,* these are the only game in town. You can reserve rooms at any of them through the main office (tel. 020/726-336, fax 020/711-746, www.korcula-hotels.com, marketing @htp-korcula.hr). I've listed peak-season prices with breakfast only; rates are progressively lower the further off-season you get. You can pay 10 percent more per person for half-board (dinner at the hotel). It's much cheaper to stay a week or longer. There's a long-term plan to renovate all of these hotels, but so far the Marko Polo is the only one that's seen any progress (and the only one that has air-con).

$$$ Hotel Korčula has by far the best location, right on the waterfront alongside the Old Town. It has a fine seaside terrace restaurant and friendly staff, even if the 20 rooms are outmoded and waaay overpriced. The rooms are on two floors: The more expensive "first-floor" rooms (actually on the third floor) have big windows and sea views; the cheaper "second-floor" rooms (actually on the fourth floor) have tiny windows and no views (July–Aug: Sb-€120, Db-€160; June and Sept: Sb-€90, Db-€130; cheaper Oct–May; reception tel. 020/711-078).

$$$ Hotel Marko Polo, the only one of the chain that has been renovated, has 94 crisp rooms, air-conditioning, and an elevator. All of this makes it the town's only real "splurge"...and it's priced accordingly (July–Aug: Sb-€150, Db-€200; June and Sept: Sb-€105, Db-€150; cheaper Oct–May; reception tel. 020/726-004).

$$$ Other Hotels: Three more hotels cluster a 15-minute walk away, around the far side of Shell Bay. All are poorly maintained, overpriced, and relatively inconvenient to the Old Town, but they share a nice beach. **Hotel Liburna,** with a clever split-level design that reflects the skyline of the Old Town, has 109 rooms, most of them accessible by elevator; half the rooms face the sea and cost an additional 10 percent (July–Aug: Sb-€120, Db-€160; June and Sept: Sb-€90, Db-€130; cheaper Oct–May; reception tel. 020/726-006). Dreary **Hotel Park** has 153 cheaper rooms (reception tel. 020/726-100). The fifth hotel, **Hotel Bon Repos**—another 15 minutes by foot from the Old Town—is, in every sense, the last resort.

EATING

Korčula is awash in interchangeable seafood restaurants. These are all good options, but (with the exception of Fresh) everything in town is pretty similar—make your decision based on atmosphere and what looks best to you. The price ranges given here don't include top-end seafood splurges (which are normally listed in menus by the 100-gram unit or by the kilogram). Note that almost all of these eateries close from about November to Easter.

Pizzeria Amfora, on a side lane off the people-parade up Korčula's main drag in the Old Town, features delicious and well-priced pastas and pizzas. Squeeze into the small dining room or enjoy the sidewalk tables (50–60-kn pizzas and pastas, 60–100-kn main dishes, daily 11:00–24:00, closed 15:00–18:00 and Sun dinner in shoulder season, ulica od Teatra 4, tel. 020/711-739).

Adio Mare, with fine seafood, may have the best decor in town: a cavernous stone dining room with long shared tables and a thick vine scaling one wall. Or climb the stairs and cross the little bridge to the delightful rooftop garden terrace (50–100-kn main dishes, well-described menu, daily 17:30–24:00, sometimes also 12:00–14:00 in peak season, on the main drag just past Marco Polo's House, tel. 020/711-253).

Konoba Marinero has pleasantly nautical decor, outdoor tables on an atmospherically tight lane, and a simple menu of Dalmatian specialties (60–100-kn main dishes, Easter–Oct daily 11:00–24:00, closed Nov–Easter, Marka Andrijića 13, tel. 020/711-170).

Konoba Morski Konjic ("Moorish Seahorse") has tables spilling along the eastern seawall, offering al fresco dining with salty views. Even though the crank-'em-out food is disappointing and the service is jaded, this is the best option for romantic harborside dining (60–100-kn main dishes, 10-kn cover, daily 8:00–24:00). A small second location is right at the tip of town, across from the Buffet Massimo tower (see below).

Cheaper Options Around Shell Bay: Prices inside the Old Town are the highest in Korčula. But several cheaper eateries lie just outside the Old Town. Window-shop menus along the harbor, then hang a left at the bus station and continue up the road toward the big resort hotels. You'll find plenty of cafés, pizzerias, and *konobas* (traditional restaurants), most with outdoor seating.

Quick and Tasty: **Fresh,** an innovative and youthful spot run by a Canadian-Croatian couple, offers 30-kn wraps and 20-kn smoothies. If you want a break from grilled seafood and pizza, this is the place (July–Aug daily 9:00–1:00 in the morning, until 19:00 in shoulder season, closed in winter, along Shell Bay behind the sunken-ship playground on the way to the bus station).

Picnics: Just outside the main gate, you'll find a lively produce market and a big, modern, air-conditioned **Konzum** supermarket (Mon–Sat 7:00–20:30, Sun 8:00–20:00, next to Marko Polo Tours). A short stroll from there, down Put Sv. Nikola, takes you to beach perches with the best Korčula views. Otherwise, there are many inviting picnic spots along the Old Town embankment.

A Scenic Drink: The best setting for drinks is at **Buffet "Massimo,"** a youthful-feeling cocktail bar in a city-wall tower at the very tip of the Old Town peninsula. You can have a drink on one of three levels: the downstairs bar, the main-floor lounge, or climb the ladder (at your own risk) to the tower-top terrace (terrace is only for cocktail-sippers—no beer or wine). If you're up top, notice the simple dumbwaiter for hauling up drinks (35–50-kn cocktails, daily in summer 18:00–2:00 in the morning, shoulder season 17:30–1:00 in the morning, closed Nov–April, tel. 020/715-073).

Sweet Shop: For some good (if pricey) local sweets, stop by **Cukarin,** which sells tasty traditional cookies such as the *amareta* almond cake and the walnut cream–filled *klašun*. They also sell homemade wine, liqueur, honey, and jam (Mon–Sat 8:30–12:00 & 17:30–20:00, closed Sun and Jan–Feb, a block behind the Jadrolinija office on ulica Hrvatske Bratske Zajednice, tel. 020/711-055).

Ice Cream: My favorite *sladoled* in Korčula is at **Kiwi** (just up the lane across from Konzum supermarket, open long hours daily).

TRANSPORTATION CONNECTIONS

Korčula is reasonably well connected to the rest of the Dalmatian Coast by boat, but service becomes sparse in the off-season. If you're here during a lull in the sailing schedule, buses are your ticket out of town. No matter when you travel, it's smart to carefully study current boat schedules when planning your itinerary, as they are always subject to change.

Korčula Boat Connections

Boats big and small depart from the embankment surrounding Korčula's Old Town peninsula. Which side of the peninsula a boat uses can depend on the weather—be flexible and inquire locally about where to meet your boat. Some boats leave from other parts of the island, most notably the town of Vela Luka (at the opposite tip of the island, a 1-hour bus ride from Korčula town—described below). Other boats, including the car ferry to Orebić (described under "Route Tips for Drivers" at the end of this chapter), leave from the Dominče dock, about a five-minute drive east of Korčula town.

Big Jadrolinija Car Ferries: From Korčula town, these huge, handy vessels go north, to **Stari Grad** on Hvar Island (20-min bus ride from Hvar town; 2/week year-round, 3.5 hrs; the catamaran described next is faster and takes you right to Hvar town) and **Split** (3/week July–mid-Sept, 2/week mid-Sept–June, 3.5–6 hrs); or south, to **Sobra** on Mljet Island (1.25-hr bus ride from the national park, 3/week July–Sept, 2/week June, none Oct–May, 2 hrs; for details, see next) and **Dubrovnik** (5/week July–Sept, 4/week June, 2/week Oct–May, 3–4 hrs).

Speedy *Krilo* Catamaran from Korčula Town to Hvar Town and Split: A speedy catamaran called *Krilo* leaves Korčula town at 6:00 and zips to Hvar town and Split (daily June–Sept, daily except Sun Oct–May, 2 hrs to Hvar, 3 hrs to Split, some summer boats stop at Prigradica on Korčula Island—in which case these times are longer). In Korčula, tickets for the *Krilo* boat are sold at Marko Polo Tours—not the Jadrolinija office (35 kn one-way to Hvar, 55 kn to Split). Since it returns from Split and Hvar the same afternoon, this extremely handy catamaran allows you to effortlessly day-trip to either place (see "Transportation Connections" for Split). For the latest schedule, see www.krilo.hr.

Speedy *Nona Ana* Catamaran to Mljet and Dubrovnik: From June through September, this convenient boat zips travelers from Korčula to Polače (on Mljet Island, handy to the national park there), then to Sobra (a less-appealing spot on Mljet) and on to Dubrovnik (4/week, generally departs Korčula at 16:00, 1 hr and 30 kn to Polače, 2.75 hrs and 55 kn to Dubrovnik). Unfortunately, the boat doesn't serve Korčula in the winter (Oct–May). Confirm schedules at www.gv-line.hr, and buy tickets at Marko Polo Tours.

From Vela Luka to Hvar Town and Split: There are additional boats to points north, but they usually require a very early bus from Korčula town (departing at 4:00) to the port at Vela Luka, an hour away at the other end of the island. A Jadrolinija **fast catamaran** goes daily from Vela Luka to both Hvar town and Split (Mon–Sat departs at 5:30, Sun at 8:00, 45 min to Hvar, 2 hrs to Split). A much slower **car ferry** also travels daily from Vela Luka to Split (departs June–Sept 2/day at 6:15 and 13:45— take the 12:15 bus from Korčula to catch the later boat; different schedule Oct–May; 2.75 hrs, does not stop at Hvar town). Since reaching Vela Luka from Korčula town is a hassle, carefully confirm these boat schedules and understand all your options (at the Korčula TI or Jadrolinija office) before you get up early to make the trip.

The Excursion Loophole: If you're desperate to reach a particular place (such as Mostar or Mljet National Park) from Korčula, and too impatient to wait for regularly scheduled service, consider paying for an excursion...then "forgetting" to return with the rest of your group (but tell your guide so no one waits around for you). Sometimes you'll pay full price, but occasionally you'll only be charged half. Be warned that this is far from a sure thing: Sometimes the agencies aren't willing to let you do it, and excursions can be sold out. And obviously it's much more expensive than a boat ticket (especially if they charge you full price). But, if you're in need, it's worth a try. Ask at Atlas and Marko Polo travel agencies, and try to look as pathetic as possible.

Korčula Bus Connections

All buses from Korčula town (except those to Vela Luka) first drive to Dominče, where they meet the car ferry to cross over to Orebić, on the Pelješac Peninsula. Don't be surprised if you have to get off the bus, walk onto the ferry, and meet a different bus across the channel. It takes just over an hour to drive the length of the Pelješac Peninsula and meet the main coastal road.

From Korčula Town by Bus to: Dubrovnik (peak season: 2/day, 3.5 hrs; off-season: Mon–Sat 1/day with an early departure, Sun 2/day; about 100 kn), **Zagreb** (1/day, 9–13.5 hrs depending on route), **Split** (1/day, 5 hrs, same bus goes to Zagreb), **Vela Luka** (at far end of island, Mon–Fri 7/day, Sat 6/day, Sun 4/day, 1 hr, first bus at 4:00 gets you to the early-morning ferries—see above).

Shuttle Bus to Dubrovnik: Korkyra Travel Agency runs a handy minibus that costs only slightly more than the bus, and takes you right to your accommodations in Dubrovnik (120 kn one-way, runs Mon–Fri at 7:00 year-round, also at 8:00 with demand, Sat–Sun by request only, 2 hrs, includes light breakfast and room-finding help if needed, reserve ahead, mobile 091-571-4355, www.korkyra.info, info@korkyra.info).

Route Tips for Drivers:
Between Korčula and the Mainland

The island of Korčula is connected to the mainland by a small car ferry that runs between Dominče—about a mile east of Korčula town—and Orebić, across the channel on the Pelješac Peninsula (50 kn/car, 12 kn/passenger, 15-min crossing, departs Dominče at the top of most but not all hours—check carefully in Korčula, departs Orebić at :30 past most hours).

If you're driving via the mainland, you'll first cross on this car ferry to Orebić on the vineyard-strewn Pelješac Peninsula. The Pelješac Peninsula is extremely long and narrow, and the roads are very rough, so it can take longer than you'd expect to reach the main coastal road (figure 1–1.5 hrs). Where the peninsula meets the mainland, you'll see the cute little "Great Wall of Croatia" town of Ston.

If you're heading south to **Dubrovnik,** the coastal road zips you right there (about an hour from Ston). If you're heading north to **Split,** soon after joining the coastal road you'll actually pass through Bosnia-Herzegovina for a few miles (around the town of Neum—just stop and flash your passport as you enter and exit the country).

Because of the ferry crossing and the long drive along the Pelješac Peninsula, driving **between Split and Korčula** is time-consuming and tiring. Instead, I prefer to take the longer car ferry the whole way between Split and Vela Luka, at the far end of Korčula Island (described above; allow 1 hour for the drive from Korčula town to Vela Luka, about 300 kn per car). The scenic and relaxing 2.75-hour boat ride saves you more than that much driving time.

ROVINJ

Pula • Motovun

Rising dramatically from the Adriatic as though being pulled up to heaven by its grand bell tower, Rovinj (roh-VEEN; Rovigno/roh-VEEN-yoh in Italian) is a welcoming Old World oasis in a sea of tourist kitsch. Among the villages of Croatia's coast, there's something particularly romantic about Rovinj—the most Italian town in Croatia's most Italian region. Rovinj's streets are delightfully twisty, its ancient houses are characteristically crumbling, and its harbor—lively with real-life fishermen—is as salty as they come. Like a little Venice on a hill, Rovinj is the stage set for your Croatian seaside dreams.

Rovinj was wealthy and well-fortified in the Middle Ages. It boomed in the 16th and 17th centuries, when it was flooded with refugees fleeing both the Ottoman invasions and the plague. Because the town was part of the Republic of Venice for five centuries (13th to 18th centuries), its architecture, culture, and even dialect is strongly Venetian. The local folk groups sing in a dialect actually considered more Venetian than the Venetians themselves speak these days. (You can even see Venice from Rovinj's church bell tower on a very clear day.)

After Napoleon seized the region, then was defeated, Rovinj became part of Austria. While the Venetians had neglected the town, the Austrians invested in it, bringing the railroad, gas lights, and a huge Ronhill tobacco factory (recently replaced by an enormous, state-of-the-art facility farther inland). The Austrians chose Pula and Trieste to be the empire's major ports—cursing those cities with pollution and sprawl, while allowing Rovinj to linger in its trapped-in-the-past quaintness.

Before long, Austrians discovered Rovinj as a handy escape for

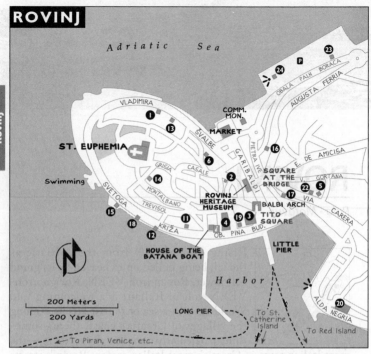

ROVINJ

Adriatic Sea

VLADIMIRA

COMM. MON.

MARKET

ST. EUPHEMIA

ŠVALBE

GARIBALDI

PIETRA IN.

Swimming

GRISIA

CASALE

MONTALBANO

SVETOGA

TREVISOL

KRIŽA

ROVINJ HERITAGE MUSEUM

OB. PINA BUD.

BALBI ARCH

TITO SQUARE

SQUARE AT THE BRIDGE

E. DE AMICISA

GORTANA

VIA

CARERA

OBALA PALIH BORACA

AUGUSTA FERRIA

LITTLE PIER

HOUSE OF THE BATANA BOAT

Harbor

200 Meters

200 Yards

LONG PIER

To St. Catherine Island

To Red Island

ALDA NEGRIA

To Piran, Venice, etc.

a beach holiday. Tourism came to town in the late 1890s, when a powerful Austrian baron bought one of the remote, barren islands offshore and brought it back to life with gardens and a grand villa. Before long, another baron bought another island...and a tourist boom was underway. In more recent times, Rovinj has become a top destination for nudists. The resort of Valalta, just to the north, is a popular spot for those seeking "southern exposure"... as a very revealing brochure at the TI explains (www.valalta.hr). Whether you want to find PNBs (pudgy nude bodies), or avoid them, remember that the German phrase *FKK* (*Freikörper Kultur,* or "free body culture") is international shorthand for nudism.

Rovinj is the star attraction of Croatia's wedge-shaped Istrian Peninsula. With more time in Istria (EE-stree-ah; "Istra" in Croatian), visit the striking Roman ruins in urban Pula and the laid-back hill town of Motovun (both described later in this chapter; for more on Istria, see page 746).

Rovinj is the most atmospheric of Croatia's small coastal towns. Unfortunately, it's also one of the most over-promoted—as you approach, you pass endless billboards touting hotels, restaurants, and tour companies. But if you survive this tacky gauntlet, the commercialism melts away as soon as you set foot in Rovinj's Old Town.

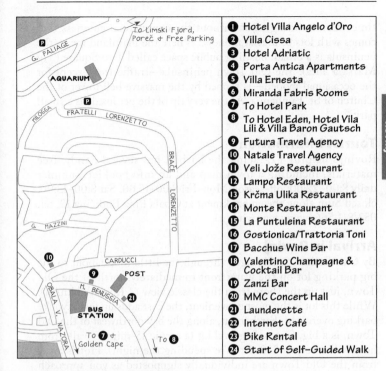

To Limski Fjord, Poreč & Free Parking

G. PALIAGE

AQUARIUM

MILOSSA

FRATELLI LORENZETTO

BRACE

LORENZETTO

G. MAZZINI

CARDUCCI

POST

OBALA V. NAZORA

M. BENUSSIA

BUS STATION

To **7** & Golden Cape

To **8**

❶ Hotel Villa Angelo d'Oro
❷ Villa Cissa
❸ Hotel Adriatic
❹ Porta Antica Apartments
❺ Villa Ernesta
❻ Miranda Fabris Rooms
❼ To Hotel Park
❽ To Hotel Eden, Hotel Vila Lili & Villa Baron Gautsch
❾ Futura Travel Agency
❿ Natale Travel Agency
⓫ Veli Jože Restaurant
⓬ Lampo Restaurant
⓭ Krčma Ulika Restaurant
⓮ Monte Restaurant
⓯ La Puntuleina Restaurant
⓰ Gostionica/Trattoria Toni
⓱ Bacchus Wine Bar
⓲ Valentino Champagne & Cocktail Bar
⓳ Zanzi Bar
⓴ MMC Concert Hall
㉑ Launderette
㉒ Internet Café
㉓ Bike Rental
㉔ Start of Self-Guided Walk

Planning Your Time

While you can reach Rovinj by bus (see "Transportation Connections" on page 745), it's most worthwhile by car (which allows you to easily visit nearby destinations, such as Pula and Motovun). For drivers, Rovinj fits neatly between Slovenia and Croatia (for example, on a Ljubljana-Lake Bled-Julian Alps-Rovinj-Plitvice-Split itinerary).

Rovinj is hardly packed with diversions. You can get the gist of it in a one-hour wander, but the town deserves the better part of a day to enjoy its ambience and pedal a rental bike to a nearby beach for swimming or sunbathing.

With a second day, side-trip to Pula and Motovun; to fill a lazy afternoon on a single day, choose just one of these attractions.

Be aware that much of Rovinj closes down from November through Easter.

ORIENTATION

(area code: 052)

Rovinj, once an island, is now a peninsula. The Old Town is divided in two parts: a particularly charismatic chunk on the oval-shaped peninsula, and the rest on the mainland (with similarly time-worn buildings, but without the commercial cuteness that comes with lots of tourist money). Where the mainland meets the peninsula is a broad, bustling public space called Tito Square (Trg Maršala Tita). The Old Town peninsula—traffic-free except for the occasional moped—is topped by the massive bell tower of the Church of St. Euphemia. At the very tip of the peninsula is a small park.

Tourist Information

Rovinj's helpful TI, facing the harbor, has several handy, free materials, including a town map and an info booklet (summer daily 8:00–22:00; off-season Mon–Fri 8:00–15:00, Sat 8:00–13:00, closed Sun; along the embankment at Obala Pina Budičina 12, tel. 052/811-566, www.tzgrovinj.hr).

Arrival in Rovinj

By Car: Follow *Centar* signs through the little roundabout to the big parking lot on the waterfront immediately north of the Old Town, just up the shore from the classic view of Rovinj (5 kn/hr). While this lot is the most convenient, the cost adds up fast if you're parking overnight. Farther out, along the bay northwest of the Old Town, is a big, free, safe gravel lot (a scenic 15-minute walk from here will save you $20 if you're spending the night). Hotels away from the Old Town are individually signposted as you approach the town center.

By Bus: The bus station is on the south side of the Old Town, close to the harbor. Leave the station to the left, then walk on busy Carera street directly into the center of town.

By Boat: The few boats connecting Rovinj to Venice, Piran, and other towns dock at the long pier protruding from the Old Town peninsula. Simply walk up the pier, and you're in the heart of town.

Helpful Hints

Laundry: The full-service **Galax** launderette hides up the street beyond the bus station (10 kn per kilogram for wash and dry, Mon–Fri 7:00–19:00, Sat–Sun 7:00–15:00, closed Sun Nov–Easter, up Istarska street past the bus station, on the left after the post office, tel. 052/816-130).

Internet Access: A-Mar Internet Club has several terminals and long hours (40 kn/hr, Mon–Fri 8:00–22:00, Sat–Sun 8:00–23:00, on the main drag in the mainland part of the Old Town, Carera 26, tel. 052/841-211).

Local Guides: Vukica Palčić is a very capable guide who knows her town intimately and loves to share it with visitors (€50 for a 2-hour tour, mobile 098-794-4003, vukica.palcic@pu.t-com.hr).

Renato Orbanić is a laid-back musician (sax) who also enjoys wandering through town with visitors. While light on heavy-hitting facts, his casual tour somehow suits this easygoing little town (€60 for a 2-hour tour, mobile 091-521-6206, rorbanic@inet.hr).

Best Views: The town is full of breathtaking views. Photography buffs will be busy in the "magic hours" of early morning and evening, and even by moonlight. The postcard view of Rovinj is from the parking lot embankment at the north end of the Old Town (at the start of the "Self-Guided Walk," below). For a different perspective on the Old Town, head for the far side of the harbor on the opposite (south) end of town. The church bell tower provides a virtual aerial view of the town and a grand vista of the outlying islands.

SELF-GUIDED WALK

▲▲▲Rovinj Ramble

This orientation walk introduces you to Rovinj in about an hour. Begin at the parking lot just north of the Old Town.

Old Town View

Many places offer fine views of Rovinj's Old Town, but this is the most striking. Boats bob in the harbor, and behind them Venetian-

looking homes seem to rise from the deep. (For an aerial perspective, notice the big billboard overhead and to the left.)

The Old Town is topped by the church, whose bell tower is capped by a weathervane in the shape of Rovinj's patron saint, Euphemia. Local fishermen look to this saintly weathervane for direction: When Euphemia is looking out to sea, it means the stiff, fresh Bora wind is blowing, bringing dry air from the interior...a sailor's delight. But if she's facing the land, the humid Jugo wind will soon bring bad weather from the sea. After a day or so, even a tourist learns to look to St. Euphemia for the weather report.

As you soak in this scene, ponder how the town's history created its current shape. The town was first mentioned in the fifth century. In the Middle Ages, Rovinj was an island, rather than a peninsula, and it was surrounded by a double wall—a protective inner wall and an outer seawall. Because it was so well defended against pirates and other marauders (not to mention the plague), it was extremely desirable real estate. And yet, it was easy to reach from the mainland, allowing it to thrive as a trading town. With more than 10,000 residents at its peak, Rovinj became immensely crowded, explaining today's pleasantly claustrophobic Old Town.

Over the centuries—as demand for living space trumped security concerns—the town walls were converted into houses, with windows grafted onto their imposing frame. Gaps in the wall, with steps that seem to end at the water, are where fishermen would pull in to unload their catch directly into the warehouse on the bottom level of the houses. (Later you can explore some of these lanes from inside the town.) Today, if you live in one of these houses, the Adriatic is your backyard.

• *Now head into town. In the little park near the sea, just beyond the end of the parking lot, look for the big, blocky...*

Communist-Era Monument

Dating from the time of Tito, this celebrates the Partisan Army's victory over the Nazis in World War II, and commemorates the victims of fascism. The minimal-ist reliefs on the ceremonial tomb show a slow prisoners' parade of victims prodded by a gun in the back from a figure with a Nazi-style helmet. Notice that one side of the monument is in Croatian, and the other is in Italian. With typical Yugoslav grace and subtlety, this jarring block shatters the otherwise

harmonious time-warp vibe of Rovinj. Fortunately, it's the only modern structure anywhere near the Old Town.

• *Now walk a few more steps toward town, stopping to explore the covered...*

Market

The front part of the market, near the water, is for souvenirs. But natives delve deeper in, to the local produce stands. Separating the gifty stuff from the nitty-gritty produce is a line of merchants aggressively pushing free samples. Everything is local and mostly homemade. Consider this snack-time tactic: loiter around, joking with the farmers while sampling their various tasty walnuts, figs, cherries, olive oils, *rakija* (the powerful schnapps popular through-out the Balkans), and more. If the sample is good, buy some more for a picnic. In the center of the market, a delightful and practical fountain from 1908 reminds locals of the infrastructure brought in by their Hapsburg rulers a century ago. The hall labeled *Ribarnica/Pescheria* at the back of the market is where you'll find fresh, practically wriggling fish. This is where locals gather ingredients

Italo-Croatia

Apart from its tangible attractions, one of the Istrian Peninsula's hallmarks is its biculturalism: It's an engaging hybrid of Croatia and Italy. Like most of the Croatian Coast, Istria has variously been controlled by Illyrians, Romans, Byzantines, Slavs, Venetians, and Austrians. After the Hapsburgs lost World War I, most of today's Croatia joined Yugoslavia—but Istria became part of Italy. During this time, the Croatian vernacular was suppressed, while the Italian language and culture flourished. This extra chapter of Italian rule left Istrians with an identity crisis. After World War II, Istria joined Yugoslavia, and Croatian culture and language returned. But many people here found it difficult to abandon their ties to Italy.

Today, depending on who you ask, Istria is the most Italian part of Croatia...or the most Croatian part of Italy. Istria pops up on Italian weather reports. Not long ago, Italy's then-Prime Minister Silvio Berlusconi declared that he still considered Istria part of Italy—and he wanted it back. When I wrote an article about Istria for a newspaper recently, some Italian readers complained that I made it sound "too Croatian," while some Croatians claimed my depiction was "too Italian."

People who actually live here typically don't worry about the distinction. Locals insist that they're not Croatians and not Italians—they're Istrians. They don't mind straddling two cultures. Both languages are official (and often taught side-by-side in schools), street signs are bilingual, and most Istrians dabble in each tongue—often seeming to foreign ears as though they're mixing the two at once.

As a result of their tangled history, Istrians have learned how to be mellow and take things as they come. They're gregarious, open-minded, and sometimes seem to thrive on chaos. A twentysomething local told me, "My ancestors lived in Venice. My great-grandfather lived in Austria. My grandfather lived in Italy. My father lived in Yugoslavia. I live in Croatia. My son will live in the European Union. And we've all lived in the same town."

for their favorite dish, *brodet*—a stew of various kinds of seafood mixed with olive oil and wine...all of this region's best bits rolled into one dish. It's slowly simmered and generally served with polenta (unfortunately, it's rare in restaurants).

• *Continue up the broad street, named for* **Giuseppe Garibaldi**—*one of the major players in late-19th-century Italian unification. Imagine: Even though you're in Croatia, Italian patriots are celebrated in this very Italian-feeling town (see the "Italo-Croatia" sidebar above). After one long block, you'll come to the wide cross-street called...*

Square at the Bridge (Trg na Mostu)

This marks the site of the medieval bridge that once connected the fortified island of Rovinj to the mainland (as illustrated in the small painting above the door of the Kavana al Ponto—"Bridge Café"). Back then, the island was populated mostly by Italians, while the mainland was the territory of Slavic farmers. But as Rovinj's strategic importance waned, and its trading status rose, the need for easy access became more important than the canal's protective purpose—so in 1763, it was filled in. The two populations integrated, creating the bicultural mix that survives today.

Notice the breeze? Via Garibaldi is nicknamed Val de Bora ("Valley of the Bora Wind") for the constant cooling wind that blows here. Nearby (on the left), the Viecia Batana Café (named for Rovinj's unique, flat-bottomed little fishing boats) has a retro interior with a circa-1960 fishermen mural that evokes an earlier age. The café is popular for its chocolate cake and "Batana" ice cream. On the island side of Trg na Mostu is the Rovinj Heritage Museum (described under "Sights," page 738). Next door, the town's cultural center posts lovingly hand-lettered signs in Croatian and Italian announcing upcoming musical events (generally free, designed for locals, and worth noting and enjoying).

• *Now proceed to the little fountain in the middle of the square (near Hotel Adriatic)...*

Tito Square (Trg Maršala Tita)

This wide-open square at the entrance to the Old Town is the crossroads of Rovinj. The **fountain,** with a little boy holding a water-spouting fish, celebrates the government-funded water system that finally brought running water to the Old Town in 1959. Walk around the fountain, with your eyes on the relief, to see a successful socialist society at the inauguration of this new water system. Despite the happy occasion, the figures are pretty stiff—conformity trumped most other virtues in Tito's world.

Now walk out to the end of the concrete pier, called the **Mali Molo ("Little Pier").** From here, you're surrounded by Rovinj's crowded harbor, with fishing vessels and excursion boats that shuttle tourists out to the offshore islands. If the weather's good, a boat trip can be a memorable way to get out on the water for a different angle on Rovinj. In Rovinj's own little archipelago, the two most popular islands to visit are St. Catherine (Sv. Katarina—the lush, green island just across the harbor, about a 5-min trip, boats run 2/hr in summer, 15 kn) and Red Island (Crveni Otok—farther out, about a 15-min trip, boats run hourly in summer, 30 kn). Each island has a hotel and its own share of beaches. If you're more interested in the boat trip than the destination, it's also fun to simply go for a cruise to the various coves and islands around Rovinj—to figure out your options, chat with the captains nearby hawking excursions. You'll also see kitschy trinket-laden souvenir boats bobbing precariously in the surf.

Scan the **harbor.** On the left is the MMC, the local concert hall (see "Nightlife," page 739). Above and behind the MMC, the highest bell tower inland marks the Franciscan monastery, which was the only building on the mainland back before the island town was connected to shore. Along the waterfront to the right of the MMC is Hotel Park, a typical monster hotel from the communist era, now tastefully renovated on the inside (see "Sleeping," page 743). A recommended bike path starts just past this hotel, leading into a nature preserve and the best nearby beaches (which you can see in the distance; for more on bike rental, see page 739).

Now head back to the base of the pier. If you were to walk down the **embankment** between the harbor and the Old Town (past Hotel Adriatic), you'd find the TI and a delightful "restaurant row" with several tempting places for a drink or a meal. Many fishermen pull their boats into this harbor, then simply walk their catch across the street to a waiting restaurateur. (This self-guided walk finishes with a stroll down this lane.)

Backtrack 10 paces past the fountain and face the Old Town entrance gate, called the **Balbi Arch.** The winged lion on top is a reminder this was Venetian territory for centuries.

• *Head through the gate into the Old Town. Inside and on the left is the...*

Town Hall

On the old Town Hall, notice another Venetian lion, as well as other historic crests embedded in the wall. The town hall actually sports an Italian flag (along with ones for Croatia and Rovinj) and faces a square named for Giacomo Matteotti, a much-revered Italian patriot. Nearby, with a *batana* boat out front, is the Italian Union building—even more reminders of how Istria has an important bond with Italy.

A few more steps in, Trattoria Cisterna faces the square that once functioned as a cistern (collecting rainwater, which was pulled from a subterranean reservoir through the well you see today).

• *Now begin walking up the street to the left of Trattoria Cisterna...*

Rovinj

Grisia Street

The main "street" (actually a tight lane) leading through the middle of the island is choked with tourists during the midday rush and lined with art galleries. This inspiring town has attracted many artists, some of whom display their works along this colorful stretch. Notice the rusty little nails speckling the walls—each year in August, an art festival invites locals to hang their best art on this street. With paintings lining the lane, the entire community comes out to enjoy each other's creations.

As you walk, keep your camera cocked and ready, as you can find delightful scenes down every side lane. Remember that, as crowded as it is today, little Rovinj was even more packed in the Middle Ages. Keep an eye out for arches that span narrow lanes (such as on the right, at Arsenale street)—the only way a walled city could grow was up. Many of these additions created hidden little courtyards, nooks, and crannies that make it easy to get away from the crowds and claim a corner of the town for yourself. Another sign of Rovinj's overcrowding are the distinctive chimneys poking up above the rooftops. These chimneys, added long after the buildings were first constructed, made it possible to heat previously underutilized rooms...and squeeze in even more people.

• *At the top of town is the can't-miss-it...*

▲Church of St. Euphemia (Sv. Eufemija)

Rovinj's landmark Baroque church dates from 1754. It's watched over by an enormous 190-foot-tall campanile, a replica of the famous bell tower on St. Mark's Square in Venice. The tower is topped by a copper weathervane with the weather-predicting St. Euphemia, the church's namesake (described below).

Go inside (free, generally open May–Sept daily 10:00–19:00, less off-season). The vast, somewhat gloomy interior boasts some fine altars of Carrara marble (a favorite medium of Michelangelo's). Services here are celebrated using a combination of Croatian and Italian, suiting the town's mixed population.

To the right of the main altar is the church's highlight: the chapel containing the relics of St. Euphemia. Before stepping into the chapel, notice the altar featuring Euphemia—depicted, as she usually is, with her wheel (a reminder of her torture) and a palm frond (symbolic of her martyrdom), and holding the fortified town of Rovinj, of which she was the protector.

St. Euphemia was the virtuous daughter of a prosperous

early-fourth-century family in Chalcedon (near today's Istanbul). Euphemia used her family's considerable wealth to help the poor. Unfortunately, her pious philanthropy happened to coincide with anti-Christian purges by the Roman Emperor Diocletian. When she was 15 years old, Euphemia was arrested for refusing to worship the local pagan idol. She was brutally tortured, her bones broken on a wheel. Finally she was thrown to the lions as a public spectacle. But, the story goes, the lions miraculously refused to attack her—only nipping her gently on one arm. The Romans murdered Euphemia anyway, and her remains were later rescued by Christians. In the year 800, a gigantic marble sarcophagus containing St. Euphemia's relics somehow found its way into the Adriatic and floated all the way up to Istria, where Rovinj fishermen discovered it bobbing in the sea. They towed it back to town, where a crowd gathered. The townspeople realized what it was, and wanted to take it up to the hilltop church (an earlier version of the one we're in now). But nobody could move it...until a young boy with two young calves showed up. He said he'd had a dream of St. Euphemia—and, sure enough, he succeeded in dragging her relics to where they still lie.

The small chapel behind the altar is dominated by Euphemia's famous sarcophagus. The front panel (behind the glass) is opened with much fanfare every September 16, St. Euphemia's feast day, to display the small, withered, waxen face of Rovinj's favorite saint. The sarcophagus is flanked by frescoes depicting her most memorable moment (protected by angels, as a bored-looking lion tenderly nibbles at her right bicep), and her arrival here in Rovinj (with burly fishermen looking astonished as the young boy succeeds in moving the giant sarcophagus). Note the depiction of Rovinj fortified by a double crenellated wall—looking more like a castle than like the creaky fishing village of today. At the top of the hill is an earlier version of today's church.

• *If you have time and energy, consider climbing the...*

Bell Tower

Scaling the church bell tower's creaky wooden stairway requires an enduring faith in the reliability of wood. It rewards those who brave the climb with a commanding view of the town and surrounding islands (10 kn, same hours as church, enter from inside church—to the left of the main altar). The climb doubles your altitude, and from this perch you can also look down—taking advantage of the quirky little round hole in the floor to photograph the memorable staircase you just climbed.

• *As you leave the church, dead ahead is a peaceful café on a park terrace (once a cemetery). To the right, a winding lane leads down toward the water, then zigzags left past a WWII pillbox and back into town past the "restaurant row." As you stroll back toward the main square, survey the various restaurants and bars (described under "Eating," page 744).*

SIGHTS

▲House of the Batana Boat (Kuća o Batani)—Rovinj has a long, noble shipbuilding tradition, and this tiny but interesting museum gives you the story of the town's distinctive *batana* boats...and lets you feel the soul of this town. These flat-bottomed vessels are favored by local fishermen for their ability to reach rocky areas close to shore that are rich with certain shellfish. The museum explains how the boats are built, with the help of an entertaining elapsed-time video showing a boat built from scratch in five minutes. You'll also meet some of the salty old sailors who use these vessels (find the placemat with wine stains, and put the glass in different red circles to hear various seamen talk in the Rovinj dialect). Upstairs is a wall of photos of *batana* boats still in active use, a tiny library (peruse photos of the town from a century ago), and a video screen displaying *bitinada* music—local music with harmonizing voices that imitate instruments. Sit down and listen to several (there's a button for skipping ahead). The museum has no posted English information, so pick up the comprehensive English flyer as you enter (10 kn; June–Sept daily 9:00–13:00 & 19:00–22:00; Oct–Dec and March–May Tue–Sun 10:00–13:00 & 15:00–17:00, closed Mon; closed Jan–Feb; Obala Pina Budicina 2, tel. 052/812-593, www.batana.org).

Rovinj Heritage Museum (Zavičajni Muzej Grada Rovinja)—This ho-hum museum combines art old (obscure classic painters) and new (obscure contemporary painters from Rovinj) in an old mansion. Rounding out the collection are some model ships and a small archaeological exhibit (15 kn; summer Tue–Fri 9:00–15:00 & 19:00–22:00, Sat–Sun 9:00–14:00 & 19:00–22:00, closed Mon; winter Tue–Sat 9:00–15:00, closed Sun–Mon; Trg Maršala Tita 11, tel. 052/816-720, www.muzej-rovinj.com).

Aquarium (Akvarij)—This century-old collection of local sealife is one of Europe's oldest aquariums (15 kn, daily in summer 9:00–21:00, progressively shorter hours off-season, a 10-min walk up the coast from the parking lots, Obala G. Paliage 5, tel. 052/804-712).

ACTIVITIES

▲Swimming and Sunbathing—The most central spot to swim or sunbathe is on the rocks along the embankment on the south side of the Old Town peninsula. For bigger beaches, go to the wooded Golden Cape (Zlatni Rat) south of the harbor (past the big, waterfront Hotel Park). This cape is lined with walking paths and beaches, and shaded by a wide variety of trees and plants. For a scenic and memorable sunbathing spot, choose a perch facing Rovinj on the north side of the Golden Cape. To get away from it all, take a boat to an island on Rovinj's little archipelago (described on page 734). (There are no showers at any of the town's public beaches.)

▲**Bike Ride**—The TI's free, handy biking map suggests a variety of short and long bike rides. The easiest and most scenic is a quick loop around the Golden Cape (Zlatni Rat, described above). You can do this circuit and return to the Old Town in about an hour (without stops). Start by biking south around the harbor and past the waterfront Hotel Park, where you leave the cars and enter the wooded Golden Cape. Peaceful miniature beaches abound (see above). The lane climbs to a quarry (much of Venice was paved with Istrian stone), where you're likely to see beginning rock climbers inching their way up and down. Cycling downhill from the quarry and circling the peninsula, you hit the Lovor Grill (open daily in summer 10:00–16:00 for drinks and light meals)—simple restaurant housed in the former stables of the Austrian countess who planted what today is called "Wood Park." From there, you can continue farther along the coast, or return to town (backtrack two minutes and take the right fork through the woods back to the waterfront path).

Bike Rental: Bikes are rented at a subsidized price from the city parking lot kiosk (5 kn/hr, open 24 hours daily, fast and easy process; choose a bike with enough air in its tires or have them pumped up, as the path is rocky and gravelly). Or pay four times as much at the kiosk near Hotel Park (20 kn/hr, daily 9:00–19:00).

NIGHTLIFE

Rovinj After Dark

Rovinj is a delight after dark. Views that were great by day become magical in the moonlight and floodlight. The streets of the Old Town are particularly inviting when empty and under stars.

Concerts—Lots of low-key, small-time music events take place right in town (check at the TI, and look for handwritten signs on Garibaldi street near the Square at the Bridge). Groups perform on the harborfront (you'll see the bandstand set up) or at the Multi-Media Center (a.k.a. the "MMC," which locals call "Cinema Belgrade"—its former name). The MMC concerts—in a cute little hall above a bank—generally have plenty of seats, and free or nearly free admission.

Wine Bar—**Bacchus Wine Bar** is *the* place to sample Istrian and Croatian wine in Rovinj. Owner Paolo is happy to explain how the local wine has improved since communist times, when wine production stagnated (10–25 kn per deciliter, also serves Istrian cheese and prosciutto-like *pršut,* open long hours daily, Carera 5, tel. 052/812-154). While they offer full-bodied reds from farther south, be sure to give the very local whites a chance. Istrian vintners are particularly proud of their *malvazija* (mahl-VAH-zee-yah; sometimes spelled Malvasia in English)—a light white wine that can be either sweet *(slatko)* or dry *(suho).*

Lounging—**Valentino Champagne and Cocktail Bar** is a memorable, romantic place for a late-night waterfront drink with jazz. Fish, attracted by its underwater lights, swim by from all over the bay...to the enjoyment of those nursing a cocktail on the rocks (literally—you'll be given a small seat cushion and welcomed to find your own seaside niche). Or you can choose to sit on one of the terraces. Patricia opens her bar nightly from 19:00 until as late as there's any action (45–65-kn cocktails, 40-kn non-alcoholic drinks, Via Santa Croce 28, tel. 052/830-683). **Zanzi Bar,** while named for an African archipelago, has a Havana ambience. Stepping over its threshold, you enter a colonial Caribbean world, with seating indoors or out on the tropical veranda (30–50-kn cocktails, nightly until 1:00 in the morning, near the TI on Obala Pina Budicina).

SLEEPING

Most Rovinj accommodations (both hotels and *sobe*) prefer longer stays of at least four or five nights, so in peak season (mid-July–mid-Sept), you'll likely run into strict minimum-stay requirements or high fees for shorter stays. Unfortunately, you'll probably have to simply eat this extra cost for a short stay. Hoteliers and *sobe* hosts are somewhat more flexible in the shoulder season.

In Rovinj's Old Town

All of these accommodations (except Villa Ernesta) are on the Old Town peninsula, rather than the mainland section of the Old Town. While Rovinj has no hostel, *sobe* are a good budget option.

$$$ Hotel Villa Angelo d'Oro is your top Old Town splurge. The location—on a peaceful street just a few steps off the water—is ideal, and the public spaces (including a serene garden bar and sauna/whirlpool area) are rich and inviting. The 23 rooms don't quite live up to the fuss, but if you want your money to talk your way into the Old Town, this is the place (Aug: Sb-1,000 kn, Db-1,600 kn; June–July and Sept: Sb-800 kn, Db-1,400 kn; cheaper Oct–Dec and March–May, closed Jan–Feb, pricier suites also available, no elevator, air-con, dinner in their restaurant-205 kn per person, Vladimira Švalbe 38–42, tel. 052/840-502, fax 052/840-111, www.angelodoro.hr, hotel.angelo@vip.hr).

Sleep Code

(5 kn = about $1, country code: 385, area code: 052)
S = Single, **D** = Double/Twin, **T** = Triple, **Q** = Quad, **b** = bathroom.
The modest tourist tax (7 kn or €1 per person, per night, lower off-season) is not included in these rates. Hotels accept credit cards and include breakfast in their rates, while most *sobe* accept only cash and don't offer breakfast. Everyone listed here speaks at least enough English to make a reservation (or knows someone nearby who can translate).

To help you sort easily through these listings, I've divided the rooms into three categories based on the price for a standard double room with bath in peak season:

$$$ **Higher Priced**—Most rooms 700 kn or more.
$$ **Moderately Priced**—Most rooms between 500–700 kn.
$ **Lower Priced**—Most rooms 500 kn or less.

$$$ **Villa Cissa,** run by Zagreb transplant Veljko Despot (who looks a bit like Robin Williams), has three apartments with tastefully modern, artistic decor above an art gallery in the Old Town. Because this place is designed for longer stays, you'll pay a premium for a short visit (50 percent more for 2-night stays, prices double for 1-night stays), and it comes with some extra one-time fees, such as for cleaning (June–Sept: Db-750 kn, May: Db-650 kn, April and Oct: Db-600 kn, Nov–March: Db-500 kn, big apartment more expensive, air-con, Zdenac 14, tel. 052/813-080, mobile 091-481-4018, www.villacissa.com, info@villacissa.com).

$$$ **Hotel Adriatic,** a lightly renovated holdover from the communist days, features 27 rooms overlooking the main square, where the Old Town peninsula meets the mainland. The quality of the drab, worn rooms doesn't justify the high prices...but the location does. Of the big chain of Maistra hotels, this is the only one in the Old Town (rates flex with demand, in top season figure Sb-700 kn, Db-1,100 kn; all Sb are non-view, most Db are twins and have views—otherwise 10 percent less, 15 percent more for 1-night stays, closed mid-Oct–March, no elevator, air-con, Trg Maršala Tita, tel. 052/803-510, fax 052/813-573, www.maistra.hr, adriatic@maistra.hr).

$$ **Porta Antica** is an agency renting five nicely decorated apartments over a restaurant facing the harbor. While the location is excellent, this place might be closing in the near future (mid-July–mid-Sept: 400–650 kn for no view, 750 kn for seaview, 900 kn for seaview and terrace, 5-night minimum during peak season only; June–mid-July: 350–500 kn for no view, 550 kn for

seaview, 650 kn for seaview and terrace; mid-Sept–May: 260–350 kn for no view, 400 kn for seaview, 500 kn for seaview and terrace; outside of mid-July–mid-Sept, shorter stays are allowed with an extra charge: 200 kn for 1 night, 150 kn per night for 2 nights, 110 kn per night for 3 nights, 40 kn per night for 4 nights; prices are for 2 people—90 kn more per extra person, no breakfast, cash only, open year-round, next door to TI, www.portaantica.com. If Porta Antica is closed, contact **Loredana Poretti,** who also rents apartments in and out of the Old Town (be clear on location before you book; mobile 099-206-5600, lporetti@yahoo.co.uk).

$$ **Villa Ernesta** has six apartments in the thick of the Old Town, on a tranquil courtyard just off of the bustling Carera street (though not on the peninsula). While communication can be challenging (limited English), the apartments are modern and beautifully appointed, with artwork decorating the hallways (July–Aug: Db-500–750 kn, shoulder season: Db-400–650 kn, surcharge for short stays, air-con, Carera 22, tel. 052/813-543, mobile 091-481-7969, villa-ernesta@inforovinj.com).

$ **Miranda Fabris** is a charming local woman renting four fine apartments with little kitchenettes (Db-300 kn, or 370 kn in July–Aug, no extra charge for 1- or 2-night stays, lots of steep stairs, across from Villa Val de Bora at Chiurca 5, mobile 091-881-8881, miranda_fabris@yahoo.com).

$ *Other Sobe:* Try looking for your own room online (www .inforovinj.com is helpful). Several agencies rent private rooms in the Old Town for good prices (figure Db-150–300 kn, depending on season, location, and size). But remember that in peak season, you'll pay double for a one-night stay, and 20–50 percent extra for a two- or three-night stay. Just about everyone in town has a line on rooms. These two agencies are English-friendly and handy to the bus station (open sporadic hours, based on demand): **Futura Travel** (across from bus station at Benussi 2, tel. 052/817-281, fax 052/817-282, www.futura-travel.hr) and **Natale** (Carducci 4, tel. & fax 052/813-365, www.rovinj.com).

On the Mainland

To escape the high prices of Rovinj's Old Town, consider the resort neighborhood just south of the harbor. While the big hotels themselves are an option, I prefer cheaper alternatives in the same area. The big hotels are signposted as you approach town (follow signs for *hoteli,* then your specific hotel). Once you're on the road to Hotels Eden and Park, the other two are easy to reach: Villa Baron Gautsch is actually on the road to Hotel Park (on the right, brown *pansion* sign just before Hotel Park itself); Hotel Vila Lili is a little farther on the main road toward Eden (to the left just after turnoff for Hotel Park, look for *Vila Lili* sign). All of these options are about a 15-minute uphill walk from the Old Town.

$$$ *Maistra Hotels:* The local hotel conglomerate, Maistra, has several hotels in the lush parklands just south of the Old Town. Most of my readers—looking for proximity to the Old Town rather than plush rooms, a big lounge, and hotel-based activities—will prefer to save money and stay at one of my other listings. These hotels have extremely slippery pricing, based on the type of room, the season, and how far ahead you book. Both of the hotels listed here have similar rates (July–Aug: Sb-850 kn, Db-1,500 kn, cheaper off-season), but you'll have to check the website for specifics (www.maistra.hr). **Hotel Park** has 202 thoroughly renovated but boring rooms in a colorized communist-era hull, and a seaside swimming pool with sweeping views to the Old Town. From here, you can walk along the scenic harborfront promenade into town (tel. 052/811-077, fax 052/816-977, park@maistra.hr). **Hotel Eden** offers 325 upscale, imaginatively updated rooms with oodles of contemporary style behind a brooding communist facade. This flagship hotel is the fanciest one in the Maistra chain, but it's a bit farther from the Old Town—frustrating without a car (10 percent extra for fancier rooms, tel. 052/800-400, fax 052/811-349, eden@maistra.hr). Both hotels have air-conditioning, elevators, and free parking. The Maistra chain also has several other properties (including the Old Town's Hotel Adriatic, described on page 741, and other more distant, cheaper options). Only one branch of the Maistra chain remains open through the winter.

$$$ Hotel Vila Lili is a charming, family-run hotel over a restaurant on a quiet lane in a modern part of town. Its 20 pleasant rooms are comfortable (July–Aug: Sb-450 kn, Db-800 kn; shoulder season: Sb-260 kn, Db-550 kn; pricier suites also available, 10 percent discount with this book except in July–Aug, cheaper off-season, no extra charge for 1-night stays, elevator, air-con, parking-30 kn/day, Mohorovičića 16, tel. 052/840-940, fax 052/840-944, www.hotel-vilalili.hr, vila-lili@pu.t-com.hr, Petričević family).

$ Villa Baron Gautsch, named for a shipwreck, is a German-owned pension with 17 simple but comfortable rooms (Aug: Db-500 kn, July and Sept: Db-450 kn, shoulder season: Db-350 kn, they also have two Sb for half the Db price, fancier rooms with balcony and newer bathroom not worth the 80 kn extra, 20 percent more for 1- or 2-night stays, closed Nov–Easter, cash only, no elevator, shared terrace with great views, Ronjgova 7, tel. 052/840-538, fax 052/840-537, www.baron-gautsch.com, baron.gautsch @gmx.net).

EATING

Interchangeable restaurants cluster where Rovinj's Old Town peninsula meets the mainland, and all around the harbor. Choose the

place with the view or menu you like best—or delve a bit farther into the heart of the peninsula to one of my other recommendations. Be warned that most of these eateries—like much of Rovinj—close for the winter (roughly November to Easter).

Along Rovinj's "Restaurant Row": The easiest dining option is to stroll the Old Town embankment overlooking the harbor (Obala Pina Budičina), which changes its name to Svetoga Križa and cuts behind the buildings after a few blocks. While these restaurants are all about the same, a few are notable (all open long hours daily). **Veli Jože,** with reliably good food and a rollicking, folksy interior decorated to the hilt, is in all the guidebooks (Sv. Križa 1). **Lampo** has scenic seating right on the water—fine for a big salad, pizza, or pasta at a reasonable price (Sv. Križa 22).

Krčma Ulika, a truly classy hole-in-the-wall run by Inja Tucman, has a mellow, cozy interior strewn with art. The simple menu, featuring creative Mediterranean cuisine, changes based on what's fresh. The food is prepared right in a corner of the tight six-table dining room. Explore your options with the help of friendly Inja before ordering. If you don't need a sea view, you'll find the value hard to beat (12-kn cover, 50–80-kn main dishes, Wed–Mon 18:00–2:00 in the morning, closed Tue except in peak season, closed off-season, Vladimira Švalbe 34, tel. 052/818-089).

Monte Restaurant is your upscale, white-tablecloth splurge. With tables strewn around a covered terrace just under the town bell tower, this atmospheric place features inventive international cuisine. Don't go here on a budget (as the high cover, and charges for bread, water, and so on really pad the bill). But if you enjoy mod, well-presented dishes and dressy service, this may be the best in town (plan to spend at least 300 kn per person for dinner, daily 12:00–15:00 & 19:00–23:00, reserve ahead in peak season, Montalbano 75, tel. 052/830-203, Đekić family).

La Puntuleina is a fancy spot near the tip of the Old Town peninsula with perhaps the most scenic seafront settings in town. This restaurant, cocktail bar, and wine bar features pricey Italo-Mediterranean cuisine served in the contemporary dining room or outside on tables literally scattered along the rocks overlooking a swimming hole. The menu is short, and the selection each day is even less, since Miriam insists on serving only what's fresh in the market. Reservations are recommended (100-kn pastas, 120–200-kn main dishes, Thu–Tue 12:00–15:00 & 18:00–22:00, closed Wed except in peak season, closed Nov–Easter, on the Old Town embankment past the harbor at Sv. Križa 38, tel. 052/813-186). If the food is priced too steeply for your budget, consider dropping by for a drink.

Gostionica/Trattoria Toni is a more affordable option buried in the mainland part of the Old Town. This hole-in-the-wall serves unpretentious fare in a cozy interior, or out on a terrace on a bustling mostly-pedestrian street (40–60-kn pastas, 50–120-kn main dishes, Thu–Tue 12:00–15:00 & 18:00–22:30, closed Wed, just up ulica/via Driovier on the right, tel. 052/815-303).

Breakfast: Most rental apartments come with a kitchenette handy for breakfasts (stock up at a neighborhood grocery shop). Cafés and bars along the waterfront serve little more than an expensive croissant with coffee. The best budget breakfast (and a fun experience) is a picnic. Within a block of the market, you have all the necessary stops: the Brionka bakery (fresh-baked cheese or apple strudel); mini-grocery stores (juice, milk, drinkable yogurt, and so on); market stalls (cherries, strawberries, walnuts, and more, as well as an elegant fountain for washing); an Albanian-run bread kiosk/café between the market and the water...plus benches with birds chirping, children playing, and fine Old Town views along the water.

TRANSPORTATION CONNECTIONS

From Rovinj by Bus to: Pula (about hourly, 45 min), **Poreč** (6–8/day, 1 hr), **Umag** (5/day, 1.5 hrs), **Rijeka** (6/day, 1–3 hrs), **Zagreb** (8/day, 5–8 hrs), **Split** (1/day, 11 hrs), **Dubrovnik** (nightly, 15 hrs), **Piran** (1/day June–mid-Oct, 1.5 hrs; otherwise transfer in Umag and Portorož), **Ljubljana** (1/day in season, 5.5 hrs), **Venice** (1/day early in the morning, 8 hrs). Bus information: tel. 052/811-453.

Pula

Pula (Pola in Italian) isn't quaint. Istria's biggest city is an industrial port town with traffic, smog, and sprawl...but it has the soul of a Roman poet. Between the shipyards, you'll discover some of the top Roman ruins in Croatia, including its stately amphitheater—a fully intact mini-Colosseum that marks the entry to a seedy Old Town with ancient temples, arches, and columns.

Strategically situated at the southern tip of the Istrian

Pula

Istria

Rovinj is just one of many worthwhile attractions on the peninsula called Istria. In Istria, pungent truffles, Roman ruins, cute hill towns, quaint coastal villages, carefully cultivated food and wine, and breezy Italian culture all compete for your attention.

While you could spend days exploring Istria, two destinations outside Rovinj are especially worthwhile (each one deserves a half-day side-trip). Down at the tip of Istria is big, industrial Pula, offering a bustling urban contrast to the rest of the time-passed coastline, plus some remarkable Roman ruins (including an amphitheater so intact, you'll marvel that you haven't heard of it before). The charming hill town of Motovun—with sweeping views over the surrounding terrain, including a truffle-packed forest—is one of the country's most appealing reasons to head inland.

Getting Around Istria

Istria is a cinch for **drivers,** who find distances short and roads and attractions well marked (though summer traffic can be miserable, especially on weekends). Istria is neatly connected by a speedy two-lane highway nicknamed the *ipsilon* (the Croatian word for the letter Y, which is what the highway is shaped like). One branch of the "Y" (A-9) runs roughly parallel to the coast from Slovenia to Pula, about six miles inland; the other branch (A-8) cuts diagonally northeast to the Učka Tunnel (leading to Rijeka). You'll periodically come to toll booths, where you'll pay a modest fee for using the *ipsilon*. Following road signs here is easy (navigate by town names), but if you'll be driving a lot, pick up a good map to more easily navigate the back roads. My favorite is the Kod & Kam 1:100,000 *Istra* map (available in local bookstores and some TIs).

If you're relying on **public transportation,** Istria is frustrating. While it may be possible to patch together some of the better sights (such as Rovinj and Motovun) by bus, it's probably not worth the hassle. Even if you're doing the rest of your trip by public transportation, consider renting a car for a day or two in Istria.

By Boat to Venice: Venezia Lines connects Venice with Rovinj and Pula, as well as Poreč (in Istria), Piran (in Slovenia), and other Adriatic destinations (such as Ravenna and Ramini in Italy, and Opatija in Croatia). While designed for day-trippers from Istria to Venice, this service can also be used one-way. For details, see www.venezialines.com.

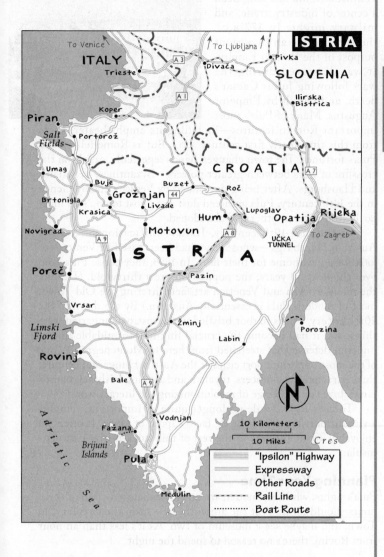

ISTRIA

To Venice
To Ljubljana
ITALY
Trieste
A 3
Divača
Pivka
SLOVENIA
Ilirska
Bistrica
Koper
Piran
Salt
Fields
Portorož
Umag
Buje
Buzet
Roč
CROATIA
A 7
Brtonigla
Grožnjan
44
Livade
Krasica
Hum
Lupoglav
Opatija
Rijeka
Novigrad
A 9
Motovun
A 8
UČKA
TUNNEL
To Zagreb
Poreč
ISTRIA
Pazin
Vrsar
Žminj
Porozina
Limski
Fjord
Labin
Rovinj
Bale
A 9
Fažana
Vodnjan
10 Kilometers
10 Miles
Cres
Brijuni
Islands
Pula
Adriatic
Sea
Medulin

N

"Ipsilon" Highway
Expressway
Other Roads
Rail Line
Boat Route

Pula

Peninsula, Pula has long been a center of industry, trade, and military might. In 177 B.C., the city became an important outpost of the Roman Empire. It was destroyed during the wars following Julius Caesar's death, and rebuilt by Emperor Augustus. Many of Pula's most  important Roman features—including its amphitheater—date from this time (early first century A.D.). But as Rome fell, so did Pula's fortunes. The town changed hands repeatedly, caught in the crossfire of wars between greater powers—Byzantines, Venetians, and Hapsburgs. After being devastated by Venice's enemy Genoa in the 14th century, Pula gathered dust as a ghost town...still militarily strategic, but otherwise abandoned.

In the mid-19th century, Italian unification forced the Austrian Hapsburgs—whose navy had been based in Venice—to look for a new home for their fleet. In 1856, they chose Pula, and over the next 60 years, the population grew thirtyfold. (Despite the many Roman and Venetian artifacts littering the Old Town, most of modern Pula is essentially Austrian.) By the dawn of the 20th century, Pula's harbor bristled with Austro-Hungarian warships, and it had become the crucial link in a formidable line of imperial defense that stretched from here to Montenegro. As one of the most important port cities of the Austro-Hungarian Empire, Pula attracted naval officers, royalty...and a young Irishman named James Joyce on the verge of revolutionizing the literary world.

Today's Pula, while no longer quite so important, remains a vibrant port town and the de facto capital of Istria. It offers an enjoyably urban antidote to the rest of this stuck-in-the-past peninsula.

Planning Your Time

Pula's sights, while top-notch, are quickly exhausted. Two or three hours should do it: Visit the amphitheater, stroll the circular Old Town, and maybe see a museum or two. As it's less than an hour from Rovinj, there's no reason to spend the night.

ORIENTATION

(area code: 052)
Although it's a big city, the tourist's Pula is compact: the amphitheater and, beside it, the ring-shaped Old Town circling the base of an old hilltop fortress. The Old Town's main square, the Forum, dates back to Roman times.

Tourist Information

Pula's well-organized TI overlooks the Old Town's main square, the Forum. It offers a free map and information on the town and all of Istria (May–Oct daily 9:00–20:00, July–Aug until 22:00; Nov–April Mon–Sat 9:00–19:00, Sun 10:00–16:00; Forum 3, tel. 052/219-197, www.pulainfo.hr).

To **rent a car** in Pula, consider **Avis** (Riva 14, tel. 052/224-350), which is the most central. **Europcar** (tel. 052/530-351) and **Hertz** (tel. 052/210-868) are at the airport (3.5 miles northeast of the center; figure an 80-kn taxi trip).

Arrival in Pula

By Car: Pula is about a 45-minute drive south of Rovinj. Approaching town, follow *Centar* signs, then look for the amphitheater. You'll find a large pay lot just below the amphitheater, toward the waterfront (4 kn/hr, 20 kn/all day).

By Bus: The bus station is just up the street and around the corner from the amphitheater. Exit the station to the left and walk up the busy street (ulica 43 Istarske Divizije) about 10 minutes, bearing left to the amphitheater.

By Train: The train station is a 15-minute walk from the amphitheater, near the waterfront (in the opposite direction from the Old Town). Walk with the coast on your right until you see the amphitheater.

SELF-GUIDED WALK

Welcome to Pula

This walk is divided between Pula's two most interesting attractions: The Roman amphitheater, and the circular Old Town. About an hour for each is plenty. More time can be spent sipping coffee *al fresco* or dipping into museums.

• *Begin at Pula's landmark...*

Amphitheater (Amfiteatar)

Of the dozens of amphitheaters left around Europe and North Africa by Roman engineers, Pula's is the sixth-largest (435 feet long and 345 feet wide), and one of the best-preserved anywhere.

Cost and Hours: 30 kn, daily April–Oct 8:00–21:00, Nov–March 9:00–16:00. The 30-kn audioguide narrates 20 stops with 30 minutes of flat, basic data on the structure.

Self-Guided Tour: Go inside and explore the interior, climbing up the seats as you like. An "amphi-theater" is literally a "double theater"—imagine two theaters, without the back wall behind the stage, stuck together to maximize seating. Pula's amphitheater was built over several decades (first century A.D.) under the reign of three of Rome's top-tier emperors: Augustus, Claudius, and Vespasian. It was completed around 80 A.D., about the same time as the Colosseum in Rome. It remained in active use until the beginning of the fifth century, when gladiator battles were outlawed. The location is unusual but sensible: It was built just outside town (too big for tiny Pula, with just 5,000 people) and near the sea (so its giant limestone blocks could more easily be transported here from the quarry six miles away).

Notice that the amphitheater is built into the gentle incline of a hill. This economical plan, unusual for Roman amphitheaters, saved on the amount of stone needed, and provided a natural foundation for some of the seats (notice how the upper seats incorporate the slope). It may seem like the architects were cutting corners, but they actually had to raise the ground level at the lower end of the amphitheater to give it a level foundation. The four rectangular towers anchoring the amphitheater's facade are also unique (two of them are mostly gone). These once held wooden staircases for loading and unloading the amphitheater more quickly. At the top of each tower was a water reservoir, used for powering fountains that sprayed refreshing scents over the crowd to mask the stench of blood.

And there was plenty of blood. Imagine this scene in the days of the gladiators. More than 25,000 cheering fans from all social classes filled the seats. The Romans made these spectacles cheap or even free—distracting commoners with a steady diet of mindless entertainment prevented discontent and rebellion. (Hmm... *American Idol*, anyone?) Canvas awnings rigged around the top of the amphitheater shaded many seats. The fans surrounded the "slaying field," which was covered with sand to absorb blood spilled by man and beast, making it easier to clean up after the fight. This sand *(harena)* gave the amphitheater its nickname...arena.

The amphitheater's "entertainers" were gladiators. Some gladiators were criminals, but most were prisoners of war from lands conquered by Rome, who dressed and used weapons according to their country of origin. A colorful parade kicked off the spectacle, followed by simulated fights with fake weapons. Then the real battles began. Often the fights represented stories from mythology or Greek or Roman history. Most ended in death for the loser. Sometimes gladiators fought exotic animals—gathered at great expense from far corners of the empire—which would enter the arena from the two far ends (through the biggest arches).

While the life of a gladiator seems difficult, consider that it wasn't such a bad gig—compared to, say, being a soldier. Gladiators were often better paid than soldiers, enjoyed terrific celebrity (both in life and in death), and only had to fight a few times each year.

Ignore the modern seating, and imagine when the arena (sandy oval area in the center) was ringed with two levels of stone seating and a top level of wooden bleachers. Notice that the outline of the arena is marked by a small moat—just wide enough to keep the animals off the laps of those with the best seats, but close enough so that blood still sprayed their togas.

After the fall of Rome, builders looking for ready-cut stone picked apart structures like this one—scraping it as clean as a neat

slice of cantaloupe. Sometimes the scavengers were seeking the iron hooks that were used to connect the stone—in those oh-so "Dark Ages," the method for smelting iron from ore was lost. Most of this amphitheater's interior structures—such as steps and seats—are now in the foundations and walls of Pula's buildings...not to mention palaces in Venice, across the Adriatic. In fact, in the late 16th century, the Venetians planned to take this entire amphitheater apart, stone by stone, and reassemble it on the island of Lido on the Venetian lagoon. A heroic Venetian senator—still much revered in Pula—convinced them to leave it where it is.

Despite these and other threats, the amphitheater's exterior has been left gloriously intact. The 1999 film *Titus* (with Anthony Hopkins and Jessica Lange) was filmed here, and today the amphitheater is still used to stage spectacles—from Placido Domingo to Marilyn Manson—with seating for about 5,000 fans.

Before leaving, don't miss the museum exhibit (in the "subterranean hall," down the chute marked #17). This takes you down to the lower level of the amphitheater, where gladiators and animals were kept between fights. When the fight began, gladiators would charge up a chute and burst into the arena, like football players being introduced at the Super Bowl. As you go down the passage, you'll walk on a grate over an even lower tunnel. Pula is honeycombed with tunnels like these, originally used for sewers and as a last-ditch place of refuge in case of attack. Inside, the exhibit—strangely dedicated to "viniculture and olive-oil production in Istria in the period of antiquity" instead of, you know, gladiators—is surprisingly interesting. Browse the impressive collection of amphorae (see sidebar), find your location on the replica of a fourth-century Roman map (oriented with east on top), and

Amphorae

In museums, hotels, and restaurants all along the Croatian coast, you'll see amphorae. An amphora is a jug that was used to transport goods when the ancient Greeks ruled the seas, through about the seventh century B.C. Later, the Romans also used their own amphorae. These tall and skinny ceramic jugs—many of them lost in ancient shipwrecks—litter the Adriatic coastline.

Amphorae were used to carry oil, wine, and fish on long sea journeys. They're tapered at the bottom because they were stuck into sand (or placed on a stand) to keep them upright in transit. They also have a narrow neck at the top, often with two large handles. In fact, the name comes from the Greek *amphi pherein,* "to carry from both sides." The taller, skinnier amphorae were generally used for wine, while the fat, short ones were for olive oil. Because amphorae differ according to their purpose and nationality, archaeologists find them to be a particularly useful clue for dating shipwrecks and determining the country of origin of lost ships. This is made easier by later Roman amphorae, which are actually stamped with the place they came from and what they held.

ogle the gigantic grape press and two olive-oil mills.

• *From the amphitheater, it's a few minutes' walk to Pula's Old Town, where more Roman sights await. Exit the amphitheater to the left and walk one long block up the busy road (Amfiteatarska ulica) along the small wall, bearing right at the fork. When you reach the big park on your right, look for the car-sized...*

Town Model

Use this handy model of Pula to get oriented. Next to the amphitheater, the little water cannon spouting into the air marks the blue house nearby, the site of a freshwater spring (which makes this location even more strategic). The big star-shaped fortress on the hill is Fort Kaštel, designed by a French architect but dating from the Venetian era (1630). Read the street plan of the Roman town into this model: At the center (on the hill) was the *castrum,* or military base. At the base of the hill (the far side from the amphitheater) was the forum, or town square. During Pula's Roman glory days, the hillsides around the *castrum* were blanketed with the villas of rich merchants. The Old Town, which clusters around the base of the fortress-topped hill, still features many fragments of the Roman period, as well as Pula's later occupiers. We'll take a counterclockwise stroll around the fortified old hill through this ancient zone.

The huge anchor across the street from the model celebrates the number-one employer of Pula—its shipyards.

• Continue along the street. At the fork, again bear right (on Kandlerova ulica—level, not uphill). Notice the Roman ruins on your right. Just about any time someone wants to put up a new building, they find ruins like these. Work screeches to a halt while the valuable remains are excavated. In this case, they've discovered three Roman houses, two churches, and around 2,000 amphorae. I guess the new parking garage has to wait.

After about three blocks, on your right-hand side, you'll see Pula's...

Cathedral (Katedrala)

This church combines elements of the two big Italian influences on

Pula: Roman and Venetian. Dating from the fifth century, the Romanesque core of the church (notice the skinny, slit-like windows) marks the site of an early-Christian seafront settlement in Pula. The Venetian Baroque facade and bell tower are much more recent (early 18th century). Typical of the Venetian style, notice how far away the austere bell tower is from the body of the church. The bell tower's foundation is made of stones that were scavenged from the amphitheater. On the square is an instructive poster illustrating the physical

development of the town through the ages. The church's interior features a classic Roman-style basilica floor plan, with a single grand hall—the side naves were added in the 15th century, after a fire (free, generally open daily 7:00–12:00 & 16:00–18:00, but often closed).

• Keep walking through the main pedestrian zone, past all the tacky souvenir shops and Albanian-run fast-food and ice-cream joints. After a few more blocks, you emerge into the...

Forum

Every Roman town had a forum, or main square. Twenty centuries later, Pula's Forum still serves the same function, and has kept the old Roman name.

Two important buildings front the north end of the square, where you entered. The smaller building (on the left, with the columns) is the first-century A.D. Roman **Temple of Augustus** (Augustov Hram). Built during the reign of, and dedicated to, Augustus Caesar, this temple took a direct hit from an Allied bomb in World War II, but was rebuilt after the war—notice the patchwork repair job. (When I asked my guide if it was an American bomb that destroyed the temple, he answered sheepishly, "Yes, a little bit.") It's the only one remaining of three such temples that once lined this side of the square. Inside the temple is a single room

with fragments of ancient sculptures (10 kn, Mon–Sat 9:00–21:00, Sun 9:00–15:00, shorter hours off-season, sparse English labels). The statue of Augustus, which likely stood on or near this spot, dates from the time of Christ. Other evocative chips and bits of Roman Pula include the feet of a powerful commander with a pathetic little vanquished barbarian obediently at his knee (perhaps one of the Histri—the indigenous Istrians that the Romans conquered in 177 B.C.).

Head back out onto the square. As Rome fell, its long-subjugated subjects in Pula had little respect for the former empire's symbols, and many temples didn't survive. Others were put to new use: Part of an adjacent temple (likely dedicated to Diana) was incorporated into the bigger building on the right, Pula's medieval **Town Hall** (Gradska Palača). (If you circle around behind this building, you can still see Roman fragments embedded in the back.) The Town Hall encapsulates many centuries of Pula architecture: Romanesque core, Gothic reliefs, Renaissance porch, Baroque windows...and a few Roman bits and pieces. Notice the interesting combination of flags above the door: Pula, Croatia, Istria (with its mascot goat), and Italy (for the large ethnic minority here). No European Union...yet.

• *Consider dropping by the* **TI** *on this square before continuing our circular stroll down the main drag, Sergijevaca. You'll pass by a small park on your right, then a block of modern shops. Immediately after the Kenvelo shop on the right (with a red-and-black* K *sign), turn right into the white, unmarked doorway. Emerging on the other side, turn left, walk to the metal grill, and look down to see the...*

Roman Floor Mosaic (Rimski Mozaik)

This hidden mosaic is a great example of the Roman treasures that lie below the old center of Pula. Uncovered by locals who were cleaning up from World War II bombs, this third-century floor was carefully excavated and cleaned up for display right where it was laid nearly two millennia ago. (Notice that the Roman floor level was about six feet below today's.) The centerpiece of the mosaic depicts the punishment of Dirce. According to the ancient Greek legend, King Lykos of Thebes was bewitched by Dirce and abandoned his pregnant queen. The queen gave birth to twin boys (depicted in this mosaic), who grew up to kill their deadbeat dad and tie Dirce to the horns of a bull to be bashed against a mountain. This same story is famously depicted in the twisty *Toro Farnese* sculpture partly carved by Michelangelo (on display in Naples' Archaeological Museum).

• *For an optional detour to Byzantine times, walk into the parking lot just beyond the mosaic. Near the end of the lot, on the left-hand side, is a fenced-off grassy field. At the far end of the field is the small...*

Basilica of St. Mary Formosa (Kapela Marije Formoze)

We've seen plenty of Roman and Venetian bric-a-brac, but this chapel survives from the time of another Istrian occupier: Byzantium. For about 170 years after Rome fell (the sixth and seventh centuries A.D.), this region came under the control of the Byzantine Empire, and was ruled from Ravenna (across the Adriatic, south of Venice). Much of this field was once occupied by a vast, richly decorated basilica. This lonely chapel is all that's left, but it still gives a feel for the architecture of that era—including the Greek cross floor plan (with four equal arms) and heavy brick vaulting. An informational sign posted nearby outlines the original basilica and floor plan.

• *Back on the main drag (Sergijevaca), continue a few more blocks through Pula's most colorful and most touristy neighborhood, until you arrive at the...*

Arch of Sergius (Slavoluk Sergijevaca)

This triumphal arch was Michelangelo's favorite of Pula's many Roman remains. Marking the edge of the original Roman town, it

was built during the time of Emperor Titus to honor Lucius Sergius Lepidus. He fought on the side of Augustus in the civil wars that swept the empire after Julius Caesar's assassination. The proto-feminist inscription proudly explains, "Silvia of the Sergius family paid for this with her own money." Statues of Lucius and two of his relatives once stood on the three blocks at the top of the arch. (Squint to see the *Sergivs* name on each block.) On the underside of the arch is a relief of an eagle (Rome) clutching an evil snake in its talons.

• *Before going under the arch, look to your left to see a famous Irishman appreciating the view from the terrace of...*

Café Uliks

In October of 1904, a young writer named James Joyce moved from Dublin to Pula with his girlfriend, Nora Barnacle. By day, he taught English to Austro-Hungarian naval officers at the Berlitz language school (in the building marked by the plaque). By night, he imagined strolling through his hometown as he penned short stories that would eventually become the collection *Dubliners*. But James and Nora quickly grew bored with little Pula, and moved to Trieste in March of 1905. Even so, Pula remains proud of its literary connections.

• *Now pass through the arch, into a square next to remains of the town wall. Continue straight ahead (up two bustling blocks, along the in-love-with-life Flanatička street) to...*

National Square (Nardoni Trg) and Market Hall

Pula's market hall was an iron-and-glass marvel when inaugurated in the 19th century. This structure is yet another reminder of the way the Austro-Hungarian Empire modernized Pula with grace and gentility. You'll find smelly fish on the ground floor (Mon–Sat 7:00–13:30, Sun 7:00–12:00) and an inviting food circus upstairs (Mon–Fri 7:00–15:00, Sat 7:00–14:00, Sun 7:00–12:00). All around is a busy and colorful farmers' market that bustles until about 13:00, when things quiet down.

• *Our tour is finished. If you're ready for lunch, consider one of the cheap options inside the market hall, or walk one block to Kantina (see "Eating," next page). When you're done here, backtrack to the town wall. Standing with the Arch of Sergius at your back, take a left and walk under the leafy canopy next to the wall. Keep an eye out (mostly on your left, along the wall) for more Roman remains. Among these are the* **Twin Gates** *(Porta Gemina), marking the entrance to a garden that's home to the* **Archaeological Museum of Istria** *(listed under "Sights," on next page). With more time, you can also consider a trip to the hilltop fortress,* **Fort Kaštel.** *Otherwise, we've completed our circular tour—the amphitheater is just around the corner.*

SIGHTS

Archaeological Museum of Istria (Arheološki Muzej Istre)—If Pula's many ruins intrigue you, here's the place to scratch your Roman itch. This museum, over a century old, shows off some of what you've seen in the streets, plus lots more—stone monuments, classical statues, ancient pottery...you name it (12 kn; summer Mon–Sat 9:00–12:00, Sun 10:00–15:00; winter Mon–Fri 9:00–15:00, closed Sat–Sun; Carrarina 3, tel. 052/218-603, www.mdc .hr/pula).

On the hill behind the museum (and free to visit) is its highlight, the remains of a **Roman Theater** (Rimsko Kazalište). Part of the stage is still intact, along with the semicircle of stone seats (some of which are still engraved with the names of the wealthy theatergoers who once sat there). To find it, go up the hill around the right side of the museum. This was the smaller of the two theaters in Roman Pula; the second was south of the center (and is no longer intact today).

Fort Kaštel—For a bird's-eye view over the town, head up to its centerpiece fortress. This deserted-feeling place, hosting the Historical Museum of Istria, is worth visiting only for the chance to wander the ramparts. While neither the museum nor the fortress is worth the hike up here, it's a good way to kill some extra time in Pula, and sample the views over the town and amphitheater (various trails lead up from the streets below).

EATING

The best lunch options are in and near the town's **market hall** (which is also where my self-guided walk ends). The top floor of the market is a food circus with a number of cheap and tempting eateries with both indoor and terrace seating (Mon–Fri 7:00–15:00, Sat 7:00–14:00, Sun 7:00–12:00).

Kantina Restaurant, a block away, serves good lunches (including veggie and vegan options) and hearty, creative 30-kn salads both in an elegant vaulted cellar and on a lazy shady terrace. The service can be slow—if you're in a rush, eat at the market hall instead (40–70-kn pastas, 80–100-kn meat dishes, daily 12:00–23:00, at the end of the pedestrian zone at Flanatička 16, tel. 052/214-054).

TRANSPORTATION CONNECTIONS

By Bus from Pula to: Rovinj (about hourly, 45 min), **Poreč** (12/day, 1 hr), **Opatija** (almost hourly, 2 hrs), **Rijeka** (almost hourly, 2.5 hrs), **Zagreb** (almost hourly, 3.75–6 hrs), **Split** (3/day, 10 hrs),

Dubrovnik (nightly, 14 hrs), **Piran** (2/day in summer only, 3.5 hrs), **Portorož** near Piran (2/day in summer, 1/day off-season, 3.5 hrs), **Venice** (1/day with early departure, 5 hrs). Be aware that bus connections are more frequent on weekdays (fewer departures Sat–Sun).

By Train to: Zagreb (3/day, 6 hrs, transfer in Rijeka; in summer also 1 night train with very early arrival in Zagreb, 8 hrs), **Ljubljana** (1/day, 6 hrs, transfer in Rijeka; plus 1 more Mon–Fri, 5.5 hrs).

Motovun

Most tourists in Croatia focus on the coast. For a dash of variety, head inland. Some of the best bits of the Croatian interior lie just a short drive from Rovinj. Dotted with picturesque hill towns, speckled with wineries and olive-oil farms, embedded with precious truffles, and grooved by meandering rural roads, the Istrian interior is worth a visit.

Dramatically situated high above vineyards and a truffle-filled forest, Motovun (moh-toh-VOON, Montona in Italian, pop. about 300) is the best-known and most-touristed of the Istrian hill towns. And for good reason: Its hilltop Old Town is particularly evocative, with a colorful old church and a rampart walk with spine-tingling vistas across the entire region. It's hard to believe that race-car driver Mario Andretti was born in such a tranquil little traffic-free hamlet. Today Motovun's quiet lanes are shared by locals, tourists, and artists—who began settling here a generation ago, when it was nearly deserted.

Getting There

While it's possible to reach Motovun by public transportation (by bus from Pazin), the rewards are not worth the headaches. Drivers find it worth a quick detour from the Istrian coast: From Rovinj or Pula, take the fast *ipsilon* highway north to Buje (between the *ipsilon* and Buje, consider stopping for a meal in Brtonigla). From Buje, continue eastward through Krasica and take road #44 that follows the Mirna River Valley farther eastward, to Motovun (well signed off the main road).

ORIENTATION

(area code: 052)

Motovun is steep. Most everything of interest to tourists is huddled around its tippy-top. The one and only entrance gate into town deposits you at the main square, with the church on your left and Hotel Kaštel on the right. From there, you're just about two blocks in every direction from a sheer drop-off. This hilltop zone is circled by an old rampart that today offers Motovun's most scenic stroll.

Tourist Information

Motovun doesn't have an official TI, but the gang at Hotel Kaštel dispenses tourist information. During the day, you can drop into their travel agency on the main square, called Istria Magica (Mon–Fri 8:00–16:00, closed Sat–Sun, to the right as you face Hotel Kaštel, at Trg Andrea Antico 8, tel. 052/681-750); at other times, ask at the hotel reception desk (listed under "Sleeping" later in this section).

Arrival in Motovun

Motovun's striking hilltop setting comes with a catch: Visitors usually have to hike up part of the way. A steep, twisty road connects the base of the hill with the Old Town up top. If it's not too crowded, drive as far up this road as possible until you're directed to park in the lot partway up (near the lower church, a steep 10-min uphill walk to the main square, 15 kn/day). In busier peak times, this lot might be full, so you may have to wait a few minutes for a car to leave; or you can park in the big lot at the foot of the hill and walk all the way up (during very busy times, such as the Film Festival, a shuttle bus may be taking visitors up the hill). If you're staying at Hotel Kaštel, follow the procedure explained in "Sleeping".

SELF-GUIDED WALK

Welcome to Motovun

The following commentary will bring some meaning to your Motovun hilltop stroll.

The street leading up into town is lined with wine-and-truffle shops. My favorite is the Lanča family's **Etnobutiga ČA,** a restored 17th-century house with a beautiful view terrace and a wide selection of local wines, brandies, and truffle products (all of them by Zigante, just across the valley; daily in season 10:00–20:00, slightly shorter hours off-season, closed Nov–mid-March, just above the parking lot on the right at Gradiziol 33, tel. 052/681-767). Like many people around here, Livio Lanča makes his own mistletoe brandy laced with honey.

Walking along the base of the town's wall, you'll go through the first of two **defensive gateways.** Inside this passage (under the fortified gate), notice the various insignias from Motovun's history lining the walls—look for the Venetian lion, the Latin family tombstone, and the seal of Motovun (with five towers being watched over by an angel). The area above the gate was a storehouse for weapons in the 15th century, when Motovun first flourished.

Emerging from the gateway, you're greeted by sweeping views of the valley below on your right-hand side. (A coffee or meal with this view is unforgettable.) Just up and to the left, you'll find the second defensive gateway, which leads to the heart of the **Old Town.**

To your left as you come through the main gate is the yellow town church, **St. Stephen's.** The crenellated tower is a reminder of

a time when this hilltop town needed to be defended. While unassuming from the outside, this austere house of worship has an impressive pedigree: It was designed by the famous Venetian architect Andrea Palladio (1508–1580), who greatly influenced the Neoclassical architecture of Washington, DC. The interior is a little gloomy but refreshingly lived-in—used more by locals than by tourists. On the left, notice a painting of the heart of Jesus, its eyes following you around the church (free, generally open daily 10:00–18:00 and during frequent services).

As you stand on the square in front of the church, imagine Motovun during its annual **film festival,** when it's filled with 20,000 movie-lovers from throughout the region and around the world—often including a minor celebrity or two. This square fills to capacity, and films are projected on a giant screen at the far end (generally late July or early Aug, www.motovunfilmfestival.com).

At the other end of the square is a leafy little piazza dominated by the big **Hotel Kaštel**—the main industry in town. In addition to its rooms and restaurant, Hotel Kaštel serves as the town TI. This is also where bigwigs in town for the local film festival stay—ask the staff about recent star-sightings of B-, C-, and D-list celebrities. (For example, if you're staying here, you may be showering in the same bathroom once graced by Jason Biggs, star of *American Pie*.) In the fall, they can also arrange truffle-finding excursions for tourists (about 700 kn/person).

Between the church and Hotel Kaštel, follow the lane to the **ramparts**. Take the five-minute stroll around the Old Town on these fortifications. As you breathe in the stunning panorama, notice that well-defended Motovun has been fortified three times—two layers of wall up top, and a third down below.

Motovun

SLEEPING

In Motovun

$$ Hotel Kaštel, the only big-hotel-in-a-small-town option in the Istrian interior, is a pleasant family-run place dominating Motovun's hilltop. The 30 rooms (most of which have views) are colorful and simple, and the location couldn't be better in this little burg. As the building used to be a castle, the floor plan can be confusing (July–Aug: Sb-400 kn, Db-650 kn, Tb-850 kn; June and Sept: Sb-350 kn, Db-600 kn, Tb-800 kn; May and Oct: Sb-300 kn, Db-550 kn, Tb-700 kn; Igor and Natasha promise a 10 percent discount with this book, pricier apartments available, cheaper off-season, no elevator, cheap laundry—do it by the kilo not by the piece, Trg Andrea Antico 7, tel. 052/681-607, fax 052/681-652, www.hotel-kastel-motovun.hr, info@hotel-kastel-motovun.hr). The hotel also has a small massage room where guests can get a good rub-down (100 kn/30 min, 200 kn/1 hr). If you're driving, tell the attendant at the gate that you're staying here. If there's room on top, he'll let you pass. Otherwise he'll instruct you where to park and call the hotel, which will send down a car to shuttle you up.

$ Pension Miro, just below and across from the gate to the main square, is a low-key, simply furnished, no-frills guest house renting 10 rooms (six have private bathrooms, while four top-floor rooms share one bathroom). As the guest house is operated by a local travel agency, it has no real reception—so you're on your own (when you reserve, clearly communicate your arrival time). Enjoy the beautiful view terrace (D-400 kn for 1 night, 375 kn for 2 nights, 330 kn for 3 or more nights; Db-440 kn for 1 night, 420 kn for 2 nights, 355 kn for 3 or more nights; singles pay about 275 kn no matter how many nights; includes minimal self-service breakfast, cash only, Bargo 4, tel. 052/681-970, fax 052/616-409, mobile 095-832-1795, www.montonatours.com, info@montonatours.com, Barbara). This agency also rents rooms elsewhere in town, including five above a café (Antica) in the heart of the Old Town, behind the town church (Db-350 kn).

Motovun

Truffle Mania

A mysterious fungus with a pungent, unmistakable flavor has been all the rage in Istria for the last decade or so. Called *tartufi* in both Croatian and Italian, these precious tubers have been gathered here since Roman times, and were favored by the region's Venetian and Austrian rulers. More recently, local peasants ate them as a substitute for meat (often mixed with polenta) during the lean days after World War II.

In 1999, local entrepreneur Giancarlo Zigante discovered a nearly three-pound white truffle. In addition to making Giancarlo Zigante a very wealthy man (see "Zigante Tartufi" listing, below), this giant truffle legitimized Istria on the world truffle scene. Today, Istria is giving France's Provence and Italy's Piedmont a run for their money in truffle production. Most of Istria's truffles are concentrated in the Motovun Forest, the damp, oak tree–filled terrain surrounding Motovun, Livade, and Buzet.

A truffle is a tuber that grows entirely underground, usually at a depth of eight inches near the roots of oak trees. Since no part of the plant grows aboveground, they're particularly difficult to find...and, therefore, valuable. Traditionally, Istrian truffle-gatherers use specially trained dogs to find truffles. This is most productive at night, when the darkness forces the dog to rely more on its sense of smell rather than sight. Once a truffle is located, the gatherer digs it up with a specially designed spade that looks like a wooden handgun with a long, narrow shovel at the end. There are two general types of truffles: white (more valuable and

$ At Bella Vista, on the steep road leading up to town, the Kotiga family rents two apartments with cute decor and balconies that offer sweeping views across the countryside (Db-300 kn, cash only, on the way up to the main gate at Gradiziol 1, tel. & fax 052/681-724, mobile 091-523-0321, www.apartmani-motovun .com, info@apartmani-motovun.com, Mirjana).

EATING

In Motovun

Considering this is a small hill town with just three real restaurants, all of them are impressively good. The first two listings are particularly notable.

Barbakan Konoba, just below the first town gate (on the left, at the base of the wall), features delicious Istrian cuisine with an emphasis on truffles. The beloved dog Nero, who finds the truffles, has earned a special place in the restaurant and might pay a visit with a milder flavor—*Tuber magnatum,* known as the "Queen of the Truffles") and black. Each type of truffle has a "season"—a specific time of year when its scent is released, making it easier to find (May–Nov for black, Oct–Jan for white). Once dug up, they look pretty unassuming—like a tough, dirty pinecone.

Truffles can be eaten in a variety of ways. Thanks to their powerful and distinctive kick, they're often used sparingly for flavor—grated like parmesan cheese, or truffle oil sprinkled over a dish. But you'll also find them in cheese, salami, olive oil, pâté,

and even ice cream. Some people find that the pungent, musty aftertaste follows them around all day...and all night, when its supposed aphrodisiac qualities kick in. Because they're so rare and difficult to find, truffles are incredibly expensive—but many people are more than happy to pay royally for that inimitable flavor.

If you're a truffle nut, you'll find yourself in heaven here; if not, you may still appreciate the chance to sample a little taste of truffle. While you do that, ponder how one giant tuber changed the economy of an entire region.

while you dine (80–140-kn pastas, 100–150-kn main dishes, Wed–Sun 12:30–15:30 & 18:30–23:30, closed Mon–Tue).

Taverna, actually inside the town's main gate itself (on the right, marked *Konoba pod Voltom*), serves excellent, well-presented Istrian food in a cozy dining room. In good weather, it's hard to beat their view loggia, just below and outside the gate (40–60-kn pastas, 50–100-kn main dishes, 140–200-kn truffle splurges, Thu–Tue 12:00–22:00, closed Wed, tel. 052/681-923).

Hotel Kaštel has its own restaurant, with good food and fine seating on the leafy main square of town (also listed under "Sleeping," page 761; daily 7:00–10:00 & 13:00–15:00 & 19:00–21:00).

The simple **Montona Gallery** café, with tables along the rampart between the two gates, serves drinks and ice cream with mammoth views (open long hours daily).

For a pricey truffle feast, head across the valley to **Zigante** in Livade (described next).

Near Motovun

To round out your Istrian interior experience, consider a meal in one of the villages near Motovun.

In Livade: Zigante Tartufi

The little crossroads village of Livade, sitting in the valley facing the back of Motovun's hill, is home to the first and last name in Istrian truffles. In 1999, Giancarlo Zigante unearthed the biggest white truffle the world had ever seen—2.9 pounds, as verified by *The Guinness Book of World Records*. (In 2007, the record was broken by a 3.3-pound Tuscan truffle.) This single hunk of fungus—now revered as if a religious relic—kicked off a truffle craze that continues in Istria today (see sidebar). Today Zigante has a virtual monopoly on Istria's truffle industry, producing a wide range of truffle goodies. If you're a connoisseur, or just curious, make a pilgrimage to this truffle mecca.

Zigante's large facility here is divided into two parts:

The **Zigante Tartufi shop** offers a big room with shelves upon shelves of both fresh and packaged truffle products (plus local wines, olive oils, brandies, and more). There's also a little tasting table where you can sample the earthy goods, and a brain-sized replica of that famously massive chunk of white truffle. A small jar of preserved truffles will run you 50–130 kn, depending on the size, type of truffle, and preparation. You can even pick up a recipe sheet telling you what to do with the precious stuff once you get it home (daily 9:00–21:00, Livade 7, tel. 052/664-030, www.zigantetartufi.com).

The adjacent **Restaurant Zigante,** one of Istria's fanciest (and most expensive), dishes up all manner of truffle specialties. The decor—inside or out on the terrace—is white-tablecloth classy, the service is deliberate but friendly, and the truffles, as if on a cooking game show, are prepared in a dizzying variety of ways. If you want the full dose of this local delicacy from a place that knows its truffles, this is a worthwhile splurge (150–300-kn main dishes, 400–500-kn fixed-price meals, daily 12:00–23:00, Livade 7, tel. 052/664-302).

In Brtonigla, Between Motovun and Rovinj

Brtonigla (bur-toh-NEEG-lah, Verteneglio in Italian, literally "black soil") is a tiny wine village surrounded by vineyards. Brtonigla is well-marked off the main *ipsilon* highway (coming north from Rovinj, but still south of Buje). Once in town, you'll find just a handful of haphazard streets, and this fine restaurant.

Konoba Astarea is a local favorite for traditional, take-your-time Istrian cuisine with a focus on fish and lamb. Anton and Alma Kernjus don't print an English menu, but they'll explain your options. As for seating, choose between the warmly cluttered, borderline-kitschy dining room huddled around the blazing open fire, where Alma does a lot of the cooking, or the cool and welcoming terrace with faraway sea views. It's smart to reserve ahead (60–100-kn meals, daily 11:00–23:00, closed Nov, tel. 052/774-384).

ZAGREB

While Zagreb doesn't have the urban bustle of Split or the stay-awhile charm of Ljubljana, the Croatian capital offers historic neighborhoods, worthwhile museums, a thriving café culture, and an illuminating contrast to the beaches. As a tourist destination, Zagreb pales in comparison to the sparkling coastal towns. But you can't get a complete picture of modern Croatia without a visit here—away from the touristy resorts, in the lively and livable city that is home to one out of every six Croatians (pop. 780,000).

Zagreb began as two walled medieval towns, Gradec and Kaptol, separated by a river. As Croatia fell under the control of various foreign powers—Budapest, Vienna, Berlin, and Belgrade—the two hill towns that would become Zagreb gradually took on more religious and civic importance. Kaptol became a bishopric in 1094, and it's still home to Croatia's most important church. In the 16th century, the Ban (Croatia's governor) and the Sabor (parliament) called Gradec home. The two towns officially merged in 1850, and soon after, the railroad connecting Budapest with the Adriatic port city of Rijeka was built through the city. Zagreb prospered.

After centuries of being the de facto religious, cultural, and political center of Croatia, Zagreb officially became a European capital when the country declared its independence in 1991. In the ensuing war with Serbia, Zagreb was hardly damaged—Serbian bombs hit only a few strategic targets. Today, just over a decade later, Zagreb has long since repaired the minimal damage, and the capital is safe, modern, lively, and fun.

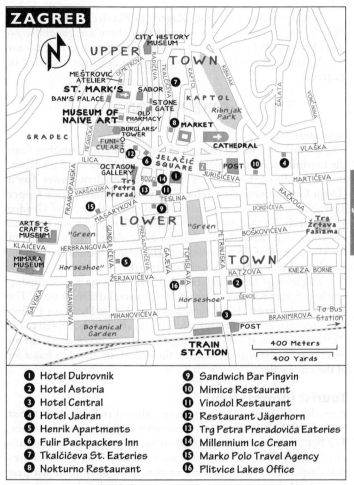

❶	Hotel Dubrovnik	❾	Sandwich Bar Pingvin
❷	Hotel Astoria	❿	Mimice Restaurant
❸	Hotel Central	⓫	Vinodol Restaurant
❹	Hotel Jadran	⓬	Restaurant Jägerhorn
❺	Henrik Apartments	⓭	Trg Petra Preradovića Eateries
❻	Fulir Backpackers Inn	⓮	Millennium Ice Cream
❼	Tkalčićeva St. Eateries	⓯	Marko Polo Travel Agency
❽	Nokturno Restaurant	⓰	Plitvice Lakes Office

Planning Your Time

Most visitors just pass through Zagreb, but the city is worth a look. Check your bag at the station and zip into the center for a quick visit—or consider spending the night.

You can get a decent sense of Zagreb in just a few hours. With whatever time you have, make a beeline for Jelačić Square to visit the TI and get oriented. Take the funicular up to Gradec, visit the excellent Museum of Naive Art, and stroll St. Mark's Square. Then wander down through the Stone Gate to the lively Tkalčićeva scene (good for a drink or meal), through the market (closes at 14:00), and on to Kaptol and the cathedral.

With more time, visit some of Zagreb's museums or wander the series of parks called the "Green Horseshoe."

If you're moving on from Zagreb to Plitvice Lakes National Park (see next chapter), be warned that there are generally no buses between 15:00 and 22:00 (or sometimes later). Confirm your bus departure carefully to ensure that you don't get stranded in Zagreb.

ORIENTATION

(area code: 01)

Zagreb, just 30 minutes from the Slovenian border, stretches from the foothills of Medvednica ("Bear Mountain") to the Sava River. In the middle of the sprawl, you'll find the modern **Lower Town** (Donji Grad, centered on **Jelačić Square**) and the historic **Upper Town** (Gornji Grad, comprising the original hill towns of **Gradec** and **Kaptol**). To the south is a U-shaped belt of parks, squares, and museums that make up the "Green Horseshoe." The east side of the U is a series of three parks, with the train station at the bottom (south) and Jelačić Square at the top (north).

Zagrebians have devised a brilliant scheme for confusing tourists: Street names can be depicted several different ways. For example, the street that is signed as ulica Kralja Držislava ("King Držislav Street") is often called by locals simply Držislavova ("Držislav's"). So if you're looking for a street, don't search for an exact match—be willing to settle for something that just has a lot of the same letters.

Tourist Information

Zagreb's TI is at Jelačić Square (Mon–Fri 8:30–20:00, Sat 9:00–17:00, Sun 10:00–14:00, sometimes longer hours in summer, Trg bana Jelačića 11, tel. 01/481-4052, www.zagreb-touristinfo .hr). The TI offers piles of free, well-produced tourist brochures that desperately try to convince visitors to do more than just pass through. Pick up the one-page city map (with handy transit map and regional map on back), the *Zagreb Info A–Z* booklet (including accommodations and restaurant listings), the monthly events guide, the great *City Walks* brochure (with a couple of mildly diverting self-guided walking tours), the museum guide, the booklet about the surrounding region, and more.

The **Zagreb Card** gives you free transportation and 50 percent discounts at most Zagreb museums, plus other deals (60 kn/24 hrs, 90 kn/72 hs, sold at TI). This usually doesn't make sense for folks who are day-tripping here—to break even, you'd have to take the city walking tour (see below) and visit at least four museums in one day. If you do the city bus-plus-walking tour, the card is a better deal.

To get oriented, consider the fun daily **city tours** (2-hour

Zagreb Essentials

English	Croatian	Pronounced
Jelačić Square	Trg bana Jelačića	turg BAH-nah YEH-lah-chee-chah
Gradec (original civic hill town)	Gradec	GRAH-dehts
Kaptol (original religious hill town)	Kaptol	KAHP-tohl
Café street between Gradec and Kaptol	Tkalčićeva (or "Tkalči" for short)	tuh-KAHL-chee-chay-vah (tuh-KAHL-chee)
Main Train Station	Glavni Kolodvor	GLAHV-nee KOH-loh-dvor
Bus Station	Autobusni Kolodvor	OW-toh-boos-nee KOH-loh-dvor

walking tour: 95 kn, usually Mon–Thu at 10:00 or 16:00; 3-hr bus-plus-walking tour: 150 kn, usually Fri–Sun; 25 percent discount on either tour with Zagreb Card). For either tour, call the TI by 14:00 the day before to confirm the schedule, reserve a space, and request an English guide. The same company runs theme tours and excursions into the surrounding countryside (about 2/month, mobile 091-370-3092, www.event.hr).

Arrival in Zagreb

By Train: Zagreb's Main Train Station (Glavni Kolodvor) is conveniently located a few blocks south of Jelačić Square on the Green Horseshoe. The straightforward arrivals hall has a train information desk, ticket windows, ATMs, WCs, and newsstands. The left-luggage office is at the left end of the station, with your back to the tracks (look for low-profile *garderoba* sign, open daily 24 hours). To reach the city center, go straight out the front door. You'll run into a taxi stand, and then the tracks for tram #6 (buy 6.50-kn ticket from kiosk, then hop on: direction Črnomerec zips you to Jelačić Square; direction Sopot takes you to the bus station—the third stop, just after you turn right and go under the big overpass). If you walk straight ahead through the long, lush park, you'll wind up at the bottom of Jelačić Square in 10 minutes.

By Bus: The user-friendly but inconveniently located bus station (Autobusni Kolodvor) is a few long blocks southeast of the Main Train Station. The station has all the essentials—ATMs, post office, mini-grocery store, left-luggage counter...everything from a smut store to a chapel. Upstairs, you'll find ticket windows and access to the buses (follow signs to *perone;* wave ticket in front of turnstile to open gate). Tram #6 (in direction Črnomerec) takes you to the Main Train Station, then on to Jelačić Square. Walking to Jelačić Square from the bus station takes about 25 minutes.

By Plane: Zagreb's small airport is 10 miles south of the center (tel. 01/626-5222, www.zagreb-airport.hr). Once you get through security, your only food and drink option is one very expensive bar. While a shuttle bus connects the airport to the bus station (2/hr, 30 min, 30 kn), it's more convenient to pay the 150 kn for a taxi right to your hotel (30 min; confirm price, as some crooked cabbies will attempt to get 200 kn).

Getting Around Zagreb

The main mode of public transportation is the **tram,** operated by ZET (Zagreb Electrical Transport). A single ticket (good for 90 min in one direction, including transfers) costs 8 kn if you buy it from the driver (6.50 kn at kiosk, ask for *ZET karta*—zeht KAR-tah). A day ticket *(dnevna karta)* costs 18 kn. The most useful tram for tourists is #6, connecting Jelačić Square with the train and bus stations.

Taxis start at 19 kn, then run 7 kn per kilometer (20 percent more Sun and at night, 3 kn extra for each piece of baggage; beware of corrupt cabbies—ask for an estimate up front, or call Radio Taxi, tel. 01/970). A typical ride within the city center shouldn't run more than about 30 kn, and the trip to the airport should cost about 150 kn (agree on a price first).

Helpful Hints

Schedule Quirks: Virtually all of Zagreb's museums are closed on Sunday afternoon and all day Monday. Some museums stay open until 22:00 one night a week in summer. On Sunday morning, the city is thriving—but by afternoon, it's extremely quiet.

Ferry Tickets: If you're heading for the Dalmatian Coast, note that there isn't a Jadrolinija ferry office in the center. But you can reserve and buy tickets at the **Marko Polo** travel agency (Mon–Fri 9:00–17:00, Sat 9:00–13:00, closed Sun, Masarykova 24, tel. 01/481-5216).

Plitvice Lakes Office: If you're going to Plitvice Lakes National Park, you can get a preview and ask any questions at their information office in Zagreb (Mon–Fri 8:00–16:00, closed Sat–Sun, a block in front of Main Train Station at Trg Kralja Tomislava 19, tel. 01/461-3586).

SELF-GUIDED WALK

▲▲Zagreb's Upper Town

The following one-way circular orientation walk begins at Jelačić Square. The entire route takes about an hour at a leisurely pace (not counting museum stops).

▲Jelačić Square (Trg bana Jelačića)

The "Times Square" of Zagreb bustles with life. It's lined with cafés, shops, Baroque buildings, and the TI. Watching the crowds

pile in and out of trams and seeing the city buzz with activity, you feel the energy of capitalism, freedom, and a new country on the go. People-watching is one of the treats of Zagreb.

When Zagreb consisted of the two hill towns of Gradec and Kaptol, this Donji Grad ("lower town") held the townspeople's farm fields. Today, it features a prominent equestrian statue of national hero **Josip Jelačić** (YOH-seep YEH-lah-cheech, 1801–1859), a 19th-century governor who extended citizens' rights and did much to unite the Croats within the Hapsburg Empire. In Jelačić's time, the Hungarians were exerting extensive control over Croatia, even trying to make Hungarian the official language. Meanwhile, Budapesters revolted against Hapsburg rule in 1848. Jelačić, ever mindful of the need to protect Croatian cultural autonomy, knew that he'd have a better shot at getting his way from Austria than from Hungary. Jelačić chose the lesser of two evils, and fought alongside the Hapsburgs to put down the Hungarian uprising. In the Yugoslav era, Jelačić was considered a dangerously nationalistic symbol, and this statue was dismantled and stored away. But when Croatia broke away in 1991, Croatian patriotism was in the air, and Jelačić returned. Though Jelačić originally faced his Hungarian foes to the north, today he's staring down the Serbs to the south.

Get oriented. If you face Jelačić's statue, down a long block to your left is a funicular that takes you up to one of Zagreb's original villages, Gradec. To the right, look for the TI. If you leave the square ahead and to the right, you'll reach the other original village, Kaptol, and the cathedral (you can't miss its huge, pointy, Neo-Gothic spires—visible from virtually everywhere in Zagreb). If you leave the square ahead and to the left, you'll come to the market (Dolac) and the lively café street, Tkalčićeva.

For now, we'll head up to Gradec. Go a long block down the busy Ilica. On the way, consider ducking inside the big **shopping**

gallery on the left (at #5). This was the ultimate in iron-and-glass shopping elegance a century ago. Look for the tie shop from the chain called Croata (for the story, see page 693).

Continue up Ilica and turn right on Tomićeva, where you'll see a small **funicular** (ZET Uspinjača) crawling up the hill. Dating from the late 19th century, this funicular is looked upon fondly by Zagrebians—both as a bit of nostalgia and as a way to avoid some steps. You can walk up if you want, but the ride is more fun and takes only 55 seconds (3 kn, validate ticket in orange machine before you board, leaves every 10 min daily 6:30–21:00).

Gradec

From the top of the funicular, you'll enjoy a fine panorama over Zagreb. The tall tower you face as you exit is one of Gradec's original watchtowers, the **Burglars' Tower** (Kula Lotršćak). After the Tatars ransacked Central Europe in the early 13th century, King Béla IV decreed that towns be fortified—so Gradec built a wall and guard towers (just like Kraków and Budapest did). Look for the little cannon in the top-floor window. Every day at noon, this cannon fires a shot, supposedly to commemorate a 15th-century victory over the besieging Ottomans. Zagrebians hold on to other traditions, too—the lamps on this hill are still gas-powered, lit by a city employee every evening.

Head up the street next to the tower. Little remains of medieval Gradec. When the Ottomans overran Europe, they never managed to take Zagreb—but the threat was enough to scare the nobility into the countryside. When the Ottomans left, the nobles came back, and replaced the medieval buildings here with Baroque mansions. At the first square, to the right, you'll see the Jesuit **Church of St. Catherine.** It's not much to look at from the outside, but the interior is intricately decorated. The same applies to several mansions on Gradec. This simple-outside, ornate-inside style is known as "Zagreb Baroque."

As you continue up the street, notice that the old-timey **street signs** are a holdover from the Austro-Hungarian era: in both Croatian (Gospodska ulicza) and German (Herren Gasse).

On the left you'll see the **Croatian Museum of Naive Art**—Zagreb's best museum, and well worth a visit (listed under "Sights," page 774). In the next block, on the left, look for the monument to Nikola Tesla (1856–1943), a prominent Croatian-born Serb scientist who championed alternating current as an alternative to Thomas Edison's direct current.

At the end of the block, you'll come to the low-key **St. Mark's Square** (Markov trg), centered on the **Church of St. Mark.** The original church here was from the 12th century, but only a few fragments remain. The present church's colorful tile roof, from

1880, depicts two coats of arms. On the left, the red-and-white checkerboard symbolizes north-central Croatia, the three lions' heads stand for the Dalmatian Coast, and the marten (*kuna,* like the money) running between the two rivers (Sava and Drava) represent Slavonia—Croatia's northern, inland panhandle. On the right is the seal of Zagreb: a walled city with wide-open doors (strong, but still welcoming to visitors...like you). The interior is a bit stark, livened up by a few sculptures by Ivan Meštrović, whose former home is about a block straight ahead (go down the street behind the church on the left-hand side, and you'll see the museum on the right; see listing under "Sights").

As you face the church, to the right is the **Sabor,** or parliament. From the 12th century, Croatian noblemen would gather here to make important decisions regarding their territories. This gradually evolved into today's modern parliament. (If you walk along the front of the Sabor and continue straight ahead two blocks, you'll run into the excellent Zagreb City Museum, described under "Sights.")

Across the square from the Sabor (to your left as you face the church) is the **Ban's Palace** (Banski Dvori), today the offices for the president and prime minister. This was one of the few buildings in central Zagreb destroyed in the recent war. In October of 1991, the Serbs shelled it from afar, knowing that Croatian President Franjo Tuđman was inside...but Tuđman survived.

Walk from Gradec to Kaptol

For an interesting stroll from St. Mark's Square to the cathedral, head down the street (Kamenita ulica) to the right of the parliament building. Near the end of the street, you'll see the oldest **pharmacy** in town—recently restored and gleaming (c. 1355, on the right, marked *gradska ljekarna*).

Just beyond, you'll reach Gradec's oldest surviving gate, the **Stone Gate** (Kamenita Vrata). Inside is an evocative chapel. The focal point is a painting of Mary that miraculously survived a major fire in 1731. When this medieval gate was reconstructed in the Baroque style, they decided to turn it into a makeshift chapel. The candles (purchased in the little shop and lit in the big metal bin) represent Zagrebians' prayers. Notice the soot-blackened ceiling over the forest fire of blazing candles in the bin. The stone plaques on the wall give thanks *(Hvala)* for prayers that were answered. You may notice people making the sign of the cross as they walk through here, and often a crowd of worshippers gather, staring intently at the painting. Mary was made the official patron saint of Zagreb in 1990.

As you leave the Stone Gate and come to Radićeva, turn right and walk downhill. Take the next left, onto the street called **Krvavi Most**—"Blood Bridge." At the end of Krvavi Most, you'll come to **Tkalčićeva.** This lively café-and-restaurant street used to be a river—the natural boundary between Gradec and Kaptol. The two towns did not always get along, and sometimes fought against each other. Blood was spilled, and the bridge that once stood here between them became known as Blood Bridge. By the late 19th century, the towns had united, and the river began to stink—so they covered it over with this street.

As you cross Tkalčićeva, you enter the old town of Kaptol. You'll come to the **market** *(dolac)*, packed with colorful stalls selling produce of all kinds (Mon–Sat 7:00–14:00, Sun 7:00–13:00). At the back-left corner is the fragrant fish market *(ribarnica)*, and under your feet is an indoor part of the market *(tržnica)*, where farmers sell farm-fresh eggs and dairy products (same hours as outdoor market, entrance down below in the direction of Jelačić Square).

Your walk is over. On the other side of the market, visit the cathedral (see description in "Sights").

SIGHTS

Museums in Gradec

▲▲Croatian Museum of Naive Art (Hrvatski Muzej Naivne Umjetnosti)—This remarkable spot, founded in 1952 as the "Peasant Art Gallery," is one of the most enjoyable little museums in Croatia. It features expressionistic paintings by untrained peasant artists (called "autodidacts" because they are self-taught). On one easy floor, the museum displays 80 paintings made mostly by Croatians from the 1930s to the 1980s. These stirring images—lyrical landscapes and fantasy dreamscapes rich with detail—really leave an impression. The movement's star is Ivan Generalić. Mijo Kovačić's paintings are particularly striking, with hauntingly detailed layers of twisted tree branches. The works by Ivan Večenaj are similar, but even more grotesque (20 kn, pick up the English explanations as you enter, Tue–Fri 10:00–18:00, Sat–Sun 10:00–13:00, closed Mon, ulica Sv. Čirila i Metoda 3, tel. 01/485-1911, www.hmnu.org).

▲Ivan Meštrović Atelier—Ivan Meštrović, the only Croatian artist worth remembering, designed, built, decorated, and lived in this house from 1922 until 1942 (before he fled to the US after World War II). The house has been converted into a delightful gallery of the artist's works, displayed in two parts: residence and studio. Split's Meštrović Gallery is the definitive museum of the 20th-century Croatian sculptor, but if you're not going there, Zagreb's gallery is a convenient place to gain an appreciation for the prolific, thoughtful artist (20 kn, 20-kn English catalog, Tue–Fri 10:00–18:00, Sat–Sun 10:00–14:00, closed Mon, behind St. Mark's Square at Mletačka 8, tel. 01/485-1123). For more on Meštrović, see page 695.

▲**Zagreb City Museum (Muzej Grada Zagreba)**—This collection, with a modern, well-presented exhibit that sprawls over two floors of an old convent, traces the history of the city through town models, paintings, furniture, clothing, and lots of fascinating artifacts. After buying your ticket, head through the door and turn left, then work your way up through the ages. Each display has a fine English description. The 19th-century wing is like a folk museum. Find the giant map on the floor, punctuated with models of key buildings. The coverage of the tumultuous 20th century is perhaps most engaging, with an understandably bad attitude about the Serb-dominated first Yugoslav period, followed by stirring videos, a hall of propaganda posters, and artifacts from World War II and the Tito period (when Croatia was a player in Belgrade). The finale is a room dedicated to the creation of independent Croatia, including an exhibit on damage sustained during the warfare (20 kn, Tue–Fri 10:00–18:00, likely open later on Thu, Sat–Sun 10:00–14:00, closed Mon, at north end of Gradec at Opatička 20, tel. 01/485-1361, www.mdc.hr/mgz).

▲**Cathedral (Katedrala)**

By definition, Croats are Catholics. Before the recent war, relatively few people practiced their faith. But as the Croats fought with their Orthodox and Muslim neighbors, Catholicism took on a greater importance. Today, more and more Croats are attending Mass. This is Croatia's single most important church.

In 1094, when a diocese was established at Kaptol, this church quickly became a major center of high-ranking church officials. In the mid-13th century, the original cathedral was destroyed by invading Tatars, who actually used it as a stable. It was rebuilt, only to be destroyed again by an earthquake in 1880. The current version—undergoing yet another renovation for the last several years—is Neo-Gothic (about a hundred years old inside and out). Surrounding the church are walls with pointy-topped towers (part of a larger archbishop's palace) that were built for protection against the Ottomans. The full name is the Cathedral of the Assumption of the Blessed Virgin Mary and the Saintly Kings Stephen and Ladislav (whew!)—but most locals just call it "the cathedral."

Standing out front, appreciate the gorgeous facade and modern tympanum (carved semi-circular section over the door). Then step inside (free, Mon–Sat 10:00–17:00, Sun 13:00–17:00). Look closely at the silver relief on the main **altar:** a scene of the Holy Family doing chores around the house (Mary sewing, Joseph and Jesus building a fence...and angels helping out).

In the front-left corner (on the wall, between the confessionals), find the modern tombstone of **Alojzije Stepinac.** He was the Archbishop of Zagreb in World War II, when he shortsightedly supported the Ustaše (Nazi puppet government in Croatia)—thinking, like many Croatians, that this was the ticket to greater independence from Serbia. When Tito came to power, he put Stepinac on trial and sent him to jail for five years. But Stepinac never lost his faith, and remains to many the most important inspirational figure of Croatian Catholicism. (He's also respected in the US, where some Catholic schools bear his name. But many Serbs today consider Stepinac a villain who cooperated with the brutal Ustaše.)

As you leave the church, look high on the wall to the left of the door. This strange script is the **Glagolitic alphabet** *(glagoljca)*, invented by Byzantine missionaries Cyril and Methodius in the ninth century to translate the Bible into Slavic languages. Though these missionaries worked mostly in Moravia (today's eastern Czech Republic), their alphabet caught on only here, in Croatia. (Glagolitic was later adapted in Bulgaria to become the Cyrillic alphabet—still used in Serbia, Russia, and other parts east.) In 1991, when Croatia became its own country and nationalism surged, the country flirted with the idea of making this the official alphabet.

The Green Horseshoe

With extra time, stroll around the Green Horseshoe (the U-shaped belt of parks and museums in the city center). The museums here aren't nearly as interesting as those on Gradec, but may be worth a peek on a rainy day.

Mimara Museum (Muzej Mimara)—This grand, empty-feeling building displays the eclectic collection of a wealthy Dalmatian, ranging from ancient artifacts to paintings by European masters. While the names are major—Rubens, Rembrandt, Velázquez, Renoir, Manet—the paintings themselves are minors. Still, art buffs may find something to get excited about (20 kn, 90-kn English guidebook, otherwise virtually no English, Tue–Sat

10:00–17:00, Thu until 19:00, Sun 10:00–14:00, closed Mon, Rooseveltov trg 5, tel. 01/482-8100).

Arts and Crafts Museum (Muzej za Umjetnost i Obrt)—This decorative arts collection of furniture, ceramics, and clothes is well-displayed. From the entry, go upstairs, then work your way clockwise and up to the top floor—passing through each artistic style, from Gothic to the present. It's mostly furniture, with a few paintings and other items thrown in (20 kn, some rooms have laminated English descriptions to borrow, otherwise very limited English, Tue–Sat 10:00–19:00, Sun 10:00–14:00, closed Mon, Trg Maršala Tita 10, tel. 01/488-2111, www.muo.hr).

Botanical Garden (Botanički Vrt)—For a back-to-nature change of pace from the urban cityscape, wander through this relaxing garden, run by the University of Zagreb (free, Mon–Tue 9:00–14:30, Wed–Sun 9:00–18:00—or until 19:00 in summer, at southwest corner of the Green 'Shoe).

SLEEPING

Hotels in central Zagreb are very expensive—you won't get much for your money. I prefer sleeping in Ljubljana or at Plitvice Lakes National Park, both of which offer better values. But if you must stay in Zagreb, these are the best deals right in the main tourist zone. If you show up without a reservation, the TI can help you find a hotel room or *sobe* for no charge.

$$$ Hotel Dubrovnik has an ideal location (at the bottom of Jelačić Square) and 268 business-class rooms (small Sb-800 kn, bigger Sb-1,000 kn, Db with 1 big bed-1,100 kn, twin Db-1,200 kn, suite-1,400–1,600 kn, extra bed-250 kn, rooms overlooking the

---

Sleep Code

(5 kn = about $1, country code: 385, area code: 01)
S = Single, **D** = Double/Twin, **T** = Triple, **Q** = Quad, **b** = bathroom. English is spoken at each place. Unless otherwise noted, credit cards are accepted, breakfast is included, and the modest tourist tax (7 kn per person, per night) is not.

To help you sort easily through these listings, I've divided the rooms into three categories based on the price for a standard double room with bath:

   $$$ **Higher Priced**—Most rooms 800 kn or more.
    $$ **Moderately Priced**—Most rooms between
                                500–800 kn.
     $ **Lower Priced**—Most rooms 500 kn or less.

square don't cost extra—try to request one, often cheaper on weekends, prices soft, non-smoking floors, elevator, Gajeva 1, tel. 01/486-3555, fax 01/486-3506, www.hotel-dubrovnik.hr, reservations @hotel-dubrovnik.hr).

$$$ **Hotel Astoria,** a Best Western, was recently renovated from top to bottom. Now it offers 102 smallish but plush rooms and a high-class lobby. It's on a grimy street near the train station, so I wouldn't splurge here unless I were in town on a weekend, when rates drop by a third (Sb-700–850 kn, Db-900–1,100 kn; Fri–Sun: Sb-600 kn, Db-760 kn; price depends on demand, can be soft on some weekdays, fancier suites also available, elevator, Petrinjska 71, tel. 01/480-8900, fax 01/480-8908, www.bestwestern.com, sales @hotelastoria.hr).

$$ **Hotel Central**'s 76 overly perfumed rooms are comfortable and modern, and the price is right. This place seems to get a little better every year, and the location—right across from the Main Train Station—is convenient for rail travelers (Sb-580, larger Sb-650 kn, Db with one big bed-750 kn, twin Db-820 kn, extra bed-130 kn, elevator, Branimirova 3, tel. 01/484-1122, fax 01/484-1304, www.hotel-central.hr, info@hotel-central.hr).

$$ **Hotel Jadran** has 49 decent rooms near the cathedral, a few blocks east of Jelačić Square (Sb-520 kn, Db-730 kn, Tb-900 kn, some street noise—request quiet room, elevator, Vlaška 50, tel. 01/455-3777, fax 01/461-2151, www.hup-zagreb.hr, jadran @hup-zagreb.hr).

$ **Henrik Apartments** has seven rooms over a neighborhood tavern on a drab urban street several blocks from Jelačić Square (Sb-250 kn, Db-300 kn, apartment-400 kn, no breakfast, cash only, Gundulićeva 39, tel. 01/485-6171, mobile 098-994-6014, www.apartmanihenrik.com, henrikmarinsek@gmail.com).

$ **Fulir Backpackers Inn,** a funky slumbermill named for a legendary Zagrebian bon vivant, is loosely run by Davor and Leo, a pair of can-do Croats who lived in Ohio. It's colorful and friendly, with a big 12-bunk dorm and a smaller four-bed room sharing two bathrooms. Just a few steps from Jelačić Square, this hostel puts you in the heart of Zagreb (150 kn/bunk, includes sheets, no breakfast, free lockers, pay Internet access, upstairs at the end of the courtyard at Radićeva 3a, tel. 01/483-0882, mobile 098-193-0552, www.fulir-hostel.com).

EATING

For the perfect place to sip a lazy cup of coffee, look no further than Jelačić Square—Zagreb's heart and soul. To venture a little farther, try these places.

On Tkalčićeva: This is Zagreb's main café street, "restaurant row," and urban promenade rolled into one. It's a parade of fashionable locals, and *the* place to see and be seen. Wander here and choose your favorite spot (starts a block behind Jelačić Square, next to the market). For good pizza and pasta, walk a few feet up Skalinska (near the Jelačić Square end of the street) to find **Nokturno,** with a lively interior and ample outdoor seating on a terrace cascading down the street (20–30-kn pizzas, pastas, and salads, 30–50-kn meat and fish dishes, daily 9:00–1:00 in the morning, Skalinska 4, tel. 01/481-3394).

At the Market **(Dolac):** Zagreb's busy market offers plenty of options (Mon–Sat 7:00–14:00, Sun 7:00–13:00). Buy a fresh picnic direct from the producers. Or, for something already prepared, duck into one of the many cheap restaurants and cafés on the streets around the market. The middle level of the market, facing Jelačić Square, is home to a line of places with cheap food and indoor or outdoor seating.

Sandwich Bar Pingvin, busy with locals dropping by for take-away, is a favorite for quick, cheap, tasty sandwiches. The photo menu—featuring sandwiches with chicken, turkey, steak, fish, even salmon—makes ordering easy. They'll wrap it all in a piece of grilled bread and top it with your choice of veggies and sauces. Or sit at one of the few tiny tables or stools (20–25 kn, open long hours daily, Teslina 7).

Mimice is a local institution and an old-habits-die-hard favorite of the older generation. While a bit tired and dreary, it's a cheap and memorable time-warp serving up simple fish dishes (20–30 kn, order starches and sauces separately). Choose what you want from the limited menu (if confused, survey the room for a plate that looks good and ask what it is), pay, and take your receipt to the next counter to claim your food. Order the smelt to get a plate of tiny deep-fried fish (Mon–Sat 7:00–22:00, closed Sun, Jurišićeva 21). As Zagreb is a Catholic town, you'll have to wait in line if you're here on a Friday.

Vinodol is your white-tablecloth classy dinner spot, with a peaceful covered terrace and a smartly appointed dining room under an impressive vaulted ceiling. The good cuisine includes veal prepared *peka*-style, in a pot covered with hot coals (60–100-kn main dishes, daily 10:00–24:00, Teslina 10, tel. 01/481-1427).

Restaurant Jägerhorn is an oasis in the heart of the city, sharing a delightful garden courtyard with a serene waterfall. The menu includes game and grilled dishes (50–100 kn; daily 10:00–22:30, at the end of a courtyard a block from Jelačić Square at Ilica 14—go down passage marked *Lovački Rog,* tel. 01/483-3877). They also rent 13 small, musty, overpriced rooms.

On Trg Petra Preradovića: This inviting square, just a short walk from Jelačić Square, bustles with appealing restaurants featuring outdoor tables and good food. It's a fine place to compare menus and choose the food and ambience you like best.

Ice Cream!: Zagreb's favorite *sladoled* (Italian gelato-style ice cream) is at **Millennium,** just a block from Jelačić Square. With giant mounds of the widest variety of flavors I've seen in Croatia, this is the city's top dessert stop (Mon–Sat 8:00–23:00, Sun 9:00–23:00, Bogovićeva 7, tel. 01/481-0850).

TRANSPORTATION CONNECTIONS

From Zagreb by Train to: Rijeka (3/day, 4 hrs), **Split** (3/day, 5.5 hrs, plus 1 direct night train, 8 hrs), **Ljubljana** (8/day, 2.5 hrs), **Vienna** (4/day, 5.5–7 hrs, 2 direct, others with 1–2 changes), **Budapest** (2/day, 5 or 7 hrs), **Lake Bled** (via Lesce-Bled, 5/day, 3.5 hrs).

By Bus to: Plitvice Lakes National Park (about hourly until around 15:00, 2–2.5 hrs; then none until about 22:00), **Rijeka** (hourly, 3.5 hrs), **Rovinj** (8/day, 5–8 hrs), **Pula** (almost hourly, 3.75–6 hrs), **Split** (about 2/hr, 5–9 hrs), **Dubrovnik** (2 in the early morning, sometimes 1–2 midday, then 4–6 overnight, 11–12.5 hrs), **Korčula** (1/night, 13.5 hrs).

Bus schedules can be sporadic (e.g., several departures clustered around the same time, then nothing for hours)—confirm carefully locally (schedules online at www.akz.hr). The TI is very helpful with providing bus information. Popular buses, such as the afternoon express to Split, can fill up quickly in peak season. Unfortunately, it's impossible to buy bus tickets anywhere in the center, so to guarantee a seat, you'll have to get to the station early (locals suggest even two hours in advance). Better yet, call the central number for the bus station to check schedules and reserve the bus you want: tel. 060-313-333 (from abroad, dial +385-1-611-2789). If you can't get an English-speaker on the line, and the TI isn't too busy, they might be able to call for you.

PLITVICE LAKES NATIONAL PARK

Nacionalni Park Plitvička Jezera

Plitvice (PLEET-veet-seh) is one of Europe's most spectacular natural wonders. Imagine Niagara Falls diced and sprinkled over a heavily forested Grand Canyon. There's nothing like this lush valley of 16 terraced lakes, laced together by waterfalls and miles of pleasant plank walks. Countless cascades and water that's both strangely clear and full of vibrant colors make this park a misty natural wonderland. Years ago, after eight or nine visits, I thought I really knew Europe. Then I discovered Plitvice, and realized you can never exhaust Europe's surprises.

Planning Your Time

Plitvice deserves at least a few good hours. Since it takes some time to get here (two hours by car or bus from Zagreb), the most sensible plan is to spend the night in one of the park's hotels (no character, but comfortable and convenient) or a nearby private home (cheaper, but practical only if you're driving). If you're coming from the north (e.g., Ljubljana), take the train to Zagreb in the morning, spend a few hours seeing the Croatian capital, then take the bus (generally no buses 15:00–22:00) or drive to Plitvice in the late afternoon to spend the night at the park. Get up early and hit the trails (ideally by 8:30); by early afternoon, you'll be ready to move on (by bus to the coast, or back to Zagreb). Two nights and a full day at Plitvice

The Science of Plitvice

Virtually every visitor to Plitvice eventually asks the same question: How did it happen? A geologist once explained to me that Plitvice is a "perfect storm" of unique geological, climatic, and biological features you'll rarely find elsewhere on earth.

Plitvice's magic ingredient is calcium carbonate ($CaCO_3$), a mineral deposit from the limestone. Calcium is the same thing that makes "hard water" hard. If you have hard water, you may get calcium deposits on your cold-water faucet. But these deposits build up only at the faucet, not inside the pipes. That's because when hard water is motionless (as it usually is in the pipes), it holds on to the calcium. But at the point where the water is subjected to pressure and movement—as it pours out of the faucet—it releases the calcium.

Plitvice works the same way. As water flows over the park's limestone formations, it dissolves the rock, and the water becomes supersaturated with calcium carbonate. When the water is still, it holds on to the mineral—which creates the beautiful deep-blue color of the pools. But when the water speeds up and spills over the edge of the lakes, it releases carbon dioxide gas. Without the support of the carbon dioxide, the water can't hold on to the calcium carbonate, so it gets deposited on the lake bed and at the edges of the lakes. Eventually, these deposits build up to form a rock called travertine (the same composition as the original limestone, but formed in a different way). The travertine coating becomes thicker, and barriers—and eventually dams and new waterfalls—are formed. The ongoing process means that Plitvice's landscape is always changing.

And why is the water so clear? For one thing, it comes directly from high-mountain runoff, giving it little opportunity to become polluted or muddy. Also, the calcium carbonate in the water both gives it more color and makes it highly basic, which prevents the growth of plantlife (such as certain algae) that could cloud the water.

Wildlife found in the park includes deer, wolves, wildcats, lynx, wild boar, voles, otters, and more than 160 species of birds (including eagles, herons, owls, grouse, and storks). The lakes (and local menus) are full of trout, and you'll also see smaller, red-finned fish called klen ("chub" in English). Perhaps most importantly, Plitvice is home to about 50 brown bears—a species now extremely endangered in Europe. You'll see bears, the park's mascot, plastered all over the tourist literature (and in the form of a scary representative in the lobby of Hotel Jezero).

is probably overkill for all but the most avid hikers.

Crowd-Beating Tips: Plitvice is swamped with international tour groups, many of whom aren't shy about elbowing into position for the best photos. It's essential to get an early start to get in front of the hordes.

Getting to Plitvice

Plitvice Lakes National Park, a few miles from the Bosnian border, is two hours by car south of Zagreb on National Road #1 (a.k.a. D-1).

By **car** from Zagreb, you'll take the expressway south for about an hour, exiting at Karlovac (marked for *1* and *Plitvice*). From here, D-1 takes you directly south about another hour to the park. For information about driving onward from Plitvice, see "Route Tips for Drivers" at the end of this chapter.

Buses leave from Zagreb's main bus station in the direction of Plitvice. Various bus companies handle the route; just go to the ticket window and ask for the next departure (about 75 kn, trip takes 2–2.5 hours). Buses run from Zagreb about hourly until 15:00, and then there are generally no departures until 22:00 (or sometimes later). Confirm that your bus will actually stop at Plitvice. (The driver may be willing to take you to your specific hotel, or, worst-case scenario, he'll drop you at the official Plitvice bus stop, which is a 10-min walk beyond the hotels.) Confirm the schedule online (www.akz.hr) or at the Plitvice office in Zagreb (Mon–Fri 8:00–16:00, closed Sat–Sun, Trg Kralja Tomislava 19, tel. 01/461-3586).

By car or bus, you'll see some thought-provoking terrain between Zagreb and Plitvice. As you leave Karlovac, you'll pass through the village of **Turanj,** part of the war zone just a decade ago. The destroyed, derelict houses belonged to Serbs who have not come back to reclaim and repair them. Farther along, about 25 miles before Plitvice, you'll pass through the striking village of **Slunj,** picturesquely perched on travertine formations (like Plitvice's) and surrounded by sparkling streams and waterfalls. If you're in a car, this is worth a photo stop. This town, too, looks very different than it did before the war—when it was 30 percent Serb. As in countless other villages in the Croatian interior, the Orthodox church has been destroyed...and locals still seethe when they describe how occupying Serbs "defiled" the town's delicate beauty.

ORIENTATION

(area code: 053)
Plitvice's 16 lakes are divided into the Upper Lakes (Gornja Jezera) and the Lower Lakes (Donja Jezera). The park officially has two entrances *(ulaz),* each with ticket windows and snack and gift

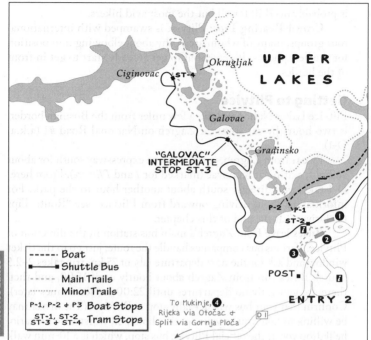

UPPER LAKES

Ciginovac · ST-4 · Okrugljak

Galovac

"GALOVAC" INTERMEDIATE STOP ST-3

Gradinsko

P-2 P-1

ST-2

POST

ENTRY 2

----- Boat
▪——▪ Shuttle Bus
----- Main Trails
········· Minor Trails
P-1, P-2 & P3 **Boat Stops**
ST-1, ST-2
ST-3 & ST-4 **Tram Stops**

To Mukinje, ❹
Rijeka via Otočac &
Split via Gornja Ploča

shops. Entrance 1 is at the bottom of the Lower Lakes, across the busy D-1 road from the park's best restaurant, Lička Kuća (see "Eating," page 790). Entrance 2 is about 1.5 miles south, at the cluster of Plitvice's three hotels (Jezero, Plitvice, and Bellevue; see "Sleeping," page 788). There is no town at Plitvice. The nearest village, Mukinje, is a residential community mostly for park workers (boring for tourists, but has some good private room options).

Cost and Hours: The price to enter the park during peak season (April–Oct) is a hefty 110 kn (70 kn Nov–March, ticket good for entire stay, including park entry, boat, shuttle bus, and parking). Park hours vary (generally from 7:00 in summer, 8:00 in spring and fall, and 9:00 in winter; closes at dusk). Night owls should note that the park never "closes"; these hours are for the ticket booths and the boat and shuttle bus system. You can just stroll right into the park at any time, provided that you aren't using the boat or bus. Again, for fewer tour-group crowds, visit early or late in the day.

Tourist Information

A handy map of the trails is on the back of your ticket, and big maps are posted all over the park. The big map is a good investment; the various English-language guidebooks are generally

PLITVICE LAKES NATIONAL PARK

L O W E R   L A K E S

Kozjak

P-3

**BIG
WATERFALL**

Korana River

**ŠUPLJARA
CAVE**

Milanovac

To Zagreb

ST-1

Gavanovac   Kaluđerovac

D 1

6

7

E N T R Y 1

P

5

6

500 Meters
500 Yards

❶ Hotel Jezero
❷ Hotel Plitvice
❸ Hotel Bellevue &
    Restaurant Poljana
❹ To Knežević Guest House
❺ Lička Kuća Restaurant
❻ Grocery Stores (2)

Plitvice Lakes

poorly translated and not very helpful (both sold at entrances, hotels, and shops throughout the park). The park has a good website: www.np-plitvicka-jezera.hr.

Getting Around Plitvice

Of course, Plitvice is designed for hikers. But the park has a few ways (included in entry cost) to help you connect the best parts.

By Shuttle Bus: Buses connect the hotels at Entrance 2 (stop ST2, below Hotel Jezero) with the top of the Upper Lakes (stop ST4) and roughly the bottom of the Lower Lakes (stop ST1, a 10-min walk from Entrance 1). Between Entrance 2 and the top of the Upper Lakes is an intermediate stop (ST3, at Galovac lake)—designed for tour groups, available to anyone, and offering a convenient way to skip the less interesting top half of the Upper Lakes. Buses start running early and continue until late afternoon (frequency depends on demand—generally 3–4/hr; buses run from March until the first snow—often Dec). Note that the park refers to its buses as "trains," which confuses some visitors. Also note that no local buses take you along the major road (D-1) that connects the entrances. The only way to get between them without a car is by shuttle bus (inside the park) or by foot (about a 40-min walk).

By Boat: Low-impact electric boats ply the waters of the biggest lake, Kozjak, with three stops: below Hotel Jezero (stop P1), the bottom of the Upper Lakes (P2), and at the far end of Kozjak, at the top of the Lower Lakes (P3). From Hotel Jezero to the Upper Lakes, it's a quick five-minute ride; the boat goes back and forth continuously. The trip from the Upper Lakes to the Lower Lakes takes closer to 20 minutes, and the boat goes about twice per hour—often at the top and bottom of every hour. (With up to 10,000 people a day visiting the park, you might have to wait for a seat on this boat.) Unless the lake freezes (about every five years), the boat also runs in the off-season—though frequency drops to hourly, and it stops running earlier.

SIGHTS AND ACTIVITIES

Plitvice is a refreshing playground of 16 terraced lakes, separated by natural travertine dams and connected by countless waterfalls. Over time, the water has simulta-neously carved out, and, with the help of mineral deposits, built up this fluid landscape.

Plitvice became Croatia's first national park in 1949. On Easter Sunday in 1991, the first shots of Croatia's war with Yugoslavia were fired right here—in fact, the war's first casualty was a park policeman, Josip Jović. The Serbs occupied Plitvice until 1995, and most of the Croatians you'll meet here were evacuated and lived near the coastline as refugees. Today, the war is a fading memory, and the park is again a popular tourist destination, with nearly a million visitors each year (though relatively few are from the US).

▲▲▲Hiking the Lakes

Plitvice's system of trails and boardwalks makes it possible for visi-tors to get immersed in the park's beauty. (In some places, the path leads literally right up the middle of a waterfall.) The official park map and signage recommend a variety of hikes, but there's no need to adhere strictly to these suggestions; invest in the big map and create your own route.

Most visitors stick to the main paths, and choose between two basic plans: uphill or downhill. Each one has pros and cons. Park officials generally recommend hiking uphill, from the Lower Lakes to the Upper Lakes, which offers slightly better head-on views of the best scenery (this is the route described below). It also saves the most scenic stretch of lakes and falls—the Upper Lakes—for last. Hiking downhill, from Upper to Lower, is easier (though you'll have to hike steeply up out of the canyon at the end), and since most groups go the opposite way, you'll be passing—but not stuck behind—the crowds. Either way you go, walking briskly and with a few photo stops, figure on an hour for the Lower Lakes, an hour for the Upper Lakes, and a half-hour to connect them by boat.

Lower Lakes (Donja Jezera)—The lower half of Plitvice's lakes are accessible from Entrance 1. If you start here, the route marked *G2* (intended for groups, but doable for anyone) leads you along the boardwalks to Kozjak, the big lake that connects the Lower and the Upper Lakes (see below).

From the entrance, you'll descend down a steep path with lots of **switchbacks,** as well as thrilling views over the canyon of the Lower Lakes. As you reach the lakes and begin to follow the boardwalks, you'll have great up-close views of the travertine formations that make up Plitvice's many waterfalls. Count the trout. If you're tempted to throw in a line, don't. Fishing is strictly forbidden. (Besides, they're happy.)

After you cross the path over the first lake, an optional 10-minute detour (to the right) takes you down to the **Big Waterfall** (Veliki Slap). It's the biggest of Plitvice's waterfalls, where the Plitvica River plunges 250 feet over a cliff into the valley below. Depending on recent rainfall, the force of the Big Waterfall varies from a light mist to a thundering deluge.

If you're a hardy hiker, consider climbing the steep steps from the Big Waterfall up to a **viewpoint** at the top of the canyon (marked *Sightseeing Point/ Vidikovac;* it's a strenuous 10-min hike to the top). Take the stairs up, bearing to the right at the top (near the shelter) to find a nice viewpoint overlooking the Big Waterfall. From here, you can carry on along the road that actually goes up over the top of the Big Waterfall, offering more views over the park. (Go as far as you like, then return the way you came.)

After seeing the Big Waterfall, backtrack up to the main trail and continue on the boardwalks. After you pass another bank of waterfalls, a smaller trail branches off (on the left) toward **Šupljara Cave.** You can actually climb through this slippery cave all the way up to the trail overlooking the Lower Lakes (though it's not recommended). This unassuming cavern is a surprisingly big draw. In the 1960s, several German and Italian "Spaghetti Westerns" were filmed at Plitvice and in other parts of Croatia (which, to European eyes, has terrain similar to the American West). The most famous, *Der Schatz im Silbersee (The Treasure in Silver Lake)*, was filmed here at Plitvice, and the treasure was hidden in this cave. The movie—complete with *Deutsch*-speaking "Native Americans"—is still a favorite in Germany, and popular theme tours bring German tourists to movie locations here in Croatia. (If you drive the roads near Plitvice, keep an eye out for strange, Native American–sounding names such as Winnetou—fictional characters from these beloved stories of the Old West, by the German writer Karl May.)

After Šupljara Cave, you'll stick to the east side of the lakes, then cross over one more time to the west, where you'll cut though a comparatively dull forest. You'll emerge at a pit-stop-perfect clearing with WCs, picnic tables, a souvenir shop, and a self-service restaurant. Here you can catch the shuttle boat across Lake Kozjak to the bottom of the Upper Lakes (usually every 30 min).

Lake Kozjak (Jezero Kozjak)—The park's biggest lake, Kozjak, connects the Lower and Upper Lakes. The 20-minute boat ride between Plitvice's two halves offers a great chance for a breather. You can hike between the lakes along the west side of Kozjak, but the scenery's not nearly as good as in the rest of the park.

Upper Lakes (Gornja Jezera)—Focus on the lower half of the Upper Lakes, where nearly all the exotic beauty is. From the boat dock, signs for *C* and *G2* direct you up to Gradinsko Lake through the most striking scenery in the whole park. Enjoy the stroll, taking your time...and lots of photos.

After Gradinsko Lake, when you reach the top of Galovac Lake, you'll have three options:

1. Make your hike a loop by continuing around the lake (following *H* and *G1* signs back to the P2 boat dock), then take the boat back over to the hotels (P1 stop).

2. Hike a few steps up to the ST3 bus stop to catch the shuttle bus back to the hotels (more efficient, but doesn't give you a second look at the lakes).

3. Continue hiking up to the top of the Upper Lakes; you'll get away from the crowds and feel like you've covered the park thoroughly. From here on up, the scenery is less stunning, and the waterfalls are fewer and farther between. At the top, you'll finish at shuttle bus stop ST4 (with food stalls and a WC), where the bus zips you back to the entrances and hotels.

Nice work!

SLEEPING

At the Park

The most convenient way to sleep at Plitvice is to stay at the park's lodges. Book any of these hotels through the same office

---

Sleep Code

(€1 = about $1.40, country code: 385, area code: 053)
English is spoken, credit cards are accepted, and breakfast is included at each place. The tourist tax (€1 per person, per day) is not included in these prices.

To help you sort easily through these listings, I've divided the rooms into three categories based on the price for a standard double room with bath in peak season:

$$$ Higher Priced—Most rooms €100 or more.
$$ Moderately Priced—Most rooms between €50–100.
$ Lower Priced—Most rooms €50 or less.

(reservation tel. 053/751-015, fax 053/751-013, www.np-plitvicka -jezera.hr, info@np-plitvicka-jezera.hr; reception numbers for each hotel listed next). Because of high volume in peak season, the hotels often don't return emails; it's better to call or fax for a reservation—they speak English.

$$$ Hotel Jezero is big and modern, with all the comfort—and charm—of a Holiday Inn. It's well-located right at the park entrance, and offers 200 rooms that feel newish, but generally have at least one thing that's broken. Rooms facing the park have big glass doors and balconies (July–Aug: Sb-€83, Db-€118; May–June and Sept–Oct: Sb-€76, Db-€108; Nov–April: Sb-€61, Db-€86, elevator, reception tel. 053/751-400).

$$ Hotel Plitvice, a better value than Jezero, offers 50 rooms and mod, wide-open public spaces on two floors with no elevators. For rooms, choose from economy (fine, older-feeling; July–Aug: Sb-€72, Db-€96; May–June and Sept–Oct: Sb-€65, Db-€82; Nov–April: Sb-€50, Db-€70), standard (just a teeny bit bigger; July–Aug: Sb-€77, Db-€106; May–June and Sept–Oct: Sb-€70, Db-€96; Nov–April: Sb-€55, Db-€74), or superior (bigger still, with a sitting area; July–Aug: Sb-€82, Db-€116; May–June and Sept–Oct: Sb-€75, Db-€106; Nov–April: Sb-€60, Db-€84, reception tel. 053/751-100).

$$ Hotel Bellevue is simple and bare-bones (no TVs or elevator). It has an older feel to it, but the price is right and the 80 rooms are perfectly acceptable (July–Aug: Sb-€55, Db-€74; May–June and Sept–Oct: Sb-€50, Db-€68; Nov–April: Sb-€40, Db-€54, reception tel. 053/751-700).

Near the Park

While the park's lodges are the easiest choice for non-drivers, those with a car should consider these cheaper alternatives.

$ Knežević Guest House, with 11 bright, modern rooms, is a family-run hotel a five-minute drive south of the park in the nondescript workers' town of Mukinje. The street is modern and dull, but the yard is peaceful, with an inviting hammock (Db-€40, Tb-€60, family room-€70, breakfast-€5, dinner-€10; driving south from the park, take first right turn into Mukinje and you'll see #57; tel. 053/774-081, mobile 098-168-7576, www.knezevic.hr, guest_house@vodatel.net, daughter Kristina speaks English).

$ *Sobe:* Drivers looking for character and preferring to spend €40, rather than €80, should simply find a room in a private home, advertised with *sobe* signs for miles on either side of the park. For details, see page 616.

EATING

The park runs all of the restaurants at Plitvice. These places are handy, and the food is affordable and reasonably good. If you're staying at the hotels, you have the option of paying for half-board with your room (lunch or dinner, €12 each). This option is designed for the restaurants inside hotels Jezero and Plitvice, but you can also use the voucher at other park eateries (you'll pay the difference if the bill is more). The half-board option is worth doing if you're here for dinner, but don't lock yourself in for lunch—you'll want more flexibility as you explore Plitvice (excellent picnic spots and decent food stands abound inside the park).

Hotel Jezero and **Hotel Plitvice** both have big restaurants with decent food and friendly, professional service (half-board for dinner, described above, is a good deal; or order à la carte; both open daily until 23:00).

Lička Kuća, across the pedestrian overpass from Entrance 1, has a wonderfully dark and smoky atmosphere around a huge open-air wood-fired grill (pricey, daily 11:00–24:00, tel. 053/751-024).

Restaurant Poljana, behind Hotel Bellevue, has the same boring, park-lodge atmosphere in both of its sections: cheap, self-service cafeteria and sit-down restaurant with open wood-fired grill (same choices and prices as the better-atmosphere Lička Kuća, above; both parts open daily but closed in winter, tel. 053/751-092).

For **picnic** fixings, there's a small grocery store at Entrance 1, and another one with a larger selection across road D-1 (use the pedestrian overpass). At the P3 boat dock, you can buy grilled meat and drinks. Friendly old ladies sell homemade goodies (such as strudel or hunks of cheese) throughout the park, including at Entrance 1.

TRANSPORTATION CONNECTIONS

To reach the park, see "Getting to Plitvice," earlier in this chapter. Moving on from Plitvice is trickier. Buses pass by the park in each direction—northbound (to **Zagreb,** 2–2.5 hrs) and southbound (to coastal destinations such as **Split,** 4–6 hrs, and **Dubrovnik,** 9–10 hrs).

There is no bus station—just a low-profile *Plitvice Centar* bus stop shelter. To reach it from the park, go out to the main road from either Hotel Jezero or Hotel Plitvice, then turn right; the bus stops are just after the pedestrian overpass. The one on the hotel side of the road is for buses headed for the coast; the stop on the opposite side is for Zagreb. But here's the catch: Many buses that pass through Plitvice don't stop (either because they're full, or because they don't have anyone to drop off there). You can stand at the bus stop and try to flag one down, but it's safer to get help from the park's hotel staff. They can help you figure out which bus suits your schedule, then they'll call ahead to be sure the bus stops for you. If you don't want to make the 10-minute walk out to the bus stop, someone at the hotel can usually drive you out for a modest fee.

Route Tips for Drivers

Plitvice's biggest disadvantage is that it's an hour away from the handy A-1 expressway that connects northern Croatia to the Dalmatian Coast. You have three ways to access this expressway from Plitvice, depending on which direction you're heading.

Going North: If you're heading north (to Zagreb or Slovenia), you'll get on the expressway at **Karlovac:** From Plitvice, drive about one hour north on D-1 to the town of Karlovac, where you can access A-1 northbound. Alternatively, you can take A-1 southbound to A-6, which leads west to Rijeka, Opatija, and Istria (though this route is more boring and only slightly faster than the route via Otočac, described next).

Going to Central Croatia: If you're going to central destinations, such as Istria or Rijeka, get on the expressway at **Otočac.** From Plitvice, go south on D-1, then go west on road #52 to the town of Otočac (about an hour through the mountains from Plitvice to Otočac). After Otočac, you can get on A-1 (north to Zagreb, south to the Dalmatian Coast); or continue west and twist down the mountain road to the seaside town of Senj, on the main coastal road of the Kvarner Gulf. From Senj, it's about an hour north along the coast to Rijeka, then on to Opatija or Istria.

During the recent war, the front line between the Croats and Serbs ran just east of **Otočac** (OH-toh-chawts), and bullet holes still mar the town's facades. (Watch for minefield warning signs just east of Otočac, but don't be too nervous—it's safe to drive here, but not safe to get out of your car and wander through the fields.) Today Otočac is putting itself back together, and it's a fine place to drop into a café for a coffee, or pick up some produce at the outdoor market. The Catholic church in the center of town, destroyed in the war but now rebuilt, has a memorial out back with its damaged church bells. Notice that the crucifix nearby is made of old artillery shells. Just up the main street, beyond the big, grassy park, is the Orthodox church. Otočac used to be about one-third Serbian, but the Serbs were forced out during the war, and this church fell into disrepair. But, as Otočac and Croatia show signs of healing, about two dozen Serbs have returned to town and re-opened their church—if the door's open, take a look inside (for more on the Serbian Orthodox Church, see page 659).

Going South: If you're heading south (to Dalmatia) from Plitvice, catch the expressway at **Gornja Ploča.** Drive south from Plitvice on D-1, through Korenica, Pećane, and Udbina, then follow signs for the A-1 expressway (and *Lovinac*) via Kurjak to the Gornja Ploča on-ramp. Once on A-1, you'll twist south through the giant Sveti Rok tunnel to Dalmatia.

BOSNIA-HERZEGOVINA

MOSTAR

I know what you're thinking: War. Bloodshed. Destruction. The early 1990s weren't kind to Bosnia-Herzegovina. But apart from its tragic separation from Yugoslavia, the country has long been—and still remains—a remarkable place, with ruggedly beautiful terrain, a unique mix of cultures and faiths, kind and welcoming people who pride themselves on their hospitality, and some of the most captivating sightseeing in southeastern Europe. After all, little Bosnia-Herzegovina—with fewer than four million people—is a country with three faiths, three languages, and two alphabets.

There's so much to see in this country. But for the scope of this book, I've selected just one destination: Mostar. Safe, stable, and within easy reach of the Dalmatian Coast, Mostar is worth considering as a detour—both geographical and cultural—from the Croatian mainstream. In Mostar's cobbled Old Town, you can poke into several mosques, tour old-fashioned Turkish-style houses, shop your way through a bazaar of souvenir stands, and hear the call to prayer echoing across the rooftops. For me, it's the single best side-trip from Dubrovnik.

Mostar represents the best and the worst of Yugoslavia. During the Tito years, it was an idyllic mingling of cultures—Catholic Croats, Orthodox Serbs, and Muslim Bosniaks living together in harmony, their differences spanned by an Old Bridge that epitomized an optimistic vision of a Yugoslavia where ethnicity didn't matter. And yet, as the country unraveled in the early 1990s, Mostar was gripped by a gory three-way war among those same peoples...and that famous bridge crumbled into the Neretva River.

More than any other destination in this book, Mostar rearranges your mental furniture. Most startling are the many vivid and thought-provoking signs of the war. The Old Town has been mostly restored. But a few steps outside this tourist zone, burned-out husks of buildings, unmistakable starburst patterns in the pavement, and bullet holes everywhere are a constant reminder that the city is still recovering—physically and psychologically. In an age when we watch TV news coverage of conflicts abroad with the same detachment we give Hollywood blockbusters, Mostar provides an unpleasant but essential reminder of how real and how destructive war truly is.

Western visitors may also be struck by the immediacy of the Muslim culture that permeates Mostar. Here at a crossroads of

civilizations, minarets share the skyline with church steeples. During the Ottomans' 400-year control of this region, many Slavic subjects converted to Islam (see sidebar on page 808). And, although the Ottomans retreated in the late 19th century, they left behind a rich architectural, cultural, and religious legacy that has forever shaped Mostar. Five times each day, loudspeakers on minarets crackle to life, the call to prayer warbles through the streets, and Mostar's Muslim residents flock into the mosques. In many parts of the city, you'd swear you were in Turkey.

If these factors intrigue you, read on—Mostar has so much more to offer. Despite the scars of war, its setting is stunning: straddling the banks of the gorgeous Neretva River, with tributaries and waterfalls carving their way through the rocky landscape. The sightseeing—mosques, old Turkish-style houses, and that spine-tingling Old Bridge—is more engaging than much of what you'll find in Croatia or Slovenia. And it's cheap—hotels, food, and museums are less than half the prices you'll pay in Croatia.

Planning Your Time

Because of its cultural hairiness, a detour into Bosnia-Herzegovina feels like a real departure from a Dalmatian vacation. But actually, Mostar is easier to reach from Dubrovnik or Split than many popular Dalmatian islands (it's just a three-hour drive or bus ride from either city).

The vast majority of tourists in Mostar are day-trippers from the coast, which means the Old Town is packed midday, but empty in the morning and evening. You can get a good feel for

Bosnia-Herzegovina Almanac

Official Name: Bosna i Hercegovina (abbreviated "BiH"); the *i* means "and"—Bosnia *and* Herzegovina (the country's two regions—see "Geography," on next page). The tongue-twisting name "Herzegovina" (hert-seh-GOH-vee-nah) comes from the German word for "dukedom" (*Herzog* means "duke").

Snapshot History: Bosnia-Herzegovina's early history is similar to the rest of the region: Illyrians, Romans, and Slavs (oh, my!). The country's story parts ways with Croatia's in the late 15th century, when Turks from the Ottoman Empire began a 400-year domination of the country. Many of the Ottomans' subjects converted to Islam, and their descendants remain Muslims today. After the Hapsburgs forced out the Ottomans in 1878, Bosnia-Herzegovina became part of the Austro-Hungarian Empire, then Yugoslavia, until it declared independence in October of 1991. The bloody war that ensued came to an end in 1995. (For details, see the Understanding Yugoslavia chapter near the end of this book.)

Population: Because no census has been conducted since the recent war, the population can only be estimated at about four million. (There were about 100,000 identified casualties of the war, but many estimates of total casualties are double that number.) Someone who lives in Bosnia-Herzegovina, regardless of ethnicity, is called a "Bosnian." A southern Slav who practices Islam is called a "Bosniak." Today, about half of all Bosnians are Bosniaks (Muslims), about a third are Orthodox Serbs, and about 15 percent are Catholic Croats. Traditionally, Bosniaks lived in the towns and cities, while Serbs and Croats farmed the countryside.

Political Divisions: As a part of the Dayton Peace Accords that ended the conflict here in 1995, the nation is divided into three separate regions: The Federation of Bosnia and Herzegovina (FBiH, shared by Bosniaks and Croats, very roughly in the western and central parts of the country), the Republika Srpska (RS, dominated by Serbs, generally to the north and east), and the Brčko District (BD, a tiny corner of the country, with a mix of the ethnicities). For the most part, each of the three native ethnic groups stay in "their" part of this divided country, but tourists can move freely between them.

Language: Technically, Bosnia-Herzegovina has three languages—Bosnian, Serbian, and Croatian. But all three are mutually intelligible dialects of what was recently considered a single language: Serbo-Croatian. Bosniaks and Croats use basically the same Roman alphabet we do, while Serbs generally use the

Cyrillic alphabet. You'll see both alphabets on currency and other official documents. Many people also speak English.

Area: 19,741 square miles (like Vermont and New Hampshire combined, or slightly larger than Slovakia).

Geography: Bosnia and Herzegovina are two distinct regions that share the same mountainous country. Bosnia constitutes the majority of the country (in the north, with a continental climate), while Herzegovina is the southern tip (about a fifth of the total area, with a hotter Mediterranean climate). Mostar is the biggest city and unofficial capital of Herzegovina—so saying you're in "Bosnia" while you're here is actually incorrect.

Red Tape: To enter Bosnia-Herzegovina, Americans and Canadians need only a passport (no visa required).

Economy: Bosnia-Herzegovina is struggling. Officially, there's a 45 percent unemployment rate, but in reality it's likely closer to 25 or 30 percent. The per capita GDP is $6,800.

Currency: The official currency is the Convertible Mark (Konvertibilna Marka, abbreviated KM locally, BAM internationally). The official exchange rate is $1 = about 1.40 KM. But merchants in these destinations are willing to take (and may actually prefer) euros or Croatian kunas, converting prices with a simple formula:

2 KM = €1 = 8 kunas (= about $1.40)

Even though you can get by without Convertible Marks, consider making a small withdrawal to get a sense of them. Notice that to satisfy the country's various factions, the currency uses both the Roman and the Cyrillic alphabets, and bills have different figureheads and symbols (some bills feature Bosniaks, others Serbs).

Telephones: Bosnia-Herzegovina's country code is 387. If calling from another country, first dial the international access code (00 in Europe, 011 in the US), then 387, then the area code (minus the initial zero), then the number.

Flag: The flag of Bosnia-Herzegovina, adopted after the recent war, is a blue field with a yellow triangle along the top edge. The three points of the triangle represent Bosnia-Herzegovina's three peoples (Bosniaks, Croats, Serbs), and the triangle also resembles the physical shape of the country. A row of white stars underscores the longest side of the triangle. These stars—and the yellow-and-blue color scheme—resemble the flag of the European Union (a nod to the EU's efforts to bring peace to the region).

Mostar

Mostar in just a few hours, but a full day gives you time to linger and ponder.

You have three basic options: take a package tour from Dalmatia; rent a car for a one-day side-trip into Mostar; or (my favorite) spend the night here en route between Croatian destinations. To work a Mostar overnight into your itinerary, consider a round-trip plan that takes you south along the coast, then back north via Bosnia-Herzegovina (for example, Split–Korčula–Dubrovnik–Mostar–back to Split).

Getting to Mostar

By Package Tour: Taking an excursion from a Dalmatian resort town is the most efficient and accessible—but least rewarding—way to visit Mostar. These all-day tours are sold from Split, Korčula, Dubrovnik, and other Croatian coastal destinations for about €50–60. The best tours max out their time in Mostar itself (it still won't be enough); avoid the tours that include a pointless boat trip on the Neretva River. Those that add on a quick visit to the worthwhile town of Počitelj are a better deal. Atlas and Elite are the biggest operators; ask for details at any travel agency in Dalmatia (or visit www.atlas-croatia.com and www.elite.hr).

By Car: Coming with your own car gives you maximum flexibility, but you may find Mostar—which has poor signage—stressful. For specific route information, see "Route Tips for Drivers" on page 816. If you do plan to drive here, let your car-rental company know in advance to ensure you have the appropriate paperwork for crossing the border.

By Bus: Bus connections are sparse but possible (see page 815).

ORIENTATION

(country code: 387; area code: 036)
Mostar—a mid-sized city, with just over 100,000 people—is situated in a basin surrounded by mountains and split down the middle by the emerald-green Neretva River. Bosniaks live mostly on the east side of the river, and Croats on the west (though increasingly the populations are mixing again). Visitors move freely throughout the city, and most don't even notice the division. The cobbled, Turkish-feeling Old Town (called the "Stari Grad" or—borrowing a Turkish term—the "Stara Čaršija") surrounds the town's centerpiece, the Old Bridge. Timid tourists feel most comfortable in the Old Town sector, and that's where I've focused my sightseeing and hotel recommendations.

The skyline is pierced by the minarets of various mosques, but none is as big as the two major Catholic (Croat) symbols in

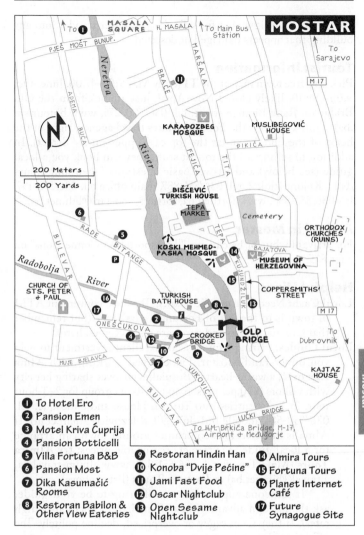

MOSTAR

- ❶ To Hotel Ero
- ❷ Pansion Emen
- ❸ Motel Kriva Ćuprija
- ❹ Pansion Botticelli
- ❺ Villa Fortuna B&B
- ❻ Pansion Most
- ❼ Dika Kasumačić Rooms
- ❽ Restoran Babilon & Other View Eateries
- ❾ Restoran Hindin Han
- ❿ Konoba "Dvije Pećine"
- ⓫ Jami Fast Food
- ⓬ Oscar Nightclub
- ⓭ Open Sesame Nightclub
- ⓮ Almira Tours
- ⓯ Fortuna Tours
- ⓰ Planet Internet Café
- ⓱ Future Synagogue Site

Mostar

town, both erected since the recent war: The giant white cross on the hilltop (placed where Croat forces shelled the Bosniak side of the river, including the Old Bridge); and the enormous (almost 100-foot-tall) bell tower of the Church of Sts. Peter and Paul. A monumental Orthodox Church once stood on the hillside across the river, but it was destroyed in the war when the Serbs were forced out, and never rebuilt.

A note about safety: Mostar is as safe as any city its size—but it doesn't always *feel* safe. You'll see bombed-out buildings everywhere, even in the core of the city. Some are marked with *Warning!*

Dangerous Ruin signs, but for safety's sake, never wander into any building that appears damaged or deserted.

Tourist Information

Pick up a free town map at the **TI** (daily May 9:00–17:00, June–Oct 9:00–20:00, likely closed Nov–April, just a block from the Old Bridge on Rade Bitange street, tel. 036/580-275, www.bhtourism .ba). More central is the **Fortuna Tours** travel agency, right in the heart of the Old Town (at the top of Coppersmiths' Street). In addition to selling all the tourist stuff, they can book you a local guide (see below) and answer basic questions (open long hours daily, Kujundžiluk 2, tel. 036/551-887, main office tel. 036/552-197, fax 036/551-888, www.fortuna.ba, fortuna_mostar1@bih.net.ba).

Arrival in Mostar

For arrival by **bus** or by **car,** see "Transportation Connections" on page 815.

Helpful Hints

Local Cash: Need Convertible Marks? The most convenient ATM in town is to the left of Fortuna Tours' door (but remember that Croatian kunas and euros are also accepted here).

Local Guides: Hiring a guide is an excellent investment to help you understand Mostar. I've enjoyed working with **Alma Elezović,** a warm-hearted Bosniak who loves sharing her city with visitors (€20 per person up to €70 per group for 2–3-hour tour, includes entries into Turkish House and a mosque, tel. 036/550-514, mobile 061-467-699, aelezovic@gmail.com). If Alma is busy, various companies around town can arrange for a local guide at extremely reasonable prices; try **Almira Tours** (Mala Tepa 9, tel. 036/551-873, www.almira-travel.ba, a.travel@bih.net.ba) or **Fortuna Tours** (listed above).

    If someone approaches you offering to be your guide, ask the price in advance (they often charge ridiculously high rates). If they seem cagey or overpriced, decline politely. The official guides are better anyway.

Internet: Internet cafés can be found all over town. **Planet Internet** is a slick, upscale place with six fast terminals and good prices (4 KM/hr, daily 9:00–22:00, near the Old Town at Husnije Rebca 44, tel. 036/580-092).

SIGHTS

Mostar's major sights line up along a handy L-shaped axis. I've laced them together as an enjoyable orientation walk: From the Franciscan Church, you'll walk straight until you cross the Old

Bridge. Then you'll turn left and walk basically straight (with a couple of detours) to the big square at the far end of town.
• *Begin at the...*

▲Franciscan Church

In a town of competing religious architectural "exclamation points," this spire is the tallest. The church, which adjoins a work-

ing Franciscan monastery, was built after the fighting subsided in 1997 (the same year as the big cross on the hill). The tower, which looks at first glance like a minaret on steroids, is actually modeled after the typical Croatian/Venetian *campanile* bell towers. Step inside to see how the vast and coarse concrete shell awaits completion. Until the church is finished, Mostar's Catholic community fills the temporary sanctuary in the basement. (Sunday Mass here is an inspiration.)
• *The church fronts the busy boulevard called...*

▲Bulevar

This "Boulevard" was once the modern main drag of Mostar. Today much of it is in ruins. In the early 1990s, this city of Bosniaks,

Croats, and Serbs began to groan under the pressure of politicians' propaganda. In October of 1991, Bosnia-Herzegovina—following Croatia's and Slovenia's example, but without the blessing of its large Serb minority—declared independence from Yugoslavia. Soon after, the Serb-dominated Yugoslav National Army invaded.

Mostar's Bosniaks and Croats joined forces to battle the Serbs, and succeeded in claiming the city as their own and forcing out the Serb residents.

But even as they defended their city from the final, distant bombardments of Serb forces, the Bosniaks and Croats began to squabble. Neighbors, friends, and even relatives took up arms against each other. As fighting raged between the Croat and Bosniak forces, this street became the front line—and virtually all of its buildings were destroyed. Then as now, the area to the east of here (toward the river) was controlled by Bosniaks, while the western part of town was Croat territory.

Stroll a bit, imagining the hell of a split community at war. Mortar craters in the asphalt leave poignant scars. (In Sarajevo, these have been filled with red resin to create monuments called "Sarajevo roses.") During those dark war years, the Croats on this side of the city were laying siege to the Bosniaks (Muslims) on the other side. Through '93 and '94, when the Bosniaks went out, they sprinted past exposed places, for fear of being picked off by a sniper. Local Bosniaks explain, "Night was time to live" (in black clothes). When people were killed along this street, their corpses were sometimes left here for months (because it wasn't safe to retrieve the bodies). Since there was no electricity, the Bosniaks had no choice but to listen to the Croatian rabble-rousing pop music and Tokyo Rose–type propaganda speeches blaring from loudspeakers. Tens of thousands left (Scandinavian countries were the first to open their doors, but many Bosnians ended up elsewhere in Europe, and in the US and Canada).

Cross the boulevard and head down Onešćukova street. A few steps down, the vacant lot with the menorah-ornamented metal fence will someday be the Mostar Synagogue. While the town's Jewish population has dwindled to a handful of families since World War II, many Jews courageously served as aid workers and intermediaries when Croats and Bosniaks were killing each other. In recognition of their loving help, the community of Mostar gave them this land for a new synagogue.

• Continue past the synagogue, entering the Old Town and following the canyon with the small river...

Radobolja River Valley

The creek called Radobolja winds over waterfalls and several mills on its way to join the Neretva. As you step upon cobbles, you suddenly become immersed in the Turkish heritage of Mostar. From the arrival of the Ottomans all the way through the end of World War II, Mostar had fewer than 15,000 residents. This compact central zone was pretty much all there was to the city until it became industrialized and grew like crazy during the Tito years. The historic core is cobbled with smooth river stones. Until 2004, the stones were simply embedded in loose sand, but now they're held together with concrete.

Near the beginning of the pedestrian area, you'll pass the inviting white lounge chairs of Oscar's Bar on the right—a fun place to suck on a water pipe (either now or later this evening).

Walk straight ahead until you reach a small square view platform on your right. It's across from a sweet little mosque and above a stream. The mosque is one of 10 in town. Before the recent war, there were 36. Many mosques were actually damaged or destroyed in World War II, but were never repaired or replaced (since Tito's communist Yugoslavia discouraged religion). But the recent war inspired Muslims to finally rebuild. Each of the town's newly reconstructed mosques has been financed by a Muslim nation or organization (this one was a gift from an international association for the protection of Islamic heritage). Around you are several fine examples of Mostar's traditional heavy limestone-shingled roofs.

• *Spanning the river below the mosque is the...*

▲Crooked Bridge (Kriva Ćuprija)

This miniature Old Bridge was built nearly a decade before its more famous sibling, supposedly to practice for the real deal.

Damaged—but not destroyed—during the war, the bridge was swept away several years later by floods. The bridge you see today is a recent reconstruction.

• *Continue deeper on the same street into the city center. After a few steps, a street to the left (worth a short detour) leads to the TI, then a copper-domed* hammam, *or Turkish bath house, which was also destroyed in World War II and only recently rebuilt. A happening nightlife and restaurant scene tumbles downhill toward the river from here, offering great views of the Old Bridge.*

As you walk through the Old Town, you may want to survey restaurants to choose a spot for dinner (my recommendations are all within a few steps of here—see "Eating," page 814).

Back on the main drag, continue along the main shopping zone, past several market stalls, to the focal point of town, the...

▲▲▲Old Bridge (Stari Most)

One of the most evocative sights in the former Yugoslavia, this iconic bridge confidently spanned the Neretva River for more than four centuries. Mostarians of all faiths love the bridge, and speak of "him" as an old friend. Traditionally considered the point where East meets West, the Old Bridge is as symbolic as it is beautiful. Dramatically arched and flanked by two boxy towers, the bridge is striking—even if you don't know its history.

Before the Old Bridge, the Neretva was spanned only by a rickety suspension bridge, guarded by *mostari* ("watchers of the bridge") who gave the city its name. Commissioned in 1557 by the Ottoman sultan Süleyman the Magnificent, and completed just nine years later, the Old Bridge was a technological marvel for its time..."the longest single-span stone arch on the planet." (In other words, it's the granddaddy of the Rialto Bridge in Venice.) Because of its graceful keystone design—and the fact that there are empty spaces inside the structure—it's much lighter than it seems. And yet, nearly four hundred years after it was built, the bridge was still strong enough to support the weight of Nazi tanks that rolled in to occupy Mostar. Over the centuries, it became the symbol for the town and region—a metaphor in stone for the way that the diverse faiths and cultures here were able to bridge the gaps that divided them.

All of that drastically changed in the early 1990s. When the city became engulfed in war, the Old Bridge frequently got caught in the crossfire. Old tires were slung over its sides to absorb some of the impact from nearby artillery or shrapnel. In November of 1993, Croats began shelling the bridge from the top of the mountain (where the cross is now—you can just see its tip peeking over the hill from the top of the bridge). Several direct hits caused the venerable Old Bridge to lurch, then tumble in pieces into the river. The mortar inside, which contained pink bauxite, turned the water red as it fell in. Locals said that their old friend was bleeding.

The decision to destroy the bridge was partly strategic—to cut off a Bosniak-controlled strip on the west bank from Bosniak forces on the east. (News footage from the time shows Bosniak soldiers scurrying back and forth over the bridge.) But there can be no doubt that, like the siege of Dubrovnik, the attack was also partly symbolic: the destruction of a bridge representing the city's Muslim legacy.

After the war, city leaders decided to rebuild the Old Bridge. Chunks of the original bridge were dredged up from the river. But the stone had been compromised by soaking in the water for so long, so it couldn't be used (you can still see these pieces of the old Old Bridge on the riverbank below). Staying true to their pledge to do it authentically, restorers quarried new stone (a limestone called *tenelija*) from the original quarry, and each stone was hand-carved.

Then they assembled the stones with the same technology used by the Ottomans 450 years ago: Workers erected wooden scaffolding and fastened the stones together with iron hooks cast in lead. The project cost over $13 million, funded largely by international donors and overseen by UNESCO.

It took longer to rebuild the bridge in the 21st century than it did to build it in the 16th century. But on July 23, 2004, the new Old Bridge was inaugurated with much fanfare, and was immediately embraced by both the city and the world as a sign of reconciliation. Feel the shivers run down your spine as you walk over the Old Bridge today, and ponder its troubled yet inspirational past.

On a lighter note: One of Mostar's favorite traditions is for young men to jump from the bridge 75 feet down into the Neretva (which remains icy cold even in summer). Done both for the sake of tradition, and to impress girls, this custom was carried on even during the time the destroyed bridge was temporarily replaced by a wooden one. Now the tower on the west side of the bridge houses the office of the local "Divers Club," a loosely run organization that carries on this longstanding ritual. On hot summer days, you'll see divers making a ruckus and collecting donations at the top of the bridge. They tease and tease, standing up on the railing and pretending they're about to jump...then getting down and asking for more money. (If he's wearing trunks rather than a Speedo, he's not a diver—just a teaser.) Once they collect about €30, one of them will take the plunge.

Before moving on, see how many of the town's 10 mosques you can see from the top of the bridge (I counted eight minarets).

• *Continue over the Old Bridge and drop into the free photo exhibition on the right. Inside this former mosque for soldiers who guarded the bridge, you'll see powerful images of war-torn Mostar. Then turn left with the street and walk along...*

▲▲Coppersmiths' Street (Kujundžiluk)

This lively strip, with the flavor of a Turkish bazaar, offers some of the most colorful shopping this side of Istanbul. You'll see Mostar's characteristic bridge depicted in every possible way, along with blue-and-white "evil eyes" (believed in the Turkish culture to keep bad spirits at bay), old Yugoslav army kitsch, and hammered-copper decorations (continuing the long tradition that gave the street its name). Partway up, the homes with the colorfully painted facades double as galleries for local artists. The artists live and work upstairs, then sell their work right on this street. Pop into the *atelier d'art* ("Đul Emina") on the right to meet Sead Vladović and enjoy his impressive iconographic work (daily 9:00–20:00). This is the most touristy street in all of Bosnia-Herzegovina, so don't expect any bargains. Still, it's fun. As you stroll, check out the fine views of the Old Bridge.

• *Continue uphill. About halfway along this street, on the left-hand side, look for the entrance to the...*

▲Koski Mehmed-Pasha Mosque (Koski Mehmed-Paša Džamija)

Mostar's Bosniak community includes many practicing Muslims. Step into this courtyard for a look at one of Mostar's many mosques (3 KM to enter mosque, 5 KM includes mosque and minaret, open long hours daily). This mosque, dating from the early 17th century, is notable for its cliff-hanging riverside location, and because it's particularly accessible for tourists. The information here generally applies to the other mosques in Mostar, as well:

The fountain *(šadrvan)* in the courtyard allows worshippers to wash before entering the mosque, as directed by Islamic law. This practice, called ablution, is both a literal and a spiritual cleansing in preparation for being in the presence of Allah. It's also refreshing in this hot climate, and the sound of running water helps worshippers concentrate.

The minaret—the slender needle jutting up next to the dome—is the Islamic equivalent of the Christian bell tower, used to call people to prayer. In the old days, the *muezzin* (prayer leader) would climb the tower five times a day and chant, "There is only one God, and Muhammad is his prophet." In modern times, loudspeakers are used instead. Climbing the minaret, despite its claustrophobic staircase, is a memorable experience rewarding you with a grand view at the top (entrance to the right of mosque entry).

Because this mosque is accustomed to tourists, you don't need to take off your shoes to enter (there's a special covering on the floor), women don't need to wear scarves, and it's fine to take photos inside. Near the front of the mosque, you may see some of the small, overlapping rugs that are below the floor covering (reserved for shoes-off worshippers).

Once inside, notice the traditional elements of the mosque. The niche *(mihrab)* across from the entry is oriented toward Mecca

(the holy city in today's Saudi Arabia)—the direction all Muslims face to pray. The small stairway *(mimber)* that seems to go nowhere is symbolic of the growth of Islam—Muhammad had to stand higher and higher to talk to his growing following. This serves as a kind of pulpit, where the cleric gives a speech, similar to a sermon or homily in Christian church services. No priest ever stands on the top stair, which is symbolically reserved for Muhammad.

The balcony just inside the door is traditionally where women worship. For the same reason I find it hard to concentrate on God at aerobics classes, Muslim men decided prayer would go better without the enjoyable but problematic distraction of bent-over women between them and Mecca. These days, women can also pray on the main floor with the men, but they still must avoid physical contact.

Muslims believe that capturing a living creature in a painting or a sculpture is inappropriate. (In fact, depictions of Allah and the prophet Muhammad are strictly forbidden.) Instead, mosques are filled with ornate patterns and calligraphy (of the name "Muhammad" and important prayers and sayings from the Quran). Some of the calligraphy is in Arabic, and some is in Bosnian. You'll also see some floral and plant designs, which you'd never see in a more conservative, Middle Eastern mosque.

Before leaving, ponder how progressive the majority of Mostar's Muslims are. Most of them drink alcohol, wear modern European clothing (you'll see virtually no women wearing head scarves or men with beards), and almost never visit a mosque to pray. In so many ways, these people don't fit our preconceived notions of Islam...and yet, they consider themselves Muslims all the same.

The mosque's courtyard is shared by several merchants. When you're done haggling, head to the terrace behind the mosque for the best view in town of the Old Bridge.

• *Just beyond this mosque, the traffic-free cobbles of the Old Town end. Take a right and leave the cutesy tourists' world. Walk up one block to the big...*

▲▲New Muslim Cemetery

In this cemetery, which was a park before the war, every tomb is dated 1993, 1994, or 1995. As the war raged, more-exposed cem-

eteries were unusable. But this tree-covered piece of land was relatively safe from Croat snipers. As the casualties mounted, locals buried their loved ones here under cover of darkness. Many of these people were soldiers, but some were

civilians. Strict Muslim graves don't display images of people, but here you'll see photos of war dead who were young, less-traditional members of the Muslim community. The fleur-de-lis shape of many of the tombstones is a patriotic symbol for the nation of Bosnia. The Arabic writing is the equivalent of an American having Latin on his or her tombstone—old-fashioned and formal.

• *Go up the wide stairs to the right of the cemetery (near the mosque). Three doors up on the right, you'll find the...*

The Muslims of Mostar

While recent Muslim immigrants are becoming a fixture in many European cities, Bosnia-Herzegovina is one place where Muslims have continuously been an integral part of the cultural tapestry for centuries.

During the more than 400 years that Mostar was part of the Ottoman Empire, the Muslim Turks (unlike some Catholic despots at the time) did not forcibly convert their subjects. However, it was advantageous for non-Turks to adopt Islam (for lower taxes and better business opportunities), so many Slavs living here became Muslims. In fact, within 150 years of the start of Ottoman rule, half of the population of Bosnia-Herzegovina was Muslim.

The Ottomans became increasingly intolerant of other faiths as time went on, and uprisings by Catholics and Orthodox Christians eventually led to the end of Ottoman domination in the late 19th century. But even after the Ottomans left, many people in this region continued practicing Islam, as their families had been doing for centuries. These people constitute an ethnic group called "Bosniaks," and many of them are still practicing Muslims today (following the Sunni branch of the Muslim faith). Keep in mind that most Bosniaks are Slavs—of the same ethnic stock as Croats and Serbs—and look pretty much the same as their neighbors, although some Bosniaks have ancestors who married into Turkish families, and may have some Turkish features.

Due to the recent actions of a small but attention-grabbing faction of Muslim extremists, Islam is burdened with a bad reputation in the Western world. But

Museum of Herzegovina (Muzej Hercegovine)

This humble but worthwhile little museum collects fragments of this region's rich history, including historic photos and several items from its Ottoman period. There's no English (in fact, there's barely any Bosnian), and without a tour guide the exhibits are difficult to appreciate—especially the small room commemorating the house's former owner, Dzemal Bijedić. It feels like a lesser version of Mostar's Turkish House, described on page 810. But the museum is made worthwhile by a deeply moving film, rated ▲▲, that traces the history of the town through its Old Bridge: fun circa-1957 footage of the diving contests; harrowing scenes of the bridge being pummeled, and finally toppled, by artillery; and a stirring sequence showing the bridge's reconstruction and grand judging Islam based on Osama bin Laden and al-Qaeda is like judging Christianity based on Timothy McVeigh and the Ku Klux Klan. Visiting Mostar is a unique opportunity to get a taste of a fully Muslim society, made a bit less intimidating because it wears a more-familiar European face.

Here's an admittedly basic and simplistic outline (written by a non-Muslim) designed to help travelers from the Christian West understand a very rich but often misunderstood culture worthy of respect:

Muslims, like Christians and Jews, are monotheistic. They call their god Allah. The most important person in the Islamic faith is Muhammad, Allah's most important prophet, who lived in the sixth and seventh centuries A.D.

The "five pillars" of Islam are the same among Muslims in Bosnia-Herzegovina, Turkey, Iraq, Indonesia, the US, and everywhere else. Followers of Islam should:

1. Say and believe, "There is only one God, and Muhammad is his prophet."

2. Pray five times a day, facing Mecca. Modern Muslims explain that it's important for this ritual to include several elements: washing, exercising, stretching, and thinking of God.

3. Give to the poor (one-fortieth of your wealth, if you are not in debt).

4. Fast during daylight hours through the month of Ramadan. Fasting is a great social equalizer and helps everyone to feel the hunger of the poor.

5. Visit Mecca. This is interpreted by some Muslims as a command to travel. Muhammad said, "Don't tell me how educated you are, tell me how much you've traveled."

Good advice for anyone, no matter what—or if—you call a higher power.

Mostar

re-opening on that day in 2004—with high-fives, Beethoven's *Ode to Joy,* fireworks, and more divers (2 KM, 12 min, no narration—works in any language, ask about "film?" as you enter, daily 8:00–16:00, Bajatova 4—walking up these stairs, it's the second door that's marked for the museum, under the overhanging balcony).

• *Backtrack to where you left the Old Town. Notice the* **Tepa Market,** *with locals buying produce, in the area just beyond the pedestrian zone. Now walk (with the produce market on your left) along the lively street called* **Braće Fejića.** *(There's no sign, but the street is level and busy with cafés.) You're in the "new town," where locals sit out in front of boisterous cafés sipping Turkish (or "Bosnian") coffee while listening to the thumping beat of distinctly Eastern-sounding music.*

Stroll down this street for a few blocks. At the palm trees (about 50 yards before the minaret), side-trip a block to the left to reach...

▲Bišćević Turkish House (Bišćevića Kuća)

This is your best city-center look at a traditional Turkish home (2 KM, generally open daily March–Oct 8:00–20:00, Nov–Feb 9:00–15:00, Bišćevića 13). Dating from 1635, this is typical of old houses in Mostar, which mix Oriental style with Mediterranean features. Notice that it's surrounded by a high wall—protection from the sun's rays, from thieves...and from prying eyes. First you'll step through the outer (or men's) garden, then into the inner (or women's) garden. Notice how the smooth river stones are set in geometrical forms in the floor (for example, the five-sided star, representing the five times a day Muslims pray), and keep an eye out for the house's pet turtle. It's

no coincidence that the traditional fountain *(šadrvan)* resembles those at the entrance to a mosque—a reminder of the importance of running water in Muslim culture. The little white building is a kitchen—cleverly located apart from the house so that the heat and smells of cooking didn't permeate the upstairs living area.

Buy your ticket and take off your shoes before you climb up the wooden staircase. Imagine how this stairway could be pulled up for extra protection in case of danger. The cool, shady, and airy living room is open to the east—from where the wind rarely blows. The overhanging roof also prevented the hot sun from reaching this area. The loom in the corner was the women's workplace—the carpets you're standing on would have been woven there. The big chests against the wall were used to bring the dowry when the homeowner took a new wife. The privacy latticework allowed the women to peek down discreetly to see what was happening in the courtyard. Study the fine wood carving and the heavy stonework of the roof.

Continue back into the main gathering room *(divanhan)*. This space—designed in a circle so people could face each other, cross-legged, for a good conversation—has a dramatic view overlooking the Neretva. The room comes with a box of traditional costumes—great for photo fun. Put on a pair of baggy pants and a fez and really lounge.

If you're intrigued by this, consider dropping by Mostar's two other Turkish houses (both charge a modest entry fee). The **Kajtaz House** (Kajtazova Kuća), hiding up a very residential-feeling alley a few blocks from the Old Bridge, feels lived-in because it still is (in the opposite direction from most of the other sights, at Gaše Ilića 21). The grander, more ornamental **Muslibegović House** (Muslibegovića Kuća) is a bit more recent and modern-feeling, and therefore less homey and colorful (just two blocks uphill from the Karađozbeg Mosque).

• *Go back to the main café street and continue to the...*

▲Karađozbeg Mosque (Karađozbegova Džamija)

The city's main mosque was completed in 1557, the same year work began on the Old Bridge. This mosque, which welcomes visitors, feels less touristy than the one back in the Old Town (3 KM to enter, 5 KM includes mosque entry and minaret, daily May–Sept 9:00–19:30, Oct–April 10:00–15:00). Before entering the gate into the complex, look for the picture showing the recent war damage sustained by this mosque (which has since been repaired). You'll see that this mosque has most of the same elements as the one we saw earlier (read the description for the Koski Mehmed-Pasha Mosque,

page 806). But here, some of the decorations are original. Across the street is another cemetery with tombstones from that terrible year, 1993.

• *Now continue into modern, urban Mostar along the street called...*

▲Braće Fejića

Walking along the modern town's main café strip, enjoy the opportunity to observe this workaday Bosniak town. You'll see the offices of the humble Bosna Airlines; a state-run gambling office taxing its less-educated people with a state lottery; and lots of cafés that serve drinks but no food. People generally eat at home before going out to nurse an affordable drink. (Café ABC has good cakes and ice cream; the upstairs is a popular pizza hangout for students and families.)

Obituary announcements are tacked to trees by the mosque, listing the bios and funeral times for locals who have recently died. A fig tree grows out of the minaret in the small mosque—just an accident of nature illustrating how that plant can thrive with almost no soil.

Walking farther, you see ruins still ugly a decade and a half after the war. There's a messy confusion about who owns what. Surviving companies have no money. Yugo Bank, which held the mortgages, is defunct. No one will invest until clear ownership is established. Until then, the people of Mostar will sip their coffee and rip up their dance clubs in the shadow of these jagged reminders of the warfare less than 15 years ago.

Jami, a wonderful local-style fast-food joint, is at #15 at the end of the pedestrian zone (daily 8:00–23:00). Lots of savory pies are sold here—fresh, tasty, and extremely cheap by the gram. Even if you're not hungry, buy a mini-*burek* (savory phyllo-dough pastry) and a refreshing cup of kefir (liquid yogurt). Beyond Jami on the right stands a ruined mall. It's strewn with communist-era reliefs of Bogomil tomb decor from the 12th century, remembering the indigenous culture before the arrival of the Ottomans.

When you finally hit the big street (with car traffic), head left one block to the big **Masala Square** (literally, "Place for Prayer"). Historically this was where pilgrims gathered before setting off for Mecca on their hajj. This is a great scene on balmy evenings, when it's a rendezvous point for the community.

• *For a finale, you can continue one block more out onto the bridge to survey the town you just explored. From here, you can backtrack to linger in the places you found most inviting.*

NIGHTLIFE

Be sure to enjoy the local scene after dark in Mostar. While the town is touristy, it's also a real urban center with a young population riding a wave of raging hormones. The meat market in the courtyard next to the old Turkish bathhouse near the TI is fun to observe. The Old Bridge is a popular meeting place for locals as well as tourists (and pickpockets).  A stroll from the Old Bridge down the Braće Fejića café-lined boulevard, to the modern Masala Square at the far end of town (described above) gives a great peak at Mostarians socializing.

Oscar Nightclub is a caravanserai for lounge lizards—an exotic world mixing babbling streams, terraces, lounge chairs, and big sofas where young and old enjoy 5-KM cocktails and hubbly-bubblies (*šiša*, SHEE-shah). Ask to have one of these big water pipes fired up for you and choose your perfumed tobacco—apple, cappuccino, banana, or lemon (10 KM per pipe per group, open daily, drop by late, up from the Old Bridge on Onešćukova street, near the Crooked Bridge at the end of the pedestrian zone).

The perfectly named **Open Sesame,** across the Old Bridge, is a cave featuring a fun, atmospheric, and youthful party scene (open late daily, cross the old bridge and head up Coppersmiths' Street, look for it on the right).

SLEEPING

Mostar has a surprising concentration of new, friendly, accessible, and very affordable hotels right in the city center. Each of these places is small, with English-speaking staff, and will provide a comfortable home base for your time here. None of these is a full-service hotel, so don't expect an all-night reception desk. (If you want more service, I've also included one big hotel on the edge of the center, Hotel Ero.) Mostar's Old Town can be very noisy on weekends, with nightclubs and outdoor restaurants rollicking into the wee hours. If you're a light sleeper, consider Villa Fortuna and Pansion Most, which are quieter than the norm.

$$$ Hotel Ero, a 20-minute walk north of the Old Town, is your big-hotel option, with 140 fine rooms and a professional staff. This was one of the only big buildings in the center not damaged during the war, since it hosted journalists and members of the international community and was therefore off-limits (Sb-€50, Db-€85, suite-€110, air-con, elevator, some street noise, ulica Dr. Ante Starčevića, tel. 036/386-777, fax 036/386-700, www.ero.ba, hotel.ero@ero.ba).

$$$ Pansion Emen has six modern, sleek rooms overlooking a busy café street a few cobbled blocks from the Old Bridge (Sb-€30, Db-€45–60 depending on size, air-con, Onešćukova 32, tel. 036/581-120, www.pansion-emen.com, info@pansion-emen.com).

$$$ Motel Kriva Ćuprija ("Crooked Bridge"), by the bridge of the same name, is tucked between waterfalls in a picturesque valley a few steps from the Old Bridge. It's an appealing oasis with seven rooms, three apartments, and a restaurant with atmospheric outdoor seating (Db-€60, apartment-€65–80 depending on size, extra bed-€20, 10 percent discount with this book, air-con, can

---

Sleep Code

(€1 = about $1.40, country code: 387, area code: 036)
S = Single, **D** = Double/Twin, **T** = Triple, **Q** = Quad, **b** = bathroom.
To help you sort easily through these listings, I've divided the rooms into three categories based on the price for a standard double room with bath in peak season:

$$$ **Higher Priced**—Most rooms €45 or more.
　$$ **Moderately Priced**—Most rooms between €35–45.
　　$ **Lower Priced**—Most rooms €35 or less.

be noisy, Kriva Ćuprija 2, tel. 036/550-953, mobile 061-135-286, www.motel-mostar.ba, info@motel-mostar.ba, Sami).

$$ Pansion Botticelli, just up the valley from the Crooked Bridge, has five colorful, artsy rooms (Sb-€30, Db-€40, breakfast-€3, air-con, Muje Bjelavca 6, mobile 063-319-057, botticelli@bih .net.ba, Snježana and Zoran). You can also book through Fortuna Tours (see next), where Snježana works.

$$ Villa Fortuna B&B, in a nondescript urban neighborhood a few minutes' walk farther away from the Old Bridge, has five tasteful, modern, air-conditioned rooms. The rooms are just above the main office of Fortuna Tours, and you'll reserve through them (Sb-€30, Db-€40, breakfast-€5, tel. 036/552-197, fax 036/551-888, fortuna_mostar@bih.net.ba). Fortuna Tours can also put you in touch with locals renting rooms and apartments.

$$ Pansion Most rents eight older-feeling rooms a few minutes' walk farther from the Old Bridge, above a sports book and a travel agency (Sb-€25, Db-€40, air-con, Adema Buća 100, tel. 036/552-528, www.pansionmost.dzaba.com, pansion_most @yahoo.com).

$ Dika Kasumačić has five basic, inexpensive rooms on a quiet lane just above the Crooked Bridge action (S-€15, D-€30, cash only, follow blue *pansion* signs from near Pansion Botticelli to Kapetanovina 16, mobile 061-506-443, sanjink@hotmail.com).

EATING

Most of Mostar's tourist-friendly restaurants are conveniently concentrated in the Old Town. If you walk anywhere that's cobbled,

you'll stumble onto dozens of tempting restaurants charging about the same reasonable prices and serving traditional food. Grilled meats are especially popular—read "Balkan Flavors," on page 627, before you dine. Another specialty here is *dolma*—a pepper stuffed with minced meat, vegetables, and rice. The local Sarajevsko Pivo beer is on tap. Bosnian cuisine is pretty rustic, and trying to find variety or exceptional quality may just lead to frustration. Don't bother looking for pork.

On the Embankment, with Old Bridge Views

For the best atmosphere, find your way into the several levels of restaurants that clamber up the riverbank with perfect views of the Old Bridge. To reach these, go over the Old Bridge to the west side of the river, and bear right on the cobbles until you get to the old Turkish bathhouse, or *hammam* (with the copper humps on the roof). To the right of the bathhouse is the entrance to a lively courtyard surrounded with cafés and restaurants. Continuing toward the river from the courtyard, stairs lead down to several riverfront terraces. While you'll have menus pushed in your face as you walk, don't hesitate—poke around to find your favorite bridge view before settling in for a drink or a meal. If you want a good perch, it's fun and smart to drop by during the day and personally reserve the table of your choice. Of the many restaurants with prime Old Bridge–view tables, I ate well at **Restoran Babilon.** Its prices are essentially the same as restaurants *without* Mostar's best views (5–15-KM grilled meats, 25-KM "Babilon Plate" sampler, open long hours daily, mobile 061-164-912).

In the Old Town, Away from the Old Bridge

Restoran Hindin Han lacks the famous Old Bridge views, but comes with its own appealing ambience with a woody terrace over a rushing stream. It's respected locally for its good cooking and fair prices (big 9-KM salads, 5–10-KM dinner plates, steak and trout, Sarajevsko beer on tap, daily 11:00–24:00, Jusovina 10, tel. 036/581-054). To find it, walk west from the Old Bridge, bear left at the Šadrvan restaurant, cross the bridge, and you'll see it on the left.

Konoba "Dvije Pećine" ("The Two Caves") is a mom-and-pop place woven into a tangle of terraces over a rushing little stream facing the Crooked Bridge. It's known for its home-cooking (*domaće*—"homemade"—is the key word) and the food does taste a cut above the norm (5–10-KM plates, splittable mixed grill for 15 KM, daily 11:00–24:00, on Jusovina street, mobile 061-558-228, Nuna and Jusa Dizdarević, and Čako, the charming head waiter). To get here, cross the Crooked Bridge and turn right.

TRANSPORTATION CONNECTIONS

From Mostar by Bus: Not surprisingly for a divided city, Mostar has two different bus terminals, each served by different companies. The main bus station (called Autobuska Stanica) is on the east (Bosniak/Muslim) side of the river (about an 8-KM taxi ride from the Old Town). On the west (Croat/Catholic) side, the situation is less predictable: Some buses leave from a bus stop near the cathedral, while others use a bus station on Vukovarska street. As this information is particularly subject to change, carefully confirm schedules—and precisely where your bus leaves from.

Buses go to **Međugorje** (7/day Mon–Fri, 3/day Sat, none Sun, 50 min, mostly from the west side, 3 KM), **Sarajevo** (about hourly,

2.5 hrs, from main bus station, 15 KM), **Zagreb** (1 night bus/day, 9.5 hrs, 70 KM), **Split** (7/day, 4–4.5 hrs, can be from either side— ask locally about your specific bus, 20 KM), **Dubrovnik** (3–4/day, 4 hrs, from main bus station, 20 KM—but note that except for some weekends, most Dubrovnik buses leave early in the day, making an afternoon return from Mostar to Dubrovnik impossible). Service to **Korčula** is sporadic—sometimes once per week, sometimes none at all.

By Train: Mostar is on the train line that runs from Ploče (on the Croatian coast between Split and Dubrovnik) to Zagreb, via Mostar and Sarajevo. This train generally runs once daily, leaving **Ploče** soon after 6:00, with stops at **Mostar** (1.5 hours), **Sarajevo** (4.25 hours), and **Zagreb** (13.5 hours). Going the opposite direction, the train leaves Zagreb at about 9:00. Additional trains may also follow this route.

Route Tips for Drivers

You have two ways to drive between Mostar and Dubrovnik: easy and straightforward, or adventurous and off the beaten path.

Between Mostar and the Main Coastal Road

The most convenient entry point into Bosnia-Herzegovina from the Dalmatian Coast is the town of **Metković,** about halfway between Dubrovnik and Split. (If you're driving there from Dubrovnik or Korčula, you'll actually cross into Bosnia-Herzegovina twice— including the short stretch of coastline that Bosnia-Herzegovina still controls, with the town of **Neum.**)

Near Metković, the main coastal road jogs away from the coast and around the striking **Neretva River Delta**—the extremely fertile "garden patch of Croatia," which produces a significant portion of Croatia's fruits and vegetables. The Neretva is the same river that flows under Mostar's Old Bridge upstream—but in Metković, it spreads out into 12 branches as it enters the Adriatic, flooding a vast plain and creating a bursting cornucopia in the middle of an otherwise rocky and arid region. Enjoying some of the most plentiful sunshine on the Croatian coast, as well as a steady supply of irrigation water, the Neretva Delta is as productive as it is beautiful.

After passing through Metković, you'll cross the border into **Bosnia-Herzegovina,** then continue straight on the main road (M-17) directly into Mostar. As you drive, you'll see destroyed buildings and occasional roadside memorials bearing the likenesses of fresh-faced soldiers who died in the recent war.

Along the way are a few interesting detours: In Čapljina, you can turn off toward **Međugorje.** At this popular Catholic pilgrimage site, six residents have reported seeing visions of the Virgin

Enter the Dragon

Reconciliation works in strange and unexpected ways. In the early 2000s, idealistic young Mostarians formed the Urban Movement of Mostar, which searched for a way to connect the still-feuding Catholic and Muslim communities. As a symbol of their goals, they chose the deceased kung-fu movie star Bruce Lee, who is beloved by both Croats and Bosniaks for his characters' honorable struggle against injustice. A life-size bronze statue of Lee was unveiled with fanfare in November of 2005 in Veliki Park. Unfortunately, soon after, the statue was damaged. Whether or not the vandalism was ethnically motivated is unclear, but many locals hope the ideals embodied in the statue will continue to bring the city together.

Mary. While this can be a powerful experience for pilgrims, non-believers generally find it underwhelming (aside from the thriving zone of kitschy restaurants, hotels, and rosary shops surrounding the town church).

Soon after, a mountaintop castle tower on the right side of the road marks the medieval town of **Počitelj**—an artists' colony (both

before and after the war) with a compelling mix of Christian and Muslim architecture, including a big mosque and a multi-domed bathhouse. It's well worth pulling over and strolling around this steep village.

With extra time, just before Mostar (in Buna), you can detour a few miles along the Buna River into **Blagaj**—the historical capital of the region until the arrival of the Ottomans. This is the site of a mountain called Hum, which is topped by the ruins of a hilltop castle that once belonged to Herzog ("Duke") Stjepan, who gave Herzegovina its name. Deep in Blagaj is an impressive cliff face with a scenic house marking the source of the Buna River. The building, called the Tekija, is actually a former monastery for Turkish dervishes (an order that emphasizes poverty and humility, and is famous for the way they whirl when in a worshipful trance); inside is a modest museum with the graves of two important dervishes. Today the area is surrounded by gift shops and a big restaurant with fine views over the river and cliff.

Approaching **Mostar** on M-17, you'll pass the airport, then turn left at your first opportunity to cross the river. After crossing the bridge, bear right onto Bulevar street, and continue on that main artery for several blocks (passing several destroyed buildings). At the street called Rade Bitange (just after the giant church bell tower), turn right to find the public parking lot—less than a 10-minute walk from the Old Bridge. Be warned that signage is poor; if you get lost, try asking for directions to "Stari Most" (STAH-ree most)—the Old Bridge.

Rugged-but-Scenic Backcountry Route Through Serbian Herzegovina

If you're visiting Mostar round-trip from Dubrovnik, consider coming back a different route, mostly through Herzegovina. This feels much more remote and takes an hour or two longer, but the roads are good and the occasional gas station and restaurant break up the journey. Since this route takes you through the Republika Srpska part of Herzegovina, most road signs are exclusively in the Cyrillic alphabet—though, interestingly, much of the advertising you'll see uses the more familiar Roman alphabet. (Because this road goes through the Serbian part of Herzegovina, it's not popular among Bosniaks or Croats—in fact, locals might tell you this road "does not exist." It does.)

This route is narrated from Dubrovnik to Mostar, but you can do it in reverse—just hold the book upside-down. If you want a little taste of Republika Srpska, consider just day-tripping into Trebinje—especially on Saturday, when the produce market is at its liveliest.

From Dubrovnik, head south toward Cavtat, the airport, and Montenegro. Shortly after leaving Dubrovnik, watch for signs on the left directing you to *Ivanica*. Follow this road to the border of Bosnia-Herzegovina, cross the border, and carry on about 20 minutes into **Trebinje** (Требиње). Consider stopping for a break in Trebinje, a pleasant and relatively affluent town with a leafy main square that hosts a fine Saturday market. Then continue north toward **Bilećko Lake**—a vast, aquamarine lake you'll see on your right (the Vikiovac Restaurant offers a great viewpoint). Then you'll go through the town of **Bileća** (Билећа), turning west at the gloomy industrial town of **Gacko** (Гацко, with a giant coal mine), and onward to the humble but proud little town of **Nevesinje** (Невесиње). From Nevesinje, it's a quick drive up over the mountains, then down into Mostar—passing more familiar Roman-alphabet road signs, then spectacular views of Herzog Stjepan's imposing castle over the town of Buna. Follow signs on into Mostar.

AUSTRIA

AUSTRIA

Österreich

Most people wouldn't consider Austria "Eastern Europe." The country barely slipped out of communism's clutches in 1955, when it became an independent country with the Soviet Union's blessing...provided it remained neutral (it never joined NATO).

Cold War blinders have forced us to separate the communist East from the capitalist West. But consider this part of Europe in the days before Hitler. A hundred years ago, Austria was the head of an enormous empire that encompassed virtually every destination in this book. In the big picture, no other city had more of a cultural and political impact in Eastern Europe than Vienna. In fact, the German name for Austria—Österreich—literally means "the Kingdom of the East."

From a practical standpoint, Vienna serves as a prime "gateway" city. The location is central and convenient for most major Eastern European destinations. Actually farther east than Prague, Ljubljana, and Zagreb, and just upstream on the Danube from Budapest and Bratislava, Vienna is an ideal launchpad for a journey into the East.

In its 18th- and 19th-century glory days, the Austrian Empire (a.k.a. the Austro-Hungarian Empire, a.k.a. the Hapsburg Empire) was arguably the most powerful European entity since Rome. The

Key German Phrases

English	German	Pronounced*
Hello.	*Guten Tag.*	GOO-tehn tahg
Do you speak English?	*Sprechen Sie Englisch?*	SHPREHKH-ehn zee ENG-lish
yes / no	*ja / nein*	yah / nīn
Please. / You're welcome. / Can I help you?	*Bitte.*	BIT-teh
Thank you.	*Danke.*	DAHNG-keh
I'm sorry.	*Es tut mir leid.*	ehs toot meer līd
Excuse me. (to pass or to get attention)	*Entschuldigung.*	ehnt-SHOOL-dig-oong
Good.	*Gut.*	goot
Goodbye.	*Auf Wiedersehen.*	owf VEE-der-zayn
one / two	*eins / zwei*	īns / tsvī
three / four	*drei / vier*	drī / feer
five / six	*fünf / sechs*	fewnf / zehks
seven / eight	*sieben / acht*	ZEE-behn / ahkht
nine / ten	*neun / zehn*	noyn / tsayn
hundred	*hundert*	HOON-dert
thousand	*tausend*	TOW-sehnd
How much?	*Wie viel?*	vee feel
local currency	*euro (€)*	OY-roh
Where is...?	*Wo ist...?*	voh ist
...the toilet	*...die Toilette*	dee toy-LEH-teh
men	*Herren*	HEHR-ehn
women	*Damen*	DAH-mehn
water / coffee	*Wasser / Kaffee*	VAH-ser / kah-FAY
beer / wine	*Bier / Wein*	beer / vīn
Cheers!	*Prost!*	prohst
the bill	*die Rechnung*	dee REHKH-noong

*When using the phonetics, pronounce ī as the long i sound in "light."

Hapsburg family built this giant kingdom of more than 60 million people by making love, not war—having lots of children and marrying them into the other royal houses of Europe.

Today, this small, landlocked country (with just 8 million people) does more to cling to its elegant past than any other nation in Europe. The waltz is still the rage. Austrians are very sociable; it's important to greet people in the breakfast room and those you pass on the streets or meet in shops. The Austrian version of "Hi" is a cheerful *"Grüss Gott"* ("May God greet you"). You'll get the correct pronunciation after the first volley—listen and copy.

While they speak German and talked about unity with Germany long before Hitler ever said *Anschluss,* the Austrians cherish their distinct cultural and historical traditions. They are not Germans. Austria is mellow and relaxed compared to Deutschland—but stiff and formal compared to most Eastern Europeans (except maybe the Hungarians). *Gemütlichkeit* is the word most often used to describe this special Austrian cozy-and-easy approach to life. It's good living—whether engulfed in mountain beauty or bathed in lavish high culture. The people stroll as if every day were Sunday, topping things off with a cheerful visit to a coffee or pastry shop.

It must be nice to be past your prime—no longer troubled by being powerful, able to kick back and celebrate life in the clean, untroubled mountain air. While the Austrians make more money than their Eastern European neighbors, they enjoy a short workweek and a long life span. And compared to much of Eastern Europe, which only recently joined the European Union, Austria is a long-established EU member that adopted the euro as its currency years ago.

Austrians eat on about the same schedule we do. Treats include Wiener schnitzel (breaded veal cutlet), *Knödel* (dumplings), *Apfelstrudel,* and fancy desserts like the *Sachertorte,* Vienna's famous chocolate cake.

In Austria, all cars must have a ***Vignette*** toll sticker stuck to the inside of their windshield to legally drive on the freeways. These are sold at all border crossings (24 hours a day), big gas stations near borders, and car-rental agencies. Stickers cost €8 for 10 days (€22 for 2 months). Not having one earns you a stiff fine.

VIENNA

Wien

Vienna is a head without a body. The capital of the once-grand Hapsburg Empire for 640 years, Vienna started and lost World War I, and with it its far-flung holdings. Culturally, historically, and from a sightseeing point of view, this city is the sum of its illustrious past. The home of Freud, Brahms, Maria Theresa's many children, a gaggle of Strausses, and a dynasty of Holy Roman Emperors ranks right up there with Paris, London, and Rome.

Vienna has always been the easternmost city of the West. In Roman times, it was Vindobona, on the Danube facing the Germanic barbarians. In the Middle Ages, Vienna was Europe's bastion against the Ottomans—a Christian breakwater against the riding tide of Islam (hordes of up to 200,000 Ottomans were repelled in 1529 and 1683). During this period, as the Ottomans dreamed of conquering what they called "the big apple" for their sultan, Vienna lived with a constant fear of invasion (and the Hapsburg court ruled from safer Prague). You'll notice none of Vienna's great palaces were built until after 1683, when the Ottoman threat was finally over.

The Hapsburgs, who ruled the enormous Austrian Empire from 1273 to 1918, shaped Vienna. Some ad agency has convinced Vienna to make Elisabeth, wife of Emperor Franz Josef—with her narcissism and struggles with royal life—the darling of the local tourist scene. You'll see images of "Sisi" (SEE-see) all over town. But stay focused on the Hapsburgs who mattered: Maria Theresa (ruled 1740–1780, see page 861) and Franz Josef (ruled 1848–1916, see page 853).

After Napoleon's defeat and the Congress of Vienna in 1815

(which shaped 19th-century Europe), Vienna enjoyed its violin-filled belle époque, giving us our romantic image of the city: fine wine, chocolates, cafés, waltzes, and the good life.

In 1900, Vienna's 2.2 million inhabitants made it the world's fifth-largest city—after New York, London, Paris, and Berlin.

While Vienna's old walls had held out would-be invaders (including the Ottomans), they were no match for WWII bombs, which destroyed nearly a quarter of the city's buildings. In modern times, neutral Austria took a big bite out of the USSR's Warsaw Pact buffer zone. Today, Vienna is a springboard for newly popular destinations in Eastern Europe.

Vienna's population has dropped to 1.6 million, with dogs being the preferred "child" and the average Viennese mother having only 1.3 children. Even with fewer residents, Vienna is still a grand and elegant capital containing one-fifth of Austria's population.

The truly Viennese person is not Austrian, but a second-generation Hapsburg cocktail, with grandparents from the distant corners of the old empire—Hungary, the Czech Republic, Slovakia, Poland, Slovenia, Croatia, Bosnia-Herzegovina, Serbia, Romania, and Italy. Vienna is the melting-pot capital of a now-collapsed empire that, in its heyday, consisted of 60 million people—only eight million of whom were Austrian.

Planning Your Time

For a big city, Vienna is pleasant and laid-back. Packed with sights, it's worth two days and two nights on the speediest trip. To be grand-tour efficient, you could sleep in and sleep out on the train (Berlin, Kraków, Venice, Rome, the Swiss Alps, Paris, and the Rhine Valley are each handy night trains away).

The Hofburg and Schönbrunn are both world-class palaces, but seeing both is redundant—with limited time or money, I'd choose just one. The Hofburg comes with the popular new Sisi Museum and is right in the town center, making for an easy visit. With more time, a visit to Schönbrunn—set outside town amid a grand and regal garden—is also a great experience. (For efficient sightseeing, drivers should note that Schönbrunn Palace is conveniently on the way out of town toward Salzburg.)

If you have two days for Vienna, here's a great way to spend them:

Day 1

9:00   Circle the Ringstrasse by tram, following my self-guided tram tour (page 832).

10:00   Drop by the TI for any planning and ticket needs, then see the sights in Vienna's old center (using my

self-guided commentary): Monument Against War
and Fascism, Kaisergruft crypt, Kärntner Strasse,
St. Stephen's Cathedral (nave closed 11:30–13:30), and
the Graben pedestrian zone.

12:00 Lunch of finger sandwiches at Buffet Trzesniewski.

13:00 Tour the Hofburg Palace and Treasury.

16:00 Hit one more museum, or shop, browse, and people-
watch.

19:30 Choose classical music (concert or opera), Haus der
Musik, Heuriger wine garden, or any sight listed
under "Sightseeing After Dark," below.

Day 2

Morning Choose between Schönbrunn Palace (which could
be redundant if you've seen the Hofburg Palace
yesterday) or the Lipizzaner Stallions. If you choose
Schönbrunn Palace, arrive by 9:00 and return to
central Vienna by noon. The Lipizzaner Stallions'
practice starts at 10:00 (about Feb–June and Sept–Oct
Tue–Sat 10:00–12:00, no practice Sun–Mon or
July–Aug).

12:00 Have lunch at Naschmarkt.

13:00 Tour the Opera (check red sign on door for today's
schedule).

14:00 Visit the Kunsthistorisches Museum.

16:00 Choose from the many sights left to see in Vienna.

Evening See Day 1 evening options.

Sightseeing After Dark

Several of Vienna's sights are open late one or more evenings a
week.

Haus der Musik: Nightly until 22:00.

KunstHausWien: Nightly until 19:00.

Mozart Haus Museum: Nightly until 19:00.

Museum of Applied Art (MAK): Tue until 24:00.

Albertina Museum: Wed until 21:00.

Natural History Museum: Wed until 21:00.

Kunsthistorisches Museum: Thu until 21:00.

The Secession: Thu until 20:00.

Other late-night activities include: going to an opera (see page
845), a concert (see page 889), or a free, open-air cultural event
on the Rathausplatz (see page 896). Also remember that Vienna's
coffee shops (see page 892) and wine gardens (see page 894) are
generally open late.

ORIENTATION

(area code: 01)

Vienna—Wien in German (pronounced "veen")—sits between the Vienna Woods (Wienerwald) and the Danube (Donau). To the southeast is industrial sprawl. The Alps, which arc across Europe from Marseille, end at Vienna's wooded hills, providing a popular playground for walking and sipping new wine. This greenery's momentum carries on into the city. More than half of Vienna is parkland, filled with ponds, gardens, trees, and statue-maker memories of Austria's glory days.

Think of the city map as a target with concentric sections: The bull's-eye is St. Stephen's Cathedral, the towering cathedral south of the Danube; the first circle is the Ringstrasse; and the second is the Gürtel outerbelt. The old town—snuggling around St. Stephen's—is bound tightly by the Ringstrasse, marking what used to be the city wall. The Gürtel, a broader ring road, contains the rest of downtown.

Addresses start with the district, or *Bezirk,* followed by street and building number. The Ringstrasse (a.k.a. the Ring) circles the first *Bezirk.* Any address higher than the ninth *Bezirk* is beyond the Gürtel, far from the center. The middle two digits of Vienna's postal codes show the *Bezirk.* The address "7, Lindengasse 4" is in the seventh district, #4 on Linden street. Its postal code would be 1070.

Nearly all your sightseeing will be done in the core first district or along the Ringstrasse. As a tourist, concern yourself only with this compact old center. When you do, sprawling Vienna suddenly becomes manageable.

Tourist Information

Vienna's one real tourist office is a block behind the Opera at Albertinaplatz (daily 9:00–19:00, tel. 01/24555, press 2 for English info, www.vienna.info).

Confirm your sightseeing plans and pick up the free and essential city map with a list of museums and hours (also available at most hotels), the monthly program of concerts (called *Wien-Programm*—details below), the *Vienna from A to Z* booklet (details on next page), the biannual city guide *(Vienna Journal),* and the youth guide *(Vienna Hype).* If you're visiting in summer, pick up the *KlangBogen* brochure, which lists the summer symphony schedule (runs June–Sept; see page 891). The TI also books rooms for a €2.90 fee. While hotel and ticket-booking agencies at the train stations and airport can answer questions and give out maps and brochures, I'd rely on the official TI if possible.

The ***Wien-Programm*** monthly entertainment guide is particularly important in Europe's music capital. It includes a daily

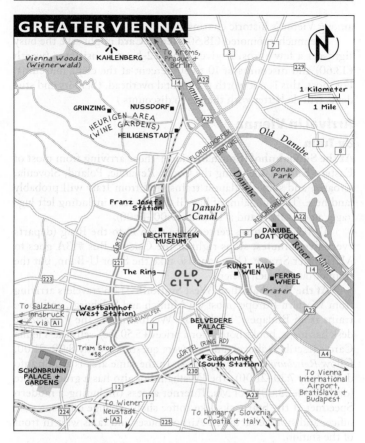

calendar and information on the contemporary cultural scene, including live music, jazz, walks, expositions, and evening museum options. First you see the month's events, then guided walks offered (*E* means in English), then the opera schedule, followed by other theaters and concert halls (with phone numbers to call direct to check seat availability, and to save the 20 percent booking fees you'll pay for buying tickets through an agency). Last is the calendar section (with codes for venues that are all listed—with their phone numbers—on the first page of the section).

Consider the TI's handy €3.60 *Vienna from A to Z* booklet. Every important building sports a numbered flag banner that keys into this guidebook. *A to Z* numbers are keyed into the TI's city map. When lost, find one of the "famous-building flags" and match its number to your map. If you're at a famous building, check the map to see what other key numbers are nearby, then check the *A to Z* book description to see if you want to go in. This system is especially helpful for those just wandering aimlessly among Vienna's historic charms.

The much-promoted €18.50 **Vienna Card** might save the busy sightseer a few euros. It gives you a 72-hour transit pass (worth €13.60) and discounts of 10 to 50 percent at the city's museums. For most, this is not worth the mental overhead. (Seniors and students will do better with their own discounts.)

Arrival in Vienna

By Train

At the Südbahnhof (South Station): Those arriving from most of Eastern Europe (including the Czech Republic, Poland, Slovenia, Croatia, and some Budapest trains) and from Italy will probably land here. The Südbahnhof has all the services, including left luggage, a post office, and a TI (daily 9:00–19:00).

To reach Vienna's center, take tram D to the Ring (departs every five minutes, stops right at the Opera). Bus #13A goes to Mariahilfer Strasse. (You can also take the S- or U-Bahn, but the tram or bus is much easier.)

At the Westbahnhof (West Station): Train travelers arriving from Western Europe (most via Munich and Salzburg), and some trains from Budapest, land at the Westbahnhof. The *Verkersbüro* desk has maps, books hotels (for a pricey €5.50 fee), sells the Vienna Card (described above), and answers questions (daily 8:00–21:00, follow *Reisebüro am Bahnhof* signs). In the same area is a train info desk (daily 7:30–21:00). The Westbahnhof also has a grocery store (daily 5:30–23:00), ATMs, Internet access (including a modern Speednet at the Starbucks-like coffee shop), change offices, a post office, and storage facilities. Airport buses and taxis wait in front of the station.

To get to the city center (and most likely, your hotel), take the U-Bahn (subway) on the U-3 line (buy your ticket or transit pass—described under "Getting Around Vienna," below—from a *Tabak* shop in the station or from a machine). *U-3* signs lead down to the tracks (for Mariahilfer Strasse hotels or the center, direction: Simmering). If your hotel is along Mariahilfer Strasse, your stop is on this line (see page 901). If you're sleeping in the center or just sightseeing, ride five stops to Stephansplatz, escalate in the exit (direction: Stephansplatz), and you'll hit St. Stephen's Cathedral. From the cathedral, the TI is a five-minute stroll down the busy Kärntner Strasse pedestrian street.

By Plane

Vienna International Airport: The airport (tel. 01/700-722-233, www.viennaairport.com), 12 miles from the center, is connected to the central Wien-Mitte Bahnhof by S-Bahn (S-7 yellow, €3, price includes any bus or S- or U-Bahn transfers, 2/hr, 24 min) and the newer City Airport Train (CAT, follow green signs, €8, 2/hr, usually departs at :05 and :35, 16 min, www.cityairporttrain.com).

Express airport buses (parked immediately in front of the arrival hall, €6, 2/hr, 30 min, buy ticket from driver, note time to destination on curbside TV monitors) go conveniently to the Schwedenplatz U-Bahn station (for city-center hotels), Westbahnhof (for Mariahilfer Strasse hotels), and Südbahnhof, where it's easy to continue by taxi or public transportation (see above).

Taxis into town cost about €35 (including the €11 airport surcharge); taxis also wait at the downtown terminus of each airport transit service. Hotels arrange for fixed-rate car service to the airport (€30, 30-min ride).

Some budget carriers—especially SkyEurope—fly into nearby **Bratislava Airport.** For details, see page 167.

Helpful Hints

Money: ATMs are everywhere. Banks are open weekdays roughly from 8:00 to 15:00 (until 17:30 on Thu). After hours, you can change money at train stations, the airport, post offices, or the American Express office (Mon–Fri 9:00–17:30, Sat 9:00–12:00, closed Sun, Kärntner Strasse 21–23, tel. 01/5124-0040).

Internet Access: The TI has a list of Internet cafés. **BigNet** is the dominant outfit (www.bignet.at), with lots of stations at Hoher Markt 8–9 (daily 9:00–23:00). **Surfland Internet Café** is near the Opera (daily 10:00–23:00, Krugerstrasse 10, tel. 01/512-7701).

Post Offices: Choose from the main post office (Postgasse in center, daily 6:00–22:00, handy metered phones), Westbahnhof (Mon–Fri 7:00–22:00, Sat–Sun 9:00–20:00), Südbahnhof (daily 7:00–22:00), near the Opera (Mon–Fri 7:00–19:00, closed Sat–Sun, Krugerstrasse 13), and many other locations scattered around town.

English Bookstores: Consider the **British Bookshop** (Mon–Fri 9:30–18:30, Sat 9:30–18:00, closed Sun, at corner of Weihburggasse and Seilerstätte, tel. 01/512-1945; same hours at branch at Mariahilfer Strasse 4, tel. 01/522-6730) or **Shakespeare & Co.** (Mon–Sat 9:00–19:00, closed Sun, north of Hoher Markt, Sterngasse 2, tel. 01/535-5053).

Keeping Up with the News: Don't buy newspapers. Read them for free in Vienna's marvelous coffee houses. It's much classier.

Travel Agency: Intropa is convenient, with good service for flights and train tickets (Mon–Fri 9:00–18:00, Sat 10:00–13:00, closed Sun, Spiegelgasse 15, tel. 01/513-4000). Train tickets come with a €7 service charge when purchased from an agency rather than at the station—but, for many, the convenience is worth it.

Getting Around Vienna

By Public Transportation: Take full advantage of Vienna's simple, cheap, and super-efficient transit system, which includes trams, buses, U-Bahn (subway), and S-Bahn (faster suburban trains). I use the tram mostly to zip around the Ring (tram #1 or #2) and take the U-Bahn to outlying sights or hotels. Numbered lines (such as #38) are trams, and numbers followed by an *A* (such as #38A) are buses. The smooth, modern trams are Porsche-designed, with "backpack technology" locating the engines and mechanical hardware on the roofs for a lower ride and easier entry. Lines that begin with U (e.g., U-3) are U-Bahn lines (directions are designated by the end-of-the-line stops). Blue lines are the speedier S-Bahns. Take a moment to study the eye-friendly city-center map on station walls to internalize how the transit system can help you. The free tourist map has essentially all the lines marked, making the too-big €1.50 transit map unnecessary (info tel. 01/790-9105).

Trams, buses, the U-Bahn, and the S-Bahn all use the same tickets. Buy your tickets from *Tabak* shops, station machines, marked *Vorverkauf* offices in the station, or on board (just on trams, single tickets only, more expensive). You have lots of choices:

- Single tickets (€1.70, €2.20 if bought on tram, good for one journey with necessary transfers);
- 24-hour transit pass (€5.70);
- 72-hour transit pass (€13.60);
- 7-day transit pass (*Wochenkarte*, €14, pass always starts on Mon); or
- 8-day card *(Acht Tage Karte)*, covering eight full days of free transportation for €27.20 (can be shared—for example, 4 people for 2 days each). With a per-person cost of €3.50/day (compared to €5.70/day for a 24-hour pass), this can be a real saver for groups. Kids under 15 travel free on Sundays and holidays.

Stamp a time on your ticket as you enter the Metro system, tram, or bus (stamp it only the first time for a multiple-use pass). Cheaters pay a stiff €50 fine if caught—and then they make you buy a ticket. Rookies miss stops because they fail to open the door. Push buttons, pull latches—do whatever it takes. Study the excellent wall-mounted street map before you exit the U-Bahn station. Choosing the right exit—signposted from the moment you step off the train—saves lots of walking.

Cute little electric buses wind through the tangled old center (bus #1A is best for a joy ride—hop on and see where it takes you).

By Taxi: Vienna's comfortable, civilized, and easy-to-flag-down taxis start at €2.50. You'll pay about €10 to go from the Opera to the Westbahnhof. Pay only what's on the meter—any surcharges (other than the €2 fee added to fares when you telephone them, or €10 for the airport) are just crude cabbie rip-offs.

By Car with Driver: Consider the luxury of having your own car and driver. Johann (a.k.a. John) Lichtl is a kind, honest, English-speaking cabbie who can take up to four passengers in his car (€25/1 hr, €20/hr for 2 or more hours, €23 to or from airport, mobile 0676-670-6750). Consider hiring gentle Johann for a day trip to the Wachau Valley (up the Danube from Vienna, €130, up to 8 hours), or to drive you to Salzburg with Wachau sightseeing en route (€300, up to 14 hours; other trips by negotiation).

By Bike: Vienna is a great city for biking—*if* you own a bike. The bike path along the Ring is wonderfully entertaining. But bike rental is a hassle (get list at TI). Your best biking is likely up and down the traffic-free and people-filled Donauinsel (Danube Island). Weather permitting from March through October, you can rent a bike all day (about 9:30 until dusk) from one of two shops near these bridges: **Floridsdörferbrücke** (€3.60/hr, €18/day, near tram #31 stop, tel. 01/278-8698) and **Reichsbrücke** (€5.40/hr, €27/day, tel. 01/263-5242).

American Rick Watts runs **Pedal Power,** and will deliver your bike to your hotel and pick it up when you're done (€32/day including delivery, Ausstellungsstrasse 3, tel. 01/729-7234, www.pedalpower.at).

Crazy Chicken bike rental, a short tram ride from the Westbahnhof, is less convenient but a bit cheaper (€15/half-day, €22/day, daily 8:30–19:00, near recommended Pension Fünfhaus at Grangasse 8—see page 905 for directions, tel. 01/892-2134, mobile 0664-421-4789).

Citybikewien, which has bikes parked in public racks all over town, is a clever program that works fine for locals and technically works for tourists (but the complexity of the credit-card forms befuddled me). The bikes lock in their stalls (50 of which are scattered through the city center) and are released when you insert your credit card and log on. Figure it out, and you have a bike for €2 per hour (first hour free, fliers explain the process in English, www.citybikewien.at).

TOURS

Walking Tours—The TI's *Walks in Vienna* brochure describes Vienna's many guided walks. The basic 90-minute "Vienna First Glance" introductory walk is offered daily throughout the summer (€12, leaves at 14:00 from near the Opera, in English and German, tel. 01/894-5363, www.wienguide.at). Various specialized tours go once a week and are listed on their website.

Hop-On, Hop-Off Bus Tours—Vienna Sightseeing operates hop-on, hop-off tours (departures from the Opera at top of each hour 10:00–17:00, recorded commentary). The schedule is posted curbside (three different routes, €13 for one, €16 for two). You could pay much more to get 24 hours of hop-on and hop-off privileges, but given the city's excellent public transportation and this outfit's meager one-bus-per-hour frequency, I'd take this not to hop on and off, but only to get the narrated orientation drive through town.

City Bus Tour—Vienna Sightseeing offers a basic three-hour city tour, including a tour of Schönbrunn Palace (€35, 3/day, call 01/7124-6830 or go to www.viennasightseeingtours.com, which also lists their many other tours).

Horse and Buggy Tour—These traditional horse-and-buggies, called *Fiakers*, take rich romantics on clip-clop tours lasting 20 minutes (€40–old town), 40 minutes (€65–old town and the Ring), or one hour (€95–all of the above, but more thorough). You can share the ride and cost with up to five people. Because it's a kind of guided tour, before settling on a carriage, talk to a few drivers and pick one who's fun and speaks English.

Local Guides—The tourist-board website (www.vienna.info) has a long list of local guides with their specialties and contact information. Lisa Zeiler is an excellent English-speaking guide (two-hour walks for €130—if she's booked up, she can set you up with another guide, tel. 01/402-3688, lisa.zeiler@gmx.at). Ursula Klaus, an art scholar specializing in turn-of-the-20th-century Vienna, music, art, and architecture, also offers two-hour tours for €130 (mobile 0676-421-4884, ursula.klaus@aon.at). Lisa and Ursula are both top-notch, bring art museums to life masterfully, and can tailor tours to your interests.

SELF-GUIDED TRAM TOUR

▲▲Around the Ringstrasse

In the 1860s, Emperor Franz Josef had the city's ingrown medieval wall torn down and replaced with a grand boulevard 190 feet wide. The road, arcing nearly three miles around the city's core, predates all the buildings that line it—so what you'll see is very "Neo": Neoclassical, Neo-Gothic, and Neo-Renaissance. One of Europe's great streets, the Ringstrasse is lined with many of the city's top sights. Trams #1 and #2 and a great bike path circle the whole route—and so should you.

This self-guided tram tour gives you a fun orientation and a ridiculously quick glimpse of the major sights as you glide by (€1.70, €2.20 if bought on tram, 30-min circular tour). Tram #1 goes clockwise; tram #2, counterclockwise. Most sights are on the outside, so use tram #2 (sit on the right, ideally in the front seat of the front car). Start immediately across the street from the Opera. You can (and should) jump on and off as you go (trams come every 5 min). Read ahead and pay attention—these sights can fly by. While this works best in the daylight, this tram ride is still worthwhile after dark, when nearly every sight on the route is well-lit. Let's go:

◗ Immediately on the left: The city's main pedestrian drag, Kärntner Strasse, leads to the zigzag-mosaic roof of **St. Stephen's Cathedral.** This tram tour makes a 360-degree circle around the cathedral, staying about this same distance from it.

◗ At first bend (before first stop): Look right, toward the tall fountain and the guy on a horse. Schwarzenberg Platz shows off its **equestrian statue** of Prince Charles Schwarzenberg, who fought Napoleon. Behind that is the Russian monument (behind the fountain with the Soviet soldier holding a flag), which was built in 1945 as a forced thanks to the Soviets for liberating Austria from the Nazis. Formerly a sore point, now it's just ignored. Beyond that (out of sight, on tram D route) is Belvedere Palace (see page 882).

● Going down Schubertring, you reach the huge **Stadtpark** (City Park) on the right, which honors many great Viennese musicians and composers with statues. At the beginning of the park, the gold-and-cream concert hall behind the trees is the **Kursalon,** opened in 1867 by the Strauss brothers, who directed many waltzes here. The touristy Strauss concerts are held in this building (see "Music Scene," page 889). If you'd like, hop off here for a stroll in the park.

● Immediately after the next stop, look right: In the same park, the gilded statue of "Waltz King" **Johann Strauss** holds a violin as he did when he conducted his orchestra, whipping his fans into a three-quarter-time frenzy.

● Just after the next stop, at end of park: On the left, a green statue of **Dr. Karl Lueger** honors the popular man who was mayor of Vienna until 1910. Coming up, on the right, the big red-brick building is the **Museum of Applied Art** (MAK, showing furniture and design through the ages; described on page 886).

● At next bend: On the right, the quaint white building with military helmets decorating the windows was the **Austrian Ministry of War**—back when that was a big operation. Field Marshal Radetzky, a military big shot in the 19th century under Franz Josef, still sits on his high horse. He's pointing toward the Post Office Savings Bank, the only Art Nouveau building facing the Ring.

The architecture along the Ring is known as **"Historicism"** because it's all Neo-this and Neo-that—generally fitting the purpose of the particular building. For example, farther along the Ring, we'll see a Neoclassical parliament building—celebrating ancient Greek notions of democracy; the Neo-Gothic City Hall—recalling when medieval burghers ran the city government in Gothic days; Neo-Renaissance museums—celebrating learning; and the Neo-Baroque National Theater—recalling the age when opera and theater flourished.

● At next corner: The white-domed building over your right shoulder as you turn is the **Urania,** Franz Josef's 1910 observatory. Lean forward and look behind it for a peek at the huge red cars of the giant 100-year-old Ferris wheel in Vienna's Prater Park (fun for families, described on page 887).

● Now you're rolling along the **Danube Canal.** This "Baby Danube" is one of the many small arms of the river that once made up the Danube at this location. The rest have been gathered together in a mightier modern-day Danube, farther away. This neighborhood was thoroughly bombed in World War II. The buildings across the canal are typical of postwar architecture (1960s). They were built on the cheap, and are now being replaced by sleek, futuristic buildings. On your left was the site of the original Roman town, Vindobona.

In three long blocks, on the left (opposite the BP station, be ready—it passes fast), you'll see the ivy-covered walls and round Romanesque arches of **St. Ruprecht's** (Ruprechtskirche), the oldest church in Vienna (built in the 11th century on a bit of Roman ruins). Remember, medieval Vienna was defined by the long-gone wall that you're tracing on this tour. Across the river is an OPEC headquarters, where oil ministers often meet to set prices. Relax for a few stops (or marvel at the public-transit infrastructure Vienna enjoys) until the corner.

➋ Leaving the canal, turning left up Schottenring, at first corner: A block down on the right, you can see a huge red-brick **castle**—actually high-profile barracks built here at the command of a nervous Emperor Franz Josef (who found himself on the throne as an 18-year-old in 1848, the same year people's revolts against autocracy were sweeping across Europe).

➋ At next stop: On the left, the orange-and-white, Neo-Renaissance temple of money—the **Börse**—is Vienna's stock exchange.

➋ Next stop, at corner: The huge, frilly, Neo-Gothic church on the right is a **"votive church,"** a type of church built to fulfill a vow in thanks for God's help—in this case, when an 1853 assassination attempt on Emperor Franz Josef failed. Ahead on the right (in front of tram stop) is the **Vienna University** building (Universität, established in 1365, it has no real campus as the buildings are scattered around town). It faces (on the left, behind a gilded angel across the Ring) a chunk of the old **city wall.** Beethoven lived and composed in the building just above the piece of wall.

➋ At next stop, on right: The Neo-Gothic **City Hall** (Rathaus), flying the flag of Europe, towers over Rathausplatz. This square is a festive site in summer, with a huge screen showing outdoor movies, operas, and concerts and a thriving food circus (see page 896—or, if you're hungry and it's thriving, hop off now). In the winter, the City Hall becomes a huge Advent calendar, with 24 windows opening—one each day—as Christmas approaches.

Immediately across the street (on left) is the **Burgtheater,** Austria's national theater. Behind that is the Landtmann Café (the only café built with the Ringstrasse buildings, and one of the city's finest).

➋ At next stop, on right: The Neo-Greek temple of democracy houses the **Austrian Parliament.** The lady with the golden helmet is Athena, goddess of wisdom. Across the street (on left) is

Vienna at a Glance

▲▲▲**Opera** Dazzling, world-famous opera house. **Hours:** Visit the Opera by guided 35-minute tour only, daily in English; generally July–Aug at 11:00, 13:00, 14:00, 15:00, and often at 10:00 and 16:00; Sept–June fewer tours, afternoon only; call ahead to confirm tour times or check out daily schedule in red on door. Opera Museum open Tue–Sun 10:00–18:00, closed Mon. See page 845.

▲▲▲**Hofburg Palace's Imperial Apartments** Lavish main residence of the Hapsburgs. **Hours:** Daily 9:00–17:00, July–Aug until 17:30. See page 850.

▲▲▲**Hofburg Palace's Treasury** The Hapsburgs' collection of jewels, crowns, and other valuables—the best on the Continent. **Hours:** Wed–Mon 10:00–18:00, closed Tue. See page 855.

▲▲▲**Kunsthistorisches Museum** World-class exhibit of the Hapsburgs' art collection, including Raphael, Titian, Caravaggio, Bosch, and Bruegel. **Hours:** Tue–Sun 10:00–18:00, Thu until 21:00, closed Mon. See page 863.

▲▲▲**Schönbrunn Palace** Spectacular summer residence of the Hapsburgs, similar in grandeur to Versailles. **Hours:** Daily July–Aug 8:30–18:00, April–June and Sept–Oct 8:30–17:00, Nov–March 8:30–16:30, reservations recommended. See page 884.

▲▲**St. Stephen's Cathedral** Enormous, historic Gothic cathedral in the center of Vienna. **Hours:** Church doors open Mon–Sat 6:00–22:00, Sun 7:00–22:00; nave open for tourists only Mon–Sat 9:00–11:30 & 13:30–16:30, Sun 13:00–16:30. Tower open July–Aug 8:30–18:00, April–June and Sept–Oct 8:30–17:30, Nov–March 8:30–17:00. See page 846.

▲▲**Hofburg's New Palace Museums** Uncrowded collection of armor, musical instruments, and ancient Greek statues, in the elegant halls of a Hapsburg palace. **Hours:** Wed–Mon 10:00–18:00, closed Tue. See page 857.

▲▲**Albertina Museum** Hapsburg residence with decent apartments and world-class temporary exhibits. **Hours:** Daily 10:00–18:00, Wed until 21:00. See page 860.

▲▲**Kaisergruft** Crypt for the Hapsburg royalty. **Hours:** Daily 10:00–18:00. See page 860.

▲▲**Haus der Musik** Modern museum with interactive exhibits on Vienna's favorite pastime. **Hours:** Daily 10:00–22:00. See page 874.

▲▲**Belvedere Palace** Elegant palace of Prince Eugene of Savoy, with a collection of 19th- and 20th-century Austrian art (including Klimt). **Hours:** Daily 10:00–18:00. See page 882.

▲**Monument Against War and Fascism** Powerful four-part statue remembering victims of the Nazis. **Hours:** Always open. See page 840.

▲**Lipizzaner Museum** Displays dedicated to the regal Lipizzaner Stallions; horse-lovers should check out their practice sessions. **Hours:** Museum open daily 9:00–18:00; stallions practice across the street roughly Feb–June and Sept–Oct Tue–Sat 10:00–12:00 when the horses are in town—call to confirm. See page 858.

▲**Imperial Furniture Collection** Eclectic collection of Hapsburg furniture. **Hours:** Tue–Sun 10:00–18:00, closed Mon. See page 862.

▲**Natural History Museum** Big building facing Kunsthistorisches Museum, featuring the ancient *Venus of Willendorf*. **Hours:** Wed–Mon 9:00–18:30, Wed until 21:00, closed Tue. See page 872.

▲**Academy of Fine Arts** Small but exciting collection with works by Bosch, Botticelli, Rubens, Guardi, and Van Dyck. **Hours:** Tue–Sun 10:00–18:00, closed Mon. See page 877.

▲**The Secession** A great chance to see Klimt *in situ*. **Hours:** Tue–Sun 10:00–18:00, Thu until 20:00, closed Mon. See page 877.

▲**Naschmarkt** Sprawling, lively, people-filled outdoor market. **Hours:** Mon–Fri 6:00–18:30, Sat 6:00–17:00, closed Sun, closes earlier in winter. See page 880.

▲**Liechtenstein Museum** Impressive Baroque collection. **Hours:** Fri–Mon 10:00–17:00, closed Tue–Thu. See page 880.

▲**KunstHausWien** Modern art museum dedicated to zany local artist/environmentalist Hundertwasser. **Hours:** Daily 10:00–19:00. See page 881.

Vienna

the imperial park called the **Volksgarten,** with a fine rose garden (free and open to the public).

⊙ After the next stop on the right is the **Natural History Museum** (Naturhistorisches Museum)**,** the first of Vienna's huge twin museums. It faces the **Kunsthistorisches Museum,** containing the city's greatest collection of paintings (see page 863). The **MuseumsQuartier** behind them completes the ensemble with a collection of mostly modern art museums (see page 872). A hefty statue of Empress Maria Theresa squats between the museums, facing the grand gate to the **Hofburg,** the emperor's palace (on left, across the Ring, described on page 849). Of the five arches, only the center one was used by the emperor. (Your tour is essentially finished. If you want to jump out here, you're at many of Vienna's top sights.)

⊙ Fifty yards after the next stop, on the left through a gate in the black-iron fence, is a statue of Mozart. It's one of many charms in the **Burggarten,** which until 1918 was the private garden of the emperor. Vienna had more than its share of intellectual and creative geniuses. A hundred yards farther (on left, just out of the park), the German philosopher Goethe sits in a big, thought-provoking chair playing trivia with Schiller (across the street on your right). Behind the statue of Schiller is the **Academy of Fine Arts** (see listing on page 877; and next to it is the Burg Kino, which plays the movie *The Third Man* three times a week in English—see page 897).

⊙ Hey, there's the **Opera** again. Jump off the tram and see the rest of the city.

SELF-GUIDED WALK

Welcome to Vienna

This walk connects the top three sights in Vienna's old center: the Opera, St. Stephen's Cathedral, and the Hofburg Palace. Along the way, you'll get a glimpse of Vienna past and present. The total trip takes about an hour, not counting sightseeing stops (which could be lengthy).

• *Begin by standing on the square in front of Vienna's landmark Opera.*

Opera

This is regarded by music-lovers as one of the planet's premier houses of music. If you're a fan, consider taking a guided tour of the Opera, or spring for a performance (standing-room tickets are surprisingly cheap; for information on all your Opera options, see page 845). The U-Bahn station in front of the Opera is actually a huge underground shopping mall with fast food, newsstands, lots of pickpockets, and even an

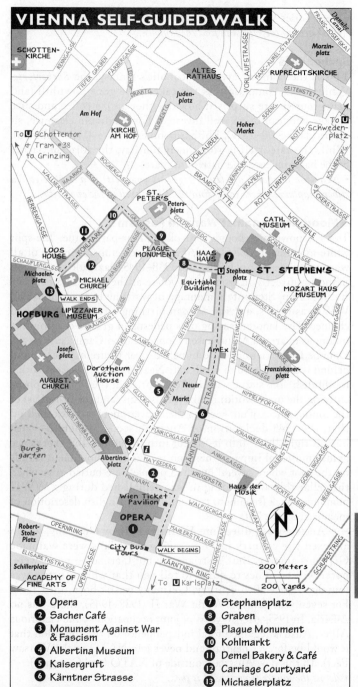

VIENNA SELF-GUIDED WALK

SCHOTTEN-KIRCHE

REINGASSE

TIEFER GRABEN

FÄRBERGASSE

LEID.HOF

DRAHTG.

ALTES RATHAUS

VORLAUFSTRASSE

MARC-AUREL-STRASSE

FRANS-JOSEFS-KAI

Danube Canal

Morzin-platz

RUPRECHTSKIRCHE

Juden-platz

NURBERT G.

SEITENSTETTG.

Am Hof

KIRCHE AM HOF

To U Schottentor + Tram #38 to Grinzing

WALLNERSTRASSE

HAARHOF

NAGLERGASSE

BOGNERGASSE

Hoher Markt

JUDENG.

ROTG.

To U Schweden-platz

TUCHLAUBEN

BRANDSTÄTTE

BAUERNMARKT

KRAMERG.

ROTENTURMSTRASSE

LICHTENSTEG

WOLLZEILE

HERRENGASSE

ST. PETER'S

Peters-platz

GOLDSCHMIEDG.

CATH. MUSEUM

SCHULERSTRASSE

WÄCKERSTRASSE

LOOS HOUSE

KOHLMARKT

GRABEN

PLAGUE MONUMENT

HAAS HAUS

ST. STEPHEN'S

SCHAUFLERGASSE

HABSBURGERGASSE

Michaeler-platz

MICHAEL CHURCH

WALK ENDS

Stephans-platz

MOZART HAUS MUSEUM

HOFBURG

LIPIZZANER MUSEUM

BRÄUNERSTRASSE

Equitable Building

SINGERSTRASSE

BLUTG.

GRÜNANGERG.

KUMPFGASSE

Josefs-platz

DOROTHEERGASSE

PLANKENGASSE

SEILERGASSE

RAUHENSTEINGASSE

WEIHBURGGASSE

BALLGASSE

Franziskaner-platz

AUGUST. CHURCH

Dorotheum Auction House

SPIEGELGASSE

GLUCKG.

TEGETTHOFSTR.

Neuer Markt

KÄRNTNER STRASSE

HIMMELPFORTGASSE

AmEx

Burg-garten

AUGUSTINERBASTEI

FÜHRICHGASSE

JOHANNESGASSE

SEILERSTÄTTE

SCHELLINGGASSE

Albertina-platz

MAYSEDERG.

KRUGERSTR.

ANNAGASSE

FICHTEGASSE

PHILHARM.

Haus der Musik

Wien Ticket Pavilion

WALFISCHGASSE

Robert-Stolz-Platz

OPERNRING

OPERA

MAHLERSTRASSE

AKADEMIESTRASSE

SCHWARZENBERGSTR.

SCHUBERTRING

City Bus Tours

WALK BEGINS

N

ELISABETHSTRASSE

OPERNGASSE

KÄRNTNER RING

Schillerplatz

ACADEMY OF FINE ARTS

To U Karlsplatz

200 Meters

200 Yards

Vienna

❶ Opera	❼ Stephansplatz
❷ Sacher Café	❽ Graben
❸ Monument Against War & Fascism	❾ Plague Monument
❹ Albertina Museum	❿ Kohlmarkt
❺ Kaisergruft	⓫ Demel Bakery & Café
❻ Kärntner Strasse	⓬ Carriage Courtyard
	⓭ Michaelerplatz

Opera Toilet Vienna experience (€0.60, *mit Musik*).
• *Walk behind the Opera to find the famous...*

Sacher Café

This is the home of every chocoholic's fantasy, the *Sachertorte*. While locals complain that the cakes have gone downhill (and many tourists are surprised how dry they are), a coffee and slice of cake here can be €8 well invested. For maximum elegance, sit inside (daily 8:00–23:30, Philharmoniker Strasse 4, tel. 01/51456). While the café itself is grotesquely touristy, the adjacent Sacher Stube has ambience and natives to spare.
• *Near the Sacher Café (turn right as you exit) is a square called Albertinaplatz, where you'll find the TI, as well as the evocative...*

▲Monument Against War and Fascism

This is a powerful, thought-provoking, four-part statue. The split white monument, *The Gates of Violence,* remembers victims of all wars and violence, including the 1938–1945 Nazi rule of Austria. Standing directly in front of it, you're at the gates of a concentration camp. Step into a montage of wartime images: clubs and WWI gas masks, a dying woman birthing a future soldier, and chained slave laborers sitting on a pedestal of granite cut from the infamous quarry at Mauthausen Concentration Camp (just up the Danube from Vienna). The hunched-over figure on the ground behind is a Jew forced to scrub anti-Nazi graffiti off a street with a toothbrush. The statue with its head buried in the stone (Orpheus entering the underworld) reminds Austrians (and the rest of us) of the consequences of not keeping their government on track. Behind that, the 1945 declaration of Austria's second republic—with human rights built into it—is cut into the stone. The experience gains emotional impact when you realize this monument stands on the spot where several hundred people were buried alive when the cellar they were hiding in was demolished during a WWII bombing attack (see photo to right of park, English description of memorial on the left).

Austria was pulled into World War II by Germany, which annexed the country in 1938, saying Austrians were wannabe Germans anyway. But Austrians are not Germans—never were, never will be. They're quick to tell you that while Austria was founded in the 10th century, Germany wasn't born until 1870. For seven years during World War II (1938–1945), there was no Austria. In 1955, after 10 years of joint occupation by the victorious Allies, Austria regained total independence on the condition that it would be forever neutral (and never join NATO or the Warsaw Pact). To this day, Austria is outside of NATO (and Germany).
• *Across the square from the TI is the...*

Albertina Museum

Overlooking Albertinaplatz is what looks like a big terrace. This was actually part of Vienna's original defensive rampart. Later, it was the home to Empress Maria Theresa's daughter Maria Christina. And today, it's topped by a sleek, controversial titanium canopy (called the "diving board" by critics) that welcomes visitors into a recently restored museum. For details on the Albertina Museum, see page 860.

• *Across Albertinaplatz from the Albertina Museum (beyond the memorial photo plaque) is the street called Tegetthoffstrasse. Walk down this street a block to the square called Neuer Markt. Fronting the square is the...*

Kaisergruft

This church has a crypt filled with the fancy coffins of the Hapsburgs. Before moving on, consider paying your respects here (described on page 860).

• *After visiting the Kaisergruft, cross to the center of the square.*

The **fountain,** with the "four rivers" of the Hapsburg Empire (only the Danube is famous), dates from the mid-1700s. The original nude statues were replaced with more modest versions by Maria Teresa (originals are in the Lower Belvedere Palace). The buildings all around you were rebuilt after World War II, when half of the first district was intentionally destroyed by Churchill to demoralize the Viennese, who were disconcertingly enthusiastic about the Nazis.

• *Atop the fountain is a statue of Providence. Her one bare breast points to Kärntner Strasse (50 yards away). Go there and turn left.*

Kärntner Strasse

This grand, mall-like street (traffic-free since 1974) is the people-watching delight of this in-love-with-life city. While it's mostly a crass commercial pedestrian mall with its famed elegant shops now long gone, locals know it's the same road Crusaders marched down as they headed off for the Holy Land in the 12th century. Its name indicates that it points south, in the direction of the region of Kärnten (Carinthia, a province that today is divided between Austria and Slovenia).

Along this drag, you'll find lots of action: shops, street music, the city casino (at #41), the venerable Lobmeyr Crystal shop (#26—climb up the classic Old World interior to the glass museum), and American Express (#21). Note the minimalism of the **American Bar,** designed by Modernist master Adolf Loos (see sidebar on next page). It's dark, plush, and small, with great €8 cocktails (Kärntner Durchgang 10, tel. 01/512-3283). At the end of this street, you'll come to the cathedral. Where Kärntner Strasse

Adolf Loos
(1870–1933)

"Decoration is a crime," wrote Adolf Loos, the turn-of-the-20th-century architect who was Vienna's answer to Frank Lloyd Wright. Foreshadowing the Modernist style of "less is more" and "form follows function," Loos stripped buildings down to their structural skeleton.

In his day, most buildings were plastered with fake Greek columns, frosted with Baroque balustrades, and studded with statues. Even the newer buildings featured flowery Art Nouveau additions. Loos' sparse, geometrical style stood out at the time—and still does a century later. Loos was convinced that unnecessary ornamentation was a waste of workers' valuable time and energy, and was a symbol of an unevolved society. (He even went so far as to compare decoration on a facade with a lavatory wall smeared with excrement.) On this Self-Guided Walk through Vienna, you'll see four examples of his work:

American Bar (Kärntner Durchgang 10): Built the same year Loos published his famous essay *Ornament and Crime*, this tiny bar features Loos' specialties. The facade is cubical, with square columns and crossbeams (and no flowery capitals). The interior is elegant and understated, with rich marble and mirrors that appear to expand the small space.

Public WCs on the Graben: Yes, these modern loos are by Loos.

Manz Bookstore: The facade is a perfect cube, divided into other simple, rectangular shapes.

Loos House on Michaelerplatz: The facade is a perfectly geometrical grid of square columns and windows. Compare it with the Hofburg's ornate, Neo-Rococo look (done only a few decades earlier) to see how revolutionary Loos was. An anti–Art Nouveau statement (inspired by Frank Lloyd Wright and considered Vienna's first "modern" building), this was actually considered shocking. The building's trapezoidal footprint makes no attempt to hide the awkward street corner it's placed on. This "house without eyebrows" features windows without the customary cornice framing the top. The 10 flower boxes beneath the windows (the "moustaches") were only added by Loos reluctantly, after citizens protested that the building was just too stark.

hits Stephansplatz (at #3), the Equitable Building (filled with law-yers, bankers, and insurance men) is a fine example of historicism from the turn of the 20th century. Look up and imagine how slick Vienna must have felt in 1900.

Across the street on the corner, facing St. Stephen's, is the sleek concrete-and-glass **Haas Haus** by noted Austrian architect Hans Hollein (finished in 1990). The curved facade is supposed to echo the Roman fortress of Vindobona (whose ruins were found near here)...but the Viennese, who protested having this stark modern tower right next to their beloved cathedral, were not con-vinced. Since then, it's become a fixture of Vienna's main square. Notice how the smooth, rounded glass reflects St. Stephen's pointy Gothic architecture, providing a great photo opportunity. The café and pricey restaurant inside offer a nice perch, complete with a view of Stephansplatz below.

• *At the end of Kärntner Strasse, you'll wander into...*

Stephansplatz

Vienna's fun and colorful main square is also home to its cathedral, St. Stephen's. Now's the time to visit this massive church (see page 846).

• *When you're finished on Stephansplatz, head for the Hofburg. At the bottom of the square (near the start of Kärntner Strasse) is the street called...*

Graben

This was once a *Graben,* or ditch—originally the moat for the Roman military camp. In the middle of this pedestrian zone (at the intersection with Bräuner Strasse), top-notch street entertainers dance around an extravagant **plague monument,** officially called

the Trinity Column (step back to notice the wonderful gilded "Father, Son, and Holy Ghost" at its top). In the Middle Ages, peo-ple didn't understand the causes of plagues, and figured they were a punishment from God. It was common for survivors—and their rulers—to bribe or thank God with a monument like this one (c. 1690). One-third of Vienna died; this column is thanks from the other two-thirds. Find Emperor Leopold I, who ruled during the plague and ordered this statue created in gratitude. (Hint: The typical inbreeding of royal families left him with a gaping under-bite.) Below Leopold, Faith (with the help of a disgusting little cupid) tosses an old naked woman—symbolizing the plague—into the abyss.

Just before the plague monument is Dorotheergasse, leading to the Dorotheum auction house (see page 875). Just beyond the monument, you'll pass a fine set of **public WCs.** Around 1900, a local chemical-maker needed a publicity stunt to prove that his chemicals really got things clean. He purchased two wine cellars under the Graben and had them turned into classy WCs in the Modernist style (by Loos, see sidebar), complete with chandeliers and finely crafted mahogany. The restrooms remain clean to this day—in fact, they're so inviting that they're used for poetry readings. Locals and tourists happily pay €0.50 for a quick visit.

• *The Graben dead-ends at the aristocratic supermarket Julius Meinl am Graben (see page 910). At the end of the Graben, turn left onto...*

Kohlmarkt

This is Vienna's most elegant shopping street (except for "American Catalog Shopping" at #5, second floor), with the emperor's palace at the end. Strolling Kohlmarkt, daydream about the edible window displays at **Demel** (#14, daily 10:00–19:00). Demel is the ultimate Viennese chocolate shop. The room is filled with Art Nouveau boxes of Empress Sisi's choco-dreams come true: *Kandierte Veilchen* (candied violet petals), *Katzenzungen* (cats' tongues), and so on. The cakes here are moist (compared to the dry *Sachertortes*). The delectable window displays change about monthly, reflecting current happenings in Vienna. Inside, an impressive cancan of cakes is displayed to tempt visitors into springing for the €10 cake-and-coffee deal (point to the cake you want). You can sit inside, with a view of the cake-making, or outside, with the street action. (Upstairs is less crowded.) Shops like this boast "K.u.K."—good enough for the *König und Kaiser* (king and emperor—same guy).

Next to Demel, the **Manz Bookstore** has a Loos-designed facade (see sidebar on page 842). Just beyond Demel and across the street, at #1152, you can pop into a charming little Baroque **carriage courtyard,** with the surviving original carriage garages.

• *Kohlmarkt ends at...*

Michaelerplatz

In the center of this square, a scant bit of Roman Vienna lies exposed. On the left are the fancy Loden Plankl shop, with traditional formal wear, and the stables of the Spanish Riding School. Study the grand entry facade to the Hofburg Palace—it's Neo-Baroque from around 1900. The four heroic giants illustrate Hercules wrestling with his great challenges (much like the Hapsburgs, I'm sure). Opposite the facade, notice the modern

Loos House (now a bank, described in sidebar on page 842); it was built at about the same time.

• *You've made it to the Hofburg Palace. To get to the sights inside, simply walk through the gate, under the dome, and into the first square (In der Burg). For details on all the sights here, see page 836.*

SIGHTS

For a self-guided walk connecting these first three landmark sights, see page 838.

▲▲▲Opera (Staatsoper)

The Opera, facing the Ring and near the TI, is a central point for any visitor. While the critical reception of the building 130 years ago led the architect to commit suicide, and though it's been rebuilt since being destroyed by WWII bombs, it's still a sumptuous place.

Tours: Unless you're attending a performance, you can enter the Opera only with a guided 50-minute tour, offered daily in English (€6.50; generally July–Aug at 11:00, 13:00, 14:00, 15:00, and often at 10:00 and 16:00; Sept–June fewer tours, afternoons only, tel. 01/514-442-606). Tour times are often changed or cancelled due to rehearsals and performances. The opera posts a monthly schedule (blue, on the wall), but the more accurate schedule is the daily listing (red, posted on the door on the Operngasse side of building, farthest from St. Stephen's Cathedral). Tour tickets include the tiny and disappointing Opera Museum (across the street toward the Hofburg), except on Monday, when the museum is closed.

Opera Museum: New and included in your opera tour ticket (whether you like it or not), the Opera Museum is a let-down, with descriptions only in German and rotating six-month-long special exhibits (€3, or included in the €6.50 tour ticket, Tue–Sun 10:00–18:00, closed Mon, a block away from the Opera, near Albertina Museum, tel. 01/514-442-100).

Performances: The Vienna State Opera—with musicians provided by the Vienna Philharmonic Orchestra in the pit—is one of the world's top opera houses. There are 300 performances a year, but in July and August the singers rest their voices (or go on tour). Since there are different operas nearly nightly, you'll see big trucks out back and constant action backstage—all the sets need to be switched each day. Even though the expensive seats normally sell out long in advance, the opera is perpetually in the red and subsidized by the state.

Opera Tickets: To buy tickets in advance, call 01/513-1513 (phone answered daily 10:00–21:00, www.wiener-staatsoper.at).

The theater's box office is open from 9:00 until two hours before each performance. Unless Placido Domingo is in town, it's easy to get one of 567 **standing-room tickets** (*Stehplätze*, €2.50 at the top or €3.50 downstairs). While the front doors open one hour before the show starts, a side door (middle of building, on the Operngasse side) opens 80 minutes before curtain time, giving those in the know an early grab at standing-room tickets. Just walk in straight, then head right until you see the ticket booth marked *Stehplätze* (tel. 01/514-442-419). If fewer than 567 people are in line, there's no need to line up early. If you're one of the first 160 in line, try for the "Parterre" section and you'll end up directly under the Emperor's Box. You can even buy standing-room tickets after the show has started—in case you want only a little taste of opera. Dress is casual (but do your best) at the standing-room bar. Locals save their spot along the rail by tying a scarf to it.

Rick's Crude Tips: For me, three hours is a lot of opera. But just to see and hear the Opera in action for half an hour is a treat. You can buy a standing-room spot and just drop in for part of the show. Ushers don't mind letting tourists with standing-room tickets in for a short look. Ending time is posted in the lobby—you could stop by for just the finale. If you go at the start or finish, you'll see Vienna dressed up. Of the 567 people with cheap standing-room tickets, invariably many will not stand through the entire performance. You can drop by at about 21:30, ask for standing-room tickets, and if none are available, just wait for tourists to leave and bum their tickets off them. Guards don't care. Even those with standing-room tickets are considered "ticket-holders," and are welcome to explore the building. As you leave, wander around the first floor (fun if leaving early, when halls are empty) to enjoy the sumptuous halls (with prints of famous stage sets and performers) and the grand entry staircase. The last resort (and worst option) is to drop into the Opera Café and watch the opera live on TV screens (reasonable menu and drinks).

▲▲St. Stephen's Cathedral (Stephansdom)

This massive church is the Gothic needle around which Vienna spins. According to the medieval vision, it stands like a giant jeweled reliquary, offering praise to God from the center of the city. It has survived Vienna's many wars and today symbolizes the city's freedom.

Cost: Entering the church is free (except July–mid-Oct, when it's €3 to get past the rear of the nave). Going up the towers costs €3 (by stairs, south tower) or €4 (by elevator, north tower). For more information, see "Towers" below.

Hours: The church doors are open Mon–Sat 6:00–22:00, Sun 7:00–22:00, but the nave is only open for tourists Mon–Sat 9:00–11:30 & 13:30–16:30, Sun 13:30–16:30. During services, you can't enter the main nave (unless you're attending Mass), but you can go into the back of the church to reach the north tower elevator (€4, daily July–Aug 8:30–18:00, April–June and Sept–Oct 8:30–17:30, Nov–March 8:30–16:30). The stairs up to the south tower (enter from outside) are open daily 9:00–17:30.

Tours: The €4 tours in English are entertaining (daily April–Oct at 15:45, check information board inside entry to confirm schedule). Audioguides may be available.

❍ Self-Guided Tour: This is the third church to stand on this spot. The church survived the bombs of World War II, but, in the last days of the war, fires from the ruins leapt to the rooftop. The original timbered Gothic rooftop burned, and the cathedral's huge bell crashed to the ground. With a financial outpouring of civic pride, the roof was rebuilt in its original splendor by 1952. The ceramic tiles are purely decorative (locals who contributed to the postwar reconstruction each "own" one for their donation). Dramatic photos show WWII damage (with bricks neatly stacked and ready).

The **grounds** around the church were a cemetery until Josef II emptied it as an "anti-plague" measure in 1780. All the tombs were removed, and the remains were dumped into mass graves outside of town (as was the case when Mozart died here in 1791). A few of the most important tombstones decorate the church walls (see west facade flanking entry). You can still see the footprint of the old cemetery church in the pavement, today ignored by the buskers and human statues. Remains of the earlier Virgil Chapel (dating from the 13th century) are immediately under this (actually on display underground, in the U-Bahn station).

Study the church's **main entrance** (west end). You can see the original Romanesque facade (c. 1240) with classical Roman statues embedded in it. Above are two stubby towers nicknamed "pagan towers" because they're built with a few Roman stones (flipped over to hide the inscriptions and expose the smooth sides). The two 30-foot-tall columns flank the main entry. If you stand back and look at the tops, you'll see that they symbolize creation (one's a penis, the other's a vagina).

Stepping inside, you'll find a Gothic nave with a Baroque overlay. While the columns support the roof, they also tell a story. Richly populated with statues, the columns make a saintly parade leading to the high altar. Near the church's right rear, find the "Madonna with the Protective Mantle"—showing people of all walks of life seeking and finding refuge in the holy mother. The Tupperware-colored glass windows date from 1950. Before World War II, the entire church was lit with windows like the richly colored ones behind the altar. Those, along with the city's top art treasures, were hidden safely from the Nazis in cellars and mines. The altar painting of the stoning of St. Stephen is early Baroque, painted on copper.

St. Stephen's is proud to be Austria's national church. A **plaque** (10 feet up, three pillars in front of the main altar) explains how each region contributed to the rebuilding after World War II: windows from Tirol, furniture from Vorarlberg (westernmost Austrian state), the floor from Lower Austria, and so on.

The Gothic sandstone pulpit in the rear of the nave (on left) is a realistic masterpiece carved from three separate blocks (find the seams). A spiral stairway winds up to the lectern, surrounded and supported by the four Latin Church fathers: Saints Ambrose, Jerome, Gregory, and Augustine. The railing leading up swarms with symbolism: lizards (animals of light) and toads (animals of darkness). The "Dog of the Lord" stands at the top, making sure none of those toads pollutes the sermon. Below the toads, wheels with three parts (the Trinity) roll up, while wheels with four parts (the four seasons, symbolizing mortal life) roll down. This work, attributed by most  scholars to Anton Pilgram, has all the elements of the Flamboyant Gothic style—in miniature. Gothic art was done for the glory of God. Artists were anonymous. But this was around 1500, and the Renaissance was going strong in Italy. While Gothic persisted in the North, the Renaissance spirit had already arrived. In the more humanist Renaissance, humanity was allowed to shine—and artists became famous. So Pilgram included a rare self-portrait bust in his work (the guy with sculptor's tools, in the classic "artist observing the world from his window" pose under the stairs). A few steps farther ahead on the left wall, you'll see a similar self-portrait of Pilgram in color (symbolically supporting the heavy burden of being a master builder of this huge place).

Towers: You can ascend both towers—the south (outside right transept, by spiral staircase) and the north (via crowded elevator inside on the left). The 450-foot-high south tower, called St. Stephen's Tower, offers the far better view, but you'll earn it by hiking 343 tightly wound steps up the spiral staircase (€3, daily 9:00–17:30, this hike burns about one *Sachertorte* of calories). From the top, use your city map to locate the famous sights. The north tower elevator takes you to a mediocre view and a big bell: the 21-ton Pummerin, cast from the cannon captured from the Ottomans in 1683, and supposedly the second biggest bell in the world that rings by swinging (locals know it as the bell that rings in the Austrian New Year; elevator-€4, daily July–Aug 8:30–18:00, April–June and Sept–Oct 8:30–17:30, Nov–March 8:30–17:00).

Cathedral Museum (Dom Museum): This forlorn museum (outside left transept, past the horses) gives a close-up look at piles of religious paintings, statues, and a treasury (€7, Tue–Sat 10:00–17:00, closed Sun–Mon, Stephansplatz 6, tel. 01/515-523-689).

Hofburg Palace

The complex, confusing, and imposing Imperial Palace, with 640 years of architecture, demands your attention. This first Hapsburg residence grew with the family empire from the 13th century until 1913, when the last "new wing" opened. The winter residence of the Hapsburg rulers until 1918, it's still the home of the Spanish Riding School, the Vienna Boys' Choir, the Austrian president's office, 5,000 government workers, and several important museums.

Rather than lose yourself in its myriad halls and courtyards, focus on three sections: the Imperial Apartments, Treasury, and New Palace (Neue Burg). Note that Hapsburg sights not actually inside the Hofburg (including the Lipizzaner Stallions, the Augustinian Church, and the Albertina Museum) are covered on page 860.

Orientation from In der Burg

Begin at the square called In der Burg (enter through the gate from Michaelerplatz). The statue is of Emperor Franz II, grandson of Maria Theresa, grandfather of Franz Josef, and father-in-law of Napoleon. Behind him is a tower with three kinds of clocks (the yellow disk shows the stage of the moon tonight). On the right, a door leads to the Imperial Apartments. Franz faces the oldest part of the palace. The colorful gate (behind you), which used to have a drawbridge, leads to the 13th-century Swiss Court (named for the Swiss mercenary guards once stationed here), the Treasury (Schatzkammer), and the Imperial Chapel (Hofburgkapelle, where the Boys' Choir sings the Mass—see page 889). For the Heroes' Square and the New Palace, continue opposite the way you entered In der Burg, passing through the left-most tunnel.

Eating at the Hofburg: Down the tunnel to Heroes' Square is a tiny but handy sandwich bar called **Hofburg Stüberl** (same €2 sandwich price whether you sit or go, Mon–Fri 7:00–18:00, Sat–Sun 10:00–16:00). For a cheap, quick meal, duck into **Restaurant zum Alten Hofkeller** in a cellar under the palace (€5 plates,

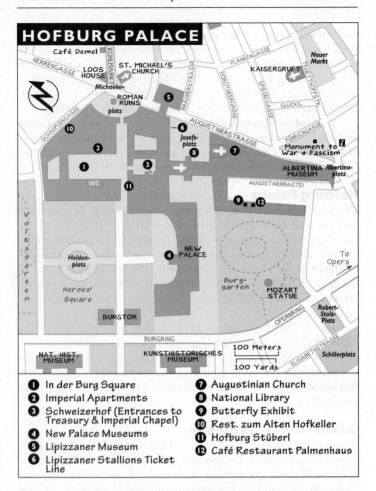

HOFBURG PALACE

1. In der Burg Square
2. Imperial Apartments
3. Schweizerhof (Entrances to Treasury & Imperial Chapel)
4. New Palace Museums
5. Lipizzaner Museum
6. Lipizzaner Stallions Ticket Line
7. Augustinian Church
8. National Library
9. Butterfly Exhibit
10. Rest. zum Alten Hofkeller
11. Hofburg Stüberl
12. Café Restaurant Palmenhaus

Mon–Fri 11:00–13:30, closed Sat–Sun and in Aug, breakfast from 7:30, cafeteria-style, mod and efficient, Schauflergasse 7).

▲▲▲Imperial Apartments (Kaiserappartements)

These lavish, Versailles-type, "wish-I-were-God" royal rooms are the downtown version of the grander Schönbrunn Palace. If you're rushed and have time for only one palace, do this. Palace visits are a one-way romp through 20 rooms. You'll find some helpful posted English information, and the included audioguide brings the exhibit to life. With those tools and the following description, you won't need the €8 *Imperial Apartments and Sisi* museum guidebook. Your ticket also gets you into the royal silver and porcelain collection *(Silberkammer)* near the turnstile. If touring the silver and porcelain, do it first to save walking.

Sisi
(1837–1898)

Empress Elisabeth—Franz Josef's mysterious, narcissistic, and beautiful wife—is in vogue. Sisi was mostly silent. Her main goals in life seem to have been preserving her reputation as a beautiful empress, maintaining her Barbie Doll figure, and tending to her fairy-tale, ankle-length hair. In spite of severe dieting and fanatic exercise, age took its toll. After turning 30, she allowed no more portraits to be painted and was generally seen in public with a delicate fan covering her face (and bad teeth).

Complex and influential, Sisi was adored by Franz Josef, whom she respected. Her personal mission and political cause was promoting Hungary's bid for nationalism. Her personal tragedy was the death of her son Rudolf, the crown prince, an apparent suicide (an incident often dramatized as "The Mayerling Affair," after the royal hunting lodge where it happened).

Disliking Vienna and the confines of the court, Sisi traveled more and more frequently. Over the years, the restless Sisi and her hardworking husband became estranged. In 1898, while visiting Geneva, Switzerland, she was murdered by an Italian anarchist.

Sisi has been compared to Princess Diana because of her beauty, bittersweet life, and tragic death. Her story is wonderfully told in the new Sisi Museum, now part of the Hofburg Imperial Apartments tour.

Cost, Hours, Location: €10, daily July–Aug 9:00–17:30, Sept–June 9:00–17:00, last entry 30 min before closing, from courtyard through St. Michael's Gate—just off Michaelerplatz, tel. 01/533-7570, www.hofburg-wien.at.

 Self-Guided Tour: Get your ticket, tour the silver and porcelain collection, climb the stairs, go through the turnstile, consider the WC, and use the big model of the palace complex to understand the complex lay of the imperial land. Then head into the...

Sisi Museum: The first six rooms tell the life story of Empress Elisabeth's fancy world—her luxury homes and fairy-tale existence (see sidebar above). While Sisi's life story is the perfect stuff of legends, the exhibit tries to keep things from getting too giddy, and doesn't add to the sugary, kitschy image that's been created. The exhibit starts with her assassination (see her death mask) and traces the development of her legend, analyzing how her fabulous but tragic life could create a 19th-century Princess Diana from a rocky start (when she was disdained for abandoning Vienna and her husband, the venerable Emperor Franz Josef). You'll read bits of her poetic writing, see exact copies of her now-lost jewelry, and learn about her escapes, dieting mania, and chocolate bills. Admire Sisi's hard-earned thin waist (20 inches at age 16, 21 inches at age 50...after giving birth to four children). The black statue in the dark room represents the empress after the suicide of her son—aloof, thin, in black, with her back to the world. At the end, ponder the crude knife that killed Sisi.

A special exhibit opened in August 2006 to celebrate the 50th anniversary of the films that made Sisi a household name (at least in Austria): *Sisi* (1955); *Sisi: The Young Empress* (1956); *Sisi: Fateful Years of an Empress* (1957); and the condensed English version, *Forever My Love* (1962). The exhibition showcases the furniture borrowed from the palace for the movies, along with photographs and props from the filming.

After the Sisi Museum, a one-way route takes you through a series of royal rooms. The first room—as if to make clear that there was more to the Hapsburgs than Sisi—shows a family tree tracing the Hapsburgs from 1273 to their messy WWI demise. From here you enter the private apartments of the royal family (Franz Josef's first, then Sisi's).

Waiting Room for the Audience Room: A map and manne-quins from the many corners of the Hapsburg realm illustrate the multi-ethnicity of the vast empire. Every citizen had the right to meet privately with the emperor. Three huge paintings entertained guests while they waited. They were propaganda, showing crowds of commoners enthusiastic about their Hapsburg rulers.

On the right: an 1809 scene of the emperor returning to Vienna, celebrating news that Napoleon had begun his retreat.

Left: the return of the emperor from the 1814 Peace of Paris, the treaty that ended the Napoleonic wars. The 1815 Congress of Vienna that followed was the greatest assembly of diplomats in European history. Its goal: to establish peace through a "balance of power" among nations. While rulers ignored nationalism in favor of continued dynastic rule, it worked for about a century, until a colossal war—World War I—wiped out the Hapsburgs and the rest of Europe's royal families.

Center: Less important, the emperor makes his first public appearance to adoring crowds after recovering from a life-threat-ening illness (1826). The chandelier—considered the best in the palace—is Baroque, made of Bohemian crystal.

Audience Room: Suddenly, you were face-to-face with the emp himself. The portrait on the easel shows Franz Josef in 1915, when he was over 80 years old. Famously energetic, he lived a spartan life dedicated to duty. He'd stand at the high table here

Emperor Franz Josef
(1830–1916)

Franz Josef I—who ruled for 68 years (1848–1916)—was the embodiment of the Hapsburg Empire as it finished its six-century-long ride. Born in 1830, Franz Josef had a stern upbringing that instilled in him a powerful sense of duty and—like so many men of power—a love of things military.

His uncle, Ferdinand I, was a dimwit. As the revolutions of 1848 were rattling royal families throughout Europe, the Hapsburgs replaced Ferdinand, putting 18-year-old Franz Josef on the throne. FJ put down the revolt with bloody harshness and spent the first part of his long reign understandably paranoid as social discontent simmered.

FJ was very conservative. But worse, he figured wrongly that he was a talented military tactician, leading Austria into catastrophic battles against Italy (which was fighting for its unification and independence) in the 1860s. As his army endured severe, avoidable casualties, it became clear: FJ was a disaster as a general.

Wearing his uniform to the end, he never saw what a dinosaur his monarchy was becoming, and never thought it strange that the majority of his subjects didn't even speak German. He had no interest in democracy and pointedly never set foot in Austria's parliament building. But, like his contemporary Queen Victoria, he was the embodiment of his empire—old-fashioned but sacrosanct. His passion for low-grade paperwork earned him the nickname "Joe Bureaucrat." Mired in these petty details, he missed the big picture. In 1914, he helped start a Great War that ultimately ended the age of monarchs. The year 1918 marked the end of Europe's big royal families: Hohenzollerns (Prussia), Romanovs (Russia), and Hapsburgs (Austria).

to meet with commoners, who came to show gratitude or make a request. (Standing kept things moving.) On the table, you can read a partial list of 56 appointments he had on January 3, 1910 (three columns: family name, meeting topic, and *Anmerkung*—the emperor's "action log").

Conference Room: The emperor presided here over the equivalent of cabinet meetings. After 1867, he granted Hungary some authority over his sprawling and suddenly unruly lands (creating the "Austro-Hungarian Empire")—so Hungarians also attended these meetings. The paintings on the wall show the military defeat of a popular Hungarian uprising...subtle.

Emperor Franz Josef's Study: This room evokes how seriously the emperor took his responsibilities as the top official of a vast empire. The desk was originally between the windows. Franz Josef could look up from his work and see his lovely, long-haired, tiny-waisted Empress Elisabeth's reflection in the mirror. Notice the trompe l'oeil paintings above each door, giving the believable illusion of marble relief. Notice also all the family photos—the perfect gift for the dad/uncle/hubby who has it all.

The walls between the rooms are wide enough to hide servants' corridors (the hidden door to his valet's room is in the back left corner). The emperor lived with a personal staff of 14: "three valets, four lackeys, two doormen, two manservants, and three chambermaids."

Emperor's Bedroom: Franz Josef famously slept on this no-frills iron bed, and used the portable washstand until 1880 (when the palace got running water). While he had a typical emperor's share of mistresses, his dresser was always well-stocked with photos of Sisi. Franz Josef lived here after his estrangement from Sisi. An etching shows the empress—a fine rider and avid hunter—sitting sidesaddle while jumping a hedge.

Large Salon: This room was for royal family gatherings, and went unused after Sisi's death. The big, ornate stove in the corner was fed from behind. Through the 19th century, this was a standard form of heating.

Small Salon: This room is dedicated to the memory of the assassinated Emperor Maximilian of Mexico (bearded portrait, Franz Josef's brother, killed in 1867). It was also a smoking room—necessary in the early 19th century, when smoking was newly fashionable (but only for men—never done in the presence of women). Left of the door is a small button the emperor had to buzz before entering his estranged wife's quarters. You, however, can go right in.

Empress' Bedroom and Drawing Room: This was Sisi's, refurbished in the Neo-Rococo style in 1854. She lived here—the bed was rolled in and out daily—until her death in 1898.

Sisi's Dressing/Exercise Room: Servants worked two hours a day on Sisi's famous hair here. She'd exercise on the wooden structure. You can psychoanalyze Sisi from the people and photos she hung on her walls. It's mostly her favorite dogs, her Bavarian family, and several portraits of the romantic and anti-monarch poet Heinrich Heine. Her infatuation with the liberal Heine caused a stir in royal circles.

Sisi's Bathroom: Detour into the behind-the-scenes palace. In the narrow passageway, you'll walk by Sisi's hand-painted-porcelain, dolphin-head WC (on the right). In the main bathroom, you'll see her huge copper tub (with the original wall coverings behind it). Sisi was the first Hapsburg to have running water in her bathroom (notice the hot and cold faucets). You're walking on the first linoleum ever used in Vienna (c. 1880).

Servants' Quarters: Next, enter the servants' quarters, with tropical scenes painted by Bergl in 1766. Take time to enjoy Bergl's playful details. As you leave these rooms and re-enter the imperial world, look back to the room on the left.

Empress' Great Salon: The room is painted with Mediterranean escapes, the 19th-century equivalent of travel posters. The statue is of Elisa, Napoleon's oldest sister (by the Neoclassical master Canova). A print shows how the emperor and Sisi would share breakfast in this room. Turn the corner and pass through the anterooms of Alexander's apartments.

Small Salon: The portrait is of Crown Prince Rudolf, Franz Josef and Sisi's son, who supposedly committed suicide at age 30. The mysterious circumstances around his death at Mayerling hunting lodge have been dramatized in numerous movies, plays, opera—and even a ballet.

Red Salon: The Gobelin wall hangings were a 1776 gift from Marie-Antoinette and Louis XVI in Paris to their Viennese counterparts.

Dining Room: It's dinnertime, and Franz Josef has called his extended family together. The settings are modest...just silver. Gold was saved for formal state dinners. Next to each name card was a menu with the chef responsible for each dish. (Talk about pressure.) While the Hofburg had tableware for 4,000, feeding 3,000 was a typical day. The cellar was stocked with 60,000 bottles of wine. The kitchen was huge—50 birds could be roasted on the hand-driven spits at once. (Drop off your audioguide in this room.)

Zip through the shop, go down the stairs, and you're back on the street. Two quick lefts take you back to the palace square (In der Burg), where the Treasury awaits just past the black, red, and gold gate on the far side.

▲▲▲Treasury (Weltliche und Geistliche Schatzkammer)

This "Secular and Religious Treasure Room" contains the best jewels on the Continent. Slip through the vault doors and reflect on the glitter of 21 rooms filled with scepters, swords, crowns, orbs, weighty robes, double-headed eagles, gowns, gem-studded bangles, and a unicorn horn.

Cost, Hours, Information: €10, Wed–Mon 10:00–18:00, closed Tue, follow *Schatzkammer* signs to the Schweizerhof, tel. 01/525-243-410, www.hofburg-wien.at. While no English descriptions are provided within the Treasury, the well-produced, €3 audioguide provides a wealth of information and is worth renting.

❸ **Self-Guided Tour:** Here's a basic rundown of the highlights (the audioguide listed above is much more complete).

Vienna

Room 2: The personal crown of Rudolf II has survived since 1602—it was considered too well-crafted to cannibalize for other crowns. It's a big deal because it's the adopted crown of the Austrian Empire, established in 1806 after Napoleon dissolved the Holy Roman Empire (an alliance of Germanic kingdoms so named because it wanted to be considered the continuation of the Roman Empire). Pressured by Napoleon, the Austrian Francis II—who had been Holy Roman Emperor—became Francis I, Emperor of Austria. Francis I/II (the stern guy on the wall, near where you entered) ruled from 1792 to 1835. Look at the crown. Its design symbolically merges the typical medieval king's crown and a bishop's miter.

Rooms 3 and 4: These contain some of the coronation vestments and regalia needed for the new Austrian emperor.

Room 5: Ponder the Throne Cradle. Napoleon's son was born in 1811 and made king of Rome. The little eagle at the foot is symbolically not yet able to fly, but glory-bound. Glory is symbolized by the star, with dad's big *N* raised high.

Room 8: The eight-foot-tall, 500-year-old unicorn horn (possibly a narwhal tusk) was considered incredibly powerful in the old days, giving its owner the grace of God. This was owned by the Holy Roman Emperor—clearly a divine monarch.

Room 11: The collection's highlight is the 10th-century crown of the Holy Roman Emperor (HRE). The imperial crown swirls with symbolism "proving" that the emperor was both holy and Roman. The jeweled arch over the top is reminiscent of the parade helmet of ancient Roman emperors whose successors the HRE claimed to be. The cross on top says the HRE ruled as Christ's representative on earth. King Solomon's portrait (on the crown, right of cross) is Old Testament proof that kings can be wise and good. King David (next panel) is similar proof that they can be just. The crown's eight sides represent the celestial city of Jerusalem's eight gates. The jewels on the front panel symbolize the 12 apostles.

The nearby 11th-century Imperial Cross preceded the emperor in ceremonies. Encrusted with jewels, it carried a substantial chunk of *the* cross and *the* holy lance (supposedly used to pierce the side of Jesus while on the cross; both items displayed in the same glass case). This must be the actual holy lance, as Holy Roman Emperors actually carried this into battle in the 10th century. Look behind the cross to see how it was a box that could be clipped open and shut, used for holding holy relics. You can see bits of the "true cross" anywhere, but this is a prime piece—with the actual nail hole.

The other case has jewels from the reign of Karl der Grosse (Charlemagne), the greatest ruler of medieval Europe. Notice Charlemagne modeling the crown (which was made a hundred years after he died) in the tall painting adjacent.

Room 12: The painting shows the coronation of Maria Theresa's son Josef II in 1764. In a room filled with the literal big wigs of the day, Josef is wearing the same crown and royal garb you've just seen.

Room 16: Most tourists walk right by perhaps the most exquisite workmanship in the entire Treasury, the royal vestments (15th century). Look closely—they're painted with gold and silver threads.

▲New Palace (Neue Burg)

This last grand addition to the palace, from the early 20th century, was built for the Hapsburg heir Franz Ferdinand (it was tradition

for rulers not to move into their predecessor's quarters). But—while he was waiting politely for his long-lived uncle, Emperor Franz Josef, to die so he could move into his new digs—Franz Ferdinand was assassinated in Sarajevo in 1914, sparking the beginning of World War I.

The palace's grand facade arches around **Heroes' Square** (Heldenplatz). Notice statues of two great Austrian heroes on horseback: Prince Eugene of Savoy (who defeated the Ottomans that had earlier threatened Vienna) and Archduke Charles (first to beat Napoleon in a battle, breaking Nappy's image of invincibility and heralding the end of the Napoleonic age). The frilly spires of Vienna's Neo-Gothic City Hall break the horizon, and a line of horse-drawn carriages await their customers.

▲▲New Palace Museums: Armor, Music, and Ancient Greek Statues

—The New Palace (Neue Burg)—technically part of the Kunsthistorisches Museum across the way—houses three fine museums (same ticket): an armory (with a killer collection of medieval weapons), historical musical instruments, and classical statuary from ancient Ephesus. The included audioguide brings the exhibits to life and lets you actually hear the collection's fascinating old instruments being played. An added bonus is the chance to wander all alone among those royal Hapsburg halls, stairways, and painted ceilings (€10, Wed–Mon 10:00–18:00, closed Tue, almost no tourists, tel. 01/525-243-430).

More Hapsburg Sights near the Hofburg

Central Vienna has plenty more sights associated with the Hapsburgs. With the exception of the last one (on Mariahilfer

Strasse), these are all near the Hofburg. Remember that the biggest Hapsburg sight of all, Schönbrunn Palace, makes a great half-day trip (four miles from the center—see page 884).

Palace Garden (Burggarten)

This greenbelt, once the backyard of the Hofburg and now a people's park, welcomes people to loiter on the grass. On nice days, it's lively with office workers enjoying a break. The statue of Mozart facing the Ringstrasse is popular. The iron-and-glass pavilion now houses the recommended Café Restaurant Palmenhaus (see page 911) and a small but fluttery butterfly exhibit (€5; April–Oct Mon–Fri 10:00–16:45, Sat–Sun 10:00–18:15; Nov–March daily 10:00–15:45). The butterfly zone is delightfully muggy on a brisk off-season day, but trippy any time of year. If you tour it, notice the butterflies hanging out on the trays with rotting slices of banana. They lick the fermented banana juice as it beads, and then just linger there in a stupor...or fly giddy loop-de-loops.

▲ Lipizzaner Museum

While the famous court horses of the Hapsburg emperors were originally from Spain, by the 16th century they were moved closer to Vienna (to the Slovenian town of Lipica). For four centuries, the "Lipizzaner Stallions" have been bred, raised, and trained in Lipica. They actually have "surnames" that can be traced to the original six 16th-century stallions that made the trip from Spain. A must for horse-lovers, this tidy museum in the Renaissance Stallburg Palace shows (and tells in English) the 400-year history of the famous "Spanish Riding School" and the Lipizzaner Stallions.

Cost, Hours, Location: €5, €15 combo-ticket includes training sessions—see below, daily 9:00–18:00, between Josefsplatz and Michaelerplatz at Reitschulgasse 2, tel. 01/525-243-450, www.lipizzaner.at. Ask about the next English showing of the film, which plays in the basement.

❷ Self-Guided Tour: This commentary will make your visit more meaningful.

First Room: One horse's family tree—Conversano Toscana (born 1984)—is shown, tracing his father's line (Conversano) back to 1767. Paintings show how horses were bred for small heads and legs, but massive bodies. The three-minute video is quite graphic, starting with a horse worked up and ready to "joust," followed by a horse giving birth, then a wobbly baby—just minutes old—taking its first steps.

Downstairs: Videos clearly illustrate how the traditional moves so appreciated today evolved. After horses became antiquated on the battlefield, dressage morphed from no-nonsense military moves to court entertainment. The "dancing" originated as battle moves: *pirouette* (quick turns for surviving in the thick of battle) and *courbette* (on hind legs, to make a living shield for the knight). The *capriole* is a strong back-kick that could floor any enemy.

Theater: A 45-minute movie with great horse footage runs constantly (showings alternate between German and English).

Back Upstairs: Here an exhibit retells the dramatic WWII Lipizzaner rescue story. Lipizzaner fans have a warm spot in their hearts for General Patton, who, at the end of World War II—knowing that the Soviets were about to take control of Vienna—ordered a raid on the stable to save the horses and ensure the survival of their fine old bloodlines.

If all this horse information gets you fired up for more, consider...

Seeing the Lipizzaner Stallions—Seats for performances by Vienna's prestigious Spanish Riding School book up months in advance, but standing room is often available the same day (tickets-€45–160, standing room-€28, Feb–June and Sept–Oct Sun at 11:00, sometimes also Fri at 18:00, no shows July–Aug, fewer Nov–Jan, tel. 01/533-9031, www.srs.at). Luckily for the masses, training sessions with music in a chandeliered Baroque hall are open to the public (€12 at the door, roughly Feb–June and Sept–Oct Tue–Sat 10:00–12:00—but only when the horses are in town).

Tourists line up early at Josefsplatz, gate 2. Save money and avoid the wait by buying the €15 combo-ticket that covers both the museum and the training session (and lets you avoid that ticket line). If you want to hang out with Japanese tour groups, get there early and wait for the doors to open at 10:00. Better yet, simply show up late. Almost no one stays for the full two hours—except for the horses. As people leave, new tickets are printed continuously, so you can just waltz in with no wait at all. Don't have high expectations, as the horses often do little more than trot and warm up.

With the riding school enduring financial problems, other ways to see the horses and their stables are now possible (pricey, but for some a good value, details online at www.lipizzaner.at).

▲Augustinian Church (Augustinerkirche)

This is the Gothic and Neo-Gothic church where the Hapsburgs latched, then buried, their hearts (weddings took place here, and the royal hearts are in the vault). Don't miss the exquisite, tomb-like Canova memorial (Neoclassical, 1805) to Maria Theresa's favorite daughter, Maria Christina, with its incredibly sad white-marble procession. The church's 11:00 Sunday Mass is a hit with music-lovers—both a Mass and a concert, often with an orchestra accompanying the choir. To pay, contribute to the offering plate and buy a CD afterwards. Programs are available at the table by the entry all week (church open long hours daily, Augustinerstrasse 3).

The church faces Josefsplatz, with its statue of the great reform emperor Josef II. Next to the Augustinian Church, the **National Library** and its State Hall are impressive (€5, Tue–Sun 10:00–18:00, Thu until 21:00, closed Mon).

▲▲Albertina Museum

This building, at the southern tip of the Hofburg complex (near the Opera), was the residence of Maria Teresa's favorite daughter: Maria Christina, who was the only one allowed to marry for love rather than political strategy. Her many sisters were jealous. (Marie-Antoinette had to marry the French king...and lost her head over it.) Maria Christina's husband, Albert of Saxony, was a great collector of original drawings. He amassed an enormous assortment of works by Dürer, Rembrandt, Rubens, and others. Today, the Albertina allows visitors to tour its elegant state rooms, which hold reproductions of some of these works, and presents temporary exhibits of other artists.

First, head up the central staircase and stroll through the Hapsburg staterooms *(Prunkräume)*, decorated in the French Classicist style—lots of white marble. Top-quality facsimiles of the collection's greatest pieces hang in these rooms. Then browse the modern gallery, featuring special exhibitions well-described in English.

Cost, Hours, Location: €9.50, price can vary based on special exhibits, audioguide-€4, daily 10:00–18:00, Wed until 21:00, overlooking Albertinaplatz across from the TI and Opera, tel. 01/534-830, www.albertina.at.

▲▲Kaisergruft, the Remains of the Hapsburgs

Visiting the imperial remains is not as easy as you might imagine. These original organ donors left their bodies—about 150 in all—in the unassuming Kaisergruft (Capuchin Crypt), their hearts in the Augustinian Church (described above; church open long hours daily, but to see the goods you'll have to talk to a priest), and their entrails in the crypt below St. Stephen's Cathedral. Don't tripe.

Cost, Hours, Location: €4, daily 10:00–18:00, last entry at 17:40, behind the Opera on Neuer Markt, tel. 01/512-685-316.

Empress Maria Theresa (1717–1780)
and Her Son, Emperor Josef II (1741–1790)

Maria Theresa was the only woman to officially rule the Hapsburg Empire in that family's 640-year reign. She was a strong and effective empress (r. 1740–1780). People are quick to remember Maria Theresa as the mother of 16 children (10 survived). Imagine that the most powerful woman in Europe either was pregnant or had a newborn for most of her reign. Maria Theresa ruled after the Austrian defeat of the Ottomans, when Europe recognized Austria as a great power. (Her rival, the Prussian emperor, said, "When at last the Hapsburgs get a great man, it's a woman.")

The last of the Baroque imperial rulers, and the first of the modern rulers of the Age of Enlightenment, Maria Theresa marked the end of the feudal system and the beginning of the era of the grand state. During her reign, she avoided wars and expanded her empire by skillfully marrying her children into the right families. For instance, after daughter Marie-Antoinette's marriage into the French Bourbon family (to Louis XVI), a country that had been an enemy became an ally. (Unfortunately for Marie-Antoinette, Maria Theresa's timing was off.)

Maria Theresa was a great reformer and in tune with her age. She taxed the Church and the nobility, provided six years of obligatory education to all children, and granted free health care to all in her realm. Maria Theresa also welcomed the boy genius Mozart into her court.

The empress' legacy lived on in her son, Josef II, who ruled as emperor himself for a decade (1780–1790). He was an even more avid reformer, building on his mother's accomplishments. An enlightened monarch, Josef mothballed the too-extravagant Schönbrunn Palace, secularized the monasteries, established religious tolerance within his realm, freed the serfs, made possible the founding of Austria's first general hospital, and promoted relatively enlightened treatment of the mentally ill. Josef was a model of practicality (for example, reusable coffins à la *Amadeus,* and no more than six candles at funerals)—and very unpopular with other royals. But his policies succeeded in preempting the revolutionary anger of the age, enabling Austria to avoid the turmoil that shook so much of the rest of Europe.

Upon entering the Kaisergruft, buy the €0.50 map with a Hapsburg family tree and a chart locating each coffin.

Highlights: The double coffin of **Maria Theresa** (1717–1780) and her husband, **Franz I** (1708–1765), is worth a close look for its artwork. Maria Theresa outlived her husband by 15 years—which she spent in mourning. Old and fat, she installed a special lift enabling her to get down into the crypt to be with her dear, departed Franz (even though he had been far from faithful). The couple recline—Etruscan-style—atop their fancy lead coffin. At each corner are the crowns of the Hapsburgs—the Holy Roman Empire, Hungary, Bohemia, and Jerusalem. Notice the contrast between the Rococo splendor of Maria Theresa's tomb and the simple box holding her more modest son, **Josef II** (at his parents' feet; for more on Maria Theresa and Joe II, see the sidebar on page 861).

Franz Josef (1830–1916; see sidebar on page 853) is nearby, in an appropriately austere military tomb. Flanking Franz Josef are the

tombs of his son, the archduke **Rudolf,** and Empress Elisabeth. Rudolf and his teenage mistress supposedly committed suicide together in 1889 at Mayerling hunting lodge and—since the Church figured he forced her and was therefore a murderer—it took considerable legal hair-splitting to win Rudolf this spot (after examining his brain, it was determined that he was mentally disabled and therefore incapable of knowingly killing himself and his girl). *Kaiserin* Elisabeth (1837–1898), a.k.a. **Sisi,** always gets the "Most Flowers" award (see sidebar on page 851).

In front of those three is the most recent Hapsburg tomb. **Empress Zita** was buried in 1989. Her burial procession was probably the last such Old Regime event in European history. The monarchy died hard in Austria.

While it's fun to chase down all these body parts, remember that the real legacy of the Hapsburgs is the magnificence of this city. Step outside. Pan up. Watch the clouds glide by the ornate gables of Vienna.

▲Imperial Furniture Collection (Kaiserliches Hofmobiliendepot)

Bizarre, sensuous, eccentric, or precious, this collection is your peek at the Hapsburgs' furniture—from grandma's wheelchair to the emperor's spittoon—all thoughtfully described in English. The Hapsburgs had many palaces, but only the Hofburg was permanently furnished. The rest were furnished on the fly—set up and taken down by a gang of royal roadies called the "Depot of Court Movables" (Hofmobiliendepot). When the monarchy was dissolved in 1918, the state of Austria took possession of the Hofmobiliendepot's inventory—165,000 items. Now this royal storehouse is open to the public in a fine and sprawling museum. Don't go here for the Jugendstil furnishings. The older Baroque, Rococo, and Biedermeier pieces are the most impressive and tied most intimately to the royals. Combine a visit to this museum with a stroll down the lively shopping boulevard, Mariahilfer Strasse.

Cost, Hours, Location: €7, Tue–Sun 10:00–18:00, closed Mon, Mariahilfer Strasse 88, U-3: Zieglergasse, tel. 01/5243-3570.

▲▲▲Kunsthistorisches Museum

This exciting museum, across the Ring from the Hofburg Palace, showcases the grandeur and opulence of the Hapsburgs' collected

artwork in a grand building (built as a museum in 1888). There are European masterpieces galore, all well-hung on one glorious floor, plus a fine display of Egyptian, classical, and applied arts.

Cost, Hours, Location: €10, audioguide-€3, Tue–Sun 10:00–18:00, Thu until 21:00, closed Mon, on the Ringstrasse at Maria-Theresien-Platz, U-2 or U-3: Volkstheater/Museumsplatz, tel. 01/525-240, www.khm.at.

 Self-Guided Tour: Thanks to Gene Openshaw for writing the following tour.

The Kunsthistorwhateveritis Museum—let's just say "Koonst"—houses some of the most beautiful, sexy, and fun-loving art from two centuries (c. 1450–1650). The collection reflects the *joie de vivre* of Austria's luxury-loving Hapsburg rulers. At their peak of power in the 1500s, the Hapsburgs ruled Austria, Germany, northern Italy, the Netherlands, and Spain—and you'll see a wide variety of art from all these places and beyond.

Of the museum's many exhibits, we'll tour only the Painting Gallery (Gemäldegalerie) on the first floor. Climb the main staircase, featuring Antonio Canova's statue of *Theseus Clubbing the Centaur*. Italian Art is in the right half of the building (as you face Theseus), and Northern Art to the left. Notice that the museum labels the largest rooms with Roman numerals (Saal I, II, III), and the smaller rooms around the perimeter with Arabic (Rooms 1, 2, 3).

• *Enter Saal I and walk right into the High Renaissance.*

Venetian Renaissance (1500–1600)—Titian, Veronese, Tintoretto: Around the year 1500, Italy had a Renaissance, or

KUNSTHISTORISCHES MUSEUM

↑ To Opera

VAN DER WEYDEN, BOSCH & VAN EYCK

COREGGIO & PARMIGIANINO

DÜRER

EARLY NORTHERN

MANTEGNA

RAPHAEL

17   16   14   1   2   3   4

RINGSTRASSE

X

WC   WC   TITIAN   VERO-NESE   TINTO-RETTO

BRUEGEL

THESEUS STATUE

I   II   III

MORE NORTHERN ART

NORTHERN ART

STAIRS

ITALIAN ART

RUBENS

BAROQUE   CARA-VAGGIO

XIII   XIV   XV

VI   V

VELÁZ-QUEZ   10

21   22 VERMEER 23 STEEN

REMBRANDT

BOOKS

ENTRANCE
(on ground level)

MARIA-THERESIEN-PLATZ

Not to Scale

"rebirth," of interest in the art and learning of ancient Greece and Rome. In painting, that meant that ordinary humans and Greek gods joined saints and angels as popular subjects.

Saal I spans the long career of **Titian** the Venetian (that rhymes)—who seemed particularly intimate with the pre-Christian gods and their antics. In *Mars, Venus, and Amor,* a busy cupid oversees the goddess of love making her case that war is not the answer. Mars—his weapons blissfully discarded—sees her point.

Danae with Nursemaid (also usually in Saal I, but may be out for renovation in 2008) features more pre-Christian mythology. Zeus, the king of the gods, was always zooming to earth in the form of some creature or other to fool around with mortal women. Here, he descends as a shower of gold to consort with the willing Danae. You can almost see the human form of Zeus within the cloud. Danae is helpless with rapture, opening her legs to receive him, while her servant tries to catch the heavenly spurt with a towel. Danae's rich, luminous flesh on the left of the canvas is set off by the dark servant at right and the threatening sky above. The white sheets beneath her make her glow even more. This is more than a classic nude—it's a Renaissance Miss August. How could ultra-conservative Catholic emperors have tolerated such a down-right pagan and erotic painting? Apparently, without a problem.

In *Ecce Homo* (just to the right), Titian tackles a Christian theme. A crowd mills about, when suddenly there's a commotion. They nudge each other and start to point. Follow their gaze diagonally up the stairs to a battered figure entering way up in the corner. "Ecce Homo!" says Pilate. "Behold the man." And he presents Jesus to the mob. For us, as for the unsympathetic crowd, the humiliated Son of God is not the center of the scene, but almost an afterthought.

In the next large galleries (Saal II and Saal III), the colorful works by Paolo Veronese and Tintoretto reflect the wealth of

Venice, the funnel where luxury goods from the exotic East flowed into northern Europe. In **Veronese's** *Adoration of the Magi (Anbetung der Könige),* these-Three-Kings-from-Orient-are dressed not in biblical costume, but in the imported silks of Venetian businessmen. Tintoretto's many portraits give us a peek at the movers and shakers of the Venetian Empire.

• *Find the following paintings in Rooms 1–4, the smaller rooms that adjoin Saals I, II, and III.*

Italian Renaissance and Mannerism: *St. Sebastian (Der Hl. Sebastian),* by **Mantegna,** is shot through with arrows. Sebastian was an early Christian martyr, but he stands like a Renaissance statue—on a pedestal, his weight on one foot, displaying his Greek-god anatomy. Mantegna places the three-dimensional "statue" in a three-dimensional setting, using floor tiles and roads that recede into the distance to create the illusion of depth.

In **Correggio's** *Jupiter and Io,* the king of the gods appears in a cloud—see his foggy face and hands?—to get a date with a beautiful nymph named Io. ("Io, Io, it's off to earth I go.") Correggio tips Renaissance "balance"—the enraptured Io may be perched vertically in the center of the canvas right now, but she won't be for long.

Find the little round painting nearby. In his *Self-Portrait in a Convex Mirror (Selbstbildnis im Konvexspiegel),* 21-year-old **Parmigianino** (like the cheese) gazes into a convex mirror and perfectly reproduces the curved reflection on a convex piece of wood. Amazing.

The 22-year-old **Raphael** (roff-eye-EL) captured the spirit of the High Renaissance, combining symmetry, grace, beauty, and emotion. His *Madonna of the Meadow (Die Madonna im Grünen)* is a mountain of motherly love—Mary's head is the summit and her flowing robe is the base—enfolding baby Jesus and John the Baptist. The geometric perfection, serene landscape, and Mary's adorable face make this a masterpiece of sheer grace...but then you get smacked by an ironic fist: The cross the little tykes play with foreshadows their gruesome deaths.

• *Find Caravaggio in Saal V.*

Caravaggio: Caravaggio (karra-VAH-jee-oh) shocked the art world with brutally honest reality. Compared with Raphael's super-sweet *Madonna of the Meadow*, Caravaggio's *Madonna of the Rosary* (*Die Rosenkranzmadonna*, the biggest canvas in the room) looks perfectly ordinary, and the saints kneeling around her have dirty feet.

In *David with the Head of Goliath (David mit dem Haupt des Goliath)*—in the corner near the window—Caravaggio turns a third-degree-interrogation light on a familiar Bible story. David shoves the dripping head of the slain giant right in our noses. The painting, bled of color, is virtually a black-and-white crime-scene photo—slightly overexposed. Out of the deep darkness shine only a few crucial details. This David is not a heroic Renaissance Man like Michelangelo's famous statue, but a

homeless teen that Caravaggio paid to portray God's servant. And the severed head of Goliath is none other than Caravaggio himself, an in-your-face self-portrait.

• *Find Room 10, in the corner of the museum.*

Velázquez: When the Hapsburgs ruled both Austria and Spain, cousins kept in touch through portraits of themselves and their kids. Diego Velázquez (veh-LOSS-kehs) was the greatest of Spain's "photo-journalist" painters: heavily influenced by Caravaggio's realism, capturing his subjects without passing judgment, flattering, or glorifying them.

Watch little Margarita Hapsburg grow up in three different *Portraits of Margarita Theresa (Die Infantin Margarita Teresa)*, from

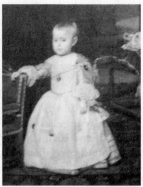

age two to age nine. Margarita was destined from birth to marry her Austrian cousin, the future Emperor Leopold I. Pictures like these, sent from Spain every few years, let her pen-pal/fiancé get to know her. Also see a portrait of Margarita's little brother, *Philip Prosper,* looking like a tiny priest. The kids' oh-so-serious faces, regal poses, and royal trappings are contradicted by their cuteness. No wonder Velázquez was so popular.

• *Complete the Italian Art wing by passing through several rooms of Baroque art, featuring large, colorful canvases showcasing over-the-top emotions and the surefire mark of Baroque art—pudgy, winged babies. If you don't have time to get out to Schönbrunn Palace on this visit, you can get a good look at it here—find Canaletto's* Schloss Schönbrunn, *which also shows the Viennese skyline in the distance. Then head to the east wing, opposite the Titian Room, to see some...*

Early Northern Art: The "Northern Renaissance," brought on by the economic boom of Dutch and Flemish trading, was more secular and Protestant than Catholic-funded Italian art. We'll see fewer Madonnas, saints, and Greek gods and more peasants, landscapes, and food. Paintings are smaller and darker, full of down-to-earth objects. Northern artists sweated the details, encouraging the patient viewer to appreciate the beauty in everyday things.

In the three sections of Room 14 are three early northern painters. **Rogier van der Weyden**'s *Triptych: The Crucifixion*

(Kreuzigungsaltar) strips the Crucifixion down to the essential characters, set in a sparse landscape. The agony is understated, seen in just a few solemn faces and dramatically creased robes. Just to the left, in the painstakingly detailed *Portrait of Cardinal Niccolo Albergati,* **Jan van**

Eyck refuses to airbrush out the jowls and wrinkles, showcasing the quiet dignity of an ordinary man. And in the freestanding case, **Hieronymous Bosch**'s *Christ Carrying the Cross (Kreuztragung Christi)* is crammed with puny humans, not supermen.

• *Room X contains the largest collection of Bruegels in captivity. Linger. If you like it, linger longer.*

Pieter Bruegel (c. 1525–1569)—Norman Rockwell of the 16th Century: The undisputed master of the slice-of-life village scene was Pieter Bruegel the Elder. (His name is pronounced "BROY-gull," and is sometimes spelled *Brueghel*. Don't confuse Pieter Bruegel the Elder with his sons, Pieter Brueghel the Younger and Jan Brueghel, who added luster and an "h" to the family name.) Despite his many rural paintings, Bruegel was actually an urban metrosexual who liked to wear peasants' clothing to observe country folk at play (a trans-fest-ite?). He celebrated their simple life, but he also skewered their weaknesses—not to single them out as hicks, but as universal examples of human folly.

The Peasant Wedding (Bauernhochzeit), Bruegel's most famous work, is less about the wedding than the food. It's a farmers' feeding frenzy as the barnful of wedding guests scramble to get their share of free eats. Two men bring in the next course, a tray of fresh pudding. The bagpiper pauses to check it out. A guy grabs bowls and passes them down the table, taking our attention with them. Everyone's going at it, including a kid in an oversized red cap who licks the bowl with his fingers. In the middle of it all, look who's been completely forgotten—the demure bride sitting in front of the blue-green cloth. (One thing: The guy carrying the front end of the food tray—is he stepping forward with his right leg, or with his left, or with...all three?)

Speaking of two left feet, Bruegel's *Peasant Dance (Bauerntanz)* shows peasants happily clogging to the tune of a lone bagpiper who wails away while his pit crew keeps him lubed with wine. The three Bruegel landscape paintings are part of an original series of six "calendar" paintings, depicting the seasons of the year. *The Gloomy Day (Der düstere Tag)* opens the

cycle, as winter turns to spring... slowly. The snow has melted, flooding the distant river, the trees are still leafless, and the villagers stir, cutting wood and mending fences. We skip ahead to autumn *(The Return of the Herd)*—still sunny, but winter's storms are fast approaching. We see the scene from above, empha-sizing the landscape as much as the people. Finally, in *Hunters*

in Snow (Jäger im Schnee) it's the dead of winter, and three dog-tired hunters with their tired dogs trudge along with only a single fox to show for their efforts. As they crest the hill, the grove of bare trees opens up to a breathtaking view—they're almost home,

where they can join their mates playing hockey. Birds soar like the hunters' rising spirits—emerging from winter's work and looking ahead to a new year.

• *Linger among the Bruegels, then head for the nearby Room 16.*

Albrecht Dürer: As the son of a goldsmith and having trav-eled to Italy, Dürer (DEW-rer) combined meticulous Northern

detail with Renaissance symmetry. So his *Landauer Altarpiece of the Trinity (Allerheiligenbild)* may initially look like a complex pig-pile of saints and angels, but it's perfectly geometrical. The cru-cified Christ forms a triangle in the center, framed by triangular clouds and flanked by three-sided crowds of peo-ple—appropriate for a painting about the Trinity. Dürer practically invented the self-portrait as an art form, and he included himself, the lone earthling in this heavenly vision (bot-tom right), with a plaque announcing that he, Albrecht Dürer, painted this in 1511.

• *Locate these paintings scattered through Rooms 17–21.*

More Northern Art: Contrast Dürer's powerful Renaissance Christ with **Lucas Cranach**'s all-too-human *Crucifixion (Die Kreuzigung)*—twisted, bleeding, scarred, and vomiting blood, as the storm clouds roll in.

Albrecht Altdorfer's garish *Resurrection (Die Auferstehung Christi)* looks like a poster for a bad horror film: "Easter Sunday III. He's back from the dead...and he's ticked!" A burning Christ ignites the dark cave, tingeing the dazed guards.

Hans Holbein painted *Jane Seymour,* wife number III of the VI wives of Henry

VIII. The former lady in waiting—timid and modest—poses stiffly, trying very hard to look the part of Henry's queen. Next.

Giuseppe Arcimboldo's *Summer*—a.k.a "Fruit Face"—is one of four paintings the Hapsburg court painter did showing the seasons (and elements) as people. With a pickle nose, pear chin, and corn-husk ears, this guy literally is what he eats.

In *Flowers in a Wooden Vessel (Der Grosse Blumenstrauss),* **Jan Brueghel,** the son of the famous Bruegel, puts meticulously painted flowers from different seasons together in one artfully arranged vase.

• *Leaving the simplicity of Northern Art—small canvases, small themes, attention to detail—reenter the big-canvased, bright-colored world of Baroque in Saal XIII.*

Peter Paul Rubens: Stand in front of Rubens' *Self-Portrait (Selbstbildnis)* and admire the darling of Catholic-dominated Flanders (Belgium) in his prime: famous, wealthy, well traveled,

eled, the friend of kings and princes, an artist, diplomat, man about town, and—obviously—confident. Rubens' work runs the gamut, from realistic portraits to lounging nudes, Greek myths to altarpieces, from pious devotion to violent sex. But, can we be sure it's Baroque? Ah yes, I'm sure you'll find a pudgy, winged baby somewhere.

The 53-year-old Rubens married Hélène Fourment, this dimpled girl of 16. She pulls the fur around her ample flesh, simultaneously covering herself and exalting her charms. Rubens called both this painting and his young bride "The Little Fur" *(Das Pelzchen).* Hmm. Hélène's sweet cellulite was surely an

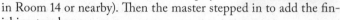

inspiration to Rubens—many of his female figures have Helene's gentle face and dimpled proportions.

In the large *Ildefonso Altarpiece*, a glorious Mary appears (with her entourage of p.w.b.'s) to reward the grateful Spanish saint with a chasuble (priest's smock).

• *Saal XIV features more big Rubens canvases.*

How could Rubens paint all these enormous canvases in one lifetime? He didn't. He kept a workshop of assistants busy painting backgrounds and minor figures, working from Rubens' small sketches (often displayed in Room 14 or nearby). Then the master stepped in to add the finishing touches.

• *From there, find Room 23.*

Jan Steen: In *The World Upside-Down (Die Verkehrte Welt)*, Steen (1626–1679) gives us an intimate look into Dutch life. Not everyone could afford a masterpiece, but even the poorer people wanted works of art for their own homes (like a landscape from Sears for over the sofa). Steen painted humorous scenes from the lives of the lower classes. As a tavern owner, he observed society firsthand. In this scene, everything's going wrong.

• *In the adjoining Room 22:*

Jan Vermeer: In his small canvases, the Dutch painter Jan Vermeer quiets the world down to where we can hear our own heartbeat, letting us appreciate the beauty in common things.

The curtain opens and we see *The Art of Painting (Die Malkunst)*, a behind-the-scenes look at Vermeer at work. He's painting a model dressed in blue, starting with her laurel-leaf headdress. The studio is its own little dollhouse world framed by a chair in the foreground and the wall in back. Then Vermeer fills this space with the few gems he wants us to focus on—the chandelier, the map, the painter's costume. Everything is lit by a crystal-clear light, letting us see these everyday items with fresh eyes.

The painting is also called *The Allegory of Painting.* The model has the laurel leaves, trumpet, and book that symbolize fame. The artist—his back to the public—earnestly tries to capture fleeting fame with a small sheet of canvas.

• *Finish your tour in the corner room.*

Rembrandt van Rijn: Rembrandt got wealthy painting

portraits of Holland's upwardly-mobile businessmen, but his greatest subject was himself. In the *Large Self-Portrait (Grosses Selbstbildnis)* we see the hands-on-hips, defiant, open-stance determination of a man who will do what he wants, and if they don't like it, tough.

In typical Rembrandt style, most of the canvas is a dark, smudgy brown, with only the side of his face glowing from the darkness. (Remember Caravaggio? Rembrandt did.) Unfortunately, the year this was painted, Rembrandt's fortunes changed. Looking at the *Small Self-Portrait (Kleines Selbstbildnis)* from 1657, consider Rembrandt's last years. His wife died, his children died young, and commissions for paintings dried up as his style veered from the common path. He had to auction off paintings to pay his debts, and died a poor man. Rembrandt's numerous self-portraits painted from youth until old age show a man always changing—from wide-eyed youth to successful portraitist to this disillusioned, but still defiant, old man.

The Rest of the Kunst: We've seen only the "Kunst" (art) half of the Kunst-"Historisches" (history) Museum. The collections on the ground floor are among Europe's best, filled with ancient treasures and medieval curios. Highlights include a statue of the Egyptian pharaoh Thutmosis III, and the Gemma Augustea, a Roman cameo kept by Julius Caesar on his private desk. Happily, one of the glittering jewels in the museum's crown is now back, after being stolen several years ago (see sidebar). The *Salt Cellar,* a divine golden salt bowl by Renaissance sculptor Benvenuto Cellini, will be the centerpiece of a new "Kunstkammer"—a section dedicated to Hapsburg medieval and Renaissance jeweled wonders.

Near the Kunsthistorisches Museum

▲**Natural History Museum**—In the twin building facing the Kunsthistorisches Museum, you'll find moon rocks, dinosaur stuff, and a copy of the fist-sized *Venus of Willendorf*—at 25,000 years old, the world's oldest sex symbol, found in the Danube Valley (the original is in the museum's vault). This museum is a hit with children (€8, Wed–Mon 9:00–18:30, Wed until 21:00, closed Tue, tel. 01/521-770).

MuseumsQuartier—The vast grounds of the former imperial stables now corral several impressive, cutting-edge museums. Walk into the complex from the Hofburg side, where the main entrance (with visitors center) leads to a big courtyard with cafés, fountains,

The Case of the *Salt Cellar* Stealer

In the middle of the night of May 11, 2003, someone broke into the Kunsthistorisches Museum, smashed the glass case containing Cellini's *Salt Cellar (Saliera)*, and set off the alarm. The thief grabbed the $60 million gold-plated salt bowl and ran, scrambling through a second-story window and down some construction scaffolding. The security guard, assuming it was a false alarm, simply turned it off and went back to sleep.

For the next two years, the Kunsthistorisches' prize possession vanished from sight. Police looked everywhere—including a foray into Italy, chasing a tip from a prankster—but came up empty. Meanwhile, the 10-inch-high masterpiece lay hidden right nearby, tucked under a bed in a Vienna apartment.

Then, in October of 2005, a ransom note arrived at the insurance company: Pay $12 million and the statue will be returned. The thief even sent proof he really had it, enclosing the tiny pickle-fork trident held by Neptune. An exchange was arranged, but on the appointed day, the thief suddenly got suspicious. He called it off by sending a text message from his cell phone. Crafty police traced the cell phone, and located the Vienna store where it had been purchased. They pored over the store's security camera footage until they found who had bought it. When they published the images in the media, the thief turned himself in. He was an otherwise ordinary security-alarm salesman who'd almost pulled off the art crime of the century.

Police found the salt cellar carefully wrapped, boxed, and buried in the woods near Vienna, with only a few scratches on it. The 1,000-day ordeal was over, and Cellini's one-of-a-kind masterpiece was home.

and ever-changing "installation lounge furniture," all surrounded by the quarter's various museums (behind Kunsthistorisches Museum, U-2 or U-3: Volkstheater/Museumsplatz). Various combo-tickets are available for those interested in more than just the Leopold and Modern Art museums (visit www.mqw.at).

The **Leopold Museum** features several temporary exhibits of modern Austrian art, and a top floor that holds the largest collection of works by Egon Schiele (1890–1918; many Americans are offended by Schiele's relaxed comfort with human nudity) and a few paintings by Klimt and Kokoschka (€9, €2.50 audioguide—worth it only for enthusiasts, daily 10:00–18:00, Thu until 21:00, tel. 01/525-700, www.leopoldmuseum.org). Note that for these three artists, you'll do better in the Belvedere Palace (described on page 882).

The **Museum of Modern Art** (Museum Moderner Kunst Stiftung Ludwig, a.k.a. "MUMOK") is Austria's leading modern-art gallery. It's the striking lava-paneled building—three stories tall and four stories deep, offering seven floors of far-out art that's hard for most visitors to appreciate. This huge, state-of-the-art museum displays revolving exhibits showing off art of the last generation—including Klee, Picasso, and Pop Art (€9, €2 audioguide has more than you probably want to hear, Tue–Sun 10:00–18:00, Thu until 21:00, closed Mon, tel. 01/52500, www.mumok.at).

Rounding out the sprawling MuseumsQuartier are an architecture museum, Transeuropa, Electronic Avenue, children's museum, and the Kunsthalle Wien—an exhibition center for contemporary art (€7.50, Thu–Tue 10:00–19:00, Thu until 22:00, closed Wed, tel. 01/521-8933, www.kunsthallewien.at).

Central Vienna, Inside the Ring

▲▲**Haus der Musik**—Vienna's "House of Music" has a small first-floor exhibit on the Vienna Philharmonic, and upstairs you'll enjoy fine audiovisual exhibits on each of the famous hometown boys (Haydn, Mozart, Beethoven, Strauss, and Mahler). But the museum is unique for its effective use of interactive touch-screen computers and headphones to actually explore the physics of sound. You can twist, dissect, and bend sounds to make your own musical language, merging your voice with a duck's quack or a city's traffic roar. Wander through the "sonosphere" and marvel at the amazing acoustics—I could actually hear what I thought only a piano tuner could hear. Pick up a virtual baton to conduct the Vienna Philharmonic Orchestra (each time you screw up, the musicians put their instruments down and ridicule you). Really experiencing the place takes time. It's open late and makes a good evening activity (€10, €15 combo-ticket with Mozart Haus Museum, daily 10:00–22:00, last entry 1 hour before closing, 2 blocks from the Opera at Seilerstätte 30, tel. 01/51648, www.hdm.at).

Mozart Haus Museum—Opened in 2006 to commemorate Wolfgang's 250th birthday, this museum is easy to get excited about, but it disappoints. Exhibits fill the only surviving Mozart residence in Vienna, where he lived from 1784 to 1787, when he had lots of money. You'll learn his life story, with an emphasis on his most creative years...when he lived here. Included is a rundown on the Vienna music scene during the Mozart years, a quirky look at his gambling habits and his interest in crudely erotic peep shows, and a four-minute montage of his most famous arias in a mini-theater. Unfortunately, visiting the museum is like reading a book standing up—rather than turning pages, you climb stairs. There are almost no real artifacts. Wolfie would have found the audio-guide dreadful. While the museum might be worth the time and money for Mozart enthusiasts, the Mozart sights in Salzburg are more gratifying. In Vienna, I enjoy the Haus der Musik (above) much more (€9, €15 combo-ticket with Haus der Musik, daily 10:00–19:00, a block behind the cathedral, go through arcade at #5 and walk 50 yards to Domgasse 5, tel. 01/512-1791, www.mozarthausvienna.at).

▲**Vienna's Auction House, the Dorotheum**—For an aristocrat's flea market, drop by Austria's answer to Sotheby's, the Dorotheum. Its five floors of antique furniture and fancy knickknacks have been put up either for immediate sale or auction, often by people who inherited old things they don't have room for. Wandering through here, you feel like you're touring a museum with exhibits you can buy (Mon–Fri 10:00–18:00, Sat 9:00–17:00, closed Sun, classy little café on second floor, between the Graben and Hofburg at Dorotheergasse 17, tel. 01/51560, www.dorotheum.com). The info desk at the ground floor has a building map and schedule of upcoming auctions. Labels on each item predict the auction value. Continue your hunt for the perfect curio on the streets around the Dorotheum, lined with many fine antique shops.

Judenplatz Memorial and Museum—The square called Judenplatz marks the location of Vienna's 15th-century Jewish

community, one of Europe's largest at the time. The square, once filled with a long-gone synagogue, is now dominated by a blocky memorial to the 65,000 Austrian Jews killed by the Nazis. The memorial—a library turned inside out—symbolizes Jews as "people of the book" and causes viewers to ponder the huge loss of culture, knowledge, and humanity that took place between 1938 and 1945.

The Judenplatz Museum, while sparse, has displays on medieval Jewish life and a well-done video re-creating community scenes from five centuries ago. Wander the scant remains of the medieval synagogue below street level—discovered during the construction of the Holocaust memorial. This was the scene of a medieval massacre. Since Christians weren't allowed to lend money, Jews were Europe's moneylenders. As so often happened in Europe, when Viennese Christians fell too deeply into debt, they found a convenient excuse to wipe out the local ghetto—and their debts at the same time. In 1421, 200 of Vienna's Jews were burned at the stake. Others who refused a forced conversion committed mass suicide in the synagogue (€4, €10 combo-ticket includes synagogue and Jewish Museum of the City of Vienna—see page 887, Sun–Thu 10:00–18:00, Fri 10:00–14:00, closed Sat, Judenplatz 8, tel. 01/535-0431, www.jmw.at).

Near Karlsplatz

These sights cluster around Karlsplatz, just southeast of the Ringstrasse (U-1, U-2, or U-4: Karlsplatz).

Karlsplatz—This picnic-friendly square, with its Henry Moore sculpture in the pond, is ringed with sights. The Art Nouveau station pavilions—from the late 19th-century municipal train system *(Stadtbahn)*—are textbook Jugendstil by Otto Wagner, with iron frames, decorative marble slabs, and painted gold ornaments. One of Europe's first subway systems, this precursor to today's U-Bahn was built with a military purpose in mind: to move troops quickly in time of civil unrest—specifically, out to Schönbrunn Palace. One of the pavilions is open as an exhibit on Otto Wagner (€2, June–Oct Tue–Sun 9:00–18:00, closed Mon and Nov–May).

Charles Church (Karlskirche)—Charles Borromeo, a 16th-century bishop from Milan, was an inspiration during plague times. This "votive church" was dedicated to him in 1713, when an epidemic spared Vienna. The church offers the best Baroque in Vienna, with a unique combination of columns (showing scenes from the life of Charles Borromeo, à la Trajan's Column in Rome), a classic pediment, and an elliptical dome. But this church is especially worthwhile for the chance (probably through 2008) to see restoration work in progress and up close (€6 includes a skippable one-room museum, audioguide, and visit to renovation site; Mon–Sat 9:00–12:30 & 13:00–18:00, Sun 13:00–17:45, last entry 30 min before closing). The entry fee may seem steep, but remember that it funds the restoration.

Visitors ride the industrial lift to a platform at the base of the dome. (Consider that the church was built and decorated with a scaffolding system essentially the same as this one.) Once up there, you'll climb stairs to the steamy lantern at the extreme top of the church. At that dizzying height, you're in the clouds with cupids and angels. Many details that appear smooth and beautiful from ground level—such as gold leaf, rudimentary paintings, and fake

marble—look rough and sloppy up close. It's surreal to observe the 3-D figures from an unintended angle. Faith, Hope, Charity, and Borromeo triumph and inspire—while Protestants and their stinkin' books are trashed. Borromeo lobbies heaven for plague relief. At the very top, you'll see the tiny dove representing the Holy Ghost, surrounded by a cheering squad of nipple-lipped cupids.

Historical Museum of the City of Vienna (Wien Museum Karlsplatz)—This under-appreciated museum walks you through the history of Vienna with fine historic artifacts. You'll work your way up, chronologically: The ground floor exhibits Roman artifacts and original statues from St. Stephen's Cathedral (c. 1350), with various Hapsburgs showing off the slinky hip-hugging fashion of the day. The first floor features old city maps, booty from an Ottoman siege, and an 1850 city model showing the town just before the wall was replaced by the Ring. Finally, the second floor displays a city model from 1898 (with the new Ringstrasse), sentimental Biedermeier paintings and objets d'art, and early 20th-century paintings (including some by Gustav Klimt). The museum is worth the €6 admission (free Sun and Fri morning, open Tue–Sun 9:00–18:00, closed Mon, www.wienmuseum.at).

▲Academy of Fine Arts (Akademie der Bildenden Künste)—This small but exciting collection includes works by Bosch, Botticelli, and Rubens (quick, sketchy cartoons used to create his giant canvases); a Venice series by Guardi; and a self-portrait by a 15-year-old van Dyck. It's all magnificently lit and well-described by the €2 audioguide, and comes with comfy chairs.

The fact that this is a working art academy gives it a certain realness. As you wander the halls of the academy, ponder how history might have been different if Hitler—who applied to study architecture here but was rejected—had been accepted as a student. Before leaving, peek into the ground floor's central hall—textbook Historicism, the Ringstrasse style of the late 1800s.

Cost, Hours, Location: €7, Tue–Sun 10:00–18:00, closed Mon, 3 blocks from the Opera at Schillerplatz 3, tel. 01/5881-6225, www.akademiegalerie.at.

▲The Secession—This little building, behind the Academy of Fine Arts, was created by the Vienna Secession movement, a group of non-conformist artists led by Gustav Klimt, Otto Wagner, and friends. (For more on the art movement, see the sidebar on page 878.)

The young trees carved into the walls and its bushy "golden cabbage" rooftop (see photo) are

Art Nouveau (a.k.a. Jugendstil or the Vienna Secession), c. 1896–1914

As Europe approached the dawn of a new (nouveau) century, it embraced a new art: Art Nouveau.

On the one hand, Art Nouveau was very forward-looking and modern, embracing the new technology of iron and glass. But it was also a reaction against the sheer ugliness of the mass-produced, boxy, rigidly geometrical art of the Industrial Age. Art Nouveau artists returned to nature (which abhors a straight line), and were inspired by the curves of plants. And as in nature, no two objects are exactly the same, leaving the artist free to make his work unique.

Art Nouveau street lamps twist and bend like flower stems. Ironwork fountains sprout buds that squirt water. Dining rooms are paneled with leafy garlands of carved wood. Advertising posters feature flowery typefaces and beautiful young women rendered in pure, curving lines. A hit with interior decorators, Art Nouveau was a total "look" that could be applied to furniture, jewelry, paintings, and the building itself.

Though the Art Nouveau movement began in Paris and Belgium, each country gave it its own spin. In German-speaking lands (including Austria), Art Nouveau was called Jugendstil (meaning "youth style").

The innovators in Vienna called their particular Jugendstil movement the Secession, named for the daring artists who "seceded" from tradition. They turned their backs on Vienna's centuries-long love affair with Baroque, Rococo, and Neoclassical styles. They preferred buildings that were simple and geometrically pure, which they then decorated with a few unadulterated Art Nouveau touches. Various artists were part of this movement. Architects, painters, and poets had no single unifying style, except a commitment to what was new. The Secessionist motto

symbolic of the renewal cycle. Today, the Secession continues to showcase cutting-edge art, as well as one of Gustav Klimt's most famous works, the *Beethoven Frieze*.

While the staff hopes you take a look at the temporary exhibits (and the ticket includes this whether you like it or not), most tourists head directly for the basement, home to a small exhibit about the history of the building and the museum's highlight: Klimt's classic *Beethoven Frieze* (a.k.a. the "Searching Souls").

One of the masterpieces of Viennese Art Nouveau, this 105-foot-long fresco was a centerpiece of a 1902 "homage to Beethoven" exhibition. Sit down and read the free flier, which explains Klimt's still-powerful work. The theme, inspired by Beethoven's *Ninth Symphony*, features floating female figures "yearning for happiness."

was: "To each age its art, and to art its liberty."

The TI has a brochure laying out Vienna's 20th-century architecture. Here are some of the best of Vienna's scattered Jugendstil sights:

The Secession: This clean-lined building at the Ring end of the Naschmarkt (see page 880) was the headquarters of the group of artists calling themselves the Secession. It's nicknamed the "golden cabbage" for its bushy gilded rooftop designed by the painter Gustav Klimt. It was here that young artists first exhibited their "youth-style" art in 1897. In the basement is Klimt's *Beethoven Frieze* (see page 877).

Belvedere Palace: This museum's collection includes work by Secessionist leader and poster boy Gustav Klimt (1862-1917). He gained fame painting slender young women entwined together in florid embrace, exploring the highly charged erotic terrain of his contemporary, Sigmund Freud. Klimt took the decorative element of Art Nouveau to extremes. In many of his paintings, only the face and bits of body show through gilded ornamental friezes. The two lovers of *The Kiss* are wrapped up in the colorful gold-and-jeweled cloak of bliss (for more about the palace, see page 882).

The Anchor Clock on Hoher Markt: This mosaic-decorated clock (1911-1917) spans two buildings and does a musical act at noon. The clock honors 12 great figures from Vienna's history, from Marcus Aurelius to Joseph Haydn. While each gets his own top-of-the-hour moment, all parade by at high noon. A plaque on the left names each figure. Notice the novel way to mark the time.

Karlsplatz: Otto Wagner (1841-1918), Vienna's premier Jugendstil architect, designed several structures for Vienna's subway system, including the original arched entrances (see page 876).

They drift and weave and search—like most of us do—through internal and external temptations and forces, falling victim to base and ungodly temptations, and losing their faith. Then, finally, they become fulfilled by poetry, music, and art as they reach the "Ideal Kingdom" where "True Happiness, Pure Bliss, and Absolute Love" are found in a climactic embrace.

Glass cases show sketches Klimt did in preparation for this work. The adjacent room tells the history of this masterpiece, and how the building was damaged in World War II.

Cost, Hours, Location: €6, Tue–Sun 10:00–18:00, Thu until 20:00, closed Mon, Friedrichstrasse 12, tel. 01/587-5307, www.secession.at.

▲**Naschmarkt**—In 1898, the city decided to cover up its Vienna River. The long, wide square they created was filled with a lively produce market that still bustles most days (closed Sun). It's long been known as *the* place to get exotic far-away foods. In fact, locals say, "From here start the Balkans."

From near the Opera, the Naschmarkt (roughly, "Munchies Market") stretches along Wienzeile Street. This "Belly of Vienna" comes with two parallel lanes—one lined with fun and reasonable eateries, and the other featuring the town's top-end produce and gourmet goodies. This is where top chefs like to get their ingredients. At the gourmet vinegar stall, you sample the vinegar like perfume—with a drop on your wrist (see photo). Farther from the center, the Naschmarkt becomes likeably seedy and surrounded by sausage stands, Turkish Döner Kebab stalls, cafés, and theaters. At the market's far end is a

line of buildings with fine Art Nouveau facades. Each Saturday, the Naschmarkt is infested by a huge flea market where, in olden days, locals would come to hire a monkey to pick little critters out of their hair (Mon–Fri 6:00–18:30, Sat 6:00–17:00, closed Sun, closes earlier in winter, U-4: Kettenbruckengasse). For a picnic in the park, pick up your grub here and walk over to Karlsplatz (described on page 876).

Beyond the Ring

▲Liechtenstein Museum

The noble Liechtenstein family (who own only a tiny country, but whose friendship with the Hapsburgs goes back generations) amassed an incredible private art collection. Their palace was long a treasure for Vienna art-lovers. Then, in 1938—knowing Hitler was intent on plundering artwork to create an immense "Führer Museum"—the family fled to their tiny homeland with their best art. Since the museum reopened in 2004, attendance has been disappointing, and each year the museum cuts back its hours. The problem is its location...not its worthiness.

The Liechtensteins' "world of Baroque pleasures" includes the family's rare French Rococo carriage (which was used for their grand entry into Paris; it had to be carted to the edge of town and assembled, as nearly all such carriages were destroyed in the French Revolution), a plush Baroque library, an inviting English Garden, and an impressive collection of paintings including a complete cycle of early Rembrandts.

Cost, Hours, Location: €10, audioguide-€1, Fri–Mon 10:00–

Vienna

17:00, closed Tue–Thu, tram D to Bauernfeldplatz, Fürstengasse 1, tel. 01/319-5767-252, www.liechtensteinmuseum.at.

▲KunstHausWien: Hundertwasser Museum

This "make yourself at home" museum and nearby apartment complex is a hit with lovers of modern art. It mixes the work and philosophy of local painter/environmentalist Friedensreich Hundertwasser (1928–2000). Stand in front of the colorful checkerboard building and consider Hundertwasser's style. He was against "window racism": Neighboring houses allow only one kind of window, but $100H_2O$'s windows are each different—and he encouraged residents in the Hundertwasserhaus (a 5–10 minute walk away, see below) to personalize them. He recognized "tree tenants" as well as human tenants.  His buildings are spritzed with a forest and topped with dirt and grassy little parks—close to nature and good for the soul.

Floors and sidewalks are irregular—to "stimulate the brain" (although current residents complain it just causes wobbly furniture and sprained ankles). Thus $100H_2O$ waged a one-man fight—during the 1950s and 1960s, when concrete and glass ruled—to save the human soul from the city. (Hundertwasser claimed that "straight lines are godless.")

Inside the museum, start with his interesting biography. His fun-loving paintings are half Jugendstil and half just kids' stuff. Notice the photographs from his 1950s days as part of Vienna's bohemian scene. Throughout the museum, keep an eye out for the fun philosophical quotes from an artist who believed, "If man is creative, he comes nearer to his creator."

Cost, Hours, Location: €9 for Hundertwasser Museum, €12 combo-ticket includes special exhibitions, half-price on Mon, open daily 10:00–19:00, extremely fragrant and colorful garden café, Weissgerberstrasse 13, U-3: Landstrasse, tel. 01/712-0491, www .kunsthauswien.com.

Hundertwasserhaus: The KunstHausWien provides by far the best look at Hundertwasser, but for an actual lived-in apartment complex by the green master, walk five minutes to the one-with-nature Hundertwasserhaus (free, at Löwengasse and Kegelgasse). This complex of 50 apartments, subsidized by the government to provide affordable housing, was built in the 1980s as a breath of architectural fresh air in a city of boring, blocky apartment complexes. While not open to visitors, it's worth visiting for its fun-loving and colorful patchwork exterior and the Hundertwasser festival of shops across the street. Don't miss the view from Kegelgasse to see the "tree tenants" and the internal winter garden residents enjoy.

Hundertwasser detractors—of which there are many—remind visitors that $100H_2O$ was a painter, not an architect. They describe the Hundertwasserhaus as a "1950s house built in the 1980s," and colorfully painted with no real concern about the environment, communal living, or even practical comfort. Nearly all the original inhabitants got fed up with the novelty and moved out.

▲▲Belvedere Palace

This is the elegant palace of Prince Eugene of Savoy (1663–1736), the still-much-appreciated conqueror of the Ottomans. Eugene, a Frenchman considered too short and too ugly to be in the service of Louis XIV, offered his services to the Hapsburgs. While he was indeed short and ugly, he became the greatest military genius of his age. When you conquer cities, as Eugene did, you get really rich. He had no heirs, so the state got his property and Emperor Josef II established the Belvedere as Austria's first great public art gallery. Today, his palace boasts sweeping views and houses the Austrian gallery of 19th- and 20th-century art.

The palace is actually two grand buildings separated by a fine garden. For our purposes, the **Upper Belvedere Palace** is what matters. The Upper Palace was Eugene's party house. Today, like the Louvre in Paris (but much easier to enjoy), this palace contains a fine collection of paintings. The collection is arranged chronologically: on the first floor, you'll find Historicism, Romanticism, Impressionism, Realism, tired tourism, Expressionism, Art Nouveau, and early modernism. Each room tries to pair Austrian works from that period with much better-known European works. It's fun to see the original work of artists like Van Gogh, Munch, and Monet hung with their lesser-known Austrian contemporaries.

As Austria becomes a leader in art around 1900, the collection gets stronger, with fine works by late-19th-century Romantics Gustav Klimt and Egon Schiele.

In the two rooms full of sumptuous paintings by Klimt (facing the city center, on the far right) you can get caught up in his fascination with the beauty and danger he saw in women. To Klimt, all art was erotic art. He painted during the turn of the century, when Vienna was a splendid laboratory of hedonism. For Klimt, Eve was the prototypical woman; her body, not the apple, provided the seduction. Frustrated by the censorship of his age, Klimt refused every form of state support. While he couldn't paint nudes, he managed to paint a fully clothed yet bewitching eroticism in a world full of pollen and pistils.

Restitution of Art Stolen by Nazis

The Austrian government has worked diligently to fairly reimburse victims of the Nazis, whose buildings, businesses, personal belongings, and art were taken after the 1938 *Anschluss* (when Germany annexed Austria).

A fund of over $200 million was established by both the Austrian government and corporations who profited through their collaboration with the Nazis. Surviving locals (mostly Jews) who paid a *Reichsfluchtsteuer* ("tax for fleeing the country") were located and given some money. Former slave laborers were also tracked down and given €5,000 each. (Imagine what an amazing windfall that would be for an 80-year-old Romanian peasant woman.)

Most significantly for sightseers, great art was returned to its rightful owners. The big news for the Vienna art world was the return of several Gustav Klimt paintings, most notably his *Golden Adele,* from Vienna's Belvedere Palace collection to a Jewish woman in California. In 2006, *The Golden Adele* was auctioned off for $135 million, the highest price ever paid for a painting. While the Austrian government wanted to buy it back, it figured she was asking too much for the art and refused to get into a bidding war. Fortunately for art-lovers, the most famous Klimt *(The Kiss)* was not involved in the restitution and remains in Vienna's Belvedere Palace.

The famous painting of Judith shows no biblical heroine—Klimt paints her as a high-society Vienna woman with an ostentatious dog-collar necklace. With half-closed eyes and slightly parted lips, she's dismissive...yet mysterious and bewitching. Holding the head of her biblical victim, she's the modern femme fatale.

In what is perhaps his most well-known painting, *The Kiss,* Klimt's woman is no longer dominating, but submissive, abandoning herself to her man in a fertile field and a vast universe. In a glow emanating from a radiance of desire, the body she presses against is a self-portrait of the artist himself.

Don't miss the poignant Schiele family portrait from 1918—his wife died while he was still working on it. (Schiele and his child were soon taken by the influenza epidemic that swept through Europe after World War I.)

The upper floor shows off early 19th-century Biedermeier paintings (hypersensitive, super-sweet, uniquely Viennese Romanticism—the poor are happy, things are lit impossibly well, and folk life is idealized). Your ticket also includes the Austrian Baroque and Gothic art in the Lower Belvedere Palace. Prince

Eugene lived in that palace, but he's long gone, and I wouldn't bother to visit.

Cost, Hours, Location: €9.50 for Upper Belvedere Palace only, €12 for Upper and Lower palaces—not worth it, audioguide-€3, daily 10:00–18:00, entrance at Prinz-Eugen-Strasse 27, tel. 01/7955-7134, www.belvedere.at. To get here from the center, catch tram D at the Opera (direction Südbahnhof, it stops at the palace gate).

View: *Belvedere* means "beautiful view." Sit at the top palace and look over the Baroque gardens, the mysterious sphinxes (which symbolized solving riddles and the finely educated mind of your host, Eugene), the lower palace, and the city. The spire of St. Stephen's Cathedral is 400 feet tall, and no other tall buildings are allowed inside the Ringstrasse. The hills—covered with vineyards—are where the Viennese love to go to sample the new wine. You can see Kahlenberg, from where you can walk down to several recommended *Heurigen* (wine gardens) beyond the spire (see page 894). These are the first of the Alps, which stretch from here all the way to Marseilles, France. The square you're overlooking was filled with people on May 15, 1955, as local leaders stood on the balcony of the Upper Palace (behind you) and proclaimed Austrian independence following a decade-long Allied occupation after World War II.

▲▲▲Schönbrunn Palace (Schloss Schönbrunn)

Among Europe's palaces, only Schönbrunn rivals Versailles. This former summer residence of the Hapsburgs, located four miles from the center, is big, with 1,441 rooms. But don't worry—only 40 rooms are shown to the public. (Today the families of 260 civil servants rent simple apartments in the rest of the palace, enjoying rent control and governmental protections so they can't be evicted.)

Getting There: Take U-4 to Schönbrunn and walk 400 yards (just follow the crowds). The main entrance is in the left side of the palace as you face it.

Royal Apartments

While the exterior is Baroque, the interior was finished under Maria Theresa in let-them-eat-cake Rococo. The chandeliers are either of Bohemian crystal or of hand-carved wood with gold-leaf gilding. Thick walls hid the servants as they ran around stoking the ceramic stoves from the back, and attending to other behind-the-scenes matters. Most of the public rooms are decorated in Neo-Baroque, as they were under Franz Josef (r. 1848–1916). When WWII bombs rained on the city and the palace grounds, the palace itself took only one direct hit. Thankfully, that bomb, which crashed through three floors—including the sumptuous central ballroom—was a dud.

Cost: The admission price is based on which route you select (each one includes an audioguide): the 22-room **Imperial Tour** (€9.50, 45 min, Grand Palace rooms plus apartments of Franz Josef and Elisabeth—mostly 19th-century and therefore least interesting) or the 40-room **Grand Tour** (€13, 60 min, includes Imperial tour plus Maria Theresa's apartments—18th-century Rococo). A combo-ticket called the **Schönbrunn Pass Classic** includes the Grand Tour, as well as other sights on the grounds: the Gloriette viewing terrace, maze, privy garden, and court bakery—complete with *Apfelstrudel* demo and tasting (€17, available April–Oct only). I'd go for the Grand Tour.

Hours: Daily July–Aug 8:30–18:00, April–June and Sept–Oct 8:30–17:00, Nov–March 8:30–16:30. Information: www.schoenbrunn.at.

Crowd-Beating Tips: Schönbrunn suffers from crowds. It can be a jam-packed sauna in the summer. It's busiest from 9:30 to 11:30, especially on weekends and in July and August; it's least crowded from 12:00 to 14:00 and after 16:00, when there are no groups. To avoid the long delays in summer, make a reservation by telephone (tel. 01/8111-3239, answered daily 8:00–17:00, wait through the long message for the operator). You'll get an appointment time and a ticket number. Check in at least 30 minutes early. Upon arrival, go to the "Group and Reservations" desk (immediately inside the gate on the left at the gate house—long before the actual palace), give your number, pick up your ticket, and jump in ahead of the masses. If you show up in peak season without calling first, you deserve the frustration. (In this case, you'll have to wait in line, buy your ticket, and wait until the listed time to enter—which could be tomorrow.) If you have any time to kill, spend it exploring the gardens or Coach Museum.

Palace Gardens

If you've visited the Kaisergruft and strolled by the Hapsburgs (tucked neatly into their crypts), enjoy a walk with the commoners, just to mix things up. This emperor's garden is a celebration of the evolution of civilization from autocracy into real democracy. As a civilization, we're doing well.

Most of the park itself is free, as it has been since the 1700s (open daily sunrise to dusk, entrance on either side of the palace). The small side-gardens are the most elaborate. The Kammergarten on the left was a fancy private garden for the Hapsburgs (now

Vienna

restored and with a fee). The so-called Sisi Gardens on the right are free. Inside are several other sights, including a **palm house** (€4, daily May–Sept 9:30–18:00, Oct–April 9:30–17:00); Europe's oldest **zoo,** or *Tiergarten,* built by Maria Theresa's husband for the entertainment and education of the court in 1752 (€12, May–Sept daily 9:00–18:30, less off-season, tel. 01/8779-2940); and—at the end of the gardens—the **Gloriette,** a purely decorative monument celebrating an obscure Austrian military victory and offering a fine city view (viewing terrace-€2, included in €17 Schönbrunn Pass Classic, daily April–Sept 9:00–18:00, July–Aug until 19:00, Oct 9:00–17:00, closed Nov–March). A touristy choo-choo train makes the rounds all day, connecting Schönbrunn's many attractions.

Coach Museum Wagenburg

The Schönbrunn coach museum is a 19th-century traffic jam of 50 impressive royal carriages and sleighs. Highlights include silly sedan chairs, the death-black hearse carriage (used for Franz Josef in 1916, and most recently for Empress Zita in 1989), and an extravagantly gilded imperial carriage pulled by eight Cinderella horses. This was rarely used other than for the coronation of Holy Roman Emperors, when it was disassembled and taken to Frankfurt for the big event (€4.50; April–Oct daily 9:00–18:00; Nov–March Tue–Sun 10:00–16:00, closed Mon; last entry 30 min before closing, 200 yards from palace, walk through right arch as you face palace, tel. 01/525-240).

"Honorable Mentions": More Vienna Museums

These museums, scattered around the city, are worth a peek if you have a special interest.

Museum of Applied Art—The Österreichisches Museum für Angewandte Kunst, or MAK, is Vienna's answer to London's Victoria and Albert Museum. It shows off the fancies of local aristocratic society, including a fine Jugendstil collection.

The MAK is more than just another grand building on the Ringstrasse. It was built to provide models of historic design for Ringstrasse architects, and is a delightful space in itself (many locals stop in to enjoy a coffee on the plush couches in the main lobby). Each wing is dedicated to a different era. Exhibits, well-described in English, come with a playful modern flair—notable modern designers were assigned various spaces.

Cost, Hours, Location: €8, €10 includes a big English guidebook, free on Sat, open Tue–Sun 10:00–18:00, Tue until 24:00, closed Mon, Stubenring 5, tel. 01/711-360, www.mak.at.

The associated **Restaurant Österreicher im MAK** is named for a chef renowned for his classic and modern Viennese cuisine.

Classy and mod, it's trendy for locals (open daily, reserve for evening, €10–15 plates).

Sigmund Freud Museum—Freud enthusiasts travel to Vienna just to see this humble apartment and workplace of the man who fundamentally changed our understanding of the human psyche. Freud established his practice here in 1891, and it was here that he wrote his work on the interpretation of dreams. Freud, who was Jewish, fled with the rise of Nazism, and took most of his furniture with him. You won't see "the couch," but you will see his waiting room, along with three rooms packed with papers, photos, mementos, and documents. These, along with a family video from the 1930s, give an intimate peek at Freud's life. The old-fashioned exhibit is tediously described in a three-ring info binder loaned to visitors, which complements the more general audioguide.

Cost, Hours, Location: €7, daily 9:00–18:00, cool shop, half a block from a tram D stop at Berggasse 19, tel. 01/319-1596, www.freud-museum.at.

More Museums—There's much, much more. The city map lists everything. If you're into Esperanto, undertakers, tobacco, clowns, firefighting, or the homes of dead composers, you'll find them all in Vienna.

These good museums try very hard but are submerged in the greatness of Vienna: **Jewish Museum of the City of Vienna** (€6.50, or €10 combo-ticket includes synagogue and Judenplatz Memorial and Museum—described on page 875, Sun–Fri 10:00–18:00, closed Sat, Dorotheergasse 11, tel. 01/535-0431, www.jmw.at), **Folkloric Museum of Austria** (Tue–Sun 10:00–17:00, closed Mon, Laudongasse 15, tel. 01/406-8905), and **Museum of Military History,** one of Europe's best if you like swords and shields (Heeresgeschichtliches Museum, €5.10, includes audioguide, Sat–Thu 9:00–17:00, closed Fri, Arsenal district, Objekt 18, tel. 01/795-610).

ACTIVITIES

People-Watching and Strolling

These activities allow you to take it easy and enjoy the Viennese good life.

▲**Stadtpark (City Park)**—Vienna's major park is a waltzing world of gardens, memorials to local musicians, ponds, peacocks, music in bandstands, and Viennese escaping the city. Notice the Jugendstil entrance at the Stadtpark U-Bahn station. The Kursalon, where Strauss was the violin-toting master of waltzing ceremonies, hosts daily touristy concerts in three-quarter time.

▲**Prater**—Since the 1780s, when the reformist Emperor Josef II gave his hunting grounds to the people of Vienna as a public

888 Rick Steves' Eastern Europe

park, this place has been Vienna's playground. While tired and a bit run-down these days, Vienna's sprawling amusement park still tempts visitors with its huge 220-foot-tall, famous, and lazy Ferris wheel *(Riesenrad),* roller coaster, bumper cars, Lilliputian railroad, and endless eateries. Especially if you're traveling with kids, this is a fun, goofy place to share the evening with thousands of Viennese (daily 9:00–24:00 in summer, but quiet after 22:00, U-1: Praterstern). For a local-style family dinner, eat at Schweizerhaus (good food, great Czech "Budweiser" beer, classic conviviality).

Donauinsel (Danube Island)—In the 1970s, the city dug a canal parallel to the mighty Danube River, creating both a flood barrier and a much-loved island escape from the city (easy U-Bahn access on U-1 to Donauinsel). This skinny, 12-mile-long island provides a natural wonderland. All along the traffic-free, grassy park you'll find Viennese—especially immigrants and those who can't afford their own cabin or fancy vacation—at play. The swimming comes tough, though, with rocky entries rather than sand. The best activity here is a bike ride (see "Getting Around Vienna—By Bike," page 831). Be careful—if you venture too far from the crowds, you're likely to encounter nudists on rollerblades.

A Walk in the Vienna Woods (Wienerwald)—For a quick side-trip into the woods and out of the city, catch the U-4 to Heiligenstadt, then bus #38A to Kahlenberg, where you'll enjoy great views and a café overlooking the city. From there, it's a peaceful 45-minute downhill hike to the *Heurigen* of Nussdorf or Grinzing to enjoy some new wine (see "Vienna's Wine Gardens," page 894). Your free TI-produced city map can be helpful...just go downhill. For the very best views, stay on bus #38A to Leopoldsberg, where you'll find a lovely Baroque church, a breezy *Weinstube* (pub), and shady tables with expansive panoramas of the city and the Danube. While it seems like a long way to go for a big view, buses are cheap (or free with a transit pass) and go twice an hour until 22:00.

Naschmarkt—Vienna's busy produce market is a great place for people-watching (see page 880).

Shopping

For Traditional Austrian Clothing—Two famous shops are fun to visit if you're interested in picking up a classy felt suit or dirndl. Most central is the fancy **Loden Plankl** shop (across from the Hofburg, at Michaelerplatz 6). But the **Tostmann Trachten** shop is the ultimate for serious shopping. Mrs. Tostmann powered the resurgence of this style. Her place is like a shrine to traditional Austrian and folk clothing—handmade and very expensive (Schottengasse 3A, 3-min walk from Am Hof, tel. 01/533-5331, www.tostmann.at).

Vienna

Day-Tripping to Slovakia

Fast Boat to Bratislava—The generally overlooked (I've long thought for good reason) capital of Slovakia is suddenly on the radar screen for Vienna travelers for three reasons: its newly lively economy (thanks to its recent EU membership and intense foreign investment); its popular discount airport (see page 167); and the new, fast, catamaran day trip. The DDSG line offers several daily boat trips from Schwedenplatz (where Vienna's old town hits the canal) to Bratislava in 75 minutes with good views (€25 each way, cheaper at less convenient times). For a fine day trip, you can depart at 8:30, arrive at 9:45 in Bratislava's Old Town, explore Bratislava, and return to Vienna at 14:30 or 18:15 (departures daily June–Oct only, tel. 01/58880, www.ddsg-blue-danube.at). The train makes the trip a bit faster and much cheaper (2–3/hr, 1-hour trip). For more on Bratislava, see page 164.

EXPERIENCES

Music Scene

As far back as the 12th century, Vienna was a mecca for musicians—both sacred and secular (troubadours). The Hapsburg emperors of the 17th and 18th centuries were not only generous supporters of music, but fine musicians and composers themselves. (Maria Theresa played a mean double bass.) Composers like Haydn, Mozart, Beethoven, Schubert, Brahms, and Mahler gravitated to this music-friendly environment. They taught each other, jammed together, and spent a lot of time in Hapsburg palaces. Beethoven was a famous figure, walking—lost in musical thought—through Vienna's woods. In the city's 19th-century belle époque, "Waltz King" Johann Strauss and his brothers kept Vienna's 300 ballrooms spinning.

This musical tradition continues into modern times, leaving some prestigious Viennese institutions for today's tourists to enjoy: the Opera (see page 845), the Boys' Choir, and the great Baroque halls and churches, all busy with classical and waltz concerts. As you poke into churches and palaces, you may hear groups practicing. You're welcome to sit and listen.

Vienna is Europe's music capital. It's music *con brio* (with brilliance) from October through June, reaching a symphonic climax during the Vienna Festival each May and June. Sadly, in July and August, the Boys' Choir, the Opera, and many more music companies are—like you—on vacation. But Vienna hums year-round with live classical music. Except for the Boys' Choir, the musical events listed below are offered in summer.

Vienna Boys' Choir—The boys sing (from a high balcony, where they are heard but not seen) at the 9:15 Sunday Mass from

September through March in the Hofburg's Imperial Chapel (Hofburgkapelle; entrance at Schweizerhof, from Josefsplatz go through tunnel). Reserved seats must be booked two months in advance (€5–29; reserve by fax, email, or mail: fax from the US 011-431-533-992-775, whmk@chello.at, or write Hofmusikkapelle, Hofburg-Schweizerhof, 1010 Wien; call 01/533-9927 for information only—they can't book tickets at this number). Much easier, standing room inside is free and open to the first 60 who line up. Even better, rather than line up early, you can simply swing by and stand in the narthex just outside, where you can hear the boys and see the Mass on a TV monitor. Boys' Choir concerts (on stage at the Musikverein) are also given Fridays at 16:00 in May, June, September, and October (€35–48, standing room goes on sale at 15:30 for €15, Karlsplatz 6; U-1, U-2, or U-4: Karlsplatz; tel. 01/5880-4141). They're nice kids, but, for my taste, not worth all the commotion. Remember, many churches have great music during Sunday Mass. Just 200 yards from the Boys' Choir chapel, Augustinian Church has a glorious 11:00 service each Sunday (see page 859).

Touristy Mozart and Strauss Concerts—If the music comes to you, it's touristy—designed for flash-in-the-pan Mozart fans.

Powdered-wig orchestra performances are given almost nightly in grand traditional settings (€25–50). Pesky wigged-and-powdered Mozarts peddle tickets in the streets. They rave about the quality of the musicians, but you'll get second-rate chamber orchestras, clad in historic costumes, performing the greatest hits of Mozart and Strauss. These are casual, easygoing concerts with lots of tour groups. While there's not a Viennese person in the audience, the tourists generally enjoy the evening. To sort through all your options, check with the ticket office in the TI (same price as on the street, but with all venues to choose from). Savvy locals suggest getting the cheapest tickets, as no one seems to care if cheapskates move up to fill unsold pricier seats. Critics explain that the musicians are actually very good (often Hungarians, Poles, and Russians working a season here to fund an entire year of music studies back home), but that they haven't performed much together so aren't "tight." Of the many fine venues, the Mozarthaus is a small room richly decorated in Venetian Renaissance style with intimate chamber-music concerts (€35–42, almost nightly at 19:30, Sat at 18:00, near St. Stephen's Cathedral at Singerstrasse 7, tel. 01/911-9077).

Strauss Concerts in the Kursalon—For years, Strauss concerts have been held in the Kursalon, where the "Waltz King" himself

directed wildly popular concerts 100 years ago (€38–54, concerts nightly generally at 20:15, tel. 01/512-5790 to reserve). Shows last 1.75 hours and are a mix of ballet, waltzes, and a 15-piece orchestra. It's touristy—tour guides holding up banners with group numbers wait out front after the show. Even so, the performance is playful, visually fun, fine quality for most, and with a tried-and-tested, crowd-pleasing format. The conductor welcomes the crowd in German (with a wink) and English; after that...it's English only.

Serious Concerts—These events, including the Opera, are listed in the monthly *Wien-Programm* (available at TI, described on page 826). Tickets run from €36 to €75 (plus a stiff 22 percent booking fee when booked in advance or through a box office like the one at the TI). While it's easy to book tickets online long in advance, spontaneity is also workable, as there are invariably people with tickets they don't need selling them at face value or less outside the door before concert time. If you call a concert hall directly, they can advise you on the availability of (cheaper) tickets at the door. Vienna takes care of its starving artists (and tourists) by offering cheap standing-room tickets to top-notch music and opera (generally an hour before each performance).

Theater an der Wien—Considered the oldest theater in Vienna, this venue was designed in 1801 for Mozart operas—intimate, with just a thousand seats. Reopened in 2006 for Mozart's 250th birthday, it treats Vienna's music lovers to a different opera every month—generally Mozart with a contemporary setting and modern interpretation—with the top-notch Vienna Radio Orchestra in the pit. With the reopening of Theater an der Wien, Vienna now supports three opera companies. This one is the only company playing through the summer (facing the Naschmarkt at Linke Wienzeile 6, tel. 01/5818-1110 for information, tickets available at www.theater-wien.at).

Summer of Music Festival (a.k.a. "KlangBogen")—This annual festival assures that even from June through September, you'll find lots of great concerts, choirs, and symphonies (special *KlangBogen* brochure at TI; get tickets at Wien Ticket pavilion off Kärntner Strasse next to the Opera, or go directly to location of particular event; Summer of Music tel. 01/42717, www.klangbogen.at).

Vienna

Musicals—The Wien Ticket pavilion sells tickets to contemporary American and British musicals done in the German language (€10–95, €2.50 standing room), and offers these tickets at half price from 14:00 until 17:00 the day of the show. Or you can reserve (full-price) tickets for the musicals by phone (call combined office for the three big theaters at tel. 01/58885).

Films of Concerts—To see free films of great concerts in a lively, outdoor setting near City Hall, check "Nightlife," page 896.

Dance Evening—If you'd like to actually dance (waltz and ballroom), or watch people who are really good at it, consider the Dance Evening at the Tanz Café in the Volksgarten (€5–6, May–Sept Sat from 19:00 and Sun from 18:00, www.volksgarten.at).

Classical Music to Go—To bring home Beethoven, Strauss, or the Wiener Philharmonic on a top-quality CD, shop at Gramola on the Graben or EMI on Kärntner Strasse.

Vienna's Cafés

In Vienna, the living room is down the street at the neighborhood coffee house. This tradition is just another example of Viennese expertise in good living. Each of Vienna's many long-established (and sometimes even legendary) coffee houses has its individual character (and characters). These classic cafés are a bit tired, with a shabby patina and famously grumpy waiters who treat you like an uninvited guest invading their living room. Still, it's a welcoming place. They offer newspapers, pastries, sofas, quick and light workers' lunches, elegance, smoky ambience, and "take all the time you want" charm for the price of a cup of coffee. Order it *melange* (like a cappuccino), *brauner* (strong coffee with a little milk), or *schwarzer* (black). Americans who ask for a latte are mistaken for Italians and given a cup of hot milk. Rather than buy the *International Herald Tribune* ahead of time, spend the money on a cup of coffee and read the paper for free, Vienna-style, in a café.

These are my favorites:

Café Hawelka has a dark, "brooding Trotsky" atmosphere, paintings by struggling artists who couldn't pay for coffee, a saloon-wood flavor, chalkboard menu, smoked velvet couches, an international selection of newspapers, and a phone that rings for regulars. Mrs. Hawelka died just a couple weeks after Pope John Paul II. Locals suspect the pontiff wanted her much-loved *Buchteln* (marmalade-filled doughnuts) in heaven. Mr. Hawelka, now alone and understandably a bit forlorn, still oversees the action (Wed–Mon 8:00–2:00 in the morning, Sun from 10:00, closed Tue, just off the Graben, Dorotheergasse 6).

Café Sperl dates from 1880, and is still furnished identically to the day it opened—from the coat tree to the chairs (Mon–Sat 7:00–23:00, Sun 11:00–20:00 except closed Sun July–Aug, just

Vienna 893

Viennese Coffee:
From Ottomans to Starbucks

The story of coffee in Vienna is steeped in legend. In the 17th century, the Ottomans (invaders from the Turkish Empire) were laying siege to Vienna. A spy working for the Austrians who infiltrated the Ottoman ranks got to know the Turkish lifestyle...including their passion for a drug called coffee. After the Austrians persevered, the ecstatic Hapsburg emperor offered the spy anything he wanted. The spy asked for the Ottomans' spilled coffee beans, which he gathered up to start the first coffee shop in town. (It's a nice story. But actually, there was already an Armenian in town running a coffee house.)

In the 18th century, coffee boomed as an aristocratic drink. In the 19th-century Industrial Age, people were expected to work 12-hour shifts, and coffee became a hit with the working class, too. By the 20th century, the Vienna coffee scene became so refined that old-timers remember when waiters brought a sheet with various shades of brown (like paint samples) so a customer could make clear exactly how milky she wanted her coffee.

In 2003, Vienna's first Starbucks boldly opened next to the Opera—across the street from the ultimate Old World coffee house, the Sacher Café. The locals like the easy-chair ambience and quality of Starbucks coffee, but think it's overpriced. Viennese coffee connoisseurs aren't impressed by quantity, can't relate to flavored coffee, and think drinking out of a paper cup is really trashy. The consensus: For the same price, you can have an elegant and traditional experience in a top Vienna-style coffee shop instead. While the "coffee to go" trend has been picked up by many bakeries and other joints, the Starbucks invasion has stalled, with nowhere near as many outlets as the Seattle-based coffee empire had planned.

off Naschmarkt near Mariahilfer Strasse, Gumpendorfer 11, tel. 01/586-4158).

Café Braunerhof, between the Hofburg and the Graben, offers a classic ambience with no tourists and live music on weekends (light classics, no cover, Sat–Sun 15:00–18:00), and a practical menu with daily specials (open long hours daily, Stallburgasse 2).

Other Classics in the Old Center: All of these places are open long hours daily: **Café Pruckel** (at Dr.-Karl-Lueger-Platz, across from Stadtpark at Stubenring 24); **Café Tirolerhof** (2 blocks from the Opera, behind the TI on Tegetthoffstrasse, at Führichgasse 8); and **Landtmann Café** (directly across from the City Hall on the Ringstrasse at Dr.-Karl-Lueger-Ring 4). The Landtmann is

Vienna

unique, as it's the only grand café built along the Ring with all the other grand buildings.

Vienna's Wine Gardens *(Heurigen)*

The *Heuriger* (HOY-rih-gur; plural is *Heurigen,* HOY-rih-gehn) is a uniquely Viennese institution. When the Hapsburgs let Vienna's vintners sell their own new wine (called *Sturm*) tax-free, several hundred families opened *Heurigen* (wine-garden restaurants clustered around the edge of town)—and a tradition was born. Today they do their best to maintain the old-village atmosphere, serving the homemade new wine (the last vintage, until November 11, when a new vintage year begins) with light meals and strolling musicians. Most *Heurigen* are decorated with enormous antique presses from their vineyards. Wine gardens might be closed on any given day; always call ahead to confirm, if you have your heart set on a particular place. (For a near-*Heuriger* experience right downtown, drop by Gigerl Stadttheuriger—see page 906.)

At any *Heuriger,* fill your plate at a self-serve cold-cut buffet (€6–9 for dinner). Food is sold by the *"10 dag"* unit. (A *dag* is a decigram, so *10 dag* is 100 grams...about a quarter-pound.) Dishes to look for...or look out for: *Stelze* (grilled knuckle of pork), *Fleischlaberln* (fried ground-meat patties), *Schinkenfleckerln* (pasta with cheese and ham), *Schmalz* (a spread made with pig fat), *Blunzen* (black pudding...sausage made from blood), *Presskopf* (jellied brains and innards), *Liptauer* (spicy cheese spread), *Kornspitz* (whole-meal bread roll), and *Kummelbraten* (crispy roast pork with caraway). Waitresses will then take your wine order (€2.20 per quarter-liter, about 8 oz). Many locals claim it takes several years of practice to distinguish between the *Sturm* wine and vinegar.

There are more than 1,700 acres of vineyards within Vienna's city limits, and countless *Heuriger* taverns. For a *Heuriger* evening, rather than go to a particular place, take a tram to the wine-garden district of your choice and wander around, choosing the place with the best ambience.

Getting to the *Heurigen:* You have three options: a 15-minute taxi ride, trams and buses, or a goofy tourist train.

Trams make a trip to the Vienna Woods quick and affordable. The fastest way is to ride U-4 to its last stop, Heiligenstadt, where trams and buses in front of the station fan out to the various neighborhoods. Ride tram D to its end point for Nussdorf. Ride bus #38A for Grinzing and on to the Kahlenberg viewpoint—#38A's end station. (Note that tram #38—different from bus #38A—starts at the Ring and finishes at Grinzing.) To get to Neustift am Walde, ride U-6 to Nussdorfer Strasse and catch bus #35A. Connect Grinzing and Nussdorf with bus #38A and tram D (transfer at Grinzinger Strasse).

The **Heurigen Express** tourist train is tacky but handy and relaxing, chugging you on a hop-on, hop-off circle from Nussdorf through Grinzing and around the Vienna Woods with light narration (€7.50, buy ticket from driver, 1 hour, daily April–Oct 12:00–18:00, departs from end station of tram D in Nussdorf at the top of the hour, tel. 01/479-2808).

Here are a couple of good *Heuriger* neighborhoods:

Grinzing—Of the many *Heuriger* suburbs, Grinzing is the most famous, lively...and touristy. Many people precede their visit to Grinzing by riding tram #38 from Schottentor (on the Ring) to its end (up to Kahlenberg for a grand Vienna view), and then ride 20 minutes back into the *Heuriger* action. From the Grinzing tram stop, follow Himmelgasse uphill toward the onion-top dome. You'll pass plenty of wine gardens—and tour buses—on your way up. Just past the dome, you'll find the heart of the *Heurigen*.

Heiligenstadt (Pfarrplatz)—Between Grinzing and Nussdorf, this area features several decent spots, including the famous and touristy Mayer am Pfarrplatz (a.k.a **Beethovenhaus,** Mon–Sat 16:00–24:00, Sun 11:00–23:00, bus #38A stop: Fernsprechamt/Heiligenstadt, walk 5 min uphill on Dübling Nestelbachgasse to Pfarrplatz 2, tel. 01/370-1287). This place has a charming inner courtyard with an accordion player and a sprawling backyard with a big children's play zone. Beethoven lived—and composed his *Sixth Symphony*—here in 1817. He hoped the local spa would cure his worsening deafness. **Weingut and Heuriger Werner Welser,** a block uphill from Beethoven's place, is lots of fun, with music nightly from 19:00 (open daily 15:30–24:00, Probusgasse 12, tel. 01/318-9797).

Nussdorf—A less-touristy district, characteristic and popular with the Viennese, Nussdorf has plenty of *Heuriger* ambience. Right at the end station of tram D, you'll find three long and skinny places side by side: **Schübel-Auer Heuriger** (Tue–Sat 16:00–24:00, closed Sun–Mon, Kahlenberger Strasse 22, tel. 01/370-2222) is my favorite. Also consider **Heuriger Kierlinger** (daily 15:30–24:00, Kahlenberger Strasse 20, tel. 01/370-2264) and **Steinschaden** (daily 15:00–24:00, Kahlenberger Strasse 18, tel. 01/370-1375). Walk through any of these and you pop out on Kahlenberger Strasse, where a walk 20 yards uphill takes you to some more eating and drinking fun: **Bamkraxler** ("Tree Jumper"), the only beer garden amid all these vineyards. It's a fun-loving, youthful place with fine keg beer and a regular menu—traditional, ribs, veggie, kids' menu—rather than the *Heuriger* cafeteria line (€6–10 meals, kids' playground, Tue–Sat 16:00–24:00, Sun 11:00–24:00, closed Mon, Kahlenberger Strasse 17, tel. 01/318-8800).

Sirbu Weinbau *Heuriger*—This option is actually in the vineyards, high above Vienna with great city and countryside views, a top-notch buffet, a glass veranda, and a traditional interior for cool weather. It's a bit more touristy, and dinner reservations are often required, since it's more upmarket and famous as "the ultimate setting" (April–Oct from 15:00, closed Sun, big children's play zone, Kahlenberger Strasse 210, tel. 01/320-5928). It's high above regular transit service, but fun to incorporate into a little walking. Ideally, ride bus #38A to the end at Kahlenberg, and ask directions to the *Heuriger* (a 20-min walk downhill; if you prefer an uphill walk, take tram D from the Ring to Nussdorf Platz and walk up Kahlenberger Strasse for 25 min).

NIGHTLIFE

If old music and new wine aren't your thing, Vienna has plenty of alternatives. For an up-to-date rundown on fun after dark, get the TI's free *Vienna Hype* booklet.

Open-Air Classical Music Cinema and Food Circus—A thriving people scene erupts each evening in July and August at the park in front of City Hall (Rathaus, on the Ringstrasse). Thousands of people keep a food circus of 24 simple stalls busy. There's not a paper plate or plastic cup anywhere, just real plates and glasses—Vienna wants the quality of eating to be as high as the music that's about to begin. About 3,000 folding chairs face a 60-foot-wide

screen up against the City Hall's Neo-Gothic facade. When darkness falls, an announcer explains the program, and then the music starts. The program is different every night—mostly movies of opera and classical concerts, with some films. The schedule is at the TI (programs generally last around two hours, starting when it's dark—between 21:30 in July and 20:30 in August).

Since 1991, the city has paid for 60 of these summer event nights each year. Why? To promote culture. Officials know the City Hall Music Festival is mostly a "meat market" where young people come to hook up. But they believe many of these people will develop a little appreciation of classical music and high culture on the side.

Bermuda Triangle (Bermuda Dreieck)—The area known as the "Bermuda Triangle"—north of St. Stephen's Cathedral, between Rotenturmstrasse and Judengasse—is the hot local nightspot. You'll find lots of music clubs and classy pubs, or *Beisl* (such as Krah Krah, Salzamt, Bermuda Bräu, and First Floor—for cocktails with live fish). The serious-looking guards have nothing to do with the bar scene—they're guarding the synagogue nearby.

Gürtel—The Gürtel is Vienna's outer ring road. The arches of a lumbering viaduct (which carries a train track) are now filled with trendy bars, sports bars, dance clubs, strip clubs, antique shops, and restaurants. To experience—or simply see—the latest scene in town, head out here. The people-watching—the trendiest kids on the block—makes the trip fun even if you're looking for exercise rather than a drink. Ride U-6 to Nussdorfer Strasse or Thaliastrasse and hike along the viaduct.

English Cinema—Two great theaters offer three or four screens of English movies nightly (€6–9): **English Cinema Haydn,** near my recommended hotels on Mariahilfer Strasse (Mariahilfer Strasse 57, tel. 01/587-2262, www.haydnkino.at); and **Artis International Cinema,** right in the town center a few minutes from the cathedral (Schultergasse 5, tel. 01/535-6570).

***The Third Man* at Burg Kino**—This movie, voted the best British film ever by the British Film Institute, takes place in 1949 Vienna—when it was divided like Berlin between the four victorious Allies. With a dramatic Vienna cemetery scene, coffeehouse culture surviving amid the rubble, and Orson Welles being chased through the sewers, the tale of a divided city about to fall under Soviet rule and rife with smuggling is an enjoyable two-hour experience while in Vienna (€8, in English with German subtitles; three or four showings weekly: Fri at 22:45, Tue and Sun afternoons depending on other film times; Opernring 19, tel. 01/587-8406, www.burgkino.at).

SLEEPING

As you move out from the center, hotel prices drop. My listings are in the old center (figure at least €100 for a decent double), along the likeable Mariahilfer Strasse (around €90), and near the Westbahnhof (around €70). While few accommodations in Vienna are air-conditioned (they are troubled by the fact that, per person, Las Vegas expends more energy keeping people cool than arctic Norway does to keep people warm), you can generally get fans on request. Places with elevators often have a few stairs to climb, too.

In June 2008, the European soccer championships come to town, driving up hotel prices for most of the month. Since some places will raise their rates much more than others, it's worth calling around.

These hotels lose big and you pay more if you find a room through Internet booking sites. Book direct by phone, fax, or email and save. The city has deliberately created an expensive hell for cars in the center. Don't even try. If you must bring a car into Vienna, leave it at an expensive garage.

Sleep Code

(€1 = about $1.40, country code: 43, area code: 01)
S = Single, **D** = Double/Twin, **T** = Triple, **Q** = Quad, **b** = bathroom, **s** = shower only. English is spoken at each place. Unless otherwise noted, credit cards are accepted, rooms have no air conditioning, and breakfast is included.

To help you sort easily through these listings, I've divided the rooms into three categories, based on the price for a standard double room with bath:

$$$ **Higher Priced**—Most rooms €120 or more.
 $$ **Moderately Priced**—Most rooms between €75–120.
  $ **Lower Priced**—Most rooms €75 or less.

Within the Ring, in the Old City Center

You'll pay extra to sleep in the atmospheric old center, but if you can afford it, staying here gives you the best classy Vienna experience.

$$$ Hotel am Stephansplatz is a four-star business hotel with 56 rooms. It's plush but not over-the-top, and reasonably priced for its incredible location—literally facing the cathedral—and sleek comfort. Every detail is modern and quality; breakfast is superb, with a view of the city waking up around the cathedral; and the staff is always ready with a friendly welcome (Db-€210–250, Tb-€250, €20 less July–Aug and in winter, €15 less Fri–Sun, children free or very cheap, air-con, free Internet access, Wi-Fi in lobby, sauna, elevator, Stephansplatz 9, U-1 or U-3: Stephansplatz, tel. 01/534-050, fax 01/5340-5710, www.hotelamstephansplatz.at, office@hotelamstephansplatz.at).

$$$ Pension Pertschy, circling an old courtyard, is bigger and more hotelesque than the options below. Its 50 rooms are huge, but well-worn and a bit musty. Those on the courtyard are quietest (Sb-€93, Db-€134–167 depending on room size, €20–30 cheaper off-season, extra bed-€34, non-smoking rooms, elevator, Habsburgergasse 5, U-1 or U-3: Stephansplatz, tel. 01/534-490, fax 01/534-4949, www.pertschy.com, pertschy@pertschy.com).

$$$ Pension Aviano is another peaceful place, with 17 comfortable rooms on the fourth floor above lots of old center action (Sb-€99, Db-€144–165 depending on size, cheaper in July–Aug and Nov–March, extra bed-€33, non-smoking rooms, fans, elevator, between Neuer Markt and Kärntner Strasse at Marco d'Avianogasse 1, tel. 01/512-8330, fax 01/5128-3306, www.secrethomes.at, aviano@secrethomes.at).

$$$ Hotel Schweizerhof is classy, with 55 big rooms, all the comforts, shiny public spaces, and a more formal ambience. It's

Vienna

HOTELS IN CENTRAL VIENNA

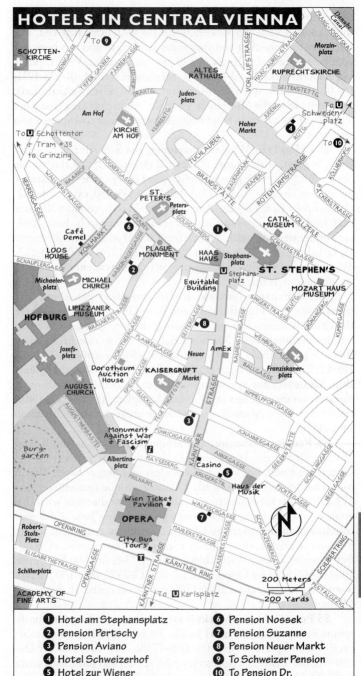

1. Hotel am Stephansplatz
2. Pension Pertschy
3. Pension Aviano
4. Hotel Schweizerhof
5. Hotel zur Wiener Staatsoper
6. Pension Nossek
7. Pension Suzanne
8. Pension Neuer Markt
9. To Schweizer Pension
10. To Pension Dr. Geissler

centrally located midway between St. Stephen's Cathedral and the Danube Canal (Sb-€84–95, Db-€113–140, extra bed-€32, low prices are for July–Aug and slow times, with cash and this book get your best price and then claim a 10 percent discount, Wi-Fi, elevator, Bauernmarkt 22, U-1 or U-3: Stephansplatz, tel. 01/533-1931, fax 01/533-0214, www.schweizerhof.at, office@schweizerhof.at). Since this is in the "Bermuda Triangle" nightclub area (see page 896), it can be noisy on weekends. Ask for a quiet room when you reserve.

$$$ Hotel zur Wiener Staatsoper, the Schweizerhof's sister hotel, is quiet, with a more traditional elegance. Its 22 tidy rooms come with high ceilings, chandeliers, and fancy carpets on parquet floors (tiny Sb-€79–86, Db-€113–128, Tb-€135–150, extra bed-€22, cheaper prices are for July–Aug and Dec–March, rooms €30 more than high season rates during soccer championship in June 2008, fans on request, elevator, a block from the Opera at Krugerstrasse 11, U-1, U-2, or U-4: Karlsplatz, tel. 01/513-1274, fax 01/513-127-415, www.zurwienerstaatsoper.at, office@zurwienerstaatsoper .at, manager Claudia).

$$ At Pension Nossek, an elevator takes you above any street noise into Frau Bernad's and Frau Gundolf's world, where the children seem to be placed among the lace and flowers by an interior designer. With 30 rooms right on the wonderful Graben, this is a particularly good value (S-€50–58, Ss-€60, Sb-€73–77, Db-€115, prices won't go up during June 2008 soccer championship, €28 extra for sprawling suites, extra bed-€35, cash only, elevator, Graben 17, U-1 or U-3: Stephansplatz, tel. 01/5337-0410, fax 01/535-3646, www.pension-nossek.at, reservation@pension -nossek.at).

$$ Pension Suzanne, as Baroque and doily as you'll find in this price range, is wonderfully located a few yards from the Opera. It's small, but run with the class of a bigger hotel. The 25 rooms are packed with properly Viennese antique furnishings (Sb-€79, Db-€100–121 depending on size, 4 percent discount with this book if you pay cash, prices won't go up during June 2008 soccer championship, extra bed-€20–25, spacious apartment for up to 6 also available, discounts in winter, fans on request, elevator, free Internet access, Walfischgasse 4, U-1, U-2, or U-4: Karlsplatz and follow signs for Opera exit, tel. 01/513-2507, fax 01/513-2500, www.pension-suzanne.at, info@pension-suzanne.at, manager Michael).

$$ Pension Neuer Markt is family-run, with 37 quiet, comfy rooms in a perfectly central locale. Its hallways have the ambience of a cheap cruise ship (Ss-€60–77, Sb-€90–130, smaller Ds-€80–96, Db-€110–135, prices vary with season and room size, extra bed-€19–22, request a quiet room when you reserve, fans, elevator,

Seilergasse 9, tel. 01/512-2316, fax 01/513-9105, www.hotelpension
.at/neuermarkt, neuermarkt@hotelpension.at).

$$ Schweizer Pension has been family-owned for three generations. The current owners, Anita and Gerhard, run an extremely
tight ship, offering 11 homey rooms for a great price, with parquet
floors and lots of tourist info (S-€42–47, big Sb-€55–67, D-€58–68,
Db-€78–92, Tb-€102–114, Qb-€126–131, prices depend on season
and room size, cash only, entirely non-smoking, elevator, laundry-
€16/load, Heinrichsgasse 2, U-2 or U-4: Schottenring, tel. 01/533-
8156, fax 01/535-6469, www.schweizerpension.com, schweizer
.pension@chello.at).

$$ Pension Dr. Geissler has 23 comfortable rooms on the
eighth floor of a modern, nondescript apartment building about
10 blocks northeast of St. Stephen's, near the canal (S-€48, Ss-
€68, Sb-€76, D-€65, Ds-€77, Db-€95, 20 percent less in winter,
elevator, Postgasse 14, U-1 or U-4: Schwedenplatz, tel. 01/533-
2803, fax 01/533-2635, www.hotelpension.at/dr-geissler, dr.geissler
@hotelpension.at).

Hotels and Pensions Along Mariahilfer Strasse

Lively Mariahilfer Strasse connects the Westbahnhof (West
Train Station) and the city center. The U-3 line, starting at the
Westbahnhof, goes down Mariahilfer Strasse to the cathedral.
This very Viennese street is a tourist-friendly and vibrant area filled
with shopping malls, simpler storefronts, and cafés. Its smaller
hotels and private rooms are generally run by people from the
non-German-speaking part of the former Hapsburg Empire (i.e.,
Eastern Europe). Most hotels are within a few steps of a U-Bahn
stop, just one or two stops from the Westbahnhof (direction from
the station: Simmering). The nearest place to do laundry is **Schnell
& Sauber Waschcenter** (wash-€4.50 for small load or €9 for large
load, plus a few euros to dry, daily 6:00–23:00, a few blocks north
of Westbahnhof on the east side of Urban-Loritz-Platz).

$$$ NH Hotels, a Spanish chain, runs two stern, passion-
less business hotels a few blocks apart on Mariahilfer Strasse.
Both rent ideal-for-families suites, each with a living room, two
TVs, bathroom, desk, and kitchenette (rack rate: Db suite-€155,
going rate usually closer to €110, plus €15 per person for optional
breakfast, apartments for 2–3 adults, kids under 12 free, non-
smoking rooms, elevator). The 78-room **NH Atterseehaus** is at
Mariahilfer Strasse 78 (U-3: Zieglergasse, tel. 01/5245-6000, fax
01/524-560-015, nhatterseehaus@nh-hotels.com), and the slightly
pricier **NH Wien** has 106 rooms at Mariahilfer Strasse 32 (U-3:
Neubaugasse—follow *Stiftgasse* signs to exit and turn left from top
of escalator; from Mariahilferstrasse, enter through shop passage-
way between Nordsee and Edusco—or from Lindergasse 9, tel.

HOTELS AND RESTAURANTS OUTSIDE THE RING

❶ Hotel NH Atterseehaus
❷ Hotel NH Wien
❸ Pension Corvinus & Haydn Hotel
❹ Pension Mariahilf

❺ Hotel Admiral
❻ Hotel Kugel
❼ Pension Hargita
❽ K&T Boardinghouse
❾ Pension Lindenhof
❿ Budai Ildiko Rooms
⓫ Hotel Mercure Wien Europaplatz
⓬ Hotel Ibis Wien
⓭ To Pension Fünfhaus, Wombat's City Hostel & Hostel Ruthensteiner
⓮ Jugendherberge Myrthengasse

⓯ Westend City Hostel
⓰ Lauria Rooms & Hostel
⓱ Spittelberg Quarter Eateries
⓲ Buffet Trzesniewski
⓳ Schnitzelwirt
⓴ Café Sperl
㉑ City Hall Food Circus
㉒ Landtmann Café
㉓ Launderette
㉔ British Bookshop
㉕ Imperial Furniture Collection

01/521-720, fax 01/521-7215, nhwien@nh-hotels.com). The website for both is www.nh-hotels.com.

$$ Pension Corvinus is bright, modern, and proudly and warmly run by a Hungarian family: Miklós, Judit, Anthony, and Zoltan. Its 12 comfortable rooms are spacious, and some are downright sumptuous (Sb-€55–65, Db-€89–99, Tb-€105–115, these prices promised with current edition of this book except during soccer championship in June, extra bed-€26, also has apartments with kitchens, most rooms non-smoking, air-con, elevator, free Internet access and Wi-Fi, parking garage-€11/day, on the third floor at Mariahilfer Strasse 57–59, U-3: Neubaugasse, tel. 01/587-7239, fax 01/587-723-920, www.corvinus.at, hotel@corvinus.at).

$$ Pension Mariahilf offers a clean, aristocratic air in an affordable and cozy pension package. Its 12 rooms are spacious but outmoded, with an Art Deco flair. Book direct and ask for a Rick Steves discount (Sb-€60–70, twin Db €80–95, Db-€90–106, Tb-€105–134, five-person apartment with kitchen-€120–150, lower prices are for off-season or longer stays, elevator, Mariahilfer Strasse 49, U-3: Neubaugasse, tel. 01/586-1781, fax 01/586-178-122, www.mariahilf-hotel.at, office@mariahilf-hotel.at).

$$ Haydn Hotel is big and formal, with masculine public spaces and 50 spacious rooms (Sb-€80–90, Db-€110–120, suites and family apartments, extra bed-€30, ask for a 10 percent Rick Steves discount, all rooms non-smoking, air-con, elevator, Internet access, parking-€14/day, Mariahilfer Strasse 57–59, U-3: Neubaugasse, tel. 01/5874-4140, fax 01/586-1950, www.haydn-hotel.at, info@haydn-hotel.at, Nouri).

$$ Hotel Admiral is huge and practical, with 80 large, workable rooms (Sb-€68, Db-€92, extra bed-€23, manager Alexandra promises these prices with cash and this book, cheaper in winter, breakfast-€6 per person, free Internet access, limited free parking if you call to reserve it—otherwise €10/day, a block off Mariahilfer Strasse at Karl-Schweighofer-Gasse 7, U-2 or U-3: Volkstheater, tel. 01/521-410, fax 01/521-4116, www.admiral.co.at, hotel@admiral.co.at).

$$ Hotel Kugel is run with pride and attitude. "Simple quality and good value" is the motto of the hands-on owner, Johannes Roller. It's a big 34-room hotel with simple Old World charm, offering a fine value (S-€35, Sb-€55, D-€48, Db-€83, supreme Db with canopy beds-€100, prices about 10 percent higher during June 2008 soccer championship, Siebensterngasse 43, at corner with Neubaugasse, U-3: Neubaugasse, tel. 01/523-3355, fax 01/5233-3555, www.hotelkugel.at, office@hotelkugel.at). Herr Roller is happy to offer his cheaper rooms for backpackers.

$ Pension Hargita rents 24 generally small, bright, and tidy rooms (mostly twins) with Hungarian decor. This spick-and-span, well-located place is a good value (S-€38, Ss-€45, Sb-€55, D-€52, Ds-€58, Db-€66, Ts-€73, Tb-€80, Qb-€110, extra bed-€12, breakfast-€5, reserve with credit card but pay with cash to get these rates, corner of Mariahilfer Strasse and Andreasgasse, Andreasgasse 1, U-3: Zieglergasse, tel. 01/526-1928, fax 01/526-0492, www.hargita.at, pension@hargita.at, Erika and Tibor). While the pension is on a bustling street, its windows block noise well.

$ K&T Boardinghouse is a top value, renting four big, bright, airy, and comfortable rooms facing the bustling Mariahilfer

Strasse (Db-€69, Tb-€89, Qb-
€109, €20–30 more in June 2008,
2-night minimum, no breakfast,
air-con-€10/day, cash only, non-
smoking, Internet access, coffee
in rooms, 3 flights up, no elevator, Mariahilfer Strasse 72, U-3:
Neubaugasse, tel. 01/523-2989,
fax 01/522-0345, www.kaled.at,
k.t@chello.at, Tina).

$ Pension Lindenhof rents 19 very basic, very worn but clean
rooms. It's a dark and mysteriously dated time-warp filled with
plants; rooms have outrageously high ceilings and teeny bathrooms (S-€32, Sb-€40, D-€54, Db-€72, hall shower-€2, cash
only, elevator, Lindengasse 4, U-3: Neubaugasse, tel. 01/523-0498,
fax 01/523-7362, pensionlindenhof@yahoo.com, Gebrael family,
Keram and his father speak English).

$ *Private Room:* If you're on a tight budget and wish you
had a grandmother to visit in Vienna, stay with English-speaking
Budai Ildiko. She rents high-ceilinged rooms with Old World
furnishings out of her dark and homey apartment. Two cavernous rooms, which sleep two to four, and a skinny twin room all
share one bathroom (S-€35–39, D-€46–49, T-€65–68, Q-€79, no
breakfast but free coffee, cash only, lots of tourist information,
classic old elevator, laundry-€4, Lindengasse 39, apartment #5,
U-3: Neubaugasse, tel. 01/523-1058, tel. & fax 01/526-2595, www
.wienwien.de, budai@hotmail.com).

Near the Westbahnhof (West Station)

$$$ Hotel Mercure Wien Europaplatz offers high-rise modern
efficiency and comfort in 210 air-conditioned rooms, directly
across from the Westbahnhof (Db-€130–170 depending on sea-
son, online deals as cheap as Db-€70 if you book well in advance,
breakfast-€14, elevator, parking-€15/day, Matrosengasse 6, U-3:
Westbahnhof, tel. 01/5990-1181, fax 01/597-6900, www.mercure
.com, h1707@accor.com).

$$ Hotel Ibis Wien, a modern high-rise hotel with American
charm, is ideal for anyone tired of quaint old Europe. Its 340
cookie-cutter rooms are bright, comfortable, and modern, with all
the conveniences (Sb-€71, Db-€88, Tb-€103, €5 cheaper in July,
€10–20 more during soccer championship in June 2008, breakfast-
€9, non-smoking rooms, air-con, elevator, parking garage-€11/day;
exit Westbahnhof to the right and walk 400 yards, Mariahilfer
Gürtel 22–24, U-3: Westbahnhof; tel. 01/59998, fax 01/597-9090,
www.ibishotel.com, h0796@accor.com).

$ Pension Fünfhaus is big, plain, clean, and stark—almost institutional. The neighborhood is run-down (with a few ladies loitering late at night) and the staff can be grouchy, but this 47-room pension offers the best doubles you'll find for around €50 (S-€34, Sb-€42, D-€47, Db-€57, T-€70, Tb-€85, 4-person apartment-€98, prices promised with current edition of this book, cash only, closed mid-Nov–Feb, Sperrgasse 12, U-3: Westbahnhof, tel. 01/892-3545 or 01/892-0286, fax 01/892-0460, www.pension5haus.at, pension5haus@tiscali.at, Frau Susi Tersch). Half the rooms are in the main building and half are in the annex, which has good rooms but is near the train tracks and a bit scary on the street at night. From the station, ride tram #52 or #58 two stops down Mariahilfer Strasse away from center, and ask for Sperrgasse. Crazy Chicken bike rental, listed on page 831, is just a block farther down Sperrgasse.

Cheap Dorms and Hostels near Mariahilfer Strasse

$ Jugendherberge Myrthengasse is your classic huge and well-run youth hostel, with 260 beds (€16–17 per person in 4- to 6-bed rooms, Db-€38–40, extra bed-€15, includes sheets and breakfast, non-members pay €3.50 extra, always open, no curfew, lockers and lots of facilities, Myrthengasse 7, tel. 01/523-6316, fax 01/523-5849, hostel@chello.at).

$ Westend City Hostel, just a block from the Westbahnhof and Mariahilfer Strasse, is well run and well located, with 180 beds in 4- to 12-bed dorms (€17–25 per person, depending on season and how many in the room—prices may go up during June 2008 soccer championship; includes sheets, breakfast, and locker; cash only, Internet access, laundry, Fügergasse 3, tel. 01/597-6729, fax 01/597-672-927, www.westendhostel.at, westendcityhostel@aon.at).

$ Lauria Rooms and Hostel is a creative little place run by friendly Gosha, with two 10-bed coed dorms with lockers for travelers ages 17 to 30 (€15/bed), plus several other rooms sleeping two to six each (any age, €24/bed, D-€48; Kaiserstrasse 77, tram #5 or a 10-min walk from Westbahnhof, tel. 01/522-2555, lauria_vienna @hotmail.com).

$ *More Hostels:* Other hostels with €17 beds and €40 doubles near Mariahilfer Strasse are **Wombat's City Hostel** (near tracks behind the station at Grangasse 6, tel. 01/897-2336, www .wombats-hostels.com, office@wombats-vienna.at) and **Hostel Ruthensteiner** (leave the Westbahnhof to the right and follow Mariahilferstrasse behind the station, then left on Haidmannsgasse for a block, then turn right and find Robert-Hamerling-Gasse 24, tel. 01/893-4202, www.hostelruthensteiner.com, info @hostelruthensteiner.com).

EATING

The Viennese appreciate the fine points of life, and right up there with waltzing is eating. The city has many atmospheric restaurants. As you ponder the Eastern European specialties on menus, remember that Vienna's diverse empire may be gone, but its flavor lingers.

While cuisines are routinely named for countries, Vienna claims to be the only *city* with a cuisine of its own: Vienna soups come with fillings (semolina dumpling, liver dumpling, or pancake slices). *Gulasch* is a beef ragout of Hungarian origin (spiced with onion and paprika). Of course, Viennese schnitzel *(Wiener Schnitzel)* is traditionally a breaded and fried veal cutlet (though pork is more common these days). Another meat specialty is boiled beef *(Tafelspitz)*. While you're sure to have *Apfelstrudel,* try the sweet cheese strudel, too *(Topfenstrudel*—wafer-thin strudel pastry filled with sweet cheese and raisins). The *dag* you see in some prices stands for "decigram" (10 grams). Therefore, *10 dag* is 100 grams, or about a quarter-pound.

On nearly every corner, you can find a colorful *Beisl* (BYE-zul). These uniquely Viennese taverns are a characteristic cross between an English pub and a French brasserie—filled with poetry teachers and their students, couples loving without touching, housewives on their way home from cello lessons, and waiters who enjoy serving hearty food and good drink at an affordable price. Ask at your hotel for a good *Beisl.*

Near St. Stephen's Cathedral

Each of these eateries is within about a five-minute walk of the cathedral.

Gigerl Stadtheuriger offers a friendly near-*Heuriger* experience (à la Grinzing—see "Vienna's Wine Gardens," page 894), often with accordion or live music, without leaving the city center. Just point to what looks good. Food is sold by the weight; 100 grams *(10 dag)* is about a quarter-pound (cheese and cold meats cost about €3 per 100 grams, salads are about €2 per 100 grams; price sheet is posted on the wall to right of buffet line). The *Karree* pork with herbs is particularly tasty and tender. They also have menu entrées, spinach strudel, quiche, *Apfelstrudel,* and, of course, casks of new and local wines (sold by the *Achtel*). Meals run €7 to €12 (daily 15:00–24:00, indoor/outdoor seating, behind cathedral, a block off Kärntner Strasse, a few cobbles off Rauhensteingasse on Blumenstock, tel. 01/513-4431).

Am Hof Eateries: The square called Am Hof (U-3: Herrengasse) is surrounded by a maze of atmospheric medieval lanes; the following eateries are all within a block of the square.

RESTAURANTS IN CENTRAL VIENNA

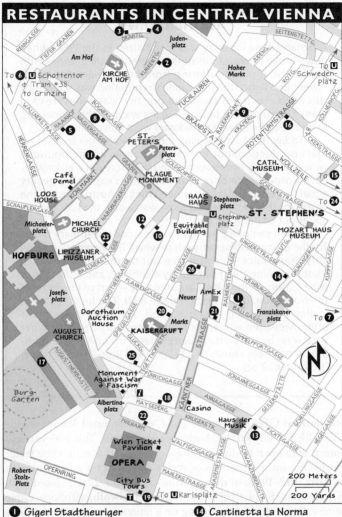

1. Gigerl Stadtheuriger
2. Restaurant Ofenloch
3. Brezel-Gwölb
4. Beisl "Zum Scherer"
5. Esterhazykeller
6. To Melker Stiftskeller
7. To Zu den Drei Hacken
8. Zum Schwarzen Kameel
9. Wrenkh Restaurant & Bar
10. Buffet Trzesniewski
11. Julius Meinl am Graben Deli
12. Café Hawelka & Reinthaler's Beisl
13. Gyros
14. Cantinetta La Norma
15. To Plachutta Restaurant
16. Zanoni & Zanoni Gelateria
17. Café Rest. Palmenhaus
18. Rosenberger Markt Rest.
19. Ruckenbauer (in underpass)
20. Kurkonditorei Oberlaa & Le Bol Patisserie Bistro
21. Danieli Ristorante
22. Sacher Café
23. Café Braunerhof
24. To Café Pruckel
25. Café Tirolerhof
26. American Bar

Austrian Wines

Austrian's wine industry was scandalized in the 1980s when news broke of major vintners sweetening their wines with antifreeze. Already suffering from being characterized as "sweet and light," the local wine's reputation was scarred by this news. Austrians claim the practice was widespread in many countries, and believe Austria was just the scapegoat. Regardless, the local wine industry went into a tailspin.

Today the Austrian wine industry no longer focuses on mass production, but instead specializes in fine boutique wines (generally not exported, and therefore not well known). Locals order white or red Austrian wines expecting quality equal to French and Italian wines. When in Austria, I go for the better local wines when dining—well worth the cost (generally about €4 per small glass).

When sampling Austrian wine, some vocabulary helps. Try the *grüner Veltliner* (dry white wine), *Traubenmost* (a heavenly grape juice—alcohol-free but on the verge of wine), *Most* (the same thing but lightly alcoholic), and *Sturm* ("new wine," stronger than *Most,* autumn only—part of the *Heuriger* phenomenon, described on page 894). The local red wine (called *Portugieser*) is pretty good. Since Austrian wine is often sweet, remember the word *trocken* (dry). You can order your wine by the *Viertel* (quarter-liter, 8 oz) or *Achtel* (eighth-liter, 4 oz). Beer comes in a *Krügel* (half-liter, 17 oz) or *Seidel* (third-liter, 10 oz).

Restaurant Ofenloch serves good, old-fashioned Viennese cuisine with friendly service, both indoors and out. This 300-year-old eatery, with great traditional ambience, is dressy (with white tablecloths) but intimate and woodsy. It's central but not overrun with tourists (€12–19 main dishes, Mon–Sat 12:00–22:45, closed Sun, Kurrentgasse 8, tel. 01/533-8844). **Brezel-Gwölb,** a Tolkien-esque wine cellar with outdoor dining on a quiet square, serves delicious light meals, fine *Krautsuppe* (cabbage soup), and old-fashioned Viennese dishes. It's ideal for a romantic late-night glass of wine (daily 11:30–23:30; leave Am Hof on Drahtgasse, then take first left to Ledererhof 9; tel. 01/533-8811). Around the corner, **Beisl "Zum Scherer"** is untouristy and serves traditional plates for €10. Sitting outside, you'll face a stern Holocaust memorial. Inside comes with a soothing woody atmosphere and intriguing decor (Mon–Sat 11:30–22:00, closed Sun, Judenplatz 7, tel. 01/533-5164). Just below Am Hof, the ancient and popular **Esterhazykeller** has traditional fare deep underground. For a cheap and sloppy buffet, climb down to the lowest cellar. For table service on a pleasant square, sit outside (Mon–Sat 11:00–23:00, Sun 16:00–23:00, Haarhof 1, tel. 01/533-3482).

Wine Cellars: These wine cellars are fun and touristy but typical, in the old center, with reasonable prices and plenty of smoke: **Melker Stiftskeller,** less touristy, is a *Stadtheuriger* in a deep and rustic cellar with hearty, inexpensive meals and new wine (Tue–Sat 17:00–24:00, closed Sun–Mon and July–mid-Aug, between Am Hof and Schottentor U-Bahn stop at Schottengasse 3, tel. 01/533-5530). **Zu den Drei Hacken** is famous for its local specialties (€10 plates, Mon–Sat 11:00–23:00, closed Sun, indoor/outdoor seating, Singerstrasse 28, tel. 01/512-5895).

Zum Schwarzen Kameel ("The Black Camel") is popular for its two classy but very different scenes: a tiny, elegant restaurant and a trendy wine bar. The small, dark-wood, 12-table, Art Nouveau restaurant serves fine gourmet Viennese cuisine (three-course dinner-€45–60 plus pricey wine). The wine bar is filled with a professional local crowd enjoying small plates from the same kitchen at a better price. This is *the* place for horseradish and thin-sliced ham (*Beinschinken mit Kren,* €7 a plate, *Achtung*—the horse-radish is *hot*). I'd order the *Vorspeisenteller* (a great antipasti dish that comes with ham and horseradish) and their *Tafelspitz* (boiled ham and vegetable, €15). Stand, grab a stool, or sit anywhere you can—it's customary to share tables in the wine-bar section. Fine Austrian wines are sold by the *Achtel* (eighth-liter glass) and listed on the board; Aussie bartender Karl can help you choose. They also have a buffet of tiny €1–2 sandwiches, warmly served by Mario, who calls himself the "best waiter in Vienna" (daily 8:30–22:00, Bognergasse 5, tel. 01/533-8125).

Wrenkh Restaurant and Bar is well liked for its vegetarian cuisine (though it does serve some meat dishes as well). Chef Wrenkh offers daily €8 lunch *menus* and €8 to €15 dinner plates in a bright, mod bar or in a dark, fancier restaurant (Mon–Fri 12:00–16:00 & 18:00–23:00, Sat 18:00–23:00, closed Sun, can be smoky, Bauernmarkt 10, tel. 01/533-1526).

Buffet Trzesniewski is an institution—justly famous for its elegant and cheap finger sandwiches and small beers (€1 each). Three different sandwiches and a *kleines Bier (Pfiff)* make a fun, light lunch. Point to whichever delights look tasty (or grab the English translation sheet and take time to study your 21 sandwich options). The classic favorites are *Geflügelleber* (chicken liver), *Matjes mit Zwiebel* (herring with onions), and *Speck mit Ei* (bacon and eggs). Pay for your sandwiches and a drink. Take your drink tokens to the lady on the right. Sit on the bench and scoot over to a tiny table when a spot opens up. Trzesniewski has been a Vienna favorite for a century...and many of its regulars seem to have been here for the grand opening (Mon–Fri 8:30–19:30, Sat 9:00–17:00,

Wieners in Wien

For hardcore Viennese cuisine, drop by a *Würstelstand*. The local hot-dog stand is a fixture on city squares throughout the old center, serving a variety of hot dogs and pickled side dishes with a warm corner-meeting-place atmosphere. The *Wiener* we know is named for Vienna, but the guy who invented the weenie studied in Frankfurt. Out of nostalgia for his school years, he named his fun fast food for that city... a Frankfurter. Only in Vienna are *Wieners* called *Frankfurters*. (Got that?)

Explore the fun menus. Be adventurous. The many varieties of hot dogs cost €2–3 each. Key words: *Weisswurst*—boiled white sausage, *Bosna*—with onions and curry, *Käsekrainer*—with melted cheese inside, *Debreziner*—spicy Hungarian, *Frankfurter*—our weenie, *frische*—fresh ("eat before the noon bells"), *Kren*—horseradish, and *Senf*—mustard (ask for *süss*—sweet or *scharf*—sharp). Generally, the darker the weenie, the spicier it is. Only a tourist puts the sausage in a bun like a hot dog. Munch alternately between the meat and the bread ("that's why you have two hands"), and you'll look like a native.

You'll find particularly good stands on Hoher Markt, the Graben, and in front of the Albertina Museum.

closed Sun; 50 yards off the Graben, nearly across from brooding Café Hawelka, Dorotheergasse 2; tel. 01/512-3291). In the fall, this is a good opportunity to try the fancy grape juices—*Most* or *Traubenmost* (described on page 908). Their other location, at Mariahilfer Strasse 95, serves the same sandwiches with the same menu in the same ambience, and is near many recommended hotels.

Reinthaler's Beisl is a time-warp serving simple, traditional *Beisl* fare all day. It's handy for its location (a block off the Graben, across the street from Buffet Trzesniewski) and because it's a rare restaurant in the center that's open on Sunday. Its fun, classic interior winds way back (use the handwritten daily menu rather than the printed English one, €6–10 plates, daily 11:00–22:30, at Dorotheergasse 4, tel. 01/513-1249).

Julius Meinl am Graben, a posh supermarket right on the Graben, has been famous since 1862 as a top-end delicatessen with all the gourmet fancies. Along with the picnic fixings on the shelves, there's a café with light meals and great outdoor seating, a stuffy and pricey restaurant upstairs, and a take-away counter (shop open Mon–Fri 8:30–19:30, Sat 9:00–18:00, closed Sun; restaurant open Mon–Sat until 24:00, closed Sun; Am Graben 19, tel. 01/532-3334).

Vienna

Akakiko Sushi: If you're just schnitzeled out, this small chain of Japanese restaurants with an easy sushi menu may suit you. The €9 bento box meals are a tasty value. Three locations have no charm but are fast, reasonable, and convenient (€7–10 meals, all open daily 10:30–23:30): Singerstrasse 4 (a block off Kärntner Strasse near the cathedral), Heidenschuss 3 (near other recommended eateries just off Am Hof), and Mariahilfer Strasse 42–48 (fifth floor of Kaufhaus Gerngross, near many recommended hotels).

Gyros is a humble little Greek/Turkish joint run by Yilmaz, a fun-loving Turk from Izmir. He simply loves to feed people—the food is great, the price is cheap, and you almost feel like you took a quick trip to Turkey (daily 10:00–21:30, a long block off Kärntner Strasse at corner of Fichtegasse and Seilerstätte, tel. 01/228-9551).

Cantinetta La Norma, a short walk from the cathedral, serves Italian dishes amid a cozy ambience that's both elegant and energetic. Even on weeknights the small dining area is abuzz with friendly chatter among its multinational, extremely loyal regulars. Owner Paco and his staff Hany and Novka will happily show you their snapshots of the notables who've dined here (€7–18 entrées, daily 11:00–24:00, Franziskaner Platz 3, tel. 01/512-8665).

Plachutta Restaurant, with a stylish green-and-crème, elegant-but-comfy interior and breezy covered terrace, is famous for the best beef in town. You'll find an enticing menu with all the classic Viennese beef dishes, fine desserts, attentive service, and an enthusiastic and sophisticated local clientele. They've developed the art of beef to the point of producing popular cookbooks. Their specialty is a page-long list of *Tafelspitz*—a traditional copper pot of boiled beef with broth and vegetables. Treat the broth as your soup course. A chart on the menu lets you choose your favorite cut. Make a reservation for this high-energy Vienna favorite (€16–21 per pot, daily 11:30–23:30, 10-min walk from St. Stephen's Cathedral to Wollzeile 38, U-3: Stubentor, tel. 01/512-1577).

Ice Cream!: **Zanoni & Zanoni** is a very Italian *gelateria* run by an Italian family. They're mobbed by happy Viennese hungry for their huge €2 cones to go. Or, to relax and watch the thriving people scene, lick your gelato in their fun outdoor area (daily 7:00–24:00, 2 blocks up Rotenturmstrasse from cathedral at Lugeck 7, tel. 01/512-7979).

Near the Opera

Café Restaurant Palmenhaus overlooks the Palace Garden (Burggarten—see page 858). Tucked away in a green and peaceful corner two blocks behind the Opera in the Hofburg's back yard, this is a world apart. If you want to eat modern Austrian cuisine with palm trees rather than tourists, this is it. And, since it's at the edge of a huge park, it's great for families. Their fresh fish with generous vegetables specials are on the board (€8 two-course lunches available Mon–Fri, €15–18 entrées, open daily 10:00–24:00, serious vegetarian dishes, fish, extensive wine list, indoors in greenhouse or outdoors, tel. 01/533-1033).

Rosenberger Markt Restaurant is mobbed with tour groups. Still, if you don't mind a freeway cafeteria ambience in the center of the German-speaking world's classiest city, this self-service eatery is fast and easy. It's just a block toward the cathedral from the Opera. The best cheap meal here is a small salad or veggie plate stacked high (daily 10:30–23:00, lots of fruits, veggies, fresh-squeezed juices, addictive banana milk, ride the glass elevator downstairs, Maysedergasse 2, tel. 01/512-3458).

Ruckenbauer, a fast-food kiosk in a transit underpass (under the street in front of the Opera), is a favorite for a quick bite (Mon–Fri 6:00–20:00, Sat–Sun 9:00–20:00). Their €1.50 *Tramezzini* sandwiches and fine pastries make a classy, quick picnic lunch or dinner before the Opera (just 100 yards away).

Kurkonditorei Oberlaa may not have the royal and plush fame of Demel (see page 844), but this is where Viennese connoisseurs serious about the quality of their pastries go to get fat. With outdoor seating on Neuer Markt, it's particularly nice on a hot summer day (€10 daily three-course lunches, great selection of cakes, daily 8:00–20:00, Neuer Markt 16, tel. 01/5132-9360). Next door, **Le Bol Patisserie Bistro** satisfies your need for something French. The staff speaks to you in French, serving fine €8 salads, baguette sandwiches, and fresh croissants (daily 8:00–22:00, Neuer Markt 14).

Danieli Ristorante is your best classy Italian bet in the old center. White-tablecloth dressy, but not stuffy, it has reasonable prices (€8–13 pizza and pastas, fresh fish, open daily, 30 yards off Kärntner Strasse opposite Neuer Markt at Himmelpfortgasse 3, tel. 01/513-7913).

City Hall (Rathausplatz) Food Circus: During the summer, scores of outdoor food stands and hundreds of picnic tables are set up in the park in front of the City Hall. Local mobs enjoy mostly ethnic meals on disposable plates for decent-but-not-cheap prices. The fun thing here is the energy of the crowd, and a feeling that you're truly eating as the Viennese do...not schnitzel and quaint traditions, but trendy "world food" with young people out having fun in a fine Vienna park setting (July–Aug daily from 11:00 until late, in front of City Hall on the Ringstrasse).

Spittelberg Quarter

A charming cobbled grid of traffic-free lanes and Biedermeier apartments has become a favorite neighborhood for Viennese wanting a little dining charm between the MuseumsQuartier and Mariahilfer

Strasse (handy to many recommended hotels; take Stiftgasse from Mariahilfer Strasse, or wander over here after you close down the Kunsthistorisches Museum). Tables tumble down sidewalks and into breezy courtyards filled with appreciative natives enjoying dinner or a relaxing drink. It's only worth the trip on a balmy summer evening, as it's dead in bad weather. Stroll Spittelberggasse, Schrankgasse, and Gutenberggasse and pick your favorite. Don't miss the vine-strewn wine garden at Schrankgasse 1.

Amerlingbeisl, with a casual atmosphere both on the cobbled street and in its vine-covered courtyard, is a great value (€7 plates, €6–8 daily specials, salads, veggie dishes, traditional specialties, daily 9:00–24:00, Stiftgasse 8, tel. 01/526-1660).

Plutzer Bräu, next door, is also good (ribs, burgers, traditional dishes, Tirolean beer from the keg, daily 11:00–2:00 in the morning, food until 22:30, Schrankgasse 4, tel. 01/526-1215).

Witwe Bolte is classier and a good choice for uninspired Viennese cuisine with tablecloths. Its tiny square has wonderful leafy ambience (daily 11:30–23:30, closed 15:00–17:30 in winter, Gutenberggasse 13, tel. 01/523-1450).

Zu Ebener Erde und Erster Stock is a charming little restaurant with a near-gourmet menu. The upstairs is Biedermeier-style, with violet tablecloths and seating for about 20. The downstairs is more casual and woody. Reservations are smart (modern Viennese seasonal fixed-price meal-€45, traditional three-course fixed-price meal-€34, Tue–Sat from 18:00, closed Sun–Mon, Burggasse 13, tel. 01/523-6254).

Near Mariahilfer Strasse

Mariahilfer Strasse is filled with reasonable cafés serving all types of cuisine. For a quick yet traditional bite, consider the venerable **Buffet Trzesniewski** sandwich bar at Mariahilfer Strasse 95 (see page 909).

Schnitzelwirt is an old classic with a 1950s patina and a clientele to match. In this smoky, working-class place, no one finishes their schnitzel ("to go" for the dog is wrapped in newspaper, "to go" for you is wrapped in foil). You'll find no tourists, just cheap €6 schnitzel meals (Mon–Sat 10:00–23:00, closed Sun, Neubaugasse 52, tel. 01/523-3771).

Naschmarkt (described on page 880) is Vienna's best Old World market, with plenty of fresh produce, cheap local-style eateries, cafés, *Döner Kebab* and sausage stands, and the best-value sushi in town (Mon–Fri 6:00–18:30, Sat 6:00–17:00, closed Sun, closes earlier in winter, U-4: Kettenbrückengasse). Survey the lane of eateries at the end of the market nearest the Opera. The circa 1900 pub is inviting. Picnickers can buy supplies at the market and eat on nearby Karlsplatz (plenty of chairs facing the Charles Church).

TRANSPORTATION CONNECTIONS

Vienna has two main train stations: the Westbahnhof (West Station), serving Munich, Salzburg, Melk, and some Budapest-bound trains; and the Südbahnhof (South Station), serving the Czech Republic, Poland, Slovenia, Croatia, other Budapest-bound trains, and usually Italy (though some Italy-bound trains go from the Westbahnhof). A third station, Franz Josefs, serves Austria's Danube Valley (including Krems, but Melk is served by the Westbahnhof). There are exceptions, so always confirm which station your train leaves from. Metro line U-3 connects the Westbahnhof with the center, tram D takes you from the Südbahnhof and the Franz Josefs station to downtown, and tram #18 connects Westbahnhof and Südbahnhof stations. Train info: tel. 051-717 (to get an operator, dial 2, then 2).

To Eastern Europe: Vienna is a handy springboard for a quick trip to Prague or Budapest—it's three hours by train to Budapest (€40 one-way; covered by any railpass that includes both Austria and Hungary) and four hours to Prague (€44 one-way, €88 round-trip). Purchase tickets at the station or at most travel agencies.

From Vienna by Train to: Bratislava (2–3/hr, 1 hr; or try the new boat trip described on page 889), **Budapest** (6/day, 3 hrs), **Prague** (6/day direct, 4.5 hrs, more with 1 change, 5–6 hrs), **Český Krumlov** (5/day, 5–6 hrs, 1–2 changes, connections from all three Vienna stations depending on time of day), **Kraków** (4/day, 6.5–7.5 hrs, 2 direct including a night train departing at about 22:30, arriving around 6:00), **Warsaw** (3/day direct including 1 night train, 8–9 hrs), **Ljubljana** (6/day, 6–7 hrs, convenient early-morning direct train, others change in Villach or Maribor), **Zagreb** (7/day, 6–8 hrs, 2 direct, others with up to 4 changes including Villach and Ljubljana), **Krems** (hourly, 1 hr), **Melk** (2/hr, 1.25 hrs, some with change in St. Pölten), **Salzburg** (1–2/hr, 3 hrs), **Innsbruck** (every 2 hrs, 5 hrs), **Munich** (2/day direct, 4 hrs; otherwise about hourly, 4.75–5.75 hrs, transfer in Salzburg), **Dresden** (2/day, 7 hrs; plus 1 night train/day, 9 hrs), **Berlin** (5/day, 9–9.5 hrs, longer on night train), **Zürich** (3/day, 9 hrs, 1 with changes in Innsbruck and Feldkirch), **Rome** (1/day, 13 hrs), **Venice** (2 direct/day, 7–8.5 hrs; plus 1 direct night train, 12 hrs), **Frankfurt** (3/day direct, 2 more with change in Munich or Würzburg, 7–8 hrs), **Amsterdam** (2/day, 11.5 hrs, 1–2 changes).

Excursions by Car with Driver: Those wishing they had wheels may consider hiring Johann (see page 831) for Danube excursions from Vienna or en route to Salzburg (particularly economic for groups of 3–4).

UNDERSTANDING YUGOSLAVIA

Americans struggle to understand the complicated breakup of Yugoslavia—especially when visiting countries that rose from its ashes, such as Croatia and Slovenia. Talking to the locals can make it even more confusing: Everyone in the former Yugoslavia seems to have a slightly different version of events. A very wise Bosniak told me, "Listen to all three sides—Muslim, Serb, and Croat. Then decide for yourself what you think." That's the best advice I can offer. But since you likely won't have time for that on your brief visit, here's an admittedly oversimplified, as-impartial-as-possible history to get you started.

Balkan Peninsula 101

To begin, it helps to have a handle on the different groups who've lived in the Balkans—the southeastern European peninsula between the Adriatic and the Black Sea, stretching from Hungary to Greece. The Balkan Peninsula has always been a crossroads of cultures. The Illyrians, Greeks, and Romans had settlements here before the Slavs moved into the region from the north around the seventh century. During the next millennium and a half, the western part of the peninsula—which would become Yugoslavia—was divided by a series of cultural, ethnic, and religious fault lines.

The most important influences were three religions: **Western Christianity** (i.e., Roman Catholicism, first brought to the western part of the region by Charlemagne, and later reinforced by the Austrian Hapsburgs), **Eastern Orthodox Christianity** (brought to the east from the Byzantine Empire), and **Islam** (in the south, from the Ottomans).

Two major historical factors made the Balkans what they are today: The first was the **split of the Roman Empire** in the fourth century A.D., dividing the Balkans down the middle into Roman

Who's Who in Yugoslavia

Yugoslavia was made up of six republics, which were inhabited by eight different ethnicities (not counting small minorities such as Jews, Germans, and Roma). This chart shows each ethnicity, and in which republic(s) they were most concentrated. Not coincidentally, the more ethnically diverse a region was, the more conflict it experienced.

	Serbia*	Croatia	Bosnia-Herz.	Slovenia	Montenegro	Macedonia
Serbs (Orthodox)	x	x	x		x	
Croats (Catholic)		x	x			
Bosniaks (Muslims)			x			
Slovenes (Catholic)				x		
Macedonians (like Bulgarians)						x
Montenegrins (like Serbs)					x	
Albanians	x		x			x
Hungarians	x	x		x		

*Within Serbia were two "autonomous provinces," each of which was dominated by a non-Slavic ethnic group: Hungarians in Vojvodina and Albanians in Kosovo. Tito intentionally set up these two autonomous provinces to prevent Serbia from becoming too powerful. Tito was right: Slobodan Milošević's annexation of Kosovo is precisely what tipped the balance of power in Yugoslavia, sparking the Balkan wars of the 1990s.

Catholic (west) and Byzantine Orthodox (east)—roughly along today's Bosnian-Serbian border. The second was the **invasion of the Islamic Ottomans** in the 14th century. The Ottoman victory at the Battle of Kosovo (1389) began five centuries of Islamic influence in Bosnia-Herzegovina and Serbia, further dividing the Balkans into Christian (north) and Muslim (south).

Because of these and other events, several distinct ethnic identities emerged. Confusingly, the major "ethnicities" of Yugoslavia are all South Slavs—they're descended from the same ancestors, and speak essentially the same language, but they practice different religions. Catholic South Slavs are called **Croats** or **Slovenes**

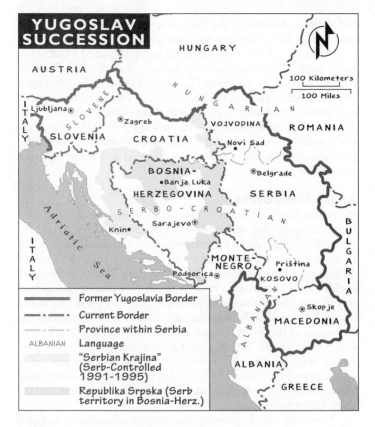

YUGOSLAV SUCCESSION

Former Yugoslavia Border

Current Border

Province within Serbia

ALBANIAN Language

"Serbian Krajina" (Serb-Controlled 1991-1995)

Republika Srpska (Serb territory in Bosnia-Herz.)

(mostly west of the Dinaric Mountains: Croats along the Adriatic coast, and Slovenes farther north, in the Alps); Orthodox South Slavs are called **Serbs** (mostly east of the Dinaric range); and Muslim South Slavs are called **Bosniaks** (whose ancestors converted to Islam under the Ottomans, mostly living in the Dinaric Mountains). To complicate matters, the region is also home to several non-Slavic minority groups, including **Hungarians** (in the northern province of Vojvodina) and **Albanians,** concentrated in the southern province of Kosovo (descended from the Illyrians, who lived here long before the Greeks and Romans).

Of course, these geographic divisions are extremely general. The groups overlapped a lot—which is exactly why the breakup of Yugoslavia was so contentious. One of the biggest causes of this ethnic mixing came in the 16th century. The Ottomans were threatening to overrun Europe, and the Austrian Hapsburgs wanted a buffer zone—a "human shield." The Hapsburgs encouraged Serbs who were fleeing from Ottoman invasions to settle along today's Croatian-Bosnian border (known as *Vojna Krajina*, or "Military Frontier"). The Serbs stayed after the Ottomans left, establishing homes in predominantly Croat communities.

After the Ottoman threat subsided in the late 17th century, some of the Balkans (basically today's Slovenia and Croatia) became part of the Austrian Hapsburg Empire. The Ottomans stayed longer in the south and east (today's Bosnia-Herzegovina and Serbia)—making the cultures in these regions even more different. Serbia finally gained its independence from the Ottomans in the mid-19th century, but not long before World War I erupted... after a disgruntled Bosnian Serb nationalist killed the Austrian archduke.

South Slavs Unite

When the Austro-Hungarian Empire fell at the end of World War I, the European map was redrawn for the 20th century. After centuries of being governed by foreign powers, the South Slavs began to see their shared history as more important than their minor differences. A tiny country of a few million Croats or Slovenes couldn't have survived on its own. Rather than be absorbed by a non-Slavic power, the South Slavs decided that there was safety in numbers, and banded together as a single state—first called the "Kingdom of the Serbs, Croats, and Slovenes" (1918), later known as the Kingdom of Yugoslavia ("Land of the South Slavs"—*yugo* means "south"). "Yugoslav unity" was in the air, but this new union was fragile and ultimately bound to fail (not unlike the partnership between the Czechs and Slovaks, formed at the same time and for much the same reasons).

From the very beginning, the various ethnicities struggled for power within the new union of Yugoslavia. The largest group was the Serbs (about 45 percent), followed by the Croats (about 25 percent). Croats often felt they were treated as lesser partners under the Serbs. For example, many Croats objected to naming the country's official language "Serbo-Croatian"—why not "Croato-Serbian?" Serbia already had a very strong king, Alexander Karađorđević, who immediately made attempts to give his nation a leading role in the federation. A nationalistic Croatian politician named Stjepan Radić, pushing for a more equitable division of powers, was shot by a Serb during a parliament session in 1928. Karađorđević abolished the parliament and became dictator. Six years later, infuriated Croatian separatists killed him.

Many Croat nationalists sided with the Nazis in World War II in the hopes that it would be their ticket to independence from Serbia. The Nazi puppet government in Croatia (called the Ustaše) conducted an extermination campaign, murdering many Serbs (along with Jews and Roma) living in Croatia; other Serbs were forced to flee the country or convert to Catholicism. Most historians consider the Ustaše concentration camps to be the first instance of "ethnic cleansing" in the Balkans...and the Serbs' long memory of it may go far in explaining their own ethnic cleansing of the Croats in the 1990s.

At the end of World War II, the rest of Eastern Europe was "liberated" by the Soviets—but the Yugoslavs regained their independence on their own, as their communist Partisan Army forced out the Nazis. After the short but rocky Yugoslav union between the World Wars, it seemed that no one could hold the southern Slavs together in a single nation. But there was one man who could, and did: Tito.

Tito's Yugoslavia

Communist Party president and war hero Josip Broz (a.k.a. Tito) emerged as a political leader after World War II. With a Slovene for a mother, a Croat for a father, a Serb for a wife, and a home in Belgrade, Tito was a true Yugoslav. Tito had a compelling vision that this fractured union of the South Slavs could function. And, under him, it did.

Tito's new incarnation of Yugoslavia aimed for a more equitable division of powers. It was made up of six republics, each with its own parliament and president: **Croatia** (mostly Catholic Croats), **Slovenia** (mostly Catholic Slovenes), **Serbia** (mostly Orthodox Serbs), **Bosnia-Herzegovina** (the most diverse—mostly Muslim Bosniaks, but with very large Croat and Serb populations), **Montenegro** (mostly Serb-like Montenegrins), and **Macedonia** (with about 25 percent Albanians and 75 percent Macedonians—who share similarities with both Bulgarians and Serbs). There were also two autonomous provinces, each one dominated by an ethnicity that was a minority in greater Yugoslavia: Albanians in **Kosovo** (to the south) and Hungarians in **Vojvodina** (to the north). Tito hoped that by allowing these two provinces some degree of independence—including voting rights—they could balance the political clout of Serbia, preventing a single republic from dominating the union.

Each republic managed its own affairs...but always under the watchful eye of president-for-life Tito, who said that the borders between the republics should be "like white lines in a marble column." Nationalism was strongly discouraged, and Tito's tight control—though sometimes oppressive—kept the country from unraveling. For more on Tito, see the sidebar.

Tito's Yugoslavia was communist, but it wasn't Soviet communism; you'll find no statues of Lenin or Stalin here. Despite strong pressure from Moscow, Tito refused to ally himself with the Soviets—and therefore received good will (and $2 billion) from the United States. Tito's vision was for a "third way," where Yugoslavia

Tito
(1892–1980)

The Republic of Yugoslavia was the vision of a single man, who made it reality. Josip Broz—better known as Maršal Tito—presided over the most peaceful and prosperous era in this region's long and troubled history. Nearly three decades after his death, Tito is beloved by many of his former subjects...and yet, he was a communist dictator known for torturing and executing his political enemies. This love-him-and-hate-him autocrat is one of the most complex and quixotic figures in the history of this very complicated land.

Josip Broz was born in 1892 to a Slovenian mother and a Croatian father in the northern part of today's Croatia, which then belonged to the Austro-Hungarian Empire. After growing up in the rural countryside, Tito was trained as a metalworker. He was drafted into the Austro-Hungarian army, went to fight on the Eastern Front during World War I, and was captured and sent to Russia as a prisoner of war. Freed by Bolsheviks, Broz fell in with the Communist Revolution...and never looked back.

At war's end, Broz returned home to the newly independent Kingdom of Yugoslavia, where he worked in conjunction with the Soviets to build a national Communist Party. As a clandestine communist operative, he adopted the codename with which he would always be associated: Tito. (Some people half-joke that the name came from Tito's authoritarian style: *"Ti, to!"* means "You, do this!")

When the Nazis occupied Yugoslavia, Tito became the commander of a homegrown, communist Partisan Army. Through guerilla tactics, Tito's clever maneuvering, and sheer determination, the Partisans liberated their country. And, because they did so mostly without support from the USSR's Red Army, Yugoslavia could set its own course after the war.

The war hero Tito quickly became the "president for life" of postwar Yugoslavia. But even as he introduced communism to his country, he retained some elements of a free-market economy—refusing to become a satellite of Moscow. He also led the creation of the worldwide Non-Aligned Movement, joining with nations in Africa, the Middle East, Asia, and Latin America in refusing to ally with the US or USSR. Stubborn but suitably cautious, Tito expertly walked a tightrope between East and West.

There was a dark side to Tito. In the early years of his regime, Tito resorted to brutal, Stalin-esque tactics to assert his control. Immediately following World War II, the Partisan Army massacred tens of thousands of soldiers who had supported the Nazis. Then Tito ruthlessly and systematically routed out other Nazi supporters, arresting, trying, torturing, or executing those who did not accept his new regime. One of his highest-profile enemies was the Croatian archbishop Alojzije Stepinac, whom Tito imprisoned for five years (see page 776).

But once he had gained full control, Tito moved away from strong-arm tactics and into a warm-and-fuzzy era of Yugoslav brotherhood. Tito believed that the disparate peoples of Yugoslavia could live in harmony...and, under him, they did. For example, every Yugoslav had to serve in the National Army, and Tito made sure that each unit was a microcosm of the complete Yugoslavia—with equal representation from each ethnic group. This meant that Yugoslavs from diverse backgrounds were forced to work together and socialize, and as a result, became friends.

Tito's reign is a case study in the power of the cult of person-ality. Rocks on hillsides throughout Yugoslavia were rearranged to spell "TITO," and his portrait hung over every family's dinner table. Each of the six republics renamed one of its cities for their dictator (such as Titograd for Montenegro's Podgorica, or Titovo Velejne in Slovenia). The main street and square in virtually every town was renamed for Tito (and many have kept the name). Tito also had vacation villas in all of Yugoslavia's most beautiful areas, including Lake Bled (see page 568), Croatia's Brijuni Islands, and the Montenegrin Coast. People sang patriotic anthems to their Druža (Comrade) Tito: "Comrade Tito, we bow to you."

Tito died in 1980 in a Slovenian hospital. His body was loaded onto his Blue Train and went on a grand tour of the Yugoslav capitals: Ljubljana, Zagreb, Sarajevo, and Belgrade, where he was buried before hundreds of thousands of mourners—including more heads of state than any other funeral in history.

The genuine outpouring of support at Tito's death might seem unusual for a man who was, on paper, an authoritarian communist dictator. But even today, many former Yugoslavs have forgiven him for governing with an iron fist, believing that this was a necessary evil to keep the country strong and united. The eventual balance Tito struck between communism and capitalism, and between the competing interests of his ethni-cally diverse nation, led to this region's most stable and prosper-ous era. Pictures of Tito still hang in many Croatians' homes. In a recent poll in Slovenia, Tito had a higher approval rating than any present-day politician, and 80 percent of Slovenes said they had a positive impression of him.

And yet, the Yugoslavs' respect for their former leader was not enough to keep them together. Tito's death began a long, slow chain reaction that led to the end of Yugoslavia. As the decades pass, the old joke seems more and more appropriate: Yugoslavia had eight distinct peoples in six republics, with five languages, three religions (Orthodox, Catholic, and Muslim), and two alphabets (Roman and Cyrillic), but only one Yugoslav—Tito.

Yugoslavia

could work with both East and West, without being dominated by either. Yugoslavia was the most free of the communist states: While large industry was nationalized, Tito's system allowed for small businesses. This experience with a market economy benefited Yugoslavs when Eastern Europe's communist regimes eventually fell. And even during the communist era, Yugoslavia remained a popular tourist destination for visitors from both East and West, keeping its standards more in line with Western Europe than the Soviet states.

Things Fall Apart

With Tito's death in 1980, Yugoslavia's six constituent republics gained more autonomy, with a rotating presidency. But before long, the fragile union Tito had held together started to unravel.

The breakup began in the late 1980s, with squabbles in the province of Kosovo between the Serb minority and the ethnic-Albanian majority. While technically part of Serbia, Kosovo had been awarded partial autonomy by Tito. But, even though 9 out of every 10 Kosovars were Albanian, the region remained important to the Serbs, who consider Kosovo the cradle of their civilization—the site of their most important monasteries and historic battlefields. (One Serb told me, "Kosovo is the Mecca and Medina of the Serb people.")

Serbian politician Slobodan Milošević saw how the conflict could be used to Serbia's (and his own) advantage. Milošević went to Kosovo, where he delivered a rabble-rousing speech, pledging that Serbia would come to the aid of their Kosovar-Serb brothers. In this one visit, Milošević upset the delicate balance that Tito had so carefully sought to attain. (He had also set the stage for his own rise to the Serbian presidency.) The end was near.

When Milošević annexed Kosovo soon after, other republics (especially Slovenia and Croatia) feared that he would gut their nation to create a "Greater Serbia," instead of a friendly coalition of diverse Yugoslav republics. Some of the leaders—most notably Milan Kučan of Slovenia—tried to avoid warfare by suggesting a plan for a loosely united Yugoslavia, based on the Swiss model of independent yet confederated cantons. But other parties, who wanted complete autonomy, refused. Over the next decade, Yugoslavia broke apart, with much bloodshed.

The Slovene Secession

Slovenia was the first Yugoslav republic to hold free elections, in the spring of 1990. The voters wanted the communists out—and their own independent nation. Along with being the most ethnically homogeneous of the Yugoslav nations, Slovenia was also the most Western-oriented, most prosperous, and most geographically isolated—so secession just made sense. But that didn't mean that there was no violence.

After months of stockpiling weapons, Slovenia closed its borders and declared independence from Yugoslavia on June 25, 1991. Belgrade sent in the Yugoslav National Army to take control of Slovenia's borders with Italy and Austria, figuring that whoever controlled the borders had a legitimate claim on sovereignty. Fighting broke out around these borders. Because the Yugoslav National Army was made up of soldiers from all republics, many Slovenian soldiers found themselves fighting their own countrymen. (The army had cut off communication between these conscripts and the home front, so they didn't know what was going on—and often didn't realize they were fighting their friends and neighbors until they were close enough to see them.)

Slovenian civilians bravely entered the fray, blockading the Yugoslav barracks with their own cars and trucks. Most of the Yugoslav soldiers—now trapped—were young and inexperienced, and were terrified of the ragtag (but relentless) Slovenian militia even though their own resources were far superior.

After 10 days of fighting and fewer than a hundred deaths, Belgrade relented. The Slovenes stepped aside and allowed the Yugoslav National Army to take all of the weapons with them back into Yugoslavia, and destroy all remaining military installations. When the Yugoslav National Army had cleared out, they left the Slovenes with their freedom.

The Croatian Conflict

In April of 1990, a historian named Franjo Tuđman—and his highly nationalistic, right-wing party, the HDZ (Croatian Democratic Union)—won Croatia's first free elections (for more on Tuđman, see page 624). Like the Slovenian reformers, Tuđman and the HDZ wanted more autonomy from Yugoslavia. But Tuđman's methods were more extreme than those of the gently progressive Slovenes. Tuđman immediately invoked the spirit of the last group that led an "independent" Croatia—the Ustaše, who had ruthlessly run Croatia's puppet government under the Nazis. Tuđman reintroduced the Ustaše's red-and-white checkerboard flag and their currency (the *kuna*). The 600,000 Serbs living in Croatia, mindful of their grandparents who had been massacred by the Ustaše, saw the writing on the wall and began to rise up.

The first conflicts were in the Serb-dominated Croatian city of Knin. Among Tuđman's reforms was the decree that all of Croatia's policemen wear a new uniform, which bore a striking resemblance to Nazi-era Ustaše uniforms. Infuriated by this slap in the face, and prodded by Slobodan Milošević's rhetoric, Serb police officers in Knin refused. Over the next few months, tense

Yugoslavia

negotiations ensued. Serbs from Knin and elsewhere began the so-called "tree trunk revolution"—blocking important tourist roads to the coast with logs and other barriers. Meanwhile, the Croatian government—after being denied support from the United States—illegally purchased truckloads of guns from Hungary. Tensions escalated, and the first shots of the conflict were fired on Easter Sunday of 1991 at Plitvice Lakes National Park, between Croatian policemen and Serb irregulars from Knin.

By the time Croatia declared its independence (on June 25, 1991—the same day as Slovenia), it was already embroiled in the beginnings of a bloody war. Croatia's more than half-million Serb residents immediately declared their own independence from Croatia. The Serb-dominated Yugoslav National Army swept in, supposedly to keep the peace between Serbs and Croats—but it soon became obvious that they were there to support the Serbs. The ill-prepared Croatian resistance, made up mostly of police-men and a few soldiers who defected from the Yugoslav National Army, were quickly overwhelmed. The Serbs gained control over a large swath of inland Croatia, mostly around the Bosnian bor-der (including Plitvice) and in Croatia's inland panhandle (the region of Slavonia). They called this territory—about a quarter of Croatia—the **Republic of Serbian Krajina** (*krajina* means "bor-der"). This new "country" (hardly recognized by any other nations) minted its own money and had its own army, much to the con-sternation of Croatia—which was now worried about the safety of Croats living in Krajina.

As the Serbs advanced, hundreds of thousands of Croats fled to the coast and lived as refugees in resort hotels. The Serbs began a campaign of ethnic cleansing, systematically removing Croats from their territory—often by murdering them. The bloodiest siege was at the town of **Vukovar,** which the Yugoslav army surrounded and shelled relentlessly for three months. At the end of the siege, thousands of Croat soldiers and civilians mysteriously disappeared. Many of these people were later discovered in mass graves; hun-dreds are still missing, and bodies are still being found. In a sur-prise move, Serbs also attacked the tourist resort of **Dubrovnik** (see page 632). By early 1992, both Croatia and the Republic of Serbian Krajina had established their borders, and a tense ceasefire fell over the region.

The standoff lasted until 1995, when the now well-equipped Croatian Army retook the Serbian-occupied areas in a series of two offensives—**"Lightning"** *(Blijesak),* in the northern part of the country, and **"Storm"** *(Oluja),* farther south. Some Croats retaliated for earlier ethnic cleansing by doing much of the same to Serbs—torturing and murdering them, and dynamiting their homes. Croatia quickly established the borders that exist today, and the Erdut Agreement brought peace to the region—but most of the 600,000 Serbs who once lived in Croatia/Krajina were forced into Serbia or were killed. While Serbs have long since been legally invited back to their ancestral Croatian homes, relatively few have returned—afraid of the "welcome" they might receive from the Croat neighbors who killed their relatives or blew up their houses just a few years ago.

The War in Bosnia-Herzegovina

Bosnia-Herzegovina declared its independence from Yugoslavia four months after Croatia and Slovenia did. But Bosnia-Herzegovina was always at the crossroads of Balkan culture, and therefore even more diverse than Croatia—populated predominantly by Muslim Bosniaks (mostly in the cities), but also by large numbers of Serbs and Croats (many of them farmers).

The fighting in Bosnia-Herzegovina began for similar reasons as fighting in Croatia did: As soon as Bosnia-Herzegovina declared independence, the Bosnian Serb minority seceded as their own "state," called the Republic of the Serb People of Bosnia-Herzegovina. To legitimize their claim on this land, the Serbs began a campaign of ethnic cleansing against Bosniaks and Croats in the spring of 1992.

At first, the Bosniaks and Croats teamed up to fight against the Serbs. But even before the first wave of fighting had subsided, Croats and Bosniaks turned their guns on each other. The Croats split off their own mini-state, which they called the Croatian Republic of Herzeg-Bosnia. A bloody war raged for years between the three groups: the Serbs (with support from Serbia proper), the Croats (with support from Croatia proper), and—squeezed between them—the internationally recognized Bosniak (Muslim) government, led by President Alija Izetbegović, who desperately worked for peace.

Bosnia-Herzegovina was torn apart. Even the many mixed families were forced to choose sides. If you had a Serb mother and a Croat father, you were expected to pick one ethnicity or the other—and your brother might choose the opposite. As families and former neighbors trained their guns on each other, proud and beautiful cities such as Sarajevo and Mostar were turned to rubble, and people throughout Bosnia-Herzegovina lived in a state of constant terror.

Serb sieges of Bosnian Muslim cities—such as the notorious siege of Srebrenica in July of 1995, which ended with a massacre of about 8,000 Bosniak civilians—brought the ongoing atrocities to the world's attention. The methods of the aggressors were intentionally gruesome and violent. Perhaps most despicable was the establishment of so-called "rape camps"—concentration camps

Yugoslavia

where Bosniak women were imprisoned and systematically raped by Serb soldiers. It was the aggressors' goal not only to remove people from "their" land (which could have been done more peacefully), but to ensure that the various groups could never tolerate living together again. The two men considered most responsible for the worst atrocities in Bosnia-Herzegovina—the Bosnian Serb President Radovan Karadžić and his general, Ratko Mladić—are (as of this writing) still at large and wanted to stand trial.

The United Nations Protection Force (UNPROFOR)—dubbed "Smurfs" both for their light-blue helmets and for their ineffectiveness—exercised their very limited authority to try to suppress the violence. But because they were not allowed to use force, even in self-defense, they became impotent witnesses to atrocities. This ugly situation was brilliantly parodied in the film *No Man's Land* (which won the Oscar for Best Foreign Film in 2002), a very dark comedy about the absurdity of the Bosnian war.

Finally, in 1995, the Dayton Peace Accords carefully divided Bosnia-Herzegovina among the different ethnicities. According to this compromise, the country is split into three different units: the Federation of Bosnia and Herzegovina (shared by Bosniaks and Croats), the Serb-dominated Republika Srpska, and the Brčko District (a tiny corner of the country, with a mix of the ethnicities).

Kosovo

The ongoing Yugoslav crisis finally concluded in the place where it began: the Serbian province of Kosovo. After years of poor treatment by Serbia, the Albanians in Kosovo rebelled in 1998. Milošević sent in the army, and in March 1999, they began a campaign of ethnic cleansing. Thousands of Kosovars were murdered, and hundreds of thousands fled into Albania and Macedonia. NATO planes, under the command of US General and Supreme Allied Commander Wesley Clark, bombed Serb positions for two months, forcing the Serb army to leave Kosovo in the summer of 1999.

The Fall of Milošević

After years of bloody conflicts, public opinion among Serbs had decisively swung against their president. The transition began gradually in early 2000, spearheaded by Otpor, a nonviolent, grassroots, student-based opposition movement, and aided by similar groups. These organizations used clever PR strategies to gain support and convince Serbians that real change was possible. As anti-Milošević sentiments gained momentum, opposing political parties banded together and got behind one candidate, Vojislav Koštunica. Public support for Koštunica mounted, and when the arrogant Milošević called an early election in September 2000, he was soundly defeated. Though Milošević tried to claim that the election results were invalid, determined Serbs streamed into their capital, marched on their parliament, and—like the Czechs and Slovaks a decade before—peacefully took back their nation.

In 2001, Milošević was arrested and sent to The Hague, in the Netherlands, to stand trial before the International Criminal Tribunal for the Former Yugoslavia (ICTY). Milošević served as his own attorney as his trial wore on for five years, frequently delayed due to his health problems. Then, on March 11, 2006—as his trial was coming to a close—Milošević was found dead in his cell. Ruled a heart attack, Milošević's death, like his life, was controversial. His supporters alleged that Milošević had been denied suitable medical care while on trial, some speculated that he'd been poisoned, and others suspected that he'd intentionally worsened his heart condition to avoid the completion of his trial. Whatever the cause, in the end Milošević avoided coming to justice—he was never found guilty of a thing.

Finding Their Way: The Former Yugoslav Republics

Today, Slovenia and Croatia are as stable as Western Europe, Bosnia-Herzegovina is slowly putting itself back together, Macedonia feels closer to Bulgaria than to Belgrade, and the last two united parts of "Yugoslavia"—Serbia and Montenegro—have peacefully parted ways, leaving six independent countries where once there was one.

And yet, nagging questions remain. Making the wars even more difficult to grasp is the fact that there were no "good guys" and no "bad guys"—just a lot of ugliness on all sides. When considering specifically the war between the Croats and the Serbs, it's tempting for Americans to take Croatia's "side"—because we saw them in the role of victims first; because they're Catholic, so they seem more "like us" than the Orthodox Serbs; and because we admire their striving for an independent nation. But in the streets and the trenches, it was never that clear-cut. The Serbs believe that *they* were the victims first—back in World War II, when their grandparents were executed in Croat-run Ustaše concentration camps. And when Croatians retook the Serb-occupied areas in 1995, they were every bit as brutal as the Serbs had been a few years before. Both sides resorted to ethnic cleansing, both sides had victims, and both sides had victimizers.

Even so, many can't help but look for victims and villains. During the conflict in Bosnia-Herzegovina, several prominent and respected reporters began to show things from one "side" more than the others—specifically, depicting the Bosniaks (Muslims) as victims. This re-awakened an old debate in the journalism community: Should reporters above all be impartial, even if "showing

Yugoslavia

all sides" might make them feel complicit in ongoing atrocities?

As for villains, it's easy to point a finger at Slobodan Milošević, Radovan Karadžić, Ratko Mladić, and other military leaders who are wanted or standing trial at The Hague. Others condemn the late Croatian President Franjo Tuđman, who, it's becoming increasingly clear, secretly conspired with Milošević to redraw the maps of their respective territories throughout the course of the war (for more on Tuđman, see page 624).

Finally comes the inevitable question: Why did any of it happen in the first place? Explanations tend to gravitate to two extremes. Some observers say that in this inherently warlike part of the world, deep-seated hatreds and age-old tribal passions between the various ethnic groups have flared up at several points throughout history. According to these people, there's an air of inevitability about the recent wars...and about the potential for future conflict. Others believe that this theory is an insulting oversimplification. Sure, animosity has long simmered in this region—but it takes a selfish leader to exploit it to advance his own interests. It wasn't until Milošević, Tuđman, and others expertly manipulated the people's grudges that the country fell into war. By vigorously fanning the embers of ethnic discord, and carefully controlling media coverage of the escalating violence, these leaders turned what could have been a healthy political debate into a holocaust.

Tension still exists throughout the former Yugoslavia—especially areas that were most war-torn. Croatians and Slovenes continue to split hairs over silly border disputes, and Serbs ominously warn that they'll take up arms to defend their claim on Kosovo. When the people of this region encounter other Yugoslavs in their travels, they immediately evaluate each other's accent to determine: Are they one of us, or one of them?

But, with time, these hard feelings are fading. The younger generations don't look back—teenaged Slovenes no longer learn Serbo-Croatian, can't imagine not living in an independent little country, and get bored (and a little irritated) when their old-fashioned parents wax nostalgic about the days of a united Yugoslavia. A middle-aged Slovene friend of mine thinks fondly of his months of compulsory service in the Yugoslav National Army, when his unit was made up of Slovenes, Croats, Serbs, Bosniaks, Albanians, Macedonians, and Montenegrins—all of them countrymen, and all good friends. To these young Yugoslavs, minor ethnic differences didn't matter. He still often visits with his army buddy from Dubrovnik—600 miles away, not long ago part of the same nation—and wishes there had been a way to keep it all together. But he says, optimistically, "I look forward to the day when the other former Yugoslav republics also join the European Union. Then, in a way, we will all be united once again."

APPENDIX

CONTENTS

RESOURCES

Tourist Information Offices

In the US

Each country's national tourist office is a wealth of information. Before your trip, get the free general information packet and request any specifics you may want (such as regional and city maps and festival schedules).

Czech Republic: Basic information and a map are free; additional materials are $4 (prepaid by czech...er, check). Call 212/288-0830 or visit www.czechtourism.com (info-usa@czechtourism.com).

Poland: Ask for Warsaw and Kraków information, regional brochures, maps, and more. Call 201/420-9910 or visit www.polandtour.org (pntonyc@polandtour.org).

Hungary: Request the *Budapest Guide* and any specifics (such as horseback-riding info or "Routes to your Roots" booklet for those of Hungarian descent). Call 212/695-1221 or visit www.gotohungary.com (info@gotohungary.com).

Slovakia: Call 212/679-7045 or visit www.cometoslovakia
.com (slovakoffice@nyc.rr.com).

Slovenia: They have a *Slovenia Invigorates* brochure, map, and
information on various regions, hiking, biking, winter travel, and
tourist farms. From the US, call Slovenian tel. 011-386-1-560-8823
or visit www.slovenia.info (info@slovenia.info).

Croatia: Ask for their free brochures and maps. In the US,
call 800-829-4416 or visit http://us.croatia.hr (cntony@earthlink
.net).

Austria: Ask for their "Austria Kit" with a map, and get information on cities, hiking, the wine country, and more (tel. 212/944-
6880, www.austria.info).

In Europe

The local tourist information office is your best first stop in any new
city. In this book, I'll refer to a tourist information office as a **TI.**
Throughout Eastern Europe, you'll find TIs are usually well organized and always have an English-speaking staff. They hand out
free maps of the town and have information on events, activities,
and bus and train schedules. Try to arrive, or at least telephone,
before they close. Most TIs in Eastern Europe are run by the government, which means their information isn't colored by a drive
for profit. This also means they're not allowed to make money by
running a room-booking service—though they can almost always
give you a list of local hotels and private rooms, and if they're not
too busy, can call around for you to check on availability.

Resources from Rick

Guidebooks and Online Updates

I've done my best to make sure that the information in this book
is up-to-date—but things change. For the latest, visit www
.ricksteves.com/update. Also at my website, you'll find a valuable list of reports and experiences—good and bad—from fellow
travelers who have used this book (www
.ricksteves.com/feedback).

This book is one of more than 30 titles
in my series on European travel, which
includes country guidebooks, city and
regional guidebooks, and my budget-travel
skills handbook, *Rick Steves' Europe Through
the Back Door.* My phrase books—for
German, French, Italian, Spanish, and
Portuguese—are practical and budget-
oriented. My other books are *Europe 101*
(a crash course on art and history, newly
expanded and in full color), *European*

Begin Your Trip at www.ricksteves.com

At our travel website, you'll find a wealth of free information on European destinations, including fresh monthly news and helpful tips from thousands of fellow travelers.

Our **online Travel Store** offers travel bags and accessories specially designed by Rick Steves to help you travel smarter and lighter. These include Rick's popular carry-on bags (wheeled and rucksack versions), money belts, totes, toiletries kits, adapters, other accessories, and a wide selection of guidebooks, planning maps, and DVDs.

Choosing the right **railpass** for your trip—amidst hundreds of options—can drive you nutty. We'll help you choose the best pass for your needs, plus give you a bunch of free extras.

Rick Steves' Europe Through the Back Door travel company offers **tours** with more than two dozen itineraries and 450 departures reaching the best destinations in this book... and beyond. We offer a 17-day Best of Eastern Europe tour that visits the Czech Republic, Poland, Hungary, Croatia, and Slovenia, as well as a 14-day Adriatic tour that focuses on Slovenia, Croatia, and a bit of Bosnia-Herzegovina. You'll enjoy great guides, a fun bunch of travel partners (with small groups of generally around 25), and plenty of room to spread out in a big, comfy bus. You'll find European adventures to fit every vacation length. For all the details, and to get our Tour Catalog and a free Rick Steves Tour Experience DVD (filmed on location during an actual tour), visit www.ricksteves.com or call the Tour Department at 425/608-4217.

Christmas (on traditional and modern-day celebrations), and *Postcards from Europe* (a fun memoir of my travels over 25 years). For a complete list of my books, see the inside of the last page of this book.

Public Television and Radio Shows

My TV series, *Rick Steves' Europe*, covers European destinations in 70 shows, including five different episodes that explore Eastern Europe. My weekly public radio show, *Travel with Rick Steves*, features interviews with travel experts from around the world, including several from Eastern Europe. All the TV scripts and radio shows (which are easy and free to download to an MP3 player) are at www.ricksteves.com.

Maps

The black-and-white maps in this book, designed by my well-traveled staff, are concise and simple. The maps are intended to help you locate recommended places and get to local TIs, where you can pick up a more in-depth map of the city or region (usually free).

Better maps are sold at newsstands and bookstores in Europe—take a look before you buy to be sure the map has the level of detail you want. Train travelers can usually manage fine with the freebies they get at the local tourist offices. Hikers will find no shortage of excellent, very detailed maps locally. For drivers, I'd recommend a 1:200,000- or 1:300,000-scale map for each country. Since new expressways are constantly being built in these countries, an up-to-date map is essential—it can mean the difference between choosing an old, slow road or saving an hour by finding the brand-new highway. In Croatia and Slovenia, my favorite maps of the region are by the Slovenian cartographer Kod & Kam (they have a store in Ljubljana—see page 537—but you can find these maps everywhere).

Other Guidebooks

Especially if you'll be traveling beyond my recommended destinations, you may want some supplemental information. When you consider the improvements that they'll make in your $3,000 vacation, $30 for extra maps and books is money well spent. Particularly for several people traveling by car, the extra weight and expense of a small trip library are negligible. One budget tip can save the price of an extra guidebook. Note that none of the following books are updated annually; check the publication date before you buy.

The Rough Guides, which individually cover the countries in this book, are packed with historical and cultural insight. The Lonely Planet guides are similar, but are designed more for travelers than for intellectuals. If choosing between these two titles, I buy the one that was published most recently. Lonely Planet's fat, far-ranging *Eastern Europe* overview book gives you little to go on for each destination, though their country- and city-specific guides are more thorough.

Students, backpackers, and nightlife-seekers should consider the Let's Go guides (by Harvard students, has the best hostel listings). Dorling Kindersley publishes snazzy Eyewitness Guides, covering Prague, the Czech Republic, Slovakia, Budapest, Hungary, Kraków, Warsaw, Poland, Dubrovnik and the Dalmatian Coast, Croatia, and Vienna. While pretty to look at, the Eyewitness Guides weigh a ton and are skimpy on actual content.

In Your Pocket publishes regularly updated magazines on major Eastern European cities (especially useful in Poland, including editions for Kraków, Warsaw, and Gdańsk). These handy guides are especially good for their up-to-date hotel, restaurant, and nightlife recommendations (available locally, usually for a few dollars, but often free; condensed versions available free online at www.inyourpocket.com). The British entertainment publication *Time Out* sells a similarly well-researched annual magazine with up-to-date coverage on Croatia (look for it at newsstands, www.timeout.com).

For more extensive coverage of this region and neighboring countries, consider *Rick Steves' Croatia & Slovenia, Rick Steves' Prague & the Czech Republic,* and *Rick Steves' Germany & Austria.*

Recommended Books and Movies

For information on Eastern Europe past and present, consider these books and films.

Non-Fiction

Lonnie Johnson's *Central Europe: Enemies, Neighbors, Friends* is the best history overview of the countries in this book. Rebecca West's classic, bricklike *Black Lamb and Grey Falcon* is the definitive travelogue of the Yugoslav lands (written during a journey between the two World Wars). For a more recent take, Croatian journalist Slavenka Drakulić has written a trio of insightful essay collections from a woman's perspective: *Café Europa: Life After Communism; The Balkan Express;* and *How We Survived Communism and Even Laughed.* Timothy Garton Ash has written several good "eyewitness account" books analyzing the transition in Eastern Europe over the last two decades, including *History of the Present* and *The Magic Lantern.* For information on Eastern European Roma (Gypsies), consider the textbook-style *We Are the Romani People* by Ian Hancock, and the more literary *Bury Me Standing* by Isabel Fonseca. Tina Rosenberg's dense but thought-provoking *The Haunted Land* asks how those who actively supported communism in Eastern Europe should be treated in the post-communist age.

Fiction

The most prominent works of Eastern European fiction have come from the Czechs. These include *I Served the King of England* (Bohumil Hrabal), *The Unbearable Lightness of Being* (Milan Kundera), and *The Good Soldier Švejk* (Jaroslav Hašek). The Czech existentialist writer Franz Kafka wrote many well-known novels, including *The Trial* and *The Metamorphosis.* Bruce Chatwin's *Utz* is set in communist Prague. James Michener's *Poland* is a hefty look into the history of the Poles. Joseph Roth's *The Radetzky March* details the decline of an aristocratic family in the Austro-Hungarian Empire. *Zlateh the Goat* (Isaac Bashevis Singer) includes seven folktales of Jewish Eastern Europe.

Films

Each of these countries has produced fine films. Here are a few highlights:

• **Czech Republic:** *Kolya* (1996); *The Trial* (1993); *Kouř* (*Smoke*, 1991); *The Unbearable Lightness of Being* (1988); *The Firemen's Ball* (1967); *Closely Watched Trains* (1966); *The Loves of a Blonde* (1965).

• **Poland:** *Karol: A Man Who Became Pope* (2005); *The Pianist* (2002, multiple-Oscar winner); *Schindler's List* (1993, multiple-Oscar winner); *The Wedding* (1972).

• **Hungary:** *Kontroll* (2003); *Csinibaba* (1997); *Time Stands Still* (1981); *The Witness* (1969).

• **Croatia:** *How the War Started on My Island* (1996); *Underground* (1995); *Tito and Me* (1992); *When Father Was Away on Business* (1985).

• **Slovenia:** *No Man's Land* (2002, Slovenian-produced, but deals with Bosnian war; Oscar winner for Best Foreign Film).

The BBC produced a remarkable (but difficult-to-find) six-hour documentary series called *The Death of Yugoslavia*, featuring interviews with all of the key players. For a funny and nostalgic look at Eastern Europe's fitful transition to capitalism, the 2003 German film *Good Bye Lenin!* can't be beat.

MONEY MATTERS

Damage Control for Lost Cards

If you lose your credit, debit, or ATM card, you can stop people from using it by reporting the loss immediately to the respective global customer-assistance centers. Call these 24-hour US numbers collect: Visa (410/581-9994), MasterCard (636/722-7111), and American Express (623/492-8427).

At a minimum, you'll need to know the name of the financial institution that issued you the card, along with the type of card (classic, platinum, or whatever). Providing the following information will allow for a quicker cancellation of your missing card: full card number, whether you are the primary or secondary cardholder, the cardholder's name exactly as printed on the card, billing address, home phone number, circumstances of the loss or theft, and identification verification (your birth date, your mother's maiden name, or your Social Security number—memorize this, don't carry a copy). If you are the secondary cardholder, you'll also need to provide the primary cardholder's identification-verification details. You can generally receive a temporary card within two or three business days in Europe.

If you promptly report your card lost or stolen, you typically won't be responsible for any unauthorized transactions on your account, although many banks charge a liability fee of $50.

Tipping

A decade ago, tipping was unheard of in Eastern Europe. But then came the tourists. Today, especially in big cities such as Prague and Budapest, some waiters and taxi drivers are beginning to expect Yankee-sized tips when they spot an American. Tipping the appropriate amount—without feeling stingy, but also avoiding contributing to the overtipping epidemic—is nerve-wracking to conscientious visitors. Relax! Many locals still don't tip at all, so any tip is appreciated. As in the US, the proper amount depends on your resources, tipping philosophy, and the circumstances, but the following guidelines should help you out.

Restaurants: Tipping is an issue only at restaurants that have table service. If you order your food at a counter, don't tip.

At restaurants that have a waitstaff, round up the bill 5–10 percent after a good meal. My rule of thumb is to estimate about 10 percent, then round down slightly to reach a convenient total (for a 370-Kč meal, I pay 400 Kč—a tip of 30 Kč, or about 8 percent). I'm a little more generous in Hungary, where a minimum 10 percent tip is expected (I'll hand over 4,000 Ft for a 3,600-Ft bill—that's a 400-Ft tip, or 11 percent). A 15 percent tip is overly generous, verging on extravagant, anywhere in Eastern Europe. At some tourist-oriented restaurants, a 10 percent "service charge" may be added to your bill, in which case an additional tip is not necessary. (More commonly, menus or bills remind you that the tip is *not* included.) If you're not sure whether your bill includes the tip, just ask.

Taxis: To tip the cabbie, round up about five percent (for a 71-kn fare, pay 75 kn). If the cabbie hauls your bags and zips you to the airport to help you catch your flight, you might want to toss in a little more. But if you feel like you're being driven in circles or otherwise ripped off, skip the tip.

Special Services: Tour guides at public sites sometimes hold out their hands for tips after they give their spiels. If I've already paid for the tour, I don't tip extra. I don't tip at hotels, but if you do, give the porter the local equivalent of 50 cents for carrying bags, and, at the end of your stay, leave a dollar's worth of local cash for the maid if the room was kept clean. In general, if someone in the service industry does a super job for you, a small tip (the equivalent of a dollar) is appropriate...but not required.

VAT Rates and Minimum Purchases Required to Qualify for Refunds

Country of Purchase	VAT Standard Rate*	Minimum in Local Currency	Approx. Min. in US Dollars
Austria	20%	€75.01	$100
Croatia	18.5%	501 kn	$100
Czech Republic	19%	2,000 Kč	$200
Hungary	25%	45,000 Ft	$225
Poland	22%	200 zł	$70
Slovakia	19%	5,000 Sk/€150	$200
Slovenia	20%	€63	$85

* The VAT Standard Rates listed above—while listed as exact amounts—are intended to give you an idea of the rates and minimums involved. But VAT rates fluctuate based on many factors, including what kind of item you are buying. Your refund will also likely be less than the above rate, especially if it's subject to processing fees.

When in doubt, ask: If you're not sure whether (or how much) to tip for a service, ask your hotelier or the TI; they'll fill you in on how it's done on their turf.

VAT Refunds for Shoppers

Wrapped into the purchase price of your souvenirs is a Value Added Tax (VAT) that varies per country. If you spend a minimum amount—which also differs per country—at a store that participates in the VAT refund scheme, you're entitled to get most of that tax back (see chart for VAT rates and minimum amounts).

Getting your refund is usually straightforward and, if you buy a substantial amount of souvenirs, well worth the hassle. If you're lucky, the merchant will subtract the tax when you make your purchase. (This is more likely to occur if the store ships the goods to your home.) Otherwise, you'll need to:

Get the paperwork. Have the merchant completely fill out the necessary refund document, called a "cheque." You'll have to present your passport at the store.

Get your stamp at the border or airport. Process your cheque(s) at your last stop in the country with the customs agent who deals with VAT refunds. It's best to keep your purchases in your carry-on for viewing, but if they're too large or dangerous (such as knives) to carry on, track down the proper customs agent to inspect them before you check your bag. To qualify, your purchased goods should be unused. If you show up at customs wearing your chic Czech shirt, officials might look the other way—or deny you a refund.

Collect your refund. You'll need to return your stamped document to the retailer or its representative. Many merchants work with a service that has offices at major airports, ports, and border crossings, such as Global Refund (www.globalrefund.com) or Premier Tax Free (www.premiertaxfree.com). These services, which extract a 4 percent fee, usually can refund your money immediately in your currency of choice or credit your card (within two billing cycles). If the retailer handles VAT refunds directly, it's up to you to contact the merchant for your refund. You can mail the documents from home, or quicker, from your point of departure (using a stamped, addressed envelope you've prepared or one that's been provided by the merchant)—and then wait. It could take months.

Customs for American Shoppers

You are allowed to take home $800 worth of items per person duty-free, once every 30 days. The next $1,000 is taxed at a flat 3 percent. After that, you pay the individual item's duty rate. You can also bring in duty-free a liter of alcohol (slightly more than a standard-size bottle of wine; you must be at least 21), 200 cigarettes, and up to 100 non-Cuban cigars. Food in cans or sealed jars is permissible as long as no meat is included. Some, but not all, types of cheese are allowed. Fresh fruits and vegetables are prohibited. (Hungarian paprika is OK as long as it's in a sealed container.) Note that you'll need to carefully pack any bottles of wine and other liquid-containing items in your checked luggage, due to the three-ounce limit on liquids in carry-on baggage. To check customs rules and duty rates before you go, visit www.cbp .gov, and click on "Travel," then "Know Before You Go."

TELEPHONES, EMAIL, AND MAIL

Telephones

Smart travelers learn the phone system and use it daily to reserve or reconfirm rooms, get tourist information, reserve restaurants, confirm tour times, or phone home.

Types of Phones

You'll encounter various kinds of phones on your trip:

Card-operated phones—in which you insert a locally bought phone card into a public pay phone—are common in Eastern Europe.

Hurdling the Language Barrier

The language barrier in Eastern Europe is no bigger than in the West. In fact, I find that it's much easier to communicate in Hungary or Croatia than in Italy or Spain. Since the Eastern European countries are small and not politically powerful, their residents realize that it's unreasonable to expect visitors to learn Hungarian (with only 12 million speakers worldwide), Croatian (5 million), or Slovene (2 million). It's essential to find a common language with the rest of the world—so they learn English early and well. In Croatia, for example, all schoolchildren start learning English in the third grade. (I've had surprisingly eloquent conversations with Croatian grade-schoolers.) You'll find that most people in the tourist industry—and virtually all young people—speak excellent English.

Of course, not *everyone* speaks English. You'll run into the most substantial language barriers in situations when you need to deal with a lesser-educated clerk or service person (train stations and post-office counters, maids, museum guards, bakers, and so on). Be reasonable in your expectations. Museum ticket-sellers in Hungary are every bit as friendly and multilingual as they are in the US. Luckily, it's relatively easy to get your point across in these places. I've often bought a train ticket simply by writing out the name of my destination (preferably with the local spelling—for example, "Praha" instead of "Prague"); the time I want to travel (using the 24-hour clock); and, if I'm not traveling on the same day I'm buying the ticket, I include the date I want to leave (day first, then the month as a Roman numeral, then the year). Here's an example of what I'd show a ticket-seller at a train station: "Warszawa, 17:30, 15.VII.08."

Eastern Europeans, realizing that their language intimidates Americans, often invent easier nicknames for themselves—so Šárka goes by "Sara," András becomes "Andrew," and Jaroslav tells you, "Call me Jerry."

Most of the destinations in this book—the Czech Republic, Slovakia, Poland, Slovenia, Croatia, and Bosnia-Herzegovina—speak Slavic languages. These languages are closely related to each other and to Russian, and are, to varying degrees, mutually intelligible (though many spellings change—for example, Czech *hrad,* or "castle," becomes Croatian *grad*). Slavic languages have simple vocabularies but are highly inflected—that is, the meaning of a sentence depends on complicated endings that are tacked onto the ends of the words (as in Latin).

Slavic words are notorious for their seemingly unpronounceable, long strings of consonants. Slavic pronunciation can be tricky. In fact, when the first Christian missionaries, Cyril and Methodius, came to Eastern Europe a millennium ago, they invented a whole new alphabet to represent these strange Slavic sounds. A modified version of that alphabet—called Cyrillic—is still used today in the eastern Slavic countries (such as Serbia and Russia).

Fortunately, the destinations covered in this book all use the same Roman alphabet we do, but they add lots of different diacritics—little markings below and above some letters—to represent a wide range of sounds (for example, č, ą, ó, đ, ł). I explain each of these diacritics in this book's various country introductions.

Hungarian is another story altogether—it's completely unrelated to Slavic languages, German, or English. For more on the challenging Magyar tongue, see page 398.

German is spoken in Vienna. As part of the same language family as English, German sounds noticeably more familiar to American ears than the Slavic languages. Throughout Eastern Europe, German can be a handy second language (especially in Croatia, which is popular among German-speaking tourists). And a few words of Italian can come in handy in Slovenia and Croatia.

There are certain universal English words all Eastern Europeans know: hello, please, thank you, super, pardon, stop, menu, problem, and no problem. Another handy word that people throughout the region will understand is *Servus* (SEHR-voos)—the old-fashioned greeting from the days of the Austro-Hungarian Empire. If you draw a blank on how to say hello in the local language, just offer a cheery, *"Servus!"*

Learn the key phrases (see each country introduction) and travel with a phrase book. Consider Lonely Planet's good *Eastern Europe Phrasebook,* which covers all of the destinations in this book (except Vienna).

Don't be afraid to interact with locals. Eastern Europeans can initially seem shy or even brusque—a holdover from the closed communist society—but often a simple smile is the only icebreaker you need to make a new friend. You'll find that doors open a little more quickly when you know a few words of the language. Give it your best shot. The locals will appreciate your efforts.

Coin-operated phones, the original kind of pay phone (but now increasingly rare), require you to have enough change to complete your call.

Hotel room phones are sometimes cheap for local calls (confirm at the front desk first), but can be a rip-off for long-distance calls unless you use an international phone card (described below). But incoming calls are free, making this a cheap way for friends and family to stay in touch, provided they have a good long-distance plan for calls to Europe.

American mobile phones work in Europe if they're GSM-enabled, tri-band, or quad-band, and on a calling plan that includes international calls. They're convenient, but pricey. For example, with a T-Mobile phone, you'll pay $1 per minute for calls.

European mobile phones run about $75 (for the most basic models, but it's often easy to find phones for much less) and come without contracts. These phones are loaded with prepaid calling time that you can recharge as you use up the minutes. As long as you're not "roaming" outside the phone's home country, incoming calls are free. For more information on mobile phones, see www.ricksteves.com/plan/tips/mobilephones.htm.

Using Phone Cards

Get a phone card for your calls. Prepaid cards come in two types: insertable phone cards (usable only in pay phones) and international phone cards (usable from any phone). Both are described below.

Insertable phone cards are a convenient way to pay for calls from public pay phones and can be purchased at any post office, newsstand, or tobacco shop. Simply take the phone off the hook, insert the prepaid card, wait for a dial tone, and dial away. The price of the call (local or international) is automatically deducted while you talk. These cards only work in the country where you buy them (so your Czech phone card is worthless in Poland). Insertable phone cards are a good deal for calling within Europe, but calling the US can be more expensive (at least 50 cents/min) than if you use an international phone card. Be aware that with the prevalence of mobile phones, public phones are getting harder to find.

Prepaid **international phone cards,** which are popular and easy to buy in Western Europe, are still relatively rare (and more expensive) in the East. Look for fliers advertising long-distance rates, or ask about the cards at Internet cafés, newsstands, souvenir shops, youth hostels, and post offices. If you can snare one of these cards, your calls to the US will generally cost around 25–50 cents per minute (and they also work for domestic calls).

Before buying a card, make sure the access number you dial is toll-free, not a local number (or else you'll be paying for a local call *and* deducting time from your calling card). These cards usually work only in the country where you buy them, but some brands work internationally. Buy a lower denomination in case the card is a dud.

To use a card, scratch off the back to reveal your code. After you dial the access phone number, the message tells you to enter your code and then dial the phone number you want to call. A voice may announce how much is left in your account before you dial. Usually you can select English, but if the prompts are in another language, experiment: Dial your code, followed by the pound sign (#), then the number, then pound again, and so on, until it works.

To call the US, see "Dialing Internationally," page 944. To make calls within the country you're in, dial the area code plus the local number; when using an international phone card, the area code must be dialed even if you're calling across the street.

Using Hotel-Room Phones, VoIP, or US Calling Cards

The phone in your **hotel room** is convenient...but costly. While incoming calls can be the cheapest way to keep in touch (explained below), charges for *outgoing* calls can be a very unpleasant surprise. Make sure you understand all the charges and fees associated with outgoing calls before you pick up that receiver. I find hotel room phones handy for making local calls, but dialing direct from your hotel room is usually quite pricey for international calls. If your family has an inexpensive way to call Europe, either through a long-distance plan or prepaid calling card, have them call you in your hotel room. Give them a list of your hotels' phone numbers before you go. Then, as you travel, send them an email or make a quick pay-phone call to set up a time for them to give you a ring.

Metered phones are available in phone offices and sometimes in bigger post offices. You can talk all you want, then pay the bill when you leave—but be sure you know the rates before you have a lengthy conversation.

If you're traveling with a laptop, consider trying **VoIP (Voice over Internet Protocol)**. With VoIP, two computers act as the phones, allowing for a free Internet-based call. The major providers are Skype (www.skype.com) and Google Talk (www.google.com/talk).

US Calling Cards (such as the ones offered by AT&T, MCI, or Sprint) are the worst option. You'll nearly always save a lot of money by paying with a phone card (see earlier in "Telephones").

How to Dial

Calling from the US to Europe, or vice versa, is simple—once you break the code. The European calling chart on page 942 will walk you through it.

European Calling Chart

Just smile and dial, using this key:
AC = Area Code, LN = Local Number.

European Country	Calling long distance within ...	Calling from the US or Canada to ...	Calling from a European country to ...
Austria	AC + LN	011 + 43 + AC (without the initial zero) + LN	00 + 43 + AC (without the initial zero) + LN
Belgium	LN	011 + 32 + LN (without initial zero)	00 + 32 + LN (without initial zero)
Bosnia-Herzegovina	AC + LN	011 + 387 + AC (without initial zero) + LN	00 + 387 + AC (without initial zero) + LN
Britain	AC + LN	011 + 44 + AC (without initial zero) + LN	00 + 44 + AC (without initial zero) + LN
Croatia	AC + LN	011 + 385 + AC (without initial zero) + LN	00 + 385 + AC (without initial zero) + LN
Czech Republic	LN	011 + 420 + LN	00 + 420 + LN
Denmark	LN	011 + 45 + LN	00 + 45 + LN
Estonia	LN	011 + 372 + LN	00 + 372 + LN
Finland	AC + LN	011 + 358 + AC (without initial zero) + LN	999 + 358 + AC (without initial zero) + LN
France	LN	011 + 33 + LN (without initial zero)	00 + 33 + LN (without initial zero)
Germany	AC + LN	011 + 49 + AC (without initial zero) + LN	00 + 49 + AC (without initial zero) + LN
Greece	LN	011 + 30 + LN	00 + 30 + LN
Hungary	06 + AC + LN	011 + 36 + AC + LN	00 + 36 + AC + LN
Ireland	AC + LN	011 + 353 + AC (without initial zero) + LN	00 + 353 + AC (without initial zero) + LN

European Country	Calling long distance within ...	Calling from the US or Canada to ...	Calling from a European country to ...
Italy	LN	011 + 39 + LN	00 + 39 + LN
Montenegro	AC + LN	011 + 382 + AC (without initial zero) + LN	00 + 382 + AC (without initial zero) + LN
Netherlands	AC + LN	011 + 31 + AC (without initial zero) + LN	00 + 31 + AC (without initial zero) + LN
Norway	LN	011 + 47 + LN	00 + 47 + LN
Poland	LN	011 + 48 + LN (without initial zero)	00 + 48 + LN (without initial zero)
Portugal	LN	011 + 351 + LN	00 + 351 + LN
Slovakia	AC + LN	011 + 421 + AC (without initial zero) + LN	00 + 421 + AC (without initial zero) + LN
Slovenia	AC + LN	011 + 386 + AC (without initial zero) + LN	00 + 386 + AC (without initial zero) + LN
Spain	LN	011 + 34 + LN	00 + 34 + LN
Sweden	AC + LN	011 + 46 + AC (without initial zero) + LN	00 + 46 + AC (without initial zero) + LN
Switzerland	LN	011 + 41 + LN (without initial zero)	00 + 41 + LN (without initial zero)
Turkey	AC (if no initial zero is included, add one) + LN	011 + 90 + AC (without initial zero) + LN	00 + 90 + AC (without initial zero) + LN

- The instructions above apply whether you're calling a land line or mobile phone.
- The international access codes (the first numbers you dial when making an international call) are 011 if you're calling from the US or Canada, or 00 if you're calling from virtually anywhere in Europe (except Finland, where it's 999).
- To call the US or Canada from Europe, dial 00, then 1 (the country code for the US and Canada), then the area code and number. In short, 00 + 1 + AC + LN = Hi, Mom!

Dialing Domestic Calls

About half of all European countries use area codes; the other half use a direct-dial system without area codes.

In countries that use area codes (such as Slovakia, Hungary, Slovenia, Croatia, and Austria), you dial the local number when calling within a city, and you add the area code if calling long distance within the same country. For example, Dubrovnik's area code is 020, and the number of one of my recommended Dubrovnik B&Bs is 453-834. To call the B&B within Dubrovnik, just dial 453-834. To call it from Split, dial 020/453-834.

Hungary is a special case: For long distance within Hungary, you have to dial "06" before the number. For example, to call a hotel in Eger, I'd dial 411-711 if I'm calling from within Eger; but from Budapest, I'd have to dial 06, then 36 (Eger's area code), then 411-711. For more on the confusing Hungarian phone system, see page 388.

To make calls within a country that uses a direct-dial system (such as the Czech Republic or Poland), you dial the same number whether you're calling across the country or across the street.

Don't be surprised that in some countries, local phone numbers have different numbers of digits within the same city, or even the same hotel (e.g., a hotel can have a 6-digit phone number, a 7-digit mobile phone number, and an 8-digit fax number).

Dialing Internationally

If you want to make an international call, follow these three steps:

1. Dial the international access code (00 if you're calling from Europe, 011 from the US or Canada).

2. Dial the country code of the country you're calling (see chart on page 942).

3. Dial the entire phone number, keeping in mind that calling many countries requires dropping the initial zero of the phone number (see the calling chart on page 942). For example, to call the Dubrovnik B&B from the US, dial 011, 385 (Croatia's country code), 20 (Dubrovnik's area code without the initial zero), and 453-834.

To call my office in Edmonds, Washington, from the Czech Republic, I dial 00 (Europe's international access code), 1 (the US country code), 425 (Edmonds' area code), and 771-8303.

Europeans often write their phone numbers with + at the front—it's just a placeholder for the international access code (again, that's 011 from the US or Canada, 00 from Europe).

Useful Phone Numbers

Emergency

Emergencies: Dial 112 in any of the countries in this book (except

Bosnia-Herzegovina, where it's 124).
Police: In Slovakia, Hungary, Poland, or Austria, dial 112. In the Czech Republic, dial 158. In Slovenia, dial 113. In Croatia, dial 92. In Bosnia-Herzegovina, dial 122.

Directory Assistance
Dial 1188 in the Czech Republic, 913 in Poland, 198 in Hungary, 988 in Croatia or Slovenia, 1181 in Slovakia, and 16 in Austria.

US Embassies
Austria: Boltzmanngasse 16, Vienna, tel. 01/313-390, www .usembassy.at
Bosnia-Herzegovina: Alipašina 43, Sarajevo, tel. 033/445-700, on weekends and after hours call the same number and press 0 after the recording, www.usembassy.ba; also a branch office in Mostar (Mostarskog Bataljona b.b., tel. 036/580-580)
Croatia: Ulica Thomasa Jeffersona 2, Zagreb, tel. 01/661-2200, consular services tel. 01/661-2300, www.usembassy.hr.
Czech Republic: Tržiště 15, Prague, tel. 257-022-000, www .usembassy.cz
Hungary: Szabadság tér 12, Budapest, tel. 1/475-4400, after-hours emergency tel. 1/475-4703 or 1/475-4924, www.usembassy.hu
Poland: Aleja Ujazdowskie 29/31, Warsaw, tel. 022/504-2000, www.usinfo.pl; also a US Consulate in Kraków at ulica Stolarska 9, tel. 012/424-5100
Slovakia: Bratislava, tel. 02/5443-3338, http://slovakia.usembassy .gov
Slovenia: Prešernova 31, Ljubljana, tel. 01/200-5500, www .usembassy.si

Email and Mail
Email: Many travelers set up a free Web-based email account with Yahoo, Microsoft (Hotmail), or Google (Gmail). Internet cafés are easy to find in big cities. Most of the towns where I've listed accommodations in this book also have Internet cafés. Look for the places listed in this book, or ask the local TI, computer store, or your hotelier. Some hotels have a dedicated computer for guests' email needs—sometimes free, sometimes for a fee. Small places are accustomed to letting clients (who've asked politely) sit at their desk for a few minutes just to check their email.

Internet access for laptop users is becoming commonplace at most hotels and B&Bs (except in Croatia). Most hotels that offer this do so for free, but some (especially fancier chain hotels) charge by the minute. You'll either access the hotel's wireless Internet (Wi-Fi, sometimes called "WLAN" in Europe), sometimes using a password provided by the hotelier; or plug your computer directly into an Internet wall socket (they can usually loan you a cable). These days, I can get online at most hotels in this book, and I've noted this in each listing. If I say "Internet access," there's a public terminal in the lobby for guests to use. If I say "Wi-Fi" or "cable Internet," you can access it in your room, but only if you have your own laptop.

Mail: Get stamps at the neighborhood post office, newsstands within fancy hotels, and some mini-marts and card shops. While you can arrange for mail delivery to your hotel (allow 10 days for a letter to arrive), phoning and emailing are so easy that I've dispensed with mail stops altogether.

TRANSPORTATION

By Car or Public Transportation?

In Eastern Europe, I travel mostly by public transportation. For long distances between big cities (such as Prague to Kraków, Warsaw to Budapest, or Vienna to Dubrovnik), I prefer to take a cheap flight or a night train. For shorter distances (like Gdańsk to Warsaw or Ljubljana to Zagreb), I take a daytime train or bus. In areas with lots of exciting day-trip possibilities, such as the Czech or Slovenian countryside, I rent a car for a day or two—or hire a local with a car to drive me around (which can be cheaper than you might think; I recommend several drivers and tour guides with cars).

If you're debating between public transportation and car rental, consider these factors: Trains, buses, and boats are best for single travelers; those who'll be spending more time in big cities; those with an ambitious, multi-country itinerary; and those who don't want to drive in Europe. While a car gives you more freedom—enabling you to search for hotels more easily and carrying your bags for you—trains, buses, and boats zip you effortlessly from city to city, usually dropping you in the center, near the tourist office. Cars are great in the countryside, but a worthless headache in places like Prague, Budapest, and Dubrovnik. If you're lacing the big cities together, the last thing you want is a car.

Public Transportation

Trains

Trains are punctual and cover cities well, but frustrating schedules make a few out-of-the-way recommendations difficult—or impossible—to reach (usually the bus will get you there instead; see "Buses" on page 949).

Schedules: For timetables, the first place to check is Germany's excellent all-Europe timetable at http://bahn.hafas .de/bin/query.exe/en. Individual countries also have their own

PUBLIC TRANSPORTATION IN EASTERN EUROPE

To Copenhagen

To Rødby (Denmark)

To Ystad (Sweden)

To Ystad & Copenhagen

Baltic Sea

Lübeck

Puttgarten

Sassnitz

Gdynia

Gdańsk

Sopot

Hamburg

Swinoujście

Tczew

To Vilnius & Riga

To Amsterdam

Szczecin

Malbork

Frankfurt an der Oder

Toruń

To Brest & Moscow

To Amsterdam

Berlin

Poznań

Warsaw

Forst

GERMANY

POLAND

Leipzig

Görlitz

Zgor.

Wrocław

Częstochowa

Dresden

Schona

Opole

Lichkov

Katowice

Oswięcim (Auschwitz)

To Frankfurt

Karlovy Vary

Prague

Zeb.

Kraków

Medyka

Cheb

Plzeň

CZECH. REP.

Žil.

Zak.

Plaveč

To L'viv

Nürnberg

Česky Krum.

České Bud.

Brno

SLO.

Levoča

UKR.

To Frankfurt

Sum.

Břeclav

Spišská Nova Ves

Košice

Passau

Gmünd

Bratislava

Cana

Munich

Linz

Vienna

Heg.

Eger

Miskolc

Salzburg

Graz

Györ

Füzesabony

Inns.

Sopron

Budapest

To Zürich

Villach

Klag.

Spiel.

Siofok

Curtici

AUSTRIA

Taravisio

Jes.

Mar.

Hodos

HUNGARY

ITALY

Bled

SLOV.

Kop.

Pécs

To Bucharest

To Milan

Verona

Trieste

V.O.

Ljub.

Zagreb

Subotica

Venice

Koper

Rijeka

CROATIA

Šid

ROMANIA

Piran

Zadar

Plitvice

Belgrade

Rovinj

Pula

BOSNIA-- HERZ.

SERBIA

Bologna

Split

Sarajevo

Niš

Kalo.

ITALY

Adriatic Sea

Mostar

Florence

Korčula

Ploče

MONT.

Pres.

To Sofia & Istanbul

Rome

Dubrovnik

Kotor

MACE- DONIA

To Naples

Not to Scale

A. L. B.

To Athens

- - - - - Bus Route .... Ferry Route

- - - - - Railway - - - o - - - Border Station

train timetable websites:
- **Czech Republic:** http://jizdnirady.idnes.cz
- **Slovakia:** http://cp.atlas.sk
- **Poland:** http://rozklad.pkp.pl/bin/query.exe/en
- **Hungary:** www.elvira.hu
- **Slovenia:** www.slo-zeleznice.si
- **Croatia:** www.hznet.hr
- **Austria:** www.oebb.at

Tickets: Buy tickets at the train station (or on board, if the station is unstaffed)—you rarely need a reservation, except for night trains.

Night Trains: To cover the long distances between the major destinations in this book, consider using night trains (or taking an inexpensive flight—see "Cheap Flights," on page 954). Remember, each night on the train saves a day for sightseeing. Fortunately, most of Eastern Europe's big cities are connected by night trains. I appreciate the convenience of night trains, and take them routinely. Still, some of my readers have complained that Eastern European night trains aren't as new, plush, and comfy as those they've used in the West. Expect a bumpy, noisy ride and gross WCs. In general, if you're accustomed to a higher degree of comfort, fly or take a day train.

One more thing: No matter how many times you hear "totally true" stories of train cars being "gassed" with a sleep-inducing drug by thieves, it's an urban legend, most likely invented by travelers who felt foolish for sleeping through a theft. But as on Western European night trains, thefts do occur, so lock the door and secure your belongings (to make it difficult—or at least noisy—for thieves to rip you off). When sleeping on a night train, I wear my money belt.

Railpasses: While railpasses can be a good deal in Western Europe, they usually aren't the best option in the East for two reasons: Point-to-point tickets are cheap and simple here, and most railpasses don't conveniently combine Eastern European countries. For example, with the Eurail Selectpass, you can buy unlimited travel for up to 15 travel days (within a two-month period) in three, four, or five adjacent countries; but of the countries in this book, only Hungary, Austria, and Slovenia/Croatia are eligible. Another option is the European East Pass, covering the Czech Republic, Hungary, Poland, Slovakia, and Austria—but not Slovenia or Croatia. The Czech Republic, Hungary, Slovenia, and Austria have their own individual railpasses, valid for trips only within their country. And three different combo-passes combine various countries: one for Austria and the Czech Republic; another for Austria, Slovenia, and Croatia; and another for Hungary, Slovenia, and Croatia. Again, none of these passes is likely to save you much money, but if a pass matches your itinerary, give it a look and crunch the numbers. For all of the options, including approximate point-to-point train fares, visit my online Eurail Pass guide at www.ricksteves.com/rail.

Language Barrier: For tips on buying train tickets from monolingual staff in Eastern European stations, see "Hurdling the Language Barrier" on page 938.

Buses

While the train can get you most places faster than a bus can, this book covers a few areas where buses are worth considering. For example, Ljubljana and Lake Bled are connected by both train and bus—but the bus station is right in the town center of Bled, while the train station is a few miles away. And a few destinations, including Croatia's Plitvice Lakes National Park and Rovinj, are accessible only by bus. In general, trains are best in Poland and Hungary; buses are often better in Slovakia and Croatia; and it's a toss-up in the Czech Republic and Slovenia. Throughout this book, I'll suggest whether trains or buses are better for a particular destination (in the "Transportation Connections" section at the end of each chapter). When in doubt, ask at the local TI for advice.

Boats

Once you get to the Croatian coast, boats can be your best option. For details, see "Getting Around the Dalmatian Coast" on page 618.

Cars

Car Rental

It's cheaper to arrange long-term European car rentals in the US than in Europe. For short rentals of a day or two, I usually have no problem finding an affordable car on the spot (I've listed car-rental companies in this book)—but if your itinerary is set, it doesn't hurt to book ahead. All of the big American companies have offices throughout Eastern Europe. Comparison-shop on the Web to find the best deal, or ask your travel agent. For a longer trip, look into leasing (see page 952).

Allow about $750 per person (based on two people sharing the car) to rent a small economy car for three weeks with unlimited mileage, including gas, tolls, and insurance. I normally rent a small, inexpensive model like a Ford Fiesta or Škoda Fabia. You'll pay extra for Collision Damage Waiver (CDW) insurance (described below). Be warned that dropping a car off in a different country—say, picking up in Prague and dropping in Croatia—can be prohibitively expensive (depends on distance, but the extra fee averages a few hundred dollars, and can exceed $1,000). If you're doing a multi-country trip by car, find out what the international drop-off fee will be. If it's exorbitant, consider doing a round-trip itinerary instead...or using public transportation. Again, I prefer to connect long distances by train or bus, then rent cars for a day or two where they're most useful (I've noted these places throughout this book).

If you want an automatic, reserve the car at least a month in advance and specifically request an automatic. You'll pay about 40 percent more to rent a car with an automatic instead of a manual transmission.

As a rule, always tell your car-rental company up front exactly which countries you'll be entering. Some companies levy extra insurance fees for trips taken with certain types of cars (such as BMWs, Mercedes, and convertibles) in certain countries. More importantly, as you cross borders you may need to show the proper paperwork, such as proof of insurance (called a "green card"). Double-check with your rental agent that you have all the documentation you need before you drive off. For more on borders, see "Borders," page 11.

When you pick up the car, check it thoroughly and make sure any damage is noted on your rental agreement. Find out how your car's lights, turn signals, wipers, and gas cap function.

If you drop your car off early or keep it longer, you'll be credited or charged at a fair, prorated price. But always keep your receipts in case any questions arise about your billing.

Returning a car at a big-city train station can be tricky; get precise details on the car drop-off location and hours. When you return the car, make sure the agent verifies its condition with you.

Car Insurance Options

When you rent a car, you are liable for a very high deductible, sometimes equal to the entire value of the car. There are various ways you can limit your financial risk in case of an accident. You have three options: buy Collision Damage Waiver (CDW) coverage from the car-rental company, get coverage through your credit card (free, if your card automatically includes zero-deductible coverage), or buy coverage through Travel Guard.

CDW includes a very high deductible (typically $1,000–1,500). When you pick up the car, you'll be offered the chance to "buy down" the deductible to zero (for $7–15/day; this is often called "super CDW").

If you opt instead for credit-card coverage, there's a catch. You'll technically have to decline all coverage offered by the car-rental company, which means they can place a hold on your card for the full deductible amount. In case of damage, it can be time-consuming to resolve the charges with your credit-card

DRIVING: DISTANCE AND TIME

DANUBE BEND DETAIL

15m · .5h — Visegrád
Esztergom ● — 15m .5h
25m · 1h — Szentendre — 15m .5h
Budapest ●

To Gdańsk

Berlin ● —180m · 3.75h— Poznań —190m · 4h— Warsaw

120m · 2.25h   365m 8h   140m · 2.75h   185m · 4h   220m · 4.5h
215m · 5h
120m · 3h
POLAND

GERMANY
Dresden ●

390m · 8h   Częstochowa ●   80m · 1.75h
65m 1.75h   40m 1.5h — Kraków

65m 1.5h   290m · 5.5h   100m · 4h
Terezín ●   Auschwitz ●   80m · 2h
140m · 1.5h   40m 1.25h — Kutná Hora   115m · 4h

Prague ●
25k · .75h   **CZECH REPUBLIC**   45m · 1h
Karlštejn Castle   130m · 2.5h   Zakopane ●
175m · 3h   200m · 4h   Poprad ●
100m · 2.25h   180m · 3.5h   Brno ●   200m · 3.5h   **SLOVAKIA**
240m · 4h   135m · 2.5h   80m · 1.5h   240m · 5.5h   115m · 4h
Český Krumlov ●
Vienna ●   Bratislava ●   Eger ●
Munich ●   40m · 1h   90m · 2.5h   80m · 2h
90m · 1.5h   140m · 3h   125m · 2h   150m · 2.5h   Detail Above   Budapest ●
Salzburg ●   235m · 4h   240m · 4h
145m · 3h   275m · 5.75h

AUSTRIA   **HUNGARY**
220m · 5h
SLOV.
Bled ●   90m · 2h
30m · 1h   Ljubljana ●
ITALY   60m 1.5h   Zagreb ●
140m   240m · 5h   **CROATIA**
100m · 1.75h   75m · 2h   100m 2h
Trieste ●   50m · 1.5h   Rijeka ●   90m · 2.5h
Venice ●   Rovinj ●   85m 4h
30m · .75h   55m   140m · 3h   Plitvice ●
Pula ●   **BOSNIA-HERZEGOVINA**
85m 1.75h
Mostar ●
Zadar ●   110m · 5h
Adriatic Sea   100m · 2h   65m · 1.5h

m = miles
h = hours
- - - = car ferry

N

Note: Your times may vary based on traffic, construction, and road conditions.

50 Kilometers
50 Miles

105m   Split ●   2h   Ston ●
3.5h   35m · 1h
35m · 1h
Korčula ●   3-4h
Dubrovnik ●

company. Before you decide on this option, quiz your credit-card company about how it works and ask them to explain the worst-case scenario.

Buying CDW insurance (plus "super CDW") is the easier but pricier option. Using the coverage that comes with your credit card saves money, but can involve more hassle.

Finally, you can buy CDW-type insurance from Travel Guard ($9/day plus a one-time $3 service fee covers you up to $35,000, $250 deductible, tel. 800-826-4919, www.travelguard.com). It's valid throughout Europe, but some car-rental companies refuse to honor it (especially in Italy and in the Republic of Ireland). Oddly, residents of Washington State aren't allowed to buy this coverage.

For more fine print about car-rental insurance, see www.ricksteves.com/cdw.

Leasing

For trips of two and a half weeks or more, leasing (which automatically includes CDW-type insurance with no deductible) is the best way to go. By technically buying and then selling back the car, you save lots of money on tax and insurance, but you may have to pick up and drop off the car in Germany or Austria. Leasing provides you a new car with unlimited mileage and a 24-hour emergency assistance program. You can lease for as little as 17 days to as long as six months. Car leases must be arranged from the US. A reliable company offering 17-day lease packages for about $850 is Europe by Car (US tel. 800-223-1516, www.europebycar.com).

Driving

If you'll be driving in Eastern Europe, be sure to bring along your valid US driver's license. Given the language barrier, it can also be helpful to get an International Driving Permit ahead of time at your local AAA office ($15 plus two passport-type photos, www.aaa.com).

During the communist era, Eastern Europe's infrastructure lagged far behind the West's. Now that the Iron Curtain is long gone, superhighways are being rolled out like crazy. Since construction is ongoing, it's not unusual to discover that a not-yet-finished expressway ends, requiring a transfer to an older, slower road. Likewise, you'll sometimes discover that a much faster road has been built between major destinations since your three-year-old map was published. (This is another good reason to travel with the most up-to-date maps available and study them before each drive.) New superhighways recently opened between Dresden and Prague (A17), and from Zagreb to Budapest (to the north) and Zagreb to Split (to the south). As soon as a long-enough section is completed, the roads are opened to the public.

Occasionally backcountry roads are the only option (especially in Poland and Slovakia). These can be bumpy and slow, but they're almost always paved (or, at least, they once were). In Poland, where the network of new expressways is far from complete, locals travel long distances on two-lane country roads. Since each lane is about a lane and a half wide, passing is commonplace. Slower drivers should keep to the far-right of their lane, and not be surprised when faster cars zip past them.

Tolls: In many countries, driving on highways requires a toll sticker (generally available at the border, post offices, gas stations, and sometimes car-rental agencies): the **Czech Republic** (*dálniční známka,* 200 Kč/15 days, 300 Kč/2 months); **Slovakia** (*úhrada,* 150 Sk/7 days); **Hungary** (*autópálya matrica,* 1,170–1,530 Ft/4 days depending on season, 2,550 Ft/10 days, 4,200 Ft/month, www .motorway.hu); and **Austria** (*Vignette,* €8/10 days, €22/2 months). Fines for not having a toll sticker can be stiff. Note that you don't need a toll sticker if you'll be dipping into the country on minor roads—only for major highways. Your rental car may already come with the necessary sticker—ask. In **Slovenia** and **Croatia,** you'll take a toll-ticket as you enter the expressway, then pay when you get off, based on how far you've traveled (figure about 5 cents per kilometer). In **Poland,** drivers also pay tolls to use completed expressway segments.

Learn the universal road signs. Seat belts are required, and

two beers under those belts are enough to land you in jail. (In Croatia, it's illegal to have any alcohol at all in your system if you're driving.) More and more European countries—including Slovenia, Croatia, and the Czech Republic—require you to have your headlights on any time you're driving, even in broad daylight. (I've been pulled over more than once for having my lights off.) The lights of many newer cars automatically turn on and off with the engine—ask when you pick up your car.

Parking: Parking is a costly headache in big cities. You'll pay about $10–20 a day to park safely. Rental-car theft can be a problem in cities (especially Prague), so ask at your hotel for advice.

Cheap Flights

Low-cost airlines have arrived in Eastern Europe, allowing you to cheaply connect many of the destinations in this book. One of the biggest Eastern Europe–based budget airlines, **SkyEurope** (www.skyeurope.com), has hubs in Prague, Kraków, Košice (eastern Slovakia), Bratislava, and Vienna, with flights to various destinations in both Eastern Europe (including Warsaw, Dubrovnik, and Split) and Western Europe. **Wizz Air** (www.wizzair.com) has hubs in Budapest, Warsaw, Gdańsk, and Katowice (near Kraków), but most of their flights go to Western Europe rather than destinations within Eastern Europe. **Smart Wings** (www.smartwings.net), based in Prague, has a few flights to Western Europe. And LOT, Poland's biggest carrier, has a low-cost subsidiary called **Centralwings** (www.centralwings.com).

Several of the more established Western European budget airlines have expanded their offerings eastward. For example, **easyJet** (www.easyjet.com) and **Ryanair** (www.ryanair.com) fly from Western hubs to several major Eastern European cities (including Prague, Kraków, Warsaw, Gdańsk, Budapest, Bratislava, and Ljubljana). And **Air Berlin** (www.airberlin.com) connects Budapest and Vienna to the West. To search several budget airlines at once, check out www.skyscanner.net.

Prices are cheap, but there are some trade-offs: minimal customer service, non-refundable tickets, and strict restrictions on the amount of baggage you're allowed to check without paying extra. In general, you'll be nickel-and-dimed every step of the way (e.g., no free drinks). Also note that you'll sometimes fly out of less convenient, secondary airports. For example, Wizz Air's flights from "Kraków" actually depart from Katowice, 50 miles away (see page 208). Finally, be warned that many no-frills airlines save money by scheduling flights on the same plane extremely close together—so they can pack more flights into one day. But this means that a delay early in the day can trickle down and cause major delays later.

Now that the established airlines in Eastern Europe face more competition, they've been forced to adapt. Many national carriers sell a handful of seats on certain flights at super-cheap promotional rates, which sell out quickly; for example, check out Croatia Airlines (www.croatiaairlines.com) and Slovenia's Adria Airways (www.adria-airways.com).

Europe by Air offers a Flight Pass, charging $99 per leg (plus taxes and airport fees) for flights within Europe. They partner with various well-established airlines, providing good coverage for low prices (most useful for Croatia Airlines flights to and from

the Dalmatian Coast; tickets can be purchased only in US, www
.europebyair.com, US tel. 888-321-4737).

HOLIDAYS AND FESTIVALS

This is a partial list of holidays and festivals—in these countries,
holidays can strike without warning. Catholic holidays are celebrated in Poland, Slovakia, Croatia, and Slovenia (and to a lesser
extent in Hungary and the Czech Republic). For more information, contact the tourist information offices listed at the beginning
of this chapter.

Jan 1	New Year's Day, all countries
Jan 6	Epiphany, Catholic countries
Jan 19	Anniversary of Jan Palach's Death, Prague (flowers in Wenceslas Square)
Feb 8	National Day of Culture, Slovenia (celebrates Slovenian culture and national poet France Prešeren)
Early March	One World International Human Rights Film Festival, Prague (1 week, www .oneworld.cz)
March 15	National Day, Hungary (celebrates 1848 Revolution)
Late March	Budapest Spring Festival (2 weeks, www .festivalcity.hu)
Late March	Ski Flying World Championships, Planica, Slovenia (3 days, www.planica .info)
Easter	(March 23 in 2008, April 12 in 2009) all countries
April 27	National Resistance Day, Slovenia
April 30	Witches' Night, Czech Republic (similar to Halloween, with bonfires)
May	Vienna Festival of Arts and Music
May 1	Labor Day, all countries
Ascension	(May 1 in 2008, May 21 in 2009) Catholic countries
May 3	Constitution Day, Poland (celebrates Europe's first constitution)
May 8	Liberation Day, Czech Republic and Slovakia
Pentecost	(May 11 in 2008, May 31 in 2009) Catholic countries
Whitmonday	(May 12 in 2008, June 1 in 2009) Hungary

Mid-May	Prague International Marathon (www.pim.cz)
Late May	"Prague Spring" Music Festival (3 weeks, www.festival.cz)
Corpus Christi	(May 22 in 2008, June 11 in 2009) Catholic countries
Early June	Dance Week Festival, Zagreb, Croatia (www.danceweekfestival.com)
June 22	Antifascist Struggle Day, Croatia
June 25	National Day, Slovenia; Statehood Day, Croatia
Late June	Celebration of the Rose, Český Krumlov, Czech Republic (3 days, medieval festival, music, theater, dance, knights' tournament)
Late June	Floating of the Wreaths Midsummer Festival, Kraków, Poland (1 weekend, wreaths on rafts in Vistula River, fireworks, music)
Late June	Jewish Culture Festival, Kraków, Poland (1 week, www.jewishfestival.pl)
Late June	Midsummer Eve Celebrations, Austria
July 5	Sts. Cyril and Methodius Day, Czech Republic and Slovakia
July 6	Jan Hus Day, Czech Republic
July 10–Aug 25	(every year) Dubrovnik Summer Festival, Croatia (www.dubrovnik-festival.hr)
Early July–late Aug	Ljubljana Summer Festival, Slovenia (www.festival-lj.si)
Late July	Marco Polo Festival, Korčula, Croatia (3 days, www.marcopolofest.hr)
Late July–late Aug 25	International Music Festival, Český Krumlov, Czech Republic (www.czechmusicfestival.com)
Late July	International Folklore Festival, Zagreb, Croatia (5 days, costumes, songs, dances from all over Croatia, www.msf.hr)
Aug 5	National Thanksgiving Day, Croatia
Early Aug	Formula 1 races, Budapest (1 day, www.hungaroinfo.com/formel1)
Early Aug	Sziget Festival, Budapest (1 week, rock and pop music, www.sziget.hu)
Aug 15	Assumption of Mary, Catholic countries
Aug 20	Constitution Day and St. Stephen's Day, Hungary (fireworks, celebrations)

Aug 29	National Uprising Day, Slovakia (commemorates uprising against Nazis)
Late Aug–early Sept	Jewish Summer Festival, Budapest (2 weeks, www.jewishfestival.hu)
Early Sept	Marco Polo Naval Battle Reenactment, Korčula, Croatia
Sept 1	Constitution Day, Slovakia
Late Sept	Prague Autumn Music Festival (2 weeks, www.pragueautumn.cz)
Sept 28	St. Wenceslas Day, Czech Republic (celebrates national patron saint and Czech statehood)
Oct 8	Independence Day, Croatia
Oct 23	Republic Day, Hungary (remembrances of 1956 Uprising)
Mid-Oct	Budapest Autumn Festival (1 week, music, www.festivalcity.hu)
Oct 28	Independence Day, Czech Republic
Oct 31	Reformation Day, Slovenia
Nov 1	All Saints' Day/Remembrance Day, Catholic countries (religious festival, some closures)
Nov 11	Independence Day, Poland; St. Martin's Day (official first day of wine season), Slovenia and Croatia
Nov 17	Velvet Revolution Anniversary, Czech Republic and Slovakia
Dec 5	St. Nicholas Eve, Prague (St. Nick gives gifts to children in town square)
Dec 24–25	Christmas Eve and Christmas Day, all countries
Dec 26	Boxing Day/St. Stephen's Day; Independence and Unity Day, Slovenia
Dec 31	St. Sylvester's Day, Prague and Vienna (fireworks)

CONVERSIONS AND CLIMATE

Numbers and Stumblers

- Europeans write a few of their numbers differently than we do. 1 = 1, 4 = 4, 7 = 7.
- In Europe, dates appear as day/month/year, so Christmas is 25/12/09.
- Commas are decimal points and decimals commas. A dollar and a half is 1,50, and there are 5.280 feet in a mile.
- When counting with fingers, start with your thumb. If you

hold up your first finger to request one item, you'll probably get two.
- What Americans call the second floor of a building is the first floor in Europe.
- On escalators and moving sidewalks, Europeans keep the left "lane" open for passing. Keep to the right.

Metric Conversions (approximate)

1 foot = 0.3 meter	1 square yard = 0.8 square meter
1 yard = 0.9 meter	1 square mile = 2.6 square kilometers
1 mile = 1.6 kilometers	1 ounce = 28 grams
1 centimeter = 0.4 inch	1 quart = 0.95 liter
1 meter = 39.4 inches	1 kilogram = 2.2 pounds
1 kilometer = 0.62 mile	32°F = 0°C

Climate

The first line is the average daily high; the second line, the average daily low. The third line shows the average number of days without rain. For more detailed weather statistics for destinations in this book (as well as the rest of the world), check www.worldclimate .com.

J	F	M	A	M	J	J	A	S	O	N	D

AUSTRIA • Vienna

34°	38°	47°	58°	67°	73°	76°	75°	68°	56°	45°	37°
25°	28°	30°	42°	50°	56°	60°	59°	53°	44°	37°	30°
15	14	13	13	13	14	13	13	10	13	14	15

CROATIA • Dubrovnik

53°	55°	58°	63°	70°	78°	83°	82°	77°	69°	62°	56°
42°	43°	57°	52°	58°	65°	69°	69°	64°	57°	51°	46°
13	13	11	10	10	6	4	3	7	11	16	15

CZECH REPUBLIC • Prague

31°	34°	44°	54°	64°	70°	73°	72°	65°	53°	42°	34°
23°	24°	30°	38°	46°	52°	55°	55°	49°	41°	33°	27°
13	11	10	11	13	12	13	12	10	13	12	13

HUNGARY • Budapest

34°	39°	50°	62°	71°	78°	82°	81°	74°	61°	47°	39°
25°	28°	35°	44°	52°	58°	62°	60°	53°	44°	38°	30°
13	12	11	11	13	13	10	9	7	10	14	13

J F M A M J J A S O N D

POLAND • Kraków

32°	34°	45°	55°	67°	72°	76°	73°	66°	56°	44°	37°
22°	22°	30°	38°	48°	54°	58°	56°	49°	42°	33°	28°
16	15	12	15	12	15	16	15	12	14	15	16

SLOVENIA • Ljubljana

36°	41°	50°	60°	68°	75°	80°	78°	71°	59°	47°	39°
25°	25°	32°	40°	48°	54°	57°	57°	51°	43°	36°	30°
13	11	11	13	16	16	12	12	10	14	15	15

Temperature Conversion: Fahrenheit and Celsius

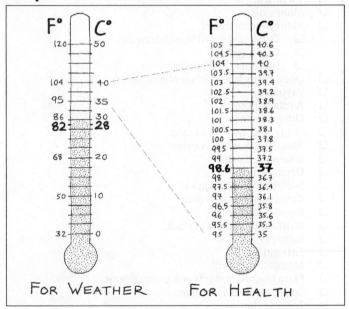

Europe takes its temperature using the Celsius scale, while we opt for Fahrenheit. For a rough conversion from Celsius to Fahrenheit, double the number and add 30. For weather, remember that 28°C is 82°F—perfect. For health, 37°C is just right.

Essential Packing Checklist

Whether you're traveling for five days or five weeks, here's what you'll need to bring. Remember to pack light to enjoy the sweet freedom of true mobility. Happy travels!

- ❏ 5 shirts
- ❏ 1 sweater or lightweight fleece jacket
- ❏ 2 pairs pants
- ❏ 1 pair shorts
- ❏ 1 swimsuit (women only—men can use shorts)
- ❏ 5 pairs underwear and socks
- ❏ 1 pair shoes
- ❏ 1 rainproof jacket
- ❏ Tie or scarf
- ❏ Money belt
- ❏ Money—your mix of:
  - ❏ Debit card for ATM withdrawals
  - ❏ Credit card
  - ❏ Hard cash in US dollars
- ❏ Documents (and backup photocopies)
- ❏ Passport
- ❏ Airplane ticket
- ❏ Driver's license
- ❏ Student ID and hostel card
- ❏ Railpass/car-rental voucher
- ❏ Insurance details
- ❏ Daypack
- ❏ Sealable plastic baggies
- ❏ Camera and related gear
- ❏ Empty water bottle
- ❏ Wristwatch and alarm clock
- ❏ Earplugs
- ❏ First-aid kit
- ❏ Medicine (labeled)
- ❏ Extra glasses/contacts and prescriptions
- ❏ Sunscreen and sunglasses
- ❏ Toiletries kit
- ❏ Soap
- ❏ Laundry soap (if liquid and carry-on, limit to 3 oz.)
- ❏ Clothesline
- ❏ Small towel
- ❏ Sewing kit
- ❏ Travel information
- ❏ Necessary map(s)
- ❏ Address list (email and mailing addresses)
- ❏ Postcards and photos from home
- ❏ Notepad and pen
- ❏ Journal

Hotel Reservation

To: _____ _____
           hotel   *email or fax*

From: _____ _____
           name   *email or fax*

Today's date: _____ / _____ / _____
                        day   *month*   *year*

Dear Hotel _____ ,
Please make this reservation for me:

Name: _____

Total # of people: _____ # of rooms: _____ # of nights: _____

Arriving: _____ / _____ / _____   My time of arrival (24-hr clock): _____
                 day *month* *year*   (I will telephone if I will be late)

Departing: _____ / _____ / _____
                   day *month* *year*

Room(s): Single____ Double ____ Twin ____ Triple ____ Quad____

With: Toilet ____ Shower_____ Bath ____ Sink only____

Special needs: View____ Quiet____ Cheapest____ Ground Floor____

Please email or fax confirmation of my reservation, along with the type of room reserved and the price. Please also inform me of your cancellation policy. After I hear from you, I will quickly send my credit-card information as a deposit to hold the room. Thank you.

_____
Name

_____
Address

_____
City   *State*   *Zip Code*   *Country*

Before hoteliers can make your reservation, they want to know the information listed above. You can use this form as the basis for your email, or you can photocopy this page, fill in the information, and send it as a fax (also available online at www.ricksteves.com/reservation).

INDEX

Travel smart…carry on!

The latest generation of Rick Steves' carry-on travel bags is easily the best—benefiting from two decades of on-the-road attention to what really matters: maximum quality and strength; practical, flexible features; and no unnecessary frills. You won't find a better value anywhere!

Rick Steves' Convertible Carry-On $99.⁹⁵

Our roomy, versatile 9" x 21" x 14" carry-on has a large 2600 cubic-inch main compartment, plus four outside pockets (small, medium and huge) that are perfect for often-used items. Wish you had even more room to bring home souvenirs? Pull open the full-perimeter expando-zipper and its capacity jumps from 2600 to 3000 cubic inches. When you want to use it as a suitcase or check it as luggage (required when "expanded"), the straps and belt hide away in a zippered compartment in the back. It weighs just 3 lbs.

Rick Steves' Classic Back Door Bag $79.⁹⁵

This ultra-light (1½ lbs.) version of our Convertible Carry-On features the same 9" x 21" x 14" dimensions and hideaway straps, but does not include a waistbelt or expandability. This is the bag that Rick lives out of for three months a year!

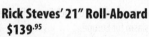

Rick Steves' 21" Roll-Aboard $139.⁹⁵

Our sturdy 21" Roll-Aboard is rucksack-soft in front, but the rest is lined with a hard ABS-lexan shell to give maximum protection to your belongings. We've spared no expense on moving parts, splurging on an extra-long button-release handle and big, tough inline skate wheels for easy rolling on rough surfaces. It features the same 9" x 21" x 14" carry-on dimensions, pocket configuration and expandability as our Convertible Carry-On—and at 7 lbs. it's the lightest roll-aboard in its class.

Prices and features are subject to change.

For great deals on a wide selection of travel goodies, begin your next trip at the Rick Steves Travel Store!

Visit the Rick Steves Travel Store at
www.ricksteves.com

Start your trip at
www.ricksteves.com

Rick Steves' website is packed with over 3,000 pages of timely travel information. It's also your gateway to getting FREE monthly travel news from Rick—and more!

Free Monthly Travel News

Fresh articles on Europe's most interesting destinations and happenings. Rick will even send you an email every month (often direct from Europe) with his latest discoveries!

Timely Travel Tips

Rick Steves' best money-and-stress-saving tips on trip planning, packing, transportation, hotels, health, safety, finances, hurdling the language barrier...and more.

Travelers' Graffiti Wall

Candid advice and opinions from thousands of travelers on everything listed above, plus whatever topics are hot at the moment (discount flights, politics, nude beaches, scams...you name it).

Rick's Guide to Eurail Passes

The clearest, most comprehensive guide to the confusing array of railpass options out there, and how to choo-choose the railpass that best fits your itinerary and budget.

Great Gear at Our Travel Store

In the past year alone, more than 50,000 travelers have enjoyed great online deals on Rick's guidebooks, maps, DVDs—and his custom-designed carry-on bags, day packs, and light-packing accessories.

Rick Steves Tours

This year, 12,000 lucky travelers will explore Europe on a Rick Steves tour. Learn about our 28 different one- to three-week itineraries, read uncensored feedback from our tour alums, and get our free Tour Experience DVD.

Rick on TV, Radio and Podcasts

Read the scripts from the popular Rick Steves' Europe TV series, and listen to or download your choice of over 100 hours of our Travel with Rick Steves radio show.

Respect for Your Privacy

Whether you buy something from us or subscribe to Rick's monthly Travel News emails, we'll never share your name or email address with anyone else. You won't be spammed!

Have fun raising your Travel I.Q. at
www.ricksteves.com

Rick Steves®

More *Savvy*. More *Surprising*. More *Fun*.

COUNTRY GUIDES

Croatia & Slovenia
England
France
Germany & Austria
Great Britain
Ireland
Italy
Portugal
Scandinavia
Spain
Switzerland

CITY GUIDES

Amsterdam, Bruges & Brussels
Florence & Tuscany
Istanbul
London
Paris
Prague & The Czech Republic
Provence & The French Riviera
Rome
Venice

BEST OF GUIDES

Eastern Europe
Best of Europe

PHRASE BOOKS & DICTIONARIES

French
French, Italian & German
German
Italian
Portuguese
Spanish

MORE EUROPE FROM RICK STEVES

Europe 101
Europe Through the Back Door
Postcards from Europe

RICK STEVES' EUROPE DVDs

All 70 Shows 2000–2007
Britain
Eastern Europe
France & Benelux
Germany, The Swiss Alps & Travel Skills
Ireland
Italy
Spain & Portugal

PLANNING MAPS

Britain & Ireland
Europe
France
Germany, Austria & Switzerland
Italy
Spain & Portugal

CREDITS

Contributor

Gene Openshaw

Gene is the co-author of seven Rick Steves books. For this book, he wrote material on Europe's art, history, and contemporary culture. When not traveling, Gene enjoys composing music, recovering from his 1973 trip to Europe with Rick, and living everyday life with his daughter.

IMAGES

Location	Photographer
Title Page: Széchenyi Baths, Budapest, Hungary Cameron Hewitt	
Full-Page Color: Ulica Długa, Gdańsk, Poland	Cameron Hewitt
Czech Republic (full-page image): Charles Bridge, Prague	Cameron Hewitt
Prague: Vltava River, Charles Bridge, and Prague Castle	Cameron Hewitt
Český Krumlov: View of City	David C. Hoerlein
Slovakia (full-page image): St. Michael's Gate, Bratislava	Cameron Hewitt
Bratislava: Bratislava Castle	Cameron Hewitt
The Spiš Region: Spiš Castle	Cameron Hewitt
Poland (full-page image): Old Town Square, Warsaw	Cameron Hewitt
Kraków: Main Market Square	Cameron Hewitt
Auschwitz-Birkenau: Birkenau Guard Tower	Rick Steves
Warsaw: Castle Square and the Old Town	Rick Steves
Gdańsk: Artus Court on Ulica Długa	Cameron Hewitt
Pomerania: Malbork Castle	Cameron Hewitt
Hungary (full-page image): Parliament, Budapest	Cameron Hewitt
Budapest: Chain Bridge Panorama	Cameron Hewitt
The Danube Bend: View from Visegrád Citadel	Cameron Hewitt
Eger: View from the Castle	Cameron Hewitt
Slovenia (full-page image): Soča River Valley	Cameron Hewitt

Location	Photographer
Slovenia (full-page image): Soča River Valley	Cameron Hewitt
Ljubljana: Ljubljana Castle overlooking Prešeren Square	Cameron Hewitt
Lake Bled: Pletna Boat on Lake Bled	Cameron Hewitt
The Julian Alps: Mountain Hut	Cameron Hewitt
Croatia (full-page image): Dubrovnik	Cameron Hewitt
Dubrovnik: View of Old Town	Cameron Hewitt
Split: Riva Promenade and Old Town	Cameron Hewitt
Korčula: Korčula Old Town	Cameron Hewitt
Rovinj: Rovinj Harbor	Cameron Hewitt
Zagreb: Jelačić Square	Cameron Hewitt
Plitvice Lakes National Park: Plitvice	Rick Steves
Bosnia-Herzegovina (full-page image): Coppersmiths' Street, Mostar	Cameron Hewitt
Mostar: Old Bridge	Cameron Hewitt
Austria (full-page image): St. Peter's Church, Vienna	Cameron Hewitt
Vienna: Schönbrunn Palace	Cameron Hewitt

Rick Steves' Guidebook Series

Country Guides
Rick Steves' Best of Europe
Rick Steves' Croatia & Slovenia
Rick Steves' Eastern Europe
Rick Steves' England
Rick Steves' France
Rick Steves' Germany & Austria
Rick Steves' Great Britain
Rick Steves' Ireland
Rick Steves' Italy
Rick Steves' Portugal
Rick Steves' Scandinavia
Rick Steves' Spain
Rick Steves' Switzerland

City and Regional Guides
Rick Steves' Amsterdam, Bruges & Brussels
Rick Steves' Florence & Tuscany
Rick Steves' Istanbul
Rick Steves' London
Rick Steves' Paris
Rick Steves' Prague & the Czech Republic
Rick Steves' Provence & the French Riviera
Rick Steves' Rome
Rick Steves' Venice

Rick Steves' Phrase Books
French
German
Italian
Spanish
Portuguese
French/Italian/German

Other Books
Rick Steves' Europe Through the Back Door
Rick Steves' Europe 101: History and Art for the Traveler
Rick Steves' Postcards from Europe
Rick Steves' European Christmas

(Avalon Travel Publishing)

Avalon Travel
a member of the Perseus Books Group
1700 Fourth Street
Berkeley, CA 94710, USA

Special thanks to Ian Watson for his innumerable contributions. Many thanks also to Honza Vihan, the co-author of *Rick Steves' Prague & the Czech Republic*, for his help with all things Czech. *Danke* to Gene Openshaw for his *wunderbar* tour of the Kunsthistorisches Museum in Vienna.

Portions of this book were originally published in *Rick Steves' Germany & Austria* © 2008, 2007, 2006, 2005, by Rick Steves; in *Rick Steves' Germany, Austria & Switzerland* © 2004, 2003, 2002, 2001, 2000, 1999, by Rick Steves; in *Rick Steves' Prague & the Czech Republic* © 2008, 2007, 2006, 2005, by Rick Steves and Honza Vihan; and in *Rick Steves' Croatia & Slovenia* © 2008, 2007 by Rick Steves and Cameron Hewitt.

For the latest on Rick Steves' lectures, guidebooks, tours, public radio show, and public television series, contact Europe Through the Back Door, Box 2009, Edmonds, WA 98020, tel. 425/771-8303, fax 425/771-0833, www.ricksteves.com, rick@ricksteves.com.

ISBN (10) 1-56691-851-0
ISBN (13) 978-1-56691-851-0
ISSN 1547-8505

Europe Through the Back Door Senior Editor: Cameron Hewitt
ETBD Editors: Gretchen Strauch, Jennifer Madison Davis, Cathy McDonald, Jennifer Hauseman (Senior Editor)
ETBD Managing Editor: Risa Laib
Avalon Travel Senior Editor & Series Manager: Madhu Prasher
Avalon Travel Project Editor: Kelly Lydick
Avalon Travel Editorial Assistant: Jamie Andrade
Copy Editor: Amy Scott
Proofreader: Janet Walden
Indexer: Claire Splan
Production & Typesetting: McGuire Barber Design
Cover Design: Kari Gim, Laura Mazer
Cover Art Manager: Laura VanDeventer
Maps & Graphics: David C. Hoerlein, Laura VanDeventer, Lauren Mills, Barb Geisler, Mike Morgenfeld, Chris Markiewicz, Brice Ticen, Albert Angulo
Photography: Cameron Hewitt, Rick Steves, David C. Hoerlein
Front Matter Color Photos: page i: Széchenyi Baths, Budapest, Hungary © Cameron Hewitt; page ii: Ulica Długa, Gdańsk, Poland © Cameron Hewitt
Cover Photos: front: Main Market Square, Kraków, Poland © Cameron Hewitt; back: Plitvice Lakes National Park, Croatia © Mike Potter